abled. Plaintiffs primarily used the Rehabilitation Act of 1973 (29 U.S.C.A. § 701 et seq.), the earliest law of this type. But the Rehabilitation Act has a limited scope: it applies only to federally funded workplaces and institutions, and says nothing about those that do not receive government money.

With passage of the ADA in 1990, Congress gave broad protection to people with AIDS who work in the private sector. In general, the ADA is designed to increase access for disabled persons, and it also forbids discrimination in hiring or promotion in companies with fifteen or more employees. Specifically, employers may not discriminate if the person in question is otherwise qualified for the job. Moreover, they cannot use tests to screen out disabled persons, and they must provide reasonable accommodation for disabled workers. The ADA, which took effect in 1992, has quickly emerged as the primary means for bringing AIDS-related discrimination lawsuits.

AIDS and Health Care Closely related to work is the issue of health care. In some cases, the two overlap: health insurance, Social Security, and disability benefits for AIDS victims were often hard to obtain during the 1980s. Insurance was particularly difficult because employers feared rising costs and insurance companies did not want to pay claims. To avoid the costs of AIDS, insurance companies used two traditional industry techniques: they attempted to exclude AIDS coverage from general policies, and they placed caps (limits on benefits payments) on AIDS-related coverage.

In January 1995, the settlement in a lawsuit brought by a Philadelphia construction worker with AIDS illustrated that the ADA can be used to fight caps on coverage. In 1992, the joint union-management fund for the Laborers' District Council placed a $10,000 limit on AIDS benefits, in stark contrast to the $100,000 allowed for other catastrophic illnesses. At that time, the fund said the cap on AIDS benefits was designed to curb all health costs. In 1993, the EEOC ruled that it violated the ADA, and, backed by the AIDS Law Project of Philadelphia, the worker sued. Rather than fight an expensive lawsuit, the insurance fund settled.

AIDS and Education Issues in the field of education include the rights of HIV-positive students to attend class and of HIV-positive teachers to teach, the confidentiality of HIV records, and how best to teach young people about AIDS. A few areas have been settled in court: for instance, the right of students to attend classes was of greater concern in the early years of the epidemic, and no longer remains in dispute.

Certain students with AIDS may assert their right to public education under the Education for All Handicapped Children Act of 1975 (EAHCA), but the law is only relevant in cases involving special education programs. More commonly, students' rights are protected by the Rehabilitation Act.

Schools play a major role in the effort to educate the public on AIDS. Several states have mandated AIDS prevention instruction in their schools. But the subject is controversial: it evokes personal, political, and moral reactions to sexuality. During the 1980s, those who often criticized liberal approaches to sex education argued that AIDS materials should not be explicit, encourage sexuality, promote the use of contraceptives, or favorably portray gays and lesbians.

Civil Litigation TORT law has seen an explosion of AIDS-related suits. This area of law is used to discourage individuals from subjecting others to unreasonable risks, and to compensate those who have been injured by unreasonably risky behavior. The greatest number of AIDS-related LIABILITY lawsuits has involved the receipt of HIV-infected blood and blood products. A second group has concerned the sexual transmission of HIV. A third group involves AIDS-related psychic distress. In these cases, plaintiffs have successfully sued and recovered damages for their fear of having contracted HIV.

CROSS-REFERENCES
Disabled Persons; Discrimination; Food and Drug Administration; Gay and Lesbian Rights; Health Care; Patients' Rights; Physicians and Surgeons; Privacy.

Cross-references at end of article

BIOGRAPHY

Gloria Allred

Biography of contributor to American law

ALLRED, GLORIA Gloria Allred, born July 3, 1941, in Philadelphia, is a flamboyant, widely recognized lawyer, feminist, activist, and radio talk show host. Though her critics dismiss her as a publicity monger and a dilettante, Allred has received praise from others who believe that she is a master at using the power of the news media to draw attention to the day-to-day struggles of ordinary people.

Born Gloria Rachel Bloom, Allred grew up in Philadelphia with her parents, Morris Bloom, a door-to-door salesman, and Stella Davidson Bloom, a homemaker. Her conventional middle-class childhood gave no hint of the outspoken activist to come. Allred graduated with honors from the University of Pennsylvania in 1963 with a bachelor's degree in English. She moved to New York to pursue a master's degree in teaching at New York University. Wh[...] interested in the CIVIL RIGHT[...] was beginning to gain mom[...] her master's degree in 19[...]

GLORIA ALLRED 1941–

Timeline for subject of biography, including general historical events and life events

Philadelphia to teach at a high school with a predominantly black enrollment.

Allred says her interest in the struggle for equal rights arose from personal experiences. While she was in college, she married, gave birth to a daughter, and divorced. Unable to collect CHILD SUPPORT from her former husband, she was forced to return to her parents' home. She also recalls being paid less than a man for what she considered equal work. The reason given was that the man had a family to support, but at the time, Allred was the single mother of an infant.

After moving to California, Allred taught in the turbulent Watts section of Los Angeles and became the first full-time female staff member in United Teachers of Los Angeles, the union representing Los Angeles teachers. The experience stirred her interest in CIVIL RIGHTS and collective bargaining and prompted her to go to law school. She received her law degree, with honors, from Loyola Marymount University, Los Angeles, Law School in 1974. Soon after, she entered a law firm partnership with her classmates Nathan Goldberg and Michael Maroko.

Allred is probably the most flamboyant and well known member of her firm. She has achieved notoriety and name recognition through staged press conferences and demonstrations publicizing and dramatizing the cause she is championing at the time. She also accepts controversial cases that naturally attract media attention. During her years in practice, she has successfully sued Los Angeles County to stop the practice of shackling and chaining pregnant inmates during labor and delivery; put a halt on the city of El Segundo's quizzing job applicants about their sexual histories (*Thorne v. City of El Segundo*, 802 F.2d 1131 [9th Cir. 1986]); represented a client who was turned down for a job as a police officer after a six-hour lie detector exam that included questions about her sex life; and sued a dry cleaning establishment for discrimination because it charged more to launder women's shirts than men's.

Allred relishes confrontation, and her showy tactics have earned her both praise and criticism.

Internal cross references

Quotation from subject of biography

Full cite for case

"THERE ARE ENOUGH HIGH HURDLES TO CLIMB, AS ONE TRAVELS THROUGH LIFE, WITHOUT HAVING TO SCALE ARTIFICIAL BARRIERS CREATED BY LAW OR SILLY REGULATIONS."

Defending what many have called self-promoting publicity stunts, Allred says she tries to use the few moments she is in the spotlight to make her point as forcefully as possible. Her detractors say that she wastes her time and energy on trivial issues that do not advance any worthwhile cause and deflect attention away from serious issues. Yet, she points out, she is often stopped on the street by people who recognize her and want to thank her for taking on the small fights that no one else wants.

Some critics say she is all show and no substance. But Allred has many supporters as well. Among them is Justice Joan Dempsey Klein, of the California Court of Appeal, who credits Allred with moving women's issues forward. Klein also points out that Allred saves her dramatics for outside the courtroom and always observes proper decorum when before the bench. According to Klein, Allred is always well-prepared and, for that reason, is quite successful.

Dressed in her trademark reds and electric blues, her striking black hair set off by deep red lipstick, Allred is a potent combination of scholarship and theatrics. Her keen intelligence and shrewd understanding of the power of the media have made her a contemporary success story in the world of law and politics.

ARBITER [*Latin, One who attends something to view it as a spectator or witness.*] Any person who is given an absolute power to judge and rule on a matter in a dispute.

Definition enclosed in book logos with Latin translation provided

WEST'S
ENCYCLOPEDIA
of
AMERICAN
LAW

WEST'S ENCYCLOPEDIA of AMERICAN LAW

Volume 7

WEST GROUP

This encyclopedia is the result of efforts by numerous individuals and entities from the Twin Cities and around the United States. West Group wishes to thank all who made this publication, its quality and content, a priority in their lives.

In addition to the individuals who worked on *West's Encyclopedia of American Law*, West Group recognizes Harold W. Chase (1922–1982) for his contributions to *The Guide to American Law: Everyone's Legal Encyclopedia.*

COPYRIGHT ©1998 By
    WEST GROUP
    610 Opperman Drive
    P.O. Box 64526
    St. Paul, MN 55164-0526
All rights reserved
Printed in the United States of America
05 04 03 02 01 00 99 98   8 7 6 5 4 3 2 1 0
Library of Congress Cataloging in
    Publication Data
ISBN: 0-314-20160-2 (Hard)

West's encyclopedia of American law.
    p.   cm.
    Includes bibliographical references and
       indexes.
    ISBN 0-314-20160-2 (hard   :
       alk. paper)
    1. Law—United States—Encyclopedias.
    2. Law—United States—Popular works.
    I. West Publishing Company.
KF154.W47   1997
348.73'03 —dc20
[347.30803]   96-34350
                                          CIP

PRODUCTION CREDITS

Cover, interior design, and page layout:
    David J. Farr, ImageSmythe
Composition: Carlisle Communications
Proofreading: Maureen Meyer
Photo research: Elsa Peterson Ltd.
Art research: Nanette E. Bertaut
Editorial research: Pat Lewis
Artwork: Patricia Isaacs, Parrot Graphics
Indexing: Schroeder Indexing Services

This publication is designed to provide information on the subjects covered. It is sold with the understanding that the publisher is not engaged in rendering legal or other professional advice. If legal advice or other professional assistance is required, the services of a competent professional person should be sought.

WEST'S COMMITMENT TO THE ENVIRONMENT

In 1906, West Publishing Company began recycling materials left over from the production of books. This began a tradition of efficient and responsible use of resources. Today, 100 percent of our legal bound volumes are printed on acid-free, recycled paper consisting of 50 percent new paper pulp and 50 percent paper that has undergone a de-inking process. We also use vegetable-based inks to print all of our books. West recycles nearly 27,700,000 pounds of scrap paper annually—the equivalent of 229,300 trees. Since the 1960s, West has devised ways to capture and recycle waste inks, solvents, oils, and vapors created in the printing process. We also recycle plastics of all kinds, wood, glass, corrugated cardboard, and batteries, and have eliminated the use of polystyrene book packaging. We at West are proud of the longevity and the scope of our commitment to the environment.

West pocket parts and advance sheets are printed on recyclable paper and can be collected and recycled with newspapers. Staples do not have to be removed. Bound volumes can be recycled after removing the cover.

Production, printing, and binding by West Group.

PREFACE

The legal system of the United States is admired around the world for the freedoms it allows the individual and the fairness with which it attempts to treat all persons. On the surface, it may seem simple. Yet, those who have delved into it know that this system of federal and state constitutions, statutes, regulations, and common-law decisions is elaborate and complex. It derives from the English common law, but includes principles older than England, and from other lands. Many concepts are still phrased in Latin. The U.S. legal system, like many others, has a language all its own. Too often it is an unfamiliar language.

In 1983, West published *The Guide to American Law: Everyone's Legal Encyclopedia*, in response to a dearth of reference sources weaving the language of the law into the language of everyday life. *West's Encyclopedia of American Law (WEAL)*, developed with generous feedback from users of *The Guide*, replaces that set as an improved and updated legal encyclopedia. *WEAL* is a reference source devoted to the terms and concepts of U.S. law. It also covers a wide variety of persons, entities, and events that have shaped the U.S. legal system. *WEAL* contains thousands of entries, and a number of unique features and visual aids. It is the most complete reference source of its kind.

Main Features of This Set

Entries This encyclopedia contains over 4,000 entries devoted to terms, concepts, events, movements, cases, and persons significant to U.S. law. Entries on legal terms contain a definition of the term, followed by explanatory text if necessary. Entries are arranged al-phabetically in standard encyclopedia format for ease of use. A wide variety of additional features, listed later in this preface, provide interesting background and supplemental information.

Definitions Every entry on a legal term is followed by a definition, which begins and ends with the symbol of an open book (📖). The appendix volume includes a glossary containing all the definitions from the *WEAL*.

Cross-References To facilitate research, *WEAL* provides two types of cross-references, within and following entries. Within the entries, terms are set in small capital letters—for example, LIEN—to indicate that they have their own entry in the encyclopedia. At the end of the entries, related entries the reader may wish to explore are listed alphabetically by title.

In Focus Pieces In Focus pieces accompany related entries and provide additional facts, details, and arguments on particularly interesting, important, or controversial issues raised by those entries. The subjects covered include hotly contested issues, such as abortion, capital punishment, and gay rights; detailed processes, such as the Food and Drug Administration's approval process for new drugs; and important historical or social issues, such as debates over the formation of the U.S. Constitution. In Focus pieces are marked by the symbol that appears in the margin.

Sidebars Sidebars provide brief highlights of some interesting facet of accompanying entries. They complement regular entries and In Focus pieces by adding informative details. Sidebar topics include the Million Man March, in Washington, D.C., and the branches of the

IN FOCUS

U.S. armed services. Sidebars appear at the top of a text page and are set in a blue box.

Biographies WEAL profiles a wide variety of interesting and influential people—including lawyers, judges, government and civic leaders, and historical and modern figures—who have played a part in creating or shaping U.S. law. Each biography includes a time line, which shows important moments in the subject's life as well as important historical events of the period. Biographies appear alphabetically by the subject's last name.

Additional Features of This Set

Milestones in the Law A special section, Milestones in the Law, appearing at the end of selected volumes, allows readers to take a close look at landmark cases in U.S. law. Readers can explore the reasoning of the judges and the arguments of the attorneys that produced major decisions on important legal and social issues. Included in the Milestones section are the opinions of the lower courts; the briefs presented by the parties to the U.S. Supreme Court; and the decision of the Supreme Court, including the majority opinion and all concurring and dissenting opinions for each case.

Enhancements Throughout WEAL, readers will find a broad array of photographs, charts, graphs, manuscripts, legal forms, and other visual aids enhancing the ideas presented in the text.

Tables and Indexes WEAL features several detailed tables and indexes at the back of each volume, as well as a cumulative index contained in a separate volume.

Appendixes An appendix volume included with WEAL contains hundreds of pages of documents, laws, manuscripts, and forms fundamental to and characteristic of U.S. law.

Citations Wherever possible, WEAL entries include citations for cases and statutes mentioned in the text. These allow readers wishing to do additional research to find the opinions and statutes cited. Two sample citations, with explanations of common citation terms, can be seen below and opposite.

Bibliography A bibliography is included at the end of each book and in the index volume.

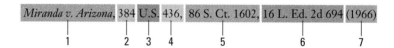

Miranda v. Arizona, 384 U.S. 436, 86 S. Ct. 1602, 16 L. Ed. 2d 694 (1966)
     1   2 3   4   5   6   7

1. *Case title.* The title of the case is set in italics and indicates the names of the parties. The suit in this sample citation was between Ernesto A. Miranda and the state of Arizona.
2. *Reporter volume number.* The number preceding the reporter name indicates the reporter volume containing the case. (The volume number appears on the spine of the reporter, along with the reporter name.)
3. *Reporter name.* The reporter name is abbreviated. The suit in the sample citation is from the reporter, or series of books, called *U.S. Reports,* which contains cases from the U.S. Supreme Court. (Numerous reporters publish cases from the federal and state courts.)

4. *Reporter page.* The number following the reporter name indicates the reporter page on which the case begins.
5. *Additional reporter citation.* Many cases may be found in more than one reporter. The suit in the sample citation also appears in volume 86 of the *Supreme Court Reporter,* beginning on page 1602.
6. *Additional reporter citation.* The suit in the sample citation is also reported in volume 16 of the *Lawyer's Edition,* second series, beginning on page 694.
7. *Year of decision.* The year the court issued its decision in the case appears in parentheses at the end of the cite.

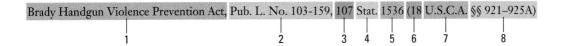

Brady Handgun Violence Prevention Act, Pub. L. No. 103-159, 107 Stat. 1536 (18 U.S.C.A. §§ 921–925A)

     1   2   3 4 5 6   7   8

1. *Statute title.*
2. *Public law number.* In the sample citation, the number 103 indicates that this law was passed by the 103d Congress, and the number 159 indicates that it was the 159th law passed by that Congress.
3. *Reporter volume number.* The number preceding the reporter name indicates the reporter volume containing the statute.
4. *Reporter name.* The reporter name is abbreviated. The statute in the sample citation is from *Statutes at Large.*
5. *Reporter page.* The number following the reporter name indicates the reporter page on which the statute begins.
6. *Title number.* Federal laws are divided into major sections with specific titles. The number preceding a reference to the *U.S. Code Annotated* is the title number. Title 18 of the U.S. Code is Crimes and Criminal Procedure.
7. *Additional reporter.* The statute in the sample citation may also be found in the *U.S. Code Annotated.*
8. *Section numbers.* The section numbers following a reference to the *U.S. Code Annotated* indicate where the statute appears in that reporter.

continued

LEGAL REPRESENTATION 📖 The legal work that a licensed ATTORNEY performs on behalf of a CLIENT. 📖

Licensed attorneys have the authority to represent persons in court proceedings and in other legal matters. Many persons need an attorney to handle a legal problem or dispute at some point in their life.

When hiring an attorney, a careful consumer considers a number of variables, including the nature and importance of the case, the attorney's fee and payment arrangement, personal chemistry with the attorney, and the attorney's reputation.

Advertising Many attorneys advertise their services. Attorneys must obey all applicable advertising laws and must follow rules of professional conduct related to advertising. Under these rules they may not make false or misleading claims, create unjustified expectations, or compare the services of another attorney unless the comparison can be factually substantiated. An attorney may not make in-person or live telephone solicitations unless the attorney is related to the person or has a professional relationship with the person. An attorney may not contact a person after the person indicates a desire that the solicitations cease, and an attorney may not coerce or harass prospective clients. Aside from these and similar restrictions, attorneys generally are free to use the various media to promote their services.

Self-Representation If a case is simple, a person may wish to represent herself, or proceed PRO SE. The courts usually discourage self-representation because legal practice re-

quires special skills, and an unschooled pro se party is usually at a disadvantage in court. Even attorneys are well advised to hire another attorney for personal legal problems.

Duties and Obligations Legal representation places duties on both the client and the attorney. The client should provide the attorney with all information relevant to the case and keep the attorney apprised of new information. The client should be completely honest about the case with the attorney. The client also should follow the attorney's directives.

The client has an obligation to pay the attorney for the representation. If the client does not make timely payment, the attorney may decline to perform further work for the client. An attorney also may discontinue representation if the client wants the attorney to perform an unethical or illegal act, the client lies and refuses to correct the lie, the client makes representation unreasonably difficult, or the attorney discovers a CONFLICT OF INTEREST.

Generally, a conflict of interest is any circumstance that adversely affects a client, or limits the loyalty of the attorney to a client. For example, assume that an attorney regularly represents a corporation. A new client seeks the attorney's representation in a suit against the same CORPORATION. Representing the new client would be a conflict of interest. Generally, the attorney would not be able to take the case or continue representation after the conflict was discovered. However, the attorney may continue representation if he does not believe that the conflict would adversely affect the relationship with the corporation, and if both the corporation and the client agree to the attorney's representation. In practice, continued representation where there is a conflict of interest is rare.

If an attorney must withdraw from representation, he must act to protect the interests of the client. This may involve helping the client find another attorney, postponing court dates, and surrendering papers and documents relevant to the case. The attorney must return to the client any money owed to the client under the fee agreement.

An attorney has many obligations to her client. She must zealously defend the interests of the client and respond to the client's concerns. She must communicate with the client and work diligently on the client's case. She must keep the client informed about the status of the case and explain developments so that the client can make informed tactical decisions. She must abide by the client's decisions regarding the objectives of the representation. With few exceptions an attorney may not divulge client communications to outside parties without the client's consent.

Attorneys are OFFICERS OF THE COURT, and as such they must follow the law and obey ethical constraints. They may not harass persons in the course of representation. They may not assist a client who they know will not tell the truth about the case. An attorney should not begin a romantic affair with the client during the course of legal representation. In most states such behavior is an ethical violation. No attorney in any state may perform legal services in exchange for sexual relations.

Fees Attorneys' fees vary by attorney and by case. An attorney may charge a client in several different ways. The most common forms of billing include flat fees, hourly rates, contingent fees, and retainers.

A flat fee is a dollar amount agreed to by the attorney and the client before the attorney begins work on the case. The flat fee is favored by many attorneys because it is a simple transaction and because the attorney is paid at the beginning of the representation. The attorney identifies the amount of work that the case will require and calculates a reasonable fee based on the time and effort involved. If the attorney spends less time on the matter than anticipated, the attorney may keep the excess payment, unless the attorney and client agree otherwise. Conversely, the attorney who charges a flat fee may not later demand more money if the case requires more time and effort than originally anticipated.

An hourly rate is a predetermined amount charged for each hour of the attorney's work. The attorney and client may agree that hourly fees are to be paid periodically, or in one lump sum at the end of the case. The time that an attorney charges for legal work is called billable time, or billable hours. Hourly rates vary according to the attorney's expertise and experience. Some critics have argued that hourly rates discourage quick work and expedited resolutions. Before agreeing to an hourly rate, prospective clients should ask for a written estimate of the number of billable hours that the attorney anticipates will be necessary to complete the matter.

A CONTINGENT FEE is a percentage of the amount recovered by the client. A contingent fee is not paid by the client until the client wins money DAMAGES from a defendant. Attorneys offer such a fee if the client stands a good chance of winning a sizable cash settlement or JUDGMENT. Contingent fees cannot be used in DIVORCE cases, CHILD CUSTODY cases, and criminal cases.

Contingent fees are a gamble for the attorney. If the client does not win the case or wins less money than anticipated, the attorney may work for no or little pay. Common contingent fees range from 20 to 40 percent of the client's recovery. For PERSONAL INJURY and MEDICAL MALPRACTICE cases, laws in all states limit the percentage that an attorney may receive from a client's recovery. For other cases the percentage is negotiable between the client and attorney.

A client may retain an attorney for a specific period of time rather than for a specific project. In return for regular payment, the attorney agrees to be on call to handle the day-to-day legal affairs of the client. Most individuals do not have enough legal matters to keep an attorney on RETAINER.

The term *retainer* also refers to an initial fee paid by the client. Retainers often are used by attorneys who charge an hourly rate, and some attorneys add an initial retainer to a contingent fee.

Pro Bono Services The term *pro bono* means "for the good." In practice pro bono describes legal work performed free of charge. Pro bono work is not required of attorneys in most jurisdictions, but courts occasionally appoint attorneys to represent an indigent client free of charge. Under Rule 6.2 of the ABA's Model Rules of Professional Conduct, a lawyer may refuse an appointment, but only if: (1) the appointment would somehow violate another rule of conduct (such as conflicts of

HIRING AN ATTORNEY

The first task in hiring an attorney is to find one who can manage the particular legal problem at issue. All attorneys are not equally skilled in every area of the law. Like many other professionals, attorneys tend to specialize in certain areas of practice such as contracts, patents, family matters, taxes, personal injuries, criminal matters, and business matters. A person facing criminal charges, for example, will want to contact an attorney who specializes in criminal defense work, not a patent attorney.

Some attorneys are known for their skill in certain types of cases within a specialty. For example, a criminal defense attorney may be competent to handle any criminal case, but may be especially proficient in drunk driving cases or homicide cases. Attorneys who specialize in certain types of cases often have developed a network of helpful contacts and have a great deal of experience with the kinds of issues involved in these cases.

Some attorneys are general practitioners, proficient in a broad range of legal topics. These attorneys are generally less expensive than specialists. However, if a general practitioner is not competent in a particular area, she may need to put more time and effort into the case than would a specialist, and the client will have to pay for this extra work.

IN FOCUS

Many businesses specialize in making attorney referrals at no charge to the consumer. They offer lists of attorneys categorized by area of expertise or type of client. For example, some referral services list attorneys who specialize in representing persons of color, women, or gay men and lesbians.

After obtaining a list of qualified attorneys, the consumer should have an initial consultation with several attorneys if possible. Some attorneys offer such a consultation at no cost, whereas others may charge a nominal fee. In either case the initial consultation does not obligate the consumer to hire that attorney or firm.

At the initial consultation, the potential client should provide the attorney with as much information as possible about the case. Relevant information may include pictures, witness statements, and other documents. This information helps the attorney make an informed judgment about the case.

The attorney generally does not give legal advice at the initial consultation. Instead, the attorney will ask questions to determine whether he is able to represent the consumer. The attorney will not begin to work on the case until a fee arrangement has been reached with the consumer.

In deciding whether to retain a particular attorney, the consumer should look at a number of issues. If money is a consideration, the consumer should weigh the attorney's fee against the importance of the case. For example, the consumer may be willing to spend more money on an attorney if facing criminal charges than if involved in a minor civil matter.

If the consumer and the attorney will need to meet frequently during the representation, the consumer should consider the location of the attorney's office and required travel time.

Another consideration is personal chemistry. Attorneys and clients do not have to be friends, but they should have some rapport so that they can work together. If the consumer does not feel comfortable with an attorney, she should find another attorney.

If time is a consideration, the consumer should ask how long the attorney expects the case to last. Some attorneys work more quickly than others.

A consumer should also consider the reputation of the attorney. Attorneys usually are willing to provide a list of previous clients as references. All states have a professional responsibility board that oversees the conduct of attorneys in the state. These boards may be able to give consumers information regarding ethical violations by attorneys. The consumer also may want to ask if an attorney has malpractice insurance, which compensates clients who are victims of incompetent legal work.

interest) or law; (2) the appointment would unreasonably burden the lawyer; or (3) the lawyer finds the appointment so repugnant that he would not be able to effectively represent the client. Attorneys often perform pro bono work in order to contribute to their community and create goodwill for the firm.

Public Legal Services Legal services organizations exist in all states to provide free or low-cost legal services to qualified persons. Legal services offices are funded by a variety of sources, including private businesses, private individuals, and federal, state, and local govern-

ments. Civil matters such as bankruptcies, divorces, and landlord-tenant disputes are handled by legal aid agencies. Criminal matters are handled by state PUBLIC DEFENDERS.

Private Legal Services Some organizations sell "legal insurance" for a fee. Legal insurance is a form of prepaid legal service in which the consumer pays a premium to cover future legal needs. Such a service may be offered through LABOR UNIONS, employers, or other private businesses. Most legal insurance policies do not cover all types of legal matters, and the policyholder may not be entitled to choose his lawyer. The consumer should determine the scope and nature of the legal representation offered in legal insurance packages.

Other Considerations If a client does not believe she has received competent legal representation, the client has several options. In a criminal case, if a convicted defendant believes she received incompetent representation, the defendant can address the issue on APPEAL, and the APPELLATE COURT may reverse the VERDICT. If a client believes that an attorney has committed misconduct, the client may contact the board of professional responsibility in the state in which the attorney practices. If an attorney is found to have violated the law or the applicable professional conduct code, the attorney is subject to discipline by the board. Discipline can range from a reprimand to revocation of the attorney's LICENSE.

In some states if an attorney and client have a dispute over fees, the attorney may place a LIEN on the client's money or PERSONAL PROPERTY. There are two types of attorney liens: a retaining lien and a charging lien. A retaining lien gives the attorney the right to retain money or property belonging to the client until the client pays the bill. The attorney does not have to go to court to do this, but the judge may order a hearing at the request of the client to determine whether the attorney has good reason to keep the money or property.

A charging lien gives an attorney the right to be paid from the proceeds of a lawsuit. For example, if an attorney charges a client a contingency fee and the attorney wins a large monetary award for the client, the attorney is entitled to a predetermined share of the award. Generally, the attorney may keep a certain amount for services rendered even if he was fired by the client. However, if a court finds that the client properly fired the attorney for misconduct, the attorney may not be entitled to any portion of the client's award.

CROSS-REFERENCES

Attorney-Client Privilege; Attorney Misconduct; Attorney's Lien; Ethics; Legal Advertising; Malpractice; Pro Bono Publico; Right to Counsel.

LEGAL REPRESENTATIVE In its broadest sense, one who stands in place of, and represents the interests of, another. A person who oversees the legal affairs of another. Examples include the EXECUTOR or administrator of an ESTATE and a court appointed GUARDIAN of a MINOR or incompetent person.

This term is almost always held to be synonymous with the term *personal representative*. In accident cases, the member of the family

The board of directors of the Legal Services Corporation directs the distribution of grants to legal services programs around the country. These programs provide financial support for legal assistance in civil matters to people who are poor.

entitled to benefits under a WRONGFUL DEATH statute.

LEGAL RESERVE Liquid assets that life INSURANCE companies are required by statute to set aside and maintain to assure payment of claims and benefits. In banking, that percentage of bank deposits that must by law be maintained in cash or equally liquid assets to meet the demands of depositors.

LEGAL RESIDENCE The place of domicile—the permanent dwelling—to which a person intends to return despite temporary ABODES elsewhere or momentary absences.

A person can have several transitory residences, but is deemed to have only one legal RESIDENCE.

LEGAL RIGHT An interest that the law protects; an enforceable CLAIM; a PRIVILEGE that is created or recognized by law, such as the constitutional right to FREEDOM OF SPEECH.

LEGAL SERVICES CORPORATION The Legal Services Corporation (LSC) is a private, nonprofit organization established by Congress in 1974 to provide financial support for legal assistance in civil matters to people who are poor (Legal Services Corporation Act of 1974, 42 U.S.C.A. § 2996 et seq.). The LSC receives funds from Congress and makes grants to local nonprofit programs run by boards of directors made up of local lawyers, community leaders, and client representatives. LSC support is the backbone of legal aid funding in the United States. The organization has attracted opposition from conservatives who wish to abolish it.

The federal government began to make direct grants to legal aid organizations in 1965, during President LYNDON B. JOHNSON's war on poverty. Studies revealed that states were doing an inadequate job of providing legal assistance to people who were poor, especially in the South, the Southwest, and much of the Mid-

west. The LSC was established in 1974, during President RICHARD M. NIXON's administration, to establish a structure for distributing funds to qualified local providers of legal aid that was permanent and immune to political pressure.

The LSC is governed by an eleven-member board of directors, appointed by the president of the United States with the advice and consent of the Senate. No more than six members may be of one political party, and at least two members must be eligible clients. Through its Office of Field Services and its regional offices, the LSC distributes grants to legal services programs operating in neighborhood offices in all fifty states, the District of Columbia, Puerto Rico, the Virgin Islands, and Micronesia. Only three percent of its budget is spent on the administration costs for the home office; the rest goes to community programs.

The LSC supports local legal aid programs through training, research, sharing of information, and technical assistance. It also funds sixteen national support centers that provide specialized assistance to attorneys in representing their clients. Most of these support centers specialize in substantive areas of the law, such as housing, administrative benefits, and health. Others specialize in the unique legal problems of particular groups, such as Native Americans, migrant farmworkers, immigrants, and older people. Staff members of the support centers may become directly involved in litigation on behalf of their clients.

General research is conducted by the LSC's Institute on Legal Assistance. The institute is devoted to substantive study of the broad range of legal problems encountered by poor people that relate to the services provided by legal aid programs. The research projects of the institute are in five broad categories: problems posing the most serious consequences to people who are poor, such as income security and health benefit programs; gaps in substantive poverty law, such as rural issues; studies of agencies that provide benefits to people who are poor, such as welfare agencies and public hospitals; projects to prevent legal controversies and to create new procedures for settling disputes; and ways to evaluate how special legal institutions such as housing and small-claims court affect people who are poor. The institute also conducts seminars and holds meetings on these topics and others that deal with the effect of the law on poor people.

The LSC's 1995 budget of $415 million provided services directly to 1.7 million people and benefited some 5 million, mostly children living in poverty.

Legal tender includes all U.S. coins and currencies.

The LSC has been under attack for many years by conservative politicians and groups that allege that the legal aid programs it funds have engaged in political and lobbying activities, often at the expense of providing legal services needed by people who are poor. Critics argue that the LSC has been the legal pillar of the welfare state, opposing efforts by conservatives to rein in government programs. Congressional Republicans have sought either to drastically reduce funding of the LSC or to abolish the LSC altogether.

LEGAL TENDER ◫ All U.S. coins and currencies—regardless of when coined or issued—including (in terms of the Federal Reserve

System) Federal Reserve NOTES and circulating notes of Federal Reserve banks and national banking associations that are used for all debts, public and private, public charges, taxes, duties, and dues. ◫

LEGAL TITLE ◫ Ownership of PROPERTY that is cognizable or enforceable in a court of law, or one that is complete and perfect in terms of the apparent right of ownership and possession, but that, unlike equitable TITLE, carries no BENEFICIAL INTEREST in the property. ◫

BIOGRAPHY

Hugh Swinton Legare

LEGARE, HUGH SWINTON Hugh Swinton Legare was a lawyer, a legal scholar, and an attorney general of the United States under President JOHN TYLER.

Born January 2, 1797, in Charleston, South Carolina, to a wealthy French Huguenot father, both Legare and his sister, Mary, enjoyed a privileged upbringing and social advantages. But the family's money and influence could not change the physical handicap with which Legare was born. Prevented by his handicap from strenuous physical activity, Legare turned his attention to scholarly pursuits, and in these, he excelled.

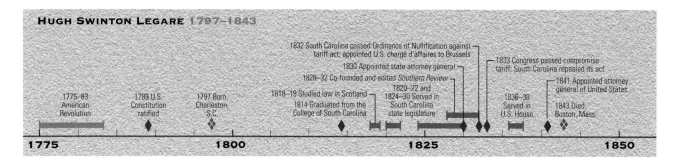

Hugh Swinton Legare 1797–1843

1832 South Carolina passed Ordinance of Nullification against tariff act; appointed U.S. charge d'affaires to Brussels

1830 Appointed state attorney general

1833 Congress passed compromise tariff; South Carolina repealed its act

1828–32 Co-founded and edited *Southern Review*

1841 Appointed attorney general of United States

1818–19 Studied law in Scotland

1820–22 and 1824–30 Served in South Carolina state legislature

1775–83 American Revolution

1789 U.S. Constitution ratified

1797 Born, Charleston, S.C.

1814 Graduated from the College of South Carolina

1836–38 Served in U.S. House

1843 Died, Boston, Mass.

1775   1800   1825   1850

He studied at Moses Waddel's Academy and the College of South Carolina, and graduated in 1814. He worked toward degrees in law and languages in the United States (1814–17) and in Scotland (1818–19). Legare's interest in Roman and CIVIL LAW was developed at Edinburgh University under the tutelage of Professor Dugald Stewart. Stewart, a disciple of legal philosopher Friedrich von Savigny, praised the systematic character of ROMAN LAW, and argued that Anglo-American COMMON LAW could be made more precise and scientific by the application of the principles of deductive reasoning.

The notion that law—like geometry—could be treated as a deductive science was embraced by Legare and became a lifelong interest. He amassed a large personal library containing works on Roman and civil law, and he encouraged legal and philosophical discussions on the subjects by making his library available to practicing attorneys and professional academics. This library, which contained the works of Johan Gottlieb Heineccius, a German jurist and philosopher, Jacques Cujas, a pre-revolutionary French jurist, and Savigny, was among the best in the United States. Both Heineccius and Cujas were legal scholars who wrote about the relationship between Roman law and their own legal systems. At the time, Legare's library contained more Roman and civil law volumes than did the Library of Congress, which had inherited THOMAS JEFFERSON's collection of books on Roman law.

Legare wrote extensively on law, legal philosophy, and classical literature throughout his life. As a young man, he partnered with botanist Steven Elliot, Sr., and other prominent Charleston intellectuals to establish a quarterly magazine devoted to all disciplines of scholarly writing. According to its masthead, the *Southern Review* proposed "to offer to our fellow citizens one Journal in which they may read without finding themselves the objects of perpetual sarcasm." Legare was a principal contributor until the death of his partner and the demands of his political career caused the magazine to fold.

Legare entered politics shortly after his return to the United States in 1819. He settled on

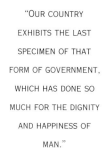

"OUR COUNTRY EXHIBITS THE LAST SPECIMEN OF THAT FORM OF GOVERNMENT, WHICH HAS DONE SO MUCH FOR THE DIGNITY AND HAPPINESS OF MAN."

St. John's Island, off the South Carolina coast, with the intention of developing a cotton plantation, but his physical limitations soon forced a change of plans. Within a year, he was elected to represent St. John's Island in the South Carolina state legislature.

In 1822 Legare gave up his plantation and moved back to his family home in Charleston. He practiced law and campaigned for reelection to the state legislature—this time as a representative from Charleston. He was elected in 1824 and served until 1830, when he was named state attorney general.

During Legare's tenure as state attorney general, the nullification crisis in South Carolina came to a head. (Nullification is a doctrine asserting the right of a state to prevent within its borders the enforcement of an act of the federal government not authorized by the U.S. Constitution as interpreted by the highest legislative authority of the state.) Convinced that the 1828 and 1832 federal TARIFF laws favored Northern industry and threatened Southern SLAVERY, the South Carolina legislature declared them to be unconstitutional, and threatened to secede from the Union if the federal government moved to enforce them. Legare opposed the nullification group, spoke on behalf of the Union, and cautioned the federal government against any exercise of authority that "might tip the political balance . . . toward the nullifiers" and stir the citizens to secession. For his efforts, he was rewarded with a diplomatic post in Brussels. Legare was named U.S. chargé d'affaires in 1832.

After fulfilling his obligations in Brussels and enjoying an extended tour of Europe, Legare returned to the United States in the fall of 1836. On his return, he was elected as a Union Democrat to represent South Carolina in the U.S. Congress. He was defeated in the 1838 election when his view of fiscal policy did not coincide with that of his constituents.

Following his defeat, Legare returned to Charleston and, for the first time in his career, concentrated on the practice of law. He tried a number of important cases and made his mark in the South Carolina and federal courts. U.S.

Supreme Court justice Joseph Story said, "His argumentation was marked by the closest logic; at the same time he had a presence in speaking I have never seen excelled."

Legare also returned to writing, authoring articles on Demosthenes, Athenian democracy, and Roman law. During the presidential campaign of 1840, Legare affiliated with the Whig party, and he began a series of articles in support of William Harrison, and later Tyler, which appeared in the *New York Review*.

In appreciation for his support, President Tyler named Legare attorney general of the United States in 1841. Because of Legare's foreign service experience in Belgium and his thorough knowledge of both civil and international law, he was a highly regarded member of the cabinet. As attorney general, Legare replaced Daniel Webster on the Ashburton Treaty Commission; he is credited with contributing important portions of the treaty related to the right of search.

When Webster resigned as secretary of state in May 1843, Legare assumed a number of his duties and was named secretary ad interim. A month later, on June 2, 1843, Legare died suddenly while accompanying President Tyler to the dedication of the monument at Bunker Hill, in Boston.

LEGATEE A person who receives PERSONAL PROPERTY through a WILL.

The term *legatee* is often used to denote those who inherit under a will without any distinction between REAL PROPERTY and personal property, but technically, a *devisee* inherits real property under a will.

LEGATION The persons commissioned by one government to exercise diplomatic functions at the court of another, including the minister, secretaries, attachés, and interpreters, are collectively called the *legation* of their government. The word also denotes the official residence of a foreign minister.

LEGES HENRICI [*Latin, Laws of Henry.*] A book written between 1114 and 1118 containing Anglo-Saxon and Norman law. It is an invaluable source of knowledge of the period preceding the full development of the Norman law.

LEGISLATE To enact laws or pass resolutions by the lawmaking process, in contrast to law that is derived from principles espoused by courts in decisions.

LEGISLATION Lawmaking; the preparation and enactment of laws by a LEGISLATIVE body.

Legislative bodies exist to enact legislation. The legislative process is a series of steps that a legislative body takes to evaluate, amend, and

vote on proposed legislation. The U.S. Congress, state legislatures, county boards, and city councils engage in the legislative process. Most legislation is enacted by Congress and state legislatures.

Legislative Bills A formal work of a LEGISLATURE begins with the submission of a bill to the legislature for consideration. A bill is a draft, or tentative version, of what might become part of the written law. A bill that is enacted is called an ACT or STATUTE. The entire legislative process is concerned with the words used in the bill to communicate the values, judgments, and purposes of the proposal. Legislators need to understand what is intended by the bill and who will be affected by it.

A legislature decides whether certain words should be enacted and have the force of law. Implementation of legislation is left to other entities, both public and private, such as law enforcement agencies, the courts, community leaders, and government agencies.

The selection of appropriate language for legislation is critical. An idea becomes an item of legislative business when it is written as a bill. A bill is amended to accommodate interested and affected groups and to eliminate technical defects. More legislative attention is generally devoted to decisions on AMENDMENTS than to disputes over whether a bill will be passed. An able legislator or supporter of a piece of legislation constantly seeks ways to silence opposition or convert opponents into supporters. Many important provisions that finally become law are adjusted by amendments in order to accommodate conflicting viewpoints.

Sources of Legislation Ideas for legislation come from many sources. Legislators who have experience and knowledge in a particular field introduce bills that they think will improve or correct that field. Legislators often copy legislation because an idea that works well in one jurisdiction can be useful to its neighbors. For example, in the 1970s legislation that created "no-fault" divorces was copied state by state.

Legislators receive proposals from the National Conference of Commissioners on Uniform State Laws. This conference of 250 lawyers, which is appointed by governors to represent the states, proposes UNIFORM ACTS that are of scholarly quality. Uniform acts, such as the Uniform Probate Code, have been widely enacted. See also COMMISSIONERS ON UNIFORM LAWS.

The Council of State Governments, the American Law Institute, the AMERICAN BAR ASSOCIATION, and numerous other organizations all produce MODEL ACTS for legislatures. Even if a uniform or model act or a law used in a neighboring state is not totally applicable, it is easier to edit and revise it than to draft a new one.

Legislation is not motivated solely by ideas. Modern legislation is often concerned with changing or protecting social and economic interests. Interest groups usually become involved in the legislative process through lobbyists, who are persons they hire to act for them. Often lobbyists work to protect the status quo by defensive lobbying, that is, arguing against a piece of legislation. Other times lobbyists propose a bill. Whether opposing or proposing change, lobbyists typically inform legislators about the expected effect of legislation on their particular interest group. Lobbyists also influence legislation through financial contributions to the political campaign committees of legislators.

Legislators and executives win their office by promising programs during election campaigns. Public opinion is focused on an executive (PRESIDENT or governor), so he is under special pressure to propose legislation. The president's State of the Union speech, usually given in January each year, is both a report on the current state of affairs and a call for certain legislative action. State governors typically give a similar speech to their citizens each year as well.

Modern legislatures have a large staff that helps prepare legislation. On occasion studies are authorized when a problem is recognized and no solution is readily available. Major legislation often starts with a blue-ribbon legislative commission, which might include citizen members and an independent staff from the academic community. A handful of states have created permanent law revision commissions, which operate independently of the legislature.

In addition, most states have independent offices that act as editors, putting legislative ideas into formal, statutory language that conforms to current usage in the JURISDICTION. Modern legislation has become increasingly lengthy and complex, making it difficult for a single legislator to craft a bill alone.

Legislative Procedure The procedure by which legislation is enacted varies within the following general structure.

A CONSTITUTION is the basic charter for governments in the U.S. legal system. Constitutions typically specify that some kinds of legislation, like a capital expenditure, require an extraordinary vote, such as passage by two-thirds rather than by a simple majority. Three separate readings, or announcements, of a bill to the full house, are commonly required before a vote can be taken. Some constitutions require a detailed reading each time, but legislatures have found ways to circumvent this mandate.

Constitutions often require an affirmative vote by a majority of all the members of a house, not merely those present, in order to pass a bill. They can also require that the names of members voting aye and nay be recorded in the journal of the legislative body. Constitutions can authorize the executive to VETO legislation, and establish a procedure for the legislature to override a veto. Sometimes a specific period of time is prescribed for the legislative session or term, and all work must be completed before expiration of the session.

It is common for a constitution to require that a bill pertain to only one subject, which must be expressed in the title of the bill. For example, An Act to Increase the State Sales Tax from Six to Seven Percent is a proper title for a bill that does exactly that and nothing else. This requirement efficiently packages legislative work, significantly affecting procedure, order, and efficiency. It does not apply to the U.S. Congress, but often applies to state and local legislatures.

Measures Introduced and Enacted in U.S. Congress, 1977 to 1994

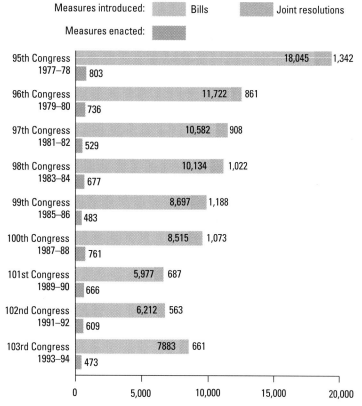

Source: U.S. Congress, Congressional Record and Daily Calendar, selected issues.

Each legislature adopts its own rules to detail the organization and procedure of its body. A standard version of legislative rules is often adopted to cover any situation not governed by a specific rule. Legislatures frequently need to depart from regular procedure in order to accomplish tasks. Therefore, special rules usually provide for the suspension of normal procedure, when necessary. A rules suspension can be allowed only by a two-thirds vote, so that minorities are better insulated from retaliatory or unforeseen abandonment of regular procedure.

Some of the work of the legislature can be accomplished by RESOLUTION rather than by bill. A resolution is used to settle internal matters or to make a public pronouncement without enacting a law. Resolutions are used to adopt the rules of the house, to establish committees, to initiate investigations, and to authorize and hire legislative employees. Even more mundane daily work can be accomplished by a MOTION on the floor. A motion lacks the formality of a resolution in that it cannot be formally announced and printed in the record.

A resolution takes one of several forms. A senate resolution or assembly resolution is adopted by only one house. A JOINT RESOLUTION originates in one house and then is passed in the other house, having the full force of official legislative action. This is the customary form for proposing state CONSTITUTIONAL AMENDMENTS and ratifying amendments to the U.S. Constitution. A CONCURRENT RESOLUTION, like a joint resolution, originates in one house and is assented to by the other. It lacks the legal effect of a normally adopted joint resolution, and is often used to express an opinion. Petitions from state legislatures to the president or to the U.S. Congress are drawn as concurrent resolutions. Commendations to persons who have performed socially significant deeds and to victorious athletic teams are typical concurrent resolutions.

The Enactment of a Bill A bill must follow certain customary steps through a legislature. It is introduced by an elected member who acts as a sponsor. The chief sponsor, who might or might not be the author of the bill, is the legislator who manages the bill as it progresses through the body and who explains it to other legislators. The bill may also have cosponsors, who attach their names to the bill to add support.

When the bill is introduced, it is referred to a standing committee. Whenever possible the bill's sponsors and the legislative leadership attempt to steer the bill to a particular committee. In most legislatures there is room for discretion in the reference of bills. Major legislation might have to be referred to several committees, so the issue might be who receives it first.

Once the bill is referred, the committee must be convinced to place it on the agenda so that it can be considered and passed. The committee chair is in charge of the committee, and requests for a slot on the agenda of the committee must be directed to the chair and the chair's staff. An autocratic chair can decide which bills to consider without consulting committee members, but much of the work of a committee is done by consensus.

Competition for committee time is generally intense. Usually bills that are heard are essential, popular, or generally beneficial. Occasionally they are noncontroversial or not especially appealing to the chair. A bill can even be scheduled merely to impede another, unfavorable proposal. If a spot cannot be attained on the agenda, a sponsor can seek consideration by a subcommittee so that a rough proposal can be polished into a draft that will be more appealing to the full committee.

Legislative procedure is designed so that a bill is heard when a need for it is demonstrated. Unnecessary or poorly drafted bills are bottled up in committees where no one takes time to consider them. As a bill approaches passage, it becomes more difficult to amend it or kill it. Efforts made early in the history of the bill are generally more effective. For example, fewer members have to be persuaded when a bill is still being considered by a committee, and fewer compromises have to be made.

If a committee decides not to act on a bill and tables it, that bill is effectively stopped for that session of the legislature. If the committee recommends that the bill be indefinitely postponed, the bill is formally killed and that recommendation is reported to the floor as a committee report to be confirmed by house vote. Adoption of the committee report officially kills the bill. If the committee recommends that the bill be passed, the bill is submitted to the floor with a favorable report, which is essential to its passage. If the bill must go through more than one committee, the first committee must then refer it to the second, and the first favorable decision gives it some momentum toward success.

After a legislative body approves a favorable committee report, the bill is placed on the agenda for floor action, or action by the full body. The agenda can be lengthy. During its wait for floor action, the bill is subject to a motion to refer it again to the same committee or any other committee for reconsideration. Making a successful motion to refer it again is a classic method of defeating a bill without taking the difficult step of going on record against it on a final vote.

In most state legislatures, a bill is first considered on the floor in a committee of the whole, in which every member of the house sits as a committee to debate the bill. A committee of the whole is derived historically from the desire of early English parliaments to act in semisecrecy, without recorded votes that the queen or king could monitor. The idea has survived, and legislators continue to act without suffering the political consequences of an unpopular vote on the record.

Procedurally, the consideration of a bill by a committee of the whole allows debate without limits on the duration of time or number of times a member can speak. It also provides an interval between the first formal floor consideration and final passage of the bill, which permits more time for careful deliberation.

The use of the committee of the whole has, however, declined. More bills are submitted for deliberation by the legislative body and final vote while the subject is still fresh in the members' minds. A legislature can, therefore, eliminate use of the committee of the whole for some types of bills, for special circumstances, or altogether.

Almost every legislature has a consent calendar for bills identified by committee reports as noncontroversial. Each such bill is read at the appointed time and briefly explained, and a vote is taken. If even a few votes dissent, the bill is returned to the regular calendar for examination. The consent calendar permits a legislature to dispose of a host of minor bills expeditiously.

As a general practice, the legislative leadership uses a special order to schedule debate, amendment, and passage of a bill at a single session. A bill can be designated for special order by a vote of two-thirds, or more commonly by selection by a priority-setting or policy committee. Bills from APPROPRIATIONS and tax committees might receive automatic special order privileges because of the necessity for their enactment.

Some constitutions, including that of the United States, permit a vote on the final passage of a bill to be oral and unrecorded unless a member calls for the ayes and nays. Ordinarily, a member is entitled to do this on any motion, including final passage.

Immediately following a vote on final passage, a motion to reconsider can be made. In effect this motion requests another vote on the bill. Although the number of successful reconsiderations is small, the device can facilitate additional compromise to accommodate competing interests on the issue. Generally, only one reconsideration of any vote is allowed, so both sides endeavor to gather switch votes after a close vote. The victorious side attempts to conduct the vote on the reconsideration immediately, so that the losers do not have time to marshal strength. In the U.S. Congress, a motion to reconsider is made routinely after every vote, to give the vote a finality by precluding such a motion at a later time.

In a BICAMERAL legislature, once a bill is passed in one house, the chances for success in the second house are good because the bill has become a product of compromise. There is no concern about wasting time on a bill that can never succeed, because the bill has already cleared the other house. Busy legislators prefer not to repeat debates that have already been extensive in the first house, and they respect the value of cooperation between the two houses.

A single bill must be passed by both houses of a bicameral legislature and be signed by the executive. If the houses pass identical but separate bills, one of the houses must approve the official bill from the other house. The presiding officer and the chief clerical official must verify passage of a bill by signing the official or enrolled copy before the bill is ready for the executive's signature. After the final affirmative vote for passage in the first house, the bill is put into an official engrossment, or formal final copy, and transmitted to the other house for consideration.

Since each house must pass the exact same bill, the form that is passed in the first house can be substituted for a parallel or companion bill in the second house. If the second house accepts the version that is adopted in the first house, it returns the bill with a message to that effect. The first house then enrolls, transcribes, and registers the bill on a roll of bills and submits it to the executive for signature.

If the second house amends the bill, it returns the bill to the first house with a message requesting agreement on the changes. If the amendments are acceptable, a motion is made to concur and to place the bill on repassage. If the motion passes, all the formalities of a final vote are repeated for the bill in its amended form. If repassed the bill is enrolled in its amended form, signed by the legislative officers, and submitted to the executive for signature.

When the two houses cannot agree on a final form for a bill, a complex procedure of compromise is attempted in a conference committee comprising usually three to five members from each house. If the conferees can reach agreement, a conference committee report is filed in both houses that reflects the final changes. Both houses must approve the report, without amendment, for the bill to be passed.

Once the bill is approved by both houses, it is put into final form and transmitted to the executive. If the executive signs the enrolled bill, it is filed with the secretary of state. The enrolled bill is then an act, a written law. Depending on the bill, the act may become effective upon signature of the executive or at some date specified in the bill.

Executive Veto Power An executive can refuse to sign a bill and can return it to the legislature with a veto message explaining why. The legislature can attempt, first in the house where the bill originated, to override the veto by an extraordinary vote, usually a two-thirds majority.

State governors in forty-three states also have the authority to select particular items from an appropriations bill and individually veto them. This authority, called the line-item veto, became popular because it allowed the executive to cancel specific appropriations items from bills that were hundreds of pages long. Congress enacted the federal line-item veto authority in 1996 (2 U.S.C.A. §§ 691, 692) to give the president the ability to impose cuts on the FEDERAL BUDGET. However, a federal district court ruled the law, the Line Item Veto Act, unconstitutional in *Byrd v. Raines*, 965 F. Supp. 25 (1997). The Supreme Court agreed to hear an appeal of the decision. The line-item veto, like a regular veto, can be overridden at the state and federal levels by a two-thirds majority vote.

If the executive does not sign a bill or return it to the legislature with a message of disapproval, the bill becomes law within a prescribed number of days. At the state level, the governor turns the bill over to the office of the secretary of state, and the fact that it became law without the governor's signature is noted. If the legislature adjourns before the governor's time for signing expires, the bill does not become law without this signature. The governor's time for consideration has been curtailed, and the adjournment prevents the governor from returning the bill with a veto message. In this case the governor can defeat the bill by refusing to act, which produces a pocket veto.

The veto power gives the executive a pivotal role in the legislative process, if the executive cares to assert her authority. Use of the veto power varies considerably, depending on the personality of the executive, the political allegiances of house members and independence of legislative leaders, local customs, and the quality of the work produced by the legislature.

CROSS-REFERENCES

Congress of the United States; Engrossed Bill; Enrolled Bill; House of Representatives; Legislative History; Lobbying; Senate.

LEGISLATIVE Pertaining to the governmental function of lawmaking or to the process of enacting laws.

LEGISLATIVE ACTS STATUTES passed by lawmakers, as opposed to court-made laws.

LEGISLATIVE COURT The term *legislative court* was coined in 1828 by Chief Justice JOHN MARSHALL, who wrote the opinion in *American Insurance Co. v. Canter*, 26 U.S. (1 Pet.) 516, 7 L. Ed. 242 (1828). In *Canter*, the High Court ruled that the U.S. Congress had the power to establish a FEDERAL COURT in the U.S. territory of Florida. Marshall held that Congress had this power under Article I, Section 8, Clause 9, of the U.S. Constitution. Marshall called courts created under this provision "legislative courts, created in virtue of the general right of sovereignty, which exists in the government."

On the federal level, the congressional authority to create courts is found in two parts of the U.S. Constitution. Under Article III, Section 1, "The judicial Power of the United States, shall be vested in one supreme Court, and in such inferior Courts as the Congress may from time to time ordain and establish." Article III, Section 1, also provides that the judges in the Supreme Court and in the inferior courts will not have their pay diminished and will hold their office during GOOD BEHAVIOR. This section establishes an independent JUDICIARY that cannot be influenced by threats of pay cuts or of removal without cause. Article III courts are called constitutional courts.

Article I, Section 8, Clause 9, confers on Congress the power to "constitute Tribunals inferior to the supreme Court." This authority is not encumbered by a clause requiring lifetime tenure and pay protection, so judges sitting on Article I courts do not have lifetime tenure, and Congress may reduce their salaries. Article I courts are called legislative courts.

According to the U.S. Supreme Court, under Article I, the Framers of the Constitution intended to give Congress the authority to create a special forum to hear matters concerning congressional powers, and to further the congressional powers over U.S. territories under Article IV, Section 3. This authority allowed the government to create special courts that can quickly resolve cases that concern the government. This is considered a benefit to society at large because it facilitates the efficient functioning of government.

The distinction between legislative courts and constitutional courts lies in the degree to which those courts are controlled by the legislature. Control of the judiciary by the legislature is forbidden under the SEPARATION-OF-POWERS doctrine. This doctrine states that the three branches of government—executive, legislative, and judicial—have separate-but-equal powers. Legislative courts challenge this doctrine because the pay rates and job security of their judges are controlled by a legislature.

The U.S. Supreme Court has identified three situations in which Congress may create legislative courts. First, Congress may create legislative courts in U.S. territories. This is because Congress has an interest in exercising the general powers of government in U.S. territories that do not have their own government. Such legislative courts exist in Guam, the U.S. Virgin Islands, and the Northern Mariana Islands. The local courts of the District of Columbia are also considered legislative courts.

Second, Congress may create legislative courts to hear military cases. This is because Congress has traditionally maintained extraordinary control over military matters. The U.S. Court of Military Appeals is such a legislative court.

Third, Congress may create legislative courts to hear cases involving public rights. Generally, these are rights that have historically been determined exclusively by the legislative or EXECUTIVE BRANCH. The government is always a party in such cases, and such cases generally involve matters of government administration. On the federal level, the only Article I court established under the public rights doctrine is the U.S. TAX COURT. This court hears cases involving federal taxes, brought by or against the INTERNAL REVENUE SERVICE or another federal agency.

Some scholars maintain that the public rights category of legislative courts could pose a threat to the independence of the federal judiciary. Because Congress is involved in many facets of life, these analysts fear that Congress could create an unacceptable number of courts that are not sufficiently independent. For the most part, that fear has not been realized. Congress has not created an inordinate number of Article I courts, and the U.S. Supreme Court has at times been vigilant in protecting the independence of Article III courts.

In 1982 the U.S. Supreme Court struck down a federal statute on the ground that it gave too much power to a legislative court (*Northern Pipeline Construction Co. v. Marathon Pipe Line Co.*, 458 U.S. 50, 102 S. Ct. 2858, 73 L. Ed. 2d 598). At issue in *Northern Pipeline* was the Bankruptcy Reform Act of 1978 (11 U.S.C.A. § 101 et seq.). This act created federal BANKRUPTCY courts to hear bankruptcy cases. Before the act bankruptcy cases were heard by U.S. district courts, which were independent Article III courts. The new bankruptcy judges were given a tenure of fourteen years, and their salaries were subject to adjustment. The new bankruptcy courts had the authority to decide contract and tort cases related to bankruptcy.

According to the Supreme Court, the bankruptcy courts had been given the authority to decide issues of private rights, which generally concern the rights of one private party in relation to another private party. Under the Supreme Court's interpretation of Article I, Section 8, Clause 9, legislative courts cannot decide issues of private rights, so the bankruptcy courts were declared unconstitutional.

Two years after the Supreme Court's decision in *Northern Pipeline*, Congress passed the Bankruptcy Amendments and Federal Judgeship Act of 1984 (28 U.S.C.A. § 1408 et seq.). This act created a distinction between core and noncore bankruptcy proceedings. Core proceedings were matters directly related to bankruptcy; noncore proceedings involved ancillary issues such as personal injury and wrongful death claims. Bankruptcy courts maintained jurisdiction in core proceedings. In noncore proceedings bankruptcy courts were limited to proposing findings of fact that could be thoroughly reviewed by a federal district court.

LEGISLATIVE FACTS Matters of such general knowledge that they need not be proven to an ADMINISTRATIVE AGENCY that is deciding a question of policy.

General information and ideas affecting a blanket increase in PROPERTY valuations are an illustration of legislative facts, as distinguished from individual grounds for the assessment of each parcel of property, which are ADJUDICATIVE FACTS—information pertaining to the businesses and activities of parties to administrative proceedings.

LEGISLATIVE HISTORY The discussions and documents, including committee reports, hearings, and floor debates, surrounding and preceding the enactment of a law.

Legislative history includes earlier, similar bills introduced but not passed by the LEGISLATURE; legislative and executive reports and studies regarding the legislation; transcripts from legislative committee hearings and reports from the committees; and floor debates on the bill.

The legislative history of a STATUTE is a unique form of secondary legal authority. It is not binding on courts in the way that PRIMARY AUTHORITY is. Federal and state constitutions, statutes, CASE LAW (judicial decisions), and agency regulations form the body of primary authority that courts use to resolve disputes. As SECONDARY AUTHORITY, legislative history is used only to decipher the precise meaning behind an ambiguous statute or statutory provision.

For example, suppose Congress passes a criminal law requiring that all persons under age eighteen who appear in public after sundown must carry a federal identification card, which must be produced for law enforcement officers on demand. If the statute contains no definition of the phrase "in public," a court faced with a case brought under it may have to consult the legislative history to determine precisely where minors may venture without the identification card.

The value of legislative history in the law is similar to that of academic TREATISES: both are extrinsic aids. Lawyers may use favorable language from legislative history and academic treatises when they are presenting arguments to a court, and courts may use it when they are attempting to interpret a statute.

In some countries, such as England, courts may not consider secondary sources in making any decision. In these countries the potential for judicial abuse of a secondary source such as legislative history is considered an unacceptable risk to the legislative and judicial processes. The fear is that a judge could use one particularly unrepresentative statement from a lengthy legislative debate to incorrectly interpret a statute. *North Haven Board of Education v. Bell*, 456 U.S. 512, 102 S. Ct. 1912, 72 L. Ed. 2d 299 (1982), illustrates why legislative history is of secondary importance. The question in *Bell* was whether a federal statute (Title IX of the Education Amendments of 1972, 86 Stat. 373, 20 U.S.C.A. § 1681 et seq.) barred gender-based discrimination in employment by educational institutions. In answering the question in the affirmative, the majority opinion relied heavily on the remarks of Senator Birch Bayh, the sponsor of the legislation. The dissenting opinion relied heavily on remarks by the same senator in reaching a different conclusion.

Not all legislative history in the United States has the same value. Generally, committee reports have the most weight with the judiciary. Remarks of legislators during floor debates have the least value. Committee hearings and reports from the president or governor are given varying weight, according to the court's need for the information.

Legislative history is never the only consideration in a case. In all cases courts examine the plain meaning of the words in the statute before looking at any legislative history. See also PLAIN-MEANING RULE.

The legislative history of federal statutes can be found in the various publications of special legislative commissions and legislative committee hearings, and in the *Congressional Record.* The *Congressional Record* is published by Congress each day that it is in session. It summarizes the proceedings of the previous day in both the Senate and the House of Representatives. Members of Congress also may publish unspoken remarks and all or part of their floor speeches. Collections of federal legislative history are maintained in law libraries and state government libraries. West Group issues a compilation of the statutes passed in each session of Congress and their legislative history. This compilation, called the *United States Code Congressional and Administrative News,* is available in state government libraries, in law libraries, and on West's on-line computer service, WESTLAW.

Legislative materials on the state level are more difficult to acquire. In most states committee reports and transcripts of floor debates are stored at the state government library at the state capitol for a certain period of time, such as two years. After that period of time, they may be shipped to a state archives office. Some well-stocked law libraries may have history on state legislation.

The availability of the history of local laws varies from JURISDICTION to jurisdiction. Some large cities preserve committee reports and legislative comments on local laws; most small towns leave no trace of the intent behind their laws.

Methods for storing state and local legislative history vary widely. To find the legislative history of a particular state or local statute, consult the reference librarian at the appropriate state government library or at a law library.

See also CANONS OF CONSTRUCTION.

LEGISLATURE ◫ A representative assembly of persons that makes statutory laws for a municipality, state, or nation. ◫

A legislature is the embodiment of the doctrine of popular sovereignty, which recognizes that the people are the source of all political power. Citizens choose by popular vote the legislators, or REPRESENTATIVES, they want to serve them. The representatives are expected to be sensitive to the needs of their constituents and to represent their constituents' interests in the legislature.

Structure   The federal legislature, the U.S. Congress, is BICAMERAL in structure, meaning that it consists of two chambers, in this case the House of Representatives and the Senate.

Each state has a legislature, and all state legislatures have two houses, except the Nebraska Legislature, which has only one. State legislative bodies have various official designations, including *state legislature*, *general assembly*, *general court*, and *legislative assembly*. Local legislatures are generally structured differently from the state and national model. They may be called city councils, or boards of aldermen and alderwomen.

The traditional bicameral structure of state and national legislatures developed out of early U.S. societal distinctions between the public in general and the propertied, wealthy class. This structure provided for a lower house and an upper house. The lower-house legislators were elected by the general voting public, and it was believed that their votes were likely to be radical. The upper-house legislators were elected by voters who owned more property, and it was believed that they would be more mindful of concerns to property owners.

Traditional bicameralism is still supported for various reasons. It is believed that because both houses must separately pass a BILL in order for the bill to become law, bicameral legislatures are less likely to pass hasty, ill-considered laws or to be subject to public passions. Proponents of unicameralism (a one-chamber system) cite lower costs, simpler procedures, better executive-legislative relationships, and legislative developments that are easier for the public to follow.

Federal and state legislatures range in size from the U.S. Congress, consisting of 535 members, to the Delaware state legislature, with fewer than 100 members. Legislatures organize themselves into a number of committees and subcommittees, which undertake in-depth study of issues within their area of expertise and focus. Each committee addresses the issues presented to it, recommends action, and changes bills before they are passed on for consideration by the full house. Once a bill is passed by the members of one house, it must go to the other house for approval. After both houses have approved a bill, it is presented to the president or governor to be signed into law or vetoed.

U.S. state legislatures and the U.S. Congress organize their members according to political party affiliations. The political party that represents the majority of a particular house of the legislature is able to organize and control the actions of that house. The lower house of the legislature chooses a member of the dominant political party to serve as Speaker. The upper house chooses a member of the dominant political party to serve as president. Generally, the members of the different political parties meet separately to determine what actions their party will take in the upcoming session of the legislature. Though there are exceptions, legislators tend to vote along party lines. Political parties are less able to command party loyalty from individual legislators in state legislatures than in the U.S. Congress.

The Speaker of the lower house is the presiding officer of that house and is generally the most powerful member of the house. The full membership of the house chooses the Speaker. The duties of the Speaker include appointing members of the standing committees in the lower house. The speaker typically considers party membership, seniority, and the opinions of other party members in making these appointments. Unless there are house rules to the contrary, the Speaker may also refer bills to committee. It is the role of the Speaker to interpret and apply the rules of procedure that govern the actions of the house.

In accordance with the U.S. Constitution, the VICE PRESIDENT of the United States officially presides over the U.S. Senate. Most state constitutions have similar rules, charging the lieutenant governor with the duty of presiding over the state's upper legislative house. In states that do not have a lieutenant governor, or do not give that individual power to preside over the upper house of the state legislature, a member of the upper house is selected by other members to serve as president of the house. The duties of the president of the upper house are similar to those of the Speaker of the lower house, although they generally do not include appointing members to committees. Some states that do permit the president of the upper house to appoint committee members diminish that power by making the appointments subject to approval by the whole membership of the house. In a state where the lieutenant governor serves as president of the upper house, if there is a tie on a vote in the upper house, the president of the house must cast the deciding vote. In the U.S. Senate and in states where the lieutenant governor presides over the upper house, the house selects one member to serve as president pro tem (for the time being) when the president of the house is absent.

Legislative sessions are the periods of time in which a legislature conducts its business. Each legislative session of the U.S. Congress is called a "Congress," lasts for two years, and is numbered consecutively. For example, the 104th Congress began in January of 1995 and ended in December of 1996. The 105th Congress

GALE ZUCKER/STOCK BOSTON

began in January of 1997. Each Congress begins in the year following a biennial election of members and is divided into two one-year "sessions." Most states have annual sessions, each lasting perhaps only a few months. The governor of a state may call a special session of the state legislature, outside of its normal meeting times, to address issues that require immediate attention.

Qualifications, Terms, and Compensation of Legislators
Members of the U.S. Congress are chosen to represent a particular state. Each state may elect two U.S. senators. The number of U.S. representatives a state may elect is determined by the population of the state, with a minimum of one.

Every state uses a district system to choose its state legislators. Under this system the state is divided into districts, often along county lines, with one or more legislators representing each district.

The Connecticut State legislature meets in Hartford, Connecticut. The relationship of state legislatures to state judicial and executive branches is very similar to the relationships among the three federal branches of government.

The applicable national or state constitution sets the qualifications for individuals who are eligible to serve as legislators. These rules are generally not restrictive, including only age, citizenship, and residency requirements. U.S. citizenship is a universal requirement, as is a certain period of state residency. A legislator must live in the state or district from which he or she is elected. Every state requires that members of the lower house of the state legislature be at least twenty-one years old. The U.S. Constitution requires members of the House of Representatives to be at least twenty-five years old, and members of the Senate to be at least thirty years old.

Congressional terms are six years for senators and two years for representatives. Terms for state legislators vary, but generally are either two or four years. Recent years have seen a push toward setting term limits in the U.S. Congress—that is, restricting the number of terms a U.S. legislator may serve. State legislatures have a higher rate of turnover and therefore do not generally face this issue.

Legislators are compensated for their services at various rates, and many state legislators are considered underpaid. Legislators also receive reimbursement for their expenses, including mileage to and from their home district and the location of the legislature. Legislators usually have the authority, by virtue of powers given to the legislature, to raise their own salaries. But they are often reluctant to do so for fear of a negative public reaction.

Relationship with Executive and Judicial Branches
The purpose of a legislature is to make, alter, amend, and repeal laws. Legislatures are empowered to enact laws by virtue of legislative jurisdiction, which is the authority vested in them by the national or state CONSTITUTION. The enumerated powers of Congress are provided for in Article I of the U.S. Constitution. In addition to their lawmaking duties, members of Congress also have the power to appropriate funds for government functions, institute taxes, regulate commerce, declare war, raise and support a military, approve presidential appointments, and impeach executive officers. Like the national model, each state legislature derives its powers from the state constitution.

In addition to the legislative branch, national and state governments include executive and judicial branches. The head of the EXECUTIVE BRANCH at the national level is the president of the United States, and at the state level is the governor. The executive branch enforces the laws enacted by the legislature. It can do so in a number of ways, including policing the streets and prosecuting those who violate laws.

The judicial branch interprets the laws passed by the legislature. The courts first look to the exact language of a particular law. Sometimes the meaning of the statutory language is not clear to the court, or the application of the language to the particular case before the court is doubtful. In such a circumstance, the court tries to determine what the legislature intended when it enacted the statute. Legislative intent can often be determined by looking to the history of the particular law and reading committee notes or congressional debates regarding the law. The judicial branch has developed many maxims of statutory interpretation over many years to help the courts carry out legislative intent when interpreting laws.

See also CONGRESS OF THE UNITED STATES; JUDICIAL REVIEW; LEGISLATIVE HISTORY.

LEGITIMATE 📖 To make lawful, such as when a child is born prior to the parents' marriage and they subsequently wed and thereby confer upon the child the same legal status as those born in lawful wedlock. See also ILLEGITIMACY.

That which is lawful, legal, recognized by law, or in accordance with law, such as legitimate children or legitimate authority; real, valid, or genuine. 📖

LEMON LAWS 📖 Laws governing the rights of purchasers of new and used motor vehicles that do not function properly and which have to be returned repeatedly to the dealer for repairs. 📖

Laws in all fifty states and the District of Columbia provide remedies to purchasers of defective new vehicles, often called lemons. These so-called lemon laws protect consumers from substantial defects occurring within a specified period after purchase, and provide that a manufacturer must either replace the lemon with a new, comparable car or refund the full purchase price. According to the consumer advocate group Consumers for Auto Reliability and Safety, automakers repurchase fifty thousand vehicles a year, about .33 percent of the 15 million vehicles sold annually.

California and Connecticut passed the first lemon laws in 1982, in response to dissatisfaction with remedies in state sales laws and the 1975 federal Magnuson-Moss Warranty Act (15 U.S.C.A. § 2301 et seq.). Magnuson-Moss and other laws previously in effect provided remedies for the breach of full warranties, but the automobile industry typically provided only limited warranties. Other states quickly followed California and Connecticut in an effort to provide relief to new-car buyers under limited warranties.

Lemon laws typically provide CONSUMER PROTECTION for owners of new cars, trucks, and vans. A significant minority of states also provide coverage for leased vehicles. Many states specify coverage for one year from delivery or for the written WARRANTY period, whichever is shorter; a handful of states mandate coverage for the shorter of two years or twenty-four thousand miles.

Lemon laws cover only substantial defects, meaning defects that substantially impair the use, value, or safety of the vehicle. If a defect is safety related, the manufacturer is usually allowed just one chance to fix it before the owner may invoke the lemon law; if a defect impairs the use or value of a vehicle, the manufacturer is usually permitted three or four attempts to repair it. A consumer may also invoke the law if a vehicle is out of service for a certain number of days because of any combination of substantial defects. The time out of service is cumulative, not consecutive, and ranges from fifteen to forty days. Paint defects, rattles, cosmetic flaws, jumpy suspensions, premature wear of the tires, and the like are not normally considered substantial defects.

The purchaser of a new car typically returns to the dealership to have repair work done. Therefore, the dealer knows that a defect exists. However, lemon laws generally require that the purchaser give the manufacturer written notification of a problem within a specific time frame. The manufacturer then has a final opportunity to repair the vehicle before a lawsuit may be commenced. It has been argued that this notice requirement is unduly burdensome for consumers, who are often unaware of it. Consumer advocates have also argued that such notice is redundant. A substantial defect means that the defect would be covered by the automobile's warranty. If a car requires repair for an item covered by warranty, it is done at no cost to the consumer. The manufacturer reimburses the dealer for the warranty repair; the manufacturer would have notice of the defect when the dealer requests reimbursement from the manufacturer for the repair.

After a consumer invokes the lemon law, the parties arbitrate the matter in an attempt to resolve it. Some statutes provide for a state-run ARBITRATION process. Others provide for arbitration provided by private groups such as the Better Business Bureau, or even a manufacturer-sponsored panel. Arbitration is an informal trial with a panel or individual deciding the matter. Each side tells its story. Mechanics might testify on behalf of either side. Lawyers are not required but may increase a consumer's likelihood of prevailing or settling prior to the arbitration hearing.

According to one report, fewer than 10 percent of the cases handled by a manufacturer-sponsored panel are decided in the consumer's favor. Consumers tend to fare slightly better in cases handled by the Better Business Bureau, and fare best of all under state-run arbitration procedures. An early 1990s survey of three states with state-run arbitration found that consumers were awarded a full refund or replacement car in at least half of the cases. Many states make the arbitrator's decision binding on the manufacturer but not on the consumer.

During arbitration automakers frequently argue that the consumer abused the car or failed to service the vehicle properly, or that the defect does not substantially affect the car's safety or value. For this reason consumers should save all documentation about a vehicle, as well as keep meticulous records of any service problems. One owner of a top-of-the-line luxury car succeeded in arbitration for a whining noise in the air conditioner because an advertising brochure promised that the car would be a soothing and calming haven.

States vary on whether the manufacturer or the consumer chooses the remedy. A lemon owner is entitled to a refund of the vehicle's purchase price, including sales tax, license, and fees, or a new, comparable car—minus a deduction for the value of the owner's use of the lemon. Some states also provide that the manufacturer reimburse the owner's attorneys' fees and costs for bringing the lawsuit.

Used-car purchasers must also be wary of lemons. Once a lemon has been repurchased by the manufacturer, either voluntarily or pursuant to an arbitrator's or judge's decision, scant protections prevent its resale elsewhere. States vary greatly on how much information must be disclosed to subsequent purchasers. Some states require the title of a lemon to carry a notation reflecting the lemon status. The notation varies from "nonconforming vehicle" to "defect substantially impairs use, value, or safety." A handful of states require that buyback stickers be placed on the vehicle. However, enforcement of such requirements is often a low priority for state governments, and enforcement of lemon laws effectively ends at a state's border. In response to complaints about resold lemons, in 1996 the Federal Trade Commission began investigating the possibility of imposing a national standard for the resale of lemons.

See also AUTOMOBILES.

LEND-LEASE ACT 📖 Legislation enacted by Congress in 1941 that empowered the president to sell, transfer, lend, or lease war supplies—

Under the Lend-Lease Act, the United States sent equipment, food, and weapons to its allies during World War II. Thousands of bags of sugar were stored in Casablanca, Morocco.

such as equipment, food, and weapons—to American allies during World War II.

In exchange for the valuable assistance provided under the Lend-Lease Act (55 Stat. 31 [1941]), the Allies were to comply with the terms set by the president for repayment. The Office of Lend-Lease Administration was created pursuant to the act to oversee the implementation of the program, but this function was later transferred to the Department of State.

Although the Lend-Lease Act was enacted to provide aid to China and the British Empire, eligibility under its provisions was expanded to include all Allies who were essential to the maintenance of the security of the United States. Subsequent reciprocal agreements with countries where American troops were stationed provided that the troops would receive comparable aid while stationed there.

President Harry Truman ended the lend-lease program in 1945.

LENIN, VLADIMIR ILYICH Vladimir Ilyich Lenin founded the Russian Communist party and led the 1917 Russian Revolution, which placed the Bolshevik party in charge of the government. The establishment of the Soviet Union can be traced to Lenin's study of revolution and the ruthless imposition of a one-party state based on Lenin's interpretation of Marxism. The Russian Revolution also profoundly affected U.S. society and politics.

Lenin was born Vladimir Ilyich Ulyanov on April 22, 1870, in Simbirsk, a town on the Volga River. The son of a government official, Lenin was a bright student. He entered Kazan University at Kazan in 1887. That same year his brother Alexander Ulyanov was hanged for taking part in an unsuccessful plot to kill Czar Alexander III, of Russia. Lenin was deeply influenced by his brother's actions. Within three months, he was expelled from school for protesting the lack of freedom in the university. He moved to St. Petersburg and entered St. Petersburg University, from which he graduated with a law degree in 1891.

During his academic period, Lenin studied the works of Karl Marx and his political philosophy, Marxism. In 1893 Lenin joined the Social Democratic group, which believed in Marxist principles. A gifted writer and speaker, Lenin soon traveled to Western Europe to meet with other Marxists. He was arrested by the czar's police in 1896 for revolutionary activities and sent into Siberian exile in 1897. During his exile Lenin wrote one of his most important works, *The Development of Capitalism in Russia* (1899).

Lenin was allowed to leave Russia in 1900. He traveled to Germany, where he began writing for a revolutionary newspaper called *Zarya* (Dawn), which was smuggled into Russia. He took the pen name Lenin at this time, hoping to confuse the police. In 1902 he wrote what is considered a masterpiece of revolutionary organization, *What Is to Be Done?* In this work Lenin advocated the use of a highly disciplined party of professional revolutionaries to lead the masses in an uprising against czarist Russia. This revolutionary party would serve as the "vanguard of the proletariat." It would also assume supreme control during this revolutionary period.

Disputes within Russian revolutionary circles over Lenin's ideas led to a split in 1903 between Lenin's Bolshevik party and the Menshevik party, which favored moderation. Bolsheviks followed Lenin's instructions to commit acts of terrorism within Russia. They also worked hard to organize TRADE UNION members and Russian sailors and soldiers.

During most of World War I, Lenin stayed in Switzerland. When revolution broke out in Russia in March 1917, Lenin returned with the aid of Germany, which hoped he would gain power and agree to a peace treaty. Accused of being a German agent by the provisional government, Lenin fled to Finland. He returned to Russia secretly in October 1917 and led the

Vladimir Ilyich Lenin led the 1917 Russian Revolution and established the Soviet Union, a one-party Communist state. Fear in the United States of further Communist revolutions in Europe led to the Red scare of 1919 and 1920.

CORBIS-BETTMANN

October Revolution, which toppled the provisional government and placed the Bolsheviks in charge.

Once in power Lenin moved quickly to eliminate all political opposition. He organized the Red Army (named after the color of the flag of the world Communist movement). The Red Army fought a civil war with the Whites, who opposed one-party and one-man rule by Lenin. The civil war ended in 1922, with the defeat of the White Army. During this period the U.S. government supported the Whites, fearing that the Russian Revolution was a prelude to further Communist revolutions in Europe. This fear seemed confirmed in 1919 when Lenin formed the Communist International to export revolution to the rest of the world.

In 1919 and 1920, U.S. anxiety about the Russian Revolution and the dictatorship of Lenin produced a national hysteria that has come to be known as the first RED SCARE. President WOODROW WILSON's attorney general A. MITCHELL PALMER created an antiradicalism unit and appointed J. EDGAR HOOVER to run it. In late 1919 and early 1920, Palmer raided suspected revolutionaries and subversives. Most of these suspects were not U.S. citizens. The largest "Palmer raid" occurred on January 2, 1920, when six thousand people were arrested. Palmer's agents abused the constitutional rights of these people, searching homes without warrants, holding individuals without giving specific charges, and refusing access to legal counsel. Many aliens were deported because of their radical political views.

Lenin's revolutionary zeal was tempered by the need to defeat the Whites and to establish a national government in the wake of the loss of lives and resources in World War I. Faced with economic ruin, Lenin instituted in March 1921 his New Economic Policy. This policy abandoned many socialist measures and permitted the growth of small businesses. Lenin also tried to get the United States and Europe to invest in the Soviet Union, but was refused because the Soviets had repudiated all foreign debts. The United States did, however, through its Commission for Relief, provide large amounts of food that may have helped save hundreds of thousands of lives.

Lenin's last years were marked by failing health and a concern about the direction of the Communist party and the Soviet Union. He worried about the increasing strength of the political bureaucracy and about JOSEPH STALIN's plottings to succeed him. In May 1922 he suffered a stroke, then returned to work against his doctor's advice. He suffered additional strokes in November 1922 and March 1923, the last one destroying his ability to speak clearly. Lenin died January 24, 1924, physically unable to appoint his successor. His body was preserved using special chemicals and placed in a tomb on Red Square in Moscow.

See also COMMUNISM.

LEOPOLD (NATHAN) AND LOEB (RICHARD)

In 1924, the city of Chicago, Illinois, was shocked by the brutal and senseless MURDER of adolescent Bobby Franks. The crime resulted in a sensational murder trial wherein eminent attorney CLARENCE DARROW achieved a brilliant victory despite an overwhelming amount of incriminating EVIDENCE.

Nathan Leopold (*b.* November 19, 1904, in Chicago, Illinois; *d.* August 29, 1971, in San Juan, Puerto Rico), age nineteen, and Richard Loeb (*b.* June 11, 1905, in Chicago, Illinois; *d.* January 28, 1936, in Joliet, Illinois), age eighteen, college students from wealthy families, were regarded as unusually intelligent. Their extraordinary reasoning powers compelled them to construct and execute the perfect crime. They decided that KIDNAPPING and murder would challenge their mental capacities to the fullest.

The two young men plotted their crime in 1923. They chose the names Louis Mason and Morton Ballard as aliases and successfully stole a typewriter from the University of Michigan to type a ransom note that would be difficult, if not impossible, to trace. By 1924 they had perfected their plan and accumulated their other necessities, including a chisel and acid.

Leopold and Loeb chose their victim by chance. The ransom note, already typed, had not been addressed to anyone in particular, since the abduction of their victim would be a spontaneous happening. On May 21, 1924, Leopold and Loeb drove around in a rented car near the Harvard School, a private preparatory school in the Kenwood area of Chicago's south side. The first possible victim was a youth named Levinson, who was an acquaintance of the two kidnappers. They drove around the block but lost sight of him. The next student they saw was fourteen-year-old Bobby Franks. Bobby Franks knew Leopold and Loeb from the neighborhood, and when the two college students offered Bobby a ride home, the boy accepted. Once he was in the car he was bludgeoned to death with a chisel. On the way to dispose of the body, the two killers stopped for something to eat. They then proceeded to a deserted area of Chicago, where they dumped

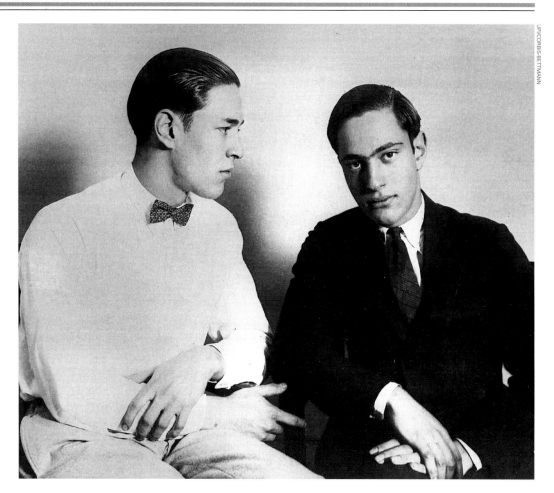

Richard Loeb and Nathan Leopold committed a nearly perfect crime that shocked Chicago in the 1920s. They later confessed but prominent lawyer Clarence Darrow won life sentences rather than the death penalty for both of them.

Bobby's body. They buried his clothes and poured acid on his face to hinder positive identification.

The Franks family was frantic with worry over their missing son. Leopold and Loeb began a ritual of telephone calls promising Bobby's safe return upon receipt of $10,000. A ransom note delivered the next day confirmed this demand.

As Mr. Franks was leaving to deliver the ransom money as directed by the kidnappers, he was notified that his son's body had been found. An extensive police investigation ensued, but Leopold and Loeb had cleverly disposed of all evidence. The two men followed the events of the frustrating investigation and joined in local discussions concerning the case.

There was one flaw in the perfect crime, and that was human frailty. A pair of glasses had been discovered near the site of the murdered boy's body, and the prescription was traced to Nathan Leopold. Unperturbed, Leopold stated that he had been with his friend Richard Loeb on the day of the murder, and they had spent the day driving around Chicago in the car owned by the Leopold family. The glasses were lost during a day of birdwatching, which Leopold often pursued in conjunction with an ornithology class he was teaching. Since they were seldom used, he had not noticed that the glasses were missing. Leopold's story was feasible, and his upstanding family and educational background added to his credibility; he was released.

More evidence began to emerge against Leopold and Loeb as the investigation continued. A paper typed by Leopold for a class was discovered, and when it was compared to the typewritten ransom note, the type was suspiciously similar. Further investigation revealed that the Leopold family car, which Leopold and Loeb supposedly used the day of the murder, had not left the garage; this information was corroborated by the family chauffeur.

Loeb panicked and confessed, forcing Leopold to do the same. They admitted that they had killed the boy for the excitement of committing a crime.

The case against Leopold and Loeb was airtight. The CONFESSIONS were authentic, and further evidence was elicited from the two men. The families of the killers appealed to prominent lawyer Clarence Darrow to defend the accused murderers.

Darrow opposed the idea at first, but felt that Leopold and Loeb would be convicted more on an emotional level than on legal expertise. Darrow knew they were guilty but agreed to attempt to secure a sentence other than the applicable death penalty.

The case came to court on July 21, 1924. Darrow requested that the case be decided solely by a judge, without a jury. Judge John R. Caverly consented.

Leopold and Loeb pleaded guilty. They had been examined by psychiatrists and declared legally sane. Darrow decided that since he could not argue that they were insane, he would try to prove that the two men were mentally diseased, which would not excuse their guilt but could be a mitigating factor in their sentencing. Darrow appealed to the mercy of the court in deciding the punishment for Leopold and Loeb.

The judge deliberated for ten days before rendering his decision. Leopold and Loeb were spared the death sentence and received sentences of life imprisonment.

LESSEE 📖 One who rents REAL PROPERTY or PERSONAL PROPERTY from another. 📖

A lessee of land is a tenant. See also LANDLORD AND TENANT.

LESSER INCLUDED OFFENSE 📖 A lesser crime whose elements are encompassed by a greater crime. 📖

A lesser included offense shares some, but not all, of the elements of a greater criminal offense. Therefore, the greater offense cannot be committed without also committing the lesser offense. For example, MANSLAUGHTER is a lesser included offense of MURDER, ASSAULT is a lesser included offense of RAPE, and unlawful entry is a lesser included offense of BURGLARY.

The rules of CRIMINAL PROCEDURE permit two or more offenses to be charged together, regardless of whether they are misdemeanors or felonies, provided that the CRIMES are of a similar character and based on the same act or common plan. This permits prosecutors to charge the greater offense and the lesser included offense together. Although the offenses can be charged together, the accused cannot be found guilty of both offenses because they are both parts of the same crime (the lesser offense is part of the greater offense).

When a defendant is charged with a greater offense and one or more lesser included offenses, the trial court is generally required to give the jury instructions as to each of the lesser included offenses as well as the greater offense. However, a defendant may waive his or her right to have the jury so instructed. If the jury finds guilt BEYOND A REASONABLE DOUBT as to a lesser included offense, but finds reasonable doubt as to the defendant's guilt with regard to the greater offense, the court should instruct the jury that it may convict on the lesser charge.

It is not uncommon for a prosecutor and defendant to negotiate an agreement by which the defendant pleads guilty to the lesser included offense either before the trial begins or before the jury returns a VERDICT. Such a plea negotiation is generally acceptable to the prosecuting attorney because the EVIDENCE establishing guilt for the lesser included offense is usually strong. The defendant is generally willing to make such an agreement because the lesser included offense carries a less severe sentence.

The notion of lesser included offenses developed from the COMMON-LAW doctrine of MERGER. In the past, FELONY and MISDEMEANOR trials involved different procedural rights. The merger doctrine determined an individual's procedural rights at trial if the individual was charged with both a felony and a lesser included misdemeanor. In that circumstance the misdemeanor was considered to have merged with the felony, and felony procedural rights applied. The merger doctrine has been repudiated in modern U.S. law because an accused's procedural rights are essentially the same whether the accused is charged with a misdemeanor or a felony.

See also CRIMINAL LAW; PLEA BARGAINING.

LESSOR 📖 One who rents REAL PROPERTY or PERSONAL PROPERTY to another. 📖

A lessor of land is a landlord. See also LANDLORD AND TENANT.

LET 📖 To award a contract, such as for the erection of public works, to one of several bidders. See also PUBLIC CONTRACT.

To lease certain property. 📖

LETTER OF CREDIT 📖 A written instrument from a bank or merchant in one location that requests that anyone or a specifically named party advance money or items on CREDIT to the party holding or named in the document. 📖

When a letter of credit is used, repayment of the DEBT is guaranteed by the bank or merchant issuing it. For example, if a bank is aware that a prominent citizen is trustworthy and can safely be relied upon to settle the debts which he or she incurs, then a letter of credit will be offered to that person on the basis of his or her good reputation so the person can travel without carrying large sums of money.

A sample
irrevocable letter
of credit

_____ Bank

__ Street, __ , __

CABLE ADDRESS _____

IRREVOCABLE CREDIT   DATE

> ALL DRAFTS DRAWN MUST BE MARKED:
> DRAWN UNDER CREDIT NO.

DEAR SIRS:

WE HEREBY AUTHORIZE YOU TO VALUE ON

FOR ACCOUNT OF

UP TO THE AGGREGATE AMOUNT OF

AVAILABLE BY YOUR DRAFT(S) AT   FOR   INVOICE COST TO BE

ACCOMPANIED BY

BILLS OF LADING MUST BE DATED NOT LATER THAN
BILLS OF EXCHANGE MUST BE NEGOTIATED NOT LATER THAN
EXCEPT AS OTHERWISE EXPRESSLY STATED HEREIN, THIS CREDIT IS
SUBJECT TO THE UNIFORM CUSTOMS AND PRACTICE FOR COMMERCIAL
DOCUMENTARY CREDITS AS SET FORTH IN THE INTERNATIONAL CHAM-
BER OF COMMERCE PUBLICATION NO. 290.
WE HEREBY AGREE WITH THE DRAWERS, ENDORSERS AND BONA FIDE
HOLDERS OF DRAFTS DRAWN UNDER AND IN COMPLIANCE WITH THE
TERMS OF THIS CREDIT THAT SUCH DRAFTS WILL BE DULY HONORED ON
DUE PRESENTATION TO THE DRAWEE.
                                    YOURS VERY TRULY,
                                         ASSISTANT CASHIER

Letters of credit were used frequently before credit cards and travelers' checks were in common usage.

LETTER OF THE LAW ▨ The strict and exact force of the language used in a statute, as distinguished from the spirit, general purpose, and policy of the statute. ▨

LETTER RULING ▨ In tax law a written interpretation of certain provisions of federal statutes by the Office of the Assistant Commissioner of the INTERNAL REVENUE SERVICE. ▨

Tax laws are often the subject of dispute between U.S. taxpayers and the Internal Revenue Service (IRS). Authority for interpreting the laws, which are found in the INTERNAL REVENUE CODE, rests with regional IRS agents, who have the power to review TAX RETURNS through an AUDIT. If a taxpayer disagrees with an interpretation of the law, she or he may ask the national IRS office to issue a ruling on the point of contention. This statement is called a private letter ruling.

Because of the time and expense involved in preparing a request for a letter ruling, such a request is seldom made. The taxpayer must submit a complete record of the transaction in dispute, including a justification for the transaction, all pertinent documents, the section of the tax code in question, and any relevant IRS regulations, rulings, and court PRECEDENTS.

Letter rulings are issued by the Office of the Assistant Commissioner of the IRS. They are numbered—for example, Private Letter Ruling 8616003. Each discusses the applicable facts before the IRS as well as the IRS ruling, but does not name the individual or organization that requested the ruling. After the ruling is issued to the regional office and the taxpayer, it is published by the IRS. Several thousand letter rulings are issued annually.

The legal value of a letter ruling is extremely limited. The ruling applies only to the taxpayer who requested it and only for the year in which it is issued; federal tax law states that a letter ruling may not be used or cited by another taxpayer (I.R.C. § 6110(j)(3)). If the ruling favors the taxpayer, the regional IRS agent is bound by it. If the ruling is adverse, the taxpayer can submit the issue to a tax court.

Since the 1930s courts have refused to give precedential weight to letter rulings. In the 1989 case of *Phi Delta Theta Fraternity v. Commissioner of Internal Revenue*, 887 F.2d 1302 (6th Cir.), a national fraternity appealing an order of the U.S. Tax Court based part of its argument on several letter rulings. In affirming the Tax Court's decision, the APPELLATE COURT described the weight courts are to give letter rulings: "Although private letter rulings are helpful in determining the contours of tax statutes and may be considered when evaluating the consistency of application of statutes, such letter rulings have no precedential effect."

Despite the limited application of letter rulings, they are widely read by tax attorneys. Specialists use them to keep abreast of IRS interpretation, and the documents are available from electronic databases.

See also INCOME TAX; TAXATION.

LETTERS OF ADMINISTRATION 📖 A formal document issued by a court of PROBATE appointing a manager of the ASSETS and liabili-

A sample decree granting letters of administration

At a Surrogate's Court held in and for the County of _____ , at _____ , in said County, on the _____ day of _____ , 19__ .

Present: Hon. _____ , Surrogate.
[Add title of proceeding]

DECREE
File No. _____

On reading and filing the petition of _____ and _____ praying for a decree awarding letters of administration of the goods, chattels and credits of the said deceased to them or to such other person or persons who have an equal or prior right thereto, and proving also to the Surrogate the existence of all the jurisdictional facts,

And, the said _____ and _____ having appeared by _____ , Esq., their attorney in support of said petition,

And, _____ , the Public Administrator of _____ County, having appeared by _____ , Esq., his attorney, and having filed an answer to the petition of the said _____ and _____ , denying that the petitioners are distributees of the decedent presently entitled to share in his estate, and alleging that in the absence of proof by the said petitioners that they are distributees of the decedent presently entitled to share in his estate, he has a right to letters of administration of said decedent's estate prior to the petitioners,

And the matter having come regularly on before the Surrogate for a hearing on the _____ day of _____ , 19__ ,

And satisfactory proof having been made of the due service of the citation herein upon, and the due appearance herein by all the persons entitled to notice of this proceeding;

And the Surrogate having duly made and filed his decision in writing on the _____ day of _____ , 19__ .

Now, on motion of _____ , Esq., attorney for _____ , as Public Administrator of _____ County, it is

ORDERED, ADJUDGED AND DECREED that letters of administration of the goods, chattels and credits which were of _____ , deceased, be awarded to _____ , as Public Administrator of _____ County, upon his qualifying hereunder as prescribed by statute; and it is further

ORDERED, ADJUDGED AND DECREED that upon the judicial settlement of the account of proceedings of the Public Administrator, as administrator of the estate of the said deceased, _____ , _____ , _____ and _____ be cited.

_____
Surrogate

ties of the ESTATE of the deceased in certain situations. 📖

Courts are often asked to rule on the management of a deceased person's estate. Generally, this is a routine matter for probate courts, which are created specifically for this purpose. Individuals generally determine the distribution of their estate in a WILL, which usually specifies an executor to carry out its directions. But where the DECEDENT has left no will or the executor named in a will is unable or unwilling to serve, the courts must appoint an administrator. This appointment is made by issuing a short document called letters of administration, which is a decree that serves as evidence of the administrator's authority.

When an individual dies INTESTATE (without a valid will or with no will at all), issues must be resolved involving the disposal of the decedent's PROPERTY, the settlement of DEBTS and CLAIMS against the estate, the payment of estate taxes, and in particular the distribution of the estate to HEIRS who are legally entitled to receive it. These matters are resolved by following the laws of DESCENT AND DISTRIBUTION, which are found in the statutes of all states. Essentially, these laws divide the decedent's property according to well-established rules of INHERITANCE based on blood relations, ADOPTION, or MARRIAGE. In the case of a person who has died intestate, the probate court appoints an administrator to distribute the property according to the relevant descent and distribution statutes.

Even though a decedent may leave a valid will that names an executor, there is no guarantee that the executor will carry out the duties involved. An executor may be unable or unwilling to serve, for example, because of illness or other commitments. For this reason wills often name an alternate executor as a safeguard. When the named executor cannot or will not serve and there is no alternate executor, the court will intervene to appoint an administrator. Generally, one or more relatives of a decedent will submit their name in a petition for letters of administration, and the court will rule on each submitter's fitness for the duty and on the merits of competing claims, if any.

Until the court can appoint someone with full responsibility for the estate, it may choose to appoint a temporary special administrator. This individual is granted limited authority over specified property of the decedent, as opposed to having the authority to direct the disposition of the entire estate. When a valid will exists, any administrator appointed by the court is bound to direct the estate according to the terms of the will.

See also EXECUTORS AND ADMINISTRATORS.

LETTERS ROGATORY 📖 A formal written request made by one judicial body in which an action is pending to another court in a different, independent JURISDICTION that a WITNESS who resides in that jurisdiction be examined through the use of INTERROGATORIES accompanying the request.

A device used in INTERNATIONAL LAW by which the courts of one country ask the courts of another to utilize their procedure to assist the country making the request in the administration of justice within its borders. 📖

The use of letters rogatory can be traced to early American legal history when they facilitated cooperation between the courts of the several states of the Union. Their continued use is based primarily upon the COMITY of courts towards each other. Rule 28 of the Federal Rules of Civil Procedure provides for letters rogatory to be used in FEDERAL COURTS to obtain the TESTIMONY of a witness who resides in a foreign country through a number of different DISCOVERY devices and the Convention on the Taking of Evidence Abroad in Civil or Commercial Matters (28 U.S.C.A. § 1781 [1948]) sets out the procedures to be followed in the use of letters rogatory by the countries who are parties to the treaty.

See also CIVIL PROCEDURE.

LETTERS TESTAMENTARY 📖 The formal instrument of authority and appointment

A sample letters testamentary

THE PEOPLE OF THE STATE OF _____

To: _____

WHEREAS, the Last Will and Testament of _____ , deceased, was duly admitted to probate by decree of the Surrogate's Court of _____ County on the _____ day of _____ , 19___ , which decree directed the issuance to you of letters testamentary upon you qualifying according to the law,

NOW THEREFORE, KNOW YE that you are hereby authorized to administer the estate of said deceased subject to the jurisdiction and supervision of this court.

WITNESS Hon. _____ , a Surrogate of the County of _____ , this _____ day of _____ , 19___ .

_____
Clerk

granted by the proper court to an EXECUTOR (one designated in a WILL to manage the ESTATE of the deceased) empowering that person to execute the functions of the office. 📖

LEVEES AND FLOOD CONTROL 📖 The system constructed and maintained by government to prevent the overflow of water. 📖

A levee is an embankment constructed by the states along a body of water to prevent the flooding of lands adjacent to the water. The federal government also has power, by virtue of the COMMERCE CLAUSE, to prevent and control flooding, since flood control protects NAVIGABLE WATERS.

A levee prevents a body of water from overflowing into the adjacent land.

As a general rule, the power to construct or establish levees is VESTED in public authorities and not in individuals. Levee districts are the public agencies most frequently involved in the creation of flood control projects for the purpose of constructing and maintaining flood control improvements for the protection of the general public. The state legislature has power to create levee districts. Subject to constitutional limitations, a tax can be imposed for levees and for general flood control improvements. A state legislature can LEVY, assess, and tax directly, or it can DELEGATE the power to local levee districts. Generally, only property which is benefited by the flood control project can be subject to a tax assessment.

See also RIVERS.

LEVERAGE 📖 A method of financing an investment by which an investor pays only a small percentage of the purchase price in cash, with the balance supplemented by borrowed funds, in order to generate a greater rate of return than would be produced by paying primarily cash for the investment; the economic benefit gained by such financing. 📖

REAL ESTATE syndicates and promoters commonly use leverage financing. A leveraged investor builds up EQUITY or ownership in the investment by making payments on the amount of PRINCIPAL borrowed from a third person. The money allotted to the repayment of interest charged on the borrowed principal is treated typically as a deduction that reduces TAXABLE INCOME. The greater the amount of principal borrowed, the larger the interest payments and the resulting deductions. Obviously, a taxpayer who pays cash is not entitled to deductions for interest payments. In many cases, deductions for the DEPRECIATION of the CAPITAL ASSET constituting the investment are also permitted.

Any investor receives an anticipated rate of return from the investment although the rate may fluctuate depending upon the economic climate and the management of the investment. Because of the favorable tax treatment enjoyed as a result of this method of financing, the leveraged investor keeps more of the income generated by the investment than an investor who financed the investment mainly through cash. There is, however, risk involved in leverage financing. If the income generated by the investment decreases, there might not be adequate funds available to meet payment of the outstanding principal and interest, leading to substantial losses for the investor.

LEVI, EDWARD HIRSCH   Edward Hirsch Levi served as U.S. attorney general from 1975 to 1976. A prominent and respected lawyer, scholar, and teacher, Levi became attorney general following the WATERGATE scandals and the resignation of President RICHARD M. NIXON. Levi helped restore respect and public confidence in the Justice Department, which had become deeply politicized during the Nixon administration.

Levi was born June 26, 1911, in Chicago. He graduated from the University of Chicago in 1932 and earned a law degree there in 1935. He received a doctor's degree in 1938 from Yale University, where he had been a Sterling Fellow in 1935 and 1936.

Levi was named an assistant professor of law at the University of Chicago in 1936, the year he was admitted to the Illinois bar. From 1940 to 1945, he took a leave of absence from the university to be a special assistant to the U.S. attorney general. During this period he served in the Antitrust and War Divisions, and was chairman of the Interdepartmental Committee on Monopolies and Cartels. His time in government service helped make him an expert on ANTITRUST LAW.

He returned to the University of Chicago Law School in 1945 as a professor. In 1949 he

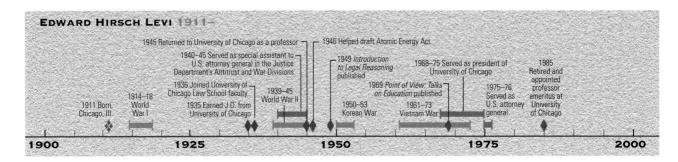

1945 Returned to University of Chicago as a professor
1946 Helped draft Atomic Energy Act
1940–45 Served as special assistant to U.S. attorney general in the Justice Department's Antitrust and War Divisions
1949 *Introduction to Legal Reasoning* published
1968–75 Served as president of University of Chicago
1936 Joined University of Chicago Law School faculty
1969 *Point of View: Talks on Education* published
1985 Retired and appointed professor emeritus at University of Chicago
1939–45 World War II
1975–76 Served as U.S. attorney general
1914–18 World War I
1935 Earned J.D. from University of Chicago
1950–53 Korean War
1961–73 Vietnam War
1911 Born, Chicago, Ill.

1900   1925   1950   1975   2000

published *Introduction to Legal Reasoning*, a classic work of legal education that has been used by thousands of students. He was named dean of the law school in 1950 and provost of the university in 1962, and was appointed president of the university in 1968.

During these years Levi remained an active participant in government. He was an adviser and counsel to the Federation of Atomic Scientists and in 1946 helped draft the Atomic Energy Act (60 Stat. 755 [42 U.S.C.A. § 2011 et seq.]), which led to the establishment of the Atomic Energy Commission. In 1950 he was appointed chief counsel to the Subcommittee on Monopoly Power of the House Judiciary Committee. In this position he conducted hearings on monopolistic practices in the steel and newsprint industries. During the administration of President LYNDON B. JOHNSON, Levi was a member of the White House Central Group on Domestic Affairs and of the White House Task Force on Education.

In February 1975 President GERALD R. FORD appointed Levi attorney general of the United States. Ford had assumed the presidency after Nixon resigned August 9, 1974, in the wake of the Watergate scandals. These scandals initially revolved around Nixon's role in covering up a break-in and electronic bugging of Democratic National Committee headquarters in the Watergate office building complex in Washington, D.C. But investigations soon revealed that Nixon had used the Federal Bureau of Investigation (FBI), Internal Revenue Service, and Central Intelligence Agency to pursue his political enemies. During this period the Justice Department came under heavy attack. It appeared that the department either was aiding the cover-up or was incompetent in pursuing the truth.

The appointment of Levi restored confidence in the department. Because of his impeccable credentials and lack of partisanship, Levi was able to restore morale to the shaken organization and to institute internal reforms that might prevent future scandals. He issued policies that restricted the FBI's ability to be ex-

BIOGRAPHY

APWIDE WORLD PHOTOS

Edward Hirsch Levi

"THE BASIC PATTERN OF LEGAL REASONING IS REASONING BY EXAMPLE . . . IN WHICH A PROPOSITION DESCRIPTIVE IN THE FIRST CASE IS MADE INTO A RULE OF LAW AND THEN APPLIED TO A NEXT SIMILAR SITUATION. A METHOD . . . NECESSARY FOR THE LAW, BUT [WITH] CHARACTERISTICS WHICH UNDER OTHER CIRCUMSTANCES MIGHT BE CONSIDERED IMPERFECTIONS."

ploited for political investigations. While in office Levi also pursued enforcement of antitrust laws, an area in which he had a great deal of expertise.

Following JIMMY CARTER's defeat of Ford in the 1976 presidential election, Levi returned to the University of Chicago as a professor of law. He retired from full-time teaching in 1985 and was appointed professor emeritus.

LEVY 📖 To assess; raise; execute; exact; tax; collect; gather; take up; seize. Thus, to levy a tax; to levy a NUISANCE; to levy a fine; to levy war; to levy an EXECUTION, *i.e.*, to levy or collect a sum of money on an execution.

A SEIZURE. The obtaining of money by legal process through seizure and sale of property; the raising of the money for which an execution has been issued. 📖

A SHERIFF or other officer of the law can be ordered by a court to make a levy against any property not entitled to an exemption. The court can do this with an order of ATTACHMENT, by which the court takes CUSTODY of the property during pending litigation, or by execution, the process used to enforce a JUDGMENT. The order directs the sheriff to take and safely keep all non-exempt property of the defendant found within the county or as much property as is necessary to satisfy the plaintiff's demand plus costs and expenses. The order also directs the sheriff to make a written statement of efforts and to return it to the clerk of the court where the action is pending. This report, called a RETURN, lists all the property seized and the date of seizure.

The sheriff's act in taking custody of the defendant's property is the levy. A levy on REAL PROPERTY is generally accomplished by giving the defendant and the general public notice that the defendant's property has been ENCUMBERED by the court order. This can be done by filing a notice with the clerk who keeps real estate MORTGAGES and DEEDS recorded with the county. A levy of tangible PERSONAL PROPERTY usually requires actual seizure. If the goods are capable of being moved around, most states insist that the sheriff actually take them into custody or remove them to another place for safekeeping with an independent person. If the property is bulky or cumbersome and removal would be impracticable and expensive, actual seizure is not necessary. The levy can be accomplished by removing an essential piece, such as the pinsetter in a bowling alley, or by services of the court demanding preservation of the property. The order can be served on the defendant or anyone else in possession of the property, and disobedience of it then can be punished as a CONTEMPT of court.

Often the order will permit levy against any property belonging to the defendant, but it will specify seizure of a unique item and allow something else of comparable value to be substituted only if the unusual item cannot be found.

An attempt to attach a debtor's property is effective only after a levy, and from that time on there is a LIEN on the attached property. This gives the plaintiff some security that he or she will be able to collect what is owed and, if first in time, establishes the plaintiff's priority at the head of the line of the defendant's creditors who might subsequently seek a levy upon a debtor's property. It can strengthen the plaintiff's bargaining position if the plaintiff is trying to settle the dispute with the defendant, and it may even create JURISDICTION for the court over the defendant, but only to the extent of the value of the property subject to levy.

LEWDNESS Behavior that is deemed morally impure or unacceptable in a sexual sense; open and public indecency tending to corrupt the morals of the community; gross or WANTON indecency in sexual relations.

An important element of lewdness is openness. Lewdness is sometimes used interchangeably with LICENTIOUSNESS or LASCIVIOUSNESS, which both relate to debauchery and MORAL TURPITUDE. It is a specific offense in certain state statutes and is included in general provisions in others.

LEX [*Latin, Law.*] In medieval JURISPRUDENCE, a body or collection of various laws peculiar to a given nation or people; not a code in the modern sense, but an aggregation or collection of laws not codified or systematized. Also, a similar collection of laws relating to a general subject, and not peculiar to any one people.

In modern U.S. and English jurisprudence this term signifies a system or body of laws, written or unwritten, applicable to a particular case or question regarded as local or unique to a particular state, country, or JURISDICTION.

LEX FORI [*Latin, The law of the forum, or court.*] The POSITIVE LAW of the state, nation, or JURISDICTION within which a lawsuit is instituted or REMEDY sought.

The *lex fori*, or law of the jurisdiction in which relief is pursued, governs all procedural matters as distinguished from substantive rights.

LEXIS® An on-line legal information service that provides the full text of opinions and statutes in electronic format. Subscribers use their personal computers to search the LEXIS database for relevant cases. They may download or print the legal information they retrieve.

The LEXIS service began in 1973. In 1979 the LEXIS service was joined by the companion NEXIS® news and information service. LEXIS contains about 4,800 legal sources, and NEXIS contains 8,700 news and information sources. The services add approximately 9.5 million documents each week to their more than one billion documents on-line.

The LEXIS service contains major archives of federal and state CASE LAW, statutes of all fifty states, state and federal regulations, and public records from major U.S. states. The LEXIS service has forty-one specialized libraries covering all major fields of practice, including tax, securities, banking, environmental, energy, and international law. Group files combine legal information from all JURISDICTIONS and, where appropriate, add sources of relevant business, financial, or general news.

LEXIS also has a public records service that provides on-line access to information from selected states about real and personal property ASSETS, Uniform Commercial Code LIENS, secretary of state corporation filings, a VERDICTS and settlements library, and court indices and DOCKETS.

The company is a division of Reed Elsevier Inc., part of Reed Elsevier plc, a group of international publishing and information businesses with headquarters in London. LEXIS-NEXIS is based in Dayton, Ohio.

See also COMPUTER-ASSISTED LEGAL RESEARCH; WESTLAW.

LEX LOCI [*Latin, The law of the place.*] The law of the state or the nation where the matter in litigation transpired.

The term *lex loci* can be employed in several descriptions, but, in general, it is used only for *lex loci contractus* (the law of the place where the contract was made), which is usually the law that governs the contract.

LIABILITY A comprehensive legal term that describes the condition of being actually or potentially subject to a legal obligation.

JOINT *liability* is an obligation for which more than one person is responsible.

JOINT AND SEVERAL LIABILITY refers to the status of those who are responsible together as one unit as well as individually for their conduct. The person who has been harmed can institute a lawsuit and recover from any or all of the wrongdoers—but cannot receive double compensation, for instance, the full amount of recovery from each of two wrongdoers.

Primary liability is an obligation for which a person is directly responsible; it is distinguished from *secondary liability* which is the responsibility of another if the party directly responsible fails or refuses to satisfy his or her obligation.

LIBEL AND SLANDER Two TORTS that involve the communication of false information about a person, a group, or an entity such as a corporation. Libel is any DEFAMATION that can be seen, such as a writing, printing, effigy, movie, or statue. Slander is any defamation that is spoken and heard.

Collectively known as defamation, libel and slander are civil wrongs that harm a reputation; decrease respect, regard, or confidence; or induce disparaging, hostile, or disagreeable opinions or feelings against an individual or entity. The injury to good name or reputation is effected through written or spoken words or visual images. The laws governing these torts are identical.

To recover in a libel or slander suit, the plaintiff must show evidence of four elements: that the defendant conveyed a defamatory message; that the material was published, meaning that it was conveyed to someone other than the plaintiff; that the plaintiff could be identified as the person referred to in the defamatory material; and that the plaintiff suffered some injury to her reputation as a result of the communication.

To prove that the material was defamatory, the plaintiff must show that at least one other person who saw or heard it understood it as having defamatory meaning. It is necessary to show not that all who heard or read the statement understood it to be defamatory, only that one person other than the plaintiff did so. Therefore, even if the defendant contends that the communication was a joke, if one person other than the plaintiff took it seriously, the communication is considered defamatory.

Defamatory matter is published when it is communicated to someone other than the plaintiff. This can be done in several different ways. The defendant might loudly accuse the plaintiff of something in a public place where others are present, or make defamatory statements about the plaintiff in a newsletter or an on-line bulletin board. The defamation need not be printed or distributed. However, if the defendant does not intend it to be conveyed to anyone other than the plaintiff, and conveys it in a manner that ordinarily would prevent others from seeing or hearing it, the requirement of publication has not been satisfied even if a third party inadvertently overhears or witnesses the communication.

LIABILITY for republication of a defamatory statement is the same as for original publication, provided the defendant had knowledge of the contents of the statement. Thus, newspapers, magazines, and broadcasters are liable for republication of a libel or slander because they have editorial control over their communications. On the other hand, bookstores, libraries, and other distributors of material are liable for republication only if they knew or had reason to know the statement was defamatory. COMMON CARRIERS such as telephone companies are not liable for defamatory material they convey, even if they know it is defamatory, unless they know or have reason to know that the sender does not have a PRIVILEGE to communicate the material. Suppliers of communications equipment are never liable for defamatory material transmitted through the equipment they provide.

In general, there are four defenses to libel or slander: truth, consent, accident, and privilege. The fact that the allegedly defamatory communication is essentially true is usually an absolute defense; the defendant need not verify every detail of the communication, as long as its substance can be established. If the plaintiff consented to publication of the defamatory material, recovery is barred. Accidental publication of a defamatory statement does not constitute publication. Privilege confers immunity on a small number of defendants who are directly involved in the furtherance of the public's business—for example, attorneys, judges, jurors, and witnesses whose statements are protected on PUBLIC POLICY grounds.

Before 1964 defamation law was determined on a state-by-state basis, with courts applying the local COMMON LAW. Questions of FREEDOM OF SPEECH were generally found to be not relevant to libel or slander cases, and defendants were held strictly liable even if they had no idea that the communication was false or defamatory, or had exercised reasonable caution in ascertaining its truthfulness. This deference to state protection of personal reputation was confirmed in *Chaplinsky v. New Hampshire*, 315 U.S. 568, 62 S. Ct. 766, 86 L. Ed. 1031 (1942), in which the Supreme Court stated, "There are certain well-defined and narrowly limited classes of speech, the prevention and punishment of which have

Richard Jewell and the Olympic Park Bombing

When a bomb exploded at Atlanta's Olympic Park in the early morning hours of July 27, 1996, the 1996 Summer Olympics suffered a terrible blow. Two people died and over one hundred people were injured as a result of the blast at the outdoor entertainment center. Richard Jewell, a security guard at the park, was at first lauded as a hero for discovering the suspicious package containing the bomb. By July 30 he had become the Federal Bureau of Investigation's (FBI's) prime suspect.

The information that Jewell was a suspect reached the news media, which widely publicized Jewell's shift in status. The *Atlanta Journal–Constitution* published an extra edition on July 30, with a headline that read "FBI Suspects 'Hero' May Have Planted Bomb." It was reported that Jewell had approached the news media seeking publicity for his actions, and that persons at Piedmont College, where he had been employed, had made allegations to the FBI about Jewell's character and conduct. On NBC's nightly news program, Tom Brokaw stated that "they probably have got enough to arrest him. They probably have got enough to try him." It was commonly asserted that Jewell fit the profile of a lone bomber.

Jewell maintained his innocence and pointed out that he had not approached the news media. It was quickly confirmed that he had not sought out media attention, and on October 26, 1996, the FBI cleared him as a suspect. Jewell's attorneys then announced they would seek damages from the persons and news organizations that had libeled Jewell. In December 1996 NBC negotiated a settlement with Jewell for a reported $500,000. In January 1997 CNN reached a settlement as well. In that same month, Jewell filed a libel lawsuit against the *Atlanta Journal–Constitution,* listing nineteen allegedly libelous headlines and excerpts from articles. He also sued Piedmont College for allegedly supplying false information.

never been thought to raise constitutional problems." The Court in *Chaplinsky* held that defamatory speech is not essential to the exposition of ideas and can be regulated without raising constitutional concerns. This reasoning was confirmed in *Beauharnais v. Illinois,* 343 U.S. 250, 72 S. Ct. 725, 96 L. Ed. 919 (1952), where the Court held again that libelous speech is not protected by the Constitution.

In 1964 the Supreme Court changed the direction of libel law dramatically with its decision in *New York Times v. Sullivan,* 376 U.S. 254, 84 S. Ct. 710, 11 L. Ed. 2d 686 (1964). In *Sullivan,* for the first time, the Court placed some libelous speech under the protection of the FIRST AMENDMENT. The plaintiff, a police official, had claimed that false ALLEGATIONS about him were published in the *New York Times* and sued the newspaper for libel. The Supreme Court balanced the plaintiff's interest in preserving his reputation against the public's interest in freedom of expression in the area of political debate. The Court decided that "libel can claim no talismanic immunity from constitutional limitations. It must be measured by standards that satisfy the First Amendment." It held that to protect the free flow of ideas in the political arena, the law requires that a public official alleging libel must prove actual malice

in order to recover DAMAGES. The First Amendment protects open and robust debate on public issues even when such debate includes "vehement, caustic, unpleasantly sharp attacks on government and public officials."

Since *Sullivan* a public official or other person who has voluntarily assumed a position in the public eye must prove that a libelous statement "was made with 'actual malice'—that is, with knowledge that it was false or with reckless disregard of whether it was false or not" (*Sullivan*). The actual-malice standard does not require any ill will on the part of the defendant. Rather, it merely requires that the defendant be aware that the statement is false or is very likely false. Reckless disregard is present if the plaintiff can show that the defendant had "serious doubts as to the truth of [the] publication" (see *St. Amant v. Thompson,* 390 U.S. 727, 88 S. Ct. 1323, 20 L. Ed. 2d 262 [1968]).

Also since *Sullivan* the question of who is a public official has often been raised. In *Rosenblatt v. Baer,* 383 U.S. 75, 86 S. Ct. 669, 15 L. Ed. 2d 597 (1966), the Court found that a nonelected official "among the hierarchy of government employees who have, or appear to have, substantial responsibility for or control over the conduct of public affairs" was a public official within the meaning of *Sullivan.* Similarly, in *Monitor Patriot Co. v. Roy*, 401 U.S. 265, 91 S. Ct. 621, 28 L. Ed. 2d 35 (1971), the Court found that a candidate for public office fell within the category of public officials who must prove actual malice in order to recover.

Eventually, *Sullivan*'s actual-malice requirement was extended to include defendants accused of defaming public figures who were not government officials. In the companion cases of *Curtis Publishing Co. v. Butts* and *Associated Press v. Walker*, 388 U.S. 130, 87 S. Ct. 1975, 18 L. Ed. 2d 1094 (1967), the Court held that a football coach at the University of Georgia and a retired Army general were similar to public officials in that they enjoyed a high degree of prominence and access to the mass media that allowed them to influence policy and counter criticisms leveled against them.

The Court refined its definition of PUBLIC FIGURE in *Gertz v. Robert Welch, Inc.*, 418 U.S. 323, 94 S. Ct. 2997, 41 L. Ed. 2d 789 (1974), where it held that public figures are those who thrust themselves into the public eye and invite close scrutiny. The Court also recognized two types of public figures: those who are "public figures for all purposes" and those who are public figures for limited purposes. For an individual to be considered a public figure in all situations, the person's name must be so familiar as to be a household word—for example, Johnny Carson. A limited-purpose public figure is one who voluntarily injects himself into a public controversy and becomes a public figure for a limited range of issues. Limited-purpose public figures have at least temporary access to the means to counteract false statements about them. By voluntarily placing themselves in the public eye, they relinquish some of their PRIVACY rights. For these reasons, false statements about limited-purpose public figures that relate to the public controversies in which they are involved are not considered defamatory unless they meet the actual-malice test set forth in *Sullivan*.

Defining who is a limited-purpose public figure has been compared with trying to nail a jellyfish to a wall. Nonetheless, the Court has attempted this feat on several occasions. In *Time, Inc., v. Firestone*, 424 U.S. 448, 96 S. Ct. 958, 47 L. Ed. 2d 154 (1976), it held that a wealthy socialite involved in a widely publicized divorce was not a public figure because she had not thrust herself into the public eye in order to influence the resolution of any public issue. Her divorce was not a public controversy, although it had undeniable PUBLIC INTEREST. Likewise, in *Hutchinson v. Proxmire*, 443 U.S. 111, 99 S. Ct. 2675, 61 L. Ed. 2d 411 (1979), a scientist whose research was subjected to ridicule when he received a Golden Fleece Award from Senator William Proxmire was not a public figure because he had neither thrust himself into the public spotlight nor sought to influence public opinion. Proxmire gave these awards to people he felt were fleecing the public by using tax dollars on frivolous or useless causes. The Court found that the scientist's notoriety arose strictly from Proxmire's libelous statements about him and his research. Proxmire's claim that Hutchinson was a public figure was rejected because Proxmire's libelous actions were responsible for thrusting Hutchinson into the public eye.

A 1991 case made it somewhat easier for public figures to sue authors and publishers for libel. *Masson v. New Yorker Magazine*, 501 U.S. 496, 111 S. Ct. 2419, 115 L. Ed. 2d 447 (1991), held that a plaintiff alleging libel satisfies the actual-malice standard if it can be proved that the author deliberately altered the plaintiff's words and that the alteration resulted in a material change in the meaning conveyed by the plaintiff in the original statement. Jeffrey M. Masson, a prominent psychoanalyst, had sued Janet Malcolm, the author of an article and book about him, as well as the *New Yorker* magazine and Knopf publishers, which had published the article and book, respectively. Masson claimed that quotations attributed to him in those publications were false and libelous. Malcolm conceded that she had altered quotations in order to make the finished product more readable, but maintained that the essence of Masson's words had not been changed. The Court held that quotation marks around a passage "indicate to the reader that the passage reproduces the speaker's words verbatim." The Court was careful to protect journalistic freedom, and went on to say that deliberate alteration of quotations does not automatically prove actual malice:

> We conclude that a deliberate alteration of the words uttered by a plaintiff does not equate with knowledge of falsity for purposes of *New York Times Co. v. Sullivan* . . . and *Gertz v. Robert Welch, Inc.* . . . unless the alteration results in a material change in the meaning conveyed by the statement. The use of quotations to attribute words not in fact spoken bears in a most important way on that inquiry, but it is not dispositive in every case.

The tremendous growth of electronic communications networks during the 1990s has raised numerous questions about liability for

THE PUBLIC FIGURE DOCTRINE: AN UNWORKABLE CONCEPT?

The "public figure" doctrine announced by the Supreme Court in *Curtis Publishing v. Butts*, 388 U.S. 130, 87 S. Ct. 1975, 18 L. Ed. 2d 1094 (1967), held that prominent public persons had to prove actual malice (knowledge of falsity or reckless disregard of whether a statement is true or false) on the part of the news media in order to prevail in a libel lawsuit. Prior to *Butts* only public officials had to prove actual malice. In the years since this decision, the public figure doctrine has proved a troublesome area of the law, primarily because it is difficult to apply with any consistency. Some, generally from the news media, have called for making it easier to classify a person as a public figure. Others believe that a strict line must be maintained between public and private figures, so as to prevent the damaging of personal reputations by the media. Both sides agree that greater clarity is needed in defining what constitutes a public figure.

Those who favor a less restrictive definition of public figure argue that freedom of the press requires such a definition. It is in the public interest to encourage the reporting of news without fear that the subject of a story will sue the news organization for libel. Without adequate safeguards news editors may resort to self-censorship to avoid the possibility of a lawsuit. In a democratic society, self-censorship would prove to be a damaging restriction on the public's right to information.

For these advocates the Supreme Court's decision in *Gertz v. Robert Welch, Inc.*, 418 U.S. 323, 94 S. Ct. 2997, 41 L. Ed. 2d 789 (1974), signified a step away from the protections of the First Amendment. The Court held that a person who "voluntarily injects himself or is drawn into a particular public controversy" becomes a public figure "for a limited range of issues." The Court also held that there are persons who "occupy positions of such persuasive power and influence that they are deemed public figures for all purposes."

This category would include, for example, a national labor or civil rights leader.

Critics of *Gertz* argue that these two categories make little sense and are of no help to a court in determining whether a person is a public figure. For example, should a Hollywood entertainer or a professional athlete be cast as a public person in a libel suit? Do these persons have "persuasive power and influence"? As for persons who become involved in public events, courts have been unable to articulate a consistent standard for measuring whether a person "thrust" himself or herself into the status of a public figure. Studies have revealed contradictory ways of applying the *Gertz* standard.

Some commentators have advocated abandoning *Gertz* and replacing it with a "subject matter" test. Under this test if an article or story involves public policy or the functioning of government, it should be protected by the public figure doctrine. Therefore, if a story discusses a relatively unknown person's divorce proceeding or supposed Communist political leanings, this would be a matter of public policy (divorce law or political parties) that invokes the actual-malice standard in a libel suit.

The use of subject matter analysis would give public figures more protection than they currently have under *Gertz*. A story about the private life of an entertainer or professional athlete would generally not involve a public issue under even the broadest definition. Under the subject matter test, the celebrity would not be forced to prove actual malice.

Defenders of the *Gertz* decision admit that the public figure concept has been difficult to apply, but argue that the subject matter test is not a good alternative. They note that although freedom of the press is an important value, the need to protect the reputation of private citizens is also an important societal value. Citizens are encouraged to participate in public affairs, yet

a liberal reading of the public figure doctrine could discourage participation if there is no redress for injury to reputation. In addition, private citizens who are deemed public figures could never match the news media's power and pervasiveness in telling one side of the story.

Even with the difficulties inherent in *Gertz*, defenders note that it narrowed the public figure category in ways that protect the public. Simply appearing in the newspapers in connection with some newsworthy story or stories does not make one a public figure. Forced involvement in a public trial does not by itself make one a public figure. Most important, those charged with libel cannot create their own defense by converting a private citizen into a public figure solely by virtue of their news coverage.

Defenders of *Gertz* are leery of the subject matter test. They contend this test is too one-sided in favor of the news media. Almost any topic in human affairs can be generalized into a public policy issue or one that involves the government. It would be unfair to allow a publication to falsely brand a relatively unknown person a Communist and then assert the person is a public figure because radical political parties are a matter of public concern. The victim of this charge would have a difficult time proving actual malice to win a libel suit.

Those who favor a restrictive definition of the public figure doctrine also note that a libel action serves as a private means of controlling irresponsible journalism. *Gertz*, even with its difficulties in application, has allowed private persons a better chance of success in libel suits, which in turn sends a strong message to the media to be more careful in their reporting. As to the concerns about self-censorship, defenders of *Gertz* point out that journalists make choices every day about what is published. Falsely tarnishing the reputation of a person should be the object of self-censorship in professional news-gathering organizations.

IN FOCUS

defamation. Suddenly, it is possible to commit libel and instantly communicate a libelous statement to thousands of people. When libel is perpetrated in cyberspace, who is responsible? Are on-line information providers considered publishers, distributors, or common carriers? What level of First Amendment protection should be afforded to defamatory statements transmitted electronically?

By 1996 only a handful of cases had tackled these thorny issues. In *Cubby, Inc. v. CompuServe*, 776 F. Supp. 135 (S.D.N.Y. 1991), the plaintiff sued CompuServe, an online computer service company, for libel because of statements that appeared in a newsletter written and uploaded by an independent company and transmitted through CompuServe's network. The court found that CompuServe had no editorial control over the contents of the newsletter and was therefore only a distributor of the newsletter. CompuServe could not be held liable for the newsletter's contents unless it knew or had reason to know that the newsletter contained defamatory statements. Conversely, in *Stratton Oakmont v. Prodigy Services Co.*, 63 U.S.L.W. 2765, 23 Media L. Rep. 1794, 1995 WL 323710 (N.Y. Sup. Ct. 1995); *reh'g denied*, 24 Media L. Rep. 1126 (N.Y. Sup. Ct. 1995), the court found that Prodigy, an on-line provider similar to CompuServe, was a publisher rather than a distributor, and was liable for the defamatory material in question because it exercised considerable editorial control over what appeared on its system.

See also FREEDOM OF THE PRESS; NEW YORK TIMES V. SULLIVAN.

LIBELANT 📖 Formerly the party who filed an initiatory PLEADING (a formal declaration of a claim) in an ecclesiastical or religious matter or in an admiralty case, corresponding to the plaintiff in actions at law. 📖

Since 1966, the Federal Rules of Civil Procedure and Supplementary Admiralty Rules have governed admiralty actions, which are presently commenced by COMPLAINT.

See also ADMIRALTY AND MARITIME LAW; CIVIL PROCEDURE.

LIBELOUS 📖 In the nature of a written DEFAMATION, a communication that tends to injure reputation. 📖

LIBERTARIANISM 📖 A political philosophy that advocates free will, individual rights, and voluntary cooperation. 📖

The core doctrine of libertarianism begins with the recognition that people have certain natural rights and that deprivation of these rights is immoral. Among these natural rights are the right to personal autonomy and PROPERTY RIGHTS, and the right to the utilization of previously unused resources. These two basic assumptions form the foundation of all libertarian ideals.

Libertarianism can be traced back to ancient China, where philosopher Lao-tzu advocated the recognition of individual liberties. The modern libertarian theory emerged in the sixteenth century through the writings of Etienne de La Boetie (1530–1563), an eminent French theorist. In the seventeenth century, JOHN LOCKE and a group of British reformers known as the Levellers fashioned the classical basis for libertarianism with well-received philosophies on human nature and economics. Since the days of Locke, libertarianism has attracted pacifists, utopianists, utilitarianists, anarchists, and fascists. This wide array of support demonstrates the accessibility and elasticity of the libertarian promotion of natural rights.

Essential to the notion of natural rights is respect for the natural rights of others. Without a dignified population, voluntary cooperation is impossible. According to the libertarian, the means to achieving a dignified population and voluntary cooperation is inextricably tied to the promotion of natural rights.

Libertarianism holds that people lose their dignity as government gains control of their body and their life. The abdication of natural rights to government prevents people from living in their own way and working and producing at their own pace. The result is a decrease in self-reliance and independence, which results in a decrease in personal dignity, which in turn depresses society and necessitates more government interference.

Thus, the libertarian views government as both the cause and the effect of societal ills. Government is the cause of crime and prejudice because it robs people of their independence and frustrates initiative and creativity. Then, having created the sources of crime and prejudice by depriving individuals of their natural rights, government attempts to exorcise the evils with more controls over natural rights.

Libertarians believe that government should be limited to the defense of its citizens. Actions such as MURDER, RAPE, ROBBERY, THEFT, EMBEZZLEMENT, FRAUD, ARSON, KIDNAPPING, BATTERY, TRESPASS, and POLLUTION violate the rights of others, so government control of these actions is legitimate. Libertarians acknowledge human imperfection and the resulting need for some government deterrence and punishment of violence, NUISANCE, and harassment. However, government control of human activity should be limited to these functions.

CROSS-REFERENCES

Anarchism; Independent Parties; Natural Law; Utilitarianism.

LIBERTARIAN PARTY   The Libertarian party was founded in Colorado in 1971 and held its first convention in Denver in 1972. In 1972 it fielded John Hospers for president and Theodora Nathan for vice president in the U.S. general ELECTION. It appeared on two state ballots, receiving a total of 2,648 votes in Colorado and Washington. In the 1976 elections, the party's 176 candidates garnered 1.2 million votes across the United States.

The Libertarian party believes that people have certain natural, individual rights and that deprivation of those rights is unjust. Two basic rights—the right to personal autonomy and the right to utilize previously unused resources—form the foundation of the party's ideals.

The Libertarian party views government as both the cause and the effect of societal ills. Government causes crime and prejudice because excessive laws divide society, rob people of their independence, and frustrate initiative and creativity. It then attempts to eradicate crime and prejudice by exercising more control over individual rights.

Libertarians believe that government should be limited to the defense of its citizens. Actions such as MURDER, RAPE, ROBBERY, THEFT, EMBEZZLE-MENT, FRAUD, ARSON, KIDNAPPING, BATTERY, TRESPASS, and POLLUTION violate the rights of others, so government control of these actions is legitimate. The party acknowledges human imperfection and the resulting need for some government deterrence and punishment of violence, nuisance, and harassment. However, the party holds that government control of human activity should be limited to these functions.

The Libertarian party promotes the abolition of compulsory military service, government control of television and other media, laws regarding sexual activity between consenting adults, laws against the use of mood-altering substances, and government control of migration and immigration. Under its leadership farming quotas and subsidies would be eliminated, there would be no mandatory schooling and no MINIMUM WAGE, and defense spending would be drastically reduced. According to the party, the form of government it promotes would be less expensive than the current system of federal, state, and local governance.

The Libertarian party has achieved a small measure of electoral success. In 1980 Ed Clark received over 1 million votes in his bid for the presidency. Having failed to win the popular vote in any state, however, Clark received no electoral votes. Andre Marrou garnered slightly less support as the party's presidential candidate in 1984, 1988, and 1992. In 1992 Marrou and his running mate Nancy Lord received approxi-

Economist and author Harry Browne ran for president in 1996 as the Libertarian party candidate. He and his running mate, Jo Jorgensen, won 0.5 percent of the national vote.

mately 291,000 votes. Although the party has yet to be a factor in national politics, it has had some success locally. In 1994 it had state representatives in New Hampshire and Alaska, mayors in California, and over thirty city council members in cities across the country.

In 1996 the party held its national convention in Washington, D.C., over the Fourth of July holiday. At the convention it nominated economist and author Harry Browne as its presidential candidate. In his acceptance speech, Browne presented a number of controversial ideas, including making a sizable reduction in the federal government, abolishing the federal INCOME TAX, abolishing federal drug and seizure laws, and increasing recognition of individual rights. Browne and running mate Jo Jorgensen appeared on the election ballot in all fifty states, along with approximately one thousand Libertarian party candidates for various public offices. Browne and Jorgensen won 485,759 votes, 0.5 percent of the national vote.

See also INDEPENDENT PARTIES.

LIBERTY Liberty is the concept that forms the core of all democratic principles. Yet, as a legal concept, it defies clear definition.

The modern conception of liberty as implying certain fundamental or basic rights dates back to the writings of seventeenth- and eighteenth-century theorists such as Francis Hutcheson and JOHN LOCKE. Hutcheson believed that all people are equal and possess certain basic rights that are conferred by NATURAL LAW. Locke postulated that humans are born with an innate tendency to be reasonable and tolerant. He also believed that all individuals are entitled to liberty under the natural law that governed them before they formed societies. Locke's concept of natural law required that no one should interfere with another's life, health, liberty, or possessions. According to Locke, governments are necessary only to protect those who live within the laws of nature from those who do not. For this reason he believed that the power of government and the rule of the majority must be kept in check, and that they are best controlled by protecting and preserving individual liberties. Locke's philosophies gave rise to the SEPARATION OF POWERS and the system of checks and balances that are the basis of U.S. government.

Limitless freedom is untenable in a peaceful and orderly society. Yet, the founders of the United States were concerned that individual liberty interests be adequately protected. Echoing Locke's natural-law theory, the DECLARATION OF INDEPENDENCE states that all people have inalienable rights, including the right to life, liberty, and the pursuit of happiness. Similarly, the preamble to the Constitution outlines the Framers' intent to establish a government structure that ensures liberty from oppression. It reads, in part, "We the People . . . in Order to . . . secure the Blessings of Liberty to ourselves and our Posterity. . . ." The Bill of Rights sets forth a number of specific protections of individual liberties.

Through these documents U.S. citizens are guaranteed freedom of speech, press, assembly, and religion; freedom from unreasonable SEARCHES AND SEIZURES; and freedom from SLAVERY or INVOLUNTARY SERVITUDE. CRIMINAL LAW and procedure require that a person may not be detained unlawfully and that a person accused of a crime is entitled to reasonable BAIL and a SPEEDY TRIAL. The right to be free from unlawful detention has been interpreted to mean not only that the government may not deprive a person of liberty without DUE PROCESS OF LAW, but also that a citizen has a right "to be free in the enjoyment of all his faculties; to be free to use them in all lawful ways; to live and work where he will; to earn his living by any lawful calling; to pursue any livelihood or vocation" (*Allgeyer v. Louisiana*, 165 U.S. 578, 17 S. Ct. 427, 41 L. Ed. 832 [1897]). State governments may not regulate individual freedom except for a legitimate public purpose and only by means that are rationally designed to achieve that purpose (see *Nebbia v. New York*, 291 U.S. 502, 54 S. Ct. 505, 78 L. Ed. 940 [1934]).

The liberties guaranteed to individuals are not granted without restriction. Throughout history the Supreme Court has held that individual freedom may be restricted when necessary to advance a compelling government interest, such as public safety, national security, or the protection of the rights of others. Countless cases have litigated the parameters of justifiable government restriction. In one such case, *Perry Education Ass'n v. Perry Local Educators' Ass'n*, 460 U.S. 37, 103 S. Ct. 948, 74 L. Ed. 2d 794 (1983), the Court found that the content of a message delivered in a PUBLIC FORUM may be restricted if the restriction serves a compelling state interest and is narrowly drawn to achieve that interest. Restrictions on speech in a public forum may also be upheld if the expressive activity being regulated is a type that is not entitled to full FIRST AMENDMENT protection, such as obscenity. If a restriction on speech deals only with the time, place, and manner of the activity, it need only serve a significant government interest and allow ample alternative channels of communication (see *Perry*). In that instance the law does not need to be the least restrictive alternative; it is necessary only that the government's interest would be achieved less effectively without it and the means chosen are not substantially broader than necessary to achieve the interest (*Ward v. Rock against Racism*, 491 U.S. 781, 109 S. Ct. 2746, 105 L. Ed. 2d 661 [1989]).

The Court has held that the government may infringe on a person's FREEDOM OF ASSOCIATION by punishing membership in an organization that advocates illegal conduct if the defendant had knowledge of the group's illegal objectives and had specific intent to further them (see *Scales v. United States*, 367 U.S. 203, 81 S. Ct. 1469, 6 L. Ed. 2d 782 [1961]; *Noto v. United States*, 367 U.S. 290, 81 S. Ct. 1517, 6 L. Ed. 2d 836 [1961]).

The Court has also determined that when competing liberty interests clash, the majority may not necessarily impose its belief on the minority. In *School District v. Schempp*, 374 U.S. 203, 83 S. Ct. 1560, 10 L. Ed. 2d 844 (1963), the Court held that the freedom to exercise one's RELIGION does not extend to prayer sessions in public schools, even if the proposed prayer is nondenominational and favored by the majority. Justice TOM C. CLARK, writing for the majority, emphasized that the freedom to exercise one's religion ends when it infringes on another's right to be free from state-imposed religious practices. He wrote, "While the Free Exercise Clause clearly prohibits the use of state action to deny the rights of free exercise to anyone, it has never meant that a majority could use the machinery of the State to practice its beliefs." The Court reaffirmed its holding that the free exercise clause does not allow the majority to impose its beliefs on the minority in *Wallace v. Joffree*, 472 U.S. 38, 105 S. Ct. 2479, 86 L. Ed. 2d 29 (1985).

The Court has engendered bitter and sustained controversy with its defense of PRIVACY rights in cases such as *Roe v. Wade*, 410 U.S. 113, 93 S. Ct. 705, 35 L. Ed. 2d 147 (1973), which found a constitutional right to privacy that included the right to obtain an ABORTION. Critics of such decisions contend that such liberties are not enumerated in the Constitution and that the Court should uphold only rights found in the Constitution. But the Court has consistently held that the liberties enumerated in the Constitution are a continuum that, in the words of Justice JOHN MARSHALL HARLAN, "includes a freedom from all substantial arbitrary impositions and purposeless restraints . . . and which also recognizes . . . that certain interests require particularly careful scrutiny of the state needs asserted to justify their abridgement" (*Poe v. Ullman*, 367 U.S. 497, 81 S. Ct. 1752, 6 L. Ed. 2d 989 [1961]).

The Court justifies its findings of liberty rights that are not enumerated in the Constitution by stating that some rights are basic and fundamental, and that the government has a duty to protect those rights. It has held that the Constitution outlines a "realm of personal liberty which the government may not enter." As an example it notes that MARRIAGE is not mentioned in the BILL OF RIGHTS and that interracial marriage was illegal in many places during the nineteenth century, but that the Court has rightly found these activities to be within the liberty interests guaranteed by the Constitution.

The Court has repeatedly held that individual liberties must be protected no matter how repugnant some find the activity or individual involved. For example, in *Planned Parenthood v. Casey*, 505 U.S. 833, 112 S. Ct. 2791, 120 L. Ed. 28 674 (1992), the Court stated, "Some of us as individuals find abortion offensive to our most basic principles of morality, but that cannot control our decision. Our obligation is to define the liberty of all, not to mandate our own moral code." In *West Virginia State Board of Education v. Barnette*, 319 U.S. 624, 63 S. Ct. 1178, 87 L. Ed. 1628 (1943), the Court invalidated a law mandating that all students salute the FLAG, and in *Texas v. Johnson*, 491 U.S. 397, 109 S. Ct. 2533, 105 L. Ed. 2d 342 (1989), it invalidated a law prohibiting burning of the flag. In all of these cases, the Court emphasized that individuals may disagree about whether the activity is morally acceptable, but the liberty inherent in the activity may not be proscribed even if a majority of the populace thinks that it should be.

Justice LOUIS D. BRANDEIS summarized the Court's general wariness of government intrusion into liberty interests, in *Whitney v. California*, 274 U.S. 357, 47 S. Ct. 641, 71 L. Ed. 1095 (1927): "Those who won our independence believed that the final end of the state was to make men free." The Court will continue to grapple with the extent to which organized society may restrict individual liberty without violating that mandate.

CROSS-REFERENCES

Abington School District v. Schempp; Constitution of the United States; Criminal Procedure; Freedom of Speech; Freedom of the Press; *Roe v. Wade*; School Prayer.

LIBRARY OF CONGRESS   The Library of Congress, located in Washington, D.C., is the world's largest library, with nearly 110 million items in almost every language and format stored on 532 miles of bookshelves. Its collections constitute the world's most comprehensive record of human creativity and knowledge. Founded in 1800 to serve the reference needs of Congress, the library has grown from an original collection of 6,487 books to a current accumulation of more than 16 million books and almost 100 million other items and collections, from ancient Chinese wood-block prints to compact discs.

The Library of Congress was created by Act of April 24, 1800 (2 Stat. 56), which provided for the removal of the seat of government to the new capital city of Washington, D.C., and for $5,000 "for the purchase of such books as may be necessary for the use of Congress . . . and for putting up a suitable apartment for containing them therein." The library was housed in the new capitol until August 1814, when British troops invaded Washington, D.C., and burned the capitol building, destroying nearly three thousand volumes of the small congressional library. The first major book collection acquired by Congress was the personal library of former president THOMAS JEFFERSON, purchased in 1815 at a cost of $23,950. In 1851 a second fire destroyed two-thirds of the library's accumulated holdings of 35,000 volumes, including a substantial portion of the Jefferson library. Congress voted a massive appropriation to replace the lost books, and by the end of the Civil War, the collections of the library had grown to 82,000 volumes.

The librarian of Congress is appointed by the president with the advice and consent of the Senate. In 1864 President ABRAHAM LINCOLN appointed as librarian Ainsworth Rand Spofford, who opened the library to the public and greatly expanded its collections. Spofford successfully advocated a change in the COPYRIGHT law so that the library would receive two free copies of every book, map, chart, musical composition, engraving, print, and photograph submitted for copyright. Under subsequent legislation (2 U.S.C.A. §§ 131–168d) the library's acquisitions included free copies of the *Congressional Record* and of all U.S. statutes, which Spofford parlayed into document exchanges with all foreign nations that had diplomatic relations with the United States.

Soon the Capitol's library rooms, attics, and hallways were filled with the library's growing collections, necessitating construction of the library's first permanent building, the Thomas Jefferson Building, which opened in 1897. The John Adams Building was added by Congress in 1939, and the James Madison Memorial Building in 1980. These three buildings provide nearly 65 acres of floor space.

Supported mainly by appropriations from Congress, the library also uses income derived from funds received from foundations and other private sources and administered by the Library of Congress Trust Fund Board, as well as monetary gifts presented for direct application (2 U.S.C.A. §§ 154–163). Many of the greatest items in the library have come directly from individual U.S. citizens or were purchased with money donated by them. Gifts that have enriched the cultural heritage of the nation include the private papers of President Lincoln from his son ROBERT TODD LINCOLN; rare Stradivarius violins used for public performances; the Lessing J. Rosenwald collection of illustrated books and incunabula (early works of art or industry); Joseph Pennell's contribution of Whistler drawings and letters; and hundreds of thousands of letters and documents from musicians, artists, scientists, writers, and public figures.

Congressional Research Service The library's first responsibility is service to Congress. One department, the Congressional Research Service (CRS), operates exclusively for the legislative branch of the government. The CRS provides objective, nonpartisan research, analysis, and information to assist Congress in its legislative, oversight, and representative functions.

The CRS evolved from the Legislative Reference Service, a unit developed by a former librarian, Herbert Putnam, whose tenure with the library spanned forty years. The Legislative Reference Service was developed to prepare indexes, digests, and compilations of law that Congress might need, but it quickly became a specialized reference unit for information transfer and research.

The CRS's mandate has grown over the years in response to the increasing scope of PUBLIC POLICY issues on the congressional agenda. The service answers more than five hundred thousand requests for research annually. Its staff anticipates congressional inquiries and provides timely and objective information and analyses in response to those inquiries at every stage of the legislative process and in an interdisciplinary manner. The CRS also creates and maintains a number of specialized reading lists for members of Congress and their staffs, and disseminates other materials of interest. Finally, it maintains the parts of the Library of Congress's automated information system that cover legislative matters, including digests of all

KEN WINOKUR/THE PICTURE CUBE

public bills and briefing papers on major legislative issues. The CRS director, assisted by a management team, oversees and coordinates the work of seven research divisions, which span a range of public policy subjects and disciplines.

Collections The library's extensive collections include books, serials, and pamphlets on every subject, in a multitude of languages, and in various formats including map, photograph, manuscript, motion picture, and sound recording. Among them are the most comprehensive collections of Chinese, Japanese, and Russian language books outside Asia and the former Soviet Union; volumes relating to science and to U.S. and foreign law; the world's largest collection of published aeronautical literature; and the most extensive collection of incunabula in the Western Hemisphere.

The manuscript collections, numbering 46 million, relate to manifold aspects of U.S. history and civilization, and include the personal papers of most presidents, from GEORGE WASHINGTON to CALVIN COOLIDGE, as well as papers of people from many diverse arenas, such as Margaret Mead, Sigmund Freud, HENRY KISSINGER, THURGOOD MARSHALL, and thousands of others.

The library houses a perfect copy of the Gutenberg Bible, one of three such copies in the world. It also contains the oldest written material, a Sumerian cuneiform tablet dating from 2040 B.C.; the earliest known copyrighted motion picture, *Fred Ott's Sneeze*, copyrighted by Thomas Edison in 1893; and a book so small that it requires a needle to turn the pages. The musical collections contain volumes and pieces, manuscript and published, from classic works to the newest popular compositions. Other materials available for research include maps and views; photographic records from the daguerreotype to the latest news photo; musical recordings; speeches and poetry readings; prints, drawings, and posters; government documents, newspapers, and periodicals from all over the world; and motion pictures, microfilms, and audiotapes and videotapes.

Copyrights Since 1870 the Library of Congress has been responsible for copyrights registered by the U.S. Copyright Office, located in the Madison Building (Acts of July 8, 1870 [16 Stat. 212–217]; February 19, 1897 [29 Stat. 545, codified as amended at 2 U.S.C.A. 131 (1997)]; October 19, 1976 [90 Stat. 2541, codified as amended at 2 U.S.C.A. 170 (1997)]).

The Library of Congress houses more than 16 million books and nearly 100 million other items. Its collections and staff serve Congress and the public.

The Copyright Office has handled more than 20 million copyright registrations and transfers and processes six hundred thousand new registrations annually. All copyrightable works, whether published or unpublished, are subject to a system of statutory protection that gives the copyright owner certain exclusive rights, including the right to reproduce the work and distribute it to the public by sale, rental, lease, or lending. Works of authorship include books; periodicals; computer programs; musical compositions; song lyrics; dramas and dramatico-musical compositions; pictorial, graphic, and sculptural works; architectural works; pantomimes and choreographic works; sound recordings; motion pictures; and other audiovisual works.

American Folklife Center The American Folklife Center was established in the Library of Congress by Act of January 2, 1976 (20 U.S.C.A. § 2102 et seq.). Its function is to coordinate and carry out federal and nonfederal programs to support, preserve, and present American folklife through activities such as receiving and maintaining folklife collections, scholarly research, field projects, performances and exhibitions, festivals, workshops, publications, and audiovisual presentations. The center is the national repository for folk-related recordings, manuscripts, and other unpublished materials. Its reading room contains over thirty-five hundred books and periodicals; a sizable collection of magazines, newsletters, unpublished theses, and dissertations; field notes; and many textual and musical transcriptions and recordings. The center also administers the Federal Cylinder Project, which is charged with preserving and disseminating music and oral traditions recorded on wax cylinders dating from the late 1800s to the early 1940s. A cultural conservation study was developed at the center in cooperation with the Department of the Interior pursuant to congressional mandate. Various conferences, workshops, and symposia are given throughout the year, and a series of outdoor concerts of traditional music are scheduled monthly at the library, from April to September.

Center for the Book The Center for the Book was established in the Library of Congress by Act of October 17, 1977 (2 U.S.C.A. § 171 et seq.), to stimulate public interest in books, reading, and libraries and to encourage the study of books and print culture. The center is a catalyst for promoting and exploring the vital role of books, reading, and libraries throughout the world. Since 1984 twenty-nine states have established statewide book centers that are affiliated with this national center.

National Preservation Program To preserve its collections, the library uses the full range of traditional methods of conservation and binding as well as newer technologies such as the deacidification of paper and the digitization of original materials. These measures include maintaining materials in the proper environment, ensuring the proper care and handling of the collections, and stabilizing fragile and rare materials by placing them in acid-free containers to protect them from further deterioration. Research on long-standing preservation problems is conducted by the library's Preservation Research and Testing Office.

The National Film Preservation Board, established by the National Film Preservation Act of 1992 (2 U.S.C.A. § 179b), serves as a public advisory group to the librarian of Congress. The board consists of thirty-six members and alternates representing many parts of the diverse U.S. film industry, archives, scholars, and others. As its primary mission, the board works to ensure the survival, conservation, and increased public availability of the United States' film heritage. This mission includes advising the librarian on the annual selection of films to the National Film Registry and counseling the librarian on the development and implementation of the national film preservation plan.

Extension of Service The Library of Congress extends its service through an interlibrary loan system; photoduplication of books, manuscripts, maps, newspapers, and prints in its collections; a centralized cataloging program whereby the library acquires material published all over the world as well as material from other libraries and from U.S. publishers; and the development of general schemes of classification (the Library of Congress classification for law and the DEWEY DECIMAL SYSTEM), subject headings, and cataloging, embracing the entire field of printed matter.

The library also provides for the preparation of bibliographic lists responsive to the needs of government and research; the maintenance and publication of the *National Union* catalogs and other cooperative publications; the publication of catalogs, bibliographic guides, and texts of original manuscripts and rare books; the circulation in traveling exhibitions of items from the library's collections; and the provision of books in braille, talking book records, and books on tape. In addition, the library employs an optical disk system that supplies articles on public policy to Congress, and provides research and analytical services on a fee-for-service basis to the executive and judicial branches.

Users outside the library can gain free access to its on-line catalog of files through the INTER-

Library of Congress Timeline

1800	President John Adams approved act of Congress that established the Library of Congress
1801	First books for collection stored in U.S. Capitol
1802–07	John J. Beckley served as first Librarian of Congress
1807–15	Patrick Magruder served as second Librarian of Congress
1812–18	War of 1812
1814	British burned the Capitol, destroyed the Library
1815	Congress appropriated funds to buy Thomas Jefferson's personal library; Library adopted Jefferson's classification scheme
1815–29	George Watterson served as third Librarian of Congress
1829–61	John Silva served as fourth Librarian of Congress
1832	Separate department for law collection established
1846	The law establishing the Smithsonian Institution gave Smithsonian and Library of Congress one copy of each copyrighted "book, map, chart, musical composition, print, cut, or engraving."
1851	Fire destroyed 35,000 of the 55,000-volume collection, including two-thirds of Jefferson's library
1859	Copyright deposit law repealed
1861–64	John C. Stephenson served as fifth Librarian of Congress
1861–65	U.S. Civil War
1864–97	Ainsworth Rand Spofford served as sixth Librarian of Congress
1865	Library's rooms expanded and copyright privilege reinstated; collection reached 82,000 volumes
1866	Smithsonian's 40,000-volume library transferred to Library
1867	Purchase of Peter Force's library formed the foundation of the Library's Americana and incunabula (early) collections
1869	Gift of 933 volumes from emperor of China formed nucleus of Library's Chinese collection
1870	Responsibility for copyright registration and deposit centralized
1874	Library Committee authorized subscriptions to at least two newspapers from each state
1882	Donation of Dr. Joseph Toner's 40,000-volume private library marked first large—and valuable—free gift to nation's library
1886	Construction of separate building for the Library authorized
1893	Library acquired first motion pictures in the form of *Edison Kinetoscopic Records*
1897	Library staff increased from 42 to 108, separate departments for periodicals, manuscripts, music, graphic arts, and map collections established. Eight hundred tons of materials transported from Capitol across the street to new Thomas Jefferson building.
1897–99	John Russell Young served as seventh Librarian of Congress
1899–1939	Herbert Putnam served as eighth Librarian of Congress
1903	Personal papers of Benjamin Franklin and Presidents Washington, Jefferson, Madison, and Monroe, as well as Continental Congress papers transferred from State Department to Library
1904	Cylinder recording from Kaiser Wilhelm II began Library's phonograph collection; Indic collection began with purchase of Albrecht Weber's 4,000-volume library
1906	Purchase of G.V. Yudin's 80,000-volume library of Russian literature gave Library preeminence in this field
1907	Japanese collection begun; separate archives building for government administrative records authorized
1914	Hebraic section founded
1916	Two drafts of Lincoln's Gettysburg Address donated by John Hays's descendants
1917	Gift of Theodore Roosevelt's papers marked first time presidential papers received directly from former president
1921	Original copies of Declaration of Independence and U.S. Constitution transferred from State Department
1923	Robert Todd Lincoln donated the personal papers of his father, Abraham Lincoln, to the Library
1925	Library of Congress Trust Fund Board established, enabling the Library to accept gifts and bequests of personal property for the benefit of the Library
1928	American folk song project in the Music Division established to collect and preserve the folk songs and ballads "endangered by the spread of the radio and phonograph"
1930	One of three perfect vellum copies of the Gutenberg Bible purchased
1934	Putnam declared the Library of Congress the largest library in the world
1936	Gertrude Clark Whitall donated five Stradivari violins and established endowment for their use and upkeep
1938	Photoduplication Service established to supply off-site researchers with microfilm and photocopies of Library materials
1939	John Adams Building added to house Library's collections
1939–44	Archibald MacLeish served as ninth Librarian of Congress
1940	Collection of federal WPA art, music, theater, and writer's project works begun
1941	Musical autograph collection begun
1943	Rosenwald collection of illustrated books and incunabula donated
1945–53	Luther H. Evans served as tenth Librarian of Congress
1945	Purchase of Sheikh Mahumud al-Iman Mansuri's 5,000-volume library greatly strengthened the Arabic collections
1946	Edith Wilson donated Woodrow Wilson's 9,000-volume library
1952	Declaration of Independence and U.S. Constitution transferred to National Archives
1954–74	L. Quincy Mumford served as eleventh Librarian of Congress
1959	Carnegie Corporation donated fund to establish Africana section
1963	Children's Literature Center established
1964	Library received first installment of gift of NAACP records, an archive of over one million items
1966	Library's first overseas acquisitions office opened in London
1975–87	Daniel J. Boorstin served as twelfth Librarian of Congress
1975	Alexander Graham Bell's family papers donated to the Library
1976	The American Folklife Preservation Act established the American Folklife Center at the Library
1977	Center for the Book established
1978	Library received NBC Radio Collection of 175,000 transcription discs covering 80,000 hours of radio programming from 1926 to 1970
1980	Addition of James Madison Memorial Building increased Library's floor space to 65 acres
1987	James H. Billington appointed thirteenth Librarian of Congress
1988	Library established machine-readable collections reading room, including software programs and data files on microcomputer, compact, and video discs
1990	The American Memory Project established to begin sharing portions of the Library's Americana collections in electronic form
1991	LC Direct began offering state library agencies on-line access to the Library's bibliographic, subject, and name authority cards
1992	100 millionth item added to Library's collections

Source: Library of Congress.

NET. Major exhibitions of the library are available on-line, as are selected prints and photographs, historic films, and political speeches. Internet sites include the Library of Congress World Wide Web (http://www.loc.gov); THOMAS, an important legislative service containing a searchable full text of the *Congressional Record*, texts of recent bills, and congressional committee information (http://thomas.loc.gov); major exhibits from the past three years using file transfer protocol (ftp.loc.gov), LC Marvel (marvel.loc.gov), or LC WEB; existing historical collections on the LC WEB (http://lcweb2.loc.gov/ammem); pointers to external Internet resources including extensive international, national, state, and local government information; and an international electronic library of resources arranged by Library of Congress subject headings. The Library of Congress also contributes to the National Digital Library more than 40 million bibliographic records, summaries of congressional bills, copyright registrations, bibliographies and research guides, summaries of foreign laws, an index of Southeast Asian POW-MIA documents, selections from the library's unique historical collections, and more.

Reference Resources Admission to the various research facilities of the library is free, and no introduction or credentials are required for persons over high school age. A photo identification and current address are required for the library's reading rooms and collections, and additional requirements apply for entry into certain collections like those of the Manuscript Division, Rare Book and Special Collections Division, and Motion Picture, Broadcasting, and Recorded Sound Division. Priority is given to inquiries pertaining to the library's holdings of special materials or to subjects in which its resources are unique. Demands for service to Congress and federal agencies have increased, and thus reference service to others through correspondence is limited.

LICENSE ▨ The permission granted by competent authority to exercise a certain privilege that, without such authorization, would constitute an illegal act, a TRESPASS, or a TORT. The CERTIFICATE or the document itself that confers permission to engage in otherwise proscribed conduct. ▨

A license is different from a permit. The terms *license* and *permit* are often used interchangeably, but generally, a permit describes a more temporary form of permission. For example, if a homeowner seeks to make structural additions to her property, she may have to apply for permits from local land-use and zoning boards. These permits expire on a certain date or when the work is finished. By contrast, the contractor who completes the work will likely hold a local license that allows her to operate her business for a certain number of years.

Licenses are an important and ubiquitous feature of contemporary society. Federal, state, and local governments rely on licensing to control a broad range of human activity, from commercial and professional to dangerous and environmental. Licenses may also be issued by private parties and by patent or copyright holders.

Government Licenses The great many activities that require a license issued by a government authority include fishing; hunting; marrying; driving a motor vehicle; providing health care services; practicing law; manufacturing; engaging in retail and wholesale commerce; operating a private business, trade, or technical school; providing commercial services such as those offered by whitewater rafting outfitters and travel agencies; providing public services such as food and environmental inspection; and operating public pinball machines.

Not all persons engaged in a licensed activity need to obtain a license. For example, the owner of a liquor store must obtain a license to operate it, but the cashiers and stock persons need not obtain a license to work there. By contrast, not only does a dentist have to obtain a license to conduct business in a dental office, but dental hygienists and other dental assistants must have a license to work in the office.

A license gives a person or organization permission to engage in a particular activity. If the government requires a license for an activity, it may issue criminal charges if a person engages in the activity without obtaining a license. Most licenses expire after a certain period of time, and most may be renewed. Failure to abide by certain laws and regulations can result in suspension or REVOCATION of a license. Acquiring a license through FRAUD or misrepresentation will result in revocation of the license.

Licenses are issued by the ADMINISTRATIVE AGENCIES of local, state, and federal lawmaking bodies. Administrative agencies are established by legislative bodies to regulate specific government activities and concerns. For example, the U.S. Congress and state legislatures have each created an agency that exercises authority over environmental issues. This agency usually is called a department of environmental protection or of conservation. It is responsible for issuing licenses for activities such as hunting, fishing, and camping. If the same agency has authority over environmental cleanups, it also may be responsible for issuing licenses for inspectors and businesses that specialize in waste management and removal. Specific boards or divisions within an agency may be responsible for issuing licenses.

The licensing process helps to control activity in a variety of ways. License application procedures allow government authorities to screen applicants to verify that they are fit to engage in the particular activity. Before any license is issued by an agency, the applicant must meet certain standards. For example, a person who seeks a driver's license must be at least age sixteen, must have passed a driver's test and a vision test, must show proof of insurance or financial responsibility, and must pay a fee. If an applicant is under age eighteen, the state department of motor vehicles may require that the applicant obtain the signature of a parent or guardian. If the applicant seeks to drive other than a passenger vehicle, such as a motorcycle or semi-truck, the applicant has to pass tests that relate to the driving of that vehicle and obtain a separate license for driving that vehicle.

The requirements for certain business licenses can be stringent. For example, an insurance adjuster in Maine must be at least eighteen years old; be competent, trustworthy, financially responsible, and of good personal and business reputation; pass a written examination on insurance adjusting; and have been employed or have undergone special training for not less than one year in insurance adjustment (Me. Rev. Stat. Ann. tit. 24-A, § 1853 [West 1995]). The insurance board can investigate any applicant for an insurance adjuster's license, and deny an applicant a license if he does not meet the qualifications.

Such rigorous licensing procedures are usually used if the activity places the license holder, or licensee, in a FIDUCIARY relationship, that is, in a position of confidence and trust with other persons. Such activity usually involves the handling of money or health matters, and includes endeavors like medical care, legal representation, accounting, insurance, and financial investment.

Requiring a license for a certain activity allows the government to closely supervise and control the activity. The agency responsible for issuing the license can control the number of licensees. This is important for activities such as HUNTING, where the licensing of too many hunters may deplete wildlife populations and put hunters in danger of stray bullets.

A license is not a PROPERTY RIGHT. This means that no one has the absolute right to a license. The government may decline to issue a license when it sees fit to do so, provided that the denial does not violate federal or state law. No agency may decline to issue a license on the basis of race, religion, sex, national origin, or ethnic background.

The denial of a license, the requirement of a license, or the procedures required to obtain a license may be challenged in court. The most frequent court challenges involve licenses pertaining to the operation of a business. This was the case in *FW/PBS v. City of Dallas*, 493 U.S. 215, 110 S. Ct. 596, 107 L. Ed. 2d 603 (1990). In *FW/PBS* three groups of individuals and businesses in the adult entertainment industry filed suit in federal district court challenging a new ordinance passed by the Dallas City Council. The ordinance placed a number of new restrictions on sexually oriented businesses. Among other things it required that owners of sexually oriented businesses obtain a license, renew it each year, and submit to annual inspections.

On appeal to the Supreme Court, the Court upheld a requirement that hotels renting rooms for less than ten hours obtain a special license. The Court held that the city of Dallas's evidence that such motels fostered PROSTITUTION and led to a deterioration of the neighborhoods in which they existed was adequate justification for the requirement. However, the Court struck down the application of the licensing requirement to businesses engaged in sexually oriented expression, such as adult bookstores, theaters, and cabarets. The activities of these businesses are protected by the FIRST AMENDMENT, and licenses regarding activity protected by the First Amendment must be issued promptly. The Dallas ordinance failed to meet the promptness requirement because it did not limit the time for review of license applications or provide for quick judicial review of license denials. Thus, the Court declared it unconstitutional as applied to businesses engaged in expressive activity.

Private Party Licenses When a landowner allows a person to do work or perform an act on the landowner's property, the visitor has a license to enter the property. This kind of license need not be signed and formalized: it may be oral or it may be implied by the relationship or actions of the parties. For example, a public utility inspector has a license to enter private property for the purposes of maintaining the utility and gauging consumption. In such a case, the grantor of the license, or licensor, owes a duty to the licensee to make sure the premises are safe for the licensee.

Patent and Copyright Holder Licenses A license granted by the holder of a PATENT or a COPYRIGHT on literary or artistic work gives the license holder a limited right to reproduce, sell, or distribute the work. Likewise, the owner of a TRADEMARK may give another person a license to use the mark in a region where the owner's goods have not become known and associated with the owner's use of the mark. These INTELLECTUAL PROPERTY licenses usually require that the licensee pay a fee to the licensor in exchange for use of the property.

LICENTIOUSNESS 📖 Acting without regard to law, ethics, or the rights of others. 📖

The term *licentiousness* is often used interchangeably with LEWDNESS or LASCIVIOUSNESS, which relate to moral impurity in a sexual context.

LIE DETECTOR TEST See POLYGRAPH.

LIEN 📖 A right given to another by the owner of PROPERTY to secure a DEBT, or one created by law in favor of certain creditors. 📖

A lien is an encumbrance on one person's property to secure a debt the property owner owes to another person. The statement that someone's property is "tied up" describes the effect of liens on both real and PERSONAL PROPERTY. *Lien* is a French word meaning "knot or binding" that was brought to Britain with the French language during the Norman Conquest in 1066.

Real Estate Liens In many states a MORTGAGE is regarded as a lien, not a complete transfer of TITLE, and if not repaid the debt is recovered by FORECLOSURE and sale of the real estate. REAL ESTATE is also affected by liens that favor local, state, and federal governments for real estate taxes and SPECIAL ASSESSMENTS; state and federal governments for income and sales or use taxes; condominium and homeowners' associations; and general contractors, subcontractors, material suppliers, and laborers for the value of work or materials installed on real estate. The filing requirements and STATUTES OF LIMITATIONS for these liens vary according to the law of each state.

Perhaps the riskiest move a purchaser of real estate can make is to buy without making certain that there are no liens on the property or without obtaining TITLE INSURANCE against liens on the property. In many states liens are secret: that is, they are hidden from the public records until required to be filed.

The priority of liens on a construction project relates back to the first visible commencement of the work. This line of law makes the last work, perhaps landscaping, equal in priority to the first, excavating. This means that during the entire work of construction, the owner must obtain waivers of lien from each subcontractor and material supplier. Without these waivers the real estate is subject to liens of all such claimants, if the general contractor, though paid in full, fails to pay them. A waiver is a voluntary relinquishment of a known right. Waivers of lien must be in writing, give a sufficient description of the real estate, and be signed by the one claiming a lien. No payment need be made if the claimant agrees to release the land from the lien and rely only on the credit of the owner or general contractor for payment of the debt.

Lien claimants are protected in this way because all their materials and labor are "buried" in the real estate, having become part of it. They cannot be reclaimed without irreparable damage to the property. Unlike mortgage liens, the liens of these claimants, called MECHANIC'S LIENS, offer no REDEMPTION in a foreclosure JUDGMENT.

Other Liens The published statutes of a state usually have a section on the topic of liens under which is listed most or all of the liens allowed by state law. A great number of persons in trade or business obtain liens for their services to personal property: garage keepers and warehouse owners for unpaid rent for storage; automobile mechanics for repairs; jewelers; dry cleaners and furriers; artisans for restoration of art objects; bankers; factors dealing in commodities; and many others. Not to be outdone, attorneys have a lien for their fees and may retain clients' files—perhaps containing vital information or documents needed by the client for work or family affairs—until the fees are paid.

A judgment lien can, when entered by a court after a suit, affect all the real and personal property of one who fails to pay a debt, such as a PROMISSORY NOTE to a bank, credit card balance, or judgment for injury the person may have caused. In some states the lien of a properly docketed judgment affects all the debtor's property in every county where NOTICE of the judgment is filed. State law governs the length of time such liens survive—which in some states is as long as ten years. Judgments can be enforced by EXECUTIONS and sale of property until the amount due is satisfied.

Courts of EQUITY have the power to create so-called equitable liens on property to correct some injustice. For example, one whose money was embezzled may obtain a lien on the wrong-

To the Clerk of the County of _____ , State of New York and all Others Whom It May Concern.

PLEASE TAKE NOTICE, that (1) _____ , residing at _____ , in the County of _____ , State of New York, has and claims a lien for the principal and interest of the price and value of the labor and material hereinafter mentioned, upon the house, building and appurtenances, and upon the lot, premises and parcel of land upon which the same may stand, or be intended to stand, hereinafter mentioned, pursuant to the Lien Law of the State of New York and all acts amending or extending the same or providing for the filing of mechanic's liens; or in force in said County in reference to mechanic's liens; and hereby states:

(2) The name of said lienor's attorney is _____ , of _____ , New York.

(3) The name of the owner of the real property against whose interest therein a lien is claimed is _____ of _____ , New York, and the interest of the owner as far as known to the lienor is owner in fee [*or state other interest*].

(4) The name of the person by whom the lienor was employed is _____ .
The name of the person to whom the lienor furnished or is to furnish material is
_____ .
The name of the person with whom the contract was made is _____ .

(5) The labor performed was [*specify labor performed*]. The material furnished was [*specify material furnished*]. The material actually manufactured for but not delivered is [*specify*] and
The agreed price and value of the labor performed is . . . . $_____
The agreed price and value of the material furnished is . . . . _____
The agreed price and value of the material actually manufactured for
but not delivered is . . . . _____
                    Total agreed price and value . . . . $_____

(6) The amount unpaid to the lienor for said labor performed is . . . . _____
The amount unpaid to the lienor for said material furnished is . . . . _____
The amount unpaid to the lienor for the material actually manufactured
for but not delivered is . . . . _____
                    Total amount unpaid . . . . $_____

The total amount claimed for which this lien is filed is . . . . _____

(7) The time when the first items of work were performed was _____ , 19___ ; and the time when the first items of material were furnished was _____ , 19___ .
The time when the last items of work were performed was _____ , 19___ ; and the time when the last items of materials were furnished was _____ , 19___ .

(8) [*Insert description of property subject to lien.*]

(9) That said labor and materials were performed and furnished for and used in the improvement of the real property hereinbefore described.

(10) That four months have not elapsed dating from the last item of work performed, and dating from the last items of materials furnished, nor since the completion of the contract nor since the final performance of the work, nor since the final furnishing of the materials for which this lien is claimed.

Dated: _____ , N.Y., _____ , 19___ .

_____
Lienor

[*Verification*]

doer's property by suing for a CONSTRUCTIVE TRUST.

Discharging a Lien Liens are discharged after a certain length of time. The requirements for commencing their foreclosure vary among the states. If a person pays and satisfies a lien, she should be careful to obtain a written, legally sufficient release or SATISFACTION, and file or record it in the appropriate government office, so that her title and CREDIT reports no longer show the ENCUMBRANCE.

See also TITLE SEARCH.

LIFE ESTATE 📖 An ESTATE whose duration is limited to the life of the party holding it, or some other person. 📖

LIFE IN BEING 📖 A phrase used in the COMMON-LAW and statutory rules against perpetuities, meaning the remaining duration of the life of a person who is in existence at the time when the DEED or WILL takes effect. 📖

The courts developed the rule during the seventeenth century in order to limit a person's power to control the ownership and possession of property after death, and to ensure the transferability of property.

See also RULE AGAINST PERPETUITIES.

LIFE OR LIMB 📖 The phrase within the FIFTH AMENDMENT to the U.S. Constitution, commonly known as the Double Jeopardy Clause, that provides, "nor shall any person be subject for the same offence to be twice put in jeopardy of life or limb," pursuant to which there can be no second prosecution after a first trial for the same offense. 📖

The words *life or limb* are not interpreted strictly; they apply to any criminal penalty.

See also DOUBLE JEOPARDY.

LIFO 📖 An abbreviation for *last in, first out*, a method used in inventory ACCOUNTING to value the merchandise of a particular business. 📖

LIFO assumes that the last goods purchased are the first sold and, as a result, those items that remain unsold in the INVENTORY at the end of the year are assumed to be those which were purchased first.

See also FIFO.

LIFT 📖 To raise; to take up. 📖

To lift a PROMISSORY NOTE (a written commitment to pay a sum of money on a certain date) is to terminate the obligation by paying its amount.

To lift the bar of the STATUTE OF LIMITATIONS is to remove, by some sufficient act or acknowledgment, the obstruction that it interposes. For example, some states will not permit an ACTION to be instituted on a DEBT owed after ten years from the date of the debt. This is a ten-year statute of limitations. If the DEBTOR acknowledges in writing that he or she owes the debt and will pay it on a certain date, this conduct lifts the bar of the statute of limitations so that the debtor can be sued on the debt for another ten years.

LIGAN 📖 Goods cast into the sea tied to a buoy, so that they may be found again by the owners. When goods are cast into the sea in storms or shipwrecks and remain there, without coming to land, they are distinguished by the names of JETSAM, FLOTSAM, and *ligan*. 📖

LIMITATION 📖 A qualification, restriction, or circumspection. 📖

In the law of PROPERTY, a limitation on an ESTATE arises when its duration or quality is in some way restricted. For example, in the CONVEYANCE, "Owner conveys BLACKACRE to A until B leaves the country," A's estate is limited, since A is given Blackacre for only a specified length of time.

LIMITATIONS OF ACTIONS 📖 Statutes restricting the right to bring suit on certain civil CAUSES OF ACTION or criminal prosecutions, which provide that a suit may not be commenced unless it is brought within a designated period after the time that the right to sue accrued. 📖

See also STATUTE OF LIMITATIONS.

LIMITED 📖 Restricted in duration, extent, or scope; confined. 📖

Limited liability is the rule that the owners or shareholders of a CORPORATION cannot usually be sued as individuals for corporate actions unless they are involved in FRAUD or criminal conduct.

Limited is also a designation following the name of a corporation that indicates its corporate and limited liability status; it is abbreviated *Ltd.* It is found most commonly after British and Canadian corporate names, although it is sometimes used in the United States.

LIMITED LIABILITY COMPANY 📖 A noncorporate business whose owners actively participate in the organization's management and are protected against personal LIABILITY for the organization's debts and obligations. 📖

The limited liability company (LLC) is a hybrid legal entity that has characteristics of a CORPORATION and a PARTNERSHIP. An LLC provides its owners with corporate-like protection against personal liability. It is, however, usually treated as a noncorporate business organization for tax purposes.

History The LLC is a relatively new business form in the United States, although it has existed in other countries for some time. In 1977 Wyoming became the first state to enact LLC legislation: it wanted to attract capital and created the statute specifically for a Texas oil company (W.S. 1977 § 17-15-101 et seq., Laws 1977, ch. 158 § 1). Florida followed with its own LLC statute in 1982 (West's F.S.A. § 608.401, Laws 1982, c. 82-177 § 2). At this point states had little incentive to form an LLC because it remained unclear whether the INTERNAL REVENUE SERVICE (IRS) would treat an LLC as a partnership or as a corporation for tax purposes. In 1988 the IRS issued a ruling that an LLC in Wyoming would be treated as a partnership for tax purposes. This allowed the taxable profits and losses of an LLC to flow through to the LLC's individual owners; unlike a typical corporation, an LLC would not be taxed as a separate business organization. After the 1988 IRS ruling, nearly every state in the United States enacted an LLC statute, and the LLC is now a widely recognized business form.

Many legal issues concerning the LLC are still developing.

Formation State law governs the creation of an LLC. Persons form an LLC by filing required documents with the appropriate state authority, usually the secretary of state. Most states require the filing of articles of organization. These are considered public documents and are similar to ARTICLES OF INCORPORATION, which establish a corporation as a legal entity. The LLC usually comes into existence on the same day the articles of organization are filed and a filing fee is paid to the secretary of state.

The minimum information required for the articles of organization varies from state to state. Generally, it includes the name of the LLC, the name of the person organizing the LLC, the duration of the LLC, and the name of the LLC's registered agent. Some states require additional information, such as the LLC's business purpose and details about the LLC's membership and management structure. In all states an LLC's name must include words or phrases that identify it as a limited liability company. These may be the specific words *Limited Liability Company* or one of various abbreviations of those words, such as *LLC* or *Ltd. Liability Co.*

Structure The owners of an LLC are called members and are similar in some respects to shareholders of a corporation. A member can be a natural person, a corporation, a partnership, or another legal association or entity. Unlike corporations, which may be formed by only one shareholder, LLCs in most states must be formed and managed by two or more members. LLCs are therefore unavailable to sole proprietors. In addition, unlike some closely held, or S, corporations, which are allowed a limited number of shareholders, LLCs may have any number of members beyond one.

Generally, state law outlines the required governing structure of an LLC. In most states members may manage an LLC directly or delegate management responsibility to one or more managers. Managers of an LLC are usually elected or appointed by the members. Some LLCs may have one, two, or more managers. Like a general partner in a limited partnership or an officer in a corporation, an LLC's manager is responsible for the day-to-day management of the business.

A manager owes a duty of loyalty and care to the LLC. Unless the members consent, a manager may not use LLC property for personal benefit and may not compete with the LLC's business. In addition, a manager may not engage in SELF-DEALING or usurp an LLC's business opportunities, unless the members consent

to a transaction involving such activity after being fully informed of the manager's interest.

Operating Agreement Nearly every LLC maintains a separate written or oral operating agreement, which is generally defined as the agreement between the members that governs the affairs of the LLC. Some states call an operating agreement regulations or a member control agreement. Although some states do not require an operating agreement, nearly all LLCs create and maintain a written document that details their management structure.

The operating agreement typically provides the procedures for admitting new members, outlines the status of the LLC upon a member's withdrawal, and outlines the procedures for dissolution of the LLC. Unless state law restricts the contents of an operating agreement, members of an LLC are free to structure the agreement as they see fit. An LLC can usually amend or repeal provisions of its operating agreement by a vote of its members.

Membership Interests A member of an LLC possesses a membership interest, which usually includes only an economic interest. A membership interest is considered PERSONAL PROPERTY and may be freely transferred to nonmembers or to other members. The membership interest usually does not include any right to participate in the management of the LLC. Accordingly, if a member assigns or sells a membership interest to another person, that other person typically receives only the right to the assigning member's share of profits in the LLC. Persons who receive a membership interest are not able to participate as voting members or managers unless they are admitted as new members.

State law and an LLC's operating agreement or articles of organization provide the circumstances under which a person may be admitted as a new member. These circumstances vary. Usually the admission of a new member requires the consent of existing members, and in most cases the consent must be unanimous. In some cases the articles of organization do not allow for admission of new members. In others the recipient of a membership interest may be automatically admitted as a new member.

Member Contributions Members of an LLC contribute capital to the LLC in exchange for a membership interest. There is no minimum amount of capital contribution, and members usually can contribute cash, property, or services. By default, the total amount of a member's capital contribution to an LLC determines the member's voting and financial rights in the LLC. In other words, unless an LLC's

Comparison of Structures

	Sole Proprietorship	Partnership	Limited Liability Company (LLC)	S Corporation	C Corporation
Limited liability	No	Limited partners have protection from the partnership's liabilities unless provided otherwise.	All members have protection from the LLC's liabilities unless provided otherwise.	All shareholders	All shareholders
Participation in management	Yes	Participation by limited partners generally must be restricted to preserve limited liability.	No restrictions	No restrictions	No restrictions
Transferability of interests	Yes	Restrictions are imposed by state law, by securities laws, and generally by the partnership agreement.	Restrictions are imposed by state laws, securities laws and LLC operating agreement.	Restrictions are imposed by securities laws and by a shareholders' agreement, if any.	Restrictions are imposed by securities laws and by a shareholders' agreement, if any.
Continuity of life	No	Generally, no	Generally, no	Yes	Yes
Certainty of tax status	Yes	Yes. However, a limited partnership must lack two of four corporate characteristics: (i) limited liability; (ii) free transferability of interests; (iii) continuity of life and (iv) centralized management	Yes. However, an LLC must lack free transferability of interests and continuity of life. Occasionally, an LLC may lack centralized management.	Yes. However, any shareholder may cause loss of tax status.	Yes
Qualification	N/A	A limited partnership generally needs an individual general partner or a corporate general partner with substantial assets.	No restrictions	There are various eligibility requirements including a restriction on the number and type of shareholders and on the ownership of subsidiaries.	No restrictions
Number of owners	N/A	At least 2	At least 2 (no restrictions in Texas)	1 to 75	No restrictions
Types of owner	N/A	Any	Any	Ownership is limited to U.S. residents and citizens and to certain U.S. trusts.	Any
Classes of ownership interests	N/A	Multiple classes are permitted.	Multiple classes are permitted.	One. However, there can be differences in voting rights.	Multiple classes are permitted.
Ability to do business in other states	Yes	Yes	Unclear in those states that do not have the LLC form	Yes	Yes
Levels of income tax	1	Partner level only	Member level only	Generally, only shareholder level. However, former C corporations may be subject to tax. In addition, some states will tax S corporations.	Corporate and shareholder level

operating agreement provides for a different arrangement, the profits and losses of the LLC are shared proportionally in relation to the members' contributions to the LLC. For example, if a member's capital contributions constitute 40 percent of an LLC's capital, that member typically has a 40 percent stake in the LLC and has more voting power than a member with a 20 percent interest.

A member may promise a future contribution to an LLC in exchange for a membership interest. If the member later fails to make the contribution, the LLC generally may enforce the promise as a contract or sell the member's existing interest to remedy the failure.

Distributions of profits or ASSETS to members are usually governed by an LLC's operating agreement. Most state LLC laws do not require distributions to members other than when a member withdraws or terminates membership. Members vote to determine all aspects of distributions to members, including amount and timing. Because a member's share of any distribution or loss depends on the member's share

Comparison of Structures—Continued

	Sole Proprietorship	Partnership	Limited Liability Company (LLC)	S Corporation	C Corporation
Formation	N/A	Nontaxable unless disguised sale or the partner is relieved from debt	Nontaxable unless disguised sale or the member is relieved from debt	Taxable. However, if the transferors meet the 80% control test of IRC § 351, nontaxable except to the extent of debt relief.	Taxable. However, if the transferors meet the 80% control test of IRC § 351, nontaxable except to the extent of debt relief.
Special allocations of income and loss	N/A	Yes	Yes	No, all allocations are pro rata.	N/A
Deductibility of losses	No problem	Partners may deduct the partnership's losses only to the extent of their tax basis in their partnership interest which includes their allocable share of partnership debt.	Members may deduct the LLC's losses only to the extent of their tax basis in their LLC interest which includes their allocable share of LLC debt.	Shareholders may deduct the corporation's losses only to the extent of their tax basis in their stock which does not include any portion of the corporation's debt.	Shareholders may not deduct any of the corporation's losses.
At-risk limitations	Applicable	Applicable	Applicable	Applicable	Applicable, if closely held
Passive activity limitations	All "material participation" tests applicable	Limited partner can be active under only 3 of 7 tests (i.e., essentially, the limited partner must participate in the activity for 500 hours).	It is not clear whether members or managers can qualify under all 7 or only 3 tests.	All 7 tests apply.	N/A
Fiscal year	Calendar	Generally calendar	Generally calendar	Generally calender	No restrictions
Cash distributions	N/A	Nontaxable to the extent of a partner's tax basis in his [or her] partnership interest	Nontaxable to the extent of a member's tax basis in his [or her] LLC interest	Generally nontaxable to the extent of the shareholder's tax basis in his [or her] stock	Taxable as dividends to the extent of the corporation's earnings and profits and then nontaxable to the extent of the shareholder's tax basis in his or her stock.
Liquidation	N/A	Nontaxable to the extent of a partner's tax basis in his [or her] partnership interest	Nontaxable to the extent of a member's tax basis in his [or her] LLC interest	Generally, nontaxable at corporate level and taxable at shareholder level through flow-through of corporate tax items	Taxable to both corporation and shareholders

SOURCE: J. William Callison and Maureen A. Sullivan. 1994. *Limited Liability Companies: A State-by-State Guide to Law and Practice.* St. Paul: West, pp. 27–29.

of all capital contributions to an LLC, the LLC maintains records of each member's capital contribution.

Liability   State LLC statutes specifically provide that members of an LLC are not personally liable for the LLC's debts and obligations. This limited liability is similar to the liability protection for corporate shareholders, partners in a limited partnership, and partners in a LIMITED LIABILITY PARTNERSHIP. Under certain circumstances, however, a member may become personally liable for an LLC's debts.

An individual member is generally personally liable for her own TORTS and for any contractual obligations entered into on behalf of the member and not on behalf of an LLC. In addition, a member is personally liable to a third person if the member personally guarantees a debt or obligation to the third person. A person who

incurs debts and obligations on behalf of the LLC prior to the LLC's formation is jointly and severally liable with the LLC for those debts and obligations.

Members may also become personally liable for an LLC's debts or obligations under the "piercing-the-corporate-veil" theory. This doctrine imposes personal liability upon corporate shareholders and applies primarily if a corporation is undercapitalized, fails to follow corporate formalities, or engages in FRAUD. Although the law of LLCs is still developing, piercing the corporate veil is likely applicable to an LLC that fails to follow the legal formalities required to manage the LLC. LLC statutes in Colorado, Illinois, and Minnesota specifically apply the corporate veil-piercing theory to LLCs.

A member is generally considered an agent of an LLC and thus may bind the LLC for the debts and obligations of the business. When a member has apparent or actual authority and acts on behalf of an LLC while carrying on the usual business of the LLC, the member binds the LLC. If a third person knows that the member is not authorized to act on behalf of the LLC, the LLC is generally not liable for the member's unauthorized acts. Some states also limit a member's authority to act as an AGENT of an LLC.

Records and Books Many LLC statutes require an LLC to maintain sufficient books and records of its business and management affairs. This requirement varies from state to state. The books and records generally detail the members' contributions to the LLC, the LLC's financial and tax data, and other financial and management information. Like a partnership's books, an LLC's books generally must be kept at the LLC's principal place of business, and each member must have access to and must be allowed to inspect and copy the books upon reasonable demand.

Taxation The IRS generally treats an LLC as a partnership for federal INCOME TAX purposes. The LLC's members are taxed only on their share of LLC profits. Any gains, losses, credits, and deductions flow through the LLC to the members, who report them as income and losses on their personal TAX RETURN. The LLC is not taxed as a separate entity unless it fails to qualify as a partnership for tax purposes.

The IRS will examine a state's LLC statute and an LLC's operation to determine whether the LLC qualifies as a partnership for tax purposes. Essentially, if the IRS determines that the LLC resembles a corporation more than a partnership, the LLC may not qualify as a partnership for tax purposes. Under IRS regulations, an LLC must lack two of four recognized corporate characteristics before it will be treated as a partnership for tax purposes. These characteristics are limited liability, centralized management, free transferability of interests, and continuity of life. Because every LLC protects its members' liability, an LLC almost always possesses the characteristic of limited liability. Therefore, the IRS's analysis usually focuses on the last three characteristics.

Centralized Management A business organization has centralized management when one or more persons have exclusive authority to manage its day-to-day conduct. Most LLCs lack the corporate characteristic of centralized management because most state LLC statutes provide that members manage the LLC directly, and LLCs that do not have separate managers lack the corporate characteristic of centralized management. However, some states require LLCs to have one or more managers to manage the LLC. If an LLC's operating agreement or articles of organization require each and every member to be a manager, the LLC likely lacks the corporate characteristic of centralized management. If, on the other hand, the members designate nonmembers to manage the LLC or designate member-managers who do not own a substantial portion of the LLC's membership interests, the LLC may possess the corporate characteristic of centralized management.

Free Transferability of Interests A business form possesses free transferability of interests when one of its owners essentially has the power to substitute another person as a new owner of the business. Most corporate shareholders, for example, may sell their shares freely and thereby transfer their ownership interest to another person, without the consent of other shareholders. A member in an LLC, however, generally may not substitute another person as a new member unless the existing members agree to the substitution. A member typically has the power only to assign his economic rights in an LLC. Thus, members of an LLC lack the ability to freely transfer substantially all of their interest in the LLC.

Continuity of Life Continuity of life essentially means perpetual continuation without regard to the withdrawal, expulsion, or death of any member. Most state LLC statutes provide for the DISSOLUTION of an LLC upon the death, disability, BANKRUPTCY, or withdrawal of a member. Accordingly, most LLCs lack the corporate characteristic of continuity of life, unless their operating agreement substantially changes the effect of a member's withdrawal upon the continued existence of the LLC. Many state LLC statutes also limit the duration of an LLC to thirty years, but this limitation does not affect the IRS's determination of whether an LLC lacks continuity of life.

Member Withdrawal Members may withdraw from an LLC unless the operating agreement or articles of organization limit their ability to do so. A member must usually provide to the LLC written notice that she intends to withdraw. If a withdrawal violates the operating agreement, the withdrawing member may be liable to the other members or the LLC for damages associated with it. State law frequently sets forth the circumstances under which a member may withdraw from an LLC. In many states a member may withdraw only if she or he provides six months' written notice of the intent to withdraw. In a few states, an LLC cannot prevent a member's withdrawal.

A member who withdraws is usually entitled to a return of his capital contribution to an LLC, unless the withdrawal is unauthorized. Some LLCs instead pay a withdrawing member the fair market value of his or her membership interest. The operating agreement typically provides for the method and manner of payment of a withdrawing member's interest. State law also governs those issues.

Dissolution Dissolution means the legal end of an LLC's existence. In most states an LLC legally dissolves upon the death, disability, withdrawal, bankruptcy, or expulsion of a member. These occurrences are generally called disassociations. Other circumstances that bring about dissolution include bankruptcy of the LLC, a court order, or the fulfillment of the LLC's stated period of duration.

Most states provide for the continuation of an LLC after the disassociation or withdrawal of a member. Continuation after a member's disassociation usually requires the remaining members' unanimous consent. Some states require that the articles of organization or operating agreement allow for the continuation of the business after a member's disassociation. Some states allow an LLC's articles of organization or operating agreement to require the continuation of the business after a member's dissociation even if the remaining members do not provide unanimous consent.

If an LLC dissolves, state law and the LLC's operating agreement usually outline the process for winding up the LLC's business. In this process the LLC pays off its remaining CREDITORS and distributes any remaining assets to its members. The LLC's creditors receive priority. Although members may be creditors, they are not creditors in determining the members' distributive shares of any remaining assets. After the LLC pays off its creditors, and only then, it distributes the remaining assets to its members, either in proportion to the members' shares of profits or under some other arrangement outlined in the operating agreement. After an LLC winds up its business, most states require it to file articles of dissolution.

LIMITED LIABILITY PARTNERSHIP 📖 A form of general PARTNERSHIP that provides an individual partner protection against personal LIABILITY for certain partnership obligations. 📖

The Limited Liability Partnership (LLP) is essentially a general partnership in form, with one important difference. Unlike a general partnership, in which individual partners are liable for the partnership's DEBTS and obligations, an LLP provides each of its individual partners protection against personal liability for certain partnership liabilities.

In 1991 Texas enacted the first LLP statute, largely in response to the liability that had been imposed on partners in partnerships sued by government agencies in relation to massive savings and loan failures in the 1980s. The Texas statute protected partners from personal liability for claims related to a copartner's NEGLIGENCE, ERROR, omission, INCOMPETENCY, or MALFEASANCE. It also permanently limited the personal liability of a partner for the errors, omissions, incompetence, or negligence of the partnership's employees or other agents. By the mid-1990s, at least twenty-one states and the District of Columbia had adopted LLP statutes.

The limit of an individual partner's liability depends on the scope of the state's LLP legislation. Many states provide protection only against TORT claims and do not extend protection to a partner's own negligence or incompetence or to the partner's involvement in supervising wrongful conduct. Other states provide broad protection, including protection against contractual claims brought by the partnership's creditors. For example, Minnesota enacted an expansive LLP statute in 1994. This piece of legislation provided that a partner in an LLP was not liable to a CREDITOR or for any obligation of the partnership. It further provided, however, that a partner was personally liable to the partnership and copartners for any breach of duty, and also allowed a creditor or other claimant to pierce the limited liability shield of a partner in the same way a claimant may PIERCE THE CORPORATE VEIL of a corporation and personally sue an individual member of the corporation.

In states that recognize LLPs, a partnership qualifies as an LLP by registering with the appropriate state authority and fulfilling various requirements. Some states require proof that the partnership has obtained adequate liability insurance or has adequate ASSETS to satisfy potential claims. All states require a filing fee for registration and also require that an LLP include the words *Registered Limited Liability Partnership* or the abbreviation *LLP* in its name.

A partnership that renders specific professional services may form an LLP and register as a professional limited liability partnership (PLLP). A PLLP is generally the same as an LLP except that it is an association solely of professionals. Each state specifies the qualifying professions for a PLLP. This business form is typically available to attorneys, physicians, architects, dentists, engineers, and accountants. New York's LLP statute restricts eligibility solely to partnerships that render professional services.

LIMITED TEST BAN TREATY The Limited Test Ban Treaty (LTBT), sometimes called the Partial Test Ban Treaty, was first signed in 1963 by the United States, the Union of Soviet Socialist Republics (U.S.S.R.), and the United Kingdom. It prohibits the testing of nuclear weapons in the atmosphere, underwater, or in space. As the first significant arms control agreement of the COLD WAR, the LTBT set an important precedent for future arms negotiations.

The LTBT followed quickly on the heels of the 1962 CUBAN MISSILE CRISIS, in which the United States and the U.S.S.R. came to the brink of war over the Soviet Union's placement of missiles in Cuba. Alarmed at the prospect of nuclear war, President JOHN F. KENNEDY, of the United States, and Premier Nikita Khrushchev, of the Soviet Union, agreed to begin serious arms control negotiations. The LTBT was one of the first fruits of these negotiations. Proponents of the treaty claimed that it would prevent contamination of the environment by ra-

dioactive fallout from nuclear testing, slow down the arms race, and inhibit the spread of nuclear weapons to other countries.

Although Kennedy hailed the LTBT as a significant achievement of his presidency, he was disappointed that he could not secure a comprehensive test ban treaty, which would have banned all forms of nuclear testing. Lacking such a ban, the superpowers and other countries with nuclear capability continued to test nuclear weapons underground. However, article 1, section b, of the LTBT pledges that each of its signatory countries will seek "a treaty resulting in the permanent banning of all nuclear test explosions, including all such explosions underground." By 1973, a total of 106 countries had signed the LTBT, and by 1992, that number had grown to 119.

Later test ban treaties have included the Threshold Test Ban Treaty of 1974, which prohibited nuclear tests of more than 150 kilotons (the explosive force of 150,000 tons of TNT), and the Peaceful Nuclear Explosions Treaty of 1976. Although a comprehensive test ban agreement has not yet been reached, the nuclear powers and many nations without nuclear capabilities continue to negotiate the provisions of such a treaty.

See also ARMS CONTROL AND DISARMAMENT.

The Limited Test Ban Treaty was the first significant arms control agreement of the cold war. It was signed in 1963 by the United States, the Soviet Union, and the United Kingdom. Seated left to right are Secretary of State Dean Rusk, Soviet Foreign Minister Andrei Gromyko, and British Foreign Secretary Lord Home. Standing between Gromyko and Home is Soviet Premier Nikita Khrushchev.

UPI/CORBIS-BETTMANN

LINCOLN, ABRAHAM Abraham Lincoln was the sixteenth president of the United States, serving from 1861 until his ASSASSINATION in April 1865. Lincoln and his supporters preserved the Union by defeating the South in the Civil War.

Lincoln was born February 12, 1809, near Knob Creek, Kentucky. In 1816 his family moved to a farm in Indiana, where he spent the rest of his childhood. He attended school for less than a year and gained most of his education by reading books. In 1828 and 1831, he made flatboat trips down the Mississippi River to take produce to New Orleans. On these trips he was first exposed to the institution of SLAVERY.

In 1830 his family moved to Decatur, Illinois. He left his family in 1831 and moved to New Salem, Illinois, where he worked at various jobs and continued his self-education. He began to study law, then was sidetracked by political ambitions.

In 1832 he ran for the state legislature as a member of the Whig party. He aligned himself with the views of Whig party leader HENRY CLAY, who served as a U.S. senator from Kentucky. Like Clay, Lincoln promised to use the power of the government to improve the life of the people he represented. During the 1832 campaign, the Black Hawk War erupted in southern Illinois. Lincoln enlisted in the local militia and was elected captain. Though he served for eighty days, he never saw battle. His service in the military distracted him from his campaign for the legislature, and he lost his first election.

In 1834 he was elected to the state legislature. He was reelected in 1836, 1838, and 1840. John T. Stuart, a fellow legislator and also a lawyer, was impressed with Lincoln's intellectual and oratorical abilities and encouraged him to practice law. In the fall of 1836, Lincoln was admitted to the Illinois bar, and in 1837 he became Stuart's law partner in Springfield, Illinois. In 1841 the pair dissolved their partnership and Lincoln began a new partnership with Stephen T. Logan. By 1844 that arrangement

BIOGRAPHY

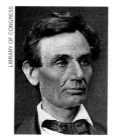

LIBRARY OF CONGRESS

Abraham Lincoln

"WHENEVER I HEAR ANYONE ARGUING FOR SLAVERY, I FEEL A STRONG IMPULSE TO SEE IT TRIED ON HIM PERSONALLY."

had dissolved and Lincoln took William H. Herndon as a partner. Lincoln was a hardworking attorney who over the years represented railroad companies and other business entities. By the 1850s he had argued many times before the Illinois Supreme Court and various federal courts.

However, his interest in politics continued. In 1847 he was elected to the U.S. House of Representatives as a member of the Whig party. His one brief term in this office was detrimental to his career, for his opposition to the Mexican War and his stand on several other issues were received unfavorably by his constituents.

He did not seek reelection in 1848, choosing instead to work on the presidential campaign of ZACHARY TAYLOR. After Taylor's victory Lincoln was severely disappointed when he failed to receive a prominent presidential appointment. He abandoned politics and devoted his energies to his law practice in Springfield.

Events involving slavery soon drew Lincoln back into the political arena. The passage in 1854 of the KANSAS-NEBRASKA ACT infuriated Lincoln. Senator STEPHEN A. DOUGLAS, of Illinois, a Democrat and rival of Lincoln's, had drafted this legislation, which revoked the MISSOURI COMPROMISE OF 1820. The repeal meant that the settlers of Kansas and Nebraska could allow slavery to exist if they so wished. This was intolerable to Lincoln and many antislavery Whigs and Democrats. Lincoln took to the political stump again, railing against slavery and the congressional actions that had placed the issue at the forefront of national policy.

The Whig party fell apart over the slavery question. In 1856 Lincoln joined others opposed to slavery from both the Whig and Democrat parties, in the newly formed REPUBLICAN PARTY. He quickly rose to prominence. The Republicans chose him as their candidate in the 1858 senatorial race against Douglas. The campaign was marked by a series of seven brilliant debates between the two contenders. Lincoln advocated loyalty to the Union, regarded slavery as unjust, and was opposed to

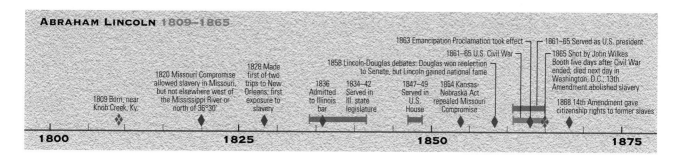

ABRAHAM LINCOLN 1809–1865

1863 Emancipation Proclamation took effect
1861–65 U.S. Civil War
1861–65 Served as U.S. president
1865 Shot by John Wilkes Booth five days after Civil War ended; died next day in Washington, D.C.; 13th Amendment abolished slavery

1858 Lincoln-Douglas debates: Douglas won reelection to Senate, but Lincoln gained national fame

1828 Made first of two trips to New Orleans; first exposure to slavery

1820 Missouri Compromise allowed slavery in Missouri, but not elsewhere west of the Mississippi River or north of 36°30'

1809 Born, near Knob Creek, Ky.

1836 Admitted to Illinois bar

1834–42 Served in Ill. state legislature

1847–49 Served in U.S. House

1854 Kansas-Nebraska Act repealed Missouri Compromise

1868 14th Amendment gave citizenship rights to former slaves

1800   1825   1850   1875

any further expansion of slavery. He opened his campaign by declaring, " 'A house divided against itself cannot stand.' I believe this government cannot endure permanently *half* slave and *half* free." Lincoln lost the election owing to an unfavorable APPORTIONMENT of legislative seats in Illinois. (At that time U.S. senators were elected by a vote of the state legislature.) Though Republicans garnered larger numbers of votes, Douglas was reelected.

Despite the Senate loss, Lincoln's national reputation was enhanced by his firm antislavery position. He was urged to run for president in 1860. At the Republican National Convention in Chicago in May 1860, Lincoln defeated William H. Seward for the nomination. A split in the Democratic party led to the fielding of two Democratic candidates, John C. Breckenridge and Douglas. This split enabled Lincoln easily to defeat his rivals, including John Bell, head of the Constitutional Union party. He would be easily reelected in 1864.

By the time Lincoln took his oath of office in March 1861, seven Southern states had seceded from the Union and had established the Confederate States of America. Jefferson Davis was elected president of the new government. Lincoln wished to find a solution short of war that would preserve the Union, but there were few options. When Lincoln allowed supplies to be sent to Fort Sumter, a Union base on an island outside Charleston, South Carolina, the new Confederate government seized the opportunity to interpret this as an act of war. On April 12, 1861, Fort Sumter was attacked by Confederate forces, and the Civil War began.

Lincoln's initial actions against this act of aggression included drafting men for military service, approving a BLOCKADE of the Southern states, and suspending the writ of HABEAS CORPUS. His troop request led to the secession of Virginia, North Carolina, Tennessee, and Arkansas. Suspending habeas corpus effectively curtailed civil liberties, as persons who were suspected of being Southern sympathizers could be held in custody indefinitely. All these actions were taken by EXECUTIVE ORDER, in Lincoln's capacity as commander in chief, because Congress was not in session at the time.

During the early stages of the war, the North suffered great losses, particularly at Bull Run. A succession of Union generals failed to achieve military success. Not until General ULYSSES S. GRANT emerged in 1863 as a strong and successful military leader did the Union army begin to achieve substantial victories. In 1864 Lincoln named Grant the commander of the Union army. In April 1865 General Robert E.

Lee surrendered his Confederate army to Grant at Appomattox, Virginia, signaling the end of the war.

Lincoln fought the Civil War to preserve the Union, not to end slavery. Though he was personally opposed to slavery, he had been elected on a platform that pledged to allow slavery to remain where it already existed. However, wartime pressures drove Lincoln toward emancipation of the slaves. Military leaders argued that an enslaved labor force in the South allowed the Confederate states to place more soldiers on the front lines. By the summer of 1862, Lincoln had prepared an EMANCIPATION PROCLAMATION, but he did not want to issue it until the Union army had better fortune on the battlefield. Otherwise the proclamation might be seen as a sign of weakness.

The Union army's victory at Antietam encouraged the president to issue on September 22, 1862, a preliminary proclamation that slavery was to be abolished in areas occupied by the Confederacy effective January 1, 1863. The wording of the Emancipation Proclamation on that date made clear that slavery was still to be tolerated in the border states and areas occupied by Union troops, so as not to jeopardize the war effort. Lincoln was uncertain that the U.S. Supreme Court would uphold the constitutionality of his action, so he lobbied Congress to adopt the THIRTEENTH AMENDMENT, which totally abolished slavery.

Lincoln's writing and speaking skills played a vital part in maintaining the resolve of the Northern states during the war and in preparing the nation for the aftermath of the war. In 1863, at Gettysburg, Pennsylvania, Lincoln delivered his poignant Gettysburg Address at the dedication of a national cemetery for soldiers who had died at the bloody battleground. The speech summarized the tragic and human aspects of Gettysburg and distilled Lincoln's resolve to protect the Union. At his second inauguration, in March 1865, Lincoln reached out to the South as the end of the war approached. He proclaimed, "With malice toward none; with charity for all."

Even before the war ended, Lincoln began to formulate a plan for Reconstruction, which included the restoration of Southern state governments and the AMNESTY of Confederate officials who vowed loyalty to the Union. These proposals met fierce opposition in Congress, as the Radical Republicans sought harsher treatment for the South and its supporters.

The war ended on April 9, 1865, but Lincoln did not have a chance to fight for his Reconstruction proposals. He was shot in the head on

THE LINCOLN ASSASSINATION: CONSPIRACY OR A LONE MAN'S ACT?

On April 14, 1865, President Abraham Lincoln was assassinated at Ford's Theater in Washington, D.C. Five days earlier, Confederate General Robert E. Lee had surrendered to Union troops. John Wilkes Booth, a well-known actor, Confederate sympathizer, and spy, has gone down in history as the lone assailant of Lincoln. However, Booth was killed by federal soldiers before he could be brought to trial. Eyewitnesses at Ford's Theater identified Booth as the man who shot the president at point-blank range with a single bullet to the back of the head. But Booth's exact motive in the killing was never established. In the wake of the first assassination of a U.S. president, eight of Booth's associates were charged as conspirators. All eight were convicted. However, since then, some modern theories have downplayed the roles of Southern radicals in the conspiracy. Some historians have even pointed fingers at the Republicans, Lincoln's own party.

Shortly before his death, Lincoln announced his Reconstruction policy for restoring the United States. He advocated "malice toward none, charity for all." However, more than a handful of Confederates distrusted Yankee politics. Confederate plots to kill the president or kidnap him had certainly existed long before April 1865. Lincoln appeared unconcerned about the threats, however, and refused to heed the advice of his advisers to take fewer risks in his public appearances. "What does anybody want to assassinate me for?" Lincoln once asked. "If anyone wants to do so, he can do it any day or night, if he is ready to give his life for mine. It is nonsense."

Booth fled Ford's Theater immediately after killing Lincoln and headed for refuge in the South. The Union cavalry, after a massive manhunt (announced throughout the nation), cornered Booth at the Garrett farm, his hiding spot in Virginia. Soldiers shot him through the neck leaving him partially paralyzed. Booth somehow managed to exit the barn when it was set on fire. He died at the feet of federal officers on the morning of April 26.

In somewhat mysterious fashion, Booth's "diary" (actually an 1864 datebook), was recovered from the site of his death. Booth wrote a running commentary, in scattered detail, on his plans before he shot Lincoln, and the developments of his final days. He wrote:

For six months we had worked to capture. But our cause, being almost lost, something decisive & great must be done. But it's failure was owing to others, who did not strike for their country with a heat. I struck boldly and not as the papers say.

Booth even described himself as a savior, claiming, "Our country owed all her trouble to him, and God simply made me the instrument of his punishment." Booth's diary would not be used directly as evidence in the trial of others with whom he had allegedly conspired. Instead, it is a primary piece of evidence to support the argument that Booth acted alone.

Booth's quick death with no trial left many in the nation questioning the circumstances surrounding the murder of the North's beloved leader. Federal investigators subsequently singled out eight Southern civilians who had, by varying accounts, associated with Booth at a boarding house in Maryland. The eight were held as prisoners, accused of assisting in the crime of the century. David Herold, Lewis Payne, George Atzerodt, Michael O'Laughlin, Samuel Arnold, Dr. Samuel Mudd, Edward Spangler, and Mary E. Surratt were charged as traitors and conspirators in a plot to kill Lincoln, Vice President Andrew Johnson, Secretary of State William H. Seward and General Ulysses S. Grant.

Lincoln's secretary of war, Edwin M. Stanton, had conducted most of the criminal investigation. Based on the charges he developed, former Confederate President Jefferson Davis was directly implicated, but not tried, in the assassination plot. Stanton and Attorney General James Speed subsequently put together a nine-man military commission of seven generals and two colonels from the Union Army to sit in judgment. All nine of the appointed officers were staunch Republicans.

In the trial of the suspects, the prosecution relied heavily on the testimony of one individual in particular, Louis Weichmann. Weichmann had been closely acquainted with most of the conspirators and had first learned of their plot, according to his testimony, at a Maryland boarding house run by Mary Surratt. The accounts Weichmann gave primarily implicated Surratt and a country doctor, Samuel Mudd. The defense noted that Weichmann had not reported any of the alleged activity at the boarding house until after the assassination. However, the evidence to which Weichmann led investigators, particularly a boot of Booth's with the inscription "J. Wilkes," found at the home of Dr. Mudd, appeared to seal the fate of the eight defendants.

On June 29 the commission met behind closed doors to consider the evidence. They deliberated for two days and then sentenced four prisoners to death and four to imprisonment and hard labor. On July 7 Surratt was the first to be led to the gallows. Atzerodt, Herold, and Payne also received the death penalty.

Though four people were sent to their deaths, and four to prison, for the crime, historians continue to debate the conspiracy to kill Lincoln. One book that stirred much discussion on the subject was Otto Eisenschiml's *Why Was Lincoln Murdered?*, published in 1937. Eisenschiml postulated that Stanton and a group of Northern industrialists plotted the death of Lincoln to secure the interests of radical Republicans who were bent on the takeover of the newly restored Union. That theory, however, has been largely rebutted by other historians.

April 14 by John Wilkes Booth during the performance of a play at Ford's Theatre, in Washington, D.C. He died the next day. After lying in state in the Capitol, his body was returned to Springfield for burial.

LINCOLN, LEVI Levi Lincoln was a U.S. attorney general under President THOMAS JEFFERSON. He held various political posts, including that of sixth governor of Massachusetts. He was among the creators of the first state constitution. As a trial lawyer, Lincoln was involved in a set of landmark cases in the struggle against SLAVERY. He was also the father of Massachusetts statesman and state supreme court justice Levi Lincoln, Jr. (1782–1868).

Lincoln was born May 15, 1749, in Hingham, Massachusetts. His father was a farmer, and as a youth Lincoln was apprenticed to a blacksmith. However, because Lincoln was an avid student, his father allowed him to continue studying in preparation for college. His initial studies were in theology, but after hearing JOHN ADAMS argue a case in Boston, his interests turned to law.

Lincoln graduated from Harvard in 1772 and then worked in the office of Joseph Hawley, in Northampton, Massachusetts. Until the outbreak of the Revolutionary War, he was active in politics and a prominent figure in the Massachusetts movement to abolish slavery. After the Battle of Lexington, in 1775, he traveled with the militia for a brief period before moving to Worcester, Massachusetts. He was admitted to the bar in 1775 and set up his law practice in Worcester, where he remained a resident for the rest of his life.

Lincoln quickly became prominent as a successful trial lawyer and served in various civil offices during the years of the Revolutionary War. In 1775 he was a state court judge, and from 1777 to 1781 he was a PROBATE court judge. In 1779 Lincoln was a delegate to the Massachusetts state constitutional convention, which drew up the first state constitution. In 1781 he married Martha Waldo, with whom he had nine children.

Also in 1781 Lincoln served as a defense counsel in three cases concerning the question of the right to hold slaves. The cases—*Walker v. Jenison*, *Jenison v. Caldwell*, and *Commonwealth v. Jenison*—addressed the issue of slavery in light of the bill of rights in the 1780 Massachusetts Constitution. Lincoln and co–defense counsel Caleb Strong argued against the legality of slavery in Massachusetts. Their position prevailed, and slavery was made illegal in the state.

Lincoln, a leading Republican, became a key adviser to President Jefferson on matters of Federalist-Republican logistics and diplomacy, specifically regarding introducing laws or policies likely to be unpopular in New England.

Lincoln served in the Massachusetts state House of Representatives in 1796 and was a state senator the following year. From 1800 to 1801, he was a member of the U.S. Congress.

Lincoln served as U.S. attorney general under President Jefferson from 1801 to 1804. Early in his term, he also fulfilled the duties of secretary of state, because personal illness and a death in the family delayed the arrival in Washington, D.C., of secretary of state appointee JAMES MADISON.

As attorney general Lincoln was one of two men to whom Jefferson frequently turned for advice regarding his New England constituency; the other was Postmaster General Gideon Granger. For example, Jefferson, a rigid secularist, drafted a letter of support in response to an appeal from a minority group in Connecticut known as the Danbury Baptists, who were seeking stronger church-state separation in their state. Jefferson's draft declared that because of the Constitution's FIRST AMENDMENT prohibitions, a "wall of separation" had been built between church and state. The draft also noted that because of this strong separation, Jefferson refrained from prescribing "even occasional performances of devotion," such as days of fasting or thanksgiving, as his predecessors had done. Before releasing the paper, Jefferson asked the advice of both Granger and Lincoln. Granger proposed leaving the draft as it was

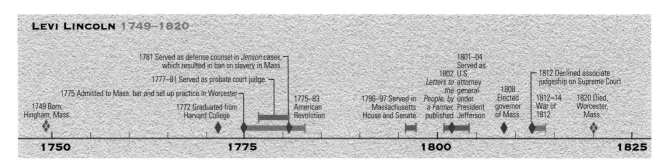

LEVI LINCOLN 1749–1820

- 1749 Born, Hingham, Mass.
- 1772 Graduated from Harvard College
- 1775 Admitted to Mass. bar and set up practice in Worcester
- 1775–83 American Revolution
- 1777–81 Served as probate court judge
- 1781 Served as defense counsel in *Jenison* cases, which resulted in ban on slavery in Mass.
- 1796–97 Served in Massachusetts House and Senate
- 1801–04 Served as U.S. attorney general under President Jefferson
- 1802 U.S. *Letters to the People, by a Farmer* published
- 1808 Elected governor of Mass.
- 1812 Declined associate judgeship on Supreme Court
- 1812–14 War of 1812
- 1820 Died, Worcester, Mass.

1750   1775   1800   1825

written. Lincoln argued that the phrase regarding days of thanksgiving might anger the eastern states because their governors frequently proclaimed such days. Based on Lincoln's advice, Jefferson removed the phrase.

Because of his Republican partisanship, Lincoln was the subject of frequent criticism by Federalist newspapers and clergy representatives. His book *Letters to the People, by a Farmer*, published in 1802, in which he attacked the political role of the clergy, was written in response to this criticism.

Lincoln resigned his post as attorney general in 1805 and resumed his political career in Massachusetts. In 1807 he served as lieutenant governor of Massachusetts. The following year he was elected governor. He was on the governor's council in 1806 and from 1810 to 1812. In 1812 he was offered a position in the U.S. Supreme Court, which he refused because of failing eyesight. In recommending Lincoln for the position to President Madison, Jefferson called Lincoln a highly desirable appointee because of his legal abilities, his integrity, and his unimpeachable character.

Lincoln spent the rest of his life on his farm in Worcester. He died there April 14, 1820.

See also MASSACHUSETTS CONSTITUTION OF 1780.

LINCOLN, ROBERT TODD Robert Todd Lincoln was a lawyer, a presidential elector for the Illinois branch of the Republican party in 1880, secretary of war in the cabinets of Presidents JAMES GARFIELD and CHESTER A. ARTHUR, U.S. minister to Great Britain from 1889 to 1893, president and chairman of the board for the Illinois-based Pullman Palace Car Company, and the son of President ABRAHAM LINCOLN.

Lincoln was born August 1, 1843, in Springfield, Illinois. At the age of thirteen, Lincoln began attending classes at Illinois State University (later Concordia College). He subsequently enrolled in the Phillips Exeter Academy, a famous preparatory school, and then went to Harvard. His years there concurred with his father's presidency, between 1861 and 1865.

"UNDERSTAND THAT I STILL DO NOT LIKE THE 'HONEST ABE' BUSINESS AT ALL, BUT I AM ACTING ON THE UNDERSTANDING THAT THERE IS NO ESCAPE FROM THAT PART OF IT."

BIOGRAPHY

Robert Todd Lincoln

Lincoln graduated from Harvard on July 20, 1864, and in September enrolled at Harvard Law School. He then opted to enlist in the Army. On February 11, 1865, Lincoln was appointed captain and assistant adjutant general of Union army volunteers. In his service, he witnessed the surrender of General Lee at Appomattox, Virginia, on April 9, 1865.

In the 1880 presidential election, Lincoln was active on behalf of the Republican party. He supported ULYSSES S. GRANT's attempt to win the presidency for a third time and was chosen to be a presidential elector. James Garfield won the presidency that year. Garfield respected Lincoln's political abilities, and on March 5, 1881, appointed him secretary of war.

In 1881 a disappointed office seeker shot President Garfield. Garfield died from his wound in September of that year, and Chester A. Arthur became president. Lincoln continued in his cabinet duties until March 1885. By then, he had reemerged as a possible Republican candidate for president. However, this was not a position Lincoln had a great interest in, and ultimately he did not run for the office.

Lincoln nevertheless continued to serve in important federal positions. In 1889 he served as minister to Britain. In 1892, he was discussed for a final time as a potential nominee for president. Lincoln appeared more interested in resuming his work as a lawyer.

Lincoln returned to private life, serving as president of the Pullman Company until 1911, and then as its board chairman. In the ensuing years his health began to fail and he made few public appearances. He did see the dedication of the Lincoln Memorial on May 30, 1922, but declined to speak.

He died July 25, 1926, in Washington, D.C.

LINDBERGH ACT The Lindbergh Act is a federal law (48 Stat. 781) that makes it a crime to kidnap—for ransom, reward, or otherwise—and transport a victim from one state to another or to a foreign country, except in the case of a MINOR abducted by his or her parent.

The Lindbergh law provides that if the victim is not released within twenty-four hours

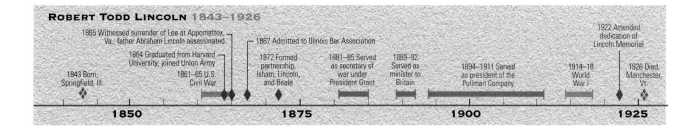

ROBERT TODD LINCOLN 1843–1926

1843 Born, Springfield, Ill.

1861–65 U.S. Civil War

1864 Graduated from Harvard University; joined Union Army

1865 Witnessed surrender of Lee at Appomattox, Va.; father Abraham Lincoln assassinated

1867 Admitted to Illinois Bar Association

1872 Formed partnership, Isham, Lincoln, and Beale

1881–85 Served as secretary of war under President Grant

1889–92 Served as minister to Britain

1894–1911 Served as president of the Pullman Company

1914–18 World War I

1922 Attended dedication of Lincoln Memorial

1926 Died, Manchester, Vt.

1850   1875   1900   1925

after being kidnapped, there is a REBUTTABLE PRESUMPTION that he or she has been transported in interstate or foreign commerce.

The punishment for violation of the Lindbergh Act is imprisonment for a term of years or for life.

See also KIDNAPPING; LINDBERGH KIDNAPPING.

LINDBERGH KIDNAPPING

The KIDNAPPING of Charles A. and Anne M. Lindbergh's twenty-month-old son horrified the United States, and even the world. In 1927, at age twenty-five, Lindbergh achieved international fame with the first solo crossing of the Atlantic Ocean by air, and in the bleak years of the late 1920s, the young aviator became a symbol of courage and success. The disappearance of Charles Augustus Lindbergh, Jr., on March 1, 1932, and the discovery of his corpse ten weeks later, led to a riotous trial, significant changes in federal law, and a tightening of courtroom rules regarding cameras.

Lindbergh's historic flight from New York to Paris in *The Spirit of St. Louis* brought him both adulation and wealth. By the end of 1930, he was estimated to be worth over $1.5 million. His was an enviable life, with more than enough justifications for the nickname Lucky Lindy: world fame; the Congressional Medal of Honor; foreign nations sponsoring his long-distance flights; positions with several airlines; a publishing career; and, in 1929, marriage to the daughter of the U.S. ambassador to Mexico, the writer Anne Spencer Morrow. The couple made their home in New Jersey, where their first child, Charles, Jr., was born in 1930.

In the context of 1930s crime, the kidnapping of Charles, Jr., was not unique. But because he was the Lindberghs' son, his disappearance provoked weeks of well-publicized agonizing. Lindbergh led the search effort and even negotiated with organized crime figures. All hopes ended when the child's body was found near the family estate.

Nearly two years passed before Bruno Richard Hauptmann, a carpenter, was arrested as the prime suspect in the murder. Hauptmann's trial, held between 1934 and 1935, was a sensation. Nearly seven hundred reporters and pho-

tographers flocked to the New Jersey town that was the site of the trial. Inside the courtroom, where flashbulbs popped and a concealed newsreel camera whirred, order was seldom possible. Equally beset were the Lindberghs themselves, and Charles Lindbergh, despite his fame, developed a hatred for the media. After Hauptmann was convicted and, in 1936, executed, the couple left the United States to live in England.

The AMERICAN BAR ASSOCIATION (ABA) viewed the trial as a media circus and called for reform. In 1937 the ABA included a prohibition on courtroom photography in its Canons of Professional and Judicial Ethics. All but two states adopted the ban, and the U.S. Congress amended the Federal Rules of Criminal Procedure to ban cameras and broadcasting from FEDERAL COURTS. The ban on photography in courtrooms prompted by the trial would last nearly four decades.

Another important result of the kidnapping was the passage of the 1932 Federal Kidnapping Act (U.S.C.A. §§ 1201–1202 [1988 & Supp. 1992]), popularly called the Lindbergh Law. This statute made it a federal offense to kidnap someone with the intent to seek a ransom or reward. The law has since been modified several times not only to increase penalties but to make the investigative work of federal agents easier.

See also CAMERAS IN COURT.

LINDSEY, BENJAMIN BARR

BIOGRAPHY

Benjamin Barr Lindsey

Benjamin Barr Lindsey achieved prominence for his work in the juvenile court. Lindsey was born November 25, 1869, in Jackson, Tennessee. He received honorary degrees from the University of Denver and Notre Dame University and was admitted to the bar in 1894. In 1928 he was also admitted to the California bar.

In 1900 Lindsey became judge of the juvenile court of Denver, remaining on the bench until 1927. He is credited with the founding of the juvenile court system in the United States. Many of his ideas were adopted internationally.

As a recognized expert in the field of juvenile delinquency, Lindsey initiated many successful programs concerned with rehabilitation of minors. For example, he introduced the honor

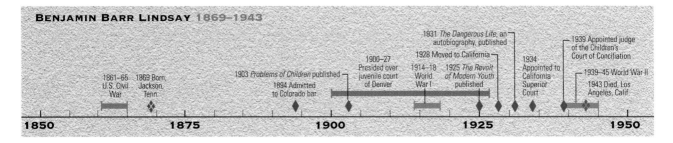

BENJAMIN BARR LINDSAY 1869–1943

1850   1861–65 U.S. Civil War   1869 Born, Jackson, Tenn.   1903 *Problems of Children* published   1894 Admitted to Colorado bar   1875   1900–27 Presided over juvenile court of Denver   1900   1914–18 World War I   1925 *The Revolt of Modern Youth* published   1928 Moved to California   1931 *The Dangerous Life*, an autobiography, published   1925   1934 Appointed to California Superior Court   1939 Appointed judge of the Children's Court of Conciliation   1939–45 World War II   1943 Died, Los Angeles, Calif.   1950

system, first used at the Industrial School in Golden, Colorado, which allowed boys the freedom to be unattended. Out of several hundred boys there, only five did not adhere to the code of honor. He was also instrumental in the enactment of legislation in Colorado that recognized the negligence of parents as a contributory factor to the delinquency of juveniles.

In 1928 Lindsey moved to California and, in 1934, sat on the bench of the superior court. In 1939 he became the first judge of the California Children's Court of Conciliation, a court he helped to create.

Lindsey was the author of many publications, including: *Problems of the Children* (1903); *The Beast and the Jungle* (1910); *The Revolt of Modern Youth* (1925); *The Companionate Marriage* (1927); and *The Dangerous Life* (a 1931 autobiography).

He died March 26, 1943, in Los Angeles, California.

See also JUVENILE LAW.

LINEAL 📖 That which comes in a line, particularly a direct line, as from parent to child or grandparent to grandchild. 📖

LINE OF CREDIT 📖 The maximum borrowing power granted to a person from a financial institution. 📖

Line of credit denotes a limit of credit extended by a bank to a customer, who can avail himself or herself of its full extent in dealing with the bank but cannot exceed this limit. It most frequently covers a series of transactions, in which case, when the customer's line of credit is nearly exhausted or not replenished, the customer is expected to reduce the indebtedness by submitting payments to the bank before making additional use of the line of credit.

LINEUP 📖 A criminal investigation technique in which the police arrange a number of individuals in a row before a WITNESS to a crime and ask the witness to identify which, if any, of the individuals committed the crime. 📖

In a police lineup, a witness to a crime, who may be the victim, observes a group of individuals that may or may not include a suspect in the crime. The witness is not visible to those in the lineup. The witness is asked to identify which, if any, of the individuals committed the crime. A lineup places greater demands on the memory of the witness than does a viewing of a single suspect, and is believed to reduce the chances of a false identification. For example, assume a witness saw a man with a beard and a cap run across an alley near a crime scene. If the police show this witness one man who has a beard and a cap, the witness might make a positive identi-

fication. If they instead show the witness several men with a beard and a cap, the witness must make a more detailed identification and may not identify the same man.

In *Schmerber v. California*, 384 U.S. 757, 86 S. Ct. 1826, 16 L. Ed. 2d 908 (1966), the U.S. Supreme Court held that the FIFTH AMENDMENT constitutional privilege against SELF-INCRIMINATION—the right not to be made a witness against oneself in a criminal case—does not apply to appearance in lineups. That privilege, held the Court, protects accused people only from being compelled to testify against themselves or to otherwise provide the state with EVIDENCE of a testimonial or communicative nature.

The Constitution does afford an accused individual the RIGHT TO COUNSEL at a post-indictment lineup, and the right not to have TESTIMONY from a suggestive lineup admitted at trial. The constitutional right to the presence of counsel at a lineup or for counsel to receive notice of a lineup attaches, or becomes available, when a formal charge, INDICTMENT, preliminary hearing, or arraignment is issued or conducted. Post-indictment lineups are considered a critical part of proceedings because the filing of a charge initiates adversary proceedings, triggering the right to counsel (*United States v. Wade*, 388 U.S. 218, 87 S. Ct. 1926, 18 L. Ed. 2d 1149 [1967]). Counsel observes the lineup to decide whether to offer information about it during trial in order to cast doubt on an in-court identification. (In an in-court identification, the prosecution asks the witness whether he or she identified anyone in a lineup prior to trial and if so, whether that person is present in the courtroom.) According to *Wade*, an "intelligent waiver" of counsel and of notice to counsel may be made by the accused.

Police lineups that are conducted prior to the filing of a formal charge or the issuance of an indictment are not regarded as occurring at a critical stage of a criminal proceeding and do not require the presence of counsel.

The Due Process Clause of the Constitution requires that a lineup not be unduly suggestive or conducive to irreparable mistaken identification. An unduly suggestive lineup might be one in which the defendant was the only female. Some characteristics that courts have considered in determining suggestiveness is whether the others in the lineup were of similar age, skin coloration, and physical characteristics such as height and weight.

Courts examine on a case-by-case basis the question of whether a lineup was unduly suggestive or created a likelihood of misidentification. In making this determination, they look at the "totality of circumstances." The totality-of-circumstances test was announced by the Supreme Court in *Manson v. Brathwaite*, 432 U.S. 98, 97 S. Ct. 2243, 53 L. Ed. 2d 140 (1977). This test considers whether the witness or victim had an opportunity to observe the criminal at the time of the crime; the accuracy of the prior description of the accused as well as the degree of attention given to that description; the level of certainty demonstrated by the victim or witness at the confrontation; and the length of time between the crime and the confrontation. Generally, if the court finds that a lineup violated due process, testimony as to the fact of identification is inadmissible. If the lineup complied with constitutional standards, a person who has identified the defendant in the lineup can testify to that fact at trial.

See also CRIMINAL LAW; CRIMINAL PROCEDURE; DUE PROCESS OF LAW.

LIQUID ASSETS ▥ Cash, or property immediately convertible to cash, such as SECURITIES, NOTES, life insurance policies with CASH SURRENDER VALUES, U.S. savings BONDS, or an ACCOUNT RECEIVABLE. ▥

Although the ownership of REAL PROPERTY is considered an ASSET, it is not a liquid asset because it cannot be readily converted into cash upon sale.

LIQUIDATE ▥ To pay and settle the amount of a DEBT; to convert ASSETS to cash; to aggregate the assets of an insolvent enterprise and calculate its liabilities in order to settle with the DEBTORS and the CREDITORS and apportion the remaining assets, if any, among the stockholders or owners of the corporation. ▥

LIQUIDATED DAMAGES ▥ Monetary compensation for a loss, detriment, or injury to a person or a person's rights or property, awarded by a court JUDGMENT or by a contract stipulation regarding breach of contract. ▥

Generally, CONTRACTS that involve the exchange of money or the PROMISE of PERFORMANCE have a liquidated damages stipulation. The purpose of this stipulation is to establish a predetermined sum that must be paid if a party fails to perform as promised.

DAMAGES can be liquidated in a contract only if (1) the injury is either "uncertain" or "difficult to quantify"; (2) the amount is reasonable and considers the actual or anticipated harm caused by the contract breach, the difficulty of proving the loss, and the difficulty of finding another, adequate remedy; and (3) the damages are structured to function as damages, not as a penalty. If these criteria are not met, a liquidated damages clause will be void.

The *American Law Reports* annotation on liquidated damages states, "Damages for breach by either party may be liquidated in the agreement but only at an amount that is reasonable in light of the anticipated or actual harm caused by the breach. . . . A term fixing unreasonably large liquidated damages is unenforceable on grounds of public policy as a penalty" (12 A.L.R. 4th 891, 899).

A PENALTY is a sum that is disproportionate to the actual harm. It serves as a punishment or as a deterrent against the breach of a contract.

The builder of the Mall of America in Bloomington, Minnesota, might have paid liquidated damages if it had failed to fulfill its contract and the mall had not opened on time. The amount to be paid would have been written in the original contract, and would approximate the amount of business lost by the delay.

Penalties are granted when it is found that the stipulations of a contract have not been met. For example, a builder who does not meet his or her schedule may have to pay a penalty. Liquidated damages, on the other hand, are an amount estimated to equal the extent of injury that may occur if the contract is breached. These damages are determined when a contract is drawn up, and serve as protection for both parties that have entered the contract, whether they are a buyer and a seller, an employer and an employee or other similar parties.

The principle of requiring payments to represent damages rather than penalties goes back to the EQUITY courts, where its purpose was to protect parties from making UNCONSCIONABLE bargains or overreaching their boundaries. Today section 2-718(1) of the UNIFORM COMMERCIAL CODE deals with the difference between a valid liquidated damages clause and an invalid penalty clause.

Liquidated damages clauses possess several contractual advantages. First, they establish some predictability involving costs, so that parties can balance the cost of anticipated performance against the cost of a breach. In this way liquidated damages serve as a source of limited insurance for both parties. Another contractual advantage of liquidated damages clauses is that the parties each have the opportunity to settle on a sum that is mutually agreeable, rather than leaving that decision up to the courts and adding the costs of time and legal fees.

Liquidated damages clauses are commonly used in REAL ESTATE contracts. For buyers, liquidated damage clauses limit their loss if they DEFAULT. For sellers, they provide a preset amount, usually the buyer's deposit money, in a timely manner if the buyer defaults.

The use and enforcement of liquidated damages clauses have changed over the years. For example, cases such as *Colonial at Lynnfield v. Sloan*, 870 F.2d 761 (1st Cir. 1989), and *Shapiro v. Grinspoon*, 27 Mass. App. Ct. 596, 541 N. E. 2d 359, 1989), have granted courts permission to compare the amount set forth in the liquidated damages provision against the actual damages caused by a breach of contract. These "second-look" rulings have led several courts to honor the liquidated damages clauses only if they are equal to, or almost equal to, the actual damages.

LIQUIDATION 📖 The collection of ASSETS belonging to a DEBTOR to be applied to the discharge of his or her outstanding DEBTS.

A type of proceeding pursuant to federal BANKRUPTCY law by which certain property of a debtor is taken into custody by a trustee to be sold, the proceeds to be distributed to the debtor's creditors in satisfaction of their claims.

The settlement of the financial affairs of a business or individual through the sale of all assets and the distribution of the proceeds to creditors, HEIRS, or other parties with a legal claim. 📖

The liquidation of a CORPORATION is not the same as its DISSOLUTION (the termination of its existence as a legal entity). Depending upon statute, liquidation can precede or follow dissolution.

When a corporation undergoes liquidation, the money received by stockholders in lieu of their stock is usually treated as a sale or exchange of the stock resulting in its treatment as a capital gain or loss for INCOME TAX purposes.

LIQUORMART v. RHODE ISLAND The U.S. Supreme Court has stringently limited government regulation of noncommercial expression, citing the FIRST AMENDMENT's guarantee of freedom of expression. Before the mid-1970s, however, the Court regarded the regulation of commercial speech as simply an aspect of economic regulation, entitled to no special First Amendment protection. Since that time the Court has made it more difficult for government to restrict advertising. In *44 Liquormart v. Rhode Island*, __U.S.__, 116 S. Ct. 1495, 134 L. Ed. 2d 711 (1996), the Court ruled that the state of Rhode Island could not prohibit the public advertising of liquor prices, as doing so would abridge the liquor retailer's right to FREEDOM OF SPEECH. After *Liquormart* the ability of the government to restrict truthful, nondeceptive advertising seemed extremely limited.

Commercial speech is a broad category including but not limited to the advertising of services and products. The constitutional protection of commercial expression emerged in the 1970s, when the Supreme Court struck down state laws that banned the advertising of ABORTION services, prescription drug prices, and attorneys' fees. Constitutional expression was not considered absolute, and the Court allowed reasonable regulation to prevent FRAUD and deception.

A standard was first set in *Central Hudson Gas & Electric Corp. v. Public Service Commission*, 447 U.S. 557, 100 S. Ct. 2343, 65 L. Ed. 2d 341 (1980). In *Central Hudson* the Court noted that commercial speech serves the economic interests of the speaker, but also helps consumers and society overall. It outlined a four-part test for evaluating regulation of commercial speech. First, if the commercial speech is to receive First Amendment protection, the Court must determine that it concerns a lawful activity and is not misleading. Second, the court must determine whether the asserted government interest is substantial. Third, if the answer to the second part of the test is yes, the court must determine if the regulation directly advances the asserted government interest. Fourth, the court must decide if the regulation is more extensive than is necessary to serve that purpose.

Central Hudson represented a compromise between one approach that emphasized CONSUMER PROTECTION and another that stressed a free marketplace of ideas. Only five justices fully joined in the majority opinion, and the viability of the test has been called into question. In *Posadas de Puerto Rico Associates v. Tourism Co. of Puerto Rico*, 478 U.S. 328, 106 S. Ct. 2698, 92 L. Ed. 2d 266 (1986), the Court upheld a law prohibiting advertisements inviting residents of Puerto Rico to gamble legally in local casinos. Justice WILLIAM H. REHNQUIST emphasized Puerto Rico's substantial interest in reducing the demand for casino gambling among its citizens, and noted that the regulation at issue directly advanced this objective. In addition, he maintained that because the legislature could have banned all gambling by local residents, this legislative power included the lesser power to ban advertising of casino gambling. Justice JOHN PAUL STEVENS dissented, arguing that Puerto Rico had blatantly discriminated in punishing speech "depending on the publication, audience, and words employed."

The *Liquormart* case raised issues regarding the viability of both the *Central Hudson* test and the *Posadas* reasoning. In 1956 the Rhode Island legislature enacted laws that prohibited the public advertising of alcoholic beverages. Prices could be advertised only inside a licensed liquor retail establishment (R.I. Gen. Laws §§ 3-8-7, 3-8-8.1). 44 Liquormart, a Rhode Island retailer of alcoholic beverages, and the Rhode Island Liquor Stores Association challenged the law in 1993, alleging that the ban violated the First Amendment.

The state of Rhode Island argued that competitive pricing would lower prices and that lower prices would produce more sales, thus encouraging ALCOHOL consumption. It claimed that under *Central Hudson* it had a substantial government interest in controlling the consumption of alcohol and in the laws that directly advance that interest. Apart from *Central Hudson*, the state asserted that under the TWENTY-FIRST AMENDMENT, which repealed the EIGHTEENTH AMENDMENT's prohibition on the sale of alcoholic beverages, the states were given the power to regulate the sale of alcohol, including the power to prohibit sales altogether. Citing *Posadas* Rhode Island said it was in the same position as the Puerto Rican legislature. Because the state could prohibit the sale of alcohol, it could restrict liquor advertising.

Though the Supreme Court unanimously agreed that Rhode Island's laws on liquor advertising were an unconstitutional restraint on protected First Amendment expression, the Court split in its reasoning for the decision. Justice Stevens, with a shifting coalition of three to four justices in various sections of the opinion, moved away from the *Central Hudson* test, indicating concern about any test that might permit a total ban on truthful, noncoercive advertising. Stevens reasoned that such a ban "usually rest[s] solely on the offensive assumption that the public will respond 'irrationally' to the truth. The First Amendment directs us to be especially skeptical of regulations that seek to keep people in the dark for what the government perceives to be their own good."

Though skeptical about *Central Hudson*, Stevens applied its four-part test and found the state's position deficient. Stevens concluded that Rhode Island had failed to provide any evidence that its advertising restrictions significantly reduced the consumption of alcohol. The state could not prove that the ban "advanced the substantial state interest," and the ban was "more extensive than necessary" to address the issue of alcohol consumption. Stevens pointed out that the state's goal of promoting temperance could be achieved through "higher prices maintained either by direct regulation or by increased taxation." Educational campaigns against excessive use might produce better results. Any of these approaches would not infringe on First Amendment expression.

Stevens also dismissed Rhode Island's use of the *Posadas* case—a move that was not surprising in light of his vigorous dissent in that case. He stated that "*Posadas* clearly erred in concluding that it was 'up to the legislature' to choose suppression over a less speech-restrictive policy." Therefore, the Court declined to give force to its "highly deferential approach."

In addition, a unanimous Court rejected the state's argument that the Twenty-first Amendment tilted the First Amendment analysis in its favor. It ruled that the Twenty-first Amendment "does not qualify the constitutional prohibition against laws abridging the freedom of speech embodied in the First Amendment."

Justice CLARENCE THOMAS, in a concurring opinion, went further than the rest of the

Court, advocating that *Central Hudson* be discarded. In Thomas's view, the four-part balancing test had no role to play when "the government's asserted interest is to keep legal users of a product or service ignorant in order to manipulate their choices in the marketplace." According to Thomas such an interest is "*per se* illegitimate and can no more justify regulation of 'commercial' speech than it can justify regulation of 'noncommercial' speech."

On the other hand, Justice SANDRA DAY O'CONNOR, in a concurring opinion joined by three other justices, argued that the case could be resolved more narrowly by applying only the *Central Hudson* test. Applying the test O'Connor concluded that the law failed because it was more extensive than necessary to serve Rhode Island's interest.

The *Liquormart* decision revealed that the Court was divided over the question of whether *Central Hudson* is the right test to apply to commercial expression cases. It also demonstrated that the Court was fully committed to First Amendment protection of commercial expression. The practical result was that Rhode Island and other states with similar laws could not prohibit liquor advertising. The decision put in doubt whether existing and proposed prohibitions on TOBACCO advertising were constitutional.

See also LEAST RESTRICTIVE MEANS TEST; LEGAL ADVERTISING.

LIS PENDENS 📖 [*Latin, Pending lawsuit.*] A reference to the JURISDICTION (or control) that courts obtain over property in a suit awaiting action.

A notice filed in the office of public records that the ownership of REAL PROPERTY is the subject of a legal controversy and that anyone who purchases it takes it subject to any claims asserted in the action and thereby its value might be diminished. 📖

LISTING 📖 An agreement that represents the right of a real estate AGENT or BROKER to handle the sale of REAL PROPERTY and to receive a fee or commission for services. 📖

There are various types of REAL ESTATE listings. A *general* or *open* listing is a right to sell that may be given to more than one agent or broker simultaneously. An *exclusive agency* listing is the right of one real estate agency to be the sole party, with the exception of the owner, who is permitted to sell the property during a particular period. Through an *exclusive authorization to sell* listing, one agency is given the sole authority to sell the property during a certain time period. The agency will receive a commis-

sion even if the owner finds the buyer during the time period.

A *multiple listing* takes place when an agent with an exclusive listing provides a number of members of a real estate association with information about the property and shares the commission with the agent who is able to find a buyer.

A *net listing* is an arrangement whereby the seller establishes a minimum price that will be taken for the property, and the agent's commission is the amount for which it sells above such minimum.

LITCHFIELD LAW SCHOOL 📖 The first law school in America, founded by Tapping Reeve (*b*. October 1744, in Southhold, Long Island, New York; *d*. December 13, 1823, in Litchfield, Connecticut) in 1784 in Litchfield, Connecticut. It continued operation until 1833. 📖

In 1778, Tapping Reeve, a young attorney recently admitted to the bar, settled in Litchfield to practice law. Born in Southhold, Long Island, New York, in 1744, the son of Reverend Abner Reeve, a Presbyterian minister, he graduated from Princeton College in 1763 and immediately taught at a grammar school affiliated with the college. He spent seven years in that position and as a tutor in the college itself. He then moved to Connecticut to study law, entering the office of Judge Elihu Root, who was at that time a practicing attorney in Hartford, and, subsequently, a judge of the Supreme Court. From Hartford, he arrived in Litchfield, after marrying Sally Burr, daughter of President Aaron Burr of Princeton and sister of AARON BURR, the later vice president.

Until the Revolutionary War ended, there was very little civil business transacted in Litchfield County, and Reeve provided legal instruction in anticipation of the conclusion of the war and the resumption of ordinary business matters. This employment augmented his legal knowledge and proficiency and enabled him to commence in 1784 a systematic course of instruction in the law, including regular classes.

The Litchfield Law School officially opened its doors to students in 1784 and continued in successful operation with annual graduating classes until 1833. Its catalog contained the names of 1,500 young men who prepared for the bar after 1798. Most graduates were admitted to the practice of law in the court at Litchfield. The roster of students prior to that date is inaccurate, but it is certain that there were at least 210. More than two-thirds of the students were from states other than Connecticut, with the original thirteen colonies amply represented. A lesser number of students came from states recently admitted to the Union. The greatest number who entered in any one year was 54 in 1813, when the law school apparently reached its zenith.

Prominent statesmen and politicians, such as Aaron Burr and JOHN C. CALHOUN, studied law at Litchfield. Two of its graduates, HENRY BALDWIN and LEVI WOODBURY, became Supreme Court justices. In addition, fifteen U.S. senators, fifty members of Congress, five cabinet members, ten governors, forty-four judges of state and lower federal courts, and seven foreign ministers graduated from the school. Georgia had the greatest number of distinguished graduates.

The term of instruction at Litchfield was completed in fourteen months, including two vacations (spring and fall) of four weeks each. No students could be admitted for a period shorter than three months. In 1828, tuition was $100 for the first year and $60 for the second year.

The curriculum covered the entire body of the law. Tapping Reeve's lectures referred to the law in general, with respect to the sources from which it is derived, such as customs or statutes, and analyzed the rules for the application and interpretation of each. Courses in real estate, rights of persons, rights of things, contracts, torts, evidence, pleading, crimes, and equity then followed. Each of these general subjects was treated under various subsidiary topics, in order to enhance the student's comprehension of the subject matter and its relation to the actual practice of law. Reeve administered the school alone until 1798, when, after his election to the Supreme Court, he invited James Gould to become his associate. They jointly operated the school until 1820, when Judge Reeve withdrew. Gould continued the classes until 1833, with the assistance of Jabez W. Huntington during the final year.

The Litchfield Law School afforded an intensive LEGAL EDUCATION because there were not as many different highly developed areas of law as there are today. In 1784, there were no printed reports of decisions of any court in the United States. The English reports contained nearly the entire body of the law. During the tenure of the law school, the COMMON-LAW system of PLEADING became so encumbered by nuances and fictions that it fell into disfavor. The renowned Rules of Hilary Term were adopted in 1834 to rectify this situation. This development proved to be the forerunner of modern legal theories, such as the merger of LAW and EQUITY and the desirability of short and plain statements of claims and defenses.

LITERAL CONSTRUCTION 📖 The determination by a court of the meaning of the language of a document by an examination of only the actual words used in it, without any consideration of the intent of the parties who signed the writing except for the fact that they chose the language now in dispute. 📖

See also CANONS OF CONSTRUCTION.

LITERARY PROPERTY 📖 The interest of an author in an original and expressive composition, that entitles the author to the exclusive use and profit thereof, with no interest vested in any other individual. The corporal property in which an intellectual production is embodied. 📖

The concept of literature as PROPERTY grew from the notion that literary works have value, and that writers deserve legal protection from unauthorized use of their work by others. Before the fifteenth century, writing generally was an activity performed for royalty and organized religion, and literature was not considered a commodity. With the invention of the printing press in the fifteenth century, along with a societal trend away from royal and religious control, literature came to be seen as an item of value that could be bought and sold.

As literature became a commodity, the law slowly moved to protect the economic interests of writers. In England the Statute of Anne was passed by Parliament in 1710 to limit the monopoly of rights that publishers held over writers. Similar COPYRIGHT laws migrated to the American colonies, and comprehensive federal copyright statutes now regulate the right to own and sell literary property in the United States. In the absence of an agreement to the contrary, copyrights to literary property now vest automatically in the author as soon as the work is affixed to a TANGIBLE medium.

A precise definition of literary property is elusive. According to Eaton S. Drone, an influential nineteenth-century treatise writer, there is no literary property

> in thoughts, conceptions, ideas, sentiments, etc., apart from their association. . . . their arrangement and combination in a definite form constitute an intellectual production, a literary composition, which has a distinct being capable of identification and separate ownership, and possessing the essential attributes of property. The property is not in the simple thoughts, ideas, etc., but in what is produced by their association. (*A Treatise*

SHOULD BIOGRAPHERS BE ALLOWED TO QUOTE UNPUBLISHED LITERARY PROPERTY?

The protection of literary property by the federal copyright statute is intended to create economic incentives that induce authors to create and disseminate new works. A copyright is a reward to an author for making a contribution to society. Nevertheless, the author's copyright monopoly is not unlimited. The doctrine of fair use permits other authors to copy or adapt limited amounts of the copyrighted material without infringing the copyright. Fair use allows someone other than the original author to make secondary use of a copyrighted work to create a new work. The creation of the new work is also viewed as a contribution to society.

The competing interests of copyright and fair use have generated conflict over the quotation of unpublished works, primarily letters, by literary biographers. The U.S. Court of Appeals for the Second Circuit's decision in *Salinger v. Random House*, 811 F.2d 90 (1987), concluded that biographers cannot invoke fair use when dealing with unpublished letters. Defenders of the decision assert that it allows authors to control material they do not want published. Critics argue that this restrictive view of fair use ignores the legitimate need of biographers, historians, and other scholars to mine rich sources of unpublished material and present their findings to the public.

Defenders of *Salinger* and its restrictions on the quotation of unpublished works note that the purpose and character of the use of unpublished material are one factor in determining fair use. For example, though a literary biography is a work of criticism and scholarship, biographical works are generally published by commercial, for-profit businesses. If previously unpublished material were used in such a book, the publisher would promote the book by emphasizing that it contained that material.

Because biographies are written for profit, supporters of restrictions argue, biographers should not be entitled to any special consideration in determining fair use. A biographer is free to read unpublished letters and extract their factual content, but copying their author's expression of particular facts is not, and should not be, permitted. The reader of the biography will still benefit from the new factual content. Therefore, it cannot be argued that banning the quotation of unpublished work defeats the advancement of knowledge and scholarship.

Supporters of restrictions further contend that unpublished works deserve heightened protection because their authors have not yet commercially exploited them. If a biographer could quote generous selections from a series of letters, the potential market for and value of these unpublished letters would likely decrease. Even if the author asserts that he has no intention of publishing the letters, the law should preserve the author's opportunity to sell the letters if a change of mind occurs. The author's copyright must be protected to allow the author the first chance to reap an economic benefit.

Critics of *Salinger* and its reasoning point out that unpublished letters are usually "public," having been donated by the recipient to an academic or research library for scholarly use. It is unfair, charge the critics, to permit persons who can travel to an academic library holding the unpublished letters of a literary figure to read those letters, while denying the rest of the public the opportunity to learn more about the letter writer.

Authors who write letters know that they surrender ownership of them when they send them. Furthermore, authors do not write letters for financial gain; they write them as a simple form of communication with another individual. Critics of *Salinger* suggest that it should

thus be fair use to quote from unpublished letters—while noting that it would not be fair use to quote from an unpublished novel or a short story without the author's permission, since such a work is generally written for economic exploitation.

Critics of the *Salinger* decision also argue that limiting biographers to reciting bland and brief digests of unpublished letters does not advance the public interest. They contend that the use of quotations is essential in literary biographies, where the biographer seeks to compare the public author and the private person. The comparison of expression between published works and letters can reveal consistency and contradiction. Further, the use of the subject's own thoughts and words demonstrates to the reader the complex relationship between art and life.

These critics also dismiss the conclusion that quotations from letters will diminish the market value of the letters for future publication. They point out that the publication of a literary biography generally sparks new interest in the subject and in the subject's works, including a collection of letters. Because of this response in academe and the marketplace, critics contend that the biographer actually enhances the status of the subject.

Critics also hold that the *Salinger* decision is motivated by privacy concerns. They note that if the author of unpublished letters does not wish to permit a biographer to investigate her life, a denial of permission to quote from the letters is an effective way of maintaining privacy. Critics are more troubled by grants of permission to quote that are accompanied by the requirement that the manuscript cannot be published without approval of the subject. Critics maintain that a subject's power to control the content of a book is antithetical to the promotion of scholarship and to the public purposes of copyright.

See also Privacy.

J. D. Salinger Biography

Biographers of living persons often encounter reluctant or hostile subjects. Such was the case for biographer Ian Hamilton, whose completed manuscript about novelist J. D. Salinger had to be rewritten because Hamilton had violated copyright law by quoting from Salinger's unpublished letters.

Salinger, the author of *The Catcher in the Rye* (1951) and several other acclaimed works, has lived reclusively since the early 1960s and did not publish any new works between 1965 and 1996. He has zealously protected his privacy, creating an aura of mystery and helping to establish his status as a cult figure.

Hamilton, a noted literary biographer, tracked down and quoted from unpublished letters that Salinger had written between 1939 and 1961. As Hamilton's book containing those quotations neared publication, Salinger sued, noting that as the author of the letters he retained the right of publication. Hamilton then eliminated direct quotations but substituted extensive paraphrases that tracked the original language very closely.

The federal courts agreed with Salinger, holding that Hamilton could write about the factual content of the letters but that Salinger retained the letters' "expressive content." According to the courts, Hamilton's paraphrasing invaded Salinger's expressive content and formed a substantial part of Hamilton's manuscript (*Salinger v. Random House*, 811 F.2d 90 [2d Cir. 1987]). Hamilton was forced to rewrite his manuscript. In the end, the book, *In Search of J. D. Salinger* (1988), was as much about the legal case and the pursuit of Salinger as it was about the novelist's life.

---

on the Law of Property in Intellectual Productions in Great Britain and the United States [1879])

Ultimately, lawmakers have left the job of determining what constitutes literary property to the courts, which have fashioned some general guidelines.

Not all literature qualifies as literary property. Furthermore, not all the content in a piece of literary property can receive protection from copying or use by other authors. Only the original expressive content of a piece of literature qualifies as literary property.

Mere ideas generally do not constitute literary property. For example, the idea of writing a novel set in Okefenokee Swamp, in Georgia, is not literary property. But if a person writes such a novel, the expressive content of the novel is literary property, and the author owns the rights to that property. After the novel is published and sold, another person may write a book set in Okefenokee Swamp. However, the writer of the second book may not use the original expressions, characters, and sequence of events created by the author of the first book.

No bright line distinguishes protected and unprotected characters and story lines. Rather, courts place these elements on a continuum from simple to complex. On this continuum general qualities and emotional features do not receive copyright protection. However, the more a character or story is developed, the more it comes to constitute literary property, and the more copyright protection it receives.

A determination of COPYRIGHT infringement also can depend on the degree of similarity between the literary property and subsequent literary works. For example, assume that a novelist has developed a character named Hijinks, a lovable pool cleaner who moonlights as a private detective and drinks only papaya juice. This is a well-defined character, so it is the property of the novelist and no one may copy it without permission. If a second author writes and sells a book that features a private detective who cleans pools part-time, this would probably not be sufficient borrowing of an original expression to constitute copyright infringement. The second author may even give the pool-cleaning private eye a penchant for fruit juice and be safe from suit. However, if the second author's main character is a papaya-juice drinking, pool-cleaning private detective named Hijinks, a judge or jury could find infringement and award DAMAGES to the first author.

Before 1976 the term *literary property* was used to describe the author's state of ownership prior to publication. When an author fixed a piece of literature in a tangible medium, such as on paper or on an audiotape, the author owned the work forever and could exclude others from using it forever. Once the author published the work, the work became governed by copyright laws, which granted exclusive rights to the author for a fixed term of years.

The effect of publication was eliminated by the Copyright Act of 1976, 17 U.S.C.A. § 101 et seq. Under this act all literary property is subject to statutory provisions from the moment it is affixed in a tangible medium.

The term *literary property* also can describe the tangible instrument that contains the words of a literary work. Novels, short stories, poems, plays, essays, letters, lectures, sermons, and songs are some basic forms of literary property. They can be contained on any tangible medium, including audiotape, videotape, and paper.

See also INTELLECTUAL PROPERTY.

LITIGATION An ACTION brought in court to enforce a particular right. The act or process of bringing a lawsuit in and of itself; a judicial contest; any dispute.

When a person begins a civil lawsuit, the person enters into a process called litigation. Under the various rules of CIVIL PROCEDURE that govern actions in state and federal courts, litigation involves a series of steps that may lead to a court TRIAL and ultimately a resolution of the matter.

Before a lawsuit is filed, the person contemplating the lawsuit (called the PLAINTIFF) typically demands that the person who caused the alleged injury (called the DEFENDANT) perform certain actions that will resolve the conflict. If the demand is refused or ignored, the plaintiff may start the lawsuit by serving copies of a SUMMONS and COMPLAINT on the defendant and filing the complaint with a civil trial court. The complaint must state the alleged injuries and attribute them to the defendant, and request money DAMAGES or equitable RELIEF.

If the service of the complaint on the defendant does not result in a settlement of the issues, the plaintiff must begin the DISCOVERY process. This involves sending to the defendant written questions (called INTERROGATORIES) that seek information involving the dispute at issue. The plaintiff may DEPOSE the defendant and others concerning the issues, with the DEPOSITION recorded by a court reporter. The plaintiff may also request copies of documents for review. Once litigation commences the defendant is also permitted to use discovery to learn more about the plaintiff's case. The discovery process may be conducted in a matter of weeks, or it may take years, depending on the complexity of the case and the level of cooperation between the parties.

After discovery is completed, most courts require the parties to attend a settlement conference to determine if the case may be resolved before trial. If the parties are unable to reach a settlement, the litigation continues to trial. Near or on the day of trial, one or both parties often make settlement offers, in the hope of avoiding court proceedings (which are often costly and protracted). Litigation ends if a settlement is reached.

If the parties are still unable to resolve their differences, a trial is held. At trial both sides are permitted to introduce relevant EVIDENCE that will help to prove to the JURY or the court the truth of their positions. If the plaintiff makes a convincing case, the defendant may seek to settle the case immediately. On the other hand, if the plaintiff presents a weak case, the defendant may ask the court to dismiss the case. If the trial proceeds to a conclusion, either the jury or the JUDGE (if a jury trial was waived) must decide which party prevails.

If the defendant loses the lawsuit, the defendant may ask the court to throw out the jury VERDICT if the evidence did not warrant the decision, or the defendant may ask that the damages awarded to the plaintiff be reduced. The court has discretion to grant or refuse these kinds of requests.

Once a final decision has been made at the trial court, the losing party may APPEAL the decision within a specified period of time. The federal courts and the states have intermediate courts of appeal that hear most civil appeals. The APPELLATE COURT reviews the arguments of the parties on appeal and determines whether the trial court conducted the proceedings correctly. Once the appellate court issues a decision, usually in opinion form, the losing party may appeal to the state supreme court if the litigation occurred in a state court, or to the U.S. Supreme Court if the litigation occurred in a FEDERAL COURT. After the supreme court rules on the case, the decision is final.

Once a decision is final, litigation ends. The prevailing party is then given the authority to collect damages or receive other REMEDIES from the losing party. After the losing party provides the relief, that party is entitled to receive from the prevailing party a SATISFACTION of JUDGMENT, which is filed with the trial court. This document attests to the satisfaction of all court-imposed relief and signifies the end of the case.

BIOGRAPHY

COURTESY RODNELL COLLINS

Ella Lee
Little-Collins

LITTLE-COLLINS, ELLA LEE Ella Lee Little-Collins (Muslim name Alziz A. Hamid) was the half sister of MALCOLM X, who credited her with playing a major role in his life. She supported the black revolutionary leader both emotionally and financially throughout his short but highly influential life. Malcolm lived with Little-Collins, who served essentially as a surrogate mother for him, off and on from 1940 until 1946, a period that left an indelible imprint on him. Little-Collins also sponsored Malcolm in his pilgrimage to Mecca in the early

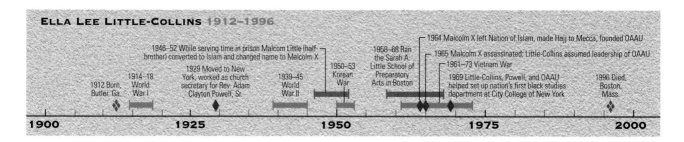

ELLA LEE LITTLE-COLLINS 1912–1996

1964 Malcolm X left Nation of Islam, made Hajj to Mecca, founded OAAU

1946–52 While serving time in prison Malcom Little (half-brother) converted to Islam and changed name to Malcolm X

1965 Malcolm X assassinated; Little-Collins assumed leadership of OAAU

1958–68 Ran the Sarah A. Little School of Preparatory Arts in Boston

1929 Moved to New York, worked as church secretary for Rev. Adam Clayton Powell, Sr.

1950–53 Korean War

1961–73 Vietnam War

1912 Born, Butler, Ga.

1914–18 World War I

1939–45 World War II

1969 Little-Collins, Powell, and OAAU helped set up nation's first black studies department at City College of New York

1996 Died, Boston, Mass.

1900 1925 1950 1975 2000

1960s—another important, formative period of his life.

Though Malcolm credited Little-Collins for being only a positive influence in his life, at least one of his biographers suggests that she was a negative influence as well, asserting that she taught Malcolm his lifestyle of petty thievery. And Malcolm's widow, Betty Shabazz, has stated that she had no respect for Little-Collins because of her poor influence on Malcolm. Little-Collins did not dispute that she had many run-ins with the law, resulting in ten convictions for offenses including petty LARCENY and ASSAULT AND BATTERY. But Little-Collins's family asserts the run-ins occurred when she was defending others who were being harassed or taken advantage of by people in positions of authority. Little-Collins emerges as a major figure in Malcolm's life, one of few people who knew him and remained by his side throughout all of his many philosophical incarnations.

Little-Collins was born December 4, 1912, in Butler, Georgia, the eldest of three children of the Reverend Earl Lee Little and his first wife, Daisy Mason. Her parents had two more children, Mary and Earl, Jr., and divorced in 1917 or 1918. Little-Collins's mother moved to Boston around 1920, taking Earl Jr. with her. Ella and Mary were left in Butler, Georgia, with Earl Sr.'s parents, John and Ella Little, who raised them to adulthood.

Little-Collins left Georgia in 1929 with very little to her name, and went to New York to earn a living. She worked at first as a church secretary at Abyssinian Baptist Church in Harlem, the parish at which the Reverend Adam Clayton Powell, Sr. was minister. This position led to a long-standing professional relationship with the minister's son, ADAM CLAYTON POWELL, JR., a CIVIL RIGHTS activist and Harlem's first African American congressional representative. After a short period in New York, Little-Collins moved to Boston to work at a grocery that her mother was running at the time. She was a hard worker, and she soon began sending money to the relatives remaining in Georgia so that they

could also come north. Her father was very proud of her for bringing many family members from Georgia to Boston. Collins's devotion to her family extended beyond bringing them out of southern poverty: she was known to support others in achieving their educational or career goals as well. Malcolm later wrote, "[I]f Ella had ever thought that she could help any member of the Little family put up any kind of professional shingle— as a teacher, a foot-doctor, anything . . . you would have had to tie her down to keep her from taking in washing."

In 1933, Little-Collins married Dr. Thomas Lloyd Oxley, a Jamaican-born follower of Marcus Garvey. (Garvey urged black Americans to return to their African roots; many members of the Little family were proponents of his philosophy.) Oxley and Little-Collins divorced in 1934. By early 1939, when Little-Collins visited her father's family in Michigan and met Malcolm for the first time, she had been married to her second husband, Frank Johnson, for nearly four years. During this visit, the seeds were planted that led to Malcolm's living with her in Roxbury, Massachusetts, later that summer. Malcolm described his first meeting with his half sister, which occurred when he was a young adolescent and she was twenty-six: "[S]he was the first really proud black woman I had ever seen in my life. She was plainly proud of her very dark skin. This was unheard of among Negroes. . . . I had never been so impressed with anybody."

Little-Collins' second husband was in the military when Malcolm arrived in the summer of 1939, after he had finished seventh grade. In his autobiography, Malcolm described Little-Collins as a community leader in Roxbury, an enclave of blacks outside of Boston, which was to Boston as Harlem was to New York. Little-Collins's standing and the Boston atmosphere impressed the young man, and after he returned home, during the next school year, when he became disenchanted with his opportunities in Michigan, he wrote to Little-Collins that he wanted to live with her permanently in Boston.

Little-Collins arranged to transfer official custody of Malcolm to Massachusetts, and he moved there upon finishing eighth grade.

Little-Collins had separated from Frank shortly before Malcolm came to live in Roxbury in 1940. They divorced in June 1942. Malcolm later wrote, "[A]ny average man would find it almost impossible to live for very long with a woman whose every instinct was to run everything and everybody she had anything to do with—including me."

Little-Collins did not approve of the lifestyle that Malcolm began to lead in Roxbury and later continued in Harlem. She was very strict, locking him out of the house if he failed to return home in time, forcing him to spend the night with other relatives who lived downstairs in the same house. She had married Kenneth Collins in June 1942. They had a child, Rodnell, in 1945. Even though Little-Collins had a family of her own, and Malcolm was in and out of trouble, she never really abandoned him. From time to time, when Malcolm returned to her household, she welcomed him with open arms.

After Malcolm was convicted of burglary and firearms charges and sent to prison in 1946, Little-Collins sent him money. In 1948, through her efforts, Malcolm was transferred from Concord Prison to the Norfolk, Massachusetts, Prison Colony, an experimental rehabilitative institution patterned after a college campus. This transfer proved to be monumental for Malcolm. The Norfolk Colony had an outstanding library, whose books Malcolm read prodigiously, and inmates were allowed to participate in cultural events such as debates, group discussions, and educational lectures. Malcolm read about history and religion, increased his vocabulary, and developed his debating skills, all of which later served him as a leader in the NATION OF ISLAM.

Little-Collins continued to have contact with Malcolm after his release from prison, as his stature as a black leader increased. She also continued working within the black community. By 1957, her third marriage had ended; by Malcolm's description, Little-Collins was "more driving and dynamic" than the sum of her three husbands. Because of her half brother's influence, Little-Collins joined the Nation of Islam, becoming a member of Boston's Mosque Eleven. However, she was thrown out, according to Malcolm, because of her tendency to take charge of any situation. She was taken back, but later left on her own, breaking with Elijah Muhammad's Black Muslims in 1959.

During this time, Little-Collins also started the Sarah A. Little School of Preparatory Arts, in Boston, where children were taught Arabic, as well as Swahili, French, and Spanish. Little-Collins herself hired the teachers, who donated their time; although she did not speak any language but English, she echoed her half brother's belief in the importance of being able to communicate with others in their native tongues. The school's curriculum also included arts and etiquette instruction. It was in existence from 1958 to 1968.

Malcolm continued to rely on Little-Collins for her support of both himself and his ministry. After he was silenced as a spokesman for the Nation of Islam, he decided that he wanted to make a pilgrimage to Mecca, but he did not have enough of his own money to pay for the trip. He flew to Boston to ask Little-Collins for help. In his autobiography, he described their meeting as follows: "I was turning again to my sister Ella. Though at times I'd made Ella angry at me . . . Ella had never once really wavered from my corner." When Malcolm announced that he wanted to make the pilgrimage, Little-Collins said only, "How much do you need?" Through the income from her real estate holdings, Little-Collins had been saving for her own trip to Mecca, but insisted that Malcolm take the money because it was more important that he go. Malcolm later credited the trip, taken in April and May 1964, with broadening his horizons and changing his entire outlook on the U.S. blacks' struggle for civil rights.

After Malcolm was assassinated in February 1965, Little-Collins accompanied his widow to the medical examiner's office in New York to identify the body. Little-Collins later returned to Boston, where she announced at a press conference that she would choose the leaders of the Organization of Afro-American Unity (OAAU), the group Malcolm had set up after his break with Elijah Muhammad, to succeed Malcolm. Little-Collins herself served as interim president and president of the OAAU for a time as well as supporting the group financially. For ten years, the OAAU sponsored workshops during the week of May 19, the anniversary of Malcolm's birth. Little-Collins, Adam Clayton-Powell, Jr., and the OAAU were instrumental in setting up what is said to be the nation's first degree-granting college black studies department, at the City College of New York, in 1969. However, perhaps owing to her domineering personality and the rift between her and Shabazz, the group's influence diminished after Malcolm's death.

Little-Collins continued supporting black causes by donating her time and money. She brought young people into her home, raised them, passed along the teachings of Malcolm, and sent several on pilgrimages to Mecca. She characterized herself as a human-rights activist rather than a civil-rights activist, because she felt that universal human rights were of primary importance. Little-Collins eventually moved to a Boston-area nursing home, where she died August 3, 1996 at the age of 84. She left one son, Rodnell Collins, who is the OAAU's current president.

See also CIVIL RIGHTS MOVEMENT.

LITTLETON, SIR THOMAS

Sir Thomas Littleton was an English judge and writer who is known for his treatise on land law, entitled *On Tenures* (1481). Littleton's work served as an inspiration and model for later English jurists, including SIR EDWARD COKE.

Littleton was born in 1422 in Frankley Manor House, Worcestershire. He became a counsel at law in 1445 and served as a recorder of Coventry in 1450. In 1455 he became a judge of ASSIZE on the Northern Circuit, and he was appointed a justice of COMMON PLEAS in 1466. In 1475 King Edward IV made him a knight of the Bath. He died in 1481 and was buried in Worcestershire Cathedral.

Littleton's *On Tenures* is regarded as a model of legal scholarship, a clear and concise classification of English land law. Its significance rests in Littleton's attempt to impose a rational and orderly arrangement on legal rights in land. At the time the work was written, English land law had become extremely complicated.

The treatise consists of three books. The first deals with various ESTATES in land; the second with the incidents of tenure (the holding of lands in subordination to some superior); and the third with co-ownership and other specialized doctrines relating to property. Unlike previous authors, Littleton did not rely on ROMAN LAW but dealt exclusively with English land law.

Littleton followed a consistent method of analysis. He first defined a particular class of rights and then analyzed the many variations and implications of that class. Having identified

BIOGRAPHY

Sir Thomas Littleton

certain key principles underlying a particular area of land law, Littleton then demonstrated how novel problems might be solved by reference to them. Modern commentators have lauded Littleton for the scientific organization of his material.

On Tenures was the first major legal treatise written in French instead of Latin and the first work on ENGLISH LAW to be printed in London. For more than three centuries, it formed the standard introduction to students of English REAL PROPERTY law. Coke, who considered it a model of clear and lucid exposition of English law, made it the subject of his First Institute, *Coke upon Littleton* (1628). It stands as an early classic of English law.

LITTORAL RIGHTS

Rights relating to the ownership of property that abuts an ocean, SEA, or lake.

Littoral proprietors are occupants of land that borders the above-named bodies of water, whereas *riparian proprietors* are those who occupy land bordering streams or RIVERS. Littoral rights are generally concerned with the use and enjoyment of the shore. See also RIPARIAN RIGHTS.

LITVINOV ASSIGNMENT OF 1933

An executive agreement made by President FRANKLIN DELANO ROOSEVELT as part of the arrangements by which the United States recognized the Soviet Union.

The Litvinov Assignment purported to transfer to the United States certain American ASSETS located in Russia that had been previously nationalized by the Soviet Union. Accordingly, the United States went to court to establish its TITLE to the assets. In the famous case of *United States v. Pink*, 315 U.S. 203, 62 S.Ct. 552, 86 L. Ed. 796 (1942), the Supreme Court upheld this title on the basis of the executive agreement. The Court saw the agreement as an integral part of the new RECOGNITION policy of the government and as a proper method of mitigating losses resulting from the nationalization of U.S. owned property in the Soviet Union. The Court held that the powers of the EXECUTIVE BRANCH in the conduct of foreign policy were not herein restricted by the need for Senate consent.

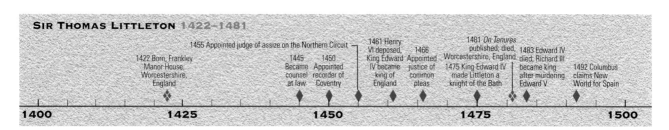

SIR THOMAS LITTLETON 1422–1481

1422 Born, Frankley Manor House, Worcestershire, England

1445 Became counsel at law

1450 Appointed recorder of Coventry

1455 Appointed judge of assize on the Northern Circuit

1461 Henry VI deposed; King Edward IV became king of England

1466 Appointed justice of common pleas

1481 *On Tenures* published; died, Worcestershire, England

1475 King Edward IV made Littleton a knight of the Bath

1483 Edward IV died; Richard III became king after murdering Edward V

1492 Columbus claims New World for Spain

1400   1425   1450   1475   1500

LIUZZO, VIOLA FAUVER GREGG CIVIL RIGHTS activist and martyr Viola Fauver Gregg Liuzzo was murdered after the 1965 VOTING rights march from Selma, Alabama, to Montgomery, Alabama. A thirty-nine-year-old wife, mother, and student, Liuzzo had spontaneously driven from her home in Detroit to help with the historic march. While transporting other participants back to Selma afterward, she was killed by members of the KU KLUX KLAN (KKK). The tragedy both shocked and inspired U.S. citizens. President LYNDON B. JOHNSON decried her slaying on national television, and her death gave impetus for passing the landmark Voting Rights Act of 1965 (42 U.S.C.A. § 1973 et seq.). Two Alabama juries failed to convict her assassins, who were ultimately found guilty of CONSPIRACY. Nearly two decades later, her family brought an unsuccessful $2 million lawsuit against the FEDERAL BUREAU OF INVESTIGATION (FBI), following congressional revelations that the bureau may have known about but done nothing to stop Klan plans to kill the marchers. Liuzzo's memory is honored by memorials in Alabama and commemorations in Detroit.

Liuzzo was born in the coal-mining town of California, Pennsylvania, on April 11, 1925. She dropped out of school in the tenth grade and worked as a waitress. In 1950, she married Anthony James Liuzzo, a business agent of the International Brotherhood of Teamsters, with whom she had three children.

Liuzzo returned to school and in 1962, she graduated with top honors from the Carnegie Institute of Detroit. She found employment as a medical laboratory assistant. Though a high school dropout, she loved reading, and introduced her children to the works of the philosopher HENRY DAVID THOREAU. She explained to them his theory of civil disobedience, a concept that would find widespread support during the CIVIL RIGHTS MOVEMENT.

Despite her lack of formal education, Liuzzo won acceptance to Wayne State University. By 1965, she was studying Shakespeare and philosophy. Like other students across the United States, she became increasingly concerned

BIOGRAPHY

Viola Fauver Gregg Liuzzo

"IT'S EVERYBODY'S FIGHT. THERE ARE TOO MANY PEOPLE WHO JUST STAND AROUND TALKING."

about violence against civil rights workers. The civil rights movement was at a crossroads: it had achieved important gains against desegregation, but now it faced resistance and violence as it sought to win voting rights for African Americans living in the South.

In early March 1965, a pivotal event in civil rights history pushed the movement forward and changed Liuzzo's life. The murder of Jimmie Lee Jackson at the hands of Alabama troopers had motivated civil rights leaders to stage a protest march from Selma, Alabama, to the capitol in Montgomery, fifty miles away. The march would be led by MARTIN LUTHER KING, JR., president of the SOUTHERN CHRISTIAN LEADERSHIP CONFERENCE (SCLC); Ralph J. Bunche, an African American Nobel laureate and diplomat to the United Nations; and other dignitaries. Once at the capitol, they planned to confront Governor GEORGE WALLACE, an unbending foe of INTEGRATION. But, as in previous civil rights protests, Wallace's state troopers struck first. On March 7, hundreds of African Americans set out from Selma, only to be stopped minutes later by club-wielding police officers and troopers. As law enforcement officers beat men, women, and children, millions of horrified U.S. citizens watched on television. Liuzzo and her family were among the viewers.

Within days, protests erupted nationwide. In Washington, D.C., some six hundred people picketed outside the White House. In Detroit, Liuzzo joined 250 students in a march on local FBI offices. Wherever protests occurred, people demanded federal protection for civil rights workers and the passage of new voting rights legislation. King announced a new march from Selma to Montgomery. Before it could begin on March 9, federal judge FRANK M. JOHNSON, fearing new violence, postponed it. Two days later, another civil rights worker—the Reverend James J. Reeb, a Unitarian minister from Boston—died at the hands of violent whites in Selma.

On March 15, President Lyndon B. Johnson appeared on television to address both houses of Congress. He called for passage of the voting rights bill and also gave his full support to the

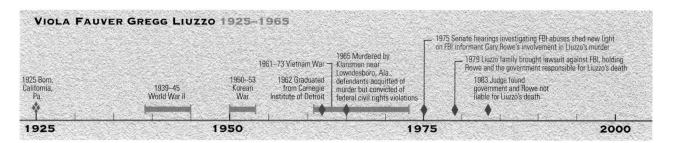

VIOLA FAUVER GREGG LIUZZO 1925–1965

1925 Born, California, Pa.

1939–45 World War II

1950–53 Korean War

1961–73 Vietnam War

1962 Graduated from Carnegie Institute of Detroit

1965 Murdered by Klansmen near Lowndesboro, Ala.; defendants acquitted of murder but convicted of federal civil rights violations

1975 Senate hearings investigating FBI abuses shed new light on FBI informant Gary Rowe's involvement in Liuzzo's murder

1979 Liuzzo family brought lawsuit against FBI, holding Rowe and the government responsible for Liuzzo's death

1983 Judge found government and Rowe not liable for Liuzzo's death

1925   1950   1975   2000

marchers in Selma. That night, Liuzzo attended a meeting at which several Wayne State students said they would join the march. She too decided to go. She packed a few clothes in a shopping bag, and by the next afternoon was driving south.

Liuzzo was one of thousands arriving at the church that served as the launching point for the march, Brown Chapel. Appointed to the reception desk to help with last-minute chores, she greeted new arrivals. As was her way, she wanted to do more, and soon she had volunteered the use of her car for transporting others.

On March 21, the journey to Montgomery began as marchers passed a vast contingent of federal security. Governor Wallace had ruled out protecting the marchers as being too expensive, but President Johnson had made available military police, FBI agents, U.S. marshals, and nineteen hundred members of the Alabama National Guard who were placed under federal control. There was to be no repeat of the violence committed two weeks earlier by Alabama troopers.

The five-day march ended in a gathering of twenty-five thousand people at the capitol in Montgomery, where King once again preached his doctrine of nonviolence. Yet he warned of further struggles ahead.

Now that the march was over, Liuzzo prepared to make good on her promise of driving people back to Selma. Staff members of the SCLC advised her that further help was unnecessary, given the buses already waiting. Liuzzo nevertheless drove three women and a man to their destination and by nightfall, was returning to Selma again, this time with nineteen-year-old Leroy Moton, an African American barber and civil rights worker. In the swamplands of Lowndes County, a car chased them down and its occupants shot and killed Liuzzo. Moton, covered with Liuzzo's blood, feigned death and then ran three miles before finding safety with other civil rights workers.

It took the FBI eight hours to arrest three suspects, all Klan members. Gary Thomas Rowe, Jr., a thirty-four-year-old Klan member who had been passing information to the FBI for five years, was riding with three others in the car from which the fatal shots were fired. Immediately, the state of Alabama indicted the other three men on first-degree murder charges. Rowe was given IMMUNITY and put in protective custody in return for testifying against Eugene Thomas, age forty-three; William Orville Eaton, age forty-one; and Collie Leroy Wilkins, Jr., age twenty-one. According

to Rowe's subsequent testimony, the men had received instructions from Klan leaders to punish one of the marchers.

A trial on state charges in May 1965 ended in a mistrial. However, a subsequent federal trial, based on a conspiracy to violate Luizzo's civil rights, brought guilty verdicts. Each of the defendants was sentenced to ten years. A subsequent appeal failed.

In 1979 the Liuzzo family filed a $2 million lawsuit against the FBI. The suit accused the bureau of NEGLIGENCE in its hiring, training, and supervision of Rowe. The informant, it alleged, was a loose gun who had actively participated in the murder. U.S. district judge Charles Joiner heard the trial without a jury and on May 30, 1983, found that Rowe did not shoot Liuzzo. He further ruled that the government was not responsible for her death.

In 1982 the Detroit City Council honored Liuzzo for her contributions to the struggle for civil and human rights. In June 1982, a mayoral proclamation made June 1–8 Viola Liuzzo Commemoration Week. Other memorials followed. In 1985, nearly one hundred marchers led by the Reverend Joseph Lowery, president of the SCLC, retraced the historic Selma-to-Montgomery march and laid a wreath at the site where she was murdered. There along U.S. Route 80, beside a swampy stretch, stands a simple stone marker, dedicated in 1991 by women members of the SCLC. It reads, In Memory of Our Sister Viola Liuzzo Who Gave Her Life in the Struggle for the Right to Vote.

LIVERY OF SEISIN 📖 A ceremony performed in medieval England that effected the transfer of land from one party to another. 📖

Livery of seisin was the dominant method of transferring land in England until 1536, and it continued to be legal until 1925. The term *livery of seisin* means simply "transfer of possession": *livery* means "delivery" and is from the Old French *livrer*; and *seisin* means "possession" and is from the Old French *saisir* or *seisir*. The concept behind livery of seisin, therefore, was the symbolic transfer of the possession of land. The entire ceremony of transfer was called FEOFFMENT with livery of seisin, with *feoffment* meaning "a gift," specifically a gift of a FREEHOLD interest in a parcel of land. The transferor was the feoffor, the transferee was the feoffee, and the land interest was the fief.

In the Middle Ages, a livery of seisin was essential to convey land from one party to another; without it no real right to land could be transferred. When performing the ceremony, the feoffor, the feoffee, and their witnesses generally stood on the land itself, though it was permissible to stand within view of the land if the feoffee made an actual entry to the land while the feoffor was still alive. During the ceremony the feoffor spoke appropriate words declaring the gift, and then handed the feoffee an object representing that gift, such as dirt, turf, or a twig, or even a ring, a cross, or a knife. If a house was being transferred, the ring of the door might be exchanged.

In addition to delivering possession of the land, the feoffor needed to vacate the land. The feoffor's tenants and others living on the land were expelled, along with their possessions. In some cases, the feoffor performed a ceremony or gesture showing abandonment of the land, such as by making a sign with the hands, jumping over a hedge, or throwing a rod to the feoffee.

A livery of seisin was sometimes accompanied by a DEED, or charter of feoffment, written in Latin, which was used to call attention to the CONVEYANCE of land. This was often the case when the transfer in question had special political significance or when it involved complex BOUNDARIES. If a charter of feoffment existed, it was read during the livery of seisin. However, such a charter did not in itself serve as a means of transferring land; rather, it was used simply as evidence that a transfer had taken place. Its language was not "I hereby give" but "Know ye that I have given." A charter of feoffment by itself was not considered an agreement to transfer land, but had to be accompanied by a livery of seisin.

During the Anglo-Saxon period in England, before the Norman Conquest of 1066, the use of writing was rare, so few charters existed. After the Norman invasion, writing was used more often, but charters were still generally short and crude. Eventually, over a period of hundreds of years, the delivery of a charter or deed came to replace the delivery of dirt, twigs, or knives that had been used to convey land in the livery-of-seisin ceremonies.

The Real Property Act of 1845 (8 & 9 Vict. ch. 106 [Eng.]) did not abolish livery of seisin, but it did allow deeds to be used freely as granting devices, which had the same effect. The Law of Property Act, passed in 1925 (15 & 16 Geo. 5, ch. 20 [Eng.]), finally abolished the livery-of-seisin ceremony.

LIVERY STABLE KEEPERS Individuals who, as a regular course of business, provide quarters for the boarding of horses and rent them for hire.

Livery stables are ordinarily subject to regulation. A MUNICIPAL CORPORATION acting subject to the authority delegated by the state legisla-

Livery stable keepers are regulated by local governments in order to ensure safety.

ture can prohibit the maintenance of such stables in particular areas of a town or city. Such regulation must be reasonable and uniform in its effect upon individual keepers as well as the general public at large. A state or a municipal corporation can require that a livery stable keeper obtain a LICENSE, or it can impose a tax upon their activities. Generally a livery stable keeper who hires out a horse makes an implied promise or warranty that it is fit for ordinary use. The livery stable keeper will be held liable in the event that the horse is vicious and, as a result, a person suffers injury as a result of the horse's behavior.

LIVINGSTON, HENRY BROCKHOLST

Henry Brockholst Livingston came from a powerful New York family. He was educated at Princeton alongside JAMES MADISON, had political ties to THOMAS JEFFERSON, and enjoyed rapid advancement through the military, private practice, and the bench. From 1802 to 1807, Livingston served on the New York Supreme Court. An outspoken anti-Federalist in his youth, Livingston grew more conservative in later life. He served as an associate justice on the U.S. Supreme Court from 1807 until his death in 1823.

Livingston was born November 25, 1757, in New York City. Established in New York in the late seventeenth century, his family also included other notable public figures: Philip Livingston (1716–78) signed the DECLARATION OF INDEPENDENCE, William Livingston (1723–90) was New Jersey's first governor, ROBERT R. LIVINGSTON (1746–1813) negotiated the LOUISIANA PURCHASE, and Edward Livingston (1764–1836) served in Congress and as secretary of state. At an early age, Livingston had several outstanding accomplishments in military service. He was commissioned a major at age

BIOGRAPHY

Henry Brockholst Livingston

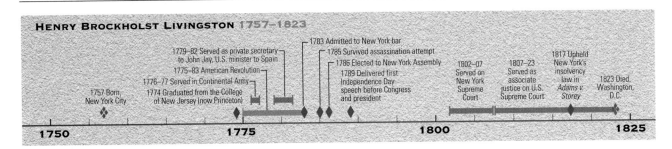

HENRY BROCKHOLST LIVINGSTON 1757–1823

1757 Born, New York City

1774 Graduated from the College of New Jersey (now Princeton)

1776–77 Served in Continental Army

1775–83 American Revolution

1779–82 Served as private secretary to John Jay, U.S. minister to Spain

1783 Admitted to New York bar

1785 Survived assassination attempt

1786 Elected to New York Assembly

1789 Delivered first Independence Day speech before Congress and president

1802–07 Served on New York Supreme Court

1807–23 Served as associate justice on U.S. Supreme Court

1817 Upheld New York's insolvency law in *Adams v. Storey*

1823 Died, Washington, D.C.

1750   1775   1800   1825

nineteen. At twenty-two he was a secretary in Spain to his brother-in-law, U.S. minister JOHN JAY. At twenty-five he helped negotiate the end of the Revolutionary War.

Livingston's legal career advanced in similar fashion. After being admitted to the New York bar in 1783, he was soon in private practice working alongside ALEXANDER HAMILTON and AARON BURR. He entered politics in 1786 when he was elected to the New York Assembly. In 1789 he delivered the first Independence Day speech in Saint Paul's Church, before Congress, President GEORGE WASHINGTON, and other distinguished leaders. During this period he became a fierce anti-Federalist and sided with Jefferson.

Livingston's outspokenness in public and in print led to conflict. He survived an ASSASSINATION attempt in 1785, and in 1798, after being punched in the nose by an angry Federalist, he killed the man in a duel. But his politics also brought rewards. In return for helping Jefferson win the state of New York in the 1800 presidential election, Livingston was appointed to the New York Supreme Court.

In four years on the New York bench, Livingston gained high distinction. He wrote 149 opinions—a prodigious number—many concerning his specialty, commercial law. He tended to favor business interests at a time when capitalism was bustling. In civil liberties he took the traditional view that truth and GOOD FAITH were not defenses against a charge of seditious libel. He was also a practitioner of the art of judicial humor. His most-quoted opinion is his dissent in the so-called *Foxhunt* case, *Pierson v. Post*, 3 Cai. R. 175 (1805), which dealt with the question of who should be entitled to claim a fox—the hunter who has pursued it up to the end, or another hunter who snatches it at the last moment. "This is a knotty point," wrote Livingston, "and should have been submitted to the arbitration of sportsmen."

In 1807 President Jefferson made Livingston his second appointee to the U.S. Supreme Court. Under Chief Justice JOHN MARSHALL, Livingston's anti-Federalism was tempered, and he generally followed the chief justice's lead. Compared with the stream of opinions he issued in

New York, his output of thirty-eight majority opinions, eight dissents, and six concurrences was minimal. He continued to write chiefly on commercial and maritime law; in the latter area, he was a specialist in PRIZE LAW, a now antiquated area of jurisprudence that dealt with the capture of goods at sea during wartime. Early Supreme Court justices, in addition to their duties on the Court, routinely travelled the circuit to which they were assigned and presided over its cases. Most scholars have found Livingston's circuit court decisions more notable than his opinions in Supreme Court cases, especially *Adams v. Storey*, 1 Fed. Cas. 141 (C.C.D.N.Y. 1817) (No. 66), in which he upheld New York's INSOLVENCY law against a challenge that it violated the Constitution's Contracts Clause and federal BANKRUPTCY jurisdiction.

Livingston suffered two ethical lapses while on the Supreme Court. He told JOHN QUINCY ADAMS the Court's decision in *Fletcher v. Peck*, 10 U.S. (6 Cranch) 87, 4 L. Ed. 629 (1810) before it was announced, when Adams was a counsel on the case. And while the Court was deciding *Dartmouth College v. Woodward*, 17 U.S. (4 Wheat.) 518, 4 L. Ed. 629 (1819), he reportedly received extrajudicial information about the case from a former colleague.

Neither incident seems to have damaged his career. He continued to serve on the Court until his death on March 18, 1823, in Washington, D.C.

LIVINGSTON, ROBERT R. Robert R. Livingston served the United States in many ways, from participating in the Continental Congress, to administering the oath of office to GEORGE WASHINGTON and negotiating the Louisiana Purchase.

Livingston was born November 27, 1746, in New York City. His great-grandfather came to America in the 1670s with little, but through hard work and a fortuitous marriage soon began building a vast empire. Livingston's father, Judge Robert R. Livingston, was called the richest landowner in New York, and real estate holdings of the influential and politically active Livingston clan eventually totaled nearly 1 million acres.

BIOGRAPHY

Robert R. Livingston

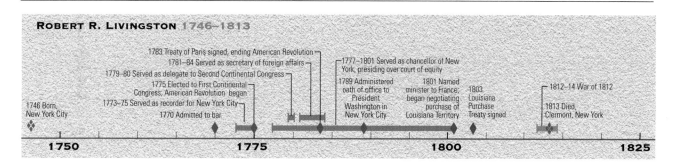

ROBERT R. LIVINGSTON 1746–1813

- 1746 Born, New York City
- 1770 Admitted to bar
- 1773–75 Served as recorder for New York City
- 1775 Elected to First Continental Congress; American Revolution began
- 1779–80 Served as delegate to Second Continental Congress
- 1781–84 Served as secretary of foreign affairs
- 1783 Treaty of Paris signed, ending American Revolution
- 1777–1801 Served as chancellor of New York, presiding over court of equity
- 1789 Administered oath of office to President Washington in New York City
- 1801 Named minister to France; began negotiating purchase of Louisiana Territory
- 1803 Louisiana Purchase Treaty signed
- 1812–14 War of 1812
- 1813 Died, Clermont, New York

1750   1775   1800   1825

After graduating from King's College (now Columbia University), Livingston studied law, and was admitted to the bar in 1770. He practiced law for a time with his college classmate and friend JOHN JAY. In 1773 he received a political appointment as recorder for New York City, wherein he presided over certain criminal trials. He held the position until 1775, when his Revolutionary sympathies made him unacceptable to the Crown.

Livingston was elected to the Continental Congress in 1775. He was soon appointed to the committee charged with drafting a declaration of independence, with ROGER SHERMAN, BENJAMIN FRANKLIN, JOHN ADAMS, and THOMAS JEFFERSON. However, Livingston was apparently not involved in the actual drafting of the document; his appointment was seemingly a political maneuver designed to encourage the equivocating province of New York into a firm commitment to independence. Livingston himself was ambivalent. He believed that autonomy from Britain was necessary and inevitable, but inexpedient at that time; in debate he advocated postponement of the issue. When the Continental Congress voted on the declaration on July 2, 1776, New York abstained, preventing a unanimous ballot. The New York delegation was forced to abstain because the New York convention had not authorized it to vote affirmatively. Within weeks a newly elected New York convention ratified the declaration, and the ratification was retroactively ruled unanimous. When the signing of the DECLARATION OF INDEPENDENCE commenced in Philadelphia on August 2, Livingston was elsewhere organizing a committee to coordinate New York's defense and conferring with General Washington on military matters.

Livingston, Jay, and Gouverneur Morris were the principal writers of New York's constitution, which was submitted for approval in 1777. Livingston's main contribution to the document was a council of revision, which could veto legislation. The council of revision was composed of the governor, chancellor, and state supreme court justices.

"ON THE WHOLE I THINK IT WOULD BE MORE DIGNIFIED AND MORE SAFE TO ACT UPON OUR GROUND AND IF WE MUST ENTER INTO THE WAR [AGAINST NAPOLEON], SECURE TO OURSELVES ALL THE ADVANTAGES THAT MAY RESULT FROM [DOING SO]."

In 1777 Livingston was appointed chancellor of New York, the state's highest legal officer, second in precedence only to the governor. In this position, which he held until 1801, he presided over the court of EQUITY. His legal abilities were highly regarded by his colleagues.

Livingston was again a delegate to the Continental Congress in 1779–80. A tireless worker, he was active on committees on financial affairs, military issues, legal organization, and foreign affairs, among others. He helped formulate a court of appeals. In 1780 he was nominated for an appellate judgeship, but declined the position.

In 1781 Livingston was appointed secretary of foreign affairs, a position he held for three years. He organized the newly established department. His most important contribution during this period was his diplomatic correspondence regarding peace with Great Britain. The Revolutionary War was over, but negotiating the peace was a lengthy endeavor. Finally, on April 19, 1783, the Treaty of Paris made it official, and Livingston had the honor of conveying the news to General Washington.

Livingston served in the Continental Congress again in 1784–85. In 1788 he was a leader in Poughkeepsie, New York, at the convention to ratify the U.S. Constitution. A staunch Federalist, he was one of the most frequent pro-Constitution speakers at the ratifying convention. Livingston, along with ALEXANDER HAMILTON, played a major role in the success of FEDERALISM in New York at that time.

By virtue of his position as chancellor, Livingston administered the oath of office to President Washington in the national capital, then New York City, on April 30, 1789. His friend Jay was appointed chief justice of the U.S. Supreme Court, and Hamilton was named secretary of the treasury. Despite Livingston's activism the new government did not reward him with an office. Possibly for this reason, and because he disagreed with Hamilton's policy of federal assumption of state debts, Livingston turned anti-Federalist and entered into a political alliance with members of the Jeffersonian opposition—then called Republicans—in about 1791.

Jefferson offered Livingston the secretaryship of the Navy in 1800, but he declined. In 1801 Jefferson named him minister to France. Once in Paris Livingston set about investigating rumors that Spain was about to cede its province Louisiana back to France, which had owned it until 1762. Livingston was charged with preventing this. If unable to do so, he was to procure parts of the province, including West Florida and New Orleans, for the United States.

Livingston soon discovered that the retrocession had already occurred. However, because of impending war with Great Britain, a French failure in Santo Domingo, and financial concerns, Napoléon suddenly offered to sell the entire Louisiana Territory to the United States. No one really knew how vast the region was, but it was generally agreed that the Mississippi River formed the eastern boundary and the Rocky Mountains the western edge. Livingston and JAMES MONROE, who had recently joined him in Paris, negotiated the final deal for $15 million—purchasing approximately 828,000 square miles for only pennies an acre. Overnight, the size of the United States doubled. The Louisiana Purchase Treaty, closing the purchase from France, signed May 2, 1803, but antedated April 30, 1803, was the triumph of Livingston's career.

Livingston resigned his diplomatic post in 1804. After touring Europe he returned to his home in Clermont, New York, and retired from politics.

Livingston had long been interested in steam navigation. While in Paris he had met Robert Fulton, and the two men had entered into a partnership to develop a commercially successful steamboat. An early venture sank on the Seine, but in 1807 a new boat sailed on the Hudson River from New York City to Albany. The running speed of the *Clermont* approached five miles an hour, and cut sailing time to a small fraction of that required by the tall-masted Hudson River sloops then in use. Livingston had used his political clout to obtain a steam navigation MONOPOLY in New York in 1798, and he and Fulton set about attempting to exploit and extend the monopoly. Protracted litigation concerning the monopoly kept Livingston occupied in his final years.

Livingston was very active in his home state as well as nationally. In addition to working on New York's constitution, he was a leader in Revolutionary organizations replacing the Crown government, and was a member of the commission that governed the state after the Revolutionary War. In 1811 he was on the first canal commission, which eventually resulted in the Erie Canal.

Livingston also had a keen interest in farming, and maintained an active correspondence with Jefferson, Washington, and others regarding the latest scientific agricultural methods. He was a leader in importing merino sheep from Spain and using gypsum as fertilizer.

Livingston died February 26, 1813, in Clermont.

See also NEW YORK CONSTITUTION OF 1777.

LIVING TRUST A PROPERTY RIGHT, held by one party for the benefit of another, that becomes effective during the lifetime of the creator and is, therefore, in existence upon his or her death.

A living trust, also known as an *inter vivos trust*, is different from a *testamentary trust*, which is created by WILL and does not take effect until the death of the SETTLOR.

LIVING WILL A written document that allows a patient to give explicit instructions about medical treatment to be administered when the patient is terminally ill or permanently unconscious; also called an advance directive.

With improvements in modern medicine, the life of persons who are terminally ill or permanently unconscious can be prolonged. For increasing numbers of persons, the decision of whether to prolong life is being made in the form of a written document called a living will. The living will is one type of advance directive that may be used by a person before incapacitation to outline a full range of treatment preferences or, most often, to reject treatment.

A living will extends the principle of consent, whereby patients must agree to any medical intervention before doctors can proceed. It allows the patient to guide health care for the future when she may be too ill to make decisions concerning care. It can be revoked by the patient at any time. For many the living will preserves personal control and eases the decision-making burden of a family.

Forty-two states and the District of Columbia have living-will statutes that make a properly executed living will legally binding. In states that do not have a statute, living wills stand as a clear expression of the patient's wishes. Living-will statutes require that the person be legally COMPETENT to execute the will and that the will be witnessed by at least one disinterested person. Once a person who has a valid living will is terminally ill, the attending physician and a second physician must certify in writing that there is no reasonable expectation for improvement in the patient's condition and that death will occur as a result of the incurable disease, illness, or injury.

Upon this certification the doctor is obligated to follow the instructions contained in the living will. This typically means the patient does not want any medical procedures that serve only to prolong but not prevent the dying process. Therefore, if the patient is unable to breathe, the doctor is not required to connect the patient to a respirator. A patient may state in a living will that he does not want a feeding tube if unable to swallow food. Another common directive is to forbid resuscitation if the patient's heart stops beating.

Living wills have been criticized because they are usually limited to the withholding or withdrawing of "life-sustaining" procedures from a patient with a "terminal condition" or "terminal illness," and thus do not accurately reflect the broad legal right to refuse treatment. In addition, by their very nature, living wills reduce the patient's wishes to writing, and thus may be too rigid (or too vague) to adapt to changing interests or anticipate future circumstances.

To overcome these problems, many states have enacted statutes that permit a competent adult to designate a surrogate decision maker (also termed a health care PROXY or AGENT) to make health care decisions for her in the event of incapacitation. The proxy's authority is usually not limited to decisions about life-sustaining treatment. A proxy can supplement a living will.

All fifty states have durable-power-of-attorney statutes that permit an individual (the principal) to designate another person (the attorney in fact) to perform specific tasks during any period of incapacity. Though most of these statutes do not expressly refer to medical care decisions, no court has ruled that they preclude the delegation of medical decision-making authority to the attorney in fact.

CROSS-REFERENCES

Death and Dying; Health Care Law; Organ Donation Law; Patients' Rights; Physicians and Surgeons; *In re Quinlan.*

BIOGRAPHY

Karl N. Llewellyn

"A COURT IS DOING ITS DUTY WHEN . . . WITH CLEAR CONSCIOUSNESS THAT IT UNDERSTANDS WHAT IT IS DOING AND WHY, AND WITH CLEAR STATEMENT OF BOTH, IT GOES TO BAT ON THE WHOLE OF A BROAD SITUATION."

LL.B. An abbreviation denoting the degree of bachelor of laws, which was the basic degree awarded to an individual upon completion of law school until the late 1960s.

The degree has been largely replaced by the J.D., JURIS DOCTOR (or doctor of jurisprudence) degree.

LLEWELLYN, KARL N.   Karl N. Llewellyn was a distinguished legal scholar and professor, and a leading proponent of LEGAL REALISM, a philosophy critical of the theory that the law operates only as a system of objective rules.

Llewellyn was born May 22, 1893, in West Seattle, Washington. His father was of Welsh ancestry and his mother's ancestors had come to the New World on the *Mayflower.* Llewellyn spent much of his youth in Brooklyn, where his family had moved during the first year of his life. Unhappy and unchallenged academically by high school in the United States, he entered the *Realgymnasium* in Mecklenburg, Germany, where he boarded with relatives of a family friend. During his three years in Germany, Llewellyn became fluent in German and demonstrated talent in mathematics and science. He left Mecklenburg in the spring of 1911, and briefly attended the University of Lausanne, in Switzerland, before returning to the United States.

In September 1911 Llewellyn entered Yale, where he compiled an outstanding academic record and excelled at athletics, especially boxing. In the spring of 1914, he entered the Sorbonne, in Paris, to study Latin, law, and French. He was still a student there when World War I broke out. Although he never officially enlisted, he fought with the Seventy-eighth Prussian Infantry on the western front, earning the Iron Cross for his service. He was wounded in battle in November 1914, and spent nearly three months in a military hospital.

Llewellyn returned to the United States and to school in 1915. During his second stint at Yale, he took his coursework even more seriously and began considering a career in teaching. He studied under William Graham Sumner, author of *Folkways* (1906), an acclaimed work concerning social practices and beliefs and

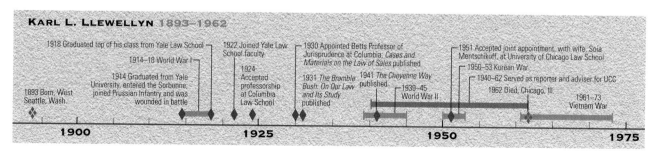

KARL L. LLEWELLYN 1893–1962

1893 Born, West Seattle, Wash.

1914 Graduated from Yale University, entered the Sorbonne, joined Prussian Infantry and was wounded in battle

1914–18 World War I

1918 Graduated top of his class from Yale Law School

1922 Joined Yale Law School faculty

1924 Accepted professorship at Columbia Law School

1930 Appointed Betts Professor of Jurisprudence at Columbia; *Cases and Materials on the Law of Sales* published

1931 *The Bramble Bush: On Our Law and Its Study* published

1939–45 World War II

1941 *The Cheyenne Way* published

1940–62 Served as reporter and adviser for UCC

1950–53 Korean War

1951 Accepted joint appointment, with wife, Soia Mentschikoff, at University of Chicago Law School

1962 Died, Chicago, Ill.

1961–73 Vietnam War

1900   1925   1950   1975

the influence of both on society and individual behavior. The ideas and theories found in Sumner's work would significantly affect the development of Llewellyn's view of the law as a social institution greatly influenced by the surrounding culture.

Later in 1915 Llewellyn entered Yale Law School. He served as editor in chief of the *Yale Law Journal* for three years and wrote many of its articles himself. In 1918 he graduated at the top of his class. He remained for two years as a part-time instructor in the law school, filling in for an ailing professor. Llewellyn mostly taught courses in commercial law, which would later become his specialty. In September 1920, thinking that practical experience was important before settling into an academic career, he took a position in the legal department of the National City Bank in New York City. Soon after he was hired, the bank dissolved its legal department and transferred its legal business to the Wall Street law firm of Shearman and Sterling. Llewellyn was also transferred, and subsequently worked almost exclusively on the bank's legal affairs. Although he enjoyed the work and gained valuable experience in legal drafting and international banking matters, two years later he decided to return to teaching, accepting a full-time position at Yale as an assistant professor.

In 1923 Llewellyn was promoted to associate professor. He stayed at Yale for only a year, before accepting a post at Columbia Law School so that his first wife could continue with her graduate studies at Columbia University. He remained at Columbia until 1951. While there he authored a number of important books, including *The Bramble Bush: On Our Law and Its Study* (1931), adapted from a series of introductory lectures he gave to first-year law students during the 1929–30 academic year, when he was appointed the first Betts Professor of Jurisprudence at Columbia. He also wrote what would eventually become a leading casebook on commercial law, *Cases and Materials on the Law of Sales*, published the same year.

Llewellyn's developing theories on legal realism, introduced in *The Bramble Bush*, brought him much attention. Llewellyn declared that legal opinions must be examined to see how judges are influenced by factors that may have nothing to do with the law. He wrote that "[f]or the long haul, for the large-scale reshaping and growth of doctrine and our legal institutions, . . . the almost unnoticed changes . . . [are] more significant than the historic key cases." Thus, he believed, lawyers should be trained to make persuasive arguments that emphasize the particular facts of a case, since those facts can sometimes have a more significant effect on the outcome than does the applicable law.

Although Llewellyn's views were considered important and innovative, they also drew criticism. Opponents of his theories argued that, for practical reasons, legal realism was difficult to apply. Under Llewellyn's system of JURISPRUDENCE, they said, a lawyer would be required to go to potentially ridiculous lengths to argue a case adequately, in an effort to learn every possible factor that could affect its outcome. As a result Llewellyn's legal realist theories never replaced the prevailing (and well-settled) view of the law as a set of well-defined rules to be applied to each individual situation.

Although Llewellyn's theories did not have quite the effect he had hoped for, he is still widely viewed as an important legal scholar and author. His writings extend to nonlegal areas, including a book on anthropology, *The Cheyenne Way* (1941). This was a study of dispute resolution among the Cheyenne Indians, which he coauthored with anthropologist E. Adamson Hoebel. Llewellyn was also active in the Legal Aid Society, the AMERICAN CIVIL LIBERTIES UNION, and the NATIONAL ASSOCIATION FOR THE ADVANCEMENT OF COLORED PEOPLE.

In 1951 Llewellyn left Columbia for the University of Chicago Law School, where he and his third wife, SOIA MENTSCHIKOFF, a commercial law scholar, accepted a joint appointment. Llewellyn taught there for nearly ten years and also served as chief reporter on the UNIFORM COMMERCIAL CODE, drafted during the early 1950s. He died in Chicago on February 13, 1962.

LL.M. An abbreviation for Master of Laws, which is an advanced degree that is awarded to an individual who already holds a J.D. upon the successful completion of a prescribed course of graduate study in law.

A candidate for an LL.M. degree must complete the program set forth by the graduate admissions department in the particular law school he or she attends. The program ordinarily entails a minimum number of credit hours, including some credits in seminar courses and courses in which the student must take an examination for grading purposes. Candidates generally must also comply with such requirements as the maintenance of a minimum grade average as well as attendance requirements.

Students enrolled in LL.M. programs may either opt for a general degree or a degree in a specialized area of law. An LL.M. is generally available in such specialized areas as international law, labor relations, and taxation.

LOAD LINES 📖 A marking indicating the extent to which the weight of a load may safely submerge a ship; also called *Plimsoll line.* 📖

The load line, or Plimsoll mark, is positioned amidships on both sides of a vessel. Its purpose is to indicate the legal limit to which a ship may be loaded for specific ocean areas and seasons of the year. The basic Load Line Certificate is issued after a complex calculation is made to determine exactly where the Plimsoll mark should be positioned. These certificates take several forms, such as international voyage, coastwise traffic, and Great Lakes operations.

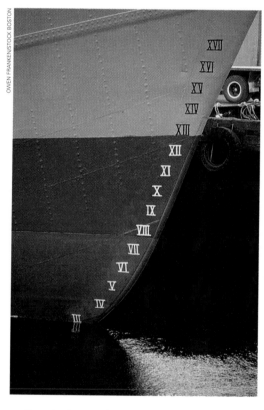

The load lines on a ship correspond to the legal limits to which a ship may be loaded.

By calculating the load line, the agency issuing a certificate has determined, among other aspects of seaworthiness, that a vessel has enough volume of ship (reserve buoyancy) above the waterline so that it will not be in danger of foundering or plunging when under way in heavy seas. In the United States the U.S. Coast Guard issues load line regulations; routine assignment of load lines is handled by the American Bureau of Shipping.

A series of multilateral treaties has been executed to impose on signatories the responsibility of seeing that ships flying under their flag have safe load lines designated and that they are observed. The principal treaty is the International Convention on Load Lines 1966. The use of load lines on vessels sailing under the flag of the United States is mandated by federal law (46 U.S.C.A. 86 [1973]). The treaties typically do not apply to ships of war, small ships, pleasure boats, and fishing vessels.

LOAN COMMITMENT 📖 Commitment to a borrower by a lending institution that it will loan a specific amount at a certain rate on a particular piece of REAL ESTATE. Such commitment is usually limited to a specified time period (e.g., four months), which is commonly based on the estimated time that it will take the borrower to construct or purchase the home contemplated by the loan. 📖

LOAN SHARK 📖 A person who lends money in exchange for its repayment at an interest rate that exceeds the percentage approved by law and who uses intimidating methods or threats of force in order to obtain repayment. 📖

In most jurisdictions USURY laws regulate the charging of interest rates. Loan sharking violates these laws, and in many states it is punishable as a criminal offense. The usual penalty imposed is a fine, imprisonment or both.

LOBBYING 📖 The process of influencing public and government policy at all levels: federal, state, and local. 📖

Lobbying involves the advocacy of an interest that is affected, actually or potentially, by the decisions of government leaders. Individuals and interest groups alike can lobby governments, and governments can even lobby each other. The practice of lobbying is considered so essential to the proper functioning of the U.S. government that it is specifically protected by the FIRST AMENDMENT to the U.S. Constitution: "Congress shall make no law . . . abridging . . . the right of the people peaceably . . . to petition the Government for a redress of grievances."

The practice of lobbying provides a forum for the resolution of conflicts among often diverse and competing points of view; provides information, analysis, and opinion to legislators and government leaders to allow for informed and balanced decision making; and creates a system of checks and balances that allows for competition among interest groups, keeping any one group from attaining a permanent position of power. Lobbyists can help the legislative process work more effectively by providing lawmakers with reliable data and accurate assessments of a bill's effect.

The role lobbyists play in the legislative arena can be compared to that of lawyers in the judicial arena. Just as lawyers provide the trier

SHOULD LOBBYISTS BE STRICTLY REGULATED?

Since the 1940s there has been continuing debate in the United States over the proper role of lobbyists in a democratic society. Lobbyists contend they offer a valuable service to legislators and government officials, providing information and raising questions about pending legislation or executive action. Critics argue that many lobbyists are nothing more than influence peddlers who seek political and legislative favors for their clients.

The perception that lobbyists and the interest groups they represent have corrupted the political process has led to state and federal legislation that regulates lobbyists. Nevertheless, a fundamental conflict remains over the extent to which government may regulate lobbyists and lobbying activities. Those opposed to restrictions on lobbying argue that the First Amendment guarantees the right of citizens to petition the government for redress of grievances. Placing restrictions on lobbyists impairs this right. On the other side, critics of lobbyists assert that regulations are needed to preserve the democratic process and to ensure the legitimacy of government. Many people have become cynical about politicians and government, perceiving that only lobbyists have access to the halls of power.

Lobbyists believe that their activities are protected by the First Amendment. Though the U.S. Supreme Court has never stated that there is a constitutional right to petition the government, supporters of lobbying note that several state supreme courts have acknowledged a fundamental right to do so. Therefore, any regulations on lobbying must be the least restrictive means to further a compelling state interest.

Lobbyists assert that regulations requiring them to name specific contacts made with legislative or congressional staff have a chilling effect and weaken relationships that have been built up over many years. Staff members are often under time pressure to find information on legislative issues, and depend on lobbyists to help them meet these demands. Disclosure of contacts with lobbyists forces staff members to refrain from making legitimate requests, out of fear that disclosure will produce political embarrassment.

Lobbyists argue they have been given an unflattering and absurd stereotype as influence peddlers. With over fourteen thousand lobbyists in Washington, D.C., representing every conceivable interest group, including environmental and consumer organizations, it is clear that there is a demand for lobbying. The size and complexity of the federal government have, in large part, driven the need for lobbyists to help define positions on issues of public policy. Moreover, on all issues of widespread concern, lobbyists are found on both sides, producing one more set of checks and balances that undercuts the simplistic picture of corruption and favoritism.

Lobbyists and their supporters main-

IN FOCUS

of fact (judge or jury) with points of view on the legal issues pertaining to a case, so do lobbyists provide local, state, and federal policymakers with points of view on PUBLIC POLICY issues.

Although lobbying as a whole serves as a checks-and-balances safeguard on the legislative process, individual lobbyists are not necessarily equal. Unlike voters, who each get one vote, lobbyists vary in their degree of influence. The level of influence a lobbyist has over the legislative process is often proportional to the resources—time and money—the lobbyist can spend to achieve its legislative goal. Some people think lobbyists in general have too much power. During his 1912 campaign for president, WOODROW WILSON remarked, "The government of the United States is a foster child of the special interests. It is not allowed to have a will of its own."

The term *lobbyist* has been traced to the mid–seventeenth century, when citizens would gather in a large lobby near the English House of Commons to express their views to members of Parliament. In the early nineteenth century, the term *lobby-agent* had come to the United States, where it was applied to citizens seeking legislative favors in the New York Capitol lobby, in Albany. By 1832 it had been shortened to *lobbyist* and was widely used at the U.S. Capitol.

Today lobbyists practice their trade not only in the halls of the U.S. Capitol and the corridors of state legislatures, but also on playgrounds, in boardrooms, in manufacturing plants, at cocktail parties, and in retirement homes. Contemporary lobbying methods include campaigns to mobilize constituents at the grassroots level, political action committees, high-tech communication techniques, and coalitions among groups and industries sharing the same political goals. Today's lobbyists include schoolchildren who want to prevent their favorite neighborhood park from becoming a shopping mall, corporations who contribute to a particular legislator's campaign, lawyers who speak with legislators on behalf of their clients' business interests, cities who lobby the state legislature for changes in transportation laws, tain that intrusive regulations on lobbying can impair the democratic process. Laws that seek to identify contributors to lobbying groups may have a chilling effect on the exercise of citizens' rights. If made public, a contribution to an unpopular lobby can discourage similar contributions by others. Because many unpopular lobbies are small and poorly funded, discouraging even a few donors may significantly affect the support for a wide variety of viewpoints.

Supporters of strict regulation of lobbyists dispute these arguments. They contend that regulation is needed to prevent special interests from controlling the political process, to ensure ethical behavior on the part of lawmakers and government officials, and to enhance the public's confidence in the government. Numerous scandals have been linked to lobbying at the federal and state levels, providing ample justification for such regulation. Lobbyists have a place in the legislative process, concede many critics, but they must be prevented from using money and favors improperly to influence legislators and their staffs.

Critics of lobbying note that the courts have generally supported reason-able regulation of lobbying activity. This type of regulation does not prevent lobbyists from openly and appropriately communicating with government in regard to legislation. The regulation does restrict traditional practices such as giving legislators and staffs tickets to sporting events, paying for meals and entertainment, and underwriting golf and skiing junkets. These practices have contributed to the public perception that gifts and favors buy access to legislators and sometimes even votes.

Critics of lobbying also support regulation that forces the public disclosure of whom lobbyists represent. Registration of lobbyists is a minimally restrictive means of serving the public interest, yet it gives the public information on which interest groups are involved in pending legislative matters. Critics argue that lobbyists should not be permitted to work their influence in anonymity. The public has a right to know what interest groups have shaped legislation.

Despite the reforms legislated in the federal Lobbying Disclosure Act of 1995, 109 Stat. 691, 2 U.S.C.A. § 1601 et seq., critics of lobbying argue that additional reform is needed. The act addresses disclosure, registration, and a ban on gifts and meals, but it leaves large loopholes, the largest being the ability of lobbyists to make large contributions to the campaign committees of members of Congress. The critics point out the irony of banning small gifts yet permitting senators and representatives to accept $5,000 donations for their campaign committees from political action committees controlled by lobbyists. Even more distressing, note critics, is the change this situation has produced in the dynamics between lobbyist and legislator: it is now the legislator who calls the lobbyist, asking for a political contribution.

Critics charge that the unceasing quest for campaign cash has distorted the political system. The only way to prevent lobbyists and the special interests they represent from dominating the legislative process is to establish the public financing of congressional campaigns. Once campaign contributions are no longer an issue, critics conclude, lobbyists will lose their last effective means of improperly influencing legislation.

presidential aides who suggest new amendment language to congressional committee members, retired persons who want to save their government benefits, and many others. Each type of lobbyist attempts to win support for a particular point of view.

Samuel Ward, a well-respected lobbyist, was so successful at influencing legislators that in the mid-1800s Congress decided to investigate him. When questioned about the elegant dinners he orchestrated for politicians, the self-described King of the Lobby said, "At good dinners people do not talk shop, but they give people a right, perhaps, to ask a gentleman a civil question and get a civil answer."

Despite the noncorrupt success of lobbyists such as Ward, lobbyists during the mid-nineteenth century were often regarded as ethically questionable individuals. This reputation was enhanced whenever lobbyists abused their position with improper practices such as bribing members of Congress.

Although lobbying is specifically protected by the Constitution, numerous attempts have been made to regulate it—attempts that, not surprisingly, lobbyists have historically resisted. Congress began efforts to reform lobbying in 1907, when it banned campaign contributions from banks and corporations. In 1911 proposed restrictions on domestic lobbying were first considered, but these were not approved until 1946, when Congress passed the Federal Regulation of Lobbying Act (2 U.S.C.A. §§ 261, 261 note, 262–270 [1946]).

In 1954 lobbyists challenged the Regulation of Lobbying Act for being unconstitutionally vague and unclear. In *United States v. Harriss*, 347 U.S. 612, 74 S. Ct. 808, 98 L. Ed. 989, the Supreme Court responded by upholding the act's constitutionality, but also by narrowing the scope and application of the act. The Court ruled that the act applies only to paid lobbyists who directly communicate with members of Congress on pending or proposed federal legislation. This means that lobbyists who visit with congressional staff members rather than members of Congress themselves are not considered lobbyists. In addition, the act covers only attempts to influence the passage or defeat of legislation in Congress, and excludes other congressional activities. Further, the act applies to and restricts only individuals who spend at least half of their time lobbying.

According to the 1946 act, lobbyists to whom the law applies are required to disclose their name and address; the names and addresses of clients for whom they work; how much they are paid and by whom; the names of all contributors to the lobbying effort and the amount of their contributions; an accounting of all money received and expended, specifying to whom it was paid and for what purposes; the names of any publications in which the lobbyists have caused articles or editorials to be published; and the particular legislation they have been hired to support or oppose. In addition, the act requires lobbyists to file registration forms with the clerk of the House of Representatives and the secretary of the Senate prior to engaging in lobbying. These forms must be updated in the first ten days of each calendar quarter for as long as the lobbying activity continues. Violation of the act is a MISDEMEANOR punishable by a fine of up to $5,000 or a jail sentence of up to twelve months, and a three-year prohibition on lobbying.

Although a number of lobbying statutes have been enacted that regulate special situations—such as lobbying by the agents of foreign governments, employees of holding companies, and firms affected by various federal shipping laws—the Federal Regulation of Lobbying Act remains the only comprehensive law governing the practice of lobbying.

Critics of the 1946 act suggest that its effectiveness is limited, since it does not apply to a large part of the population that actually lobbies the government. In fact, in 1991 the General Accounting Office found that nearly 10,000 of the 13,500 individuals and organizations listed in a popular lobbyist directory were not registered under the 1946 act.

In 1995 Congress passed a law designed to close loopholes in the 1946 law by increasing lobbyists' accountability: the Lobbying Disclosure Act of 1995 (Pub. L. No. 104-65, 109 Stat. 691). Under the new law, individuals who receive at least $5,000 in a six-month period from a single client are required to register with the clerk of the House and the secretary of the Senate, listing the congressional chambers and federal agencies they contacted, the issues they lobbied for, and how much money was spent on the effort. The reporting requirements also apply to organizations whose own employees lobby on their behalf and spend at least $20,000 in a six-month period on that effort.

Besides these federal regulations, states may separately enact their own regulations governing state lobbying. Most lobby restrictions involve reporting and registration provisions similar to those in place at the federal level.

See also ELECTION CAMPAIGN FINANCING.

LOCAL ACTION 📖 A lawsuit concerning a transaction that could not occur except in some particular place. Any type of lawsuit that can be brought only in one place. A classic example is a situation where recovery of possession of a particular parcel of land is sought. 📖

LOCHNER v. NEW YORK In *Lochner v. New York*, 198 U.S. 45, 25 S. Ct. 539, 49 L. Ed. 937 (1905), the U.S. Supreme Court struck down a state law restricting the hours employees could work in the baking industry, as a violation of the freedom of contract guaranteed by the Due Process Clause of the FOURTEENTH AMENDMENT. This seemingly minor decision spawned a new era in constitutional interpretation.

Constitutional law is often divided into three eras, the center of which is *Lochner*. In the pre-*Lochner* era (1789–1870), courts interpreted the Due Process Clause of the Fifth Amendment to have primarily a procedural content that protected persons against arbitrary governmental deprivations of life, liberty, and property. This procedural right meant that individuals were entitled to sufficient notice and a fair hearing before the government could take harmful action against them. Courts reviewed only the manner in which a particular law infringed on a substantive right, without evaluating the importance of the right or the severity of the infringement.

During the *Lochner* era (1870–1937), courts interpreted the Due Process Clauses of the Fifth and Fourteenth Amendments to have a substantive content that protected from governmental intrusion certain economic and property interests, such as the right of employers and employees to determine the terms and conditions of their employment relationship. (Though *Lochner* was decided in 1905, prior cases going back to 1870 contributed to *Lochner* and are included in the *Lochner* era.)

The post-*Lochner* era (1937–present) is marked by decreased constitutional protection for economic and PROPERTY RIGHTS, and increased recognition of "fundamental" constitutional rights that protect minorities from discrimination, safeguard the interests of criminal defendants, and delineate a sphere of private conduct upon which the state may not encroach.

The *Lochner* era was an outgrowth of the U.S. industrial revolution. During the second half of the nineteenth century, the output of manufactured goods tripled, and the value of those goods soared from $3 billion to over $13 billion. The national labor force kept pace during this period, growing from 13 million workers to 19 million. Along with the growth of industry came a large disparity in the wealth and working conditions of U.S. citizens. Although some business proprietors were working fewer hours and making more money, many of their employees were working more hours in unhealthy conditions for scant wages. The bakers of New York were one group of such workers.

New York bakers at this time reportedly worked twelve hours a day, seven days a week, in a confined and uncomfortable environment. This lifestyle left little time for rest, causing some bakers to live in their kitchen and sleep at their workbench. A number of bakers died at an early age, and others contracted debilitating diseases. In 1895 the New York state legislature unanimously passed the Bakeshop Act, which attempted to address these problems by limiting the working hours of bakers to ten a day and sixty a week.

In 1902 Joseph Lochner, who owned a small bakery in Utica, was fined $50 for permitting an employee to work more than sixty hours in a week. During the trial Lochner offered no defense, and was convicted. On appeal he challenged the constitutionality of the Bakeshop Act, claiming that it interfered with his right to pursue a lawful trade. The state defended the statute by arguing that it represented a legitimate exercise of its POLICE POWERS, pursuant to which the legislature may enact laws to preserve and promote the health, safety, and morality of society.

Lochner's claim did not lack PRECEDENT. In 1897 the Supreme Court nullified a Louisiana statute that attempted to regulate CONTRACTS between state residents and out-of-state insurance companies (*Allgeyer v. Louisiana*, 165 U.S. 578, 17 S. Ct. 427, 41 L. Ed. 832 [1897]). Holding that that statute impaired the liberty of contract guaranteed by the Due Process Clause of the Fourteenth Amendment, the Court said that the Louisiana resident had a right "to live and work where he will," "to earn a livelihood by any lawful calling," and to "enter into all contracts which may be proper, necessary, and essential to . . . carrying out . . . the purposes above mentioned."

In addition to this precedent, the general mood of the country also favored Lochner's claim. Despite the universal support for the Bakeshop Act in the New York Legislature, a large number of U.S. citizens were still committed to the idea that in a capitalistic market, a government that governs least governs best (an idea that reflects laissez-faire economics).

In a 5–4 decision, the Supreme Court upheld Lochner's due process claim, striking down the Bakeshop Act as an interference with the right of employers and employees "to make contracts regarding labor upon such terms as they may think best, or upon which they may agree." Writing for the majority, Justice RUFUS W. PECKHAM said that despite statistics indicating that the baking industry was not as healthy as some other trades, the common understanding of the Court suggested otherwise. "The trade of a baker," Peckham wrote, "is not . . . unhealthy . . . to such a degree which would authorize the legislature . . . to cripple the ability of the laborer to support himself and his family."

The Court acknowledged that state governments possess police powers to protect the health and safety of their residents. However, the Court said, a statute must have a direct relation to a material danger that would compromise the public health or the health of employees before it may restrict the hours of labor in any trade or profession. In this case, the Court concluded, the connection between the Bakeshop Act and the health and welfare of New York bakers was too remote.

Two dissenting opinions were written in *Lochner*; one by Justice OLIVER WENDELL HOLMES, JR., and the other by Justice JOHN M. HARLAN. Both dissents attacked the majority opinion as judicial activism and extolled the virtues of judicial self-restraint.

Harlan conceded that the Due Process Clause contains a substantive content that protects the liberty of contract. But this liberty, Harlan emphasized, may be circumscribed by state regulations that are calculated to promote the GENERAL WELFARE. Such regulations, Harlan argued, must be sustained by state and federal courts unless they clearly exceed legislative power, bear no substantial relation to societal welfare, or invade rights secured by FUNDAMENTAL LAW. Harlan concluded that doubts as to the validity of a statute must be resolved in favor of upholding its validity. Applying this standard, Harlan found the Bakeshop Act valid.

Holmes's dissent is considered a classic exposition of judicial self-restraint. As part of the

U.S. system of democracy, Holmes said, a majority of adults residing in any state have the "right to embody their opinions in law," even if those opinions are tyrannical or injudicious. It is the judiciary's role in this system to interpret and apply the laws passed by the coordinate branches of government.

The ideas articulated in Holmes's dissenting opinion subsequently became the law of the land when the Supreme Court overruled *Lochner* in *West Coast Hotel Co. v. Parrish*, 300 U.S. 378, 57 S. Ct. 578, 81 L. Ed. 703 (1937). *Parrish* examined the validity of a Washington state statute that established a MINIMUM WAGE for women. A hotel owner challenged the constitutionality of the statute on the grounds that it violated his liberty of contract guaranteed by the Fourteenth Amendment.

The hotel owner relied on *Lochner*, and a series of subsequent cases that nullified various state regulations as inconsistent with the substantive rights protected by the Due Process Clause. One of these cases, *Adkins v. Children's Hospital*, 261 U.S. 525, 43 S. Ct. 394, 67 L. Ed. 785 (1923), invalidated a similar minimum wage law in the District of Columbia. But the Supreme Court was no longer persuaded by the rationale underlying *Lochner*, and ruled that the Washington statute was a reasonable exercise of the state's police powers.

During the thirty-two years between *Lochner* and *Parrish*, the United States was confronted by a stock market crash in 1929, which precipitated the Great Depression of the 1930s. President FRANKLIN D. ROOSEVELT attempted to combat some of the more serious problems of the Depression by initiating a host of federal laws known as the NEW DEAL. These events made many U.S. citizens more sympathetic to governmental largesse.

The Supreme Court was also affected by these events. Where *Lochner* had underscored free-market principles of laissez-faire, *Parrish* highlighted the unequal bargaining power of employers and employees, as well as the oppression and exploitation of female workers. Freedom of contract, the Supreme Court said in *Parrish*, is not an absolute and uncontrollable liberty.

Any lingering doubts as to the validity of *Lochner* were eliminated by the Supreme Court in *United States v. Carolene Products Co.*, 304 U.S. 144, 58 S. Ct. 778, 82 L. Ed. 1234 (1938), which held that courts must sustain state and federal laws that regulate economic interests, unless there is no rational basis to support them. By contrast the Court said that legislation that "appears on its face to be within a specific

prohibition of the Constitution, . . . restricts . . . political processes . . . [or is] prejudic[ial] against discrete and insular minorities" will be subject to stricter scrutiny.

The *Carolene Products* case ushered in the post-*Lochner* era. During this era the Supreme Court has offered little constitutional protection for contract and other property rights. At the same time, the Court has offered increasing protection against legislation that touches upon a fundamental constitutional right or denies a governmental benefit to a suspect class of persons, what the Court in *Carolene Products* called "discrete and insular minorities."

Fundamental rights include most of the rights enumerated in the first ten amendments to the Constitution, as well as the right to PRIVACY, the right to travel, the right to vote, and the right to education. Suspect classes include groups of persons who are discriminated against on the basis of race, gender, national origin, or other "immutable" genetic characteristics (*Frontiero v. Richardson*, 411 U.S. 677, 93 S. Ct. 1764, 36 L. Ed. 2d 583 [1973]).

Due Process of Law; Footnote Four; Jurisprudence; Labor Law; Rational Basis Test; Substantive Law; *West Coast Hotel Co. v. Parrish*.

BIOGRAPHY

John Locke

LOCKE, JOHN John Locke was a seventeenth-century English philosopher whose writings on political theory and government profoundly affected U.S. law and society. It is chiefly from Locke's *Two Treatises of Government* (1690) that U.S. politics takes its core premises of the ultimate SOVEREIGNTY of the people, the necessity of restraints on the exercise of arbitrary power by the executive or the legislature, and the ability of the people to revoke their social contract with the government when power has been arbitrarily used against them. The DECLARATION OF INDEPENDENCE and the U.S. Constitution are testaments to many of Locke's central ideas.

Locke was born in Wrington, Somerset, England, on August 29, 1632. His father, also John Locke, was an attorney, and a Calvinist with Puritan sympathies who supported the parliamentary side in England's struggle against King Charles I and fought on that side in the English Civil War of 1642. Despite this background Locke developed monarchist leanings while attending boarding school, which remained with him throughout his life.

In 1652 Locke entered Oxford University, where he became interested in medicine and the newly developed discipline of experimental science. He collaborated with Robert Boyle, a

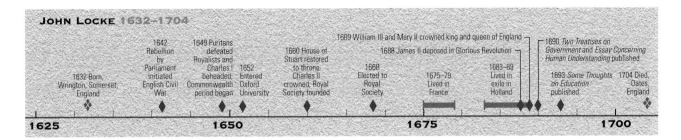

JOHN LOCKE 1632–1704

1642 Rebellion by Parliament initiated English Civil War

1649 Puritans defeated Royalists and Charles I beheaded; Commonwealth period began

1652 Entered Oxford University

1660 House of Stuart restored to throne; Charles II crowned; Royal Society founded

1689 William III and Mary II crowned king and queen of England

1688 James II deposed in Glorious Revolution

1690 Two Treatises on Government and Essay Concerning Human Understanding published

1832 Born, Wrington, Somerset, England

1668 Elected to Royal Society

1675–79 Lived in France

1683–89 Lived in exile in Holland

1693 Some Thoughts on Education published

1704 Died, Oates, England

1625   1650   1675   1700

founder of modern chemistry. Locke studied natural science and philosophy, concentrating on the principles of moral, social, and political laws. Following graduation in 1656, he earned a master of arts degree and was appointed a tutor at Oxford. He left teaching in 1662 and in 1666 decided to pursue medicine. In 1668 Locke was elected to the Royal Society.

In 1675, plagued with the symptoms of consumption, Locke moved to France in the hope of improving his health. He studied philosophy while abroad, then returned to England in 1679. His friendship with the duke of Shaftsbury made his stay in England a short one. Shaftsbury had been discovered as having been involved in a conspiracy to overthrow the king. Though Shaftsbury was acquitted of the charges, he fled to Holland in 1683. The king became suspicious of Locke and other friends of Shaftsbury, and had Locke closely watched. Knowing that his personal safety was at risk, Locke also chose exile in Holland in 1683. In 1684 his name appeared with eighty-three others on a list sent to The Hague by the English government, with the accusation that those named had committed TREASON and a demand for their EXTRADITION by the Dutch government. Locke went into hiding for a while, but soon returned to public life when the Dutch refused the extradition request.

While in Holland, Locke wrote *Essay Concerning Human Understanding* (1690) and *Two Treatises*. *Essay* set forth Locke's theory that all human knowledge comes from experience. It stated that people are born without ideas—that is, with a blank mind—directly challenging the belief that people are born with certain knowledge already implanted. It further stated that as a result people must formulate their ideas based on experience. This theory became the basis for the school of English philosophy called empiricism.

Two Treatises was written when England was divided over the rule of King James II. The Protestants wished to remove the king, who was a Roman Catholic. In the Glorious Revolution of 1688, James abdicated the throne and Parliament offered the crown to the Dutch prince

"IT IS ONE THING TO SHOW A MAN THAT HE IS IN ERROR, AND ANOTHER TO PUT HIM IN POSSESSION OF TRUTH."

William of Orange and his wife, Mary. The revolution re-formed government along the lines outlined by Locke in *Two Treatises*, which was published in 1690. England became a constitutional monarchy, controlled by Parliament, and greater measures of religious toleration and freedom of expression and thought were permitted.

Two Treatises was a blow to political absolutism. The first treatise was a refutation of the theory of the DIVINE RIGHT OF KINGS, which posits that monarchs derive their authority from God. The second treatise had the most lasting effect, for it set out a theory of politics that found its way into U.S. law.

In this second treatise, Locke maintained that people are naturally tolerant and reasonable, but that without a governing force, a certain amount of chaos and other inconvenience will occur. In his view people are basically pacific, communitarian, and good-natured. This belief contrasts with that of philosopher THOMAS HOBBES, which is that if left to their own devices, people will live in violent, selfish anarchy.

For Locke all people are inherently equal and free to pursue "life, liberty, health, and property." To do this they engage in a social contract in which they consent to give up a certain amount of power to a government dedicated to maintaining the well-being of the whole. They also give up one right, the right to judge and punish other persons, which is permitted in the state of nature. Apart from that concession to government, Locke argued, a person's individual right to freedom of thought, speech, and worship must be preserved. In addition, a person's private property must be preserved by the government. This compact between the people and their rulers legitimizes the government and explains the source of the rulers' power.

Locke believed that the people's consent to give up some power is the essential element of the social contract. Government is the trustee of the people's power, and any exercise of power by government is specifically for the purpose of serving the people. By extending the trust analogy, Locke legitimized the concept of REVOLUTION. If their trust is abused by their governors, the people—the grantors of the trust—have a right to revoke the trust. Once the trust has been revoked, the people can assume the reins of government themselves or place them in new hands.

Locke attempted to soften this justification for revolution by claiming that revolution is appropriate only as a last resort and only in extreme circumstances. But he gave no real guidance as to how the people can be trusted to distinguish between inevitable temporary aberrations, which are to be endured, and a long series of abuses that justifies rebellion.

Two Treatises was well received in England, making Locke a respected figure once more and the intellectual leader of the Whig party. He returned to England in 1689, following the Glorious Revolution. He lived in semiretirement in Essex, in the company of friends such as the scientist Sir Isaac Newton. He died October 28, 1704, in Oates, Essex.

Two Treatises commanded great interest in the eighteenth century, providing justification for the American Revolution in 1776 and the French Revolution in 1789. The U.S. Declaration of Independence uses Locke's ideas of the law of nature, popular sovereignty, and the sanctity of the right of private property to set forth the premises of U.S. political thought. The U.S. Constitution, with its separation of church and state and its guarantee of personal freedoms, draws on Locke's work.

In the United States, Lockean thought continues to justify resistance to executive tyranny, such as the despotism that was exhibited by President RICHARD M. NIXON in the WATERGATE affair in the early 1970s and led to his resignation in 1974. Locke's second treatise provides support for U.S. constitutional ideals of inalienable rights and personal liberty. The FIRST AMENDMENT would be unthinkable without Locke's philosophical foundation.

See also CONSTITUTION OF THE UNITED STATES; NATURAL LAW.

BIOGRAPHY

Belva Ann Lockwood

"I KNOW WE CAN'T ABOLISH PREJUDICE THROUGH LAWS, BUT WE CAN SET UP GUIDELINES FOR OUR ACTIONS BY LEGISLATION."

LOCKOUT 📖 Employer's withholding of work from employees in order to gain concession from them; it is the employers' counterpart of the employee's STRIKE. Refusal by the employer to furnish available work to its regular employees, whether refusal is motivated by the employer's desire to protect itself against economic injury, by its desire to protect itself at the bargaining table, or by both. 📖

See also LABOR LAW; LABOR UNION.

LOCKUP 📖 A place of detention in a police station, court or other facility used for persons awaiting trial. In corporate law, a slang term that refers to the setting aside of SECURITIES for purchase by friendly interests in order to defeat or make more difficult a takeover attempt. A lockup option is a takeover defensive measure permitting a friendly suitor to purchase divisions of a CORPORATION for a set price when any person or group acquires a certain percentage of the corporation's shares. To be legal, such agreement must advance or stimulate the bidding process, to best serve the interests of the shareholders through encouraged competition. 📖

LOCKWOOD, BELVA ANN Belva Ann Lockwood achieved prominence as the first woman to be admitted to argue cases before the U.S. Supreme Court. In addition to her legal career, she was active in many phases of the campaign for WOMEN'S RIGHTS.

Lockwood was born October 24, 1830, in Royalton, New York. A graduate of Genessee College in Lima, New York, in 1857, Lockwood received an honorary master of arts degree from Syracuse University in 1871 and a doctor of laws degree in 1908. Before her admission to the Washington, D.C., bar in 1873, Lockwood taught school from 1857 to 1868. She began her fight for women's rights with her work advocating the passage of a bill granting female government employees equal pay for equal work.

In 1879 Lockwood further advanced the cause of women to the judiciary with her participation in the enactment of a bill permitting women to practice law before the U.S. Supreme

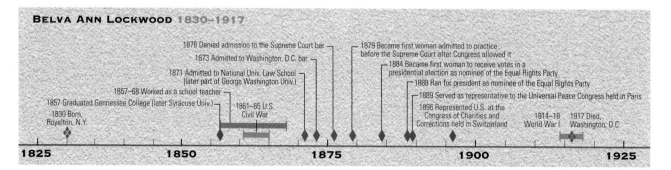

BELVA ANN LOCKWOOD 1830–1917

1876 Denied admission to the Supreme Court bar
1873 Admitted to Washington, D.C. bar
1871 Admitted to National Univ. Law School (later part of George Washington Univ.)
1857–68 Worked as a school teacher
1857 Graduated Gennessee College (later Syracuse Univ.)
1830 Born, Royalton, N.Y.
1861–65 U.S. Civil War
1879 Became first woman admitted to practice before the Supreme Court after Congress allowed it
1884 Became first woman to receive votes in a presidential election as nominee of the Equal Rights Party
1888 Ran for president as nominee of the Equal Rights Party
1889 Served as representative to the Universal Peace Congress held in Paris
1896 Represented U.S. at the Congress of Charities and Corrections held in Switzerland
1914–18 World War I
1917 Died, Washington, D.C.

1825   1850   1875   1900   1925

Court. As a result she became the first woman to be admitted to this court and was subsequently admitted to practice before the former U.S. Court of Claims.

Lockwood continued her legal career while participating in reform movements, notably those for temperance and women's suffrage. At the height of her popularity in the 1880s, Lockwood was nominated by the Equal Rights party as a candidate for president of the United States in 1884 and 1888, the first woman to receive this honor.

In 1896 Lockwood was chosen to represent the United States at the Congress of Charities and Corrections held in Switzerland. After her return she continued her work in the women's rights movement and was instrumental in the formulation of the law granting women residents of the District of Columbia equal property rights and equal claims to the custody of children. She also drafted an amendment to the statehood bills of Oklahoma, Arizona, and New Mexico, allowing women in these states the right to vote.

A staunch advocate of peace, Lockwood served as a representative to the Universal Peace Congress held in Paris in 1889 and participated at the International Peace Bureau at Bern, Switzerland, in 1892.

Lockwood died May 19, 1917, in Washington, D.C.

LOCO PARENTIS ◉ [*Latin, The place of a parent.*] A description of the relationship that an adult or an institution assumes toward an IN-FANT or MINOR of whom the adult is not a parent but to whom the adult or institution owes the obligation of care and supervision. ◉

The term is usually designated IN LOCO PARENTIS.

LOCUS ◉ *Latin, Place; place where a thing is performed or done.* ◉

For example, the *locus delicti* is the place where an accident or crime occurred.

LODGE, HENRY CABOT Henry Cabot Lodge helped write the SHERMAN ANTI-TRUST ACT of 1890 (15 U.S.C.A. § 1 et seq.). He was an enthusiastic supporter of the Spanish-

American War of 1898 and advocated military power as the United States' best tactic for peace. He believed firmly in the principles of the MONROE DOCTRINE, by which the United States sought to protect nations in the Western Hemisphere from European intrusion. Although he opposed strong control by the federal government, he believed that in some circumstances moderate government regulation was essential to prevent SOCIALISM. Lodge was a conservative Republican U.S. senator from 1893 to 1924. He successfully fought to defeat U.S. entry into President WOODROW WILSON's newly proposed LEAGUE OF NATIONS at the end of World War I. He chaired the Senate Foreign Relations Committee from 1918 to 1924 and influenced U.S. foreign policy in the first quarter of the twentieth century. He also was a prolific writer, most notably of a series of biographies, and the grandfather of Henry Cabot Lodge, Jr., a Republican senator in 1937–44 and 1947–53.

Lodge was born May 12, 1850, in Boston. The families of his father, John Ellerton Lodge, and mother, Anna Cabot Lodge, were wealthy and of high social standing. Lodge graduated from Harvard in 1871, and married Anna Cabot Mills ("Nannie") Davis the day after his graduation ceremony. He attended Harvard Law School from 1872 to 1874, and in 1874 made his first entry into politics as a delegate to the Republican state convention.

Lodge taught American colonial history at Harvard for a year and then turned to writing, producing a biography of his great-grandfather, a colonial history, and various magazine articles, among other works. He was an editor on the *International Review* magazine for four years, and wrote a set of books called the American Statesman Series, on George Washington, Washington Irving, and Daniel Webster, among others.

In the late 1870s, he wrote articles on election reform, gave an Independence Day address, and served two one-year terms in the Massachusetts General Court. In 1883 he chaired the Republican State Central Commit-

BIOGRAPHY

Henry Cabot Lodge

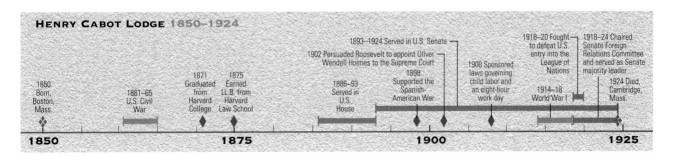

tee and met THEODORE ROOSEVELT, with whom he would remain close friends throughout his life.

Lodge was elected to the House in 1886, where he served for six years. He chaired the House Committee on Elections, sponsored the Federal Elections Bill, and introduced a bill prohibiting entry into the United States by illiterate immigrants (later vetoed by President GROVER CLEVELAND). In 1890 Lodge helped write the Sherman Anti-Trust Act, the first federal law to control growing centralization of economic power by monopolistic corporations.

In 1893 Lodge entered the Senate, where he served until his death in 1924. As a senator he was a strong supporter of the Spanish-American War, in which two of his three sons served. He supported U.S. imperialism during the presidency of Theodore Roosevelt. In 1902 he helped persuade Roosevelt to appoint OLIVER WENDELL HOLMES, JR., to the U.S. Supreme Court; Holmes's fundamentally new approach to the judicial process—which rejected the notion of legal principles as absolutes—changed U.S. law. Also in the early 1900s, he sponsored a child labor law (May 28, 1908, ch. 209, 35 Stat. 420) in Washington, D.C., and an American Federation of Labor law mandating an eight-hour workday. In 1906 Lodge worked on Roosevelt's Food and Drug Act (ch. 3915, 34 Stat. 768).

From 1918 to 1924, Lodge chaired the Senate Foreign Relations Committee and was the Senate majority leader. He also worked adamantly to foil President Wilson's efforts to establish the League of Nations. Lodge disliked both the policies and the personality of Wilson.

Wilson attempted to link the passage of his League of Nations with the signing of the peace treaty that would officially end World War I. Lodge attacked this approach, accusing Wilson of jeopardizing the peace process for the sake of his project. Lodge also was chief among Wilson's critics for two other actions by the president: First, in an era in which presidents rarely left the country, Wilson traveled to Europe to make a highly publicized case for his League of Nations. Although he was well received by the Europeans with whom he met, the trip was not favorably viewed by many in the United States. Second, he took with him a small group of men that included only Democrats, no Republicans.

In 1919 Lodge addressed the Senate about the "crudeness and looseness of expression" of the proposed League of Nations. He cited a direct conflict between Wilson's league and the Monroe Doctrine, which he said dictated that "American questions be settled by America

alone." He also questioned whether the United States could follow up on some of the promises outlined in Wilson's proposal, and cited a potential loss of U.S. control over immigration.

Lodge and two other men crafted a declaration listing their objections to the proposed League of Nations, the primary ones involving congressional rights. Lodge then circulated the declaration through the Republican senators seeking signatures of support, a process called a round-robin, and received thirty-seven signatures, more than enough to indicate strong support for the declaration. Lodge led a lengthy debate on the Senate floor, followed by hearings in which a variety of representatives from around the world were allowed to testify on a broad range of topics. Witnesses spoke, for example, on Irish independence, which had little relevance to the League of Nations but which took time on the floor. Lodge also read the entire text of Wilson's proposal, which took two weeks to complete, in order to wear down Wilson and his supporters and to encourage a deadlock.

Ultimately, Congress did deadlock on the issue, and the U.S. public decided the fate of the league with the November 1920 presidential election, when James Cox, the Democratic candidate, lost to WARREN G. HARDING, who opposed the league.

In his last years, Lodge returned to writing and spent time with his family. He died November 9, 1924, at age seventy-four.

LODGER ◻ An occupant of a portion of a dwelling, such as a hotel or boardinghouse, who has mere use of the premises without actual or exclusive possession thereof. Anyone who lives or stays in part of a building that is operated by another and who does not have control over the rooms therein. ◻

LOGAN ACT The Logan Act (18 U.S.C.A. § 953 [1948]) is a single federal statute making it a crime for a citizen to confer with foreign governments against the interests of the United States. Specifically, it prohibits citizens from negotiating with other nations on behalf of the United States without authorization.

Congress established the Logan Act in 1799, less than one year after passage of the Alien and Sedition Acts, which authorized the arrest and DEPORTATION of ALIENS and prohibited written communication defamatory to the U.S. government. The 1799 act was named after Dr. George Logan. A prominent Republican and Quaker from Pennsylvania, Logan did not draft or introduce the legislation that bears his name, but was involved in the political climate that precipitated it.

"LET EVERY MAN HONOR AND LOVE THE LAND OF HIS BIRTH . . . [BUT] IF A MAN IS GOING TO BE AN AMERICAN AT ALL LET HIM BE SO WITHOUT QUALIFYING ADJECTIVES; AND IF HE IS GOING TO BE SOMETHING ELSE, LET HIM DROP THE WORD AMERICAN FROM HIS PERSONAL DESCRIPTION."

In the late 1790s, a French trade EMBARGO and jailing of U.S. seamen created animosity and unstable conditions between the United States and France. Logan sailed to France in the hope of presenting options to its government to improve relations with the United States and quell the growing anti-French sentiment in the United States. France responded by lifting the embargo and releasing the captives. Logan's return to the United States was marked by Republican praise and Federalist scorn. To prevent U.S. citizens from interfering with negotiations between the United States and foreign governments in the future, the Adams administration quickly introduced the bill that would become the Logan Act.

The Logan Act has remained almost unchanged and unused since its passage. The act is short and reads as follows:

Any citizen of the United States, wherever he may be, who, without authority of the United States, directly or indirectly commences or carries on any correspondence or intercourse with any foreign government or any officer or agent thereof, with intent to influence the measures or conduct of any foreign government or of any officer or agent thereof, in relation to any disputes or controversies with the United States, or to defeat the measures of the United States, shall be fined under this title or imprisoned not more than three years, or both.

This section shall not abridge the right of a citizen to apply, himself or his agent, to any foreign government or the agents thereof for redress of any injury which he may have sustained from such government or any of its agents or subjects.

The language of the act appears to encompass almost every communication between a U.S. citizen and a foreign government considered an attempt to influence negotiations between their two countries. Because the language is so broad in scope, legal scholars and judges have suggested that the Logan Act is unconstitutional. Historically, the act has been used more as a threat to those engaged in various political activities than as a weapon for prosecution. In fact, Logan Act violations have been discussed in almost every administration without any serious attempt at enforcement, and to date there have been no convictions and only one recorded INDICTMENT.

One example of the act's use as a threat of prosecution involved the Reverend JESSE JACKSON. In 1984 Jackson took well-publicized trips to Cuba and Nicaragua and returned with sev-

eral Cuban political prisoners seeking asylum in the United States. President RONALD REAGAN stated that Jackson's activities may have violated the law, but Jackson was not pursued beyond a threat.

The only Logan Act indictment occurred in 1803. It involved a Kentucky newspaper article that argued for the formation in the western United States of a separate nation allied to France. No prosecution followed.

LOGGING 📖 The cutting of, or commercial dealing in, tree trunks that have been cut down and stripped of all branches. 📖

The statutes in certain JURISDICTIONS provide for the marking of logs for the purpose of identification. Once a log is marked, its mark must be recorded, as must any change in ownership of the marked logs.

Trees which are standing upon land can become objects of PERSONAL PROPERTY prior to their severance from the soil and, therefore, a change in the ownership of the land would have no effect upon ownership of the trees. Standing timber can be conveyed separately from the property upon which it was grown. If this occurs, two separate and distinct PROPERTY interests are created: one in the land and one in the timber.

A purchaser of standing timber may enter onto the land for the purpose of cutting and removing the timber. CONTRACTS for the sale of standing timber may limit the time during which the right of entry can continue.

The public may generally float logs on any stream which is capable of being so used in its natural state. When necessary, the right to use a stream includes the incidental right to use the banks, at least below the high-water mark.

In 1984 Democratic presidential candidate the Reverend Jesse Jackson met with Cuban president Fidel Castro and later described a ten-point agreement the two men had reached. His negotiations with Castro may have violated the Logan Act but he was not prosecuted.

LOGGING IN 📖 A colloquial term for the process of making the initial record of the names of individuals who have been brought to the police station upon their arrest. 📖

The process of logging in is also called BOOKING.

LOG ROLLING 📖 A legislative practice of embracing in one bill several distinct matters, none of which, perhaps, could singly obtain the assent of the legislature, and then procuring its passage by a combination of the minorities in favor of each of the measures into a majority that will adopt them all.

Practice of including in one STATUTE or CONSTITUTIONAL AMENDMENT more than one proposition, inducing voters to vote for all, notwithstanding they might not have voted for all if amendments or statutes had been submitted separately. 📖

LONG-ARM STATUTE 📖 A state law that allows the state to exercise JURISDICTION over an out-of-state defendant, provided that the prospective defendant has sufficient minimum contacts with the FORUM state. 📖

Jurisdiction over an out-of-state defendant is referred to as extraterritorial IN PERSONAM jurisdiction. In personam jurisdiction, also known as PERSONAL JURISDICTION, allows a court to exercise jurisdiction over the person, and is the fundamental requirement necessary for a court to hear the MERITS of a claim. Historically, a state could exercise jurisdiction only within its territorial boundaries; therefore, a nonresident defendant could be brought into court only when SERVICE OF PROCESS was effected while that defendant was within the boundaries of the state. The U.S. Supreme Court upheld this principle, and raised it to a constitutional level, when it stated that judgments entered by a court without such jurisdiction were violations of the Due Process Clause of the Constitution (*Pennoyer v. Neff*, 95 U.S. 714, 24 L. Ed. 565 [1877]).

The requirement of physical presence within the state's boundaries was expanded in *International Shoe Co. v. State of Washington*, 326 U.S. 310, 66 S. Ct. 154, 90 L. Ed. 95 (1945). In *International Shoe*, the Supreme Court held that DUE PROCESS required that the defendant have "certain minimum contacts" with the forum in order for a state to assert jurisdiction, and that such jurisdiction may not offend "traditional notions of fair play and substantial justice." Since *International Shoe*, the Supreme Court has set forth several criteria to be used in analyzing whether jurisdiction over a nonresident is proper. These criteria require (1) that the defendant has purposefully availed himself or herself of the benefits of the state so as to reason-ably foresee being haled into court in that state; (2) that the forum state has sufficient interest in the dispute; and (3) that haling the defendant into court does not offend "notions of fair play and substantial justice."

Following the Court's lead in *International Shoe*, individual states began enacting long-arm statutes setting forth their requirements for personal jurisdiction over nonresidents. Illinois was the first state to do so. Its statute (Ill. Rev. Stat. chap. 110, para. 17 [1955]) allowed service of process outside the state on nonresident individuals and corporations in ACTIONS arising out of (1) the transaction of any business in the state; (2) the commission of a TORTIOUS act within the state; (3) the ownership, use, or possession of REAL ESTATE in the state; or (4) a contract to insure any person, property, or risk located in the state. The Illinois statute became a template for many state long-arm statutes.

In 1963 the Uniform Interstate and International Procedure Act was promulgated by the Commission on Uniform State Laws. The Uniform Act was similar to the Illinois statute, but also included a provision authorizing jurisdiction in the event that an act or omission outside the state caused injury in the state. This Uniform Act also became a model for other states in developing their long-arm statutes.

Since 1963 all states and the District of Columbia have enacted long-arm statutes. Long-arm statutes tend to fall into one of two categories. The first enumerates factual situations likely to satisfy the minimum-contacts test of *International Shoe*, as do the Illinois statute and the Uniform Act. The second type is much broader: it provides jurisdiction over an individual or corporation as long as that jurisdiction is not inconsistent with constitutional restrictions. If such a statute enumerates requirements for jurisdiction, the facts of the situation must fall within one of those requirements. If that test is met, the court must then determine whether the procedural due process requirements of both the state and federal constitutions have been met.

Owing to the different types of long-arm statutes, as well as various court interpretations of these statutes, the relevant state laws must be examined when determining whether a prospective nonresident defendant falls under the jurisdiction of a state and may be brought into that state's court.

LOOPHOLE 📖 An omission or AMBIGUITY in a legal document that allows the intent of the document to be evaded. 📖

Loopholes come into being through the passage of statutes, the enactment of regulations, the drafting of CONTRACTS or the decisions of courts. A loophole allows an individual or group to use some gap in the restrictions or requirements of the law or contract for personal advantage without technically breaking the law or contract. In response, lawmakers and regulators work to pass reforms that will close the loophole. For example, in the federal tax code, a long-standing loophole was the so-called tax shelter, which allowed taxpayers to reduce their tax debt by making investments. Although not closed entirely, this loophole was substantially reduced by the Tax Reform Act of 1986 (Pub. L. No. 99-514, 100 Stat. 2085 [codified as amended in numerous sections of 26 U.S.C.A.]).

Loopholes exist because it is impossible to foresee every circumstance or course of conduct that will arise under, or in response to, the law. Loopholes often endure for a time because they can be difficult to close. Those who benefit from a loophole will lobby legislators or regulators to leave the loophole open. In the case of ELECTION CAMPAIGN FINANCING, it is the legislators themselves who benefit. The Federal Election Campaign Act Amendments of 1974 (Pub. L. No. 93-443, 88 Stat. 1263 [1974] [codified as amended in scattered sections of 2 U.S.C.A. §§ 431–455 (1988)]) were passed to limit private financing of federal election campaigns. But loopholes in the law allow these limits to be circumvented. Through one loophole, intermediaries can pool or "bundle" contributions so that the limit is not legally exceeded. Through another, money raised specifically for building political parties (soft money) is funneled into campaigns.

See also LOBBYING.

LOSS 📖 DIMINUTION, reduction, DEPRECIATION, decrease in value; that which cannot be recovered. 📖

The term *loss* is a comprehensive one, and relative, since it does not have a limited or absolute meaning. It has been used interchangeably with *damage*, *deprivation*, and *injury*.

In the law of INSURANCE, a loss is the ascertained LIABILITY of the insurer, a decrease in value of resources, or an increase in liabilities. It refers to the monetary injury that results from the occurrence of the contingency for which the insurance was taken out.

Loss of earning capacity is an injury to an individual's ability to earn wages at a future time and may be recovered as an element of DAMAGES in a TORT case.

LOSS OF CONSORTIUM See CONSORTIUM.

LOSS OF SERVICES 📖 A deprivation of a family member, such as a parent or spouse, of

If a family member dies because of the negligence of another, the grieving family may receive compensatory damages in the form of an award for loss of services.

the right to benefit from the performance of various duties, coupled with the privation of love and companionship, provided by the victim of a PERSONAL INJURY or WRONGFUL DEATH. 📖

Pecuniary awards for loss of services are a type of COMPENSATORY DAMAGES, intended to serve as restitution for injuries sustained by family members. Family relationships can be interfered with in various ways. Along with economic losses from medical expenses, there might exist pain and suffering as well as loss of CONSORTIUM and society.

Damages for loss of services are recoverable by a parent whose child has been killed or injured; by a husband or wife whose spouse has been killed or injured; and, in some instances, by a father whose daughter has been a victim of SEDUCTION.

The PARENT AND CHILD relationship involves many mutual duties, privileges, and obligations. A parent has the right to the services of his or her unemancipated INFANT. When a child is injured by TORT in a manner which disables the child from performing services, a parent has a cause of action to recover for the value of these services. This cause of action exists even where a child was not actually performing any services before being harmed. This right of action stems from the parental interest in the custody, society, companionship, and affection of his or her offspring.

A husband may sue for the loss of personal services of his wife, including the performance of various household duties as well as sexual relationships, companionship, and affection.

LOST INSTRUMENTS 📖 Documents that cannot be located after a thorough, careful, and diligent search has been made for them. 📖

In some JURISDICTIONS, documents that have been stolen are held to be lost. An instrument that the owner has voluntarily and intentionally destroyed in order to cancel its legal effects is not a lost instrument, nor is an instrument that has been mutilated. Generally the loss of a written instrument does not affect the validity of the transaction that it represents, since a copy can usually be established in court. An action to restore a lost instrument is not one for relief against a wrong but rather one to enforce the plaintiff's interests. It can be initiated immediately subsequent to the loss, and all interested persons should be made parties to, and should be given notice of, such proceedings.

An action to establish a lost instrument indicating ownership of land, such as a DEED, can be commenced by anyone who has an interest in the subject matter, such as an HEIR of a deceased property owner. This type of case is analogous to a QUIET TITLE ACTION.

LOT 📖 In SALES, a parcel or single article that is the subject matter of a separate sale or delivery, irrespective of whether or not it is adequate to perform the CONTRACT. In the SECURITIES and commodities market, a specific number of SHARES or a particular quantity of a commodity specified for trading. In the law of REAL ESTATE, one of several parcels into which REAL PROPERTY is divided. 📖

A lot is ordinarily one of several contiguous pieces of land of which a block is composed. Real property is commonly described in terms of lot and block numbers on recorded maps and PLATS.

LOTTERY See STATE LOTTERY.

LOUISIANA PURCHASE The Louisiana Purchase of 1803 doubled the size of the United States, gave the country complete control of the port of New Orleans, and provided territory for westward expansion. The 828,000 square miles purchased from France formed completely or in part thirteen states: Arkansas, Colorado, Iowa, Kansas, Louisiana, Minnesota, Missouri, Montana, Nebraska, North Dakota, Oklahoma, South Dakota, and Wyoming. President THOMAS JEFFERSON was unsure if the Constitution authorized the acquisition of land, but he found a way to justify the purchase.

France originally claimed the Louisiana Territory in the seventeenth century. In 1763 it ceded to Spain the province of Louisiana, which was about where the state of Louisiana is today. By the 1790s U.S. farmers who lived west of the Appalachian Mountains were shipping their surplus produce by boat down rivers that flowed into the Gulf of Mexico. In 1795 the United States negotiated a TREATY with Spain that permitted U.S. merchants the right of deposit at New Orleans. This right allowed the merchants to store their goods in New Orleans without paying duty before they were exported.

In 1800 France, under the leadership of Napoléon, negotiated a secret treaty with Spain that ceded the province of Louisiana back to France. President Jefferson became concerned that France had control of the strategic port of New Orleans, and sought to purchase the port and West Florida. When France revoked the right of deposit for U.S. merchants in 1802, Jefferson sent JAMES MONROE to Paris to help ROBERT R. LIVINGSTON convince the French government to complete the sale. These statesmen warned that the United States would ally itself with England against France if a plan were not devised that settled this issue.

Monroe and Livingston were authorized by Congress to offer up to $2 million to purchase the east bank of the Mississippi; Jefferson secretly advised them to offer over $9 million for Florida and New Orleans.

Napoléon initially resisted U.S. offers, but changed his mind in 1803. He knew that war with England was imminent, and realized that if France were tied down with a European war, the United States might annex the Louisiana Territory. He also took seriously the threat of a U.S.-English alliance. Therefore, in April 1803 he instructed his foreign minister, Charles-Maurice de Talleyrand-Périgord, to negotiate with Monroe and Livingston for the United States' purchase of the entire Louisiana Territory. Acting on their own, the U.S. negotiators agreed to the price of $15 million, with $12 million paid to France and $3 million paid to U.S. citizens who had outstanding claims against France. The purchase agreement, dated April 30, was signed May 2 and reached Washington, D.C., in July.

President Jefferson endorsed the purchase but believed that the Constitution did not provide the national government with the authority to make land acquisitions. He pondered whether a CONSTITUTIONAL AMENDMENT might be needed to legalize the purchase. After consultations Jefferson concluded that the president's authority to make treaties could be used to justify the agreement. Therefore, the Louisiana Purchase was designated a treaty and submitted to the Senate for ratification. The Senate ratified the treaty October 20, 1803, and the

United States took possession of the territory December 20, 1803.

The U.S. government borrowed money from English and Dutch banks to pay for the acquisition. Interest payments for the fifteen-year loans brought the total price to over $27 million. The vast expanse of land, running from the Mississippi River to the Rocky Mountains and from the Gulf of Mexico to the Canadian border, is the largest ever added to the United States at one time. The settling of the territory played a large part in the debate over SLAVERY preceding the Civil War, as Congress grappled with the question of whether to allow slavery in new states, such as Missouri and Kansas.

See also KANSAS-NEBRASKA ACT; MISSOURI COMPROMISE OF 1820.

LOW-TIDE ELEVATION Offshore land features such as shoals, rocks, or reefs that are exposed at low tide but submerged at high tide are referred to as low-tide elevations.

If a low-tide elevation lies at least partially within the normal breadth of the TERRITORIAL WATERS of a nation, the low-water line of that elevation may be used as a baseline for measuring the ultimate reach of the territorial sea of that nation. Those low-tide elevations lying totally outside the usual breadth of the territorial sea do not expand the reach of the territorial sea of a nation.

LOYALTY OATH An oath that declares an individual's ALLEGIANCE to the government and its institutions, and disclaims support of ideologies or associations that oppose or threaten the government.

Loyalty oaths are required of government officials, such as the president, members of Congress and state legislatures, and members of the judiciary. Naturalized citizens are required to pledge their allegiance to the United States, as are members of the ARMED SERVICES. Employees in sensitive government positions may also be required to take a loyalty oath. (See U.S.C.A. § 1448; U.S. Const. art. II, § 1, cl. 7; U.S. Const. art. VI, cl. 3.)

Requiring an employee to promise to support the government as a condition of employment is constitutional as long as the requirement is reasonably related to the employee's fitness for the particular position. Loyalty oaths that infringe on a person's ability to exercise a constitutional right must be narrowly focused to achieve a legitimate government objective. If an oath is overly broad or vague, it may be found unconstitutional.

Loyalty oaths have played a role in American history since the settlement of the colonies.

The Puritans in New England required citizens to pledge their support of the commonwealth and to report any individuals who advocated dissent against the government. To ensure unity the CONTINENTAL CONGRESS and the legislatures of the first states all enacted laws requiring citizens to pledge their allegiance to the U.S. government.

Loyalty oaths are often invoked during times of stress, such as wars, or when the government perceives an outside threat to security. For example, after the Civil War, some states enacted statutes that excluded from certain professions those who had been disloyal to the United States and had sympathized with the Confederacy. One statute that required an oath of prior loyalty for admission to the bar was found unconstitutional because it imposed a legislative punishment for past acts. (See *Ex parte Garland*, 4 Wall. 333, 71 U.S. 333, 18 L. Ed. 366 [1866]; *Cummings v. Missouri*, 4 Wall. 277, 71 U.S. 277, 18 L. Ed. 356 [1866].)

The period after World War II was the high-water mark in the history of loyalty oaths. Fear of Communist subversion affected every aspect of life in the United States. There was particular concern that Communist sympathizers were obtaining employment in the government and in public schools. This led the majority of states to enact statutes that required public employees, public school teachers, and university professors to sign a loyalty oath as a condition of employment. Under some of the statutes, schools were permitted to discharge teachers who were thought to be disloyal to the government. Most of the statutes required employees to pledge their support of the state and federal constitutions. Some also required teachers to promise to promote patriotism, pledge not to teach or advocate the forcible overthrow of the government, and swear that they did not belong to the Communist party or any other organization that advocated the overthrow of the government.

Most loyalty oaths required of public employees have been struck down by the Supreme Court, usually on the ground that they violate due process because they are vague and susceptible to wide interpretation. In *Baggett v. Bullitt*, 377 U.S. 360, 84 S. Ct. 1316, 12 L. Ed. 2d 377 (1964), the Court invalidated Washington's statute requiring teachers and state employees to take a loyalty oath. This oath stated that the employee promised to support the federal and state constitutions and promote respect for the FLAG and reverence for law and order. The Court held that the oath was unduly vague, uncertain, and broad. The Court found further that it violated due process and infringed on the teachers' FREEDOM OF SPEECH. (See also *Cramp v. Orange County, Florida*, 368 U.S. 278, 82 S. Ct. 275, 7 L. Ed. 2d 285 [1961].)

The Court expressed a particular interest in protecting ACADEMIC FREEDOM from infringements imposed by loyalty oaths, in *Keyishian v. Board of Regents*, 385 U.S. 589, 87 S. Ct. 675, 17 L. Ed. 2d 629 (1967). In declaring a New York loyalty statute unconstitutionally vague, the Court in *Keyishian* called academic freedom a "special concern of the First Amendment." It also expressed its belief that loyalty statutes that attempt to prescribe what a teacher can say threaten to "cast a pall of orthodoxy over the classroom."

Some loyalty oath statutes have been invalidated on the ground that they unconstitutionally infringe on FREEDOM OF ASSOCIATION. In *Wieman v. Updegraff*, 344 U.S. 183, 73 S. Ct. 215, 97 L. Ed. 216 (1952), the Court held that Oklahoma's loyalty oath offended due process because it indiscriminately penalized innocent association or membership in Communist or other subversive groups. That oath required public employees to deny any past affiliation with such organizations. Similarly, in *Elfbrandt v. Russell*, 384 U.S. 11, 86 S. Ct. 1238, 16 L. Ed. 2d 321 (1966), the Court invalidated Arizona's public employee loyalty oath on the ground that it infringed on the employees' freedom of association. To satisfy the Constitution, such statutes may penalize only those who join a subversive organization with knowledge of the group's illegal objectives and specific intent to further them. The Arizona statute denied public employment to anyone associated with a subversive organization, whether or not the person knew of the group's objectives or subscribed to them.

In some cases the Court has upheld loyalty oaths for government employees if the oaths meet certain requirements. The oaths may not infringe on freedom of speech or association and may not be unduly vague. According to the Court, requiring a public employee to promise to uphold and defend the Constitution and oppose the illegal overthrow of the government does not unduly burden freedom of speech or association. (See *Cole v. Richardson*, 405 U.S. 676, 92 S. Ct. 1332, 31 L. Ed. 2d 593 [1972].)

In 1994 a loyalty oath as a prerequisite for public employment was challenged on the ground that it violated religious freedom. In *Bessard v. California Community College*, 867 F. Supp. 1454 (E.D. Cal. 1994), the plaintiffs, who were Jehovah's Witnesses, stated that proclaim-ing loyalty to the government is prohibited by their RELIGION. They argued that under the Religious Freedom Restoration Act of 1993 (RFRA) (42 U.S.C.A. § 2000bb et seq.), the state could not require them to take the loyalty oath as a condition of employment unless it could prove that it had a compelling interest that could not be served except by requiring the oath. The court held that the RFRA applied to the case, that the loyalty oath unconstitutionally infringed on the plaintiffs' religious freedom, and that the defendant must make reasonable accommodations for the plaintiffs. The court further noted that the defendant could ensure the plaintiffs' loyalty by having them sign a statement that they would not act contrary to the defendant's interests. In *City of Boerne v. Flores*, 117 S. Ct. 2157 (1997), the Supreme Court struck down RFRA as exceeding Congress's authority to safeguard rights under the Fourteenth Amendment. The Court held that RFRA was an unconstitutional encroachment on state power.

Government attempts to condition the receipt of certain benefits on a declaration of loyalty have generally been found unconstitutional. In *Speiser v. Randall*, 357 U.S. 513, 78 S. Ct. 1352, 2 L. Ed. 2d 1460 (1958), the Court held that requiring veterans to take a loyalty oath as a precondition to receiving a veterans' property tax exemption impinged on their free speech rights. Justice WILLIAM J. BRENNAN, JR., writing for the majority, reasoned, "To deny an exemption to claimants who engage in certain forms of speech is in effect to penalize them for such speech." Brennan's opinion went on to say that the requirement would have a chilling effect on the claimant's exercise of free speech.

CROSS-REFERENCES

Chilling Effect Doctrine; Cold War; Communism; Compelling State Interest; Due Process of Law; Void for Vagueness.

L.S. An abbreviation for *locus sigilli*, Latin for "the place of the seal," signifying the place within a written CONTRACT where a SEAL is affixed in order to bind the agreement.

Since the use of seals is decreasing, the use of this abbreviation has declined.

LUMP-SUM SETTLEMENT The payment of an entire DEBT all at once rather than in installments; the payment of a set amount of money to satisfy a pecuniary obligation that might otherwise continue indefinitely.

Lump-sum alimony, for example, is the payment of a large sum of money upon the dissolution of a marriage in order to circumvent the obligation to pay a certain amount, fixed or fluctuating, on a regular basis, for an indefinite period of time. This type of PROPERTY SETTLE-MENT is also known as *alimony in gross.*

LURTON, HORACE HARMON

Horace Harmon Lurton epitomized late-nineteenth-century judicial conservatism. Whether he was on the state or federal bench, restraint characterized Lurton's opinions. After a successful period in private practice in the 1860s and 1870s, Lurton won election to the Tennessee Supreme Court in 1886. He was its chief justice in 1893; a federal judge on the U.S. Court of Appeals for the Sixth Circuit, in Cincinnati, from 1893 to 1909; and a professor and eventually law school dean at Vanderbilt University starting in 1898. In 1910, at age sixty-six, he became the oldest justice ever appointed to the U.S. Supreme Court.

Lurton was born in Newport, Kentucky, on February 26, 1844. The son of an itinerant physician-turned-preacher, he spent a humble childhood in Tennessee. The defining moment in his life came while he was a sixteen-year-old undergraduate studying at Douglas University, in Chicago. When the Civil War broke out, Lurton immediately left school to join the Confederate army. After refusing discharge for a lung condition, he was captured; escaped; and then, while helping conduct guerrilla raids on Union forces, imprisoned again. He was thought to be near death in the last months of the war when his mother successfully appealed to President ABRAHAM LINCOLN to release him for health reasons.

The experience of war gave Lurton new priorities. Rather than returning to finish his degree in Chicago, he chose to pursue law at Cumberland University Law School, in Lebanon, Tennessee. After graduating in 1867, he distinguished himself in private practice as a diligent, detail-oriented attorney. In 1875 he was appointed to fill a vacated judgeship in the Sixth Chancery Division of Tennessee, where he served for three years before financial pressures made him return to practicing law. The judgeship cemented his reputation, and his practice flourished over the next decade. In 1886 he ran for a seat on the Tennessee Supreme Court. Lurton won. For the next seven

BIOGRAPHY

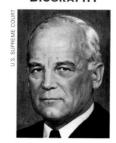

Horace Harmon Lurton

"THE DUTY OF THE COURT IS LIMITED TO THE DECISION OF ACTUAL PENDING CONTROVERSIES."

years, he was regarded as an eminently fair, patient, and courteous judge. Not the least of his admirers were his colleagues on the Tennessee high court: by a unanimous vote, they made him the court's chief justice in 1893. While on the court he also taught law at Vanderbilt University.

No sooner had Lurton been made chief justice of the Tennessee Supreme Court than President GROVER CLEVELAND tapped him for the federal bench. Lurton resigned from the Tennessee Supreme Court and took his seat on the U.S. Court of Appeals for the Sixth Circuit, in Cincinnati. On the appellate court, Lurton continued to pursue the conservative legal philosophy that had guided his earlier career. He placed extreme importance on the separation of powers, preferring to have legislatures make laws and abhorring modification of the law by the courts.

In 1905 Lurton served as dean of the Vanderbilt University law school. He was nearly appointed to the U.S. Supreme Court in 1906 by the reform-minded President THEODORE ROOSEVELT. The Republican president's selection was a measure of the respect that the Democratic judge had garnered. Roosevelt only backed off from appointing Lurton when he was persuaded to choose a Republican instead.

In 1910 President WILLIAM HOWARD TAFT had no qualms about appointing a Democrat, or about appointing the oldest candidate in Supreme Court history. Some opposition was raised over Lurton's age; more complaints were directed at the narrowness of his outlook. There proved to be no reason for worry: as an associate justice, Lurton largely followed the lead of the majority. Commentators are generally at a loss to find much of note in Lurton's tenure on the Court, which lasted four years until his death. It was the Progressive Era, and the Court was often concerned with the issue of government regulatory power, particularly in antitrust, the area of law devoted to enforcing fair competition in business. Although he had always resisted so-called judge-made law, Lurton joined in the Court's unanimous decisions in groundbreaking ANTITRUST cases such as

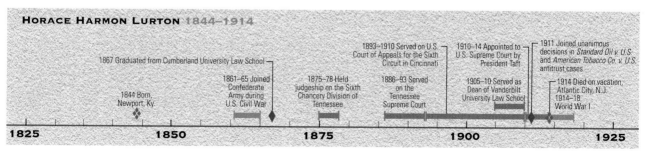

HORACE HARMON LURTON 1844–1914

1867 Graduated from Cumberland University Law School

1893–1910 Served on U.S. Court of Appeals for the Sixth Circuit in Cincinnati

1910–14 Appointed to U.S. Supreme Court by President Taft

1911 Joined unanimous decisions in *Standard Oil v. U.S.* and *American Tobacco Co. v. U.S.* antitrust cases

1861–65 Joined Confederate Army during U.S. Civil War

1844 Born, Newport, Ky.

1875–78 Held judgeship on the Sixth Chancery Division of Tennessee

1886–93 Served on the Tennessee Supreme Court

1905–10 Served as Dean of Vanderbilt University Law School

1914 Died on vacation, Atlantic City, N.J.

1914–18 World War I

1825   1850   1875   1900   1925

Standard Oil v. United States, 221 U.S. 1, 31 S. Ct. 502, 55 L. Ed. 619 (1911), and *American Tobacco Co. v. United States*, 221 U.S. 106, 31 S. Ct. 632, 55 L. Ed. 663 (1911).

Lurton died July 12, 1914, in Atlantic City, New Jersey.

MacKINNON, CATHARINE A.

Catharine A. MacKinnon is a law professor, author, and one of the leading scholars in feminist legal theory. MacKinnon's ideas about SEXUAL HARASSMENT and PORNOGRAPHY have forced courts and legal commentators to reexamine their assumptions. Her controversial proposal for suppressing pornography was enacted by the city council of Indianapolis, but the ORDINANCE was ultimately overturned by a federal appeals court.

MacKinnon was born in 1946 in Minnesota. Her father, George E. MacKinnon, was a prominent Republican party leader who served one term in Congress and later became a federal appeals court judge. MacKinnon graduated from Smith College in 1969 and then attended Yale University Law School. She received her law degree in 1977 and a Ph.D. degree in political science from Yale in 1987.

MacKinnon was admitted to the Connecticut bar in 1978, and the following year she published her first book, *Sexual Harassment of Working Women: A Case of Sex Discrimination.* She served as cocounsel for Mechelle Vinson in the groundbreaking U.S. Supreme Court case dealing with sexual harassment in the work-

BIOGRAPHY

place: *Meritor Savings Bank, FSB v. Vinson,* 477 U.S. 57, 106 S. Ct. 2399, 91 L. Ed. 2d 49 (1986). The Court agreed with MacKinnon that the concept of a "hostile work environment" was ACTIONABLE under the 1964 CIVIL RIGHTS ACT (42 U.S.C.A. § 2000e et seq.) as SEX DISCRIMINATION. The Court rejected a narrow reading of the law that would have restricted sexual harassment claims to discrimination of an economic character. Under this restrictive reading, an employer could not be held liable for harassment unless the employee's salary and promotions were affected by the actions.

Between 1979 and 1989, MacKinnon was a visiting professor at a number of prominent law schools, including her alma mater, Yale. Though she was a prolific writer and a popular teacher, her views and her actions concerning pornography made her a controversial public figure. Her radical feminist theories challenged the legitimacy of the legal system and mainstream liberal thought. She argued that men, as a class, have dominated women, creating gender inequality. This inequality is the consequence of a systematic subordination rather than a product of irrational discrimination. Thus, heterosexuality is a social arrangement with men

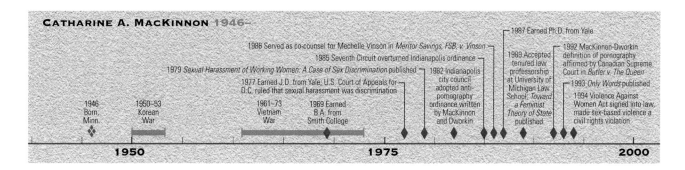

dominant and women submissive. Gender, for radical feminists, is a question of power.

In MacKinnon's view, pornography is a powerful tool of the dominant male class, subordinating women and exposing them to RAPE and other abusive behavior. In 1982 she and feminist author ANDREA DWORKIN convinced the Indianapolis city council to enact a pornography ordinance that expressed their theory of sexual subordination. The ordinance described pornography as "a discriminatory practice based on sex which denies women equal opportunity in society," and defined it as "the graphic sexually explicit subordination of women, whether in pictures or words," especially in a violent or degrading context. The ordinance made unlawful the production, sale, exhibition, and distribution of pornography and gave anyone injured by a person who has seen or read pornography the right to bring a civil suit against the maker or seller.

Supporters of the ordinance argued that the legislation was a CIVIL RIGHTS measure meant to fight sex discrimination. In their view the ordinance regulated conduct rather than free speech and thus did not violate the FIRST AMENDMENT.

The Seventh Circuit Court of Appeals, in *American Booksellers Ass'n, Inc. v. Hudnut*, 771 F.2d 323 (1985), overturned the ordinance. The court agreed that pornography affected how people view the world and their social relations but observed that the same could be said of other protected speech, including expressions of racial bigotry. To permit the MacKinnon-Dworkin approach would give the government control of "all institutions of culture" and allow it to be the "great censor and director of which thoughts are good for us." Despite the demise of the ordinance, MacKinnon has remained steadfast in her view, sometimes debating persons who defend the publication of pornography on First Amendment grounds.

In 1989 MacKinnon became a tenured law professor at the University of Michigan Law School. She has continued to write and lecture about FEMINIST JURISPRUDENCE. MacKinnon's 1993 book, *Only Words*, restated her attack on pornography, rape, and the sexual subordination of women.

MacPHERSON v. BUICK MOTOR CO.

A famous 1916 New York Court of Appeals decision, *MacPherson v. Buick Motor Co.*, 217 N.Y. 382, 111 N.E. 1050, expanded the classification of "inherently dangerous" products and thereby effectively eliminated the requirement of PRIVITY—a contractual relationship between the parties in cases that involve defective products that cause PERSONAL INJURY.

The Buick Motor Company manufactured automobiles that it sold to retailers who, in turn, sold them to consumers. The plaintiff, Donald MacPherson, bought a car from a

"PORNOGRAPHY SETS THE PUBLIC STANDARD FOR THE TREATMENT OF WOMEN IN PRIVATE AND THE LIMITS OF TOLERANCE FOR WHAT CAN BE PERMITTED IN PUBLIC."

When a wheel manufactured by a third party failed on a 1916 Buick, causing injury, the New York Court of Appeals (in MacPherson v. Buick Motor Co.) held that Buick was responsible as the seller of the finished product. This holding became the majority rule in the United States, and one of the fundamental principles of product liability law.

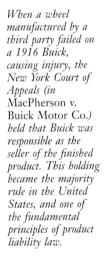

dealer and was subsequently injured when the car collapsed during a drive. The accident was due to a defective wheel, which the defendant, Buick, did not make but purchased from another manufacturer. Evidence indicated that the defect could have been discovered by reasonable inspection, but none took place. The plaintiff sued the defendant for his personal injuries, but the defendant claimed that it was not liable for the wheel manufacturer's NEGLIGENCE. The state trial and intermediate APPELLATE COURTS found for the plaintiff, and the defendant appealed to the Court of Appeals, the highest court of New York. The court narrowed the issue to whether the defendant owed a duty to anyone but the retailer to whom it sold the car.

In a majority opinion written by BENJAMIN CARDOZO, the court affirmed the JUDGMENT for the plaintiff. Since the defendant was a manufacturer of automobiles that, if defective, are inherently dangerous by virtue of their existence, it had a responsibility for the finished product, which included testing its various parts before placing it on the market for sale. The manufacturer could not avoid LIABILITY based upon the fact that it purchased the wheels from a reputable manufacturer, because it had a duty to inspect the car, which it failed to do. The defendant argued that since poisons, explosives, or comparable items that are normally used as "implements of destruction" were not involved, there was no "imminent danger" to the plaintiff's life. There was therefore, no basis for the imposition of liability upon a manufacturer to a third person, who was not a party to the contract between the manufacturer and seller of the dangerous product. The court rejected this argument, reasoning that if a product when negligently made poses a danger of personal injury, then the product is "a thing of danger," since injury is a foreseeable consequence of its use. Since the car had room for three persons and the retailer who bought the car from the manufacturer planned to resell it, ultimately to the plaintiff, it could be expected that injury could occur to persons who did not purchase the car directly from the manufacturer. The failure of the defendant—the manufacturer of the finished product for sale to the public—to inspect

the car, and in light of the other factors mentioned, rendered the company liable to the plaintiff who was not in privity with it.

The rule of *MacPherson v. Buick Motor Co.* that eliminated the need for privity between a manufacturer and an individual suffering personal injury from a defectively made product became the majority rule in the United States and one of the fundamental principles of the law of PRODUCT LIABILITY.

MacVEAGH, ISAAC WAYNE

Isaac Wayne MacVeagh served as U.S. attorney general from March to October 1881. His appointment was short because of the ASSASSINATION of President JAMES GARFIELD early in the president's term of office. MacVeagh resigned soon after Garfield's death so that President CHESTER A. ARTHUR could select his own attorney general.

MacVeagh was born on April 19, 1833, in Phoenixville, Pennsylvania. He attended school in Pottstown, Pennsylvania, before entering Yale University, where he graduated in 1853. He studied law in West Chester, Pennsylvania, and was admitted to the bar in 1856. In 1859 he became district attorney of Chester County, Pennsylvania.

During the Civil War, MacVeagh served as an infantry captain and as a major in the cavalry. He was forced to resign from the military because of ill health. He resumed his position as district attorney, but he also became active in Republican party politics. He was appointed U.S. minister to Turkey in 1870. The following year he returned to Pennsylvania and waged a failed campaign to win a U.S. Senate seat.

In 1877 President RUTHERFORD B. HAYES selected MacVeagh to direct an organization, subsequently known as the MacVeagh Commission, to arbitrate political differences in Louisiana. The actions of the commission hastened the removal of federal troops from the area and ended the last vestiges of Reconstruction in the South.

President James Garfield appointed him attorney general on March 5, 1881, but MacVeagh had little time to perform his duties. Garfield was shot on July 2, 1881, after only four months in office, at the railroad station in Washington, D.C., by Charles J. Guiteau, a

BIOGRAPHY

LIBRARY OF CONGRESS

*Isaac Wayne
MacVeagh*

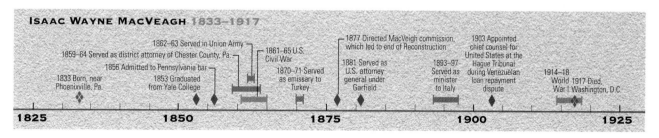

ISAAC WAYNE MACVEAGH 1833–1917

1833 Born, near Phoenixville, Pa.

1853 Graduated from Yale College

1856 Admitted to Pennsylvania bar

1859–64 Served as district attorney of Chester County, Pa.

1862–63 Served in Union Army

1861–65 U.S. Civil War

1870–71 Served as emissary to Turkey

1877 Directed MacVeigh commission, which led to end of Reconstruction

1881 Served as U.S. attorney general under Garfield

1893–97 Served as minister to Italy

1903 Appointed chief counsel for United States at the Hague Tribunal during Venezuelan loan repayment dispute

1914–18 World War I

1917 Died, Washington, D.C.

1825   1850   1875   1900   1925

disappointed office seeker. For eighty days the president lay ill and performed only one official act—the signing of an extradition paper. On September 19, 1881, Garfield died. MacVeagh submitted his resignation on October 24, 1881.

In 1882 MacVeagh decided to join the Democratic party. In 1893 President GROVER CLEVELAND, a Democrat, appointed MacVeagh minister to Italy, a post he held until 1897. Toward the end of his career, MacVeagh served as chief counsel for the United States at the Hague Tribunal during a dispute involving Venezuela's repayment of loans to several countries.

MacVeigh died on January 11, 1917, in Washington, D.C.

MADISON, JAMES James Madison was the fourth president of the United States, serving from 1809 to 1817. Before achieving the nation's highest office, he participated in the Virginia Constitutional Convention; was a delegate to the Continental Congress; drafted a proposal for the U.S. Constitution; supported ratification of the Constitution, through *The Federalist Papers*, written with ALEXANDER HAMILTON and JOHN JAY; served in the House of Representatives; helped write the BILL OF RIGHTS; and was THOMAS JEFFERSON's secretary of state.

Born March 16, 1751, in Port Conway, Virginia, Madison was the first of eleven children in his family. His father, James Madison, Sr., was the wealthiest landowner in Orange County, Virginia, and provided Madison with a stable and comfortable upbringing. Eleanor Conway Madison, his mother, was an affectionate woman who gave the family emotional support throughout her ninety-eight years of life.

Madison grew up on an isolated plantation in Montpelier, Virginia. As a teenager he attended school in King and Queen County, studying logic, philosophy, mathematics, astronomy, and French, among other subjects. Although Madison suffered from ill health during much of his youth, he developed a reputation as an intense and ambitious student at the College of New Jersey (now Princeton University), which he attended from 1769 to 1772.

James Madison

By 1774 it was becoming clear to many observers that the differences between the colonists and the British government could not be resolved peacefully. During that year Parliament passed the Coercive Acts, which closed the Boston Port, restricted town assemblies, and authorized British authorities to house their troops in private colonial residences. In September 1774 the First Continental Congress convened to discuss the emerging crisis with Great Britain. Unlike many colonists, who were reluctant to take any radical measures before Parliament could respond to the petition of grievances drafted by Congress, Madison favored immediate military preparations.

As Madison became more politically vocal, he became more politically active. In December 1774 he was elected to the Orange County Committee of Safety, one of many colonial bodies formed to carry out congressional mandates such as the American BOYCOTT of English goods. In October 1775, six months after the Revolution began in Lexington and Concord, Madison was commissioned a colonel in the county militia. In 1776, at age twenty-five, he was elected as a delegate to the Virginia Provincial Convention, where he helped draft Virginia's constitution.

In May 1776 the Virginia Provincial Convention, later known as the New House of Delegates, instructed its representatives at the Second Continental Congress to draft a declaration of independence, negotiate foreign alliances, and complete the U.S. ARTICLES OF CONFEDERATION. The Articles of Confederation empowered Congress to govern certain areas of national concern, including foreign policy. The several states retained power to govern most other issues within their own borders.

In the New House of Delegates, Madison forged a friendship with Jefferson that would leave an indelible imprint on U.S. law and U.S. history. Jefferson and Madison shared a love for books, ideas, and solitude. Jefferson had authored the DECLARATION OF INDEPENDENCE, and Madison would be considered the architect of the U.S. Constitution. But whereas Jefferson

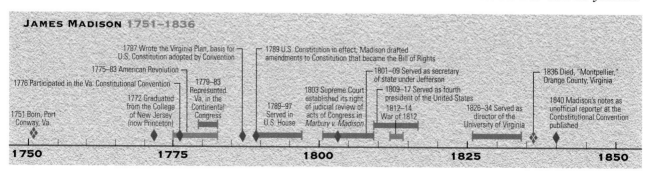

JAMES MADISON 1751–1836

1751 Born, Port Conway, Va.

1772 Graduated from the College of New Jersey (now Princeton)

1775–83 American Revolution

1776 Participated in the Va. Constitutional Convention

1779–83 Represented Va. in the Continental Congress

1787 Wrote the Virginia Plan, basis for U.S. Constitution adopted by Convention

1789 U.S. Constitution in effect; Madison drafted amendments to Constitution that became the Bill of Rights

1789–97 Served in U.S. House

1803 Supreme Court established its right of judicial review of acts of Congress in *Marbury v. Madison*

1801–09 Served as secretary of state under Jefferson

1809–17 Served as fourth president of the United States

1812–14 War of 1812

1826–34 Served as director of the University of Virginia

1836 Died, "Montpellier," Orange County, Virginia

1840 Madison's notes as unofficial reporter at the Constitutional Convention published

1750   1775   1800   1825   1850

was idealistic and impetuous, Madison was more realistic and rational. Although Madison was eight years younger than Jefferson, his thoughtful temperament often helped palliate the mercurial Jefferson. From 1777 to 1779, Madison served as a cabinet member for Jefferson, who was the governor of Virginia.

In December 1779 Virginia chose Madison as one of its five delegates to the Continental Congress. Earning respect for his sober and methodical approach to lawmaking as well as his intellectual prowess, Madison helped Congress pass a revenue measure that rescued the fledgling nation from bankruptcy. Over the next three years, Madison learned how to shape an agenda and to achieve results through compromise.

On April 15, 1783, Congress ratified a peace treaty with Great Britain that concluded the Revolutionary War, and won U.S. independence. This year also marked the end of Madison's tenure with the Continental Congress. After returning home to Virginia, Madison was elected by the voters of Orange County to the state legislature in 1784.

During the 1784 fall session, the Virginia assembly approved an act to incorporate the Episcopal Church, and postponed action on another bill that sought to subsidize Christianity by levying a tax on behalf of teachers who taught this religion. In response to this proposed bill, Madison anonymously published a short leaflet entitled *Memorial and Remonstrance against Religious Assessments.* This leaflet called for a separation of church and state, denounced government aid to religion, declared the equality of all religions, and articulated a general liberty to worship according to the dictates of one's conscience without fear of persecution. Many copies of the leaflet were distributed to the state assembly in October 1785, along with supporting signatures, which helped influence enough legislators to defeat the Christian subsidy.

The following year Madison joined Hamilton in urging Congress to summon a national convention at Philadelphia to draft a federal constitution that would replace the Articles of Confederation. Under the Articles of Confederation, Congress had no power to regulate commerce. As a result the thirteen states engaged in a series of trade wars with each other. Many states imposed discriminatory taxes and regulations on goods imported from other states, and some states refused to import any goods from neighboring states.

Also under the Articles of Confederation, Congress had no power to tax. When Congress

"BUT WHAT IS GOVERNMENT ITSELF, BUT THE GREATEST OF ALL REFLECTIONS ON HUMAN NATURE? IF MEN WERE ANGELS, NO GOVERNMENT WOULD BE NECESSARY. IF ANGELS WERE TO GOVERN MEN, NEITHER EXTERNAL OR INTERNAL CONTROLS ON GOVERNMENT WOULD BE NECESSARY."

requested money to pay for the public debt and the Continental Army, the states often failed to respond. Consequently, the national debt grew and the Continental Army suffered a rash of desertions. Congressional ability to obtain credit dwindled. Madison observed that the thirteen states would be in a precarious and vulnerable position if the country were required to defend its borders against foreign invasion.

Congress was the country's only federal government body; the Articles of Confederation did not provide for an EXECUTIVE BRANCH to enforce congressional will, or a judicial branch to resolve disputes. This single body was virtually powerless to do anything about outbreaks of rebellion that were becoming more frequent in the states. For example, it offered no reasonable resolution for SHAYS'S REBELLION of 1786, an insurrection of nearly two thousand farmers who were protesting Massachusetts's land foreclosure laws.

Fifty-five delegates representing twelve states attended the Constitutional Convention during the summer of 1787. Reaching Philadelphia on May 14, Madison was the first delegate to arrive from any state other than Pennsylvania. Business would not begin until May 25, when a quorum of seven states would first be present. Madison seized the intervening eleven days to draft a fifteen-point proposal that formed the underpinnings of the U.S. Constitution.

Known as the Virginia Plan, this proposal presented a radical departure from the Articles of Confederation. In it, with help from the other Virginia delegates, Madison suggested a constitutional system comprising a strong centralized federal government with three branches: executive, legislative, and judicial. The SOVEREIGNTY granted to each branch would be limited by the sovereignty granted to the other two branches and by the concurrent sovereignty retained by the states. This system of checks and balances had no predecessor in history.

The Virginia Plan provided the blueprint for a BICAMERAL (two-chamber) legislature, with an upper chamber known as the Senate and a lower chamber known as the House of Representatives. As originally conceived, the plan gave Congress the indefinite power to legislate in all "cases to which the states are not competent." State governments would retain authority to legislate local concerns, and to create constitutional systems of their own. However, Madison made clear that the federal government would be supreme, and that any state law in contravention of the U.S. Constitution, a congressional enactment, or a federal treaty would be void.

At the same time, Madison's proposal for a broad grant of undefined congressional power was jettisoned. Madison argued that Congress should be given more legislative authority than state legislatures because state laws had been largely responsible for the recent trade wars and farmer rebellions. However, Madison was unable to explain why the federal government, made up of representatives from the several states, should be trusted to exercise its lawmaking powers any more prudently than had the state governments. Thus, the delegates persuaded Madison that the powers of the executive and legislative branches must be limited to those expressly enumerated in the Constitution. However, one of those enumerated powers, Congress's power to make all laws "necessary and proper" in the performance of its legislative function, has provided a broad constitutional basis for federal lawmaking similar to that originally envisioned by Madison.

The Necessary and Proper Clause was only one of the constitutional provisions vigorously defended in *The Federalist Papers*, a series of essays written by Madison, Hamilton, and Jay that explained and promoted the system of government created by the Philadelphia convention. Called *The Federalist Papers* because proponents of the federal Constitution were known as Federalists, this collection of essays was circulated among the delegates to the state ratifying conventions, in an effort to win their support. Opponents of the federal Constitution, known as Anti-Federalists, published and circulated essays and leaflets of their own.

Some Anti-Federalists eventually lent their support to the ratification movement when Madison and other Federalists promised to draft a bill of rights that would protect individual liberty and state sovereignty from encroachment by the federal government. In 1788 the Constitution was adopted by the states. The next year Madison was elected to the House of Representatives, where he subsequently represented Virginia for eight years. During the First Congress, in 1789, Madison drafted twelve amendments to the U.S. Constitution, ten of which were ultimately adopted by the states, with some subtle changes in language, and now stand as the Bill of Rights.

Neither the Constitution nor the Bill of Rights expressly mentions the power of JUDICIAL REVIEW, which is the prerogative of state and federal courts to invalidate laws that violate a constitutional provision or principle. Article VI declares that the federal Constitution "shall be the supreme Law of the Land." Yet it does not state whether the executive, legislative, and judicial branches possess the power to nullify laws that are unconstitutional. Although the Framers of the Constitution recognized that courts had traditionally exercised the authority to interpret and apply the law, the power of judicial review had never been a clearly established practice in Anglo-American legal history.

In the landmark case *Marbury v. Madison*, 5 U.S. (1 Cranch) 137, 2 L. Ed. 60 (1803), the U.S. Supreme Court established the power of judicial review in the United States. While serving as secretary of state to President Jefferson (1801–1809), Madison was sued by William Marbury, a judge who had been appointed to the federal bench during the waning hours of President JOHN ADAMS's administration. Marbury argued that Madison had violated his duties as secretary of state by failing to deliver to Marbury a commission that he needed to complete his appointment to the federal judiciary.

Although the Supreme Court agreed that Madison had wrongfully withheld the commission, it denied Marbury's claim because it had been brought pursuant to an unconstitutional provision of a federal statute. By invalidating that provision, the Supreme Court established the power of judicial review. When Madison learned of the Supreme Court's decision, he criticized the judicial branch for attempting to usurp congressional lawmaking power.

Madison said that to allow unelected federal judges to overturn legislation enacted by the popularly elected branches of government makes "the judicial department paramount in fact to the legislature, which was never intended, and can never be proper." Madison changed his mind on this issue near the end of his life. As an elder statesman attending the Virginia Constitutional Convention in 1829, and as a director for the University of Virginia from 1826 to 1834, he assailed the nullification theories of southern legislators who proclaimed the prerogative to ignore federal laws in certain circumstances. Only the judiciary, Madison concluded, had the power to declare federal laws unconstitutional.

Serving as the fourth president of the United States (1809–17), Madison revealed the same propensity to reevaluate strongly held beliefs in light of experience. Earlier in his career, he had opposed the creation of a congressionally chartered national bank. He had initially believed that under no faithful interpretation of the

Constitution was Congress authorized to establish a national bank. Yet, in 1816 Madison signed a bill that established the Second Bank of the United States, agreeing that it represented a constitutional exercise of congressional power. Popular acceptance of the First Bank of the United States had altered Madison's perception.

The War of 1812 provided some of the best and worst moments of Madison's presidency. During the low point of the war with Great Britain, English troops occupied Washington, D.C., and burned down the White House. Despite other such humiliating moments for the U.S. military, Madison's troops rebounded in 1815 and soundly defeated the British in the final battle of the war at New Orleans. Although Americans gained nothing tangible from the war, they had successfully defended their soil.

The perseverance and resolve demonstrated by Madison and his troops during the war proved to be an important step in the maturation process of the young republic. By winning the War of 1812 and defeating British troops for a second time in less than half a century, John Adams remarked, Madison brought more glory to the United States than any of his three predecessors in office. Madison also unified the country like never before in its short history, allowing his successors to build upon the emerging national identity.

After the close of his second term, Madison retired from public office and returned home to Montpelier, Virginia, where he devoted long hours to farming and became president of the local agricultural society. Madison welcomed retirement, seeing it as an opportunity to renew his passion for reading and resume his correspondence with Thomas Jefferson.

He died on June 28, 1836.

CROSS-REFERENCES

Bank of the United States; Constitution of the United States; Federalism; *Federalist Papers; Marbury v. Madison;* Virginia Conventions.

MAGISTRATE

Any individual who has the power of a public civil officer or inferior judicial officer, such as a JUSTICE OF THE PEACE.

The various state judicial systems provide for judicial officers who are often called magistrates, justices of the peace, or police justices. The authority of these officials is restricted by statute, and JURISDICTION is commonly limited to the county in which the official presides. The position may be elected or appointed, depending on the governing state statute. The exact role of the official varies by state; it may include handling hearings regarding violations of motor vehicle codes or breaches of the peace, presiding over criminal preliminary hearings, officiating marriages, and dispensing CIVIL ACTIONS involving small sums of money.

U.S. magistrates are judicial officers appointed by the judges of federal district courts pursuant to the United States Magistrates Act (28 U.S.C.A. §§ 631 et seq.), enacted in 1968. This act was designed to reduce the workload of FEDERAL COURTS by replacing the old system of U.S. commissioners with a new system of U.S. magistrates. U.S. magistrates can perform more judicial functions than could U.S. commissioners. Federal magistrates may be assigned some, but not all, of the duties of a federal judge. They may serve as special masters (persons appointed by the court to carry out a particular judicial function on behalf of the court), supervise pretrial or DISCOVERY proceedings, and provide preliminary consideration of petitions for postconviction relief. U.S. magistrates generally may not decide motions to dismiss or motions for SUMMARY JUDGMENT, because these motions involve ultimate decision making, a responsibility and duty of the federal courts. However, if all the parties to a case agree, a federal magistrate may decide such motions and may even conduct a civil or MISDEMEANOR criminal trial. Federal magistrates are not permitted to preside over FELONY trials or over jury selection in felony cases.

MAGNA CHARTA

On June 15, 1215, King John (1199–1216) was surrounded on the battlefield at Runnymede by a cordon of England's most powerful barons, who demanded royal recognition for certain liberties and legal procedures they enumerated in a written document known today as the Magna Charta. Contained in the Magna Charta's sixty-three chapters are the seeds of trial by JURY, DUE PROCESS, HABEAS CORPUS, and equality under the law. The Magna Charta was reissued three times during the reign of Henry III (1216–72) with some minor alteration, and confirmed by the Crown more than thirty times thereafter.

Sometimes called the Great Charter, the Magna Charta is widely considered to be the foundation of the English and U.S. constitutional systems, representing the first time the often tyrannical power of the monarchy was restrained by law and popular resistance. The Magna Charta was cited by SIR EDWARD COKE, esteemed English jurist and member of the House of Commons, in opposition to the monarchy's assertion of absolute power in the seventeenth century. During the American Revolution, colonists relied on the Magna Charta when they convened the First Continental Congress to restore the rights lost under the coercive legislation of Parliament.

Almost from its inception, the Great Charter has been imbued with two separate meanings, one literal and the other symbolic. The literal meaning is reflected by the original understanding of the Magna Charta in the thirteenth century; the symbolic meaning was developed by subsequent generations, which interpreted its provisions in light of a changing political landscape. The literal meaning was associated with the concrete rights enforced by the barons against the monarchy; the symbolic meaning became associated with the RULE OF LAW, an impartial system of justice, and government by the consent of the people and their representatives. To understand the symbolic importance attached to the Magna Charta, one must see the literal meaning in its original context.

The Magna Charta is the product of three competing legal jurisdictions: royal, ecclesiastical, and baronial. The royal system of justice maintained JURISDICTION over all matters that affected the monarch's peace, directly or indirectly. Royal courts heard disputes at a central location in Westminster, and royal itinerant judges traveled locally to dispense the monarch's justice to communities across England.

ECCLESIASTICAL COURTS, which were run by the Catholic Church, with the pope presiding as the spiritual head in Rome, maintained jurisdiction over the discipline of the church's clergy, religious offenses such as heresy, and most moral, marital, and testamentary matters.

Baronial courts were governed by barons, powerful men who were given titles of dignity by the Crown and who held large parcels of land, known as manors, from the monarch. Each baron, as lord of his MANOR, was invested with the authority to hear disputes involving his tenants, men and women who agreed to work the land in exchange for shelter and security.

John alienated both the ecclesiastical and baronial jurisdictions during his reign as king, converting them into adversaries.

The first ten years of John's reign were consumed by controversy with the church. John considered the pope to be subordinate to the Crown and treated the archbishop as a mere civil servant. The church, on the other hand, considered itself to be a separate and independent sovereign that had shared power with the Crown since the time of Henry I (1100–1135).

Henry I and the church had agreed that the nomination of bishops in England would tacitly remain with the king. But the pope retained power to confirm bishops by conferring upon them the honorary symbols of their title, the spiritual staff and ring.

The agreement between Henry I and the church provided no resolution for the controversy between King John and Pope Innocent III at the outset of the thirteenth century. The controversy began when Innocent III rejected John's candidate for archbishop of Canterbury and substituted his own choice, Stephen Langton, a man of superior "moral and intellectual greatness" (Trevelyan 1982, 146). John responded by confiscating the church's property in England. The papacy, whose power had grown as a result of its compromise with Henry I, subsequently undertook a series of steps to damage the Crown's prestige and credibility.

The pope excommunicated King John, suspended religious sacraments in England, and declared the English empire a forfeit from God. Facing growing pressure from the church and increasing unpopularity among Catholics within his own country, John surrendered England to the papacy, receiving it back as a fief, which meant the Crown was now subordinate to Rome and was required to pay homage to the pope. These royal concessions satisfied the pope and made him a cautious ally of the Crown. Archbishop Langton was determined to achieve similar concessions for the barons.

The grievances voiced by the barons were quite different from those voiced by the church. The barons' dissatisfaction stemmed from the manner in which the royal system of justice had been abused by King John. Prior to the reign of HENRY II (1154–89), English law had comprised a loose collection of customs and traditions followed by a variety of ethnic groups scattered across the realm. Henry II created a centralized system of justice that emanated from London, which the monarch's officials administered in a uniform manner to all English people in common. Although this "COMMON LAW" established a body of rights and procedures by which all litigants appearing before the ruler's courts would theoretically be treated the same, it also vested an enormous amount of power in the Crown. The tension separating arbitrary royal power from the principle of equality under the law erupted during the struggle between King John and his baronial magnates.

King John regularly sold legal rights and privileges to the highest bidder, rewarded favorites, punished enemies, and otherwise administered justice in an erratic and unfair fashion. For a dispute to be heard by the royal courts, parties were required to pay the monarch fees, which varied from case to case depending on the circumstances. If the Crown was in need of emergency revenue—and it seemingly always was during the reign of King John—these litigation fees were increased commensurate with the urgency of a particular financial crisis. Liti-

The Magna Charta became a model for written contracts between governed and government, such as the United States Constitution.

gants in good graces with the monarch typically paid lower court fees than litigants in disfavor. A defendant who requested the postponement or suspension of a legal matter was required to pay a greater fee than the plaintiff was charged.

Such litigation fees—which were paid in all legal matters, civil, criminal, matrimonial, and probate—simply enabled parties to assert their claims and defenses before the royal court. They did not guarantee a particular outcome, although the amount paid may have influenced the outcome, and they bore no relationship to the penalty or fine imposed on the losing party. Consequently, defendants who paid an exorbitant fee just to present an unsuccessful defense often faced fines of an equally outrageous amount. Defendants who suffered incarceration for a wrongdoing were usually forced to purchase their freedom from the monarch.

The manner in which the ruler enforced and collected royal debts was no less capricious. Litigants who could not afford to pay the legal fees set by the Crown frequently borrowed money from the ruler in order to pursue a particular right or remedy. The terms of such loan agreements were typically draconian. As collateral for these loans, John required the debtors to pledge their estates, personal property, and sometimes family members. In one case, a debtor was forced to pledge his castle and four sons as collateral. On other occasions, friends and family members of the debtor were held hostage by the king until the loan was repaid in full.

In some instances, the king simply forgave a loan because the debtor was a personal friend, had promised political favors, or had provided an invaluable service. In most instances, the invaluable service was military. During the thirteenth century, each baron was required to serve as a soldier in the monarch's army, and provide the Crown with a certain number of knights for military service. A fine could be paid in lieu of the baron's military service, and a tax, known as scutage, was then paid in lieu of the knights' service. When King John launched a military campaign, he dramatically increased the fines and taxes for nonservice, and used these monies to pay mercenaries to fight his battles.

Although King John dreamed of building an English empire through military conquest on the European continent, he was an utter failure on the battlefield. With each military loss, the miscellaneous economic demands made by the Crown seemed less justified and more absurd. It is not surprising, then, that the barons renounced loyalty to the king, plotted his assassination, and ultimately compelled his capitulation to the Magna Charta.

The grievances King John promised to redress in the Magna Charta represent both the substance of the Great Charter's original meaning and its later symbolic import. The document's immediate purpose was to appease the baronial leadership. In this vein, it provided that justice would not be sold, denied, or delayed (ch. 40), and ensured that certain rights and procedures would be "granted freely" without risk of "life or limb" (ch. 36). It guaranteed the safe return of hostages, lands, castles, and family members that had been held as security by the Crown for military service and loan agreements. The Magna Charta mandated the investigation and abolition of any "ill customs" established by King John (ch. 48), and required that no "justices, constables, sheriffs, or bailiffs" be appointed unless they "know the law of the land, and are willing to keep it" (ch. 45).

The phrase "law of the land" is interspersed throughout the Magna Charta, and is emblematic of other abstract legal concepts contained in the Great Charter that outlasted the exigencies of 1215. Nowhere in the Great Charter is "law of the land" defined, but a number of sections offer an early glimpse of certain constitutional liberties in embryonic form.

For example, the American colonies equated "law of the land" with "due process of law," a legal principle that has been the cornerstone of procedural fairness in U.S. civil and criminal trials since the late 1700s. The Due Process Clause of the Fifth and Fourteenth Amendments has been relied on by the U.S. Supreme Court as a source for substantive rights as well, including the right to PRIVACY.

Chapter 39 of the Magna Charta linked the law-of-the-land principle with another important protection. It provided, "No free man shall be seized, or imprisoned, or disseised, or outlawed, or exiled or injured in any way, nor will we enter on him or send against him except by the lawful judgment of his peers, or by the law of the land." In 1215, a person obtained "lawful judgment of his peers" through a communal inquest in which twelve knights or landowners familiar with the subject matter of the dispute took an oath, and swore to testify truthfully based on their own knowledge or on knowledge gained from an eyewitness or other credible source.

This primitive form of fact-finding replaced even cruder methods—such as trial by battle, where the disputants fought savagely until one party begged for mercy or died, and the victorious party was presumed to have God and Right on his side. The process of one's peers in the community rendering judgment also presaged the modern trial by jury recognized by the SEVENTH AMENDMENT to the U.S. Constitution, which similarly entitles a defendant to be tried by a body of jurors that is a "truly representative" cross section of the community (*Glasser v. United States*, 315 U.S. 60, 62 S. Ct. 457, 86 L. Ed. 680 [1942]).

The U.S. Supreme Court has also traced the origins of modern habeas corpus law to chapter 39 of the Magna Charta (*Murray v. Carrier*, 477 U.S. 478, 106 S. Ct. 2639, 91 L. Ed. 2d 397 [1986]). Habeas corpus is a procedure that authorizes a court to determine the legality under which a person is jailed, imprisoned, or otherwise detained by the government. If the court finds that the person was deprived of liberty through "due process of law," continued detention is permissible until trial, where guilt and innocence are placed in issue. Similarly, the Magna Charta validated the continued imprisonment of persons who had been originally incarcerated by the "law of the land."

In *Harmelin v. Michigan*, 501 U.S. 957, 111 S. Ct. 2680, 115 L. Ed. 2d 836 (1991), the Supreme Court also pointed to the Magna Charta as an early source of its EIGHTH AMENDMENT proportionality analysis. Chapter 20 of the Great Charter prohibited the monarch from imposing a fine "unless according to the measure of the offense." It further provided that "for a great offense [a free man] shall be [punished] according to the greatness of the offense." Under the Eighth Amendment to the Constitution, the Supreme Court has echoed this principle by prohibiting state and federal governments from imposing fines and other forms of punishment that are disproportionate to the seriousness of the offense for which the defendant was convicted.

The contemporary significance of the Magna Charta is not confined to the areas of civil and criminal procedure. The Great Charter prohibited the government from assessing any military tax such as scutage "except by the common counsel of [the] realm" (ch. 12). The common counsel comprised persons from various classes of English society, including bishops, abbots, earls, and barons. The common counsel was a forerunner to Parliament and Congress as a representative body limiting the power of the government to pass legislation, particularly tax legislation, without popular consent.

The common counsel also proclaimed what would become a battle cry of the American colonists: No Taxation without Representation.

Indeed, some colonists decried the STAMP ACT, a statute passed by Parliament that taxed everything from newspapers to playing cards, as an illegal attempt to raise revenue in violation of the Magna Charta. Other colonists cited "the assembly of barons at Runnymede, when Magna Carta was signed" as precedent for the Continental Congress (Bailyn 1992, 173 n. 13).

The achievement of the Magna Charta, then, is found not only in the original meaning understood by Englanders of the thirteenth century, but also in the subsequent application of the document's principles. The Magna Charta began as a peace treaty between the baronial class and the king, but later symbolized a written contract between the governed and the government, a contract that included the right of rebellion when the government grew despotic or ruled without popular consent.

The Magna Charta also came to represent the notion of government bound by the law, sometimes referred to as the rule of law. The distinction between government according to law and government according to the will of the sovereign has been drawn by legal and political philosophers for thousands of years. This distinction was also made during the reign of King John. For example, Peter Fitz Herbert, an important landowner, complained that his father had been "disseised" of land "by the will of the king" despite evidence that the land belonged to his family as a matter of "right."

In another case, jurors returned a verdict against the Crown because the king had acted "by his will and without judgment" (Holt 1965, 91). For subsequent generations, in both England and the United States, the Magna Charta signified the contrast between tyrannical government unfettered by anything but the personal whims of its political leadership, and representative government limited by the letter and spirit of the law. The Magna Charta implied that no government official, not even an autocratic monarch asserting absolute power, is above the law.

Finally, the Magna Charta has come to symbolize equality under the law. Although the baronial leadership of 1215 represented a privileged class of male landowners, many provisions of the Magna Charta safeguarded the interests of women as well. For example, the Magna Charta granted women the right to refuse marriage and the option to remarry. It also protected a widow's DOWER interest in one-third of her husband's property.

Some provisions of the Magna Charta applied more broadly to all "free" individuals (ch. 39), whereas other provisions seemingly applied to every person in the realm, free or not. Chapter 16, for example, stated that "no one" shall be compelled to perform service for a knight's fee, and chapter 42 guaranteed a safe return to "anyone" who left the realm.

The most telling provision in this regard was chapter 40, which provided that "justice" will be sold to "no one." This provision embodies more than the idea that justice is cheapened when bought and sold. It also underscores the principle that all persons, rich and poor, must be treated the same under the law. An extension of this principle was captured by the Equal Protection Clause of the FOURTEENTH AMENDMENT to the U.S. Constitution, which, as interpreted by the Supreme Court, invalidates laws that discriminate on the basis of, among other things, race, gender, national origin, and illegitimacy.

See also ENGLISH LAW; FEUDALISM.

MAGNUSON-MOSS WARRANTY ACT

The first federal statute to address the law of WARRANTY. The act (15 U.S.C.A. § 2301 et seq.) mandates that a written warranty on any consumer product that costs more than $5 must completely and conspicuously disclose, in easily understood words, the terms and conditions of the warranty. A warranty may guarantee several things, such as that the item will perform in a certain way or that the manufacturer will repair or replace the item if it is defective.

The Magnuson-Moss Warranty–Federal Trade Commission Improvement Act was sponsored by Senators Warren G. Magnuson and Frank E. Moss. Congress passed the act in 1975. Its purpose was to improve the information available to consumers, prevent deception, and improve competition in the marketing of consumer products, which are defined as property distributed in commerce and actually used for personal, family, or household purposes. The act provides a federal CAUSE OF ACTION for consumers who experience problems with warranted durable goods. If a plaintiff prevails against a seller in a lawsuit brought under the act, the plaintiff is entitled to recover all litigation expenses, including attorney's fees based on actual time expended, as determined by the court.

The Act does not require that manufacturers or sellers of consumer products provide written warranties. Instead, the act requires that manufacturers and sellers who do warrant their products to clearly disclose the terms of the warranty so that the consumer understands his or her rights under the warranty.

In addition, according to the act, a written warranty on a consumer product that costs more than $10 must be clearly labeled as "full" or "limited." A full warranty means that whoever promises to fix the item must do so in cases of defect or where the item does not conform to the warranty. This action must be done within a reasonable time and without charge. A limited warranty can contain reasonable restrictions regarding the responsibilities of the manufacturer or seller for the repair or replacement of the item.

See also CONSUMER PROTECTION.

MAIL COVER 📖 The process governed by the U.S. Postal Regulations (39 C.F.R. § 233.3) that allows the recording of all the information that appears on the outside cover of mail in any class, and also allows the recording of the contents of second-, third-, and fourth-class mail, international parcel post mail, and mail on which the appropriate postage has not been paid. 📖

Mail covers may be granted by the chief postal inspector, or a delegate of the inspector's, and are allowed upon the request of a law enforcement agency. The law enforcement agency's purpose must be to protect national security, locate a fugitive, obtain evidence of the commission or attempted commission of a crime, or help identify property, proceeds or ASSETS forfeitable under law.

To obtain a mail cover, the law enforcement agency must make a request in writing to the chief postal inspector, and must specify reasonable grounds demonstrating the necessity of the mail cover. The regulations do not define reasonable grounds, but in *Vreeken v. Davis*, 718 F.2d 343 (1983), the Tenth Circuit Court of Appeals held that a statement as to why the mail cover was necessary to an investigation, and that the subjects of the mail cover were under grand jury investigation, was sufficient. In *Vreeken* the court held that a letter stating that the plaintiffs were subjects of a grand jury investigation for tax fraud, and that the mail cover was necessary to identify promoters, finders, and investors involved in the alleged scheme, was enough to meet the requirements of the mail cover regulations. The court stated that the regulations do not include a requirement that the request contain "the factual predicate upon which it concludes that the subject of the mail cover is involved in the commission of a crime."

The constitutionality of mail cover has been challenged primarily as a violation of the FOURTH AMENDMENT right against unreasonable SEARCHES AND SEIZURES. Although the U.S. Supreme Court has not addressed this issue directly, lower courts have held that such a viola-

tion does not exist. Mail cover has been compared to the use of a pen register, which is a mechanical device that records the numbers dialed on a telephone without monitoring the conversation. The Supreme Court, in *Smith v. Maryland*, 442 U.S. 735, 99 S. Ct. 2577, 61 L. Ed. 2d 220 (1979), held that pen registers do not violate an individual's Fourth Amendment right to PRIVACY. The Court concluded that there is no reasonable expectation of privacy regarding the numbers dialed on a telephone because the user knows that the phone company receives those numbers. The court in *Vreeken* compared mail covers to pen registers

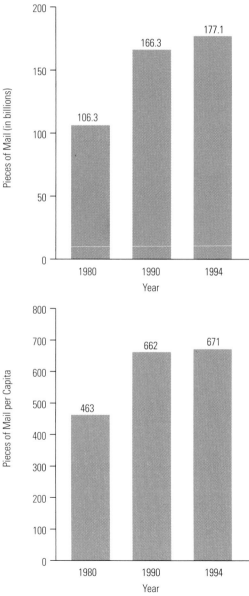

Volume of Mail Handled by U.S. Postal Service, 1980 to 1994

Source: U.S. Postal Service, *Annual Report of the Postmaster General*.

in that the contents of mail are not examined, and that a person sending or receiving mail should know that the information first goes to the post office and that the outside of the mail must be examined by employees of the post office before it can be delivered.

Mail covers also have been held not to violate the FIRST AMENDMENT, the NINTH AMENDMENT, or postal regulations.

MAIL FRAUD ◫ A crime in which the perpetrator develops a scheme using the mails to DEFRAUD another of money or property. This crime specifically requires the intent to defraud, and is a federal offense governed by section 1341 of title 18 of the U.S. Code. The mail fraud statute was first enacted in 1872 to prohibit illicit mailings with the Postal Service (formerly the Post Office) for the purpose of executing a FRAUDULENT scheme. ◫

Initially, courts strictly followed the mail fraud statute's language and interpreted it narrowly. The early decisions required a connection between the fraudulent scheme and the misuse of the mails for a violation of the mail fraud statute. Since its enactment, application of the statute has evolved to include dishonest and fraudulent activities with only a tangential relationship to the mails.

Punishment for a conviction under the mail fraud statute is a fine or imprisonment for not more than five years, or both. If, however, the violation affects a financial institution, the punishment is more severe: the statute provides that "the person shall be fined not more than $1,000,000 or imprisoned not more than 30 years, or both."

Both the Supreme Court and Congress have consistently broadened the mail fraud statute since its enactment. Prior to a 1909 amendment, a violation of the mail fraud statute required proof, among other requirements, of either opening or intending to open correspondence or communication with another person. In 1909 Congress eliminated this requirement and replaced it with the language that the mails be used "for the purpose of executing such scheme or artifice or attempting so to do." This amendment followed the Supreme Court's decision in *Durland v. United States*, 161 U.S. 306, 16 S. Ct. 508, 40 L. Ed. 709 (1896), which held that the mailing only needed to "assist" in the completion of the FRAUD. Although this amendment was the last significant change until 1988, the Supreme Court has struggled with the relationship between the mailing element and the execution of the fraud.

The Court's struggle with this relationship is illustrated by two of its decisions: *United States v. Maze*, 414 U.S. 395, 94 S. Ct. 645, 38 L. Ed. 2d 603 (1974), and *Schmuck v. United States*, 489 U.S. 705, 109 S. Ct. 1443, 103 L. Ed. 2d 734 (1989). In *Maze*, the defendant stole his roommate's credit card and car and signed his roommate's name to the charge vouchers to obtain food and lodging. The merchants mailed the invoices to a bank in Louisville, Kentucky. The Supreme Court held that this did not fall within the scope of the mail fraud statute because the mailings did not perpetuate the fraud. The Court held that the scheme did not depend on the mailings and that the fraud was completed once the defendant signed the vouchers. The Court refused to interpret the statute as merely a jurisdictional requirement and stated that "Congress could have drafted the mail fraud statute so as to require only that the mails be in fact used as a result of the fraudulent scheme."

However, in *Schmuck*, the Court did expand the mail fraud statute. In *Schmuck*, the defendant sold used cars to auto dealers in which he had rolled back the odometers to inflate the vehicles' value. The dealers sent TITLE application forms to the state department of transportation to register the cars after the dealers sold them to individual purchasers. The Court held that the sale of the vehicles depended on the TRANSFER of title and that, although the mailing of the registration may not have contributed directly to the scheme, it was necessary for the passage of title and perpetuation of the scheme.

In recent years Congress has amended the mail fraud statute twice. In 1988 Congress added section 1346, which states that the term "scheme to defraud" includes a scheme to deprive another of the intangible right of honest services. In 1994 Congress expanded the use of the mails to include any parcel that is "sent or delivered by a private or commercial interstate carrier." As a result of these amendments, the mail fraud statute has become a broad act for prosecution of dishonest and fraudulent activities, as long as those crimes involve the mails or an interstate CARRIER.

MAINE, HENRY JAMES SUMNER   Sir Henry James Sumner Maine was a leading nineteenth-century English jurist. Maine's writings on the social and historical bases of all legal systems have been recognized for their clarity of thought and style, though modern commentators have criticized him for overgeneralization.

Maine was born August 15, 1822, in Kelso, Scotland. He graduated from Cambridge University and was appointed a professor of civil law at Cambridge in 1847. He criticized legal education for teaching practical skills rather

BIOGRAPHY

*Henry James
Sumner Maine*

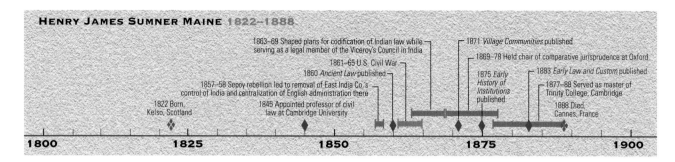

HENRY JAMES SUMNER MAINE 1822-1888

1863–69 Shaped plans for codification of Indian law while serving as a legal member of the Viceroy's Council in India

1871 *Village Communities* published

1869–78 Held chair of comparative jurisprudence at Oxford

1861–65 U.S. Civil War

1860 *Ancient Law* published

1875 *Early History of Institutions* published

1883 *Early Law and Custom* published

1857–58 Sepoy rebellion led to removal of East India Co.'s control of India and centralization of English administration there

1877–88 Served as master of Trinity College, Cambridge

1822 Born, Kelso, Scotland

1845 Appointed professor of civil law at Cambridge University

1888 Died, Cannes, France

1800   1825   1850   1875   1900

than the analysis of law as a science. His legal practice was limited, as he concentrated on publishing legal and political writings.

Maine first achieved prominence with the publication of *Ancient Law* in 1860. *Ancient Law* traced the historical development of law in the ancient world. In it Maine argued that there are two types of societies: static and progressive. Static societies include most of the non-Western world. Maine believed that countries such as India and China were locked in an unchanging world, bound by a fixed legal condition dominated by family dependency. In these societies laws had very limited application and were binding not on individuals but on families. The rule of conduct for the individual was the law of the home, as distinguished from civil law.

In contrast, Maine proposed, European societies were progressive, characterized by a desire to improve and develop. In progressive societies CIVIL LAW grew as a greater number of personal and property rights were removed from the domestic forum to the public tribunal. Maine saw the distinguishing feature in this movement as the gradual dissolution of family dependency and its replacement by individual obligation—as a movement from personal conditions to agreement, from status to contract.

Maine believed that the modern legal order would make talent and ability more important than race, sex, or family in shaping personal status. His beliefs in the evolution of Western law and progress in general struck a chord in the Anglo-American legal community. His theories were attractive to those in the United States who saw a powerful national economy reshaping society and creating opportunity for those who were willing to take risks and work hard.

Maine took a hiatus from his professorship in 1863, to serve as a legal member of the Viceroy's Council in India for six years. Upon his return to England in 1869, he resumed his legal scholarship, publishing *Village Communities* in 1871, *The Early History of Institutions* in 1875, and *Early Law and Custom* in 1883.

"EXCEPT THE BLIND FORCES OF NATURE, NOTHING MOVES ON THIS WORLD WHICH IS NOT GREEK IN ITS ORIGIN."

Maine's conclusions have been challenged in the twentieth century. Historians and social scientists have pointed out that many of his interpretations are false, based on limited information. Despite these shortcomings, Maine is still regarded as a seminal figure in JURISPRUDENCE. His use of historical and anthropological methods was groundbreaking, and his strong conceptual framework helped reshape the way legal developments are analyzed.

Maine died February 3, 1888, in Cannes, France.

MAINTENANCE Unauthorized intervention by a nonparty in a lawsuit, in the form of financial or other support and assistance to prosecute or defend the litigation. The preservation of an ASSET or of a condition of property by upkeep and necessary repairs.

A periodic monetary sum paid by one spouse for the benefit of the other upon separation or the dissolution of marriage; also called ALIMONY or spousal support.

At COMMON LAW the offense of CHAMPERTY AND MAINTENANCE arose when a stranger bargained with a party to a legal action, undertaking to pay for the litigation in exchange for a promise of a portion of the recovery. The common-law doctrines of champerty and maintenance were designed to stop vexatious and speculative litigation supported by officious intermeddlers (nonparties with improper motives). These common-law principles have been adopted in varying degrees in the United States, depending on the particular state.

The term *maintenance* is also used to describe the expenses of preserving property, which may be deductible according to the applicable state or federal tax laws. Maintenance expenses are typically recurring, with the goal of preserving the particular asset in its original condition, to prolong its useful life. Maintenance differs from a repair because a repair is an expenditure designed to return an asset to its normal operating condition.

In FAMILY LAW *maintenance* is often used as a synonym for *spousal support* or *alimony*, and the term is in fact replacing alimony. Traditionally, alimony was solely the right of the wife to be supported by the husband. In *Orr v. Orr*, 440 U.S. 268, 99 S. Ct. 1102, 59 L. Ed. 2d 306 (1979), the U.S. Supreme Court held that an Alabama statute (Ala. Code § 30-2-51 to 30-2-53 [1975]) that provided that only husbands could be required to pay alimony violated the EQUAL PROTECTION Clause of the FOURTEENTH AMENDMENT. Under current law alimony may be payment by either the wife or the husband in support of the other.

The award of spousal maintenance is generally determined based on all or some of the following guidelines: the recipient's financial needs; the payer's ability to pay; the age and health of the parties; the standard of living the recipient became accustomed to during the marriage; the length of the marriage; each party's ability to earn and be self-supporting; and the recipient's nonmonetary contributions to the marriage.

The amount and length of spousal maintenance payments may be agreed to by the parties and approved of by the court, or may be set by the court when the issue is contested. Some states have adopted financial schedules to help judges determine the appropriate level of support. Although maintenance generally takes the form of periodic payments of money directly to the recipient, it can also constitute a payment to a third party to satisfy an obligation of the receiving spouse. Maintenance may be set in a predetermined amount, such as $1,000 a month, or it may be a fluctuating percentage, such as 25 percent of the payer's gross income.

Spousal maintenance may be temporary or permanent. The parties generally may adjust its amount at a future date by returning to court and reassessing the relevant criteria at that time. In some states the parties may forever waive their right to spousal maintenance by written agreement.

Spousal maintenance payments always cease upon the death or remarriage of the recipient. Some states have adopted laws that provide for the termination of maintenance when the payer can show that the recipient is living with another person as if married, but has not remarried because he or she wants to continue to receive maintenance payments. Maintenance also generally terminates upon the death of the payer, although a minority of states will grant the receiving spouse a claim on the estate of the paying spouse. Alternatively, many states require the paying spouse to carry insurance on his or her life, payable to the recipient spouse, in lieu of granting the recipient the right to make a claim on the payer's estate.

Spousal maintenance that is periodic and made in discharge of a legal obligation is included in the gross income of the recipient and is deductible by the payer. Other voluntary payments, made by one spouse to the other, are not treated the same way by the tax code.

See also DIVORCE.

BIOGRAPHY

"THE HISTORY OF LAW MUST BE A HISTORY OF IDEAS."

MAITLAND, FREDERIC WILLIAM Frederic William Maitland pioneered the study of early English legal history. A talented and prolific scholar, Maitland imaginatively reconstructed the world of Anglo-Saxon law.

Maitland was born May 28, 1850, in London. He graduated from Cambridge University and then studied law at Lincoln's Inn. He joined the bar in 1876 and soon proved himself a skilled attorney. Maitland's interests subsequently shifted to the history of ENGLISH LAW. He set as his goal the writing of a scientific and philosophical history of English law that took into account its interaction with the social, economic, and cultural life of the English people. His first book, *Pleas of the Crown for the County of Gloucester*, was published to acclaim in 1884. In that year he left his law practice and became a reader in English law at Cambridge. In 1888 he was named a professor of law at Cambridge.

Between 1885 and 1906, Maitland published many volumes of English history, including *Justice and Police* (1885), *The History of English Law before the Time of Edward I* (with SIR FREDERICK POLLOCK, 1895), and *Domesday Book and Beyond* (1897). He also helped form the SELDEN SOCIETY, an association devoted to the preservation and analysis of Old English legal history. Maitland contributed many introductions to society publications, which mainly consisted of reprints of primary legal documents. Finally, Maitland was a popular lecturer. His published

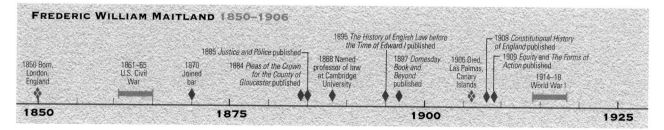

FREDERIC WILLIAM MAITLAND 1850–1906

1850 Born, London, England

1861–65 U.S. Civil War

1870 Joined bar

1884 *Pleas of the Crown for the County of Gloucester* published

1885 *Justice and Police* published

1888 Named professor of law at Cambridge University

1895 *The History of English Law before the Time of Edward I* published

1897 *Domesday Book and Beyond* published

1906 Died, Las Palmas, Canary Islands

1908 *Constitutional History of England* published

1909 *Equity* and *The Forms of Action* published

1914–18 World War I

1850   1875   1900   1925

lectures include *Constitutional History of England* (1908), *Equity* (1909), and *The Forms of Action* (1909).

As a historian, Maitland has been praised for his ability to grasp and articulate the great central themes underlying the development of the common law, and his ability to penetrate and render the inner meaning of words. He enjoyed being a historical detective, sifting through masses of often contradictory and confusing sources to find historical truth. Despite his respect for the English common-law tradition, Maitland was not an antiquarian. He actively supported the major law reform efforts of his day.

Maitland's historiography was not based on ideology or theory. History, to Maitland, was not the product of impersonal social or economic forces, but something more complex. Therefore, in the world described in his writings, individual personalities, particular events, cultural traditions, and the peculiarity of language play significant roles. Running through his work is a deep respect for the toughness, resiliency, and vitality of English COMMON LAW. Common-law lawyers and judges are intellectual and moral heroes in his evocation of medieval England.

Though many of Maitland's claims have been qualified or refuted by later research and scholarship, he is recognized as a seminal figure in the study of English legal history.

Maitland died December 19, 1906, at Las Palmas, Canary Islands.

MAJORITY Full age; legal age; age at which a person is no longer a MINOR. The age at which, by law, a person is capable of being legally responsible for all of his or her acts (e.g. contractual obligations), and is entitled to the management of his or her own affairs and to the enjoyment of civic rights (e.g. right to vote). The opposite of MINORITY. Also the *status* of a person who is a major in age.

The greater number. The number greater than half of any total.

The COMMON-LAW age of majority is twenty-one although state legislatures may change this age by statute. INFANTS reach the AGE OF MAJORITY on the first moment of the day preceding their twenty-first birthday. Minority is the period of time when a child is an infant.

MAKER One who makes, frames, executes, or ordains; as a *lawmaker;* or the *maker* of a PROMISSORY NOTE. One who signs a note to borrow and, as such, assumes the obligation to pay the note when due. The person who creates or executes a note, that is, issues it, and in signing the instrument makes the promise of payment contained therein. One who signs a CHECK; in this context, synonymous with DRAWER. One who issues a promissory note or CERTIFICATE OF DEPOSIT.

MALA FIDES [*Latin, Bad faith.*]

A *mala fide purchaser* is one who buys property from another with the knowledge that it has been stolen. In contrast, a BONA FIDE purchaser is one who does so with no knowledge that the seller lacks good TITLE to the property.

MALA IN SE Wrongs in themselves; acts morally wrong; offenses against conscience.

In criminal law, crimes are categorized as either *mala in se* or MALA PROHIBITA, a term that describes conduct that is specifically forbidden by laws. Although the distinction between the two classifications is not always clear, crimes *mala in se* are usually COMMON-LAW crimes or those dangerous to life or limb.

BATTERY and GRAND LARCENY or PETIT LARCENY are examples of offenses that courts have held to be *mala in se.*

MALA PROHIBITA [*Latin, Wrongs prohibited.*] A term used to describe conduct that is prohibited by laws, although not inherently evil.

Courts commonly classify statutory crimes as *mala prohibita.* This, however, is not a fixed rule since not all statutory crimes are classified as such.

Examples of *mala prohibita* include public intoxication and carrying a concealed weapon.

BIOGRAPHY

Malcolm X

MALCOLM X Malcolm X was a NATION OF ISLAM minister and a black nationalist leader in the United States during the 1950s and 1960s. Since his ASSASSINATION in 1965, his status as a political figure has grown considerably, and he has now become an internationally recognized political and cultural icon. The changes in Malcolm X's personal beliefs can be followed somewhat by the changes in his name, from Malcolm Little when he was a young man to Malcolm X when he was a member of the Nation of Islam to El-Hajj Malik El-Shabazz-Al-Sabann after he returned to the United States from a spiritual pilgrimage to Mecca in 1964. He was a ward of the state, a shoe shine boy in Boston, a street hustler and pimp in New York, and a convicted felon at the age of twenty. After embracing Islam in prison and directing his grassroots leadership and speaking skills to recruit members to the Nation of Islam, he ultimately became an influential black nationalist during the CIVIL RIGHTS MOVEMENT of the 1960s.

The fifth child in a family of eight children, Malcolm was born May 19, 1925, in Omaha, Nebraska. His father, Earl Little, was a Baptist

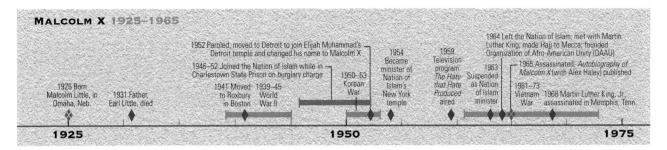

MALCOLM X 1925–1965

1925 Born Malcolm Little, in Omaha, Neb.

1931 Father, Earl Little, died

1941 Moved to Roxbury in Boston

1939–45 World War II

1946–52 Joined the Nation of Islam while in Charlestown State Prison on burglary charge

1952 Paroled; moved to Detroit to join Elijah Muhammad's Detroit temple and changed his name to Malcolm X

1950–53 Korean War

1954 Became minister of Nation of Islam's New York temple

1959 Television program *The Hate that Hate Produced* aired

1963 Suspended as Nation of Islam minister

1961–73 Vietnam War

1964 Left the Nation of Islam; met with Martin Luther King; made Hajj to Mecca; founded Organization of Afro-American Unity (OAAU)

1965 Assassinated; *Autobiography of Malcolm X* (with Alex Haley) published

1968 Martin Luther King, Jr. assassinated in Memphis, Tenn.

1925   1950   1975

minister and a local organizer for the Universal Negro Improvement Association, a black nationalist organization founded by Marcus M. Garvey in the early twentieth century. His mother, Louise Little, was of West Indian heritage. Malcom's father was killed under suspicious circumstances in 1931 and his mother had a breakdown in 1937.

After his father's death and his mother's commitment to a mental hospital, Malcolm was first placed with family friends, but the state welfare agency ultimately situated him in a juvenile home in Mason, Michigan, where he did well. Malcolm was an excellent student in junior high school, earning high grades as well as praise from his teachers. Despite his obvious talent, his status as an African American in the 1930s prompted his English teacher to discourage Malcolm from pursuing a professional career. The teacher instead encouraged him to work with his hands, perhaps as a carpenter.

In 1941, shortly after finishing eighth grade, Malcolm moved to Roxbury, a predominantly African American neighborhood in Boston. From 1941 to 1943, he lived in Roxbury with his half-sister ELLA LEE LITTLE-COLLINS. He worked at several jobs, including one as the shoe shine boy at the Roseland State Ballroom. He became what he later described as a Roxbury hipster, wearing outrageous zoot suits and dancing at local ballrooms.

Malcolm moved to Harlem in 1943, at the age of eighteen. Here, he earned the nickname Detroit Red, because of his Michigan background and the reddish hue to his skin and hair. In his early Harlem experience, Malcolm was a hustler, dope dealer, gambler, pimp, and numbers runner for mobsters.

In 1945, when his life was threatened by a Harlem mob figure named West Indian Archie, Malcolm returned to Boston, where he became involved in a burglary ring with an old Roxbury acquaintance. In 1946 he was caught attempting to reclaim a stolen watch he had left for repairs, and the police raided his apartment and arrested him and his accomplices, including two white women. He was charged with LARCENY and breaking and entering, to which he pleaded

"WE ARE NOT FIGHTING FOR INTEGRATION, NOR ARE WE FIGHTING FOR SEPARATION. WE ARE FIGHTING FOR RECOGNITION AS HUMAN BEINGS. WE ARE FIGHTING FOR . . . HUMAN RIGHTS."

guilty at trial. On February 27, 1946, he entered Charlestown State Prison to begin an eight- to ten-year sentence; he was twenty years old.

Malcolm was transferred in 1948 to an experimental and progressive prison program in Norfolk, Massachusetts. The Norfolk Prison Colony gave greater freedom to its inmates. It also had an excellent library, and Malcolm began to read voraciously. Prompted by his brother Reginald Little, Malcolm converted to Islam while in prison and became a follower of Elijah Muhammad, the leader of the Nation of Islam. The Nation of Islam, founded by Wallace D. Fard in the 1930s, advocated racial separatism and enforced a strict moral code for its followers, all of whom were African American.

Malcolm was paroled from prison in 1952. He immediately moved to Detroit, where he worked in a furniture store and attended the Nation of Islam Detroit temple. Malcolm soon abandoned the surname Little in favor of X, which represented the African surname he had never known. With his oratory skill, Malcolm X quickly became a national minister for the Nation of Islam. As a devout follower of Elijah Muhammad, he helped to establish numerous temples across the United States. He became the minister for temples in Boston and Philadelphia, and in 1954, he became minister of the New York temple. In 1958 he married Sister Betty X, who had earlier joined the Nation of Islam as Betty Sanders. Together, they had six children, including twins who were born after Malcolm's assassination.

During his early years with the Nation of Islam, Malcolm's primary role was as spokesman for Elijah Muhammad. He was a highly effective grassroots activist and successfully recruited thousands of urban blacks to join the organization. In 1959 a television program entitled *The Hate That Hate Produced* resulted in a focused public scrutiny of the Nation of Islam and its followers, who became known to many U.S. citizens as Black Muslims. Increasingly, Malcolm was seen as the national spokesman for the Black Muslims, and he was often sought out for his opinion on public issues. In vitriolic public speeches on behalf of the Nation of Islam, he described whites in the United States as devils and called for African Americans to reject any attempt to integrate them into a white racist society. As a Nation of Islam minister, he denounced Jews and criticized the more cautious mainstream civil rights leaders as traitors who had been brainwashed by a white society. He further challenged the so-called integrationist principles of recognized civil rights leaders such as MARTIN LUTHER KING, JR.

Elijah Muhammad took a somewhat less rash approach and favored a general nonengagement policy in place of more confrontational tactics. Malcolm's increasing popularity—as well as his caustic public remarks—began to create tension between him and Elijah Muhammad. Malcolm became frustrated at having to restrain his comments.

When President JOHN F. KENNEDY was assassinated on November 22, 1963, Malcolm exclaimed that Kennedy "never foresaw that the chickens would come home to roost so soon." Malcolm later regretted his comment and explained that he meant that the government's involvement in and tolerance of violence against African Americans and others had created an atmosphere that contributed to the death of the president. Nevertheless, his comments and his increasing public notoriety prompted Elijah Muhammad to "silence" Malcolm and suspend him as a minister on December 1, 1963. Members of the Nation of Islam were instructed not to speak to him.

However, by 1963, Malcolm had become disillusioned by the Nation of Islam, particularly with rumors that Elijah Muhammad had been unfaithful to his wife and had fathered several illegitimate children. On March 8, 1964—while still under suspension from the Nation of Islam—Malcolm formally announced his separation from the organization. He soon announced the creation of his own organization, Moslem Mosque, Incorporated (MMI), which would be based in New York. MMI, Malcolm stated, would be a broad-based black nationalist organization intended to advance the spiritual, economic, and political interests of African Americans. On March 26, Malcolm met for the first and only time with the Reverend King, in Washington, D.C. King at the time was scheduled to testify on the pending CIVIL RIGHTS ACT of 1964.

In April 1964, Malcolm made a spiritual pilgrimage to Mecca, the holy site of Islam and the birthplace of the prophet Muhammad. He was profoundly moved by the pilgrimage, and said later that it was the start of a radical alteration in his outlook about race relations.

Upon his return to the United States, Malcolm began to use the name El-Hajj Malik El-Shabazz Al-Sabann. He also exhibited a profound shift in political and social thinking. Whereas in the past he had advocated against cooperation with other civil rights leaders and organizations, his new philosophy was to work with existing organizations and individuals, including whites, so long as they were sincere in their efforts to secure basic CIVIL RIGHTS and freedoms for African Americans. In June 1964, he founded the secular Organization of Afro-American Unity (OAAU), which espoused a pan-Africanist approach to basic human rights, particularly the rights of African Americans. He traveled and spoke extensively in Africa to gain support for his pan-Africanist views. He pledged to bring the condition of African Americans before the General Assembly of the UNITED NATIONS and thereby "internationalize" the civil rights movement in the United States. He further pledged to do whatever was necessary to bring the black struggle from the level of civil rights to the level of human rights. When he advocated for the right of African Americans to use arms to defend themselves against violence, he not only laid the groundwork for a subsequent growth of the black power movement, but also led many U.S. citizens to believe that he advocated violence. However, in his autobiography, Malcolm said that he was not advocating wanton violence but calling for the right of individuals to use arms in self-defense when the law failed to protect them from violent assaults.

In 1965 Malcolm's increasing public criticism of Elijah Muhammad and the Nation of Islam prompted anonymous threats against his life. In his attempts to forge relationships with established civil rights organizations such as the STUDENT NON-VIOLENT COORDINATING COMMITTEE, Malcolm was criticized severely in the Nation of Islam's official publications. In a December 1964 article in *Muhammad Speaks*—the official newspaper of the Nation of Islam—Louis X (now known as Louis Farrakhan) said, "[S]uch a man as Malcolm is worthy of death, and would have met with death if it had not been for Muhammad's confidence in Allah for victory over the enemies."

On February 14, 1965, Malcolm's home in Queens, New York—which was still owned by the Nation of Islam—was firebombed while he and his family were asleep. Malcolm attributed the bombing to Nation of Islam supporters but no one was ever charged with the crime. One week later, when Malcolm stepped to the podium at the Audubon Ballroom in New York to present a speech on behalf of the OAAU, he was assassinated. The gunmen, later identified as former or current members of the Nation of Islam, were convicted and sentenced to life imprisonment in April 1966.

Malcolm left a complex political and social legacy. Although he was primarily a black nationalist in perspective, his changing philosophy and politics toward the end of his life demonstrate the unfinished development of an influential figure. Although some people point to his identification with the Nation of Islam and dismiss him as a racial extremist and anti-Semite, his later thinking reveals profound changes in his perspective and a more universal understanding of the problems of African Americans. In his eulogy of Malcolm, the U.S. actor Ossie Davis said,

> However we may have differed with him—or with each other about him and his value as a man—let his going from us serve only to bring us together, now. Consigning these mortal remains to earth, the common mother of all, secure in the knowledge that what we place in the ground is no more now a man—but a seed—which, after the winter of our discontent, will come forth again to meet us.

MALFEASANCE 📖 The commission of an act that is unequivocally illegal or completely wrongful. 📖

Malfeasance is a comprehensive term used in both civil and criminal law to describe any act that is wrongful. It is not a distinct CRIME or TORT, but may be used generally to describe any act that is criminal or that is wrongful and gives rise to, or somehow contributes to, the injury of another person.

Malfeasance is an affirmative act that is illegal or wrongful. In tort law it is distinct from MISFEASANCE, which is an act that is not illegal but is improperly performed. It is also distinct from NONFEASANCE, which is a failure to act that results in injury.

The distinctions between malfeasance, misfeasance, and nonfeasance have little effect on tort law. Whether a claim of injury is for one or the other, the plaintiff must prove that the defendant owed a duty of CARE, that the duty was breached in some way, and that the breach caused injury to the plaintiff.

One exception is that under the law of STRICT LIABILITY, the plaintiff need not show the absence of due care. The law of strict liability usually is applied to PRODUCT LIABILITY cases, where a manufacturer can be held liable for harm done by a product that was harmful when it was placed on the market. In such cases the plaintiff need not show any actual malfeasance on the part of the manufacturer. A MISTAKE is enough to create LIABILITY because the law implies that for the sake of public safety, a manufacturer warrants a product's safety when it offers the product for sale.

The actions of Los Angeles residents who rioted and looted in the wake of the 1992 Rodney King trial verdict clearly represented malfeasance, a breach of the duty of care.

CHROMOSOHM/SOHM/STOCK BOSTON

MALICE 📖 The intentional commission of a wrongful act, absent justification, with the intent to cause harm to others; conscious violation of the law that injures another individual; a mental state indicating a disposition in disregard of social duty and a tendency toward MALFEASANCE. 📖

In its legal application, the term *malice* is comprehensive and applies to any legal act that is committed intentionally without just cause or excuse. It does not necessarily imply personal hatred or ill feelings, but is the mental state that is in reckless disregard of the law in general and of the legal rights of others. An example of a malicious act would be committing the tort of slander by labeling a nondrinker an alcoholic in front of all his or her employees.

When applied to the crime of MURDER, malice is the mental condition that motivates one individual to take the life of another individual without just cause or provocation.

MALICE AFORETHOUGHT 📖 A predetermination to commit an act without legal justification or excuse. A malicious design to injure. An intent, at the time of a killing, willfully to take the life of a human being, or an intent willfully to act in callous and wanton disregard of the consequences to human life; but *malice aforethought* does not necessarily imply any ill will, spite or hatred towards the individual killed. 📖

MALICIOUS 📖 Involving MALICE; characterized by wicked or mischievous motives or intentions. 📖

An act done maliciously is one that is wrongful and performed willfully or intentionally, and without legal justification.

MALICIOUS MISCHIEF 📖 Willful destruction of PERSONAL PROPERTY of another, from actual ill will or resentment towards its owner or possessor. Though only a TRESPASS at the COMMON LAW, it is now a MISDEMEANOR in most states. 📖

MALICIOUS PROSECUTION 📖 An ACTION for DAMAGES brought by one against whom a civil suit or criminal proceeding has been unsuccessfully commenced without PROBABLE CAUSE and for a purpose other than that of bringing the alleged offender to justice. 📖

An action for malicious prosecution is the remedy for baseless and malicious litigation. It is not limited to criminal prosecutions, but may be brought in response to any baseless and malicious litigation or prosecution, whether criminal or civil. The criminal DEFENDANT or civil RESPONDENT in a baseless and malicious case may later file this claim in civil court against the parties who took an active role in initiating or encouraging the original case. The defendant in the initial case becomes the PLAINTIFF in the malicious prosecution suit, and the plaintiff or prosecutor in the original case becomes the defendant. In most states the claim must be filed within a year after the end of the original case.

A claim of malicious prosecution is a TORT action. A tort action is filed in civil court to recover money damages for certain harm suffered. The plaintiff in a malicious prosecution suit seeks to win money from the respondent as recompense for the various costs associated with having to defend against the baseless and vexatious case.

The public policy that supports the action for malicious prosecution is the discouragement of vexatious litigation. This policy must compete against one that favors the freedom of law enforcement officers, judicial officers, and private citizens to participate and assist in the administration of justice.

In most JURISDICTIONS an action for malicious prosecution is governed by the COMMON LAW. This means that the authority to bring the action lies in CASE LAW from the courts, not statutes from the legislature. Most legislatures maintain some statutes that give certain persons IMMUNITY from malicious prosecution for certain acts. In Colorado, for example, a merchant, a merchant's employee, or a police officer, who reasonably suspects that a theft has occurred, may detain and question the suspect without fear of LIABILITY for slander, false arrest, false imprisonment, unlawful detention, or malicious prosecution (Colo. Rev. Stat. Ann. § 18-4-407 [West 1996]).

An action for malicious prosecution is distinct from an action for FALSE ARREST or FALSE IMPRISONMENT. If a person is arrested by a police officer who lacks legal authority for the arrest, the proper remedy is an action for false arrest. If a person is confined against her or his will, the proper remedy is an action for false imprisonment. An action for malicious prosecution is appropriate only where the judicial system has been misused.

Elements of Proof To win a suit for malicious prosecution, the plaintiff must prove four elements: (1) that the original case was terminated in favor of the plaintiff, (2) that the defendant played an active role in the original case, (3) that the defendant did not have probable cause or REASONABLE grounds to support the original case, and (4) that the defendant initiated or continued the initial case with an improper purpose. Each of these elements presents a challenge to the plaintiff.

The Original Case Was Terminated in Favor of the Plaintiff The original case must end before the defendant or respondent in that case may file a malicious prosecution suit. This requirement is relatively easy to prove. The original case qualifies as a prosecution if the defendant or respondent had to appear in court. The original case need not have gone to trial: it is enough that the defendant or respondent was forced to answer to a COMPLAINT in court. If the original case is being appealed, it is not considered terminated, and the defendant or respondent must wait to file a malicious prosecution suit.

To proceed with a malicious prosecution claim, the plaintiff must show that the original case was concluded in her or his favor. Generally, if the original case was a criminal prosecution, it must have been dismissed by the court, rejected by the GRAND JURY, abandoned by the prosecutor, or decided in favor of the accused at trial or on APPEAL. If the original case was a civil suit, the respondent must have won at trial, or the trial court must have disposed of the case in favor of the respondent (now the plaintiff).

If recovery by the plaintiff in a CIVIL ACTION was later reversed on appeal, this does not mean that the action was terminated in favor of the respondent. However, if the plaintiff in the original case won by submitting fabricated evidence or by other fraudulent activity, a reversal on such grounds may be deemed a termination in favor of the respondent. A settlement between the plaintiff and the respondent in a civil suit is not a termination in favor of the respondent. Likewise, courts do not consider a plea bargain in a criminal case to be a termination in favor of the defendant.

The Defendant Played an Active Role in the Original Case In a malicious prosecution suit, the plaintiff must prove that the defendant played an active role in procuring or continuing the original case. The plaintiff must prove that the defendant did more than simply participate in the original case. False TESTIMONY alone, for example, does not constitute malicious prosecution. Moreover, WITNESSES are immune from suit for DEFAMATION, even if they lie on the witness stand. This is because the concept of a fair and free trial requires that witnesses testify without fear of having to defend a defamation suit owing to their testimony.

An action for malicious prosecution focuses on the abuse of legal process, not on defamatory, untruthful statements. If a person helps another person launch a baseless case or takes action to direct or aid such a case, the first person may be held liable for malicious pros-

ecution. The defendant must have been responsible in some way for the institution or continuation of the baseless case. This position of responsibility does not always include criminal prosecutors and civil plaintiffs. For example, if a prosecutor bringing criminal charges is tricked into prosecuting the case by an untruthful third party, the deceiving party is the one who may be found liable for malicious prosecution, not the prosecutor.

The Defendant Did Not Have Probable Cause to Support the Original Case The plaintiff must prove that the person who began or continued the original case did not have probable cause to do so. Generally, this means proving that the person did not have a reasonable belief in the plaintiff's guilt or liability. In examining this element, a court will look at several factors, including the reliability of any sources, the availability of information, the effort required to obtain information, opportunities given to the accused to offer an explanation, the accused's reputation, and the necessity in the original case for speedy judicial action.

A failure to fully investigate the facts surrounding a case may be sufficient to prove a lack of probable cause. The termination of the original case in favor of the original defendant (now the plaintiff) may help to prove a lack of probable cause, but it may not be decisive on the issue. The plaintiff should present enough facts to allow a REASONABLE PERSON to infer that the defendant acted without a reasonable belief in the plaintiff's guilt or liability in beginning or continuing the original case.

In a criminal case, an ACQUITTAL does not constitute a lack of probable cause. A criminal defendant stands a better chance of proving lack of probable cause if the original case was dismissed by prosecutors, a grand jury, or the court before the case went to trial. The criminal process provides several safeguards against prosecutions that lack probable cause, so a full criminal trial tends to show the presence of probable cause. Civil cases do not have the same safeguards, so a full civil trial does not tend to prove probable cause.

The Defendant Initiated or Continued the Original Case with an Improper Purpose In a malicious prosecution, the plaintiff must prove with specific facts that the defendant instituted or continued the original proceeding with an improper purpose. Sheer ill will constitutes an improper purpose, and it may be proved with facts that show that the defendant resented the plaintiff or wanted somehow to harm the plaintiff. However, the plaintiff does not have to prove that the defendant felt personal MALICE or hostility toward the plaintiff. Rather, the plaintiff need only show that the defendant was motivated by something other than the purpose of bringing the plaintiff to justice.

Few defendants admit to improper purposes, so improper purpose usually must be inferred from facts and circumstances. If the plaintiff cannot discover any apparent purpose, improper purpose can be inferred from the lack of probable cause.

Hodges v. Gibson Products Co. *Hodges v. Gibson Products Co.*, 811 P.2d 151 (Utah 1991), contained all the elements of a malicious prosecution. According to Chad Crosgrove, the manager of Gibson Discount Center in West Valley, Utah, store money was noticed missing during the afternoon of September 4, 1981. Both Crosgrove and part-time bookkeeper Shauna Hodges had access to the money, and both denied taking it. On September 9 Crosgrove and Gibson officials went to the local police station, where they lodged an accusation of theft against Hodges. Crosgrove was not accused. Hodges was arrested, handcuffed, and taken to jail. After a preliminary hearing, she was released on BAIL and ordered to return for trial on May 12, 1982.

After Hodges was formally charged, an internal audit at Gibson revealed that Crosgrove had embezzled approximately $9,000 in cash and goods from the store. The thefts had occurred over a time period that included September 4, 1981. Gibson still did not charge Crosgrove with theft. Instead, it allowed him to resign with a promise to repay the money.

The night before Hodges's trial was to begin, and almost two months after Crosgrove's EMBEZZLEMENT was discovered, management at Gibson notified Hodges's prosecutor of Crosgrove's activities. The prosecutor immediately dropped the charges against Hodges. Hodges then filed a suit for malicious prosecution against Gibson and against Crosgrove.

At trial Hodges was able to prove all the elements of malicious prosecution to the jury's satisfaction: (1) She had been subjected to prosecution for theft, and the matter had been terminated in her favor. (2) She had sued the correct parties, because Gibson and Crosgrove were responsible for instituting the original proceedings against her. (3) She had ample evidence that the original prosecution was instituted without probable cause, because Gibson failed to investigate Crosgrove until after she had been arrested, and because the prosecutor dismissed the charges against her. (4) Finally, there were enough facts for the jury to infer

that both Gibson and Crosgrove had acted with improper MOTIVE: Gibson had acted with an apparent BIAS against Hodges, and Crosgrove apparently had accused Hodges for self-preservation. The jury awarded Hodges a total of $88,000 in damages: $77,000 from Gibson, and $11,000 from Crosgrove. The verdict was upheld on appeal.

Damages The plaintiff in an action for malicious prosecution can recover money from the defendant for certain harms suffered. Typical injuries include loss of reputation and credit, humiliation, and mental suffering. If the original action was a criminal case, additional harms often include discomfort, injury to health, loss of time, and deprivation of society with family.

If the plaintiff suffered an economic loss directly related to the original action, the plaintiff can also recover the amount lost. This includes attorneys' fees and court costs incurred by the plaintiff in defending the original case.

Finally, the plaintiff may recover punitive damages. Punitive damages are imposed by judges and juries to punish misconduct by a party. Because an action for malicious prosecution requires proof of improper intent on the part of the defendant, punitive damages commonly are awarded to malicious prosecution plaintiffs who win damages awards.

Other Considerations Actions for malicious prosecution must compete against the PUBLIC INTEREST in allowing parties to pursue cases unfettered by the specter of a retaliatory case. Very few civil or criminal cases result in an action for malicious prosecution. This is because it is difficult to prove that the defendant procured or continued the original case without probable cause and with an improper purpose.

Another difficulty for the plaintiff in an action for malicious prosecution is immunity. Generally, the law protects witnesses, police officers, judges, prosecutors, and lawyers from suit for malicious prosecution. Witnesses are given immunity because justice requires that they testify without fear of reprisals. Law enforcement and judicial officers are given immunity because they must be free to perform their duties without continually defending against malicious prosecution cases.

There are exceptions. If a law enforcement or judicial official ventures outside the bounds of official duties to instigate or continue a malicious prosecution, the official may be vulnerable to a malicious prosecution suit. For example, a prosecutor who solicits fabricated testimony to present to a grand jury may be sued for malicious prosecution. The prosecutor would receive only limited immunity in this instance because the solicitation of evidence is an administrative function, not a prosecutorial function (*Buckley v. Fitzsimmons*, 509 U.S. 259, 113 S. Ct. 2606, 125 L. Ed. 2d 209 [1993]).

Private parties may also at times enjoy immunity from actions for malicious prosecution. For example, a person who complains to a disciplinary committee about an attorney may be immune. This general rule is followed by courts to avoid discouraging the reporting of complaints against attorneys.

MALPRACTICE 📖 The breach by a member of a profession of either a standard of care or a standard of conduct. 📖

Malpractice refers to NEGLIGENCE or misconduct by a professional person, such as a lawyer, a doctor, a dentist, or an accountant. The failure to meet a standard of care or standard of conduct that is recognized by a profession reaches the level of malpractice when a client or patient is injured or damaged because of error.

After the 1970s the number of malpractice suits filed against professionals greatly increased. Most malpractice suits involved doctors, especially surgeons and other specialists who performed medical procedures with a high degree of risk to their patients. Large damage awards against doctors resulted in higher malpractice INSURANCE costs. Similarly, the increase of malpractice awards against lawyers led to higher insurance PREMIUMS and caused some insurance companies to stop writing malpractice policies altogether.

The typical malpractice suit will allege the TORT of negligence by the professional. Negligence is conduct that falls below the legally established standard for the protection of others against unreasonable risk of harm. Under negligence law a person must violate a REASONABLE standard of care. Typically this has meant the customary or usual practice of members of the profession. For example, if a surgeon leaves a sponge or surgical tool inside a patient, the surgeon's carelessness violates a basic standard of care. Likewise, if an ATTORNEY fails to file a lawsuit for a client within the time limits required by law, the attorney may be charged with negligence.

Medical Malpractice Among physicians, malpractice is any bad, unskilled, or negligent treatment that injures the patient. The standard of care formerly was considered to be the customary practice of a particular area or locality. Most states have modified the "locality rule" into an evaluation of the standard of practice in the same or similar locality, combined with an examination of the state of development of medical science at the time of the incident. This modification has taken place as medicine has become increasingly uniform and national in scope. A majority of states define the standard of conduct as that degree of skill and learning ordinarily possessed and used by other members of the profession. A doctor who has met the standard, as established by expert TESTIMONY at trial, cannot generally be found negligent. Some states have passed statutes that establish the standard of the profession as the test of whether particular treatment was negligent.

Specialists within the medical field are generally held to standards of care that are higher than those for general practitioners. In addition, a specialist or anyone undertaking to perform procedures ordinarily done by a specialist will be held to the level of performance applied to that specialty, although the person may not actually be a certified specialist in that field.

A small number of states apply the "respectable minority rule" in evaluating doctors' conduct. This rule exempts a physician from LIABILITY where he chooses to follow a technique used only by a small number of respected practitioners. Courts, however, frequently have difficulty in determining what is a respectable minority of physicians or acceptable support for a particular technique.

Some states use the "error in judgment rule." This principle holds that a medical professional who otherwise subscribes to applicable professional standards should not be found to have committed malpractice merely because she committed an error in judgment in choosing among different therapeutic approaches or in diagnosing a condition.

Legal Malpractice The four general areas of legal malpractice are negligent errors, negligence in the professional relationship, fee

Dr. Richard Thompson and Beth Korinek work for Colorado Personalized Education for Physicians, an organization that assists doctors who face complaints ranging from poor bedside manner to malpractice.

disputes, and claims filed by an adversary or nonclient against a lawyer. As in the medical field, lawyers must conform to standards of conduct recognized by the profession.

A lawyer has the duty, in all dealings and relations with a client, to act with honesty, GOOD FAITH, fairness, integrity, and fidelity. A lawyer must possess the legal skill and knowledge that is ordinarily possessed by members of the profession.

Even after the lawyer and the client terminate their relationship, a lawyer is not permitted to acquire an interest that is adverse to a client, in the event that this might constitute a breach of the ATTORNEY-CLIENT PRIVILEGE. A lawyer cannot use information that he obtained from a client as a result of their relationship. For example, it would constitute unethical behavior for an attorney to first advise a client to sell a piece of property so it would not be included in the client's property settlement upon divorce and then to purchase the property from the client for half its market value.

Any dealings that a lawyer has with a client will be carefully examined. Such dealings require fairness and honesty, and the lawyer must show that no UNDUE INFLUENCE was exercised and that the client received the same benefits and advantages as if she had been dealing with a stranger. If the client had independent legal advice about any transaction, that is usually sufficient to meet the lawyer's burden to prove fairness.

A lawyer also has the duty to provide a client with a full, detailed, and accurate account of all money and property handled for her. The client is entitled to receive anything that the lawyer has acquired in violation of his duties to the client.

If a lawyer fails to promptly pay all funds to his client, the lawyer may be required to pay interest. A lawyer is liable for FRAUD—except when the client caused the attorney to commit fraud—and is generally liable for any DAMAGES resulting to the client by his negligence. In addition, a lawyer is responsible for the acts of his associates, clerks, legal assistants, and partners and may be liable for their acts if they result in losses to the client.

Negligent errors are most commonly associated with legal malpractice. This category is based on the premise that an attorney has committed an error that would have been avoided by a competent attorney who exercises a reasonable standard of care. Lawyers who give improper advice, improperly prepare documents, fail to file documents, or make a faulty analysis in examining the TITLE to REAL ESTATE may be charged with malpractice by their clients. A legal malpractice ACTION, however, is not likely to succeed if the lawyer committed an error because an issue of law was unsettled or debatable.

Many legal malpractice claims are filed because of negligence in the professional relationship. The improper and unprofessional handling of the attorney-client relationship leads to negligence claims that are not based on the actual services provided. Lawyers who fail to communicate with their clients about the difficulties and realities of the particular claim risk malpractice suits from dissatisfied clients who believe that their lawyer was responsible for losing the case.

Another area of legal malpractice involves fee disputes. When attorneys sue clients for attorneys' fees, many clients assert malpractice as a defense. As a defense, it can reduce or totally eliminate the lawyer's recovery of fees. The frequency of these claims is declining, in part perhaps because attorneys are reluctant to sue to recover their fees.

A final area of legal malpractice litigation concerns claims that do not involve a deficiency in the quality of the lawyer's legal services provided to the client, but an injury caused to a third party because of the lawyer's representation. This category includes tort claims filed against an attorney alleging MALICIOUS PROSECUTION, ABUSE OF PROCESS, DEFAMATION, infliction of emotional distress, and other theories based on the manner in which the attorney represented the client. These suits rarely are successful except for malicious prosecution. Third-party claims also arise from various statutes, such as securities regulations, and MOTIONS for SANCTIONS, such as under Federal Rule of Civil Procedure 11.

CROSS-REFERENCES

Attorney Misconduct; Ethics; Health Care Law; Medical Malpractice; Physicians and Surgeons; Privileged Communications.

MANAGED CARE A general term that refers to health plans that attempt to control the cost and quality of care by coordinating medical and other health-related services.

The U.S. health care system has undergone major structural changes since the 1970s. The traditional way of obtaining medical care has been for a patient to choose a doctor and then pay that doctor for the services provided. This "fee-for-service" model, which has been financially rewarding for doctors, gives the patient the right to choose her physician. But the fee-for-service model has undergone a rapid

Enrollment in Health Maintenance Organizations, 1976 to 1995

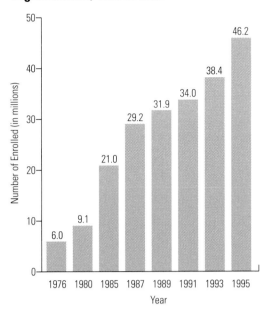

Source: *Health United States 1995*, National Center for Health Statistics, U.S. Department of Health and Human Services.

decline in the 1980s and 1990s as the concept of managed care has taken hold in the health care system.

Managed care is a new term for an old medical financing plan known as the HMO, or health maintenance organization. HMOs are not insured plans. They are prepaid health care systems, offering services to which the member is entitled, as opposed to a dollar amount guaranteed by an INSURANCE policy. Doctors are paid a set amount of money monthly for each patient regardless of the level or frequency of care provided.

HMOs emphasize preventive care and have become popular with employers who must purchase health care coverage for their employees because HMOs charge lower fees than insurance plans that reimburse patients for fee-for-service payments. Holding down the cost of medical care has been one of the chief aims of HMOs.

The first HMOs were started around 1930. The Kaiser Foundation Health Plan of California was one of the first and largest HMOs. Another large HMO is the Health Insurance Plan of Greater New York. Both Kaiser and Health Plan also have their own hospitals. The federal government has promoted HMOs since the 1970s, enacting the Health Maintenance Organization Act of 1973, 87 Stat. 931, and other legislation that allows HMOs to meet federal standards for MEDICARE and MEDICAID eligibility.

A person who participates in an HMO deals with a primary care physician, who directs the person's medical care and determines if he should be referred for specialty care. This "gatekeeper" function has drawn both criticism and praise. Critics argue that a person can be tied down to a physician not of his choosing, who has complete control over whether the person will be seen by a specialist or be given special drugs or treatments. Critics also argue that HMO physicians are not allowed to perform thorough testing procedures because of the demands of HMO management to limit costs and that this ultimately leads to rationing of medical treatment.

Advocates of HMOs and managed care argue that it is an advantage to the patient to have one physician with full responsibility for her care. With few exceptions, these primary care physicians are trained as general practitioners, family practice physicians, pediatricians, internists, or obstetrician-gynecologists.

The debate over national health care reform escalated during the first term of the Clinton administration. President BILL CLINTON sought to overhaul the U.S. health care system by guaranteeing universal coverage while simultaneously controlling costs. His plan, which emphasized the managed care model, died in Congress, yet managed care continues to grow. Medicaid, the state-operated but federally and state-funded health care plan for the poor, started in 1966 as a fee-for-service program. By the 1990s, the conversion of Medicaid to a managed care model of service delivery had grown rapidly, serving as many as ten million people.

Serious questions remain, however, about the cost and medical effectiveness of managed care. Critics worry that efforts to contain costs will come at the expense of patient care. Others argue that patients lose their freedom of choice when they cannot select their physician.

CROSS-REFERENCES

Clinton, Hillary Rodham; Health Care Law; Health Insurance; Physicians and Surgeons.

MANAGER ◨ One who has charge of a CORPORATION and control of its business, or of its branch establishments, divisions, or departments, and who is vested with a certain amount of discretion and independent judgment. A person chosen or appointed to manage, direct, or administer the affairs of another person or of a business, sports team, or the like. The designation of *manager* implies general power and permits reasonable inferences that the employee so designated is invested with the general conduct and control of the employer's business. 📖

MANDAMUS 📖 [*Latin, We comand.*] A WRIT or order that is issued from a court of superior JURISDICTION that commands an inferior tribunal, CORPORATION, MUNICIPAL CORPORATION, or individual to perform, or refrain from performing, a particular act, the performance or omission of which is required by law as an obligation. 📖

A writ or order of mandamus is an extraordinary court order because it is made without the benefit of full judicial process, or before a case has concluded. It may be issued by a court at any time that it is appropriate, but it is usually issued in a case that has already begun.

Generally, the decisions of a lower-court made in the course of a continuing case will not be reviewed by higher COURTS until there is a final JUDGMENT in the case. On the federal level,

A sample petition for writ of mandamus

IN THE SUPREME COURT OF THE STATE OF _____

STATE OF _____, Plaintiff

v.

_____ , Defendant

Criminal Action No. _____

PETITION FOR WRIT OF MANDAMUS TO THE

_____ COURT OF _____ COUNTY

On _____, 19____, in the _____ Court of _____ County, a charge or charges of _____ (offense or offenses) (was) (were) filed against me. A warrant or order for my arrest on these charges is outstanding. I was sentenced in the United States District Court for the _____ District of _____, on the date of _____ _____, _____, to a term of _____
[Month]   [Day]   [Year]
[State]

years' imprisonment and am now confined in the United States Medical Center for Federal Prisoners, Springfield, Missouri.

A request for future delivery of my person and for execution of the warrant or order of arrest mentioned above, based upon the above charges in the _____ Court of _____ County, is now lodged with the Bureau of Prisons of the United States which is adversely affecting my eligibility for release from federal custody and the conditions of my confinement. Further, I am, or have been, denied a speedy trial. Therefore, I filed in the above court, where the charges are pending against me a (motion for speedy trial or for dismissal of the charges against me) (motion to dismiss the charges against me) on _____ _____, _____, requesting such relief under the
[Month]   [Day]   [Year]

authority of Smith v. Hooey, 393 U.S. 374, 89 S. Ct. 575, 21 L. Ed. 2d 607. To date, I have received no notice of that court's having acted on that motion.

Therefore, I petition this Court for its writ of mandamus directing the _____ Court of _____ County to act upon my said motion, any other available remedy being inadequate under the circumstances of my case.

_____
[Signature of Petitioner]

} ss.

_____, being first duly sworn under oath, represents that he has subscribed to the foregoing petition and does state that the information is true and correct to the best of his knowledge and belief.

_____
[Signature of Affiant]

Subscribed and sworn to before me this _____ day of _____, _____.
[Month]   [Year]

_____
Notary Public

My commission expires: _____

for example, 28 U.S.C.A. § 1291 provides that APPELLATE review of lower-court decisions should be postponed until after a final judgment has been made in the lower court. A writ of mandamus offers one exception to this rule. If a party to a case is dissatisfied with some decision of the trial court, the party may appeal the decision to a higher court with a PETITION for a writ of mandamus before the trial proceeds. The order will be issued only in exceptional circumstances.

The writ of mandamus was first used by English courts in the early seventeenth century. It migrated to the courts in the American colonies, and the law on it has remained largely the same ever since. The remedy of mandamus is made available through court opinions, statutes, and court rules on both the federal and state levels. On the federal level, for example, 28 U.S.C.A. § 1651(a) provides that courts "may issue all writs necessary or appropriate in aid of their respective jurisdictions and agreeable to the usages and principles of law."

The Supreme Court set forth some guidelines on writs of mandamus in *Kerr v. United States District Court*, 426 U.S. 394, 96 S. Ct. 2119, 48 L. Ed. 2d 725 (1976). In *Kerr*, the Court upheld the denial of a writ of mandamus sought by prison officials to prevent the district court from compelling them to turn over personnel and inmate files to seven prisoners who had sued the prison over alleged constitutional violations. The officials argued that turning over the records would compromise prison communications and confidentiality.

The Supreme Court observed in *Kerr* that the writ of mandamus was traditionally used by FEDERAL COURTS only to confine an inferior court to a lawful exercise of its jurisdiction, or to compel an INFERIOR COURT to exercise its authority when it had a duty to do so. The Court also noted that mandamus is available only in exceptional cases because it is so disruptive of the judicial process, creating disorder and delay in the trial. The writ would have been appropriate, opined the Court, if the trial court had wrongly decided an issue, if failure to reverse that decision would irreparably injure a party, and if there was no other method for relief. Because the prison officials could claim a privilege to withhold certain documents, and had the right to have the documents reviewed by a judge prior to release to the opposing party, other remedies existed and the writ was inappropriate.

Although traditionally writs of mandamus are rare, they have been issued in a growing number of situations. They have been issued by federal courts when a trial judge refused to dismiss a case even though it lacked jurisdiction; refused to reassign a case despite a CONFLICT OF INTEREST; stopped a trial for ARBITRATION or an administrative remedy; denied a party the opportunity to intervene, to file a CROSS-CLAIM, or to amend a PLEADING; denied a CLASS ACTION; denied or allowed the consolidation or severance of two trials; refused to permit DEPOSITIONS; or entered an order limiting or denying DISCOVERY of EVIDENCE.

The writ of mandamus can also be issued in a mandamus proceeding, independent of any judicial proceeding. Generally, such a petition for a mandamus order is made to compel a judicial or government officer to perform a duty owed to the petitioner. For example, in Massachusetts, each year the commonwealth's attorney general and each district attorney must make available to the public a report on wiretaps and other interceptions of oral communications conducted by law enforcement officers. If the report is not made available, any person may compel its production by filing an ACTION for mandamus (Mass. Gen. Laws Ann. ch. 272, § 99 [West 1996]). If successful, a court would issue an order directing the attorney general and district attorneys to produce the information. The attorney general and district attorneys have a chance to defend their actions at a hearing on the action. If the parties fail to comply with a mandamus order, they may be held in CONTEMPT of court and fined or jailed.

MANDATE 📖 A judicial command, order, or precept, written or oral, from a court; a direction that a court has the authority to give and an individual is bound to obey. 📖

A mandate might be issued upon the decision of an APPEAL, which directs that a particular action be taken, or upon a disposition made of a case by an inferior tribunal.

The term *mandate* is also used in reference to an act by which one individual empowers another individual to conduct transactions for an individual in that person's name. In this sense, it is used synonymously with POWER OF ATTORNEY.

MANDATORY 📖 Peremptory; obligatory; required; that which must be subscribed to or obeyed. 📖

Mandatory statutes are those that require, as opposed to permit, a particular course of action. Their language is characterized by such directive terms as "shall" as opposed to "may." A *mandatory provision* is one that must be observed, whereas a DIRECTORY provision is optional.

An example of a mandatory provision is a law that provides that an election judge must endorse his or her initials on a ballot.

MANDATORY AUTHORITY 📖 PRECEDENTS, in the form of prior decisions by a higher court of the same state on point, statutes, or other sources of law that must be considered by a judge in the determination of a legal controversy. 📖

Mandatory authority is synonymous with BINDING AUTHORITY.

MAN-IN-THE-HOUSE RULE 📖 A regulation that was formerly applied in certain jurisdictions that denied poor families WELFARE payments in the event that a man resided under the same roof with them. 📖

Under the man-in-the-house rule, a child who otherwise qualified for welfare benefits was denied those benefits if the child's mother was living with, or having relations with, any single or married able-bodied male. The man was considered a substitute father, even if the man was not supporting the child.

Before 1968 administrative agencies in many states created and enforced the man-in-the-house rule. In 1968 the U.S. Supreme Court struck down the regulation as being contrary to the legislative goals of the Aid to Families of Dependent Children (AFDC) program. The AFDC program, established by the Social Security Act of 1935 (49 Stat. 620, *as amended* [42 U.S.C.A. § 301 et seq.]), provides benefits to the children of impoverished parents.

In *King v. Smith*, 392 U.S. 309, 88 S. Ct. 2128, 20 L. Ed. 2d 1118 (1968), the U.S. Supreme Court entertained a challenge to the man-in-the-house rule brought by the four children of Mrs. Sylvester Smith, a widow. These children were denied benefits by Dallas County, Alabama, welfare authorities based on their knowledge that a man named Williams was visiting Smith on weekends and had sexual relations with her.

The children of Smith filed a CLASS ACTION suit in federal court on behalf of other children in Alabama who were denied benefits under Alabama's "substitute father" regulation. This regulation considered a man a substitute father if (1) he lived in the home with the mother; (2) he visited the home frequently for the purpose of living with the mother; or (3) he cohabited with the mother elsewhere (*King*, citing Alabama Manual for Administration of Public Assistance, pt. I, ch. II, § VI). Testimony in the case revealed that there was some confusion among the authorities over how to interpret the regulation. One official testified that the regulation applied only if the parties had sex at least once a week, another official testified that sex every three months was sufficient, and still another placed the frequency at once every six months.

According to the High Court, Congress did not intend that the AFDC program require children "to look for their food to a man who is not in the least obliged to support them." The Court maintained that when Congress used the term *parent* in the Social Security Act, it was referring to "an individual who owed to the child a state-imposed legal duty of support." Ultimately, the Court struck down the man-in-the-house rule by holding that under the AFDC provisions in the Social Security Act, "destitute children who are legally fatherless cannot be flatly denied federally funded assistance on the transparent fiction that they have a substitute father."

MANN, HORACE Attorney, politician, and reformer of U.S. public education Horace Mann transformed the nation's schools. Mann was a gust of wind blowing through the doldrums of nineteenth-century teaching. In 1837, he left a promising career in law and politics to become Massachusetts's first secretary of education. In this capacity, he rebuilt shoddy schools, instituted teacher training, and ensured widespread access to education for children and adults. These reforms not only revived the state system but also inspired great national progress. The spirit of opportunity and the duty of citizenship guided Mann: "In a republic," he said, "ignorance is a crime." Later, he served in the

BIOGRAPHY

Horace Mann

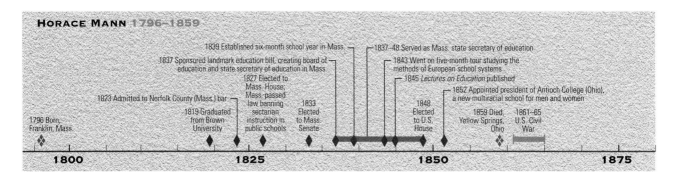

HORACE MANN 1796–1859

1796 Born, Franklin, Mass.

1819 Graduated from Brown University

1823 Admitted to Norfolk County (Mass.) bar

1827 Elected to Mass. House; Mass. passed law banning sectarian instruction in public schools

1833 Elected to Mass. Senate

1837 Sponsored landmark education bill, creating board of education and state secretary of education in Mass.

1839 Established six-month school year in Mass.

1837–48 Served as Mass. state secretary of education

1843 Went on five-month tour studying the methods of European school systems

1845 *Lectures on Education* published

1848 Elected to U.S. House

1852 Appointed president of Antioch College (Ohio), a new multiracial school for men and women

1859 Died, Yellow Springs, Ohio

1861–65 U.S. Civil War

1800   1825   1850   1875

U.S. Congress before becoming a professor at and the president of Antioch College. Besides these contributions, his legacy to U.S. education is still felt in the contemporary debate over SCHOOL PRAYER. He helped wean education from its religious origins in order to create a truly public system.

Mann was born in poverty on May 4, 1796, in Franklin, Massachusetts. His father, Thomas Mann, was a farmer in Franklin. Neither his father nor his mother, Rebecca Mann, received much formal education, which was not widely available in the years following the American Revolution. Little opportunity existed for Mann, a sensitive boy driven to tears by hellfire-and-brimstone sermons on Sundays. Although an avid reader, Mann never attended school for more than ten weeks of the year. His extraordinary mind might have gone no further than the family's ancestral farm were it not for a traveling Latin teacher who tutored him when Mann was twenty. Provided with decent instruction, Mann's gifts were revealed: he qualified for entrance as a sophomore to Brown University. He graduated with high honors in 1819; remained briefly as a tutor in Latin and Greek; enrolled in LITCHFIELD LAW SCHOOL, in Connecticut, two years later; and was admitted to the bar of Norfolk County in 1823.

Mann practiced law for fourteen years while making his name in politics. He first won election to the Massachusetts House of Representatives in 1827; election to the state senate, where he served as president, followed in 1833. He left his mark on the legislature in two ways: by seeking state help for mentally ill persons and by passing the landmark education bill of 1837. The law created a board of education at a time when Massachusetts's public schools were barely limping along. Buildings were crumbling, teachers underpaid, and teaching methods erratic. Much the same could be said of the nation's public schools. In Massachusetts, moreover, one-third of the children did not attend school at all, and one-sixth of all students attended private schools. To clean up this mess, the 1837 law called for the appointment of a state secretary of education. Mann, despite the promise of further success as a lawyer and politician, took the job.

Over the next twelve years, Mann's success was stunning. His efforts rebuilt Massachusetts's education system from the ground up: he centralized control of its schools, invested in better facilities, established institutes for teacher training, revamped the curriculum, discouraged physical punishment, and held annual education conventions for teachers and the public. Educators nationwide sought out his ideas, published in a bimonthly magazine that he founded, called the *Common School Journal*, as well as in annual reports. In 1843, pursuing new ideas for improving the quality of Massachusetts's system, he toured schools in eight European countries. His praise for the rigors of the German model brought him into open conflict with schoolteachers back home, who thought him critical of their work. Mann stood his ground; he had not spent five months abroad only to be bullied by the status quo.

Even more controversial was Mann's position on Bible reading in public schools. In the mid–nineteenth century, the practice remained a leftover from the colonial period, when schools were each run by a church of an individual sect, or group. Mann thought Bible reading useful for teaching moral instruction, and he promoted it, but only so long as it was done without comment. As a Unitarian, he did not want teachers imposing views on students of different faiths; this had often led to bitter disagreements. (In the early 1840s, disputes over classroom Bible reading would cause Catholic-Protestant riots in New York and Philadelphia.) Under Mann's influence, Massachusetts adhered to the law it had passed in 1827 banning sectarian instruction (instruction specific to or characteristic of a particular religious group) from public schools. Orthodox church leaders sharply attacked Mann, one calling his policy "a grand instrument in the hands of free thinkers, atheists and infidels." History was on Mann's side, however. The sectarian influence would continue to die out over the next half century, a historical trend culminating in the U.S. Supreme Court's landmark rulings banning school prayer in 1962 (*Engel v. Vitale*, 370 U.S. 421, 82 S. Ct. 1261, 8 L. Ed. 2d 601 [1962]) and Bible reading in 1963 (*Abington School District v. Schempp*, 374 U.S. 203, 83 S. Ct. 1560, 10 L. Ed. 2d 844 [1963]). Ironically, the prayer ban arose from an attempt by administrators of education in New York to compose a bland, inoffensive prayer in the spirit of Mann's anti-sectarianism.

Mann spent the last decade of his life in public service and education. Resigning the education secretary's post in 1848, he won election to the U.S. Congress and served there four years. A run for governor of Massachusetts failed in 1852, and he accepted the offer of the presidency of newly founded Antioch College, a multiracial school for men and women, where he also taught courses in philosophy and theology. The college suffered financially. Mann's health failed, and he died August 2, 1859, at the

"EDUCATION THEN, BEYOND ALL OTHER DEVICES OF HUMAN ORIGIN, IS A GREAT EQUALIZER OF THE CONDITIONS OF MEN,—THE BALANCE WHEEL OF THE SOCIAL MACHINERY."

age of sixty-three. Shortly before his death, at a commencement ceremony, he left the graduating class to ponder this sterling ideal: "Be ashamed to die until you have won some victory for humanity."

CROSS-REFERENCES

Abington School District v. Schempp; Education Law; *Engel v. Vitale;* Schools and School Districts.

MANN, JAMES ROBERT James Robert Mann served in the U.S. House of Representatives from 1897 to 1922. Mann, an Illinois Republican, sponsored three pieces of legislation that enlarged the power of the federal government to regulate the economy and the nation's morals. He is best remembered as the author of the MANN ACT (18 U.S.C.A. § 2421 et seq.), also known as the White Slave Traffic Act.

Mann was born October 20, 1856, in McLean County, Illinois. He graduated from the University of Illinois in 1876 and then attended the Union College of Law (now known as the Northwestern University Law School). Following his admission to the Illinois bar in 1881, Mann joined a prominent Chicago law firm and achieved success as a business attorney.

Mann became active in Chicago politics during the 1880s and was elected to the U.S. House of Representatives in 1897. As a moderate Republican, Mann believed that the federal government had a role to play in managing the national economy. His interest in reform was heightened by the work of muckraking journalists who produced sensational investigative articles exposing impure food processing and impure and often fraudulent drugs.

In response to public concerns about the quality of food and medicine, Mann sponsored a major piece of federal legislation, the PURE FOOD AND DRUG ACT OF 1906 (34 Stat. 768). This act invoked the Constitution's COMMERCE CLAUSE for authority to regulate the interstate shipment of food and medicine. The law signaled a change in the state-federal power relationship, which had previously emphasized the right of states to regulate business.

BIOGRAPHY

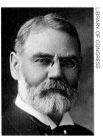

James Robert Mann

"ALL OF THE HORRORS WHICH HAVE EVER BEEN URGED, EITHER TRUTHFULLY OR FANCIFULLY, AGAINST THE BLACK-SLAVE TRADE PALE INTO INSIGNIFICANCE AS COMPARED TO THE HORRORS OF THE SO-CALLED 'WHITE-SLAVE TRAFFIC.'"

The inspection of food products and medicines by the federal government both reassured the public about the quality of what it consumed and served notice that a national economy required national regulation. Mann demonstrated his continuing interest in regulation with his sponsorship of the Mann-Elkins Act of 1910 (36 Stat. 539). Mann-Elkins gave the INTERSTATE COMMERCE COMMISSION authority to regulate and set the rates for telegraph, telephone, and railroad companies. The law recognized that these modes of communication and transportation were a vital part of the interstate economy and that their rates needed to be regulated by the federal government rather than by the states.

Mann was instrumental in the passage of the Mann Act in 1910. This act grew out of concerns of Chicago authorities that women and girls were being forced into PROSTITUTION through a variety of tricks and coercive tactics. The term *white slavery* came to symbolize the predicament of women who were kept in houses of prostitution against their will. It was alleged that "white slaves" (pimps and procurers) lured females from rural states into large cities such as Chicago and then forced them into prostitution.

Responding to pleas from Chicago prosecutors that a federal criminal law was needed, Mann introduced the Mann Act. The act prohibited the transportation of women across state lines for prostitution or "any other immoral purpose." Mann skillfully guided the legislation through the House of Representatives, overcoming congressional Democrats who argued that the act expanded federal police power. Once passed, the Mann Act became a central part of the work of the newly created Federal Bureau of Investigation.

Mann died in Washington, D.C., on November 30, 1922.

MANN ACT The Mann Act (18 U.S.C.A. § 2421 et seq.), also known as the White Slave Traffic Act, is a federal criminal statute that deals with PROSTITUTION and child PORNOGRAPHY. Enacted in 1910 and named for its sponsor, Representative JAMES R. MANN, of Illinois, it

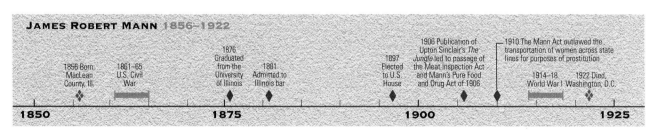

JAMES ROBERT MANN 1856–1922

1850   1875   1900   1925

1856 Born, MacLean County, Ill.

1861–65 U.S. Civil War

1876 Graduated from the University of Illinois

1881 Admitted to Illinois bar

1897 Elected to U.S. House

1906 Publication of Upton Sinclair's *The Jungle* led to passage of the Meat Inspection Act and Mann's Pure Food and Drug Act of 1906

1910 The Mann Act outlawed the transportation of women across state lines for purposes of prostitution

1914–18 World War I

1922 Died, Washington, D.C.

also was used to prosecute men who took women across state lines for consensual sex.

Representative Mann introduced the act in December 1909 at the request of Chicago prosecutors who claimed that girls and women were being forced into prostitution by unscrupulous PIMPS and procurers. The term *white slavery* became popular to describe the predicament these females faced. It was alleged that men were tricking, coercing, and drugging females to get them involved in prostitution and then forcing them to stay in brothels.

The legislation was intended to stop the interstate trafficking of women. Though federal criminal statutes were rare in 1910, and seen as an attack on state police powers, the legislation encountered little opposition. The act made it a FELONY to transport knowingly any woman or girl in interstate commerce or foreign commerce for prostitution, debauchery, or any other immoral purpose. It also made it a felony to coerce a woman or a girl into such immoral acts. President WILLIAM H. TAFT signed the bill in June 1910.

The U.S. Supreme Court upheld the constitutionality of the Mann Act in *Hoke v. United States*, 227 U.S. 308, 33 S. Ct. 281, 57 L. Ed. 523 (1913). The Court broadened the scope of the act in *Caminetti v. United States*, 242 U.S. 470, 37 S. Ct. 192, 61 L. Ed. 442 (1917), when it ruled that the act applied to noncommercial acts of immorality. In *Caminetti* the Court seized on the phrase "any other immoral purpose," concluding that Congress intended to prevent the use of interstate commerce to promote sexual immorality. This interpretation radically changed the scope of the act.

The Mann Act was used by the Federal Bureau of Investigation to curtail commercialized vice. It was also often used to prosecute prominent persons who did not conform to conventional morality. Jack Johnson, a heavyweight boxing champion, was charged with and convicted of a Mann Act violation in 1912, for taking his mistress across state lines. Over the years, similar charges were leveled against the architect Frank Lloyd Wright, the actor Charlie Chaplin, and the rock and roll singer Chuck Berry. Of these three, only Berry was convicted of a Mann Act violation.

Congress amended the act in 1978 to attack the problem of child pornography. The amendments made the act's provisions regarding this issue gender neutral, so that both boys and girls who were sexually exploited were now protected (Pub. L. No. 95-225, 92 Stat. 8–9). In 1986 the law was further amended. The new amendments made the entire act gender neutral as to victims of sexual exploitation. More important, all references to debauchery and any other immoral purpose were replaced by the phrase "any sexual activity for which any person can be charged with a criminal offense" (Pub. L. No. 99-628, 100 Stat. 3511–3512.) This change took the federal government out of the business of defining *immoral*. Because most states have repealed criminal laws against FORNICATION and ADULTERY, noncommercial, consensual sexual activity no longer is subject to prosecution.

MANOR 📖 A house, a dwelling, or a residence. 📖

Historically under ENGLISH LAW, a manor was a parcel of land granted by the king to a lord or other high ranking person. Incident to every manor was the right of the lord to hold a court called the court baron, which was organized to maintain and enforce the services and duties that were owed to the lord of the manor. The lands that constituted the manor holdings included *terrae tenementales*, Latin for "tenemental lands," and *terrae dominicales*, Latin for "demesne lands." The lord gave the tenemental lands to his followers or retainers in FREEHOLD. He retained part of the demesne lands for his own use but gave part to tenants in copyhold—those who took possession of the land by virtue of the evidence or copy in the records of the lord's court. A portion of the demesne lands, called the *lord's waste*, served as public roads and common pasture land for the lord and his tenants.

The word *manor* also meant the privilege of having a manor with the jurisdiction of a court baron and the right to receive rents and services from the copyholders.

See also FEUDALISM.

MANSFIELD, WILLIAM MURRAY, FIRST EARL OF William Murray, first earl of Mansfield, was an eighteenth-century English lawyer and judge who, along with Sir WILLIAM BLACKSTONE and SIR EDWARD COKE, played an important part in molding U.S. law. His revision of property law and his formulation of basic principles of contract law provided the basis for modern commercial law. Lord Mansfield also is remembered for his decision in *Somerset's Case*, 1 Lofft's Rep. 1, 20 Howell's State Trials 1, 98 Eng. Rep. 499 (1772), in which he held that there was no legal basis for SLAVERY in England. This case came to have great significance in the United States, as it presented a legal theory for those opposed to slavery.

BIOGRAPHY

THE GRANGER COLLECTION, NEW YORK

William Murray, First Earl of Mansfield

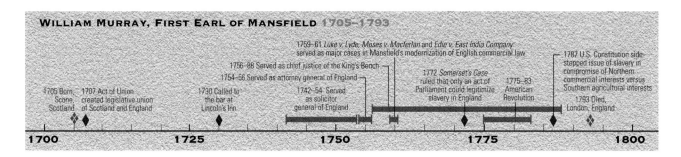

WILLIAM MURRAY, FIRST EARL OF MANSFIELD 1705–1793

1759–61 *Luke v. Lyde, Moses v. Macferlan* and *Edie v. East India Company*
served as major cases in Mansfield's modernization of English commercial law

1756–88 Served as chief justice of the King's Bench

1754–56 Served as attorney general of England

1787 U.S. Constitution side-
stepped issue of slavery in
compromise of Northern
commercial interests versus
Southern agricultural interests

1705 Born
Scone,
Scotland

1707 Act of Union
created legislative union
of Scotland and England

1730 Called to
the bar at
Lincoln's Inn

1742–54 Served
as solicitor
general of England

1772 *Somerset's Case*
ruled that only an act of
Parliament could legitimize
slavery in England

1775–83
American
Revolution

1793 Died
London, England

1700   1725   1750   1775   1800

Mansfield was born March 2, 1705, in Scone, Scotland. He was educated at Christ Church, Oxford, and was called to the bar at Lincoln's Inn in 1730. From 1742 to 1754, Mansfield acted as solicitor general of England, and from 1754 to 1756, he served as attorney general. In 1756 he became chief justice of the KING'S BENCH, and he served on the court until 1788. In recognition of these achievements, he was created first earl of Mansfield.

Mansfield departed from the traditional role of an English judge. He did not seek to formulate law solely on the basis of STARE DECISIS, which relies on the exact holdings of previous decisions. Instead, Mansfield sought to determine general principles inherent in the decisions reached by COMMON-LAW COURTS and then to apply those principles to the case at hand. This gave Mansfield great flexibility in responding to new varieties of litigation that came with the development of English commerce. Also, Mansfield educated himself about commercial practices. Because of his growing sensitivity to their interests, members of the English commercial classes were encouraged to bring more of their disputes to his court and to let their affairs be governed by his common-law principles.

In deciding commercial-law cases, Mansfield adopted the guiding principle of GOOD FAITH, which demanded an adherence to moral obligations. In contract law he believed that the parties' intentions—rather than out-of-date, rigid common-law rules—ought to be used to set the scope of agreements and to settle disputes. In the area of REAL PROPERTY, Mansfield tried, against much resistance, to update and modify a species of law that was both archaic and arcane. Throughout his tenure on the bench, Mansfield demonstrated a consistent desire to modernize the law of commerce.

Mansfield's decision in *Somerset's Case* dealt a fatal blow to English slaveholding interests. In this 1772 case, a slave brought to England by his master had escaped and had been recaptured. Antislavery activists demanded his release

"I DESIRE NOTHING SO MUCH AS THAT ALL QUESTIONS OF MERCANTILE LAW BE FULLY SETTLED AND ASCERTAINED; AND IT IS OF MUCH MORE CONSEQUENCE THAT THEY SHOULD BE SO, THAN WHICH WAY THE DECISION IS."

and sought a writ of HABEAS CORPUS (an order of protection against illegal imprisonment), arguing that England did not have a law permitting slavery. Mansfield ordered that the slave be released, holding that slavery was "so odious, that nothing can be suffered to support it but positive law." Mansfield did not rule that slavery was always illegal, only that it would take a positive law (an act of Parliament) to legitimate it. Absent a positive law that would recognize the powers of a slave owner over a slave, English courts would not uphold a slaveholder's claim to a slave. This decision was embraced by opponents of U.S. slavery in nonslaveholding states. *Somerset's Case* ultimately shaped the federal system in the United States, making slavery there a product of state, not federal, statutory law. It also permitted runaway slaves in the United States to claim legal protection if they escaped to a nonslaveholding state.

Mansfield died March 20, 1793, in London.

MANSLAUGHTER The unjustifiable, inexcusable, and intentional killing of a human being without deliberation, premeditation, and MALICE. The unlawful killing of a human being without any deliberation, which may be involuntary, in the commission of a lawful act without due caution and circumspection.

Manslaughter is a distinct crime and is not considered a lesser degree of MURDER. The essential distinction between the two offenses is that MALICE AFORETHOUGHT must be present for murder, whereas it must be absent for manslaughter. Manslaughter is not as serious a crime as murder. On the other hand, it is not a justifiable or excusable killing for which little or no punishment is imposed.

At COMMON LAW, as well as under current statutes, the offense can be either voluntary or involuntary manslaughter. The main difference between the two is that voluntary manslaughter requires an intent to kill or cause serious bodily harm while INVOLUNTARY MANSLAUGHTER does not. Premeditation or deliberation, however, are elements of murder and not of manslaughter. Some states have abandoned the use of adjectives to describe different forms of the offense and, instead, simply divide the offense into varying degrees.

Voluntary Manslaughter In most jurisdictions, voluntary manslaughter consists of an intentional killing that is accompanied by additional circumstances that mitigate, but do not excuse, the killing. The most common type of voluntary manslaughter occurs when a defendant is provoked to commit the HOMICIDE. It is sometimes described as a HEAT OF PASSION killing. In most cases, the PROVOCATION must induce rage or anger in the defendant, although some cases have held that fright, terror, or desperation will suffice.

If adequate provocation is established, a murder charge may be reduced to manslaughter. Generally there are four conditions that must be fulfilled to warrant the reduction: (1) the provocation must cause rage or fear in a reasonable person; (2) the defendant must have actually been provoked; (3) there should not be a time period between the provocation and the killing within which a reasonable person would cool off; and (4) the defendant should not have cooled off during that period.

Provocation is justifiable if a REASONABLE PERSON under similar circumstances would be induced to act in the same manner as the defendant. It must be found that the degree of provocation was such that a reasonable person would lose self-control. In actual practice, there is no precise formula for determining reasonableness. It is a matter that is determined by the trier of fact, either the jury or the judge in a nonjury trial, after a full consideration of the EVIDENCE.

Certain forms of provocation that frequently arise have traditionally been considered reasonable or unreasonable by the courts. A killing that results from anger that is induced by a violent blow with a fist or weapon might constitute sufficient provocation, provided the accused did not incite the victim. It is not reasonable, however, to respond similarly to a light blow. A killing that results from mutual combat is often considered manslaughter, provided it was caused by the heat of passion aroused by the combat. An illegal arrest of one who knows of or believes in his or her innocence may provoke a reasonable person, although cases are in dispute on the issue of whether such an arrest would justify a killing. An attempt to make a legal arrest in an unlawful manner by the use of unnecessary violence might also constitute a heat of passion killing that will mitigate an intentional killing. Some cases have held that a reasonable belief that one's spouse is committing ADULTERY will suffice. An injury to persons in a close relationship to the accused, such as a spouse, child, or parent, is often held to constitute reasonable provocation, particularly when the injury occurs in the accused's presence.

Mere words or gestures, although extremely offensive and insulting, have traditionally been viewed as insufficient provocation to reduce murder to manslaughter. There is, however, a modern trend in some courts to hold that words alone will suffice under certain circumstances, such as instances in which a present intent and ability to cause harm is demonstrated.

The reasonable person standard is generally applied in a purely objective manner. Unusual mental or physical characteristics are not taken into consideration. The fact that a defendant was more susceptible to provocation than an average person because he or she had a previous head injury is not relevant to a determination of whether the person's conduct was reasonable. There has, however, been a recent trend in some cases that indicates a willingness to consider some subjective factors.

If a reasonable period of time passed between the provocation and the killing so that the defendant had sufficient time to cool off, a homicide will not be reduced to manslaughter. Most courts will reduce the charge if a reasonable person would not have cooled off. Some, however, look solely at the defendant's temperament and make a subjective decision as to whether the person had sufficient time to regain self-control.

In some states, there is a case-law trend in which a killing that is committed under a mistaken belief that one is justified constitutes voluntary manslaughter. It is reasoned that although the crime is not justifiable, it is not serious enough to be murder.

It is a general rule that a defendant who acts in SELF-DEFENSE may only use force that is reasonably calculated to prevent harm to himself or herself. If the person honestly, but unreasonably, believes DEADLY FORCE is necessary and, therefore, causes another's death, some courts will consider the crime voluntary manslaughter. Similarly when a defendant acts under an honest but unreasonable belief that he or she has a right to kill another to prevent a FELONY, some courts will find the person guilty of voluntary manslaughter. Although it is generally considered a crime to kill another in order to save oneself, the justification of COERCION or NECESSITY may, likewise, reduce murder to manslaughter in some JURISDICTIONS.

Involuntary Manslaughter Involuntary manslaughter is the unlawful killing of another human being without intent. The absence of the intent element is the essential difference between voluntary and involuntary manslaughter. Also in most states, involuntary manslaughter does not result from a heat of passion but from an improper use of reasonable care or skill while in the commission of a lawful act, or while in the commission of an unlawful act not amounting to a felony.

Generally there are two types of involuntary manslaughter: (1) criminal-negligence manslaughter; and (2) unlawful-act manslaughter. The first occurs when death results from a high degree of NEGLIGENCE or RECKLESSNESS, and the second occurs when death is caused by one who commits or attempts to commit an UNLAWFUL act, usually a MISDEMEANOR.

Although all jurisdictions punish involuntary manslaughter, the statutes vary somewhat. In some states, the CRIMINAL NEGLIGENCE type of manslaughter is described as GROSS NEGLIGENCE or culpable negligence. Others divide the entire offense of manslaughter into degrees, with voluntary manslaughter constituting a more serious offense and carrying a heavier penalty than involuntary manslaughter.

Many statutes do not define the offense or define it vaguely in common-law terms. There are, however, a small number of modern statutes that are more specific. Under one such statute, the offense is defined as the commission of a lawful act without proper caution or requisite skill, in which one unguardedly or undesignedly kills another, or the commission of an unlawful act that is not felonious or tends to inflict great bodily harm.

Criminally Negligent Manslaughter A homicide resulting from the taking of an unreasonable and high degree of risk is usually considered criminally negligent manslaughter. Jurisdictions are divided on the question of whether or not the defendant must be aware of the risk. Modern criminal codes generally require a consciousness of risk, although, under some codes, the absence of this element makes the offense a less serious homicide.

There are numerous cases in which an omission to act or a failure to perform a DUTY constitutes criminally negligent manslaughter. The existence of a duty is essential. Since the law does not recognize that an ordinary person has a duty to aid or rescue another in distress, an ensuing death from failure to act would not be manslaughter. On the other hand, an omission in which one has a duty, such as the failure of a lifeguard to attempt to save a drowning person, might constitute the offense.

When the failure to act is reckless or negligent, and not intentional, it is usually manslaughter. If the omission is intentional and death is likely or substantially likely to result, the offense might be murder. When neither an intent to kill nor recklessness or negligence are present, no offense is committed.

In many jurisdictions, death that results from the operation of a vehicle in a criminally negligent manner is punishable as a separate offense. Usually it is considered a less severe crime than involuntary manslaughter. Although criminal negligence is an element, it is generally not the same degree of negligence as that which is required for involuntary manslaughter. For example, some vehicular homicide statutes have been construed to require only ordinary negligence while, in a majority of jurisdictions, a greater degree of negligence is required for involuntary manslaughter.

Unlawful-Act Manslaughter In many states, unlawful-act manslaughter is committed when death results from an act that is likely to cause death or serious physical harm to another person. In a majority of jurisdictions, however, the offense is committed when death occurs during the commission or attempted commission of a misdemeanor.

In some states, a distinction is made between conduct that is *malum in se*, bad in itself, and conduct that is *malum prohibitum*, bad because prohibited by law. In these states, the act that causes the death must be *malum in se* and a felony in order for the offense to constitute manslaughter. If the act is *malum prohibitum*, there is no manslaughter unless it was foreseeable that death would be a direct result of the act. In other states that similarly divide the offense, the crime is committed even though the act was *malum prohibitum* and a misdemeanor, especially if the unlawful act was in violation of a statute that was intended to prevent injury to other persons.

Punishment The penalty for manslaughter is imprisonment. The precise term of years depends upon the applicable statute. Usually the sentence that is imposed for voluntary manslaughter is greater than that given for involuntary manslaughter. In most states, a more serious penalty is imposed for criminally negligent manslaughter than for unlawful-act manslaughter.

MANUFACTURES 📖 Items of trade that have been transformed from raw materials, either by labor, art, skill, or machine into finished articles that have new forms, qualities, or properties. 📖

For example, a blouse that is made of raw silk would be considered a manufacture, whereas fresh vegetables sold on a farm would not.

The videotapes rolling off this packaging line are considered manufactures, that is, finished articles of trade transformed from raw materials.

Whether particular products are within the definition of manufactures becomes significant with respect to taxes and other regulations imposed upon manufacturers.

MAPP v. OHIO A landmark Supreme Court decision, *Mapp v. Ohio*, 367 U.S. 643, 81 S. Ct. 1684, 6 L. Ed. 2d 1081 (1961), established the rule that EVIDENCE that has been obtained by an illegal SEARCH AND SEIZURE cannot be used to prove the guilt of a defendant at a state criminal trial.

Police officers went to the home of Dollree Mapp in an attempt to find someone who was wanted for questioning about a recent bombing. When they demanded entrance to the house, Mapp called her attorney and refused to allow the police to enter without a SEARCH WARRANT. Subsequently the police officers became rough with Mapp and handcuffed her. Upon a search of the house, they found obscene books, pictures, and photographs for the possession of which the defendant was subsequently prosecuted and convicted.

The defendant brought an unsuccessful action challenging the constitutionality of the search. An appeal was made to the Ohio Supreme Court, which affirmed the judgment. The defendant appealed to the U.S. Supreme Court, which reversed the decision on the ground that evidence obtained by an unconstitutional seizure was inadmissible.

The Court was extremely critical of the actions of the police and held that the defendant's PRIVACY had been unconstitutionally in-vaded. The police tactics were deemed comparable to a confession forced out of a fearful prisoner. The Court ruled that to compel respect for the constitutional right of the people to be secure in their persons, houses, papers, and effects against unreasonable searches and seizures, it was necessary to exclude illegally obtained evidence from the consideration of the trial court.

The Supreme Court had ruled, as early as 1886, that any illegally obtained evidence could not be introduced in FEDERAL COURTS. This principle, known as the EXCLUSIONARY RULE, was initially applied to state criminal prosecutions in *Mapp.* The Court made note of the fact that, in other instances, various states had attempted to prevent illegal police searches by other means, but the exclusionary rule is, in the opinion of the Supreme Court, the only effective means of protecting citizens from illegal searches conducted by government agents.

See also CRIMINAL LAW; CRIMINAL PROCEDURE.

MARBURY v. MADISON   *Marbury v. Madison*, 5 U.S. (1 Cranch) 137, 2 L. Ed. 60 (1803), established the power of JUDICIAL REVIEW in the U.S. Supreme Court. This power, which was later extended to all FEDERAL COURTS, authorizes the federal JUDICIARY to review laws enacted by Congress and the president and to invalidate those that violate the Constitution.

The power of judicial review also permits federal courts to compel government officials to take action in accordance with constitutional principles, as the Supreme Court did when it ordered President RICHARD M. NIXON to release tapes he had made of conversations at the White House regarding a series of scandals that began with the burglary of the Democratic party's national headquarters in the WATERGATE office complex in June 1972. Finally, judicial review empowers federal courts to decide legal issues raised by state constitutions, statutes, and common-law decisions that touch upon a federal constitutional provision.

Judicial review is also routinely exercised by state courts over state and federal constitutional questions. Unlike the federal power of judicial review, which derives from *Marbury*, the state power of judicial review usually derives from an express provision in a state constitution.

Marbury was an outgrowth of political struggles between the Federalist and Republican parties during the late eighteenth and early nineteenth centuries in the United States. These struggles began as a dispute between the Federalists and Anti-Federalists over the ratification of the Constitution.

The Federalists, including ALEXANDER HAMILTON and JOHN JAY, supported ratification

ED LALLO/THE PICTURE CUBE

of the Constitution as a means of creating a stronger national government that would replace the feeble central government formed under the ARTICLES OF CONFEDERATION. The Federalists believed that a strong national government was necessary to promote economic growth and geographic expansion and to protect U.S. citizens from internal and external aggression. The Anti-Federalists, including GEORGE MASON and PATRICK HENRY, opposed ratification because they feared it would create a despotic national government that would vitiate state sovereignty and be unresponsive to local interests.

After the Constitution was ratified by the states, many disgruntled Anti-Federalists joined the Republican party. Like their Anti-Federalist predecessors, the Republicans worked to curtail further growth of the national government, drawing their constituency from farmers and mechanics. The Federalists, meanwhile, sought an increased role for the national government, including the establishment of a federal bank, and drew their constituency from wealthy property owners and mercantilists.

During the administration of JOHN ADAMS (1797–1801), Federalists controlled the executive and legislative branches of the federal government, and permeated the federal judiciary as well. However, the political tides turned against the Federalists during the elections of 1800, when the Republicans wrested control of both houses of Congress and THOMAS JEFFERSON, their party leader, was elected president. Determined not to lose all its influence over the national government, the lame-duck Federalist Congress passed legislation that created a host of new federal judgeships, and called for the

appointment of forty-two justices of the peace in the District of Columbia.

In the haste of filling these vacancies during the waning hours of his last night in office, President Adams neglected to deliver the commissions (warrants issued by the government authorizing a person to perform certain acts) of several appointees. One of the so-called midnight appointees who did not receive his commission was William Marbury. After Jefferson ordered Secretary of State JAMES MADISON to withhold Marbury's commission, Marbury petitioned the Supreme Court for a writ of MANDAMUS (a court order requiring an official to perform his duties) to compel Madison to deliver the commission.

The case was heard before Chief Justice JOHN MARSHALL and four associate justices. Marshall was one of the "midnight judges" President Adams had appointed to the federal bench during his last few months in office. Prior to his appointment to the Supreme Court, Marshall had served as secretary of state for the Adams administration. Ironically, it was Marshall who, serving in a dual capacity as the secretary of state and chief justice, had failed to deliver the commission to Marbury. None of these facts presented a sufficient CONFLICT OF INTEREST for Marshall to disqualify himself from hearing the dispute.

Marshall's opinion, written for a unanimous Court, was divided into five parts, the first three being the least controversial. First, the Court held that Marbury had a legal right to serve as JUSTICE OF THE PEACE, and was entitled to receive the commission memorializing that right. Marbury had been nominated for the office by the president and confirmed by the Senate, in accordance with the procedures set forth in the Constitution. When President Adams signed the commission and affixed the SEAL of the United States to it, the appointment was "complet[e]." Delivery of the commission was a mere "convenience" that did not interfere with Marbury's legal right.

Second, the Court ruled it was a "plain violation" of this right for Madison to withhold the commission. When a commission has been signed and sealed by the EXECUTIVE BRANCH following a nominee's appointment and confirmation, the secretary of state, Marshall said, has a "duty" to "conform to the law" and deliver it as part of his "ministerial" responsibilities.

Third, the Marshall opinion said a writ of mandamus was the proper remedy because mandamus is a "command" directing "any person, corporation or inferior court of judicature

Outgoing President John Adams appointed several judges in the last days of his term in office in an effort to continue Federalist party influence after the Republican party had won a majority of seats in Congress and the presidency.

NATIONAL ARCHIVES

... to do some particular thing ... which appertains to their office and duty."

Marshall's opinion next addressed the question of whether the Supreme Court had the power to issue Marbury the WRIT. This question turned on the Court's JURISDICTION. Article III of the U.S. Constitution confers upon the Supreme Court two types of jurisdiction: original and appellate. ORIGINAL JURISDICTION gives courts the power to hear lawsuits from their inception, when a complaint or petition is "originally" filed with the tribunal. APPELLATE jurisdiction gives courts the power to review decisions that were made by lower courts and have been "appealed" to reverse a purported error. Under Article III, the Supreme Court has original jurisdiction over politically sensitive disputes such as those "affecting ambassadors" or those in which one of the fifty states is named as a party. In all other cases, the Supreme Court retains appellate jurisdiction.

In petitioning the Supreme Court directly for a writ of mandamus, Marbury was asking the Court to invoke its original jurisdiction pursuant to section 13 of the JUDICIARY ACT OF 1789, which authorized all federal courts to issue such writs "in cases warranted by the principles and usages of law." Yet Marbury was not an ambassador or state government entitled to have the Supreme Court hear the case under its original jurisdiction. As a consequence, Marshall opined that section 13 impermissibly attempted to enlarge the Supreme Court's original jurisdiction to include disputes such as those presented by Marbury and Madison, in contravention of the constitutional limitations placed on that jurisdiction by Article III.

However, Marshall suggested that merely because a piece of legislation violates a constitutional principle does not necessarily mean that the legislation is unenforceable. "[W]hether an act repugnant to the constitution can become law of the land," Marshall noted, "is a question deeply interesting to the United States." Observing that the Constitution expressly delegates and limits the powers of Congress, Marshall asked, "To what purpose are powers limited, and to what purpose is that limitation committed to writing, if these limits may, at any time, be passed by those intended to be restrained?"

Marshall argued that the "distinction between a government with limited and unlimited powers is abolished if those limits do not confine the persons on whom they are imposed, and if acts prohibited and acts allowed are of equal obligation." Marshall continued,

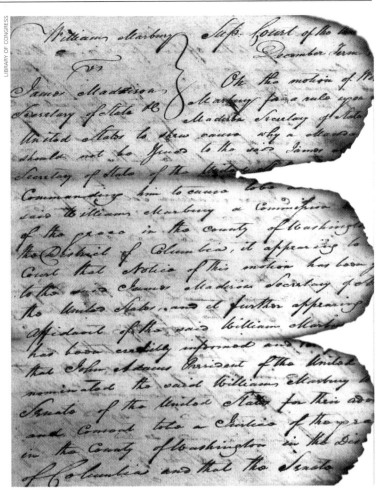

It is a proposition too plain to be contested, that the constitution controls any legislative act repugnant to it; or, that the legislature may alter the constitution by an ordinary act. ... Between these alternatives there is no middle ground. The constitution is either a superior, paramount law, unchangeable by ordinary means, or it is on a level with ordinary legislative acts, and like other acts, is alterable when the legislature shall please to alter it. ... If the former part of the alternative be true, then a legislative act contrary to the constitution is not law: if the latter part be true, then written constitutions are absurd attempts, on the part of the people, to limit a power in its own nature illimitable.

For Marshall, the idea that an unconstitutional act of legislature could "bind the courts and oblige them to give it effect" was "an absurdity too gross to be insisted on." Thus, Marshall concluded that congressional legislation contrary to the federal Constitution is null and void and cannot be enforced by a court of law.

When Secretary of State James Madison, on President Thomas Jefferson's order, refused to deliver William Marbury's commission as justice of the peace (issued by outgoing President John Adams), Marbury sued to obtain it. The Supreme Court's decision in Marbury v. Madison *established the principle of judicial review. The show-cause order served on Madison was damaged in the Capitol fire of 1898.*

Having ruled that the Judiciary Act of 1789 was invalid and unenforceable, Marshall next asked whether the judiciary was the appropriate branch to be vested with authority to overturn unconstitutional legislation. Although it is commonly accepted today that the power to nullify state and federal statutes falls within the purview of the judicial branch of government, the Constitution does not specifically delegate this power to any one branch. Under the explicit provisions of the Constitution, then, the executive and legislative branches might have argued in 1803 that they were no less entitled than the judicial branch to be entrusted with the power of judicial review.

The Court rejected this idea:

> It is emphatically the province and duty of the judicial department to say what the law is. Those who apply the rule to particular cases, must of necessity expound and interpret that rule. If two laws conflict with each other, the courts must decide on the operation of each. So if a law be in opposition to the constitution: if both the law and the constitution apply to a particular case, so that the court must either decide that case conformably to the law, disregarding the constitution; or conformably to the constitution, disregarding the law: the court must determine which of these conflicting rules governs the case. This is of the very essence of judicial duty.

Marshall was arguing that it was the historical role of courts to settle legal disputes by interpreting and applying the law. In some instances, the applicable statutory or COMMON LAW has conflicted with other laws, Marshall said, and it has been the obligation of courts to resolve "the operation of each."

Earlier in his opinion, the chief justice had described the federal Constitution as a special kind of law that was "paramount" to all other laws in the United States. It then followed, the chief justice reasoned, that courts carried the responsibility to interpret and apply the Constitution's provisions. This responsibility inevitably entailed review of cases where laws passed by the legislative and executive branches conflicted with the strictures of the Constitution. By resolving such conflicts, Marshall maintained, courts were doing nothing more than fulfilling their traditional role of settling legal disputes.

Marshall also questioned whether members of the legislative and executive branches could objectively evaluate the constitutionality of legislation they passed. It is sometimes said that a diner, not the cook, is the best judge of a meal. Following the same reasoning, Marshall hinted that the legislative and executive branches could not impartially review legislation that they had helped prepare or enact. It is far from clear, for example, whether the Federalists in Congress who supported the Judiciary Act of 1789 could have put aside their partisan views long enough to exercise the power of judicial review over the *Marbury* dispute in a fair and neutral manner.

Chief Justice Marshall's opinion in *Marbury* has been the object of much criticism. Constitutional historians claim that *Marbury* represents a paradigm of judicial activism, which is marked by judges who decide cases based on issues not argued before them. This criticism seems to be particularly apt when applied to *Marbury* because, as constitutional scholar Leonard W. Levy has pointed out, "[In] no other case in our constitutional history has the Court held unconstitutional an act of Congress whose constitutionality was not at issue." Neither Marbury nor Madison had attacked the constitutionality of the Judiciary Act.

Against this criticism, historians have weighed the dilemma confronting Chief Justice Marshall. As a Federalist appointed to the Supreme Court, Marshall attempted to facilitate the growth of the national government through his judicial opinions. To achieve this end, Marshall aspired to establish the Constitution as the supreme law of the land, under which the executive, legislative, and judicial branches of both state and federal governments would be subordinate. He also hoped to establish the Supreme Court as the ultimate arbiter of the Constitution, providing the final word on the meaning and application of any constitutional principles.

Marshall realized that none of these aspirations would be realized unless the Supreme Court gained respect and acceptance from Congress and the president. After all, the Supreme Court depended on the executive branch to enforce its decisions. President ANDREW JACKSON once underscored this point when he exclaimed, "John Marshall has made his decision [in *Worcester v. Georgia*, 31 U.S. (6 Pet.) 515, 8 L. Ed. 483 (1832)], now let him enforce it!" (as quoted in *Coleman v. United States Bureau of Indian Affairs*, 715 F.2d 1156 [7th Cir. 1983]).

Marshall also needed to curry the favor of Congress, which possessed the power to limit the appellate jurisdiction of the Supreme Court under Article III, Section 2, of the Constitution. In addition, Congress possessed the power to IMPEACH the Supreme Court justices, a power that it unsuccessfully exercised in 1805 when the Senate acquitted Federalist justice SAMUEL CHASE of wrongdoing.

Marbury was the powder keg threatening to upset the delicate relationships between the coordinate branches of the federal government. Marshall understood that if the Court ordered Madison to deliver the commission to Marbury, the Jefferson administration might ignore the order and tarnish the Court's reputation by exposing it as an impotent institution. On the other hand, if the Court ruled in favor of Madison, Marbury and the Federalists who had appointed and confirmed him would suffer a humiliating defeat. In either instance, the executive branch would be perceived as preeminent.

The chief justice's solution to this dilemma was what one constitutional scholar has called a "masterwork of indirection, a brilliant example of Marshall's capacity to sidestep danger while seeming to court it, to advance in one direction while his opponents are looking in another" (McCloskey 1960, 40). Marshall's opinion in *Marbury* denied a lilliputian power to the Supreme Court with one hand, while grabbing a titanic power for the judicial branch with the other.

By rejecting Marbury's claim on the ground that the Supreme Court did not have original jurisdiction to issue the writ of mandamus under the Constitution, Marshall established the power of judicial review in the nation's highest court. While appeasing the Jeffersonian Republicans with a victory over President Adams in the battle over the president's midnight appointments, Marshall introduced the idea that the federal Constitution is the fundamental law underlying both the state and federal governments. In striking down a section of the Federalist-supported Judiciary Act, Marshall identified the Supreme Court as the authoritative interpreter of the Constitution.

Each of these accomplishments set the stage for a gradual accretion of power, respect, and prestige in the federal judiciary. As the power of the federal judiciary increased, so did the power of the entire federal government, something that proved important in President ABRAHAM LINCOLN's efforts to preserve the Union during the Civil War.

CROSS-REFERENCES

Congress of the United States; Constitution of the United States; Separation of Powers; Supreme Court of the United States.

MARGIN   The edge or border; the edge of a body of water where it meets the land. As applied to a boundary line of land, the *margin* of

a river, creek, or other watercourse means the center of the stream. But in the case of a lake, bay, or natural pond, the *margin* means the line where land and water meet.

In finance, the difference between MARKET VALUE of loan COLLATERAL and FACE VALUE of loan.

A sum of money, or its equivalent, placed in the hands of a BROKER by the principal or person on whose account a purchase or sale of SECURITIES is to be made, as a security to the former against losses to which he or she may be exposed by subsequent fluctuations in the market value of the stock. The amount paid by the customer when he uses a broker's CREDIT to buy a security.

In commercial transactions the difference between the purchase price paid by an intermediary or retailer and the selling price, or difference between price received by manufacturer for its goods and costs to produce. Also called gross profit margin.

MARGIN CALL A demand by a BROKER that an investor who has purchased SECURITIES using CREDIT extended by the broker (on MARGIN) pay additional cash into his or her brokerage account to reduce the amount of debt owed.

A broker makes a margin call when the stocks in the account of the client have fallen below a particular percentage of their market price at the time of purchase, thereby increasing the outstanding debt and the broker's LIABILITY should the client become unable to pay. This process is also known as remargining.

A broker might also make a margin call when a client desires to make additional purchases of stock and securities.

MARIS, ALBERT BRANSON   Albert Branson Maris, a federal judge for fifty years, brought his quiet, scholarly leadership to the 1947 and 1948 recodifications of the U.S. Criminal and Judicial Codes. Because of his ongoing commitment to the revision and modernization of civil, criminal, bankruptcy, and judicial codes, Maris is often called the father of modernized judicial procedure in the United States. He not only helped to shape federal JURISPRUDENCE in this country but also was instrumental in the development of the laws and judicial systems of Guam and the U.S. Virgin Islands.

Maris was born in Philadelphia on December 19, 1893. Descendants of Quaker colonists, Maris and his family were also members of the Society of Friends. Maris studied at the Friends Select School, and later the Westtown School, attended by his father and grandfather.

Albert Branson Maris

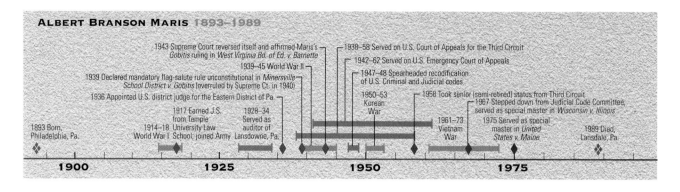

ALBERT BRANSON MARIS 1893–1989

1943 Supreme Court reversed itself and affirmed Maris's
Gobitis ruling in *West Virginia Bd. of Ed. v. Barnette*

1939–45 World War II

1939 Declared mandatory flag-salute rule unconstitutional in *Minersville
School District v. Gobitis* (overruled by Supreme Ct. in 1940)

1936 Appointed U.S. district judge for the Eastern District of Pa.

1938–58 Served on U.S. Court of Appeals for the Third Circuit

1942–62 Served on U.S. Emergency Court of Appeals

1947–48 Spearheaded recodification
of U.S. Criminal and Judicial codes

1950–53
Korean
War

1958 Took senior (semi-retired) status from Third Circuit

1967 Stepped down from Judicial Code Committee;
served as special master in *Wisconsin v. Illinois*

1917 Earned J.S.
from Temple

1914–18 University Law
World War I School; joined Army

1928–34
Served as
auditor of
Lansdowne, Pa.

1961–73
Vietnam
War

1975 Served as special
master in *United
States v. Maine*

1893 Born,
Philadelphia, Pa.

1989 Died,
Lansdale, Pa.

1900   1925   1950   1975

Mindful of his responsibility to his widowed mother and younger siblings, Maris made no plans to attend college after graduating from Westtown. He enrolled in a business course offered by a Scranton, Pennsylvania, correspondence school and entered the workforce as a clerk for an insurance company. He then took night courses at Temple University, passed the college entrance exam, and went on to study law.

Maris received his law degree from Temple University Law School—and married Edith Robinson on the same day—in 1917. The escalation of World War I delayed the practice of law for Maris. He served in an Army artillery unit as an enlisted man and later became an officer.

After the war, Maris entered private practice near Philadelphia. He also returned to school and earned a diploma from Drexel University Engineering School in 1926. He served as auditor of the borough of Lansdowne, Pennsylvania, from 1928 to 1934 and as councilman of the borough of Yeadon, Pennsylvania, from 1935 to 1936. After eighteen years of private practice and community service, Maris was appointed U.S. district judge for the Eastern District of Pennsylvania by President Franklin D. Roosevelt on June 22, 1936. Two years later, he was elevated to the U.S. Court of Appeals for the Third Circuit, which handles appeals of federal cases from Pennsylvania, New Jersey, Delaware, and the Virgin Islands.

Maris's decisions were rarely appealed and almost never overturned. *Minersville School District v. Gobitis*, 108 F.2d 683 (3d Cir. 1939), was among the few cases in which his ruling was challenged. In 1938, the children of William Gobitis and Lily Gobitis were expelled from school for refusing, on religious grounds, to recite the Pledge of Allegiance. The Gobitises filed a lawsuit in federal court, claiming that local regulations enforcing recitation of the pledge violated their FIRST AMENDMENT rights. Maris declared the school district's regulations unconstitutional. But when the case was ap-

"TO PERMIT PUBLIC OFFICERS TO DETERMINE WHETHER THE VIEWS OF INDIVIDUALS SINCERELY HELD AND THEIR ACTS SINCERELY UNDERTAKEN ON RELIGIOUS GROUNDS ARE IN FACT BASED ON CONVICTION RELIGIOUS IN CHARACTER WOULD BE TO SOUND THE DEATH KNELL OF RELIGIOUS LIBERTY."

pealed to the Supreme Court, the justices overruled Maris by an 8–1 vote. An opportunity to challenge the *Gobitis* ruling eventually made its way through the courts when two sisters faced a similar issue in West Virginia (*West Virginia State Board of Education v. Barnette*, 319 U.S. 624, 63 S. Ct. 1178, 87 L. Ed. 1628 [1943]). When that case reached the Supreme Court, two justices who had participated in the *Gobitis* decision were now retired. With two new justices, the High Court reversed itself, ruling as Maris had in the *Gobitis* case. See also FLAG.

In addition to his Third Circuit duties, Maris served on the Temporary Emergency Court of Appeals during World War II and the postwar years. (This court decided cases throughout the United States that arose from temporary legislation enacted by Congress to facilitate the war effort.) Maris served the temporary court as needed for the next twenty years and eventually became its chief judge. His work on this court broadened his interest in the crafting of legislation and the CODIFICATION of laws. This interest led to an appointment as chairman of the U.S. Judicial Conference Committee on Revision of the Laws in 1944.

His committee spearheaded the much-needed recodifications of the U.S. Criminal and Judicial Codes in 1947 and 1948. As committee chairman, he oversaw the ongoing revision and modernization of civil, criminal, bankruptcy, and appellate rules of procedure until 1967, when he stepped down. Even the modest Maris admitted that the adoption of his committee's work in 1947 and 1948 was a milestone in the improvement of JUDICIAL ADMINISTRATION.

In the early 1950s, Maris began to cultivate an interest in INTERNATIONAL LAW. Shortly after World War II, the U.S. Department of the Interior asked Maris to study the legal and judicial systems of the islands and trust territories of the South Pacific. He did, and he made recommendations that were well received at home and abroad. Throughout the 1950s, he worked tirelessly with the Virgin Islands, Guam, the Trust Territory of the Pacific Islands, and American Samoa to draft and enact legislation creating and revising their court systems and procedures. In conjunction with his international work, he served as a member of the U.S. Advisory Committee on International Rules of Judicial Procedure from 1959 to 1963, and as a member of the Advisory Committee to the Secretary of State on Private International Law from 1964 to 1967.

Maris took senior (or semiretired) status on December 31, 1958. As a senior judge, he served as special master under appointment of the U.S. Supreme Court in a number of significant and complex cases—including land and water claims cases between states and between states and the federal government (see, e.g., *Wisconsin v. Illinois*, 388 U.S. 426, 87 S. Ct. 1774, 18 L. Ed. 2d 1290 [1967]; *United States v. Maine*, 420 U.S. 515, 95 S. Ct. 1155, 43 L. Ed. 2d 363 [1975]). He continued to hear and rule on almost one hundred cases a year for the next twenty-five years.

Maris died on February 7, 1989, in Lansdale, Pennsylvania.

MARITAL 📖 Pertaining to the relationship of HUSBAND AND WIFE; having to do with MARRIAGE. 📖

Marital agreements are CONTRACTS that are entered into by individuals who are about to be married, are already married, or are in the process of ending a marriage. They ordinarily govern the division and ownership of marital property.

MARITAL COMMUNICATIONS PRIVILEGE 📖 The right given to a HUSBAND AND WIFE to refuse to TESTIFY in a trial as to confidential statements made to each other within and during the framework of their spousal relationship. 📖

The marital communications privilege is a right that only legally married persons have in court. Also called the husband-wife privilege, it protects the PRIVACY of communications between spouses. The privilege allows them to refuse to testify about a conversation or a letter that they have privately exchanged as marital partners.

The marital privilege is an exception to the general rule that all relevant EVIDENCE is admissible at trial. Similar privileges exist for communications between priest and penitent (one who has confided in the priest), attorney and client, and doctor and patient. Privileges exclude evidence from trial in order to advance some social goal. With the marital privilege, the goal of free and open communication between spouses, which is believed to strengthen and further the marital relationship, is given greater weight than the need for evidence (the information

exchanged by the spouses) to resolve a legal dispute.

The marital communications privilege originated at COMMON LAW. It was made formal in the English Evidence Amendment Act of 1853, which said that neither husbands nor wives could be forced to disclose any communication made to the other during the marriage. In the United States, the privilege came to be recognized in state and federal rules of evidence. By the twentieth century, the U.S. Supreme Court said that it was "regarded as so essential to the preservation of the marriage relationship as to outweigh the disadvantages to the administration of justice" (*Wolfle v. United States*, 291 U.S. 7, 54 S. Ct. 279, 78 L. Ed. 617 [1934]).

The marital communications privilege is available in most JURISDICTIONS. Most jurisdictions offering it allow a WITNESS spouse to choose whether to testify; some automatically disqualify evidence from a spouse.

The privilege is not absolute. Because its effect is to deny evidence at trial, courts generally interpret it narrowly.

The most important condition for its use is a legal MARRIAGE. Courts will not permit its use by partners who merely live together or by those who have a COMMON-LAW MARRIAGE or a sham, or false, marriage. Moreover, the communication must have taken place while the marriage existed, not after a DIVORCE. Generally, the determination of whether a marriage is legal depends on state law.

The privilege also cannot be claimed in certain situations, such as where one spouse is subject to prosecution for crimes committed against the other or against the children of the couple. In addition, the presence of third persons at the time of the communication usually eliminates confidentiality and thus destroys the privilege, although courts have granted exceptions for the presence of children.

Many jurisdictions make the distinction of which spouse "holds," and may therefore assert, the privilege—the defendant spouse or the witness spouse. In these jurisdictions, the spouse who holds the privilege may waive it and testify against the other spouse.

See also ATTORNEY-CLIENT PRIVILEGE; PRIVILEGED COMMUNICATIONS; TESTIMONY.

MARITIME LIEN 📖 The right of a particular individual to compel the sale of a ship because he or she has not been paid a debt owed to him or her on account of such vessel. 📖

A maritime lien is designed to furnish security to a CREDITOR and to enable a person to obtain repairs and supplies even in the event that the ship is a distance away from its owners and no significant amount of money is on board

A maritime lien would furnish security to a creditor who asserted a claim against this ship, no matter where the ship might sail.

to pay for the goods and services that are provided.

Maritime liens are distinguishable from a majority of other types of LIENS since the creditor need not retain possession of the boat before asserting a claim. They can exist only on movable objects that bear some relationship to navigation or COMMERCE on NAVIGABLE WATERS: for example, every part of a vessel, such as the hull, engine and tackle; as well as flatboats, lighters, scows, and dredges used to deepen harbors and channels. Controversy exists concerning whether a maritime lien can attach to a raft; however, courts have not recognized maritime liens for repairs done on a seaplane while it is in a hangar on dry land or for bridges, dry docks, wharves, or floating structures permanently moored to shore, such as barges that are used for restaurants.

The amount of a maritime lien equals the reasonable value of services that are performed in maintaining the ship, coupled with supplies that are furnished plus interest, less any SET-OFF for claims the ship has against the lienholders. The amount ordinarily arises out of a contract; however, a maritime lien can also be created for DAMAGES that are attributable to injuries that are caused by the ship.

An individual who is entitled to a maritime lien may forfeit his or her right if he or she delays in enforcing it or does something inconsistent with the lien. Allowing the ship to depart does not affect the lien; however, the complete destruction of a vessel extinguishes it.

A lienholder must sue in FEDERAL COURT in order to enforce a maritime lien, and anyone holding a lien against the ship can intervene in the action. See also INTERVENTION. The court may order a sale of the ship and its cargo and distribute the proceeds to those who establish a valid claim against the ship. Where there are insufficient funds to satisfy every claim, the court determines which liens have priority, and the percentage of recovery that each claimant is entitled to collect.

See also ADMIRALTY AND MARITIME LAW.

MARKETABLE TITLE ▥ Ownership and possession of REAL PROPERTY that is readily transferable since it is free from valid claims by outside parties. ▥

The concept of marketability of TITLE refers to ownership of real estate. Under law, titles are evidence of ownership. Selling real estate (land and the property attached to it) involves transferring its title. A marketable title is one that can be transferred to a new owner without the likelihood that claims will be made on it by another party. The concept is crucial in all real estate transactions because buyers generally expect to receive property to which no one else can lay CLAIM; they do not expect that their ownership will later be challenged. Marketability of title is addressed in the contract for sale. Unless a contract for sale specifies that a third party has claims on the real estate, there is an implied provision that the seller has a good or marketable title, which the buyer will receive.

However, some real estate that is for sale will

have outside claims against it. These claims are known as clouds and ENCUMBRANCES. For instance, the owner of the title may have outstanding debts or owe interest that has resulted in a LIEN being placed on the property. The lien gives the owner's CREDITOR a qualified legal right to the property in question, which remains in effect until the DEBT is settled. Because liens are long-lived (they can remain in force across generations), many states have tried to simplify land transactions by adopting marketable title acts. Generally, these laws limit the duration of a lien to a period of years during which the lien holder must take some action to satisfy the lien, or it is extinguished. Typically these laws apply to liens in existence at the time of the law's creation, as well as to future liens.

Ordinarily, CONTRACTS for the sale of real estate provide a REMEDY for a buyer who later discovers that the title is not marketable. If the seller has failed to provide marketable title, the buyer is permitted to RESCIND the sale—that is, to back out of the contract and receive a refund of the money paid for the property. Suppose, for example, that Mary buys land from Bob. The contract of sale declares that Bob holds marketable title to the land. After paying Bob, Mary receives a letter from an attorney saying that a business called Lou's Used Cars holds a lien on the property because Bob is using it as COLLATERAL for a car loan. In this case Bob has failed to provide Mary with marketable title. He will soon be hearing from her attorney, who will say that Mary is rescinding and wants her money back.

CROSS-REFERENCES

Cloud on Title; Real Property; Title Insurance; Title Search.

MARKET VALUE
The highest price a willing buyer would pay and a willing seller would accept, both being fully informed, and the property being exposed for sale for a reasonable period of time. The market value may be different from the price a property can actually be sold for at a given time (market price). The market value of an article or piece of property is the price that it might be expected to bring if offered for sale in a fair market; not the price that might be obtained on a sale at public auction or a sale forced by the necessities of the owner, but such a price as would be fixed by negotiation and mutual agreement, after ample time to find a purchaser, as between a vendor who is willing (but not compelled) to sell and a purchaser who desires to buy but is not compelled to take the particular article or piece of property.

MARQUE AND REPRISAL
A commission by which the head of a government authorizes a private ship to capture enemy vessels.

The authority to do such capturing is granted to private vessels in letters of marque and reprisal. In the technical sense, a *letter of marque* is permission to cross over the frontier into another country's territory in order to take a ship; a *letter of reprisal* authorizes taking the captured vessel to the home port of the capturer.

Since letters of marque and reprisal allowed privately owned and operated vessels to carry out acts of war, the practice came to be known as *privateering*. Privateering was frequently encouraged from the period between 1692 to 1814, at which time weaker countries used privateers to hurt a stronger country in the way guerrilla warfare is currently used. Privateers operated concomitant to regular navies. Their main purpose was to annoy the enemy; however, an enemy's merchant vessels were often seized in retaliation for acts of hostility.

The system of privateering was subject to extensive abuses. In the absence of proper letters, a PRIVATEER was tantamount to a pirate. PIRACY is subject to severe punishment throughout the world. Although privateers allegedly existed in order to support the defense of their sovereigns, they frequently acquired much personal wealth through their activities. In addition, since privateers were not subject to the same discipline as a regular navy, they yielded to the temptation to seize ships beyond the scope of their authority.

Such abuses, and new theories of naval warfare led civilized nations, in 1856, to sign an agreement outlawing privateering. The agreement does not prohibit a state from organizing a voluntary navy of private vessels, which are under the dominion and control of the state.

The U.S. Constitution provides that no state can grant letters of marque and reprisal. The federal government is not limited in this right by the Constitution; however, modern custom and treaties prevent it from granting the letters.

See also ADMIRALTY AND MARITIME LAW.

MARRIAGE
The legal status, condition, or relationship that results from a CONTRACT by which one man and one woman, who have the CAPACITY to enter into such an agreement, mutually promise to live together in the relationship of HUSBAND AND WIFE in law for life, or until the legal termination of the relationship.

Marriage is a legally sanctioned contract between a man and a woman. Entering a marriage contract changes the legal status of both parties, giving husband and wife new rights and obligations. PUBLIC POLICY is strongly in favor of marriage based on the belief that it preserves the family unit. Traditionally marriage has been viewed as vital to the preservation of morals and civilization.

The traditional principle upon which the institution of marriage is founded is that a husband has the obligation to support a wife and a wife has the duty to serve. In the past this has meant that the husband has the duty to provide a safe house, pay for necessities such as food and clothing, and live in the house. A wife's obligation has traditionally entailed maintaining a home, living in the home, having sexual relations with her husband, and rearing the couple's children. Changes in society have modified these marital roles to some degree as married women have joined the workforce in large numbers and some married men have become more involved in child rearing.

Individuals who seek to alter marital rights and duties are permitted to do so only within legally prescribed limits. Antenuptial agreements are entered into before marriage, in contemplation of the marriage relationship. Typically these agreements deal with property rights and the terms that will be in force if a couple's marriage ends in DIVORCE. Separation agreements are entered into during the marriage prior to the commencement of an action for a SEPARATION or divorce. These agreements are concerned with CHILD SUPPORT, visitation, and temporary maintenance of a spouse. The laws governing these agreements are generally concerned with protecting every marriage for social reasons whether the parties desire it or not. Couples should try to resolve their own difficulties because that is more efficient and effective than placing their problems before the courts.

In the United States, marriage is regulated by the states. At one time most states recognized COMMON-LAW MARRIAGE, which is entered into by agreement of the parties to be husband and wife. No marriage LICENSE is required nor is a wedding ceremony necessary. The parties are legally married when they agree to marry and subsequently live together, publicly holding themselves out as husband and wife. The public policy behind the recognition of common-law marriage is to protect the parties' expectations, if they are living as husband and wife in every way except that they never participated in a formal ceremony. By upholding a common-law marriage as valid, children are legitimized, surviving spouses are entitled to receive SOCIAL SECURITY benefits, and families are entitled to inherit property. These public policy reasons have declined in popularity. Most states have abolished common-law marriage, in large part because of the legal complications that arose concerning property and INHERITANCE.

The U.S. Supreme Court has held that states are permitted to reasonably regulate marriage by prescribing who can marry and the manner in which marriage can be dissolved. States may grant an ANNULMENT or divorce on terms they conclude are proper, because no one has the constitutional right to remain married. There is a right to marry, however, that cannot be casually denied. States are proscribed from absolutely prohibiting marriage in the absence of a valid reason.

The Supreme Court, for example, struck down laws in southern states that prohibited racially mixed marriages. These antimiscegenation statutes were held to be unconstitutional in the 1967 case of *Loving v. Virginia*, 388 U.S. 1, 87 S. Ct. 1817, 18 L. Ed. 2d 1010, because they violated EQUAL PROTECTION of the laws.

On the other hand, the Supreme Court ruled in 1878 that polygamous marriages (having more than one spouse simultaneously) are illegal. The requirement that marriage involve one man and one woman was held to be essential to Western civilization and the United States in *Reynolds v. United States*, 98 U.S. 145, 25 L. Ed. 244. Chief Justice MORRISON R. WAITE, writing for a unanimous court, concluded that a state (in this case Utah) may outlaw POLYGAMY for everyone, regardless of whether it is a religious duty, as the Mormons claimed it was.

Marriages and Marriage Rate in the United States, 1900 to 1995

Source: U.S. National Center for Health Statistics, *Vital Statistics of the United States*, annual.

Percent Distribution of Marriages, by Marriage Order, 1970 and 1988

1970

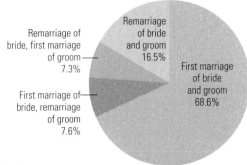

- Remarriage of bride and groom 16.5%
- First marriage of bride and groom 68.6%
- Remarriage of bride, first marriage of groom 7.3%
- First marriage of bride, remarriage of groom 7.6%

1988

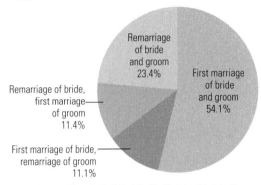

- Remarriage of bride and groom 23.4%
- First marriage of bride and groom 54.1%
- Remarriage of bride, first marriage of groom 11.4%
- First marriage of bride, remarriage of groom 11.1%

Source: U.S. National Center for Health Statistics, *Vital Statistics of the United States*, annual.

All states limit people to one living husband or wife at a time and will not issue marriage licenses to anyone who has a living spouse. Once someone is married, the person must be legally released from his or her spouse by death, divorce, or annulment before he or she may legally remarry. Persons who enter into a second marriage without legally dissolving a first marriage may be charged with the crime of BIGAMY.

The idea that marriage is the union of one male and one female has been thought to be so basic that it is not ordinarily specifically expressed by statute. This traditional principle has been challenged by gays and lesbians who, until recently, have unsuccessfully sought to legalize their relationships. In *Baker v. Nelson*, 291 Minn. 310, 191 N.W.2d 185 (1971), *cert. denied*, 409 U.S. 810, 93 S. Ct. 37, 34 L. Ed. 2d 65 (1972), the Minnesota Supreme Court sustained the clerk's denial of a marriage license to a homosexual couple.

The 1993 decision of the Hawaii Supreme Court in *Baehr v. Lewin*, 852 P.2d 44, 74 Haw. 530, revived the possibility of homosexual marriage. In *Baehr*, the court held that the state law restricting legal marriage to parties of the op- posite sex establishes a sex-based classification, which is subject to strict constitutional scrutiny when challenged on equal protection grounds. Although the court did not recognize a constitutional right to same-sex marriage, it indicated that the state would have a difficult time proving that the gay and lesbian couples were not being denied equal protection of the laws. On remand the Circuit Court of Hawaii found that the state did not meet its burden and enjoined the state from denying marriage applications solely because the applicants were of the same sex (*Baehr v. Miike*, 1996 WL 694235 [Hawaii Cir. Ct., Dec. 3, 1996]). However, this decision was stayed pending another appeal to the Hawaii Supreme Court. In the wake of *Baehr*, a number of states prepared legislation to ban same-sex marriage and prohibit recognition of such marriages performed in Hawaii. In 1996 Congress enacted the Defense of Marriage Act, which defines marriage as a legal union between one man and one woman and permits states to refuse same-sex marriages performed in other states.

Each state has its own individual requirements concerning who can marry. Before a state will issue a marriage license, a man and a woman must meet certain criteria. Some states prohibit marriage for those judged mentally ill or mentally retarded. In other states, however, a judge may grant permission to mentally retarded persons to marry.

Every state proscribes marriage between close relatives. The prohibited degree of relationship is fixed by state law. Every state forbids marriage to a child or grandchild, parent or grandparent, uncle or aunt, and niece or nephew, including illegitimate relatives and relatives of half blood, such as a half brother who has the same father but a different mother. A number of states also prohibit marriage to a first cousin, and some forbid marriage to a more distant relative, in-law, stepparent, or stepchild.

Age is an additional requirement. Every JURISDICTION mandates that a man and a woman must be old enough to wed. In the 1800s the legal age was as low as twelve years old for females. Modern statutes ordinarily provide that females may marry at age sixteen and males at age eighteen. Sometimes a lower age is permitted with the written consent of the parents. A number of states allow for marriage below the minimum age if the female is pregnant and a judge gives permission.

Every couple that wishes to marry must comply with a state's formal requirements. Many states require a blood test or a blood test

A sample marriage license

Source: Reprinted through the courtesy of the District Court of Ramsey County, Minnesota.

STATE OF MINNESOTA   **MARRIAGE LICENSE**   DISTRICT COURT
COUNTY OF RAMSEY   2nd Judicial District

To any person lawfully authorized to solemnize marriages within the State of Minnesota:
License is hereby granted to join in marriage, within six months from the date hereof,

_____ *of the County of* _____ *State of* _____ , *and*
_____ *of the County of* _____ *State of* _____
The names of the parties after their marriage, shall be: _____ ,
and _____
Wherefore, this shall be your authority for solemnizing the marriage of said parties, and making return thereof within five days as provided by law.

In Testimony Whereof, I have hereunto set my hand and affixed the seal of the said Court, at
_____ , *on* _____ , 19_____

_____

By: _____
                                      Deputy
To be Kept by Party Performing Marriage Ceremony

and physical examination before marriage to show whether one party is infected with a venereal disease. In some statutes, for example, the clerk is forbidden to issue a marriage license until the parties present the results of the blood test.

Most states impose a waiting period between the filing of an application for a license and its issuance. The period is usually three days, but in some states the period may reach five days. Other states mandate a waiting period between the time the license is issued and the date when the marriage ceremony can take place. Many states provide that the marriage license is valid for a certain period of time. If the ceremony does not take place during this period, a new license must be obtained.

It has been customary to give notice of an impending marriage to the general public. The old form of notice was called "publication of the banns," and the upcoming marriage was announced in each party's church three Sundays in a row before the marriage. This informed the community of the intended marriage and gave everyone the opportunity to object if any knew of a reason why the two persons could not be married. Today the names of applicants for marriage licenses are published in local newspapers.

Once a license is issued, the states require that the marriage commence with a wedding ceremony. The ceremony may either be civil or religious because states cannot require religious observances. Ceremonial requirements are very simple and basic to accommodate everyone. In some states nothing more is required than a declaration by each party in the presence of an authorized person and one additional WITNESS that he or she takes the other in marriage.

CROSS-REFERENCES

Celebration of Marriage; Domestic Violence; Family Law; Gay and Lesbian Rights; Miscegenation; Necessaries; Privileged Communications.

MARSHAL 📖 A federal court officer whose job entails maintaining the peace, delivering legal papers, and performing duties similar to those of a state SHERIFF. 📖

The term *marshal* originated in Old English law, where it was used to describe a variety of law enforcement officers with responsibilities to the courts and the king or queen. In contemporary U.S. law, it refers primarily to the chief law officers for the FEDERAL COURTS (28 U.S.C.A. §§ 561 et seq.). U.S. marshals execute federal laws within the states under the instructions of the courts. Their chief duty is to enforce legal orders; they have no independent authority to question whether a judge is right or wrong. Their responsibilities include delivering WRITS and PROCESSES and carrying out other orders, which range from making arrests to holding property in the CUSTODY of the court. Marshals may exercise the same powers as a state sheriff.

The chain of command for U.S. marshals begins in the White House. The president appoints to a four-year term one marshal for each judicial district. Each appointment is subject to confirmation by the U.S. Senate. Once an appointment is confirmed, the president retains the power to remove the marshal at any time. In the Department of Justice, the U.S. attorney general designates where each marshal's office is located. Each marshal appoints her or his own deputies and staff, with salaries based on schedules in federal law.

At the state and local levels, the term *marshal* is also used to describe police officers whose job is similar to that of a CONSTABLE or sheriff. It can also denote the head of a city police or fire department.

MARSHALING ASSETS AND SECURITIES

The process of organizing, ranking, and distributing funds in a manner set forth by law as being the most effective way to discharge DEBTS that are owed to various CREDITORS.

When ASSETS and SECURITIES are marshalled, the *two-fund doctrine* is frequently applied. It provides that when one claimant has two possible funds in the hands of a debtor to whom the claimant is able to resort to satisfy his or her demand, and a second claimant has an interest in only one of the funds, the second claimant can force the first to satisfy the claims out of the fund in which he or she, the second claimant, has no LIEN.

MARSHALL, JOHN

John Marshall presided over the U.S. Supreme Court from 1801 to 1835. Appointed by President JOHN ADAMS, Marshall assumed leadership during a pivotal era. The early nineteenth century saw tremendous political battles over the future of the United States and its Constitution, often with the Court at the center of controversy. By the force of personality, argument, and shrewdness, Marshall steered it through this rocky yet formative period. He weathered harsh criticism as the Court set important PRECEDENTS that increased its power and defined its role in government. Historians credit him with establishing what has been called the American judicial tradition, in which the Supreme Court acts as an independent branch of government endowed with final authority over constitutional interpretation.

Marshall was born September 24, 1755, near Germantown (now Midland), Virginia. He was the son of Thomas Marshall, a wealthy landowner, justice of the peace, and sheriff. Like his father he fought in the Revolutionary War and married into a prominent family. His father's tutoring significantly enhanced his mere two years of formal education, which were augmented in 1780 by a brief attendance at lectures in law at the College of William and Mary.

Marshall was also influenced by GEORGE WASHINGTON. Because of his service to General Washington in the war, Marshall became a strong Federalist. He later wrote about his mentor in his book *Life of George Washington* (1805–7).

Marriage ties made Marshall a relative of a leading Virginia political family. This helped secure his place in society, paving the way for an early legal and political career in the 1780s. He specialized in APPELLATE cases and quickly distinguished himself in the Virginia state bar. He also served in Virginia's council of state from 1782 to 1784, and in its house of delegates four times between 1782 and 1795. But it was as a partisan of the Federalists—the opponents of the states' rights–minded Republicans—that he came to wide acclaim. The struggle between the Federalists and the Jeffersonian Republicans was the most important political contest of the day. Marshall served as a devoted publicist and organizer for the Federalist cause in Virginia, and this work earned him various offers to serve as U.S. attorney general and as an associate justice of the Supreme Court. It also earned him the animosity of his distant cousin, Republican THOMAS JEFFERSON, who soon became U.S. president and was his lifelong political adversary.

In 1798 Marshall agreed to serve Federalist president John Adams as one of three U.S.

BIOGRAPHY

John Marshall

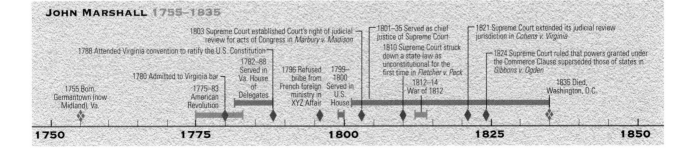

ministers to France during one of the Napoleonic Wars between France and Great Britain. In a scandal known as the XYZ AFFAIR, the French foreign ministry attempted to solicit a bribe from the U.S. emissaries, and Marshall became a national hero for refusing. He quickly emerged as the leading spokesman for Federalism in Washington, D.C., as a member of Congress from 1799 to 1800 and briefly as secretary of state under Adams in 1800. Then Adams lost the 1800 presidential election to Jefferson, and the Republicans won control of Congress. In a desperate attempt to preserve the Federalists' power, Adams spent the remaining days of his administration making judicial appointments. Sixteen new positions for judges on federal circuit courts and dozens for justices of the peace in the District of Columbia were handed out during the final days of Adams's administration. These last-minute appointees came to be known as MIDNIGHT JUDGES. One of these seats went to Marshall, who was appointed chief justice of the Supreme Court.

On March 4, 1801, Marshall assumed his duties as the head of the Court. Jefferson and the Republicans were furious over Adams's court stacking, and they swiftly quashed the appointments—except that, inexplicably, they did not challenge Marshall's. Marshall kept the Court out of the fray. He feared that in a conflict between the JUDICIARY and the EXECUTIVE BRANCH, the Court would lose.

Marshall again faced political conflict when in 1803 the Court ruled on a case brought by William Marbury, whose appointment as a D.C. JUSTICE OF THE PEACE had been one of those barred by the Republicans. Marshall's opinion for the unanimous Court in *Marbury v. Madison*, 5 U.S. (1 Cranch) 137, 2 L. Ed. 60, dismissed Marbury's suit on the ground that the Supreme Court lacked JURISDICTION to rule on it. But at the same time, the Court restated the position that it had the power to rule on questions of constitutionality. By striking down a section of the JUDICIARY ACT OF 1789 (1 Stat. 73), Marshall's opinion marked the first time that the Court overturned an act of Congress. Not for more than fifty years would it exercise this power again. Marshall asserted the right of the Supreme Court to engage in JUDICIAL REVIEW of the law, writing, "It is emphatically the province and duty of the judicial department to say what the law is." *Marbury* was the crucial first step in the evolution of the Supreme Court's authority as it exists today.

Marshall emphasized the need to limit state power by asserting the primacy of the federal government over the states. In 1819, as Mar-

"IT IS, EMPHATICALLY, THE PROVINCE AND DUTY OF THE JUDICIAL DEPARTMENT TO SAY WHAT THE LAW IS."

shall reached the height of his influence, he cited the Contracts Clause of the U.S. Constitution (art. 1, § 10) as a basis for protecting corporate CHARTERS from state interference (*Trustees of Dartmouth College v. Woodward*, 17 U.S. [4 Wheat.] 518, 4 L. Ed. 629). That year he also struck a blow to STATES' RIGHTS in *McCulloch v. Maryland*, 17 U.S. (4 Wheat.) 316, 4 L. Ed. 579, where he noted that the Constitution is not a "splendid bauble" that states can abridge as they see fit. In 1821 he advanced the theory of judicial review, rejecting a challenge by the state of Virginia to the appellate authority of the Supreme Court (*Cohens v. Virginia*, 19 U.S. [6 Wheat.] 264, 5 L. Ed. 257).

In his written opinions, Marshall typically relied on the power of logic and his own forceful eloquence, rather than citing law. This approach was noted by Associate Justice JOSEPH STORY: "When I examine a question, I go from headland to headland, from case to case. Marshall has a compass, puts out to sea, and goes directly to the result."

Marshall was not without opponents. Foremost among them was Jefferson. In 1810 Jefferson wrote to President JAMES MADISON that "[t]he Chief Justice's leadership was marked by "cunning and sophistry" and displayed "rancourous hatred" of the democratic principles of the Republicans. Jefferson led the Republican attack on Marshall with the accusation that he twisted the law to suit his own biases.

Although Marshall weathered the attacks, his authority, and the Court's, was ultimately affected. Not all his decisions were enforced; some were openly resisted by the president. New appointments to the Court brought states' rights advocates onto the bench, and Marshall began to compromise as a leader and to make concessions to ideological opponents.

Marshall died in office on July 6, 1835.

CROSS-REFERENCES

Constitution of the United States; *Fletcher v. Peck; Gibbons v. Ogden; Marbury v. Madison; McCulloch v. Maryland;* Supreme Court of the United States; *Trustees of Dartmouth College v. Woodward.*

BIOGRAPHY

Thurgood Marshall

MARSHALL, THURGOOD Thurgood Marshall, the first African American to serve on the U.S. Supreme Court, saw law as a catalyst for social change. For nearly sixty years as a lawyer and a jurist, Marshall worked to dismantle the system of segregation and improve the legal and social position of minorities.

Marshall was born July 8, 1908, in Baltimore, the son of a Pullman porter and a schoolteacher. He was a graduate of Lincoln University, a small, all-black college in Pennsylvania,

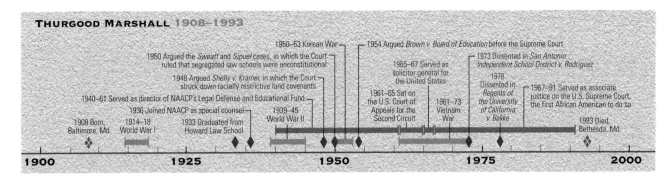

THURGOOD MARSHALL 1908–1993

1950–53 Korean War — 1954 Argued *Brown v. Board of Education* before the Supreme Court

1950 Argued the *Sweatt* and *Sipuel* cases, in which the Court ruled that segregated law schools were unconstitutional

1965–67 Served as solicitor general for the United States — 1973 Dissented in *San Antonio Independent School District v. Rodriguez*

1948 Argued *Shelly v. Kramer*, in which the Court struck down racially restrictive land covenants

1978 Dissented in *Regents of the University of California v. Bakke* — 1967–91 Served as associate justice on the U.S. Supreme Court, the first African American to do so

1940–61 Served as director of NAACP's Legal Defense and Educational Fund

1961–65 Sat on the U.S. Court of Appeals for the Second Circuit

1936 Joined NAACP as special counsel — 1939–45 World War II

1908 Born, Baltimore, Md.   1914–18 World War I   1933 Graduated from Howard Law School

1961–73 Vietnam War

1993 Died, Bethesda, Md.

1900   1925   1950   1975   2000

and Howard University Law School in Washington, D.C. At Howard, Marshall excelled under the guidance of Vice Dean CHARLES HAMILTON HOUSTON, the first African American to win a case before the U.S. Supreme Court. Houston encouraged his students to become not just lawyers but "social engineers" who could use the legal system to improve society. Marshall graduated first in his law class in 1933.

Marshall's attendance at predominantly black Howard University illustrates the barriers faced by African Americans during the early twentieth century. Although Marshall wished to attend law school at the University of Maryland (a public institution in his hometown of Baltimore), he was prohibited by law from doing so because of his race. The injustice helped set Marshall on a course of opposing all forms of official segregation that denied equal opportunities to African Americans.

After law school, Marshall set up a practice in Baltimore, representing indigent clients in civil rights cases. In 1936 his mentor Houston offered him a position with the NATIONAL ASSOCIATION FOR THE ADVANCEMENT OF COLORED PEOPLE (NAACP), and in 1940, Marshall became director of the NAACP Legal Defense and Education Fund, a position he held until 1961. Determined to eliminate segregation, Marshall coordinated a nationwide campaign to integrate higher education. He filed several successful lawsuits against public graduate and professional schools that refused to accept African American students. These suits paved the way for similar cases at the high school and elementary level. Marshall also journeyed throughout the deep South, traveling fifty thousand miles a year to fight JIM CROW LAWS (a series of laws that provided for racial segregation in the South) and represent criminal defendants.

Marshall argued thirty-two cases before the U.S. Supreme Court and won twenty-nine of them. No doubt his most famous and far-reaching triumph before the High Court was *Brown v. Board of Education of Topeka, Kansas,*

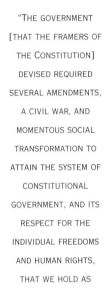

"THE GOVERNMENT [THAT THE FRAMERS OF THE CONSTITUTION] DEVISED REQUIRED SEVERAL AMENDMENTS, A CIVIL WAR, AND MOMENTOUS SOCIAL TRANSFORMATION TO ATTAIN THE SYSTEM OF CONSTITUTIONAL GOVERNMENT, AND ITS RESPECT FOR THE INDIVIDUAL FREEDOMS AND HUMAN RIGHTS, THAT WE HOLD AS FUNDAMENTAL TODAY."

347 U.S. 483, 74 S. Ct. 686, 98 L. Ed. 873 (1954). In that case, the father of African American student Linda Brown sued the school board of Topeka, Kansas, over its segregation policy. Brown was required by law to attend an all African American school several blocks from her home even though an all white public school was located in her own neighborhood. Under Kansas law, cities of more than fifteen thousand people, such as Topeka, could choose to operate segregated schools. Marshall argued that these segregated schools, defended by officials as "SEPARATE BUT EQUAL," were unconstitutional.

The separate-but-equal doctrine originated in *Plessy v. Ferguson*, 163 U.S. 537, 16 S. Ct. 1138, 41 L. Ed. 256 (1896), a case allowing segregated public accommodations for whites and blacks. In a plainspoken argument, Marshall dismissed as sheer fallacy the notion that segregated schools offered the same educational experiences to black and white students. Sociological and psychological studies demonstrated that black children were in fact harmed by the policy of school segregation. The students' self-esteem was damaged and their future diminished when they were forced to accept inadequate facilities, equipment, and educational opportunities. Marshall argued that the only purpose segregation served was to perpetuate the myth of African Americans' inferiority. A unanimous Court agreed and struck down the separate-but-equal doctrine, a momentous victory for Marshall, affecting public schools in twenty-one states.

Marshall was appointed to the U.S. Court of Appeals for the Second Circuit in 1961 and served there until 1965 when he was named solicitor general for the United States. He was appointed to the U.S. Supreme Court in 1967 by President LYNDON B. JOHNSON and served as an associate justice for twenty-four years.

While on the Supreme Court, Marshall was known more for his impassioned dissents than for his majority opinions. In particular, as a staunch opponent of CAPITAL PUNISHMENT, he regularly voiced his disagreement with the majority in death penalty cases. He was also a firm backer of AFFIRMATIVE ACTION and contributed one of his most famous dissents in *Regents of the University of California v. Bakke*, 438 U.S. 265, 98 S. Ct. 2733, 57 L. Ed. 2d 750 (1978). In that case, Marshall criticized the High Court's ruling that a public medical school's policy of reserving sixteen of one hundred spots for minority students was unconstitutional. Marshall also dissented in *San Antonio Independent School District v. Rodriguez*, 411 U.S. 1, 93 S. Ct. 1278, 36 L. Ed. 2d 16 (1973), disagreeing with the majority view that a Texas property tax system used to fund public education was acceptable even though it allowed wealthier districts to provide a better school system for students in those districts than less wealthy districts could provide. Marshall objected strongly to the property tax arrangement, claiming that it deprived poor children of an equal education.

Marshall wrote the majority opinion in *Amalgamated Food Employees Union v. Logan Valley Plaza*, 391 U.S. 308, 88 S. Ct. 1601, 20 L. Ed. 2d 603 (1968), in which the Court declared that a shopping center was a PUBLIC FORUM from which picketers could not be barred by private owners.

Marshall retired from the Court in 1991, but continued his criticism of government policies that were detrimental to African Americans or other disenfranchised groups.

Marshall died January 25, 1993, in Bethesda, Maryland. Upon Marshall's death, nearly twenty thousand mourners filed by his casket during the twelve hours it lay in state in the Great Hall of the Supreme Court.

CROSS-REFERENCES

Brown v. Board of Education of Topeka, Kansas; Civil Rights Movement; Integration; *Plessy v. Ferguson; Regents of the University of California v. Bakke;* School Desegregation.

MARSHALL PLAN

After World War II, Europe was devastated and urgently needed an organized plan for reconstruction and economic and technical aid. The Marshall Plan was initiated in 1947 to meet this need.

The originator of the plan, U.S. Secretary of State George C. Marshall, introduced it in a speech at Harvard University on June 5, 1947. He pointed out two basic reasons for providing aid to Europe: the United States sought the reestablishment of the European countries as independent nations capable of conducting valuable trade with the United States; and the threat of a Communist takeover was more prevalent in countries that were suffering economic depression.

In the aftermath of World War II, Congress established the Economic Cooperation Administration to distribute aid to Europe under the aegis of the Marshall Plan. In 1950, laborers in Berlin work on the construction of new apartments funded by the Plan.

In 1947 a preliminary conference to discuss the terms of the program convened in Paris. The Soviet Union was invited to attend but subsequently withdrew from the program, as did other Soviet countries.

Sixteen European countries eventually participated and, in July 1947, the Committee for European Economic Cooperation was established to allow representatives from member countries to draft a report that listed their requirements for food, supplies, and technical assistance for a four-year period.

The Committee for European Economic Cooperation subsequently became the Organization of European Economic Cooperation, an expanded and permanent organization that was responsible for submitting petitions for aid. In 1948, Congress passed the Economic Cooperation Act (62 Stat. 137), establishing funds for the Marshall Plan to be administered under the Economic Cooperation Administration, which was directed by Paul G. Hoffman.

Between 1948 and 1952, the sixteen-member countries received over $13 billion dollars in aid under the Marshall Plan. The plan was generally regarded as a success that led to industrial and agricultural production, while stifling the Communist movement. The plan was not without its critics, however, and many Europeans believed the COLD WAR hostilities between the Soviet nations and the free world were aggravated by it.

MARTIAL LAW 📖 The exercise of government and control by military authorities over the civilian population of a designated territory. 📖

Martial law is an extreme and rare measure used to control society during war or periods of civil unrest or chaos. According to the Supreme Court, the term *martial law* carries no precise meaning (*Duncan v. Kahanamoku*, 327 U.S. 304, 66 S. Ct. 606, 90 L. Ed. 688 [1946]). However, most declarations of martial law share some common features. Generally, the institution of martial law contemplates some use of military force. To a varying extent, depending on the martial law order, government military personnel have the authority to make and enforce civil and criminal laws. Certain civil liberties may be suspended, such as the right to be free from unreasonable SEARCHES AND SEIZURES, FREEDOM OF ASSOCIATION, and freedom of movement. And the writ of HABEAS CORPUS may be suspended (this writ allows persons who are unlawfully imprisoned to gain freedom through a court proceeding).

In the United States, martial law has been instituted on the national level only once, during the Civil War, and on a regional level only once, during World War II. Otherwise, it has been limited to the states. Uprisings, political protests, labor strikes, and RIOTS have, at various times, caused several state governors to declare some measure of martial law.

Martial law on the national level may be declared by Congress or the president. Under Article I, Section 8, Clause 15, of the Constitution, Congress has the power "[t]o provide for calling forth the Militia to execute the Laws of the Union, suppress insurrections and repel Invasions." Article II, Section 2, Clause 1, of the Constitution declares that "[t]he President shall be Commander in Chief of the Army and Navy of the United States, and of the Militia of the several States, when called into the actual Service of the United States." Neither constitutional provision includes a direct reference to martial law. However, the Supreme Court has interpreted both to allow the declaration of martial law by the president or Congress. On the state level, a governor may declare martial law within her or his own state. The power to do so usually is granted in the state constitution.

Congress has never declared martial law. However, in July 1861, Congress ratified most of the martial law measures declared by President ABRAHAM LINCOLN during the Civil War. Its martial law declaration gave the Union military forces the authority to arrest persons and conduct trials. However, Congress initially refused to ratify Lincoln's suspension of the writ of habeas corpus. This created friction between Congress and the president, and raised the question of whether unilateral suspension of the writ under martial law was within the president's power. The Supreme Court reviewed the issue and ruled in *Ex parte Merryman*, 17 F. Cas. 144 (1861) (No. 487), that only Congress had the power to suspend the writ of habeas corpus. After Congress approved Lincoln's suspension of the writ in 1863, Union forces were authorized to arrest and detain Confederate soldiers and sympathizers, but only until they could be tried by a court of law.

The martial law declared by Lincoln during the Civil War spawned another legal challenge, this one to the military courts: *Ex parte Milligan*, 71 U.S. (4 Wall.) 2, 18 L. Ed. 281 (1866). Lamdin Milligan, a civilian resident of Indiana, was arrested on October 5, 1864, by the Union military forces. Milligan was charged with five offenses: conspiring against the United States, affording aid and comfort to rebels, inciting INSURRECTION, engaging in disloyal practices, and violating the laws of war. Milligan was tried, found guilty, and sentenced to prison by a military court.

Although the habeas corpus petition had been suspended, the Supreme Court accepted Milligan's petition for a writ of habeas corpus. The Supreme Court held that neither the president nor Congress could give federal military forces the power to try a civilian who lived in a state that had federal courts. *Milligan* firmly established the right of the U.S. Supreme Court to review the propriety of martial law declarations.

The next large-scale martial law declaration took place eighty years later. On December 7, 1941, the day that Japanese warplanes bombed Pearl Harbor in what was then the territory of Hawaii, Governor Joseph B. Poindexter, of Hawaii, declared martial law on the Hawaiian Islands. The governor also suspended the writ of habeas corpus. The commanding general of the Hawaiian military assumed the position of military governor. All courts were closed by order of the military governor, and the military was authorized to arrest, try, and convict persons. Under Poindexter's martial law order, approved by the president, the military courts were given the power to decide cases without following the rules of EVIDENCE of the courts of law, and were not limited by sentencing laws in determining penalties.

In February 1942 the Department of War appointed General John L. De Witt to carry out martial law in California, Oregon, Washington, and the southern part of Arizona. In March 1942 De Witt announced that the entire Pacific Coast of the United States would be subject to additional martial law measures. Later that month he declared that all alien Japanese, Germans, and Italians, and all persons of Japanese descent, on the Pacific Coast were to remain inside their home between 8:00 P.M. and 6:00 A.M.

These martial law measures were challenged by criminal defendants shortly after they were put in force. In *Duncan v. Kahanamoku*, 327 U.S. 304, 66 S. Ct. 606, 90 L. Ed. 688 (1946), the Supreme Court held that the military tribunals established under martial law in Hawaii did not have JURISDICTION over common criminal cases, because the Hawaiian Organic Act (31 Stat. 141 [48 U.S.C.A. § 532]) did not authorize the governor to close the courts of law when they were capable of functioning. In *Duncan* the Court ordered the release of two prisoners who had been tried and convicted of EMBEZZLEMENT and ASSAULT by military courts.

In other cases the High Court was more tolerant of CIVIL RIGHTS deprivations under martial law. In *Hirabayashi v. United States*, 320 U.S. 81, 63 S. Ct. 1375, 87 L. Ed. 1774 (1943), the Court upheld a curfew placed on Japanese Americans during the war, on the ground of military necessity, and in *Korematsu v. United States*, 323 U.S. 214, 65 S. Ct. 193, 89 L. Ed. 194 (1944), the Court justified the random internment (imprisonment) of over 110,000 Japanese Americans during the war.

At least one governor has used martial law to enforce state agency regulations. In 1931 Governor Ross S. Sterling, of Texas, sent Texas National Guard troops into east Texas oil fields to force compliance with limits on the production of oil and an increase in the minimum number of acres required between oil wells. The regulations had been drawn up by the Texas Railroad Commission with the approval of the Texas Legislature, but similar regulations had been enjoined (stopped) by a federal court just four months earlier. In 1932 the Supreme Court invalidated Sterling's use of martial law, holding that it violated the constitutional DUE PROCESS rights of the property owners (*Sterling v. Constantin*, 287 U.S. 378, 53 S. Ct. 190, 77 L. Ed. 375 [1932]).

Another governor declared martial law in response to an ASSASSINATION and rumors of political corruption. In June 1954 Albert Patterson, a nominee for state attorney general in

Alabama, was shot to death on a street in Phenix City. Governor Gordon Persons, of Alabama, declared martial law in Phenix City, and dispatched General Walter J. ("Crack") Hanna and the Alabama National Guard to take over the city. Hanna appointed a military mayor, and the troops took control of the county courthouse and city hall. The troops physically removed certain officials from the courthouse and city hall, seized gambling equipment, and revoked liquor licenses.

Martial law usually is used to try to restore and maintain peace during civil unrest. It does not always yield the desired results. In May 1970, for example, Governor James Rhodes, of Ohio, declared limited martial law by sending in National Guard troops to contain a protest of the VIETNAM WAR at Kent State University. Four protestors were shot and killed by the troops. In a case brought by their survivors, the Supreme Court held that the governor and other state officials could be sued if they acted beyond the scope of state laws and the federal Constitution (*Scheuer v. Rhodes*, 416 U.S. 232, 94 S. Ct. 1683, 40 L. Ed. 2d 90 [1974]).

Martial law is generally a last resort. Courts will uphold a decision to use troops only if it was necessary and proper.

CROSS-REFERENCES

Japanese American Evacuation Cases; *Korematsu v. United States*; Military Law; Military Occupation; Militia; *Milligan, Ex Parte*; National Guard.

BIOGRAPHY

LIBRARY OF CONGRESS

Luther Martin

MARTIN, LUTHER Luther Martin was a distinguished lawyer and statesman who played an influential role in U.S. law and politics during the early years of the republic. During most of his legal career, he served as Maryland's attorney general.

Martin was born on February 9, 1748, near New Brunswick, New Jersey. He graduated from the College of New Jersey (now known as Princeton University) in 1766 and then taught school in Maryland for three years. In 1770 he began studying law and was admitted to the Virginia bar in 1771. He established a successful law practice in Maryland and Virginia and became known for his superior legal talents.

In 1774 Martin entered politics as a member of the Annapolis Convention, which was convened to formulate a list of grievances against the British government. In 1778 he was appointed Maryland's first attorney general, a position he would retain for most of the next forty years. He attended the Continental Congress in 1785 and the Constitutional Convention in 1787. Martin was against a strong federal government, preferring that power reside

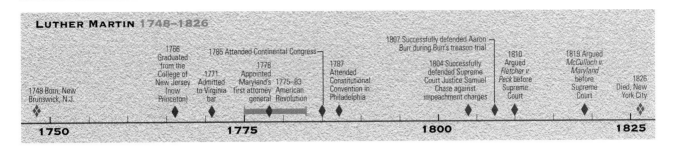

1748 Born, New Brunswick, N.J.

1766 Graduated from the College of New Jersey (now Princeton)

1771 Admitted to Virginia bar

1778 Appointed Maryland's first attorney general

1775–83 American Revolution

1785 Attended Continental Congress

1787 Attended Constitutional Convention in Philadelphia

1804 Successfully defended Supreme Court Justice Samuel Chase against impeachment charges

1807 Successfully defended Aaron Burr during Burr's treason trial

1810 Argued *Fletcher v. Peck* before Supreme Court

1819 Argued *McCulloch v. Maryland* before Supreme Court

1826 Died, New York City

1750   1775   1800   1825

in the states. Unhappy with the final version of the Constitution, he opposed its ratification.

As an attorney, Martin achieved a prestigious reputation and argued several landmark cases before the U.S. Supreme Court. In *Fletcher v. Peck*, 10 U.S. (6 Cranch) 87, 3 L. Ed. 162 (1810), the Court for the first time invalidated a state law as contrary to the Constitution. The Georgia legislature had revoked a land grant originally permitted by a CONTRACT. The Court ruled that public grants were contractual obligations and could not be abrogated without fair compensation. Chief Justice JOHN MARSHALL based the decision on the Contract Clause of the Constitution (Art. I, Sec. 10, Cl. 1), which provides that no state shall impair the obligations of contract.

Martin also appeared before the Supreme Court in *McCulloch v. Maryland*, 17 U.S. (4 Wheat.) 316, 4 L. Ed. 579 (1819), where he argued that Maryland had the right to impose a tax on a federally chartered bank. Chief Justice Marshall ruled against Maryland, finding that the state had no authority under the Constitution to tax any agency that has been authorized by the federal government. In Marshall's words, "the power to tax is the power to destroy." Such a power did not comport with the allocation of powers under the Constitution.

Martin also served as counsel in two politically charged cases. In 1804 he helped successfully defend Supreme Court Justice SAMUEL CHASE against IMPEACHMENT. Chase, a Federalist judge who had outraged Democrats with several decisions that appeared to be based as much on politics as law, was acquitted at his Senate trial after Martin convinced senators that the impeachment itself was politically motivated.

In 1807 Martin represented AARON BURR, who was accused of treason. Martin argued that the charge was baseless and was motivated by President THOMAS JEFFERSON's personal and political dislike of Burr. His indictment of the Jefferson administration helped convince the jury to acquit Burr.

Martin suffered a stroke in 1820, shortly after arguing *M'Culloch v. Maryland*. Despite his

"... IN A FEDERAL GOVERNMENT, THE PARTIES TO THE COMPACT ARE NOT THE PEOPLE, AS INDIVIDUALS, BUT THE STATES, AS STATES; AND ... [IT IS] BY THE STATES AS STATES, ... THAT THE SYSTEM OF GOVERNMENT OUGHT TO BE RATIFIED, AND NOT BY THE PEOPLE, AS INDIVIDUALS."

stature and his successful law practice, Martin was insolvent. The Maryland legislature levied a $5 license fee on every attorney to help support Martin. In 1823 Aaron Burr took Martin into his home, where he lived for three years. Martin died on July 10, 1826, in New York City.

CROSS-REFERENCES

Bank of the United States; Constitution of the United States; *Fletcher v. Peck*; *McCulloch v. Maryland*.

MARTINDALE-HUBBELL LAW DIRECTORY A database containing information about attorneys and law firms around the world.

Primarily lawyers use the *Martindale-Hubbell Law Directory* to assist them in the practice of their profession. An attorney may use the directory, for example, to find out more information about a lawyer or law firm that has filed a lawsuit against her client or to find an attorney in another JURISDICTION to assist in a case.

James B. Martindale published his first legal directory in 1868. In 1874 he published *Martindale's United States Law Directory*, a selective listing of attorneys that made no attempt to include complete information on all attorneys. The 1885–1886 biannual edition was renamed *Martindale's American Law Directory*. The first attempt to publish a complete roster of all attorneys in the United States and Canada, this edition listed each attorney and law firm in alphabetical order by state and city and the laws of each state and all Canadian provinces. In 1896 annual publication of the directory began, and a section listing foreign attorneys and law firms was added. The 1896 edition also introduced the basic information format for attorneys that continues to the present: date of birth, date of admission to the bar, and a rating, if any, of legal ability.

In 1930 the Martindale Company purchased the publishing rights of *Hubbell's Legal Directory* issued by J. H. Hubbell & Company from 1870 to 1930. The company was purchased from Edwin Powell Hubble (a variant spelling of the family name), the astronomer for whom the Hubble Space Telescope is named. The merged publications, renamed the *Martindale-Hubbell Law Directory*, appeared as a two-volume set in 1931.

The size of the directory has grown steadily as more attorneys have joined the profession. In 1948 the directory went to three volumes. By 1968 it had increased to five volumes. The first eight-volume set was published in 1987, and the 1991 edition was made up of sixteen smaller volumes. In 1996 the directory consisted of twenty-five volumes and contained listings for more than 900,000 attorneys and law firms in the United States, Canada, and throughout the world.

The directory is now available on CD-ROM, through LEXIS-NEXIS, and through the Martindale-Hubbell site on the World Wide Web. It has become a standard reference publication for law libraries. The Martindale Company was purchased by Reed Elsevier in 1990 and is part of Reed Reference Publishing.

MARX, KARL HEINRICH   Karl Heinrich Marx was a nineteenth-century German intellectual whose works have had great influence on the world. Largely ignored during his lifetime, Marx's writings on economics, politics, social science, and revolution eventually led to the founding of two political movements, SOCIALISM and COMMUNISM. In addition, his views have influenced many legal philosophers.

Marx was born May 5, 1818, in Trier, in what was then the state of Prussia. His father was a successful lawyer. A bright student, Marx studied law at the University of Bonn in 1835. The following year he transferred to the University of Berlin, where he studied philosophy. While at Berlin, Marx joined a group of students and teachers who were opposed to the Prussian government. At that time citizens of Prussia enjoyed few civil liberties and were

Karl Marx's writings led to the founding of socialism and Communism, though they were largely ignored during his lifetime.

LIBRARY OF CONGRESS

prevented from participating fully in public affairs.

Marx's political activity proved harmful for his academic career. After obtaining his doctorate in philosophy in 1841, he tried to get a teaching job. The Prussian government barred him from teaching. He then became a freelance journalist.

Following his marriage to Jenny von Westphalen in 1843, Marx moved to Paris. In 1845 he moved to Brussels, where he remained until 1848. In 1848 he returned to Germany to become the editor of a radical paper in Cologne. He used the newspaper to rail against the Prussian government, and he encouraged the German Revolution of 1848, which failed to topple the regime.

During the days leading up to the revolution, Marx first articulated his political and historical theories. In the *Communist Manifesto* (1848), a pamphlet written with his friend Friedrich Engels, Marx argued that history is a series of conflicts between economic classes. He predicted that the ruling middle class would be overthrown by the working class, and a classless society would be created. This classless society would be characterized by the public ownership of all means of economic production. Marx and Engels had previously written *The German Ideology* (1845–46), a seven-hundred-page book that dealt in more philosophic terms with economics and politics.

Marx's participation in the failed revolution forced him to flee Germany. In 1849 he settled in London, where he remained for the rest of his life. He and his family lived in abject poverty. He refused to work, except for a stint as a political reporter for the *New York Tribune*. Instead, he spent his time researching at the British Museum library. Friends contributed to his support, especially Engels, who owned a textile manufacturing plant in England. In 1864 Marx founded the International Workingmen's Association, a group dedicated to preparing the way for a socialist REVOLUTION. He died in London on March 14, 1883.

Marx spent most of his life in England working on *Das Kapital* (Capital). The first volume was published in 1867, the second and third volumes after his death. He considered *Das Kapital* to be his major work, because it described the functioning of industrial capitalism. Marx saw capitalism as an efficient way of producing wealth, but also saw a fatal flaw in how this wealth was distributed: those who owned the means of production retained most of the wealth, whereas the working class had to get by on fluctuating wages. Marx argued that this inequality would eventually lead the working class to revolt.

Marx's writings had a great effect on the socialist and Communist revolutionary movements of the nineteenth and twentieth centuries. He cast his theories as historically inevitable, providing revolutionaries with a way of explaining the world that appeared to be scientific.

Marxist ideas became the core intellectual tradition for Communist countries in the twentieth century. Social science, history, and philosophy were shaped by his views. U.S. intellectuals generally ignored Marxism until the 1960s, in part because many people believed that it was a subversive political doctrine.

In law, the field of Marxist jurisprudence has grown significantly. A Marxist analysis of law places more importance on the power of economic forces in society rather than on the concept of an impartial, neutral rule of law. Marxists believe that the material forces of a society and those that control these forces shape the society's legal system.

CROSS-REFERENCES

Cold War; Hegel, Georg Wilhelm Friedrich; Lenin, Vladimir Ilych; Stalin, Joseph.

MASON, GEORGE

George Mason was an eighteenth-century statesperson who in 1776 wrote the Declaration of Rights for the State of Virginia and who later helped write the U.S. Constitution. Mason was a champion of liberty whose opposition to SLAVERY and a strong federal government led him to refuse to sign the Constitution.

Mason was born on October 7, 1725, in Fairfax County, Virginia, the son of a wealthy commercial and agricultural family. Mason studied law but was primarily a plantation owner and real estate speculator. He was a neighbor of GEORGE WASHINGTON. Mason was deeply interested in western expansion, and in 1749 he became a member of the Ohio Company, which developed land and trade on the upper Ohio River.

At about this time, Mason helped found the city of Alexandria, Virginia. Because he suffered

BIOGRAPHY

George Mason

from chronic poor health, Mason avoided public office, serving only a short time in the Virginia House of Burgesses. Yet he did not shun the political debate over British interference with the colonies. British attempts at taxing and controlling the colonies through the STAMP ACT of 1765 and the TOWNSHEND ACTS led many colonial leaders to consider political independence.

In 1775 Mason attended the Virginia convention, where he helped write most of the Virginia constitution. In June 1776 he wrote the VIRGINIA DECLARATION OF RIGHTS. THOMAS JEFFERSON was probably familiar with Mason's concepts and language when he wrote the DECLARATION OF INDEPENDENCE later that year, and other states soon copied Mason's work. French revolutionaries also showed they had been influenced by Mason's declaration in their Declaration of the Rights of Man, which was composed in 1789.

The Virginia Declaration of Rights stated that government derived from the people, that individuals were created equally free and independent, and that they had INALIENABLE rights that the government could not legitimately deny them.

As a delegate to the Constitutional Convention of 1787, Mason was called on to write part of the first draft. By the end of the convention, however, he had become deeply alienated by the result. Although he came from a slaveholding state, Mason opposed slavery on both moral and economic grounds. He sought an end to the slave trade and the manumission of all slaves. Instead, the Constitution allowed the slave trade to continue for twenty years, and it said nothing about the institution of slavery.

Mason also objected to the lack of provision for individual rights, believing that the Constitution gave too much power to the federal government. His criticism contributed to the enactment and ratification of the BILL OF RIGHTS in 1791, portions of which were modeled on Mason's Declaration of Rights.

Mason died on October 7, 1792, at his estate in Fairfax County, Virginia.

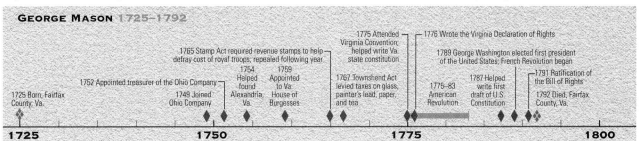

GEORGE MASON 1725–1792

1725 Born, Fairfax County, Va.

1752 Appointed treasurer of the Ohio Company

1749 Joined Ohio Company

1754 Helped found Alexandria, Va.

1759 Appointed to Va. House of Burgesses

1765 Stamp Act required revenue stamps to help defray cost of royal troops; repealed following year

1767 Townshend Act levied taxes on glass, painter's lead, paper, and tea

1775 Attended Virginia Convention; helped write Va. state constitution

1775–83 American Revolution

1776 Wrote the Virginia Declaration of Rights

1789 George Washington elected first president of the United States; French Revolution began

1787 Helped write first draft of U.S. Constitution

1791 Ratification of the Bill of Rights

1792 Died, Fairfax County, Va.

1725   1750   1775   1800

MASON, JOHN YOUNG

John Young Mason served as a U.S. attorney general under President JAMES POLK. He was secretary of the Navy during the Mexican War, chair of the House committee on foreign affairs, and an ambassador to France. While serving as ambassador, Mason was one of three U.S. ministers to sign the Ostend Manifesto, a written proposal to buy or seize Cuba from Spain that was later dismissed as an effort to extend SLAVERY in the United States.

Mason was born in Greensville County, Virginia, on April 18, 1799. His father was Edmunds Mason, and his mother was Frances Ann Young Mason. His grandfather was Captain James Mason of the Fifteenth Virginia Line. Mason graduated from the University of North Carolina in 1816 and attended the law school at Litchfield, Connecticut, for three years. In 1819 he was admitted to the Virginia bar and began practice at Hicksford in Greensville County. See also LITCHFIELD LAW SCHOOL.

In 1822 Mason moved to Southampton County, Virginia, and began a law practice that quickly became lucrative. In 1823 he was elected as a Democrat to the Virginia General Assembly, where he served until 1827. He served in the Virginia Senate from 1827 to 1831. Mason was also a member of the 1829 state constitutional convention.

In 1831 Mason was elected to the U.S. House of Representatives. While serving as a representative, Mason supported most of President ANDREW JACKSON's measures. He refused to vote to recharter the National Bank, even when the Virginia General Assembly pressed him to do so. As chair of the House committee on foreign affairs, Mason introduced a bill recognizing independence for Texas. He also supported naval preparedness during a time of adversarial relations between the United States and France. Mason served in the House until 1837, when he accepted a position as judge of the U.S. district for Virginia.

President JOHN TYLER appointed Mason secretary of the Navy in March 1844, and President Polk appointed Mason attorney general in

1845. Mason was the only member of Tyler's cabinet to be retained by the new president. He served as attorney general until 1846 when Polk reappointed him as secretary of the Navy. He served in that position until 1849.

Mason was secretary of the Navy during the years of the Mexican War. Although he was an expansionist, he opposed incorporating Mexico into the United States and supported U.S. acceptance of the treaty signed with Mexico.

At the end of the Polk administration, Mason returned to his law practice in Richmond. He was elected president of the James River and Kanawha Company in 1849 and became an active advocate of efforts to rapidly extend the canal system in Virginia. In the 1852 presidential campaign, Mason publicly supported FRANKLIN PIERCE.

In 1853 President Pierce appointed Mason U.S. minister to France. In 1854, at the request of Secretary of State William L. Marcy, Mason met with JAMES BUCHANAN, U.S. minister to Great Britain, and Pierre Soulé, U.S. minister to Spain, in Ostend, Belgium, to discuss the issue of Cuban uprisings. During this period U.S. leaders were bitterly debating the circumstances under which slavery should or should not be extended into new states. On October 18, 1854, Mason, Buchanan, and Soulé—who were pro-slavery—signed the Ostend Manifesto, a secret document proclaiming that Spain should sell Cuba to the United States and that, if it refused to do so, the United States had the right to take the island by force. The press published the document and ridiculed it as a clumsy plot to add new slave territory to the United States. Marcy subsequently dismissed the document on behalf of the Pierce administration.

Mason was reappointed U.S. minister to France when Buchanan became president, and he remained in that position, living abroad, until his death in Paris on October 18, 1859.

MASSACHUSETTS CONSTITUTION OF 1780

In 1630, John Winthrop and his associates in the Massachusetts Bay Company established the Great and General Court of Massa-

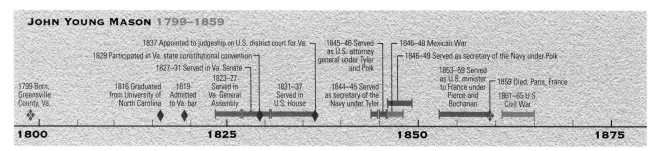

JOHN YOUNG MASON 1799–1859

1837 Appointed to judgeship on U.S. district court for Va.

1829 Participated in Va. state constitutional convention

1827–31 Served in Va. Senate

1845–46 Served as U.S. attorney general under Tyler and Polk

1846–48 Mexican War

1846–49 Served as secretary of the Navy under Polk

1799 Born, Greensville County, Va.

1816 Graduated from University of North Carolina

1819 Admitted to Va. bar

1823–27 Served in Va. General Assembly

1831–37 Served in U.S. House

1844–45 Served as secretary of the Navy under Tyler

1853–59 Served as U.S. minister to France under Pierce and Buchanan

1859 Died, Paris, France

1861–65 U.S. Civil War

1800   1825   1850   1875

chusetts to provide a form of local government for the Puritans who had settled the Boston area. During the American Revolution, the General Court produced an initial draft of a state constitution for Massachusetts. The citizens of Massachusetts refused to accept this constitution as law, however, due to their non-participation in the process by which it was formed; instead they elected representatives to meet at a constitutional convention to determine the nature of their government. In 1779, the representatives convened in Cambridge and designated JOHN ADAMS to be the primary drafter of the constitution. This constitution was ratified in 1780.

Among the terms of the Massachusetts Constitution of 1780 is the provision that empowers the governor and his or her council or the legislature to obtain advisory opinions from the Supreme Judicial Court on questions relating to the scope of the power of the governor or legislature of the Commonwealth. Presently Massachusetts is the only one of the thirteen original states that has retained its first constitution. The constitution has, however, been subject to numerous amendments, the most extensive of which were made by the Massachusetts Constitutional Convention that was convened from 1917 to 1919.

MASSACHUSETTS TRUST A business arrangement that is used in place of a CORPORATION or PARTNERSHIP in which trustees hold TITLE to property for the advantage of beneficiaries for investment purposes.

A Massachusetts trust is another name for a *common-law trust* or a BUSINESS TRUST, which offers its beneficiaries limited financial liability in transactions in which it engages.

MASS COMMUNICATIONS LAW A body of primarily federal statutes, regulations, and judicial decisions that govern radio; broadcast, cable, and satellite TELEVISION; and other means of electronic communication.

Since the introduction of the radio in the early twentieth century, sophisticated technological devices have been developed to facilitate the transmission of ideas, information, and entertainment throughout the United States and the world. The federal government has taken an active role in regulating the means of communication that involve the interstate transmittal of information. Government regulation was needed to create a coherent plan for radio and television BROADCASTING and to ensure that these facilities are used responsibly. The passage of the Telecommunications Act of 1996 (Pub. L. No. 104-104), however, signals a decline in

government regulation. This massive deregulation allows companies involved with mass communications to compete and combine more freely.

Early History Government regulation of radio began in 1910 at a time when radio was regarded primarily as a device to bring about safe maritime operations and as a potential advancement in military technology. Persons seeking to use radio frequencies would register with the Department of Commerce to have a frequency assigned to them. During World War I, entrepreneurs began to recognize the commercial possibilities of radio.

By the mid-1920s, commercial radio stations were operating, and the secretary of commerce set aside frequencies for commercial application. The regulatory powers of the secretary were uncertain because the secretary was authorized under law only to record applications and grant frequencies. The Federal Radio Commission was created in 1927 to assign applicants designated frequencies under specific engineering rules and to create and enforce standards for the broadcasters' privilege of using the public's airwaves.

The commission later became the FEDERAL COMMUNICATIONS COMMISSION (FCC), which was established by the Communications Act of 1934 (47 U.S.C.A. § 151 et seq.). The 1934 act set out a regulatory structure that would govern mass communications law for more than sixty years, with the FCC as the governing regulatory body. The law also made clear that the federal government has sole JURISDICTION over modern mass communication.

The FCC The FCC establishes the requirements for the licensing of stations and sets

The development of new methods of mass communication, such as satellite television and the Internet, has led to a reevaluation of the laws governing the transmission of information and entertainment. The Telecommunications Act of 1996, signed into law by President Bill Clinton, lessened the regulations governing many vehicles of mass communication.

up a framework that tries to ensure some competition for licenses. The FCC allows the free market to determine such matters as advertising costs, expenses, cost of equipment, and choice of programming by broadcasters.

In addition to regulating commercial and educational broadcasting, the FCC has pervasive power to govern nonbroadcast use of communications facilities, such as interstate commerce CARRIER systems, radio systems for truck-to-truck communication, taxicab networks, marine and ship radio, aviation frequencies, citizens band radio, international "ham" communication, police and fire communications networks, and cable and satellite television. All radio stations owned and operated by the United States, however, are exempt from regulation by the FCC.

The FCC cannot decide whether a particular advertising message is false and misleading. This subject matter is delegated by law to the Federal Trade Commission (FTC). The FCC can act when a licensee continues to broadcast an advertisement that the FTC has determined to be false and misleading. The FCC does not set advertising rates or oversee ordinary and usual business practices, such as production charges, commission arrangements, and salaries of artists.

Although government regulation of broadcasting appears to conflict with the FIRST AMENDMENT's guarantee of FREEDOM OF SPEECH and press, such regulation is often justified in terms of the limited number of available broadcast frequencies. Unlike the print media, which can physically coexist in the same community at the same time, broadcasting requires the government to make a choice between two or more potential broadcasters that wish to use the same broadcast space. In broadcasting, two or more radio or television stations cannot physically operate on the same frequency, because neither would be heard. Because it is important to the general public that someone be heard, the FCC must choose who that will be.

The FCC is not always faced with the necessity of choice. Only one broadcaster might apply for a particular open frequency. The FCC must determine, no matter how many applicants, whether a potential broadcaster has the proper qualifications and will operate "in the public interest" before the applicant will be permitted to broadcast.

Licensing Congress has devised a procedure by which broadcasters are granted an exclusive right or LICENSE to broadcast over a particular frequency for a statutory maximum number of years. Under the Telecommunica-

tions Act of 1996, new licenses and renewals are granted for eight years. The FCC classifies different types of stations and the particular services they provide and assigns the band of frequencies for each individual station. The three sets of broadcast frequencies are the AM band, the FM band, and a third set used for television. Licenses are issued only on a showing that public convenience, interest, and necessity will be served and that an applicant satisfies certain requirements, such as citizenship, character, financial capability, and technical expertise.

Citizenship A noncitizen, foreign government, or CORPORATION of which any officer or DIRECTOR is an alien or where more than one-fifth of the stock is owned by ALIENS or representatives of foreign governments cannot receive a broadcasting license. These restrictions are mandatory and cannot be waived by the FCC. Only Congress can pass legislation making an exception to the citizenship rule. There are no similar restrictions on foreign ownership of cable television systems.

Character Applicants must possess the essential character qualifications of honesty and candor. However, the FCC evaluates the applicant based on information that the applicant provides. The FCC relies on the honesty of applicants because it has neither the staff nor the budget to verify the representations made by license applicants or its licensees. Any intentional misrepresentation by an applicant will seriously jeopardize the license application, regardless of the significance of the matter.

A license may be denied for violations of CRIMINAL LAW, but disqualification does not automatically occur for minor offenses. An applicant convicted of violating federal regulatory laws in a business not involving communications might have a license application denied because the conviction indicates an intentional disregard for government regulations.

When faced with a choice between an applicant against whom no character question is raised and one who has violated a law, but not one that results in an automatic denial, the FCC is most likely, all other things being equal, to grant the license to the non-lawbreaker.

Financial Qualifications An applicant must demonstrate the financial capability to construct and operate the proposed facility for one year. If the person intends to rely on anticipated revenue, she or he must file evidence that these revenues will, in fact, be earned. Evidence may include AFFIDAVITS from prospective advertisers indicating their plan to contract with the station for advertising time.

An applicant who wants to buy an existing profit-making station need only show the financial ability to maintain operations without revenues for the first three months. A station that has earned profits in the past is considered to be likely to continue to earn profits in the future. Where a station that is already in financial difficulty is being sold, the applicant-purchaser must demonstrate a capability to produce a profit in the first year of operation.

Technical Expertise A broadcaster must comply with all the technical requirements imposed by the FCC, such as the use of transmitting equipment that is the type approved by the FCC and the operation of broadcast facilities during the hours appropriate for the frequency sought.

Ownership of More than One Station Before 1996 the FCC enforced its "multiple ownership rule," which restricted persons or entities from acquiring excessive power through ownership of a number of radio and television facilities. The rule was based on the assumption that if one person or company owned most or all of the media outlets in an area, the diversity of information and programming on these stations would be restricted. The rule meant that a single entity could not own more than one station in the same market, such as two AM stations in the same community, or in adjacent communities when the stations' signals would overlap to a certain designated extent. In addition, the FCC restricted the total number of licenses one entity could own to twelve AM, twelve FM, and seven television stations anywhere in the United States.

The Telecommunications Act of 1996 eliminated the restrictions limiting the number of AM and FM stations that may be owned by one entity nationally. The FCC was directed to reduce the restrictions on locally owned AM and FM stations as well. The act eliminated the restriction on the number of television stations that an entity can own directly or indirectly and increased the ceiling on permissible national audience reach from 25 to 35 percent. The FCC was directed to permit entities to have cross-ownership in network and cable systems. The act also removed the prohibition on cable operators from owning or controlling local television broadcast systems.

Procedure for Obtaining a License A license can be granted without a hearing. Where there are substantial and material questions of fact, or the FCC does not find that the issuance of a license would be in the PUBLIC INTEREST, a hearing must be held to review the application. Other broadcast stations might intervene in the application process, particularly where a grant of a license to another applicant could affect their licenses or seriously impair their economic well-being. In cases of such intervention, a hearing is usually required.

Representatives of the public can participate in the licensing process where a grant of a license would have a particular, definable effect upon them. A citizen cannot participate by merely asserting a general listenership interest without alleging a specific injury to himself or herself. A representative group that suffers a particular injury may file a petition with the FCC to deny the application. If there is a substantial or material question of fact, a hearing is justified.

License Renewal and Revocation A broadcasting entity must renew its license during the time set by statute to continue operating on that frequency, and no guarantee exists that such renewal is automatic.

A license is revocable during its term, but the FCC must notify the licensee and give it a full opportunity to be heard prior to revocation. There must be reasonable grounds to warrant revocation of the license. The FCC decision must be embodied in written findings that contain a full explanation of its reasoning and actions. Such decisions are reviewable by the U.S. court of appeals.

Regulation of Licensees Although the primary responsibility of the FCC is the licensing of broadcasting stations, it also regulates, to a certain extent, the manner in which stations operate.

Political Broadcasts Congress has long recognized the potential of using various broadcast media to influence the outcome of an election. A candidate with access to broadcasting facilities has a greater chance of reaching more voters than a candidate who lacks such access. Congress has mandated that any licensee that permits a legally qualified candidate for public office to use its facilities to campaign must give all other candidates for that position equal opportunities to use the broadcast station. This requirement, sometimes called the "equal time doctrine," does not apply to news broadcasts or advertisements on behalf of the candidate in which the candidate does not appear.

Equal rates must be charged to each candidate. During election campaigns candidates must be given the "lowest unit charge" that is offered by the station to commercial advertisers for comparable time. The FCC is the regulatory agency that ensures licensee compliance with this law. Stations cannot censor political advertisements, even if the candidate makes libelous or scandalous charges. Stations cannot be sued, however, for libel or slander based on a candidate's remarks.

When a licensee either endorses or opposes a legally qualified candidate in an editorial, the other candidate must be notified within twenty-four hours of the date and time of the editorial, be given a script or videotape or audio tape of the editorial, and be furnished with a reasonable opportunity to respond. If the editorial is broadcast within seventy-two hours of the ELEC-TION, the licensee must provide the material in sufficient time prior to the broadcast to enable candidates to have a reasonable opportunity to present a reply. These requirements exist only when a station endorses a particular candidate. They do not apply to editorials on public issues, such as funding for public education.

The FCC has developed a "quasi equal opportunity doctrine" that governs appearances by representatives for candidates who are not covered by the equal time doctrine. When supporters of a candidate purchase time from a broadcaster during an election campaign, the licensee must make comparable time available to the supporters of the opponent.

Fairness Doctrine   From 1959 to 1987, the FCC enforced the "FAIRNESS DOCTRINE," which required that broadcasters provide reasonable opportunity for the discussion of opposing views on controversial issues that affect the public. The doctrine proved controversial, and in 1987 the FCC rescinded it, concluding that it was a restriction on the First Amendment and that the growth of electronic media provided adequate means for presenting diverse opinions on issues of public policy.

Personal Attack Rule   Though the FCC repealed the fairness doctrine, it left intact the "personal attack rule," which is an aspect of the fairness doctrine that concerns the right of a person criticized in a broadcast to gain access to the broadcast facility to defend herself or himself. When, during the presentation of views on a controversial issue of public importance, the honesty, character, or integrity of an identified person or group is impugned, the licensee must, within one week after the attack, notify the subject of the attack of the date, time, and identification of the broadcast and provide a script or videotape or audio tape of the attack and a reasonable opportunity to reply using the licensee's facilities. This rule does not apply to attacks on foreign groups or foreign public figures, or personal attacks made by legally qualified candidates, their authorized representatives, or persons associated with them. Attacks

occurring during bona fide newscasts, news interviews, or on-the-air coverage of bona fide news events are not covered by the personal attack rule.

This rule does not cover every personal attack carried on a station—only personal attacks broadcast during the presentation of views on a controversial issue of public importance. A person attacked at some other time will have no redress from the FCC but might have grounds to seek relief under the law governing LIBEL AND SLANDER. If the personal attack rule is applicable, the person attacked has an absolute right to appear in his or her own defense, and the station cannot require that a different person make the defense.

Broadcasting Content   Unlike print media, radio and television broadcasts may be regulated for content. Typically this has involved broadcasts of allegedly OBSCENE or indecent material. The U.S. Supreme Court has upheld regulations banning obscene material because OBSCENITY is not protected by the First Amendment. It has also permitted the FCC to prohibit material that is "patently offensive," and either "sexual" or "excretory," from being broadcast during times when children are presumed to be in the audience (*FCC v. Pacifica Foundation*, 438 U.S. 726, 98 S. Ct. 3026, 57 L. Ed. 2d 1073 [1978]). The courts rejected FCC attempts to interpret the indecency standard more broadly. Congressional legislation that expanded the standard also was ruled unconstitutional. The Telecommunications Act of 1996 contained the Communications Decency Act (CDA), codified at 47 U.S.C.A. § 223 (a) to (h), which makes it a federal crime to use telecommunications to transmit "any comment, request, suggestion, proposal, image, or other communication which is obscene or indecent, knowing that the recipient of the communication is under 18 years of age, regardless of whether the maker of such communication placed the call or initiated the communication." A three-judge panel, in *American Civil Liberties Union v. Reno*, 929 F. Supp. 824 (E.D. Pa.1996) held that the CDA was unconstitutional because it violated the First Amendment. The U.S. Supreme Court later agreed to review the decision, (*Reno v. American Civil Liberties Union*, __U.S.__, 117 S. Ct. 554, 136 L. Ed. 2d 436 [1996]).

The Telecommunications Act of 1996 also mandates the establishment of an advisory committee to rate video programming that contains indecent material to warn parents of its content. The act also requires that by 1998, all manufactured televisions with screens thirteen inches or

Cable TV and the "Must Carry" Law

Since the 1970s the Federal Communications Commission (FCC) has required cable television systems to dedicate some of their channels to local broadcasting stations. For many years cable operators did not challenge the constitutionality of these "must carry" provisions, believing that compliance was necessary to obtain operating licenses. With the dramatic growth in the cable industry, however, cable operators argued that they should be able to use these channels for more profitable programming. In the late 1980s, as a result of challenges by cable operators, the courts struck down must carry rules as a violation of the First Amendment.

Congress replied in the Cable Television Consumer Protection and Competition Act of 1992 (47 U.S.C.A. § 151 et seq.), providing that cable systems with twelve or fewer channels must carry at least three local broadcast signals and that larger systems must carry all local signals up to a maximum of one-third of the system's total number of channels.

Turner Broadcasting System, a leading cable operator, filed suit, claiming that the must carry law violated the First Amendment by suppressing and burdening free speech. The Supreme Court, on a 5–4 vote, in *Turner Broadcasting System v. FCC*, 117 S. Ct. 1174 (1997), rejected these arguments, finding that Congress had substantial evidence to justify the must carry provisions and that the provisions advanced important governmental interests unrelated to the suppression or burdening of free speech.

The Court noted that the must carry provisions preserve the benefits of free, over-the-air local broadcast television, promote the widespread dissemination of information from many sources, and advance fair competition in the television programming market. The Court was reluctant to abandon the law when 40 percent of U.S. households still rely on over-the-air signals for television programming. The Court found that when local broadcasters are denied cable access, audience size and advertising revenues decline, station operations are restricted, and bankruptcy may result.

Conversely, the Court determined that the must carry provisions had not burdened cable operators, with the vast majority unaffected in a significant manner. Most systems had enough channels to accommodate local stations and their own programming. Therefore, Congress had not overstepped the First Amendment in mandating the must carry requirement.

---

larger must be equipped with a "V-chip" to allow parents to block programs with a predesignated rating for sex and violence.

Public Broadcasting Public broadcasting systems are noncommercial television and radio stations that are financed by viewer and private contributions, in addition to funding by federal, state, and local governments, as an alternative to the programming aired by commercial channels. The Corporation for Public Broadcasting, a private, independent, nonprofit corporation established in 1967 by the Public Broadcasting Act (47 U.S.C.A. § 390 et seq.), is also involved in the creation and development of public stations.

Cable Television CABLE TELEVISION has grown tremendously since the 1980s. By 1996 cable was available to more than 96 percent of U.S. homes, and 60 percent were subscribers to cable. Cable originally served communities in mountainous regions that had difficulty receiving broadcast transmissions. Many communities solved this problem by erecting tall receiving towers at the highest point in the area to capture broadcast signals and retransmit them over wires running from the tower to various homes that subscribed to this service. This service is called community antenna television system, popularly known as CATV, or cable television.

During the 1970s and 1980s, large corporations installed cable systems in every large metropolitan area in the United States, as well as in rural areas. Independent programming was transmitted on cable systems by companies such as Home Box Office (HBO) and Cable News Network (CNN).

The FCC adopted the first general federal regulation of cable systems, although cable television could not be categorized as broadcasting in the traditional sense. Local government also became involved because each municipality had to award a cable system FRANCHISE to one vendor. Cable operators negotiated system requirements and pricing with local government. Concerns about rate regulation led Congress to enact the Cable Television Consumer Protection and Competition Act of 1992 (Pub. L. No. 102-385). The act gave the FCC greater control of the cable television industry, mandated improved customer service, and sought to improve the competitive position of broadcast stations. It also set rate structures to control the price of cable subscriptions. However, the Telecommunications Act of 1996 reversed the 1992 act by ending all rate regulation. This meant that cable operators were free to charge what they wished.

Congress deregulated cable television rates in part because of increased interest by telephone companies to enter the cable market by sending programming through existing phone lines. The 1996 act permits phone companies to provide video programming directly to subscribers in their service areas. Congress believed that competition between phone companies and cable operators would improve service and hold down subscription rates.

New Technology The development of satellite and direct broadcast television, along with the growth of the INTERNET, has demonstrated the continuing vitality of electronic communication technology. The 1996 act moved to deregulation and competition as ways of exploiting the new vehicles of mass communication.

CROSS-REFERENCES

Election Campaign Financing; Entertainment Law; Federal Election Commission; Movie Rating; Music Publishing; Telecommunications.

MASSIAH v. UNITED STATES In *Massiah v. United States*, 377 U.S. 201, 84 S. Ct. 1199, 12 L. Ed. 2d 246 (1964), the Supreme Court held that in addition to the RIGHT TO COUNSEL at the trial stage, the SIXTH AMENDMENT also affords a defendant the right to legal counsel in pretrial stages. The Court held that this right attaches once the accused has been indicted and that the accused is protected from deliberate elicitation of information, including face-to-face encounters with police officers and approaches by unknown government informants.

Winston Massiah was a merchant sailor who was arrested, arraigned, and indicted for possession of narcotics and for conspiring to possess narcotics aboard a U.S. vessel and to import, conceal, and facilitate the sale of narcotics. Massiah retained a lawyer, pleaded not guilty, and was released on BAIL. One of the accused coconspirators, Jesse Colson, also retained a lawyer and pleaded not guilty. A few days later, unbeknownst to Massiah, Colson decided to cooperate with the government. Colson and Massiah met in Colson's automobile where Massiah made several incriminating statements during the course of their conversation. A radio transmitter had been secretly installed under the front seat of Colson's car, and a government agent listened to and recorded the conversation. At trial Massiah's incriminating statements were admitted into EVIDENCE, and the jury convicted him of several narcotics offenses.

The *Massiah* Court held that Massiah's basic protections of the Sixth Amendment were violated when his statements were surreptitiously and "deliberately elicited from him after he had been indicted and in the absence of his counsel." In essence, the *Massiah* doctrine activates the Sixth Amendment right to counsel once the criminal suspect reaches the status of accused and restricts the use of covert tactics by the government in obtaining incriminating evidence.

Since announcing the *Massiah* doctrine, the Supreme Court has attempted to limit its effect by requiring the accused to show that the government participated in active interrogation. The cases that follow *Massiah* help determine what constitutes active interrogation.

The Supreme Court held that when an inmate working for the government actively prompts an accused to make incriminating statements, this involves active interrogation and is a violation of the accused's Sixth Amendment right to counsel (*United States v. Henry*, 447 U.S. 264, 100 S. Ct. 2183, 65 L. Ed. 2d 115 [1980]). However, when a government agent passively listens to the accused's incriminating statements, there is no violation of the accused's Sixth Amendment right to counsel (*Kuhlmann v. Wilson*, 477 U.S. 436, 106 S. Ct. 2616, 91 L. Ed. 2d 364 [1986]). In *Kuhlmann*, the Court held that, to prove a violation of the Sixth Amendment, "the defendant must demonstrate that the police and their informant took some action, beyond merely listening, that was designed deliberately to elicit incriminating remarks."

The *Massiah* doctrine effectively limits the types of tactics law enforcement may use in obtaining evidence. Under this doctrine once formal charges have been initiated, the right to counsel attaches and law enforcement may not elicit information, either face-to-face, covertly, or through an undercover agent, without the presence of an attorney.

See also CRIMINAL LAW; CRIMINAL PROCEDURE.

MASTER An individual who hires employees or servants to perform services and who directs the manner in which such services are performed.

A court officer appointed by a judge to perform such jobs as examining WITNESSES, taking TESTIMONY, computing DAMAGES, or taking OATHS, AFFIDAVITS, or acknowledgments of DEEDS. ◫

A master makes a report of his or her findings to the judge so a decree can be formulated. A *master in chancery* was an officer in Chancery Court in England. In the U. S. these duties may be rendered by a court clerk, commissioner, auditor, or referee.

MASTER AND SERVANT ◫ An archaic generic legal phrase that is used to describe the relationship arising between an employer and an employee. ◫

A *servant* is anyone who works for another individual, the *master*, with or without pay. The master and servant relationship only arises when the tasks are performed by the servant under the direction and control of the master and are subject to the master's knowledge and consent.

A servant is unlike an AGENT, since the servant has no authority to act in his or her employer's place. A servant is also distinguishable from an INDEPENDENT CONTRACTOR, who is an individual entering into an agreement to perform a particular job through the exercise of his or her own methods and is not subject to the control of the individual by whom he or she was hired.

The master and servant relationship arises out of an express CONTRACT; the law, however, will sometimes imply a contract when none exists if a person was led to believe there was one by the conduct of both the employer and the employee. No contract exists, however, unless both master and servant consent to it. The contract can contain whatever terms and conditions the parties agree to, provided they are legal. It is essential that the terms be sufficiently definite so as to be enforceable by a court in the event that the contract is breached. An employment contract is legally enforceable by the award of DAMAGES against either party who breaks it. No employment contract, however, can be enforced by compelling the employee to work, since that would constitute INVOLUNTARY SERVITUDE, which is proscribed by the U.S. Constitution.

Federal and state laws regulate certain conditions of employment, such as minimum wages, maximum hours, overtime pay, time off for religious observances, and the safety of the work environment. Statutes ordinarily restrict employment of children, and federal CIVIL RIGHTS laws prohibit employment discrimination based upon race, color, religion, sex, or national origin. Employment agencies are gen-

erally licensed and regulated, due to the risk that dishonest agencies might come into existence.

Duties of Master and Servant The general rule is that a master may hire and fire servants; however, this is limited to a certain extent by the law. An employee cannot be discharged for a reason not permitted by his or her employment contract or the COLLECTIVE BARGAINING AGREEMENT that may govern the employment; nor can the person be fired because of race, color, religion, sex, or national origin. In addition, an employer cannot fire an employee who is exercising certain rights, such as filing a discrimination complaint with a governmental agency or filing for WORKER'S COMPENSATION benefits.

An employee can be discharged for misappropriating funds, being unfaithful to his or her employer's interest, refusing to perform services that were agreed upon in a contract, or for being habitually late or absent. An employee cannot be fired for insubordination for refusing to subscribe to unlawful directives from his or her employer, nor can the employee be required to perform such illegal tasks as committing PERJURY or handling stolen property. A suit for damages may be brought against an employer who wrongfully discharges an employee.

An employee has the obligation to be honest and faithful in the performance of duties. When TRADE SECRETS are disclosed to an employee, he or she must not reveal them to others either prior or subsequent to employment. In some cases, an employment contract specifies that the employer owns any new ideas or inventions created by the employee during the period of employment. When this is true, the employee

United Auto Workers Vice President Richard Shoemaker (left) and Gerald Knechtel of General Motors shake hands at a contract-signing ceremony. Workers may unionize in an effort to assert their rights—and wishes—in a master-servant relationship; over 215,000 UAW workers were affected by this contract.

has no rights in the idea or invention nor any right to ask for additional compensation.

Compensation An employee can enter into an agreement to work without compensation, but in the absence of such an agreement, an employer must pay an employee at the agreed rate. The employer cannot delay payment of wages or substitute something other than money unless the employee assents. The employee is entitled to his or her wages as long as the work is completed. If an employer wrongfully discharges an employee, the employee can collect all the money the employer had agreed to pay him or her.

The amount and type of compensation is ordinarily regulated by agreement; however, it is affected by a number of statutes. Employers are required to pay at least a certain prescribed MINIMUM WAGE under most state laws, which must be no less than the amount set by federal law, unless it is a type of employment that is excluded under the law or the employer is small enough in size to be exempt from the minimum wage laws. Other state and federal laws mandate employers to allow for paid sick time and additional wages for overtime or holiday work. It constitutes a violation of federal law, the Equal Pay Act (29 U.S.C.A. § 206 [1963]) to pay men and women different wages for substantially similar work. Special laws protect IN-FANTS (individuals under the age of majority) by restricting the hours they can work at certain ages and proscribing their employment in certain kinds of jobs.

CROSS-REFERENCES

Child Labor Laws; Employment at Will; Employment Law; Labor Law; Labor Union.

MATERIAL 📖 Important; affecting the MERITS of a case; causing a particular course of action; significant; substantial. A description of the quality of EVIDENCE that possesses such substantial probative value as to establish the truth or falsity of a point in issue in a lawsuit. 📖

A *material fact* is an occurrence, event, or information that is sufficiently significant to influence an individual into acting in a certain way, such as entering into a CONTRACT. In formal court procedures, a material fact is anything needed to prove one party's case, or tending to establish a point that is crucial to a person's position.

A *material issue* is a question that is in dispute between two parties involved in litigation, and that must be answered in order for the conflict to be resolved.

A *material witness* is a person whose TESTI-MONY is a necessary element of a lawsuit. An individual who is considered a material witness can be compelled to appear in court and provide testimony. In the event that the person's safety is endangered as a result of his or her planned or actual testimony, he or she may be given legal protection or held in PROTECTIVE CUSTODY.

MATTER OF FACT 📖 That which is to be determined by the senses or by the TESTIMONY of WITNESSES who describe what they have perceived through the senses of sight, smell, touch, taste, and hearing. 📖

Trials are highly complex forums for the consideration of FACT, opinion, and LAW. Each area is distinct in its type and in who has responsibility for evaluating it. Courts use the term *matter of fact* to distinguish a particular kind of information. A fact is a thing done—an actual occurrence or event—and it is presented during a trial in the form of testimony and EVIDENCE. The rules of evidence generally allow witnesses to testify as to what they personally know about the facts in dispute, but do not allow witnesses to testify as to their opinions (i.e., thoughts, beliefs, or inferences) in regard to those facts. An exception is made for expert witnesses, whose technical or scientific specialty is considered sufficient to allow them to state their opinion on relevant and material matters.

Facts are often difficult to ascertain because the record is unclear or because competing interpretations of the facts are presented. Questions of fact are for the JURY, which must weigh their validity in reaching a VERDICT. The jury's role is kept distinct from that of the court, which has the authority to rule on all matters of law.

See also MATTER OF LAW.

MATTER OF LAW 📖 That which is determined or ascertained through the use of statutes, rules, court decisions, and interpretations of legal principles. 📖

In legal actions the term *matter of law* is used to define a particular area that is the responsibility of the court. Matter of law is distinguished from *matter of fact*. All questions concerning the determination of FACT are for the JURY, though a judge may determine the facts if a jury trial is waived or is not permitted under the law.

The designation of matters of law to the judge and matters of fact to the jury did not develop, however, until the late eighteenth century. Until that time a jury could exercise its judgment over matters of fact and law. Jury INSTRUCTIONS, which in modern law are technical and specific about which law to apply, were informal and general. A jury was free to accept the instructions, modify them, or ignore them completely.

By the middle of the nineteenth century, courts had acquired authority over matters of law and confined juries to matters of fact. Commercial lawyers were particularly influential in bringing about this change, as greater judicial control over matters of law helped produce a stable legal system in which business could prosper.

Today courts rule on all matters of law, including pretrial motions, trial OBJECTIONS to the introduction of particular EVIDENCE or TESTIMONY, proposed jury instructions, and posttrial motions. Their decisions are based on statutes, rules of evidence and procedure, and the body of relevant CASE LAW.

When the facts in a CIVIL ACTION are not in dispute, one or both of the parties may request a court to make a summary JUDGMENT. Summary judgment is purely a matter of law; the court accepts the relevant facts as presented by the party opposing summary judgment and renders a decision based on the applicable legal principles.

A matter of law can be the basis for an APPEAL, but generally a MATTER OF FACT cannot. Though an appeals court can reverse a decision because of a mistaken matter of law, it will not reverse if the mistake did not affect the VERDICT. This "HARMLESS ERROR" rule developed, in part, from the recognition that during a trial the court often must make hundreds of decisions based on matters of law.

MATTER OF RECORD Anything that has been entered in the formal written record of a court, which can be proved by the production of that record.

A court produces a lengthy written record of a trial. A *matter of record* is anything entered in the official court record, including PLEADINGS, TESTIMONY, EVIDENCE, MOTIONS, OBJECTIONS, RULINGS, and the VERDICT. Any matter of record can be proved by producing the relevant document from the trial court record.

Proving matters of record is especially important in petitions for APPEAL. When appellate

courts determine whether to hear an appeal, the existence of a matter of record can be decisive: the record can conclusively refute ALLEGATIONS contained in the PETITION. Thus, for example, an appeal based on something said in testimony must be supported by the record; if it is not, the court may deny the petition without any further consideration. An APPELLATE COURT in most instances will not consider evidence, issues, or objections that were not made a part of the record at trial. Getting an issue into the record at trial is said to preserve the issue for appeal.

In general, matters of record are available to the public unless state law or court order prevents them from being released. For example, courts typically refuse to release the names of MINORS who are victims of sexual assault. Rhode Island's family court rules of practice provide another example; matters of record "involving scandal or immoral practices" are kept private except from the parties in interest or their representatives (R.I. R. Fam. Ct. Prac. Rule 3.3).

MATTHEWS, STANLEY Stanley Matthews served as associate justice of the U.S. Supreme Court from 1881 to 1889. A longtime friend and adviser to President RUTHERFORD B. HAYES, Matthews proved an effective and hardworking member of the Court during his brief tenure. His 1859 prosecution of a reporter for aiding the escape of two fugitive slaves proved politically embarrassing in later years. On the other hand, his opinion in *Yick Wo v. Hopkins*, 118 U.S. 356, 6 S. Ct. 1064, 30 L. Ed. 220 (1886), established an enduring principle of EQUAL PROTECTION analysis under the FOURTEENTH AMENDMENT.

Matthews was born July 21, 1824, in Cincinnati. He preferred his middle name and dropped his first name, Thomas, in his adult life. He graduated from Kenyon College in 1840 and then studied law in Cincinnati. He was admitted to the Tennessee bar in 1842 and began a law practice in Columbia, Tennessee. Matthews also devoted himself to journalism, editing the *Tennessee Democrat* newspaper. He returned to Ohio in 1845 to become editor of the *Cincinnati Morning Herald.*

BIOGRAPHY

Stanley Matthews

ARTIST C. GREGORY STAPKO. COLLECTION OF THE SUPREME COURT OF THE UNITED STATES.

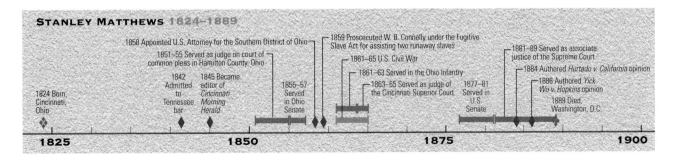

STANLEY MATTHEWS 1824–1889

1824 Born, Cincinnati, Ohio

1842 Admitted to Tennessee bar

1845 Became editor of *Cincinnati Morning Herald*

1851–55 Served as judge on court of common pleas in Hamilton County, Ohio

1855–57 Served in Ohio Senate

1858 Appointed U.S. Attorney for the Southern District of Ohio

1859 Prosecuted W. B. Connelly under the Fugitive Slave Act for assisting two runaway slaves

1861–65 U.S. Civil War

1861–63 Served in the Ohio Infantry

1863–65 Served as judge of the Cincinnati Superior Court

1877–81 Served in U.S. Senate

1881–89 Served as associate justice of the Supreme Court

1884 Authored *Hurtado v. California* opinion

1886 Authored *Yick Wo v. Hopkins* opinion

1889 Died, Washington, D.C.

1825   1850   1875   1900

Soon Matthews was drawn into politics and public service. He became clerk of the Ohio House of Representatives in 1848, then left in 1851 to sit as judge on the court of common pleas in Hamilton County, Ohio. He was elected to the Ohio Senate in 1855, where he served until 1857.

Matthews was appointed U.S. attorney for the Southern District of Ohio in 1858. In 1859 he prosecuted W. B. Connelly, a local reporter, under the federal FUGITIVE SLAVE ACT, for assisting two runaway slaves. Though Matthews was an abolitionist, he duly enforced the law. Critics charged him with forsaking his conscience in the hope of furthering his legal and political careers. Matthews never escaped the taint of these accusations.

When the Civil War broke out, Matthews enlisted in the Twenty-third Ohio Infantry as a lieutenant colonel, under the command of Hayes, a college classmate and friend. He left the army in 1863, following his election as a judge of the Cincinnati Superior Court. He held that post until 1865, when he resumed his private law practice.

Matthews aided his friend Hayes in the 1876 presidential election, against SAMUEL J. TILDEN, the Democratic governor of New York. An electoral commission was formed by Congress in early 1877 to resolve disputes over the electoral votes in several states. Matthews represented Hayes and the Republican party, successfully arguing that Hayes should be awarded all the disputed votes and thus become president.

Matthews was elected to the U.S. Senate in 1877. In 1880 Hayes nominated him to the Supreme Court. The Senate rejected his nomination, in part because of his 1859 prosecution of Connelly under the fugitive slave law and also because he had represented railroads and corporations in his law practice. Some senators argued that this would affect Matthews's judgment in cases on these issues.

In 1881 President JAMES GARFIELD nominated Matthews to the Court. This time he was confirmed by one vote.

During his nearly eight years on the Court, Matthews authored 232 opinions and five dissents. In *Hurtado v. California*, 110 U.S. 516, 4 S. Ct. 111, 28 L. Ed. 232 (1884), Matthews rejected the idea that the Fifth and Fourteenth Amendments' DUE PROCESS provisions required states to prosecute citizens solely through the GRAND JURY indictment process. Matthews wrote that as long as the defendant had notice and an opportunity to prepare a defense to the charges, due process was provided.

Matthews is most famous for his opinion in *Yick Wo*. In this opinion Matthews invalidated a San Francisco ORDINANCE requiring owners of laundries housed in wooden buildings to obtain permission from the city government to continue the operation of their business. Although the language of the ordinance was neutral, it was administered in such a way that Chinese laundry owners were denied LICENSES and nearly all non-Chinese applicants were granted licenses. Matthews looked past the neutral language to strike down the ordinance as a violation of the Fourteenth Amendment's Equal Protection Clause, concluding that unequal application of the ordinance furthered "unjust and illegal discrimination." Matthews's opinion became the foundation for modern CIVIL RIGHTS cases involving disparate impact, in which discrimination is established by statistical inequality rather than through proof of intentional DISCRIMINATION.

Matthews died March 22, 1889, in Washington, D.C.

MAXIM A broad statement of principle, the truth and reasonableness of which are self-evident. A rule of EQUITY, the system of justice that complements the COMMON LAW.

Maxims were originally quoted in Latin, and many of the Latin phrases are still familiar to lawyers today. The maxims were not written down in an organized CODE or enacted by legislatures, but they have been handed down through generations of judges. As a result, the wording of a maxim may vary from case to case. For example, it is a general rule that *equity does not aid a party at fault*. This has been variously expressed as:

> No one is entitled to the aid of a court of equity when that aid has become necessary through his or her own fault.
> Equity does not relieve a person of the consequences of his or her own carelessness.
> A court of equity will not assist a person in extricating himself or herself from the circumstances that he or she has created.
> Equity will not grant relief from a self-created hardship.

The principles of equity and justice are universal in the common-law courts of the world. They are flexible, seeking justice for both sides in each case. No maxim is ever absolute, but all of the principles must be weighed and fitted to the facts of an individual controversy. A rule does not apply when it would produce an unfair result. A party cannot insist that a strict technicality be enforced in his or her favor when it would create an injustice, because equity will instead balance the interests of the different parties and the convenience of the public.

"THE EXERCISE OF FUNDAMENTAL RIGHTS, INCLUDING THE RIGHT TO PURSUE A PROFESSION OR TRADE [MUST] NOT BE MADE SUBJECT TO THE EXERCISE OF ARBITRARY GOVERNMENTAL POWER."

The Foundations of Equity Two maxims form the primary foundations of equity: *Equity will not suffer an injustice* and *equity acts in personam*. The first explains the whole purpose of equity, and the second highlights the personal nature of equity. Equity looks at the circumstances of the individuals in each case and fashions a remedy that is directed at the person of the defendant who must act accordingly to provide the plaintiff with the specified relief. Unless a statute expands the powers of an equity court, it can make decrees that concern property only indirectly, phrasing them as decrees against persons. It is said that these are the oldest two maxims of equity. All others are consistent with them.

He who seeks equity must do equity. This maxim is not a moral persuasion but an enforceable RULE OF LAW. It does not require every plaintiff to have an unblemished background in order to prevail, but the court will refuse to assist anyone whose cause of action is founded on his or her own misconduct toward the other party. If, for example, a wealthy woman tricks her intended spouse into signing a prenuptial agreement giving him a token $500 should they divorce and after marriage she engages in a consistent pattern of conduct leading to a divorce, a court could refuse to enforce the agreement.

This maxim reflects one aspect of the principle known as the *clean hands doctrine.*

He who comes into equity must come with clean hands. This maxim bars relief for anyone guilty of improper conduct in the matter at hand. It operates to prevent any affirmative recovery for the person with "unclean hands" no matter how unfairly the person's adversary has treated him or her. The maxim is the basis of the *clean hands doctrine.* Its purpose is to protect the integrity of the court. It does not disapprove only of illegal acts but will deny relief for bad conduct that, as a matter of PUBLIC POLICY, ought to be discouraged. A court will ask whether the bad conduct was intentional. This rule is not meant to punish carelessness or a mistake. It is possible that the wrongful conduct is not an act but a failure to act. For example, someone who hires an AGENT to represent him or her and then sits silently while the agent misleads another party in negotiations is as much responsible for the false statements as if he himself or she herself had made them.

The bad conduct that is condemned by the clean hands doctrine must be a part of the transaction that is the subject of the lawsuit. It is not necessary that it actually have hurt the other party. For example, equity will not relieve a plaintiff who was also trying to evade taxes or DEFRAUD creditors with a business deal, even if that person was cheated by the other party in the transaction.

Equity will always decline relief in cases where both parties have schemed to circumvent the law. In one very old case, a robber filed a bill in equity to force his partner to account for a sum of money. When the real nature of the claim was discovered, the bill was dismissed with costs, and the lawyers were held in CONTEMPT of court for bringing such an action. This famous case has come to be called *The Highwayman* (*Everet v. Williams*, Ex. 1725, 9 L.Q. Rev. 197), and judges have been saying ever since that they will not sit to take an account between two robbers.

Equity aids the vigilant, not those who slumber on their rights. This principle recognizes that an adversary can lose EVIDENCE, WITNESSES, and a fair chance to defend himself or herself after the passage of time from the date that the wrong was committed. If the defendant can show disadvantages because for a long time he or she relied on the fact that no lawsuit would be started, then the case should be dismissed in the interests of justice. The law encourages a speedy resolution for every dispute. It does not favor the cause of someone who suddenly wakes up to enforce his or her rights long after discovering that they exist. A long unreasonable delay like this is called LACHES, and it is a defense to various forms of equitable relief.

Equity follows the law. Equity does not replace or violate the law, but it backs it up and supplements it. Equity follows appropriate rules of law, such as the rules of evidence and pretrial DISCOVERY.

Equity acts specifically. This maxim means that a party who sues in equity can recover the precise thing that he or she seeks rather than monetary DAMAGES as a substitute for it. This is the remedy of SPECIFIC PERFORMANCE.

Equity delights to do justice and not by halves. It is the purpose of equity to find a complete answer to the issues that are raised in a lawsuit. It will bring in all the necessary parties, balance their rights, and give a decree that should protect all of them against further litigation on the subject. Whenever necessary, the court will retain JURISDICTION in order to supervise enforcement of relief. For example, a lawsuit remains alive as long as an INJUNCTION is in force. Either party may come back into court and apply for reconsideration of the order if circumstances change. Courts also retain jurisdiction when CHILD SUPPORT payments are ordered. The amount can be changed if the child's needs require an increase or if the supporting parent becomes ill, unemployed, or retired.

Equity will not suffer a wrong to be without a remedy. It is the traditional purpose of equity to find solutions in lawsuits. Where money will not pay for the injury, equity has the authority to find another remedy.

This maxim is a restatement of the broad legal principle: *Ubi jus, ibi remedium,* "Where there is a right, there is a remedy." The maxim is applied in equity in an orderly way. It does not mean that anything goes. It calls forth recognized remedies for well-established wrongs, wrongs that are invasions of PROPERTY RIGHTS or personal or CIVIL RIGHTS and that the law considers ACTIONABLE. A court will not listen to complaints about every petty annoyance or immoral act.

Equity regards substance rather than form. Equity will not permit justice to be withheld just because of a technicality. Formalities that frustrate justice will be disregarded and a better approach found for each case. Equity enforces the spirit rather than the letter of the law alone.

Equity is equality. This maxim means that equity will not play favorites. For example, a RECEIVER who has been appointed to collect the ASSETS of a business in financial trouble must use the income to pay every CREDITOR an equal share of what is owed to him or her. If a pension fund loses a large amount of money through poor investment, then everyone who is entitled to benefits must suffer a fair share of the loss. Three adult children of a woman who is killed in an auto accident should share equally in any money that is recovered in a WRONGFUL DEATH action if the children are the woman's only surviving close relatives.

A judge will depart from this principle only under compelling circumstances, but the rule applies only to parties who are on an equal footing. If, for example, the woman in an auto accident died leaving three young children, then the money that is recovered might be distributed in proportion to each child's age. A younger child will have lost his or her mother for more years than an older brother or sister. Also, a receiver would have to prefer a SECURED CREDITOR over those creditors who had no enforceable interest in a particular asset of the company. Unless there is proof that one person in a group is in a special position, the law will assume that each should share equally in proportion to his or her contribution or loss.

Between equal equities the law will prevail. When two parties want the same thing and the court cannot in good conscience say that one has a better right to the item than the other, the court will leave it where it is. For example, a company that had been collecting sales tax and turning it over to the state government found that it had overtaxed and overpaid by 2 percent. It applied for a refund, but the state refused. The court upheld the state on the ground that the money really belonged to the customers of the company. Since the company had no better right to the money than the state, the court left the money with the state.

Between equal equities the first in order of time shall prevail. When two parties each have a right to possess something, then the one who acquired an interest first should prevail in equity. For example, a man advertises a small boat for sale in the classified section of the newspaper. The first person to see the ad offers him twenty dollars less than the asking price, but the man accepts it. That person says he or she will pick up the boat and pay for it on Saturday. Meanwhile another person comes by, offers the man more money, and the man takes it. Who owns the boat? Contract law and equity agree that the first buyer gets the boat, and the second buyer gets his or her money back.

Equity abhors a forfeiture. A FORFEITURE is a total loss of a right or a thing because of the failure to do something as required. A total loss is usually a rather stiff penalty. Unless a penalty is reasonable in relation to the seriousness of the fault, it is too harsh. In fairness and good conscience, a court of equity will refuse to permit an unreasonable forfeiture. This maxim has particularly strong application to the ownership of land, an interest for which the law shows great respect. TITLE to land should never be lost for a trivial reason—for example, a delay of only a few days in closing a deal to purchase a house.

Generally equity will not interfere with a forfeiture that is required by statute, such as the loss of an airplane illegally used to smuggle drugs into the country. Unless the statute violates the DUE PROCESS requirements of the Constitution, the penalty should be enforced. *Equity abhors a forfeiture* does not overcome the maxim that *equity follows the law.*

Neither will equity disregard a contract provision that was fairly bargained. Generally it is assumed that a party who does most of what is required in a business contract, and does it in a reasonable way, should not be penalized for the violation of a minor technicality. A contractor who completes work on a bridge one day late, for example, should not be treated as though he or she had breached the entire contract. If the parties, however, include in their agreement an express provision, such as TIME IS OF THE ESSENCE, this means that both of the parties understand that performance on time is essential. The party who fails to perform on time would forfeit all rights under the contract.

MAYHEM 📖 Mayhem at COMMON LAW required a type of injury that permanently rendered the victim less able to fight offensively or defensively; it might be accomplished either by the removal of (dismemberment), or by the disablement of, some bodily member useful in fighting. Today, by statute, permanent disfigurement has been added; and as to dismemberment and disablement, there is no longer a requirement that the member have military significance. In many states the crime of mayhem is treated as AGGRAVATED ASSAULT. 📖

McCARRAN, PATRICK ANTHONY

Patrick Anthony McCarran was born August 8, 1876, in Reno, Nevada. He graduated from the University of Nevada in 1901 and took up farming for a few years before his admission to the Nevada bar in 1905.

McCarran's career as a jurist was centered in Nevada. He practiced law from 1905 to 1907 in Tonopah and Goldfield, two areas that experienced prosperity due to mining successes. He served as district attorney of Nye County for the next two years before establishing a law practice in Reno. He entered the judiciary in 1912, presiding as associate justice of the Nevada Supreme Court; he rendered decisions as chief justice during 1917 and 1918. He subsequently practiced law until 1926, when he was defeated in an attempt to win election to the U.S. Senate.

In 1932, McCarran again sought a Senate seat and was successful. He represented Nevada until 1954, serving as chairman of the Judiciary Committee, from 1943 to 1946 and from 1949 to 1953, and of the Subcommittee on Foreign Economic Cooperation from 1950 to 1952.

During his lengthy participation in the Senate, McCarran was known for his outspoken beliefs. Most notable was his support of two pieces of controversial legislation that were passed despite the opposition of President

BIOGRAPHY

CULVER PICTURES

*Patrick Anthony
McCarran*

HARRY S. TRUMAN. The McCarran Internal Security Act of 1950 (50 U.S.C.A. § 781 et seq.) declared that all members of the Communist party must register with the attorney general; it also prohibited anyone with Communist connections to become involved in the government. The McCarran-Walter Act of 1952 (8 U.S.C.A. § 1101 et seq.) imposed stricter restrictions on immigration.

McCarran died September 28, 1954, in Hawthorne, Nevada.

See also COMMUNISM; McCARRAN INTERNAL SECURITY ACT.

McCARRAN-FERGUSON ACT OF 1945

📖 A federal law (15 U.S.C.A. § 1011 et seq.) that gives states the authority to regulate the "business of insurance" without interference from federal regulation, unless federal law specifically provides otherwise. 📖

The McCarran-Ferguson Act of 1945 provides that the "business of insurance, and every person engaged therein, shall be subject to the laws of the several States which relate to the regulation or taxation of such business." Congress passed the McCarran-Ferguson Act primarily in response to the Supreme Court case of *United States v. South-Eastern Underwriters Ass'n*, 322 U.S. 533, 64 S. Ct. 1162, 88 L. Ed. 1440 (1944). Before the *South-Eastern Underwriters* case, the issuing of an INSURANCE policy was not thought to be a transaction in commerce, which would subject the insurance industry to federal regulation under the COMMERCE CLAUSE. In *South-Eastern Underwriters*, the Court held that an insurance company that conducted substantial business across state lines was engaged in interstate commerce and thus was subject to federal antitrust regulations. Within a year of *South-Eastern Underwriters*, Congress enacted the McCarran-Ferguson Act in response to states' concerns that they no longer had broad authority to regulate the insurance industry in their boundaries.

The McCarran-Ferguson Act provides that state law shall govern the regulation of insurance and that no act of Congress shall invalidate any state law unless the federal law specifically

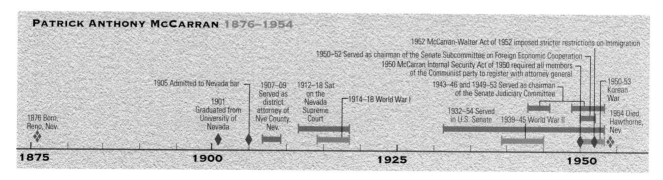

PATRICK ANTHONY McCARRAN 1876–1954

1952 McCarran-Walter Act of 1952 imposed stricter restrictions on immigration
1950–52 Served as chairman of the Senate Subcommittee on Foreign Economic Cooperation
1950 McCarran Internal Security Act of 1950 required all members of the Communist party to register with attorney general

1905 Admitted to Nevada bar
1907–09 Served as district attorney of Nye County, Nev.
1912–18 Sat on the Nevada Supreme Court
1914–18 World War I
1943–46 and 1949–53 Served as chairman of the Senate Judiciary Committee
1950–53 Korean War

1876 Born, Reno, Nev.
1901 Graduated from University of Nevada
1932–54 Served in U.S. Senate
1939–45 World War II
1954 Died, Hawthorne, Nev.

1875   1900   1925   1950

relates to insurance. The act thus mandates that a federal law that does not specifically regulate the business of insurance will not preempt a state law enacted for that purpose. A state law has the purpose of regulating the insurance industry if it has the "end, intention or aim of adjusting, managing, or controlling the business of insurance" (*United States Department of Treasury v. Fabe*, 508 U.S. 491, 113 S. Ct. 2202, 124 L. Ed. 2d 449 [1993]).

The act does not define the key phrase "business of insurance." Courts, however, analyze three factors when determining whether a particular commercial practice constitutes the business of insurance: whether the practice has the effect of transferring or spreading a policyholder's RISK, whether the practice is an integral part of the policy relationship between the INSURER and the INSURED, and whether the practice is limited to entities within the insurance industry (*Union Labor Life Insurance Co. v. Pireno*, 458 U.S. 119, 102 S. Ct. 3002, 73 L. Ed. 2d 647 [1982]).

The McCarran-Ferguson Act does not prevent the federal government from regulating the insurance industry. It provides only that states have broad authority to regulate the insurance industry unless the federal government enacts legislation specifically intended to regulate insurance and to displace state law. The McCarran-Ferguson Act also provides that the SHERMAN ANTI-TRUST ACT of 1890, 15 U.S.C.A. § 1 et seq., the Clayton Anti-Trust Act of 1914, 15 U.S.C.A. § 12 et seq., and the Federal Trade Commission Act of 1914, 15 U.S.C.A. §§ 41–51, apply to the business of insurance to the extent that such business is not regulated by state law.

Courts have distinguished between the general regulatory exemption of the McCarran-Ferguson Act and the separate exemption provided for the Sherman Act, which is the federal ANTITRUST LAW. Cases involving the applicability of the Sherman Act to state-regulated insurance practices take a narrower approach to the phrase "business of insurance" and apply the three criteria set forth in the *Pireno* case. In other cases that do not involve the federal antitrust exemption of the McCarran-Ferguson Act, the Supreme Court takes a broader approach. It has thus defined laws enacted for the purpose of regulating the business of insurance to include laws "aimed at protecting or regulating the performance of an insurance contract" (*Fabe*). Insurance activities that fall within this broader definition of the business of insurance include those that involve the relationship between insurer and insured, the type of policies issued, and the policies' reliability, interpreta-

tion, and enforcement (*Securities & Exchange Commission v. National Securities*, 393 U.S. 453, 89 S. Ct. 564, 21 L. Ed. 2d 668 [1969]).

See also CLAYTON ACT.

McCARRAN INTERNAL SECURITY ACT

Legislation proposed by Senator PATRICK ANTHONY McCARRAN and enacted by Congress in 1950 that subjected alleged members of designated Communist-action organizations to regulation by the federal government.

The McCarran Internal Security Act, also known as the Subversive Activities Control Act of 1950 (50 U.S.C.A. § 781 et seq.), was part of a legislative package that was designated as the Internal Security Act of 1950. Congress passed such statutes in response to the post-World War II COLD WAR during which many public officials perceived a threat of violent and forcible overthrow of the U.S. government by U.S. Communist groups that advocated this objective. Among other things, the legislation required members of the Communist party to register with the attorney general, and the named organizations had to provide certain information, such as lists of their members. It established the Subversive Activities Control Board to determine which individuals and organizations had to comply with the law and the procedures to be followed. Failure to satisfy the statutory requirements subjected the individual or organization to criminal prosecution and stiff fines.

Congress repealed the registration requirements of the law in 1968 as a result of a number of decisions by the U.S. Supreme Court that declared certain aspects of the law unconstitutional.

See also COMMUNISM.

BIOGRAPHY

McCARTHY, EUGENE JOSEPH

Eugene Joseph McCarthy served as a member of the U.S. House of Representatives from 1949 to 1959 and as a U.S. senator from 1959 to 1971. He was a liberal Democrat who served in the shadow of his fellow Minnesota senator, HUBERT H. HUMPHREY. His opposition to the VIETNAM WAR led to his candidacy for the Democratic presidential nomination in 1968. Though ultimately unsuccessful his candidacy galvanized the antiwar constituency and helped persuade President LYNDON B. JOHNSON not to seek reelection.

McCarthy was born March 29, 1916, in Watkins, Minnesota, the son of a livestock buyer. He graduated from Saint John's University, in Collegeville, Minnesota, in 1935, and worked on a master's degree at the University of Minnesota during the late 1930s while he was a high school teacher in Mandan, North Dakota. McCarthy returned to Saint John's in

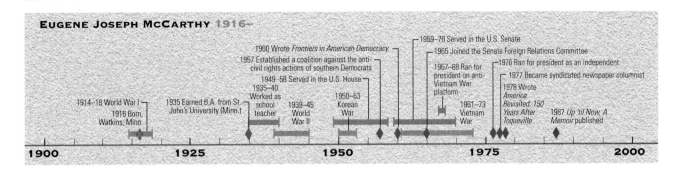

EUGENE JOSEPH McCARTHY 1916-

1959–70 Served in the U.S. Senate
1965 Joined the Senate Foreign Relations Committee
1960 Wrote *Frontiers in American Democracy*
1957 Established a coalition against the anti-civil rights actions of southern Democrats
1976 Ran for president as an independent
1977 Became syndicated newspaper columnist
1949–58 Served in the U.S. House
1967–68 Ran for president on anti-Vietnam War platform
1935–40 Worked as school teacher
1978 Wrote *America Revisited: 150 Years After Toqueville*
1914–18 World War I
1935 Earned B.A. from St. John's University (Minn.)
1939–45 World War II
1950–53 Korean War
1961–73 Vietnam War
1987 *Up 'til Now, A Memoir* published
1916 Born, Watkins, Minn.

1900   1925   1950   1975   2000

1940 to teach economics. After deciding not to join the priesthood, McCarthy left Saint John's in 1943 and served in the War Department's Intelligence Division until the close of World War II in 1945.

After the war McCarthy joined the faculty at the College of St. Thomas, in St. Paul, and taught sociology. In 1948 he was elected to the U.S. House of Representatives, beginning a twenty-two-year political career in Washington, D.C. During the 1950s McCarthy worked on labor and agricultural issues and maintained a liberal Democratic voting record. In 1957 he established an informal coalition of members of Congress, later formally organized as the House Democratic Study Group, to counter anti–civil rights actions of southern Democrats.

McCarthy was elected to the U.S. Senate in 1958 and became a respected member of the body. His wit and scholarly, understated manner became recognized nationally, but his demeanor was no match for that of Humphrey, his energetic and voluble colleague. In 1964 President Johnson generated publicity during the Democratic National Convention by floating both senators' names for the vice presidential slot on his reelection ticket. In the end he chose Humphrey.

In 1965 McCarthy joined the Senate Foreign Relations Committee, which was to become the center of congressional opposition to the Vietnam War. Though in 1964 McCarthy had voted for the TONKIN GULF RESOLUTION (78 Stat. 384), which gave President Johnson the power to wage war in Vietnam, he soon had doubts about the wisdom of U.S. involvement. In January 1966 McCarthy and fourteen other senators signed a public letter urging Johnson not to resume bombing of North Vietnam after a brief holiday truce. From this first public criticism of the Vietnam War, McCarthy became a consistent, vocal opponent, making speeches against the war in 1966 and 1967.

In November 1967 McCarthy announced his candidacy for president based specifically on Johnson's Vietnam policies. Though McCarthy's campaign was not taken seriously at first,

"THE WAR IN VIETNAM IS OF QUESTIONABLE LOYALTY AND CONSTITUTIONALITY . . . DIPLOMATICALLY INDEFENSIBLE . . . EVEN IN MILITARY TERMS [AND] MORALLY WRONG."

an outpouring of support by largely unpaid, politically inexperienced student volunteers on college campuses across the country captured national attention and gave his candidacy political momentum.

This momentum was demonstrated when McCarthy won twenty of the twenty-four New Hampshire delegates in the state's March 1968 primary. President Johnson narrowly won the popular vote in New Hampshire, but the delegates' response was a devastating blow for an incumbent president.

Encouraged by McCarthy's success, Senator ROBERT F. KENNEDY, of New York, joined the race. McCarthy was embittered by Kennedy's decision, because McCarthy had wanted Kennedy to run all along, but because Kennedy had refused, McCarthy had run instead. Kennedy had refused to contest Johnson's reelection when the odds appeared in the president's favor. Johnson, sensing the difficulty of his reelection, dropped out of the race in March. Vice President Humphrey entered the race after Johnson's withdrawal.

From April to June 1968, McCarthy and Kennedy waged a series of primary battles. McCarthy won the first three, then lost four of the next five to Kennedy. Humphrey refused to run in the primaries, collecting his delegates through state political conventions and the cooperation of local party leaders.

Kennedy was assassinated in June 1968, and the race now centered on McCarthy and Humphrey. Humphrey won the nomination, but unprecedented violence at the Democratic National Convention in Chicago helped doom his candidacy against RICHARD M. NIXON. McCarthy refused to campaign for Humphrey, largely because Humphrey was reluctant to articulate a proposal to end the Vietnam War. Humphrey lost the November election to Nixon by a smaller margin than predicted, leading some Democratic leaders to complain that McCarthy's unwillingness to campaign for the ticket cost Humphrey the election.

McCarthy declined to run for reelection to the Senate in 1970. Humphrey ran successfully in his place. McCarthy ran a lackluster presidential campaign in 1972 and a better organized independent presidential campaign in 1976. He lost both races and subsequently retired from the political arena. Since leaving politics he has concentrated on teaching, political commentary, and poetry writing.

McCARTHY, JOSEPH RAYMOND

Joseph Raymond McCarthy was a U.S. senator who during the early 1950s conducted a highly controversial campaign against supposed Communist infiltration of the U.S. government. His accusations and methods of interrogation of witnesses came to be called "McCarthyism," a term that remains a part of the U.S. political vocabulary. Though he was ultimately censured for his activities by the Senate, McCarthy was, between 1950 and 1954, the most powerful voice of anti-Communism in the United States.

McCarthy was born November 14, 1908, in Grand Chute, Wisconsin. He graduated from Marquette University in 1935 with a bachelor of laws degree. He practiced law in Wisconsin until 1939, when he was elected a circuit court judge. During World War II, McCarthy served in the Marine Corps as a tailgunner. He progressed to the rank of captain and was awarded several commendations for his military achievements.

McCarthy used his wartime record as "Tailgunner Joe" to help upset Republican Senator Robert M. LaFollette, Jr., in the 1946 Wisconsin primary election. McCarthy was elected to the Senate in 1946 and reelected in 1952.

During his first three years in office, McCarthy was an undistinguished and relatively unknown senator. He catapulted to public attention, however, after giving a speech in Wheeling, West Virginia, in February 1950. In the speech, McCarthy charged that 205 Communists had infiltrated the State Department. He claimed that Communist subversion had led to the fall of China to the Communists in October 1949. A Senate investigating committee ordered McCarthy to produce evidence of

his accusations, but he was unable to produce the names of any Communists.

Despite this failure to produce evidence, McCarthy escalated his anti-Communist crusade. He accused Democratic President HARRY S. TRUMAN's administration of harboring Communists and of failing to stop Communist aggression. His accusations struck a chord with many U.S. citizens, who were fearful of the growth of Communism and the menace of the Soviet Union as well as angry at the U.S. government's apparent inability to prevent the spread of Communism.

In 1953 McCarthy became the chair of the Senate's Government Committee on Operations and head of its permanent subcommittee on investigations. Though DWIGHT D. EISENHOWER, a Republican, became president in 1953, McCarthy used the investigations subcommittee to continue his campaign against Communist subversion in the federal government. McCarthy brought persons before his committee who he claimed were "card-carrying" Communists. He made colorful and clever accusations against these witnesses, who, as a result, often lost their jobs and were labeled as subversive. Evidence that a person had briefly joined a left-wing political group during the 1930s was used by McCarthy to suggest that the person was a Communist or a Communist sympathizer.

McCarthy attacked some of the policies of President Eisenhower, yet the president was reluctant to criticize the popular senator. In April 1954 McCarthy leveled charges against the U.S. Army, claiming the secretary of the army had concealed foreign ESPIONAGE activities. Thirty-six days of televised hearings ensued, known as the "Army-McCarthy hearings." McCarthy was unable to substantiate any of his ALLEGATIONS. During the course of the hearings, McCarthy's aggressive and intimidating tactics backfired, turning public opinion against him.

After the Democrats regained control of the Senate in the November 1954 elections, McCarthy was replaced as chair of the investigat-

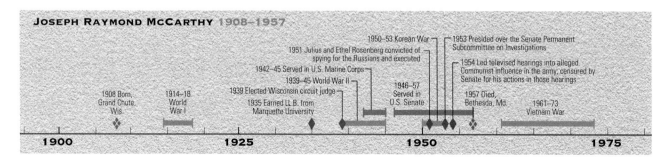

JOSEPH RAYMOND MCCARTHY 1908–1957

1908 Born, Grand Chute, Wis.

1914–18 World War I

1935 Earned LL.B. from Marquette University

1939 Elected Wisconsin circuit judge

1939–45 World War II

1942–45 Served in U.S. Marine Corps

1946–57 Served in U.S. Senate

1950–53 Korean War

1951 Julius and Ethel Rosenberg convicted of spying for the Russians and executed

1953 Presided over the Senate Permanent Subcommittee on Investigations

1954 Led televised hearings into alleged Communist influence in the army; censured by Senate for his actions in those hearings

1957 Died, Bethesda, Md.

1961–73 Vietnam War

1900   1925   1950   1975

ing committee by Senator JOHN L. McCLELLAN of Arkansas. McClellan, who had been critical of McCarthy's approach, helped lead an effort to censure McCarthy for his methods and for his abuse of other senators. In 1955, the Senate, on a vote of 67 to 22, moved to censure McCarthy.

The censure vote marked the decline of McCarthy's political influence. He died on May 2, 1957 in Bethesda, Maryland.

CROSS-REFERENCES

Cohn, Roy Marcus; Cold War; Communism; Welch, Joseph Nye.

McCLELLAN, JOHN LITTLE John Little McClellan served as a U.S. senator from 1942 to 1977. During the 1950s, McClellan rose to national prominence for his opposition to the methods used by Senator JOSEPH R. McCARTHY in investigating alleged Communist subversion. McClellan succeeded McCarthy as chair of the investigating subcommittee and conducted probes of union corruption, GRAFT, and ORGANIZED CRIME between 1955 and 1973.

McClellan was born on February 25, 1896, in Sheridan, Arkansas. He was admitted to the Arkansas bar in 1913 and served a tour of military duty in World War I. He maintained a private law practice in Arkansas before becoming a prosecuting attorney in 1927. McClellan left the post in 1930 to resume private practice, but abandoned law for Democratic party politics in 1935, when he was elected to the U.S. House of Representatives. In 1942 he began a career in the U.S. Senate that would span thirty-five years.

McClellan was largely unknown outside of Arkansas until the 1950s. In 1953, he was named to the special investigating subcommittee headed by Republican Senator Joseph R. McCarthy of Wisconsin. McCarthy had become a national figure for his controversial charges of Communist subversion in the State Department and other divisions of the federal government. McCarthy was a master of the media, attracting front-page coverage for his ALLEGATIONS. However, his use of the investigat-

John Little McClellan

"MOUNTING CRIME AND CORRUPTION ARE INSIDIOUSLY GNAWING AT THE VITALITY AND STRENGTH OF OUR REPUBLIC."

ing committee angered McClellan, who objected to McCarthy's unsubstantiated accusations and to his brow-beating of witnesses.

In 1954, following a contentious, thirty-six day televised hearing dealing with the Army's alleged concealment of foreign ESPIONAGE, McCarthy's popularity declined. McClellan served on a committee that investigated McCarthy's actions during these hearings. The committee concluded McCarthy should be censured by the Senate for his abusive methods and for his "contemptuous" conduct toward a subcommittee that had investigated his finances in 1952. McClellan and an overwhelming majority of his colleagues censured McCarthy on these charges.

After the Democrats regained control of the Senate in the November 1954 elections, McClellan replaced McCarthy as chair of the investigating committee. In 1957 he drew national attention as chair of the Senate Select Committee on Improper Activities in the Labor or Management Field. As presiding officer, he directed investigations of several powerful LABOR UNIONS. He forcefully questioned the leadership of the Teamsters Union, including Dave Beck and JAMES (Jimmy) HOFFA. The McClellan Committee's investigation revealed that the Teamsters Union and other groups had taken union funds for private use and that there were clear links between the Teamsters and organized crime. One result of the probe was the expulsion of the Teamsters and two other unions from the American Federation of Labor and Congress of Industrial Organizations (AFL-CIO).

The corruption uncovered by McClellan's committee also led to the passage of the Labor-Management Reporting and Disclosure Act of 1959, commonly known as the LANDRUM-GRIFFIN ACT (29 U.S.C.A. § 401 et seq.). This act sought to prevent union corruption and to guarantee union members that unions would be run democratically.

In 1961 McClellan investigated the fraudulent agricultural dealings of Texas businessman

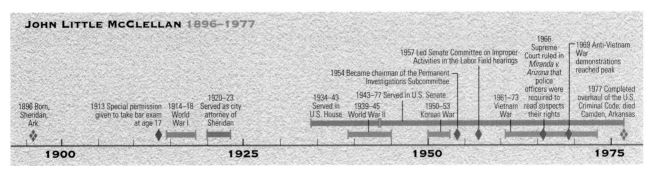

JOHN LITTLE McCLELLAN 1896–1977

1896 Born, Sheridan, Ark

1913 Special permission given to take bar exam at age 17

1914–18 World War I

1920–23 Served as city attorney of Sheridan

1934–43 Served in U.S. House

1939–45 World War II

1943–77 Served in U.S. Senate

1950–53 Korean War

1954 Became chairman of the Permanent Investigations Subcommittee

1957 Led Senate Committee on Improper Activities in the Labor Field hearings

1961–73 Vietnam War

1966 Supreme Court ruled in *Miranda v. Arizona* that police officers were required to read suspects their rights

1969 Anti-Vietnam War demonstrations reached peak

1977 Completed overhaul of the U.S. Criminal Code; died Camden, Arkansas

1900   1925   1950   1975

Billy Sol Estes. In 1963 McClellan was involved with the investigation of organized crime. During the hearings, Joseph Valachi, a member of an organized crime family, gave graphic testimony of its inner workings. McClellan continued to organize investigations as part of the Permanent Investigations Subcommittee until 1973, when he became head of the Senate Appropriations Committee.

McClellan died on November 28, 1977 in Little Rock, Arkansas.

McCULLOCH v. MARYLAND *McCulloch v. Maryland* is a keynote case, 17 U.S. (4 Wheat.) 316, 4 L.Ed. 579 (1819), decided by the U.S. Supreme Court that established the principles that the federal government possesses broad powers to pass a number of types of laws, and that the states cannot interfere with any federal agency by imposing a DIRECT TAX upon it.

This case represents another illustrative example of the ongoing debate among the founders of the U.S. constitutional government regarding the balance of powers between the states and the federal government. The Federalists were in favor of a strong central government, whereas the Republicans wanted the states to retain most powers. Those who wrote and ratified the U.S. Constitution ultimately agreed to grant the federal government certain specific powers known as the enumerated powers—listed in the Constitution—and concluded with a general provision that permitted Congress to make all laws that are necessary and proper for the carrying out of the foregoing powers, as well as all other powers vested in the U.S. government by the Constitution. Some people were fearful that such a provision, which is called the Necessary and Proper Clause of the Constitution, was a blanket authorization for the federal government to regulate the states.

Subsequently, a series of articles—which came to be called the *Federalist Papers*—were published in New York newspapers. These articles defended the clause on the basis that any power only constitutes that ability to do something, and that the power to do something is the power to utilize a means of doing it. It is necessary for a legislature to have the power to make laws; therefore, the proper means of exercising that power is by making "necessary and proper" laws. The Constitution was, therefore, ratified in 1789 with the Necessary and Proper Clause.

In exercise of the power conferred by that clause, the first Congress enacted a law in 1791 that incorporated a national bank called the BANK OF THE UNITED STATES, which operated as a private bank, took deposits of private funds, made private loans, and issued bank notes that could be used like money. In addition, wherever branches were established, it operated as a place for the federal government to deposit its funds. The legislation that incorporated the bank stated in its preamble that it would be extremely conducive to the successful operation of the national finances, would aid in the obtaining of loans for the use of the government in sudden emergencies, and would produce considerable advantages to trade and industry in general.

That bank charter was allowed to expire in 1811; however, a second Bank of the United States was incorporated in 1816 with one-fifth of its stock owned by the United States, and it became extremely unpopular. This was particularly true in the South and West, where it first overexpanded credits and then drastically limited them, thereby contributing to the failure of many state-chartered banks. A number of states attempted to keep branches of the national bank out of their states by passing laws proscribing any banks not chartered by the state or by imposing heavy taxes on them. The only bank affected by these laws was the Bank of the United States. The tremendous dispute that subsequently arose between the federal and state governments required resolution by the Supreme Court.

Maryland had one of the least stringent rules against the bank, which required that any bank or branch that was not established subject to the authority of the state must use special stamped paper for its bank notes and, in effect, pay 2 percent of the value of the notes as a tax or pay a general tax of $15,000 a year. Maryland brought suit against McCulloch, cashier of the Bank of the United States, for not paying the tax and won a JUDGMENT for the amount of the penalties. An appeal was brought to the Supreme Court by McCulloch.

Chief Justice JOHN MARSHALL wrote the majority opinion of the Court, which reversed the Maryland judgment. The Court held that the federal government has the power to do what is necessary and proper, which included the grant of authority to establish a national bank. Maryland, therefore, had no right to tax the bank, a conclusion which was based upon the theory that "the power to tax is the power to destroy." A state cannot have authority under the Constitution to destroy or tax any agency that has been properly set up by the federal government. On that basis, the law that was passed by the legislature of Maryland that imposed a tax on the Bank of the United States was unconstitutional and void.

CROSS-REFERENCES

Constitution of the United States; Federalism; *Federalist Papers.*

McGRAIN v. DAUGHERTY

McGRAIN v. DAUGHERTY A landmark decision of the Supreme Court, *McGrain v. Daugherty,* 273 U.S. 135, 47 S.Ct. 319, 71 L.Ed. 580 (1927), recognized the implicit power of either House of Congress to hold a witness in a congressional investigation in CONTEMPT for a refusal to honor its summons or to respond to its questions.

During the mid-1920s, there were numerous allegations that the Federal Department of Justice was being mismanaged by its administrator, Harry Daugherty, the attorney general of the United States. In response to the charges, the Senate passed a resolution that empowered an investigatory committee to hear EVIDENCE as to whether Daugherty failed to prosecute various violations of the ANTITRUST LAWS. Mally S. Daugherty, who was a bank president as well as the brother of the attorney general, refused to respond to a SUBPOENA that was issued by the committee on two occasions ordering him to appear and to bring designated bank ledgers. The president pro tempore of the Senate issued a WARRANT to his sergeant at arms that Mally Daugherty be taken into custody. A deputy of the sergeant at arms took Daugherty into custody in Cincinnati, Ohio. Daugherty brought a HABEAS CORPUS action for his release in federal district court in Ohio. The court declared that the attachment and detention of the witness was void on the ground that the Senate exceeded its powers in directing the investigation and in ordering the seizure of Daugherty. The deputy made a direct appeal to the Supreme Court, which accepted the case for review.

The Court defined two issues: whether the Senate or House of Representatives has authority to use its own process to compel a private person to appear as a witness and to testify before it or one of its committees in order that Congress can perform a legislative function that it has under the Constitution; and whether the process that was used in this case was directed toward that purpose. Before addressing those questions, however, the Court reviewed some of Daugherty's assertions. Daugherty argued that there was no statutory provision for a deputy and that even if there were, the deputy had no power to execute the warrant, since it was addressed to the sergeant at arms. The Court disagreed. It explained that deputies were au-thorized to act for the sergeant at arms by virtue of a standing order adopted by the Senate and that Congress recognized their status by establishing and making appropriations for their compensation.

Daugherty also used the FOURTH AMENDMENT provision that "no warrants shall issue, but upon probable cause, supported by oath or affirmation," to assert that the warrant was void because its basis was an unsworn committee report. The Court rejected this argument on the ground that the committee members were acting pursuant to their OATH as Senators when they issued the warrant. When committee members act on matters within their knowledge, PROBABLE CAUSE exists for the action of the committee. The warrant withstood constitutional muster.

Daugherty also claimed that the warrant was deficient because it stated that he be "brought before the bar of the Senate then and there" to testify. It was not a subpoena to appear before the Senate, nor did he refuse to do so. The Court dismissed this assertion, because it considered the warrant an auxiliary process used by the committee that was acting for the Senate to compel the witness to provide testimony sought by the subpoena.

The Court finally addressed the central issues of the case: the constitutional authority of the Senate to act in such a manner; and whether the warrant in this case was appropriate. It reasoned that while the power to investigate was not explicitly given to Congress by the Constitution, it was traditionally recognized as implicit in the legislative function since it is a means to obtain necessary information. The Court also referred to various federal laws that demonstrated that either house of Congress has the power to commence investigations and gather evidence concerning activities within its JURISDICTION; that committees may conduct such investigations; that in order to fully implement the power to investigate, either house may punish uncooperative witnesses; and witnesses may be given IMMUNITY from criminal prosecutions that derive from their testimonies before the committees. Based upon tradition and statutes, the Court concluded that each house of Congress has auxiliary powers that are essential in order to effectuate its express powers, but neither house has unlimited "general" power to investigate private matters and force testimony. The Senate acted within its powers when it authorized a committee to investigate Daugherty. When the committee sought Daugherty's testimony, it was as a means to perform a legislative function since the purpose of the inquiry was to determine whether the attorney general and the Department of Justice—subjects of congressional regulations and appropriations—were properly performing their duties. The Court deemed that Daugherty's seizure and detention were appropriate because of his wrongful refusal to appear and testify before a lawful congressional committee. It reversed the order of the district court that released Daugherty from custody.

See also CONGRESS OF THE UNITED STATES.

McGRANERY, JAMES PATRICK

James Patrick McGranery was a U.S. representative and a federal judge prior to his appointment as attorney general of the United States. He served as attorney general under President HARRY S. TRUMAN from April 1952 to January 1953.

McGranery was born July 8, 1895, in Philadelphia. His Irish Catholic parents, Patrick McGranery and Bridget Gallagher McGranery, were devout, hardworking, and practical. They sent McGranery to local parochial schools, and they did not discourage him when he chose to quit school and enter the workforce. McGranery was a high school student when he landed his first full-time job at a Philadelphia printing plant. He remained a card-carrying member of a Philadelphia printer's union for most of his life.

When the United States entered World War I, McGranery left his job to enlist in the Army. He served as a balloon observation pilot and as adjutant with the 111th Infantry. At the end of the war, he returned home with a broader view of the world and a strong determination to resume his education. He entered Philadelphia's Maher Preparatory School in 1919 to complete the entrance requirements for Temple University.

The war experience also sparked McGranery's interest in law and government. While at Temple, and later Temple Law School, he became active in local ward politics. Soon after graduating and passing the bar in 1928, he was tapped by Philadelphia ward bosses to manage the local campaign of Democratic presidential

James Patrick McGranery

candidate Alfred E. Smith, of New York. Smith ultimately lost his presidential bid, but McGranery was exhilarated by the political process and eager to attempt his own run for office. He hastily made a bid for a vacant clerk-of-court seat, and was defeated.

McGranery's introduction to the political process showed him the need for a solid political base, and convinced him that a base of supporters could be cultivated through the practice of law. To that end, he established the firm of Masterson and McGranery. He started to represent clients with known political influence, including police officers and firefighters, and leaders of their unions. While building his practice, McGranery made two more failed attempts at elected office—as a candidate for district attorney in 1931, and as a candidate for the U.S. Congress in 1934.

Finally in 1936, McGranery had paid his dues and curried the favor he needed. He was elected as a Democrat to represent Pennsylvania's Second Congressional District, by a margin of almost twenty-five thousand votes over his Republican opponent. He was reelected in 1938, 1940, and 1942. Just before his second term in Congress, McGranery married Attorney Regina T. Clark, of Philadelphia, with whom he had three children: James Patrick, Jr., Clark, and Regina.

During his years in Congress, McGranery served on the House Banking and Currency, Interstate, Foreign Commerce, and Ways and Means Committees. His voting record was consistent with his allegiance to President FRANKLIN D. ROOSEVELT and the Democratic party.

McGranery resigned his seat in the fall of 1943 when his congressional district was eliminated by reapportionment. Roosevelt was reluctant to lose McGranery's longtime support, so he offered to create a position for McGranery in the Justice Department as assistant to Attorney General FRANCIS BIDDLE. McGranery accepted. He served as the Justice Department's chief administrative officer and chief liaison with Congress and other federal departments and agencies during the World War II years.

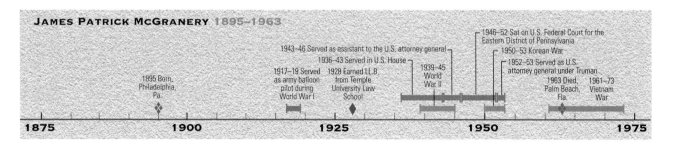

JAMES PATRICK MCGRANERY 1895–1963

1946–52 Sat on U.S. Federal Court for the Eastern District of Pennsylvania
1950–53 Korean War
1943–46 Served as assistant to the U.S. attorney general
1936–43 Served in U.S. House
1939–45 World War II
1952–53 Served as U.S. attorney general under Truman
1895 Born, Philadelphia, Pa.
1917–19 Served as army balloon pilot during World War I
1928 Earned LL.B. from Temple University Law School
1963 Died, Palm Beach, Fla.
1961–73 Vietnam War

1875　　1900　　1925　　1950　　1975

He also reviewed board of appeals findings under the Selective Service Act (50 U.S.C.A. App. 451-471a). His work was chronicled in a paper entitled "The Department of Justice and the War," which appeared in the October 1944 issue of the *Pennsylvania Bar Association Quarterly*. McGranery was later honored for his wartime service in the department.

After the war, McGranery remained in the Justice Department to serve as chief assistant to Truman's first attorney general, Tom C. Clark. Though McGranery held a position of prominence, he was not as involved or influential under Clark as he had been under Biddle. History suggests that Clark shut McGranery out of high-profile or sensitive cases, including one involving a vote fraud allegation in the president's home district; a mail fraud case against a bond dealer who raised funds for Truman, which was dismissed; and an investigation of *Amerasia*.

On June 6, 1945, six employees of *Amerasia*, a left-wing magazine devoted to Asian affairs, were arrested by the Federal Bureau of Investigation (FBI) and charged with conspiring to pass U.S. government documents to Chinese officials. A number of top secret government documents had been seized from the magazine office during an FBI raid that was later ruled to be illegal. Two magazine staff members were eventually charged with possessing illegal documents and were fined. Four others were never charged, including John Stewart Service, a State Department official well-known for his opposition to U.S. foreign policy toward China. The Justice Department was accused of bungling the case and initiating a cover-up to protect Service and other government officials.

Through years of scrutiny, the general consensus was that McGranery had little or no involvement in the case. Testifying before a House investigating committee, McGranery said only that the case could not be prosecuted fully because of the FBI's illegal search. In any case, the *Amerasia* incident precipitated McGranery's departure from the Justice Department. He resigned his post in October 1946 to accept an appointment from Truman to the federal bench in the Eastern District of Pennsylvania.

Judge McGranery quickly established a reputation as a tough jurist. Critics described him as high-handed, autocratic, and inclined to favor the government's position on any given issue. Even former attorney general Biddle acknowledged that McGranery was essentially an advocate rather than a judge.

In one celebrated pronouncement, McGranery ruled in 1949 that Representative Earl Chudoff (D-Pa.) could not appear as a defense attorney in McGranery's court because, as a government employee, the congressman had an inherent conflict in representing a client in a federal proceeding (*Chudoff v. McGranery*, 179 F.2d 869).

During his years on the federal bench, McGranery's name was often mentioned in connection with nominations to Democratic party and government posts including chairman of the Democratic National Committee, postmaster general, and attorney general. It was just as often discounted because of McGranery's personal reputation. It was well-known that he was given to emotional outbursts, and that he had a history of erratic behavior going back to his early days in the Justice Department.

Despite warnings from a number of quarters, Truman asked McGranery to fill the attorney general post in the spring of 1952, following the departure of J. HOWARD McGRATH. Truman had reluctantly asked for McGrath's resignation after McGrath failed to cooperate with, and later fired, a special assistant named to investigate corrupt practices inside the Department of Justice and the Bureau of Internal Revenue. A confirmation committee in Congress briefly raised the issue of McGranery's participation in the *Amerasia* incident and speculated that he might try to block the ongoing Justice Department investigation just as McGrath had. Nevertheless, after some discussion, McGranery was confirmed as attorney general. To the surprise of many of his longtime critics, he oversaw a thorough inquiry that led to numerous dismissals and prosecutions in both the Justice Department and the Bureau of Internal Revenue.

McGranery made a number of other contributions as attorney general, including the initiation of antitrust cases in the oil and steel industries, the diamond trade, and magazine wholesaling; the prosecution of American Communist party leaders; the deportation of Mafia crime figures; and the instigation of Justice Department support for the cause of school integration in *Brown v. Board of Education of Topeka, Kansas* (347 U.S. 483, 74 S. Ct. 686, 98 L. Ed. 873 [1954]). His office helped to provide the basis for that decision overruling the "SEPARATE-BUT-EQUAL" doctrine.

At the close of the Truman administration, McGranery practiced law in Washington, D.C., and Philadelphia. He died on April 1, 1963, in Palm Beach, Florida.

"NO SPECIFIC INTENT TO MONOPOLIZE IS NECESSARY; THE ONLY RELEVANT INTENT IS THE INTENT TO ENTER INTO THE BUSINESS ARRANGEMENTS WHICH GIVE RISE TO THE POWER."

McGRATH, JAMES HOWARD James Howard McGrath, a three-term governor and U.S. senator from Rhode Island, served as solicitor general and attorney general of the United States under President HARRY S. TRUMAN.

McGrath was born November 28, 1903, in Woonsocket, Rhode Island, and reared in nearby Providence. His father, James J. McGrath, worked as a knitter in a woolen mill before venturing into real estate and insurance. He rose to prominence through his association with the Independent Order of Foresters (a fraternal insurance organization), handling the company's affairs in the New England states. His mother, Ida E. May McGrath, used her training as a bookkeeper to manage the family's financial affairs while her husband was on the road.

As a young boy, McGrath set out to win a subscription contest at a Providence newspaper by targeting his father's business colleagues as potential subscribers. He sold a record number of new subscriptions and, in the process, captured the attention of the newspaper's owner, Rhode Island senator Peter G. Gerry.

When he was not selling newspapers, McGrath attended Providence's La Salle Academy. He completed his undergraduate studies in 1922 and enrolled at Providence College. During his college years, McGrath was a founding member and the first president of the Young Men's Democratic League of Rhode Island.

By graduation day in 1926, McGrath knew he wanted a career in politics. While waiting to attend law school, McGrath approached Senator Gerry and asked for a summer job. Gerry remembered the young man and put him to work in his senate office. McGrath worked for Gerry until his graduation from Boston University Law School in 1929. Following his admission to the bar, McGrath joined a Providence law firm and decided to marry. He and his wife, Estelle A. Cadorette McGrath, had one son, James David McGrath, in 1930.

Though 1929 and 1930 were years of change

BIOGRAPHY

James Howard McGrath

"[COMMUNISTS] ARE EVERYWHERE—IN FACTORIES, OFFICES, BUTCHER SHOPS, ON STREET CORNERS, IN PRIVATE BUSINESS—AND EACH CARRIES IN HIMSELF THE GERMS OF DEATH FOR SOCIETY."

and new beginnings for McGrath, his interest in politics remained constant. He had been named vice chairman of the Rhode Island Democratic State Committee in 1928; by 1930, he was chairman of the committee and ready to make his own place in the political arena. McGrath's first political appointment came in late 1930 when he was named city solicitor of Central Falls, Rhode Island. He served in that post for four years before resigning to accept a second appointment as U.S. district attorney for Rhode Island in 1934.

With McGrath's growing prominence in legal and business circles came growing influence in Rhode Island's Democratic party. From his position as chairman of the Rhode Island Democratic State Committee, he rose to chairman of the Rhode Island delegation at the Democratic National Convention in 1932. Age twenty-eight at the time, he was the youngest man ever to hold the job.

By 1940, he had laid the foundation for a successful bid for the state's highest office. He sought and received the gubernatorial nomination from the Democratic party, and he defeated Republican incumbent William H. Vanderbilt by a large margin.

McGrath served as governor of Rhode Island for three consecutive terms. In that office, he revised the state tax structure, reorganized the juvenile court system, established a labor relations board, and started a workers' compensation fund. During World War II, he continued to serve as governor while chairing the Rhode Island State Council of Defense and assisting the U.S. Treasury Department with war financing activities.

McGrath's work was noticed by national Democratic leaders including President FRANKLIN D. ROOSEVELT. It was not long before he was asked to serve on a committee to organize the 1944 Democratic National Convention and to help secure the presidential nomination for Roosevelt's vice president, Truman. McGrath, who had seconded Truman's vice presidential nomination at the previous convention, was an

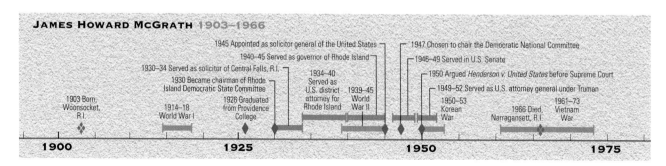

JAMES HOWARD McGRATH 1903–1966

- 1903 Born, Woonsocket, R.I.
- 1914–18 World War I
- 1926 Graduated from Providence College
- 1930 Became chairman of Rhode Island Democratic State Committee
- 1930–34 Served as solicitor of Central Falls, R.I.
- 1934–40 Served as U.S. district attorney for Rhode Island
- 1939–45 World War II
- 1940–45 Served as governor of Rhode Island
- 1945 Appointed as solicitor general of the United States
- 1946–49 Served in U.S. Senate
- 1947 Chosen to chair the Democratic National Committee
- 1949–52 Served as U.S. attorney general under Truman
- 1950 Argued *Henderson v. United States* before Supreme Court
- 1950–53 Korean War
- 1966 Died, Narragansett, R.I.
- 1961–73 Vietnam War

1900   1925   1950   1975

eager and hardworking member of the committee. He liked Truman—and the feeling was mutual.

After Truman's election, in October 1945, McGrath was rewarded with an appointment to the post of solicitor general of the United States. As solicitor general, he successfully defended the constitutionality of the Public Holding Company Act (15 U.S.C.A. § 79 et seq.) and fully supported an international military tribunal's conviction of Japan's General Tomoyuki Yamashita for war crimes.

In 1946 McGrath was elected to the U.S. Senate. While in office, McGrath fought the removal of wartime economic controls and the reduction of income taxes instituted during the war years. He thought the additional money should be used to broaden Social Security initiatives, underwrite national health insurance, and fund education. He also encouraged his colleagues to speak out on human rights issues, charging that in the years before World War II, the United States almost encouraged the Nazis by not speaking out against them.

In September 1947, McGrath became Truman's handpicked candidate to chair the Democratic National Committee and to orchestrate the president's reelection bid. McGrath was formally elected to the post a month later.

Under McGrath's leadership, the party in 1948 waged a tough, and sometimes divisive, national effort that carried many state and local Democratic candidates into office and resulted in Truman's narrow victory over THOMAS E. DEWEY.

After the election, McGrath returned to the Senate. Almost immediately, the Rhode Island Charities Trust came under investigation by a Senate subcommittee. As a trustee, McGrath was called to explain the organization's financial practices. The investigation ran its course without result, but a cloud remained over McGrath's personal finances.

McGrath's declining sphere of influence was most evident when he tried to find support for his legislative initiatives. He continued to sponsor unpopular measures addressing social issues, including a CIVIL RIGHTS bill supported by the administration in late 1949. His efforts to push the bill through the Senate further angered powerful southern Democrats he had offended during the presidential campaign by ending a policy of racially segregating the staff at Democratic national headquarters. (Though this change in policy had caused tremendous turmoil within the party and precipitated a loss of support in many southern states, it had also

helped to deliver the crucial black vote needed in 1948 to carry Illinois, New York, and Ohio.)

It was in this climate that McGrath was appointed to replace TOM C. CLARK as U.S. attorney general after Truman named Clark to the U.S. Supreme Court. The press blasted McGrath's appointment, saying it demonstrated a terrible lack of judgment on Truman's part. McGrath resigned his Senate seat in December 1949 to accept the appointment.

With Truman's blessing, McGrath continued to be a strong advocate for civil rights. During his term as attorney general, the Justice Department first challenged the constitutionality of racial segregation. McGrath argued a number of important cases before the U.S. Supreme Court in the spring of 1950, including a landmark case in which the High Court outlawed discriminatory dining arrangements in railroad cars (*Henderson v. United States*, 339 U.S. 816, 70 S. Ct. 843, 94 L. Ed. 1302).

Though he had a few bright moments, McGrath's subordinates and colleagues did not consider him a particularly effective attorney general. His most egregious error occurred when a House Ways and Means subcommittee uncovered evidence of corruption in the Bureau of Internal Revenue and in the Tax Division of the Justice Department. Truman's initial response, in January 1952, was to announce that the Justice Department would investigate and clean up any corruption in the government. When critics objected to the Justice Department's investigating itself, the president appointed New York Republican Newbold Morris to conduct an independent investigation of the charges.

Initially, McGrath promised full cooperation, but he had second thoughts when Morris asked him and other top Justice Department officials to complete a detailed financial questionnaire. Calling the questionnaire a violation of individual rights and an invasion of PRIVACY, McGrath refused to complete or submit the document—or to order his subordinates to do so. Three days later, McGrath forced Truman's hand by firing the special investigator and resuming charge of the investigation. In the political uproar that followed, the president had no choice but to ask for McGrath's resignation.

After leaving office, McGrath continued to be active in Democratic politics. In 1956 he managed Senator Estes Kefauver's vice presidential campaign, and in 1960, he made an unsuccessful attempt to regain his old Senate seat. After retiring from politics, he practiced law and managed his many business interests.

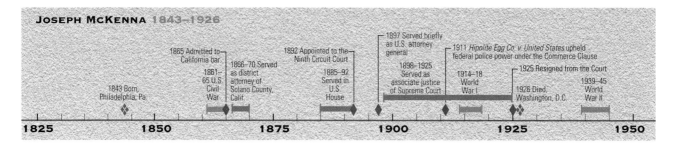

JOSEPH MCKENNA 1843–1926

1843 Born,
Philadelphia, Pa

1861–65 U.S. Civil War

1865 Admitted to California bar

1866–70 Served as district attorney of Solano County, Calif.

1885–92 Served in U.S. House

1892 Appointed to the Ninth Circuit Court

1897 Served briefly as U.S. attorney general

1898–1925 Served as associate justice of Supreme Court

1911 *Hipolite Egg Co. v. United States* upheld federal police power under the Commerce Clause

1914–18 World War I

1925 Resigned from the Court

1926 Died, Washington, D.C.

1939–45 World War II

1825   1850   1875   1900   1925   1950

McGrath died on September 2, 1966, in Narragansett, Rhode Island.

M.C.J. 📖 An abbreviation for master of comparative jurisprudence, a degree awarded to foreign lawyers trained in CIVIL LAW countries who have successfully completed a year of full-time study of the Anglo-American legal system. 📖

The M.C.J. degree is ordinarily offered by universities and law schools that have comparative law departments. It is awarded to highly qualified foreign lawyers who intend to return to the legal profession in a foreign country after completion of their studies in the United States.

McKENNA, JOSEPH Joseph McKenna rose from humble immigrant roots as a baker's son to a position of prominence in California Republican politics. McKenna served as county district attorney (1866–1870), U.S. Congressman, justice of the Ninth U.S. Circuit court (1892–1897), and, briefly, U.S. attorney general (1897). His controversial nomination to the Supreme Court in 1897 led to a twenty-seven-year tenure.

McKenna was born in Philadelphia on August 10, 1843, to Irish immigrant parents. He became head of the family at age fifteen when his father died shortly after moving the eight-member household to California. By age twenty-two, and while working several jobs, McKenna had studied enough law on his own to pass the California bar. One year later, despite little experience, he was elected district attorney for Solano County. He owed his rapid success to help from railroad baron LELAND STANFORD, the state's governor. In time, his loyalty to Stanford earned him three straight Republican nominations for Congress. He finally won in 1885. In Washington, D.C., McKenna opposed business regulations, supported federal land grants to the RAILROADS, and sponsored legislation that would have made Chinese immigrants carry identification cards.

In 1892, on the urging of Stanford, who had become a U.S. senator, President BENJAMIN HARRISON appointed McKenna to the Ninth Circuit Court of Appeals. Opponents protested that McKenna was unqualified and, moreover, beholden to railroad interests, but the nomina-

BIOGRAPHY

Joseph McKenna

BIOGRAPHY

John McKinley

tion succeeded. He held the seat for four years, largely without incident or note; yet occasionally he proved his critics right about his allegiances. In *Southern Pacific Co. v. Board of Railroad Commissioners*, 78 F. 236 (C.C.N.D. Cal. 1896), for example, he blocked the California legislature's attempt to set railroad fares, arguing that the proposed rates were unfair to the railroads.

While serving on the Ways and Means Committee in Congress, McKenna had befriended fellow Republican WILLIAM MCKINLEY. McKinley became president in 1896 and in 1897 made McKenna U.S. attorney general. Only a few months later, McKinley nominated McKenna to fill a vacancy on the U.S. Supreme Court created by the departure of Justice Stephen Field. Again, there was opposition, with newspapers and lawmakers calling him unfit for the responsibility. However, the nomination succeeded.

Of McKenna's 633 opinions, only a handful were majority opinions. These came in important cases, however, such as *Hipolite Egg Co. v. United States*, 220 U.S. 45, 31 S. Ct. 364, 55 L. Ed. 364 (1911), one of the decisions during the era that upheld federal POLICE POWER under the Constitution's COMMERCE CLAUSE. Generally regarded as a hard-working justice, his body of opinions shows that he developed a pragmatism and clarity of expression in his twenty-seven years on the bench. Slowed by age, he resigned in 1925 under the advice of Chief Justice WILLIAM HOWARD TAFT. He died several months later on November 21, 1926, in Washington, D.C.

McKINLEY, JOHN John McKinley served on the U.S. Supreme Court as an associate justice from 1837 to 1852. In the 1820s McKinley built his career in the Alabama legislature and later served in both the U.S. Senate and the House of Representatives. At a time when westward expansion brought federal and state governments into conflict over the use of land, he was a strong advocate of STATES' RIGHTS and affordable land for settlers. In 1837 President Martin Van Buren appointed McKinley to the Supreme Court, where he sat for fifteen years.

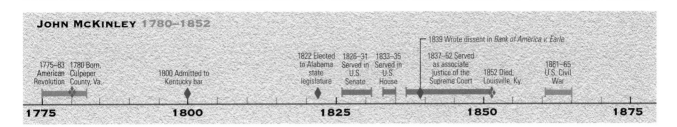

1839 Wrote dissent in *Bank of America v. Earle*

1775–83
American
Revolution

1780 Born,
Culpeper
County, Va.

1800 Admitted to
Kentucky bar

1822 Elected
to Alabama
state
legislature

1826–31
Served in
U.S.
Senate

1833–35
Served in
U.S.
House

1837–52 Served
as associate
justice of the
Supreme Court

1852 Died,
Louisville, Ky.

1861–65
U.S. Civil
War

1775   1800   1825   1850   1875

McKinley complained endlessly about the great deal of travel required by Supreme Court justices at that time. He produced only twenty opinions and two concurrences during his tenure, and is largely remembered for his dissent on behalf of states' rights in *Bank of Augusta v. Earle*, 38 U.S. (13 Pet.) 519, 10 L. Ed. 274 (1839).

Born in Culpeper County, Virginia, on May 1, 1780, McKinley studied law in Kentucky and passed the bar in 1800. While practicing law in Kentucky and later Alabama over the next twenty years, McKinley developed an interest in politics. He won election to the state legislature in 1822. Later, by shrewdly changing political allegiances from presidential candidate HENRY CLAY to the more popular ANDREW JACKSON, he was elected to the U.S. Senate in 1826. His chief concern in office was land legislation. As settlers pushed westward, McKinley favored the interests of small land buyers over those of big speculators. He also argued for the primacy of state control over land within state borders, taking the traditional states' rights view that denied the validity of federal authority. As his political fortunes rose and fell, he lost reelection to the Senate in 1830 and then alternated between serving terms in the Alabama legislature and the U.S. House of Representatives.

In 1837 McKinley had returned to the Alabama legislature as a representative when Congress increased the number of seats on the U.S. Supreme Court from seven to nine. President Van Buren first offered one of the seats to another Alabama lawmaker, William Smith, who declined. McKinley accepted, but not without reservation. He was chiefly bothered by the need to travel upwards of five thousand miles every year.

In McKinley's time justices had responsibility not only over the Court itself but also over the federal CIRCUIT COURTS, which required them to travel in a practice known as *circuit riding*. In charge of the largest circuit, the Ninth, McKinley hated this obligation. Twice, in 1838 and 1842, McKinley asked Congress to absolve him of the responsibility, which he said exposed him to undue personal expense and the risk of yellow fever. Embittered by lack of sympathy

"THE NATURAL SOCIETY OF NATIONS CANNOT SUBSIST, IF THE RIGHTS WHICH EACH HAS RECEIVED FROM NATURE ARE NOT RESPECTED."

BIOGRAPHY

William McKinley

for his complaints, he sometimes neglected to visit all of the courts in his circuit, a failure that brought him criticism.

In 1839 McKinley wrote his most notable opinion in the case of *Bank of Augusta v. Earle*. Rooted in a state banking dispute, the case dealt with the constitutional limitations of state power to regulate business—specifically, how far a state could go in excluding a corporation from doing business within its borders. On the circuit court, McKinley ruled that states have broad powers, and the opinion provoked outrage from CORPORATIONS, attorneys, and even McKinley's colleague, Supreme Court Justice JOSEPH STORY. When the case reached the Supreme Court, the 8 to 1 majority took a far more moderate view. In dissent, McKinley held to his position: a state could properly limit business activity to corporations that were chartered in it and should be free to reject the business of any outside corporation.

As McKinley's health deteriorated in his later years, he did less circuit riding, and after 1845 he played a very limited role in the Court's affairs. He remained on the Court until his death in Louisville, Kentucky, on July 19, 1852.

McKINLEY, WILLIAM   William McKinley served as the twenty-fifth president of the United States, from 1897 until his death from an assassin's bullet in 1901. A conservative Republican who advocated high TARIFFS to protect U.S. industry, McKinley waged the Spanish-American War and at the end of it gained overseas territories for the United States.

McKinley was born January 29, 1843, in Niles, Ohio. As a young man, he briefly attended Allegheny College, in Meadville, Pennsylvania; taught school; and fought in the Union army during the Civil War, attaining the rank of major. McKinley was aide-de-camp to the regimental commander, RUTHERFORD B. HAYES, who was later governor of Ohio and the nineteenth U.S. president. After the war McKinley studied law with an attorney and attended Albany Law School, in New York. He was admitted to the Ohio bar in 1867, and established a law practice in Canton, Ohio,

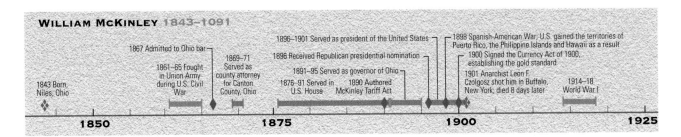

WILLIAM McKINLEY 1843–1091

1843 Born,
Niles, Ohio

1861–65 Fought
in Union Army
during U.S. Civil
War

1867 Admitted to Ohio bar

1869–71
Served as
county attorney
for Canton
County, Ohio

1876–91 Served in
U.S. House

1890 Authored
McKinley Tariff Act

1891–95 Served as governor of Ohio

1896 Received Republican presidential nomination

1896–1901 Served as president of the United States

1898 Spanish-American War; U.S. gained the territories of
Puerto Rico, the Philippine Islands and Hawaii as a result

1900 Signed the Currency Act of 1900,
establishing the gold standard

1901 Anarchist Leon F.
Czolgosz shot him in Buffalo,
New York; died 8 days later

1914–18
World War I

1850   1875   1900   1925

which remained his official residence for the rest of his life. From 1869 to 1871, he served as county attorney.

McKinley's political ambitions were nurtured by Hayes. McKinley became active in Ohio Republican politics and was elected to the U.S. House of Representatives in 1876. McKinley was an outspoken advocate of higher tariffs, believing that U.S. industry and U.S. workers were protected by the taxation of imported foreign goods. His stand on tariffs culminated in the McKinley Tariff Act of 1890, which raised duties on many imports to the highest levels up to that time. The act was an unpopular measure, and McKinley was voted out of office in the election of 1890.

McKinley returned to Ohio, where he was elected governor in 1891 and reelected governor in 1893. Mark Hanna, a wealthy Ohio industrialist and a leader in national Republican politics, became McKinley's benefactor and helped him secure the 1896 Republican presidential nomination. The Democratic candidate was WILLIAM JENNINGS BRYAN, who supported free coinage of silver, arguing that it would increase the money supply and thus help farmers and small-business owners. McKinley, who advocated retaining the gold standard, defeated Bryan, with Hanna raising large sums of money from big business to support the campaign. The money was used to help fund more than three hundred delegations and more than 750,000 people who traveled to McKinley's front porch in Canton to hear him campaign.

As president, McKinley signed the Currency Act of 1900 (31 Stat. 45), institutionalizing the gold standard until the 1930s. However, his first term was dominated by foreign affairs and overseas territorial expansion. When McKinley took office, a national independence movement had arisen in Cuba, seeking freedom from Spain. The United States tried to remain neutral while negotiating a solution acceptable to both sides. On February 15, 1898, the U.S. warship *Maine* blew up in the Havana harbor. Though later investigation suggested that a boiler explosion sank the *Maine* and killed its crew, immediate public reaction, inflamed by

"LET US REMEMBER THAT OUR INTEREST IS IN CONCORD, NOT IN CONFLICT, AND THAT OUR REAL EMINENCE AS A NATION LIES IN THE VICTORIES OF PEACE, NOT THOSE OF WAR."

the newspapers owned by William Randolph Hearst, blamed Spain for the attack. At McKinley's request Congress approved a declaration of war.

The Spanish-American War was brief, with Spain agreeing to terms in August 1898. Cuba gained its independence, though the United States reserved the right to intervene to ensure stability. Under the peace treaty, Spain transferred to the United States its claims to Puerto Rico and the Philippine Islands. In addition, the U.S. Congress voted in July 1898 to take possession of the Hawaiian Islands. This territorial expansion increased the United States' international prestige as a imperialist power, but some citizens questioned its constitutionality and whether it fit with the U.S. national character. The U.S. Supreme Court decided the legal question in 1901 in a set of decisions known as the *Insular* cases. The Court held that these new possessions were domestic territory of the United States, under the full control of Congress, and the residents of these new dependencies did not have the rights of citizens (*De Lima v. Bidwell*, 182 U.S. 1, 21 S. Ct. 743, 45 L. Ed. 1041; *Downes v. Bidwell*, 182 U.S. 244, 21 S. Ct. 770, 45 L. Ed. 1088).

In the 1900 presidential election, McKinley easily again defeated Bryan, who continued to campaign for free silver and against U.S. imperialism.

On September 6, 1901, McKinley was shot by Leon F. Czolgosz, an anarchist who had dreamed of killing a prominent person, at the Pan-American Exposition, in Buffalo, New York. An infection set into McKinley's wound, and he died September 14, in Buffalo. Vice President THEODORE ROOSEVELT succeeded McKinley as president.

McKINNEY ACT The Stewart B. McKinney Homeless Assistance Act, 42 U.S.C.A. 11301 et seq. (1989 Supp.), was named after the Republican congressman from Connecticut. It authorizes the Department of Housing and Urban Development to coordinate the disbursement of unused federal property to community groups interested in providing shelter to HOMELESS PERSONS, especially elderly persons, handicapped persons, families with children, Native Americans, and veterans. The Interagency Council on the Homeless (Pub. L. No. 100-77, 101 Stat. 484, 42 U.S.C.A. 11301 (b) (1) [1989]) distributes information on how to use benefits under the act.

Initially, priority to receive excess properties was given to homeless providers rather than local communities. However, the Base Closure and Community Redevelopment Act of 1994 (Pub. L. No. 103-421, Oct. 25, 1994, 108 Stat. 4346) amended the McKinney Act by eliminating homeless providers' priority. The result is that homeless providers' needs are considered simultaneously in a community's reuse planning.

Funding and support for the McKinney Act has been reduced, especially with the 1996 WELFARE reform, because the act functions in connection with other related legislation. In one recent funding cycle, nearly three thousand requests for transitional housing were submitted, but only 818 proposals could be funded under the act.

In 1996, to assist homeless individuals, the 104th Congress appropriated $823 million for the emergency shelter grants program (as authorized under subtitle B of title IV of the McKinney Act), the supportive housing program (as authorized under subtitle C of title IV of the McKinney Act), the section 8 moderate rehabilitation single room occupancy program (as authorized under the United States Housing Act of 1937 [Sept. 1, 1937, ch. 896, 50 Stat. 888], as amended, pursuant to section 441 of the McKinney Act), and the shelter plus care program (as authorized under subtitle F of the title IV of the McKinney Act) (110 Stat 2874).

McLEAN, JOHN John McLean served as associate justice on the U.S. Supreme Court for thirty-two years, one of the longest tenures in the history of the Court.

McLean was born on March 11, 1785, in New Jersey but was raised primarily near Lebanon, Ohio, where his father staked out land that later became the family farm. McLean attended a county school and later was tutored by two

schoolmasters, Presbyterian ministers, and paid them with money he earned working as a farm hand. In 1804, at the age of nineteen, he began working as an apprentice to the clerk of the Hamilton County Court of Common Pleas in Cincinnati and also studied law with Arthur St. Clair and John S. Gano, two distinguished Cincinnati lawyers.

In 1807 McLean was admitted to the bar, married, and returned to Lebanon to open a printing office. He began publishing the Lebanon *Western Star,* a partisan journal supporting the Jeffersonian party. Three years later McLean gave his newspaper and printing business to his brother to concentrate full-time on the practice of law. At the same time, McLean, who had been raised Presbyterian, converted to Methodism, an experience that would have a strong impact throughout his life. He was active in church affairs and wrote articles about the Bible, and in 1849 he was named honorary president of the American Sunday School Union.

In 1812, after a year serving as examiner in the U.S. Land Office in Cincinnati, McLean was elected to the U.S. House of Representatives at the age of twenty-seven and was re-elected two years later. During his two terms in the House, McLean was a staunch supporter of President JAMES MADISON and his efforts to wage the War of 1812. McLean, unhappy with the salary paid to members of Congress and wanting to be closer to his wife and children, chose not to run again in 1816 and returned home. Back in Ohio, McLean easily won election to one of four judgeships on the Ohio Supreme Court, a demanding position that required him to "ride the circuit," or hear cases throughout the state.

In 1822 McLean was again drawn to politics and made an unsuccessful bid for the U.S. Senate. Shortly after McLean lost the election, President JAMES MONROE appointed him commissioner of the General Land Office in Washington, a direct result of McLean's earlier hard work to secure Monroe's nomination for the presidency. The position meant a large increase

BIOGRAPHY

ARTIST, JOHN WESLEY JARVIS. COLLECTION OF THE SUPREME COURT OF THE UNITED STATES.

John McLean

JOHN MCLEAN 1785–1861

1811 Served as examiner in the U.S. Land Office in Cincinnati

1812 Elected to U.S. House

1804 Apprenticed to the clerk of the Hamilton County Court of Common Pleas in Cincinnati

1812–14 War of 1812

1822 Appointed commissioner of the General Land Office in Washington

1775–83 American Revolution

1785 Born, Morris County, N.J.

1797 Family moved to Ohio

1807 Admitted to Ohio bar

1816–22 Served on Ohio's Supreme Court

1823 Appointed postmaster general

1834 Wrote majority opinion in *Wheaton v. Peters*

1828–61 Served as associate justice of the U.S. Supreme Court

1857 Wrote strong dissent opinion in *Dred Scott v. Sandford*

1861 Died, Washington, D.C.

1861–65 U.S. Civil War

1775   1800   1825   1850   1875

in salary and led to McLean's appointment the next year to the position of postmaster general. During his six years as postmaster general, McLean expanded the number of routes and deliveries, established thousands of new post offices, and increased the size of the U.S. Postal Service to almost 27,000 employees.

Though he served as postmaster under JOHN QUINCY ADAMS, McLean used his considerable political skills to establish ties with ANDREW JACKSON, who defeated Adams for the presidency in 1828. As a result, McLean was appointed to the U.S. Supreme Court, winning confirmation easily.

McLean remained interested in politics during his tenure on the Supreme Court and was even seriously considered as a nominee for the presidency at several national conventions, though his name was withdrawn from consideration each time. His last bid came in 1860, a year before his death, when he was one of the Republican party's candidates. The nomination instead went to ABRAHAM LINCOLN.

While an associate justice on the High Court, McLean wrote a number of significant opinions, including a strong dissent in the *Dred Scott* case of 1857 (*Dred Scott v. Sandford*, 60 U.S. 393 (Mem), 19 How. 393, 15 L. Ed. 691). In *Dred Scott*, a slave sued his master for freedom after he had been taken to live on free soil for several years. The Supreme Court held that African Americans could not be U.S. citizens and that Congress could not pass legislation preventing SLAVERY. McLean, however, who had long opposed slavery, argued that Congress could exclude slavery from the territories and could also liberate slaves living in "free" states. McLean's most significant majority opinion came in 1834 in *Wheaton v. Peters*, a dispute between two of the Court's REPORTERS of decisions (33 U.S. 591, 8 Pet. 591, 8 L. Ed. 1055 (Mem.) (U.S. Pa., Jan. Term 1834)). Richard Peters sought to republish decisions that had previously been published by HENRY WHEATON, his predecessor. Wheaton, worried that he would sell fewer opinions and thus lose profits, sued Peters, alleging COPYRIGHT infringement. McLean, writing for the Court, held that the opinions were in the public domain and thus no copyright had been violated.

Though McLean enjoyed a long and distinguished career as a jurist, his personal life was less happy. Three of his four daughters died young, as did a brother, and he also lost his first wife in 1840. He and his second wife had one son who died only a few weeks after birth. Though McLean's own health began to fail as early as 1859, he continued to serve on the

Court until his death from pneumonia April 4, 1861.

See also DRED SCOTT V. SANDFORD; WHEATON V. PETERS.

McNABB-MALLORY RULE

A federal judicial doctrine that operates to exclude from EVIDENCE a CONFESSION that is obtained from a person who was not brought before a judicial officer promptly after the person's arrest.

The McNabb-Mallory rule, which is applicable only in federal prosecutions, derives from the U.S. Supreme Court cases of *McNabb v. United States*, 318 U.S. 332, 63 S. Ct. 608, 87 L. Ed. 819 (1943), and *Mallory v. United States*, 354 U.S. 449, 77 S. Ct. 1356, 1 L. Ed. 2d 1479 (1957). The McNabb-Mallory rule is not a constitutional rule but is based on federal law and on the federal judiciary's authority to oversee the administration of criminal justice within the FEDERAL COURTS. The purpose of the rule is to provide protection against an arresting officer's "secret interrogation" of a suspect prior to the suspect's appearance before a judicial officer. Before *McNabb*, authorities could effectively and without penalty delay a suspect's presentment before a judicial officer in order to obtain a confession. *McNabb* held that the penalty for obtaining confessions as a result of such a delay is the exclusion of the confession at trial.

In *McNabb*, a federal revenue agent was killed when agents attempted to arrest members of the McNabb family, a clan of Tennessee mountaineers. The agents subsequently arrested three of the McNabbs and placed them in a detention cell for more than fourteen hours. Over the course of the next two days, federal agents interrogated the McNabbs and finally obtained confessions from them. Based primarily on these confessions, which were admitted into evidence at trial, a jury convicted the McNabbs of second-degree murder. On appeal, however, the U.S. Supreme Court held that the McNabbs' confessions should have been excluded from trial because the federal agents had improperly obtained the confessions by delaying their appearance before a judicial officer. A federal law at the time required federal law officers to take a person charged with any crime before the nearest U.S. commissioner or judicial officer. Relying on this law and on the Court's supervisory authority to oversee justice in the federal court system, the Court held that the confessions should have been excluded from evidence at trial. The Court noted in its decision that the arresting officers had "subjected the accused to the pressures of a procedure which is wholly incompatible with the vital but very restricted duties of the investigating and arresting officers of the Government and which tends to undermine the integrity of the criminal proceeding."

Federal courts questioned whether the *McNabb* EXCLUSIONARY RULE applied only in determining whether a confession was voluntary or whether it applied only when the presentation of the arrested person before a federal MAGISTRATE was unnecessarily delayed. Subsequently, the Supreme Court in *Upshaw v. United States*, 335 U.S. 410, 69 S. Ct. 170, 93 L. Ed. 100 (1948), clarified that a confession was "inadmissible if made during the illegal detention due to failure promptly to carry a prisoner before a committing magistrate."

The *McNabb* case preceded the adoption of the Federal Rules of Criminal Procedure in 1944. Rule 5(a) provided that an arresting officer must bring an arrested person "without unnecessary delay" before the nearest available federal magistrate. In *Mallory*, the Court held that the *McNabb* ruling concerning exclusion of improperly obtained confessions applied equally to rule 5(a). Justice FELIX FRANKFURTER, writing for the Court, stated:

> The scheme for initiating a federal prosecution is plainly defined. The police may not arrest upon mere suspicion but only on "probable cause." The next step in the proceeding is to arraign the arrested person before a judicial officer as quickly as possible so that he may be advised of his rights and so that the issue of probable cause may be promptly determined. The arrested person may, of course, be "booked" by the police. But he is not to be taken to police headquarters in order to carry out a process of inquiry that lends itself, even if not so designed, to eliciting damaging statements to support the arrest and ultimately his guilt.

Because the defendant in *Mallory* had been interrogated for more than seven hours, during which time a judicial officer was readily available for arraignment, the Court held that the defendant's confession should have been excluded from evidence at trial.

The McNabb-Mallory rule is not mandated by the Constitution. As a result, Congress frequently attempted to repeal the McNabb-Mallory rule by legislative act. Finally, in 1968, Congress passed the Omnibus Crime Control and Safe Streets Act (42 U.S.C.A. § 3701 et seq.), which allowed the admission of a confession at trial as long as the confession was "voluntary." The act made the delay in an arrested person's appearance before a judicial officer one of several factors for the courts to consider in determining whether the person's confession was voluntary and therefore ADMISSIBLE. Nevertheless, Supreme Court cases since *McNabb* and *Mallory* have mandated the McNabb-Mallory rule in certain cases, such as requiring that a person be brought before a federal magistrate promptly after arrest in a case of an arrest without a WARRANT. The McNabb-Mallory rule stands for the proposition that the federal JUDICIARY may supervise the administration of justice in the federal courts and, in the exercise of that function, exclude evidence obtained in violation of federal law.

Although the McNabb-Mallory rule is not applicable to prosecutions of individuals in state court proceedings, some states have a similar rule. Other states exclude confessions of a defendant only if the confession was involuntarily made during the period of pre-arraignment detention.

See also CRIMINAL LAW; CRIMINAL PROCEDURE.

McREYNOLDS, JAMES CLARK

James Clark McReynolds served as an associate justice of the U.S. Supreme Court from 1914 to 1941. McReynolds was a very conservative justice who gained prominence for his opposition to the NEW DEAL legislation of the 1930s and for his unprecedented number of opinions declaring acts of Congress unconstitutional.

McReynolds was born on February 3, 1862, in Elkton, Kentucky, the son of a prominent surgeon. McReynolds graduated from Vanderbilt University in 1882 and then attended the

BIOGRAPHY

ARTIST, BJORN EGELI, COLLECTION OF THE SUPREME COURT OF THE UNITED STATES.

James Clark McReynolds

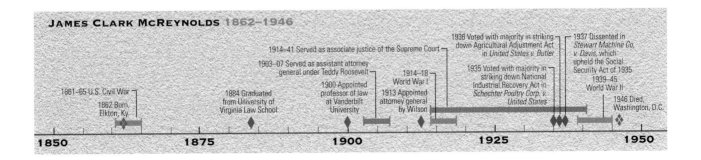

JAMES CLARK McREYNOLDS 1862–1946

- 1861–65 U.S. Civil War
- 1862 Born, Elkton, Ky.
- 1884 Graduated from University of Virginia Law School
- 1900 Appointed professor of law at Vanderbilt University
- 1903–07 Served as assistant attorney general under Teddy Roosevelt
- 1913 Appointed attorney general by Wilson
- 1914–41 Served as associate justice of the Supreme Court
- 1914–18 World War I
- 1935 Voted with majority in striking down National Industrial Recovery Act in *Schechter Poultry Corp. v. United States*
- 1936 Voted with majority in striking down Agricultural Adjustment Act in *United States v. Butler*
- 1937 Dissented in *Stewart Machine Co. v. Davis*, which upheld the Social Security Act of 1935
- 1939–45 World War II
- 1946 Died, Washington, D.C.

1850   1875   1900   1925   1950

University of Virginia law school, graduating in 1884. He established a law practice in Nashville and became a successful business attorney. In 1900 he was appointed a professor of law at Vanderbilt.

During the period 1886 to 1900, McReynolds established himself as a conservative Democrat, running unsuccessfully in 1886 for Congress despite substantial Republican support. Although a Democrat, he found favor with Republican president THEODORE ROOSEVELT, who appointed McReynolds assistant U.S. attorney general in 1903. He remained in the Justice Department until 1907.

In that year he moved to New York and joined a large law firm. In 1913 Democratic president WOODROW WILSON appointed McReynolds attorney general. He gained prominence for his prosecution of ANTITRUST cases but left the post in 1914 when Wilson appointed him to the Supreme Court.

McReynolds's conservatism was consistent and unbending. He believed in a restricted role for the federal government, which meant that he opposed federal social and economic regulation. His views matched those of most of his fellow justices during the 1920s and 1930s, but the Great Depression and the New Deal legislation of President FRANKLIN D. ROOSEVELT soon put McReynolds in the spotlight. McReynolds, along with Justices GEORGE SUTHERLAND, WILLIS VAN DEVANTER, and PIERCE BUTLER, a group known as the "Four Horsemen," became the core of opposition to federal efforts to revitalize the economy and create a social safety net. McReynolds voted with the majority to strike down as unconstitutional the National Industrial Recovery Act, 48 Stat. 195 (1933), in *Schechter Poultry Corporation v. United States*, 295 U.S. 495, 55 S. Ct. 837, 79 L. Ed. 1570 (1935), and the Agricultural Adjustment Act, 7 U.S.C.A. § 601 et seq., in *United States v. Butler*, 297 U.S. 1, 56 S. Ct. 312, 80 L. Ed. 477 (1936).

As McReynolds and the Court struck down each new piece of New Deal legislation, Roosevelt became frustrated. He proposed a "court-packing" plan that would have added additional justices to the Court, in hope of gaining a more sympathetic majority. Although Congress rejected Roosevelt's plan, the national debate over the role of the federal government and the recalcitrance of the Supreme Court led more moderate members of the Court to change their positions and vote in favor of New Deal proposals.

McReynolds was outraged at this switch and the resulting expansion of the federal government. Now in the minority, he issued stinging dissents against what he believed were uncon-

stitutional acts by the national government. In *Steward Machine Co. v. Davis*, 301 U.S. 548, 57 S. Ct. 883, 81 L. Ed. 1279 (1937), he dissented from a decision that upheld the SOCIAL SECURITY ACT OF 1935, 42 U.S.C.A. § 301 et seq., castigating the idea that the Constitution gave the federal government the right to provide "public charity throughout the United States."

On a personal level, McReynolds ranks as one of the most troubling figures ever to sit on the Court. A virulent anti-Semite, McReynolds treated Justices LOUIS D. BRANDEIS and BENJAMIN N. CARDOZO, both Jews, with undisguised contempt. He refused to sign joint opinions with Brandeis or sit next to Brandeis at official Court ceremonies.

Increasingly isolated, McReynolds retired in 1941. He died on August 24, 1946, in Washington, D.C.

MECHANIC'S LIEN A charge or claim upon the PROPERTY of another individual as security for a DEBT that is created in order to obtain priority of payment of the price or value of work that is performed and materials that are provided in the erection or repair of a building or other structure.

See also LIENS.

MEDIATION A settlement of a dispute or controversy by setting up an independent person between two contending parties in order to aid them in the settlement of their disagreement.

In INTERNATIONAL LAW, mediation is the friendly interference of one state in the controversies of nations. It is recognized as a proper action to promote peace among nations.

The individual who intervenes in order to help the other parties settle their dispute is called a *mediator.*

See also ALTERNATIVE DISPUTE RESOLUTION.

MEDIATION, INTERNATIONAL LAW One of the procedures for the peaceful settlement of international disputes is mediation, which is the direct participation by a third country, individual, or organization in resolving a controversy between states. The mediating state may become involved at the request of the parties to the dispute or on its own initiative. In its role as mediator the intervening state will take part in the discussions between the other states and may propose possible solutions. A related procedure is the offer of good offices, where a state will take various actions to bring the conflicting states into negotiations, without necessarily taking part in the discussions leading to settlement.

MEDICAID A joint federal-state program that provides health care insurance to low-income persons.

Medicaid was enacted in 1965 as an amendment to the SOCIAL SECURITY ACT OF 1935 (title XIX, 42 U.S.C.A. § 1396), entitling low-income persons to medical care. The program is a joint federal-state endeavor, with the federal government providing money to the states, which provide additional financing and administer medical programs for the poor that satisfy federal standards. Medicaid has become a major social welfare program. By 1995 thirty-four million people were covered by Medicaid, including seventeen million children.

Before 1965 a patchwork of programs financed by state and local governments, along with charities and community hospitals, provided indigent persons with limited health care. Most of these programs provided emergency health care services. President LYNDON B. JOHNSON supported Medicaid as well as MEDICARE legislation for retired persons in 1965. The enactment of Medicaid meant that persons who met federal financial eligibility requirements were entitled to health care.

Medicaid furnishes at least five general categories of treatment: inpatient hospital services, outpatient hospital services, laboratory and X-ray services, skilled nursing home services, and physicians' services. Generally each of these services is available to treat conditions that cause acute suffering, endanger life, result in illness or infirmity, interfere with the capacity for normal activity, or present a significant handicap. In addition, all states provide eye and dental care, and prescription drugs. Almost all states provide physical therapy, hospice care, and rehabilitative services.

Medicaid is a "vendor" plan because payment is made directly to the vendor (the person or entity that provides the services) rather than to the patient. Only approved nursing homes, physicians, and other providers of medical care are entitled to receive Medicaid payments for their services. Since the early 1970s, rising medical costs have placed financial pressures on the Medicaid program. Consequently, health care providers are not fully reimbursed for the services they provide to Medicaid patients. Because of lower reimbursement payments, one-third of physicians limit the number of Medicaid patients they see, and one-quarter of them refuse to accept any Medicaid patients.

The federal government, through statutes and regulations, has enacted an increasing number of criteria for the states to follow in administering the Medicaid program. For example, from 1987 to 1992, the federal government imposed thirty mandates on states that related to eligibility, reimbursement, and services. The intent of these mandates was to reduce varia-

Medicaid Recipients and Payments, in 1993

Includes Puerto Rico and outlying areas

Recipients

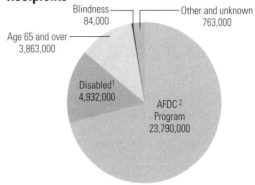

Payments

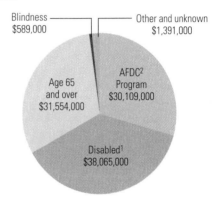

[1]Permanently and totally disabled.

[2]Aid to Families with Dependent Children.

Source: U.S. Health Care Financing Administration, Health Care Financing Review.

tions among the states and to create more consistency in the coverage to low-income persons.

Under federal law states cannot reduce other WELFARE benefits people receive when they become eligible for Medicaid. State plans cannot impose a citizenship or RESIDENCY requirement other than requiring that an applicant be a resident of the state. No age requirement exists, and everyone receiving welfare may apply for Medicaid. People who are "medically needy" because they are unable to cover costs for their medical care are also eligible, even if their incomes or resources exceed the level that would qualify them for welfare. Beginning in 1988, Medicaid was extended to the "working poor"—low-income persons who have jobs with no health coverage.

When Medicaid began, persons who were eligible had the right to select their own doctors, hospitals, or other medical facilities. Because of skyrocketing medical expenditures, almost all states have received waivers from the federal government concerning the choice of physician. These states now direct most of their Medicaid clients to private, MANAGED CARE programs. *Managed care* is a general term that refers to health plans that attempt to control the cost and quality of care by coordinating medical and other health-related services.

The federal government has also granted waivers to states that prefer to pay for home and community care for elderly beneficiaries who otherwise would end up in nursing homes. This type of care is less expensive than nursing home care and allows state funds to be stretched further.

The federal government reimburses states based mainly on their per capita income. States with high per capita incomes, such as New York and Illinois, receive fifty cents from the federal government for every dollar they spend on Medicaid. Poorer states receive more, with Mississippi receiving reimbursement of 79 percent. The average reimbursement level is 57 percent.

Medicaid FRAUD has plagued the program. The size and complexity of the system, with each state administering Medicaid differently, create opportunity for health care providers and state employees to engage in abuse. It is estimated that 10 percent of Medicaid expenditures are paid on fraudulent claims by vendors. Relatively little fraud is attributable to individuals who provide false information to receive Medicaid benefits.

Another problem for Medicaid has been the growing number of elderly middle-class persons who divest their ASSETS, usually to their children, to meet the Medicaid financial guidelines and qualify for state-paid nursing home care. This results in cases where the truly needy cannot find a bed in a nursing home. In addition, the divestiture of assets imposes additional financial pressures on a program that already has difficulty meeting the demands of the truly needy. If an individual or couple gives away or sells a resource at less than fair market value the Social Security Administration must report such a transfer to the state Medicaid agency. A transfer of assets may result in a period of ineligibility for certain Medicaid-covered nursing home services.

The seriousness of these fraudulent transfers led Congress in 1996 to make a person criminally liable who "knowingly and willfully disposes of assets (including by any transfer in trust) in order for an individual to become eligible for medical assistance" (42 U.S.C.A. § 1320a–7b(a)). A person convicted of this offense may be fined $25,000 and imprisoned for five years.

The increase in state and federal expenditures on Medicaid and in federal mandates to states on administration of the program have led to calls for reform. Reform efforts, which have been based on the payment to the states of block grants for medical assistance, have been unsuccessful.

See also HEALTH CARE LAW; HEALTH INSURANCE.

MEDICAL MALPRACTICE 📖 Improper, unskilled, or negligent treatment of a patient by a physician, dentist, nurse, pharmacist, or other health care professional. 📖

Physicians and other health care professionals may be held liable for their failure to exercise the ordinary care a reasonably prudent qualified person would exercise under the same or similar circumstances. NEGLIGENCE is the predominant theory of LIABILITY concerning ALLEGATIONS of medical malpractice, making this type of litigation part of TORT law. Since the 1970s medical malpractice has been a controversial social issue. Physicians have complained about the large number of MALPRACTICE suits and have urged legal reforms to curb large damage awards, whereas tort attorneys have argued that negligence suits are an effective way of compensating victims of negligence and of policing the medical profession.

A person who alleges negligent medical malpractice must prove four elements: (1) a DUTY OF CARE was owed by the physician; (2) the physician violated the applicable standard of care; (3) the person suffered a compensable injury; and (4) the injury was caused in fact and proximately caused by the substandard conduct. The burden of proving these elements is on the plaintiff in a malpractice lawsuit.

Physicians, as professionals, owe a duty of care to those who seek their treatment. This element is rarely an issue in malpractice litigation, because once a doctor agrees to treat a patient, he or she has a professional duty to provide competent care. The plaintiff must show some actual, compensable injury that is the result of the alleged negligent care. Proof of injury can include the physical effects of the treatment performed by the physician, but it can also include emotional effects. The amount of compensation at issue is usually a highly contested part of the litigation. Causation may also be a vigorously litigated issue because a physician may allege that the injuries were caused by physical factors unrelated to the allegedly negligent medical treatment. For example, assume that a physician is sued for the negligent prescription of a drug to a patient with coronary artery disease and that the patient died of a heart attack. The plaintiff's estate cannot recover damages for the heart attack unless there is sufficient proof to show that the medication was a contributing cause.

The critical element is standard of care, which is concerned with the type of medical care that a physician is expected to provide. Until the 1960s the standard of care was traditionally regarded as the customary or usual practice of members of the profession. This standard was referred to as the "locality rule," because it recognized the custom within a particular geographic area. This rule was criticized for its potential to protect a low standard of care as long as it was embraced by the local medical community. The locality rule also was seen as a disincentive for the medical community to adopt better practices.

Most states have modified the locality rule to include both an evaluation of the customary practices of local physicians and an examination of national medical standards. Physicians are called to testify as expert WITNESSES by both sides in medical malpractice trials because the jury is not familiar with the intricacies of medicine. Standards established by medical specialty organizations, such as the American College of Obstetricians and Gynecologists, are often used by these expert witnesses to address the alleged negligent actions of a physician who practices in that specialty. Nonconformance to these standards is evidence of negligence, whereas conformance supports a finding of due care.

Other rules govern the standard of care evaluation. A few states apply the "respectable minority rule" in evaluating a physician's conduct. This rule holds that a physician is not negligent merely by electing to pursue one of several recognized courses of treatment. Some states use the "error in judgment rule." This principle exempts a physician from liability if the malpractice is based on the physician's error in judgment in choosing among different methods of treatment or in diagnosing a condition.

Medical malpractice litigation began to increase in the 1960s. Tort lawyers were able to break the traditional "conspiracy of silence" that discouraged physicians from testifying about the negligence of colleagues or serving as expert witnesses. By the 1970s physicians alleged that malpractice claims were interfering with their medical practices, with INSURANCE companies either refusing to write malpractice policies for them or charging inflated PREMIUMS. Since then physicians and health care providers have argued that malpractice claims drive up the cost of health care. Jury VERDICTS in the millions of dollars must be passed on to the consumer in the form of higher insurance premiums and physician fees. In addition, many physicians now practice "defensive medicine" to guard against malpractice claims. Defensive medicine refers to the conducting of additional tests and procedures that are not medically necessary but that would assist in defeating a negligence claim.

Many states have enacted damage award limits that are intended to limit the amount of recovery for noneconomic losses, such as pain and suffering, and punitive damages. Plaintiffs attorneys have contested these changes, arguing that medical malpractice awards account for only one percent of the total yearly national health care expenditures. In addition, they note that malpractice claims are the only effective tool to identify incompetent physicians because the medical profession has refused to aggressively discipline its members.

CROSS-REFERENCES

Health Care Law; Managed Care; Patients' Rights; Physicians and Surgeons.

MEDICARE ▨ A federally funded system of health and hospital insurance for persons age sixty-five and older and for disabled persons. ▨

The Medicare program provides basic health care benefits to recipients of SOCIAL SECURITY and is funded through the Social Security Trust Fund. President HARRY S. TRUMAN first proposed a medical care program for the aged in the late 1940s, but Medicare was not enacted until 1965, as one of President LYNDON B. JOHNSON's Great Society programs (42 U.S.C.A. § 1395 et seq.).

Medicare went into effect in 1966 and was first administered by the Social Security Administration. In 1977 the Medicare program was transferred to the newly created HEALTH CARE FINANCING ADMINISTRATION (HCFA). The HCFA is concerned with the development of policies, programs, procedures, and guidance regarding Medicare recipients, the providers of services—such as hospitals, nursing homes, and physicians—and other organizations that are closely related to the Medicare program.

Unlike other federal programs, Medicare is not supported by a large federal organizational hierarchy. The federal government enters into CONTRACTS with private INSURANCE companies for the processing of Medicare claims. Health care providers must meet state and local licensing laws and standards set by the HCFA to qualify for Medicare payments for their services.

Eligibility for Medicare does not depend on income. Almost everyone age sixty-five and older is entitled to Medicare coverage. DISABLED PERSONS under age sixty-five can receive Medicare benefits after they have been collecting Social Security or railroad disability payments for at least two years. Workers do not have to retire at age sixty-five to be protected by Medicare. People who have not worked long enough under Social Security to receive retirement benefits may enroll in the plan by paying a monthly PREMIUM. For those individuals who are

not covered under Social Security and who are too poor to pay the monthly premium, MEDIC-AID, the state and federal program for low-income persons, is available.

Medicare is divided into a hospital insurance program and a supplementary medical insurance program. The Medicare hospital insurance plan is funded through Social Security payroll taxes. It covers REASONABLE and medically necessary treatment in a hospital or skilled nursing home, meals, regular nursing care services, and the cost of necessary special care. Medicare also pays for home health services and hospice care for terminally ill patients.

The hospital insurance program extends coverage based on "benefit periods." An episode of illness is termed a benefit period and starts when the patient enters the hospital or nursing home facility and ends sixty days after the patient has been discharged from the facility. A new benefit period starts with the next hospital stay, and there is no limit to the number of benefit periods a person can have. In any benefit period, Medicare will pay the cost of hospitalization for up to ninety days. The patient must pay a one-time DEDUCTIBLE fee for the first sixty days in a benefit period and an additional daily fee called a copayment for hospital care for the following thirty days. Apart from these payments, Medicare covers the full cost of hospital care.

Medicare also pays for the first twenty days of care in a skilled nursing home and for expenses exceeding a daily minimum amount for the next eighty days when certain conditions show that such care is necessary. Payment can also be made for up to one hundred home health visits provided by a home health agency for up to twelve months after the patient's discharge from a hospital or nursing home, provided certain conditions apply.

Medicare's supplementary medical insurance program is financed by monthly insurance premiums paid by people who sign up for coverage, combined with money contributed by the federal government. The government contributes the major portion of the cost of the program, which is funded out of general tax revenues. Persons who enroll pay a small annual deductible fee for any medical costs incurred above that amount during the year and also pay a regular monthly premium. Once the deductible has been paid, Medicare pays 80 percent for any bills incurred for physicians' and surgeons' services, diagnostic and laboratory tests, and other services. Doctors are not required to accept Medicare patients, but almost all do. Payments cannot be made for routine physical

Medicare Utilization and Charges, 1970 to 1993

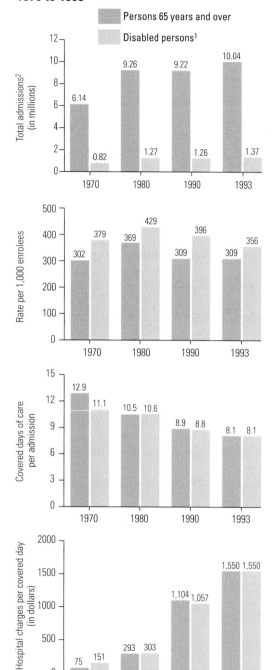

[1]Disabled persons under age 65 and persons enrolled solely because of end-stage renal disease.
[2]Beginning in 1990, represents number of discharges.

Source: U.S. Health Care financing Administration, *Medicare Program Statistics* and unpublished data.

checkups, drugs and medicines, eyeglasses, hearing aids, dentures, or orthopedic shoes.

Medicare bases its 80 percent payment for medical expenses on what is considered to be a reasonable charge for each kind of service. The reasonable charge is an amount determined by the insurance organizations that handle Medicare claims for the federal government, based on the customary charge for that service in that part of the country.

Medicare payments can be sent directly to the doctor or provider of the service or to the patient. In 1994, 93 percent of all charges to Medicare patients for covered physician services were billed directly to the insurance systems rather than to the patients themselves. This means that few patients need to be reimbursed for payments they made directly to the physician or provider of services. Under either method the patient receives a notice after the doctor or provider files a medical insurance claim. The notice details the medical service and explains which expenses are covered by Medicare and are approved, how much of the charge is credited toward the annual deductible amount, and how much Medicare has paid. A person who disagrees with the decision on the claim may ask the insurance company to review the decision. A formal hearing can be held on claims that, if paid, would total at least $100. Cases that involve $1,000 or more can eventually be appealed to a FEDERAL COURT.

The financial future of Medicare has been a hotly debated issue since the 1980s. Medicare spending reached $178 billion in 1995 and, under current laws, is expected to grow to $345 billion in 2002. In 1995, 37 million people were covered by Medicare. The number of people eligible for Medicare will continue to rise as the post–World War II baby boom generation begins to retire in 2010.

Other factors have had an impact on the financial future of Medicare. The quality of medical care has increased life expectancies. Nearly three years have been added to life expectancies since Medicare was created. Modern medicine is likely to continue this trend,

which means that Medicare will be taking care of people longer. Another factor is the increased cost of medical care itself, which takes more resources out of the system.

Medicare's hospital insurance is financed by a payroll tax of 2.9 percent, divided equally between employers and workers. The money is placed in a trust fund and invested in U.S. Treasury securities. A surplus accumulated during the 1980s and early 1990s, but the program's outlays are projected to rise more rapidly than the future payroll tax revenues, depleting the fund by 2002.

Changing the financing of Medicare has proved difficult. In 1988 Congress passed legislation to expand Medicare to cover the health care costs associated with catastrophic illnesses. The new coverage was to be financed by a surtax on the incomes of taxpayers over the age of sixty-five. Elderly citizens and organizations such as the American Association of Retired Persons vigorously protested the tax. In the face of this opposition, Congress repealed the law in 1989.

CROSS-REFERENCES
Elder Law; Health Care Law; Health Insurance; Managed Care; Physicians and Surgeons; Senior Citizens.

BIOGRAPHY

Edwin Meese III

MEESE, EDWIN III Edwin Meese III served as U.S. attorney general from 1985 to 1988. A close and trusted advisor to President RONALD REAGAN, Meese sought to advance the president's conservative agenda. His tenure, however, was clouded by allegations of ethical violations that eventually led to his resignation.

Meese was born on December 2, 1931, in Oakland. He graduated from Yale University in 1953 and received his law degree from the University of California Law School in 1958. From 1958 to 1967, Meese worked as a deputy district attorney for Alameda County, California.

From 1967 to 1969 Meese served then California governor Ronald Reagan as secretary of legal affairs. In 1969 Meese became executive assistant to the governor, and the following year he was made chief of staff. After Reagan left

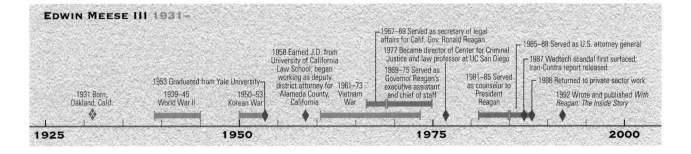

EDWIN MEESE III 1931–

1931 Born, Oakland, Calif.

1939–45 World War II

1950–53 Korean War

1953 Graduated from Yale University

1958 Earned J.D. from University of California Law School; began working as deputy district attorney for Alameda County, California

1961–73 Vietnam War

1967–69 Served as secretary of legal affairs for Calif. Gov. Ronald Reagan

1969–75 Served as Governor Reagan's executive assistant and chief of staff

1977 Became director of Center for Criminal Justice and law professor at UC San Diego

1981–85 Served as counselor to President Reagan

1985–88 Served as U.S. attorney general

1987 Wedtech scandal first surfaced; Iran-Contra report released

1988 Returned to private sector work

1992 Wrote and published *With Reagan: The Inside Story*

1925   1950   1975   2000

office, Meese worked in business and law, becoming the director of the Center for Criminal Justice and professor of law at the University of California at San Diego in 1977.

When President Reagan took office in 1981, he appointed Meese as counselor to the president. In this role Meese became an important advisor on domestic policy. Meese and Reagan shared a common agenda on legal topics. They sought to make ABORTION illegal and to restrict criminal rights, AFFIRMATIVE ACTION, and judicial activism. Meese helped reshape the federal judiciary by advising the president on the appointments for more than half the federal judgeships.

In 1984 Reagan nominated Meese to be U.S. attorney general. Meese encountered fierce opposition from Senate Democrats, who questioned his commitment to CIVIL RIGHTS and his personal ethics. Meese admitted he had paid no interest over 20 months on a $60,000 unsecured loan from a trust headed by John McKean, a California accountant he barely knew. McKean was later appointed, with the help of Meese, to the U.S. Postal Service board of governors, a part-time position that paid $10,000 a year. This apparent deal and other charges concerning Meese's personal finances contributed to a thirteen-month delay in his confirmation. The Senate eventually confirmed Meese, who became attorney general in March 1985.

As attorney general, Meese served as Chairman of the Domestic Policy Council and the National Drug Policy Board and was a member of the NATIONAL SECURITY COUNCIL. Meese sought to establish tough policies against PORNOGRAPHY. He appointed a Commission on Pornography, which issued a controversial two-volume report in 1986 that stated that there was a causal link between violent pornography and aggressive behavior toward women. The report also claimed that nonviolent sexually explicit material contributed to sexual violence, a conclusion challenged by many social scientists. The report broke new ground in its exploration of the problem of child pornography.

In 1987 Meese came under scrutiny for his role in the IRAN-CONTRA scandal, which involved a 1985 arms-for-hostages deal with Iran. The key issue in this scandal, which involved presidential aides Oliver L. North and John M. Poindexter, and other administration officials, was whether President Reagan was aware of these activities in 1985. Meese announced on November 24, 1986, that the president had not known about the deal.

A congressional Iran-Contra committee issued its report in November 1987, in which it stated that Meese had failed to give the president sound legal advice and that he had abetted the Reagan administration's alleged disdain for the law. The report suggested that Meese had not fully investigated the scandal and that he might have participated in a cover-up. In addition, the committee determined that he had failed to take appropriate steps to prevent North and Poindexter from destroying critical evidence. Independent Counsel Lawrence Walsh, who investigated Iran-Contra, issued a report in 1993 that stated Meese had made a false statement in 1986 when he said that Reagan did not know about the 1985 deal. Walsh did not seek a criminal charge against Meese because he did not have a key piece of evidence, the notes of former defense secretary Caspar W. Weinberger, until 1991.

While Iran-Contra plagued Meese, a more serious problem arose, known as the Wedtech scandal. The scandal began in February 1987 and grew to involve other highly placed members of the Reagan administration, as well as government officials in New York, where the Wedtech Corporation was located. The Wedtech Corporation sought Defense Department contracts in the early 1980s. It hired E. Robert Wallach, Meese's former law school classmate and personal attorney, to lobby the government on its behalf. In 1982 Meese helped Wedtech, at Wallach's urging, to get a special hearing on a $32 million Army engine contract, which the Army considered Wedtech unqualified to perform. Soon after the meeting, the contract was awarded to Wedtech, and one of Meese's top deputies went to work for the corporation. A federal criminal investigation unraveled a string of illegal conduct that led to the conviction of Wallach and other public officials.

Independent Counsel James C. McKay investigated the Wedtech contract and other allegations of misconduct by Meese. In July 1988 he issued his report, which did not call for the filing of any criminal charges against Meese for his actions in Wedtech or his failure to file an INCOME TAX return on capital gains. McKay did conclude, however, that Meese may have been "insensitive to the appearance of impropriety."

Following the filing of McKay's 830-page report, Meese announced his resignation, effective at the end of August 1988. Meese claimed that the report vindicated his actions.

MEETING OF CREDITORS 📖 One of the first steps in federal BANKRUPTCY proceedings whereby the CREDITORS of a DEBTOR meet in court to present their claims against him or her and a TRUSTEE is named to handle the application of the debtor's ASSETS to pay his or her DEBTS.

MEETING OF MINDS The mutual agreement and assent of the parties to a CONTRACT to its substance and terms.

The "meeting of the minds" that is required to make a contract is not predicated on the subjective purpose or intention of one of the parties that is not brought to the attention of the other party, but it is based on the purpose and intention that has been made known or that, from all the circumstances, should be known.

MEMBERSHIP CORPORATION A company or organization that is formed for purposes other than generating a profit.

Common examples of membership corporations are religious societies and TRADE UNIONS. See also BENEFICIAL ASSOCIATIONS.

MEMORANDUM An informal record, in the form of a brief written note or outline, of a particular legal transaction or document for the purpose of aiding the parties in remembering particular points or for future reference.

A memorandum may be used in court to prove that a particular CONTRACT was made. For instance, in a REAL ESTATE transaction, a memorandum can be used to show that the parties to a sale have entered into an agreement to sell a particular parcel at an indicated price, in addition to other details of the agreement. This type of memorandum is also referred to as a BINDER.

An attorney might use a memorandum to explain and summarize a specific point of law for a judge or for another attorney.

A MEMORANDUM DECISION is a written decision, issued by a court, which reports the RULING, and the decisions and orders of the court. It does not, however, contain an OPINION, which is an explanation of the rationale upon which the decision was based.

MEMORANDUM DECISION A court's decision that gives the RULING (what it decides and orders done), but no OPINION (reasons for the decision).

A memorandum decision is not subject to appeal by the dissatisfied party.

MENSA ET THORO [*Latin, From bed and board.*] A type of DIVORCE that is a partial termination of the duties of a marital relationship.

A divorce *mensa et thoro* is one that does not provide a husband and wife with the right to remarry but that permits them to live separately. Such a divorce does not dissolve the marriage but amounts to a *legal separation*.

MENS REA As an element of criminal responsibility, a guilty mind; a guilty or wrongful purpose; a criminal INTENT. Guilty knowledge and wilfulness.

A fundamental principle of CRIMINAL LAW is that a crime consists of both a mental and a physical element. Mens rea, a person's awareness of the fact that his or her conduct is criminal, is the mental element, and *actus reus*, the act itself, is the physical element.

The concept of mens rea developed in England during the latter part of the COMMON-LAW era (about the year 1600) when judges began to hold that an act alone could not create criminal LIABILITY unless it was accompanied by a guilty state of mind. The degree of mens rea required for a particular common-law crime varied. MURDER, for example, required a malicious state of mind, whereas LARCENY required a felonious state of mind.

Today most crimes, including common-law crimes, are defined by statutes that usually contain a word or phrase indicating the mens rea requirement. A typical statute, for example, may require that a person act knowingly, purposely, or recklessly.

Sometimes a statute creates criminal liability for the commission or omission of a particular act without designating a mens rea. These are called STRICT LIABILITY statutes. If such a statute is construed to purposely omit criminal intent, a person who commits the crime may be guilty even though he or she had no knowledge that his or her act was criminal and had no thought of committing a crime. All that is required under such statutes is that the act itself is voluntary, since involuntary acts are not criminal.

Occasionally mens rea is used synonymously with the words *general intent*, although GENERAL INTENT is more commonly used to describe criminal liability when a defendant does not intend to bring about a particular result. SPECIFIC INTENT, another term related to mens rea, describes a particular state of mind above and beyond what is generally required.

MENTAL ANGUISH When connected with a physical injury, includes both the resultant mental sensation of pain and also the accompanying feelings of distress, fright, and anxiety. As an element of DAMAGES implies a relatively high degree of mental pain and distress; it is more than mere disappointment, anger, worry, resentment, or embarrassment, although it may include all of these, and it includes mental sensation of pain resulting from such painful emotions as grief, severe disappointment, indignation, wounded pride, shame, despair, and/or public humiliation. In other connections, and as a ground for DIVORCE or for compensable damages or an element of damages, it includes the mental suffering resulting from the excitation of the more poignant and painful emotions, such as grief, severe disappointment, indignation, wounded pride, shame, public humiliation, despair, etc. 📖

MENTAL CRUELTY 📖 A course of conduct on the part of one spouse toward the other spouse that can endanger the mental and physical health and efficiency of the other spouse to such an extent as to render continuance of the marital relation intolerable. As a ground for DIVORCE, it is conduct that causes embarrassment, humiliation, and anguish so as to render life miserable and unendurable or to cause a spouse's life, person, or health to become endangered. 📖

MENTSCHIKOFF, SOIA Soia Mentschikoff was a distinguished legal scholar and educator whose career encompassed several "firsts" for women in the legal profession.

Mentschikoff was born April 2, 1915, in Russia where her father, a resident of New York City, was working. In 1918 her family returned to New York where Mentschikoff graduated from Hunter College in 1934 and from Columbia Law School in 1937.

At Columbia Mentschikoff met KARL LLEWELLYN, a professor of law and the chief reporter, or drafter, of the UNIFORM COMMERCIAL CODE (UCC) for the American Law Institute (the Uniform Commercial Code is a model for laws dealing with business and commercial transactions that has been adopted, at least in part, by all the states, except Louisiana, and the District of Columbia). Initially, Mentschikoff worked with Llewellyn on the UCC as his research assistant; from 1949 through 1954 she was the associate chief reporter of the code. Subsequently, she became a consultant to the Permanent Editorial Board for the UCC.

After the UCC was completed, Mentschikoff became increasingly interested in the international aspects of commercial law. In 1964 she was one of the U.S. representatives at a diplomatic conference held at The Hague to consider a uniform law on the international sale of goods. She later became an adviser to the

BIOGRAPHY

Soia Mentschikoff

Department of State on matters involving international sales and international arbitration.

In 1947 Mentschikoff joined the faculty at the Harvard Law School, the first time a woman had taught at that school. Three years earlier in 1944, she had achieved another first by becoming the first woman partner at a major Wall Street firm. In 1951 Mentschikoff and Llewellyn, whom she had married in 1947, joined the faculty at the University of Chicago Law School. To satisfy the school's anti-nepotism rule, Llewellyn was named a "professor" while Mentschikoff was a "professorial lecturer" until his death in 1962 when she became a professor. In 1974 Mentschikoff became the dean of the University of Miami School of Law, a position that she held until 1982.

Mentschikoff died June 18, 1984, in Coral Gables, Florida.

MERCANTILE 📖 Relating to trade or COMMERCE; commercial; having to do with the business of buying and selling; relating to merchants. 📖

A *mercantile agency* is an individual or company in the business of collecting data about the financial status, ability, and CREDIT of individuals who are engaged in business. Once this information is compiled, it is sold by the agency to its customers, who are known as subscribers. Mercantile agencies are known as CREDIT BUREAUS in current usage.

MERCHANTABLE 📖 Salable; of quality and type ordinarily acceptable among vendors and buyers. 📖

An item is deemed merchantable if it is reasonably fit for the ordinary purposes for which such products are manufactured and sold. For example, soap is merchantable if it cleans. In general, a seller or manufacturer is required by law to make products of merchantable quality. In the event that the items do not meet with the proper standards, a suit can be brought against the seller or manufacturer by anyone who is injured as a result.

See also PRODUCT LIABILITY; SALES.

MERCIAN LAW 📖 A major body of Anglo-Saxon customs that, along with the Dane law

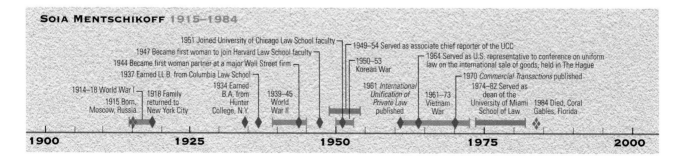

SOIA MENTSCHIKOFF 1915–1984

1951 Joined University of Chicago Law School faculty
1947 Became first woman to join Harvard Law School faculty
1944 Became first woman partner at a major Wall Street firm
1937 Earned LL.B. from Columbia Law School

1949–54 Served as associate chief reporter of the UCC
1950–53 Korean War
1964 Served as U.S. representative to conference on uniform law on the international sale of goods; held in The Hague
1970 *Commercial Transactions* published

1914–18 World War I
1915 Born, Moscow, Russia
1918 Family returned to New York City
1934 Earned B.A. from Hunter College, N.Y.
1939–45 World War II
1961 *International Unification of Private Law* published
1961–73 Vietnam War
1974–82 Served as dean of the University of Miami School of Law
1984 Died, Coral Gables, Florida

1900   1925   1950   1975   2000

and the West Saxon law, continued to constitute the law in England in the days immediately following the Norman Conquest. 📖

MERCY KILLING See DEATH AND DYING.

MEREDITH, JAMES HOWARD CIVIL RIGHTS pioneer and activist James Howard Meredith put his life at risk by being the first African American to attend the University of Mississippi in 1962. After the state repeatedly blocked his attempts to register at the university, a legal battle waged by Meredith and the NATIONAL ASSOCIATION FOR THE ADVANCEMENT OF COLORED PEOPLE (NAACP) achieved a landmark victory for integration. When violence erupted on the day that Meredith enrolled, President JOHN F. KENNEDY sent several thousand U.S. Army troops to the campus to quell bloody rioting. Armed federal marshals protected Meredith in every classroom until he graduated in 1963. In 1966 the James Meredith March against Fear united traditional and radical civil rights leaders in a voter registration march across Mississippi. Meredith was shot, but he recovered and joined MARTIN LUTHER KING, JR., and others in a month-long demonstration that marked a turning point in the civil rights struggle. In later years, Meredith, who had always maintained independence from the inheritors of the CIVIL RIGHTS MOVEMENT, became one of their sharpest critics.

Meredith was born June 25, 1933, in Kosciusko, Mississippi. He was one of ten children of Roxy Patterson Meredith and Moses Cap, a poor farmer in Kosciusko, in Attala County. As a young child, Meredith became aware of racism. He would refuse the nickels and dimes that a local white man regularly gave to black children, calling the gifts degrading. More painful was the realization he made as a young man on a trip to visit relatives in Detroit, where he saw blacks and whites sharing the same public facilities. Riding the train home from this brush with INTEGRATION, when he arrived in Memphis, the conductor told him to leave the whites-only car. "I cried all the way home," Meredith later recalled, "and vowed to devote myself to changing the degrading conditions of black people." He also had other ambitions and goals. Ever

BIOGRAPHY

"THERE IS NO WAY FOR ONE NEGRO TO CHANGE HIS BASIC STATUS WITHOUT FIRST CHANGING THAT OF ALL NEGROES."

since a childhood visit to a white doctor's office, he had harbored a dream of attending the University of Mississippi, the physician's alma mater.

After high school, in 1951, Meredith joined the U.S. Air Force. He rose to the rank of staff sergeant, earned credits toward a college degree, and served in the Korean War. Following his discharge in 1960, he attended all-black Jackson State College. But the courses he wanted to take were offered only at the state university. As a twenty-eight-year-old, he followed with hopefulness the speeches of John F. Kennedy, which promised greater enjoyment of opportunity for all U.S. citizens. Change was in the air, and many African Americans were heartened by the portents in Kennedy's 1961 inaugural address. On the same day that Kennedy became president, Meredith applied to the University of Mississippi.

The school turned down his application. Mississippi still practiced segregation, and that meant no African Americans could attend the all-white university. Even seven years after *Brown v. Board of Education* (1954), southern states resisted complying with the U.S. Supreme Court's decision that compulsory segregation was unconstitutional. Knowing that he had a constitutional right that the state refused to recognize, Meredith turned to the NAACP Legal Defense and Education Fund. This arm of the civil rights organization, accustomed to fighting segregation cases, extended help to him. Meredith and his attorneys fought some thirty court actions against the state.

At last, a federal court ruled that a qualified student could not be denied admission on the ground of race. Meredith had won, but the court order infuriated segregationists. Playing to popular sentiment, Governor Ross Barnett, of Mississippi, promised to stop Meredith. Barnett pressured the state legislature to give him authority over university admissions, a power usually exercised by the state college board.

As Meredith's enrollment date, September 20, 1962, approached, death threats were made against him, Barnett continued to promise to prevent his enrollment, and segregationists

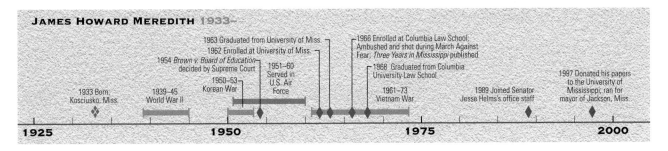

JAMES HOWARD MEREDITH 1933–

1933 Born, Kosciusko, Miss.

1939–45 World War II

1950–53 Korean War

1951–60 Served in U.S. Air Force

1954 *Brown v. Board of Education* decided by Supreme Court

1962 Enrolled at University of Miss.

1963 Graduated from University of Miss.

1961–73 Vietnam War

1966 Enrolled at Columbia Law School; Ambushed and shot during March Against Fear; *Three Years in Mississippi* published

1968 Graduated from Columbia University Law School

1989 Joined Senator Jesse Helms's office staff

1997 Donated his papers to the University of Mississippi; ran for mayor of Jackson, Miss.

1925   1950   1975   2000

spread the word to be at "Ole Miss" to save it from integration. On the day Meredith arrived to register, white students massed around a Confederate flag chanting anti-integration slogans. Barnett stood blocking the door to the admissions office. A university official read a proclamation naming Barnett acting registrar, by order of the university's board of trustees, and a satisfied Barnett told Meredith that his application was denied.

The governor's action was good politics in his home state. Across the South, leaders such as Governor GEORGE WALLACE, of Alabama, were prospering politically by staging similar acts of defiance. However, Barnett's refusal to let Meredith in was a serious problem for Washington, D.C. It represented a challenge to the authority of the FEDERAL COURTS, and in a short time, the U.S. Department of Justice entered the dispute. Attorney General ROBERT F. KENNEDY confronted Barnett, demanding assurances that Meredith's next attempt to register would be successful and that the student would be protected. Barnett gave none. He replied that the situation was beyond his control. Where civil rights were concerned, the young attorney general was quickly learning that only federal intervention could bring the southern states under the mandate of the courts. He sent five hundred federal marshals to the University of Mississippi campus with strict orders: they were to protect Meredith, but not to shoot anyone. Only tear gas and clubs were to be used for their own defense.

On September 30, Meredith arrived at Ole Miss to try to enroll for a second time. Protected by the marshals, he finally registered, and then took refuge in his dormitory. As students and outsiders began gathering, an angry mob shouted attacks on Meredith. Whites began throwing rocks at the outnumbered marshals, who were soon besieged by thousands of new protesters streaming onto the campus. A vicious riot erupted, the armed agitators firing shots and hurling rocks, bricks, bottles, flaming gas, and acid. By late evening on the same day Meredith registered, a French journalist and an onlooker were dead. More than 160 marshals were wounded, the rest were exhausted and their tear gas was running out. Reluctantly, Kennedy dispatched five thousand Army troops to Ole Miss; their numbers were finally enough to disperse the mob and regain control of the battered campus.

Meredith attended classes under armed guard, but persevered, graduating in August 1963. By the summer of 1966, Meredith was enrolled at Columbia University Law School. But he interrupted his studies to launch a bold personal demonstration for civil rights. Meredith announced plans to march across the state of Mississippi, covering the 220 miles from Memphis to Jackson in sixteen days. The James Meredith March against Fear would show African Americans that they could safely assert their right to vote, despite years of legal obstruction, harassment, and murder. As he had at Ole Miss, Meredith ignored several death threats, proclaiming that he would survive his long march along the state's back roads.

On June 5, 1966, Meredith set out from Memphis with an ebony walking stick that had been given to him by an African chieftain. When he crossed into Mississippi the following morning he was ambushed and shot; remarkably, he survived. His assailant, an unemployed member of the KU KLUX KLAN, pleaded guilty and received a five-year prison sentence (of which three years were suspended). While Meredith recovered in his hospital bed, he was visited by the leaders of major civil rights organizations. A group including STOKELY CARMICHAEL, of the STUDENT NON-VIOLENT COORDINATING COMMITTEE (SNCC), and King wanted to stage a protest. Meredith wanted to go on. He continued the march joined by other civil rights workers.

The marchers completed their journey by late June against often violent opposition. It was a great symbolic victory for civil rights, but the movement itself had begun to factionalize. King and his supporters, who advocated peaceful resistance, were at odds with Carmichael's Black Power movement, which advocated violence if necessary to secure equal rights for African Americans.

Meredith returned to Columbia, completing his law degree in 1968. In the years that followed, Meredith embarked on a series of pursuits. He studied economics at a Nigerian university, established the African Development and Reunification Association, and worked as a consultant, financial planner, tree farmer, and educator.

In the 1980s, Meredith returned to the public eye, this time as a critic of integration, WELFARE, and AFFIRMATIVE ACTION, programs that he believed did more to hurt black people than to help them. He joined the staff of conservative senator JESSE HELMS and later supported former Ku Klux Klan member David Duke, whose welfare views he praised, in Duke's campaign for governor of Louisiana. He also took a series of walks, reminiscent of his 1966 march, to promote his conservative vision. Meredith is the author of *Three Years in Mississippi* (1966).

MERGER 📖 The combination or fusion of one thing or right into another thing or right of greater or larger importance so that the lesser thing or right loses its individuality and becomes identified with the greater whole. 📖

In CONTRACT law, agreements are merged when one contract is absorbed into another. The merger of contracts is generally based on the language of the agreement and the intent of the parties. The merger of contracts is not the same as a merger clause, which is a provision in a contract stating that the written terms cannot be varied by prior or oral agreements.

ESTATES affecting ownership of land are merged where a greater estate and a lesser estate coincide and are held by the same individual. For example, merger occurs when a person who leases land from another subsequently is given ownership of it upon the death of the lessor who has so provided in his will.

In CRIMINAL LAW, the commission of a major crime that includes a lesser offense results in the latter being merged in the former. For example, the crime of rape includes the lesser offense of sexual abuse which is merged into one prosecution for rape.

See also LESSER INCLUDED OFFENSE; MERGERS AND ACQUISTIONS.

MERGERS AND ACQUISITIONS

📖 Methods by which CORPORATIONS legally unify ownership of ASSETS formerly subject to separate controls. 📖

A merger or acquisition is a combination of two companies where one corporation is completely absorbed by another corporation. The less important company loses its identity and becomes part of the more important corporation, which retains its identity. A merger extinguishes the merged corporation, and the surviving corporation assumes all the rights, privileges, and liabilities of the merged corporation. A merger is not the same as a consolidation, in which two corporations lose their separate identities and unite to form a completely new corporation.

Federal and state laws regulate mergers and acquisitions. Regulation is based on the concern that mergers inevitably eliminate competition between the merging firms. This concern is most acute where the participants are direct rivals, because courts often presume that such arrangements are more prone to restrict output and increase prices. The fear that mergers and acquisitions reduce competition has meant that the government carefully scrutinizes proposed mergers. On the other hand, since the 1980s the federal government has become less aggressive in seeking the prevention of mergers.

Despite concerns about a lessening of competition, U.S. law has left firms relatively free to buy or sell entire companies or specific parts of a company. Mergers and acquisitions often result in a number of social benefits. Mergers can bring better management or technical skill to bear on underused assets. Mergers can also produce economies of scale and scope that reduce costs, improve quality, and increase output. The possibility of a TAKEOVER can discourage company managers from behaving in ways that fail to maximize profits. A merger can enable a business owner to sell the firm to someone who is already familiar with the industry and who would be in a better position to pay the highest price. The prospect of a lucrative sale induces entrepreneurs to form new firms. Finally, many mergers pose few risks to competition.

Antitrust merger law seeks to prohibit transactions whose probable anticompetitive consequences outweigh their likely benefits. The critical time for review usually is when the merger is first proposed. This requires enforcement agencies and courts to forecast market trends and future effects. Merger cases examine past events or periods to understand each merging party's position in its market and to predict the merger's competitive impact.

Types of Mergers There are three types of mergers, based on the competitive relationships between the merging parties. In a horizontal merger, one firm acquires another firm that produces and sells an identical or similar product in the same geographic area and thereby elimi-

A merger can have effects that reach beyond the entities involved. A proposed merger between freight railroads Norfolk Southern Corp. and CSX Corp. threatened to reduce rail access for commuter trains operated by Virginia Railway Express.

AP/WIDE WORLD PHOTOS

nates competition between the two firms. In a vertical merger, one firm acquires either a customer or a supplier. CONGLOMERATE mergers encompass all other acquisitions, including pure conglomerate transactions where the merging parties have no evident relationship (a shoe producer buys an appliance manufacturer), geographic extension mergers, where the buyer makes the same product as the target firm but does so in a different geographic market (a baker in Chicago buys a bakery in Miami), and product extension mergers, where a firm producing one product buys a firm that makes a different product that requires the application of similar manufacturing or marketing techniques (a producer of household detergents buys a producer of liquid bleach).

Corporate Merger Procedures State statutes establish procedures to accomplish corporate mergers. Generally, the BOARD OF DIRECTORS for each corporation must initially pass a resolution adopting a plan of merger that specifies the names of the corporations that are involved, the name of the proposed merged company, the manner of converting shares of both corporations, and any other legal provision to which the corporations agree. Each corporation notifies all its shareholders that a meeting will be held to approve the merger. If the proper number of shareholders approves the plan, the directors sign the papers and file them with the state. The secretary of state issues a certificate of merger to authorize the new corporation.

Some statutes permit the directors to abandon the plan at any point up to the filing of the final papers. States with the most liberal corporation laws permit a surviving corporation to absorb another company by merger without submitting the plan to its shareholders for approval unless otherwise required in its certificate of incorporation.

Statutes often provide that corporations formed in two different states must follow the rules in their respective states for a merger to be effective. Some corporation statutes require the surviving corporation to purchase the shares of stockholders who voted against the merger.

Competitive Concerns Horizontal, vertical, and conglomerate mergers each raise distinctive competitive concerns.

Horizontal Mergers Horizontal mergers raise three basic competitive problems. The first is the elimination of competition between the merging firms, which, depending on their size, may be significant. The second is that the unification of the merging firms' operations may create substantial market power and could enable the merged entity to raise prices by reducing output unilaterally. The third problem is that, by increasing concentration in the relevant market, the transaction may strengthen the ability of the market's remaining participants to coordinate their pricing and output decisions. The fear is not that the entities will engage in secret collaboration but that the reduction in the number of industry members will enhance tacit coordination of behavior.

Vertical Mergers Vertical mergers take two basic forms: forward integration, by which a firm buys a customer, and backward integration, by which a firm acquires a supplier. Replacing market exchanges with internal transfers can offer at least two major benefits. First, the vertical merger internalizes all transactions between manufacturer and its supplier or dealer, thus converting a potentially adversarial relationship into something more like a partnership. Second, internalization can give management more effective ways to monitor and improve performance.

Vertical integration by merger does not reduce the total number of economic entities operating at one level of the market, but it may change patterns of industry behavior. Whether a forward or backward integration, the newly acquired firm may decide to deal only with the acquiring firm, thereby altering competition among the acquiring firm's suppliers, customers, or competitors. Suppliers may lose a market for their goods, retail outlets may be deprived of supplies, or competitors may find that both supplies and outlets are blocked. This raises the concern that vertical integration will foreclose competitors by limiting their access to sources of supply or to customers. Vertical mergers may also be anticompetitive because their entrenched market power may impede new businesses from entering the market.

Conglomerate Mergers Conglomerate transactions take many forms, ranging from short-term joint ventures to complete mergers. Whether a conglomerate merger is pure, geographical, or a product line extension, it involves firms that operate in separate markets. Therefore, a conglomerate transaction ordinarily has no direct effect on competition. There is no reduction or other change in the number of firms in either the acquiring or acquired firm's market.

Conglomerate mergers can supply a market or "demand" for firms, thus giving entrepreneurs liquidity at an open market price and with a key inducement to form new enterprises. The threat of takeover may force existing managers to increase efficiency in competitive markets.

Conglomerate mergers also provide opportunities for firms to reduce capital costs and overhead and achieve other efficiencies.

Conglomerate mergers, however, may lessen future competition by eliminating the possibility that the acquiring firm would have entered the acquired firm's market independently. A conglomerate merger also may convert a large firm into a dominant company with a decisive competitive advantage or otherwise make it difficult for other companies to enter the market. This type of merger may also reduce the number of smaller firms and increase the merged firm's political power, thereby impairing the social and political goals of retaining independent decision-making centers, guaranteeing small business opportunities, and preserving democratic processes.

Federal Antitrust Regulation   Since the late nineteenth century, the federal government has challenged business practices and mergers that create or may create a monopoly in a particular market. Federal legislation has varied in effectiveness in preventing anticompetitive mergers.

Sherman Anti-Trust Act of 1890   The Sherman Act (15 U.S.C.A. § 1 et seq.) was the first federal antitrust statute. Its application to mergers and acquisitions has varied, depending on its interpretation by the U.S. Supreme Court. In *Northern Securities Co. v. United States*, 193 U.S. 197, 24 S. Ct. 436, 48 L. Ed. 679 (1904), the Court ruled that all mergers between directly competing firms constituted a COMBINATION IN RESTRAINT OF TRADE and therefore violated section 1 of the Sherman Act. This decision hindered the creation of new monopolies through horizontal mergers.

In *Standard Oil Co. of New Jersey v. United States*, 221 U.S. 1, 31 S. Ct. 502, 55 L. Ed. 619 (1911), however, the Court adopted a less stringent "rule of reason test" to evaluate mergers. This rule meant that the courts must examine whether the merger would yield MONOPOLY control to the merged entity. In practice this resulted in the approval of many mergers that approached but did not achieve monopoly power.

Clayton Anti-Trust Act of 1914   Congress passed the CLAYTON ACT (15 U.S.C.A. § 12 et seq.) in response to the *Standard Oil Co. of New Jersey* decision, which it feared would undermine the Sherman Act's ban against trade restraints and monopolization. Among the provisions of the Clayton Act was section 7, which barred anticompetitive stock acquisitions.

The original section 7 was a weak antimerger safeguard because it banned only purchases of stock. Businesses soon realized that they could evade this measure simply by buying the target firm's assets. The Supreme Court, in *Thatcher Manufacturing Co. v. Federal Trade Commission*, 272 U.S. 554, 47 S. Ct. 175, 71 L. Ed. 405 (1926), further undermined section 7 by allowing a firm to escape LIABILITY if it bought a controlling interest in a rival firm's stock and used this control to transfer to itself the target's assets before the government filed a

The federal government has historically discouraged mergers and acquisitions that may create a monopoly in a particular market. After careful examination, the Federal Trade Commission cleared the way for the horizontal merger between the Boeing Company and rival McDonnell Douglas Corp., which created the world's largest aerospace company.

COMPLAINT. Thus, a firm could circumvent section 7 by quickly converting a stock acquisition into a purchase of assets.

By the 1930s section 7 was eviscerated. Between the passage of the Clayton Act in 1914 and 1950, only fifteen mergers were overturned under the antitrust laws, and ten of these dissolutions were based on the Sherman Act. In 1950 Congress responded to post–World War II concerns that a wave of corporate acquisitions was threatening to undermine U.S. society by passing the Celler-Kefauver Antimerger Act, which amended section 7 of the Clayton Act to close the assets loophole. Section 7 now prohibited a business from purchasing the stock or assets of another entity if "the effect of such acquisition may be substantially to lessen competition, or to tend to create a monopoly."

Congress intended the amended section to reach vertical and conglomerate mergers, as well as horizontal mergers. The U.S. Supreme Court, in *Brown Shoe Co. v. United States*, 370 U.S. 294, 82 S. Ct. 1502, 8 L. Ed. 2d 510 (1962), interpreted the amended law as a congressional attempt to retain local control over industry and to protect small business. The Court concluded that it must look at the merger's actual and likely effect on competition. In general, however, the Court relied almost entirely on market share and concentration figures in evaluating whether a merger was likely to be anticompetitive. Nevertheless, the general PRE-SUMPTION was that mergers were suspect.

In *United States v. General Dynamics*, 415 U.S. 486, 94 S. Ct. 1186, 39 L. Ed. 2d 530 (1974), the Court changed direction. It rejected any antitrust analysis that focused exclusively on market share statistics, cautioning that although statistical data can be of great significance, they are "not conclusive indicators of anticompetitive effects." A merger must be viewed in the context of its particular industry. Therefore, the Court held that "only a further examination of the particular market—its structure, history, and probable future—can provide the appropriate setting for judging the probable anticompetitive effect of the merger." This totality-of-the-circumstances approach has remained the standard for conducting an antitrust analysis of a proposed merger.

Federal Trade Commission Act of 1975
Section 5 of the Federal Trade Commission Act (15 U.S.C.A. § 45), prohibits "unfair method[s] of competition" and gives the Federal Trade Commission (FTC) independent JURISDICTION to enforce the antitrust laws. The law provides no criminal penalties and limits the FTC to issuing prospective decrees. The Justice Department and the FTC share enforcement of the Clayton Act. Congress gave this authority to the FTC because it thought an administrative body would be more responsive to congressional goals than the courts.

Hart-Scott-Rodino Antitrust Improvements Act of 1976 The Hart-Scott-Rodino Antitrust Improvements Act (HSR) (15 U.S.C.A. § 18a) established a mandatory premerger notification procedure for firms that are parties to certain mergers. The HSR process requires the merging parties to notify the FTC and the Justice Department before completing certain transactions. In general, an HSR premerger filing is required when (a) one of the parties to the transaction has annual net sales (or revenues) or total assets exceeding $100 million and the other party has annual net sales (or revenues) or total assets exceeding $10 million, and (b) the acquisition price or value of the acquired assets or entity exceeds $15 million. Failure to comply with these requirements can result in the rescission of completed transactions and can be punished by a civil penalty of up to $10,000 per day.

HSR also established mandatory waiting periods during which the parties may not "close" the proposed transaction and begin joint operations. In transactions other than cash tender offers, the initial waiting period is thirty days after the merging parties have made the requisite premerger notification filings with the federal agencies. For cash tender offers, the waiting period is fifteen days after the premerger filings. Before the initial waiting periods expire, the federal agency responsible for reviewing the transaction can request the parties to supply additional information relating to the proposed merger. These "second requests" often include extensive INTERROGATORIES (lists of questions to be answered) and broad demands for the production of documents. A request for further information can be made once, and the issuance of a second request extends the waiting period for ten days for cash TENDER OFFERS and twenty days for all other transactions. These extensions of the waiting period do not begin until the merging parties are in "substantial compliance" with the government agency's request for additional information.

If the federal government decides not to challenge a merger before the HSR waiting period expires, a federal agency is highly unlikely to sue at a late date to dissolve the transaction under section 7 of the Clayton Act. The federal government is not legally barred from bringing such a lawsuit, but the desire of the federal agencies to increase predictability for business planners has made the HSR process the critical period for federal review. However, the decision of a federal agency not to attack a merger during the HSR waiting period does not preclude a lawsuit by a state government or a private entity. To facilitate analysis by the state attorneys general, the National Association of Attorneys General (NAAG) has issued a Voluntary Pre-Merger Disclosure Compact under which the merging parties can submit copies of their federal HSR filings and the responses to second requests with NAAG for circulation among states that have adopted the compact.

Merger Guidelines In the vast majority of antitrust challenges to mergers and acquisitions, the matters have been resolved by consent order or decree. The Justice Department and the FTC have sought to clarify how they analyze mergers through merger guidelines issued May 5, 1992 (4 Trade Reg. Rep. [CCH] ¶ 13,104). These guidelines are not "law" but enforcement policy statements. Nevertheless, the antitrust enforcement agencies will use them to analyze proposed transactions.

The 1992 merger guidelines state that most horizontal mergers and acquisitions aid competition and are beneficial to consumers. The intent of issuing the guidelines is to "avoid unnecessary interference with the larger universe of mergers that are either competitively beneficial or neutral."

The guidelines prescribe five questions for identifying hazards in proposed horizontal mergers: Does the merger cause a significant increase in concentration and produce a concentrated market? Does the merger appear likely to cause adverse competitive effects? Would entry sufficient to frustrate anticompetitive conduct be timely and likely to occur? Will the merger generate efficiencies that the parties could not reasonably achieve through other means? Is either party likely to fail, and will its assets leave the market if the merger does not occur?

The guidelines essentially ask which products or firms are now available to buyers and where could buyers turn for supplies if relative prices increased by five percent (the measure for assessing a merger-generated price increase). The guidelines redraw market boundaries to cover more products and a greater area, which tends to yield lower concentration increases than Supreme Court merger decisions of the 1960s.

The Future of Mergers and Acquisitions Beginning in 1980, with President RONALD REAGAN's administration, the federal government has adjusted its policies to allow more horizontal mergers and acquisitions. The states have responded by invoking their anti-

trust laws to scrutinize these types of transactions. Nevertheless, mergers and acquisitions have increased throughout the U.S. economy, including the health care industry, electric utilities, TELECOMMUNICATIONS corporations, and national defense contractors.

CROSS-REFERENCES

Antitrust Law; Bonds *Sidebar*: Michael R. Milken: Genius, Villain, or Scapegoat?; Golden Parachute; Junk Bond; Restraint of Trade; Scorched-Earth Plan; Sherman Anti-Trust Act; Unfair Competition.

MERITS ◫ The strict legal rights of the parties to a lawsuit. ◫

The word *merits* refers to the substance of a legal dispute and not the technicalities that can affect a lawsuit. A JUDGMENT on the merits is the final resolution of a particular dispute.

MERIT SYSTEM ◫ System used by federal and state governments for hiring and promoting governmental employees to CIVIL SERVICE positions on the basis of competence. ◫

The merit system uses educational and occupational qualifications, testing, and job performance as criteria for selecting, hiring, and promoting civil servants. It began in the federal government circa 1883. The merit system was established to improve parts of the governmental work force previously staffed by the political patronage or spoils system, which allowed the political party in power the opportunity to reward party regulars with government positions. The merit system has been adopted by state and local governments as well.

MERIT SYSTEMS PROTECTION BOARD The Merit Systems Protection Board (MSPB) ensures that federal civil servants are hired and retained based on merit. In overseeing the personnel practices of the federal government, the board conducts special studies of the merit systems, hears and decides charges of wrongdoing and employment appeals of adverse agency actions, and orders corrective disciplinary actions against an executive agency or employee when appropriate. The board's independent special counsel investigates, among other things, prohibited personnel practices and allegations of activities proscribed by CIVIL SERVICE laws, rules, and regulations and prosecutes officials who violate civil service rules and regulations.

The MSPB is a successor agency to the U.S. Civil Service Commission, established by act of Congress on January 16, 1883. The duties and authority of the board are specified in 5 U.S.C.A. §§ 1201–1206 (1978).

The board has responsibility for hearing and adjudicating appeals by federal employees of adverse personnel actions, such as removals, suspensions, and demotions. It also resolves cases involving reemployment rights, the denial of periodic step increases in pay, actions against administrative law judges, charges of merit system violations, and prohibited personnel practices, including charges in connection with WHISTLE-BLOWING (the reporting of illegal acts). When President BILL CLINTON reauthorized the MSPB and the Office of Special Counsel in 1994, he directed that federal employee whistle-blowers and other victims of prohibited personnel practices receive additional protections. Clinton instructed the agencies to follow appropriate procedures to protect the constitutional rights of such federal employees.

The board has the authority to enforce its decisions and to order corrective and disciplinary actions. An employee or applicant for employment who is involved in an appealable ACTION that also involves an ALLEGATION of DISCRIMINATION may ask the EQUAL EMPLOYMENT OPPORTUNITY COMMISSION to review a board decision. Final decisions and orders of the board are appealable to the U.S. Court of Appeals for the Federal Circuit.

The board reviews regulations issued by the Office of Personnel Management and has the authority to require agencies to cease compliance with any regulation that could constitute a prohibited personnel practice. It also conducts special studies on the civil service and other EXECUTIVE BRANCH merit systems and reports to the president and the Congress on whether the federal workforce is being adequately protected against political abuses and prohibited personnel practices.

The Office of the Special Counsel is responsible for investigating allegations and other information concerning prohibited personnel practices, prohibited political activities by federal and certain state and local employees, arbitrary or capricious withholding of information in violation of the FREEDOM OF INFORMATION ACT (5 U.S.C.A. § 552 et seq.) (1986), prohibited discrimination when found by appropriate authority, and other activities that are prohibited by any civil service law, rule, or regulation. The special counsel initiates disciplinary and corrective actions before the board when warranted.

The special counsel is also responsible for receiving and referring to the appropriate agency information that evidences a violation of any law, rule, or regulation; mismanagement; gross waste of funds; abuse of authority; or substantial and specific danger to public health or safety.

CROSS-REFERENCES

Administrative Agency; Administrative Law and Procedure; Bureaucracy; Merit System.

MESNE 📖 Intermediate; intervening; the middle between two extremes, especially of rank or time. In feudal law, an intermediate lord; a lord who stood between a tenant and the chief lord; a lord who was also a tenant. 📖

See also FEUDALISM.

METES AND BOUNDS 📖 The boundary lines of land, with their terminal points and

Using a precise system of compass directions and distances, a survey team describes the metes and bounds—that is, the boundary lines—of a parcel of land. Such surveys are of great use in the sale and purchase of land, and in settling real property disputes.

JON GOELL/THE PICTURE CUBE

angles. A way of describing land by listing the compass directions and distances of the BOUND-ARIES. It is often used in connection with the Government Survey System. 📖

MEXICO AND THE UNITED STATES

Relations between the United States and Mexico are among the most important and complex that each nation maintains. They are shaped by a mixture of mutual interests, shared problems, and growing interdependence. The United States is particularly concerned with illegal immigration, narcotics trafficking, environmental POLLUTION, and economic stability.

The scope of U.S.-Mexican relations goes far beyond diplomatic and official contacts, entailing extensive commercial, cultural, and educational ties. In 1995 nearly 290 million legal crossings were made from Mexico to the United States. Along the two thousand-mile shared border, state and local governments interact closely. The two countries seek to resolve many issues, ranging from combating narcotics trafficking to improving and protecting the shared environment.

The U.S. government has long recognized that a stable and economically prosperous Mexico is fundamental to U.S. interests. Since 1981 the United States-Mexico Binational Commission, composed of numerous U.S. cabinet members and their Mexican counterparts, has met annually to discuss an array of topics, including trade and investment opportunities, financial cooperation, anti-narcotics cooperation, and migration.

Mexico is a major trading partner with the United States. Mexican exports in 1995 totaled $80 billion, with $67 billion in exports going to the United States. Of Mexico's 1995 imports totaling $72 billion, $54 billion in imports were from the United States. In January 1994 Mexico joined Canada and the United States in the NORTH AMERICAN FREE TRADE AGREEMENT (NAFTA), which will phase out all TARIFFS among the nations over a fifteen-year period. U.S. LABOR UNIONS and some businesses were concerned that the lower tariffs would induce more U.S. companies to relocate factories to Mexico because of its lower labor costs.

The United States played a major role in stabilizing the Mexican economy in 1995. The Mexican government, unable to meet its foreign debt obligations, devalued the peso in December 1994. The resulting financial crisis threatened the stability of other emerging market economies in Latin America. The United States led a group of international lenders that made available to Mexico more than $40 billion in international financial assistance, including

$20 billion from the United States. Although Mexico suffered a severe recession in 1995, the Mexican government's implementation of tough stabilization measures averted an even more serious collapse. The economy began to recover in 1996, and by 1997 Mexico was able to repay the United States the $12.5 billion in loans it actually used.

A major concern of the United States has been illegal immigration from Mexico. The desire of Mexicans to leave their country is fueled by a large population (92 million in 1997) and a shortage of high-paid jobs. The U.S. Border Patrol has grown in response to the large number of Mexicans crossing the border illegally. More than four thousand agents police the border, an increase of 50 percent from 1993, and the number is expected to grow. Parts of the two thousand-mile border have become militarized zones. Steel fences run through deserts and up over hillsides. Border Patrol agents use high-technology surveillance equipment to track the movement of illegal aliens. In some sectors the National Guard and Army personnel assist the Border Patrol.

The Mexican-U.S. border is also the leading entry point into the United States for illegal narcotics. It is estimated that drug traffickers smuggle about $10 billion worth of narcotics into the United States each year, making marijuana, heroin, cocaine, and methamphetamines some of Mexico's most lucrative exports. U.S. and Mexican officials offer differing explanations for the trafficking. U.S. officials blame the alleged corruption of Mexican law enforcement officials for allowing large-scale traffickers to continue their operations. Mexican officials argue that the problem lies on the other side of the border, where the appetite of U.S. drug users drives the trafficking.

The United States has steadily restricted the Mexican drug trade through aggressive patrol of the borders and searches at border checkpoints. Nevertheless, NAFTA has increased legitimate border traffic, overwhelming U.S. customs officers at the checkpoints. It is estimated that officers can only search about seven percent of all vehicles crossing the border.

In response, the U.S. Drug Enforcement Administration has sought to develop closer ties with Mexican drug enforcement officials. Concerns about the corruption of government officials, however, has hurt relations between the countries. Mexico has failed to arrest several drug lords that the United States has long sought and has failed to implement anti-narcotics legislation passed in 1996. In February 1997 the official in charge of Mexico's

A. RAMEY/PHOTOEDIT

While millions of legal border crossings between Mexico and the United States are made every year, more than four thousand U.S. Border Patrol agents police the border, seeking to prevent Mexicans from entering the United States illegally.

antidrug war, General Jesus Gutierrez Rebollo, was arrested for allegedly being on the payroll of the leader of the Juárez, Mexico, drug CAR-TEL. Though the United States stood by the Mexican government, it made clear that Mexico must make progress in arresting major drug lords, extraditing drug criminals to the United States, prosecuting MONEY LAUNDERING, and fighting internal corruption. With some experts claiming that Mexico is responsible for 70 percent of the illegal drugs in the United States, the war against drugs remains a source of friction between the two countries.

The United States and Mexico have sought to resolve common environmental issues, particularly in border areas where rapid population growth, urbanization, and industrialization have caused serious problems. In 1992 the United States and Mexico developed the Integrated Border Environment Plan, under which the two countries have worked to construct wastewater treatment plants, strengthen cooperative planning and enforcement efforts, reduce pollution, develop planning, training, and education, and improve understanding of the border environment.

The second phase of the 1992 border plan, called Border XXI, will promote environmental and sustainable development in the U.S.-Mexican border region through increased public participation and improved coordination among local, state, and federal agencies to maximize cooperative and effective use of limited resources. In addition, the plan will encom-

pass environmental health issues and natural resource protection.

As part of NAFTA's environmental agreement, the United States, Mexico, and Canada have created a North American Commission on Environmental Cooperation. This commission is charged with strengthening environmental laws and addressing common environmental concerns.

In 1993 the United States and Mexico established two institutions to address the environmental infrastructure needs of the border region. The Border Environmental Cooperation Commission (BECC) works with local communities to develop plans for better meeting their need for environmental facilities, including wastewater treatment plants, drinking water systems, and solid waste disposal facilities. In addition, the two countries created the North American Development Bank to obtain private sector capital to finance the construction of border environmental facilities certified by the BECC.

The International Boundary Commission, which was established as a permanent, joint commission by treaty in 1889, is responsible for solving U.S.-Mexican water and boundary problems. These include distribution between the two countries of the waters of the Colorado and Rio Grande Rivers, and joint operation of international dams on the Rio Grande to control floods, conserve water, and generate electricity. Since the early 1980s, the commission has focused on border sanitation problems and has studied groundwater resources along the boundary.

CROSS-REFERENCES

Aliens; Drugs and Narcotics; Environmental Law; Water Rights.

MICHIGAN v. TUCKER

Michigan v. Tucker, 417 U.S. 433, 94 S. Ct. 2357, 41 L. Ed. 2d 182, was a critical 1974 Supreme Court decision that limited the constitutional authority of the *Miranda* rights that the Court had developed in the landmark decision in *Miranda v. Arizona,* 384 U.S. 436, 86 S. Ct. 1602, 16 L. Ed. 2d 694 (1966). In *Michigan v. Tucker,* the Court concluded that the *Miranda* rights were procedural safeguards and not rights protected by the Constitution.

The FIFTH AMENDMENT to the Constitution contains the Self-Incrimination Clause, which guarantees a person the right to refuse to answer questions that might implicate the person in a crime. The Court in *Miranda* announced a set of warnings that law enforcement officers must give a suspect before an interrogation. These well-known warnings direct that a suspect be advised of the right to remain silent, be warned that any statement the suspect makes may be used as EVIDENCE against the person, be told of the right to have a lawyer present during interrogation, and if the suspect cannot afford an attorney, the right to have a lawyer appointed to represent the suspect. The Court believed that this set of warnings would create a uniform policy for all law enforcement officers to follow. The penalty for ignoring the *Miranda* warning was the exclusion at trial of any statements or CONFESSIONS made by the defendant.

In *Michigan v. Tucker,* the Court was confronted with a suspect in a brutal RAPE whose interrogation had occurred prior to the Court's ruling in *Miranda.* Nevertheless, the police officers who interrogated Thomas W. Tucker advised him of his right to remain silent and his right to an attorney. They did not advise him, however, that he had a right to a free lawyer. Tucker waived his rights and proceeded to name a person who he claimed could provide an alibi. That person, however, provided incriminating evidence against Tucker. Tucker objected to the admission of his statements and sought the protection of the *Miranda* rights that the Court had announced after his arrest but prior to his trial. Tucker also asked that the alibi WITNESS not be allowed to testify because Tucker had provided that information during his interrogation.

The trial judge excluded all of Tucker's statements but allowed the alibi witness to testify. A jury convicted Tucker, and his APPEALS were denied by the Michigan courts. He then filed a HABEAS CORPUS action in FEDERAL COURT, alleging that the admission of the alibi witness's TESTIMONY was tainted by the failure of the police to give him his full *Miranda* rights. Both the federal district court and the court of appeals agreed with Tucker, reversing the conviction.

The U.S. Supreme Court disagreed with the lower courts. Justice WILLIAM H. REHNQUIST, writing for the majority, articulated in general terms the difference between a *Miranda* violation and a constitutional violation of a defendant's Fifth Amendment right against SELF-INCRIMINATION. The Court found that there was a difference between incriminating statements that are actually "coerced" or "compelled" and those obtained merely in violation of the *Miranda* warning. The former are violations of the Fifth Amendment, whereas the latter are violations of a set of procedural safeguards. Violations of the procedural safeguards, by themselves, will not result in the suppression of the defendant's statements. In this case Tucker's statements had not been coerced, and therefore the testimony of the alibi witness was permissible.

Rehnquist noted that *Miranda*

> recognized that these procedural safeguards [the warnings] were not themselves rights protected by the Constitution but were instead measures to insure that the right against compulsory self-incrimination was protected. . . . The suggested safeguards were not intended to "create a constitutional straitjacket," but rather to provide practical reinforcement for the right against compulsory self-incrimination.

This meant that the failure of police to provide a complete set of warnings, by itself, would not taint the interrogation and force the suppression of the statements. A court had to then look at the conduct of the police to determine if the suspect had been coerced into making incriminating statements.

In this case Rehnquist found that Tucker's interrogation did not bear "any resemblance to the historical practices at which the right against compulsory self-incrimination was aimed. . . . [H]is statements could hardly be termed involuntary as that term has been defined in the decisions of this Court." Rehnquist emphasized that the Court's determination that the case did not involve compulsion sufficient to breach the right of self-incrimination did not mean that police could disregard the *Miranda* warning. The question was "how sweeping

[were] the judicially imposed consequences of this disregard." Absent evidence that a defendant's statement was coerced, the Court was not willing to exclude evidence because the police failed to follow the procedures set out in *Miranda*.

The distinction in *Tucker* between what Rehnquist called "prophylactic rules" and constitutional rights reappeared in *New York v. Quarles*, 467 U.S. 649, 104 S. Ct. 2626, 81 L. Ed. 2d 550 (1984), and *Oregon v. Elstad*, 470 U.S. 298, 105 S. Ct. 1285, 84 L. Ed. 2d 222 (1985). In *Quarles* the Court recognized a "public safety" exception to the requirement that the *Miranda* warning be given, reasoning that "the need for answers to questions in a situation posing a threat to the public safety outweighs the need for the prophylactic rule protecting the Fifth Amendment's privilege against self-incrimination."

In *Elstad* the Court held that a second confession, immediately preceded by the *Miranda* warning, was ADMISSIBLE, although an earlier statement from the defendant had been obtained in violation of *Miranda*. The Court noted that suppression of a defendant's statements assumes a "constitutional violation" but that unwarned questioning in itself violated only prophylactic standards laid down to safeguard against such a violation. Using *Tucker's* reasoning the Court ruled that a noncoercive *Miranda* violation will not result in the suppression of the "accused's own voluntary testimony." The implication of *Tucker* and the two later decisions is that all types of evidence will not be suppressed because of *Miranda* violations.

CROSS-REFERENCES

Criminal Law; Criminal Procedure; Custodial Interrogation; Due Process of Law; *Miranda v. Arizona*; Right to Counsel.

MIDNIGHT JUDGES

Presidents throughout history have sought to influence law through their judicial appointments. However, the skirmish involving the midnight judges had a much broader significance: it belonged to a fight that had begun shortly after the War of Independence between the leaders of the new nation. The argument pitted the Federalists (led by JOHN ADAMS) against the Republicans (led by THOMAS JEFFERSON) over a fundamental problem: how much power should be given to the federal government and, in particular, the federal JUDICIARY? The answer would influence the course of U.S. law for generations to come.

When Adams lost the 1800 election, the nation was only twenty-four years old. The Constitution, ratified in 1789, was even younger. For more than two decades, the Federalists and the Republicans had argued over their competing visions of strong federal government versus STATES' RIGHTS. The 1800 election crystallized these opposing philosophies. Adams and the Federalists accused the Republicans of intending to plunder property and undermine civilized society. On the other side, Jefferson and the Republicans attacked the Federalists for trying to subvert the guarantees of the BILL OF RIGHTS. The election tipped the balance of power. With the Republicans capturing the White House and Congress, it appeared that Jefferson's party would at last have the upper hand.

But the Federalists intended to preserve their power. Just before time ran out on the Adams administration, they enacted the Judiciary Act of 1801. This sweeping law struck at a key point of contention: the JURISDICTION of the FEDERAL COURTS. The Republicans wanted the federal courts to be constrained, but the new law gave these courts increased jurisdiction over land and BANKRUPTCY cases. The federal courts now had greater authority at the expense of the states. The act added six new federal circuits with sixteen new judges. As a final measure, they also added dozens of new justices of the peace to the District of Columbia. Between December 12 and March 4, President Adams, with the approval of the Senate, busily stacked the courts with his own people. If the Federalists could not control Washington through elected office, they would at least dictate the composition of the judiciary.

The Republicans could not tolerate this bold maneuver. Enraged, Jefferson declared that "the Federalists have retired into the judiciary as a stronghold" where his own party's efforts would be "beaten down and erased." Once in power the Republicans quickly repealed the 1801 act, thus restoring the original jurisdictional authority of the federal courts. But removing the midnight judges presented a difficult constitutional question. The Constitution provided that federal judges were to hold office as long as they demonstrated good behavior—in effect, for life. The Republicans' plan was therefore to abolish the new CIRCUIT COURTS. The Federalists called this an unconstitutional attack on the independence of the judiciary and predicted that the Supreme Court—which was dominated by Federalists—would not allow it. The Republican-controlled Congress stalled a decision on their actions by eliminating the 1802 term of the Court.

The action only delayed an inevitable ruling. Fortunately for the Republicans, Adams had to leave office before he could secure commitments from his appointees, and several declined to serve. Those who accepted did not manage to challenge their removal. But one appointment of a midnight judge had gone largely unnoticed, and it proved to be one of the most important appointments in U.S. history. This was the nomination of JOHN MARSHALL as chief justice of the Supreme Court. Marshall, who was an ardent Federalist, viewed President Jefferson as nothing less than an "absolute terrorist."

In 1803, when the Court reconvened, it ruled on a case that arose from Adams's District of Columbia appointments. Prevented from receiving his commission as a JUSTICE OF THE PEACE, William Marbury asked the Court to order that his commission be honored.

The Court's landmark opinion in *Marbury v. Madison*, 5 U.S. (1 Cranch) 137, 2 L. Ed. 60 (1803), settled the immediate dispute and partially answered the constitutional question at stake. Writing for the unanimous Court, Chief Justice Marshall dismissed Marbury's suit on the grounds that the Supreme Court lacked jurisdiction. Marshall wanted to avoid an impasse between the judiciary and the White House. However, Marshall's opinion also greatly expanded the power of the Court by holding that the judiciary has the power to say what the law is, and, if necessary, to overturn acts of Congress that it finds unconstitutional. The Court did this in *Marbury* for the first time in history, striking down a section of the JUDICIARY ACT OF 1789.

The problem of the midnight judges was settled, but with unexpected results. The judges appointed by Adams could not take office, and in this way the Federalists were thwarted. Yet in an indirect way, they triumphed. Marshall would serve on the Supreme Court for the next thirty-four years and in the process become perhaps the greatest chief justice in history. Moreover, with his opinion in *Marbury v. Madison*, the Court established its power of JUDICIAL REVIEW, a principal goal of the Federalists.

CROSS-REFERENCES

Constitution of the United States; *Marbury v. Madison*; Supreme Court of the United States.

MIGRATORY BIRD TREATY OF 1918

The Migratory Bird Treaty of 1918 between the United States and Great Britain prohibited the killing of many species of birds that traversed certain parts of the United States and Canada. Such species were of great value both

as a source of food and because they destroyed insects injurious to vegetation, but they were in danger of extermination through lack of protection.

The state of Missouri sought to have the treaty declared an unconstitutional interference with the rights that are reserved to the states by the TENTH AMENDMENT to the Constitution. In *Missouri v. Holland*, 252 U.S. 416, 40 S.Ct. 382, 64 L.Ed. 641 (1920), the Supreme Court held that a valid TREATY must prevail over state law, even if a federal statute on the subject would be unconstitutional. Acts of Congress are the supreme law of the land only when made pursuant to the Constitution, and treaties are accorded the same status when made under the authority of the United States.

MILITARY GOVERNMENT

A government that is established during or after MILITARY OCCUPATION by the victorious country in an armed conflict. According to INTERNATIONAL LAW, the territory that has been placed under the authority of a hostile army continues to belong to the state that has been ousted. However, it may be ruled by the occupiers under a special regime.

When a country's army achieves decisive victory over an enemy, the victor may supplement military presence in the enemy territory with some type of government. If the victor is a signatory to certain international agreements, it must follow international RULES OF WAR that outline the rights and responsibilities when governing a territory under belligerent occupation. This military government is not the same as MARTIAL LAW, although the occupiers may impose martial law as part of maintaining order.

The rules of military government are established in various international agreements, pri-

Certain species of birds that traverse the United States and Canada are protected by the Migratory Bird Treaty of 1918. The Supreme Court held that this treaty, and others like it, must prevail over state law, even if a federal statute concerning the same matter would be held unconstitutional.

TIM DAVIS/PHOTO RESEARCHERS

marily the Hague Conference of 1907 and the Geneva Conference of 1949. These documents provide guidelines on such topics as rights and duties of the occupying power, protection of civilians, treatment of prisoners of war, coordination of relief efforts, PROPERTY RIGHTS of the ousted state, and other wartime and postwar concerns. A country that establishes a military government and steps beyond its allotted rights runs the risk of international censure or criticism. Countries sometimes try to deny that they have imposed a military government. For example, in the Persian Gulf War, Iraq claimed that Kuwait is an Iraqi province and therefore not eligible for the protections given by the law of belligerent occupation.

The U.S. Civil War (1861–1865) contributed to the development of rules for military behavior and belligerent occupation. The *Lieber Instructions* is considered a first attempt to codify the laws of WAR as they existed during the Civil War era. Columbia College Professor Francis Lieber prepared this list of laws in 1863 at the request of President ABRAHAM LINCOLN. They led in part to the Brussels Conference of 1887 and the Hague Conferences of 1899 and 1907 on land warfare. The *Lieber Instructions* included sections on military JURISDICTION, protection of persons, and public and private property of the enemy.

The U.S. Civil War pitted the Confederacy—a group of southern states that wanted to secede from the United States—against Union forces, made up of primarily northern and newly formed states. After the victory of Union forces, the U.S. government had to decide how to treat the defeated South. Some vocal members of Congress insisted that because the Confederate states had violated the Constitution by seceding, they had committed "state suicide" and should be treated like conquered provinces.

These politicians finally got their way in 1867, two years after the war ended. State governments were abolished in the rebel states, and the territory was split into five districts, each commanded by a major general of the Union army. Gradually public opinion in the North pushed for home rule for the South, and by 1870 all southern states were restored to the Union. President RUTHERFORD B. HAYES took office in 1877 and removed the army from the last three occupied southern states.

By means of the Hague and Geneva Conferences, and organizations such as the International Committee of the Red Cross, the rules of war have evolved beyond those in the *Lieber Instructions*. When following these general rules, victorious countries continue to have broad discretion in how they govern conquered

zones. The United States has used various approaches to establish postwar governments. For example, after World War II, the United States established very different types of governments to oversee the reconstruction of Germany and Japan, which were defeated by Allied forces.

After Germany surrendered in World War II, the country and its capital were each divided into four zones. Government of the zones was assigned to four different countries: the United States, Great Britain, France, and the Soviet Union. The occupiers differed in their opinions about what type of permanent government should follow military occupation, and the zones occupied by the Soviet Union became communist East Germany. The other zones became democratic West Germany. The two Germanys were reunited in October 1990.

Unlike the military government in Germany, the U.S. occupation of Japan did not involve a large military presence. After Japan surrendered, its existing civilian governing structure was left mostly intact, directed by General Douglas MacArthur and the Supreme Command of the Allied Powers (SCAP). During occupation, Japan—a nation of seventy million people—was supervised by 600,000 troops, whose number was soon reduced to 200,000.

During more than six years of U.S. occupation, the Japanese Diet (legislature) met and passed laws that were subject to veto by SCAP. The Japanese army and navy were abolished, weapons were destroyed, 4,200 Japanese were found guilty of war crimes, Shinto was disestablished as the state religion, and a new constitution—the "MacArthur Constitution"—was adopted. SCAP accomplished land reform, strengthened trade unions, and placed limits on Japan's powerful monopolistic corporations.

After World War II the international community agreed that more safeguards were necessary to protect civilians and their property in occupied territories. As a result the Fourth Geneva Conference was established in 1949 to tackle these issues.

In more recent times, the United States, after invading Grenada and Panama, established a military government in each country during a brief belligerent occupation.

See also MILITARY LAW.

MILITARY LAW ▥ The body of laws, rules, and regulations developed to meet the needs of the military. It encompasses service in the military, the constitutional rights of service members, the military criminal justice system, and the INTERNATIONAL LAW of armed conflict. ▥

Framers of the Constitution vigorously debated the necessity and advisability of a standing army. Federalists like ALEXANDER HAMILTON and JAMES MADISON argued that a standing army was needed for the maintenance of a unified defense. Others, like THOMAS JEFFERSON and GEORGE MASON, were fearful of instituting a military establishment that could be an instrument of governmental abuse. They argued that the Constitution should prohibit or at least limit the size of the armed forces. The opposing sides compromised by approving a standing army but limiting appropriations for its support to two-year terms, thereby imposing a continual check on the military's activities.

The authority of the government to maintain a military and to develop rules and regulations governing it is found in Article I, Section 8, of the Constitution, which grants Congress the power to provide for the common defense and to raise and support armed forces.

The Supreme Court confirmed the legality of the standing army in *Ex parte Milligan*, 71 U.S. 2, 18 L. Ed. 281, 4 Wall. 2 (mem.) (1866). The Court held that the Constitution allows Congress to enact rules and regulations to punish any member of the military when he or she commits a crime, in times of war or peace and in any location. The Court further confirmed the constitutionality of MARTIAL LAW in situations where ordinary law is insufficient to secure public safety and private rights.

Service in the Military Congress's duty to provide for the national defense is carried out through four basic routes into military service: enlistment, activation of reservists, conscription, and appointment as an officer.

Typically military enlistment entails a six-year service obligation, usually divided between active and reserve duty. Enlistees agree to abide by the provisions of the UNIFORM CODE OF MILITARY JUSTICE (UCMJ), obey lawful orders, serve in combat as required, and accept any changes in status or benefits brought about by war or statutory amendments. In return, the military branch agrees to provide the enlistee with compensation and to honor promises concerning assignment, education, compensation, and support of dependents.

Enlistment is open to persons who are at least seventeen years old and who enter into the enlistment agreement voluntarily. Enlistment is not available to declared homosexuals (though the military may not inquire as to sexual orientation) or to unmarried parents of children under eighteen years. Enlistees are required to sign the enlistment agreement and, in most cases, take the oath of allegiance.

Enlistment in the armed forces creates both a contractual obligation and a change in the recruit's legal status. (See *United States v. Grimley*, 137 U.S. 147, 11 S. Ct. 54, 34 L. Ed. 636 [1890].) Although personal service contracts are generally not enforceable, the courts recognize the special legal status of military enlistees and have required those who breach the enlistment contract to remain in the service or serve a prison term. However, after the institution of the all-volunteer military during the 1970s and 1980s, the courts relied more on traditional CONTRACT law when ruling on breach of enlistment suits. (See *Woodrick v. Hungerford*, 800 F.2d 1413 [5th Cir. 1986], *cert. denied*, 481 U.S. 1036, 107 S. Ct. 1972, 95 L. Ed. 2d 812 [1987], and *Cinciarelli v. Carter*, 662 F.2d 73, 213 U.S. App. D.C. 228 [D.C. Cir. 1981], where the courts applied contract law principles and found that the enlistments in question were VOID or VOIDABLE.)

Reservists or NATIONAL GUARD members are civilians who are subject to active service to execute laws, suppress INSURRECTIONS, and repel invasions. Several suits by state governors have challenged congressional power to call up reservists. In *Perpich v. Department of Defense*, 496 U.S. 334, 110 S. Ct. 2418, 110 L. Ed. 2d 312 (1990), a suit by Minnesota's governor challenging Congress's authority to call reservists to active duty, the Supreme Court confirmed that the reserve system, under which members serve in both the state National Guard and the federal National Guard, is a necessary and proper exercise of Congress's power to raise and support armies.

CONSCRIPTION, also known as the draft, is another route by which individuals are inducted into military service. The draft was the primary means of filling the ranks of the military from World War I through World War II, the Korean War, and the VIETNAM WAR. Although many cases challenged the constitutionality of conscription, the Supreme Court has consistently held that Congress's power to conscript Americans for military service is "beyond question." (See *United States v. O'Brien*, 391 U.S. 367, 88 S. Ct. 1673, 20 L. Ed. 2d 672 [1968].) Deferments and exemptions from the draft were granted for certain physical, mental, and religious reasons, or where induction would cause an undue hardship on the draftee or the draftee's family. The draft was abolished in 1972.

The final method of entry into the military is through appointment as an officer. Officer appointments are governed by the Appointments Clause of the Constitution (Art. II, Sec. 2, Cl. 2). Officers are appointed to a rank within a specific branch of the service.

Most military personnel serve their entire tour of duty and are discharged without any complications. An honorable discharge must be

opportunities or accept public office, to alleviate hardship or dependency, to accommodate the demands of pregnancy or parenthood, to address religious concerns or conscientious objections, or to deal with physical and mental conditions that interfere with assignment or performance of duty.

Administrative separation may be initiated when a service member is found to have engaged in homosexual conduct. The National Defense Authorization Act for Fiscal Year 1994, Pub. L. No. 103-160, Nov. 30, 1993, 107 Stat. 1547, states, "The presence in the armed forces of persons who demonstrate a propensity or intent to engage in homosexual acts would create an unacceptable risk to the high standards of morale, good order and discipline, and unit cohesion that are the essence of military capability." The courts have consistently upheld the congressional prerogative to discharge homosexuals from the military.

During the 1980s the military discharged service members for homosexual orientation as well as homosexual conduct. In 1993 President BILL CLINTON attempted to change the military's policy of discharging gays and lesbians because of their sexual orientation. Clinton struck a compromise with those opposed to changing the policy in the National Defense Authorization Act of 1994, which requires separation from service of individuals who voluntarily declare their homosexuality, but bars military personnel from inquiring into a service member's sexual orientation.

Two administrative bodies review military discharges: the Discharge Review Board and the Board for Correction of Military Records. Service members may also seek JUDICIAL REVIEW of a discharge, but the courts generally require exhaustion of administrative remedies before they will accept JURISDICTION over a discharge review. (See *Seepe v. Department of Navy*, 518 F.2d 760 [6th Cir. 1975], and *Woodrick v. Hungerford*, 800 F.2d 1413 [5th Cir. 1986], *cert. denied*, 481 U.S. 1036, 107 S. Ct. 1972, 95 L. Ed. 2d 812 [1987].)

Rights of Service Members In the past some legal analysts contended that those in the military receive a level of constitutional protection that is inferior to that afforded civilians. However, in *United States v. Stuckey*, 10 M.J. 347 (1981), the Court of Military Appeals (now called the U.S. Court of Appeals for the Armed Services) held that "the Bill of Rights applies with full force to men and women in the military service. . . ."

Congress, under its authority to regulate the armed forces, generally determines the due pro-

While some legal analysts contend military personnel receive a level of constitutional protection that is inferior to that granted civilians, military personnel are nevertheless afforded due process of law. These marines are on their way to a court-martial, where they face jail time and a dishonorable discharge if convicted of the charges against them.

issued when a service member's record reflects acceptable military conduct and performance of duty (32 C.F.R. pt. 41, app. A). An honorable discharge cannot be denied without DUE PROCESS OF LAW. (See *United States ex rel. Roberson v. Keating*, 121 F. Supp. 477 [D.C. Ill. 1949].) A general discharge under honorable conditions may be issued when the service member's record does not warrant an honorable discharge because of ineptitude, defective attitude, or apathy (32 C.F.R. pt. 41, app. A).

A discharge under other than honorable conditions may be issued under certain circumstances indicating that a service member's behavior is inconsistent with conduct expected of military personnel (32 C.F.R. pt. 41, app. A, pt. 2). In most cases the service member must be notified and given an opportunity to request review of the discharge by an administrative review board.

Bad-conduct and dishonorable discharges are punitive discharges that may be issued only after a full court-martial. Bad-conduct and dishonorable discharges result in loss of veterans' benefits and, in some cases, loss of CIVIL RIGHTS.

In addition to discharges, separations from military service may be accomplished through administrative proceedings (10 U.S.C.A. § 1169). The Department of Defense outlines the reasons, guidelines, and procedures for administrative separation (32 C.F.R. pt. 41, app. A). Administrative separation may be allowed to permit a service member to pursue educational cess and EQUAL PROTECTION rights of service personnel, and most courts defer to congressional authority in this area. However, the Supreme Court has made it clear that Congress must heed the Constitution when it enacts legislation dealing with the military.

Because both the FIRST AMENDMENT and the authority to regulate the military are found in the Constitution, a balance must be struck between First Amendment freedoms and the needs of the military. For example, article 88 of the UCMJ makes it a crime for a commissioned officer to use contemptuous words against the president, vice president, Congress, and other government officials. Although this would probably be a violation of First Amendment FREEDOM OF SPEECH outside the military context, constitutional challenges to article 88 have consistently failed. In *United States v. Howe*, 37 C.M.R. 555 (A.B.R. 1966), *reconsideration denied*, 37 C.M.R. 429 (C.M.A. 1967), a second lieutenant was convicted of violating article 88 when he participated in an antiwar demonstration in which he carried a sign derogating President LYNDON B. JOHNSON. The court allowed his conviction to stand, even though he was off duty and wearing civilian clothes at the time of the demonstration. Similar limitations on the speech of enlisted personnel have also been upheld.

Military personnel are entitled to certain rights and benefits by virtue of their service. They retain the right to vote and participate in the election of the government. For income and property tax purposes, they retain the domicile in which they reside at the time of enlistment and cannot be taxed by other states where they may be stationed. The Soldiers and Sailors Civil Relief Act Amendments of 1942 (SSCRA) (50 U.S.C.A. app. §§ 514–591) protects military personnel from legal or financial disadvantage that results from their being ordered to active duty. A variety of remedies to alleviate hardship are available under the SSCRA, including stays of civil proceedings; stays of EXECUTION of JUDGMENTS, ATTACHMENTS, or GARNISHMENTS; protection against FORECLOSURES on real or PERSONAL PROPERTY; a cap on interest rates charged on obligations incurred before active duty; and protection against EVICTIONS.

The Uniformed Services Employment and Reemployment Rights Act of 1994 (38 U.S.C.A. § 4301 et seq.) requires employers to rehire former employees who serve in the military for five years or less, with certain exceptions. The act also protects INSURANCE, PENSION, and fringe benefits. Also, the Veterans' Preference Act (1944) (5 U.S.C.A. §§ 2108 and 3309–3320) grants an employment preference to certain veterans and their survivors and enhances their job security.

Veterans also receive education benefits under the Post-Vietnam Era Veterans' Educational Assistance Program (1976) (38 U.S.C.A. ch. 32) and the New GI Bill (1987) (38 U.S.C.A. ch. 30). Education benefits are granted to spouses and dependent children of certain veterans in the Survivors' and Dependents' Educational Assistance Act (38 U.S.C.A. § 3501). Finally, most veterans are eligible for assistance in purchasing a home under a federal lender guarantee program that lowers the MORTGAGE interest rate and down payment a veteran must pay (38 U.S.C.A. § 3710).

Under some circumstances military personnel may seek compensation from the federal government for injury or death that occurs during service under the FEDERAL TORT CLAIMS ACT (28 U.S.C.A. §§ 2675). The most notable exceptions under the act are claims arising out of combat during time of war and claims arising while the service member is in a country outside the United States. In addition, the Military Claims Act (10 U.S.C.A. § 2733) provides an administrative remedy for those who incur damage to or loss of property, personal injury, or death caused by a civilian employee or a member of the armed services. The Military Claims Act addresses injuries not covered by the Federal Tort Claims Act.

Military Criminal Justice System

The military justice system is the primary legal enforcement tool of the armed services. It is similar to but separate from the civilian criminal justice system. The Uniform Code of Military Justice, first enacted in 1950, is the principal body of laws that apply to members of the military. Military tribunals interpret and enforce it.

There are several rationales for a separate military justice system. The system's procedures are efficient and ensure swift and certain decisions and punishments, which are essential to troop discipline. By comparison the civilian criminal justice system can be cumbersome and slow and may yield unanticipated or inconsistent results. Speedy trials and predictable decisions aid the military in its effort to maintain order and uniformity. This in turn contributes to national security. In addition, the court-martial system fulfills the civilian public's expectation of a disciplined and efficient military.

In addition to enhancing discipline, order, uniformity, efficiency, and obedience, the UCMJ addresses certain offenses unique to the military, such as desertion, insubordination, or absence without leave. Finally, the military requires a uniform system that can be administered at the location of the crime to adjudicate offenses committed by service members outside U.S. jurisdiction.

The jurisdiction of the military courts is established when the court is properly convened, the membership of the court satisfies the requirements of the UCMJ, the court has the power to try the accused, and the offense is addressed in the UCMJ. The UCMJ provides that military courts have jurisdiction over all members of the armed services and certain civilians who meet limited, well-defined criteria.

The three tiers of military courts are courts-martial, Courts of Criminal Appeals, and the United States Court of Appeals for the Armed Services.

Courts Martial The three types of courts-martial—summary, general, and special—comprise the trial level of the military justice system. Courts-martial were originally authorized by an AMENDMENT to the ARTICLES OF WAR (Act of March 3, 1863, ch. 75, sec. 30, 12 Stat. 736). The amendment gave courts-martial jurisdiction over military personnel in times of war, insurrection, or rebellion to prosecute such crimes as MURDER, robbery, ARSON, BURGLARY, RAPE, and other common crimes. The UCMJ authorizes military commanders to convene courts-martial on an ad hoc basis to try a single case or several cases of service members suspected of violating the code.

Summary Courts-Martial Summary courts-martial adjudicate minor offenses. Their jurisdiction is limited to enlisted personnel. Summary courts-martial may impose a sentence of confinement for not more than one month, hard labor without confinement for not more than forty-five days, restriction to specified limits for not more than two months, or FORFEITURE of not more than two-thirds of one month's pay (UCMJ art. 20, 10 U.S.C.A. § 820). Although the summary court-martial is intended to dispose of petty criminal cases promptly, it must fully and fairly investigate both sides of the case. Nevertheless, the protections guaranteed in special or general courts-martial are diminished in a summary hearing. Therefore, a summary court-martial may be conducted only with the consent of the accused.

The defendant in a summary court-martial may consult with military counsel before trial but is not entitled to military defense counsel at the hearing. A summary court-martial is presided over by a single commissioned officer who conducts the trial with minimal input from adversarial counsel and acts as judge, fact finder, and counsel. Thus, a summary court-martial is more similar to the inquisitorial courts of the CIVIL-LAW system than the Anglo-American adversarial model. Summary courts-martial are employed less frequently than other types of courts-martial. With increased recognition of the constitutional rights of the accused during the last part of the twentieth century, their use has greatly diminished.

Special Courts-Martial A special court-martial generally consists of a military judge and at least three armed service members. However, under article 16(2) of the UCMJ (10 U.S.C.A. § 816(2)), the members may sit without a judge, or the accused may choose to be tried by a judge alone.

The military judge position was authorized by the Military Justice Act of 1968 (UCMJ art. 26, 10 U.S.C.A. § 826). The military judge's role is similar to that of a civilian trial judge. Military judges do not determine penalties and may only instruct the members of the court, who act as a JURY, as to the kind and degree of punishment the court may legally impose, unless the accused elects to have the judge sit as both judge and jury. This dual role is permissible only in noncapital cases. In any case the judge rules on all legal questions.

The UCMJ requires that service members selected for the special court-martial be the best qualified to serve, as measured by their age, education, training, experience, length of service, and judicial temperament.

Special courts-martial have jurisdiction over most offenses under the UCMJ and may impose a range of sentences, including confinement for no longer than six months, three months of hard labor without confinement, a bad-conduct discharge, forfeiture of pay not to exceed two-thirds monthly pay, withholding of pay for no more than six months, or a reduction in rank (UCMJ art. 19, 10 U.S.C.A. § 819).

General Courts-Martial The general court-martial is the most powerful trial court in the military justice system. A general court-martial is presided over by either a military judge and at least five service members, or a judge alone if the accused so requests and the case involves a noncapital offense (UCMJ art. 16(1), 10 U.S.C.A. § 816(1)). General courts-martial may try all offenses under the UCMJ and may impose any lawful sentence, including the death penalty, dishonorable discharge, total forfeiture of all pay and allowances, and confinement. General courts-martial have jurisdiction over all persons subject to the UCMJ.

A general court-martial may be convened only by a high-ranking official, such as the

president, the secretary of a military branch, a general, or a commander of a large unit or major installation. The commander of a smaller unit may only convene a special court-martial. Trial attorneys appointed to represent the accused in a general court-martial must be certified military lawyers. Verbatim recordings of general courts-martial are required by the Rules for Court-Martial.

The constitutionality of the court-martial system has been upheld in a number of cases under the theory that the military constitutes a separate society that requires its own criminal justice system. The Supreme Court has consistently deferred to the authority of the military, as conferred by Congress, to govern its members. In *Solorio v. United States*, 483 U.S. 435, 107 S. Ct. 2924, 97 L.Ed. 2d 364 (1987), the Court held that "Congress has primary responsibility for the delicate task of balancing the rights of servicemen against the needs of the military. . . . [W]e have adhered to this principle of deference in a variety of contexts where, as here, the constitutional rights of servicemen were implicated."

Courts of Criminal Appeals The intermediate APPELLATE COURTS in the military justice system are the four Courts of Criminal Appeals (CCA), one for each branch of the armed services (Army, Navy, Air Force, Marines). Before 1995 these courts were called the Courts of Military Review (CMR).

The Military Justice Act of 1968 (10 U.S.C.A. § 866) established the CMR to review court-martial convictions. They generally have three-judge panels that review all cases in which the sentence exceeds one year of confinement, involves the dismissal of a commissioned of-

Military personnel facing a general court-martial have a right to counsel, just as any citizen in a civilian court would.

ficer, or involves the punitive discharge of an enlisted person (UCMJ art. 66, 10 U.S.C.A. § 866). Courts of Criminal Appeals may review both findings of fact and findings of law and may reduce the sentence, dismiss the charges, or order a new trial.

Review by the CCA is mandatory and automatic in cases where the sentence is death, dismissal, dishonorable or bad-conduct discharge, or imprisonment for one year or more, and the right to appellate review has not been waived or an APPEAL has not been withdrawn. CCA judges may be commissioned officers or civilians, but all must be members of a bar of a federal court or of a state's highest court. The judges are selected by the judge advocate general of the appropriate service branch. CCA judges do not have tenure or fixed terms. They serve at the pleasure of the judge advocate general. Decisions of the CCA are subject to review by the United States Court of Appeals for the Armed Forces.

U.S. Court of Appeals for the Armed Forces Congress established the U.S. Court of Appeals for the Armed Forces (USCAAF), formerly known as the Court of Military Appeals (CMA), in 1950 (10 U.S.C.A. § 867). It is the highest civilian court responsible for reviewing decisions of military tribunals. It is exclusively an appellate criminal court. The court consists of three civilian judges appointed by the president, with the advice and consent of the Senate, to serve fifteen-year terms.

The USCAAF has jurisdiction over all cases in which the death penalty is imposed, all cases sent by the judge advocate general for review after CCA review, and certain appeals petitioned by the accused that the court agrees to review. The court may only review questions of law. Decisions of the USCAAF may be appealed to the U.S. Supreme Court, which may grant or deny review.

Law of Armed Conflict The international law of armed conflict applies to situations involving an armed, hostile conflict that is not a civil or internal matter.

An armed conflict may begin by declaration of war, by the announcement of one governmental entity that it considers itself at war with another, or through the commission of hostile acts by the military forces of one entity against another. In the past a formal declaration of hostilities was required before a conflict was legally interpreted as a war. Thus, in *Savage v. Sun Life Assurance Co.*, 57 F. Supp. 620 (W.D. La. 1944), the court found that the insured, who died in the Japanese attack on Pearl Harbor during World War II, had not died as a result of war because the United States had not yet formally declared itself at war with Japan. Rather, the court found that the insured's death was accidental and that his beneficiary could collect DOUBLE INDEMNITY under an accidental death policy. In modern times the outbreak of hostilities even without a formal declaration or ultimatum is regarded as war in a legal sense, unless both parties deny the existence of a state of war.

Armed conflict may be terminated by a peace treaty, a cessation of hostilities and establishment of peaceful relations, unconditional surrender, or subjugation.

The United States, as a member of the UNITED NATIONS, is bound by the U.N. Charter, which requires that its members refrain from the threat or use of force in any manner not consistent with U.N. policies. In addition, the United States is a signatory to most major treaties relating to warfare, including the Hague Conference of 1907, the Geneva conferences of 1929 and 1949, and the Genocide Convention of 1948. All of these treaties set forth basic principles that govern the conduct of war: force should be directed only at targets directly related to the enemy's ability to wage war (military necessity); the degree of force used should be directly related to the importance of the target and should be no more than is necessary to achieve the military objective (proportionality); and the force used should cause no unnecessary suffering, destruction of civilian property, loss of civilian life, or loss of natural resources (humanitarian principle). In addition, the Hague Conference provided that captured prisoners cannot be killed, captured towns cannot be pillaged, and the property, rights, and lives of civilians in armed conflict areas must be respected.

In addition to written treaties relating to war, international armed conflict is governed by customary international law, or the COMMON LAW of armed conflict. Under this constantly evolving body of law, certain conduct is proscribed because world opinion forbids it. In *Ex parte Quirin*, 317 U.S. 1, 63 S. Ct. 2, 87 L. Ed. 3 (1942), *order modified by* 63 S. Ct. 22, the Court upheld jurisdiction of a military tribunal over German saboteurs who used civilian disguises, even though no written law or treaty justified their trial. The Court based its decision on the ground that infiltration by disguise violated the customary law of armed conflict. (See also *The Paquete Habana*, 175 U.S. 677, 20 S. Ct. 290, 44 L. Ed. 320 [1900].) The customary law of war is based on the same principles embodied in the Hague Conference and subsequent treaties and reflects international agreement that actions inconsistent with those principles should not go unpunished even in the absence of express prohibitions. Many nations, including the United States, have codified significant portions of the common law of armed conflict. (See U.S. Department of the Army, *The Law of Land Warfare* [Field Manual 27-10, 1956].)

CROSS-REFERENCES

Armed Services; Arms Control and Disarmament; Conscientious Objector; Court-Martial; Gay and Lesbian Rights; Geneva (Red Cross) Conventions, 1949; Genocide; GI Bill; Involuntary Servitude; Just War; Military Government; Military Occupation; Militia; *Milligan, Ex parte*; Nuremberg Trials; Rules of War; Selective Service System; Solomon Amendment; Veterans Affairs Department; War; War Crimes.

MILITARY OCCUPATION Military occupation occurs when a belligerent state invades the territory of another state with the intention of holding the territory at least temporarily. While hostilities continue, the occupying state is prohibited by INTERNATIONAL LAW from annexing the territory or creating another state out of it, but the occupying state may establish some form of military administration over the territory and the population. Under the MARTIAL LAW imposed by this regime, residents are required to obey the occupying authorities and may be punished for not doing so. Civilians may also be compelled to perform a variety of nonmilitary tasks for the occupying authorities, such as the repair of roads and buildings, provided such work does not contribute directly to the enemy war effort.

Although the power of the occupying army is broad, the military authorities are obligated under international law to maintain public order, respect private property, and honor individual liberties. Civilians may not be deported to the occupant's territory to perform forced labor nor impressed into military service on behalf of the occupying army. Although measures may be imposed to protect and maintain the occupying forces, existing laws and administrative rules are not to be changed. Regulations of the Hague Conventions of 1907 and, more importantly, the 1949 Geneva Convention for the Protection of Civilian Persons in Time of War have attempted to codify and expand the protection afforded the local population during periods of military occupation.

See also WAR.

MILITIA ▣ A group of private citizens who train for military duty to be ready to defend their state or country in times of emergency. A militia is distinct from regular military forces, which are units of professional soldiers maintained both in war and peace by the federal government.

In the United States, the NATIONAL GUARD currently serves as the nation's militia. Made up of volunteers, the National Guard acts under the dual authority of both the federal and state governments. According to the Constitution, Congress can call the National Guard into federal service for three purposes: to enforce federal laws, to suppress INSURRECTIONS, and to defend against invasions. State governors can call upon the National Guard for emergencies that are prescribed by state law.

Another type of militia, not recognized by the federal or state governments, is the private militia. Private militias are composed of private citizens who train for armed combat. The formation of private militias became more common in the United States in the early 1990s as some political groups armed themselves to demonstrate their opposition to certain policies and practices of the federal government. One of the most publicized private militia groups was the Montana Freemen, who were involved in a lengthy standoff with agents of the FEDERAL BUREAU OF INVESTIGATION in 1996.

The American militia system has its roots in ancient English tradition, dating back to the Anglo-Saxon militia that existed centuries before the Norman Conquest in 1066. This militia, known as the *fyrd*, consisted of every able-bodied male of military age. It was traditionally used for defense only, and the sovereign could call upon the fyrd to fight if the men would be able to return to their homes by nightfall. Fyrd members were required to supply their own weapons, which they could use only in the service of the king.

After 1066 the victorious Normans retained this militia system, and successive English monarchs continued to rely on citizen soldiers for national defense. During the reign of the Tudors (1485–1603), professional forces began to be used in England, but their main task was to train the local militias, which were much less expensive to use than their professional counterparts. The major element of training was the muster, which was a mandatory gathering of all able-bodied free males, age sixteen to sixty, for the purpose of appraising the participants, their weapons, and their horses. Mustering was an ancient ritual, but during her reign Queen Elizabeth I systematized the practice, requiring musters four times a year and authorizing payment for those attending. Even with this enhanced level of organization, however, musters were as much social occasions as they were military drills. Participants looked forward to

musters as an opportunity to eat and drink heavily before engaging in fights and mock battles.

When the English began to establish colonies in North America in the seventeenth century, the colonial governments continued to require all able-bodied free men to possess arms and to participate in the colonial militias. Each colony formed its own militia unit, appointing officers, providing training, and building its own fortifications. The function of each colonial militia was principally to defend the settlers' homes and villages against Indian raids, and at this they were largely successful.

Colonial militias were much less effective when used for offensive purposes on extended campaigns far from the militiamembers' homes. GEORGE WASHINGTON discovered this when, as a colonel in the Virginia militia, he had great difficulty recruiting enough men to fight the French and Indian War, which lasted from 1754 to 1763. Few men were willing to report for duty. Of those who did, few were well armed, and many quickly deserted the troops and returned home. Some militia officers instituted drafts to recruit more men, but even then, many of the draftees simply paid less-qualified men to report in their places. The British were finally able to win the war when Prime Minister William Pitt made changes in recruiting policies and the military bureaucracy, which made serving in the militia more palatable for the American colonists.

After Great Britain defeated France in the French and Indian War, it was left with a greatly enlarged North American empire to manage and finance. Large numbers of British troops were stationed in America, and the colonists were expected to quarter them and to pay various taxes and fees, including the well-known STAMP TAX, to finance the troops. These additional taxes were one of the principal grievances that motivated the American colonists to prepare for revolution and to form the select militia units that became known as the "Minutemen"; this name reflected the fact that the men were trained to respond instantly when called. The Minutemen first saw action when the Massachusetts unit was called to defend the colonists' military stores at Lexington and Concord on April 19, 1775.

During the Revolutionary War, American military forces were made up of a combination of state militias, specially trained militia units (such as the Minutemen), and the Continental Army, a small professional force created by Congress. The militia was much more effective than it had been during the French and Indian

APWIDE WORLD PHOTOS

The National Guard, a volunteer militia distinct from professional military forces, can be pressed into service by state governors in response to emergencies prescribed by state law. Here Guard members keep watch over a store during a civilian riot.

War because its members were fighting for a cause in which they fervently believed. In addition, the militia system had been reorganized and strengthened: there were more training days, the punishment was more severe for missing musters, and fewer men were exempted from military duty. Even so, militia forces were much less reliable than the professional army, and commanders found it difficult to plan their moves, never knowing exactly how many men would show up and how long they might stay. Ultimately, however, the militias played a critical role in helping the colonists to defeat the British, supplying enough men to keep the Continental Army going and providing, on very short notice, large numbers of armed men for brief periods of emergency service.

When state delegates met in 1787 to create the constitution for the new United States of America, the principal division was between those delegates who favored a strong central government and those who preferred to leave more power to the states. The former wanted a strong standing military, and the latter argued for greater reliance on the state militias. The issue of a standing military was particularly controversial because many Americans were suspicious of the very concept of a standing

army, associating it with the tyranny they had experienced under Great Britain. Nevertheless, because most of the delegates were more concerned about invasion than domestic tyranny, Congress was given the power to create a standing army if it so chose. Advocates of state power did achieve a partial victory, however, in that authority over the state militias was divided between the federal government and the state governments. Congress was given the authority to organize, arm, and discipline the militia, but states were given the power to appoint officers and provide training. Congress, not the president, was given the power to summon state militias into federal service for just three specific tasks: "to execute the laws of the Union, suppress insurrections, and repel invasions" (Art. I, Sec. 8, Cls. 15, 16).

During his first term as president, George Washington worked with Secretary of War Henry Knox to reorganize and strengthen the militia. They sent their plan to Congress, and after heated debate Congress, on May 9, 1792, passed what became known as the Uniform Militia Act (1 Stat. 264). This law, which remained the basic militia law until the twentieth century, stated that all free, able-bodied white men, age eighteen to forty-five, were required to serve in their state militias and that they were obligated to supply themselves with the appropriate firearms and equipment. The law provided certain specifications for how militia units were to be organized, but Congress left many details to the states and declined to include sanctions for states or individuals who failed to comply with the law. As a result, the act had little legal weight and served mostly as a recommendation to the states.

All fifteen states did pass laws in response to the Uniform Militia Act. These laws had some provisions in common, such as the right of the people to keep and bear arms and the exemption of CONSCIENTIOUS OBJECTORS from military duty; the laws varied in other areas, such as in the frequency of training and the methods for selecting officers. In general, the Uniform Militia Act and the laws passed in response to it created many strong and effective state militias; in addition to being an indispensable part of ceremonies and parades, state militia units manned coastal forts, guarded criminals, enforced quarantines, and assisted the police. On the other hand, the many state laws prevented the integration of the various state militias into a reliable force for federal purposes. The federal government often lacked even basic information about the strength and organization of the state militias, making it difficult to make full use of them for military purposes.

Despite the many weaknesses of the militia system, it continued to receive widespread support in the nineteenth century from politicians and the public, who were eager to avoid the expense of a standing army and who viewed the idea of the citizen-soldier as crucial for the maintenance of U.S. freedom and independence. In reality, however, the militia system was often ineffective and unreliable, as during the War of 1812 when militia units were chronically undermanned and poorly prepared. Despite calls for reforms, the militia system declined steadily during the nineteenth century. Less training was required, fewer men attended, and fewer still had firearms, instead showing up for training with cornstalks and broomsticks.

By the 1830s and 1840s, several states had weakened or abolished their systems of compulsory service, relying instead on volunteers. As a result, the militia units became more ceremonial and elitist in nature, as members donned expensive uniforms and equipment to march in parades and other festivals. These volunteer units were useful to state and local authorities because they often assisted the local police in maintaining law and order, which were frequently disrupted by RIOTS and protests, particularly in larger cities.

After the Civil War, in which militia units played a crucial role by supplementing the regular armies of both the Union and the Confederacy, the militia system again went into a decline. A shortage of funds required cutbacks in militia programs, and military service became more unattractive as the rapid growth of industrialism led to frequent labor strikes, which the Army was required to police. According to Russell F. Weigley, a prominent military historian, "The main effect of industrialism seems to have been to reduce inclination and time for amateur soldiering, and thus to weaken the militia institutions inherited from the rural past."

One rejuvenating factor for the militia during this time, however, was the formation of the National Guard Association (NGA) in 1879. This organization was formed to represent the militia's interests before federal and state governments and the public. The name "National Guard," borrowed from the French, was chosen because most states at the time were already using that term to designate their organized volunteer companies. The leaders of the National Guard Association insisted that their units were an integral part of the U.S. military establishment but also maintained the importance of the guard's connection to individual states. In 1887 the NGA achieved its first victory by persuading Congress to raise the federal annual appropriation to arm the guard to $400,000.

At the beginning of the twentieth century, Congress and President WILLIAM MCKINLEY began work to reform the nation's military structure and operations. Secretary of War Elihu Root saw that the United States needed a workable reserve system, rather than the militia, which still operated under the Uniform Militia Act of 1792. Root worked with leaders from the NGA to create a reorganization plan, and the result was the passage in 1903 of the Dick Act (32 Stat. 775), so named for Major General Charles Dick, who had played a large role in creating and supporting the bill. This act formally repealed the Uniform Militia Act of 1792 and extended federal involvement with the National Guard in peacetime. More federal funds were made available to state National Guard units, and in return the state units were required to drill their troops twenty-four times a year, train reservists in summer encampments, and submit to annual inspections by federal officers.

In the years leading up to World War I, professional officers in the regular army and leaders of the National Guard consistently opposed each other on the issue of establishing a national reserve free from all ties to the states. The NGA contended that National Guard units were the proper national reserve, but military professionals argued that national security could not depend on reserves that had two commanders-in-chief and two chains of command—federal and state. In congressional hearings held in 1916, then ex-Secretary of War Root argued against the guard as a reliable reserve: "The idea . . . that forty-eight different governors can be the basis for developing an efficient, mobile national army is quite absurd."

Proponents of a national reserve won the debate, and on June 3, 1916, President WOODROW WILSON signed the National Defense Act (39 Stat. 166), which for the first time created reserve components of the regular services under exclusive federal control. The act also conferred federal status on the National Guard, with the federal government providing more funding and exerting more control over it. National Guard units still reported to the state governors and served on a statewide basis, but guardsmen could now be drafted directly into federal service for the duration of an emergency. Guard members now had to take LOYALTY OATHS to the United States as well as to their home states, and the War Department could cut federal aid to the guard unit of any state that failed to comply with the mandates of the act.

This basic system established in 1916 has continued to be maintained with few changes over the course of the twentieth century. The state National Guard units report to both the state and federal governments, but when they are called into federal service, state governors lose their authority over them. This state and federal authority conflicted several times in the 1950s and 1960s, when guard units from southern states were called into federal service to enforce federal desegregation mandates over the objections of the state governors.

CROSS-REFERENCES

Armed Services; Gun Control; Military Law; Second Amendment; Second Amendment *In Focus:* Private Militias.

BIOGRAPHY

John Stuart Mill

"THE WORTH OF A STATE, IN THE LONG RUN, IS THE WORTH OF THE INDIVIDUALS COMPOSING IT."

MILL 📖 One-tenth of one cent: $0.001. 📖

A mill rate is used by many localities to compute property taxes.

MILL, JOHN STUART John Stuart Mill was the leading English political philosopher of the middle and late nineteenth century. Mill's writings on individual freedom, most notably the essay "On Liberty" (1859), have had a profound influence on U.S. constitutional law. His "libertarian theory" continues to attract those opposed to government interference in the lives of individuals.

Mill was born on May 20, 1806, in London. His father, James Mill, was a leading proponent of UTILITARIANISM, a political theory that claimed that the greatest happiness of the greatest number should be the sole purpose of all public action. James Mill provided his son with an unorthodox but extensive education. John Mill began studying Greek at the age of three, and by the age of seventeen he had completed advanced courses in science, philosophy, psychology, and law.

In 1822 Mill began working as a clerk for his father at India House, the large East Indian trading company. He rose to the position of chief of the examiner's office and stayed with the company until his retirement in 1858.

Mill's real passion, however, was political and social philosophy. In 1826 he had a personal crisis over the tenets of utilitarianism, seeing it as the empty, hedonistic pursuit of pleasure. At the same time, he became acquainted with Harriet Taylor, a gifted thinker who would become Mill's collaborator and later his wife. Largely ignored by historians, Taylor is now credited as a major contributor to Mill's published works.

Mill's essay "On Liberty" remains his major contribution to political thought. He proposed that self-protection is the only reason an individual or the government can interfere with a person's liberty of action. Outside of preventing harm to others, the state has no legitimate reason to compel a person to act in the way the government wishes. This principle has proved complex in application, because it is difficult to determine which aspects of behavior concern only individuals and which concern other members of society.

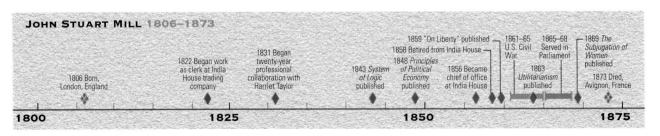

JOHN STUART MILL 1806–1873

1806 Born, London, England

1822 Began work as clerk at India House trading company

1831 Began twenty-year professional collaboration with Harriet Taylor

1843 *System of Logic* published

1848 *Principles of Political Economy* published

1856 Became chief of office at India House

1858 Retired from India House

1859 "On Liberty" published

1861–65 U.S. Civil War

1863 *Utilitarianism* published

1865–68 Served in Parliament

1869 *The Subjugation of Women* published

1873 Died, Avignon, France

1800   1825   1850   1875

In chapter two of "On Liberty," Mill considered the benefits that come from FREEDOM OF SPEECH. He concluded that, except for speech that is immediately physically harmful to others (like the classic example of the false cry of "fire" in a crowded theater, cited by OLIVER WENDELL HOLMES, JR.), no expression of opinion, written or oral, ought to be prohibited. Truth can only emerge from the clash of contrary opinions; therefore robust debate must be permitted. This "adversarial" theory of the necessary nature of the search for truth and this insistence on the free marketplace of ideas have become central elements of U.S. free speech theory.

Mill also applied his principle of liberty to action as well as speech. Mill believed that "experiments of living" maximize the development of human individuality. Restraints on action should be discouraged, even if the actions are inherently harmful to the individuals who engage in them. Mill claimed that society should not be allowed to prohibit FORNICATION, the consumption of ALCOHOL, or even POLYGAMY.

Critics have charged that Mill's liberalism condones an atomistic, fragmented society in which individuals may feel that their lives have no purpose because they do not believe that they are a meaningful part of the community. Other critics have found the same sort of hollowness that Mill ascribed to utilitarianism.

Mill's other works include *System of Logic* (1843), *Principles of Political Economy* (1848), *The Subjection of Women* (1869), and his *Autobiography* (1873).

Mill served in Parliament from 1865 to 1868. He was considered a radical because he supported the public ownership of natural resources, compulsory education, BIRTH CONTROL, and equality for women. His advocacy of women's suffrage in the Reform Bill of 1867 led to the creation of the suffrage movement.

Mill died on May 8, 1873, in Avignon, France.

See also BENTHAM, JEREMY; LIBERTARIANISM.

MILLER, LOREN Loren Miller was a municipal court judge and housing discrimination specialist whose involvement in the early stages of

"THE NEGRO HAS BEEN THE WARD OF THE SUPREME COURT OF THE UNITED STATES FOR MORE THAN A HUNDRED YEARS."

BIOGRAPHY

the CIVIL RIGHTS MOVEMENT earned him a reputation as a tenacious fighter for equal housing opportunities for minorities.

Miller was born January 20, 1903, in Pender, Nebraska, the son of a post–Civil War migrant from the South. His family moved to Kansas when he was a boy, and he graduated from high school in Highland, Kansas. Later, he attended the University of Kansas; Howard University; and Washburn University, in Topeka, Kansas, where he earned his bachelor of laws degree in 1928. He was admitted to the Kansas bar the same year, and practiced law there for one year before moving to California to pursue his first interest, journalism. He worked for the *California News*, a Los Angeles newspaper, from 1929 to 1933.

Miller returned to the field of law when he married and was admitted to the California bar in 1933. By the 1940s, he was raising his voice in protest over policies and practices that discriminated against African Americans. In the wake of World War II, many blacks had left their rural and southern homes to seek economic opportunity in California, only to face discrimination and bias, particularly in housing. By 1947, Miller had represented more than one hundred plaintiffs seeking to invalidate housing covenants that prevented blacks from purchasing or renting housing in certain areas. As a board member of the AMERICAN CIVIL LIBERTIES UNION (ACLU), he became a well-known spokesman for the rights of minorities to enjoy equal access to housing and education. He was openly critical of the Federal Housing Authority (FHA), declaring that FHA policies fostered a Jim Crow policy that kept blacks confined to "tight ghettos" and provoked racial tension. Commenting on the effect of racially restrictive covenants, he noted that contrary to the claims of those who supported the covenants, residential segregation did not preserve public peace and general welfare but rather resulted in "nothing but bitterness and strife."

In 1954 Miller's love of journalism prompted his return to the newspaper business. He became the owner and publisher of the *California*

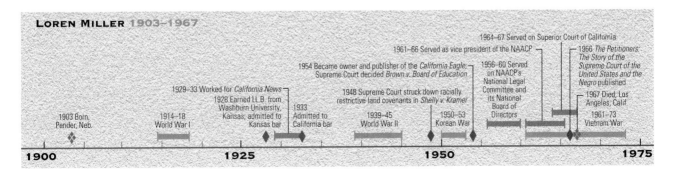

LOREN MILLER 1903–1967

1964–67 Served on Superior Court of California

1961–66 Served as vice president of the NAACP

1954 Became owner and publisher of the *California Eagle*; Supreme Court decided *Brown v. Board of Education*

1956–60 Served on NAACP's National Legal Committee and its National Board of Directors

1966 *The Petitioners: The Story of the Supreme Court of the United States and the Negro* published

1929–33 Worked for *California News*

1928 Earned LL.B. from Washburn University, Kansas; admitted to Kansas bar

1933 Admitted to California bar

1948 Supreme Court struck down racially restrictive land covenants in *Shelly v. Kramer*

1967 Died, Los Angeles, Calif.

1903 Born, Pender, Neb.

1914–18 World War I

1939–45 World War II

1950–53 Korean War

1961–73 Vietnam War

1900   1925   1950   1975

Eagle, a weekly newspaper with wide circulation in the African American community. He also contributed numerous articles to such journals as the *Crisis,* the *Nation,* and *Law in Transition.* Later, Miller was named cochair of the West Coast legal committee of the NATIONAL ASSOCIATION FOR THE ADVANCEMENT OF COLORED PEOPLE (NAACP). In that capacity, he became the first U.S. lawyer to win an unqualified verdict outlawing residential restrictive covenants in REAL ESTATE sales that involved FHA or Veterans Administration (VA) financing. Perhaps the most celebrated case Miller was involved in was *Shelley v. Kraemer,* 334 U.S. 1, 68 S. Ct. 836, 92 L. Ed. 1161 (1948), in which the U.S. Supreme Court declared that racial covenants on property cannot be enforced by the courts.

Miller was one of the first to recognize that bias in housing would be an explosive social issue in the United States. The greatest tension, he predicted, would exist where an all-white area adjoined an all-black area, because "there white Americans stand eternal guard to keep their Negro fellow Americans out." He denounced as "money lenders" and "hucksters of prejudice" the owners of slum properties where many members of minorities are forced to live under substandard conditions because of the "artificial housing shortages . . . in the Negro community."

In 1964, Governor Edmund G. Brown of California appointed Miller to the Superior Court of California, where he served until his death. He was vice president of the NAACP (1961–66); a member of the NAACP's National Legal Committee and of its National Board of Directors (1956–60); a member of the national committee of the ACLU; and vice president of the National Bar Association, an organization of African American attorneys. Miller was also a member of the California Advisory Commission on Civil Rights, vice president of the National Committee against Discrimination in Housing, and a member of the NAACP Legal Defense and Educational Fund.

In 1966, Miller wrote *The Petitioners: The Story of the Supreme Court of the United States*

Samuel Freeman Miller

PHOTOGRAPHER: HARDY STUDIOS. COLLECTION OF THE SUPREME COURT OF THE UNITED STATES

"IT DOES NOT . . . FOLLOW, THAT WHEN A WORD WAS USED IN A STATUTE . . . SEVENTY YEARS SINCE, THAT IT MUST BE HELD TO INCLUDE EVERYTHING TO WHICH THE SAME WORD IS APPLIED AT THE PRESENT DAY."

and the Negro, a book that recounts the vital role of the U.S. Supreme Court in shaping the lives of African Americans in the U.S. He and his wife, Juanita Ellsworth Miller, had two sons, Loren, Jr., and Edward. Miller died in Los Angeles on July 14, 1967.

MILLER, SAMUEL FREEMAN Samuel Freeman Miller served as an associate justice of the U.S. Supreme Court from 1862 to 1890. During his long tenure on the Court, Miller played a major role in restricting the reach of the FOURTEENTH AMENDMENT into areas of the law reserved to the states. He is most famous for writing the majority opinion in the *Slaughterhouse Cases,* 83 U.S. (16 Wall.) 36, 21 L. Ed. 394 (1873).

Miller was born on April 5, 1816, in Richmond, Kentucky, and grew up on a farm. He attended Transylvania University, where he earned a medical degree in 1838. Miller practiced medicine for ten years, and during this time he taught himself the law. In 1847 he was admitted to the Kentucky bar, and soon after he abandoned his medical practice for a law practice in Knox County, Kentucky.

He became more interested in politics after he became an attorney. A member of the Whig party, Miller was opposed to SLAVERY, which caused him difficulty in Kentucky as pro-slavery sentiment began to rise. In 1850 he moved to Iowa, which was more tolerant of his antislavery views. He established a law practice in Keokuk, Iowa, and became a prominent member of the Republican party and a supporter of ABRAHAM LINCOLN's presidential campaign in 1860.

Lincoln appointed Miller to the Supreme Court in 1862, during the most difficult period for the Union in the Civil War. Miller voted to sustain Lincoln's suspension of HABEAS CORPUS and to try civilians by military COURTS-MARTIAL. Following the war Miller voted to uphold the constitutionality of LOYALTY OATHS required of former Confederates who wished to hold public office.

Miller is best known for his majority opinion in the *Slaughterhouse Cases* in 1873. At issue was the scope of the authority in the Fourteenth Amendment, which had been passed in 1868 to

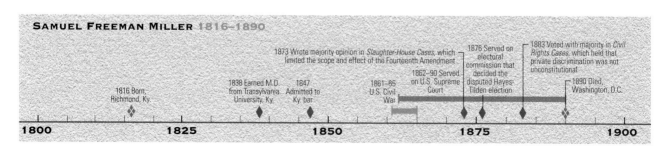

SAMUEL FREEMAN MILLER 1816–1890

1816 Born, Richmond, Ky.

1838 Earned M.D. from Transylvania University, Ky.

1847 Admitted to Ky. bar

1861–65 U.S. Civil War

1862–90 Served on U.S. Supreme Court

1873 Wrote majority opinion in *Slaughter-House Cases,* which limited the scope and effect of the Fourteenth Amendment

1876 Served on electoral commission that decided the disputed Hayes-Tilden election

1883 Voted with majority in *Civil Rights Cases,* which held that private discrimination was not unconstitutional

1890 Died, Washington, D.C.

1800   1825   1850   1875   1900

guarantee that states could not restrict the constitutional rights of citizens and businesses. The case involved a Louisiana state law that allowed one meat company the exclusive right to slaughter livestock in New Orleans. Other packing companies were required to pay a fee for using the slaughterhouses. These companies filed suit, claiming that the law violated the Privileges and Immunities Clause of the Fourteenth Amendment, which stated that "no state shall make or enforce any law which shall abridge the privileges or immunities of citizens of the United States."

Miller upheld the Louisiana monopoly law, ruling that the Privileges and Immunities Clause had limited effect because it only reached PRIVILEGES AND IMMUNITIES guaranteed by U.S. citizenship, not state citizenship. The law in question dealt with state rights; therefore the Fourteenth Amendment had no effect. In Miller's view the Fourteenth Amendment was designed to grant former slaves legal equality, not to grant expanded rights to the general population. In addition, Miller was concerned that a broad interpretation of the Fourteenth Amendment would give too much power to the federal government and distort the concept of FEDERALISM, which grants the states a large measure of power and autonomy.

Having set the standard for interpreting the Fourteenth Amendment, Miller and most members of the Court followed it during the 1870s and 1880s. Miller and the Court struck down state-sponsored racial discrimination under the amendment but refused to invoke it against private discrimination, most notably in the *Civil Rights Cases*, 109 U.S. 3, 3 S. Ct. 18, 27 L. Ed. 835 (1883). In these cases the Court held that federal laws that banned private discrimination in public transportation and public accommodation were unconstitutional because the Fourteenth Amendment only reaches state-enacted discrimination.

In a nonjudicial role, Miller served on the electoral commission that counted the electoral votes in the deadlocked and disputed presidential election of 1876 between RUTHERFORD B. HAYES and SAMUEL J. TILDEN. In the 1880s some

Republican leaders promoted Miller as a presidential candidate, but nothing came of it.

Miller died on December 13, 1890, in Washington, D.C.

CROSS-REFERENCES
Civil Rights Cases; *Slaughter-House* Cases; States' Rights.

MILLER, WILLIAM HENRY HARRISON
William Henry Harrison Miller served as U.S. attorney general from 1889 to 1893, in the administration of President BENJAMIN HARRISON. Miller, Harrison's law partner and political adviser, was recognized for his incorruptibility.

Miller was born on September 6, 1840, in Augusta, New York. His connection with Benjamin Harrison appeared preordained, because Miller was named after the ninth president, WILLIAM HENRY HARRISON, the grandfather of Benjamin. Miller attended country schools and Whitestown Seminary before enrolling at Hamilton College, from which he graduated in 1861.

He studied law in the office of future U.S. Supreme Court Chief Justice MORRISON R. WAITE and was admitted to the Indiana bar in 1865. He started a law practice in Peru, Indiana, and also held the office of county school examiner. In 1866 he moved his law practice to Fort Wayne, Indiana. He remained there until 1874, when he moved to Indianapolis and became the law partner of General Benjamin Harrison.

Harrison had achieved fame as a Civil War commander. For his heroism in leading the Seventieth Indiana Regiment, President ABRAHAM LINCOLN promoted him to brigadier general. Upon his return to Indianapolis, Harrison began to build a political career. Miller entered Harrison's law firm and the political arena. He soon became a trusted adviser to Harrison, who ran unsuccessfully for the Indiana governorship in 1876. Harrison later served in the U.S. Senate from 1881 to 1887, and in 1888 he was the Republican nominee for president. It was during the 1888 campaign that Miller served as a confidential adviser to Harrison, who defeated President GROVER CLEVELAND.

Harrison, who had promised the country a

BIOGRAPHY

William Henry Harrison Miller

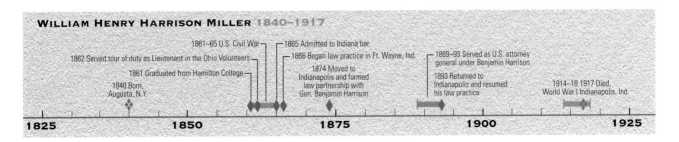

WILLIAM HENRY HARRISON MILLER 1840–1917

1862 Served tour of duty as Lieutenant in the Ohio Volunteers
1861 Graduated from Hamilton College
1840 Born, Augusta, N.Y.
1861–65 U.S. Civil War
1865 Admitted to Indiana bar
1866 Began law practice in Ft. Wayne, Ind.
1874 Moved to Indianapolis and formed law partnership with Gen. Benjamin Harrison
1889–93 Served as U.S. attorney general under Benjamin Harrison
1893 Returned to Indianapolis and resumed his law practice
1914–18 World War I
1917 Died, Indianapolis, Ind.

1825   1850   1875   1900   1925

Legal Deal, appointed six lawyers and two businessmen to his cabinet. Miller was named attorney general, a position he held for the four years of the Harrison administration. In 1890 Congress passed the SHERMAN ANTI-TRUST ACT (15 U.S.C.A. § 1 et seq.), which outlawed trusts and monopolies that restrained trade. Miller did not make any effort, however, to use the new legislation.

The Harrison administration was untouched by scandal, but an economic depression in the West severely hurt the Republican party. Democrat Grover Cleveland defeated Harrison in the 1892 election. Miller returned to Indianapolis in March 1893 and resumed his law practice.

He died on May 25, 1917, in Indianapolis.

MILLETT, KATHERINE MURRAY

Katherine Murray Millett is a writer and sculptor who is best known for her groundbreaking work of feminist literary criticism, *Sexual Politics* (1969). Though she abandoned criticism after this book, turning to works of fiction and autobiography, *Sexual Politics* became a starting point for scholars working in FEMINIST JURISPRUDENCE.

Millett was born on September 14, 1934, in St. Paul. She was educated at the University of Minnesota, Oxford University, and Columbia University. As a graduate student and part-time instructor in English at Columbia during the 1960s, she became active in the CIVIL RIGHTS MOVEMENT. Soon Millett focused her attention on sexual discrimination against women. Her dissertation shifted from traditional literary criticism to an analysis of the sexual subordination of women in the works of novelists D. H. Lawrence, Henry Miller, and Norman Mailer. She was granted her Ph.D. degree in 1970, on the heels of the publication of *Sexual Politics*, a revised version of her dissertation.

The book became a national best-seller overnight, attracting both strong support and vitriolic opposition. Millett argued that in the twentieth century, social and technological change had helped women in the United States to begin redefining gender roles. In the face of

change, the male-dominated society had sought to preserve a patriarchal social structure and the patriarchal family through an ideology of sexual domination and violence. This ideology was most fully expressed in novels written by men and acclaimed by male intellectuals and critics.

Millett charged D. H. Lawrence with glorifying masculinity, Henry Miller with exalting the sexual degradation of women, and Norman Mailer with promoting a cult of virility. These writers served as a mirror on U.S. culture and helped explain why women have been sexually subordinated. Sexual subordination, in Millett's view, is tied to the economic and political subordination of women.

Sexual Politics was published before the field of feminist jurisprudence had been started. Millett's analysis of sexual subordination in literature inspired feminist legal scholars to examine U.S. law for patriarchal influences. In their attacks on PORNOGRAPHY, law professor CATHARINE A. MACKINNON and writer ANDREA DWORKIN derived many of their ideas from Millett's work.

After writing *Sexual Politics* Millett wrote *Flying*, an autobiography (1974), and a novel, *Sita* (1976). Her personal life has been marked by periods of mental illness and institutionalization. She wrote about this part of her life in *The Loony Bin Trip* (1990). She published *The Politics of Cruelty* in 1994, which explored the use of torture in the modern world, and another memoir, *A.D.*, in 1995.

See also SEX DISCRIMINATION; WOMEN'S RIGHTS.

MILLIGAN, EX PARTE

An 1866 Supreme Court decision, *Milligan ex parte*, 71 U.S. (4 Wall.) 2, 18 L.Ed. 281, recognized that a civilian and citizen of a state that is not invaded by hostile forces during wartime is not subject to the JURISDICTION of a COURT-MARTIAL.

In 1864, Lambdin P. Milligan, a civilian, was arrested in Indiana for CONSPIRACY, INSURRECTION, and other crimes arising from his alleged involvement in organizing a secret military unit in the state to assist the Confederacy. His arrest and detention were made pursuant to the orders of General Alvin P. Hovey, commander of the

BIOGRAPHY

THE IMAGE WORKS

Katherine Murray Millett

"IT IS INTERESTING THAT MANY WOMEN DO NOT RECOGNIZE THEMSELVES AS DISCRIMINATED AGAINST; NO BETTER PROOF COULD BE FOUND OF THE TOTALITY OF THEIR CONDITIONING."

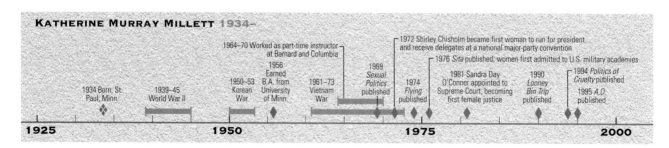

KATHERINE MURRAY MILLETT 1934–

1934 Born, St. Paul, Minn.

1939–45 World War II

1950–53 Korean War

1956 Earned B.A. from University of Minn.

1961–73 Vietnam War

1964–70 Worked as part-time instructor at Barnard and Columbia

1969 *Sexual Politics* published

1972 Shirley Chisholm became first woman to run for president and receive delegates at a national major-party convention

1974 *Flying* published

1976 *Sita* published; women first admitted to U.S. military academies

1981 Sandra Day O'Connor appointed to Supreme Court, becoming first female justice

1990 *Looney Bin Trip* published

1994 *Politics of Cruelty* published

1995 *A.D.* published

1925   1950   1975   2000

military district of Indiana. He was brought to trial before a military commission in Indianapolis, convicted, and sentenced to death. Milligan applied for a writ of HABEAS CORPUS to the Supreme Court, challenging the jurisdiction of the military commission to try and sentence him.

The Court acknowledged that Article III, Section 2, Clause 3 of the Constitution—which provides "that the trial of all crimes, except in cases of impeachment, shall be by jury"—and other constitutional provisions safeguarded this right. It recognized, however, that in times of WAR, various civil liberties and the right to challenge illegal detention by a writ of habeas corpus may be suspended. MARTIAL LAW might be imposed, however, only where an actual invasion of enemy forces effectively stopped the operation of the civil government.

The military argued that the designation of Indiana as a military district with a commander because of the constant threat of invasion by Confederate troops justified the imposition of martial law. The military commission, therefore, had lawful jurisdiction under the "laws and usages of war." The Court rejected this argument. The state of Indiana had not opposed federal authority, its civil and criminal courts continued to operate during the war, and Milligan was a civilian who was not connected to the military. Although civil liberties and habeas corpus could be suspended in wartime, to permit the military commission to determine the fate of Milligan, a civilian, in a state which was loyal to the Union, and where there was only a mere threat of invasion and the courts were open, would usurp the powers of the courts in violation of the Constitution. The Court decided that the military commission had no jurisdiction over Milligan and therefore ordered Milligan's release.

MINE AND MINERAL LAW 📖 The law governing the ownership, sale, and operation of mines, quarries, and wells, and the rights to natural resources found in the earth. 📖

The extraction of natural resources from the earth is governed by specific laws dealing with mines and minerals. Federal and state governments have mine and mineral laws to protect the health and safety of miners, encourage the efficient use of natural resources, protect the environment, and raise tax revenues.

A mine is an excavation in the soil and subsoil from which ores, coal, or other mineral substances are removed. A mineral is valuable, inert matter created by forces of nature and found either on or in the earth. A MINERAL RIGHT is the possessory interest in minerals in the ground. The owner of the mineral rights has the right to enter the land and occupy it for the purpose of removing the minerals. It is possible for someone to own the mineral rights and mine the minerals without owning the land itself.

The federal government has played a large role in the exploitation of mineral resources by granting mineral rights, called patents, to persons and companies that wish to mine on land owned by the federal government. The Mining Act of 1872 has remained unchanged since its enactment during the presidential administration of ULYSSES S. GRANT. The law tried to help small prospectors by making land more affordable. It set the price of mineral rights to federal property at between $2.50 and $5.00 an acre and gave prospectors the right to mine without paying royalties. A royalty is the payment by the LESSOR to the owner of the property of a percentage of the value of the minerals that are mined.

The Mining Act of 1872 has drawn increased criticism since the 1980s because of the small amount of money companies pay to obtain mineral rights valued at millions and even billions of dollars and because the companies do not have to pay a royalty to the federal government. Most of the federal land is located in the West. Western legislators have been unwilling to amend the law, out of fear that changes would reduce employment and depress the mining industry. Attempts to amend the act to raise the price of mineral rights and to impose a royalty have met fierce resistance by western lawmakers and the mining industry, which is dominated by companies located outside the United States.

Mining operations are considered one of the main sources of environmental POLLUTION. Under the Mining Act of 1872, mining companies are not required to clean up mining sites that are on federal property. The ENVIRONMENTAL PROTECTION AGENCY estimates that cleaning up fifty-five of the United States' most dangerous mines will cost taxpayers $32 billion. On lands that are not owned by the federal government, state and federal environmental regulations require mining companies to clean up and restore their mining sites.

Mining is a dangerous occupation. Since the late 1960s, state and federal legislation has set numerous operating standards regarding dust and gas concentrations in the mines, as well as general rules regarding roof support. These provisions attempt to prevent explosions, mine collapses, and the breathing of tainted air. The Federal Mine Safety and Health Act of 1977 (30 U.S.C.A. § 801) is a comprehensive safety and health act that applies to all metal and nonmetal mines, including coal mines.

CROSS-REFERENCES

Environmental Law; Land-Use Control *In Focus:* The West Wrestles with D.C.; Law of the Sea; Miner's Codes; Solid Wastes, Hazardous Substances, and Toxic Pollutants.

MINERAL RIGHT An interest in minerals in land, with or without ownership of the surface of the land. A right to take minerals or a right to receive a ROYALTY.

Mineral right is a term encompassing all the ways a person can have a possessory interest in minerals in the ground. It includes the right to enter the land and occupy it in order to remove the minerals. Mineral rights can be retained when land is sold or conveyed, thus making it possible for someone to own the right to mine the minerals without owning the land. A right of entry onto the land can be held by the grantor who retains the mineral rights, or other arrangements can be made to gain access to the minerals. Mineral rights can be leased or sold. A landowner who leases mineral rights often receives a royalty, or a percentage of the value of the minerals which are mined by the lease-holder.

See also MINE AND MINERAL LAW.

MINER'S CODES During the era of Western settlement in the middle of the nineteenth century, various forms of primitive legal practices were instituted to bring order to the frontier; many formal legal codes evolved from these early precepts, including the Miner's Codes.

Originally the codes were various traditional laws that were respected throughout mining camps in the West. The codes were recorded, and their purpose was to establish guidelines for filing and determining claims and arbitrating disagreements among miners. The miner's "courts" rendered decisions in disputes, and the tenets of the codes guaranteed their enforcement.

The Gregory Diggings Code of Colorado was the best example of a functioning system based on the laws of the Miner's Code. The Gregory Code successfully produced a harmonious political and judicial system that was imitated by other mining towns. Between 1861 and 1862, the legislature of the Colorado territory formally adopted the canons of the Gregory Code.

See also MINE AND MINERAL LAW.

MINIMUM CONTACTS See PERSONAL JURISDICTION.

MINIMUM WAGE The minimum hourly rate of compensation for labor, as established by federal statute and required of employers engaged in businesses that affect interstate commerce. Most states also have similar statutes governing minimum wages.

Along with a requirement for overtime pay and restrictions on child labor, the minimum wage law is one of the most significant, substantive obligations created more than fifty years ago by the FAIR LABOR STANDARDS ACT of 1938 (FLSA) (29 U.S.C.A. § 201 et seq.). The FLSA culminated a long struggle for state and federal protective legislation for workers that began in the nineteenth century.

The original campaign for minimum wage legislation in the United States began at the state level and resulted from growing public concern about the prevalence of sweatshops—workhouses where recent immigrants, women, and young children were paid substandard wages. Proponents of minimum wage legislation appealed to society's sense of obligation to act through its elected officials to ensure an adequate standard of living for all working citizens.

In 1912 Massachusetts, an industrial state, was the first state to enact minimum wage legislation. The momentum continued, and by 1920 thirteen states and Puerto Rico and the District of Columbia had enacted minimum wage programs. The Great Depression moved even more states to enact protective minimum wage legislation, and by 1938 twenty-five states

Seemingly primitive forms of legal practice can be surprisingly effective in the absence of strict legislation and governance. Such was the case with the Miner's Codes, generally respected laws of tradition that governed mining camps in the American West. Often these guidelines evolved into formally adopted legislation.

THE GRANGER COLLECTION, NEW YORK

had some form of minimum wage law. In creating minimum wage legislation, the states generally used three minimum wage models. The Massachusetts model established a wage commission that recommended voluntary minimum wage rates based on what commission members determined was the best combination of a "living wage" for employees and the "financial condition" of the employer's business. The next model established a similar wage commission but disregarded the financial conditions of the employer, made the minimum wage compulsory, and established sanctions for noncompliance. The third law, the Utah model, established a flat rate of minimum compensation for all covered workers.

Despite the success of state legislatures in creating minimum wage laws, state supreme courts and, ultimately, the U.S. Supreme Court rejected as unconstitutional any legislation that interfered with an employer's freedom to contract with employees over wages.

Under the leadership of President FRANKLIN D. ROOSEVELT, Congress passed the NATIONAL INDUSTRIAL RECOVERY ACT of 1933 (NIRA) (June 16, 1933, ch. 90, 48 Stat. 195). NIRA granted the president authority to establish minimum wage and maximum hour standards for all private industry workers; its legal basis was the federal government's power to regulate interstate commerce. The Supreme Court, however, rejected the NIRA's legal basis as unconstitutional in *ALA Schechter Poultry v. United States*, 295 U.S. 495, 55 S. Ct. 837, 79 L. Ed. 1570 (1935). In fact, from 1923 in *Adkins v. Children's Hospital*, 261 U.S. 525, 43 S. Ct. 394, 67 L. Ed. 785, to 1937 in *Morehead v. New York ex rel. Tipaldo*, 298 U.S. 587, 56 S. Ct. 918, 80 L. Ed. 1347, the Supreme Court consistently ruled against the constitutionality of all minimum wage legislation.

In his second administration, President Roosevelt worked with members of Congress to create a modified version of the labor provisions of the NIRA, and in 1937 the FLSA was introduced. Although national business lobbies and agricultural interests vigorously opposed the proposed legislation and even organized labor did not support it, Congress passed the FLSA, and it was signed into law on June 25, 1938. Referring to the FLSA the night before signing the bill into law, President Roosevelt declared, "Except perhaps for the Social Security Act, it is the most far-reaching, the most far-sighted program for the benefit of workers ever adopted." In a landmark decision in 1941 (*United States v. Darby*, 312 U.S. 100, 61 S. Ct.

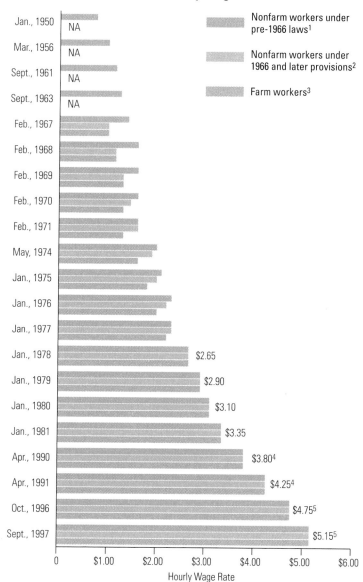

Effective Federal Minimum Hourly Wage Rates, 1950 to 1997

Legend:
- Nonfarm workers under pre-1966 laws[1]
- Nonfarm workers under 1966 and later provisions[2]
- Farm workers[3]

Date	Value
Jan., 1950	NA
Mar., 1956	NA
Sept., 1961	NA
Sept., 1963	NA
Feb., 1967	
Feb., 1968	
Feb., 1969	
Feb., 1970	
Feb., 1971	
May, 1974	
Jan., 1975	
Jan., 1976	
Jan., 1977	
Jan., 1978	$2.65
Jan., 1979	$2.90
Jan., 1980	$3.10
Jan., 1981	$3.35
Apr., 1990	$3.80[4]
Apr., 1991	$4.25[4]
Oct., 1996	$4.75[5]
Sept., 1997	$5.15[5]

Hourly Wage Rate (0 – $6.00)

[1] Applies to workers covered prior to 1961 Amendments and, after Sept. 1965, to workers covered by 1961 Amendments.
[2] Applies to workers newly covered by Amendments of 1966, 1974, 1977, and Title IX of Education Amendments of 1972.
[3] Included in coverage as of 1966, 1974, and 1978 Amendments.
[4] Training wage for workers 16–19 in first six months of first job: Apr. 1, 1990, $3.35; Apr. 1, 1991, $3.62. The training wage expired Mar. 31, 1993.
[5] A sub-minimum training wage of $4.25 was established for employees under age 20 during the first 90 consecutive calendar days of employment. The minimum wage for workers receiving gratuities remained $2.13 per hour.

Source: Bureau of Labor Statistics.

451, 85 L. Ed. 609), the Supreme Court found the FLSA constitutional:

> [I]t is no longer open to question that the fixing of a minimum wage is within the legislative power and the bare fact of its exercise is not a denial of due process under the Fifth more than under the Fourteenth Amendment.

The minimum wage law has evolved significantly since the Supreme Court declared it

Minimum wage laws attempt to ensure workers in traditionally low-paying service jobs a living wage.

constitutionally sound in *United States v. Darby.* The federal minimum wage remains the same until Congress passes a bill to raise it and the president signs the bill into law. The minimum wage started at 25¢ an hour, and Congress has increased it eighteen times. Since the law was enacted, increases to the minimum wage have been signed into law by Presidents HARRY S. TRUMAN, DWIGHT D. EISENHOWER, JOHN F. KENNEDY, LYNDON B. JOHNSON, RICHARD M. NIXON, JIMMY CARTER, GEORGE BUSH, and BILL CLINTON. The increases in the minimum wage have been sporadic. For example, the wage rose five times in the inflationary 1970s but was unchanged for the last nine years of the 1980s. In 1989 the FLSA was amended to raise the minimum wage in two steps: from $3.35 to $3.80 an hour on April 1, 1990, and from $3.80 to $4.25 an hour on April 1, 1991.

Every time Congress considers legislation to increase the minimum wage, it must ponder what constitutes a living wage—a wage sufficient to provide a worker with food, clothing, and shelter. Along those lines, the Congressional Research Service estimated that the minimum wage would have to rise to $6.75 per hour in 1996 to equal the purchasing power it represented in 1978.

Congress most recently amended the minimum wage law with the Minimum Wage Increase Act of 1996 (Pub. L. No. 104-188, sec. 2104(a), 110 Stat. 1228 [amends sec. 206]). Congress increased the minimum wage to $4.75 an hour effective October 1, 1996, and increased it to $5.15 an hour effective September 1, 1997.

The minimum wage is the most direct and definitive measure to guarantee workers a living wage, but the FLSA (and thus, its minimum wage provisions) does not protect all employees. In 1988, of the approximately 110 million wage and salary earners in the United States, the FLSA did not cover about 8 million workers because of coverage limits, nor another 28 million workers because of exemptions.

The minimum wage law can be enforced by employees themselves, by the secretary of labor, or by the attorney general. Under section 216(b) of the FLSA, employees can file suit in federal or state court to enforce their rights to minimum wages and overtime compensation. Employees can also seek redress if employers retaliate against them for trying to enforce their rights under the FLSA. The secretary of labor can also enforce the act on behalf of employees under sections 216(c) and 217 by either filing a wage suit on behalf of the employees or by seeking an INJUNCTION.

If a suit by either the employees or the secretary of labor is successful, the FLSA authorizes recovery of any unpaid minimum wages and/or overtime compensation; with some exceptions, the injured party may also be able to recover an equal amount in liquidated damages. In addition, employees who win FLSA suits may be awarded attorneys' fees. For repeated or willful violations of the minimum wage provisions, the secretary is authorized to assess civil penalties, subject to administrative review, of up to $1,000 per violation (29 U.S.C.A. § 217(e)).

Finally, the attorney general has the authority to file criminal actions for FLSA violations, although this authority has rarely been used.

Although the FLSA is the most significant federal wage statute, a number of other laws impose minimum wage obligations on entities performing work for the federal government. For example, the DAVIS-BACON ACT (40 U.S.C.A. §§ 276a–276a–5) applies to CONTRACTS in excess of $2,000 to work on federal buildings or other public works; the Walsh-Healey Act (41 U.S.C.A. §§ 35–45) applies to employers that provide materials, supplies, and equipment to the United States under contracts exceeding $10,000; and the Service Contract Act (41 U.S.C.A. §§ 351–358) applies to contracts in excess of $2,500 to provide services to the federal government. These statutes all require contracting entities to pay workers the prevailing wage in the locality.

CROSS-REFERENCES

Child Labor Laws; Employment Law; Labor Law; National Recovery Administration; New Deal; *Schechter Poultry Corp. v. United States.*

MINISTER See AMBASSADORS AND CONSULS; DIPLOMATIC AGENTS.

MINISTERIAL 📖 Done under the direction of a supervisor; not involving discretion or policymaking. 📖

Ministerial describes an act or a function that conforms to an instruction or a prescribed procedure. It connotes obedience. A *ministerial act* or *duty* is a function performed without the use of judgment by the person performing the act or duty.

MINOR 📖 An INFANT or person who is under the age of legal competence. A term derived from the CIVIL LAW, which described a person under a certain age as *less than* so many years. In most states, a person is no longer a minor after reaching the age of 18 (though state laws might still prohibit certain acts until reaching a greater age; e.g., purchase of liquor). Also, less; of less consideration; lower; a person of inferior condition. 📖

MINORITY 📖 The state or condition of a MINOR; INFANCY. Opposite of MAJORITY. The smaller number of votes of a deliberative assembly; opposed to majority. In context of the Constitution's guarantee of EQUAL PROTECTION, *minority* does not have merely numerical denotation but refers to identifiable and specially disadvantaged groups such as those based on race, religion, ethnicity, or national origin. 📖

MINTON, SHERMAN Sherman Minton served as an associate justice of the U.S. Supreme Court from 1949 to 1956. A strong supporter of President FRANKLIN D. ROOSEVELT's New Deal policies when he served as a U.S. senator from Indiana, Minton maintained a consistent judicial philosophy that allowed the legislative and executive branches wide discretion without judicial interference.

Minton was born on October 20, 1890, in Georgetown, Indiana. He graduated from Indiana University in 1915 and earned a law degree from Yale Law School in 1916. He entered the private practice of law in Indiana but also devoted himself to Democratic party politics. In 1934 he was elected to the U.S. Senate, where he served one term. While in the Senate, Minton was a staunch supporter of Roosevelt's

"ONE'S ASSOCIATES, PAST AND PRESENT, . . . MAY PROPERLY BE CONSIDERED IN DETERMINING FITNESS AND LOYALTY [FOR A JOB]."

BIOGRAPHY

Sherman Minton

legislative efforts, including the president's plan to "pack" the Court with extra justices to break the conservative majority that had ruled many pieces of NEW DEAL law unconstitutional. Minton lost his seat in the 1940 election.

In 1941 President Roosevelt first appointed Minton to advise him on military agencies and planning and then nominated him to the U.S. Court of Appeals for the Seventh Circuit. President HARRY S. TRUMAN, who got to know Minton when they served in the Senate together, elevated him to the Supreme Court in 1949. During his confirmation process, Minton refused to testify before the Senate Judiciary Committee, claiming it would be improper to testify. Surprisingly, the committee did not object.

During his seven years on the Court, Minton maintained his belief that the judiciary should not intrude on the actions of the other branches unless absolutely required. His conservative view led him to support decisions that upheld anticommunist policies such as LOYALTY OATHS and restrictions on the civil liberties of subversives. Minton, writing for the majority in *Adler v. Board of Education*, 342 U.S. 485, 72 S. Ct. 380, 96 L. Ed. 517 (1952), ruled that a New York statute that prohibited members of politically subversive groups from teaching in public schools was permissible.

As a result of his deference to the other branches of government, Minton was the only dissenter in *Youngstown Sheet and Tube Co. v. Sawyer*, 343 U.S. 579, 72 S. Ct. 863, 96 L. Ed. 1153 (1952). In this case President Truman had claimed executive authority when he seized U.S. steel mills in 1952 as the steel workers union went on strike. This occurred during the second year of the Korean War. Truman needed steel for war production and wanted to make sure that a pay hike would not cause higher steel prices, which would increase inflation in the national economy. The majority rejected Truman's claim to inherent executive power in the Constitution to protect the public interest in times of crisis. Minton sided with the president's position.

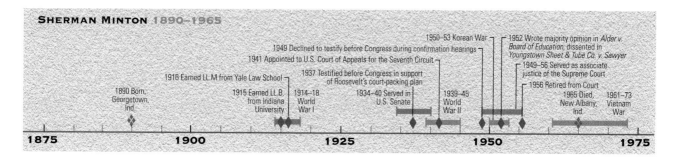

SHERMAN MINTON 1890–1965

1890 Born, Georgetown, Ind.

1915 Earned LL.B. from Indiana University

1916 Earned LL.M from Yale Law School

1914–18 World War I

1934–40 Served in U.S. Senate

1937 Testified before Congress in support of Roosevelt's court-packing plan

1939–45 World War II

1941 Appointed to U.S. Court of Appeals for the Seventh Circuit

1949 Declined to testify before Congress during confirmation hearings

1950–53 Korean War

1952 Wrote majority opinion in *Alder v. Board of Education*, dissented in *Youngstown Sheet & Tube Co. v. Sawyer*

1949–56 Served as associate justice of the Supreme Court

1956 Retired from Court

1965 Died, New Albany, Ind.

1961–73 Vietnam War

1875   1900   1925   1950   1975

Minton suffered serious health problems for several years and resigned from the Court for health reasons in 1956. He died on April 9, 1965, in New Albany, Indiana.

See also YOUNGSTOWN SHEET AND TUBE CO. V. SAWYER.

MINUTE BOOK 📖 An account where official proceedings are recorded. 📖

A minute book refers to a book kept by the CLERK of a court for recording a summary of all the judicial orders in a proceeding. The records are identified by case numbers.

It also refers to a record of official actions taken at a meeting of a BOARD OF DIRECTORS or of the stockholders of a CORPORATION.

MINUTES 📖 The written record of an official proceeding. The notes recounting the transactions occurring at a meeting or official proceeding; a record kept by courts and corporations for future reference. 📖

MIRANDA v. ARIZONA *Miranda v. Arizona* was a landmark decision, 384 U.S. 436, 86 S. Ct. 1602, 16 L. Ed. 2d 694 (1966), in the field of CRIMINAL PROCEDURE. In *Miranda*, the U.S. Supreme Court declared a set of specific rights for criminal defendants. The *Miranda* warning, named after Ernesto Miranda, one of the petitioners in the case, is a list of rights that a law enforcement officer must read to anyone arrested for a criminal act.

Before the High Court's decision in *Miranda*, the law governing CUSTODIAL INTERROGATION of criminal suspects varied from state to state. In many states statements made by criminal defendants who were in custody and under interrogation by law enforcement officials were ADMISSIBLE at trial, even though the defendants had not been advised of their legal rights. If the totality of the circumstances surrounding the statements indicated that the suspect made the statements voluntarily, it did not matter that officers had not apprised the suspect of his legal rights.

The totality of the circumstances rule was effective even if a defendant was in custody. Generally a defendant was considered in custody if she was not free to leave the presence of law enforcement officers. The basic legal rights for criminal defendants subjected to custodial interrogation included the FIFTH AMENDMENT right against SELF-INCRIMINATION and the right to an attorney, this latter right established by the Court two years earlier in *Escobedo v. Illinois*, 378 U.S. 478, 84 S. Ct. 1758, 12 L. Ed. 2d 977 (1964).

The *Miranda* case involved four criminal defendants. Each of the defendants was appealing a conviction based in part on the failure of law enforcement officers to advise him, prior to custodial interrogation, of his right to an attorney or his right to remain silent.

Ernesto Miranda, the first defendant listed in the case, was arrested on March 18, 1963, at his home in Arizona and taken to a Phoenix police station. At the station witnesses identified Miranda as a rapist. Police then brought Miranda to an interrogation room where he was questioned by two police officers.

The officers did not tell Miranda that he had a right to an attorney, and Miranda confessed to the crime in two hours. Miranda wrote a confession on a piece of paper and signed the paper. At the top of the paper was a typed statement saying that Miranda had made the CONFESSION voluntarily and with full knowledge of his legal rights. Miranda was convicted of RAPE and KIDNAPPING in an Arizona state court. The circumstances involving the other three defendants were similar, all three confessing after a period of custodial interrogation without the assistance of legal counsel.

The U.S. Supreme Court agreed to hear APPEALS from all four defendants, joining the appeals into a single review. A divided Court affirmed the California Supreme Court's decision against one of the defendants and reversed the guilty VERDICTS against Miranda and the other two.

The majority opinion, written by Chief Justice EARL WARREN, began with a review of police interrogation activities and a detailed formulation of new rules for law enforcement personnel.

The opening of the *Miranda* majority opinion set a grave tone:

> The cases before us raise questions which go to the roots of American criminal jurisprudence: the restraints society must observe consistent with the Federal Constitution in prosecuting individuals for crime. More specifically, we deal with the admissibility of statements obtained from an individual who is subjected to custodial police interrogation and the necessity for procedures which assure that the individual is accorded his privilege under the Fifth Amendment to the Constitution not to be compelled to incriminate himself.

The Court described in detail the unfairness and COERCION used by some law enforcement officers engaged in interrogation. The majority also took note of deceptive practices in interrogation. For example, officers would put a suspect in a LINEUP and tell her that she had been identified as a suspect in the instant crime as well as other crimes even though no such identifications had taken place. The suspect would confess to the instant crime to avoid being prosecuted for the fictitious crimes. The majority noted that these examples were exceptions, but it also stated that they were sufficiently widespread to warrant concern.

The Court then outlined the now-familiar procedures that law enforcement officers would have to follow thereafter. They would have to tell persons in custody that they have the right to remain silent, that they have the right to an attorney, that if they cannot afford an attorney the court will appoint an attorney, and that anything they say can be used in a criminal prosecution.

Ultimately, the Court held that statements made by a criminal suspect in custody would not be admissible at trial unless the suspect had made a knowing and intelligent WAIVER of his legal rights after being apprised of the various legal rights and after being given an opportunity to exercise those rights. The majority assured the law enforcement community that it did not intend to hamper criminal investigations and prosecutions. The Court pointed out that interrogations were still a perfectly legitimate investigative tool, that questioning a suspect without advising the suspect of legal rights before taking the suspect into custody was still legitimate, and that volunteered statements were likewise legitimate.

Justice TOM CLARK dissented to the decisions with respect to all defendants except the one whose conviction was upheld. According to Clark, the Court should continue to accept the totality of the circumstances test for determining whether a defendant's statements or confession were made voluntarily. Clark concluded that only the defendant whose conviction was upheld gave a confession that was not voluntary.

Justices JOHN M. HARLAN, POTTER STEWART, and BYRON R. WHITE dissented in all the cases. In an opinion authored by Harlan, the dissent argued that the majority had exaggerated the evils of normal police questioning. According to Harlan, "Society has always paid a stiff price for law and order, and peaceful interrogation is not one of the dark moments of the law."

Another dissent by White argued that the majority had gone too far in imposing such procedural requirements on the law enforcement community. White predicted that the new procedures would prevent the early release of

the truly innocent because they discourage statements that would quickly explain a situation. According to White, the procedures were "a deliberate calculus to prevent interrogations, to reduce the incidence of confessions and pleas of guilty and to increase the number of trials." "I have no desire whatsoever," wrote White, "to share the responsibility for any such impact on the present criminal process."

The *Miranda* case was remarkable in at least two ways. The opinion mandated important procedural changes that had to be followed by each and every law enforcement official across the country. In addition, the majority opinion's survey of interrogation tactics sent a rare notice to the law enforcement community that the Court was aware of, and would not tolerate, abuse in interrogation.

In recent years the *Miranda* holding has been pared down by the High Court. In 1985 the Court held that if a defendant makes an incriminating statement without the *Miranda* warning and then later receives the *Miranda* warning and confesses, the confession should not be excluded from trial (*Oregon v. Elstad*, 470 U.S. 298, 105 S. Ct. 1285, 84 L. Ed. 2d 222 [1985]).

In *Withrow v. Williams*, 507 U.S. 680, 113 S. Ct. 1745, 123 L. Ed. 2d 407 (1993), the Court held that a prisoner could not base a HABEAS CORPUS petition on the failure of law enforcement to give *Miranda* rights before interrogation. In *Illinois v. Perkins*, 496 U.S. 292, 110 S. Ct. 2394, 110 L. Ed. 2d 243 (1990), the Court held that the *Miranda* warning is not required when a suspect who is unaware that she is speaking to a law enforcement officer gives a voluntary statement.

In *Moran v. Burbine*, 475 U.S. 412, 106 S. Ct. 1135, 89 L. Ed. 2d 410 (1986), the Court appeared to return to the totality of the circumstances test. In *Moran*, a lawyer representing a criminal suspect, Brian Burbine, called the police station while Burbine was in custody. The lawyer was told that Burbine would not be questioned until the next day. In fact, Burbine was questioned that day, and he confessed, without requesting the lawyer and after being told his *Miranda* rights. According to the Court, the conduct of the police fell "short of the kind of misbehavior that so shocks the sensibilities of civilized society as to warrant a federal intrusion into the criminal processes of the States." Although law enforcement had not given Burbine a full opportunity to exercise his right to an attorney, a 6–3 majority of the Court concluded that, on the facts of the case, the incriminating statements were made voluntarily and that excluding them was therefore not required.

CROSS-REFERENCES

Criminal Law; Due Process of Law; Exclusionary Rule; Fruit of the Poisonous Tree; Right to Counsel.

MISCARRIAGE OF JUSTICE ◐ A legal proceeding resulting in a prejudicial outcome. ◐

A miscarriage of justice arises when the decision of a court is inconsistent with the substantive rights of a party.

MISCEGENATION ◐ Mixture of races. A term formerly applied to marriage between persons of different races. Statutes prohibiting marriage between persons of different races have been held to be invalid as contrary to the EQUAL PROTECTION Clause of the Constitution. ◐

MISDEMEANOR ◐ Offenses lower than felonies and generally those punishable by fine, penalty, FORFEITURE, or imprisonment other than in a PENITENTIARY. Under federal law, and most state laws, any offense other than a FELONY is classified as a misdemeanor. Certain states also have various classes of misdemeanors (e.g., Class A, B, etc.). ◐

MISFEASANCE ◐ A term used in TORT LAW to describe an act that is legal but performed improperly. ◐

Generally, a civil DEFENDANT will be liable for misfeasance if the defendant owed a DUTY of CARE toward the PLAINTIFF, the defendant breached that duty of care by improperly performing a legal act, and the improper performance resulted in harm to the plaintiff.

For example, assume that a janitor is cleaning a restroom in a restaurant. If he leaves the floor wet, he or his employer could be liable for any injuries resulting from the wet floor. This is because the janitor owed a duty of care toward users of the restroom, and he breached that duty by leaving the floor wet.

In theory, misfeasance is distinct from NONFEASANCE. *Nonfeasance* is a term that describes a failure to act that results in harm to another party. Misfeasance, by contrast, describes some affirmative act that, though legal, causes harm. In practice, the distinction is confusing and uninstructive. Courts often have difficulty determining whether harm resulted from a failure to act or from an act that was improperly performed.

To illustrate, consider the example of the wet bathroom floor. One court could call a resulting injury the product of misfeasance by focusing on the wetness of the floor. The washing of the floor was legal, but the act of leaving the floor wet was improper. Another court could call a resulting injury the product of nonfeasance by focusing on the janitor's failure to post a warning sign.

See also MALFEASANCE.

MISPRISION ◐ The failure to perform a public DUTY. ◐

Misprision is a versatile word that can denote a number of offenses. It can refer to the improper performance of an official duty. In Arkansas, for example, rule 60 of the Arkansas Rules of Civil Procedure provides that a JUDGMENT, DECREE, or ORDER may be vacated or modified "for misprisions of the clerk." In this sense *misprision* refers to NEGLECT, MISTAKE, or subterfuge on the part of the court CLERK who performed the paperwork for the judgment, decree, or order.

Misprision also can refer to seditious or rebellious conduct against the government or the courts. This is an archaic usage of the word. Organized rebellion against the government is now uniformly referred to as SEDITION or INSURRECTION.

The most familiar and popular use of the term *misprision* describes the failure to report a crime. In England, beginning in the thirteenth century, the failure to report a crime became itself a crime. According to tradition, it was a citizen's duty to "raise the hue and cry" by reporting crimes, especially felonies, to law enforcement authorities (*Branzburg v. Hayes*, 408 U.S. 665, 92 S. Ct. 2646, 33 L. Ed. 2d 626 [1972], quoting WILLIAM BLACKSTONE).

The crime of misprision still exists in England, but it has never been fully embraced in the United States. The first Congress passed a misprision of FELONY statute in 1789. The statute holds, "Whoever, having knowledge of the actual commission of a felony . . . conceals and does not as soon as possible make known the same to some judge or other person in civil or military authority under the United States" is guilty of misprision of felony and can be punished with up to three years in prison.

Under the federal statute, the prosecution must prove the following elements to obtain a misprision of felony conviction: (1) another person actually committed a felony; (2) the defendant knew that the felony was committed; (3) the defendant did not notify any law enforcement or judicial officer; and (4) the defendant took affirmative steps to conceal the felony. Precisely what constitutes active concealment is a QUESTION OF FACT that depends on the circumstances of the case. Lying to a police officer satisfies the requirement, but beyond that generally accepted rule, little is certain about the definition of active concealment.

Almost every state has rejected the crime of misprision of felony. Thus, persons are under no duty to report a crime. One policy reason for rejecting misprision is that the crime is vague and difficult to apply to real situations. Another reason is that the crime is seen as an unacceptable encroachment on civil freedom. In 1822 the U.S. Supreme Court cautioned against misuse of the misprision of felony statute, stating, "It may be the duty of a citizen to . . . proclaim every offense which comes to his knowledge; but the law which would punish him in every case, for not performing this duty, is too harsh" (*Marbury v. Brooks*, 20 U.S. [7 Wheat.] 556, 5 L. Ed. 522).

The Supreme Court has not completely abandoned the duty to report criminal activity. In *Roberts v. United States*, 445 U.S. 552, 100 S. Ct. 1358, 63 L. Ed. 2d 622 (1980), the High Court held that a court can increase a criminal defendant's sentence if the defendant refuses to cooperate with government officials investigating a related crime. Also, a journalist who has knowledge of a crime may be compelled to reveal the source of that knowledge (*Branzburg v. Hayes*).

The federal misprision of felony statute remains on the books, but the crime rarely has been prosecuted. On the state level, most states have either abolished or refused to enact misprision of felony laws. South Carolina is the only state that has prosecuted the misprision of a felony.

In *State v. Carson*, 262 S.E.2d 918, 274 S.C. 316 (1980), Isaac E. Carson, the eyewitness to a murder, refused to give law enforcement authorities information regarding the MURDER because he feared for his life if he cooperated with authorities. Carson was prosecuted and convicted of misprision of felony and sentenced to three years in prison.

The prosecution of Carson was based on the COMMON LAW. South Carolina did not have a misprision of felony statute. Instead the prosecution relied on title 14, chapter 1, section 50, of the Code of Laws of South Carolina. Under this statute the common law of England continues in effect in South Carolina. On appeal by Carson, the Supreme Court of South Carolina affirmed the conviction. According to the court, the prosecution was valid because misprision of felony was a crime at common law in England and because the South Carolina legislature had not taken steps to repeal the common-law crime of misprision of felony.

The crime of misprision of felony is similar to the crime of acting as an ACCESSORY after the fact because both crimes involve some affirma-

tive act to conceal a crime. Two basic differences are that the crime of misprision is committed even if the defendant does not give aid to the criminal and misprision is committed only if the underlying crime is completed.

MISREPRESENTATION An assertion or manifestation by words or conduct that is not in accord with the facts.

Misrepresentation is a tort, or a civil wrong. This means that a misrepresentation can create civil LIABILITY if it results in a pecuniary loss. For example, assume that a real estate speculator owns swampland but advertises it as valuable commercially zoned land. This is a misrepresentation. If someone buys the land relying on the speculator's statement that it is commercially valuable, the buyer may sue the speculator for monetary losses resulting from the purchase.

To create liability for the maker of the statement, a misrepresentation must be relied on by the listener or reader. Also, the speaker must know that the listener is relying on the factual correctness of the statement. Finally, the listener's reliance on the statement must have been reasonable and justified, and the misrepresentation must have resulted in a pecuniary loss to the listener.

A misrepresentation need not be intentionally false to create liability. A statement made with conscious ignorance or a reckless disregard for the truth can create liability. Nondisclosure

KENT KNUDSON/STOCK BOSTON

Would advertising this house for sale as a "fixer-upper" constitute misrepresentation? It might, if the seller failed to disclose that it had been deemed unfit for habitation.

of material or important facts by a FIDUCIARY or an expert, such as a doctor, lawyer, or accountant, can result in liability. If the speaker is engaged in the business of selling products, any statement, no matter how innocent, may create liability if the statement concerns the character or quality of a product and the statement is not true. In such a case, the statement must be one of fact. This does not include so-called PUFFING, or the glowing opinions of a seller in the course of a sales pitch (such statements as "you'll love this car," or "it's a great deal").

A misrepresentation in a CONTRACT can give a party the right to RESCIND the contract. A RESCISSION of a contract returns the parties to the positions they held before the contract was made. A party can rescind a contract for misrepresentation only if the statement was MATERIAL, or critical, to the agreement.

A misrepresentation on the part of the INSURED in an INSURANCE policy can give the INSURER the right to cancel the policy or refuse a claim. An insurer may do this only if the misrepresentation was material to the RISK insured against and would have influenced the insurer in determining whether to issue a policy. For example, if a person seeking auto insurance states that she has no major chronic illnesses, the insurer's subsequent discovery that the applicant had an incurable disease at the time she completed the insurance form probably will not give the insurer the right to cancel the auto policy. However, if the person was seeking HEALTH INSURANCE, such a misrepresentation may justify cancellation of the policy or a denial of coverage. Generally, cancellation or denial of insurance coverage for a misrepresentation can occur only if the insurance applicant was aware of the inaccuracy of the statement.

CROSS-REFERENCES
Consumer Protection; Product Liability; Sales Law; Tort Law.

MISSOURI COMPROMISE OF 1820 ◫ A
congressional agreement that regulated the extension of SLAVERY in the United States for the next thirty years. Under the agreement the territory of Missouri was admitted as a slave state, the territory of Maine was admitted as a free state, and the boundaries of slavery were limited to the same latitude as the southern boundary of Missouri: 36° 30′ north latitude. ◫

The issue of slavery had been troublesome since the drafting of the Constitution. Slaveholding states, concerned that they would be outvoted in Congress because their white population was much smaller than that of the free

states, extracted concessions. Under the Constitution representation of the U.S. House of Representatives was based on the total white population and three-fifths of the black population. The Constitution apportioned two senators for each state.

By 1820, however, the rapid growth in population in the North left Southern states, for the first time, with less than 45 percent of the seats in the House. The Senate was evenly balanced between eleven slave and eleven free states. Therefore, Missouri's 1818 application for statehood, if approved, would give slaveholding seats a majority in the Senate and reduce the Northern majority in the House.

After a bill was introduced in the House in 1818 to approve Missouri's application for statehood, Representative James Tallmadge of New York introduced an amendment that prohibited the further introduction of slavery in Missouri and required that any slave born there be emancipated at age twenty-five. The bill passed the House but was defeated in the Senate, where Southern strength was greater.

In 1819 the free territory of Maine applied for statehood. Speaker of the House HENRY CLAY of Kentucky saw this event as an opportunity to maintain the balance of free and slave states. He made it clear to Northern congressmen that Maine would not be admitted without an agreement to admit Missouri. Clay was successful, getting the Northern congressmen to drop their amendment restricting slavery while winning Southern congressmen over to the idea of limiting slavery to the 36° 30′ north latitude. This provision, in effect, left unsettled portions of the LOUISIANA PURCHASE north and west of Missouri free from slavery. The only area remaining for further expansion of slavery was the future territory of Arkansas and Oklahoma. Clay managed to pass the compromise in the House by a three-vote margin. Missouri and Maine were to be admitted to the Union simultaneously to preserve the sectional equality in the Senate.

In 1821 Missouri complicated matters, however, by inserting a provision into its state constitution that forbade any free blacks or mulattoes (people of mixed Caucasian and African-American heritage) to enter the state. Northern congressmen objected to this language and refused to give final approval for statehood until it was removed. Clay then negotiated a second compromise, removing the contested language and substituting a provision that prohibited Missouri from discriminating against citizens from other states. It left unsettled the question of who was a citizen. With this change Missouri and Maine were admitted to the Union.

The Missouri Compromise of 1820 merely postponed the conflict over slavery. As new territories were annexed to the Union, new compromises with slavery became necessary. The COMPROMISE OF 1850 redrew the territorial map of slavery and altered the 36° 30′ north latitude prescription of the Missouri Compromise. California was admitted as a free state, and the Utah and New Mexico territories were open to slavery. The KANSAS-NEBRASKA ACT of 1854 repealed the Missouri Compromise. This new law provided for the organization of two new territories that allowed slavery, Kansas and Nebraska, both north of the 1820 Missouri Compromise line of 36° 30′ north latitude. The land open to slavery drove deep into the north and west.

The constitutionality of the Missouri Compromise itself was challenged in the landmark U.S. Supreme Court case of *Dred Scott v. Sandford*, 60 U.S. (19 How.) 393, 15 L. Ed. 69 (1857). Scott, a slave, had lived with his master in the free state of Illinois and also in part of the Wisconsin territory, where slavery had been federally prohibited under the Missouri Compromise. After his master died, Scott sued in the Missouri courts for his freedom, on the grounds that he had lived in a free territory. The Supreme Court ruled against Scott, with Chief Justice ROGER B. TANEY holding that the FIFTH AMENDMENT denies Congress the right to deprive persons of their property without DUE PROCESS OF LAW. Therefore, the Missouri Compromise prohibiting slavery north of 36° 30′ was unconstitutional. The decision wiped away the Missouri Compromise but also raised the issue of whether slavery could be regulated by any government anywhere in the Union.

See also DRED SCOTT V. SANDFORD.

MISTAKE An unintentional act, omission, or error.

Mistakes are categorized as a mistake of fact, mistake of law, or mutual mistake. A mistake of fact occurs when a person believes that a condition or event exists when it does not. A mistake of law is made by a person who has knowledge of the correct facts but is wrong about the legal consequences of an act or event. A MUTUAL MISTAKE arises when two or more parties have a shared intention that has been induced by a common misbelief.

MISTAKE OF FACT An ERROR that is not caused by the neglect of a legal duty on the part of the person committing the error, but rather consists of an unconscious ignorance of a past or present material event or circumstance, or a belief in the present existence of a MATERIAL event that does not exist, or a belief in the past existence of a material event that did not exist.

Mistake of fact can be a factor in reducing or eliminating civil LIABILITY or criminal culpability. A mistake of fact is of little consequence unless it is born of unconscious ignorance or forgetfulness. A person cannot escape civil or criminal liability for intentional mistakes.

In CONTRACT law a mistake of fact may be raised as a defense by a party seeking to avoid liability under the contract. Also, a mistake of fact can be used affirmatively to cancel, RESCIND, or reform a contract. A mistake of FACT can affect a contract only if the mistaken fact was material, or important, to the agreement.

For example, assume that a bookseller has agreed to sell a copy of a Virginia Woolf novel that was signed by the late author. Assume further that the only reason the buyer is interested in buying the book is because it contains Woolf's signature. The seller knows this, and with an authentic signature the book fetches a very high price. If it is later discovered that the signature was actually forged decades earlier and neither the seller nor the buyer knew of the FORGERY, this would be a mistake of fact material to the deal, and the buyer would have the right to return the book and get her money back. This is an example of a mutual mistake, or a material fact that is mistaken by both parties. In such a case, the party who is adversely affected by the mistake has the right to cancel or rescind the contract.

Another example of mistake of fact in contract law is a unilateral mistake, where only one party to the agreement is mistaken about a material fact. In such a case, the party adversely affected by the mistake will not be able to VOID the contract unless the other party knew or should have known of the mistake, or unless the other party had a DUTY to disclose the mistaken fact. For example, assume that a person owns an expensive sports car that is in perfect condition. Assume further that a neighbor asks the owner if he will sell the car, and the owner responds, "I will sell this car for thirty bills." If the neighbor returns with $30, no contract is formed. This is because the neighbor mistakenly thought that the owner meant $30 when actually the owner was using slang for $30,000. Further, the neighbor should have known that an expensive sports car would not be sold for $30.

If a party to a contract assumes the risk that a material fact may be different than expected, that party will not be able to recover any losses when the fact turns out to be different. For example, assume that a farmer sells a horse to a buyer who wants to use the horse for polo games. Neither the farmer nor the buyer knows whether the horse will be suitable for polo, and the farmer makes no guarantees. If the horse proves unsuitable, the buyer will not be able to rescind the deal because the farmer made no warranties as to the horse's suitability for polo. To avoid such a result, parties to a contract may agree, as part of the deal, to cancel or rescind the contract if a certain fact related to the contract later proves unacceptable to one of the parties.

If a contract can be reformed, a court may not allow a party to rescind a contract on account of mistake of fact. The court reforms a contract to reflect the true intent of the parties. For example, assume that a footwear retailer offers to buy one hundred mukluks from a mukluk manufacturer for $10 a pair. Assume further that the retailer mistakenly orders one hundred mukluks for $100 a pair. If the mukluk manufacturer delivers one hundred mukluks and later demands $100 for each pair, the retailer can ask a court to reform the contract to reflect a price of $10 a pair. This generally occurs when the mistake makes the agreement UNCONSCIONABLE. If, for example, the retailer had offered to pay $101 a pair and the retailer later discovered that the standard price was $100, the retailer would likely be stuck with the contract.

A mistake involving the use of force in the defense of property can give rise to civil liability. Generally, if a person has a PRIVILEGE to enter onto PROPERTY, a landowner or TENANT has no right to use force to keep the intruder off the property. If, however, the intruder causes a reasonable, mistaken belief that the property must be defended, a landowner or tenant may have the right to use force to repel the intruder. For example, if an electricity meter reader arrives to read a meter at night wearing dark clothing and a ski mask, a resident on the property may not be liable for a REASONABLE use of force necessary to expel the intruder. The meter reader can be considered to have caused the mistaken belief on the part of the resident that the property was being invaded by someone with no privilege to enter.

In CRIMINAL LAW an honest and reasonable mistake of fact can eliminate the MENS REA element of criminal responsibility. *Mens rea* is Latin for "guilty mind," and, along with an act, a guilty mind, or a criminal intent, is required before a person can be held criminally respon-sible for most crimes. For example, assume that a person who buys stolen goods honestly and reasonably believed that the goods actually belonged to the seller. This would negate the criminal intent necessary to be convicted of receiving stolen goods, and the buyer would not be held criminally liable.

If a mistake of fact in a criminal case does not negate mens rea, it may reduce it. For example, if a person honestly and reasonably, but mistakenly, believes that DEADLY FORCE is necessary to preserve her own life, she may not be found guilty of MURDER if a death results from the deadly force. The mistake reduced the mens rea necessary to be convicted of murder. That is, the person did not have the specific intent to kill without justification or excuse. She may be found guilty of MANSLAUGHTER, a HOMICIDE less serious than murder, if her actions were unreasonable. She may even be found not guilty of any homicide if the judge or jury finds that she was not reckless or negligent in the killing. This is a question of fact to be determined by the judge or jury sitting on the case.

In some criminal and civil cases, no mens rea is required for liability. Such cases involve strict liability crimes. Statutory RAPE is an example of a strict liability crime. It does not matter whether the defendant knew that the victim was too young to have sexual relations, or whether the defendant intended to have sex with a minor. In such a case, a mistake of fact is no defense. Strict liability crimes are generally those that endanger the public welfare, such as toxic waste dumping and the sale of ALCOHOL to MINORS.

MISTAKE OF LAW 📖 A misconception that occurs when a person with complete knowledge of the facts reaches an erroneous conclusion as to their legal effect; an incorrect opinion or inference, arising from a flawed evaluation of the facts. 📖

Generally, a mistaken belief about a law is no defense to a violation of that law. All persons are presumed to know and understand the law, except MINORS, persons who lack mental CAPAC-ITY to contract with others, and, in criminal cases, persons who are insane. There are, however, a few other rare exceptions to this general rule.

A mistake of law may be helpful to criminal defendants facing prosecution for a specific-intent crime. A specific-intent crime requires that a defendant act with a criminal intent beyond the GENERAL INTENT required to commit the act. MURDER, for example, is a specific-intent crime. The prosecution must show that the defendant specifically intended to kill the victim without justification. MANSLAUGHTER, conversely, requires only a showing that the defendant intended to do those actions that caused the death. If a defendant is charged with a specific-intent crime, the defendant's REASON-ABLE mistaken belief about the law may reduce the defendant's criminal LIABILITY.

For example, assume that a defendant is accused of robbing another person. Assume further that the defendant was actually trying to retrieve money that the alleged victim owed to the defendant. A court may hold that the defendant mistakenly believed that the law allows self-help in such situations and that the mistaken belief about the law negated the specific intent required for the crime. That is, the defendant did not have the specific intent to gain control over the property of another person. Generally, a mistake of law is helpful to criminal defendants only in specific-intent cases. For general-intent and strict liability crimes, a mistake of law is no defense.

There are other exceptions to the general rule that ignorance of the law is no excuse. If a defendant relied on a statute that permitted a certain act and the act is later made illegal, the defendant cannot be prosecuted. This applies to general-intent and strict liability crimes as well as specific-intent crimes. If a defendant reasonably relies on a judicial decision, an opinion, or a JUDGMENT that is later reversed, the reversal does not retroactively make a related act illegal. Similarly, if a defendant acts with reasonable reliance on an official statement of law in an administrative order or from an official interpretation by a public officer or government agency, the defendant may use the mistake-of-law defense. Mistaken advice from an ATTORNEY, however, does not create a mistake-of-law defense.

MISTRIAL 📖 A courtroom TRIAL that has been terminated prior to its normal conclusion. A mistrial has no legal effect and is considered an INVALID or NUGATORY trial. It differs from a "new trial," which recognizes that a trial was completed but was set aside so that the issues could be tried again. 📖

A judge may declare a mistrial for several reasons, including lack of JURISDICTION, incorrect JURY selection, or a deadlocked, or hung, jury. A deadlocked jury—where the jurors cannot agree over the defendant's guilt or innocence—is a common reason for declaring a mistrial. Extraordinary circumstances, such as death or illness of a necessary juror or an attorney, may also result in a mistrial. A mistrial may also result from a fundamental ERROR so prejudicial to the defendant that it cannot be

cured by appropriate instructions to the jury, such as improper remarks made during the prosecution's summation.

In determining whether to declare a mistrial, the court must decide whether the error is so prejudicial and fundamental that expenditure of further time and expense would be wasteful, if not futile. Although the judge has the power to declare a mistrial and discharge a jury, this power should be "exercised with great care and only in cases of absolute necessity" (*Salvatore v. State of Florida*, 366 So. 2d 745 [Fla. 1978], *cert. denied*, 444 U.S. 885, 100 S. Ct. 177, 62 L. Ed. 2d 115 [1979]).

For example, in *Ferguson v. State*, 417 So. 2d 639 (Fla. 1982), the defendant moved for a mistrial because of an allegedly improper comment made by the prosecution during closing argument. The prosecution stated that not only was defense counsel asking the jury to find a scapegoat for the defendant's guilt, he was also putting the blame on someone who had already been found guilty. The APPELLATE COURT found that the lower court had properly denied the motion for a mistrial because the prosecutor's comment fell within the bounds of "fair reply."

A mistrial in a criminal prosecution may prevent retrial under the DOUBLE JEOPARDY provision of the FIFTH AMENDMENT, which prohibits an individual from being tried twice for the same offense, unless required by the interests of justice and depending on which party moved for the mistrial. Typically, there is no bar to a retrial if the defendant requests or consents to a mistrial. A retrial may be barred if the court grants a mistrial without the defendant's consent, or over his objection. If the mistrial results from judicial or prosecutorial misconduct, a

During final arguments in the second murder trial of Lyle (pictured) and Erik Menendez, a motion for mistrial was prompted by the prosecution's suggestion that there was insufficient evidence to show the brothers were abused by their parents.

retrial will be barred. In *United States v. Jorn*, 400 U.S. 470, 91 S. Ct. 547, 27 L. Ed. 2d 543 (1971), the Supreme Court held that reprosecuting the defendant would constitute double jeopardy because the judge had abused his discretion in declaring a mistrial. On his own motion, the judge had declared a mistrial to enable government witnesses to consult with their own attorneys.

CROSS-REFERENCES
Criminal Procedure; Harmless Error; Hung Jury.

MITCHELL, JOHN NEWTON
John Newton Mitchell served as U.S. attorney general from 1969 to 1972. A key political adviser to President RICHARD M. NIXON, Mitchell was later convicted of crimes associated with the WATERGATE scandal, becoming the first attorney general to serve time in a federal prison.

Mitchell was born September 5, 1913, in Detroit. He worked his way through Fordham University and Fordham Law School playing semiprofessional hockey. After graduating from law school in 1938, he was admitted to the New York bar and began work in a New York City law firm. He was made a partner in 1942. During World War II, he served as a torpedo boat commander in the U.S. Navy.

Mitchell became rich and prominent as a municipal bond lawyer, devising new ways for states and municipalities to finance construction projects. He met Richard M. Nixon in 1962, when Nixon joined a prominent New York law firm. At that time Nixon appeared to have no political future; he had lost the 1960 presidential election and the 1962 California gubernatorial election. In 1967 Mitchell's firm merged with Nixon's and the pair became confidants.

Mitchell served as Nixon's campaign manager for the presidency in 1968. He forged a conservative coalition of southern and western states that helped carry Nixon to victory over Vice President HUBERT H. HUMPHREY. During the campaign Mitchell claimed he would never accept a CABINET position if Nixon was elected. Despite these statements Mitchell accepted the post of attorney general in 1969.

BIOGRAPHY

"YOU WILL BE BETTER ADVISED TO WATCH WHAT WE DO INSTEAD OF WHAT WE SAY."

As attorney general, Mitchell led the Justice Department in a sweeping law-and-order drive that many critics believed went too far. He increased the number of telephone wiretaps on private citizens and generally clamped down on political dissenters, especially those who opposed U.S. involvement in the VIETNAM WAR. A number of these Justice Department initiatives were later ruled illegal by the courts. For example, in *Ellsberg v. Mitchell*, 353 F. Supp. 515 (D.D.C. 1973), the department sought to prosecute Daniel Ellsberg for leaking secret documents to the press regarding military involvement in Vietnam. The release of the Pentagon Papers infuriated the Nixon White House. The case was dismissed after Ellsberg's attorneys informed the court that a secret White House security group (the "plumbers") had illegally broken into the office of Ellsberg's psychiatrist in search of damaging evidence. The dismissal was also based on the Justice Department's refusal to produce wiretap records pertaining to Ellsberg.

Mitchell resigned as attorney general in February 1972 to head President Nixon's reelection committee. On June 17, 1972, five men were arrested after breaking into Democratic National Committee headquarters at the Watergate building complex in Washington, D.C. They and two other men associated with the White House and the reelection committee were charged with burglary and WIRETAPPING. Mitchell denied playing any part in the Watergate incident but resigned from the reelection committee post in July.

In May 1973 he was indicted in New York City for PERJURY and obstruction of justice in an alleged scheme to secretly contribute cash to the Nixon reelection campaign. He was acquitted of the charge in 1974. In that same year, however, he was indicted for CONSPIRACY, obstruction of justice, giving false testimony to a GRAND JURY, and perjury, for his role in the Watergate break-in and cover-up. He was convicted of these charges in 1975 and sentenced to two-and-a-half to eight years in prison. After exhausting his criminal appeals, he entered fed-

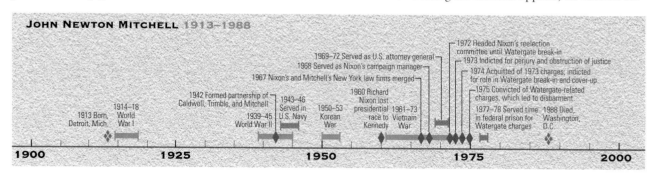

JOHN NEWTON MITCHELL 1913–1988

1900 — 1925 — 1950 — 1975 — 2000

1913 Born, Detroit, Mich.
1914–18 World War I
1942 Formed partnership of Caldwell, Trimble, and Mitchell
1939–45 World War II
1943–46 Served in U.S. Navy
1950–53 Korean War
1960 Richard Nixon lost presidential race to Kennedy
1961–73 Vietnam War
1967 Nixon's and Mitchell's New York law firms merged
1968 Served as Nixon's campaign manager
1969–72 Served as U.S. attorney general
1972 Headed Nixon's reelection committee until Watergate break-in
1973 Indicted for perjury and obstruction of justice
1974 Acquitted of 1973 charges; indicted for role in Watergate break-in and cover-up
1975 Convicted of Watergate-related charges, which led to disbarment
1977–78 Served time in federal prison for Watergate charges
1988 Died, Washington, D.C.

eral prison in June 1977. His sentence was later reduced to one to four years after he made a statement of contrition. He was paroled in January 1978.

His criminal convictions led to his disbarment in 1975. Following his release he served as an international business consultant. He died on November 9, 1988, in Washington, D.C.

MITCHELL, WILLIAM DE WITT William de Witt Mitchell was a distinguished lawyer who became the fifty-fourth attorney general of the United States.

Mitchell was born on September 9, 1874, in Winona, Minnesota. He was the son of William Mitchell, a distinguished justice of the Minnesota Supreme Court for whom the William Mitchell College of Law in St. Paul is named. The younger Mitchell left Minnesota at the age of fourteen to attend preparatory school in New Jersey. He then entered Yale University to study electrical engineering, but during vacations back in Minnesota, he pursued his interest in the law, spending time discussing legal issues with his father and with other judges and attorneys who were family friends. As a result, after two years at Yale, he transferred to the University of Minnesota for pre-law studies. After receiving his bachelor of arts degree in 1895 and his bachelor of laws degree in 1896, he was admitted to the bar and took a position as a law clerk with Stringer and Seymour, a St. Paul law firm.

When the Spanish-American War broke out in 1898, Mitchell enlisted in the Fifteenth Minnesota Volunteer Infantry, where he became a second lieutenant and served as a judge advocate for the Second U.S. Army Corp. When the war ended, he returned to St. Paul and Stringer and Seymour. After his father lost his seat on the state supreme court in an election, Mitchell and the elder Mitchell established a law partnership with two other lawyers. Though his father died in 1900, Mitchell continued to practice law until another war—World War I—intervened. Mitchell again returned to military service as an infantry officer until 1919, when he rejoined his law firm, becoming a senior partner in 1922.

In 1925, through an influential friend in

William de Witt Mitchell

"WE ARE GOING TO HAVE AN OUTBURST AGAINST THIS DISCOVERY BUSINESS UNLESS WE CAN HEDGE IT WITH SOME APPEARANCE OF SAFETY AGAINST FISHING EXPEDITIONS."

Washington, Mitchell's name was brought to the attention of President CALVIN COOLIDGE, who was seeking to fill the position of solicitor general. Coolidge, a Republican, offered Mitchell, a Democrat, the job, passing over several better-known Republican candidates. As solicitor general, under the direction of the U.S. attorney general, Mitchell was primarily responsible for representing the government of the United States before the U.S. Supreme Court in cases in which the United States had an interest. Mitchell, though he had intended to hold the position for only two years and then return to private practice, was solicitor general until 1929, appearing before the Court in thirty-four cases.

That year, upon the recommendation of several justices on the Supreme Court, newly elected President HERBERT HOOVER appointed Mitchell to be U.S. attorney general. Though his new role involved a wide and daunting range of responsibilities (including acting as a member of the president's cabinet), Mitchell continued to occasionally argue important cases himself before the High Court. One significant case was *Okanogan, Methow, San Poelis, Nespelem, Colville, and Lake Indian Tribes or Bands of State of Washington v. United States*, 279 U.S. 655, 49 S. Ct. 463, 73 L. Ed. 894 (1929), better known as the *Pocket Veto* case. In that decision the Supreme Court upheld the president's power to VETO a bill by failing to return it to Congress when Congress was in recess.

At the end of the Hoover administration, Mitchell returned to private practice, joining a New York law firm. Twelve years later, in 1945, Mitchell was appointed counsel for the Joint Congressional Committee on the Investigation of the Pearl Harbor Attack. Though he was selected unanimously and had virtually unfettered access to all departments, records, and personnel involved in the incident, Mitchell was unhappy with the slow pace of the committee's inquiry and left the position after less than three months to again return to private practice in New York. While practicing he served on several important commissions and was chairman of the Committee on Federal Rules of Civil Procedure, which was charged with re-

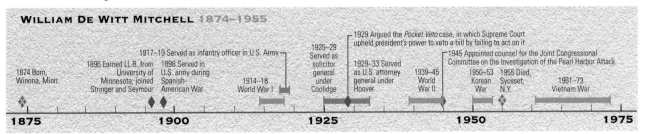

WILLIAM DE WITT MITCHELL 1874–1955

1874 Born, Winona, Minn.

1896 Earned LL.B. from University of Minnesota; joined Stringer and Seymour

1898 Served in U.S. army during Spanish-American War

1914–18 World War I

1917–19 Served as infantry officer in U.S. Army

1925–29 Served as solicitor general under Coolidge

1929 Argued the *Pocket Veto* case, in which Supreme Court upheld president's power to veto a bill by failing to act on it

1929–33 Served as U.S. attorney general under Hoover

1939–45 World War II

1945 Appointed counsel for the Joint Congressional Committee on the Investigation of the Pearl Harbor Attack

1950–53 Korean War

1955 Died, Syosset, N.Y.

1961–73 Vietnam War

1875   1900   1925   1950   1975

drafting rules governing practice in the federal courts. He died on August 24, 1955, in Syosset, New York, at the age of eighty-one.

MITIGATING CIRCUMSTANCES 📖 Circumstances that may be considered by a court in determining culpability of a defendant or the extent of DAMAGES to be awarded to a plaintiff. Mitigating circumstances do not justify or excuse an offense but may reduce the severity of a charge. Similarly, a recognition of mitigating circumstances to reduce a damage award does not imply that the damages were not suffered but that they have been partially ameliorated. 📖

In criminal cases where the death penalty may be imposed, the Supreme Court has held that, under the Eighth and Fourteenth Amendments, juries must be instructed that they may consider mitigating circumstances such as the defendant's youth, mental capacity, or childhood abuse so that they may reach a reasoned and moral sentencing decision. (See *Penry v. Lynaugh*, 492 U.S. 302, 109 S. Ct. 2934, 106 L. Ed. 2d 256 [1989].) Mitigating circumstances may be used to reduce a charge against a defendant. In *People v. Morrin*, 31 Mich. App. 301, 187 N.W.2d 434 (1971), the Michigan Court of Appeals reversed and remanded Morrin's conviction on first-degree MURDER charges because he committed the murder in the HEAT OF PASSION caused by adequate legal provocation. The court found that because of these mitigating circumstances, the evidence was insufficient to support a first-degree murder conviction, which requires MALICE AFORETHOUGHT.

In CIVIL ACTIONS mitigating circumstances may be considered to reduce damage awards or the extent of the defendant's LIABILITY. In *Cerretti v. Flint Hills Rural Electric Cooperative Ass'n*, 251 Kan. 347, 837 P.2d 330 (1992), the Supreme Court of Kansas held that a court, in reviewing a damage award, may consider any mitigating circumstances that affected the intent of the defendant, the financial worth of the defendant, or the plaintiff's expenses.

Many states allow defendants in DEFAMATION actions to prove mitigating circumstances by showing that they acted in GOOD FAITH, with honesty of purpose, and without MALICE in speaking or publishing the defamatory words. If the court is convinced that legitimate mitigating circumstances existed, it may reduce the amount of damages the defendant is required to pay. In *Roemer v. Retail Credit Co.*, 44 Cal. App. 3d 926, 119 Cal. Rptr. 82 (1975), the defendant claimed that the plaintiff defaced the wall of his office, thereby mitigating the defendant's liability for defamatory statements. However, the court did not allow the defendant to introduce this EVIDENCE because he could not prove that the plaintiff was responsible for the defacement.

See also CAPITAL PUNISHMENT; CRIMINAL LAW.

MITIGATION OF DAMAGES 📖 The use of reasonable CARE and DILIGENCE in an effort to minimize or avoid INJURY. 📖

Under the mitigation of damages doctrine, a person who has suffered an injury or loss should take REASONABLE action, where possible, to avoid additional injury or loss. The failure of a plaintiff to take protective steps after suffering an injury or loss can reduce the amount of the plaintiff's recovery. The mitigation of damages doctrine is sometimes called minimization of damages or the doctrine of AVOIDABLE CONSEQUENCES.

In CONTRACT law the non-breaching party should mitigate damages or risk a reduction in recovery for the breach. For example, assume that a property owner and home builder contract for the construction of a home in exchange for payment of $50,000. Assume further that the builder begins constructing the home but that the owner wrongfully cancels the contract before the builder has finished construction. If the builder must sue the owner to recover the unpaid portion of the contract price, a court may reduce the amount of money that the builder recovers if the builder does not try to avoid additional loss. For example, the builder could sell the materials already purchased for the job or use the materials in another job. The savings that the builder realizes will be deducted from the loss incurred on the contract in computing the builder's net recovery in court.

In TORT LAW mitigation of damages refers to conduct by the plaintiff that, although not con-

If the builder of this home were unable to complete the project due to a breach of contract by the buyer, he could seek to mitigate damages by selling the unused building materials.

stituting a civil wrong itself, may reduce the plaintiff's recovery. For example, if the victim of an ASSAULT used provocative words prior to the assault, the words may mitigate the plaintiff's damages. Most states limit mitigation of damages for provocative words to a possible reduction in PUNITIVE DAMAGES, as opposed to COMPENSATORY DAMAGES.

A tort victim also should act to mitigate damages subsequent to the wrongful acts of another. For instance, assume that the victim in the assault example suffers a broken leg. If the victim refuses to get medical treatment and the leg eventually must be amputated, the defendant may be liable only for the reasonable medical expenses to repair a broken leg. Because a reasonable person would seek medical attention after suffering a broken leg, a court could find it unreasonable to make the defendant pay for additional damage that the victim could have prevented with minimal effort.

If it is unreasonable to expect the victim to mitigate DAMAGES following the injury, the defendant may be held liable for subsequent injury to the victim that stems from the wrongful act. For example, if the assault victim lives alone in a rural area without a source of transportation, and if the leg requires amputation because the victim could not get to a hospital, the defendant may be held liable not only for a broken leg but for the medical expenses, pain and suffering, and lost wages associated with the amputation.

MITTIMUS 📖 A court order directing a SHERIFF or other police officer to escort a convict to a PRISON. 📖

A mittimus is a written document. It can command a jailer to safely keep a FELON until he or she can be transferred to a prison. A mittimus also refers to the transcript of the conviction and sentencing stages, which is duly certified by a clerk of court.

MIXED ACTIONS 📖 Lawsuits having two purposes: to recover REAL PROPERTY and to obtain monetary DAMAGES. 📖

Mixed actions take their character from REAL ACTIONS and PERSONAL ACTIONS. Originally the COMMON-LAW COURTS in England concentrated on rights involving the possession of land. The relief granted was an order to give over possession of the real property in dispute. These were the real actions. Only later were FORMS OF ACTION developed to permit a lawsuit for monetary damages in a personal or mixed action. Then the sheriff might be ordered to collect a fine and later damages, out of the loser's profits, which were the rents and income from land, and out of any PERSONAL PROPERTY. Special procedures existed for mixed actions that concerned the sort of relief sought in both real and personal actions.

M'NAGHTEN RULE 📖 A test applied to determine whether a person accused of a crime was sane at the time of its commission and, therefore, criminally responsible for the wrongdoing. 📖

The M'Naghten rule is a test for criminal insanity. Under the M'Naghten rule, a criminal defendant is not guilty by reason of insanity if, at the time of the alleged criminal act, the defendant was so deranged that she did not know the nature or quality of her actions or, if she knew the nature and quality of her actions, she was so deranged that she did not know that what she was doing was wrong.

The M'Naghten rule on criminal insanity is named for Daniel M'Naghten, who, in 1843, tried to kill England's prime minister Sir Robert Peel. M'Naghten thought Peel wanted to kill him, so he tried to shoot Peel but instead shot and killed Peel's secretary, Edward Drummond. Medical experts testified that M'Naghten was psychotic, and M'Naghten was found not guilty by reason of insanity.

The public chafed at the VERDICT, and the House of Lords in Parliament ordered the Lords of Justice of the Queen's Bench to fashion a strict definition of criminal insanity. The Lords of Justice complied and declared that insanity was a defense to criminal charges only if

> at the time of the committing of the act, the party accused was labouring under such a defect of reason, from a disease of the mind, as not to know the nature and quality of the act he was doing; or, if he did know it, that he did not know he was doing what was wrong. (*Queen v. M'Naghten*, 8 Eng. Rep. 718 [1843])

The aim of the M'Naghten rule was to limit the insanity defense to cognitive insanity, a basic inability to distinguish right from wrong. Other tests formulated by legislatures and courts since *M'Naghten* have supplemented the M'Naghten rule with another form of insanity called volitional insanity. Volitional insanity is experienced by mentally healthy persons who, although they know what they are doing is wrong, are so mentally unbalanced at the time of the criminal act that they are unable to conform their actions to the law.

The M'Naghten rule was adopted in most jurisdictions in the United States, but legislatures and courts eventually modified and expanded the definition. The definition of criminal insanity now varies from JURISDICTION to jurisdiction, but most of them have been influenced by the M'Naghten rule.

Many jurisdictions reject volitional insanity but retain cognitive insanity with a minor variation on the M'Naghten definition. Under the M'Naghten rule, a person was legally insane if she was so deranged that she did not know what she was doing. Under many current statutes, a person is legally insane if she is so deranged that she lacks substantial CAPACITY to appreciate the criminality of her conduct.

The difference between the two definitions is largely theoretical. In theory, the latter definition is more lenient because it requires only that a person lack substantial capacity to appreciate her conduct.

See also DURHAM RULE; INSANITY DEFENSE.

MODEL ACTS 📖 Statutes drafted by the National Conference of Commissioners on Uniform State Laws in cooperation with the American Law Institute. State legislatures may adopt model acts in whole or in part, or they may modify them to fit their needs. Model acts differ from uniform acts, which are adopted by the states in virtually the same form proposed by the conference and the American Law Institute. 📖

The National Conference of Commissioners on Uniform State Laws first met in 1892 in response to a perceived need for uniformity and certainty in laws among the states. Since then, the commissioners have met annually to draft model statutes that deal with a variety of topics, from ADOPTION to PARTNERSHIPS. Model acts are often proposed in controversial or complex areas of law to serve as a means of effecting a measure of agreement and uniformity of result.

The Model Business Corporation Act (MBCA) is an example of a model act that was implemented successfully. The MBCA was first adopted in 1950 and revised substantially in 1969, 1971, and 1983. It addresses all aspects of corporate legal structure, from BYLAWS to shareholder rights to FIDUCIARY responsibilities. At least eighteen states have adopted the act in its entirety. Many other states have adopted significant portions of the act. Similarly, most states have substantially adopted the Model Penal Code, first promulgated in 1960, which attempts to impose uniformity in controversial areas such as mental disease or mental defect defenses and the definition of the term *attempt* when used in the description of the commission of a crime.

Other model acts adopted in whole or in part by the states include the Model Probate Code, the Model Class Actions Act, the Model Juvenile Court Act, and the Model Survival and Death Act.

See also COMMISSIONERS ON UNIFORM LAWS; UNIFORM ACTS.

MODEL RULES OF PROFESSIONAL CONDUCT See PROFESSIONAL RESPONSIBILITY.

MODIFICATION 📖 A change or alteration in existing materials. 📖

Modification generally has the same meaning in the law as it does in common parlance. The term has special significance in the law of CONTRACTS and the law of sales.

The parties to a completed and binding contract are free to change the terms of the contract. Changes to a preexisting contract are called *contract modifications*. If the parties agree to modify the contract, the modification will be enforceable in a court of law.

A contract modification may be either written or oral, with some exceptions. An oral modification is unenforceable if the contract specifies that modifications must be in writing (*United States ex rel. Crane Co. v. Progressive Enterprises, Inc.*, 418 F. Supp. 662 [E.D. Va. 1976]). As a general rule, a modification should be in writing if it increases or decreases the value of the contract by $500 or more.

In contracts between parties who are not merchants, a modification should be supported by some CONSIDERATION, which is the exchange of value, or something to solidify an AGREEMENT. Courts impose this requirement to prevent FRAUD and deception in the modification of contracts. Consideration operates as EVIDENCE that the parties have agreed to the modification. Without the requirement of consideration, a party to a contract could declare that the contract should be modified or canceled whenever such a demand was advantageous.

In contracts between merchants, a modification need not be supported by consideration. Derived from article 2, section 209, of the UNIFORM COMMERCIAL CODE, this rule is designed to honor the intent of commercial parties without requiring the time-consuming technicalities of consideration.

Like any non-merchant, a merchant is free to reject a proposed modification, but a merchant may waive the right to reject a modification by failing to object to the modification. For example, if an electrician doing work as a subcontractor notifies the general contractor that the electrical work will be more expensive than anticipated, the general contractor may be obliged to pay for the extra expenses if she fails to object before the electrician begins the work. There must be a legitimate commercial reason for such a contract modification, and the modification must be reasonable in light of the standards within the particular industry. Courts are free to strike down contract modifications that are brought about by DURESS or BAD FAITH.

See also SALES LAW.

MODUS OPERANDI 📖 [*Latin, Method of working.*] A term used by law enforcement authorities to describe the particular manner in which a crime is committed. 📖

The term *modus operandi* is most commonly used in criminal cases. It is sometimes referred to by its initials, M.O. The prosecution in a criminal case does not have to prove modus operandi in any crime. However, identifying and proving the modus operandi of a crime can help the prosecution prove that it was the defendant who committed the crime charged.

Modus operandi evidence is helpful to the prosecution if the prosecution has EVIDENCE of crimes committed by the defendant that are similar to the crime charged. The crimes need not be identical, but the prosecution must make a strong and persuasive showing of similarity between the crime charged and the other crimes. The prosecution may introduce evidence from prior or subsequent crimes to prove modus operandi only if the other crimes share peculiar and distinctive features with the crime charged. The features must be uncommon and rarely seen in other crimes, and they must be so distinct that they can be recognized as the handiwork of the same person.

For example, assume that a defendant is on trial for armed ROBBERY. In the robbery the defendant is alleged to have brandished a pistol and ordered the victim to relinquish cash and valuables. Assume further that the defendant has committed armed robbery in the past by brandishing a pistol and demanding cash and valuables. A PROSECUTOR might be able to introduce the evidence into trial to show the defendant's MOTIVE, INTENT, or state of mind, or to identify the weapon used in the crime. However, the prosecutor could not argue to the judge or jury that the robberies were so similar as to demonstrate that it was the defendant who committed that particular robbery, because it is not unusual for a robber to brandish a pistol and demand cash and valuables in the course of an armed robbery.

Now assume that a defendant is charged with robbing a movie theater that was showing the movie *Showgirls* and that the defendant was wearing a glittering, flamboyant Las Vegas-style cabaret costume during the robbery. Assume further that the prosecution has evidence that the defendant, while dressed as a Las Vegas dancer, has robbed other movie theaters showing the movie *Showgirls*. The prosecution could introduce this evidence into trial to prove modus operandi and show that it was the defendant who committed the crime, because the method of armed robbery used in the crimes was both similar and distinctive.

When offering evidence to prove modus

During the 1982 trial of Angelo Buono, California's notorious "Hillside Strangler," the prosecution relied on modus operandi evidence to show similarities in the deaths of ten victims.

operandi, the prosecution does not have to prove BEYOND A REASONABLE DOUBT that the other crimes occurred. Rather, the prosecution simply must present sufficient evidence to show that the act took place and was committed by the defendant.

See also CRIMINAL LAW; CRIMINAL PROCEDURE.

MOIETY 🕮 One-half. 🕮

Joint tenants own their ESTATE by the moiety. See also JOINT TENANCY.

MONEY LAUNDERING 🕮 The process of taking the proceeds of criminal activity and making them appear legal. 🕮

Laundering allows criminals to transform illegally obtained money into seemingly legitimate funds. Money laundering is a worldwide problem, with approximately $300 billion going through the process annually in the United States. The sale of illegal narcotics accounts for much of this money. Those who commit the underlying criminal activity may attempt to launder the money themselves, but increasingly a new class of criminals provides laundering services to organized crime. This new class consists of lawyers, bankers, and accountants.

Criminals want their illegal funds laundered because they can then move their money through society freely, without fear that the funds will be traced to their criminal deeds. In addition, laundering prevents the funds from being confiscated by the police.

Money laundering usually consists of three steps: placement, layering, and integration. Placement is depositing funds in financial institutions or converting cash into NEGOTIABLE INSTRUMENTS. Placement is the most difficult step. The easiest way to begin laundering large amounts of cash is to deposit them into a financial institution. However, under the federal Bank Secrecy Act of 1970 (BSA) (31 U.S.C.A. § 5311 et seq.), financial institutions are required to report deposits of more than $10,000 in cash made by an individual in a single day. To disguise criminal activity, launderers route cash through a "front" operation, that is, a business such as a check cashing service or a jewelry store. Another option is to convert the cash into negotiable instruments, such as cashier's checks, money orders, or traveler's checks.

Layering involves the wire transfer of funds through a series of accounts in an attempt to hide the funds' true origins. This often means transferring funds to countries outside the United States that have strict bank secrecy laws. Such countries include the Cayman Islands, the Bahamas, and Panama. Once deposited in a foreign bank, the funds can be moved through accounts of "shell" corporations, which exist solely for laundering purposes. The high daily volume of wire transfers makes it difficult for law enforcement agencies to trace these transactions.

Integration involves the movement of layered funds, which are no longer traceable to their criminal origin, into the financial world, where they are mixed with funds of legitimate origin.

Many banks did not comply with the BSA during the 1970s and early 1980s. Following several federal investigations where it was revealed that banks had failed to report billions of dollars of cash transactions, reporting requirements were strengthened. Also, Congress enacted the Money Laundering Control Act of 1986 (MLCA) (18 U.S.C.A. § 1956 et seq.). This act criminalizes money laundering itself. It centers its attention on the criminals and conspirators who seek to launder the proceeds of illegal activity, including merchants, bankers, and members of the professions who assist criminals with money laundering. Another provision of the MLCA authorizes the government to confiscate all property traceable to violations of laws against money laundering.

See also BANKS AND BANKING.

MONEY PAID 🕮 The technical name given a declaration in ASSUMPSIT in which the plaintiff declares that the defendant had and received certain money. A COMMON-LAW PLEADING, stating that the defendant received money that, in EQUITY and good conscience, should be paid to the plaintiff. 🕮

MONOPOLY 🕮 An economic advantage held by one or more persons or companies deriving from the exclusive power to carry on a particular business or trade or to manufacture and sell a particular item, thereby suppressing competition and allowing such persons or companies to raise the price of a product or service substantially above the price that would be established by a free market. 🕮

In a monopoly one or more persons or companies totally dominates an economic market. Monopolies may exist in a particular industry if a company controls a major natural resource, produces (even at a reasonable price) all the output of a product or service because of technological superiority (called a natural monopoly), holds a PATENT on a product or process of production, or is granted government permission to be the sole producer of a product or service in a given area.

U.S. law generally views monopolies as harmful because they obstruct the channels of free competition that determine the price and quality of products and services offered to the public. The owners of a monopoly have the power, as a group, to set prices, exclude competitors, and control the market in the relevant geographic area. U.S. antitrust laws prohibit monopolies and any other practices that unduly restrain competitive trade. These laws are based on the belief that equality of opportunity in the marketplace and the free interactions of competitive forces result in the best allocation of the economic resources of the nation. Moreover, it is assumed that competition enhances material progress in production and technology while preserving democratic, political, and social institutions.

History Economic monopolies have existed throughout much of human history. In England a monopoly originally was an exclusive right expressly granted by the king or Parliament to one person or class of persons to provide some service or goods. The holders of such rights, usually the English guilds or inventors, dominated the market. By the early 1600s, the English courts began voiding monopolies because they interfered with freedom of trade. In 1623 Parliament enacted the Statute of Monopolies, which prohibited all but specifically excepted monopolies. With the industrial revolution of the early 1800s, economic production and markets exploded. The growth of capitalism and its emphasis on the free play of competition reinforced the idea that monopolies were unlawful.

In the United States during most of the 1800s, monopolies were prosecuted under common law and by statute as market-interference offenses in an attempt to stop dealers from raising prices through techniques such as buying up all available supplies of a material, or cornering the market. Courts also refused to enforce CONTRACTS with harsh provisions that were clearly unreasonable restraints on trade. These measures were largely ineffective.

Government Regulation Congress intervened after abuses became widespread. In 1887 Congress, pursuant to its constitutional power to regulate interstate commerce, passed the INTERSTATE COMMERCE ACT (49 U.S.C.A. § 1 et seq.) in response to the monopolistic practices of RAILROAD companies. Although competition among railroad companies for long-haul routes was great, it was minimal for short-haul runs. Railroad companies discriminated in the prices they charged to passengers and shippers in different localities by providing REBATES to large shippers or buyers to retain their long-haul business. These practices were especially harmful to farmers because they lacked the volume of traffic necessary to obtain more favorable rates. Although states attempted to regulate the railroads, they were powerless to act where interstate commerce was involved. The Interstate Commerce Act was intended to regulate shipping rates. It mandated that charges be fair and made it illegal to discriminate unreasonably among customers through the use of rebates or other preferential devices.

Congress soon moved ahead on another front, enacting the SHERMAN ANTI-TRUST ACT of 1890 (15 U.S.C.A. § 31 et seq.). A trust was an arrangement by which stockholders in several companies transferred their shares to a set of trustees in exchange for a CERTIFICATE entitling them to a specified share of the consolidated earnings of the jointly managed companies. The trusts came to dominate a number of major industries, destroying their competitors. The Sherman Act prohibited such trusts and their anticompetitive practices. From the 1890s through 1920, the federal government used the act to break up these trusts.

The Sherman Act provides for criminal prosecution by the federal government against corporations and individuals who restrain trade, but criminal sanctions are rarely sought. The act also provides for civil remedies for private persons who start an ACTION under it for injuries caused by monopolistic acts. The award of TREBLE DAMAGES (the tripling of the amount of DAMAGES awarded) is authorized under the act to promote the interest of private persons in safeguarding a free and competitive society and to deter violators and others from future illegal acts.

The Clayton Anti-Trust Act of 1914 (15 U.S.C.A. § 12 et seq.) was passed as an amendment to the Sherman Act. The CLAYTON ACT specifically defined which monopolistic acts were illegal but not criminal. The act proscribed price discrimination, the sale of the same product at different prices to similarly situated buyers, exclusive dealing contracts, sales on condition that the buyer stop dealing with the seller's competitors, corporate mergers, and INTERLOCKING DIRECTORATES (the same people serving on the BOARDS OF DIRECTORS of competing companies). Such practices were illegal only if, as a result, they materially reduced competition or tended to create a monopoly in trade.

The Federal Trade Commission Act of 1914 (15 U.S.C.A. § 41 et seq.) established the Federal Trade Commission, the regulatory body that promotes free and fair competitive trade in interstate commerce through the prohibition of

PRICE-FIXING arrangements, FALSE ADVERTISING, BOYCOTTS, illegal combinations of competitors, and other methods of UNFAIR COMPETITION.

Congress passed the ROBINSON-PATMAN ACT of 1936 (15 U.S.C.A. § 13 et seq.) to amend the Clayton Act. The act makes it unlawful for any seller engaged in commerce to directly or indirectly discriminate in the sale price charged on commodities of comparable grade and quality where the effect might injure, destroy, or prevent competition unless the seller discriminated in order to dispose of perishable or obsolete goods or to meet the equally low price of a competitor.

Exemptions Despite these legal prohibitions, not all industries and activities are subject to them. LABOR UNIONS monopolize the labor force and take concerted action to improve the wages, hours, and working conditions of their members. The Clayton Act and the NORRIS-LAGUARDIA ACT of 1932 (29 U.S.C.A. § 101 et seq.) recognized that unions would be powerless without this monopolistic behavior and therefore made unions immune from antitrust laws.

A government-awarded monopoly, such as the right to provide ELECTRICITY or natural gas to a region of the country, is exempt from antitrust laws. Government agencies regulate these industries and set reasonable rates that the company may charge.

Sometimes an industry is a natural monopoly. This type of monopoly is created as a result of circumstances over which the monopolist has no power. A natural monopoly may exist where a market for a particular product or service is so limited that its profitable production is impossible except when done by a single plant large enough to supply the whole demand. Natural monopolies are beyond the reach of antitrust laws.

Special interest industries, such as agricultural and fishery marketing associations, banking and insurance industries, and export trade associations, are also immune from antitrust laws. Major league BASEBALL has also been exempted from antitrust laws.

CROSS-REFERENCES

Antitrust Law; Combination in Restraint of Trade; Interstate Commerce Commission; Mergers and Acquisitions; Public Utilities; Restraint of Trade.

BIOGRAPHY

James Monroe

"LET US BY ALL WISE AND CONSTITUTIONAL MEASURES PROMOTE INTELLIGENCE AMONG THE PEOPLE AS THE BEST MEANS OF PRESERVING OUR LIBERTIES."

MONROE, JAMES James Monroe was the fifth president of the United States and a distinguished diplomat. His administration was marked by several foreign-policy accomplishments, including the MONROE DOCTRINE, and a period of domestic tranquility that has been called the Era of Good Feelings.

Monroe was born in Westmoreland County, Virginia, on April 28, 1758. He attended the College of William and Mary at the age of sixteen but left in 1776 to fight in the Revolutionary War. He was wounded at the Battle of Trenton but served until the end of the war.

During this period he became acquainted with THOMAS JEFFERSON, then governor of Virginia. Monroe soon adopted Jefferson as his teacher and mentor, a relationship that would endure throughout Monroe's life. In 1780 Monroe began studying law with Jefferson, and in 1786 he established a law practice in Fredericksburg, Virginia. Politics, however, proved a more powerful attraction than a legal career.

Monroe became a member of the Virginia House of Delegates in 1782, and from 1781 to 1786 he participated in the CONTINENTAL CONGRESS. Monroe, like Jefferson, did not favor a highly centralized federal government. He preferred a government system under the ARTICLES OF CONFEDERATION, which allocated greater powers to the states, as opposed to the Constitution, which gave the federal government more authority. He did believe in the development of the West and worked with Jefferson to enact laws to further this purpose.

In 1786 he retired from Congress. In 1788 Monroe participated in the Virginia convention that ratified the new federal Constitution. He was elected to the U.S. Senate in 1790 and served until 1794. After the expiration of his senatorial term, Monroe served as minister to France. President GEORGE WASHINGTON appointed Monroe to this position despite Mon-

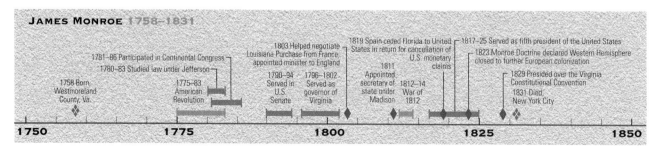

JAMES MONROE 1758–1831

1758 Born, Westmoreland County, Va.

1775–83 American Revolution

1780–83 Studied law under Jefferson

1781–86 Participated in Continental Congress

1790–94 Served in U.S. Senate

1796–1802 Served as governor of Virginia

1803 Helped negotiate Louisiana Purchase from France; appointed minister to England

1811 Appointed secretary of state under Madison

1812–14 War of 1812

1819 Spain ceded Florida to United States in return for cancellation of U.S. monetary claims

1817–25 Served as fifth president of the United States

1823 Monroe Doctrine declared Western Hemisphere closed to further European colonization

1829 Presided over the Virginia Constitutional Convention

1831 Died, New York City

1750   1775   1800   1825   1850

roe's opposition to the Washington administration's policies. When Monroe did not follow his diplomatic instructions and made intemperate remarks about policies with which he disagreed, Washington recalled him in 1796.

Monroe quickly reentered Virginia politics. He was elected governor in 1799 and served a three-year term. In 1802 President Jefferson sent Monroe back to France as a special envoy. He and Robert R. Livingston negotiated the Louisiana Purchase from France in 1803. Following this success, Jefferson named Monroe minister to England, where he served until 1806.

Again Virginia politics beckoned. Monroe served briefly as governor but left in 1811 to join the cabinet of President James Madison. He was secretary of state from 1811 to 1817 and secretary of war, during the War of 1812, from 1814 to 1815. The successful conclusion of the war and the military triumphs of General Andrew Jackson helped boost Monroe's popularity.

In 1816 he was elected president of the United States as a member of the Democratic-Republican party. The Federalist party disappeared after the election, and most politicians belonged to the Democratic-Republican party. With an end to the political feuding of the early years of the Republic, Monroe was able to promote what has been called the Era of Good Feelings. His popularity was so great that he was unopposed for reelection in 1820.

Monroe's presidency produced important domestic legislation, including the Missouri Compromise of 1820, which limited the extension of slavery into new territories. His main efforts, however, were directed at foreign affairs. The Rush-Bagot Treaty, drafted in 1817, restricted the increase of armaments in the Great Lakes area. In 1818 Great Britain agreed to the forty-ninth parallel as the boundary between the United States and Canada from Lake of the Woods on the Minnesota-Ontario border as far west as the Rocky Mountains. In 1819 U.S. diplomats convinced Spain to cede Florida to the United States in return for the cancellation of $5 million in U.S. claims against Spain.

In 1823 Monroe presented the most significant measure of his administration, the Monroe Doctrine. During the Napoleonic Wars, Spain had lost interest in its American colonies. Most of the colonies declared their independence, but the United States was concerned that Spain might try to reassert control. The Monroe Doctrine declared that the Western Hemi-

sphere was closed to further European colonization and that any European intervention would be regarded as a threat to the security of the United States. Conversely, the United States agreed not to intervene in European matters. The Monroe Doctrine would be invoked several times by future presidential administrations.

After leaving the presidency in 1824, Monroe retired to Oak Hill, his estate in Virginia that was near Jefferson's Monticello. He served as a regent of the University of Virginia and in 1829 presided over the Virginia Constitutional Convention.

Monroe's last years were difficult. He left public service a poor man and was too old to rebuild his law practice. He was forced to sell his home and move to New York City to live with his daughter. He died there on July 4, 1831.

MONROE DOCTRINE
The Founding Fathers of the United States of America sought to establish a foreign policy that was compatible with the surge of nationalism that engulfed the new country during its first century of independence. The Monroe Doctrine, proposed by President James Monroe in 1823, contributed to the formation of such a policy.

Certain events in 1821 prompted the creation of the doctrine. An insurrection in the colonies under Spanish rule in Latin America resulted in freedom for the colonies, but several European nations threatened to intervene on Spain's behalf and restore the former colonies to Spanish domination. Both the United States and Great Britain saw the advantages of trade with the new Latin American nations and feared further European interference in future disputes. As a result, British Foreign Secretary George Canning approached the U.S. emissary

Is it the folly or the efficacy of the Monroe Doctrine depicted in this 1896 F. Victor Gillam cartoon?

THE GRANGER COLLECTION, NEW YORK

KEEP OFF!
The Monroe Doctrine must be respected.

in London, Richard Rush, with a proposal for the formation of a dual alliance to protect the interests of the two countries. According to Canning's plan, the United States and Great Britain would oppose any intervention in the Spanish colonies by any European country except Spain.

President Monroe was agreeable to the terms of Canning's proposition, as were Secretary of War JOHN C. CALHOUN and former Presidents THOMAS JEFFERSON and JAMES MADISON. Secretary of State JOHN QUINCY ADAMS, however, presented an alternative view. Adams believed that Britain's interests in Latin America were sufficiently strong to encourage Britain's defense of those nations whether or not the United States agreed to Canning's proposal. Adams favored the development of a U.S. policy without alliance with Britain.

On December 2, 1823, Monroe presented the terms of the Monroe Doctrine, which Adams had helped to develop. The doctrine contained four significant elements: the American continents were to be regarded as independent, with no further settlement by European nations; the nations of the Western Hemisphere were deemed republics, as opposed to the European system of monarchies; European intervention in the affairs of nations of the Western Hemisphere was prohibited and would be viewed as a threat to the security of the United States; and, conversely the United States promised to refrain from involvement in European affairs.

MONTESQUIEU, CHARLES-LOUIS de SECONDAT, BARON de la BRÈDE et de

Charles-Louis de Secondat, Baron de la Brède et de Montesquieu was a French social and political philosopher whose ideas about laws and government had great influence on the leaders of the American Revolution and the Framers of the U.S. Constitution.

Montesquieu was born January 18, 1689, in La Brède, France, just outside of Bordeaux, to an aristocratic family with considerable land-holdings. As a young man, he studied Latin, French, history, and the law before graduating from the University of Bordeaux in 1708. In 1715 he married Jeanne Lartigue, whose family

BIOGRAPHY

CULVER PICTURES

Charles-Louis de Secondat, Baron de la Brède et de Montesquieu

brought him substantial wealth, and a year later his uncle died and left him his title and his property, making Montesquieu extremely rich. While his wife remained in La Brède managing his estate, Montesquieu traveled and enjoyed the social and intellectual life of Paris, attending fashionable salons and meeting with leading thinkers in the areas of politics and literature. He also served as *president á mortier*, or justice, of the Bordeaux *parlement*, an office he inherited from his uncle.

In 1728 Montesquieu left Paris for a three-year trip through Europe. Montesquieu closely examined the people and cultures of the countries he visited, paying particular attention to England, where he was intrigued by the level of political and religious freedom the people there enjoyed, as well as the country's bustling mercantile economy. He remained in England for eighteen months. During this time he was introduced into the most prestigious intellectual and social circles, was admitted to court, was made a fellow of the Royal Society, and attended several sessions of Parliament. Montesquieu's experience in England was critical in shaping his political philosophies because it proved to him that a society could combine the rule of law with political freedom.

After returning home in May 1731, Montesquieu spent the next fifteen years working on his masterpiece, *De l'Esprit des lois* (literally *On the Spirit of the Laws*, but usually translated as *The Spirit of the Laws*). In this immense and loosely connected work, containing more than six hundred chapters grouped into thirty-one books, Montesquieu combined a lifetime of thoughts and personal observations concerning governments, laws, and human nature. His topics ranged from detailed analyses of ancient history to the effects of climate on national character. By closely examining a wide variety of societies through time and across cultures, Montesquieu sought to identify the basic principles underlying how laws work, how they evolve, and how they differ from country to country and culture to culture.

The Spirit of the Laws was published in 1748 in Geneva. It was a huge and immediate success; by the end of 1749, twenty-two other

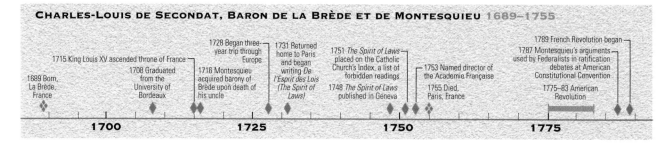

CHARLES-LOUIS DE SECONDAT, BARON DE LA BRÈDE ET DE MONTESQUIEU 1689–1755

1689 Born, La Brède, France

1715 King Louis XV ascended throne of France

1708 Graduated from the University of Bordeaux

1716 Montesquieu acquired barony of Brède upon death of his uncle

1728 Began three-year trip through Europe

1731 Returned home to Paris and began writing *De l'Esprit des Lois (The Spirit of Laws)*

1751 *The Spirit of Laws* placed on the Catholic Church's Index, a list of forbidden readings

1748 *The Spirit of Laws* published in Geneva

1753 Named director of the Académie Française

1755 Died, Paris, France

1789 French Revolution began

1787 Montesquieu's arguments used by Federalists in ratification debates at American Constitutional Convention

1775–83 American Revolution

1700   1725   1750   1775

editions, including many translations, had reached all over Europe and across the ocean to the North American colonies. The work also generated considerable controversy, particularly with church authorities. They objected to Montesquieu's intellectual approach, which was grounded in the then radical notion that laws were not divinely inspired or handed down by ancient lawgivers such as Moses but evolved naturally out of everything that influences life in a country, including traditions, habits, history, religion, economics, and climate. Laws, Montesquieu believed, could be rationally studied and then adjusted to increase liberty for all. He responded to criticisms of his work in 1750 with *Defense de l'Esprit des lois*, but the Catholic Church nevertheless put *The Spirit of the Laws* on the church's Index in 1751, which meant that Catholics were forbidden to read it. Despite this official censure, Montesquieu was named director of the Academie Française in 1753.

On January 29, 1755, Montesquieu became ill with what appears to have been influenza, and his health quickly deteriorated. His sickness generated much attention; many people viewed it as symbolic of the great conflict between established religion and the forces of reason and enlightenment that marked the eighteenth century. During his illness Montesquieu's house was filled with friends monitoring his condition, including messengers from the king. Montesquieu died on February 10, 1755, and was buried in the parish church of Saint-Sulpice.

As was the case in Europe, Montesquieu was a leading intellectual figure in the American colonies, and *The Spirit of the Laws* was a standard subject of close study for young American scholars. Figures show that Montesquieu's works, particularly *The Spirit of the Laws*, were widely disseminated through American booksellers and libraries, and Montesquieu's ideas were frequently discussed in newspapers and journals. Montesquieu's works were found in the personal libraries of nearly all of the country's founding fathers, including BENJAMIN FRANKLIN, JOHN ADAMS, THOMAS JEFFERSON, and JAMES MADISON.

Different elements of the theories Montesquieu outlined in *The Spirit of the Laws* were popular in America at different times, varying with political conditions and developments. In general, however, the most influential portions of the work were chapters 3 and 6 of book XI, in which Montesquieu analyzed the English constitution, a discussion that heavily influenced the separation of powers later enshrined in the U.S. Constitution. In his analysis Montesquieu outlined the basic principle of the

English constitution, which was—and still is—not an actual document but an unwritten consensus regarding the proper rules of governing based on such historical documents as the MAGNA CHARTA, the body of COMMON LAW, court decisions, PRECEDENTS, and tradition.

According to Montesquieu, although England did not have the perfect system of government, it was the best system to be found in modern Europe because it allowed for the greatest degree of LIBERTY, which Montesquieu defined as the right "to do what one should want to do, and not being forced to do what one should not want to do." For Montesquieu, liberty was, essentially, the right to be left alone.

This type of liberty, Montesquieu argued, was only possible under a government specifically constituted to protect citizens from the oppression of their rulers and the aggressions of each other, while allowing for the representation of a wide range of popular interests. For citizens to maintain their liberty against the encroachment of oppressive rulers, a government had to be composed of separate and balanced powers that would check and moderate each other, thus leaving the people a maximum degree of freedom under the laws.

To Montesquieu, England most closely approximated this model because its government divided the three main functions of government—the legislative, the executive, and the judicial—into three separate branches: the Parliament, the monarch, and the courts. The powers of these branches were so intertwined that the branches needed each other to operate and also served to moderate each other's actions. For example, the king or queen could VETO parliamentary legislation, but the monarch's actions were limited by Parliament's power of the purse. Because no single branch was able to dominate the other branches or the populace at large, the people were left with a large degree of political freedom. Because the branches had to operate together, their forces counterbalanced each other and resulted in a guarantee of freedom and a bulwark against political tyranny. Although Montesquieu did not present the English system as the perfect model for democratic government, he did praise it for being the only government in modern Europe constituted for the specific purpose of maximizing political liberty.

Montesquieu's description of the basic principles of the English constitution and his emphasis on political liberty held great appeal for the English colonists in North America, particularly beginning in the 1760s when those colonists were chafing under taxes and restrictions imposed by Parliament that they thought

"USELESS LAWS

WEAKEN THE

NECESSARY LAWS."

undermined their constitutional rights. Montesquieu was frequently quoted in newspapers, pamphlets, and speeches as colonists protested the oppressive powers of Parliament and defended their right to political liberty. His description of the English constitution became a model against which the colonists contrasted what they saw as the injustice and corruption of the actual English government.

After the Revolutionary War ended, Montesquieu again became a principal authority as political leaders set about to create a constitution for the new United States of America. Most of the architects of the Constitution were thoroughly acquainted with Montesquieu's ideas, and at the Constitutional Convention of 1787, *The Spirit of the Laws* was frequently cited as delegates attempted to lay down the principles for a government that would maximize political liberty while also maintaining the rule of law. The Framers followed many of Montesquieu's maxims, including his insistence upon a SEPARATION OF POWERS and his belief that a country's laws must not be imposed from above but conform to the genius, or nature, of the citizens of that country.

Montesquieu's arguments were also used in the debates over the ratification of the Constitution that followed the Constitutional Convention. He was cited with particular frequency in *The Federalist Papers*, which were written by James Madison, ALEXANDER HAMILTON, and JOHN JAY to argue in favor of the new Constitution. The writers cited Montesquieu at length in defense of the wisdom of confederating the states into a single REPUBLIC and of creating a government based upon a separation of powers. Although other scholars had also written on the separation of powers principle, Montesquieu was most closely associated with it, as James Madison noted in *The Federalist*, no. 47: "The oracle who is always consulted and cited on this subject, is the celebrated Montesquieu. If he be not the author of this invaluable precept in the science of politics, he has the merit at least of displaying and recommending it most effectually to the attention of mankind." Montesquieu's arguments were also frequently used in

the debates over the Constitution at the individual state conventions. Both proponents and opponents of the new Constitution respected him as a political authority, and both used his writings to bolster their arguments.

After the ratification of the Constitution in 1789, Montesquieu continued to remain an authority on the creation of laws and the rule of government. *The Spirit of the Laws* continued to be taught at colleges and universities, and leaders of both political parties, the Republicans and the Federalists, used his arguments to advance their own. Montesquieu's only significant detractor was Thomas Jefferson, who believed, along with friends involved in the impending revolution in France, that Montesquieu was too enamored with England and its constitution. After the French Revolution and the radical changes it wrought, Montesquieu's writings came to seem dated and less relevant, and they gradually faded from the political debates. Even so, his work continues to exert a lasting influence on the laws of the United States through the Constitution that was so significantly shaped by his ideas.

See also CONSTITUTION OF THE UNITED STATES; FEDERALIST PAPERS.

MONUMENT 📖 Anything by which the memory of a person, thing, idea, art, science or event is preserved or perpetuated. A tomb where a dead body has been deposited.

In REAL-PROPERTY law and surveying, visible marks or indications left on natural or other objects indicating the lines and BOUNDARIES of a survey. Any physical object on the ground that helps to establish the location of a boundary line called for; it may be either natural (e.g., trees, rivers, and other land features) or artificial (e.g., fences, stones, stakes, or the like placed by human hands). 📖

MOODY, WILLIAM HENRY William Henry Moody, Supreme Court appointee of THEODORE ROOSEVELT, served the Court from 1906 to 1910. The Massachusetts Republican, representative, and two-time cabinet member supported the progressive policies of his era. He was especially respected by his colleagues for his skill in the area of ANTITRUST LAW. Moody's

BIOGRAPHY

William Henry Moody

ARTIST C. GREGORY STAPKO. COLLECTION OF THE SUPREME COURT OF THE UNITED STATES

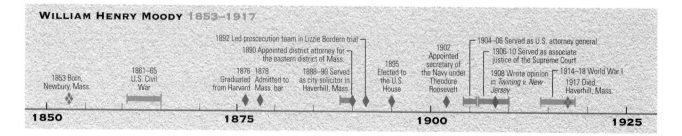

WILLIAM HENRY MOODY 1853–1917

1853 Born, Newbury, Mass.

1861–65 U.S. Civil War

1876 Graduated from Harvard

1878 Admitted to Mass. bar

1888–90 Served as city solicitor in Haverhill, Mass.

1890 Appointed district attorney for the eastern district of Mass.

1892 Led prosecution team in Lizzie Bordern trial

1895 Elected to the U.S. House

1902 Appointed secretary of the Navy under Theodore Roosevelt

1904–06 Served as U.S. attorney general

1906–10 Served as associate justice of the Supreme Court

1908 Wrote opinion in *Twining v. New Jersey*

1914–18 World War I

1917 Died, Haverhill, Mass.

1850   1875   1900   1925

service on the Court was ended prematurely due to health problems.

Moody was born on December 23, 1853, in Newbury, Massachusetts from a long line of New England, Puritan ancestry. He was educated at Phillips Academy and found his first real success in life as an athlete on the Harvard baseball team. He graduated from Harvard in 1876 with honors in history, ranking third in his class. After Harvard, he worked in the law office of Richard Dana. He was admitted to the bar in 1878.

Moody established a private practice in Haverhill, Massachusetts, and served as the city solicitor for two years (1888–1890). In 1890 he was appointed district attorney for the eastern district of Massachusetts. He was one of the state's two prosecutors in the trial of LIZZIE BORDEN, who was charged with murdering her father and stepmother with an ax in 1892. Although Borden was acquitted, Moody won respect for his performance in the trial.

Shortly after the Borden case, the Republicans nominated Moody to a seat in Congress. He was elected to the House of Representatives in November 1895 and became one of its most influential members. On April 30, 1902, he resigned from the House to become Theodore Roosevelt's secretary of the Navy.

Two years later he was appointed attorney general. He successfully argued the landmark antitrust case of *Swift and Company v. United States*, 196 U.S. 375, 25 S. Ct. 276, 49 L. Ed. 518 (1905), before the Supreme Court. The government had obtained an INJUNCTION against the trust by arguing that a combination of CORPORATIONS and individuals, after purchasing livestock and converting it to fresh meat, sold products in interstate commerce in such a manner as to suppress competition both in livestock and fresh meats. The trust appealed the injunction. Moody won a perpetual injunction, but the trust ignored it. Moody was infuriated and instigated a GRAND JURY investigation in Chicago, which led to INDICTMENT of all the major packers. Through Moody's success in prosecuting Swift and Company, the Supreme Court first formulated the "stream of commerce" doc-

trine, which held corporations responsible for all of their interstate commercial activities.

After the resignation of Associate Justice HENRY B. BROWN, Roosevelt appointed Moody to the Supreme Court in 1906. Moody's most important opinion with the Court was probably that in *Twining v. New Jersey*, 211 U.S. 78, 29 S. Ct. 14, 53 L. Ed. 97 (1908), which held that the FOURTEENTH AMENDMENT's Due Process Clause did not incorporate the FIFTH AMENDMENT right against SELF-INCRIMINATION and apply it to the states. *Twining* was overruled in 1964 by *Malloy v. Hogan*, 378 U.S. 1, 84 S. Ct. 1489, 12 L. Ed. 2d 653.

Moody continued to serve the Court until 1910, at which time acute rheumatism forced his retirement. He died July 2, 1917, in Haverhill, Massachusetts.

MOORE, ALFRED   As an associate justice, Alfred Moore served on the U.S. Supreme Court for five years. The ardent federalist, whose life and political career involved danger, controversy, and principled stands, left little mark on the Court's business during his service from 1799 to 1804. Although he fought in the Revolutionary War and later held high office in North Carolina, Moore's fire had mostly left him by the time President JOHN ADAMS appointed him to the Supreme Court. Even at a time when the Court decided major cases, he either acquiesced to the majority or did not participate in certain decisions because of poor health. He wrote just one opinion, *Bas v. Tingy*, 4 U.S. (4 Dall.) 37, 1 L. Ed 731 (1800), important only in its historical relevance to the United States' undeclared naval war with France in the last years of the eighteenth century.

Moore was a youth during the country's difficult transition from British colony to independent nation. Born on May 21, 1755, in New Hanover County, North Carolina, he was the son of Maurice Moore, a colonial judge. Moore studied in Boston before being educated in law by his father, and he was admitted to the North Carolina bar at the age of twenty in 1775. Soon after, he fought against the British, first as a soldier and then as a saboteur. During the war,

BIOGRAPHY

Alfred Moore

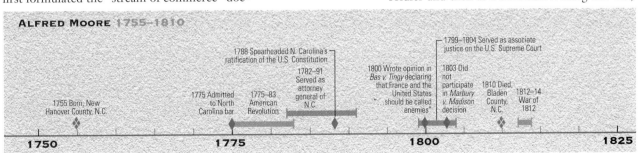

ALFRED MOORE 1755–1810

1755 Born, New Hanover County, N.C.
1775 Admitted to North Carolina bar
1775–83 American Revolution
1782–91 Served as attorney general of N.C.
1788 Spearheaded N. Carolina's ratification of the U.S. Constitution
1800 Wrote opinion in *Bas v. Tingy* declaring that France and the United States "should be called enemies"
1799–1804 Served as associate justice on the U.S. Supreme Court
1803 Did not participate in *Marbury v. Madison* decision
1810 Died, Bladen County, N.C.
1812–14 War of 1812

1750   1775   1800   1825

Moore's brother, father, and uncle were killed, the family plantation was ransacked, and their home was destroyed.

Moore was a member of the North Carolina legislature in 1782 and 1792. From 1782 to 1791, he served as the state's attorney general, arguing one particularly important case, *Bayard v. Singleton*, 1 N.C. (Mart.) 5 (1787), which marked one of the first complete discussions of the doctrine of JUDICIAL REVIEW (the authority of courts to determine the validity of legislation under the Constitution). A federalist who firmly believed in central government, he spearheaded North Carolina's ratification of the U.S. Constitution in 1788. In 1791 Moore took the strongest personal stand of his career when he resigned from the office of attorney general; he stepped down over the state legislature's creation of the office of solicitor general with powers equivalent to his, an action he saw as unconstitutional. He won reelection to the legislature but failed in a 1795 bid for the U.S. Senate by one vote.

In 1799 President John Adams nominated Moore to fill a vacancy on the U.S. Supreme Court created by the death of Associate Justice JAMES IREDELL. The next five years were pivotal ones for the Supreme Court, which expanded its powers of judicial review under the highly influential Chief Justice JOHN MARSHALL. However, failing health minimized Moore's role. He did not participate in the most important decision of his day, *Marbury v. Madison*, 5 U.S. (1 Cranch) 137, 2 L. Ed. 60 (1803).

Moore's only recorded Supreme Court opinion is a five-paragraph statement on the undeclared naval war between France and the United States. This war reached its height in 1798 and 1799 and was fought chiefly over French claims to seize all cargo of British origin from both British and U.S. ships. Although Congress passed many acts in relation to the conflict, problems arose over the ownership of goods that were recaptured, and in one instance the issue was resolved by determining whether France and the United States were enemy nations. When *Bas v. Tingy* reached the Supreme Court in 1800, each of the four justices hearing the case agreed that the two nations were indeed foes. Moore's opinion declared, "It is for the honor and dignity of both nations . . . that they should be called enemies."

In 1804 Moore resigned from the Court. He died on October 15, 1810, in Bladen County, North Carolina, leaving as part of his legacy the establishment of the University of North Carolina.

"IF WORDS ARE BUT THE REPRESENTATIVE OF IDEAS, . . . BY WHAT OTHER WORD [CAN] THE IDEA OF THE RELATIVE SITUATION OF AMERICA AND FRANCE BE COMMUNICATED, THAN BY THAT OF HOSTILITY OR WAR?"

MOOT 📖 An ISSUE presenting no real controversy. 📖

Moot refers to a subject for academic argument. It is an abstract question that does not arise from existing facts or rights.

Moot court is a cocurricular or extracurricular activity in law school where students have the opportunity to write BRIEFS and present oral arguments on hypothetical cases.

MOOT COURT 📖 A method of teaching law and legal skills that requires students to analyze and argue both sides of a hypothetical legal issue using procedures modeled after those employed in state and federal APPELLATE COURTS. 📖

In the mid-1700s moot courts in the United States had a tradition of debate and oratory revered in undergraduate institutions such as Yale College. Moot court exercises have changed in the United States since that time. Law instructors present hypothetical cases and students argue them before professors or other lawyers, who serve as judges. Hypothetical cases often address matters of current political and constitutional import.

Moot court requirements vary from law school to law school, with most schools mandating that students participate at least once in a moot court argument before receiving their law degree. Many law schools offer a series of moot court opportunities for students of differing skill levels and legal interests. The activity is competitive by nature, and students vie for honors within their school and in regional and national moot court competitions featuring teams of students from several law schools.

Moot court helps students learn to analyze legal issues; its larger purpose is to teach students the practical side of practicing law. Typically, law students are given a detailed hypothetical fact scenario that raises one or more legal issues. Often these fact patterns are based on real cases on APPEAL to a state's highest court or the U.S. Supreme Court. Students choose or are assigned the position on the issue to be argued. They then conduct legal research, finding statutes, regulations, and CASE LAW that both support their position and detract from it. An important part of the moot court process is to teach students to overcome legal authority (statutes, regulations, and cases) that cuts against their position.

Students then draft appellate briefs, which are formal legal papers combining a recital of the facts of the case with analysis and argument of the legal issues raised. As with real appellate courts, moot courts generally dictate many specific requirements for a BRIEF, including the size of the paper, the width of the margins, and the maximum number of pages. CITATIONS to legal authority must also be listed in a uniform style.

Once the briefs are written, students prepare for the second phase of moot court advocacy: oral argument. Oral argument demands preparation, organization, and the ability to think quickly and respond convincingly when questioned. The student appears before a panel of judges (typically law professors, actual judges, or other students) and presents her or his position on the legal issue. Each student has a time limit, normally five to ten minutes, to convince the panel. As with real appellate courts, judges on the panel are free to interrupt the student advocate frequently and at any time to ask questions about the facts of the case, legal authority for or against the student's position, or the student's thoughts and opinions about the case's outcome. Students learn to anticipate difficult questions about their legal position and respond intelligently and persuasively. Following oral argument, the moot court panel often will review the student's performance.

Moot court is modeled after the appellate procedure employed in state and federal courts. Moot court is sometimes confused with mock trials, a similar learning method by which students conduct a jury trial based on a hypothetical fact pattern. Where moot court emphasizes legal research, analysis, writing, and oratory, mock trials emphasize jury persuasion techniques and a thorough familiarity with the rules of EVIDENCE.

Top moot court advocates from law schools throughout the country compete each year at a variety of national moot court competitions, many having a focus on a specific area of the law. The National Moot Court Competition is held annually in New York City and focuses on issues of CONSTITUTIONAL LAW. The Phillip C. Jessup International Law Moot Court Competition, held each spring in Washington, D.C., is sponsored by the American Society of International Law and the International Law Students' Association. The Chief Judge Conrad B. Duberstein National Bankruptcy Moot Court is an annual competition focusing on BANKRUPTCY issues.

See also LEGAL EDUCATION.

MORAL LAW 📖 The rules of behavior an individual or a group may follow out of personal conscience and that are not necessarily part of legislated law in the United States. 📖

Moral law is a system of guidelines for behavior. These guidelines may or may not be part of a religion, codified in written form, or legally enforceable. For some people moral law is synonymous with the commands of a divine being. For others, moral law is a set of universal rules that should apply to everyone.

Ethical principles held primarily by the followers of Christianity have influenced the development of U.S. secular law. As a result, Christian moral law and secular law overlap in many situations. For example, MURDER, THEFT, PROSTITUTION, and other behaviors labeled immoral are also illegal. MORAL TURPITUDE is a legal term used to describe a crime that demonstrates depravity in one's public and private life, contrary to what is accepted and customary. People convicted of this crime can be disqualified from government office, lose their LICENSE to practice law, or be deported (in the case of immigrants).

Passing laws is relatively easy when public policy makers can unanimously identify behavior that is socially unacceptable. Policy makers can then attempt to enforce socially correct behavior through legal channels. However, in many other situations, it is far more difficult to determine what behavior the government should promote, if any. When a government seeks to implement a code of conduct that may conflict with the U.S. Constitution, the courts are generally called upon to determine the law's validity.

ABORTION is an area where legal and moral principles converge and often conflict. In 1973 the U.S. Supreme Court ruled in *Roe v. Wade,* 410 U.S. 113, 93 S. Ct. 705, 35 L. Ed. 2d 147, that a woman's decision to have an abortion is a private choice that is protected by the Constitution, at least until the end of the first trimester of pregnancy. After a fetus is viable (able to survive outside the womb), the state may regulate the woman's pregnancy and prohibit abortion except if the woman's life is in danger.

Some advocates of legalized abortion as well as some critics believe that the current legal situation is inadequate. To protect either the rights of the pregnant woman or the rights of the fetus is a moral question that individuals decide for themselves. Yet the extent to which people should be allowed to act on their beliefs and exercise their rights is debated in the arena of legislative and judiciary decision making.

Medical science is a field where evolving technology can create moral crises that have legal consequences. The American Medical Association sponsors a Council on Ethical and Judicial Affairs, which debates such problems as assisted suicide, harvesting organs over the objections of family, and whether to include HIV status on autopsy reports.

Many public policy issues form a crossroad of legal and moral law, including euthanasia, assisted suicide, same-sex marriages, and CAPITAL PUNISHMENT.

CROSS-REFERENCES

Acquired Immune Deficiency Syndrome; Animal Rights; Death and Dying; Ethics; Fetal Rights; Fetal Tissue Research; Gay and Lesbian Rights; Genetic Engineering; Genetic Screening; Health Care Law; Health Insurance; Jurisprudence; Natural Law; Organ Donation Law; Organ Transplantation; Patients' Rights; Slavery; Surrogate Motherhood.

MORAL TURPITUDE ◫ A phrase used in CRIMINAL LAW to describe conduct that is considered contrary to community standards of justice, honesty, or good morals. ◫

Crimes involving moral turpitude have an inherent quality of baseness, vileness, or depravity with respect to a person's duty to another or to society in general. Examples include RAPE, FORGERY, ROBBERY, and SOLICITATION by prostitutes.

Many jurisdictions impose penalties, such as DEPORTATION of ALIENS and disbarment of attorneys, following convictions of crimes involving moral turpitude.

MORATORIUM ◫ A suspension of activity or an authorized period of delay or waiting. A moratorium is sometimes agreed upon by the interested parties, or it may be authorized or imposed by OPERATION OF LAW. The term also is used to denote a period of time during which the law authorizes a delay in payment of debts or performance of some other legal obligation. This type of moratorium is most often invoked during times of distress, such as war or natural disaster. ◫

Government bodies may declare moratoria for a broad range of reasons. For example, a local government may attempt to regulate property development by imposing a moratorium on the issuance of building permits. The legality of such a moratorium is generally determined by measuring its impact on the affected parties. In 1987 the U.S. Supreme Court held that certain moratoria on property development may be unconstitutional takings, thus making it more difficult for local governments to slow development in their communities (*First English Evangelical Lutheran Church v. Los Angeles County*, 482 U.S. 304, 107 S. Ct. 2378, 96 L. Ed. 2d 250). On the other hand, in 1995 the Court upheld a thirty-day moratorium on lawyer advertising that was challenged as an infringement of FIRST AMENDMENT rights (*Florida Bar v. Went For It, Inc.*, 515 U.S. 618, 115 S. Ct. 2371, 132 L. Ed. 2d 541).

Many state legislatures have passed moratorium legislation in response to popular demand for DEBT relief during emergencies. The constitutionality of these statutes is determined using a two-pronged analysis. First, the courts consider the effect of the moratorium on the rights of the parties to the impaired CONTRACT. If the moratorium changes only the remedy for breach and not the terms of the contract, it is generally upheld (see *Sturges v. Crowninshield*, 17 U.S. [4 Wheat.] 122, 4 L. Ed. 529 [1819]). Second, if the moratorium is a response to a bona fide emergency, it is upheld (see *Johnson v. Duncan*, 3 Mart. 530 [La. 1815], upholding a moratorium passed when the British invaded Louisiana in 1814).

As a function of its POLICE POWER, a state may suspend contractual rights when public welfare, health, or safety are threatened. However, this police power is limited by standards of reasonableness. During the World War I housing shortage, some New York landlords raised rents to exorbitant levels and evicted tenants who failed to pay. In response to what it perceived as a public health and safety emergency, the state legislature passed a law that limited rentals to reasonable amounts, gave courts authority to determine reasonableness, and prohibited landlords from evicting tenants willing to pay reasonable rents. The law was sustained by the U.S. Supreme Court in *Marcus Brown Holding Co. v. Feldman*, 256 U.S. 170, 41 S. Ct. 465, 65 L. Ed. 877 (1921).

An example of a contemporary debt moratorium is the Minnesota Mortgage Moratorium Act (1933 Minn. Laws 514), passed by the Minnesota legislature in response to a sharp rise in FORECLOSURES on mortgaged farm property. The constitutionality of the act was challenged in *Home Building & Loan Association v. Blaisdell*, 290 U.S. 398, 54 S. Ct. 231, 78 L. Ed. 413 (1934), in which the Supreme Court upheld the legislation based on five criteria: a bona fide emergency existed; the statute addressed a legitimate societal interest; debt relief was granted only under limited conditions; contractual rights were reasonably protected; and the legislation was of limited duration. This act was extended until 1942. Fifty years later the Minnesota legislature responded again to public pressure to relieve farm debts by passing another Mortgage Moratorium Act (Minn. Stat. § 583.03 [Supp. 1983]).

MORMON CHURCH The Mormon Church is a religious body founded in 1830 in Fayette, New York, by Joseph Smith. It is also known as the Church of Jesus Christ of Latter-day Saints, or LDS Church. There are 7.7 million Mormons worldwide. Approximately two-thirds reside in the United States, with the highest concentration in the western states, especially Utah. The church, which is headquartered in Salt Lake City, Utah, encountered legal difficulties during its early years because of its practice of polygamy and its opposition to the use of common law as legal precedent. The church's differences with the U.S. government led to armed conflict in the late 1800s.

Joseph Smith based his teachings on his translation of hieroglyphic messages revealed to him on several golden plates. Smith's translation of these divine messages is known as the Book of Mormon. The Book of Mormon and the Bible form the basis of Mormon belief.

During the early 1800s, Smith and his followers settled in Kirtland, Ohio, and Jackson County, Missouri, where they were persecuted because of their beliefs. They moved to Illinois and helped establish the town of Nauvoo, where the church prospered. However, local residents became inflamed over rumors that Smith and his followers were practicing PO-LYGAMY, or plural marriage. Smith and his brother Hyrum were arrested and taken to Carthage, the county seat. On June 27, 1844, they were both shot and killed by a group of townspeople.

Smith was succeeded by Brigham Young, the head of the church's Council of the Twelve Apostles. In 1846 Young organized and directed church members to follow him from Nauvoo to the Great Salt Basin in the Utah Territory. They settled there and established the headquarters of the church in Salt Lake City.

In Utah the Mormon Church prospered and grew. In addition to leading the church, Young became provisional governor of the Utah Territory in 1849. In that capacity he and the other members of the government, most of whom were Mormons, defied the U.S. government by rejecting COMMON LAW as valid legal PRECEDENT in Utah. Common law, as distinct from statutory law, is English precedent adopted by U.S. courts. Over time, common law became part of U.S. JURISPRUDENCE except where it was expressly abrogated. Although Young patterned the structure of Utah's territorial government after the other state governments, with executive, legislative, and judicial branches, he believed that the United States should abandon all vestiges of English tradition. According to Young, the application of common law allowed judges too much latitude to impose standards that did not comport with public will.

Young's opposition to the application of common law reached its nadir over the issue of

Brigham Young was the second leader of the Mormon Church. He moved the church community from Nauvoo, Illinois, to Salt Lake City, Utah.

polygamy. By the mid-1800s, the Mormon Church had acknowledged polygamy as one of its tenets. Mormon teaching of the time held that men were obligated to have multiple wives. Common law provides that marriage to more than one living husband or wife is a FELONY and that any marriages other than the first are VOID.

When President MILLARD FILLMORE assigned three federal judges to the Utah Territory in the 1850s, Young became concerned that the new judges would impose common-law precedent. He attempted to blunt their impact by urging the legislature to prohibit judges from using common-law precedent in Utah. On January 14, 1854, the legislature passed a bill that prohibited any law from being read, cited, or adopted in Utah unless it had been enacted by the legislature or the governor. This bill directly contravened the Organic Act of Utah of 1850 (9 Stat. 453) by which the U.S. Congress created the Utah Territory. The act gave the U.S. Supreme Court and the federal district courts of the territory both common-law and EQUITY jurisdiction and established that the laws of the United States applied in the territory. In 1856 the Territorial Supreme Court held that the Organic Act extended common law over the Territory of Utah and that the legislature violated the Organic Act when it forbade the use of common law in Utah (*People v. Moroni Green*, 1 Utah 11 [1856]).

Tensions continued to mount between Mormons and the federal government. In May 1857 President JAMES BUCHANAN dispatched 2,500 U.S. Army troops to Utah to remove Young from office and enforce federal authority. Anticipating the federal troops' arrival, a group of angry Mormons joined forces with a group of Paiute Indians who attacked and killed 120 settlers traveling through the territory in September 1857. Mormon leaders feared that the attack, known as the Mountain Meadows Massacre, would lead to further reprisals by the federal government. They sent sympathetic church members to destroy the Army's supplies, thereby delaying the troops' arrival. The Mormons' resistance came to be known as the Utah War. By the time the troops arrived in the summer of 1858, tensions had eased considerably, and under a negotiated settlement, troops were stationed outside Salt Lake City without incident.

The Mormon Church's resistance to the application of common law continued through the late 1800s. A number of cases reached the Territorial Supreme Court, which repeatedly affirmed that common law is valid in the territory. (See *Murphy v. Carter*, 1 Utah 17 [1868], and *Godebe v. Salt Lake City*, 1 Utah 68 [1870]). In *First National Bank of Utah v. Kinner*, 1 Utah 100 (1873), the court held that the people of the Utah territory had tacitly agreed to the application of common law. In 1878 the U.S. Supreme Court settled the question of whether the common-law prohibition of polygamy applied in the territory. In *Reynolds v. United States*, 98 U.S. (8 Otto) 145, 25 L. Ed. 244, the plaintiff argued that the common-law prohibition of polygamy was unconstitutional because it violated the FIRST AMENDMENT guarantee of freedom of RELIGION. The Court disagreed and held that religious freedom does not encompass the practice of polygamy and that laws prohibiting the practice are constitutional. The Court stated that to allow Mormons to practice plural marriage "would be to make the professed doctrines of religious belief superior to the law of the land, and in effect permit every citizen to become a law unto himself. Government could exist only in name under such circumstances."

By the 1890s the Mormon Church had officially abandoned the practice of plural marriage. In 1896 Utah became a state, and in 1898 the legislature passed a measure that declared that the common law "shall be the rule of decision in all courts of this state" (The Revised Statutes of the State of Utah, § 2488). The common law continues to carry the force of

precedent in Utah, except for the common law of crimes, which the legislature abolished in 1973 (Utah Code Ann. § 76-1-105; repealed, Utah Code Ann. § 68-2-3; replaced by Utah Code Ann. § 68-3-1).

MORTALITY TABLES A means of ascertaining the probable number of years any man or woman of a given age and of ordinary health will live. A mortality table expresses on the basis of the group studied the probability that, of a number of persons of equal expectations of life who are living at the beginning of any year, a certain number of deaths will occur within that year.

Such tables are used by INSURANCE companies to determine the PREMIUM to be charged for those in the respective age groups.

MORTGAGE A legal document by which the owner (buyer) transfers to the lender an interest in REAL ESTATE to secure the repayment of a DEBT, evidenced by a mortgage note. When the debt is repaid, the mortgage is discharged, and a satisfaction of mortgage is recorded with the register or recorder of deeds in the county where the mortgage was recorded. Because most people cannot afford to buy real estate with cash, nearly every real estate transaction involves a mortgage.

The party borrowing the money and giving the mortgage (the DEBTOR) is the mortgagor; the party paying the money and receiving the mortgage (the lender) is the mortgagee. Under early English and U.S. law, the mortgage was treated as a complete transfer of TITLE from the borrower to the lender. The lender was entitled not only to payments of interest on the debt but also to the rents and profits of the real estate. This meant that as far as the borrower was concerned, the real estate was of no value, that is, "dead," until the debt was paid in full—hence the Norman-English name "mort" (dead), "gage" (pledge).

The mortgage must be executed according to the formalities required by the laws of the state where the property is located. It must describe the real estate and be signed by all owners, including nonowner spouses if the property is a HOMESTEAD. Some states require witnesses as well as acknowledgement before a NOTARY PUBLIC.

The mortgage note, in which the borrower promises to repay the debt, sets out the terms of the transaction: the amount of the debt, the mortgage due date, the rate of interest, amount of monthly payments, whether the lender requires monthly payments to build a tax and INSURANCE reserve, whether the loan may be repaid with larger or more frequent payments without a prepayment penalty, and whether failing to make a payment or selling the property will entitle the lender to call the entire debt due.

State courts have devised varying theories of the legal effect of mortgages: some treat the mortgage as a CONVEYANCE of the title, which can be defeated on payment of the debt; others regard it as a LIEN, entitling the borrower to all the rights of ownership, as long as the terms of the mortgage are observed. In California a DEED OF TRUST to a trustee who holds title for the lender is the preferred security instrument.

At COMMON LAW, if the borrower failed to pay the debt in full at the appointed time, the borrower suffered a complete loss of title, however long and faithfully payments had been made.

Courts of EQUITY, which were originally ECCLESIASTICAL COURTS, had authority to decide cases on the basis of moral obligation, fairness, or justice, as opposed to the law courts, which were bound to decide strictly according to the common law. Equity courts softened the harshness of the common law by ruling that the debtor could regain title even after DEFAULT, but before it was declared FORFEIT, by paying the debt with interest and costs. This form of relief is known as the EQUITY OF REDEMPTION.

Now nearly all states have enacted statutes incorporating the equity of redemption, and many have also enacted periods of REDEMPTION, specifying lengths of time within which the borrower may redeem. Although some debtors, or mortgagors, are able to avoid FORECLOSURE through equity of redemption, many are not, because redeeming means coming up with the balance of the mortgage plus interest and costs, something a financially troubled debtor may not be able to accomplish. However, because foreclosure upends the agreement between mortgagor and mortgagee and creates burdens for both parties, lenders are often willing to work with debtors to help them through a period of temporary difficulty. Debtors who run into problems meeting their mortgage obligations should speak to their lender about developing a plan to avert foreclosure.

Failure to redeem results in foreclosure of the borrower's rights in the real estate, which is then sold by the county SHERIFF at a public foreclosure sale. At a foreclosure sale, the lender is the most frequent purchaser of the property.

If the bid at the sale is less than the debt, even if it is for FAIR MARKET VALUE, the lender

Mortgage Debt Outstanding, by Type of Property and Holder, in 1993
(In billions of dollars. Includes Puerto Rico and Guam.)

Type of Property

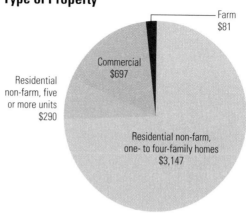

Farm $81

Commercial $697

Residential non-farm, five or more units $290

Residential non-farm, one- to four-family homes $3,147

Type of Holder

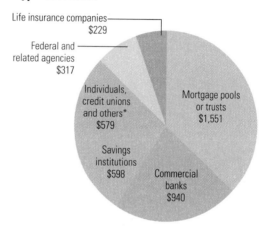

Life insurance companies $229

Federal and related agencies $317

Individuals, credit unions and others* $579

Savings institutions $598

Mortgage pools or trusts $1,551

Commercial banks $940

*Others include mortgage companies, REITs, state and local retirement funds, noninsured pension funds, state and local credit agencies, and finance companies.

Source: Board of Governors of the Federal Reserve System, *Federal Reserve Bulletin*, monthly.

may be granted a DEFICIENCY JUDGMENT for the balance of the debt against the debtor, with the right to resort to other ASSETS or income for its collection.

Often other CREDITORS bid at the sale to protect their interest as JUDGMENT CREDITORS, second mortgagees, or MECHANIC'S LIEN claimants. All such persons must be notified of the foreclosure suit and given a right to bid at the sale to protect their claims. Similar protections are afforded transactions involving deeds of trust.

Subdivision or condominium development mortgages that cover a large tract of land are blanket mortgages. A blanket mortgage makes possible the sale of individual lots or units, with the proceeds applied to the mortgage, and

A sample
plain-language
mortgage note

NOTE

US $ _____   _____ , New York

City

_____ , 19_____

1. BORROWER'S PROMISE TO PAY

In return for a loan that I have received, I promise to pay _____ Dollars (this amount will be called "principal"), plus interest, to the order of the Lender. The Lender is _____ . I understand that the Lender may transfer this Note. The Lender or anyone who takes this Note by transfer and who is entitled to receive payments under this Note will be called the "Note holder."

2. INTEREST

I will pay interest at a rate of _____ percent per year. Interest will be charged on that part of principal which has not been paid. Interest will be charged beginning on the date of this Note and continuing until the full amount of principal has been paid.

3. PAYMENTS

I will pay principal and interest by making payments every month. Each of my monthly payments will be in the amount of _____ Dollars (US $_____).

I will make my monthly payments on the _____ day of each month beginning on _____ , 19_____ . I will make these payments every month until I have paid all of the principal and interest and any other charges, described below, that I may owe under this Note. If, on _____ , I still owe amounts under this Note, I will pay all those amounts, in full, on that date.

I will make my monthly payments at _____ , or at a different place if required by the Note holder.

4. BORROWER'S FAILURE TO PAY AS REQUIRED

(A) Late Charge for Overdue Payments

If the Note holder has not received the full amount of any of my monthly payments by the end of _____ calendar days after the date it is due, I will pay a late charge to the Note holder. The amount of the charge will be _____ percent of my overdue payment of principal and interest.

(B) Notice From Note Holder

If I do not pay the full amount of each monthly payment on time, the Note holder may send me a written notice telling me that if I do not pay the overdue amount by a certain date I will be in default. That date must be at least 30 days after the date on which the notice is mailed to me or, if it is not mailed, 30 days after the date on which it is delivered to me.

(C) Default

If I do not pay the overdue amount by the date stated in the notice described in (B) above, I will be in default. If I am in default, the Note holder may require me to pay immediately the full amount of principal which has not been paid and all the interest that I owe on that amount.

Even if, at a time when I am in default, the Note holder does not require me to pay immediately in full as described above, the Note holder will still have the right to do so if, at a later time, I am in default again.

(D) Payment of Note Holder's Costs and Expenses

If the Note holder has required me to pay immediately in full as described above, the Note holder will have the right to be paid back for all of its reasonable costs and expenses. Those expenses include, for example, reasonable attorney's fees.

5. BORROWER'S PAYMENTS BEFORE THEY ARE DUE

(A) Borrower's Right to Make Prepayments

I have the right to make payments of principal before they are due. Any payment made before it is due is known as a "prepayment." A prepayment of only part of the unpaid principal is known as a "partial prepayment."

A sample
plain-language
mortgage note
(continued)

If I choose to make a partial prepayment, the Note holder may require me to make the prepayment on the same day that one of my monthly payments is due. The Note holder may also require that the amount of my partial prepayment be equal to the amount of principal that would have been part of my next one or more monthly payments. If I make a partial prepayment, there will be no delays in the due dates or changes in the amounts of my monthly payments unless the Note holder agrees in writing to those delays or changes. The Note holder will use all of my prepayments to reduce the amount of principal that I owe under this Note.

(B) Prepayment Charge

I will pay a prepayment charge to the Note holder only if a percentage and a date are filled in below *and if I make the prepayment using money lent to me by a lender other than the Note holder.* [Strike italics if not applicable.]

During any twelve-month period ending on an anniversary of the date of this Note, I may make partial prepayments of up to $ _____ without charge. This amount will be called the "free prepayment amount."

I will pay a prepayment charge if the total of my prepayments during any such twelve-month period is greater than the free prepayment amount. The prepayment charge will be a percentage of the amount by which my prepayments in any such twelve-month period are greater than the free prepayment amount. That percentage will be _____ percent until _____ ; it will change to _____ percent on that date until _____ ; and it will change to _____ percent on that date until _____ . After the last date filled in above, there will be no prepayment charge.

6. BORROWER'S WAIVERS

I waive my rights to require the Note holder to do certain things. Those things are: (A) to demand payment of amounts due (known as "presentment"); (B) to give notice that amounts due have not been paid (known as "notice of dishonor"); (C) to obtain an official certification of nonpayment (known as a "protest"). Anyone else (i) who agrees to keep the promises made in this Note, or (ii) who agrees to make payments to the Note holder if I fail to keep my promises under this Note, or (iii) who signs this Note to transfer it to someone else (known as "guarantors, sureties, and endorsers"), also waives these rights.

7. GIVING OF NOTICES

Any notice that must be given to me under this Note will be given by delivering it or by mailing it addressed to me at the Property Address below. A notice will be delivered or mailed to me at a different address if I give the Note holder a notice of my different address.

Any notice that must be given to the Note holder under this Note will be given by mailing it to the Note holder at the address stated in Section 3 above. A notice will be mailed to the Note holder at a different address if I am given a notice of that different address.

8. THIS NOTE COVERED BY A MORTGAGE

A Mortgage, dated _____ , protects the Note holder from possible losses which might result if I do not keep the promises which I make in this Note. That Mortgage describes how and under what conditions I may be required to make immediate payment in full of all amounts that I owe under this Note.

9. RESPONSIBILITY OF PERSONS UNDER THIS NOTE

If more than one person signs this Note, each of us is fully and personally obligated to pay the full amount owed and to keep all of the promises made in this Note. Any guarantor, surety, or endorser of this Note (as described in Section 6 above) is also obligated to do these things. The Note holder may enforce its rights under this Note against each of us individually or against all of us together. This means that any one of us may be required to pay all of the amounts owed under this Note.

Any person who takes over my rights or obligations under this Note will have all of my rights and must keep all of my promises made in this Note. Any person who takes over the rights or obligations of a guarantor, surety, or endorser of this Note (as described in Section 6 above) is also obligated to keep all of the promises made in this Note.

_____   _____

Property Address   (*Sign Original Only*) partial release of the mortgage recorded to clear the title for that lot or unit.

Construction mortgages need special treatment depending on state construction lien law. Often the loan proceeds are placed in ESCROW with TITLE INSURANCE companies to make certain that the mortgage remains a first lien, with priority over contractors' construction liens.

OPEN-END MORTGAGES make possible additional advances of money from the lender without the necessity of a new mortgage.

The time of repayment may be extended by a recorded extension of mortgage. Other real estate may be added to the mortgage by a spreading agreement. Mortgaged real estate may be sold, with the buyer taking either "subject to" or by "assuming" the mortgage. In the former case, the buyer acknowledges the existence of the mortgage and, upon default, may lose the title. By assuming the mortgage, the buyer promises to repay the debt and may be personally liable for a deficiency judgment if the sale brings less than the debt.

Lenders regularly assign mortgages to other investors. ASSIGNMENTS with recourse are guarantees by the one who assigns the mortgage that that party will collect the debt; those without recourse do not contain such guarantees. Assignments with recourse usually involve lower-risk properties or those of relatively stable or rising value. Assignments without recourse tend to involve riskier properties. Mortgages assigned without recourse are often sold at a price discounted well below their market value.

Before the Great Depression of the 1930s, most mortgages were "straight" short-term mortgages, requiring payments of interest and lump-sum PRINCIPAL, with the result that when incomes dropped, many borrowers lost their properties. That risk is minimized today because commercial lenders take fully amortized mortgages, in which part of the periodic payment applies first to interest and then to principal, with the balance reduced to zero at the end of the term.

Several agencies of the federal government have assisted the mortgage market by infusion of capital and by guarantees of repayment of mortgages. The Federal Housing Administration made possible purchases of real estate at low interest rates and with low DOWN PAYMENTS. The Veterans Administration also guarantees home loans to certain veterans on favorable terms. Both agencies contributed greatly to the growth of the housing market after World War II. In the late 1950s, private corporations began insuring repayment of conventional mortgages.

The GOVERNMENT NATIONAL MORTGAGE ASSOCIATION (Ginnie Mae), created by the U.S. government in 1968, makes possible trading in mortgages by investors by guaranteeing mortgages-backed securities.

The FEDERAL NATIONAL MORTGAGE ASSOCIATION (Fannie Mae) is a private CORPORATION, chartered by the U.S. government, that bolsters the supply of funds for home mortgages by buying mortgages from banks, insurance companies, and savings and loans.

Inflation in the 1970s made long-term fixed-rate mortgages less attractive to lenders. In response, lenders devised three types of mortgage loans that enable the rate of interest to vary in case of rises in rates: the variable-rate mortgage, graduated payment mortgage, and adjustable-rate mortgages. These mortgages are offered at initial interest rates that are somewhat lower than those for twenty- to thirty-year fixed-rate mortgages.

Home equity loans are typically second mortgages to the holder of the first mortgage, advancing funds based on a percentage of the owner's equity, that is, the amount by which the value of the real estate exceeds the first mortgage balance.

See also AMORTIZATION.

MORTMAIN 📖 [*French, Dead hand.*] A term to denote the CONVEYANCE of ownership of land or TENEMENTS to any corporation, religious or secular. 📖

Traditionally, such transfers were made to religious CORPORATIONS. Like any corporation, the religious society had unlimited, perpetual duration under the law. It could, therefore, hold land permanently unlike a natural person, whose property is redistributed upon his or her death. The holdings of religious corporations grew as contributions were received from their members. Because such holdings were immune from responsibilities for taxes and payment of feudal dues, greater burdens were placed on noncorporate secular property. Therefore, land in mortmain was said to be held in perpetuity in one dead hand, that of the corporation.

MORTMAIN ACTS 📖 Statutes designed to prevent lands from being perpetually possessed or controlled by religious corporations. 📖

The first MORTMAIN act in England was enacted during the reign of King Edward I. A later statute passed during the reign of King George II was the model for subsequent mortmain acts in that it prevented the transfer of lands to CHARITIES unless the gift complied with certain requirements. Mortmain acts have been abolished by statute.

In the law governing WILLS, statutes based

upon the original mortmain acts have been passed in some states to restrict the power of a TESTATOR to make gifts to charities. These modern statutes, also called mortmain acts, protect only the immediate family of a DECEDENT from disinheritance by death-bed gifts to charities when the will is executed within the statutory period.

MOSELEY-BRAUN, CAROL Carol Moseley-Braun was the first woman and first African American to serve as assistant majority leader of the Illinois House of Representatives; later, she became the first woman and first African American to hold executive office in Cook County (Chicago), Illinois; and in 1992, she became the first African American woman elected to the U.S. Senate.

Born August 16, 1947, in Chicago, the daughter of a police officer and a medical technician, Moseley-Braun grew up in Chicago. She earned her bachelor of arts degree from the University of Illinois at Chicago in 1969. Then she went to the University of Chicago Law School, where she was awarded her doctor of jurisprudence degree in 1972. While still in law school, she began her legal career as a law clerk with Mayer, Brown, and Platt (1970) and Rose, Hardies, O'Keefe, Babcock, and Parsons (1971). After earning her doctorate, she spent one year as an associate with the firm of Davis, Miner, and Barnhill.

In 1973 Moseley-Braun was appointed assistant U.S. attorney for the Northern District of Illinois, a position she held until 1977. Her election to the Illinois state legislature in 1978 started her on the road that would eventually lead to the U.S. Senate. While a member of the Illinois House, Moseley-Braun rose to the position of assistant majority leader, becoming the first African American and the first woman to do so.

Moseley-Braun's last position before being elected to the U.S. Senate was Cook County recorder of deeds and registrar of titles. She was also the first woman and first African American to hold this, or any, executive office in Cook County.

BIOGRAPHY

Carol Moseley-Braun

"HOW WE CHARACTERIZE THE DEBATE WILL HAVE A CRITICAL IMPACT ON HOW WE CHARACTERIZE THE OUTCOME."

Moseley-Braun entered the Illinois primary and upset two-term Democratic incumbent Alan J. Dixon. She then played upon voters' unhappiness with the sagging U.S. economy to clinch her victory over Republican Richard S. Williamson and become the first African American woman elected to the U.S. Senate.

Moseley-Braun's rise to national office was not without controversy. During her campaign against Williamson, it was reported that she had received over $28,000 in royalty payments from the sale of timber on land owned by her mother, a nursing home resident whose care was being paid for by MEDICAID. Moseley-Braun did not report the income either to the INTERNAL REVENUE SERVICE or to Medicaid, as required by law. She later repaid the state $15,239 for her mother's nursing home expenses.

During her first term in the Senate, Moseley-Braun was appointed to some of the most powerful and influential Senate committees: Banking, Housing and Urban Affairs, Small Business, and Judiciary. She also became a member of the Congressional Black Caucus.

In May 1993, just a few months after her induction into the Senate, she challenged Senator STROM THURMOND (R-S.C.), the Senate's most senior member at the time. The two debated a bill that would have extended the design patent on the insignia of the United Daughters of the Confederacy (UDC), which featured the Confederate flag. Arguing that the flag was a symbol of a time in U.S. history when African Americans were held as human chattel under the flag of the Confederacy, Moseley-Braun persuaded her colleagues on the Judiciary Committee not to extend the UDC patent.

The issue was not dead, however. In July 1993, Senator JESSE HELMS (R-N.C.) included the patent extension as an amendment to another bill. The Senate voted 52–48 to approve the amendment. Undaunted, Moseley-Braun vowed to FILIBUSTER to reverse the vote. She lobbied her fellow Senators to reconsider the vote on the Helms amendment. She argued that the Confederate flag had no place in our mod-

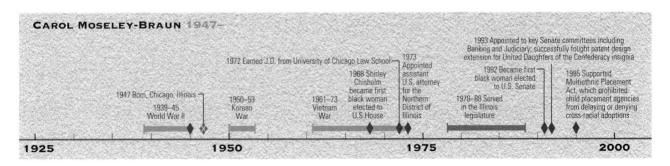

CAROL MOSELEY-BRAUN 1947–

1947 Born, Chicago, Illinois

1939–45 World War II

1950–53 Korean War

1961–73 Vietnam War

1968 Shirley Chisholm became first black woman elected to U.S. House

1972 Earned J.D. from University of Chicago Law School

1973 Appointed assistant U.S. attorney for the Northern District of Illinois

1978–88 Served in the Illinois legislature

1992 Became first black woman elected to U.S. Senate

1993 Appointed to key Senate committees including Banking and Judiciary; successfully fought patent design extension for United Daughters of the Confederacy insignia

1995 Supported Multiethnic Placement Act, which prohibited child placement agencies from delaying or denying cross-racial adoptions

1925   1950   1975   2000

ern times, no place in the Senate, and no place in our society. The Senate reconsidered its vote and finally tabled the Helms amendment, effectively killing it, by a vote of 75–25.

Moseley-Braun is a member of a new and diverse group of legislators making their mark on the national political scene in the 1990s and beyond.

MOST-FAVORED-NATION STATUS ⬚ A method of establishing equality of trading opportunity among states by guaranteeing that if one country is given better trade terms by another, then all other states must get the same terms. ⬚

In the twentieth century, the history of world trade is dominated by the move from protective TARIFFS to free trade. International agreements have permitted most of the world's nations to export their products without facing discriminatory duties. A key concept in the liberalization of trade is most-favored-nation (MFN) status.

MFN status is a method of preventing discriminatory treatment among members of an international trading organization. MFN status provides trade equality among partners by ensuring that an importing country will not discriminate against another country's goods in favor of those from a third. Once the importing country grants any type of concession to the third-party country, this concession must be given to all other countries.

For example, assume that the United States government negotiates a bilateral trade agreement with Indonesia that provides, among other things, that a duty of $1 will be charged for imported Indonesian television sets. All countries that have MFN status will pay no more than a $1 duty to export televisions to the United States. If the United States later negotiates a duty of 75¢ with Japan for imported televisions, Indonesia and all other MFN countries will pay 75¢, despite Indonesia's original agreement to pay more duty.

The number of countries with MFN status increased after World War II with the GENERAL AGREEMENT ON TARIFFS AND TRADE (GATT) treaty, which was signed by many nations in 1948. Article I of the GATT requires that exports of all contracting parties to the treaty should be treated alike by other contracting parties, immediately and without condition. Thus, each member's exports are treated on the best terms (or "most favored" terms) available to any GATT member.

The MFN status proclaimed in the GATT has been granted to about 180 countries. Only a handful of communist countries have been denied MFN status.

The United States is forbidden by law to grant MFN status to communist countries that do not have free-market economies. The practical effect is that imports from these countries are subject to much higher tariffs. An amendment to the Trade Act of 1974, however, created a loophole. The president may waive the MFN restriction on an annual basis if the communist country permits free EMIGRATION or if MFN status would lead to increased emigration. By law, the president must tell Congress each year of the administration's intention to renew or deny MFN status benefits to a communist country. Congress has sixty days to overturn the decision and would then need a two-thirds majority to override a presidential VETO.

China has been the main beneficiary of this loophole. Since 1979 China has been granted MFN status. After China suppressed its democracy movement and the Tiananmen Square protest in 1989, Congress opposed continuation of the country's MFN status, yet both President GEORGE BUSH and President BILL CLINTON renewed China's MFN benefits.

MOTION ⬚ A written or oral application made to a court or judge to obtain a RULING or ORDER directing that some act be done in favor of the applicant. The applicant is known as the moving party, or the MOVANT. ⬚

In the U.S. judicial system, procedural rules require most motions to be made in writing and can require that written NOTICE be given in advance of a motion being made. Written motions specify what action the movant is requesting and the reasons, or grounds, for the request. A written motion may contain CITATIONS to CASE LAW or statutes that support the motion. A motion almost always contains a recitation of the facts of the case or the situation prompting the movant to make the request.

For example, suppose that a plaintiff in a lawsuit has refused to submit to a DEPOSITION—questioning under oath—by the defendant. The defendant therefore files a motion with the court to compel in an effort to compel the plaintiff to attend the deposition. The written motion briefly explains the nature of the lawsuit, describes the efforts made by the defendant to get the plaintiff to submit to a deposition, addresses any known reasons for the plaintiff's failure to cooperate, and recites the statute that permits the taking of depositions in civil litigation. The motion may also request that the issue be addressed at a HEARING before the judge with all parties present.

Once the judge receives the motion, he or she may grant or deny the motion based solely on its contents. In the alternative, the judge

A sample notice of motion

> To: _____
>   Attorney for _____
>   Please take notice that the undersigned will bring the above motion on for hearing before
> this court at Room _____ , United States Courts and Post Office Building, City of
> _____ , State of _____ , on the _____ day of _____ ,
> 19_____ , at _____ o'clock in the _____ noon of that day or as soon
> thereafter as counsel can be heard.
>
>   [*Signed*] _____
>   Attorney for _____
>   Address: _____

may schedule a hearing. At a motion hearing, each party has an opportunity to argue its position orally, and the judge can ask specific questions about the facts or the law. The judge's decision on the motion is called an order.

Under some circumstances motions can be made orally. Oral motions frequently occur during trials, when it is impractical to draft a written motion. A common oral motion occurs during WITNESS testimony. Witnesses sometimes give INADMISSIBLE testimony before an attorney can object. When that happens, the attorney must object and move the court to strike the inadmissible TESTIMONY from the record. Motions for MISTRIAL—made when courtroom proceedings are fraught with errors, inadmissible evidence, or disruptions so prejudicial to a party's case that justice cannot be served—often are made orally. Sometimes judges themselves take action on behalf of a party, such as changing or adding necessary language to a PLEADING without a mo-

tion from a party. This is known as making an AMENDMENT on the court's own motion.

A motion to dismiss asks the court to dismiss an action because the initial pleading, or COMPLAINT, fails to state a CAUSE OF ACTION or CLAIM for which the law provides a REMEDY. For example, a complaint alleges that an employer unfairly fired an employee but does not allege illegal discrimination or labor practices. Merely firing an employee for unfair reasons is not illegal; thus a court may dismiss this complaint.

A motion to strike asks the court to remove from the record inadmissible EVIDENCE or language in pleadings that is redundant, immaterial, impertinent, or scandalous. A party can file a motion for a more definite statement when the language in a pleading is so vague or ambiguous that the party cannot reasonably be expected to draft a responsive pleading.

A motion for summary JUDGMENT, also known as a motion for judgment on the plead-

A sample motion

> UNITED STATES DISTRICT COURT_____
>   DISTRICT OF _____
>
> A _____ B _____ ,
>   Plaintiff,   Civil Action,
>   v.   File Number _____
> C _____ D _____ ,   Motion _____
>   Defendant.
>
>   The _____ moves the court as follows:
>   1. [*State the relief or order sought and state the grounds with particularity.*]
>   2. [*State the relief or order sought and the grounds with particularity.*]
>   [*Signed*] _____
>   Attorney for _____
>   Address: _____

ings, asks the court to make a judgment solely on the facts set forth in the pleadings, without the necessity of trial. A court will grant a summary judgment motion when the material facts of the case are not in dispute and all that remains to be determined are questions of law. For example, in *Stieber v. Journal Publishing Co.*, 120 N. M. 270, 901 P.2d 201 (App. 1995), the court found that the issue of whether a newspaper company's treatment of a reporter was extreme and outrageous was a legal question, not a factual question. In that case the reporter, Tamar Stieber, sued her employer for, among other things, intentional infliction of emotional distress. Stieber charged that the newspaper asked her to write so many daily stories that she could not perform her duties as a special projects reporter. To recover for the tort of intentional infliction of emotional distress, the court noted, Stieber had to prove that the newspaper's conduct was so extreme and outrageous as to go "beyond all possible boundaries of decency, and to be regarded as atrocious, and utterly intolerable in civilized community." The court ruled that as a matter of law, Stieber failed to prove this ALLEGATION, and the lower court's summary judgment was affirmed.

A motion in limine, also made before trial, asks the court to prohibit an opposing party from offering evidence or referring to matters that would be highly prejudicial to the movant during a trial. A motion to SUPPRESS is similar to a motion in limine but asks the court to keep out of a criminal trial evidence that was obtained illegally, usually in violation of the Fourth, Fifth, or Sixth Amendments to the U.S. Constitution. For example, a defendant in a MURDER trial may move the court to suppress her CONFESSION because she was questioned without being told of her right to have an attorney present.

Following a trial but before a jury VERDICT, a party may move for a DIRECTED VERDICT, asking the judge to make a judgment without letting the jury reach a verdict. Following a jury verdict, a party may move for JUDGMENT NOTWITHSTANDING THE VERDICT, or JNOV. This motion requests that the court enter a judgment contrary to the jury verdict, and is granted when no reasonable jury could have reached that verdict. A motion for a new trial asks the judge to order a new trial, setting aside the judgment or verdict, because the trial was improper or unfair. This motion is sometimes brought as the result of newly discovered evidence.

See also CIVIL PROCEDURE; CRIMINAL PROCEDURE.

MOTIVE 📖 An idea, belief, or emotion that impels a person to act in accordance with that state of mind. 📖

Motive is usually used in connection with CRIMINAL LAW to explain why a person acted or refused to act in a certain way—for example, to support the prosecution's assertion that the accused committed the crime. If a person accused of MURDER was the beneficiary of a life INSURANCE policy on the deceased, the prosecution might argue that greed was the motive for the killing.

PROOF of motive is not required in a criminal prosecution. In determining the guilt of a criminal defendant, courts are generally not concerned with *why* the defendant committed the alleged crime, but *whether* the defendant committed the crime. However, a defendant's motive is important in other stages of a criminal case, such as police investigation and SENTENCING. Law enforcement personnel often consider potential motives in detecting perpetrators. Judges may consider the motives of a convicted defendant at sentencing and either increase a sentence based on avaricious motives or decrease the sentence if the defendant's motives were honorable—for example, if the accused acted in defense of a family member.

In criminal law, motive is distinct from INTENT. Criminal intent refers to the mental state of mind possessed by a defendant in committing a crime. With few exceptions the prosecution in a criminal case must prove that the defendant intended to commit the illegal act. The prosecution need not prove the defendant's motive. Nevertheless, PROSECUTORS and defense attorneys alike may make an issue of motive in connection with the case.

For example, if a defendant denies commission of the crime, he may produce EVIDENCE showing that he had no motive to commit the crime and argue that the lack of motive supports the proposition that he did not commit the crime. By the same token, the prosecution may produce evidence that the defendant did have the motive to commit the crime and argue that the motive supports the proposition that the defendant committed the crime. Proof of motive, without more evidence tying a defendant to the alleged crime, is insufficient to support a conviction.

A HATE CRIME is one crime that requires proof of a certain motive. Generally, a hate crime is motivated by the defendant's belief regarding a protected status of the victim, such as the victim's religion, sex, disability, customs, or national origin. In states that PROSECUTE hate crimes, the prosecution must prove that the defendant was motivated by animosity toward a protected status of the victim. Hate-crime laws are exceptions to the general rule that proof of motive is not required in a criminal prosecution.

In CIVIL LAW a plaintiff generally need not prove the respondent's motive in acting or failing to act. One notable exception to this general rule is the TORT of MALICIOUS PROSECUTION. In a suit for malicious prosecution, the plaintiff must prove, in part, that the respondent was motivated by MALICE in subjecting the plaintiff to a civil suit. The same applies for a malicious criminal prosecution.

MOTLEY, CONSTANCE BAKER

Constance Baker Motley played an integral role in defending legislation that was created to protect the rights of all Americans. Her work on landmark CIVIL RIGHTS cases in the 1940s, 1950s, and 1960s helped abolish segregation in schools and changed the way the U.S. Constitution is interpreted. Motley was the first African American woman elected to the New York State Senate, the first African American and the first woman to be elected Manhattan borough president, and the first female African American federal judge.

Motley was born in New Haven, Connecticut, on September 14, 1921, one of nine children. The America Motley grew up in was segregated. As a child going to a beach in Milford, Connecticut, Motley was turned away because of the color of her skin. When she returned home, she asked her parents, both West Indian immigrants, why the color of her skin meant she could not go swimming. Her parents were unfamiliar with U.S. segregation and had no answer.

As a teenager Motley became fascinated with U.S. history, particularly the Civil War, ABRAHAM LINCOLN, and the EMANCIPATION PROCLAMATION. She sought out role models in her community to help her focus her interests and began attending meetings at a local adult community center. At that center, she came in contact with George W. Crawford, a prominent black lawyer in New Haven, who told her about the case of *Missouri ex rel. Gaines v. Canada*, 305 U.S. 337, 59 S. Ct. 232, 83 L. Ed. 208 (1938).

At the time of *Gaines*, Missouri was like many southern states that maintained all white professional schools, sending qualified minority law school applicants to schools in other states.

The Supreme Court ruled in *Gaines* that Missouri's admissions practice did not offer an equal educational opportunity to minority students and therefore violated the Equal Protection Clause of the FOURTEENTH AMENDMENT. That verdict meant that many states had to reevaluate their school systems and either create new schools specifically for black students or desegregate existing white graduate schools. Crawford told Motley that he believed *Gaines* would prompt states to create separate schools to avoid desegregation.

The *Gaines* case inspired Motley to attend law school. She wanted to be a lawyer to fight for civil rights as Abraham Lincoln had done. However, when she approached her father about following her dream, he told her that college was a financial impossibility on his wages as a chef at a Yale fraternity house.

After graduating from high school as an honor student in 1939, Baker spent eighteen months working for the National Youth Administration in New Haven. Disturbed by blacks' lack of interest in the community center, Motley decided to address her peers at a meeting at the center. As president of the New Haven Youth Council, Motley spoke about the apparent apathy of blacks toward the center, which she suggested stemmed from the lack of black involvement in setting policy and designing projects for the center. Clarence Blakeslee, the successful white businessman who had been the primary donor for the community center, heard Motley speak and was very impressed. He offered to pay for Motley's education.

Accepting the offer, Motley attended New York University where she received a bachelor of arts degree in economics. She then went to Columbia University School of Law where she received her law degree in 1946. While still at Columbia, Motley got a job with the NATIONAL ASSOCIATION FOR THE ADVANCEMENT OF COLORED PEOPLE (NAACP) Legal Defense and Educational Fund clerking for chief counsel THURGOOD MARSHALL, who would later sit on the U.S. Supreme Court.

Motley joined the NAACP during World War II and worked on many cases involving

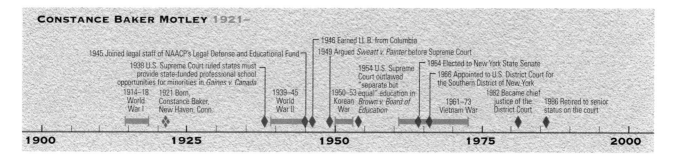

CONSTANCE BAKER MOTLEY 1921–

1946 Earned LL.B. from Columbia
1949 Argued *Sweatt v. Painter* before Supreme Court
1945 Joined legal staff of NAACP's Legal Defense and Educational Fund
1938 U.S. Supreme Court ruled states must provide state-funded professional school opportunities for minorities in *Gaines v. Canada*
1964 Elected to New York State Senate
1966 Appointed to U.S. District Court for the Southern District of New York
1954 U.S. Supreme Court outlawed "separate but equal" education in *Brown v. Board of Education*
1982 Became chief justice of the District Court
1986 Retired to senior status on the court

1914–18 World War I
1921 Born, Constance Baker, New Haven, Conn.
1939–45 World War II
1950–53 Korean War
1961–73 Vietnam War

1900   1925   1950   1975   2000

black servicemen. These soldiers told of segregation in the armed forces and protested that punishments given to black soldiers were outrageous compared with those given to white soldiers for similar infractions. Motley worked on hundreds of COURT-MARTIAL cases that earned the NAACP much notoriety. Motley's work with the NAACP enabled her to try cases in federal courts and even to try ten cases before the Supreme Court. Motley often was the first African American attorney and usually the first female African American attorney to be seen in many of those courtrooms.

In the late 1940s, the NAACP decided to focus on eliminating segregation in education. The first case Motley had after completing law school took the *Gaines* case a step further. The case involved Herman Marion Sweatt (*Sweatt v. Painter*, 339 U.S. 629, 70 S. Ct. 848, 94 L. Ed. 1114 [1949]) who was denied admission to the law school at the University of Texas solely because he was black. Under pressure from the NAACP, the school set up a makeshift classroom for Sweatt in the basement of a building, got him a few books, and assigned him four professors from the faculty. However, the Supreme Court held that the state had violated the Equal Protection Clause because Sweatt's inability to interact with fellow classmates made his education inferior. Motley tried other cases involving segregation in professional schools and was a driving force in reforming their admission practices, paving the way for minority professionals in this country.

In 1954 Motley helped write legal briefs for the landmark case *Brown v. Board of Education of Topeka, Kansas*, 347 U.S. 483, 74 S. Ct. 686, 98 L. Ed. 873 (1954). In *Brown*, the Court ruled that segregated schools were unconstitutional, violating the Equal Protection Clause of the U.S. Constitution. The case was a major victory for civil rights advocates, fueling Motley's hope for real change in U.S. attitudes toward minority groups.

In the 1960s Motley turned her attention toward minority children. She was concerned about the inadequate schooling for black children, the slum conditions in which many were forced to live, and the high rates of unemployment in black communities. She wanted new legislation to address these problems. In 1964 Motley became the first African American woman elected to the New York State Senate. In 1965 she relinquished her Senate seat when she was elected president of the borough of Manhattan. From that post she worked to revitalize Harlem and advance urban renewal.

In 1966 when President LYNDON B. JOHNSON appointed Motley to the United States District Court for the Southern District of New York, protest from southerners held up her appointment from January to August. Later, when President Johnson nominated Motley to the U.S. Court of Appeals, male opposition pressured him into withdrawing her name.

Since becoming a federal judge, Motley has ruled on more than 2,500 cases. She has urged members of other minorities to look to African Americans to witness the gains that can be made through legal action.

CROSS-REFERENCES

Brown v. Board of Education of Topeka, Kansas; Civil Rights Movement; Equal Protection; Integration; School Desegregation.

MOVANT 📖 One who makes a MOTION before a court. The applicant for a judicial rule or ORDER. 📖

Generally, it is the job of the movant to convince a judge to rule, or grant an order, in favor of the motion. Rules and legal PRECEDENT within particular jurisdictions, as well as the type of motion sought, dictate the burdens of proof and persuasion each party must meet when a court considers a motion.

For example, one common type of motion is a motion for summary JUDGMENT. This motion is made shortly before a trial commences and is granted if the PLEADINGS, DEPOSITIONS, ANSWERS to INTERROGATORIES, and AFFIDAVITS indicate that no genuine dispute as to any MATERIAL fact exists and that the movant is entitled to a favorable judgment as a MATTER OF LAW. In other words, if the facts of the case are not disputed, it is easier, faster, and less expensive for a judge to simply rule on the legal issues that apply to those facts, avoiding a trial altogether.

A summary judgment movant in most jurisdictions has the burden of showing that no genuine issue of material fact exists and that, by law, the undisputed facts support a judgment in the movant's favor. But once the movant meets this burden, the opposing party is given a chance to refute the movant's argument. The opposing party will try to establish that there is a genuine dispute about a material fact in the case and that the law does not support a judgment in the movant's favor.

For example, assume a case in which a fashion model is suing a newspaper for publishing her picture without her knowledge or permission in an advertisement for a nightclub. Shortly before trial the newspaper makes a motion for summary judgment. The movant

newspaper admits that the photograph of the model ran in the newspaper and that the newspaper did not have the model's permission to publish it. The newspaper argues, however, that the model has no right under current law to sue the newspaper, which merely sells space for advertisements, and that her only legal recourse is in suing the advertiser that placed the advertisement in the newspaper. Thus, the newspaper has argued that no material facts are in dispute. The movant has also shown that, given the incontestable material facts, the law would support a judgment in favor of the newspaper.

Now the burden shifts to the model, who must demonstrate the existence of a disputed fact that, if proven, would make the newspaper legally liable. She may do this by producing an affidavit—a sworn written statement—by a former newspaper employee alleging that the newspaper did not merely print the advertisement but actually created the advertisement with the model's picture for the nightclub. Because this material fact, if proven, could make the newspaper legally liable, the court would deny the movant's summary judgment motion.

In most jurisdictions the burden of producing EVIDENCE supporting the granting or denial of a summary judgment motion shifts between the movant and the opposing party, but the ultimate burden of persuading the court remains with the movant. A movant's burdens of proof and persuasion differ depending on the JURISDICTION and the type of motion. In Hawaii, a movant in a criminal case seeking to have the trial continued or postponed because a witness is unavailable must show that the movant has exercised due diligence in finding the WITNESS; the witness would provide substantial favorable

A cross-examining attorney who moves to have a witness's testimony stricken from the record is considered the movant in the matter.

evidence; the witness is otherwise available and willing to testify; and the movant would be materially prejudiced by a denial of the continuance (*State v. Lee*, 9 Hawai'i App. 600, 856 P.2d 1279 [1993]). In Utah a movant requesting that the court set aside its child support award because of a judicial mistake in failing to use a required joint custody worksheet in computing the amount of child support need only demonstrate the existence of a judicial mistake. A denial of the motion by the trial court, without an explanation as to why it deviated from the joint custody worksheet requirement, was an ABUSE OF DISCRETION and was reversed and remanded by an APPELLATE COURT (*Udy v. Udy*, 893 P.2d 1097 [Utah App. 1995]).

MOVE 📖 To make an application to a court for a rule or order, or to take action in any matter. The term comprehends all things necessary to be done by a litigant to obtain an order of the court directing the relief sought. To propose a resolution, or recommend action in a deliberative body. To pass over; to be transferred, as when the CONSIDERATION of a contract is said to *move* from one party to the other. To occasion; to contribute to; to tend or lead to. 📖

MOVIE RATING 📖 A classification given to a commercially released motion picture that indicates to consumers whether the film contains SEX, PROFANITY, violence, or other subject matter that may be inappropriate for persons in certain age-groups. 📖

The idea for a nationwide movie rating system took root in the late 1960s. In 1966 Jack Valenti, a former aide to President LYNDON B. JOHNSON, became president of the Motion Picture Association of America (MPAA). That same year the film *Who's Afraid of Virginia Woolf* was completed. The film used terms such as *screw* and *hump* to refer to sexual intercourse. Because these terms were considered controversial language, Valenti met with officials at Warner Brothers before the film's release, and the group decided which terms could be deleted and which ones were necessary to the film's content.

The experience led Valenti in 1968 to implement a voluntary film ratings system, which has remained in effect, in varying forms, since that time. The MPAA that year created the Classification and Ratings Administration (CARA) to designate films with one of four ratings: G (general audiences), M (mature audiences), R (children under sixteen years old not admitted without parent or guardian), and X (children under seventeen years old not admitted). Three years later M became PG (parental guidance suggested). In 1984, in response to violence in the movie *Indiana Jones and the Temple of Doom*, the film review board instituted the new PG-13 rating, which cautions parents that the film's contents may be inappropriate for children under age thirteen. In 1990 the board responded to criticism that the X rating unfairly categorized artistic adult films, such as *Midnight Cowboy*, with hard-core PORNOGRAPHY. In that year the board replaced X with NC-17.

In the movie business, a better rating is generally a lower rating. Movies typically make more money when they appeal to the widest possible audience. This rule holds true particularly with motion picture video sales. Many video outlets limit their inventory to movies with ratings no higher than PG-13 or R. Some theaters refuse to show movies with the NC-17 rating, and some newspapers refuse to carry advertisements for movies with the NC-17 rating. A movie studio therefore wants its film to earn the least restrictive rating possible.

One exception to this general rule is the marketing of pornographic films. Because studies have suggested that sexually explicit films become more desirable when they are restricted, the pornographic film industry voluntarily labels its films X or XXX in an effort to increase sales. XXX is a marketing tool, not an actual MPAA rating.

Although the MPAA publicizes the meaning of each rating, most moviegoers do not know how the ratings are assigned. A ratings board, consisting of eleven members, views approximately six hundred films a year, discusses each film's content, and chooses a rating for each film. Valenti and the board's chair choose all the board members and keep their identities secret to prevent film producers and studios from attempting to influence them. The members work full-time, serving terms of varying length. Members must be parents and cannot be involved with the motion picture industry, but they must meet no other requirements. Members base their ratings on a set of MPAA guidelines, some of which are precise whereas others call for individual taste and judgment. According to one MPAA guideline, a certain word used merely as an expletive in a film may garner a PG rating whereas the same word used to convey a sexual meaning may result in an R rating.

Directors who are unhappy with the board's rating may cut or edit objectionable film footage and resubmit the movie, or they may appeal the rating. Movie producers have the right to know the reason behind the rating their film receives. However, directors and producers have complained that the board's reasons are often unclear or lack specificity, requiring them to edit a film several times before it receives the target rating. Some directors have added especially gory scenes to the first version of a film with the idea that they will cut the gore during the ratings process, leaving the film in its intended state with the desired rating.

Because the movie ratings system is a voluntary process not under government control, FIRST AMENDMENT protections do not apply to ratings. If filmmakers believe that the rating for their film is too restrictive, they may appeal to a special board, which is composed of movie industry professionals rather than laypersons. The board screens the film, consults with the original ratings board, and listens to the complaints of the producer or director before voting. A two-thirds majority will overturn the original rating, and the decision of the appeals board is final.

No law requires filmmakers to undergo the ratings process; it is strictly voluntary. Yet, with very few exceptions, filmmakers comply. The system has the support of major film studios, theater owners, and video rental chains that rely on customer satisfaction for a healthy business. It is the movie industry that pays for the privilege of having a film rated; the producer of a film pays a fee for this service that is based on the cost of film production.

The ratings system has critics. Filmmakers complain that the system is arbitrary and point to instances in which films with similar content have different ratings. Producers and directors have also alleged racism, arguing that films depicting sexual encounters between African Americans receive more restrictive ratings than films involving sex between white characters. Critics also allege sex bias in that movies with frontal nude shots of women commonly receive R ratings, whereas movies with similar nude shots of men commonly receive X or NC-17 ratings. And major studios, say some critics, receive better treatment from the ratings board than do smaller, independent studios, which also have less money to spend to reedit and resubmit movies in the effort to achieve a better rating.

See also X OR XXX RATING.

MULTIDISTRICT LITIGATION 📖 A procedure provided by federal statute (28 U.S.C.A. § 1407) that permits civil lawsuits with at least one common (and often intricate) question of fact that have been pending in different federal district courts to be transferred and consolidated for pretrial proceedings before one judge. ◫

Congress has given the federal judicial system a mechanism to help manage complex and protracted civil lawsuits that are related to each other. Under 28 U.S.C.A. § 1407, the Judicial Panel on Multidistrict Litigation has the authority to transfer related cases to one federal judge for "coordinated and consolidated pretrial discovery" in advance of trial. The panel is composed of seven federal judges based throughout the United States, who have been appointed by the chief justice of the U.S. Supreme Court. The panel's clerk's office is located in Washington, D.C.

Certain types of litigation are good candidates for transfer and consolidation to a single judge. Torts involving a disaster (usually airplane crashes), PRODUCT LIABILITY, TRADEMARK and PATENT infringement, securities violations, and ANTITRUST issues have typically used multidistrict transfer.

Section 1407 transfers are initiated either by motion of a party or by the panel itself. The panel's decision whether to make a transfer is guided by a number of criteria: the existence of one or more common questions of fact within the group of cases being considered; whether transfer would be "for the convenience of parties and witnesses [and would] promote the just and efficient conduct of such actions" (section 1407(a)); the residence of the principal WITNESSES; the locations where the ACTIONS were initially filed; and the likelihood that transfer will avoid conflicting rulings. In general, economy and convenience become the determining factors.

Once the panel decides that a transfer is appropriate, it must select the appropriate judicial district to handle the litigation. There are no statutory guidelines governing the assignment of the consolidated case, but the panel considers the location of the judicial district in relation to the residences of the parties, the scene of the disaster (if the case involves such a situation), the business headquarters of the parties, the location with the highest concentration of relevant documents, and how easily the location of a judicial district can be reached. Apart from these factors, the panel seeks to place transferred cases in courts that have the time to oversee the complexities of the litigation.

After a district is chosen and a federal district judge is selected to manage the group of cases, the judge exercises full judicial powers over the case. The judge will enter a "practice and procedure order" that governs all matters leading to trial. During the pretrial stage, the parties use the DISCOVERY process to find out as much as they can about each other's case.

Under the statute, once all pretrial proceedings have been concluded, the judge remands the case to the panel, along with a recommendation as to how the panel should proceed in setting the cases for trial. Though the statute implies that the cases be remanded to their districts of inception for trial, the panel usually transfers a case back to the judge who handled the pretrial proceedings.

Federal multidistrict litigation is governed by the Rules of Procedure of the Judicial Panel on Multidistrict Litigation and the *Manual for Complex Litigation*. The panel's *In re Concrete Pipe*, 302 F. Supp. 244 (J.P.M.L. 1969), contains many additional factors that it may consider in deciding whether to transfer a case.

At the state level, similar transfer and consolidation methods have been employed to deal with complex litigation. States have appointed judges to oversee product liability cases involving products such as asbestos, breast implants, and tobacco.

See also CIVIL PROCEDURE; FEDERAL COURTS.

MULTILEVEL DISTRIBUTORSHIP ◫ A type of referral sales scheme by which an individual who purchases a particular item from a company agrees to solicit and provide additional buyers for the product in exchange for a commission or REBATE from the company. ◫

This type of plan is also known as a PYRAMID SALES SCHEME and is against the law in many JURISDICTIONS. See also CONSUMER PROTECTION.

MULTIPLICITY OF ACTIONS ◫ Several unnecessary attempts to litigate the same CLAIM or ISSUE. ◫

The law strongly disfavors multiplicity of actions because of the PUBLIC POLICY to promote judicial efficiency and to furnish speedy relief to an injured party. The rule against splitting a claim provides that if a plaintiff sets forth only certain aspects of the CAUSE OF ACTION in a COMPLAINT, he or she will be barred from raising the remaining aspects in a subsequent suit. If the plaintiff sues upon any portion of a particular claim, all other aspects of the claim are merged in this judgment if the plaintiff wins and are barred if the plaintiff does not win. For example, a plaintiff who claims $10,000 due under a single, indivisible CONTRACT and files two separate suits, for $5,000 each, will be permitted to litigate only the first suit, since the contract claim is a single cause of action.

MUNICIPAL 📖 In its narrower and more common sense, pertaining to a local governmental unit, commonly a city or town. In its broader sense, pertaining to the public or governmental affairs of a state, nation, or of a people. Relating to a state or nation, particularly when considered as an entity independent of other states or nations. 📖

MUNICIPAL CORPORATION 📖 An incorporated political subdivision of a state that is composed of the citizens of a designated geographic area and which performs certain state functions on a local level and possesses such powers as are conferred upon it by the state. 📖

A municipal corporation is a city, town, village, or borough that has governmental powers. A municipality is a city, town, village, or, in some states, a borough. A CORPORATION is an entity capable of conducting business. Cities, towns, villages, and some boroughs are called municipal corporations because they have the power to conduct business with the private sector.

Generally, the authority to govern the affairs within a state rests with the state legislature, the governor, and the state judicial system. However, states give localities limited powers to govern their own areas. The origin of the municipal corporation varies from state to state. Municipal corporations are given the power to govern through either the state constitution or state statutes, or through the legislative grant of a CHARTER.

States give municipalities the power to create an official governmental body, such as a board or council. Members of this body are elected by voters who live within the voting boundaries of the municipality. The local body has the power to pass ORDINANCES, or local laws. These laws may not conflict with state or federal laws.

Most states grant so-called HOME RULE powers to municipalities in the state constitution and state statutes. Home rule is a flexible grant of power from the state to the voters of a municipality. The first grant of home rule was given to the city of St. Louis in 1875 when the state of Missouri created a new state constitution that gave the city the power to create its own government.

Home rule gives municipalities the power to determine their own goals without interference from the state legislature or state agencies. It gives municipalities room to experiment with new approaches to government without first seeking approval from the state. It also allows municipalities to act more quickly on issues of local concern because they do not have to seek approval for their actions from the state legis-

lature. Although home rule powers are broad, in no event may a municipality enact a law that is specifically precluded by state law or that is contrary to state law. For example, a municipality may not vote to decriminalize narcotics that are illegal under state law. It may, however, strengthen existing state laws. For instance, a municipality may act to restrict the sale of ALCOHOL to a greater degree than is done in other municipalities.

The alternative to home rule is Dillon's Rule, a set of principles related to municipal power formulated by the influential jurist John Forest Dillon in 1872. Under Dillon's Rule, municipalities exercise only the limited powers specifically granted by the state, the powers necessary to carry out the specifically granted powers, and the powers indispensable to the declared purposes of the municipality. Few states rely on Dillon's Rule, and the trend among states is to give municipalities more power in deciding local issues.

The governmental authority most commonly exercised by municipalities is the POLICE POWER. The term *police power* does not refer to the authority to create police departments, although it does include that power. Police power is the power of state and local governments to enact laws governing health, safety, morals, and general public welfare. On the local level, such ordinances range from the provision of local police to ZONING laws to laws on domestic partnerships. The authority of states to exercise police power can be found in the TENTH AMENDMENT to the U.S. Constitution. States, in turn, grant police power to municipalities, and the municipalities exercise that power within their respective borders. The grant of police power from the state to municipalities can be found in state constitutions or state statutes.

States also commonly give their municipalities the power to enter into contracts. This power can be exercised only by action of the local governing body. The body must give notice of its intent to hire a private party for local government work. For example, if a municipality seeks a contractor to construct a building, the municipality must publish a notice of its intentions in a local newspaper and post other notices in public places. A municipality should not hire a private company if a member of the governing body has a financial interest in the company.

A municipality must exercise ordinary and REASONABLE care in providing safe public places and safe public services. If a municipality fails to exercise reasonable care, it may be held liable for resulting injuries. For example, if a person falls through a manhole and into the sewer, the city may be liable for any injuries resulting from the fall if the manhole cover was not secure. In this respect, a municipality may be liable for its negligence just like an individual. The most common TORT cases against municipalities are based on personal injuries caused by defects or obstructions in public streets, sidewalks, drains, and sewers.

Since the 1960s, cities across the United States have begun to decay because of lack of resources. To increase municipal resources, cities have imposed a variety of fees on private developers. Such fees include charges for building permit approvals, plat approvals, and water or sewer connection; impact fees that take into account future costs of a development; and special assessments for benefits given to a developer by the city. For example, a city may impose a transportation exaction fee on the developer of a residential subdivision to pay for the laying and maintenance of new roads that must be built to serve the subdivision. Developers have argued that such fees force private parties to pay for public functions, and they have attacked the fees as being beyond the power of the city government. In some cases their challenges have been upheld.

Municipal corporations are an important feature of the political structure of the United States. Incorporating a municipality gives it the freedom to form a society that is distinct from other localities in the state and around the country. This idea of local control is the same concept that animates the constitutional division of the country into a collection of smaller states. By giving municipalities some autonomy, individuals are more capable of participating in politics and gaining a measure of control over their lives than if political activity occurred only on the federal and state levels.

See also LAND-USE CONTROL.

MUNIMENTS OF TITLE 📖 Documents that serve as EVIDENCE of ownership of real or personal property. Written instruments, such as stock certificates or DEEDS to land, by which an owner is enabled to defend his or her ownership rights. 📖

The *muniment of title* doctrine provides that when ownership of property has been litigated between two parties and TITLE has been adjudicated to be held by one of the two, the loser is not able to relitigate the matter with anyone who relies upon the title of the winner.

MURDER 📖 The unlawful killing of another human being without justification or excuse. 📖

Murder is perhaps the single most serious criminal offense. Depending on the circum-

stances surrounding the killing, a person convicted of murder may be sentenced to many years in prison, a prison sentence with no possibility of parole, or death.

The precise definition of murder varies from JURISDICTION to jurisdiction. Under the COMMON LAW, or law made by courts, murder was the unlawful killing of a human being with MALICE AFORETHOUGHT. The term *malice aforethought* did not necessarily mean that the killer planned or PREMEDITATED on the killing, or that the killer felt MALICE toward the victim. Generally, *malice aforethought* referred to a level of intent or recklessness that separated murder from other killings and warranted stiffer punishment.

The definition of murder has evolved over several centuries. Under most modern statutes in the United States, murder comes in four varieties: (1) intentional murder, (2) a killing that resulted from the intent to do serious bodily injury, (3) a killing that resulted from a depraved heart or extreme RECKLESSNESS, and (4) murder committed by an ACCOMPLICE during the commission of, attempt of, or flight from certain felonies.

Some jurisdictions still use the term *malice aforethought* to define intentional murder, but many have changed or elaborated on the term to describe more clearly a murderous state of mind. California has retained the malice aforethought definition of murder (Cal. Penal Code § 187 [West 1996]). California also maintains a statute that defines the term *malice*. Under section 188 of the California Penal Code, malice is divided into two types: EXPRESS and IMPLIED. Express malice exists "when there is manifested a deliberate intention unlawfully to take away the life of a fellow creature." Malice may be implied by a judge or jury "when no considerable provocation appears, or when the circumstances attending the killing show an abandoned and malignant heart."

Murder Victims in the United States, 1980 to 1995

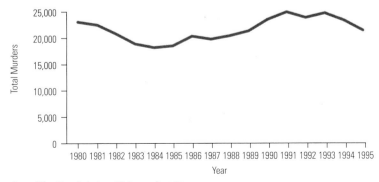

Source: Office of Juvenile Justice and Delinquency Prevention.

Murders in 1995

Victims

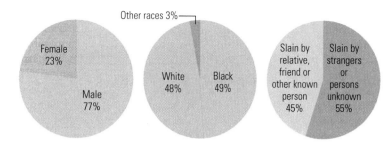

Offenders

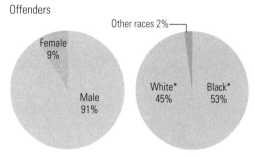

Source: Federal Bureau of Investigation, Uniform Crime Reporting Program, *Uniform Crime Reports.*

Many states use the California definition of implied malice to describe an unintentional killing that is charged as murder because the defendant intended to do serious bodily injury or acted with extreme recklessness. For example, if an aggressor punches a victim in the nose, intending only to injure the victim's face, the aggressor may be charged with murder if the victim dies from the blow. The infliction of serious bodily injury becomes the equivalent of an intent to kill when the victim dies. Although the aggressor did not have the express desire to kill the victim, the aggressor in such a case would not be charged with ASSAULT, but murder. To understand why, it is helpful to consider the alternative. When a person dies at the hands of an aggressor, it does not sit well with the public conscience to preclude a murder charge simply because the aggressor intended only to do serious bodily injury.

A person who unintentionally causes the death of another person also may be charged with murder under the depraved-heart theory. Depraved-heart murder refers to a killing that results from GROSS NEGLIGENCE. For example, assume that a man is practicing shooting his firearm in his backyard, located in a suburban area. If the man accidentally shoots and kills someone, he can be charged with murder under the depraved-heart theory.

Most states also have a felony murder statute. Under the felony murder doctrine, a person who attempts or commits a specified FELONY

may be held responsible for a death caused by an accomplice in the commission of the felony, an attempt to commit the felony, or flight from the felony or attempted felony. For example, if two persons rob a bank and during the ROBBERY one of them shoots and kills a security guard, the perpetrator who did not pull the trigger may nevertheless be charged with murder.

The felonies that most commonly give rise to a felony murder charge are murder, RAPE, robbery, BURGLARY, KIDNAPPING, and ARSON. Many states add to this list. Maine, for example, adds gross sexual assault and escape from lawful custody (Me. Rev. Stat. Ann. tit. 17-A, § 202 [West 1996]). Generally, felony murder exists only if the death was a reasonably foreseeable consequence of the felony, a felony attempt, or flight from the crime. For example, courts have held that death is a reasonably foreseeable consequence of armed robbery.

Most states divide the crime of murder into first and second degrees. In such states any intentional, unlawful killing done without justification or excuse is considered second-degree murder. The offense usually is punished with a long prison term or a prison term for life without the possibility of parole. Second-degree murder can be upgraded to first-degree murder, a more serious offense than second-degree murder, if the murder was accomplished with an aggravating or a special circumstance. An aggravating or a special circumstance is something that makes the crime especially heinous or somehow worthy of extra punishment.

California lists some twenty different special circumstances that can boost a murder from second to first degree, including murder carried out for financial gain; murder committed with an explosive; murder committed to avoid or prevent a lawful arrest; murder to perfect or attempt an escape from lawful CUSTODY; murder of a law enforcement officer, prosecutor, judge, or elected, appointed, or former government official; murder committed in an especially heinous, atrocious, or cruel fashion where the killer lay in wait for, or hid from, the victim, where the victim was tortured by the killer, where the killer used poison, or where the killing occurred during the commission of, aid of, or flight from certain felonies. These felonies include rape, robbery, kidnapping, burglary, arson, train wrecking, sodomy, the performance of a lewd or lascivious act upon a child under age fourteen, and oral copulation with a child under age fourteen (Cal. Penal Code § 190.2 [West 1996]).

If a murder does not qualify by statute for first-degree murder, it is charged as second-degree murder. A second-degree murder may

Women Murdered on the Job

The workplace can be a dangerous environment, exposing workers to hazards that can cause accidents, disease, and sometimes death. But the workplace also is a place where murders are committed. Statistics indicate that there is a large difference between the number of men and the number of women killed on the job. Fifteen percent of men who die at work are murdered, whereas 35 percent of female workplace deaths are the result of homicides.

It is believed that the high number of female workplace murders is based in part on the kinds of jobs women take in the economy. Many work in retail jobs, clerking at late-night convenience stores where robberies often occur and where security is often lacking. Analysts also believe that male perpetrators select retail stores where they believe that they can easily overpower a female employee.

Other workplace murders of women are committed by former boyfriends and husbands who are upset over a separation. Some psychologists believe that these men associate the woman's job with independence and the breakup of their relationship. Murdering a former wife or lover is a way for a man to reassert his dominance.

Finally, some murders of women appear to be committed out of resentment over the loss of a job at the workplace and the perception that women are to blame for the job loss. Roughly five percent of all the murders committed in the workplace, male and female, are committed by former or current employees.

be downgraded to MANSLAUGHTER if mitigating factors were involved in the killing, such as adequate provocation by the victim or the absence of intent or recklessness on the part of the defendant.

Maine is an example of a state that has simplified the law of murder. In Maine a person is guilty of murder if he or she intentionally or knowingly causes the death of another human being, engages in conduct that manifests a depraved indifference to the value of human life and causes death, or intentionally or knowingly causes another human being to commit suicide by the use of force, DURESS, or deception (Me. Stat. tit. 17-A § 201 [1996]). Maine also has a felony murder statute. It does not divide murder into degrees.

SENTENCING for murder varies from state to state, and according to degrees in the states that have them. Second-degree murder usually is punished with more than twenty years in prison. A person convicted of second-degree murder in Minnesota, for example, may be sentenced to prison for not more than forty years. Some states, such as California, allow a sentence up to life in prison for second-degree murder.

In some states that have a first-degree murder charge, the crime is punished with a life term in prison without the possibility of parole. In other states first-degree murder is punishable by death. A defendant's criminal history may affect sentencing for a murder conviction. The greater the criminal history, the more time the defendant is likely to serve. The criminal history of a murder defendant may even cause a

murder charge to be upgraded from second degree to first degree. In California, for example, a murder defendant who has a prior conviction for murder faces an automatic first-degree murder charge.

The best defenses to a murder charge are PROVOCATION and SELF-DEFENSE. If the defendant acted completely in self-defense, this may relieve the defendant of all criminal LIABILITY. If it does not relieve the defendant of all liability, self-defense at least may reduce the charge from murder to manslaughter. Provocation rarely results in complete absolution, but it may reduce the defendant's criminal liability. For example, assume that a family is being tormented by a neighbor for no apparent reason. The neighbor has damaged the family's property, assaulted the children, and killed the family dog. If the father kills the neighbor and is charged with murder, the father may argue that the provocation by the victim was so great that if he is to be found criminally liable at all, he should be found liable for manslaughter, not murder.

Insanity is another defense to a murder charge. If a defendant was suffering from such a defect of the mind that she did not know what she was doing, or she did not know that what she was doing was wrong, she may be found not guilty by reason of insanity. In some states the defendant may be found guilty but mentally ill. In either case the result is the same: the defendant is confined to a mental institution instead of a prison.

The modern law of murder is relatively static, but minor changes are occasionally proposed or implemented. Some legislatures have debated the idea of striking assisted suicide from murder statutes. Some have considered proposals making doctors liable for murder if they perform a third-term ABORTION. Many have made changes with respect to juveniles. Juveniles accused of murder used to be tried in juvenile courts, but in the 1980s and 1990s, legislatures passed laws to make juvenile murder defendants over the ages of fourteen or fifteen stand trial as adults. This is significant because a juvenile defendant convicted in the juvenile justice system may go free on reaching a certain age, such as twenty-one. A juvenile defendant tried in adult court does not have such an opportunity and may be sentenced to prison for many years, or for life without parole. A juvenile may be put to death on conviction for murder but only if he was age sixteen or older at the time of the offense (*Thompson v. Oklahoma*, 487 U.S. 815, 108 S. Ct. 2687, 101 L. Ed. 2d 702 [1988]).

CROSS-REFERENCES

Capital Punishment; Criminal Law; Death and Dying; Felony-Murder Rule; Homicide; Insanity Defense; Juvenile Law.

MURPHY, FRANCIS WILLIAM As a champion of civil liberties in the World War II era, Francis ("Frank") William Murphy had an extraordinary political and legal career. An associate justice of the U.S. Supreme Court from 1940 to 1949, he previously had served in local, state, and federal government. He was appointed U.S. governor general of the Philippine Islands in 1935, elected governor of Michigan in 1936, and appointed U.S. attorney general in 1939. Murphy's support for workers, women, and members of religious and racial minority groups, as well as his broad reading of the First and Fourth Amendments, distinguished him at a time when both the federal government and the Court moved slowly in upholding CIVIL RIGHTS.

Born in Harbor Beach, Michigan, April 13, 1890, Murphy was the son of an Irish Catholic country lawyer and a devoutly religious mother.

"OFFICIAL COMPULSION TO AFFIRM WHAT IS CONTRARY TO ONE'S RELIGIOUS BELIEFS IS THE ANTITHESIS OF FREEDOM OF WORSHIP."

BIOGRAPHY

Francis William Murphy

PHOTOGRAPHER, WHITMORE LIFE PHOTOGRAPHS, COLLECTION OF THE SUPREME COURT OF THE UNITED STATES

He studied at the University of Michigan before being admitted to the state bar in 1914. He then went off to fight in France and Germany in World War I. On returning to Michigan, he acquired legal experience by working in the state attorney general's office and in private practice. He next became judge for the principal criminal court in Detroit, which in turn led to a political career. A pro-labor Democrat, Murphy was mayor of Detroit from 1930 to 1933.

In the midst of the Great Depression, Murphy supported FRANKLIN D. ROOSEVELT for president in 1932. President Roosevelt rewarded him with appointment as the governor general of the Philippine Islands. Murphy enacted MINIMUM WAGE laws and supported women's suffrage while helping to effect the country's transition to independence. Returning to Michigan, he campaigned and won election as governor in 1936. That year the historic sit-down strike by 135,000 automobile workers proved to be the turning point in Murphy's career. He refused to deploy state police against the unpopular strikers and as a consequence lost his reelection bid in 1938.

President Roosevelt named him to his administration. Although Murphy wanted to be secretary of war—and, indeed, would spend several years trying to find ways to join the war effort—Roosevelt had other plans. The president made him U.S. attorney general. Murphy established the first civil liberties unit in the Department of Justice and brought suit against trust companies and a powerful Democratic party boss, Thomas J. Pendergast of Kansas City. In 1939 the death of Associate Justice PIERCE BUTLER opened the so-called Catholic seat on the Supreme Court, and Roosevelt gave it to a reluctant Murphy, who thought himself less qualified than others.

Murphy served for nine years as an associate justice. He wrote 199 opinions. Inherently suspicious of government power and passionately devoted to the rights of the weak, Murphy supported civil rights in nearly every case. He

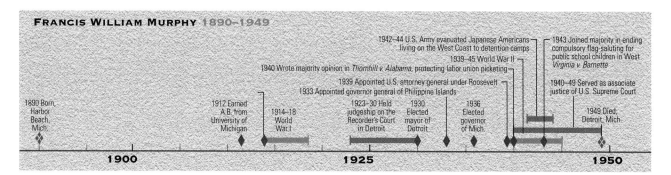

FRANCIS WILLIAM MURPHY 1890–1949

1942–44 U.S. Army evacuated Japanese Americans living on the West Coast to detention camps

1943 Joined majority in ending compulsory flag-saluting for public school children in West *Virginia v. Barnette*

1939–45 World War II

1940 Wrote majority opinion in *Thornhill v. Alabama*, protecting labor union picketing

1939 Appointed U.S. attorney general under Roosevelt

1940–49 Served as associate justice of U.S. Supreme Court

1933 Appointed governor general of Philippine Islands

1890 Born, Harbor Beach, Mich.

1912 Earned A.B. from University of Michigan

1914–18 World War I

1923–30 Held judgeship on the Recorder's Court in Detroit

1930 Elected mayor of Detroit

1936 Elected governor of Mich.

1949 Died, Detroit, Mich.

1900   1925   1950

scorned the federal government's treatment of Japanese Americans during World War II, for example, and at other times sided with the claims of workers and religious minority groups.

This philosophy found its best expression in 1944. "The law knows no finer hour," Murphy wrote in one of his many dissents, "than when it cuts through formal concepts and transitory emotions to protect unpopular citizens against discrimination and persecution" (*Falbo v. United States*, 320 U.S. 549, 64 S. Ct. 346, 88 L. Ed. 305). That case was one of several in the 1940s involving church-state issues that concerned the rights of the Jehovah's Witnesses, in this case a conscientious objector. Murphy often voted in favor of upholding FIRST AMENDMENT claims; for example, he joined the majority in ending compulsory flag-saluting for children in public schools (*West Virginia State Board of Education v. Barnette*, 319 U.S. 624, 63 S. Ct. 1178, 87 L. Ed. 1628 [1943]). In another important speech case, Murphy wrote the majority opinion protecting LABOR UNION picketing (*Thornhill v. Alabama*, 310 U.S. 88, 60 S. Ct. 736, 84 L. Ed. 1093 [1940]). Yet more often than not, his broader reading of individual rights led him into dissent against the majority.

On and off the Court, Murphy faced criticism for his idealism. He was seen as too emotional at the expense of strict legal thinking. He was the target of the popular barb, "justice tempered with Murphy." His personal life only fed his somewhat prim reputation, because he was a hypochondriac who never drank, smoked, or married. Chief Justice HARLAN F. STONE disliked him for another reason: he thought Murphy was too reliant on his law clerks.

Although Murphy occasionally seemed out of step with both the Court and his times, his broad vision of civil liberties was later vindicated. In particular, he believed in vigorous application of the FOURTH AMENDMENT's prohibition of unreasonable SEARCHES AND SEIZURES by the police. Murphy dissented in *Wolf v. Colorado*, 338 U.S. 25, 69 S. Ct. 1359, 93 L. Ed. 1782 (1949), where the Court refused to apply to the states what already existed for federal courts: the ban on admitting improperly seized EVIDENCE in a trial. He wrote that the majority, by leaving state courts out of the equation, was allowing "lawlessness by officers of the law." Twelve years later, in 1961, a different Supreme Court agreed with him and overruled *Wolf* in the landmark case *Mapp v. Ohio*, 367 U.S. 643, 81 S. Ct. 1684, 6 L. Ed. 2d 1081 (1961).

Murphy died on July 19, 1949 in Detroit, Michigan.

See also FLAG; JAPANESE AMERICAN EVACUATION CASES.

MUSIC PUBLISHING The contractual relationship between a songwriter or music composer and a music publisher, whereby the writer assigns part or all of his or her music copyrights to the publisher in exchange for the publisher's commercial exploitation of the music.

Music publishing has been an important part of the U.S. entertainment industry since the early twentieth century. Songwriters contract with music publishing companies to exploit their songs, with both parties sharing the income generated from the songs. Before the introduction of musical recordings, songwriters and publishers earned their income primarily from the sale of sheet music. In the modern era, songs can be commercially exploited in many types of media, including recordings, radio, television, film, and video. Music publishing is governed by U.S. COPYRIGHT law, but much of the law of music publishing is negotiated through private contractual agreements.

Music publishers are powerful intermediaries between songwriters and recording companies. Typically, a music publisher demands copyright ownership from the songwriter, along with half of the royalties. A publisher may make a large cash advance to a popular or promising songwriter, but often the advance is minimal. In return, the publisher seeks to place the songwriter's compositions with performers who will make a recording. In addition, a publisher will try to place songs in films, television shows, and advertisements. If the songwriter is also a performer, the publisher will assist the artist in obtaining a recording contract. The publisher also assumes the responsibility of collecting royalties and giving the songwriter his share.

Publishing income comes from various sources, but it is separate from income derived from retail sales of recordings. Income from recording sales flows to the owner of the recording (usually the record company), which then pays a contractually negotiated recording ROYALTY to the performer. The owner of the recording separately pays the publisher of the recorded compositions a mechanical royalty for the right to record, copy, and distribute copies of the composition. These royalties are called mechanical royalties because the LICENSE is for mechanical recording and reproduction of the composition.

Under U.S. copyright law, a publisher is required to grant a mechanical license to anyone wishing to record a composition that has previously been recorded and released commercially. This is called a compulsory license, and the minimum rate that must be paid to the publisher for such a license is set by Congress at a few cents for each copy made of a recording of the composition. Normally, however, a record label that wishes to record a publisher's composition will negotiate a private license with the publisher rather than follow the strict accounting and reporting rules that accompany recording under a compulsory license. Because of this situation, the statutory compulsory license rate has become the effective ceiling rate for recording a composition, because no one need pay more than the rate set by law.

A lucrative part of music publishing involves performance royalties. Performance royalties are paid when a song is played on the radio or television, used by businesses for background music, or used by clubs for dance music or by bands performing at a club. A popular song can earn thousands and sometimes millions of dollars through the collection of performance royalties. However, it would be too demanding for a publisher to sign performance licenses with every club, radio station, and business office that might use a particular song. Instead publishers and songwriters register with a performing rights organization (PRO) to collect fees on their behalf.

The three PROs in the United States are the American Society of Composers, Authors, and Publishers (ASCAP), Broadcast Music, Inc. (BMI), and the Society of European State Authors and Composers (SESAC). The PROs negotiate blanket licenses with all who use music for profit. Such fees can range from less than one hundred dollars for a small business using music to enhance its business environment, to hundreds of thousands of dollars or millions of dollars for large-scale broadcasting entities. The PROs then monitor radio and television broadcasts and, using a complex statistical model, pay publishers and songwriters based on projected actual uses of a song. When a composition is registered with a PRO, the registrant informs the PRO what percentages of royalties are to be paid to the publisher and songwriter. The PRO issues separate payments to the publisher and to the songwriter (or songwriters). A particular songwriter may only be registered with one PRO at a given time to avoid confusion as to which PRO is responsible for collecting performance royalties on the songwriter's behalf. The use of blanket licenses allows an artist to perform compositions written by another songwriter without first requesting the songwriter's permission.

As opposed to mechanical licenses, there is no statutory rate for the use of a song in films and television advertisements (synchronization licenses), in radio advertisements (transcription licenses), or for sale as sheet music (print licenses). These fees are negotiated separately between the user and the music publisher. The licensee pays the entire fee to the publisher, who then pays the songwriter's share to the songwriter.

Since the 1960s, many popular musical performers have written their own musical compositions. Some of these artists choose to "self-publish," forgoing relationships with publishers and thus retaining full ownership and control of their copyrights. These artists are more often songwriters whose compositions are so unique that they are not likely to be recorded by other performers. Therefore, this type of artist will receive little benefit from an outside publisher's marketing efforts. However, because the music industry's royalty structure assumes that publishing income will be paid to a publisher, a self-published artist often will set up her own publishing company under an assumed name to receive publishing income. A self-published artist will frequently hire an accounting firm to handle specific administrative functions such as royalty collection, for a much smaller fee than a full-service music publisher would demand.

CROSS-REFERENCES

Broadcasting; Entertainment Law; Intellectual Property.

BIOGRAPHY

Ellen Spencer Mussey

MUSSEY, ELLEN SPENCER   At a time when women in the United States were often excluded from higher education, Ellen Spencer Mussey helped found a coeducational law school to promote the social and economic advancement of women.

In 1896, Mussey and colleague EMMA M. GILLETT sponsored a series of lectures in Washington, D.C., aimed at attracting and training female lawyers. The lectures were primarily for local women whose professional goals were frustrated by the men-only admission policies of most law schools in the District. After two years of well-received lectures, Mussey and Gillett expanded their curriculum and formally established Washington College of Law, a coeducational institution that later became part of American University. Mussey was the law school's first dean; she was succeeded by Gillett in 1913.

Mussey was born May 13, 1850, in Geneva, Ohio, to Platt Rogers Spencer and Persis Duty Spencer. After attending Lake Erie Seminary, in Painesville, Ohio, and Rockford Seminary, in

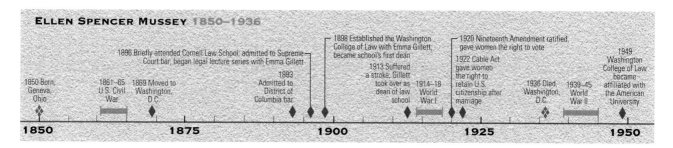

ELLEN SPENCER MUSSEY 1850–1936

1898 Established the Washington College of Law with Emma Gillett; became school's first dean

1896 Briefly attended Cornell Law School; admitted to Supreme Court bar, began legal lecture series with Emma Gillett

1920 Nineteenth Amendment ratified, gave women the right to vote

1922 Cable Act gave women the right to retain U.S. citizenship after marriage

1949 Washington College of Law became affiliated with the American University

1850 Born, Geneva, Ohio

1861–65 U.S. Civil War

1869 Moved to Washington, D.C.

1893 Admitted to District of Columbia bar

1913 Suffered a stroke; Gillett took over as dean of law school

1914–18 World War I

1936 Died, Washington, D.C.

1939–45 World War II

1850   1875   1900   1925   1950

Rockford, Illinois, Mussey moved to Washington, D.C., where she worked as a principal for the Spencerian Business College. She married lawyer Reuben Delavan Mussey in 1871 and had two children, Spencer Mussey and William Hitz Mussey. Under her husband's tutelage, Mussey read law and eventually attended the Law School of Cornell University in the summer of 1896.

When Mussey's husband became seriously ill, she took over the daily operation of his law office. After his death in 1892, Mussey was admitted to the D.C. bar. (At that time, a law degree was not required for bar admission.) She became one of very few women from her generation to be admitted to practice before the U.S. Supreme Court and the U.S. Court of Claims. In private practice, Mussey specialized in international and real estate law. At the request of American Red Cross founder Clara Barton, she became the Red Cross's first staff attorney.

A social reformer, Mussey was a major force behind new legislation giving women the same rights as men over children, property, and earnings. She also pushed for laws allowing women to keep their U.S. citizenship after marrying foreign citizens.

Mussey served as editor of *American Monthly* magazine, committee chair for the National Council of Women, and delegate to the 1911 International Council of Women held in Stockholm. She also helped organize the National Association of Women Lawyers and the Women's Bar Association of the District of Columbia.

Mussey died April 21, 1936, in Washington, D.C., at the age of eighty-five. She had overcome long-standing societal barriers to pursue her professional interests and social agenda. Washington College of Law was the crowning achievement of her illustrious career.

MUSSOLINI, BENITO   Benito Mussolini ruled as dictator of Italy from 1922 to 1943. His political philosophy, which he called fascism, was based on the total domination of the government in all spheres of political, social, eco-

nomic, and cultural life. Initially seen by the Italian people as a hero, Mussolini was driven from government before the end of World War II.

Mussolini was born in Dovia di Predappio, Italy, on July 29, 1883, the son of a socialist blacksmith. He embraced socialism as a teenager and as a young man became a schoolteacher and socialist journalist in northern Italy. In 1902 he moved to Switzerland and earned a living as a laborer. He returned to Italy in 1904 to perform his required military service and then resumed his teaching.

His wanderlust, however, resumed. He went to Trent, Austria, in 1909 and worked for a socialist newspaper. He was expelled from Austria after he publicly urged the return of Trent to Italy. In 1912 he became editor of *Avanti!*, the most important Italian socialist newspaper, with headquarters in Milan. When World War I broke out in August 1914, Mussolini proved unwilling to toe the socialist line. Socialists argued that disputes between nations were not their concern and that Italy should stay out of the conflict. Mussolini disagreed, whereupon the socialists expelled him from the party.

This expulsion radically changed Mussolini's political outlook. He founded *Il Popol d'Italia* (The People of Italy), a strident newspaper that argued that Italy should enter the war against Germany. When Italy did join the war, Mussolini enlisted in the army and served from 1915 to 1917, when he was wounded.

After the war Mussolini started his own political movement. In 1919 he formed the Fascist party, called the Fasci di Combattimento. The name *fascism* is derived from the Latin *fascis*, meaning *bundle*. The fasces is a bundle of rods strapped together around an axe. A symbol of authority in ancient Rome, it represented absolute, unbreakable power. Mussolini promised to recreate the glories of the Roman Empire in a movement that was nationalistic, antiliberal, and antisocialist.

Mussolini's movement struck a chord with lower-middle-class people. Supporters wore black shirts and formed private militias. In 1922

THE GRANGER COLLECTION, NEW YORK

Benito Mussolini formed the Fascist party in 1919 and he ruled Italy from 1922 to 1943. He and his mistress were murdered at the end of World War II.

Mussolini threatened a march on Rome to take over the government. King Victor Emmanuel capitulated to this threat and asked Mussolini to form a government. Once in power Mussolini abolished all other political parties and set out to transform Italy into a fascist state.

Initially Italians and foreign observers saw Mussolini as a strong leader who brought needed discipline to the economy and social structure of Italy. He poured money into building the infrastructure of a modern country. In a country known for disorganization, it was said that Mussolini made the trains run on time. He also, however, abolished trade unions and closed newspapers that did not follow the party line. He used the police to enforce his rule and imprisoned thousands of people for their political views.

In the 1930s Mussolini sought to make Italy an international power. In 1935 Italy invaded the East African country of Ethiopia. Mussolini ignored the LEAGUE OF NATIONS' demand that he withdraw and proceeded to conquer the country. In 1936 he sent Italian troops to support General Francisco Franco's Loyalist Army in the Spanish Civil War. By the end of the 1930s, Mussolini also moved closer to ADOLF HITLER and Nazi Germany. In 1939 he invaded nearby Albania.

Mussolini did not enter World War II until June 1940, when he invaded the south of France. At first his alliance with Hitler appeared propitious. However, the Italian army suffered defeat in North Africa, and the Allies invaded Sicily in 1943. Mussolini's regime crumbled. King Victor Emmanuel dismissed Mussolini as the head of state on July 25, 1943. Mussolini was briefly imprisoned, but German troops rescued him. Hitler directed Mussolini to head an Italian puppet state in northern Italy, then under the control of German forces. As the Allies moved north in 1945, Mussolini tried to escape to Switzerland. He was captured by Italian partisans and shot on April 28, 1945. The bodies of Mussolini and his mistress, Clara Petacci, were displayed to jeering crowds on the streets of Milan.

MUTILATION Cutting, tearing, erasing, or otherwise changing a document in a way that changes or destroys its legal effect. It is a federal crime to mutilate public records, coins, or passports.

In CRIMINAL LAW, the crime of violently, maliciously, and intentionally giving someone a serious permanent wound.

MUTINY A rising against lawful or constituted authority, particularly in the naval or ARMED SERVICES.

In the context of CRIMINAL LAW, mutiny refers to an INSURRECTION of soldiers or crew members against the authority of their commanders. The offense is similar to the crime of SEDITION, which is a revolt or an incitement to revolt against established authority, punishable by both state and federal laws.

MUTUAL COMPANY 📖 A CORPORATION in which members are the exclusive shareholders and the recipients of profits distributed as DIVIDENDS in proportion to the business that such members did with the company. 📖

The most common kind of mutual company is a mutual INSURANCE company. In this type of organization, which is a cooperative association, the members are both the insurers and the insured. Such companies exist for the purpose of satisfying the insurance needs of their members at a minimal cost. The members contribute through a system of premiums or assessments, forming a fund from which all losses and liabilities are paid. Any profits are divided among the members of the company in amounts proportionate to their individual interests.

The members of a mutual company choose the management. Professional associations that offer their members insurance coverage often form mutual insurance companies.

MUTUAL FUND 📖 A fund, in the form of an INVESTMENT company, in which shareholders combine their money to invest in a variety of STOCKS, BONDS, and money-market investments such as U.S. Treasury bills and bank CERTIFICATES OF DEPOSIT. 📖

Mutual funds provide a form of investment that is both relatively safe and relatively lucrative. Mutual funds offer investors the advantages of professional management of invested money and diversification of that investment. Mutual fund managers assume the responsibility of investigating and researching financial markets and selecting the combination of stocks, bonds, and other investment vehicles to be bought and sold. Thus, consumers purchase shares in a mutual fund and rely on the expertise of the mutual fund manager, whose job is to provide them with the highest possible return on their investments.

Investing in a mutual fund is not as safe as investing in a bank or a savings and loan association. The federal government normally insures money deposited in BANKS or SAVINGS AND LOAN ASSOCIATIONS; if one of those institutions fails, each of its deposits of up to $100,000 generally is guaranteed. This is not true of other investment vehicles such as stocks and bonds, which by their nature rise and fall in value and offer no guarantees. But investing in a mutual fund usually is considered to be safer than investing in individual stocks and bonds. Mutual fund managers observe the financial markets and take advantage of trends that affect the fund by buying and selling various components of the fund. And because a mutual fund is diverse—comprised perhaps of a hundred or more different kinds of stocks, bonds, or other investments—even the complete failure of one stock will make a relatively small impact on the fund's overall success.

There are two general types of mutual funds. An investor in an open-end fund may request at

Mutual Funds Summary, 1980 to 1994

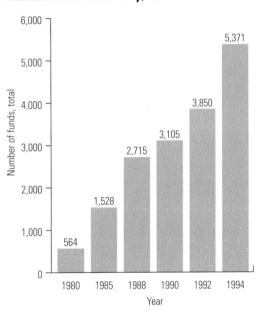

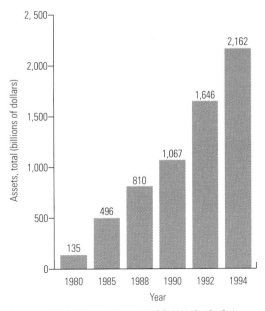

Source: Investment Company Institute, Washington, D.C., *Mutual Fund Fact Book*.

any time that the fund buy back, or redeem, that investor's shares. The price of shares in an open-end fund is based on the MARKET VALUE of the fund's portfolio of investments. Investors in open-end funds may be charged additional fees known as loads. Front-end loads are charged when the investor purchases shares in a mutual fund; back-end loads are subtracted from the redemption price. Open-end funds are sold by securities dealers and brokers and financial planners, or they are sold directly to the investor by the fund's sales staff.

Closed-end funds are traded on stock exchanges or the over-the-counter market. Unlike open-end funds, closed-end funds usually have a fixed number of shares, which are purchased and redeemed at their market price plus a commission.

Mutual funds are broadly classified according to three types of investment objectives: growth of capital, stability of capital, or current income. Most funds are geared toward one or two of these objectives. For example, money-market funds invest in instruments like U.S. Treasury bills, which are relatively safe and generally stable. Therefore many investors view money-market funds as a good alternative to a bank account. Other funds seek stability of capital by investing in blue-chip stocks and high-quality bonds. Some funds are potentially more lucrative, but far riskier. Growth funds are somewhat aggressive, investing in speculative securities that show promise over time for slow but steady long-term return. Income funds also tend to be speculative, often investing in high-risk, high-yield securities with the goal of greater short-term return.

Within the three broad categories of mutual funds are numerous subcategories. Funds that seek both growth and income are known as balanced funds. Sector funds invest in certain types of businesses, such as the computer industry. Some funds strive to fulfill a political agenda, such as investing in environmentally responsible companies or companies that actively promote women and minorities. Precious metals funds, municipal bond funds, and international stock funds are other examples of mutual fund categories. Other funds are far less specialized and allow the fund manager free reign to compile and alter the fund's portfolio.

Mutual fund shareholders receive periodic investment income, or dividends, which comes from DIVIDENDS and interest earned by the various securities that make up the fund's portfolio. Shareholders often elect to have these dividends reinvested into the mutual fund. Investors in mutual funds may choose to make monthly payments into the fund or have a specified amount automatically withdrawn from a bank account or savings and loan association account each month. Some companies offer a variety of open-end mutual funds with different investment objectives and allow investors a simple way to switch their money from one fund to another as their savings goals change.

Securities laws, both state and federal, govern mutual funds. Some statutes regulate the organization of investment companies and the sale of securities by BROKERS and dealers. Federal securities laws that regulate mutual funds include the Securities Act of 1933 (15 U.S.C.A. § 77a et seq.), the Securities Exchange Act of 1934 (15 U.S.C.A. § 78a et seq.), and the Investment Company Act of 1940 (15 U.S.C.A. § 80a–1 et seq.).

MUTUALITY OF OBLIGATION ◫ The legal principle that provides that unless both parties to a CONTRACT are bound to perform, neither party is bound. ◫

MUTUAL MISTAKE ◫ An error of both parties to a CONTRACT, whereby each operates under the identical misconception concerning a past or existing material fact. ◫

For example, a customer goes to the sample room of an interior decorator to select a carpet and asks the clerk to show him a navy carpet, which he subsequently purchases and takes with him. The sales slip notes that the carpet purchased is navy. When, upon examining the carpet in daylight, the customer discovers that it is black, not navy as he thought when he bought it, a mutual mistake would have occurred, since both the seller and buyer were in error concerning the correct color of the carpet sold. Since there had never been a true and complete meeting of the minds, no mutual assent was actually arrived at, and the buyer would be entitled to return the carpet and obtain a full refund. See also MEETING OF THE MINDS.

N

NADER, RALPH Considered the father of the CONSUMER PROTECTION movement, Ralph Nader has had a great effect on U.S. law and PUBLIC POLICY of the late twentieth century. Nader's advocacy on behalf of consumers and workers hastened into reality many features of the contemporary political landscape. The work of this lawyer and irrepressible gadfly of the powers that be, which began in the mid-1960s, has led to the passage of numerous consumer protection laws in such areas as AUTOMOBILES, mining, INSURANCE, GAS pipelines, and meatpacking, as well as the creation of government agencies such as the National Highway Traffic Safety Administration, the Occupational Safety and Health Administration, the ENVIRONMENTAL PROTECTION AGENCY, and the CONSUMER PRODUCT SAFETY COMMISSION. Nader himself has founded many well-known consumer advocacy groups, including the Public Interest Research Group, the Clean Water Action Project, the Center for Auto Safety, and the Project on Corporate Responsibility. His goal in these efforts, he has said, is "nothing less than the qualitative reform of the industrial revolution."

Ralph Nader

Nader was born February 27, 1934, in Winsted, Connecticut, to Nadra Nader and Rose Bouziane Nader, Lebanese immigrants who owned and operated a restaurant and bakery. He is the youngest of five children. He attended the Gilbert School and Princeton University on scholarships. At Princeton, he entered the Woodrow Wilson School of Public and International Affairs, and he graduated magna cum laude and Phi Beta Kappa in 1955. During an era of conformity, his challenges to school authorities and procedures at Princeton made him stand out. At one point, he protested the use of the poisonous insecticide DDT on campus trees.

After Princeton, Nader attended Harvard Law School, where he edited the *Harvard Law Record*, and graduated with distinction in 1958. It was at Harvard that he first became interested in auto safety. After studying auto injury cases, in 1958 he published his first article on the subject, "American Cars: Designed for Death," in the *Harvard Law Record*. It contained a thesis that he would bring to national attention in the mid-1960s: auto fatalities result not just from

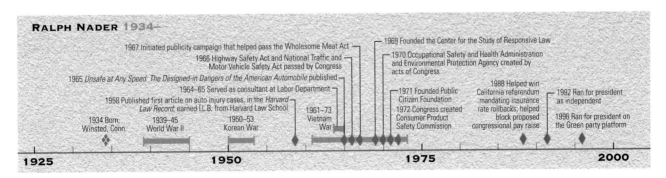

RALPH NADER 1934–

1967 Initiated publicity campaign that helped pass the Wholesome Meat Act

1966 Highway Safety Act and National Traffic and Motor Vehicle Safety Act passed by Congress

1965 *Unsafe at Any Speed: The Designed-in Dangers of the American Automobile* published

1964–65 Served as consultant at Labor Department

1958 Published first article on auto injury cases, in the *Harvard Law Record*; earned LL.B. from Harvard Law School

1934 Born, Winsted, Conn.

1939–45 World War II

1950–53 Korean War

1961–73 Vietnam War

1969 Founded the Center for the Study of Responsive Law

1970 Occupational Safety and Health Administration and Environmental Protection Agency created by acts of Congress

1971 Founded Public Citizen Foundation

1972 Congress created Consumer Product Safety Commission

1988 Helped win California referendum mandating insurance rate rollbacks; helped block proposed congressional pay raise

1992 Ran for president as independent

1996 Ran for president on the Green party platform

1925   1950   1975   2000

driver error, as the auto industry had maintained, but also from poor vehicle design. Nader followed his law degree with six months of service in the Army and then a period of personal travel through Latin America, Europe, and Africa. Upon his return, he established a private law practice in Hartford, created an informal legal aid society, and lectured from 1961 to 1963 at the University of Hartford.

Having worked on a local level for auto safety regulations in the years subsequent to his graduation from Harvard, Nader decided to go to Washington, D.C., in 1964, where he hoped to have more influence. Through his friendship with Daniel P. Moynihan, then serving as assistant secretary of labor, Nader worked as a consultant at the Labor Department and wrote a study that called for federal responsibility for auto safety.

Nader left the Labor Department in May 1965 and devoted himself to completing what would become his most celebrated book, *Unsafe at Any Speed: The Designed-in Dangers of the American Automobile.* The book was published later that year and quickly became a best-seller. In it, Nader painted a grim picture of motor vehicle injuries and fatalities, noting that 47,700 people were killed in auto accidents in 1964. He made an eloquent appeal for federal safety standards on autos that would both prevent accidents from occurring and better protect passengers in the event of an accident. The book also communicated a philosophy regarding public regulation of technology that would cause him to do battle on many another issue. "A great problem of contemporary life," he wrote, "is how to control the power of economic interests which ignore the harmful effects of their applied science and technology." Nader has devoted his life to solving this problem.

Taking some of his inspiration from the civil rights movement, Nader stood up to the most powerful companies in the world. His book targeted the safety problems of the Chevrolet Corvair, a product of the world's largest company, General Motors (GM). He convincingly marshaled evidence that the driver could lose control of the Corvair even when it was moving slowly, thus making it "unsafe at any speed." The Goliath of GM did not take kindly to the stones thrown by this David, and the company began a campaign of harassment and intimidation intended to abort Nader's efforts. Congressional committee hearings later, in 1966, revealed that GM's campaign against Nader involved harassing phone calls and attempts to lure Nader into compromising situations with

"THE MOST IMPORTANT OFFICE IN AMERICA FOR ANYONE TO ACHIEVE IS FULL-TIME CITIZEN."

women. The company formally apologized before Congress for these tactics.

Politicians in Washington, D.C., and the U.S. public were receptive to Nader's ideas. In 1966, in his State of the Union address, President LYNDON B. JOHNSON called for a national HIGHWAY safety act. Later that year, Congress passed the Highway Safety Act (80 Stat. 731 [23 U.S.C.A. § 401 note]) and the National Traffic and Motor Vehicle Safety Act (80 Stat. 718 [15 U.S.C.A. § 1381 note]). The latter created a new government body, later named the National Highway Traffic Safety Administration, that oversaw the creation of federal safety standards for automobiles and was also empowered to authorize recalls of unsafe vehicles. In subsequent years, these laws and others for which Nader had advocated helped to bring about a marked decrease in traffic fatalities per vehicle mile. As the *Washington Post* exclaimed, on August 30, 1966, "[A] one-man lobby for the public prevailed over the nation's most powerful industry."

Nader's first work in the area of auto safety remains his most famous consumer advocacy. However, he has remained a tireless proponent of consumers' and workers' rights on many different fronts. Shortly after his triumph with auto regulation, Nader initiated a publicity campaign that helped pass the Wholesome Meat Act, 81 Stat. 584, 19 U.S.C.A. 1306 (1967), which established stricter federal guidelines for meatpacking plants. By the late 1960s, he began to mobilize college students who joined him in his investigations of public policy and the effectiveness of government regulations. These young forces came to be called Nader's Raiders, and many of them eventually rose to positions of influence in the government and in public policy organizations. By the mid-1970s, the various groups Nader had created, including Public Interest Research Groups in many states, were doing research and financing legal action in relation to myriad public policy issues, including tax reform, consumer product safety, and corporate responsibility.

During RONALD REAGAN's presidency in the 1980s, Nader's influence in Washington, D.C., declined, particularly as the Reagan administration dismantled much of the government regulation Nader had helped establish. He did not give up his cause, however. In the late 1980s, he was again in the media spotlight, this time through his attempts to lower car insurance rates in California and to block a proposed congressional pay increase. During the 1980s and 1990s, he also addressed the savings and loan bailout problem, well before it became high on the nation's agenda; opposed the use of chlorinated fluorocarbons, which damage the ozone layer; and worked to prevent limitations on damages that consumers may receive from corporations through civil lawsuits.

Nader has written and edited dozens of books in his career. These include *The Consumer and Corporate Accountability* (1973), *Corporate Power in America* (1973), *Working on the System: A Comprehensive Manual for Citizen Access to Federal Agencies* (1974), *Government Regulation: What Kind of Reform?* (1976), *The Big Boys: Power and Position in American Business* (1986), and *Collision Course: The Truth about Airline Safety* (1994).

NAKED CONTRACT ◫ An agreement between two parties that is without any legal effect because no CONSIDERATION has been exchanged between the parties. ◫

The Latin term for naked contract is *nudum pactum*.

NAME ◫ The designation of an individual person or of a firm or corporation. A word or combination of words used to distinguish a person, thing, or class from others. ◫

An individual's name is comprised of a name given at birth, known as the *given name* or *first name*, selected by the parents, and the surname or last name, which identifies the family to which he or she belongs. Ordinarily an individual is not properly identified unless he or she is called or described by this given name in addition to the surname. This rule has significance, among other times, when students are designated in school records and when parties are called or referred to in legal proceedings, including CHILD CUSTODY actions. The general rule is that when identity is certain, a small variance in name, such as that caused by typographical errors, is unimportant.

The method by which an individual can change his or her name is usually prescribed by state statutes and involves filing a certificate in, or making an application to, a court. Whether or not a name change will be granted is ordinarily a matter of judicial discretion.

In recent years, some married women have begun to depart from the traditional practice of taking their husband's surname upon MARRIAGE. Instead they retain their birth names, the surnames possessed before marriage. While some states subscribe to the rule that a woman's legal name is her husband's surname, others hold that an individual can be known by whatever name he or she desires as long as such designation is used consistently and in the absence of a fraudulent purpose. A number of states have specifically provided that a wife is not required to use her husband's surname, or that she can use it in her personal life while continuing to use her birth name in her profession.

NAPOLEONIC CODE ◫ The first modern organized body of law governing France, also known as the Code Napoleon or Code Civil, enacted by Napoléon I in 1804. ◫

In 1800, Napoléon I appointed a commission of four persons to undertake the task of compiling the Napoleonic Code. Their efforts, along with those of J. J. Cambacérès, were instrumental in the preparation of the final draft. The Napoleonic Code assimilated the private law of France, which was the law governing transactions and relationships between individuals. The Code, which is regarded by some commentators as the first modern counterpart to ROMAN LAW, is currently in effect in France in an amended form.

The Napoleonic Code is a revised version of the Roman law or CIVIL LAW, which predominated in Europe, with numerous French modifications, some of which were based on the Germanic law that had been in effect in northern France. The code draws upon the Institutes of the Roman CORPUS JURIS CIVILIS for its categories of the civil law: PROPERTY RIGHTS, such as LICENSES; the acquisition of property, such as TRUSTS; and personal status, such as legitimacy of birth.

Napoléon applied the code to the territories he governed—namely, some of the German states, the low countries, and northern Italy. It was extremely influential in Spain and, eventually, in Latin America as well as in all other European nations except England, where the COMMON LAW prevailed. It was the harbinger, in France and abroad, of CODIFICATIONS of other areas of law, such as criminal law, civil procedure, and commercial law. The Napoleonic Code served as the prototype for subsequent codes during the nineteenth century in twenty-four countries; the province of Québec and the state of Louisiana have derived a substantial portion of their laws from it. Napoléon also promulgated four other codes: the Code of Civil Procedure (1807), the Commercial Code (1808), the Code of Criminal Procedure (1811), and the Penal Code (1811).

NATIONAL ASSOCIATION FOR THE ADVANCEMENT OF COLORED PEOPLE
Founded in 1909, the National Association for the Advancement of Colored People (NAACP) is the oldest and largest CIVIL RIGHTS organization in the United States. The interracial

NAACP works for the elimination of racial discrimination through lobbying, legal action, and education. With its victories in landmark Supreme Court cases such as *Brown v. Board of Education*, 347 U.S. 483, 74 S. Ct. 686, 98 L. Ed. 873 (1954), as well as its sponsorship of grassroots social programs, the NAACP has been a leader in the effort to guarantee that African Americans and members of other racial minorities receive EQUAL PROTECTION under the law.

The NAACP grew out of race riots that occurred in Springfield, Illinois, in August 1908. Shocked at the violence directed against African Americans by European American mobs in ABRAHAM LINCOLN's hometown, William English Walling, a white socialist, wrote a magazine article that called for the formation of a group to come to the aid of African Americans. The following year, Walling met with two young white social workers, Mary White Ovington and Henry Moskowitz, and began planning a course of action. They enlisted the aid of Oswald Garrison Villard, grandson of the abolitionist William Lloyd Garrison, to publicize the Conference on the Status of the Negro, to be held that May. The conference drew several hundred people, many of whom would unite a year later as the NAACP.

Although originally the NAACP's leadership was largely white, since the 1920s, it has been primarily African American. The organization drew many of its original white members from progressive and socialist ranks, and most of its first African American members through the leadership of the historian and sociologist W. E. B. DU BOIS. Du Bois and Booker T. Washington were the two principal African American leaders of the day. Du Bois had led the Niagara Movement, an African American protest organization, since 1905 and he brought the membership of that organization into the

National Association for the Advancement of Colored People

1905	W. E. B. Du Bois and others founded the Niagara Movement
1908	Race riots erupted in Springfield, Illinois, Abraham Lincoln's hometown
1909	On 100th anniversary of Lincoln's birthday, more than sixty citizens issued a "call" for a national conference to renew the struggle for civil and political liberty; the group and conference formed the foundation of the NAACP
1910	National Association for the Advancement of Colored People (NAACP) chosen as group's name at second annual conference; William Walling chosen as executive director; W. E. B. Du Bois chosen as director of publicity and research and editor of the *Crisis*
1911	NAACP incorporated
1915	In *Guinn v. United States*, the Supreme Court struck down grandfather clauses in state constitutions as unconstitutional barriers to voting rights granted under the Fifteenth Amendment
1917	Supreme Court barred municipal ordinances requiring racial segregation in housing in *Buchanan v. Warley*
1920	NAACP appointed its first African American executive director, James Weldon Johnson
1923	Supreme Court ruled in *Moore v. Dempsey* that exclusion of African Americans from a jury was inconsistent with the right to a fair trial
1931	Walter White appointed to succeed Johnson as director of the NAACP
1934	Charles Hamilton Houston hired as NAACP's first full-time attorney
1936	Thurgood Marshall joined NAACP as special counsel
1940	NAACP created separate legal arm, the NAACP Legal Defense and Educational Fund, and appointed Marshall as its director-counsel
1941	Secretary of Army authorized first segregated airman unit, the 99th Squadron, better known as the Tuskegee airmen
1948	Marshall's team argued *Shelly v. Kramer*, which struck down racially restrictive (land) covenants; President Truman abolished racial segregation in armed services by executive order
1950	In *Sweatt v. Painter*, Supreme Court ruled racially segregated professional schools inherently unequal and therefore unconstitutional; first integrated combat units saw action in Korea
1954	Marshall's team argued *Brown v. Board of Education of Topeka, Kansas,* which ruled racial segregation in public schools unconstitutional
1955	Roy Wilkins appointed to succeed White as NAACP's executive director
1961	Marshall appointed to U.S. Court of Appeals for the Second Circuit, Jack Greenberg succeeded Marshall as director of LDF
1964	NAACP lobbying led to passage of the Civil Rights Act of 1964
1965	NAACP lobbying led to passage of the Voting Rights Act of 1965
1967	Thurgood Marshall became first African American associate justice of the Supreme Court
1968	NAACP lobbying led to passage of the Fair Housing Act of 1968
1972	U.S. Supreme Court declared existing capital punishment laws unconstitutional in *Furman v. Georgia*
1974	NAACP experienced a setback when Supreme Court overturned efforts to integrate largely white suburban school districts with largely black urban districts in *Bradley v. Millikin*
1976	Georgia, Florida and Texas drafted new death penalty laws; Supreme Court upheld these new laws
1977	Benjamin Hamilton Hooks succeeded Wilkins as NAACP's executive director
1978	Supreme Court placed limits on affirmative action programs in *Regents of University of California v. Bakke*
1993	Benjamin F. Chavis, Jr. appointed to succeed Hooks as NAACP's executive director
1994	NAACP board of directors voted to oust Chavis after sexual harassment suit was filed against him
1995	Myrlie Evers-Williams replaced William F. Gibson as chairman of the NAACP board of directors
1996	NAACP board appointed Kweisi Mfume, a U.S. representative from Maryland, as president and chief financial officer; Mfume cut national staff by third as first step in returning NAACP to financial health
1997	NAACP retired debt

Sources: NAACP web page; *Simple Justice* by Richard Kluger (1975).

NAACP. He was named director of publicity and research for the NAACP in 1910, and edited the organization's highly respected journal, *The Crisis*, until 1934.

From the beginning, the NAACP made legal action on behalf of African Americans a top priority. It won early Supreme Court victories in *Guinn v. United States*, 238 U.S. 347, 35 S. Ct. 926, 59 L. Ed. 1340 (1915), which overturned the GRANDFATHER CLAUSE as a means of disfranchising black voters, and in *Buchanan v. Warley*, 245 U.S. 60, 38 S. Ct. 16, 62 L. Ed. 149 (1917), which barred municipal ordinances requiring racial segregation in housing. (The *grandfather clause* imposed a literacy test on persons who were not entitled to vote prior to 1866. This meant that all slaves and their descendants had to pass a rigorous literacy test based on knowledge of the state constitution and other highly technical documents. Few, if any, African Americans passed the test.)

The NAACP appointed its first African American executive director, JAMES WELDON JOHNSON, in 1920. Under Johnson and his successor, Walter White, who led the organization from 1931 to 1955, the NAACP worked for the passage of a federal antilynching law. Although unsuccessful in its efforts to pass a federal law, the NAACP brought public attention to the brutality of lynching and helped to significantly reduce its occurrence. As a result, lynching—which is the infliction of punishment, usually hanging, by a mob without trial—is now illegal in every state.

For its early litigation efforts, the NAACP relied on lawyers who volunteered their services. In 1934, the group hired CHARLES HAMILTON HOUSTON, an African American and dean of Howard Law School, as its first full-time attorney. The following year, Houston started a legal campaign to end school segregation. Houston was assisted by THURGOOD MARSHALL, a young lawyer who would go on to argue many cases before the Supreme Court and in 1967 would become the first African American appointed to the Court. In 1940, the NAACP appointed Marshall director-counsel of its new legal branch, the NAACP Legal Defense and Educational Fund.

After succeeding in Supreme Court cases concerning unequal salary scales for black teachers and segregation in graduate and professional schools, the NAACP achieved its most celebrated triumph before the Court in *Brown*, a decision that declared racial segregation in public schools to be unconstitutional.

The *Brown* decision sparked another civil rights initiative, the Montgomery, Alabama, bus BOYCOTT of 1955. The boycott catapulted MARTIN LUTHER KING, JR., to national recognition and spurred the creation of the SOUTHERN CHRISTIAN LEADERSHIP CONFERENCE (SCLC). By the early 1960s, the SCLC, the STUDENT NONVIOLENT COORDINATING COMMITTEE (SNCC), the Congress of Racial Equality (CORE), and the National Urban League all took the lead in promoting civil rights for African Americans. These groups adopted a direct-action approach to promoting African American interests, conducting highly publicized sit-ins and demonstrations.

The NAACP, meanwhile, drew criticism for its devotion to traditional legal and political means for seeking social change. ROY WILKINS, executive director of the NAACP from 1955 to 1975, voiced his preference for traditional tactics over "the kind that picks a fight with the sheriff and gets somebody's head beaten" (Spear 1984, 7:402). Although many viewed it as overly conservative in its civil rights approach, the NAACP helped pass important civil rights legislation such as the CIVIL RIGHTS ACT of 1964 (42 U.S.C.A. § 2000a et seq.), the Voting Rights Act of 1965 (42 U.S.C.A. § 1973 et seq.), and the Fair Housing Act of 1968 (42 U.S.C.A. § 3601 et seq.). The NAACP remained an interracial group and spurned the call for black nationalism and separatism voiced by SNCC, the Black Panthers, and other groups that turned to blacks-only membership later in the 1960s.

Unlike many of the more radical civil rights groups, the NAACP outlasted the turbulent 1960s. However, it experienced setbacks during the 1970s in Supreme Court cases such as *Bradley v. Millikin*, 418 U.S. 717, 94 S. Ct. 3112, 41 L. Ed. 2d 1069 (1974), which overturned efforts to integrate largely white suburban public school districts and largely black urban districts, and *Regents of University of California v. Bakke*, 438 U.S. 265, 98 S. Ct. 2733, 57 L. Ed. 2d 750 (1978), which placed limits on AFFIRMATIVE ACTION programs.

BENJAMIN L. HOOKS succeeded Wilkins as NAACP director in 1977. He held that office until 1993, when he was replaced by Benjamin F. Chavis, Jr. Funding and leadership problems plagued the NAACP during the mid-1990s. After a SEXUAL HARASSMENT suit was filed against Chavis in 1994, the NAACP board of directors voted to oust him as executive director. The following year, it dismissed board chairman William F. Gibson and replaced him with MYRLIE EVERS-WILLIAMS, the widow of civil rights activist MEDGAR EVERS. Seeking to put aside its troubles, on February 20, 1996, the NAACP board appointed Kweisi Mfume, a U.S. representative from Maryland and head of the Congressional Black Caucus, as the organization's new president and chief executive officer. To restore the organization's financial stability, Mfume cut back the national staff by one-third.

Among its many tasks, the NAACP works on the local level to handle cases of racial discrimination; offers referral services, tutorials, and day care; sponsors the NAACP National Housing Corporation to help develop low- and moderate-income housing for families; offers programs to youths and prison inmates; and maintains a law library. It also lobbies Congress regarding the appointment of Supreme Court justices.

The NAACP accepts people of all races and religions as members. In the mid-1990s, it had a membership of over four-hundred-thousand people, with 1,802 local groups and 132 staff. Its headquarters is in Baltimore.

CROSS-REFERENCES

Brown v. Board of Education of Topeka, Kansas; Civil Rights Movement; Integration; *Regents of University of California v. Bakke*; School Desegregation.

NATIONAL CHARACTER OF AIRCRAFT

The nationality of an aircraft is determined by the state in which the aircraft is registered. This principle was recognized by state practice soon after air flight proved feasible and was incorporated into the Convention on International Civil Aviation of December 7, 1944 (Chicago Convention). Applying the same concept of nationality to aircraft as is applied to maritime vessels provides a basis for a state to maintain JURISDICTION over an aircraft while it is flying through international airspace and establishes the power of the state to regulate what happens on board the aircraft regardless of its location. Under the Chicago Convention, contracting states register aircraft according to their domestic laws. When it registers an aircraft, the state must also certify that the craft is airworthy and has appropriate markings identifying the nationality and registration of the aircraft.

See also AIRLINES.

NATIONAL CONSUMER COOPERATIVE BANK

The National Consumer Cooperative Bank (NCCB) was created and chartered by the National Consumer Cooperative Bank Act (92 Stat. 499, 12 U.S.C.A. 3001), enacted on August 20, 1978. The bank is directed by the act to encourage the development of new and existing cooperatives. The bank provides specialized credit and technical assistance to eligible cooperatives that provide goods, services, housing, and other facilities to their members as ultimate consumers. The bank is itself structured as a cooperative financial institution. Under its congressional charter, the bank is directed to make loans and offer its services throughout the United States, its territories and possessions, and the Commonwealth of Puerto Rico.

The act provided that the federal government would contribute the initial capitalization of the bank through the purchase of the bank's Class A stock. All fifteen membersof the bank's BOARD OF DIRECTORS are appointed by the President of the United States. The act contemplated that the number of presidentially appointed directors was to decrease gradually as borrowers and cooperatives eligible to borrow purchased Class B and Class C stock in the bank.

In 1981 the act was amended by Title III, subtitle C, of the Omnibus Budget Reconciliation Act of 1981 (95 Stat. 433). The Omnibus Budget Reconciliation Act of 1981 converted the federal government's initial capitalization of the bank, formerly represented by Class A stock, into Class A capital notes, held by the secretary of the treasury. The act further mandated that after the Final Government Equity Redemption Date (FGERD), as defined by the National Consumer Cooperative Bank Act, the bank's Class B and C stockholders shall elect twelve of the bank's fifteen directors. The remaining three are appointed by the president with the advice and the consent of the Senate. The president is directed by the act, as amended, to select one member from among proprietors of small business concerns, one member from among the officers of the agencies and departments of the United States, and one member from among persons having extensive experience in the cooperative field representing low-income eligible cooperatives.

The bank is a mixed-ownership government instrumentality governed by its board of directors. It is operated by the board under bylaws and policies it prescribes consistent with the National Consumer Cooperative Bank Act.

The bank's credit and technical assistance to cooperatives is intended to improve the quality and availability of goods and services to consumers. The bank makes loans to eligible cooperatives at prevailing market interest rates.

The bank encourages broad-based ownership, control, and active participation by members in eligible cooperatives. The bank also seeks to maintain broad-based control of the bank by its voting stockholders.

The National Consumer Cooperative Bank Act established the Office of Self-Help Development and Technical Assistance within the bank. Cooperatives that are eligible to receive assistance from the bank may be eligible to qualify for financial and technical assistance from the office. The office may provide financial assistance to newly developed or established cooperatives that cannot qualify for a bank loan, or when the membership of the cooperative consists substantially of low-income persons or it provides services to low-income persons.

The Omnibus Budget Reconciliation Act of 1981 directs that as soon as practicable after the FGERD, the board of directors of the bank shall establish a nonprofit corporation under the laws of the District of Columbia to succeed the office and to carry out the functions of the office. That nonprofit corporation, the Consumer Cooperative Development Corporation, was incorporated on December 30, 1982.

NATIONAL CREDIT UNION ADMINIS-TRATION The National Credit Union Administration (NCUA) Board is responsible for chartering, insuring, supervising, and examining federal CREDIT UNIONS (FCUs) and for administering the National Credit Union Share Insurance Fund. The board also manages the Central Liquidity Facility, a mixed-ownership government corporation, the purpose of which is to supply emergency loans to member credit unions.

A credit union (CU) is a financial cooperative that aids its members by improving their economic situation through encouraging thrift among its members and providing them with a source of CREDIT for provident purposes at reasonable rates of interest. Federal CUs serve occupational, associational, and residential groups, thus benefiting a broad range of citizens throughout the country.

The NCUA was established by an act of March 10, 1970 (84 Stat. 49, 12 U.S.C.A. 1752), and reorganized by an act of November 10, 1978 (92 Stat. 3641, 12 U.S.C.A. 226 note), as an independent agency in the EXECUTIVE BRANCH of the federal government. The NCUA regulates and insures all FCUs and insures state-chartered CUs that apply and qualify for share insurance. Total assets of federally chartered CUs now exceed $172 billion, and the assets of all federally insured state-chartered CUs exceed $104 billion.

Programs and Activities The NCUA board grants FCU charters to groups sharing a common bond of occupation or association, or to groups within a well-defined neighborhood,

Summary of Federal Credit Unions, 1980 to 1996

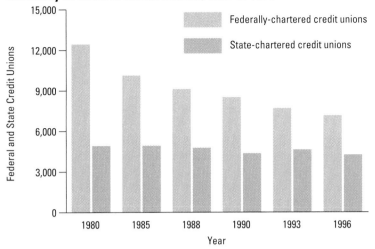

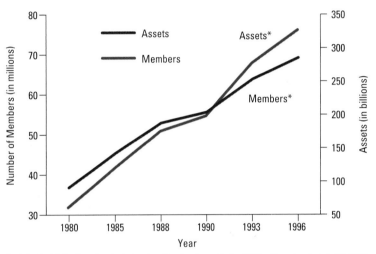

*Includes both federally and state-chartered credit unions insured by the NCUA. All numbers include District of Columbia, Puerto Rico, Canal Zone, Guam, and the Virgin Islands.

Source: National Credit Union Administration, *Annual Report of the National Credit Union Administration.*

community, or rural district. A preliminary investigation is made to determine if certain minimum standards are met before granting a federal charter.

Supervisory activities are carried out through examiner contacts and through periodic policy and regulatory releases from the administration. The administration also maintains an early warning system designed to identify emerging problems as well as to monitor operations between examinations.

The administration conducts periodic examinations of federal credit unions to determine their solvency and compliance with laws and regulations and to assist credit union management in improving operations.

The act of October 19, 1970 (84 Stat. 994, 12 U.S.C.A. 1781 et seq.), provides for a program of share insurance. The insurance is mandatory for federal credit unions and optional for state-chartered credit unions that meet NCUA standards. Credit union members' accounts are insured up to $100,000. The National Credit Union Share Insurance Fund charges each insured credit union a PREMIUM of one-twelfth of 1 percent of the total member accounts (shares) outstanding at the end of the preceding calendar year.

NATIONAL ENVIRONMENTAL POLICY ACT OF 1969

The National Environmental Policy Act of 1969 (NEPA) (42 U.S.C.A. § 4331 et seq.) was a revolutionary piece of legislation. NEPA established for the first time national policies and goals for the protection of the environment. NEPA aims to encourage harmony between people and the environment, promote efforts to prevent or eliminate damage to the environment and the biosphere, and enrich the understanding of ecological systems and natural resources important to the country.

NEPA is divided into two titles. Title I contains a basic national charter for protection of the environment. Section 101 is entitled "Declaration of the National Environmental Policy." Title II establishes the Council on Environmental Quality (CEQ), an executive branch watchdog organization that monitors the progress toward the goals set forth in Section 101 of NEPA. The CEQ advises the president on environmental issues and provides guidance to all federal agencies, which are required by NEPA to cooperate with the CEQ. The CEQ prepares an annual report on environmental quality, evaluates federal programs and activities affecting the environment, and gathers and provides statistical information.

NEPA requires that every federal agency submit an environmental impact statement (EIS) with every legislative recommendation or program proposing major federal projects that will most likely affect the quality of the surrounding environment. An EIS may be required for such projects as rerouting an interstate highway, building a new dam, or expanding a ski resort on federally owned land. The first question NEPA asks is whether the proposed action merits a "categorical exclusion." If an action has been studied in the past and does not have significant impact, or if it can be compared with different activities that the law defines as not having significant impact, then no further NEPA studies are necessary. The agency can then implement its proposed action.

If the proposed action is not excluded from further study, the next question asked is whether the action will have a significant impact on the environment. If the answer is yes, NEPA outlines a detailed process for an EIS. If the answer is unknown, a less detailed study or an environmental assessment (EA) is prepared.

An EA is an overview of potential impacts. Enough analysis is done to determine either that the more detailed EIS is necessary or that the action will not have a significant impact on the environment.

Preparing the EIS is a well-defined process. A notice of intent is published in the *Federal Register* informing the public that a study will be done. The general public, federal and state agencies, and Native American tribes are given the opportunity to comment on the proposal. Next, a draft EIS is written, and a forty-five-day period for public comment is set. At the end of the comment period, the federal agency drafts a final EIS that responds to oral and written comments received during the public review of the draft. The agency, after a thirty-day waiting period, issues its record of decision, which discusses the decision, identifies the alternatives, and indicates whether all practicable means to avoid or minimize environmental harm from the selected alternative were adopted. The federal agency may then begin to implement its decision.

The EIS is a tool to assist in decision making, providing information about the positive and negative environmental effects of the proposed undertaking and its alternatives. The EIS must also examine the impact of not implementing the proposed action. In this no-action alternative, the agency may continue to use existing approaches. Although NEPA requires agencies to consider the environmental consequences of their actions, it does not force them to take the most environmentally sound alternative nor does it dictate the least expensive alternative.

CROSS-REFERENCES

Air Pollution; Environmental Law; Environmental Protection Agency; Land-Use Control; Pollution; Solid Wastes, Hazardous Substances, and Toxic Pollutants; Water Pollution.

NATIONAL GUARD

The National Guard is the term for the state-organized units of the United States Army and Air Force, composed of citizens who undergo training and are available for service in national or local emergencies. National Guard units are organized in each of the fifty states, the District of Columbia, and Puerto Rico. The National Guard units are subject to the call of the governor of their state or territory, except when ordered into federal service by the president of the United States. Entry into the National Guard is by voluntary enlistment. The National Guard is trained to work in conjunction with the active forces of the Army and Air Force. Much of its value comes from its service in times of peace, when the Guard provides emergency aid to victims of national disasters and assists law enforcement authorities during civil emergencies.

"Citizen-soldiers" have come a long way since the American Revolution. The Army National Guard has fought in every major war in which the United States has been involved, from the American Revolution to the VIETNAM WAR. Since the end of the Vietnam War, the Guard has been engaged in all U.S. national defense missions. Not only is the National Guard devoted to the defense of the United States and its allies, it is also involved in a number of other activities, such as dealing with emergencies like civil disturbances, RIOTS, and natural disasters, and helping law enforcement agencies to keep illegal drugs off the streets.

After the American Revolution, the First Congress of the United States did not consider the formation of a MILITIA a top priority, and it disbanded the Continental Army. Congress did not officially debate the notion of a militia until the Constitutional Convention in 1787. The Constitution authorized a standing army in its Army Clause (art. I, § 8, cl. 12) and provided for a militia under the Militia Clauses (U.S. Const. art. I, § 8, cls. 15–16). Under the Constitution, the militia is to be available for federal service for three distinct purposes: "to execute the Laws of the Union, suppress Insurrections and repel Invasions." Congress is to organize and discipline the militia, and the states are to appoint officers and train the soldiers.

The National Guard, whose main responsibility since its inception had been the protection of colonial settlements, faced its first significant challenge when it tried to defend the settlements from Native American domination. In 1789, the federal government formed a War Department of approximately seven hundred men for the purpose of defending U.S. soil and its settlements from Native American attack. These small armies failed, and Congress responded to the failure of its small armies to fight off Native Americans in the West by enacting the Militia Act of 1792 (May 8, 1792, ch. 33, I Stat. 271 [repealed 1903]); this act was the militia's only permanent organizing legislation for more than one hundred years. While the act governed the militia, the United States endured three wars—the War of 1812, the Civil War, and the Spanish-American War—and the

militia was ineffective in all three. Congress replaced the act with the Dick Act of 1903 (32 Stat. 775) to transform "a frontier police force into a respected and modern fighting machine."

The Dick Act provided for an organized militia—to be named the National Guard—that would conform to the organization of the Army, be equipped through federal funds, and be trained by Army instructors. The act consisted of twenty-six sections and set forth new provisions that had previously only applied to the Army, but now also applied to the newly formed National Guard, including a nine-month limit for reservists' service on active duty, a provision that when on active duty, the reservists would be guided by Army rules and regulations and would receive the same pay as that given to Army soldiers, and a new requirement for the performance of twenty-four drills per year and a five-day summer camp. The act also gave states' governors certain powers over their Guard units, such as the power to excuse their troops from any of the drills or summer camp.

Congress amended and strengthened the Dick Act when it passed the National Defense Act of 1908, May 27, 1908, ch. 204, 35 Stat. 399 (amending Dick Act of Jan. 21, 1903, ch. 196, 32 Stat. 775), which provided that the Guard could not only be called into services within or outside of United States territory but could also be called into service for as long as the president deemed necessary, no longer subject to a nine-month limitation. The National Defense Act of 1916 (June 3, 1916, ch. 134, 39 Stat. 166) separated the Army, the reserves, and the militia and "federalized" the National Guard.

Several years later Congress declared the National Guard a part of the Army, and the National Guard became solely authorized by the Army Clause of the Constitution when

National Guard units were called to help with sandbagging efforts along the Mississippi River as waters rose in the summer of 1993. National Guard units are a part of the federal armed forces but are primarily called to service by state authorities.

National Guard, 1980 to 1993

Personnel

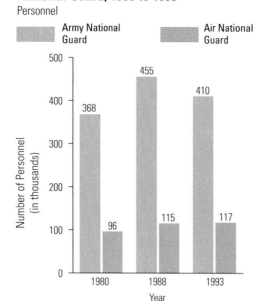

Value of Equipment

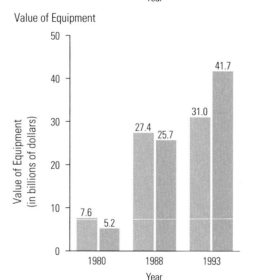

Source: National Guard Bureau, *Annual Review of the Chief, National Guard Bureau.*

Congress passed the Act of 1933 (48 Stat. 149, 155). This act provided that reserve soldiers would no longer be drafted into federal service and that they would be ordered to active duty only if "Congress declared a national emergency and authorized the use of troops in excess of those of the Regular Army."

Since 1933 federal law has provided that persons enlisting in a state National Guard unit simultaneously enlist in the National Guard of the United States, a part of the Army. The enlistees retain their status as state National Guard members unless and until ordered to active federal duty and revert to state status upon being relieved from federal service.

The authority to order the Guard to federal duty was limited to periods of national emer-

gency until Congress passed the Armed Forces Reserve Act of 1952 (66 Stat. 481), which authorized orders "to active duty or active duty for training" without any emergency requirement but provided that such orders could not be issued without the consent of the governor of the state concerned. The act also set forth the mission of the reserve components and defined some important terms. For example, the act clarified that the United States armed forces are the Army, Navy, Air Force, the Marine Corps and the Coast Guard, and that the seven reserve components are the National Guard, the Army Reserve, the Navy Reserve, the Marine Corps Reserve, the Air National Guard, the Air Force Reserve, and the Coast Guard Reserve. According to the act, the purpose of the reserve components is to provide "trained units and qualified individuals to be available for active duty in the Armed Forces of the United States in time of war or national emergency, and at such other times as the national security may require."

Further, the act declares that "the National Guard . . . [is] an integral part of the first line defenses of this Nation [and must be maintained at all times]. . . . [W]henever . . . units and organizations are needed for the national security in excess of those of the Regular components . . ., the National Guard . . . shall be ordered into the active military service of the United States and continued therein so long as such necessity exists."

The legal basis of the National Guard is founded not only in federal constitutional and statutory law but in state constitutions and statutes as well. The original "militia," which eventually became known as the Army National Guard, began as a domestic force made up of untrained men led by political generals. The Army Clause of the Constitution gives Congress the power to provide and maintain a Navy and make rules for the government and regulation of the land and naval forces. The Militia Clauses of the Constitution authorize the states to organize the National Guard but give Congress the power to employ the Guard in the service of the country.

Article II, Section 2, of the Constitution states that the president of the United States is the "Commander in Chief of the Army and Navy of the United States, and of the Militia of the several States, when called into the actual Service of the United States."

The Framers of the Constitution authorized Congress to recognize a militia that was largely controlled by the states. The states generally have maintained control over the militia during times of peace but not during war or national emergency. However, after two state governors refused to consent to federal training missions abroad for their Guard units, the gubernatorial consent requirement was partially repealed in 1986 by the Montgomery Amendment, which provides that a governor cannot withhold consent for reservists to be on active duty outside the United States because of any objection to the location, purpose, type, or schedule of such duty. The Supreme Court affirmed the constitutionality of the Montgomery Amendment in *Perpich v. Department of Defense*, 496 U.S. 334, 110 S. Ct. 2418, 110 L. Ed. 2d 312 (1990). According to the Court, the Militia Clause of the Constitution granted independent rights to both the states and the federal government to train the militia. Congress is free to train the militia as it sees fit, provided it does not prevent the states from also conducting training.

Ultimately, the National Guard enjoys a dual status as both a state militia and as an integral part of the federal armed forces. Although it continues to perform important domestic functions, the federal government has ultimate power when it requires the National Guard for national defense.

CROSS-REFERENCES
Armed Services; Military Law; Second Amendment.

NATIONAL INDUSTRIAL RECOVERY ACT OF 1933
The National Industrial Recovery Act of 1933 (NIRA) was one of the most important and daring measures of President FRANKLIN D. ROOSEVELT'S NEW DEAL. It was enacted during the famous First Hundred Days of his first term in office and was the centerpiece of his initial efforts to reverse the economic collapse of the Great Depression. NIRA was signed into law on June 16, 1933, and was to remain in effect for two years. It attempted to make structural changes in the industrial sector of the economy and to alleviate unemployment with a public works program. It succeeded only partially in accomplishing its goals, and on May 27, 1935, less than three weeks before the act would have expired, the U.S. Supreme Court ruled it unconstitutional.

Economists, scholars, politicians, and the public at large were deeply divided as to the underlying causes of the Great Depression and the best means to bring it to an end. In the months following Roosevelt's inauguration, his advisers, along with members of Congress and representatives from business and labor, drafted the legislation that was introduced in Congress on May 15, 1933, as the National Industrial Recovery Act. The division of opinions about the Depression was reflected in those who

drafted NIRA, and the act drew both praise and criticism from across the political spectrum. Nevertheless, the urgency of the economic situation (with unemployment exceeding 30 percent in many parts of the country) pressured Congress to act.

The House of Representatives passed NIRA by a vote of 325 to 76. When it reached the Senate, however, several powerful senators opposed the bill. Some favored alternative legislation authored by Alabama Senator HUGO L. BLACK (who Roosevelt would appoint to the U.S. Supreme Court in 1937), which promoted a thirty-hour work week. Some Senate progressives preferred other alternatives to NIRA. Many conservatives opposed any increase in federal powers that would result from NIRA or from other relief measures. Finally, some senators were troubled by the fact that the act suspended the enforcement of ANTITRUST LAWS at the same time that it called on businesses to play a major role in drafting "codes of fair competition." Given the benefits that business was expected to derive from NIRA, New York Senator ROBERT F. WAGNER, who had helped draft the bill, insisted that it provide a guarantee of COLLECTIVE BARGAINING for labor. That guarantee was contained in section 7(a) of title I and proved to be the most enduring legacy of NIRA. The Senate eventually approved the bill by a margin of seven votes.

NIRA was divided into three sections, or titles. Title I promoted centralized economic planning by instituting codes of fair competition for industry. Title II provided $3.3 billion for public works projects. Title III contained minor amendments to the Emergency Relief and Construction Act of 1932 (47 Stat. 709).

Title I of the act declared a "national emergency productive of widespread unemployment and disorganization of industry, which burdens interstate and foreign commerce, affects the public welfare, and undermines the standards of living of the American people." To correct this situation, NIRA proposed to "remove obstructions to the free flow of interstate and foreign commerce . . . to eliminate unfair competitive practices . . . to increase the consumption of industrial and agricultural products by increasing purchasing power, to reduce and relieve unemployment [and] to improve standards of labor." NIRA was to accomplish these goals through the codes of fair competition, which were essentially sets of rules created on an industry-by-industry basis governing wages, prices, and business practices. The codes were intended to arrest the downward spiral of the economy in which high unemployment de-

Thousands of Americans lost their jobs during the Great Depression and relied on local soup kitchens like this one in Chicago for food. The National Industrial Recovery Act attempted to introduce structural changes in the industrial sector of the economy and alleviate unemployment with a public works program.

pressed wages, which decreased public purchasing power, leading to lower prices and profits (as desperate businesses tried to undersell one another), putting further downward pressure on wages. It was hoped that organized cooperation between business and government would correct what was perceived by some to be waste and inefficiency in the free-market economy.

NIRA created the NATIONAL RECOVERY ADMINISTRATION (NRA) to oversee the drafting and implementation of the codes of fair competition. The agency was modeled, in part, after the War Industries Board, which had operated during World War I. To lead NRA, Roosevelt chose former Army General Hugh S. Johnson, who had served as a liaison between the Army and the War Industries Board during World War I. NRA began its work with great fanfare and initially received enthusiastic public support. A massive public relations campaign included the largest parade in the history of New York City. Businesses that adopted the codes were encouraged to advertise the fact by displaying the NRA blue eagle logo with its motto, "We do our part."

The NRA began to work with businesses to establish the mandated codes for fair competition, which were to be exempt from the antitrust laws. Cooperation to this extent among

competing businesses would ordinarily be prohibited. Industrial groups first submitted proposed codes to the president for his approval. The president was to approve the codes only if the submitting organization did not restrict membership and was representative of the industry and if the codes themselves promoted the policy of the act. Codes were to neither foster MONOPOLIES nor discriminate against small businesses. Once approved, the codes became legally enforceable standards for that trade or industry. Under section 3(c) of the act, federal district courts had JURISDICTION over code violations, and U.S. district attorneys were given authority to seek court orders to compel violators to comply with the codes. Section 3(f) provided that any violation affecting interstate or foreign commerce was to be treated as a MISDEMEANOR for which an offender could be fined not more than $500 for each offense; each day during which a violation occurred was to be regarded as a separate offense.

Under Section 7(a), industry codes were required to include provisions for the protection of labor. Provisions for MINIMUM WAGES and the right to collective bargaining were to increase workers' deflated purchasing power, and limits on number of work hours were to increase employment by spreading the available hours of work among more employees. Section 7(a) also provided that an employee must not be required to join a company union or be prevented from joining any other union as a condition of employment.

Section 7(a) was to have such far-reaching consequences that some labor historians have called it the Magna Charta of the labor movement. Nationwide, union membership grew dramatically. The Amalgamated Clothing Workers, for example, doubled its membership from 60,000 to 120,000 between early 1933 and mid-1934. The United Mine Workers of America quadrupled its membership, from 100,000 to 400,000, less than a year after passage of NIRA.

Under the supervision of the NRA, several hundred industry codes were rapidly enacted, but public support soon diminished. The codes tended to increase efficiency and employment, improve wages and hours, prevent price cutting and unfair competition, and encourage collective bargaining. However, they also tended to raise prices and limit production. Businesses found the codes burdensome. More than 540 codes were promulgated, and it was not unusual for one business to be governed by several, or even several dozen, codes. The codes sometimes conflicted with each other, and businesses occasionally had to pay their workers different rates of pay at different times of the day. Moreover, labor was dissatisfied with the activities of the NRA regarding unions. Although it appears that Congress had intended Section 7(a) of NIRA to assist employees in self-organizing and in discouraging company unions, the NRA interpreted the section in a manner that favored neither labor nor management. Thus, although the NRA sought to ensure that the government protected workers from discrimination resulting from union membership, it did not actively seek to prohibit the creation of company unions, nor did it satisfy many in its efforts to protect the right of individuals not to be coerced into joining a union.

In spite of some NRA successes on behalf of labor—it ended child labor in the textile industry—many in the labor community alleged that the NRA's interpretation of the labor provisions favored employers. Regardless of the NRA's intentions in any given case, few staff members were available for enforcement, and codes were often easily manipulated or avoided.

Title II of NIRA created the Public Works Administration (PWA) to award $3.3 billion in contracts for the construction of public works. (The government did not directly employ workers on PWA projects, as it did in a later New Deal program with a similar name, the Works Progress Administration (WPA).) Secretary of the Interior Harold L. Ickes ran the PWA. Ickes was scrupulously honest in choosing projects and awarding contracts, and he insisted that funds not be wasted. He was successful in that respect, with the result that the benefits of the public works provisions of NIRA were realized too slowly to have much immediate effect on national recovery.

Nevertheless, the PWA did oversee an enormous number and variety of public works projects, including schools, hospitals, post offices, courthouses, roads, bridges, water systems, and waste treatment plants. Its two most prominent projects were the construction of the Triborough Bridge in New York City and the completion of the Boulder (now called the Hoover) Dam on the Colorado River in Arizona. Ultimately the PWA completed more than 34,000 projects around the country.

In spite of the gradual success of the Public Works Administration, the NRA continued to lose the support of the public and its government sponsors. Three weeks before NIRA's two-year expiration date, the Supreme Court unanimously declared it unconstitutional in *Schechter Poultry Corp. v. United States*, 295 U.S. 495, 55 S. Ct. 837, 79 L. Ed. 1570. The Court held that the act impermissibly delegated legislative power to the NRA and that the application of the act to commerce within the state of New York exceeded the powers granted to the federal government by the Commerce Clause. (The Commerce Clause gives Congress the power to regulate commerce between states, but not within an individual state.) In response to *Schechter* and to other decisions invalidating New Deal legislation, Roosevelt delivered a famous speech on May 31, 1935, in which he criticized the Supreme Court for employing "the horse and buggy definition of interstate commerce." Subsequent New Deal legislation incorporated some elements of NIRA, most notably the labor provisions of Section 7(a), and ultimately survived the scrutiny of the Supreme Court.

CROSS-REFERENCES

Labor Law; Labor Union; *Schechter Poultry Corp. v. United States.*

NATIONALITY See Aliens.

NATIONAL LABOR RELATIONS ACT
See Labor Law; Labor Union.

NATIONAL MEDIATION BOARD ▥ A three-person board created by federal statute to resolve disputes in the railroad and airline industries that could disrupt travel or imperil the economy. The board also handles railroad and airline employee representation disputes and provides administrative and financial support in adjusting minor grievances in the railroad industry. 📖

The National Mediation Board was created in 1934 by an act amending the Railway Labor Act (45 U.S.C.A. §§ 151–158, 160–162, 1181–1188). At the time the board was created, railroads were the dominant CARRIERS of passengers and commercial goods. Railroad strikes were common, which disrupted travel and the national economy. In addition, friction between railroad companies and the railroad LABOR UNIONS made negotiation of employment issues difficult.

The National Mediation Board was created to address these issues, first for RAILROADS and later for commercial AIRLINES. The board's major responsibility is the MEDIATION of disputes over wages, hours, and working conditions that arise between rail and air carriers and organizations representing their employees. The board also investigates representation disputes and certifies employee organizations as representatives of crafts or classes of carrier employees.

The board may become involved in mediation when the parties fail to reach accord in direct bargaining. Either party may request the board's services, or the board may become involved on its own. Once the board has entered the process, negotiations continue until the board determines that its efforts to mediate have been unsuccessful, at which time it seeks to induce the parties to submit the dispute to ARBITRATION. If either party refuses arbitration, the board issues a notice stating that the parties have failed to resolve the dispute through mediation. The notice triggers a thirty-day cooling-off period, after which either side may avail itself of self-help, which may include an employee strike.

The board must notify the president when the parties have failed to reach agreement through the board's mediation efforts and when the labor dispute, in the judgment of the board, threatens substantially to interrupt interstate commerce to a degree that would deprive any section of the country of essential transportation service. In these cases the president has the discretion to appoint an emergency board to investigate and report on the dispute. In these situations self-help is barred for sixty days after the appointment of the emergency board.

If a carrier's employees cannot agree on who will represent them, the board must investigate the dispute and determine by a secret ballot election or other appropriate means to whom a representation certificate should be issued. In the course of this process, the board must determine the craft or class in which the employees seeking representation properly belong.

Disputes in the railroad industry concerning rates of pay, rules, or working conditions are referred to the National Railroad Adjustment Board. This board has four divisions, each one consisting of an equal number of representatives of the carriers and of national organizations of employees. In deadlocked cases the National Mediation Board is authorized to appoint a referee to sit with the members of the division for the purpose of making an award.

No national adjustment board has been established in the airline industry. Air carriers and employees have established bargaining relationships that create a grievance procedure with a board to resolve the conflicts. The National Mediation Board is frequently called on to name a neutral referee to serve on these kinds of boards when the parties cannot agree on such an appointment themselves.

The board consists of a chair and two other members. Its headquarters are in Washington, D.C.

See also LABOR LAW.

NATIONAL RECOVERY ADMINISTRATION (NRA)

In 1933, the United States was in the throes of a severe economic depression. Unemployment was widespread, and the economic system was in chaos. An emergency measure was needed to alleviate the situation, and the members of President FRANKLIN DELANO ROOSEVELT's New Deal administration attempted to ease the problem with the passage of the National Industrial Recovery Act (NIRA) (48 Stat. 195).

The chief provision of the act was the establishment of business codes to be enforced nationally. The codes included rules regarding fair competition, discontinuance of antitrust regulations for a two-year period, voluntary participation in unions, and establishment of shorter hours and better wages.

In June 1933, the National Recovery Administration (NRA) was created to supervise the execution of the NIRA under the direction of Hugh S. Johnson. During its first year, the NRA worked on the industrial codes; all participating businesses displayed a blue eagle, a sign of patriotism as well as acceptance of the program.

Many people regarded the NRA as too powerful, and in 1935 the U.S. Supreme Court declared the codification system of the NRA unconstitutional in *Schechter Poultry Corp. v. United States*, 295 U.S. 495, 55 S. Ct. 837, 79 L.

Ed. 1570, due to the incorrect granting of legislative authority to the EXECUTIVE BRANCH.

In 1936 the controversial NRA came to an end. During its brief existence, employment was stimulated, child labor was prohibited, and labor organization was encouraged.

See also SCHECHTER POULTRY CORP. V. UNITED STATES.

NATIONAL SECURITY COUNCIL 📖 The

PRESIDENT of the United States' principal forum for considering national security and foreign policy matters; the council comprises senior national security advisors and CABINET officials. 📖

Since its inception in 1947 under President HARRY S. TRUMAN, the function of the National Security Council (NSC) has been to advise and assist the president on national security and foreign policies. The council also serves as the president's principal arm for coordinating these policies among various government agencies.

The NSC was established by the National Security Act of 1947, as amended (50 U.S.C.A. § 402), and was placed in the Executive Office of the President by Reorganization Plan No. 4 of 1949 (5 U.S.C.A. app.). The NSC was designed to provide the president with a foreign-policy instrument independent of the STATE DEPARTMENT.

The NSC is chaired by the president. Its statutory members, in addition to the president, include the vice president and the secretaries of state and defense. The chair of the Joint Chiefs of Staff is the statutory military advisor to the council, and the director of the CENTRAL INTELLIGENCE AGENCY is the statutory intelligence advisor. The secretary of the treasury, the U.S. representative to the United Nations, the assistant to the president for national security affairs, the assistant to the president for economic policy, and the chief of staff to the president are invited to all meetings. The attorney general and the director of the Office of National Drug Control Policy attend meetings pertaining to their jurisdiction. Other officials are invited, as appropriate.

The NSC began as a small office supporting the president, but its staff has grown over the years. It is headed by the assistant to the president for national security affairs, who is also referred to as the national security advisor. The NSC staff performs a variety of activities for the president and the national security advisor. The staff participates in presidential briefings, assists the president in responding to congressional inquiries, and prepares public remarks. The NSC staff serves as an initial point of contact for departments and agencies that want to bring a national security issue to the president's atten-

tion. The staff also participates in interagency working groups organized to assess policy issues in coordinated fashion.

The issues concerning national security are wide ranging. Foreign and military relations with other countries have generally taken center stage, but international terrorism, narcotics control, and world economic issues have been brought before the NSC. In most administrations, the national security advisor has played a key role in formulating foreign policy. For example, as national security advisor during the Nixon administration, HENRY KISSINGER was the *de facto* secretary of state, developing policy on the VIETNAM WAR, the opening of relations with communist China, and negotiating with Israel and the Arab nations for a peaceful solution to problems in the Middle East.

The image of the NSC was tarnished in the 1980s during the Reagan administration. Two successive national security advisors, Robert C. McFarlane and Rear Admiral John M. Poindexter, and NSC staffer Lieutenant Colonel Oliver L. North participated in the IRAN-CONTRA Affair. They violated a congressional ban on U.S. military aid to the Nicaraguan anticommunist Contra rebels by providing the rebels with funds obtained by the secret sale of military weapons to Iran.

See also EXECUTIVE BRANCH; PRESIDENTIAL POWERS.

NATIONAL TRANSPORTATION SAFETY BOARD The National Transportation Safety Board (NTSB) is a federal investigatory board whose mandate is to ensure safe public transportation. Established in 1966 as part of the Department of Transportation, the NTSB investigates accidents, conducts studies, and

Robert Bell, director of Defense Policy and Arms Control for the National Security Council, met with reporters to discuss Anti-Ballistic-Missile Treaty agreements after a 1997 summit between U.S. president Bill Clinton and Russian president Boris Yeltsin.

makes recommendations to federal agencies and the transportation industry. It is chiefly known for its highly visible role in civil aviation accidents, which it has sole authority under federal law to investigate. Additionally, the NTSB probes certain marine accidents and accidents that occur in the use of RAILROADS, HIGHWAYS, and pipelines. The five members of the board are appointed by the president.

The NTSB grew out of the long history of federal oversight of aviation. As early as 1926, Congress required the investigation of civil aviation crashes under the Air Commerce Act (Pub. L. No. 69-254, 44 Stat. 568). Over the next three decades, lawmakers created a maze of regulatory agencies, including the Civil Aeronautics Authority and the FEDERAL AVIATION ADMINISTRATION (FAA). The Federal Aviation Act of 1958 (Pub. L. No. 85-726, 72 Stat. 731) gave duties for investigating accidents to the Civil Aeronautics Board (CAB), intending for the board to study aircraft and the actions of their pilots in the hopes of preventing future disasters.

As the airline industry grew, Congress reorganized its regulatory scheme. With passage of the Department of Transportation Act of 1966 (Pub. L. No. 89-670, 80 Stat. 935), lawmakers created the NTSB within the Department of Transportation and gave it the responsibilities formerly held by the CAB. However, the NTSB often ended up conducting investigations of the FAA. In 1974, in an attempt to avoid conflicts between agencies, Congress made the NTSB an independent board by passing the Independent Safety Board Act of 1974 (49 U.S.C.A. app. § 1901 [1982]). The act gave the NTSB sole responsibility for investigating airline crashes.

The investigatory powers of the NTSB are quite broad. Once its teams are dispatched to the site of an accident, they maintain exclusive control over the scene. Their authority includes seizing all evidence for examination, including an airline's flight recorder (the so-called black

National Transportation Safety Board

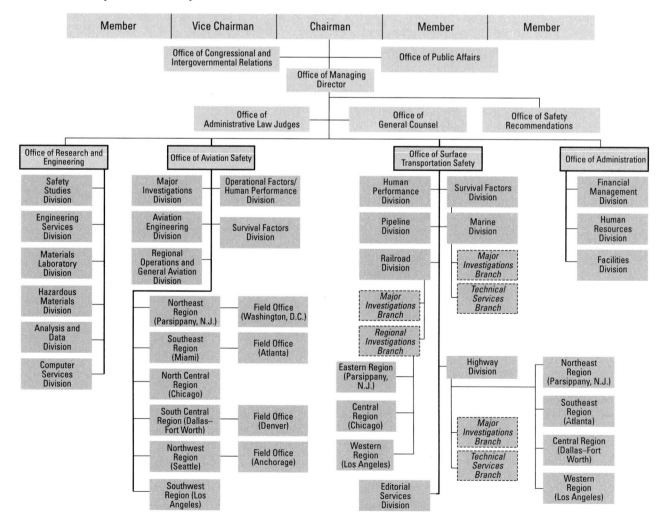

box). They can also bar other parties from their proceedings—an important element of autonomy given the inevitable litigation that follows airline accidents. In subsequent stages of an investigation, the NTSB is empowered to demand records, testimony, and other information from airline officials. The purpose of its work is to prepare public reports of two types: factual reports, and interpretive analyses of accidents to determine their PROBABLE CAUSE.

The use of NTSB reports in court is controversial. Under federal law they are intended to be used to prevent further accidents from occurring, and therefore they are released to the public. But to a certain extent, they are forbidden by law from being used in civil lawsuits. Some form of this rule has been in effect since creation of the CAB in 1958. Section 1441(e) of the Independent Safety Board Act of 1974 stated, "No part of any report or reports of the National Transportation Safety Board relating to any accident or the investigation thereof, shall be admitted as evidence or used in any suit or action for damages growing out of any matter mentioned in such report or reports." However, courts have permitted civil litigants to use some NTSB report material, and the regulations have changed in response. Only the so-called probable cause reports are strictly impermissible in civil lawsuits, and NTSB employees are permitted only to testify as to factual matters surrounding their investigations. These limitations have upset some attorneys who argue that civil litigants should have full access to all NTSB data, but defenders have argued that the standard is necessary to protect the board's autonomy.

See also AIRLINES.

NATION OF ISLAM The Nation of Islam (NOI) is a religious and political organization whose origins are somewhat mysterious. Wallace D. Fard, later known as Master Wallace Fard Muhammad, established the NOI in Detroit during the 1930s. Fard Muhammad, a traveling salesman who sold African silks and advocated self-sufficiency and independence for African Americans, taught Elijah Poole the history of what Fard Muhammad called the Lost-Found Nation of Islam—descendants of the tribe of Shabazz from the Lost Nation in Asia. Fard Muhammad taught Poole in part that Mr. Yacub, a black mad scientist, created what was called the devil race—the white race—approximately six thousand years ago, and that the devil race would rule the world for the next six thousand years.

Elijah Poole was born in Sandersville, Georgia in 1897. His father, who was a Baptist preacher, had been a slave. At the age of twenty-six, Poole moved to Detroit with his family. In 1930 in Detroit, he met W. D. Fard, the founder of the Lost-Found Nation of Islam. When Fard disappeared in 1934, Poole—then known as Elijah Muhammad—moved to Chicago, where he organized his own following and established the headquarters of the Nation of Islam. Elijah Muhammad remained the spiritual and organizational leader of the NOI from 1934 until his death in 1975. During that time, the NOI became recognized as a black nationalist religious organization that advocated racial separatism and self-sufficiency for African Americans. Often called Black Muslims, the NOI's members are required to adhere to a strict moral and disciplinary code. Men members typically wear suits and ties, and women members are required to wear modest clothing, typically white gowns or saris. The NOI's teachings forbid the eating of pork and the consumption of alcohol or tobacco.

In the early 1950s and 1960s, the NOI called for racial separatism in the United States, and at times protested against police brutality and filed suit against various police departments in response to alleged police brutality. It also frequently recruited members in large cities and prisons. In 1947, Malcolm Little—who later became MALCOLM X—converted to Islam and joined the NOI while incarcerated in a Massachusetts prison. As a national minister and spokesman for the NOI, Malcolm X was a fiery speaker and proponent of the organization's concerns. However, during the early 1960s, ideological differences developed between Malcolm X and Elijah Muhammad, and in 1964, Malcolm X formally left the NOI.

Shortly after Elijah Muhammad's death in 1975, his son Warith Deen Muhammad renounced black separatism and the origins of Black Muslims and established the World Community of Al-Islam in the West, later called the American Muslim Mission. NOI minister Louis X, who later became Louis Farrakhan, initially supported Warith Muhammad but soon reestablished the NOI. Other organizations and factions also split off from the original NOI, including the more militant Lost-Found Nation of Islam, which publishes the weekly newspaper *Muhammad Speaks*. In the mid-1990s, Farrakhan's organization was generally known as the NOI.

Like Malcolm X, Farrakhan is a fiery orator and skilled leader. Yet, he and the NOI have been criticized for anti-Semitic and antiwhite statements as well as conspiracy theories concerning Jewish American business leaders. Khalid Muhammad, a former NOI spokesman, was especially known for the excoriating statements and speeches he gave at many U.S. colleges in the late 1980s and early 1990s. Although the NOI later expelled Khalid Muhammad, his speeches contributed to a continuing debate as to whether so-called hate speech should be punished or regulated by U.S. universities. See also HATE CRIME.

During the early and mid-1990s, Farrakhan and the NOI appeared to be shifting their political focus away from black separatism and toward a more universalist or mainstream approach. The NOI also has begun to develop various major business ventures, including the operation of a restaurant in a poor neighborhood on Chicago's South Side. Its security arm—the Fruit of Islam—has been involved in providing security for housing projects in Baltimore, Chicago, and Washington, D.C., under contracts with public agencies such as the Chicago Housing Authority. In October 1995, the NOI and Farrakhan were instrumental in organizing the Million Man March, bringing together hundreds of thousands of African American men in Washington, D.C.

See also CIVIL RIGHTS MOVEMENT.

NATIVE AMERICAN RIGHTS

In the United States, persons of Native American descent occupy a unique legal position. On the one hand, Native Americans are U.S. CITIZENS and are entitled to the same legal rights and protections under the Constitution that all other U.S. citizens enjoy. On the other hand, Native Americans are members of self-governing tribes whose existence far predates the arrival of Europeans on American shores; in this capacity, they are the descendants of peoples who had their own inherent rights—rights that required no validation or legitimation from the newcomers who found their way onto their soil.

These combined, and in many ways conflicting, legal positions have resulted in a complex relationship between Native American tribes and the federal government. Although the historic events and specific details of each tribe's situation vary considerably, the legal rights and status maintained by Native Americans are the result of their shared history of wrestling with the U.S. government over such issues as tribal sovereignty, shifting government policies, treaties that were made and often broken, and conflicting latter-day interpretations of those treaties. The result today is that although Native Americans enjoy the same legal rights as every other U.S. citizen, they also retain unique rights in such areas as hunting and fishing, water use, and gaming operations. In general, these rights are based on the legal foundations of tribal sovereignty, TREATY provisions, and the "reserved rights" doctrine, which holds that Native Americans retain all rights not explicitly abrogated in treaties or other legislation.

Tribal Sovereignty Tribal SOVEREIGNTY refers to the fact that each tribe has the inherent right to govern itself. Before Europeans came to North America, Native American tribes conducted their own affairs and needed no outside source to legitimate their powers or actions. When the various European powers did arrive, however, they claimed dominion over the lands they found, thus violating the sovereignty of the tribes already living there.

The issue of the extent and limits of tribal sovereignty came before the Supreme Court in *Johnson v. McIntosh*, 21 U.S. (8 Wheat.) 543, 5 L. Ed. 681 (1823). Writing for the majority, Chief Justice JOHN MARSHALL described the effects of European incursion on native tribes, saying that although the Indians were "admitted to be the rightful occupants of the soil . . . their rights to complete sovereignty, as independent nations, were necessarily diminished, and their power to dispose of the soil, at their own will, to whomsoever they pleased, was denied by the original fundamental principle, that discovery gave exclusive title to those who made it." The European nations that had "discovered" North America, Marshall ruled, had "the sole right of acquiring the soil from the natives."

Having acknowledged this limitation to tribal sovereignty in *Johnson*, however, Marshall's opinions in subsequent cases reinforced the principle of tribal sovereignty. In *Cherokee Nation v. Georgia*, 30 U.S. (5 Pet.) 1, 8 L. Ed. 25 (1831), Marshall elaborated on the legal status of the Cherokees, describing the tribe as a "distinct political society separated from others, capable of managing its own affairs and governing itself." In *Worcester v. Georgia*, 31 U.S. (6 Pet.) 515, 8 L. Ed. 483 (1832), Marshall returned to the issue, this time in an opinion denying the state of Georgia's right to impose its laws on a Cherokee reservation within the state's borders. Marshall rejected the state's argument, saying "The Cherokee nation . . . is a distinct community, occupying its own territory, with boundaries accurately described, in which the laws of Georgia can have no force." Reviewing the history of relations between native tribes and the colonizing European powers, Marshall cited the Indians' "original natural rights," which he said were limited only by "the single exception of that imposed by irresistible

The route taken by Cherokees from southern Appalachia to Oklahoma in 1838 is called the Trail of Tears. Supreme Court decisions of that time called the native tribes "the rightful occupants of the soil" but also held that Europeans had "discovered" North America and had the right to "acquir[e] the soil from the natives."

power, which excluded them from intercourse with any other European potentate than the first discoverer of the coast of the particular region claimed."

The cumulative effect of Marshall's opinions was to position Native American tribes as nations whose independence had been limited in just two specific areas: the right to transfer land and the right to deal with foreign powers. In regard to their own internal functions, the tribes were considered to be sovereign and to be free from state intrusion on that sovereignty. This position formulated by Marshall has been modified over the years, but it continues to serve as the foundation for determining the extents and limits of Native American tribal sovereignty. Although Congress has the ultimate power to limit or abolish tribal governments, until it does so each tribe retains the right to self-government, and no state can impose its laws on the reservation. This position was reiterated in a 1978 Supreme Court case, *United States v. Wheeler*, 435 U.S. 313, 98 S. Ct. 1079, 55 L. Ed. 2d 303, in which Justice POTTER STEWART concluded that "Indian tribes still possess those aspects of sovereignty not withdrawn by treaty or statute, or by implication as a necessary result of their dependent status."

The ways that individual tribes exercise their sovereignty vary widely, but, in general, tribal authority is used in the following areas: to form tribal governments, determine tribal membership, regulate individual property, levy and collect taxes, maintain law and order, exclude non-

members from tribal territory, regulate domestic relations, and regulate commerce and trade.

Treaty Rights From the time Europeans first arrived in North America, they needed goods and services from Native Americans to survive. Often the terms of such exchanges were codified in treaties, which are contracts between sovereign nations. After the American Revolution, the federal government used treaties as its principal method for acquiring land from the Indians. From the first treaty with the Delawares in 1787 to the end of treaty making in 1871, the federal government signed more than 650 treaties with various Native American tribes. Although specific treaty elements varied, treaties commonly included such provisions as a guarantee of peace, a cession of certain delineated lands, a promise by the United States to create a reservation for the Indians under federal protection, a guarantee of Indian hunting and fishing rights, and a statement that the tribe recognized the authority or placed itself under the protection of the United States. Treaty making ended in 1871 when Congress passed a rider to an Indian appropriations act providing, "No Indian nation or tribe . . . shall be acknowledged or recognized as an independent nation, tribe, or power with whom the United States may contract by treaty . . ." (25 U.S.C.A. § 71). This rider was passed largely in response to the House of Representatives' frustration that it was excluded from Indian affairs because the constitutional power to make treaties rests exclusively with the Senate. Since 1871 the federal government has regulated Native American affairs through legislation, which does not require the consent of the Indians involved, as treaties do.

Indian treaties may seem like historical documents, but the courts have consistently ruled that they retain the same legal force they did when they were negotiated. Despite frequent challenges and intense opposition, courts have upheld guaranteed specific tribal rights, such as hunting and fishing rights. Often disputes over treaty rights arise from conflicting interpretations of the specific language of treaty provisions. In general, there are three basic principles for interpreting treaty language. First, uncertainties in Indian treaties should be resolved in favor of the Indians. Second, Indian treaties should be interpreted as the Indians signing the treaty would have understood them. Third, Indian treaties are to be liberally construed in favor of the Indians involved. Courts have consistently upheld these principles of treaty interpretation, which clearly favor the Indians, on the basis that Indian tribes were the much weaker party in treaty negotiations, signing documents written in a foreign language and often with little choice. Liberal interpretation rules are designed to address the great inequality of the parties' original bargaining positions.

Reserved Rights Doctrine Another crucial factor in the interpretation of Native American treaties is what is known as the reserved rights doctrine, which holds that any rights not specifically addressed in a treaty are reserved to the tribe. In other words, treaties outline the specific rights the tribes gave up, not those they retained. The courts have consistently interpreted treaties in this fashion, beginning with *United States v. Winans*, 198 U.S. 371, 25 S. Ct. 662, 49 L. Ed. 1089 (1905), in which the Supreme Court ruled that a treaty is "not a grant of rights to the Indians, but a grant of rights from them." Any right not explicitly extinguished by a treaty or a federal statute is considered to be "reserved" to the tribe. Even when a tribe is officially "terminated" by Congress, it retains any and all rights not specifically mentioned in the termination statute.

Federal Power over Native American Rights Although Native Americans have been held to have both INHERENT rights and rights guaranteed, either explicitly or implicitly, by treaties with the federal government, the government retains the ultimate power and authority to either abrogate or protect Native American rights. This power stems from several legal sources. One is the power the Constitu-

tion gives to Congress to make regulations governing the territory belonging to the United States (Art. IV, Sec. 3, Cl. 2), and another is the president's constitutional power to make treaties (Art. II, Sec. 2, Cl. 2). A more commonly cited source of federal power over Native American affairs is the COMMERCE CLAUSE of the U.S. Constitution, which provides that "Congress shall have the Power ... to regulate Commerce with foreign Nations, and among the several States, and with the Indian Tribes" (Art. I, Sec. 8, Cl. 3). This clause has resulted in what is known as Congress's "plenary power" over Indian affairs, which means that Congress has the ultimate right to pass legislation governing Native Americans, even when that legislation conflicts with or abrogates Indian treaties. The most well-known case supporting this congressional right is *Lone Wolf v. Hitchcock*, 187 U.S. 553, 23 S. Ct. 216, 47 L. Ed. 299 (1903), in which Congress broke a treaty provision guaranteeing that no more cessions of land would be made without the consent of three-fourths of the adult males from the Kiowa and Comanche tribes. In justifying this ABROGATION, Justice EDWARD D. WHITE declared that when "treaties were entered into between the United States and a tribe of Indians it was never doubted that the *power* to abrogate existed in Congress, and that in a contingency such power might be availed of from considerations of governmental policy."

Another source for the federal government's power over Native American affairs is what is called the "trust relationship" between the government and Native American tribes. This "trust relationship" or "trust responsibility" refers to the federal government's consistent promise, in the treaties that it signed, to protect the safety and well-being of the tribal members in return for their willingness to give up their lands. This notion of a trust relationship between Native Americans and the federal government was developed by Supreme Court Justice John Marshall in the opinions he wrote for the three cases on tribal sovereignty described above, which became known as the Marshall Trilogy. In the second of these cases, *Cherokee Nation v. Georgia*, Marshall specifically described the tribes as "domestic dependant nations" whose relation to the United States was like "that of a ward to his guardian." Similarly, in *Worcester v. Georgia*, Marshall declared that the federal government had entered into a special relationship with the Cherokees through the treaties they had signed, a relationship involving certain moral obligations. "The Cherokees," he said, "acknowledge themselves to be under the protection of the United States, and of no other power. Protection does not imply the destruction of the protected."

The federal government has often used this trust relationship to justify its actions on behalf of Native American tribes, such as its defense of Indian fishing and hunting rights and the establishment of the Bureau of Indian Affairs. Perhaps more often, however, the federal government has used the claim of a trust relationship to stretch its protective duty toward tribes into an almost unbridled power over them. The United States, for example, is the legal title-holder to most Indian lands, giving it the power to dispose of and manage those lands, as well as to derive income from them. The federal government has also used its powers in ways that seem inconsistent with a moral duty to protect Indian interests, such as terminating dozens of Indian tribes and consistently breaking treaty provisions. Because the trust responsibility is moral rather than legal, Native American tribes have had very little power or ability to enforce the promises and obligations of the federal government.

Hunting and Fishing Rights HUNTING and fishing rights are some of the special rights Native Americans enjoy as a result of the treaties signed between their tribes and the federal government. Historically, hunting and fishing were critically important to Native American tribes. Fish and wildlife were a primary source of food and trade goods, and tribes based their own seasonal movements on their migrations. In addition, fish and wildlife played a central role in the spiritual and cultural framework of Native American life. As the Supreme Court noted, access to fish and wildlife was "not much less necessary to the existence of the Indians than the atmosphere they breathed" (*United States v. Winans*).

When Native American tribes signed treaties consenting to give up their lands, the treaties often explicitly guaranteed hunting and fishing rights. When the treaties created reservations, they usually gave tribe members the right to hunt and fish on reservation lands. In many cases treaties guaranteed Native Americans the continued freedom to hunt and fish in their traditional hunting and fishing locations, even if those areas were outside the reservations. Even when hunting and fishing rights were not specifically mentioned in treaties, the reserved rights doctrine holds that tribes retain any rights, including the right to hunt and fish, that are not explicitly abrogated by treaty or statute.

Controversy and protest have surrounded Native American hunting and fishing rights, as state governments and non-Indian hunters and fishers have fought to make Native Americans subject to state hunting and fishing regulations. The rights of tribal members to hunt and fish on their own reservations have rarely been questioned, because states generally lack the power to regulate activities on Indian reservations. Tribes themselves have the right to regulate hunting and fishing on their reservations, whether or not they choose to do so. Protests have arisen, however, over the rights of Native Americans to hunt and fish off their reservations. Such rights can be acquired in one of two ways. In some instances Congress has reduced the size of a tribe's reservation, or terminated it completely, without removing the tribe's hunting and fishing rights on that land. In other cases treaties have specifically guaranteed tribes the right to hunt and fish in locations off the reservations. In the Pacific Northwest, for example, treaty provisions commonly guaranteed the right of tribes to fish "at all usual and

Controversy surrounds Native American hunting and fishing rights. Here, an Ojibwe woman counterprotests at a rally against Native American rights to spear and net fish.

accustomed grounds and stations," both on and off their reservations. Tribes in the Great Lakes area also reserved their off-reservation fishing rights in the treaties they signed.

These off-reservation rights have led to intense opposition and protests from both non-Indian hunters and fishers and state wildlife agencies. Non-Indian hunters and fishers resent the fact that Indians are not subject to the same state regulations and limits imposed on them. State agencies have protested the fact that legitimate conservation goals are compromised when Indians can hunt and fish without having to follow state wildlife regulations. The Supreme Court, however, has consistently upheld the off-reservation hunting and fishing rights of Native Americans. In the 1905 case *United States v. Winans*, the Court ruled that treaty language guaranteeing a tribe the right to "tak[e] fish at all usual and accustomed places" indeed guaranteed access to those usual and accustomed places, even if they were now on privately owned land.

The most intense opposition to Native American off-reservation hunting and fishing rights has occurred in the Pacific Northwest, where tribal members have fought to defend their right to fish in their traditional locations, unhindered by state regulations. In a series of cases involving the state of Washington and local Native American tribes, the federal courts ruled on aspects of the extent and limits of tribal fishing rights. In a 1942 case, *Tulee v. Washington*, 315 U.S. 681, 62 S. Ct. 862, 86 L. Ed. 1115, the Court ruled that tribal members could not be forced to purchase fishing LICENSES because the treaties their ancestors had signed already reserved the right to fish in the "usual and accustomed places."

This case was followed by a series of cases involving the Puyallup Indian tribe that became known as *Puyallup I*, *Puyallup II*, and *Puyallup III*. In the first of these cases, the Court ruled that the state of Washington has the right, in the interest of conservation, to regulate tribal fishing activities, as long as "the regulation meets appropriate standards and does not discriminate against the Indians" (*Puyallup Tribe v. Department of Game*, 391 U.S. 392, 88 S. Ct. 1725, 20 L. Ed. 2d 689 [1968]). In the second case, the Court ruled that the state's prohibition on net fishing for steelhead trout was discriminatory because its effect was to reserve the entire harvestable run of steelhead to non-Indian sports fishers (*Department of Game v. Puyallup Tribe*, 414 U.S. 44, 94 S. Ct. 330, 38 L. Ed. 2d 254 [1973]). In its ruling the Court declared that the steelhead "must in some man-

ner be fairly apportioned between Indian net fishing and non-Indian sports fishing." Finally, in *Puyallup III*, the Court ruled that the fish caught by tribal members on their reservation could indeed be counted against the Indian share of the fish (*Puyallup Tribe v. Department of Game*, 429 U.S. 976, 97 S. Ct. 483, 50 L. Ed. 2d 583 [1976]).

This notion of a fair apportionment of fish was clarified by *United States v. Washington*, 384 F. Supp. 312 (W.D. Wash. 1974), in which the court determined that treaty language guaranteeing tribes the right to take fish "in common with all citizens of the Territory" guaranteed the Indians not just the right to fish but the right to a certain percentage of the harvestable run, up to 50 percent. This decision set off a firestorm of controversy throughout the Pacific Northwest. Hundreds of legal disputes erupted over the allocation of individual runs of salmon and steelhead, and both state and non-Indian fishing interests attacked the decision. The Supreme Court ultimately upheld the decision in a collateral case, *Washington v. Washington State Commercial Passenger Fishing Vessel Ass'n* 443 U.S. 658, 99 S. Ct. 3055, 61 L. Ed. 2d 823 (1979). In this case the Court upheld the district court's ruling and went on to clarify the details of how the fish should be apportioned. Writing for the majority, Justice JOHN PAUL STEVENS wrote that the treaties guaranteed the tribes "so much as, but no more than, is necessary to provide the Indians with a livelihood— that is to say a moderate living." A "fair apportionment," he said, would be 50 percent of the fish, emphasizing that 50 percent was the maximum, but not the minimum, amount of fish to which the Indians were entitled.

Water Rights Access to water is another area in which Native Americans enjoy special rights. The issue of WATER RIGHTS has been most pertinent in the western part of the United States, where most Indian reservations are located and where water is the scarcest. In the West, rights to water are determined by the "appropriative" system, which holds that water rights are not connected to the land itself. Rather, the right to water belongs to the first user who appropriates it for a beneficial use. That appropriator is guaranteed the right to continue to take water from that source, unhindered by future appropriators, as long as the water continues to be put to a beneficial use; when the appropriator ceases to use the water, he or she loses the right to it. In contrast to this appropriative system, states in the East, where water is plentiful, follow the "riparian" system, which gives the owner of land bordering a body of water the right to the reasonable use of that water. All riparian owners are guaranteed the right to a continued flow of water, whether or not they use it continuously.

Native American water rights combine the features of the appropriative and riparian systems. The legal foundation for Indian water rights is the 1908 Supreme Court case *Winters v. United States*, 207 U.S. 564, 28 S. Ct. 207, 52 L. Ed. 340. This case involved a Montana Indian reservation that had a river as one of its borders. After the reservation was established, non-Indian settlers diverted the river's water, claiming that they had appropriated the water after the reservation was created but before the Indians had begun to use the water themselves. The Supreme Court ruled against the settlers, finding that when the reservation was created, reserved water rights for the Indians were necessarily implied. It was unreasonable, the Court argued, to assume that Indians would accept lands for farming and grazing purposes without also reserving the water that would make those activities possible.

A second important case involving Native American water rights is *Arizona v. California*, 373 U.S. 546, 83 S. Ct. 1468, 10 L. Ed. 2d 542 (1963). In this case, as in *Winters*, the Supreme Court held that the establishment of a reservation necessarily implied the rights to the water necessary to make the land habitable and productive. *Arizona* went beyond *Winters*, however, in also ruling on the quantity of water to which the reservation had a right. Although competing water users argued that the amount of water reserved to the reservation should be limited to the amount likely to be needed by the relatively small Indian population, the Court ruled that the Indians were entitled to enough water "to irrigate all the practicably irrigable acreage on the reservation," a much more generous allotment.

Based on *Winters* and *Arizona*, Native American water rights today are determined by a set of principles called "*Winters* rights." First, Congress has the right to reserve water for federal lands, including Indian reservations. Second, when Congress establishes a reservation, it is implied that the reservation has the right to water sources within or bordering the reservation. Third, reservation water rights are reserved as of the date of the reservation's creation. Competing users with earlier appropriation dates take precedence, but those with later dates are subordinate. Fourth, the amount of water reserved for Indian use is the amount necessary to irrigate all the practically irrigable land on the reservation. Finally, *Winters* rights

to water are not lost through non-use of the water. All of these rights apply both to surface water and to groundwater.

Even with the acknowledgement of Native Americans' *Winters* rights, water use in the West continues to be highly contested, as reservations fight to maintain their rights against the competing demands of state governments and non-Indian users. Several issues are yet to be resolved, such as the precise quantity of water needed to irrigate all "practically irrigable acreage" and the question of whether states can regulate non-Indian water users on Indian reservations. Because of the high costs and other difficulties involved in litigation, many tribes and states are choosing to try to negotiate water rights and then ask Congress or the courts to approve their agreements.

Gaming Rights In recent years GAMING has become one of the most important areas of economic development for Native American tribes. Since 1979, when the federal courts ruled that tribal-sponsored gaming activities were exempt from state regulatory law, the Indian gaming industry has grown tremendously, with more than two hundred tribes operating gaming establishments. These gaming operations have been extremely lucrative for the tribes running them; in 1993 the gross gambling revenues from class II and class III tribal gaming operations amounted to approximately $2.6 billion. By comparison, Atlantic

Native Americans enjoy the same legal rights of other U.S. citizens, but as members of self-governing tribes, they also retain unique hunting, fishing, water use, and gaming rights.

City had revenues of $3.3 billion the same year. Tribe members benefit from the creation of jobs on the reservation and from the cash generated, which some tribal governments choose to distribute through direct payments to tribe members and others choose to reinvest in improving reservation infrastructure, educational facilities, and other programs and services designed to benefit tribe members.

The impetus for the growth of Native American gaming began in the late 1970s, when the Oneida tribe in Wisconsin and the Seminole tribe in Florida sought to open high-stakes bingo operations on their reservations. The applicable laws in those states imposed limitations on the size of jackpots and the frequency of bingo games. The tribes asserted, however, that as sovereign nations, they were not bound by such limitations; they claimed that they could operate bingo games and regulate them under tribal law, deciding for themselves how large prizes could be and how often games could be played. Both suits ended up in federal court, and both tribes won (*Seminole Tribe of Florida v. Butterworth*, 658 F. 2d 310 [5th Cir. 1981]; *Oneida Tribe of Indians v. Wisconsin*, 518 F. Supp. 712 [W.D. Wis. 1981]). The rulings in both cases hinged on whether the states' laws concerning gaming were criminal laws that prohibited gaming or civil laws that regulated gaming. If the laws were criminal-prohibitory, they could be applied to activities on Indian reservations, but if they were civil-regulatory, they could not. The courts ruled that because the states allowed bingo games in some form, the laws were civil-regulatory and thus did not apply to gaming operations on Indian reservations.

Other tribes subsequently sued in federal court on the same issue and also won. The issue finally reached the Supreme Court in *California v. Cabazon Band of Mission Indians*, 480 U.S. 202, 107 S. Ct. 1083, 94 L. Ed. 2d 244 (1987). In this case the Court accepted the criminal-prohibitory/civil-regulatory distinction of the lower courts, ruling that the Cabazon Band of Mission Indians in California had the right to operate high-stakes bingo and poker games on its reservation because the state's gaming laws were civil-regulatory and thus could not be applied to on-reservation gaming activities.

Concern over Indian gaming had been building in Congress during the 1980s, and Congress responded to *California v. Cabazon* by passing the Indian Gaming Regulatory Act (IGRA), (25 U.S.C.A. § 2701 et seq.) in 1988. The IGRA specifically provides that Indian tribes "have the exclusive right to regulate gaming activity on Indian lands if the gaming activity is not spe-

cifically prohibited by Federal law and is conducted within a State which does not, as a matter of criminal law and public policy, prohibit such gaming activity." The sponsors of the IGRA claimed that one of the bill's main goals was to use gaming as a means of "promoting tribal economic development, self-sufficiency, and strong tribal governments." Many tribe leaders, nevertheless, were opposed to the provisions of IGRA, regarding them as infringements on tribal sovereignty.

The IGRA provides the general framework for regulating Indian gaming. Its principal provision is the classification of Indian gaming, with each category of games being subject to the different regulatory powers of the tribes, the states, and federal agencies, including the National Indian Gaming Commission (NIGC), which was created by the IGRA. The IGRA classifies games into three types. Class I games are traditional Indian games, such as those played in connection with tribal ceremonies or celebrations; these games are regulated exclusively by the tribes. Class II games include bingo and related games; these games are regulated by the tribes, with oversight from the NIGC. Class III games include all games that do not fall into classes I and II, including casino-style games, parimutuel wagering, slots, and dog and horse racing. Class III games, according to the IGRA, may be conducted if three conditions are met: if the state in which the tribe is located permits any such games for any purposes, if the tribe and the state have negotiated a compact that has been approved by the secretary of the interior, and if the tribe has adopted an ORDINANCE that has been approved by the chair of the NIGC.

Indian gaming and the IGRA continue to face opposition from various quarters. Tribe leaders view state regulation as a violation of their tribal sovereignty. The proprietors of non-Indian gaming establishments have attempted to slow or stop the growth of Indian gaming, viewing it as a threat to their own enterprises. In some cases tribal and state governments have had great difficulties negotiating the details of tribal-state compacts. These areas of difficulty and dissatisfaction suggest that Indian gaming may be subject to further legislation in the future.

Gaming has led to unprecedented growth for tribal economies, providing thousands of jobs for both Indians and non-Indians and drastically improving the financial well-being of the tribes operating successful gaming establishments. Although some legislators have expressed concern over the expansion of gaming activities and the problems associated with increased gambling, in general Indian gaming enjoys broad public support. Native Americans have described it as "the return of the white buffalo," a traditional Native American symbol of good fortune.

CROSS-REFERENCES

Fish and Fishing; Indian Child Welfare Act; Interior Department.

NATURAL AND PROBABLE CONSEQUENCES

Those ramifications of a particular course of conduct that are reasonably foreseeable by a person of average intelligence and generally occur in the normal course of events.

The individual who is guilty of misconduct in CONTRACT or TORT is responsible for the natural and probable consequences of the act or omission that proximately causes loss or injury to the plaintiff. Based on the usual experience of human beings, if the consequences were to be expected, a plaintiff can recover DAMAGES from a defendant who caused the injuries.

Breach of Contract Damages for breach of contractual agreement are those that result naturally from the violation of contract provisions and that are reasonably contemplated by the parties when the contract is made. Factors to be considered in determining what damages might have reasonably been considered include the nature and purpose of the contract as well as the accompanying conditions of which the parties were aware when the contract was executed. Damages that do not stem naturally from a breach of contract are not recoverable, nor are damages that are not within the reasonable contemplation of the parties. There is no requirement that the promisor compensate the injured party for harm that the promisor or any reasonable person upon making the contract would not have reason to foresee as the predictable outcome of a breach.

Torts An individual who is guilty of committing a tort is liable for loss or injury that is the natural and probable result of his or her act or omission. It is sufficient that consequences are merely possible, since they must be reasonably foreseeable in order to serve as an adequate basis for the recovery of damages.

Prospective and Anticipated Consequences In a situation where a cause of action is complete, prospective damages reasonably certain to accrue may be recovered as part of the natural and probable consequences of the defendant's action.

Breach of Contract Prospective damages are recoverable in cases involving an ANTICIPATORY REPUDIATION of contract. If the breach does not serve to discharge the entire contract but rather gives rise to subsequent actions, future damages must be recovered in successive actions. This type of situation might arise in an action for breach of a lease for the rental of an apartment in which the breach occurs during the fourth month of a twelve-month lease. Successive actions will have to be brought for the breach occurring from the fifth to twelfth months.

Torts Damages in tort actions are not limited to the period that ends with the institution of the lawsuit. In an action for PERSONAL INJURY, for example, the jury can properly consider the potential consequences of an injury that might require a major operation at some time in the future in assessing the present value of an injury as opposed to future damages. Damages can be awarded to a plaintiff who has adequately established that there will be future effects from an injury precipitated by the defendant's misconduct. The amount of certainty required in the assessment of future damages varies from one JURISDICTION to another; however, no recovery can be permitted for the mere possibility of future consequences of harm inflicted by the defendant.

Damage to Property All types of damages, including past, current, and prospective, can be recovered in a single ACTION for permanent damage to or TRESPASS on REAL ESTATE. If the cause of the injury can be abated through an expenditure of labor or money, future damages will not be recovered.

NATURAL LAW

The unwritten body of universal moral principles that underlie the ethical and legal norms by which human conduct is sometimes evaluated and governed. Natural law is often contrasted with positive law, which consists of the written rules and regulations enacted by government. The term *natural law* is derived from the Roman term *jus naturale*. Adherents to natural law philosophy are known as naturalists.

Naturalists believe that natural-law principles are an inherent part of nature and exist regardless of whether government recognizes or enforces them. Naturalists further believe that governments must incorporate natural-law principles into their legal systems before justice can be achieved. There are three schools of natural-law theory: divine natural law, secular natural law, and historical natural law.

Divine natural law represents the system of principles revealed or inspired by God, or some other supreme and supernatural being. These divine principles are typically reflected by authoritative religious writings such as Scripture. Secular natural law represents the system of principles derived from the physical, biological, and behavioral laws of nature as perceived by the human intellect and elaborated through reason. Historical natural law represents the system of principles that has evolved over time through the gradual accretion of custom, tradition, and experience. Each school of natural law influenced the Founding Fathers during the nascent years of U.S. law in the eighteenth century and continue to influence the decision-making process of state and federal courts today.

Divine Natural Law Proponents of divine natural law contend that law must be made to conform to the commands laid down or inspired by God, or some other deity, who governs according to principles of compassion, truth, and justice. These naturalists assert that the legitimacy of any enacted human law must be measured by its consonance with divine principles of right and wrong. Such principles can be found in Scripture, church doctrine, papal decrees, and the decisions of ECCLESIASTICAL COURTS and councils. Human laws that are inconsistent with divine principles of morality, naturalists maintain, are invalid and should neither be enforced nor obeyed. St. Thomas Aquinas, a theologian and philosopher from the thirteenth century, was a leading exponent of divine natural law.

Under Judeo-Christian belief, the Ten Commandments, which were delivered to Moses by God on Mount Sinai according to the Old Testament, represent one example of divine natural law. The Bible and Torah are thought by many to be other sources of divine natural law because their authors are said to have been inspired by a divine spirit. Some Christians point to the CANON LAW of the Catholic Church, which was applied by the ecclesiastical courts of Europe during the Middle Ages, as a third source of divine natural law.

Before the Protestant Reformation of the sixteenth century, Europe was divided into two separate and competing jurisdictions—secular and religious. The emperors, kings, and queens of Europe governed the secular jurisdiction, and the pope presided over the religious jurisdiction. The notion that a "higher law" transcends the rules enacted by human institutions and that government is bound by this law, also known as the rule of law, fermented during the struggle between the secular and religious powers in Europe before the U.S. Revolution. HENRY DE BRACTON, an English judge and scholar from the thirteenth century, wrote that a court's allegiance to the law and to God is above its allegiance to any ruler or lawmaker.

The influence of divine natural law was also pervasive during the colonial period of U.S. law.

Divine natural law theories influenced English philosopher John Locke. Locke wrote that all people are born with inherent rights to life, liberty, and estate.

AMERICAN PHILOSOPHICAL SOCIETY

In 1690 English philosopher JOHN LOCKE wrote that all people are born with the inherent rights to life, liberty, and estate. These rights are not unlimited, Locke said, and may only be appropriated according to the fair share earned by the labor of each person. Gluttony and waste of individual liberty are not permitted, Locke argued, because "[n]othing is made by God for man to spoil or destroy."

In the DECLARATION OF INDEPENDENCE, THOMAS JEFFERSON, borrowing from Locke, wrote that "all men are created equal ... and are endowed by their creator with certain inalienable rights ... [including] life, liberty and the pursuit of happiness." Jefferson identified the freedom of thought as one of the inalienable rights when he said, "Almighty God has created the mind free, and manifested his supreme will that free it shall remain by making it altogether insusceptible of restraint." In *Powell v. Pennsylvania*, 127 U.S. 678, 8 S. Ct. 1257, 32 L. Ed. 253 (1888), the Supreme Court recognized the importance of the divine influence in early U.S. law, stating that the "right to pursue happiness is placed by the Declaration of Independence among the inalienable rights of man, not by the grace of emperors or kings, or by the force of legislative or constitutional enactments, but by the Creator."

The U.S. Constitution altered the relationship between law and RELIGION. Article VI establishes the Constitution as the supreme law of the land. The FIRST AMENDMENT prohibits the government from establishing a religion, which means that a law may not advance one religion at the expense of another or prefer a general belief in religion to irreligion, atheism, or agnosticism. Although the Supremacy and Establishment Clauses seemingly preclude the judiciary from grounding a decision on Scripture or religious doctrine, state and federal courts have occasionally referenced miscellaneous sources of divine natural law.

For example, in *Edwards v. Aguillard*, 482 U.S. 578, 107 S. Ct. 2573, 96 L. Ed. 2d 510 (1987), the Supreme Court said that "the Founding Fathers believed devoutly that there was a God and that the unalienable rights of man were rooted in Him." In *McIlvaine v. Coxe's Lessee*, 6 U.S. 280, 2 Cranch 280, 2 L. Ed. 279 (1805), the Supreme Court relied on the Bible as "ancient and venerable" proof that expatriation had long been "practiced, approved, and never restrained."

Confronted with the question as to whether the CONVEYANCE of a particular piece of land was legally enforceable, the Supreme Court said that it would consider "those principles of abstract justice, which the Creator of all things has impressed on the mind of his creature man, and which are admitted to regulate, in a great degree, the rights of civilized nations" (*Johnson v. M'Intosh*, 21 U.S. 543, 8 Wheat. 543, 5 L. Ed. 681 [1823]). In *Dred Scott v. Sandford*, 60 U.S. 393, 19 How. 393, 15 L. Ed. 691 (1856), the Supreme Court held that slaves were the property of their owners and were not entitled to any constitutional protection. In a dissenting opinion, however, Justice John McLean wrote that a "slave is not mere chattel. He bears the impress of his Maker, and is amenable to the laws of God and man." See also DRED SCOTT V. SANDFORD; SLAVERY.

More recently, the Supreme Court relied on Judeo-Christian standards as evidence that homosexual SODOMY is a practice not worthy of constitutional protection because it has been condemned throughout the history of western civilization (*Bowers v. Hardwick*, 478 U.S. 186, 106 S. Ct. 2841, 92 L. Ed. 2d 140 [1986] [Burger, J., concurring]). State and federal courts also have considered Judeo-Christian standards when evaluating the constitutionality of statutes prohibiting BIGAMY and INCEST. For example, *Benton v. State*, 265 Ga. 648, 461 S.E.2d 202 (1995), upheld the constitutionality of a Georgia statute prohibiting incest.

Despite the sprinkling of cases that have referenced Scripture, religious doctrine, and Judeo-Christian heritage, such sources of divine natural law do not ordinarily form the express basis of judicial decisions. At the same time, it cannot be said that state and federal courts have completely eliminated any reliance on natural-law principles. To the contrary, many controversial legal disputes are still decided in accordance with unwritten legal principles that are derived not from religion, but from secular political philosophy.

Secular Natural Law The school of natural law known as secular natural law replaces the divine laws of God with the physical, biological, and behavioral laws of nature as perceived by human reason. This school theorizes about the uniform and fixed rules of nature, particularly human nature, to identify moral and ethical norms. Influenced by the rational empiricism of the seventeenth and eighteenth century Enlightenment thinkers who stressed the importance of observation and experiment in arriving at reliable and demonstrable truths, secular natural law elevates the capacity of the human intellect over the spiritual authority of religion.

Many secular-natural-law theorists base their philosophy upon hypotheses about human behavior in the state of nature, a primitive stage in human evolution before the creation of governmental institutions and other complex societal organizations. In the state of nature, John Locke wrote, human beings live according to three principles—liberty, equality, and self-preservation. Because no government exists in the state of nature to offer police protection or regulate the distribution of goods and benefits, each individual has a right to self-preservation that he or she may exercise on equal footing with everyone else.

This right includes the liberties to enjoy a peaceful life, accumulate wealth and property, and otherwise satisfy personal needs and desires consistent with the coterminous liberties of others. Anyone who deprives another person of his or her rights in the state of nature, Locke argued, violates the principle of equality. Ultimately, Locke wrote, the state of nature proves unsatisfying. Human liberty is neither equally fulfilled nor protected. Because individuals possess the liberty to delineate the parameters of their own personal needs and desires in the state of nature, greed, narcissism, and self-interest eventually rise to the surface, causing irrational and excessive behavior and rendering human safety evanescent. Thus, Locke concluded, the law of nature leads people to establish a government that is empowered to protect life, liberty, and property. See also HOBBES, THOMAS.

Lockean jurisprudence has manifested itself in the decisions of the Supreme Court. In *Powell v. Pennsylvania*, 127 U.S. 678, 8 S. Ct. 1257, 32 L. Ed. 253 (1888), Justice STEPHEN J. FIELD wrote that he had "always supposed that the gift of life was accompanied by the right to seek and produce food, by which life can be preserved and enjoyed, in all ways not encroaching upon the equal rights of others." In another case the Supreme Court said that the "rights of life and personal liberty are the natural rights of man. To secure these rights . . . governments are instituted among men" (*U.S. v. Cruikshank*, 92 U.S. 542, 2 Otto 542, 23 L. Ed. 588 [1875]).

In the spirit of Lockean natural law, the Fifth and Fourteenth Amendments to the Constitution prohibit the government from taking "life, liberty, or property without DUE PROCESS OF LAW." The concept of "due process" has been a continuing source of natural law in constitutional jurisprudence. If Lockean natural law involves theorizing about the scope of human liberty in the state of nature, constitutional natural law involves theorizing about the scope of liberty protected by the Due Process Clauses of the Fifth and Fourteenth Amendments.

On their face the Due Process Clauses appear to offer only procedural protection, guaranteeing litigants the right to be informed of any legal action being taken against them and the opportunity to be heard during an impartial hearing where relevant claims and defenses may be asserted. Over the last 150 years, however, FEDERAL COURTS have interpreted the Due Process Clauses to provide substantive protection against arbitrary and discriminatory governmental encroachment of fundamental liberties. Similar to the rational empiricism by which Enlightenment thinkers identified HUMAN RIGHTS in the state of nature, federal judges have identified the liberties protected by the Due Process Clauses through a reasoned elaboration of the Fifth and Fourteenth Amendments.

The federal judiciary has described the LIBERTY interest protected by the Due Process Clauses as an interest guaranteeing a number of individual freedoms, including the right to personal autonomy, bodily integrity, self-dignity, and self-determination (*Gray v. Romeo*, 697 F. Supp. 580 [1988]). The word *liberty*, the Supreme Court said, means something more than freedom from physical restraint. "It means freedom to go where one may choose, and to act in such manner . . . as his judgment may dictate for the promotion of his happiness . . . [while pursuing] such callings and avocations as may be most suitable to develop his capacities, and give to them their highest enjoyment" (*Munn v. Illinois*, 94 U.S. 113, 4 Otto 113, 24 L. Ed. 77 [1876] [Field, J., dissenting]).

The full breadth of constitutional liberty, the Supreme Court has said, is best explained as a rational continuum safeguarding every facet of human freedom from arbitrary impositions and purposeless restraints (*Poe v. Ullman*, 367 U.S. 497, 81 S. Ct. 1752, 6 L. Ed. 2d 989 [1961]). The government may not intrude upon this liberty unless it can demonstrate a persuasive countervailing interest. However, the more that the U.S. legal system cherishes a particular freedom, the less likely a court is to enforce a law that infringes upon it.

In this regard the Supreme Court has identified certain fundamental rights that qualify for heightened judicial protection against laws threatening to restrict them. This list of fundamental rights includes most of the specific freedoms enumerated in the BILL OF RIGHTS, as well as the FREEDOM OF ASSOCIATION, the right to vote and participate in the electoral process, the right to marry, procreate, and rear children, and the right to PRIVACY. The right to privacy, which is not expressly enumerated anywhere in the Constitution, guarantees the freedom of adults to use birth control (*Griswold v. Connecticut*, 381 U.S. 479, 85 S. Ct. 1678, 14 L. Ed. 2d 510 [1965]) and the right of women to terminate their pregnancy before the fetus becomes viable (*Roe v. Wade*, 410 U.S. 113, 93 S. Ct. 705, 35 L. Ed. 2d 147 [1973]). See also ABORTION; GRISWOLD V. CONNECTICUT; ROE V. WADE.

During the 1990s the right to privacy was enlarged to recognize the right of certain terminally ill or mentally incompetent persons to refuse medical treatment. In *Cruzan v. Missouri Department of Health*, 497 U.S. 261, 110 S. Ct. 2841, 111 L. Ed. 2d 224 (1990), the Supreme Court ruled that a person who is in a persistent vegetative state, marked by the absence of any significant cognitive abilities, may seek to terminate life-sustaining measures, including artificial nutrition and hydration equipment, through a parent, spouse, or other appropriate guardian who demonstrates that the incompetent person previously expressed a clear desire to discontinue medical treatment under such circumstances.

The Court of Appeals for the Ninth Circuit later cited *Cruzan* in support of its decision establishing the right of competent but terminally ill patients to hasten their death by refusing medical treatment when the final stages of life are tortured by pain and indignity (*Compassion in Dying v. Washington*, 79 F.3d 790 [9th Cir. 1996]). However, the Court of Appeals for the Second Circuit ruled that physicians possess no due process right to assist terminally ill patients in accelerating their death by prescribing a lethal dose of narcotics (*Quill v. Vacco*, 80 F.3d 716 [2d Cir. 1996]). Similarly, in a notorious case involving Dr. JACK KEVORKIAN, the

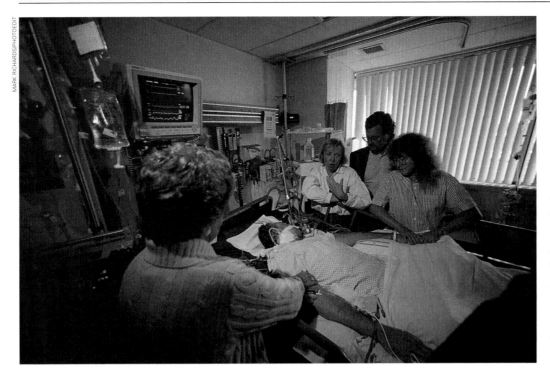

Natural law philosophy is represented in U.S. Constitutional provisions that protect individual liberty. Individual liberty includes the right of terminally ill patients to refuse medical treatment and life-sustaining nutrition and hydration.

Michigan Supreme Court ruled that patients have no due process right to physician-assisted suicide (*People v. Kevorkian*, 447 Mich. 436, 527 N. W. 2d 714 [1994]).

In the *Cruzan* decision, the manner in which the Supreme Court recognized a qualified right to die reflects the Enlightenment tradition of secular natural law. Where Locke inferred the inalienable rights of life, liberty, and property from observing human behavior, the Supreme Court said in *Cruzan* that "a Constitutionally protected liberty interest in refusing unwanted medical treatment may be inferred from our prior decisions."

For example, in *Jacobson v. Massachusetts*, 197 U.S. 11, 25 S. Ct. 358, 49 L. Ed. 643 (1905), the Supreme Court protected the constitutional right of a person to decline a smallpox vaccination that was required by state law. In *Washington v. Harper*, 494 U.S. 210, 110 S. Ct. 1028, 108 L. Ed. 2d 178 (1990), the Court ruled that the liberty interest guaranteed by the Due Process Clauses prohibits the government from compelling prisoners to take antipsychotic drugs. These cases, as well as others, the Supreme Court reasoned in *Cruzan*, establish that all U.S. citizens have a general right to refuse unwanted medical treatment, which includes the specific right of certain mentally incompetent and terminally ill persons to hasten their death. See also DEATH AND DYING.

Historical Natural Law Another school of natural law is known as historical natural law. According to this school, law must be made to

conform with the well-established, but unwritten, customs, traditions, and experiences that have evolved over the course of history. Historical natural law has played an integral role in the development of the Anglo-American system of justice. When King James I attempted to assert the absolute power of the British monarchy during the seventeenth century, for example, English jurist SIR EDWARD COKE argued that the sovereignty of the crown was limited by the ancient liberties of the English people, immemorial custom, and the rights prescribed by MAGNA CHARTA in 1215.

Magna Charta also laid the cornerstone for many U.S. constitutional liberties. The Supreme Court has traced the origins of grand juries, petit juries, and the writ of HABEAS CORPUS to Magna Charta. The EIGHTH AMENDMENT proportionality analysis, which requires that criminal sanctions bear some reasonable relationship to the seriousness of the offense, was foreshadowed by Magna Charta's prohibition of excessive fines (*Solem v. Helm*, 463 U.S. 277, 103 S. Ct. 3001, 77 L. Ed. 2d 637 [1983]). The concept of due process was inherited from the requirement in Magna Charta that all legal proceedings comport with the "law of the land" (*In re Winship*, 397 U.S. 358, 90 S. Ct. 1068, 25 L. Ed. 2d 368 [1970]).

Due process of law, the Supreme Court has observed, contains both procedural and historical aspects that tend to converge in criminal cases (*Rochin v. California*, 342 U.S. 165, 72 S. Ct. 205, 96 L. Ed. 183 [1952]). Procedurally, due process guarantees criminal defendants a fair trial. Historically, due process guarantees that no defendant may be convicted of a crime unless the government can prove his or her guilt BEYOND A REASONABLE DOUBT. Although the reasonable doubt standard can be found nowhere in the express language of the Constitution, the Supreme Court has said that the demand for a higher degree of persuasion in criminal cases has been repeatedly expressed since "ancient times" through the common-law tradition and is now "embodied in the Constitution" (*In re Winship*).

The legacy of the trial of JOHN PETER ZENGER, 17 Howell's State Trials 675, further illustrates the symbiotic relationship between history and the law. Zenger, the publisher of the *New York Weekly Journal*, was charged with libeling the governor of New York in 1735. At trial Zenger admitted that he had published the allegedly harmful article but argued that the article was not libelous because it contained no inaccurate statements. However, truth was not a defense to libel actions in the American colonies. Despite Zenger's admission of harmful publication, and lack of a cognizable legal defense, the jury acquitted him.

The Zenger acquittal spawned two ideas that have become entrenched in U.S. jurisprudence. First, the acquittal gave birth to the idea that truth should be a defense to accusations of libel. This defense received constitutional protection under the First Amendment in *New York Times v. Sullivan*, 376 U.S. 254, 84 S. Ct. 710, 11 L. Ed. 2d 686 (1964). The Supreme Court has described the Zenger trial as "the earliest and most famous American experience with freedom of the press" (*McIntyre v. Ohio Elections Commission*, 514 U.S. 334, 115 S. Ct. 1511, 131 L. Ed. 2d 426, [1995]). See also LIBEL AND SLANDER; NEW YORK TIMES V. SULLIVAN.

The Zenger trial is also the progenitor of JURY nullification, which is the power of a jury, as the conscience of the community, to acquit defendants against whom there is overwhelming evidence of guilt in order to challenge a specific law, prevent oppression, or otherwise achieve justice. For example, the Zenger jurors issued an acquittal despite what amounted to a confession by the defendant in open court. Some observers have compared the Zenger trial to the trial of O. J. Simpson, where the former football star was acquitted of a double homicide notwithstanding DNA EVIDENCE linking him to the crimes. According to these observers, JOHNNIE COCHRAN, defense attorney for Simpson, implored the jurors to ignore the evidence against his client and render a verdict that would send a message denouncing police corruption, perjury, and racism.

All three schools of natural law have influenced the development of U.S. law from colonial times to the present day. In many ways the creation and ratification of the Constitution replaced Scripture and religion as the ultimate source of law in the United States. The federal Constitution makes the people the fundamental foundation of authority in the U.S. system of government. Many of the Framers characterized the Constitution as containing "sacred and inviolate" truths. In the same vein, THOMAS PAINE described the Constitution as a "political Bible."

In 1728 many Americans understood that the COMMON LAW encompassed the Law of Nature, the Law of Reason, and the Revealed Law of God, which are equally binding at all times, in all places, and to all persons. The law of history could have been added to this litany. Between 1776 and 1784, eleven of the original thirteen states made some allowance for the adoption of the English common law. One federal court said that the Constitution "did not create any new rights to life, liberty or due process. These rights had existed for Englishmen since Magna Charta. The Declaration of Independence .. merely declared and established these rights for the American colonies" (*Screven County v. Brier Creek Hunting & Fishing Club*, 202 F. 2d 369 [5th Cir. 1953]). Thus, natural law in the United States may be best understood as the integration of history, secular reason, and divine inspiration.

See also CONSTITUTION OF THE UNITED STATES; JURISPRUDENCE.

NATURAL LAW PARTY   Citizens of Fairfield, Iowa, formed the Natural Law party in April 1992. In a few short months, the party had succeeded in placing its presidential ticket on the ballot in twenty-eight states for the 1992 ELECTION. By 1996 the party was offering candidates for elective office in all fifty states.

Fairfield, Iowa, is the site of Maharishi International University, a school that teaches students to use transcendental meditation (TM) to achieve good health and a heightened awareness and understanding of the self and the world. The school, founded by Maharishi Mahesh Yogi, has provided the Natural Law party with the inspiration and resources to enter the field of electoral politics.

The Natural Law party has fashioned an unusual and ambitious political platform. The party endorses the practice of TM as a humane and cost-effective way to rehabilitate convicted and accused criminals. The party offers a proactive alternative to the current health care system, a system that party candidates call "disease care." Instead of pouring millions of dollars each year into the creation of drugs to manage disease, the Natural Law party would promote health education and stress management, along with TM, as ways to avoid disease.

Dr. John S. Hagelin has been the standard-bearer for the Natural Law party. Hagelin, a renowned physicist, was the party's nominee for president in 1992 and 1996. Although he is a professor at the Maharishi International University and a staunch proponent of the benefits of TM, Hagelin has worked to expand the party's scope beyond the TM message. The party emphasizes the importance of social equality for all persons, and party candidates talk of world peace as a reachable goal. The party platform also stresses environmental protection. For example, the party endorses alternative methods of energy production, such as a redirection of resources away from fossil fuels and toward renewable energy.

Although party membership has grown rapidly, and may be over 100,000 members, the party's inclusion in the political process has proved elusive. In 1996 Hagelin was one of only five presidential candidates who was on enough ballots to conceivably win the election in the ELECTORAL COLLEGE and from a party that had held primaries. Hagelin, along with REFORM PARTY candidate H. Ross Perot and LIBERTARIAN PARTY candidate Harry Browne, sought to participate in the nationally televised presidential debates based on these accomplishments. However, the Commission on Presidential Debates, a private nonprofit organization formed by the Democratic and Republican National Committees, concluded that neither Hagelin, Perot, nor Browne had a realistic chance of winning the election and excluded all three from the debates. Hagelin won 113,667 votes in the national election, or about 0.12 percent of the vote.

See also INDEPENDENT PARTIES.

NAVIGABLE RIVERS   See INTERNATIONAL WATERWAYS.

NAVIGABLE WATERS   Waters that provide a channel for commerce and transportation of people and goods.

Under U.S. law, bodies of water are distinguished according to their use. The distinction is particularly important in the case of so-called navigable waters, which are used for business or transportation. JURISDICTION over navigable waters belongs to the federal government rather than states or municipalities. The federal government can determine how the waters are used, by whom, and under what conditions. It also has the power to alter the waters, such as by dredging or building dams. Generally a state or private property owner who is inconvenienced by such work has no remedy against the federal government unless state or private property itself is taken; if such property is taken, the laws of EMINENT DOMAIN would apply, which may lead to compensation for the landowner.

The basis for federal jurisdiction over navigable waters lies in the U.S. Constitution. Since the early nineteenth century, the U.S. Supreme Court has held that the COMMERCE CLAUSE (Article 1, Section 8) gives the federal government extensive authority to regulate interstate commerce. This view originated in 1824 in the landmark case of *Gibbons v. Ogden*, 22 U.S. (9 Wheat.) 1, 6 L. Ed. 23. In *Gibbons*, the Court was faced with deciding whether to give precedence to a state or federal law for the licensing of vessels. It ruled that navigation of vessels in and out of the ports of the nation is a form of interstate commerce and thus federal law must take precedence. This decision led to the contemporary exercise of broad federal power over navigable waters, and in countless other areas of interstate commerce.

In practical terms federal regulation of navigable waters takes many forms. One area of this regulation covers matters of transportation and commerce: for example, rules governing the licensing of ships and the dumping of waste. A second area applies to the alteration of the navigable waters, which is strictly controlled by federal law. The Rivers and Harbors Appropriation Act of 1899 forbids building any unauthorized obstruction to the nation's navigable waters and gives enforcement powers to the U.S. Army Corps of Engineers. A third area of regulation involves WORKERS' COMPENSATION claims. The concept of navigable waters is important in claims made under the Longshore and Harbor Workers' Compensation Act of 1988 (33 U.S.C.A. §§ 901–950). The act provides that employers are liable for injuries to sailors that occur upon navigable waters of the United States.

The vast body of federal regulation concerning navigable waters frequently gives rise to litigation, and in many cases the courts have the difficult job of determining whether particular bodies of water are navigable (and thus subject to the law or regulation in question). Lakes and RIVERS are generally considered navigable waters, but smaller bodies of water may also be navigable. Attempting to address years of problematic litigation, the U.S. Supreme Court in

Twenty Busiest U.S. Ports, 1994

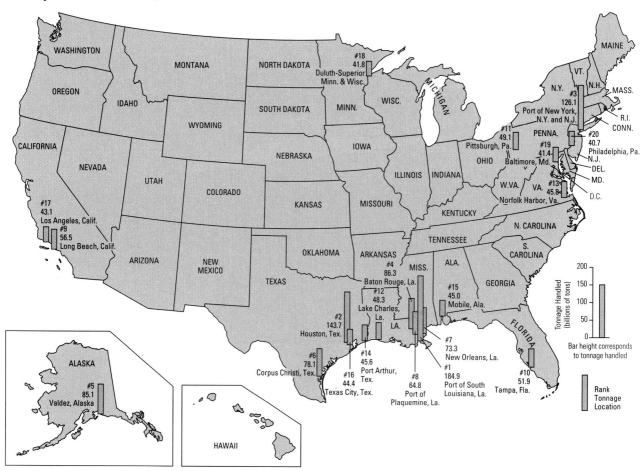

Source: U.S. Army Corps of Engineers

1979 created four tests for determining what constitutes navigable waters. Established in *Kaiser Aetna v. United States*, 444 U.S. 164, 100 S. Ct. 383, 62 L. Ed. 2d 332, the tests ask whether the body of water (1) is subject to the ebb and flow of the tide, (2) connects with a continuous interstate waterway, (3) has navigable capacity, and (4) is actually navigable. Using these tests, courts have held that bodies of water much smaller than lakes and rivers also constitute navigable waters. Even shallow streams that are traversable only by canoe have met the test.

CROSS-REFERENCES

Admiralty and Maritime Law; *Gibbons v. Ogden;* Pilot; Riparian Rights; Water Rights.

NAVY DEPARTMENT   The Navy is one of three primary components of the United States military. Incorporating the Marine Corps, it serves along with the Army and the Air Force as part of the nation's defense. The Navy's mission is to protect the United States as directed by the president or the secretary of defense by the effective prosecution of war at sea. With its Marine Corps component, the Navy's objec-

tives are to seize or defend advanced naval bases, support, as required, the forces of all military departments of the United States, and maintain freedom of the seas. The Department of the Navy includes the U.S. Coast Guard when it is operating as a service in the Navy. (The Coast Guard can come under Navy control at certain times.)

The U.S. Navy was founded on October 13, 1775, when Congress enacted the first legislation creating the Continental Navy of the American Revolution. The Department of the Navy and the Office of Secretary of the Navy were established by the act of April 30, 1798 (10 U.S.C.A. §§ 5011, 5031). For nine years before that date, by act of August 7, 1789 (1 Stat. 49), the conduct of naval affairs was under the secretary of war. The National Security Act Amendments of 1949 provided that the Department of the Navy be a military department within the Department of Defense (63 Stat. 578).

Office of the Secretary of the Navy

The secretary of the Navy is the head of the Department of the Navy. Appointed by the president of the United States, the secretary serves under the direction, authority, and control of the cabinet-level secretary of defense (10 U.S.C.A. § 5031). The secretary is responsible for the policies and control of the Navy, including its organization, administration, functioning, and efficiency. Next in succession for the position is the under secretary of the Navy, who functions as deputy and principal assistant to the secretary and has full authority in the general management of the department.

Civilian Executive Assistants The civilian executive assistants are the principal advisers and assistants to the secretary of the Navy. They include the under secretary of the Navy, the assistant secretaries of the Navy, and the general counsel of the Navy. With department-wide responsibilities for administration, the civilian executive assistants carry out their duties in harmony with the statutory positions of the chief of naval operations, who is the principal military adviser and executive to the secretary regarding naval matters, and the commandant of the Marine Corps, who is the principal military adviser and executive regarding Marine Corps matters. Each is authorized and directed to act for the secretary within his or her assigned area of responsibility.

Staff Assistants The staff assistants to the secretary of the Navy are the naval inspector general, the comptroller of the Navy, the auditor general of the Navy, and the chief of information. The secretary or the law has established the following positions and boards for administrative purposes.

Judge Advocate General The judge advocate general is the senior officer and head of the Judge Advocate General's Corps and the Office of the Judge Advocate General. The officer's primary responsibilities are to administer military justice throughout the Department of the Navy, perform functions required or authorized by the UNIFORM CODE OF MILITARY JUSTICE, and provide technical supervision for the Naval Justice School at Newport, Rhode Island. In cooperation with the general counsel to the Navy, the judge advocate general also has broad responsibility for providing legal advice and related services to the secretary of the Navy on military justice, ETHICS, ADMINISTRATIVE LAW, ENVIRONMENTAL LAW, operational and INTERNATIONAL LAW and TREATY interpretation, and litigation involving these issues. Officers of the Judge Advocate General's Corps and judge advocates of the Marine Corps provide a variety of legal services to both individual service members and naval commands, ranging from personal representation for individual service members for courts-martial to legal services for

naval commands on matters such as investigations and claims.

Naval Criminal Investigative Service The director of the Naval Criminal Investigative Service commands a worldwide organization with representation in more than 160 geographic locations to provide criminal investigation, counterintelligence, law enforcement, information, and personnel security support to the Navy and Marine Corps, both ashore and afloat.

Office of Naval Research Established by act of Congress on August 1, 1946 (10 U.S.C.A. §§ 5150–5153), the Office of Naval Research is the integrated headquarters of the Navy for science and technology investment. It manages funding for basic research, exploratory development, advanced technology development, manufacturing technologies, and small business support.

Personnel Boards The Naval Council of Personnel Boards has four components:

1. The Naval Discharge Review Board reviews, pursuant to 10 U.S.C.A. § 1553, the discharge or dismissal of former members of the Navy and Marine Corps, except in cases of COURT-MARTIAL. It determines whether, under reasonable standards of naval law and discipline, a discharge or dismissal should be changed and, if so, what change should be made.

2. The Naval Complaints Review Board reviews, upon request, decisional documents and index entries created by the Naval Discharge Review Board after April 1, 1977, to determine whether they conform to applicable regulations of the Department of Defense and the Department of the Navy.

3. The Naval Clemency and Parole Board reviews, pursuant to 10 U.S.C.A. §§ 953–954, Navy and Marine Corps court-martial cases referred to it and grants or denies CLEMENCY and, pursuant to 10 U.S.C.A. § 952, reviews and directs that PAROLE be granted or denied.

4. The Physical Evaluation Board organizes and administers disability evaluations within the Department of the Navy, pursuant to 10 U.S.C.A., ch. 61, and other applicable provisions of law and regulation.

Naval Records The Board for Correction of Naval Records is the highest echelon of review of administrative errors and injustices suffered by members and former members of the Navy and Marine Corps. Established under 10 U.S.C.A. § 1552 to give the secretary of the Navy direction on taking actions that otherwise would require congressional decision, the board relieves Congress of the need for additional legislation. This statutory civilian board reviews

Navy Department

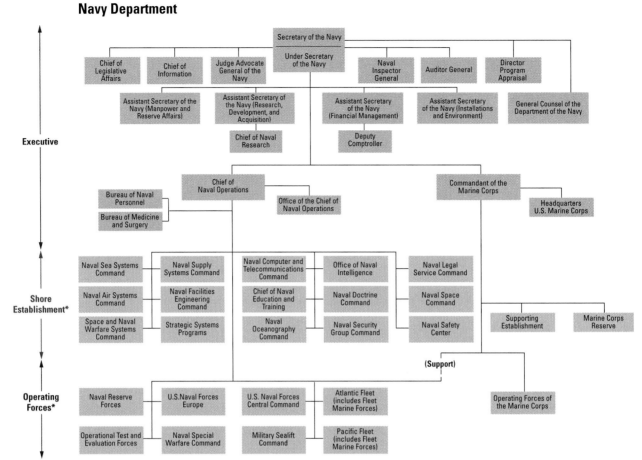

Executive

Shore Establishment*

Operating Forces*

*Also includes other designated activities not shown on the chart which are under the command or supervision of the organizations depicted.

service members' complaints about actions taken by various boards and officials in the department. The secretary of the Navy, acting through this board of civilians of the executive part of the department, is authorized to change naval or military records to correct an error or to remove an injustice.

United States Navy

Chief of Naval Operations The chief of naval operations is the highest-ranking officer of the naval service. The chief is the Navy member of the Joint Chiefs of Staff, the group of senior military officers who advise the president. Under the secretary of the Navy, the chief of naval operations exercises command over certain central executive organizations, assigned shore activities, and the Operating Forces of the Navy.

In the broadest terms, the chief of naval operations is responsible for the navy's readiness and for executing military orders. The chief plans for and provides the personnel, material, weapons, facilities, and services to support the needs of the Navy, with the exception of the

Fleet Marine Forces; maintains water transportation services, including sea transportation services for the Department of Defense; directs the Naval Reserve; and exercises authority for matters of naval administration, including matters related to customs and traditions of the naval service, security, intelligence, discipline, communications, and operations.

Operating Forces of the Navy The Operating Forces of the Navy are responsible for naval operations necessary to carry out the Department of the Navy's role in upholding and advancing the national policies and interests of the United States. The Operating Forces of the Navy include the several fleets, seagoing forces, Fleet Marine Forces and other assigned Marine Corps forces, the Military Sealift Command, and other forces and activities as may be assigned by the president or the secretary of the Navy.

The Navy's two fleets are composed of ships, submarines, and aircraft. The Pacific Fleet operates throughout the Pacific and Indian Oceans and the Atlantic Fleet operates throughout the

Atlantic Ocean and Mediterranean Sea. Additionally, the Naval Forces, Europe, is composed of forces from both fleets.

Navy Command Structure The chief of naval operations manages and supports the Operating Forces of the Navy through an organizational structure that is composed of sea systems, air systems, space and naval warfare systems, supply systems, naval facilities, strategic systems, naval personnel, naval medicine, oceanography, space command, legal services, computers and telecommunications, cryptology, intelligence, education and training, and naval doctrine command.

United States Marine Corps The United States Marine Corps was established on November 10, 1775, by resolution of the Continental Congress. The Marine Corps's composition and functions are detailed in 10 U.S.C.A. § 5063. Within the Department of the Navy, it is organized to include not less than three combat divisions and three aircraft wings, along with additional land combat, aviation, and other services. Its purpose is to provide forces necessary to seize or defend advanced naval bases and to conduct land operations essential to a naval campaign. In coordination with the Army and the Air Force, the Marine Corps develops the tactics, techniques, and equipment used by landing forces in amphibious (involving both sea and land) operations.

The Marine Corps also provides detachments and organizations for service on armed vessels of the Navy, provides security detachments for the protection of naval property at naval stations and bases, and performs such other duties as the president may direct.

The Marine Corps is composed of the Marine Corps headquarters, the Operating Forces, and the supporting establishment. The Operating Forces consist of Fleet Marine Force Atlantic, Fleet Marine Force Pacific, Marine Corps Reserve, Marine Security Forces, and Marine Detachments Afloat. The supporting establishment includes recruiting activities, training installations, reserve support activities, ground and aviation installations, and logistics bases.

Basic combat units of the Marines are deployed as Marine Air Ground Task Forces (MAGTFs). There are four types of MAGTFs: the Marine Expeditionary Force, the Marine Expeditionary Brigade, the Marine Expeditionary Unit, and the Special Purpose MAGTF. Each group has a command element, a ground combat element, an aviation combat element, and a combat service support element. Marine Expeditionary Forces are routinely deployed on amphibious ships to the Mediterranean Sea, Persian Gulf, and Pacific Ocean. Larger MAGTFs can rapidly deploy by air, sea, or any combination of means from both coasts of the United States and bases in the western Pacific to respond to emergencies worldwide.

United States Naval Academy The United States Naval Academy is the undergraduate college of the naval service. Located in Annapolis, Maryland, the academy offers a comprehensive four-year program that stresses excellence in academics, physical education, professional training, conduct, and honor. It prepares young men and women to be professional officers in the Navy and Marine Corps. All graduates receive a bachelor of science degree in one of eighteen majors.

CROSS-REFERENCES
Armed Services; Defense Department; Military Law.

NECESSARIES Things indispensable, or things proper and useful, for the sustenance of human life.

Traditional law required a husband to support his wife during their MARRIAGE irrespective of the wife's own means, her own ability to support herself, or even her own earnings, which, according to the Married Women's Property Acts passed in the mid–nineteenth century, she could do with as she pleased. The wife had no corresponding duty to support her husband. A husband owed the same support to the couple's children. He had the legal obligation to provide "necessaries" for his wife and children, which encompass food, clothing, lodging, health care, education, and comfort. Modern FAMILY LAW is now gender neutral: husbands and wives have an equal and mutual obligation to provide necessaries.

Courts rarely let themselves be involved in family disputes concerning necessaries while the marriage is ongoing. Depending on a couple's income, what is deemed "necessary" will vary widely. Although the level at which a spouse is to be maintained during marriage should correspond to the couple's station in life, successful litigation defining support obligations during marriage is rare. When a couple separates or divorces, MAINTENANCE and support become issues for the courts.

The law has recognized the wife's traditional authority to purchase necessaries. If a husband fails to fulfill his duty of support, his wife is authorized to purchase what necessaries she or their child needs, on the husband's CREDIT and even against his express wishes. Beyond the basic necessities, courts look to the couple's

Necessaries are things indispensable to sustain human life, including food, clothing, and shelter. Husbands and wives are obligated to provide necessaries for each other.

STEPHEN MCBRADY/PHOTOEDIT

circumstances. In some cases fur coats, gold watches, jewelry, and expensive furniture have been deemed necessaries. It is up to the merchant to show that the unauthorized purchases were in fact necessaries, and the merchant will not collect from the husband if the husband actually furnished appropriate necessaries to his wife and family.

The future of the necessaries rule is unclear. It may become gender neutral by evolving to protect purchases by the nonearning spouse in role-divided marriages, or it may disappear altogether because of the increasing financial independence of marriage partners and the attendant blurring of role division.

CROSS-REFERENCES

Alimony; Child Support; Divorce; Husband and Wife.

NECESSITY   A DEFENSE asserted by a criminal or civil defendant that he or she had no choice but to break the law.

The necessity defense has long been recognized at COMMON LAW and has also been made part of most states' statutory law. Although no federal statute acknowledges the defense, the Supreme Court has recognized it as part of the common law. The rationale behind the necessity defense is that sometimes, in a particular situation, a technical breach of the law is more advantageous to society than the consequence of strict adherence to the law. The defense is often used successfully in cases that involve a TRESPASS on PROPERTY to save a person's life or property. It also has been used, with varying degrees of success, in cases involving more complex questions.

Almost all common-law and statutory definitions of the necessity defense include the following elements: (1) the defendant acted to avoid a significant risk of harm; (2) no adequate lawful means could have been used to escape the harm; and (3) the harm avoided was greater than that caused by breaking the law. Some JURISDICTIONS require in addition that the harm must have been IMMINENT and that the action taken must have been reasonably expected to avoid the imminent danger. All these elements mirror the principles on which the defense of necessity was founded: first, that the highest social value is not always achieved by blind adherence to the law; second, that it is unjust to punish those who technically violate the letter of the law when they are acting to promote or achieve a higher social value than would be served by strict adherence to the law; and third, that it is in society's best interest to promote the greatest good and to encourage people to seek to achieve the greatest good, even if doing so necessitates a technical breach of the law.

The defense of necessity is considered a JUSTIFICATION defense, as compared with an EXCUSE defense such as DURESS. An action that is harmful but praiseworthy is justified, whereas an action that is harmful but ought to be forgiven may be excused. Rather than focusing on the actor's state of mind, as would be done with an excuse defense, the court with a necessity defense focuses on the value of the act. No court has ever accepted a defense of necessity to justify killing a person to protect property.

Most states that have codified the necessity defense make it available only if the defendant's value choice has not been specifically contradicted by the state legislature. For example, in 1993 the Massachusetts Supreme Judicial Court rejected the necessity defense of two people who were prosecuted for operating a needle-exchange program that was intended to reduce the transmission of AIDS through the sharing of contaminated hypodermic needles (*Massachusetts v. Leno*, 415 Mass. 835, 616 N.E.2d 453). Their actions violated a state law prohibiting the distribution of hypodermic needles without a physician's prescription. In rejecting the defense, the court held that the situation posed no clear and imminent danger. The court reasoned that citizens who disagree with the legislature's policy are not without remedy, as they can seek to have the law changed through popular INITIATIVE.

The necessity defense has been used with sporadic and very limited success in the area of civil disobedience since the 1970s. The most common circumstances involve public protests against ABORTION, NUCLEAR POWER, and nuclear weapons. Virtually all abortion protesters who have tried to avail themselves of the defense have lost. The courts have reasoned that because the right to an abortion is constitutionally protected, it cannot simultaneously be a legally recognized harm justifying illegal action. In these cases the courts have also denied the defense on the basis that the criminal act of protest would not stop abortions from occurring; that the harm caused by the act was greater than the harm of abortion; and that legal means of protest, such as demonstrating outside of the clinic rather than entering the clinic or trespassing on its property, were available. Consequently, according to the courts, there was no necessity for the protesters to break the law. In the vast majority of cases in which protesters, trespassing on property, blocked the entrance to nuclear plants, the courts have denied the necessity defense on the grounds that there was no imminent danger and that the trespassing protesters could not reasonably have believed that their actions would halt the manufacture of nuclear materials (see, e.g., *State v. Marley*, 54 Haw. 450, 509 P.2d 1095 [Haw. 1973]). The defense has also been denied in civil disobedience cases involving protests against U.S. policy abroad, the homeless problem, lack of funding for AIDS research, harmful logging practices, prison conditions, and human and animal rights violations.

Necessity has been used successfully by inmates who escape from PRISON under certain circumstances. In *Spakes v. State*, 913 S.W.2d 597 (Tex. Crim. App. 1996), the highest criminal court in Texas allowed the jury to be instructed on the necessity defense before deliberating the VERDICT for an inmate whose three cellmates had planned an escape and threatened to slit his throat if he did not accompany them. The defendant inmate argued that because of the terribly violent crimes of which his cellmates had been convicted (one had bragged about chopping his girlfriend up with an ax), he accompanied them and escaped. Even though he made no attempt to return himself to custody when he was separated from his cellmates, the court still allowed the defense. In contrast, most jurisdictions have held that an escapee must make an attempt to surrender or report to authorities as a condition for asserting the necessity defense. These courts have reasoned that once the immediate threat is no longer present, the action of escape is no longer necessary, and consequently it should end.

NEGATIVE COVENANT 📖 A provision found in an employment agreement or a contract of sale of a business that prohibits an employee or seller from competing in the same area or market. 📖

A negative covenant is commonly used by businesses, particularly those that depend upon TRADE SECRETS for their success. An employer wants to ensure that a former employee will not parlay information, skills, customer lists, and personal relationships with clients acquired on the job to gain a better position with a competitor or to start his or her own business. An employer also wants to protect his or her business in the competitive marketplace against the use of the unique personal skills of a former employee. An employer can achieve these objectives by including a negative covenant in the employment contract. Such a provision specifies that the employee will not work for a competitor or start a competing business for a period of time after leaving the employer. The covenant must be reasonable in its scope and duration. It cannot bar the employee from working at all, anywhere, or for an unreasonable length of time.

A court enforces a negative covenant by granting an INJUNCTION prohibiting the employee from working in a competitive enterprise as described in the covenant. It will do so only when necessary to protect the former employer's legitimate interests.

A contract for the sale of a business often includes a negative covenant at the insistence of the buyer. A buyer wants to protect and capitalize on the GOOD WILL of the business he or she buys. He or she must have an opportunity to get to know and serve the customers if the business is to continue to be successful. The value of the business is undermined if the seller can open a competing enterprise next door, thereby keeping some of the good will that was sold to the buyer. A negative covenant under which the seller agrees not to open a competing enterprise for a reasonable period of time within a reasonable distance from the original business is a frequent provision in a sales contract.

NEGLECT 📖 An omission to do or perform some work, duty, or act. 📖

As used by U.S. courts, the term *neglect* denotes the failure of responsibility on the part of defendants or attorneys. Neglect is related to the concept of NEGLIGENCE, but its rather limited use in the law sets it apart from that much broader doctrine. Generally speaking, neglect means omitting or failing to do something that is required. Neglect is often related to timeliness: examples include the failure of a taxpayer to file a timely income TAX RETURN and the failure of an attorney to meet a deadline for filing an APPEAL. In determining whether to rule against a party, courts consider the reason for the neglect, which can range from unavoidable accidents and hindrances to the less acceptable extreme of carelessness and indifference to duty.

Special terminology applies to some forms of neglect. CULPABLE neglect exists where a loss arises from an individual's carelessness, improvidence, or folly. WILLFUL neglect applies to marital cases; it refers to the neglect of one spouse, historically the husband, to provide such essentials as food, shelter, and clothing to the other spouse, either because of refusal or indifference. Excusable neglect is used to grant exceptions in cases where neglect was the consequence of ACCIDENT, unavoidable hindrance, reliance on legal COUNSEL, or reliance on promises made by the adverse party. Excusable neglect can serve as the basis for a MOTION to vacate a JUDGMENT, as in the case of explaining why a deadline for filing an appeal could not be met. Under the Federal Rules of Civil Procedure, excusable neglect authorizes a court to permit an act to be done after the official deadline has expired (Fed. R. Civ. P. 6(b)).

See also CHILD ABUSE; NECESSARIES.

NEGLIGENCE 📖 Conduct that falls below the standards of behavior established by law for the protection of others against unreasonable RISK of harm. A person has acted negligently if he or she has departed from the conduct expected of a reasonably prudent person acting under similar circumstances.

Negligence is also the name of a CAUSE OF ACTION in the law of TORTS. To establish negligence, a plaintiff must prove that the defendant had a DUTY to the plaintiff, the defendant breached that duty by failing to conform to the required standard of conduct, the defendant's negligent conduct was the cause of the harm to the plaintiff, and the plaintiff was, in fact, harmed or damaged. 📖

The concept of negligence developed under English law. Although English COMMON LAW had long imposed LIABILITY for the wrongful acts of others, negligence did not emerge as an independent cause of action until the eighteenth century. Another important concept emerged at that time: legal liability for a failure to act. Originally liability for failing to act was imposed on those who undertook to perform some service and breached a promise to exercise care or skill in performing that service. Gradually the law began to imply a promise to exercise CARE or skill in the performance of certain services. This promise to exercise care, whether express or implied, formed the origins of the modern concept of "duty." For example, inn-keepers were said to have a duty to protect the safety and security of their guests.

The concept of negligence passed from Great Britain to the United States as each state (except Louisiana) adopted the common law of Great Britain (Louisiana adopted the CIVIL LAW of France). Although there have been important developments in negligence law, the basic concepts have remained the same since the eighteenth century. Today negligence is by far the widest-ranging tort, encompassing virtually all unintentional, wrongful conduct that injures others. One of the most important concepts in negligence law is the "reasonable person," which provides the standard by which a person's conduct is judged.

The Reasonable Person A person has acted negligently if she has departed from the conduct expected of a reasonably prudent person acting under similar circumstances. The hypothetical REASONABLE PERSON provides an objective by which the conduct of others is judged. In law, the reasonable person is not an average person or a typical person but a composite of the community's judgment as to how the typical community member should behave in situations that might pose a threat of harm to the public. Even though the majority of people in the community may behave in a certain way, that does not establish the standard of conduct of the reasonable person. For example, a majority of people in a community may jaywalk, but jaywalking might still fall below the community's standards of safe conduct.

The concept of the reasonable person distinguishes negligence from intentional torts such as ASSAULT AND BATTERY. To prove an intentional tort, the plaintiff seeks to establish that the defendant deliberately acted to injure the plaintiff. In a negligence suit, however, the plaintiff seeks to establish that the failure of the defendant to act as a reasonable person would have acted caused the plaintiff's injury. An intoxicated driver who accidentally injures a pedestrian may not have intended to cause the pedestrian's injury. But because a reasonable person would not drive while intoxicated because it creates an unreasonable risk of harm to pedestrians and other drivers, an intoxicated driver may be held liable to an injured plaintiff for negligence despite his lack of INTENT to injure the plaintiff.

The law considers a variety of factors in determining whether a person has acted as the hypothetical reasonable person would have acted in a similar situation. These factors include the knowledge, experience, and perception of the person, the activity the person is engaging in, the physical characteristics of the person, and the circumstances surrounding the person's actions.

Knowledge, Experience and Perception The law takes into account a person's knowledge, experience, and perceptions in determining whether the person has acted as a reasonable person would have acted in the same circumstances. Conduct must be judged in light of a person's actual knowledge and observations, because the reasonable person always takes this into account. Thus, if a driver sees another car approaching at night without lights, the driver must act reasonably to avoid an accident, even though the driver would not have been negligent in failing to see the other car.

In addition to actual knowledge, the law also considers most people to have the same knowledge, experience, and ability to perceive as the hypothetical reasonable person. In the absence of unusual circumstances, a person must see what is clearly visible and hear what is clearly audible. Therefore, a driver of a car hit by a train at an unobstructed railroad crossing cannot claim that she was not negligent because she did not see or hear the train, because a reasonable person would have seen or heard the train.

Also, a person cannot deny personal knowledge of basic facts commonly known in the community. The reasonable person knows that ice is slippery, that live wires are dangerous, that alcohol impairs driving ability, and that children might run into the street when they are playing. To act as a reasonable person, an individual must even take into account her lack of knowledge of some situations, such as when walking down a dark, unfamiliar corridor.

Finally, a person who undertakes a particular activity is ordinarily considered to have the knowledge common to others who engage in that activity. A motorist must know the rules of road and a product manufacturer must know the characteristics and dangers of its product, at least to the extent they are generally known in the industry.

Special Skills If a person engages in an activity requiring special skills, education, training, or experience, such as piloting an airplane, the standard by which his conduct is measured is the conduct of a reasonably skilled, competent, and experienced person who is a qualified member of the group authorized to engage in that activity. In other words, the hypothetical reasonable person is a skilled, competent, and experienced person who engages in the same activity. Often persons practicing these special

Although many forest fires are caused by lightning strikes, they can also stem from negligence. If someone failed to put out a campfire, and if the act of putting out a campfire could be expected of a reasonably prudent person under similar circumstances, then that person was negligent.

skills must be licensed, such as physicians, lawyers, architects, barbers, pilots, and drivers. Anyone who performs these special skills, whether qualified or not, is held to the standards of conduct of those properly qualified to do so, because the public relies on the special expertise of those who engage in such activities. Thus, an unlicensed driver who takes his friends for a joyride is held to the standard of conduct of an experienced, licensed driver.

The law does not make a special allowance for beginners with regard to special skills. The learner, beginner, or trainee in a special skill is held to the standard of conduct of persons who are reasonably skilled and experienced in the activity. Sometimes the beginner is held to a standard he cannot meet. For example, a first-time driver clearly does not possess the experience and skill of an experienced driver. Although it seems unfair to hold the beginner to the standards of the more experienced person, this standard protects the general public from the risk of a beginner's lack of competence, because the community is usually defenseless to guard against such risks.

Physical Characteristics The law takes a person's physical characteristics into account in determining whether that person's conduct is negligent. Whether a person's conduct is reasonable, and therefore not negligent, is measured against a reasonably prudent person with the same physical characteristics. There are two reasons for taking physical characteristics into account. A physically impaired individual cannot be expected to conform to a standard of conduct that would be physically impossible for her to meet. On the other hand, a physically handicapped person must act reasonably in light of her handicap, and she may be negligent in taking a risk that is unreasonable in light of her known physical limitations. Thus, it would be negligent for a blind person to drive an automobile.

Mental Capacity Although a person's physical characteristics are taken into account in determining negligence, the person's mental CAPACITY is generally ignored and does not excuse the person from acting according to the reasonable person standard. The fact that an individual is lacking in intelligence, judgment, memory, or emotional stability does not excuse the person's failure to act as a reasonably prudent person would have acted under the same circumstances. For example, a person who causes a forest fire by failing to extinguish his campfire cannot claim that he was not negligent because he lacked the intelligence, judgment, or

experience to appreciate the risk of an untended campfire.

Similarly, evidence of voluntary intoxication will not excuse conduct that is otherwise negligent. Although intoxication affects a person's judgment, voluntary intoxication will not excuse negligent conduct, because it is the person's conduct, not his or her mental condition, that determines negligence. In some cases a person's intoxication is relevant to determining whether his conduct is negligent, however, because undertaking certain activities, such as driving, while intoxicated poses a danger to others.

Children Children may be negligent, but they are not held to the same standard of conduct as adults. A child's conduct is measured against the conduct expected of a child of similar age, intelligence, and experience. Unlike the standard for adults, the standard of reasonable conduct for children takes into account subjective factors such as intelligence and experience. In this sense the standard is less strict than for adults, because children normally do not engage in the high-risk activities of adults and adults dealing with children are expected to anticipate their "childish" behavior.

In many states children are presumed incapable of negligence below a certain age, usually seven years. In some states children between the ages of seven and fourteen years are presumed to be incapable of negligence, although this PRESUMPTION can be rebutted. Once a person reaches the AGE OF MAJORITY, usually eighteen years, she is held to adult standards of conduct.

One major exception to the rules of negligence exists with regard to children. If a child is engaging in what is considered an "adult activity," such as driving an automobile or flying an airplane, she will be held to an adult standard of care. The higher standard of care imposed for these types of activities is justified by the special skills required to engage in them and the danger they pose to the public.

Emergencies The law recognizes that even a reasonable person can make errors in judgment in emergency situations. Therefore, a person's conduct in an emergency is evaluated in light of whether it was a reasonable response under the circumstances, even though, in hindsight, another course of action might have avoided the injury.

In some circumstances failure to anticipate an emergency may constitute negligence. The reasonable person anticipates, and takes precautions against, foreseeable emergencies. For example, the owner of a theater must consider the possibility of a fire, and the owner of a swimming pool must consider the possibility of a swimmer drowning. Failure to guard against such emergencies can constitute negligence.

Also, a person can be negligent in causing an emergency, even if he acts reasonably during the emergency. A theater owner whose negligence causes a fire, for instance, would be liable for the injuries to the patrons, even if he saved lives during the fire.

Conduct of Others Finally, the reasonable person takes into account the conduct of others and regulates his own conduct accordingly. A reasonable person must even foresee the unlawful or negligent conduct of others if the situation warrants. Thus, a person may be found negligent for leaving a car unlocked with the keys in the ignition because of the foreseeable risk of theft, or for failing to slow down in the vicinity of a school yard where children might negligently run into the street.

Proof of Negligence In a negligence suit, the plaintiff has the burden of proving that the defendant did not act as a reasonable person would have acted under the circumstances. The court will instruct the jury as to the standard of conduct required of the defendant. For example, a defendant sued for negligent driving is judged according to how a reasonable person would have driven in the same circumstances. A plaintiff has a variety of means of proving that a defendant did not act as the hypothetical reasonable person would have acted. The plaintiff can show that the defendant violated a statute designed to protect against the type of injury that occurred to the plaintiff. Also, a plaintiff might introduce expert WITNESSES, EVIDENCE of a customary practice, or CIRCUMSTANTIAL EVIDENCE.

Statutes Federal and state statutes, municipal ordinances, and administrative regulations govern all kinds of conduct and frequently impose standards of conduct to be observed. For example, the law prohibits driving through a red traffic light at an intersection. A plaintiff injured by a defendant who ignored a red light can introduce the defendant's violation of the statute as evidence that the defendant acted negligently. However, a plaintiff's evidence that the defendant violated a statute does not always establish that the defendant acted unreasonably. The statute that was violated must have been intended to protect against the particular hazard or type of harm that caused injury to the plaintiff.

Sometimes physical circumstances beyond a person's control can excuse the violation of a statute, such as when the headlights of a vehicle suddenly fail, or when a driver swerves into oncoming traffic to avoid a child who darted into the street. To excuse the violation, the defendant must establish that, in failing to comply with the statute, she acted as a reasonable person would have acted.

In many JURISDICTIONS the violation of a statute, regulation, or ordinance enacted to protect against the harm that resulted to the plaintiff is considered *negligence per se.* Unless the defendant presents evidence excusing the violation of the statute, the defendant's negligence is conclusively established. In some jurisdictions a defendant's violation of a statute is merely evidence that the defendant acted negligently.

Experts Often a plaintiff will need an expert witness to establish that the defendant did not adhere to the conduct expected of a reasonably prudent person in the defendant's circumstances. A juror may be unable to determine from his own experience, for example, if the medicine prescribed by a physician was reasonably appropriate for a patient's illness. Experts may provide the jury with information beyond the common knowledge of jurors, such as scientific theories, data, tests, and experiments. Also, in cases involving professionals such as physicians, experts establish the standard of care expected of the professional. In the above example, the patient might have a physician offer expert testimony regarding the medication that a reasonably prudent physician would have prescribed for the patient's illness.

Custom Evidence of the usual and customary conduct or practice of others under similar circumstances can be admitted to establish the proper standard of reasonable conduct. Like the evidence provided by expert witnesses, evidence of custom and habit is usually used in cases where the nature of the alleged negligence is beyond the common knowledge of the jurors. Often such evidence is presented in cases alleging negligence in some business activity. For example, a plaintiff suing the manufacturer of a punch press that injured her might present evidence that all other manufacturers of punch presses incorporate a certain safety device that would have prevented the injury.

A plaintiff's evidence of conformity or nonconformity with a customary practice does not establish whether the defendant was negligent; the jury decides whether a reasonably prudent person would have done more or less than is customary.

Circumstantial Evidence Sometimes a plaintiff has no DIRECT EVIDENCE of how the

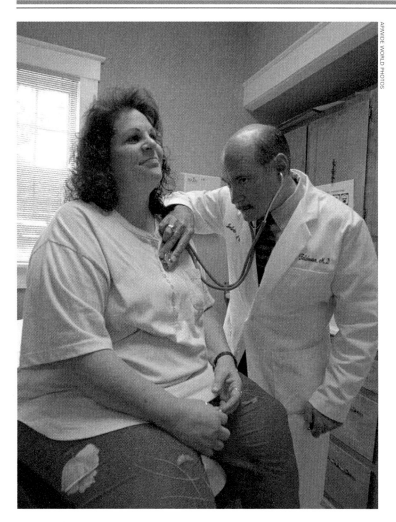

AP/WIDE WORLD PHOTOS

The law of negligence imposes higher standards on individuals who engage in activities that require special skills and training. For example, someone who engages in the practice of medicine must act as a reasonably skilled, competent, and experienced physician would.

defendant acted and must attempt to prove his case through circumstantial evidence. Of course, any fact in a lawsuit may be proved by circumstantial evidence. Skid marks can establish the speed a car was traveling prior to a collision, a person's appearance can circumstantially prove his or her age, etc. Sometimes a plaintiff in a negligence lawsuit must prove his entire case by circumstantial evidence. Suppose a plaintiff's shoulder is severely injured during an operation to remove his tonsils. The plaintiff, who was unconscious during the operation, sues the doctor in charge of the operation for negligence, even though he has no idea how the injury actually occurred. The doctor refuses to say how the injury occurred, so the plaintiff will have to prove his case by circumstantial evidence.

In cases such as this, the doctrine of RES IPSA LOQUITUR ("the thing speaks for itself") is invoked. *Res ipsa loquitor* allows a plaintiff to prove negligence on the theory that his injury could not have occurred in the absence of the defendant's negligence. The plaintiff must establish that the injury was caused by an instrumentality

or condition that was under the defendant's exclusive management or control and that the plaintiff's injury would not have occurred if the defendant had acted with reasonable care. Thus, in the above example, the plaintiff can use *res ipsa loquitor* to prove that the doctor negligently injured his shoulder.

Duty A defendant is not liable in negligence, even if she did not act with reasonable care, if she did not owe a duty to the plaintiff. In general, a person is under a duty to all persons at all times to exercise reasonable care for their physical safety and the safety of their property. This general standard of duty may lead to seemingly unjust results. For example, if a property owner leaves a deep hole in her backyard with no warnings or barriers around the hole, she should be liable if her guest falls into the hole. But what if a trespasser enters the backyard at night and falls into the hole? Although the property owner was negligent in failing to guard against someone falling into the hole, it would be unfair to require the property owner to compensate the trespasser for his injury. Therefore, the law states that a property owner does not have a duty to protect a trespasser from harm.

The law uses the concept of duty to limit the situations where a defendant is liable for a plaintiff's injury. Whether a defendant has a duty to protect the plaintiff from harm is a question decided by the court, not the jury. Over time, courts have developed numerous rules creating and limiting a person's duty to others, and sometimes duties are established or limited by statute. Whether the defendant owes the plaintiff a duty depends upon the relationship between the defendant and the plaintiff.

A preexisting relationship can create an affirmative duty to exercise reasonable care to protect another person from harm. For example, an inn has an affirmative duty to protect its guests, a school has a duty to its pupils, a store has a duty to its customers, and a lifeguard has a duty to swimmers.

One always has a duty to refrain from taking actions that endanger the safety of others, but usually one does not have a duty to render aid or prevent harm to a person from an independent cause. A common example of this limitation on duty is the lack of a duty to go to the aid of a person in peril. An expert swimmer with a boat and a rope has no duty to attempt to rescue a person who is drowning (although a hired lifeguard would). A physician who witnesses an automobile accident has no duty to offer emergency medical assistance to the accident victims.

Sometimes a person can voluntarily assume a duty where it would not otherwise exist. If the doctor who encounters an automobile accident decides to render aid to the victims, she is under a duty to exercise reasonable care in rendering that aid. As a result, doctors who have stopped along the highway to render medical assistance to accident victims have been sued for negligence. Many states have adopted "good samaritan" statutes to relieve individuals who render emergency assistance from negligence liability.

Even if a plaintiff establishes that the defendant had a duty to protect the plaintiff from harm and breached that duty by failing to use reasonable care, the plaintiff must still prove that the defendant's negligence was the PROXIMATE CAUSE of her injury.

Proximate Cause Perhaps no issue in negligence law has caused more confusion than the issue of proximate cause. The concept of proximate cause limits a defendant's liability for his negligence to consequences reasonably related to the negligent conduct. Although it might seem obvious whether a defendant's negligence has caused injury to the plaintiff, issues of causation are often very difficult. Suppose, for example, that a defendant negligently causes an automobile accident, injuring another driver. The colliding cars also knock down a utility pole, resulting in a power outage. Clearly the defendant's negligence has in fact caused both the accident and power outage. Most people would agree that the negligent defendant should be liable for the other driver's injuries, but should he also be liable to an employee who, due to the failure of her electric alarm clock, arrives late for work and is fired? This question raises the issue of proximate cause.

Actually, the term *proximate cause* is somewhat misleading because as a legal concept it has little to do with proximity (in time or space) or causation. Rather, proximate cause is related to fairness and justice, in the sense that at some point it becomes unfair to hold a defendant responsible for the results of his negligence. For example, Mrs. O'Leary's negligent placement of her lantern may have started the Great Chicago Fire, but it would be unjust to hold her responsible for all the damage done by the fire.

In determining whether a defendant's negligence is the proximate cause of a plaintiff's injury, most courts focus on the foreseeability of the harm that resulted from the defendant's negligence. For example, if a driver negligently drives his automobile, it is foreseeable that he might cause an accident with another vehicle, hit a pedestrian, or crash into a storefront. Thus, the driver would be liable for those damages. But suppose the negligent driver collides with a truck carrying dynamite, causing an explosion that injures a person two blocks away. Assuming that the driver had no idea that the truck was carrying dynamite, it is not foreseeable that his negligent driving could injure a person two blocks away. Therefore the driver would not be liable for that person's injury under this approach. When applying this approach, courts frequently instruct juries to consider whether the harm or injury was the "natural or probable" consequence of the defendant's negligence.

A minority of courts hold the view that the defendant's negligence is the proximate cause of the plaintiff's injury if the injury is the "direct result" of the negligence. Usually a plaintiff's injury is considered to be the direct result of the defendant's negligence if it follows an unbroken, natural sequence from the defendant's act and no intervening, external force acts to cause the injury.

Intervening Cause Sometimes a plaintiff's injury results from more than one cause. For instance, suppose a defendant negligently injures a pedestrian in an automobile accident. An emergency room doctor negligently treats the plaintiff, aggravating her injury. The doctor's negligence is an "intervening cause" of the plaintiff's injury. A cause of injury is an INTERVENING CAUSE only if it occurs subsequent to the defendant's negligent conduct.

Just because an intervening cause exists, however, does not mean that the defendant's negligent conduct is not the proximate cause of the plaintiff's injury. The defendant remains liable if he should have foreseen the intervening cause and taken it into account in his conduct. If a defendant negligently spills a large quantity of gasoline and doesn't clean it up, he will not be relieved of liability for a resulting fire merely because another person causes the gasoline to ignite, because it is foreseeable that the gasoline might be accidentally ignited. Also, it is foreseeable that a sudden gust of wind might cause the fire to spread quickly.

Even if an intervening cause is foreseeable, however, in some situations the defendant will still be excused from liability. If the intervening cause is the intentional or criminal conduct of a third person, the defendant is not liable for this person's negligent conduct. In the example where the defendant spilled gasoline and did not clean it up, he is not responsible for the resulting fire if someone intentionally ignites the gas. Also, sometimes a third person will discover the danger that the defendant created by his negligence under circumstances where

A bridge may collapse due to negligence.

the third person has some duty to act. If the third person fails to act, the defendant is not liable. In the gasoline example, suppose the defendant, a customer at a gas station, negligently spills a large quantity of gas near the pumps. The owner of the gas station sees the spilled gasoline but does nothing. The owner of the gas station, not the defendant, would be liable if another customer accidentally ignites the gasoline.

Sometimes, however, a completely unforeseeable event or result occurs after a defendant's negligence, resulting in harm to the plaintiff. An abnormal, unpredictable, or highly improbable event that occurs after the defendant's negligence is known as a "superseding cause" and relieves the defendant of liability. For example, suppose a defendant negligently blocks a road causing the plaintiff to make a detour in her automobile. While on the detour, an airplane hits the plaintiff's car, killing the plaintiff. The airplane was completely unforeseeable to the defendant, and thus he cannot be held liable for the plaintiff's death. The airplane was a superseding cause of the plaintiff's death.

Even great jurists have had difficulty articulating exactly what constitutes proximate cause. Although the law provides tests such as "foreseeability" and "natural, direct consequences," ultimately the issue of proximate cause is decided by people's sense of right and wrong. In the example where the defendant spills gasoline

and does not clean it up, most people would agree that the defendant should be liable if a careless smoker accidentally ignites the gasoline, even if they could not articulate that the smoker was a foreseeable, intervening cause of the fire.

Defenses to Negligence Liability
Even if a plaintiff has established that the defendant owed a duty to the plaintiff, breached that duty, and proximately caused the defendant's injury, the defendant can still raise defenses that reduce or eliminate his liability. These defenses include contributory negligence, comparative negligence, and ASSUMPTION OF RISK.

Contributory Negligence Frequently, more than one person has acted negligently to create an injury. Under the common-law rule of contributory negligence, a plaintiff whose own negligence was a contributing cause of her injury was barred from recovering from a negligent defendant. For example, a driver negligently enters an intersection in the path of an oncoming car, resulting in a collision. The other driver was driving at an excessive speed and might have avoided the COLLISION if she had been driving more slowly. Thus, both drivers' negligence contributed to the accident. Under the doctrine of contributory negligence, neither driver would be able to recover from the other, due to her own negligence in causing the accident.

The doctrine of contributory negligence seeks to keep a plaintiff from recovering from the defendant where the plaintiff is also at fault. However, this doctrine often leads to unfair results. For example, even if a defendant's negligence is the overwhelming cause of the plaintiff's injury, even slight negligence on the part of the plaintiff completely bars his recovery. Also, the negligence of many defendants such as CORPORATIONS, manufacturers, and landowners creates no corresponding risk of injury to themselves. In such cases the doctrine of contributory negligence, which can completely eliminate the liability for their negligence, reduces their incentive to act safely. As a result, courts and statutes have considerably weakened the doctrine of contributory negligence.

Comparative Negligence Most states, either by court decision or statute, have now adopted some form of comparative negligence in place of pure, contributory negligence. Under comparative negligence, or comparative fault as it is sometimes known, a plaintiff's negligence is not a complete bar to her recovery. Instead the plaintiff's damages are reduced by whatever percentage her own FAULT contributed to the injury. This requires the jury to determine, by percentage, the fault of the plaintiff and defendant in causing the plaintiff's injury. For example, suppose a plaintiff is injured in an automobile accident and sustains $100,000 in damages. The jury determines that the plaintiff was 25 percent responsible for the accident and that the defendant was 75 percent responsible. The plaintiff will then be allowed to recover 75 percent of her damages, or $75,000.

Most states have adopted the "50 percent rule" of comparative negligence. Under this rule the plaintiff cannot recover any damages if her negligence was as great as, or greater than, the negligence of the defendant. This rule partially retains the doctrine of contributory negligence, reflecting the view that a plaintiff who is largely responsible for her own injury is unworthy of compensation. A minority of states have adopted "pure comparative fault." Under that rule even a plaintiff who is 80 percent at fault in causing her injury may still recover 20 percent of damages, reflecting the defendant's percentage of fault.

Assumption of Risk Under the assumption of risk defense, a defendant can avoid liability for his negligence by establishing that the plaintiff voluntarily consented to encounter a known danger created by the defendant's negligence. Assumption of risk may be EXPRESS or IMPLIED. Under express assumption of risk, persons agree in advance that one person consents to assume the risk of the other's negligence. For example, a skier who purchases a lift ticket at a ski resort usually expressly agrees to assume the risk of any injury that might occur while skiing. Thus, even if the ski resort negligently fails to mark a hazard on a trail resulting in an injury to a skier, the ski resort may invoke the assumption of risk defense in the skier's subsequent lawsuit.

Assumption of risk may also be implied from a plaintiff's conduct. For example, the defendant gives the plaintiff, a painter, a scaffold with a badly frayed rope. The plaintiff, fully aware of the rope's condition, proceeds to use the scaffold and is injured. The defendant can raise the implied assumption of risk defense. This defense is similar to the contributory negligence defense; in the above example, the defendant might also argue that the plaintiff was contributorily negligent for using the scaffold when he knew the rope was frayed.

The implied assumption of risk defense has caused a great deal of confusion in the courts because of its similarity to contributory negligence, and with the rise of comparative fault, the defense has diminished in importance and is viable today only in a minority of jurisdictions.

CROSS-REFERENCES

Alcohol; Automobiles; Good Samaritan Doctrine; Guest Statutes; Last Clear Chance; *MacPherson v. Buick Motor Co.*; Natural and Probable Consequences; *Palsgraf v. Long Island Railroad Company*; Product Liability; Rescue; *Rylands v. Fletcher*; Strict Liability.

NEGOTIABLE INSTRUMENT 📖 A COMMERCIAL PAPER, such as a CHECK or PROMISSORY NOTE, that contains the signature of the MAKER or DRAWER; an unconditional promise or order to pay a certain sum in cash that is payable either upon demand or at a specifically designated time to the order of a designated person or to its BEARER. 📖

NEGOTIATE 📖 To conduct business transactions; to deal with another individual in regard to a purchase and sale; to bargain or trade. To conclude by way of agreement, bargain, or COMPACT. To transfer a *negotiable instrument*, such as a PROMISSORY NOTE, or other COMMERCIAL PAPER. 📖

BIOGRAPHY

NELSON, JOHN John Nelson was a prominent early U.S. lawyer, congressman, and diplomat who served as attorney general of the United States under President JOHN TYLER.

Nelson was born June 1, 1791, in Frederick County, Maryland. As a young boy, he was educated by private tutors before entering the College of William and Mary at Williamsburg, Virginia. He graduated in 1811 and went on to

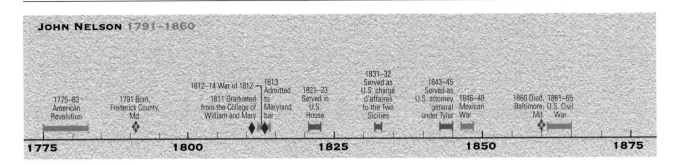

JOHN NELSON 1791–1860

1775–83 American Revolution

1791 Born, Frederick County, Md.

1812–14 War of 1812

1811 Graduated from the College of William and Mary

1813 Admitted to Maryland bar

1821–23 Served in U.S. House

1831–32 Served as U.S. charge d'affaires to the Two Sicilies

1843–45 Served as U.S. attorney general under Tyler

1846–48 Mexican War

1860 Died, Baltimore, Md.

1861–65 U.S. Civil War

1775   1800   1825   1850   1875

study law with attorneys in both Virginia and Maryland.

He was admitted to the bar in 1813 and established a practice in his hometown.

In 1820 Nelson was elected to the U.S. House of Representatives as a Democrat. He took the oath of office on March 4, 1821, and served until March 3, 1823. He did not run for reelection but did support ANDREW JACKSON's presidential bid in 1828.

Over the next two decades, Nelson served the U.S. government in a number of unofficial capacities. He received the first of his official appointments from President Jackson in 1831, when he was named to a diplomatic post in Naples. He served as U.S. charge d'affaires (*charge d'affaires* is a title accorded lower-level diplomats) to Two Sicilies from October 24, 1831, to October 15, 1832. (The Two Sicilies was an independent Bourbon/Spanish-ruled kingdom located in southern Italy prior to that country's unification in the mid-1860s. The kingdom's capital was Naples.)

When Tyler assumed the presidency following the death of President WILLIAM H. HARRISON, he named Nelson attorney general of the United States. Nelson held a cabinet post as secretary of state ad interim at the same time. (The position of attorney general was not a cabinet-level post at the time.) Nelson served in both capacities from 1843 to 1845.

In his later years, Nelson resumed the practice of law in Baltimore, Maryland. He died there on January 8, 1860, and is buried at Baltimore's Greenmount Cemetery.

BIOGRAPHY

Samuel Nelson

ARTIST: FREEMAN THORPE. COLLECTION OF THE SUPREME COURT OF THE UNITED STATES.

NELSON, SAMUEL Samuel Nelson served as an associate justice of the U.S. Supreme Court from 1845 to 1872. He brought to his position experience as a politician, lawyer, and judge, which included service as chief justice of the New York Supreme Court. His nomination to the U.S. Supreme Court by a desperate President JOHN TYLER came only after several prior nominees had declined or had been rejected by the U.S. Senate.

Nelson was born in Hebron, New York, on November 10, 1792. He entered Middlebury College, in Vermont, at the age of fifteen and graduated in 1813. Nelson chose a career in law, and in his twenties, he managed a successful private practice in real estate and commercial law that brought him political recognition. In 1821 he was the youngest delegate to serve in the New York state constitutional convention. His judicial career began in 1823 with his appointment as a judge to the Sixth Circuit. In 1831 he began a fourteen-year tenure on the New York Supreme Court, during the last four years of which he served as its chief justice, from 1836 to 1845. (Since 1847, New York's highest court has been called the New York Court of Appeals.) There Nelson developed a reputation for common sense and belief in the limits of judicial power.

In 1845 President Tyler turned to Nelson in desperation. The president's attempts to fill a vacant seat on the U.S. Supreme Court had produced more than half a dozen nominees, all of whom refused the nomination or failed to win Senate approval. Nelson, a last-minute sub-

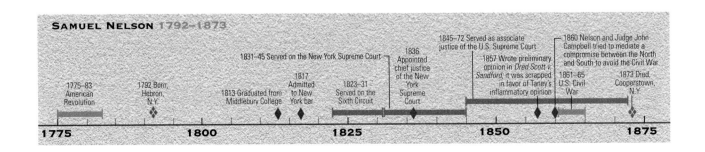

SAMUEL NELSON 1792–1873

1775–83 American Revolution

1792 Born, Hebron, N.Y.

1813 Graduated from Middlebury College

1817 Admitted to New York bar

1823–31 Served on the Sixth Circuit

1831–45 Served on the New York Supreme Court

1836 Appointed chief justice of the New York Supreme Court

1845–72 Served as associate justice of the U.S. Supreme Court

1857 Wrote preliminary opinion in *Dred Scott v. Sandford*; it was scrapped in favor of Taney's inflammatory opinion

1860 Nelson and Judge John Campbell tried to mediate a compromise between the North and South to avoid the Civil War.

1861–65 U.S. Civil War

1873 Died, Cooperstown, N.Y.

1775   1800   1825   1850   1875

stitution, sailed through the nomination process.

Nelson believed that the Court should move cautiously in matters where Congress expressed its will. He wrote the original majority opinion in the *Dred Scott* decision that upheld the institution of SLAVERY (*Dred Scott v. Sandford*, 60 U.S. [19 How.] 393, 15 L. Ed. 691 [1857]). Nelson's opinion sought to avoid answering the highly controversial question of slavery. But under political pressure from Southern justices on the Court, his opinion was scrapped and Chief Justice ROGER B. TANEY's inflammatory opinion was substituted. Taney's decision led to violent protest and deepened hostilities that ultimately led to the Civil War. Nelson died December 12, 1873.

See also DRED SCOTT V. SANDFORD.

NET ⬛ The sum that remains following all permissible deductions, including charges, expenses, discounts, commissions, or taxes. ⬛

Net assets, for example, are what remain after an individual subtracts the amount owed to creditors from his or her ASSETS. *Net pay* is the salary an individual actually receives after deductions such as INCOME TAX and SOCIAL SECURITY payments.

NET WORTH ⬛ The difference between total ASSETS and liabilities; the sum total of the assets of an individual or business minus the total amount owed to CREDITORS. ⬛

The net worth of a CORPORATION is ordinarily determined by subtracting the liabilities from the assets, or by adding the capital account to the surplus account, as shown in the balance sheet of the company.

NEUTRALITY ⬛ The state of a nation that takes no part in a WAR between two or more other nations. ⬛

Since the nineteenth century, INTERNATIONAL LAW has recognized the right of a nation to abstain from participation in a war between other states. In an international war, those taking no part are called neutrals. This means that a neutral state cannot provide assistance to the belligerents, the principal hostile powers, or to their allies, who cooperate and assist them.

The law of neutrality that emerged from the nineteenth century was codified in several of the Hague Conferences of 1907, including No. 3, Convention Relative to the Opening of Hostilities (requiring notice to neutrals of a state of war); No. 5, Convention Respecting Rights and Duties of Neutral Powers and Persons in Case of War on Land; and No. 11, Convention Relative to Certain Restrictions with Regard to the Exercise of the Right of Capture in Naval War.

Hague Convention No. 5 provided that a neutral territory cannot be used for belligerent troop movements, convoys of munitions or supplies, establishment of communications centers, or the recruitment of combatants. A neutral state need not prevent individuals from leaving its territory to enlist elsewhere in a belligerent force, nor is it obligated to prevent individuals from selling or transporting to a belligerent arms, munitions, or other goods useful to its armed forces. By implication, a neutral state may not, as a government, directly aid a belligerent state by selling or giving publicly owned munitions, military equipment, or supplies, or by providing grants, loans, or credits for their procurement. If a neutral state adopts regulations prohibiting or restricting the sale of munitions and equipment by its private citizens, it must apply them to belligerents impartially.

Once a state decides on a position of neutrality, it must take steps to prevent its territory from becoming a base for military operations of a belligerent. It must prevent the recruiting of military personnel, the organizing of military expeditions, and the constructing, outfitting, commissioning, and arming of warships for belligerent use. The neutral state therefore must prohibit by law any such activities by either its citizens or agents of foreign governments.

A neutral state is under no obligation to prevent private persons or companies from advancing credits or selling commodities to belligerents. Such sales are not illegal under the international law of neutrality. A neutral state may, if it chooses, go beyond the requirements of international law by placing an EMBARGO upon some or all sales or credits to belligerents by its nationals. If it does so, it has the obligation to see that legislation, commonly referred to as neutrality laws, is applied impartially to all belligerents. Once enacted, neutrality laws are not to be modified in ways that would advantage one party in the war.

For most of its history, the United States tried to remain a neutral during the wars among European states. President GEORGE WASHINGTON issued a neutrality proclamation in 1793 after the outbreak of war between France and the European allies. Congress enacted its first neutrality law in 1794 (1 Stat. 381), which prohibited private individuals from accepting a foreign military commission, outfitting military vessels for a foreign state, or enlisting or hiring persons for the service of a foreign state.

This legislation proved generally effective in accomplishing its objectives, but it did not deter

Germany invaded and occupied Norway during World War II even though Norway was a neutral nation and had not assisted either the Allies or the Axis.

citizens who wished to support revolutionary belligerent or insurgent movements in South and Central America during the nineteenth century. The Mexican Revolution of 1910 and the counterrevolution that followed led to the trafficking in arms and ammunition across the border. In response, Congress enacted in 1912 its first arms embargo (37 Stat. 630), a prohibition not required by international law. It authorized the president, upon finding that conditions of violence in an American country were promoted by procurement of arms or munitions of war in the United States, to prohibit further export of them.

With the rise of international conflicts around the world in the 1930s, Congress passed the Neutrality Acts of 1935, 1936, and 1937 (49 Stat. 1081, 49 Stat. 1152, 50 Stat. 121). These laws required registration and licensing by a National Munitions Control Board of all persons trading in munitions and a mandatory embargo on the export of arms, ammunition, and implements of war, and on loans and credits to all belligerents or to neutrals for transshipment to belligerents. An embargo would take effect when the president found a state of war to exist.

The desire of the United States to remain neutral has been called isolationism. During the 1930s the U.S. public did not want the United States entangled with the international strife perpetrated by Italy, Germany, and Japan. In 1935 President FRANKLIN D. ROOSEVELT invoked the arms embargo provision after the Italian invasion of Ethiopia and the consequent war.

With the outbreak of the European war in 1939, limiting the conflict by an arms embargo was no longer possible. Although isolationist sentiment was strong, there was also a growing feeling that the Allies needed support against Nazi aggression. The Roosevelt administration, with some difficulty, secured the repeal of the arms embargo in the Neutrality Act of 1939 (22 U.S.C.A. § 441). Because this repeal could work to the advantage only of Great Britain and France, it was a deliberately non-neutral act.

The United States remained a neutral state before its entry into World War II in December 1941, yet it took actions that undermined its status. In 1940 the United States entered into an agreement for the transfer of fifty old destroyers to Great Britain in exchange for leased naval and air bases in British islands off the Atlantic coast of the United States. Congress took a further step in the LEND-LEASE ACT of 1941 (55 Stat. 31) by agreeing to provide munitions, food, machinery, and services to Great Britain and the other Allies without immediate cost, thus eliminating their difficulty in finding dollar credits for purchases. Later repayment could be made in kind or property or other acceptable benefits. Under the Lend-Lease Act, the United States made huge shipments before and after entering the war.

Following the passage of the Lend-Lease Act, the United States became increasingly involved in direct military assistance, permitting U.S. merchant ships to transport war materials to the Allies, using U.S. pilots to deliver bombers to Canada and Britain, and using naval vessels for a "neutrality patrol" in the Atlantic that assisted in protecting belligerent convoys against submarines.

Much of the 1939 act remains in force (22 U.S.C.A. §§ 441–457), including the president's authority to find and proclaim a state of war, prohibition of travel by citizens in belligerent ships, and prohibition of financial transactions by persons in the United States with belligerents or solicitation or collection of contributions for a belligerent except for humanitarian purposes. The authority for an arms embargo, which was revoked in 1941, has not been reinstated. Sales by U.S. individuals and companies are governed by the international law of neutrality, unless Congress enacts a specific embargo provision.

In the post–World War II era, the U.S. government has committed several neutrality violations. Its conduct was less than disinterested and neutral in the overthrow of the Guatemalan government in 1954, in its sponsorship of the Bay of Pigs military expedition against Cuba in 1961, in its intervention in the civil war in the Dominican Republic in 1965, and in its aid to those who overthrew the Salvador Allende government in Chile in 1973.

Congress did enact the Arms Export Control Act of 1976 (22 U.S.C.A. §§ 2751–2796c [1989 Supp.]), which was designed to restrict the transfer of arms to nations that support international TERRORISM. The IRAN-CONTRA Affair that emerged as a political scandal in President Ronald Reagan's administration involved violations of this act. The transfer of arms to Iran, a nation that supported terrorism, and the financial and military support of a right-wing revolutionary group in Nicaragua violated congressional legislation and, in the case of Nicaragua, thwarted the desire of Congress to remain neutral in the conflict.

NEW DEAL "I pledge you, I pledge myself, to a new deal for the American people." In July 1932 FRANKLIN DELANO ROOSEVELT said these words to the delegates at the Democratic National Convention, who had just elected him the party's candidate for president of the United States.

Roosevelt's New Deal was a response to the tumultuous events of the years leading to his nomination. After World War I, the people of the United States experienced unprecedented prosperity. Consumers of all incomes were buying goods "on time" by putting a few dollars down and paying a few dollars a month. Record numbers of people were also using the installment buying concept to purchase stocks. The number of stockbrokers grew from fewer than

thirty thousand in 1920 to more than seventy thousand in 1929. Stockbrokers allowed their clients to "buy on MARGIN," meaning that a customer only had to pay 10–15 percent down on a stock, with the broker lending the client the rest and being repaid when the stock went up in value. By 1929 the skyrocketing prices in the stock market indicated continued prosperity to some economists, but to others it signaled impending doom. So much investment had been done on the margin that stockbrokers had borrowed money from banks that were now also heavily in debt. Stock prices began rapidly dropping in September 1929, and on "Black Thursday," October 24, 1929, they plummeted beyond all belief, devastating thousands of brokerage houses. By the following Tuesday, October 29, virtually all stocks were worthless. Millionaires became paupers overnight. People who had invested their savings woke up to find themselves penniless. This was the start of the Great Depression.

HERBERT HOOVER was the president at the time of the great stock market crash. He initially refused to believe that there was a problem, and even in April 1930, when more than three million people had lost their jobs, he continued in vain to reassure people that everything was fine. Because people were afraid of losing their jobs and running out of money, they refused to engage in the free-spending ways of the past and chose to save rather than spend their money. This in turn created a new cycle of problems. Because many banks had failed during the crash, people no longer trusted them and kept their money at home, which depleted the supply of capital that banks needed. People also refused to buy new products, and instead repaired old ones. Because few people were buying new products, companies were forced to close and to lay off employees. Many people were evicted from their homes for failing to make payments, and often several members of extended families lived together. The number of homeless soared, as did cases of malnutrition. President Hoover still remained firm in his stance that government aid was not an option. He believed that private charity could take care of those individuals who could not take care of themselves and that the ingenuity of private business would cure the ills of the country, not government intrusion. The American people resented President Hoover's attitude. The camps of makeshift shacks in which many people lived after being evicted were called Hoovervilles, and slogans such as Hard Times Are Hoover-ing over Us were heard everywhere. By December 1931 the unemployment rate was more than 13.6 million, a third of the labor force. When President Hoover called out military troops, armed with bayonets and tear gas, to disband a group of World War I veterans known as the Bonus Army that had come to Washington to seek early payment of a promised bonus for fighting in the war, the American people had had enough.

Although the Republicans knew that whomever the Democrats nominated for president would more than likely win, they nominated Hoover for president again in 1932. The Democratic nominee Franklin D. Roosevelt won all but six states and received twenty-two million votes to Hoover's fifteen million. Roosevelt came from a wealthy family, had served as assistant secretary of the Navy and as governor of New York, and had battled polio courageously. His promised "new deal" was anxiously awaited.

The day after he was inaugurated, Roosevelt requested a special session of Congress to convene and declared a bank holiday for a week. He guaranteed that at the end of one week's time banks that the government found to be sound and secure would reopen. Roosevelt also announced a moratorium on the export of gold. Because foreign investors required trading to be done in gold (paper money was believed to be too risky) the combination of the moratorium and the bank holiday effectively put the economy of the United States on hold. After the week had passed, Roosevelt held the first of his famous "fireside chats" via the radio to reassure the American people. As promised, the majority of the banks reopened. Many people followed Roosevelt's advice and again placed their money in the banks. During those same first weeks, Roosevelt and Congress worked together to repeal Prohibition, allowing the sale and consumption of ALCOHOL to resume.

These moves were only the beginning of what is referred to as the Hundred Days. More legislation was passed during the first hundred days of Roosevelt's presidency than had been passed in any similar period of any previous presidency. Roosevelt worked with young lawyers, professors, and social workers to create legislation to get people working and spending once again. To relieve the immediate need for food and shelter, Roosevelt ushered through Congress the Federal Emergency Relief Administration, which granted $500 million in aid to the states for distribution to people in need.

Next came congressional approval of Roosevelt's Civilian Conservation Corps Act (ch. 383, 50 Stat. 319). The government paid young men between the ages of eighteen and twenty-five for six months to one year to do construction or conservation work. The men built bridges, dams, and roads and planted more than seventeen million acres of new forests. They were paid $30 each month, and were required to send most of their money home to their families.

The Agricultural Adjustment Act of 1933 (AAA), 7 U.S.C.A. § 601 et seq., also was passed during these first hundred days. Farmers were growing huge surpluses of crops such as wheat and corn, and these surpluses drove prices down even though the farmers' expenses were rising. The AAA sought to reduce the surplus of crops by paying farmers not to grow them. Although some Americans questioned this practice because so many people were starving, the theory of the plan bore out, and by 1936 farmers were receiving $1.02 per bushel of wheat compared with the 38¢ per bushel they received in 1932.

Toward the end of the hundred days, Congress enacted the National Industrial Recovery Act of 1933 (NIRA), (ch. 90, 48 Stat. 195) and created the National Industrial Recovery Administration to implement the act's goals. The legislation's main goal was to stimulate dormant factories and industries and get people back to work. The National Industrial Recovery Administration believed that the best way to do this was to create a series of codes (746 in all) that companies had to follow in the marketplace. These codes regulated everything from a minimum hourly wage to the maximum number of hours a week an employee could work and controlled advertising and business production and output. Fearing a return of the high unemployment rate, one code forbade industry from developing technological advances that would lead to employee layoffs.

NIRA represents the first direct government involvement in business operations. NIRA allowed industries and business to engage in previously prohibited monopolistic PRICE-FIXING so that one manufacturer could not underprice its goods to drive a competitor out of business. The legislation allowed workers to unionize and collectively bargain for better pay and working conditions. This was all done with the goal of increasing business profits, which in turn would create more jobs and more spending. However, NIRA posed difficulties for many business owners, who were forced to restructure their business operations.

One of the most popular programs of the New Deal was the Works Progress Administration (WPA), which created more than 250,000 projects, putting millions of people to work. Most of the money and effort went to public construction of bridges, roads, and government buildings such as post offices. Writers were employed to interview town residents and compile local histories. Actors and musicians were hired to bring theater and live music to residents of rural towns, who otherwise had little opportunity to see live performances.

After the first eighteen months of the New Deal, five million previously unemployed people had found work. However, Roosevelt and his New Deal were not without their critics. When wealthy people realized that Roosevelt was not intending to return the country to the pre-crash status quo but sought to reform the entire national economic structure, they soon turned on him, calling him a traitor to his class. They disliked Roosevelt for the new taxes imposed on them, and some believed rumors that Roosevelt wanted to make the United States a socialist state under his dictatorship. The leaders of big business, once beholden to Roosevelt for getting their businesses back on track, were now among his most forceful critics.

Wealthy people were not Roosevelt's only critics. People to the political left of Roosevelt thought that he had let down the common man. Socialists such as Upton Sinclair and some Democrats such as Huey Long, the senator from Louisiana, complained that Roosevelt and his New Deal did not do enough for the lower and middle classes of society. Despite criticism from many angles, the majority of U.S. citizens loved Roosevelt, reelecting him by a landslide in 1936 over the Republican nominee, Alfred M. Landon.

A big reason for Roosevelt's huge popularity was the passage of the SOCIAL SECURITY ACT OF 1935 (42 U.S.C.A. § 301 et seq.)—the first piece of legislation in the history of the United States to deal with social welfare. The legislation provided people over the age of sixty-five with a monthly pension from the federal government. It also contained provisions for unemployment insurance and for aid for children. Though this form of government charity also had its critics, Roosevelt was pleased with it because it was proof that he had not forgotten the common man.

The early successes of the New Deal created a boldness that eventually led to its demise. The beginning of the end was Roosevelt's court packing plan. In *Schechter Poultry Corp. v. United States*, 295 U.S. 495, 55 S. Ct. 837, 79 L. Ed. 1570 (1935), the Supreme Court struck down the heart of Roosevelt's New Deal legislation, NIRA, declaring it unconstitutional. The Schechter brothers were wholesale kosher poultry distributors who did business within the state of New York. They were convicted of violating the Live Poultry Code, including wage and hour violations. The Court unanimously held that the federal government could only control trade between states, not trade within one state. Even liberal justices on the Court who had supported previous New Deal legislation found the challenged provisions unconstitutional.

Many legal actions against other New Deal legislation were piling up, and in a fast and furious move, Roosevelt proposed a restructuring of the Supreme Court through the addition of a new justice to the Court for each justice over the age of seventy. Roosevelt tried to place a nonpolitical spin on his proposal, citing instances where changes to the composition of the Court had been made before and citing the heavy workload for nine justices, but he could not disguise his blatant attempt to pack the Court with liberal justices who saw things his way. Roosevelt refused to concede, which resulted in months of Senate debates that cost him many supporters. Rather than exploding, the controversy fizzled away as the Court began supporting many pieces of New Deal legislation, including the Social Security Act. Additionally, several justices retired, allowing Roosevelt to choose their replacements. Although, in the end, the makeup of the Court was just as Roosevelt wanted, he suffered losses in support and confidence that he never regained. Many people thought that the New Deal legislation had granted labor too much power and were resentful of the unionization efforts, which led to strikes that were often violent. Finally, the unemployment rate in late 1937 to mid-1938 soared from five million to eleven million. Roosevelt and his vision for a New Deal lost Congressional support. No further reform legislation was passed during Roosevelt's time in the White House. Although the country was much better off than it had been when he took office in 1932, the Great Depression continued. It ended not by legislation, but by the coming of World War II.

The political machine of the New Deal and its dominant social policy continued for decades after the last piece of its legislation was passed. Although its demise can't be traced to one single event, by the time RONALD REAGAN was elected president in 1980, the era of the New Deal was effectively over.

CROSS-REFERENCES

Agricultural Law; Agriculture Subsidies; Banks and Banking; Labor Law; Labor Union; National Recovery Administration; *Schechter Poultry Corporation v. United States*; Social Security; Supreme Court of the United States; Welfare.

NEWS REPORTER'S PRIVILEGE See EVI-
DENCE.

NEWTON, HUEY PERCY Huey Percy
Newton was a cofounder and leader of the
BLACK PANTHER PARTY for Self-Defense, a group
formed in 1966 in Oakland to organize African
Americans against police brutality and racism.
Convicted or charged with several murders and
assaults during his life, Newton was shot and
killed in 1989 in the same poor Oakland neighborhood where he had begun mobilizing African Americans to arm themselves in self-
defense more than twenty years earlier.

Newton was born on February 17, 1942, in
New Orleans, the son of a sharecropper who
was once nearly lynched for talking back to his
white bosses. When Newton was one year old,
his family moved to Oakland. By the time he
was fourteen, Newton had been arrested for
gun possession. He was illiterate when he
graduated from high school, but he taught
himself to read before attending Merritt College in Oakland and the San Francisco School
of Law. In 1966 while at Merritt he met Bobby
Seale, with whom he formed the Black Panther
Party for Self-Defense in response to MALCOLM
X's call to African Americans to take up arms to
defend themselves against the police. The
armed and uniformed Panthers patrolled Oakland streets, interrupting arrests and other police activities when they believed that African
Americans were being mistreated.

Newton was designated minister of defense
and was a spokesperson for the party. The party
drew national attention in May 1967, when six
armed Panthers and about twenty supporters
burst into the California Assembly at Sacra-
mento to protest its plan to ban possession of
loaded firearms within city limits. Though
Newton did not participate in that event, the
Oakland police increased their surveillance on
him and his fellow Panthers.

On October 28, 1967, a scuffle during a
routine traffic check escalated into a gun battle
that left Newton with a bullet wound in his
stomach, one police officer dead, and another
wounded. Newton was convicted in 1968 of

AP/WIDE WORLD PHOTOS

Huey Percy Newton

"I SUGGESTED THAT WE
USE THE PANTHER AS
OUR SYMBOL . . .
[BECAUSE] THE
PANTHER IS A FIERCE
ANIMAL, BUT HE WILL
NOT ATTACK UNTIL HE
IS BACKED INTO A
CORNER; THEN HE WILL
STRIKE OUT."

voluntary MANSLAUGHTER, but the California
Court of Appeals overturned the conviction in
1970 because of the omission of key jury instructions. Newton's second and third trials
ended in HUNG JURIES, and the charges were
dismissed in 1972.

Newton's political agenda for the Black Panthers had moved beyond issues of police brutality to a Marxist revolutionary call for change in
U.S. society. Newton called for the release of all
African Americans from jail and for the payment of compensation to African Americans for
centuries of economic exploitation by white
America.

When Newton was released from prison in
1972 following his successful APPEAL of the
manslaughter charge, Black Panther Party
membership in forty-five cities had fallen to
fewer than one thousand people. J. EDGAR
HOOVER, head of the Federal Bureau of Investigation (FBI), had targeted the Panthers as a
dangerous, politically subversive group. The
FBI used informants and fake documents and
letters to undermine the party. Panthers in
many cities were subjected to local police harassment as well. In addition, Newton became
embroiled in a dispute over the direction of the
party with ELDRIDGE CLEAVER, the party's minister of information.

By the mid-1970s, the Black Panthers had
abandoned their violent image and had begun
community service programs, including free
health clinics, a children's breakfast program,
and drug abuse counseling. By the early 1980s,
however, the Black Panthers had effectively
disbanded.

Newton's role in the Black Panthers gradually diminished in the 1970s, as he had to
contend with new criminal charges. In 1974 he
was charged with murdering a seventeen-year-
old girl and later with pistol-whipping a tailor.
He fled to Cuba to avoid prosecution but
returned in 1977. His two murder trials ended
in hung juries, and the ASSAULT case was
dropped when the tailor refused to testify.

Newton was found guilty in 1978 of being an
ex-felon in possession of a handgun and was

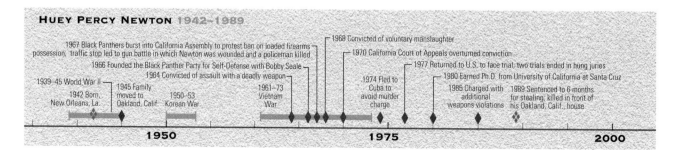

HUEY PERCY NEWTON 1942–1989

1967 Black Panthers burst into California Assembly to protest ban on loaded firearms possession; traffic stop led to gun battle in which Newton was wounded and a policeman killed
1968 Convicted of voluntary manslaughter
1966 Founded the Black Panther Party for Self-Defense with Bobby Seale
1970 California Court of Appeals overturned conviction
1964 Convicted of assault with a deadly weapon
1977 Returned to U.S. to face trial; two trials ended in hung juries
1939–45 World War II
1945 Family moved to Oakland, Calif.
1950–53 Korean War
1961–73 Vietnam War
1974 Fled to Cuba to avoid murder charge
1980 Earned Ph.D. from University of California at Santa Cruz
1942 Born, New Orleans, La.
1985 Charged with additional weapons violations
1989 Sentenced to 6 months for stealing; killed in front of his Oakland, Calif. house

1950   1975   2000

found guilty of a second count of the same charge in 1979. During this period he worked on the completion of his doctoral dissertation at the University of California at Santa Cruz. He was awarded a Ph.D. degree in 1980 for his work, "War Against the Panthers: A Study of Repression in America." After lengthy appeals Newton was sentenced in 1981. He was charged with additional weapons violations in 1985 but was acquitted by a jury in 1986. After being paroled on the earlier weapons charges, he was returned to prison twice for violation of parole following arrests for possession of narcotics paraphernalia and failure to submit to required drug testing.

Newton's downward spiral continued. In March 1989 he was sentenced to six months in jail after pleading no contest to a charge of cashing for his own use a $15,000 state aid check earmarked for the Oakland Community School, which the Black Panther party operated. The school had been closed in 1982 in the face of allegations that federal and state funds had been misused.

Newton was found shot dead on an Oakland street on August 22, 1989.

NEW YORK CONSTITUTION OF 1777

📖 The first constitution of the state of New York. It was adopted on Sunday, April 20, 1777, at Kingston, New York, by a convention of delegates empowered by the people of the colony to establish a state government. 📖

April 20, 1777, marks the birth of the state of New York. The constitution was not submitted to the people for ratification, but it became effective immediately upon its adoption by the convention.

The New York Constitution of 1777 was framed amidst the chaos of the Revolutionary War. Three men were instrumental in drafting the constitution: JOHN JAY, ROBERT R. LIVINGSTON, and Gouverneur Morris. All three were affluent young men (ages thirty, twenty-nine, and twenty-four, respectively, at the time of their appointments) with little experience in public affairs. John Jay is generally credited as being the primary author of the constitution.

The first constitution faithfully adhered in many respects to the English constitutional system of government. Some delegates, however, were incensed upon discerning minor deviations from ENGLISH LAW in the proposed constitution. The patterning of the New York Constitution of 1777 after the English governmental prototype was not actually inconsistent with the objectives of the Revolutionary War. Even though there were structural similarities between the system of government set forth in

John Jay was the primary author of the New York Constitution of 1777.

the New York Constitution of 1777 and the English system, the impact of the laws upon the lives of the people of New York and their British counterparts was different, due to the abandonment by America of the class system of government that prevailed in England. The oppressiveness of English rule was eradicated, but the valid fundamental legal principles were retained. The English constitutional system of government was applied to the extent that its principles conformed to the concept of a republican form of government. The reliance upon

Robert R. Livingston helped draft the New York Constitution of 1777.

Gouverneur Morris was instrumental in drafting the New York Constitution of 1777.

the English system was also attributable to the inexperience of the draftsmen, who felt comfortable with the basic precepts and established traditions of English law. Even they realized, however, that some changes were essential. The people of New York were permitted to choose the chief executive instead of having sovereign authority do so on their behalf. It also was deemed necessary to alter the parliamentary system, and as a result, the House of Lords and the Colonial Council were transformed into the state senate.

On April 20, the entire proposed constitution was presented, and, after several inconsequential revisions and some major ones, it was read and adopted by a vote of 32–1. John Jay was not present for the adoption of the constitution, since he had been called away as a result of his mother's death on April 17. He had wanted to include certain amendments to the constitution, and he expressed dismay over what he perceived to be its rather hasty adoption. The fact that less than one-third of the entire convention attended the discussions of the constitution was attributable to compelling personal reasons and the exigencies of the Revolutionary War. The turmoil created by the latter factor explains why the constitution was adopted on a Sunday; the delegates convened whenever possible, irrespective of weekend dates.

The New York Constitution of 1777 was a relatively brief document that covered only a few topics. Some significant provisions, particu-

larly those pertaining to the Council of Revision and the Council of Appointment, were added while the constitution was being evaluated by the convention.

The resolutions adopted by the Third Provincial Congress, providing for the election of the convention, and the DECLARATION OF INDEPENDENCE, which has been set out in its entirety, comprise the preliminary segment. The body of the constitution contains forty-five brief sections, which were labeled "articles" at that time. The powers granted to the new government are expressed in rather austere language. The framers retained the essential nature of the colonial government but removed its royal features. The judicial system of the colony and the local governments generally remained unaltered.

The constitution delineates new executive and legislative branches, administrative authority, and abstract rights, which are few in number and concise, including, but not limited to, voting rights, freedom of religion, and the right of trial by jury. Although the constitution created the legislative, executive, and judicial branches of government, the framers combined their functions due to their ignorance of the concept, significance, and ramifications of the SEPARATION OF POWERS. In addition to lawmaking power, they vested the legislature with executive authority through the Council of Appointment, which consisted of four senators selected annually by the assembly. The higher courts were granted authority over legislation through the Council of Revision, comprised by the judges of the supreme court, the chancellor, and the governor. As a result, the governor's power was severely circumscribed. Since he was under the control of the Council of Appointment, the governor was divested of the responsibility for official appointments. He also was deprived of unabridged VETO power, because the judges of the Council of Revision could overrule him.

The constitution has a few provisions pertaining to the separate powers of the senate and assembly, including the power of the assembly to issue articles of IMPEACHMENT and to choose the members of the Council of Appointment. The legislature was authorized to elect the state treasurer, administer contracts with Indians, and to naturalize ALIENS. The U.S. Constitution, however, eventually preempted this right of naturalization. The legislature was proscribed from enacting BILLS OF ATTAINDER, and from creating any courts, except COMMON LAW COURTS. The constitution fixed the terms of judicial officers and provided for the election of state and local officials. Article 35 continued the English statutory and COMMON LAW, and colonial legislation, to the extent they were applicable under the new form of government. Miscellaneous provisions established a state MILITIA, ratified English grants, and barred the clergy from holding office.

The state made tremendous progress as a result of this constitution, in spite of its inherent limitations. Its system of JURISPRUDENCE evolved and expanded. The constitution established the university and the common school, and colleges, academies, and libraries were nurtured. It provided for the administration of assistance to the indigent. A system of taxation was formulated, political subdivisions were created, and the statutory law was frequently revised. The constitution also prompted the drafting of a plan for the construction of the canals. The New York Constitution of 1777 was an extremely valuable document, and its fundamental principles became prompted in subsequent constitutions. It remained in effect until it was superseded by the Constitution of 1821.

NEW YORK TIMES v. SULLIVAN A landmark U.S. Supreme Court case, *New York Times v. Sullivan*, 376 U.S. 254, 84 S. Ct. 710, 11 L. Ed. 2d 686 (1964), extended the FIRST AMENDMENT's guarantee of free speech to libel cases brought by public officials. The Supreme Court sought to encourage public debate by changing the rules involving libel that had previously been the province of state law and state courts.

New York Times v. Sullivan grew out of events occurring during the 1960s CIVIL RIGHTS MOVEMENT in Alabama. In 1960 Dr. MARTIN LUTHER KING, JR., and other CIVIL RIGHTS leaders conducted protests against segregation in Montgomery, Alabama. Their efforts met fierce resistance from Montgomery public officials. Civil rights leaders placed a full-page advertisement in the *New York Times* seeking contributions for civil rights causes in the South. Signed by sixty-four prominent leaders in public affairs, religion, trade unions, and the performing arts, the advertisement, entitled "Heed Their Rising Voices," stated that thousands of southern African American students were engaging in nonviolent demonstrations in positive affirmation of the right to live in human dignity. The ad went on to charge that these demonstrations had been met with a "wave of terror" by state and local governments. Alleged events that backed up this charge were described, but no particular public official was named.

L. B. Sullivan, the Montgomery city commissioner responsible for supervising the city police department, filed a libel suit against four African American clergyman and the *New York Times* in Alabama state court. Sullivan alleged that the advertisement implicitly libeled him. Libel is a civil TORT and consists of injuring someone's reputation by reporting falsehoods about that person.

At trial Sullivan proved that the advertisement contained a number of minor inaccuracies about described incidents. The jury had to determine whether the statements in the advertisement were "of and concerning" Commissioner Sullivan. The judge instructed the jury that under Alabama law, the statements were libelous, falsity and MALICE were presumed, and DAMAGES could be awarded without direct proof of financial loss. The jury concluded that the statements did concern Sullivan and awarded him $500,000 for injuries to his reputation and profession.

The U.S. Supreme Court reversed, holding that the rule of law applied by Alabama violated the First Amendment. Justice WILLIAM J. BRENNAN, JR., in his majority opinion, placed the legal issues in the context of "a profound national commitment to the principle that debate on public issues should be uninhibited, robust, and wide-open, and that it may well include vehement, caustic, and sometimes unpleasantly sharp attacks on government and public officials." Brennan maintained that erroneous statements are inevitable in free debate and must be protected if freedom of expression is to have the "breathing space" it needs to survive.

The advertisement was squarely a public expression and protest and fell within constitutional protection. Neither the allegedly defamatory content of the ad, nor the falsity of some of its factual statements, nor the NEGLIGENCE of anyone in preparing or publishing it forfeited this protection. Brennan dismissed the idea that courts were free to conclude that libelous statements were made "of and concerning" a particular person when the statements on their face did not make even an oblique reference to the individual. Brennan stated that there is "no legal alchemy" by which a court constitutionally can establish that "an otherwise impersonal attack on governmental operations was a libel of an official responsible for those operations."

Brennan then set out the rule that reshaped libel law. A public official could recover in a libel action only if and when a court found that the libelous statement about the official was made with " 'actual malice'—that is, with knowledge that it was false or with reckless disregard of whether it was false or not." As long as the press has an "absence of malice," public officials are barred from recovering damages for the publication of false statements about them.

In separate concurring opinions, Justices HUGO L. BLACK and WILLIAM O. DOUGLAS differed with Justice Brennan over whether the press should ever be held liable in DEFAMATION of public officials. They concluded that the First Amendment provided an absolute IMMUNITY for criticism of the way public officials do their public duty. Anything less than absolute immunity encourages "deadly danger" to a free press by state libel laws that harass, punish, and ultimately destroy critics.

In the years since *New York Times*, some critics have argued that Black and Douglas were right. The "reckless disregard" requirement has allowed highly intrusive inquiries into the reportorial and editorial processes of the mass media. In addition, the "chilling effect" of libel suits has not been diminished because of the case. If a jury finds reckless disregard, it can award enormous damage awards against the press.

Other critics of the decision believe it affords too much protection to the press. Public officials unfairly libeled by the press rarely file libel suits because of the difficulty of proving actual malice. This prevents them from establishing in a court of law the falsity of the statements at issue.

CROSS-REFERENCES

Freedom of Speech; Freedom of the Press; Libel and Slander; Public Figure.

NEW YORK TIMES v. UNITED STATES

New York Times Co. v. United States, 403 U.S. 713, 91 S. Ct. 2140, 29 L. Ed. 2d 822 (1971), often referred to as the *Pentagon Papers* case, concerned the government's attempt to prohibit the *New York Times* and the *Washington Post* from publishing portions of a secret government study on the VIETNAM WAR. The documents in the study became known as the Pentagon Papers. The United States contended that publication of the Pentagon Papers could prolong the Vietnam War and hinder efforts to return U.S. prisoners held in Vietnam. The *Times* and the *Post* claimed that the government was engaging in CENSORSHIP. Thus, the case pitted the rights of the newspapers under the FIRST AMENDMENT against the duty of the EXECUTIVE BRANCH to protect the nation. The case drew significant national attention as it sped through the judicial system and the nation wondered what the Pentagon Papers contained.

The *Pentagon Papers* case addressed whether a PRIOR RESTRAINT on the press can be justified under the First Amendment. A "prior restraint" is the imposition of a restraint on the publication of information before the information is published. There are two basic types of prior restraints. One consists of a government order or court injunction that prohibits a person from communicating certain information. The other basic type of prior restraint occurs when a LICENSE or permit is required before a particular type of expression may be used. *New York Times v. United States* involved the first type of prior restraint, since the government sought a court INJUNCTION prohibiting the newspapers from publishing portions of the Pentagon Papers. Other than the *Pentagon Papers* case, the most important Supreme Court case discussing prior restraints is *Near v. Minnesota*, 283 U.S. 697, 51 S. Ct. 625, 75 L. Ed. 1357 (1931), which held that under the First Amendment, prior restraints on free speech are justified only in "exceptional cases," such as when the information to be published would include "the sailing dates of transports or the number and location of troops."

In the *Pentagon Papers* case a divided Supreme Court, in a decision that contains a separate opinion from each of the nine justices, refused to enjoin publication of the Pentagon Papers, emphasizing the First Amendment's strong presumption against any prior restraint on free speech. The justices' reasons for their decisions varied widely. Two justices believed that *any* prior restraint on the press amounts to censorship in clear violation of the First Amendment, whereas three justices believed that publication of the Pentagon Papers should have been delayed until the courts had more time to evaluate the impact of publication on national security. Because the case sped through the judicial system and the justices' opinions varied widely, it does not provide a clear statement of First Amendment law on prior restraint. For example, the Court failed to specify when, if ever, a prior restraint on the press might be allowed. The case is of great significance, however, as a statement that a prior restraint on the FREEDOM OF SPEECH is almost never justified.

From June 12 to 14, 1971, the *New York Times* published a series of articles about the origins of the Vietnam War. The articles were based on a forty-seven-volume Defense Department study covering the years 1945 to 1968, which had been leaked to the *Times* by Daniel Ellsberg, a former Defense Department analyst. Although the study contained only information regarding events that occurred before 1968, the government contended that the study contained "secret" and "top secret" information. Further, the government alleged that publication of the information could prolong the Vietnam War and threaten the safe return of U.S. prisoners of war. On June 15, 1971, the government sued in New York federal district court, seeking an injunction prohibiting the *Times* from continuing to publish information from the Pentagon Papers. Soon after, the *Washington Post* began publishing material from the study; accordingly, the government sought a similar injunction against the *Post* in the District of Columbia.

The actions against the *Times* and the *Post* were rushed through the courts because of the unique national importance of the issues and the widespread public attention the cases were receiving around the nation. Although the federal district courts both refused to issue a permanent injunction against publication of the Pentagon Papers, publication was temporarily enjoined pending appeals by the United States. Less than two weeks after the *Times* published its first articles, the Supreme Court heard arguments on the cases, and five days later, on June 30, 1971, issued its decision.

The Supreme Court decided on a 6–3 vote that a prior restraint could not be imposed on publication of the Pentagon Papers. In a brief opinion the whole Court noted that the government "carries a heavy burden of showing justification for the imposition of such a restraint" and stated that the government had failed to meet that burden. The brief opinion reflected the widely varying views of the nine justices. The Court could not agree on a precise standard for determining when the government may impose a prior restraint on free speech, or even whether the government could *ever* impose a prior restraint.

In concurring opinions Justices HUGO L. BLACK and WILLIAM O. DOUGLAS both stated, in very strong language, that prior restraints on the freedom of expression are never justified, no matter what the circumstances. Black, commenting on the government's argument that prior restraints might be justified in certain circumstances, stated, "I can imagine no greater perversion of history. . . . Both the history and language of the First Amendment support the view that the press must be left free to publish news, whatever the source, without censorship, injunctions or prior restraints." Black and Douglas both believed that "every moment's continuance of the injunctions . . . amounts to a flagrant, indefensible, and continuing violation of the First Amendment."

The other four justices who concurred in the judgment, Justices WILLIAM J. BRENNAN, JR., POTTER STEWART, BYRON R. WHITE, and THURGOOD MARSHALL, each believed that the government could impose a prior restraint in certain extraordinary circumstances, such as where the publication of information could endanger U.S. soldiers, but that those circumstances were not present in the *Pentagon Papers* case. Stewart was the only justice who offered a standard for determining when a prior restraint could be imposed, stating that a prior restraint would be appropriate only where publication "will surely result in direct, immediate, and irreparable damage to our Nation or its people." White, while agreeing that the circumstances did not warrant a prior restraint on the publication of the Pentagon Papers, opined that the newspapers might be criminally liable under espionage laws if they published sensitive national secrets. Marshall based his argument on the separate powers of the three branches of the government. He believed that, because Congress had declined to pass a statute authorizing the courts to enjoin publication of sensitive national secrets, the Supreme Court lacked authority to enjoin publication of the Pentagon Papers.

Chief Justice WARREN E. BURGER, Justices JOHN MARSHALL HARLAN, and HARRY A. BLACKMUN dissented, all strongly objecting to the "unseemly haste" with which the courts heard and decided the case. Harlan stated, "With all respect, I consider that the Court has been almost irresponsibly feverish in dealing with these cases." Blackmun commented,

> this, in my opinion, is not the way to try a lawsuit of this magnitude and asserted importance. It is not the way for federal courts to adjudicate, and be required to adjudicate, issues that allegedly concern the Nation's vital welfare. The country would be none the worse off were the cases tried quickly to be sure, but in the customary and properly deliberative manner.

The dissenting justices thus believed that the publication of the Pentagon Papers should have been enjoined until the courts had adequate time to evaluate carefully the legal issues and the impact of publication of the documents on the interests of the United States.

The decision was hailed as a great victory for advocates of FREEDOM OF THE PRESS. For the first time in the nation's history, the government had succeeded, if only during the appeals of the case, in precluding the press from publishing news in its possession. At least in the circumstances presented by the case, however, the Supreme Court held that such a prior restraint on freedom of speech violates the First Amendment. The practical effect of the decision, which carefully avoided any mention of the contents of the Pentagon Papers, was far less dramatic than suggested by the attention it received. The newspapers never did publish the portions of the Pentagon Papers that the government claimed were the most sensitive. In addition, further publication of the Pentagon Papers by newspapers around the country did not attract a great deal of attention or significantly affect the United States' policy on Vietnam. The *Pentagon Papers* case remains, however, an important PRECEDENT in support of freedom of the press under the First Amendment.

NEXT FRIEND An individual who acts on behalf of another individual who does not have the legal CAPACITY to act on his or her own behalf.

The individual in whose name a minor's lawsuit is brought, or who appears in court to represent such minor's interest. The French term PROCHEIN AMI has been used to designate such an individual, but the term GUARDIAN AD LITEM is more commonly used.

At COMMON LAW, when an individual was unable to look after his or her own interests or manage his or her lawsuit, the court would appoint a person to represent that individual's legal interests. In court terminology this person was called a next friend, which is derived from the French term *prochein ami*. Individuals requiring a next friend included minors, persons who were mentally ill or mentally retarded, infirm or senile persons, and others whose disabilities prevented them from managing their affairs.

State statutes now set the qualifications and duties of a person who acts as a next friend, but these laws more commonly designate this person a *guardian ad litem*, or a court-appointed special advocate. Regardless of the designation, this person's responsibilities are now confined to representing a MINOR or incompetent person in a lawsuit or court proceeding. At common law, a next friend represented a PLAINTIFF, whereas a *guardian ad litem* represented a DEFENDANT. This distinction has been removed in modern law.

A next friend is not a PARTY to a lawsuit but an OFFICER OF THE COURT. When the lawsuit is concluded, the next friend's duty ends. The next friend has no right to control the property of the person she or he represents or to assume CUSTODY of that person. These rights may be given to a person designated by a court as a minor's or incompetent person's GUARDIAN.

Guardians ad litem are commonly used in family and juvenile courts, where the best interests of the child require an independent, neutral person to safeguard the child's rights. The increased number of these representatives has

led states to develop training and certification programs for individuals wishing to serve as next friends or *guardians ad litem*. Though attorneys also may represent juveniles, next friends provide valuable assistance to the courts.

See also INFANTS.

NEXT OF KIN The blood relatives entitled by law to inherit the property of a person who dies without leaving a valid WILL, although the term is sometimes interpreted to include a relationship existing by reason of marriage.

See also DESCENT AND DISTRIBUTION.

These sisters are considered next of kin. If one of them were to die without drafting a will, the other would be entitled by law to inherit her sister's property.

NIHIL [*Latin, Nothing.*] The abbreviated designation of a statement filed by a SHERIFF or CONSTABLE with a court describing his or her unsuccessful attempts to serve a WRIT, notice, or PROCESS upon the designated person.

The complete phrase *nihil est* refers to a failure to serve any writ while the term *nihil habet* describes the failure to serve a writ SCIRE FACIAS or another writ.

The term *nil* is a contracted form of *nihil*.

NIMMER, MELVILLE BERNARD Melville B. Nimmer was a leading authority on COPYRIGHT law.

Nimmer was born June 6, 1923. He graduated from the University of California at Berkeley in 1947 and from Harvard Law School in 1950. After law school he obtained a position in the legal department at Paramount Pictures where he remained until 1957 when he entered private practice. Nimmer continued to be involved with the motion picture industry, however, and served as general counsel to the Writers Guild of America, which represents film and television writers. He was the chief negotiator for the guild during a five-month strike in 1960 where the right to receive residuals for the showing of theatrical films on television was established.

Although Nimmer's work in the film industry involved questions of copyright law, he had to learn the subject largely by reading cases on his own. At that time copyright law was a

BIOGRAPHY

Melville Bernard Nimmer

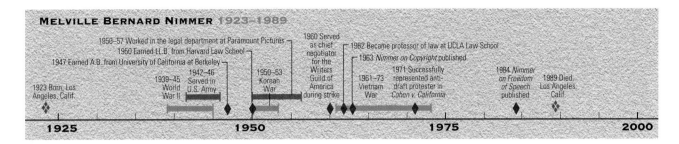

MELVILLE BERNARD NIMMER 1923–1989

1947 Earned A.B. from University of California at Berkeley
1950 Earned LL.B. from Harvard Law School
1950–57 Worked in the legal department at Paramount Pictures
1960 Served as chief negotiator for the Writers Guild of America during strike
1962 Became professor of law at UCLA Law School
1963 *Nimmer on Copyright* published

1923 Born, Los Angeles, Calif.
1939–45 World War II
1942–46 Served in U.S. Army
1950–53 Korean War
1961–73 Vietnam War
1971 Successfully represented anti-draft protester in *Cohen v. California*
1984 *Nimmer on Freedom of Speech* published
1989 Died, Los Angeles, Calif.

1925   1950   1975   2000

relatively unimportant discipline. Few lawyers specialized in it, and no law school offered courses in the subject as part of its regular curriculum. In the last decades, however, copyright questions have become a major concern for many industries, including the computer industry.

Nimmer became a leading authority in the growing field. His treatise *Nimmer on Copyright* (first published in 1963 with frequent revisions thereafter) became the standard work on the subject. A companion volume *Nimmer on Freedom of Speech* appeared in 1984. When he died, Nimmer was working on a book entitled *World Copyright*, which was to contain chapters on all significant copyright laws in the world.

In 1962 Nimmer joined the faculty at the University of California at Los Angeles School of Law and continued to teach there until his death. At the university Nimmer came into contact with the student protests and antiwar demonstrations and became increasingly interested in the FREEDOM OF SPEECH issues that the demonstrations raised. In *Cohen v. California*, 403 U.S. 15, 91 S. Ct. 1780, 29 L. Ed. 2d 284 (1971), Nimmer represented a protestor who was charged with disturbing the peace because he entered a courthouse wearing a jacket inscribed with a vulgar protest against the draft. The U.S. Supreme Court ruled in favor of the protester on the ground that the words presented no danger of violence and that the state therefore had no compelling reason to suppress them.

Nimmer died November 23, 1985, in Los Angeles, California.

NINETEENTH AMENDMENT   The Nineteenth Amendment to the U.S. Constitution reads:

> The right of citizens of the United States to vote shall not be denied or abridged by the United States or by any State on account of sex. Congress shall have power to enforce this article by appropriate legislation.

The Nineteenth Amendment was enacted in 1920, after a seventy-year struggle led by the women's suffrage movement.

The groundwork for the suffrage movement was laid in 1848 in Seneca Falls, New York, now considered the birthplace of the women's movement. Here ELIZABETH CADY STANTON drafted the Declaration of Rights and Sentiments, which demanded VOTING rights, PROPERTY RIGHTS, educational opportunities, and economic equity for women.

Rather than face the difficult task of obtaining approval of an AMENDMENT to the U.S. Constitution from an all-male Congress preoccupied with the question of SLAVERY, the suffragists decided to focus their attention on the separate states and seek state constitutional amendments. The state-by-state effort began in 1867 in Kansas with a REFERENDUM to enfranchise women. The referendum was defeated, but that same year the western territories of Wyoming and Utah provided the first victories for the suffragists.

The movement then suffered a series of setbacks beginning in January 1878 when the voting rights amendment was first introduced in Congress. The full Senate did not consider the amendment until 1887 and voted to defeat the bill. The suffragists continued their state-

The Nineteenth Amendment granted women the right to vote.

CORBIS-BETTMANN

PRESIDENT WILSON SAYS: This is the time to support Woman Suffrage.

Women in U.S. Congress: 1917 to 1997

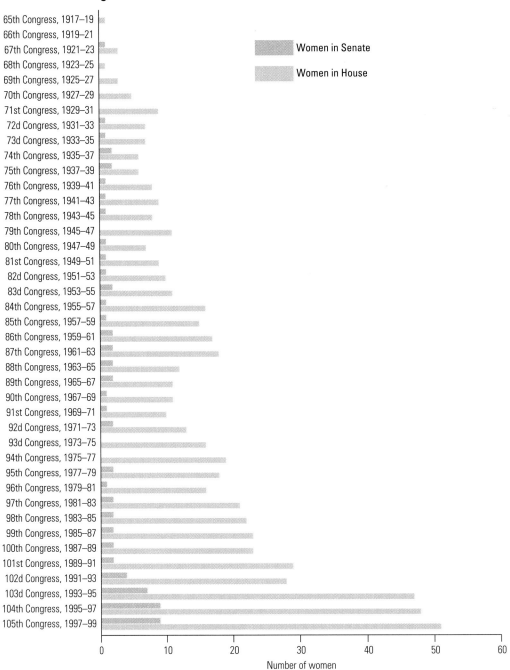

Table shows maximum number of women elected or appointed to serve in that Congress at one time. (A total of three women served in the 75th Congress, but no more than two served together at any one time.) Numbers do include those who filled expired terms and those never sworn in. Numbers do not include the delegate from pre-statehood Hawaii and current non-voting delegates from the Virgin Islands and Washington, D.C.

Source: Fact sheet from the Center for the American Woman and Politics, Eagleton Institute of Politics, Rutgers University.

by-state strategy and won a referendum ballot in Colorado in 1893 and Idaho in 1896.

The suffragists mounted a final and decisive drive in the second decade of the 1900s with victories in Washington in 1910 and California in 1911. The following year Arizona, Kansas, and Oregon gave women the right to vote, and in 1913 Illinois also passed measures supporting suffrage as did Montana and Nevada in 1914. Women in eleven states voted in the 1916 presidential election. By this time the United States was also involved in World War I, which brought national attention to the suffrage movement as well as to the important role women played in the war effort. During the war, an unprecedented number of women joined the depleted industrial and public service workforce. Women became an active and visible population of the labor sector that benefited the national economy. By the end of 1918 four more states—Michigan, Oklahoma, New York, and South Dakota—had approved women's suffrage.

With the requisite two-thirds majority, the U.S. House of Representatives introduced the amendment in January 1918. The vote was initially postponed, and the amendment was later defeated in October 1918 and again in February 1919. On June 4, 1919, almost seventeen months after its introduction by the House of Representatives, the amendment was finally passed by the Senate. Having already considered and debated the voting rights issue for several years, the states ratified the amendment quickly. In August 1920 Tennessee became the thirty-sixth and last state necessary to ratify the enactment. With ratification complete, the Nineteenth Amendment was added to the U.S. Constitution on August 18, 1920.

CROSS-REFERENCES

Anthony, Susan Brownell; Equal Rights Amendment; Women's Rights.

NINETY-DAY LETTER 📖 The name given to a written notice sent to a taxpayer by the INTERNAL REVENUE SERVICE regarding a deficiency in the payment of tax (26 U.S.C.A. § 6212 et seq.). 📖

The ninety-day letter, also known as the statutory notice of deficiency, suspends the running of the STATUTE OF LIMITATIONS regarding tax ASSESSMENT for ninety days. During the ninety days following the mailing of a ninety-day letter, the taxpayer may consent to the assessment and pay the tax but later seek a refund in U.S. district court. If the taxpayer disputes the assessment or refuses to pay the additional amount, he or she may challenge the deficiency by filing a petition with the U.S. Tax Court. The ninety-day letter, sent by certified or registered mail, gives the taxpayer an opportunity to challenge an alleged deficiency before paying it. If the taxpayer neither pays the tax nor files a Tax Court petition within the ninety-day period, the additional tax liability may be assessed promptly.

For taxpayers who reside outside the United States, the time period is extended to 150 days.

See also TAXATION.

NINTH AMENDMENT The Ninth Amendment to the U.S. Constitution reads:

The enumeration in the Constitution, of certain rights, shall not be construed to deny or disparage others retained by the people.

The Ninth Amendment to the U.S. Constitution is somewhat of an enigma. It provides that the naming of certain rights in the Constitution does not take away from the people rights that are not named. Yet neither the language nor the history of the Ninth Amendment offers any hints as to the nature of the rights it was designed to protect.

Although the U.S. Supreme Court has never based a ruling exclusively upon it, the Ninth Amendment has played a significant role in establishing a constitutional right to PRIVACY. Every year FEDERAL COURTS are asked to recognize new unenumerated rights "retained by the people." Typically the federal judiciary has declined to rely on the Ninth Amendment as an independent source of constitutional rights. However, federal courts continue to cite the Ninth Amendment as a secondary source of fundamental liberties.

Ratified in 1791, the Ninth Amendment is an outgrowth of a disagreement between the Federalists and the Anti-Federalists over the importance of attaching a BILL OF RIGHTS to the Constitution. When the Constitution was initially drafted by the Framers in 1787, it contained no Bill of Rights. The Anti-Federalists, who generally opposed RATIFICATION because they believed that the Constitution conferred too much power on the federal government, supported a Bill of Rights to serve as an additional constraint against despotism. The Federalists, on the other hand, supported ratification of the Constitution without a Bill of Rights because they believed that any enumeration of fundamental liberties was unnecessary and dangerous.

The Federalists believed that a Bill of Rights was unnecessary because in their view the federal government possessed only limited powers that were expressly delegated to it by the Constitution. The Federalists believed that all powers not constitutionally delegated to the federal government were inherently reserved to the people and the states. Nowhere in the Constitution, the Federalists pointed out, is the federal government given the power to trample on individual liberties. The Federalists feared that if the Constitution were to include a Bill of Rights that protected certain liberties from government encroachment, an inference would be drawn that the federal government could exercise an implied power to regulate such liberties.

ALEXANDER HAMILTON, one of the leading Federalists, articulated this concern in *The Federalist* No. 84. Why should a Bill of Rights, Hamilton asked, "declare that things shall not be done which there is no power to do?" For instance, Hamilton said it was unnecessary for a Bill of Rights to protect the FREEDOM OF THE PRESS when the federal government is not granted the power to regulate the press. A provision "against restraining the liberty of the press," Hamilton said, "afford[s] the clear implication that a power to prescribe proper regulations concerning it was intended to be vested in the national government."

The Federalists were also concerned that any constitutional enumeration of liberties might imply that other rights, not enumerated by the Constitution, would be surrendered to the government. A Bill of Rights, they feared, would quickly become the exclusive means by which the American people could secure their freedom and stave off tyranny. Federalist JAMES MADISON argued that any attempt to enumerate fundamental liberties would be incomplete and might imperil other freedoms not listed. A "positive declaration of some essential rights could not be obtained in the requisite latitude," Madison said. "If an enumeration be made of all our rights," Madison queried, "will it not be implied that everything omitted is given to the general government?"

Anti-Federalists and others who supported a Bill of Rights attempted to mollify the Federalists' concerns with three counterarguments. First, the Anti-Federalists underscored the fact that the Constitution guarantees certain liberties even without a Bill of Rights. For example, Article I of the Constitution prohibits Congress from suspending the writ of HABEAS CORPUS and from passing BILLS OF ATTAINDER and EX POST FACTO LAWS. If these liberties could be enumerated without endangering other unenumerated liberties, Anti-Federalists reasoned, additional liberties, such as freedom of press and RELIGION, could be safeguarded in a Bill of Rights.

Second, while acknowledging that it would be impossible to enumerate every human liberty imaginable, supporters of a Bill of Rights maintained that this obstacle should not impede the Framers from establishing constitutional protection for certain essential liberties. THOMAS JEFFERSON, responding to Madison's claim that no Bill of Rights could ever be exhaustive, joked that "[h]alf a loaf is better than no bread. If we cannot secure all of our rights, let us secure what we can."

Third, Anti-Federalists argued that if there was a genuine risk that naming certain liberties would imperil others, then an additional CONSTITUTIONAL AMENDMENT should be drafted to offer protection for all liberties not mentioned in the Bill of Rights. Such an amendment, the Anti-Federalists argued, would protect those liberties that might fall through the cracks of written constitutional provisions. This idea became the Ninth Amendment.

Unlike every other provision contained in the Bill of Rights, the Ninth Amendment had no predecessor in English law. It stemmed solely from the genius of those who framed and ratified the Constitution. Ironically, Madison, who opposed a Bill of Rights in 1787, was the chief architect of the Ninth Amendment during the First Congress in 1789.

After reconsidering the arguments against a Bill of Rights, Madison said he was now convinced that such concerns could be overcome. It was still plausible, Madison believed, that the enumeration of particular rights might disparage other rights that were not enumerated. Yet Madison told Congress that he had attempted to guard against this danger by drafting the Ninth Amendment, which he submitted in the following form:

> The exceptions [to power] here or elsewhere in the constitution made in favor of particular rights, shall not be so construed as to diminish the just importance of other rights retained by the people, or as to enlarge the powers delegated by the constitution; but either as actual limitations on such powers, or as inserted merely for greater caution.

The House Select Committee, consisting of one representative from each state in the Union, reviewed and revised Madison's proposal until it gradually evolved into its present form. The debates in both houses of Congress add little to the original understanding of the Ninth Amendment. The Senate conducted its sessions in secret, and the House debates failed to offer a glimmer as to what unenumerated rights are protected by the Ninth Amendment, how such rights might be identified, or by what branch of government they should be enforced.

The Supreme Court did not attempt to answer these questions for more than 170 years. Until 1965 no Supreme Court decision made more than a passing reference to the Ninth Amendment. In 1958 Supreme Court Justice ROBERT H. JACKSON wrote that the rights protected by the Ninth Amendment "are still a mystery." However, the dormant Ninth Amendment experienced a renaissance in *Gris-*

wold v. Connecticut, 381 U.S. 479, 85 S. Ct. 1678, 14 L. Ed. 2d 510 (1965).

In *Griswold* the Supreme Court was asked to review the constitutionality of a Connecticut law that banned adult residents from using BIRTH CONTROL and prohibited anyone from assisting others to violate this law. In the majority opinion, Justice WILLIAM O. DOUGLAS, writing for the Court, rejected the notion that the judiciary is obligated to enforce only those rights that are expressly enumerated in the Constitution. On several occasions in the past, Douglas wrote, the Court has recognized rights that cannot be found in the written language of the Constitution.

Only briefly discussed in Douglas's majority opinion, the Ninth Amendment was the centerpiece of Justice ARTHUR GOLDBERG's concurring opinion. The language and history of the Ninth Amendment, Goldberg wrote, demonstrate that the Framers of the Constitution intended the judiciary to protect certain unwritten liberties with the same zeal that courts must protect those liberties expressly referenced in the Bill of Rights. The Ninth Amendment, Goldberg emphasized, reflects the Framers' original understanding that "other fundamental personal rights should not be denied protection simply because they are not specifically listed" in the Constitution.

Justices HUGO L. BLACK and POTTER STEWART criticized the Court for invoking the Ninth Amendment as a basis for its decision in *Griswold*. The Ninth Amendment, the dissenting justices said, does not explain what unenumerated rights are retained by the people or how these rights should be identified. Nor does the Amendment authorize the Supreme Court, in contrast to the president or Congress, to enforce these rights. By reading the Ninth and other amendments in the Bill of Rights to create a general right to privacy, Black and Stewart suggested, the unelected justices of the Supreme Court had substituted their own subjective notions of justice, liberty, and reasonableness for the wisdom and experience of the elected representatives in the Connecticut state legislature who were responsible for passing the birth control regulation.

The *Griswold* decision was the starting point of a continuing debate over the proper role of the Ninth Amendment in constitutional JURISPRUDENCE. One side of the debate reads the Ninth Amendment to mean that the Constitution protects not only those liberties written into the Bill of Rights but some additional liberties found outside the express language of any one provision. The other side

sees no way to identify the unenumerated rights protected by the Ninth Amendment and no objective method by which to interpret and apply such rights. Under this view, courts that interpret and apply the Ninth Amendment do so in a manner that reflects the political and personal preferences of the presiding judge. Federal courts have attempted to reach a middle ground.

A number of federal courts have ruled that the Ninth Amendment is a rule of judicial CONSTRUCTION, or a guideline for interpretation, and not an independent source of constitutional rights (*Mann v. Meachem*, 929 F. Supp. 622 [N.D.N.Y. 1996]). These courts view the Ninth Amendment as an invitation to liberally interpret the express provisions of the Constitution. However, federal courts will not recognize constitutional rights claimed to derive solely from the Ninth Amendment (*United States v. Vital Health Products*, 786 F. Supp. 761 [E.D. Wis. 1992]). By itself, one court held, the Ninth Amendment does not enunciate any substantive rights. Instead the amendment serves to protect other fundamental liberties that are implicit, though not mentioned, in the Bill of Rights (*Rothner v. City of Chicago*, 725 F. Supp. 945 [N.D. Ill. 1989]).

After *Griswold*, federal courts were flooded with novel claims based on unenumerated rights. Almost without exception, these novel Ninth Amendment claims were rejected.

For example, the Sixth Circuit Court of Appeals ruled that there is no Ninth Amendment right to possess an unregistered submachine gun (*United States v. Warin*, 530 F.2d 103 [1976]). The Fourth Circuit court held that the Ninth Amendment does not guarantee the right to produce, distribute, or experiment with mind-altering drugs such as marijuana (*United States v. Fry*, 787 F.2d 903 [1986]). The Eighth Circuit court denied a claim asserting that the Ninth Amendment guaranteed Americans the right to a radiation-free environment (*Concerned Citizens of Nebraska v. U.S. Nuclear Regulatory Commission*, 970 F.2d 421 [1992]). The Ninth Circuit court found no Ninth Amendment right to resist the draft (*United States v. Uhl*, 436 F.2d 773 [1970]).

This series of cases has led some scholars to conclude that the Ninth Amendment may be returning to a constitutional hibernation. Yet the Ninth Amendment retains some vitality. In *Roe v. Wade*, the federal District Court for the Northern District of Texas ruled that a state law prohibiting ABORTION in all instances except to save the life of the mother violated the right to privacy guaranteed by the Ninth Amendment (314 F. Supp. 1217 [1970]).

On appeal the Supreme Court affirmed the district court's ruling, stating that the right to privacy, "whether it be founded in the Fourteenth Amendment's concept of personal liberty and restrictions upon state action, as we feel it is, or, as the District Court determined, in the Ninth Amendment's reservation of rights to the people, is broad enough to encompass a woman's decision whether or not to terminate her pregnancy" (*Roe v. Wade*, 410 U.S. 113, 93 S. Ct. 705, 35 L. Ed. 2d 147 [1973]). Federal courts continue to rely on the Ninth Amendment in support of a woman's constitutional right to choose abortion under certain circumstances.

CROSS-REFERENCES

Constitution of the United States; *Federalist Papers; Griswold v. Connecticut*; Penumbra; *Roe v. Wade.*

NIRA See NATIONAL INDUSTRIAL RECOVERY ACT.

NISI PRIUS 📖 [*Latin, Unless before.*] 📖

A court of *nisi prius* is a court that tries questions of fact before one judge and, in some cases, a JURY. In the United States, the term ordinarily applies to the trial level court where the case is heard by a jury, as opposed to a higher court that entertains APPEALS where no jury is present.

NIXON, RICHARD MILHOUS Richard Milhous Nixon was the thirty-seventh president of the United States. Though he made several major breakthroughs in his presidency, his involvement with the Watergate affair proved his undoing. In 1974 he became the only president ever to resign from office. Late in life Nixon's advice as a political analyst and foreign affairs expert was sought by both parties.

Nixon was born January 9, 1913, in Yorba Linda, California, the second of five sons of Francis A. Nixon and Hannah Milhous Nixon. His father had grown up on a farm in Ohio and arrived in California in 1907. He worked as a trolley car motorman in Whittier, where he met Hannah Milhous. They were married in 1908.

BIOGRAPHY

Richard Milhous Nixon

In 1922 they bought the grocery store and gas station where Nixon grew up. Nixon was a disciplined student who worked hard and received superior grades. He enjoyed playing football and participating in music, acting, and debating. A devout Quaker during his youth, he attended church four times a week.

When Nixon was twelve, his younger brother Arthur died of tubercular encephalitis. His older brother, Harold, died when Nixon was twenty, after a ten-year battle with tuberculosis. Harold's death was particularly traumatic for the family, as it had poured much of its limited resources into his treatment.

After graduating from high school, Nixon wanted to attend an Ivy League college but instead entered Whittier College, a small Quaker school close to home and within his family's financial means. He graduated second in his class and won a scholarship to Duke University Law School. At Duke, he was elected president of the Duke Bar Association and graduated third in his class.

In 1937, Nixon was admitted to the California bar and joined the firm of Wingert and Bewley in Whittier. He participated in civic groups; taught Sunday school; and acted in a community theater troupe, where he met Thelma Catherine Ryan, who was known as Patricia or Pat. They were married June 21, 1940, and had two children, Patricia ("Tricia") Nixon Cox and Julie Nixon Eisenhower. The Nixons would celebrate fifty-three years of marriage before Pat's death in 1993.

In 1941, Nixon took a job as an attorney with the Office of Price Administration in Washington, D.C. Seven months later, he applied for and received a Navy commission. He served as an operations officer with the South Pacific Combat Air Transport Command during World War II.

Shortly after his return from the service, Nixon ran for Congress against incumbent California Democratic representative Jerry Voorhis. Nixon's campaign literature portrayed him as a returning veteran who had defended

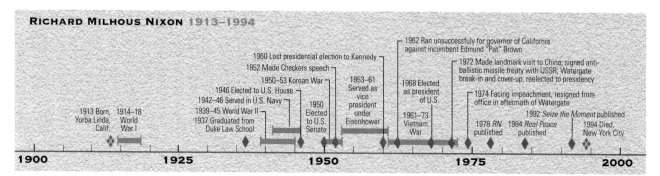

RICHARD MILHOUS NIXON 1913–1994

1913 Born, Yorba Linda, Calif.

1914–18 World War I

1937 Graduated from Duke Law School

1939–45 World War II

1942–46 Served in U.S. Navy

1946 Elected to U.S. House

1950–53 Korean War

1950 Elected to U.S. Senate

1952 Made Checkers speech

1953–61 Served as vice president under Eisenhower

1960 Lost presidential election to Kennedy

1961–73 Vietnam War

1962 Ran unsuccessfuly for governor of California against incumbent Edmund "Pat" Brown

1968 Elected as president of U.S.

1972 Made landmark visit to China; signed antiballistic missile treaty with USSR; Watergate break-in and cover-up; reelected to presidency

1974 Facing impeachment, resigned from office in aftermath of Watergate

1978 *RN* published

1984 *Real Peace* published

1992 *Seize the Moment* published

1994 Died, New York City

1900   1925   1950   1975   2000

his country in the mud and jungles of the Solomon Islands while his opponent never left Washington, D.C. It also implied that Voorhis was endorsed by a Communist-supported political action committee. At a time when fear of Communist subversion was widespread, Nixon's strategy worked. He came from behind in a race no one expected him to win to defeat Voorhis with 57 percent of the votes.

Nixon quickly made his mark in Washington, D.C. He became a vocal member of the House Committee on Un-American Activities, which investigated U.S. citizens suspected of having ties with or sympathies for the Communist party. One such case brought Nixon into the national spotlight. In 1948, ALGER HISS, a former State Department official, was investigated for allegedly passing secret information to the Communist government in the former Soviet Union. Nixon's determined pursuit of the case led to Hiss's INDICTMENT and eventual conviction for PERJURY.

In 1950 Nixon ran for the U.S. Senate against Democratic Representative Helen Gahagan Douglas. In an effort to discredit Douglas, he circulated a campaign flyer indicating that she had voted 354 times with Representative Vito Marcantonio of New York, a member of the Communist Workers party. The flyer, printed on pink paper, was known as the pink sheet, and Nixon often referred to Douglas as the pink lady, a link to the color red associated with Communism. Nixon defeated Douglas by a secure margin of 680,000 votes, raising speculation that his strident campaign may have been unnecessary.

In 1952 Republicans chose World War II hero General Dwight D. Eisenhower as their nominee for president. Eisenhower chose Nixon as his running mate. The campaign encountered a crisis almost immediately. In September 1952, several newspapers disclosed that Nixon had received financial support from a secret fund raised by wealthy California business owners. This offense was viewed as shocking, and many people called for Nixon to withdraw from the ticket. Instead, he took the offensive and pleaded his case on national television, delivering what came to be known as the "Checkers Speech." Nixon maintained his innocence, disclosed his financial situation to show he was in debt, and pointed out that his wife did not have a mink coat but rather wore "a respectable Republican cloth coat." He went on to say that a supporter in Texas had given the family a gift, a dog named Checkers, and that "the kids love the dog, and . . . we're going to keep it." The public's response was overwhelm-

"THERE IS ONE THING SOLID AND FUNDAMENTAL IN POLITICS—THE LAW OF CHANGE. WHAT'S UP TODAY IS DOWN TOMORROW."

ingly positive and Nixon remained on the Republican ticket. Nixon had discovered the enormous power of television and had utilized it to his advantage, reaching a large audience without the need to endure press scrutiny.

Eisenhower and Nixon received 55.1 percent of the popular vote in the 1952 election. Nixon served two terms as an unusually active vice president, honing his foreign policy skills during trips to fifty-six countries. Among the most famous of these journeys was a 1959 visit to Moscow, where he engaged in the celebrated Kitchen Debate with Soviet leader Nikita Khrushchev. The two men informally debated the merits of capitalism versus Communism while they toured the kitchen of a model home at a U.S. fair. Nixon's willingness to confront critics and his ability to turn adversity to his advantage earned him praise and acclaim.

In 1960 delegates at the Republican convention in Chicago nominated Nixon for president on the first ballot. He faced another young, energetic, popular contender, Democratic senator JOHN F. KENNEDY of Massachusetts. In the first of four televised debates with Kennedy, Nixon, who had been ill and was exhausted from campaigning, appeared haggard, strained, and tense. His appearance cost him many votes even though he had a keen command of the facts and debated well—indeed, those who listened to the debates on radio rather than watching them on television felt that Nixon had outdone Kennedy. Nixon lost the election, suffering his first political defeat, by a mere 119,000 votes, the slimmest margin in modern history. In spite of allegations of voting irregularities, particularly in Chicago, Nixon decided not to demand a recount and instead gracefully conceded to Kennedy.

After losing the 1960 election, Nixon ran for governor of California against Edmund "Pat" Brown in 1962 but was unable to unseat the incumbent. He moved to New York to practice law and almost immediately began preparing his comeback. In January 1968, he announced his candidacy for the presidency and was nominated on the Republicans' first ballot, defeating Governor Nelson A. Rockefeller of New York, and Governor RONALD REAGAN of California.

The Democratic party was in a shambles in 1968. President LYNDON B. JOHNSON withdrew as a candidate because of growing domestic unrest and opposition to the VIETNAM WAR. Senator ROBERT F. KENNEDY was assassinated in June 1968 while campaigning for the Democratic nomination. The Democrats nominated HUBERT H. HUMPHREY, Johnson's vice president. Nixon defeated Humphrey by a narrow margin.

During his first term, Nixon appointed a broad-based CABINET that included both conservatives and liberals. In his inaugural speech, he said that he hoped to "bridge the generation gap" and bring the country back together after years of unrest over Vietnam and racial discrimination. While he continued to pursue foreign policy goals, he also achieved much on the domestic front. He responded to strong public demand for expanded government services, and proposed a family assistance program that, had it not been voted down by Congress, would have been the most far-reaching WELFARE reform in modern history. He supported health and safety protection on the job and housing allowances for disadvantaged people. Nixon's administration built more subsidized housing units than any administration before or since. He expanded the Food Stamp Program and began the federal revenue-sharing program for local governments. Another lasting legacy was the creation of the ENVIRONMENTAL PROTECTION AGENCY.

Nixon also reshaped the Supreme Court. Under Chief Justice EARL WARREN, who had been appointed by President Eisenhower, the Court had taken what many felt was an ideologically liberal turn. During his presidency, Nixon appointed four members to the court: WARREN E. BURGER, as chief justice; and HARRY A. BLACKMUN, LEWIS F. POWELL, JR., and WILLIAM H. REHNQUIST, as associate justices. The Burger Court began a retreat from liberalism and judicial activism that continued through the 1980s and 1990s.

Perhaps Nixon's most noteworthy triumphs were in foreign policy. In 1972 Nixon and his chief foreign affairs adviser, HENRY KISSINGER, traveled to Communist China to begin the process of reestablishing diplomatic relations with the Beijing government. The visit marked a major shift in U.S. policy toward China. The two governments shared a history of animosity, and the United States had long recognized the Nationalist Chinese government of Chiang Kai-shek, based on the island of Taiwan, as the official government of China. After Nixon's visit, the door was opened to diplomatic and trade dealings. Formal diplomatic relations with Communist China were established in 1978.

Nixon also opened negotiations with the Communist government in the former Soviet Union. He initiated the process known as détente by holding three summit meetings with Soviet leader Leonid Brezhnev. His efforts culminated in a breakthrough agreement in 1972 limiting the use of antiballistic missiles.

One major goal that eluded Nixon in foreign policy was a quick end to the Vietnam War. After promising "peace with honor" during his campaign in 1968, he saw the war continue through his first term.

Though the war would end in January 1973, an event in June of 1972 marked the beginning of Nixon's downfall. At that time, during Nixon's campaign for reelection, a group of men working for the Committee to Reelect the President broke into the Democratic party headquarters in the Watergate office complex in Washington, D.C. It was a crime that would be traced back to the president.

In November, Nixon won a sweeping victory over his Democratic challenger, Senator George S. McGovern, of South Dakota, receiving 60.7 percent of the vote and carrying every state except Massachusetts. The following March, testimony before the Senate select committee investigating the incident implicated the White House. In televised hearings John W. Dean III, Nixon's White House counsel, told the Senate committee that Nixon had been involved from the start.

Further testimony revealed that Nixon had secretly recorded all conversations that took place in the Oval Office of the White House. Congress and prosecutors began efforts to obtain the tapes. In October 1973, his reputation in jeopardy, Nixon carried out what came to be called the Saturday Night Massacre. Angered by Watergate special prosecutor ARCHIBALD COX, Nixon ordered Attorney General Elliot L. Richardson to dismiss Cox. Richardson refused and resigned. Deputy Attorney General William D. Ruckelshaus also refused to carry out the task and was dismissed. Finally, Solicitor General ROBERT H. BORK, appointed acting attorney general, dismissed Cox.

Calls for Nixon's resignation mounted, and IMPEACHMENT resolutions were referred to the House Judiciary Committee. On March 1, 1974, a federal GRAND JURY indicted seven former Nixon aides in the continuing cover-up of Watergate. Nixon was named as an unindicted coconspirator.

Nixon responded to pressure from both those who wanted him to prove himself innocent and those who believed him guilty, by announcing in April 1974 that he would release to the House Judiciary Committee edited transcripts of conversations regarding Watergate culled from his library of tape recordings. Though the committee responded that it would need the tapes themselves, Nixon refused to supply them. The edited transcripts alone were tremendously damaging. The transcripts implicated the Nixon White House not only in burglaries and cover-ups, but also illegal wiretaps, corruption of government agencies, domestic ESPIONAGE, unfair campaign tactics, and abuse of campaign funds. Eventually, nineteen Nixon aides and associates served prison terms for their roles in these illegal activities.

By late July 1974, the House Judiciary Committee, in televised hearings, was deliberating ARTICLES OF IMPEACHMENT against Nixon. The articles charged him with obstruction of justice, ABUSE OF POWER, and defiance of congressional SUBPOENAS. It became clear that the full House would impeach him, and he would probably face conviction by the Senate. In early August, in response to a Supreme Court ruling (*United States v. Nixon*, 418 U.S. 683, 94 S. Ct. 3090, 41 L. Ed. 2d 1039 [1974]), Nixon released the contested tape recordings that showed conclusively that he had been involved in the effort to halt the FEDERAL BUREAU OF INVESTIGATION's probe of Watergate.

On August 7, 1974, facing certain impeachment, Nixon met with his family and aides and informed Secretary of State Kissinger of his decision to resign. He made this announcement to the nation in a television broadcast the evening of August 8. The following day, with his family around him, he bade an emotional farewell to his staff, boarded *Air Force One* with his wife, and flew home to San Clemente, California. Vice President GERALD R. FORD was sworn in to serve the remainder of Nixon's term. On September 8, President Ford granted Nixon an unconditional PARDON for all federal crimes he "committed or may have committed or taken part in" while in office, thus ending the crisis that had gripped the nation for more than two years.

After his resignation Nixon published eight books and numerous newspaper and magazine articles. He traveled again to China, where he was warmly received, and in 1994, shortly before his death, he returned to Russia. Nixon came to be considered an elder statesman and political analyst. As an expert in foreign policy his advice and counsel were sought by Senator and presidential candidate BOB DOLE and President BILL CLINTON.

Nixon died April 22, 1994. All five living presidents—Clinton, GEORGE BUSH, Reagan, JIMMY CARTER, and Ford—and their wives attended Nixon's funeral. Clinton delivered a eulogy in which he said:

> He suffered defeats that would have ended most political careers, yet he won stunning victories that many of the world's most popular leaders have failed to attain.

CROSS-REFERENCES

Arms Control and Disarmament; Cold War; Communism; Ervin, Samuel James, Jr.; Executive Privilege; Independent Counsel; Jaworski, Leon; Mitchell, John Newton; *New York Times v. United States*; *United States v. Nixon*; Watergate.

NLRB   See LABOR LAW; LABOR UNION.

NO BILL   A term that the foreman of the GRAND JURY writes across the face of a BILL OF INDICTMENT (a document drawn up by a prosecutor that states formal criminal charges against a designated individual) to indicate that the criminal charges alleged therein against a suspect have not been sufficiently supported by the EVIDENCE presented before it to warrant his or her criminal prosecution.

When the grand jury agrees that the evidence is sufficient to establish the commission of a crime, it returns an indictment endorsed by the grand jury foreman with the phrase *true bill* to indicate that the information presented before it is sufficient to justify the trial of the suspect.

NO CONTEST   The English translation of a NOLO CONTENDERE plea used in criminal cases. Generally the terms *nolo contendere* and *no contest* are used interchangeably in the legal community. The operation of a no contest plea is similar to a plea of guilty. A defendant who enters a no contest plea concedes the charges alleged without disputing or admitting guilt and without offering a defense. No contest has a different meaning in the context of a will.

The modern no contest plea originated during the reign of Henry IV in England in the early 1400s. It was considered a prisoner's implied CONFESSION. In cases where a death sentence was not a possibility, a prisoner was allowed simply to ask the court for mercy rather than contest the issue of guilt or innocence. Today the no contest plea is defined by statute and is available in almost every state. Such a plea is considered a PRIVILEGE and not an automatic right of a defendant. Consequently, a no contest plea is accepted only with the consent of the court, and a judge is vested with discretion to accept or reject the plea. A plea of no contest usually is not allowed in death penalty cases.

The court must address several procedural concerns before accepting a no contest plea. If it appears from the facts presented that the defendant did not commit the offense charged, the trial court will refuse a no contest plea. Generally, a defendant must also tender a no contest plea knowingly and voluntarily. A plea is not deemed knowing and voluntary unless the defendant has a full understanding of the charges alleged and the legal ramifications of pleading no contest. To ensure that the plea is freely tendered, the court will also inquire whether the defendant has received any threats or promises. The adherence to these standards varies among courts and JURISDICTIONS. Some courts operate under the assumption that a no contest plea should be accepted in the absence of some reason to the contrary, whereas others require the defendant to strictly observe every legal requirement before they will accept the plea.

A plea of no contest is advantageous for defendants where the effects of a plea of guilty are too harsh. For example, a defendant might choose to enter a no contest plea to avoid the expense and publicity of a trial. Another procedural advantage of a no contest plea is that it cannot be used against the accused in any civil suit for the same act. For example, if a motorist pleads no contest to a criminal ASSAULT charge against a hitchhiker, the hitchhiker cannot introduce EVIDENCE of that plea in a related civil proceeding for assault to IMPEACH the motorist's CREDIBILITY.

One disadvantage of a no contest plea is that it carries the same legal effect as a conviction for SENTENCING purposes. Though a defendant may hope for leniency during sentencing for saving the court the time and costs of a trial or because of a bargain worked out with the prosecutors, the full range of penalties remain available to the court for the given crime. Thus, a defendant risks receiving the same punishment without the opportunity to offer a defense or a chance for an ACQUITTAL from a jury.

A second meaning of no contest relates to WILLS and the intentions of the TESTATOR. A no contest provision in a will provides that the GIFT or DEVISE is given on the condition that no legal action is taken to challenge the will. If a legal challenge to the will is pursued, the no contest provision provides that the person bringing the action forfeits the gift or devise. The purpose of no contest clauses is to carry out the express wishes of the testator and to discourage litigation. Nonetheless, many courts refuse to enforce no contest clauses if the challenge is brought in GOOD FAITH and on PROBABLE CAUSE.

NO FAULT 📖 A kind of automobile INSURANCE that provides that each driver must collect the allowable amount of money from his or her own insurance carrier subsequent to an accident regardless of who was at fault. 📖

No-fault insurance is required by statute in a number of states. See also AUTOMOBILES.

The term *no fault* is also used colloquially in reference to a type of DIVORCE in which a MARRIAGE can be dissolved on the basis of irretrievable breakdown or IRRECONCILABLE DIFFERENCES, without a requirement that either party prove that the spouse was guilty of any misconduct causing the end of the marriage.

NO FAULT DIVORCE See DIVORCE.

NOLLE PROSEQUI 📖 [*Latin, Will not prosecute.*] 📖

The term *nolle prosequi* is used in reference to a formal entry upon the record made by a plaintiff in a civil lawsuit or a prosecutor in a criminal action in which that individual declares that he or she wishes to discontinue the action as to certain defendants, certain issues, or altogether. A *nolle prosequi* is commonly known as *nol pros.*

NO-LOAD FUND 📖 A type of MUTUAL FUND that does not impose extra charges for administrative and selling expenses incurred in offering its shares for sale to the public. 📖

NOLO CONTENDERE 📖 [*Latin, I will not contest it.*] A PLEA in a criminal case by which the defendant answers the charges made in the INDICTMENT by declining to dispute or admit the fact of his or her guilt. 📖

The defendant who pleads *nolo contendere* submits for a JUDGMENT fixing a fine or sentence the same as if he or she had pleaded guilty. The difference is that a plea of *nolo contendere* cannot later be used to prove wrongdoing in a civil suit for monetary DAMAGES, but a plea of guilty can. *Nolo contendere* is especially popular in ANTITRUST actions, such as PRICE-FIXING cases, where it is very likely that CIVIL ACTIONS for TREBLE DAMAGES will be started after the defendant has been successfully prosecuted.

Spiro Agnew, who served as vice president under President Richard Nixon, pleaded nolo contendere in 1973 to charges of income tax evasion.

A plea of *nolo contendere* may be entered only with the permission of the court, and the court should accept it only after weighing its effect on the parties, the public, and the administration of justice.

NOMINAL 📖 Trifling, token, or slight; not real or substantial; in name only. 📖

Nominal capital, for example, refers to extremely small or negligible funds, the use of which in a particular business is incidental.

NOMINAL DAMAGES 📖 Minimal money damages awarded to an individual in an action where the person has not suffered any substantial injury or loss for which he or she must be compensated. 📖

This kind of DAMAGES reflects a legal recognition that a plaintiff's rights have been violated through a defendant's breach of duty or wrongful conduct. The amount awarded is ordinarily a trifling sum, such as a dollar, which varies according to the circumstances of each case. In certain JURISDICTIONS, the amount of the award might include the costs of the lawsuit.

In general, nominal damages may be recovered by a plaintiff who is successful in establishing that he or she has suffered a loss or injury as a result of the defendant's wrongful conduct but is unable to adequately set forth proof of the nature and extent of the injury.

NON 📖 [*Latin, Not.*] A common prefix used to indicate negation. 📖

For example, the term *non sequitur* means "it does not follow."

NONAGE 📖 INFANCY or MINORITY; lack of requisite legal age. 📖

Nonage entails various contractual disabilities and is a ground for ANNULMENT in some JURISDICTIONS.

NONCOMPETE AGREEMENT 📖 A contract limiting a party from competing with a business after termination of employment or completion of a business sale. 📖

Found in some business CONTRACTS, noncompete agreements are designed to protect a business owner's investment by restricting potential competition. Generally, businesses pursue these agreements in two instances: when hiring new employees, or when purchasing an established business. The noncompete agreement is a form of RESTRICTIVE COVENANT, a clause that adds limitations to the employment or sale contract. These agreements protect the business by restricting the other party from performing similar work for a specific period of time within a certain geographical area. First used in the nineteenth century, and common today in certain professions, noncompete agreements sometimes have an uncertain legal status. Courts do not always uphold them. Generally, courts evaluate such clauses for their reasonableness to determine whether they constitute an unfair restraint on trade.

The rationale behind noncompete agreements is an employer's self-interest. Typically, companies invest heavily in the training of their employees. Similarly, they have an interest in protecting their customer base, trade secrets, and other information vital to their success. The noncompete agreement is a form of protection against losses. The company does not wish to invest in an employee only to see the employee take the skills acquired, or the company's customers, to another employer. Thus, when hiring a new employee, the company may make her sign a noncompete agreement as part of a condition of employment. Likewise, the prospective purchaser of an established business may only buy it if the current owner is willing to sign a noncompete agreement.

In practice, such agreements are very specific in several respects. Usually the agreement will define a length of time, geographic radius in miles, and type of activity in which the employee promises to refrain from working after leaving her or his job. This is often the case in businesses that depend on an established group of customers. A hair salon, for example, may require its stylists to agree not to compete against it in neighboring hair salons. Noncompete agreements are also well established in fields where an individual is associated with a product or service. High-profile positions in the media typically require them. A television anchorwoman, for example, will typically be contractually bound not to work for a competing news channel in the same market for a period of time following the termination of her contract.

In legal challenges courts use a standard of reasonableness in deciding whether to uphold a noncompete agreement. Most states use a three-part test: the agreement must be REASONABLE in terms of length of time, size of geographical territory included, and the business's necessity for the agreement. Covenants restricting the sellers of businesses typically receive a lower level of scrutiny, whereas restrictions on the behavior of former employees are closely scrutinized.

Courts are primarily concerned with preventing unfair restraints on trade. In a free market, most businesses cannot reasonably assert a need to restrict competition. Many states will evaluate each separate part of an agreement using the so-called blue pencil doctrine of severability, under which certain parts of the agreement can be upheld as enforceable and others can be found unenforceable. A few states, however, throw out an entire agreement if any part of it is found to be an unfair restraint on trade.

See also RESTRAINT OF TRADE.

NONCONFORMING USE 📖 Continuing use of REAL PROPERTY, permitted by ZONING ordinances, in a manner in which other similar plots of land in the same area cannot ordinarily be used. 📖

Most municipal governments have enacted zoning ORDINANCES that regulate the development of REAL ESTATE within the municipality.

If this neighborhood is zoned residential after the gas station is already in existence, the station is considered a nonconforming use site that is permitted to remain as long as it is not substantially altered or replaced by a different type of business.

The municipality is divided into zoning districts that permit a particular use of property: residence, business, or industry. Within these three main types of zoning districts, population density and building height may also be restricted. Zoning attempts to conserve the value of property and to encourage the most appropriate use of land throughout a particular locality.

When zoning is established, however, the ordinance cannot eliminate structures already in existence. Thus, if a district is zoned residential, the corner grocery store and neighborhood service station become nonconforming use sites. These businesses may remain even though they do not fit the predominant classification of real property in the zoning district.

As long as the property having nonconforming use status does not change, its status is protected. Problems arise, however, when change occurs. In general, substantial alterations in the nature of the business, new equipment that is not a replacement but a subterfuge to expand the use of the property, or a new structure amount to illegal expansion or extension. These types of actions will result in the loss of the nonconforming use status and the closing of the business. For example, if the corner grocery builds an addition to house a restaurant, that would be a significant change. If, however, the grocery updates its refrigeration equipment, that would not be an illegal change.

If a nonconforming use structure is destroyed or partially destroyed by fire or similar occurrences, zoning ordinances generally provide that if it is destroyed beyond a certain percentage, it cannot be rebuilt. Usually the owner loses the right to rebuild if 50 percent or more of the structure is damaged.

If a business stops operating at the nonconforming use site, zoning ordinances generally classify this as a discontinuance and revoke the nonconforming use status. The owner of the business must intend to abandon the use. Discontinuance due to repairs, acts of war or nature, government controls, FORECLOSURE, CONDEMNATION, or INJUNCTIONS are not regarded as manifesting intent to abandon the nonconforming use status if the situation is beyond the business owner's control.

Another tool to end nonconforming use situations is AMORTIZATION, where the nonconforming use of a structure must cease within a zoning district at the end of the structure's estimated useful economic life. This device often is used in connection with billboards and junkyards.

Though municipalities may seek to end nonconforming use status through these various approaches, landowners usually retain this status until it becomes economically undesirable.

See also LAND-USE CONTROL.

NONFEASANCE ▥ The intentional failure to perform a required duty or obligation. ▥

Nonfeasance is a term used in TORT law to describe inaction that allows or results in harm to a person or to PROPERTY. An act of nonfeasance can result in LIABILITY if (1) the actor owed a DUTY of CARE toward the injured person, (2) the actor failed to act on that duty, and (3) the failure to act resulted in injury.

Originally the failure to take affirmative steps to prevent harm did not create liability, and this rule was absolute. Over the years courts have recognized a number of situations in which a person who does not create a dangerous situation must nevertheless act to prevent harm.

Generally a person will not be held liable for a failure to act unless he or she had a preexisting relationship with the injured person. For example, if a bystander sees a stranger drowning and does not attempt a rescue, he cannot be liable for nonfeasance because he had no preexisting relationship with the drowning person. The bystander would not be liable for the drowning even if a rescue would have posed no risk to him.

However, if the victim is drowning in a public pool and the bystander is a lifeguard employed by the city, and if the lifeguard does not act to help, she may be held liable for the drowning because the lifeguard's employment places her in a relationship with swimmers in the pool. Because of this relationship, the lifeguard owes a duty to take affirmative steps to prevent harm to the swimmers.

Courts have found a preexisting relationship and a duty to act in various relationships, such as the relationship between husband and wife, innkeeper and guest, employer and employee, jailer and prisoner, CARRIER and passenger, parent and child, school and pupil, and host and guest. A person who renders aid or protection to a stranger also may be found liable if the rescuer does not act reasonably and leaves the stranger in a more dangerous position, even if the rescuer had nothing to do with the initial cause of the stranger's dilemma. See also GOOD SAMARITAN DOCTRINE.

Courts have found a duty to act if a person does something innocuous that later poses a threat and then fails to act to prevent harm. For example, assume that Johnny loans a powerful circular saw to Bobby. If Johnny later remembers that the bolt securing the blade is loose and that the blade will dislodge in a dangerous manner when the saw is used, Johnny must try to warn Bobby. If Bobby is injured because Johnny failed to act, Johnny can be held liable for nonfeasance.

In theory nonfeasance is distinct from MISFEASANCE and MALFEASANCE. Malfeasance is any act that is illegal or wrongful. Misfeasance is an act that is legal but improperly performed. Nonfeasance, by contrast, is a failure to act that results in harm.

In practice the distinctions between the three terms are nebulous and difficult to apply. Courts in various JURISDICTIONS have crafted different rules relating to the terms. The most difficult issue that faces courts is whether to imply a duty to act and find liability for the failure to act.

Originally courts used the term nonfeasance to describe a failure to act that did not give rise to liability for injuries. The meaning of the term reversed direction over time, and most courts now use it to describe inaction that creates liability.

NON OBSTANTE VEREDICTO See JUDGMENT NOTWITHSTANDING THE VERDICT.

NONPROFIT 📖 A corporation or an association that conducts business for the benefit of the general public without shareholders and without a profit motive. 📖

Nonprofits are also called not-for-profit CORPORATIONS. Nonprofit corporations are created according to state law. Like for-profit corporations, nonprofit corporations must file a statement of corporate purpose with the secretary of state and pay a fee, create ARTICLES OF INCORPORATION, conduct regular meetings, and fulfill other obligations to achieve and maintain corporate status.

Nonprofit corporations differ from profit-driven corporations in several respects. The most basic difference is that nonprofit corporations cannot operate for PROFIT. That is, they cannot distribute corporate income to shareholders. The funds acquired by nonprofit corporations must stay within the corporate accounts to pay for reasonable salaries, expenses, and the activities of the corporation. If the income of a corporation inures to the personal benefit of any individual, the corporation is considered to be profit driven. Salaries are not considered personal benefits because they are necessary for the operation of the corporation. An excessive salary, however, may cause a corporation to lose its nonprofit status.

Nonprofit corporations are exempt from the INCOME TAXES that affect other corporations but only if they conduct business exclusively for the benefit of the general public. State laws on corporations vary from state to state, but generally states give tax breaks and exemptions to nonprofit corporations that are organized and operated exclusively for either a religious, charitable, scientific, public safety, literary, or educational purpose, or for the purpose of fostering international sports or preventing cruelty to children or animals. Nonprofit organizations may charge money for their services, and contributions to tax-exempt nonprofit organizations are tax deductible. The INTERNAL REVENUE SERVICE must approve the tax-exempt status of all nonprofit organizations except churches.

A vast number of organizations qualify for nonprofit status under the various definitions. Nonprofit organizations include churches, soup kitchens, CHARITIES, political associations, business leagues, fraternities, sororities, sports

National Nonprofit Associations, by Number and Type, in 1994

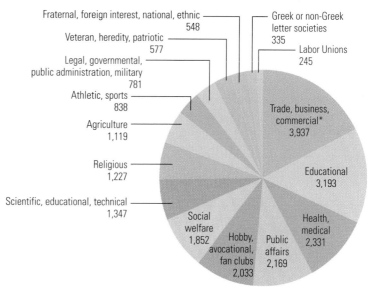

Fraternal, foreign interest, national, ethnic 548
Veteran, heredity, patriotic 577
Legal, governmental, public administration, military 781
Athletic, sports 838
Agriculture 1,119
Religious 1,227
Scientific, educational, technical 1,347
Greek or non-Greek letter societies 335
Labor Unions 245
Trade, business, commercial* 3,937
Educational 3,193
Health, medical 2,331
Public affairs 2,169
Hobby, avocational, fan clubs 2,033
Social welfare 1,852

*Includes national and binational chambers of commerce.

Source: Gale Research Inc., Detroit, Mich. Compiled from *Encyclopedia of Associations*, annual (copyright)

leagues, COLLEGES AND UNIVERSITIES, hospitals, museums, television stations, symphonies, and public interest law firms.

A nonprofit corporation with a public purpose is just one organization that qualifies for tax-exempt status. Under Section 501 of the INTERNAL REVENUE CODE (26 U.S.C.A. § 501), more than two dozen different categories of income-producing but not-for-profit organizations are exempt from federal income taxes. These other tax-exempt organizations include CREDIT UNIONS, civic leagues, recreational clubs, fraternal orders and societies, labor, agricultural, and horticultural organizations, small INSURANCE companies, and organizations of past or present members of the armed forces of the United States.

The number of nonprofit corporations in the United States has increased over the last half of the twentieth century. Although nonprofit corporations cannot produce DIVIDENDS for investors, they provide income for the employees, and they foster work that benefits the public.

The activities of nonprofit corporations are regulated more strictly than the activities of other corporations. Nonprofit corporations cannot contribute to political campaigns, and they cannot engage in a substantial amount of legislative LOBBYING.

NON PROSEQUITUR 📖 [*Latin, He does not pursue, or follow up.*] The name of a JUDGMENT rendered by a court against a plaintiff because he or she fails to take any necessary steps, in legal proceedings, within the period prescribed for such proceedings by the practice of court. 📖

When a judgment of *non prosequitur* is entered against the plaintiff, he or she has failed to properly pursue the lawsuit and cannot subsequently obtain a judgment against the defendant. A failure of such nature would result in a dismissal of the action or in a DEFAULT JUDGMENT in favor of the defendant.

NON SUI JURIS 📖 [*Latin, Not his own master.*] A term applied to an individual who lacks the legal CAPACITY to act on his or her own behalf, such as an INFANT or an insane person. 📖

NONSUIT 📖 A broad term for any of several ways to terminate a legal ACTION without an actual determination of the controversy on the MERITS. 📖

For instance, a *judgment of nonsuit* may be granted against a plaintiff who either fails to pursue, or abandons, the action.

NONSUPPORT 📖 The failure of one individual to provide financial maintenance for another individual in spite of a legal obligation to do so. 📖

Nonsupport of a spouse or child is a CRIME in some states and a ground for DIVORCE in certain JURISDICTIONS. See also CHILD SUPPORT.

NON VULT CONTENDERE 📖 [*Latin, He does not wish to contest it.*] A type of PLEA that can be entered by a defendant who is unwilling to admit guilt but is willing to submit to the court for sentencing. 📖

The term, sometimes abbreviated *non vult*, is a variation of NOLO CONTENDERE, which has the same meaning.

NORRIS, GEORGE WILLIAM George William Norris was born July 11, 1861, in Sandusky County, Ohio. He graduated from Indiana Normal College in 1881 and pursued a career in law and politics.

After admission to the Ohio and Indiana bars in 1883, Norris established a law practice in Nebraska, where he also served as prosecuting attorney. He presided as a Nebraska district court judge from 1895 to 1902.

In 1903, Norris was elected to the U.S. House of Representatives. During his tenure in the House, he was instrumental in modifying the House rules in 1910 so as to diminish the excessive powers of House Speaker Joseph Gurney Cannon.

Norris left the House of Representatives in 1913 when he was elected to the Senate, where he served for the next thirty years. He opposed the entry of the United States into World War I but generally supported the policies of President FRANKLIN DELANO ROOSEVELT. During Roosevelt's administrations, Norris was involved in several important activities. In 1932, he drafted the TWENTIETH AMENDMENT to the Constitution, which designated January 20 as the date of a presidential inauguration instead of the traditional March 4, thus eliminating the

George William Norris

UPI/CORBIS-BETTMANN

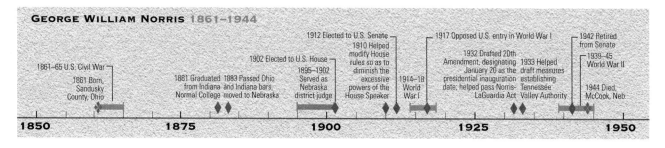

GEORGE WILLIAM NORRIS 1861–1944

1861–65 U.S. Civil War

1861 Born, Sandusky County, Ohio

1881 Graduated from Indiana Normal College

1883 Passed Ohio and Indiana bars, moved to Nebraska

1895–1902 Served as Nebraska district judge

1902 Elected to U.S. House

1910 Helped modify House rules so as to diminish the excessive powers of the House Speaker

1912 Elected to U.S. Senate

1914–18 World War I

1917 Opposed U.S. entry in World War I

1932 Drafted 20th Amendment, designating January 20 as the presidential inauguration date; helped pass Norris-LaGuardia Act

1933 Helped draft measures establishing Tennessee Valley Authority

1939–45 World War II

1942 Retired from Senate

1944 Died, McCook, Neb.

1850   1875   1900   1925   1950

need for a "LAME DUCK" congressional session. In that same year, he was instrumental in the passage of the NORRIS-LaGUARDIA ACT (29 U.S.C.A. § 101 et seq.), which restricted the use of INJUNCTIONS in labor disagreements. He also helped draft measures for the establishment of the TENNESSEE VALLEY AUTHORITY in 1933 and advocated programs for farm relief.

Norris died September 3, 1944, in McCook, Nebraska.

NORRIS-LaGUARDIA ACT ▧ One of the initial federal labor laws in favor of organized labor. It was enacted in 1932. ▧

The Norris-LaGuardia Act (29 U.S.C.A. § 101 et seq.) provides that CONTRACTS that limit an employee's right to join a LABOR UNION are unlawful. Such contracts are commonly known as YELLOW DOG CONTRACTS. Initially the law was known as the anti-INJUNCTION act since its numerous restrictions had the effect of stopping any federal court from issuing an injunction to end a labor dispute. In one part of the act, for example, there is a provision that an injunction prohibiting a STRIKE cannot be issued unless the local police are either unwilling or unable to prevent damage or violence.

See also LABOR LAW.

NORTH AMERICAN FREE TRADE AGREEMENT ▧ A trade agreement between the United States, Canada, and Mexico, which took effect January 1, 1994. Its purpose is to increase the efficiency and fairness of trade between the three nations. ▧

At the heart of the North American Free Trade Agreement (NAFTA) is a simple goal: the elimination of TARIFFS—the taxes each nation imposes on the others' imports—and other bureaucratic and legal barriers to trade. In addition to its central terms, the massive, highly detailed agreement also includes so-called side agreements intended to ensure that each nation enforces its own labor and ENVIRONMENTAL LAWS. The bulk of its regulations are to be phased in over the course of fifteen years.

The impetus for NAFTA developed in the 1980s. Its roots lie in the United States-Canada Free Trade Agreement of 1988—implemented by the United States-Canada Free Trade Agreement Implementation Act (19 U.S.C.A. § 2112 note [Supp. 1993])—which, by the mid-1990s, had already eliminated most trade barriers between the United States and Canada. With the world gradually becoming divided into large regional trading blocs where goods and services move freely, as in the European Union, NAFTA's supporters saw the inclusion of Mexico as necessary for North America to compete internationally.

In the United States, debate over NAFTA threatened to derail it. Proponents saw economic benefits for all three nations in the agreement. But opponents concentrated their attack on the implications for the relationship between the United States and Mexico. They feared two potential outcomes if NAFTA were signed: the loss of U.S. jobs, and damage to the environment as a result of economic growth in Mexico and the likelihood that U.S. safety regulations would be challenged as barriers to free trade.

In 1993 a coalition of consumer and environmental groups brought suit in an attempt to block congressional consideration of the agreement. In *Public Citizen v. United States Trade Representative*, 5 F.3d 549 (D.C. Cir. 1993), the coalition argued that the administration of President BILL CLINTON had failed to comply with the NATIONAL ENVIRONMENTAL POLICY ACT (42 U.S.C.A. § 4321 et seq. [1977]), which requires all federal agencies to submit environmental impact statements for all legislation or actions that affect the environment. The suit failed when a federal APPELLATE COURT ruled that it had no authority to review the president's actions.

In response to anti-NAFTA criticisms, the White House negotiated three side agreements that were signed on September 14, 1993. The side agreements attempted to ensure that the three countries comply with their own labor and environmental laws; established fines and limited trade sanctions for violations; and called for consultations by the members if increases in imports from one country appeared to be having a devastating effect on an industry in one of the other countries. Two months later NAFTA won congressional approval. The House of Representatives narrowly passed the implementing legislation (North American Free Trade Implementation Act [19 U.S.C.A. § 3314 et seq., Pub. L. No. 103-182, 107 Stat. 2057]), and the Senate also passed it.

NAFTA specifies a timetable for its changes. When the agreement went into effect on January 1, 1994, the United States eliminated all tariffs on 60 percent of imports from Mexico that previously were subject to tariffs. On January 1, 2003, more U.S. tariffs on Mexico's imports will be removed, with the result that 92 percent of previously taxed Mexican goods will be able to enter the United States without tariffs. Finally, on January 1, 2008, all remaining tariffs on the three countries' goods will be eliminated. Other barriers are to be removed by January 1, 2000. U.S. banks, which have hitherto been shut out of Mexico, will be free to take over as much as 15 percent of the Mexican financial market. At the same time, Mexican and U.S. truck drivers will be allowed to haul goods across the border and deliver them anywhere in either country.

See also CANADA AND THE UNITED STATES; PROTECTIONISM.

NORTH ATLANTIC TREATY ORGANI-ZATION 📖 A collective security group that was established by the North Atlantic Treaty (34 U.N.T.S. 243) in 1949 to block the threat of military aggression in Europe by the Soviet Union. 📖

The North Atlantic Treaty Organization (NATO) united Western Europe and North America in a commitment of mutual security and collective self-defense. Its sixteen members—Belgium, Canada, Denmark, France, Germany, Greece, Iceland, Italy, Luxembourg, the Netherlands, Norway, Portugal, Spain, Turkey, the United Kingdom, and the United States—have used NATO as a framework for cooperation in military, political, economic, and social matters.

NATO's military forces are organized into three main commands: the Atlantic Command, the Channel Command, and the Allied Command Europe. During peacetime, the three commands plan the defense of their areas and oversee and exercise the forces of member nations. The supreme Allied commander in Europe directs these units. Every supreme Allied commander through 1997 has been a U.S. general.

NATO established the North Atlantic Council, a nonmilitary policy group, in the 1950s. It is composed of permanent delegates from all member nations and is headed by a secretary-general. It is responsible for general policy, budget issues, and administrative actions. The Military Committee, consisting of the chiefs of staff of the member nations' armed forces, meets twice a year to define military policies and offer advice to the council.

The North Atlantic Treaty calls for the peaceful resolution of disputes, but article 5 pledges the use of the member nations' forces for collective self-defense. During the 1950s Western Europe was concerned about Soviet aggression. Though U.S. troops had been stationed in Europe since the end of World War II, the United States and European nations did not have the resources to match the Soviet Army soldier for soldier. Instead the United States stated that it would use nuclear weapons against Soviet aggression in Europe.

In the 1960s the alliance was tested. President Charles de Gaulle of France complained about U.S. domination and control of NATO. In 1966 France expelled NATO troops from its soil and removed its troops from NATO command, but it remained a member of the organization. This led to the relocation of NATO headquarters from Paris to Brussels.

With the collapse of communism in Eastern Europe and the Soviet Union and the reunification of Germany, NATO has undergone a reassessment period. Though 300,000 U.S.

North Atlantic Treaty Organization

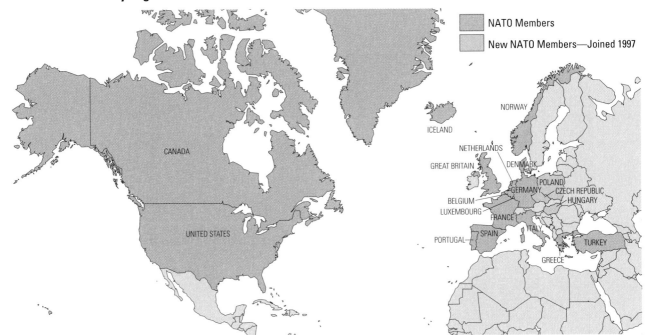

troops remain stationed in Europe, questions have been raised about the need for NATO in a post-cold-war world. Few U.S. leaders have expressed the desire to dismantle NATO, seeking instead a new mission for the organization. Some have suggested that the United States must keep a foothold in Europe to insure political stability and to prevent Germany from dominating the continent. Others have argued for using NATO as a tool to defend western interests outside of Europe. More importantly, NATO has discussed opening its membership to the former Communist bloc countries of Eastern Europe. Russia, under the leadership of Boris Yeltsin, has objected to this idea, seeing it as an attempt to end a Russian sphere of influence that has existed for fifty years.

See also COLD WAR; COMMUNISM.

NORTH PACIFIC FISHERIES CONVENTION, 1952

In the 1952 International Convention for the High Seas Fisheries of the North Pacific Ocean, Canada, Japan, and the United States joined together to establish cooperative measures for the conservation of the fishery stock of the North Pacific. The tripartite negotiations resulted in the creation of the International North Pacific Fisheries Commission, which, in addition to its duty to gather and compile information, is responsible for recommending changes in any conservation measures already in place. In limited situations, conservation measures may entail abstention from harvesting some stocks of fish. See also FISH AND FISHING.

NORTHWEST ATLANTIC FISHERIES CONVENTION, 1949

The Northwest Atlantic Fisheries Convention was held in Washington, D.C., in 1949. Its purpose was to conserve the fishery resources of the North Atlantic. The convention established the International Commission for Northwest Atlantic Fisheries. See also FISH AND FISHING.

NORTHWEST ORDINANCE

An agreement adopted in 1787 by the Congress of the Confederation of States that created the Northwest Territory, organized its governing structure, and established the procedures by which territories were admitted as states to the Union.

The Northwest Ordinance, officially known as the Ordinance of 1787, was derived from a proposal by THOMAS JEFFERSON concerning the formation of states from the territory acquired as a result of the Revolutionary War. The territory stretched from the Ohio River to the Mississippi River to the area around the Great Lakes and encompassed what is today Ohio, Indiana, Illinois, Michigan, Wisconsin, and part

of Minnesota. The reaction to Jefferson's proposal was mixed, and it was only when the Ohio Company of Associates expressed interest in purchasing the land that Congress took action.

The ordinance, passed by Congress in July 1787, was significant in providing a framework for the admission of territories into the Union as states. A government composed of a governor, a secretary, and three judges appointed by Congress was established in the region north of the Ohio River. When the population of the territory reached 5,000, the inhabitants were authorized to elect a legislature and to be represented in the House of Representatives by a nonvoting member. When a designated area of the territory had 60,000 residents, that area could seek to become a state by complying with the requirements of the ordinance. Congress required that the territory be divided into at least three but not more than five states. Five states were eventually carved out of the territory.

Aside from the provisions concerning statehood, the Northwest Ordinance had two distinct prohibitions. There was to be no SLAVERY within the boundaries of the territory, and no law could be enacted that would impair a contract.

The Northwest Ordinance was important because it provided the foundation for the creation of later territories within the Union and established the process by which territories became states.

Eleanor Holmes Norton

NORTON, ELEANOR HOLMES

Eleanor Holmes Norton is a politician, lawyer, educator, and CIVIL RIGHTS activist. As the District of Columbia's delegate to the U.S. Congress, she expanded the district's power over its own affairs.

Norton, the eldest of three daughters, was born to Coleman Holmes and Vela Holmes on June 13, 1937, in Washington, D.C. Her father was a government employee in the District of Columbia, and her mother was a schoolteacher. Norton grew up in the segregated Washington, D.C., of the 1940s and 1950s and was a member of the last segregated class at Dunbar High School. Norton attended Antioch College, where she participated in many civil rights protests, and she graduated from Yale Law School.

In 1965 Norton became an attorney with the AMERICAN CIVIL LIBERTIES UNION (ACLU), seeking to defend the freedoms of speech, press, and assembly. The clients she represented were not always those she had imagined. Among the people she represented were former Alabama governor GEORGE WALLACE, an avowed segrega-

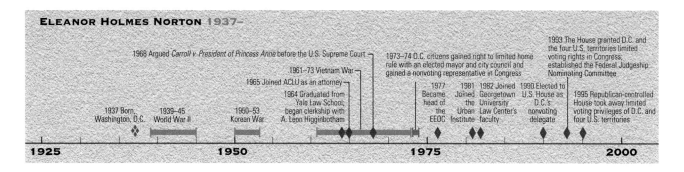

ELEANOR HOLMES NORTON 1937–

1968 Argued *Carroll v. President of Princess Anne* before the U.S. Supreme Court

1961–73 Vietnam War

1965 Joined ACLU as an attorney

1964 Graduated from Yale Law School, began clerkship with A. Leon Higginbotham

1937 Born, Washington, D.C.

1939–45 World War II

1950–53 Korean War

1973–74 D.C. citizens gained right to limited home rule with an elected mayor and city council and gained a nonvoting representative in Congress

1977 Became head of the EEOC

1981 Joined the Urban Institute

1982 Joined Georgetown University Law Center's faculty

1990 Elected to U.S. House as D.C.'s nonvoting delegate

1993 The House granted D.C. and the four U.S. territories limited voting rights in Congress; established the Federal Judgeship Nominating Committee

1995 Republican-controlled House took away limited voting privileges of D.C. and four U.S. territories

1925   1950   1975   2000

tionist, who had been denied a permit to speak at New York's Shea Stadium, and a group of white supremacists who had been barred from holding a rally. The white supremacists' suit eventually went to the U.S. Supreme Court, where Norton argued it and won (*Carroll v. President of Princess Anne*, 393 U.S. 175, 89 S. Ct. 347, 21 L. Ed. 2d 325 [1968]).

In 1970 Norton became head of the New York City Commission on Human Rights. In 1977 President JIMMY CARTER appointed her to run the federal EQUAL EMPLOYMENT OPPORTUNITY COMMISSION (EEOC), which was facing a backlog of nearly one-hundred thousand unsettled AFFIRMATIVE ACTION and discrimination complaints. At the EEOC, Norton initiated a system known as rapid charge processing, which provided for informal settlement procedures. By late 1980, the backlog had dropped to thirty-two thousand complaints. The NATIONAL ASSOCIATION FOR THE ADVANCEMENT OF COLORED PEOPLE criticized the agency's emphasis on settling individual complaints rather than attacking broad patterns of discrimination. But Norton said that only by wiping out the backlog could the EEOC get to these broader issues. By the time she left the agency, it was taking on more sweeping investigations, anti-discrimination guidelines for employers were in place, and the Carter administration was enforcing workplace laws such as the Equal Pay Act of 1963 (29 U.S.C.A. 206) and the Age Discrimination in Employment Act of 1967 (29 U.S.C.A. 621).

Following Carter's defeat in 1980, Norton moved on to the Urban Institute. In 1982, she joined the law faculty at Georgetown University Law Center, where she wrote widely on civil rights and education issues. In 1990 Norton was elected the nonvoting D.C. delegate in the U.S. House of Representatives. In her first term, she helped the district government obtain $300 million in new federal aid and a guarantee of steady increases in future aid. She secured seats on three House committees that greatly affect the district's economy, and

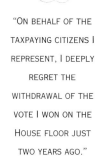

"ON BEHALF OF THE TAXPAYING CITIZENS I REPRESENT, I DEEPLY REGRET THE WITHDRAWAL OF THE VOTE I WON ON THE HOUSE FLOOR JUST TWO YEARS AGO."

she was the only first-year legislator invited on a congressional fact-finding mission to the Middle East following the Persian Gulf War.

Norton also sought to increase the power of the D.C. delegate position. The district's delegate to Congress is prohibited by the U.S. Constitution from becoming a full member of the House of Representatives, and had been allowed to vote only in legislative committees. Norton argued that because she could vote in other committees, she should also be allowed to vote in the committee of the whole where most of the business of the full House is conducted. In February 1993, the House granted Norton and the representatives of four U.S. territories—Puerto Rico, Guam, the U.S. Virgin Islands, and American Samoa—a limited vote in the committee of the whole. The voting limitations included a provision that any time the delegates provided a margin of victory for legislation, a second vote would be held, from which the delegates would be excluded. Despite these restrictions, House Republicans filed suit in federal district court asking that the delegates' right to vote be taken away. In March 1993, U.S. district judge Harold Greene rejected the challenge (*Michel v. Anderson*, 817 F. Supp. 126 [D.D.C.]). The Republicans then appealed the decision to the U.S. Court of Appeals, which upheld the lower court (14 F. 3d 623 [D.C. Cir. 1994]). Norton and the four territorial representatives retained their voting privileges until January 1995, when a new House took them away.

Norton's efforts on behalf of the District of Columbia extended outside the House of Representatives. Traditionally, the senior senator from each state, if a member of the president's party, recommends to the president candidates for federal judgeships and U.S. attorney positions. Because the district has no senators, the president alone has made these appointments for it. In 1993, Norton convinced President BILL CLINTON to give her the advisory powers reserved for senators and to allow her to nominate candidates for a U.S. attorney position and five federal judgeships—becoming the first district congressional delegate to do so. Norton established the Federal Judicial Nominating Commission, composed of members from the district, to forward recommendations to her. All five of the judges Norton ultimately recommended to the president had been active in D.C. legal circles, and four of the five lived in the district.

Norton also continued her predecessors' efforts to obtain statehood for the district. After a three-year effort to bring the issue to the House floor, the measure failed by a vote of 277–153. But Norton said she would continue her efforts and would put new emphasis on gaining support for legislation that would expand the district's limited HOME RULE. Norton also worked for increased federal contributions to the city's pension system, for an end to congressional review of the city's budget, and for the right of D.C. residents to choose local judges.

In 1994, Norton was elected to a third term in the House of Representatives.

See also DISTRICT OF COLUMBIA.

NOTARY PUBLIC 📖 A public official whose main powers include administering oaths and attesting to signatures, both important and effective ways to minimize FRAUD in legal documents. 📖

The origin of notaries public can be traced to ancient Rome, where a notarius was held in high regard as legal counsel. During that era only the few people who knew how to write were qualified to serve as a notarius. A notarius wrote legal documents, including contracts and wills, and retained them for safekeeping. A small fee was charged for those services, a tradition that continues today.

As colonists settled in the New World, most transactions that required an OATH or SIGNATURE attestation were handled in the courts. During that period the few notaries who existed were appointed or elected in a manner similar to the election or appointment of judges. However, as trade with Europe began, the demand for notaries increased because of the large number of BILLS OF EXCHANGE that needed to be witnessed. The authority to appoint notaries was transferred to the states, where the secretary of state (or another nonjudicial office) usually acted as the appointer.

In 1983 the Commission on Uniform State Laws passed the Uniform Law on Notarial Acts (14 U.L.A. 125), which covered nearly all aspects of the office of notary public, from the definition of duties to appointment policies. Today most states use this model law as a basis for their own notary public statutes. These laws vary from state to state, and the amount of power that a state gives to notaries can depend on its history. States that are French in origin, such as Louisiana, tend to give their notaries broad powers—almost equal to those of a JUSTICE OF THE PEACE. In Louisiana notaries' powers include making "inventories, appraisements, and partitions; . . . all contracts and instruments of writing; [and holding] family meetings and meetings of creditors . . ." (La. Rev. Stat. Ann. § 35:2 [1996]).

California also gives notaries additional powers, allowing them to "demand acceptance and payment of foreign and inland bills of exchange, or promissory notes, to protest them for nonacceptance and nonpayment" (Cal. Gov't. Code § 8205 [West 1997]).

In some cases the notary responsible for a transaction has an invalid commission because of a technicality. If the notary already witnessed and completed the transaction before becoming aware of the problem, the transaction is still considered valid.

Notaries public have two main duties that remain consistent from state to state. Perhaps the most important duty of a notary public is attesting to signatures on documents. This duty is important because it aids in minimizing fraud; signature ATTESTATION must be done with the notary and the signatory in a face-to-face setting.

The process of notarizing a signature is simple. The person who wants his or her signature notarized must present sufficient EVIDENCE to prove his or her identity and sign the necessary document. The notary completes the process by stamping or sealing, dating, and signing the document. This face-to-face procedure helps ensure the authenticity of the signature.

A notary public may also administer oaths in DEPOSITIONS or other situations. Even though this type of oath may not take place in court, the WITNESS can still be held accountable and be punished for PERJURY.

In Ohio a notary can also hold an affiant in CONTEMPT if he or she is a reluctant witness. In the U.S. Supreme Court case of *Bevan v. Krieger*, 289 U.S. 459, 53 S. Ct. 661, 77 L. Ed. 1316 (1933), a notary public held a witness in contempt because he refused to comply with the requirements of the SUBPOENA he was served. The court ruled that the notary was acting within his powers when he held the witness in contempt.

To become a notary, a candidate must complete several steps. A candidate must fill out an application and submit it to the appropriate government agency, usually the respective state's department of the secretary of state or the U.S. Department of State. As part of the application procedure, the candidate must also take an oath of office and submit a BOND. The purpose of the bond is to offer a small amount of monetary insurance in case the notary is sued. On average, notarial bonds are less than $5,000. If a notary is sued for more money than the amount of the bond, the notary is still personally liable for the difference between the bond and the sum awarded to the plaintiff.

Once an application is approved and the notary is commissioned, the notary must register in the county in which he or she resides and pay a registration fee. The commission itself has a time limit, which can range from two to ten years, with an average limit of four years. To renew the commission, the notary must repeat the application process.

Most states require that a notary be at least eighteen years old and be able to read and write English. However, the latter requirement may change in the future because of the increasing number of transactions that take place in languages other than English. Some states require potential notaries to pass an exam as part of the application process. Others may require a notary to keep a detailed journal of the transactions he or she officiates.

Until 1984 many states required that a notary be a U.S. citizen or a resident of the state in which he or she would serve as a notary, or both. However, in *Bernal v. Fainter*, 467 U.S. 216, 104 S. Ct. 2312, 81 L. Ed. 2d 175 (1984), the U.S. Supreme Court ruled that requiring a notary to be a U.S. CITIZEN was unconstitutional under the FOURTEENTH AMENDMENT'S EQUAL PROTECTION Clause. Therefore, even though the plaintiff in the case was actually a Mexican native and longtime resident ALIEN, it was unconstitutional to deny him a notarial commission simply because he was not a U.S. citizen. Despite this ruling many states have kept the U.S. citizenship requirement in their statutes.

Another challenge to the procedure for becoming a notary occurred in the case of *Torasco v. Watkins*, 367 U.S. 488, 81 S. Ct. 1680, 6 L. Ed. 2d 982 (1961). In this case, an atheist objected to Maryland's notary public oath, which required him to acknowledge a belief in God. When his notary commission was denied, he sued. The case went to the U.S. Supreme Court, which ruled that, under both the Maryland Constitution and the U.S. Constitution, it was "repugnant" for an oath to require a belief in God.

Notaries can only be held liable for actions they take while performing the notary function.

For example, although notaries are responsible for attesting to the validity of a signature, they are not responsible for the validity of the document. It is not considered MALPRACTICE for a notary to attest to a signature on a document that he or she knows is invalid.

A notary must "act as a reasonably prudent notary would act in the same situation." In an action against a notary, the burden of proof is on the plaintiff to show that the notary acted negligently. If the plaintiff meets this burden, the notary can be held personally liable for DAMAGES to all parties involved, including third parties.

NOTE To take notice of. A COMMERCIAL PAPER that contains an express and absolute promise by the MAKER to pay to a specific individual, to order, or to BEARER a definite sum of money on demand or at a specifically designated time.

NOTES OF DECISIONS ANNOTATIONS; concise summaries and references to the printed decisions of cases that are designed to explain particular rules of law or applicable sections of statutes.

NOTICE Information; knowledge of certain facts or of a particular state of affairs. The formal receipt of papers that provide specific information.

There are various types of notice, each of which has different results. In general, notice deals with information that a party knows or should have known. In this context notice is an essential element of due process. Notice can also refer to commonly known facts that a court or ADMINISTRATIVE AGENCY may take into EVIDENCE.

ACTUAL NOTICE is information given to the party directly. The two kinds of actual notice are EXPRESS notice and IMPLIED notice. An individual is deemed to have been given express notice when he or she actually hears it or reads it. Implied notice is deduced or inferred from the circumstances rather than from direct or explicit words. Courts will treat such information as though actual notice had been given.

CONSTRUCTIVE notice is information that a court deems that an individual should have known. According to a rule of law that applies in such cases, the court will presume that a person knows the information because she could have been informed if proper diligence had been exercised. Constructive notice can be based on a legal relationship as well. For example, in the law governing partnerships, each partner is deemed to have knowledge of all the PARTNERSHIP business. If one partner engages in dishonest transactions, the other partners are presumed to know, regardless of whether they had actual knowledge of the transaction. The term *legal notice* is sometimes used interchangeably with constructive notice.

In certain cases involving the purchase of REAL PROPERTY, an individual is charged with inquiry notice. When an individual wishes to purchase land, he ordinarily has the duty under the recording acts to check the TITLE to the property to determine that the land is not subject to any ENCUMBRANCES, which are claims, LIENS, MORTGAGES, LEASES, EASEMENTS or RIGHT OF WAYS, or unpaid taxes that have been lodged against the real property. In some situations, however, the individual must make a reasonable investigation outside of the records, such as in cases involving recorded but defective documents. This type of notice is known as inquiry notice.

Some states have notice recording statutes that govern the recording of land titles. Whereas inquiry notice deals with looking closely at documents that have been recorded, notice recording statutes state that an unrecorded CONVEYANCE of property is invalid against the title bought by a subsequent bona fide purchaser for value and without notice. This means that if John purchases a piece of land on a contract for deed from Tom and does not record the contract for deed, and if Tom resells the land to Jill, who has no notice of the prior sale, then Jill as a bona fide purchaser will prevail, and John's conveyance will be invalid.

The concept of notice is critical to the integrity of LEGAL PROCEEDINGS. Due process requires that legal action cannot be taken against anyone unless the requirements of notice and an opportunity to be heard are observed.

Legal proceedings are initiated by providing notice to the individual affected. If an individual is accused of a crime, he has a right to be notified of the charges. In addition, formal papers must be prepared to give the accused notice of the charges.

An individual who is being sued in a CIVIL ACTION must be provided with notice of the nature of the suit. State statutes prescribe the method of providing this type of notice. Courts are usually strict in requiring compliance with these laws, and ordinarily a plaintiff must put this information into a COMPLAINT that must be served upon the defendant in some legally adequate manner. The plaintiff may personally serve the complaint to the defendant. When that is not practical, the papers may be served through the mail. In some cases a court may allow, or require, service by posting or attaching the papers to the defendant's last known address or to a public place where the defendant is likely to see them. Typically, however, notice is given by publication of the papers in a local newspaper. When the defendant is not personally served, or is formally served in another state, the method of service is called SUBSTITUTED SERVICE.

Notice is also critical when suing a state or local government. Many states and municipalities have notice of CLAIM provisions in their statutes and ordinances that state that, before a lawsuit is started, a notice of claim must be filed within a reasonable time, usually three to six months after the injury occurs. The notice must contain the date of injury, how it occurred, and other facts that establish that the prospective plaintiff has a viable CAUSE OF ACTION against the government. Failure to file a notice of claim within the prescribed time period prevents a plaintiff from filing a lawsuit unless exceptions to this requirement are provided by statute or ORDINANCE.

Notice is also an important requirement in ending legal relationships. For example, a notice to quit is a written notification given either by the TENANT to the LANDLORD, or vice versa, indicating that either the tenant intends to surrender possession of the premises on a certain day or that the landlord intends to regain possession of the premises on a certain day. Many kinds of CONTRACTS require that similar notice be given to either renew or end the contractual relationship.

Notice may also refer to commonly known facts that a court or ADMINISTRATIVE AGENCY may take into evidence during a trial or hearing. JUDICIAL NOTICE is a doctrine of EVIDENCE that allows a court to recognize and accept the existence of a commonly known fact without the need to establish its existence by the admission of evidence. Courts take judicial notice of historical events, federal, state, and international laws, business customs, and other facts that are not subject to reasonable dispute.

Administrative proceedings use the term *official notice* to describe a doctrine similar to judicial notice. A presiding administrative officer recognizes as evidence, without proof, certain kinds of facts that are not subject to reasonable dispute. Administrative agencies, unlike courts, have an explicit legislative function as well as an adjudicative function: they make rules. In rule making, agencies have wider discretion in taking official notice of law and policy, labeled *legislative facts*.

CROSS-REFERENCES

Due Process of Law; Legislative Facts; Personal Service; Recording of Land Titles; Registration of Land Titles; Service of Process; Title Search.

A sample novation

Agreement made this _____ day of _____ , 19___ , between _____
(Original

_____ , of _____ , and _____
contractor)   (Address, City, State, Zip)   (Substituted contractor)

of _____ , and _____ , of _____ .
(Address, City, State, Zip)   (Contractee)   (Address, City, State, Zip)

Whereas, an agreement dated the _____ day of _____ , 19___ , was made between

_____ and _____ , and _____ desires to be released
(Original contractor)   (Contractee)   (Original contractor)

and discharged from the contract contained in said agreement, and _____ has
(Contractee)

agreed to release and discharge _____ therefrom upon the terms of
(Original contractor)

_____ undertaking to perform the said contract and to be bound by its terms;
(Substituted contractor)

It is agreed as follows:

1. Undertaking of Substituted Contractor. _____ undertakes to perform said
(Substituted contractor)

contract and to be bound by the terms thereof in all respects as if _____
(Substituted contractor)

were a party to said agreement in lieu of _____ .
(Original contractor)

2. Release of Original Contractor and Agreement for Acceptance of Substituted Contrac-

tor. _____ releases and discharges _____ from all claims and
(Contractor)   (Original contractor)

demands in respect to said agreement, and accepts the liability of _____
(Substituted contractor)

upon the said agreement in lieu of the liability of _____ , and agrees to be
(Original contractor)

bound by the terms of the said agreement in all respects as if _____ were
(Substituted contractor)

named therein in place of _____ .
(Original contractor)

In Witness Whereof, the parties have signed this agreement on the day and year first above written.

[*Signatures*]

NOVATION 📖 The substitution of a new CONTRACT for an old one. The new agreement extinguishes the rights and obligations that were in effect under the old agreement. 📖

A novation ordinarily arises when a new individual assumes an obligation to pay that was incurred by the original party to the contract. It is distinguishable from the situation that occurs when another individual makes a guarantee that a DEBTOR will pay what he or she owes to a CREDITOR. In the case of a novation, the original debtor is totally released from the obligation, which is transferred to someone else. The nature of the transaction is dependent upon the agreement between the parties.

A novation also takes place when the original parties continue their obligation to one another, but a new agreement is substituted for the old one.

NUCLEAR NONPROLIFERATION TREATY The Nuclear Nonproliferation Treaty (NPT), formally titled the Treaty on the Nonproliferation of Nuclear Weapons, is the cornerstone of the international effort to halt the proliferation, or spread, of nuclear weapons (Department of State, *United States Treaties and Other International Agreements*, Vol. 21, part 1 [1970], pp. 483–494). The NPT was first signed in 1968 by three states possessing nuclear weapons—the United States, the Soviet Union, and the United Kingdom—and by nearly one hundred states without nuclear weapons. It came into force in 1970, and by the mid-1990s had been signed by 168 countries.

The NPT distinguishes between nuclear-weapon states and non-nuclear-weapon states. It identifies five nuclear-weapon states: China, France, the Soviet Union, the United Kingdom, and the United States.

Article II forbids non-nuclear-weapon states that are parties to the treaty to manufacture or otherwise acquire nuclear weapons or nuclear explosive devices. Article III deals with controls and inspections that are intended to prevent the

The Nuclear Nonproliferation Treaty permits signing states to conduct nuclear research and development for peaceful purposes. The scientists shown here test nuclear weapons in an explosive chamber.

diversion of nuclear energy from peaceful uses to nuclear weapons or explosive devices. These safeguards are applied only to non-nuclear-weapon states and only to peaceful nuclear activities. The treaty contains no provisions for verification of the efforts by nuclear-weapon states to prevent the proliferation of nuclear weapons.

Under the provisions of article IV, all parties to the treaty, including non-nuclear-weapon states, may conduct nuclear research and development for peaceful purposes. In return for agreeing not to develop nuclear weapons, non-nuclear-weapon states receive two promises from nuclear-weapon states: the latter will help them develop nuclear technology for peaceful purposes (art. IV), and the latter will "pursue negotiations in good faith on effective measures relating to cessation of the nuclear arms race at an early date and to nuclear disarmament" (art. VI) (as quoted in U.S. Arms Control and Disarmament Agency 1982, 93).

Since 1975, NPT signatory countries have held a review conference every five years to discuss treaty compliance and enforcement.

See also ARMS CONTROL AND DISARMAMENT.

NUCLEAR POWER 📖 A form of energy produced by an atomic reaction, capable of producing an alternative source of electrical power to that supplied by coal, gas, or oil. 📖

The dropping of the atom bomb on Hiroshima, Japan, by the United States in 1945 initiated the atomic age. Nuclear energy immediately became a military weapon of terrifying magnitude. For the physicists who worked on the atom bomb, the promise of nuclear energy was not solely military. They envisioned nuclear power as a safe, clean, cheap, and abundant source of ENERGY that would end society's dependence on fossil fuels. At the end of World War II, leaders called for the peaceful use of nuclear energy.

Congress passed the Atomic Energy Act of 1946 (42 U.S.C.A. § 2011 et seq.), which shifted nuclear development from military to civilian government control. Very little development of commercial nuclear power occurred from 1946 to 1954 because the 1946 law maintained a federal government MONOPOLY over the control, use, and ownership of nuclear reactors and fuels.

Congress amended the Atomic Energy Act in 1954 (68 Stat. 919) to encourage the private commercial development of nuclear power. The act ended the federal government's monopoly over nonmilitary uses of nuclear energy and allowed private ownership of reactors under licensing procedures established by the Atomic Energy Commission (AEC). Private power companies did not rush to build nuclear power plants because they feared the financial consequences of a nuclear accident. Congress responded by passing the Price-Anderson Act of 1957 (42 U.S.C.A. § 2210), which limited the liability of the nuclear power industry and assured compensation for the public. With the passage of the Price-Anderson Act, power companies began to build nuclear plants. By the 1990s approximately 110 nuclear plants were operating in the United States, supplying 20 percent of the nation's ELECTRICITY.

A nuclear reactor produces energy through a chain reaction that splits a uranium nucleus, releasing energy in the form of heat. Fast breeder reactors, which use plutonium as fuel, generate more energy than they expend. Plutonium is not a natural element. It must be recycled from the excess uranium produced from a chain reaction. The radioactivity of plutonium is higher and its life is longer than that of any other element. Because of these characteristics, the public has been concerned about the safety of its development and use.

Nuclear power plants were built in the United States largely because the demand for electricity grew at a steady rate in the 1960s and coal-burning facilities were an environmentally unattractive alternative. The high price of oil during the mid-1970s continued to make nuclear power economically desirable and helped keep nuclear energy a prominent part of national energy plans.

Until 1969 the AEC did not have a formal process for evaluating the environmental impact of building nuclear power plants. In that year Congress passed the NATIONAL ENVIRONMENTAL POLICY ACT of 1969 (42 U.S.C.A. §§ 4321–4370), which required environmental impact statements for all major federal activities. In the 1970s the temper of nuclear regulation changed. People were no longer complacent about nuclear power safety or convinced by environmental claims made by industry and government.

This lack of public trust centered on the role of the AEC as both a promoter of nuclear technology and a regulator of the nuclear power industry. In 1974, realizing the cross purposes of promotion and safety, Congress passed the Energy Reorganization Act (42 U.S.C.A. §§ 5801–5879), which created two agencies with different missions. The NUCLEAR REGULATORY COMMISSION (NRC) is an independent agency responsible for safety and licensing. The Energy Research and Development Administration (ERDA), later absorbed into the Department of Energy, is responsible for promotion and development of nuclear power. This alignment did not completely remove fundamental regulatory conflict for the NRC, because the agency is responsible both for licensing plants and for safety oversight. If the NRC is too vigorous in exercising its safety role, the resulting compliance costs act as a disincentive to invest in nuclear plants.

A nuclear facility cannot be built without a construction permit issued by the NRC. An environmental impact statement that assesses the effect the facility will have on the environment must also be filed with the ENVIRONMENTAL PROTECTION AGENCY (EPA). Once built, a nuclear plant must operate pursuant to a LICENSE from the NRC. A license requires that the facility use the lowest levels of radiation necessary to reasonably and efficiently maintain operations. The NRC also issues licenses for the use of nuclear materials, for transportation of nuclear materials, and for the export and import of nuclear materials, facilities, and components.

Nuclear power regulation is highly centralized in the federal government when nuclear safety and radiological hazards are at issue. States may address the financial capability of power companies to dispose of waste and may define state TORT liability for injuries suffered at nuclear facilities.

Public confidence in the nuclear power industry suffered a major blow in 1979 when an accident occurred at the Three Mile Island Nuclear Station near Harrisburg, Pennsylvania. No one was hurt during the accident although radioactive gases did escape through the plant's ventilating system. The accident did reveal, however, the nuclear power industry's lack of emergency preparedness.

Following the incident at Three Mile Island, the NRC increased safety inspections, stepped up enforcement, required the retrofitting of systems to enhance safety, and developed emergency preparedness rules. These regulations delayed the opening of new nuclear plants during the early 1980s.

Nuclear power became less attractive to energy companies in the 1980s. The problem of disposing of nuclear waste became the focal point for the industry. Congress passed the Nuclear Waste Policy Act of 1982 (42 U.S.C.A. §§ 10101–10226), which directed the Department of Energy to formally begin planning the disposal of nuclear wastes and imposed most of the costs of disposal on the industry. The escalating costs of waste disposal helped bring construction of new nuclear facilities to a stop.

The problem of what to do with nuclear waste has proved to be difficult to solve. Nuclear material is contained in fuel rods. When spent fuel rods and other waste products fill the storage capacity at utility plants, the plants must either expand their storage capacity or find permanent off-site storage. Developing permanent nuclear waste sites is imperative because nuclear waste continues to accumulate. In addition, more than one hundred of the nuclear power facilities must be permanently shut down between 2010 and 2025 because

Nuclear Power Generation in the U.S., 1965 to 1995

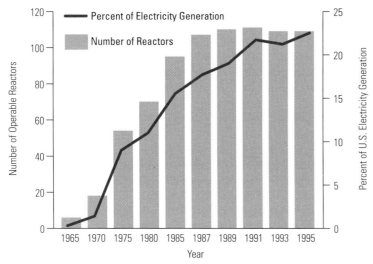

Source: U.S. Energy Information Administration, *Annual Energy Review.*

Nuclear Power Plants: Net Generation by Region in 1993

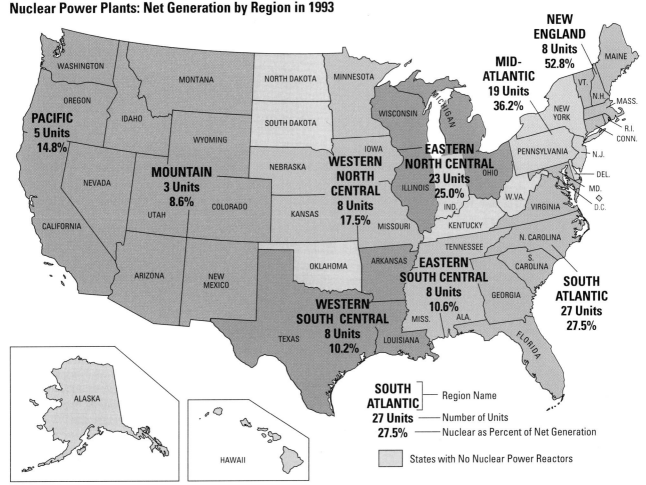

All three "mountain" region nuclear power reactors are located in Arizona.
There are no nuclear power reactors located in Oregon.

Source: U.S. Energy Power Administration, Electric Power Annual.

their equipment and infrastructure will no longer be safe. This will entail removing most radioactive elements within each plant's nuclear reactor and then razing the entire plant.

The federal government has encountered political controversy and public opposition when it has sought to identify potential permanent nuclear waste sites. Since 1986 it has been unsuccessful in finding an acceptable site. Yucca Mountain, Nevada, is the only place earmarked for a site study. Once a site is selected, opponents of the selection will likely challenge it in court, delaying the process even further.

The commercial prospects for nuclear energy have faded. The decommissioning of nuclear plants in the early twenty-first century will be a huge undertaking. The cost, per plant, will be more than one billion dollars. Utility customers will pay for the costs in higher utility rates, but power companies will have to devote significant amounts of time, energy, and money to complete the process.

Public confidence in the safety of nuclear energy has declined as well. The 1986 explosion of a nuclear reactor at Chernobyl in the Ukraine was devastating. Radiation fifty times higher than that at Three Mile Island exposed people nearest the reactor, and a cloud of radioactive fallout spread to Western Europe, causing the deaths of more than thirty people.

CROSS-REFERENCES

Energy Department; Environmental Law; Public Utilities; Solid Wastes, Hazardous Substances, and Toxic Pollutants.

NUCLEAR REGULATORY COMMISSION ▥ An independent regulatory agency that oversees the civilian use of NUCLEAR POWER in the United States. ▥

The Nuclear Regulatory Commission (NRC) licenses and regulates the uses of nuclear energy to protect the public health and safety and the environment. The NRC's prime responsibility is to ensure that the more than one hundred commercial nuclear power plants in the United

States conform to its regulations. It also regulates the use of nuclear materials used in the diagnosis and treatment of cancer, in sterilizing instruments, in smoke detectors, and in gauges used to detect explosives in luggage at airports.

The NRC was established under the provisions of the Energy Reorganization Act of 1974 (42 U.S.C.A. 5801) and Executive Order No. 11,834 of January 15, 1975 (40 F. R. 2971). These actions dissolved the Atomic Energy Commission (AEC) and transferred the AEC's licensing and regulatory functions to the NRC. The AEC, which had both regulated and promoted nuclear power, fell out of favor because of these conflicting roles. Congress believed that the NRC, which has only a regulatory function, would better protect public health and safety, because it has no direct interest in the promotion of nuclear energy. The 1974 act also created the Energy Research and Development Administration to handle the promotion of nuclear energy. This agency became part of the Department of Energy in 1977.

The major components of the NRC are the Office of Nuclear Reactor Regulation, the Office of Nuclear Material Safety and Safeguards, the Office of Nuclear Regulatory Research, and the Office of Enforcement. The agency has its headquarters in Rockville, Maryland, and it has four regional offices. The president appoints the five members of the commission.

NRC fulfills its responsibilities through a system of licensing and regulation. The Office of Nuclear Reactor Regulation licenses the construction and operation of nuclear reactors and other nuclear facilities. It regulates site selection, design, construction, operation maintenance, and the decommissioning of facilities.

The Office of Nuclear Material Safety and Safeguards licenses and regulates the processing, handling, and transportation of nuclear materials. This office ensures the safe disposal of nuclear waste and is responsible for reviewing and assessing the safeguards against potential threats, thefts, and sabotage for all licensed facilities.

The Office of Nuclear Regulatory Research performs research to confirm reactor safety and to confirm the implementation of established safeguards and environmental protection policies. This office develops regulations, criteria, guides, standards, and codes that govern health, safety, the environment, and safeguards that pertain to all aspects of nuclear facilities.

The Office of Enforcement develops policies and programs that ensure the enforcement of NRC requirements. The office has the power to give violation notices, enforce fines, and order license modification, suspension, or revocation.

In the 1979 accident at the Three Mile Island nuclear power plant near Harrisburg,

Nuclear Regulatory Commission

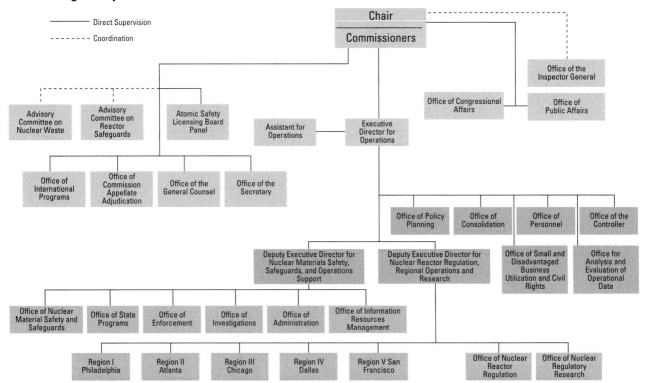

Pennsylvania, almost half of the reactor's core melted. Radioactive steam escaped, but no major injuries were reported. The credibility of the nuclear industry and the NRC fared badly after the accident. NRC responded by reexamining safety requirements and imposing new regulations to correct deficiencies. It also required each nuclear plant to create a plan for evacuating the population within a ten-mile radius of the plant in the event of a reactor accident. Plant owners must work with state and local police, fire, and civil defense authorities to devise an emergency plan that is then tested and evaluated by the NRC and the FEDERAL EMERGENCY MANAGEMENT AGENCY.

CROSS-REFERENCES

Energy Department; Public Utilities; Solid Wastes, Hazardous Substances, and Toxic Pollutants.

NUDUM PACTUM 📖 [*Latin, Naked pact.*] A promise to pay or provide or perform something without receiving anything in return, but merely out of affection or good will. 📖

Nudum pactum is another name for a NAKED CONTRACT.

NUGATORY 📖 Invalid; lacking legal force. 📖

A statute is nugatory if it has been declared unconstitutional.

NUISANCE 📖 A legal ACTION to redress harm arising from the use of one's PROPERTY. 📖

The two types of nuisance are private nuisance and public nuisance. A private nuisance is a civil wrong; it is the unreasonable, unwarranted, or unlawful use of one's property in a manner that substantially interferes with the enjoyment or use of another individual's property, without an actual TRESPASS or physical invasion to the land. A public nuisance is a criminal wrong; it is an act or omission that obstructs, damages, or inconveniences the rights of the community.

Public Nuisance   The term *public nuisance* covers a wide variety of minor crimes that threaten the health, morals, safety, comfort, convenience, or welfare of a community. Violators may be punished by a criminal sentence, a fine, or both. A defendant may also be required to remove a nuisance or to pay the costs of removal. For example, a manufacturer who has polluted a stream might be fined and might also be ordered to pay the cost of cleanup. Public nuisances may interfere with public health, such as in the keeping of diseased animals or a malarial pond. Public safety nuisances include shooting fireworks in the streets, storing explosives, practicing medicine without a license, or harboring a vicious dog. Houses of PROSTITUTION, illegal liquor establishments, GAMING houses, and unlicensed prizefights are examples of nuisances that interfere with public morals. Obstructing a highway or creating a condition to make travel unsafe or highly disagreeable are examples of nuisances threatening the public convenience.

A public nuisance interferes with the public as a class, not merely one person or a group of citizens. No civil REMEDY exists for a private citizen harmed by a public nuisance, even if her harm was greater than the harm suffered by others; a criminal prosecution is the exclusive remedy. However, if the individual suffers harm that is different from that suffered by the general public, she may maintain a tort action for DAMAGES. For example, if dynamiting has thrown a large boulder onto a public highway, those who use the highway cannot maintain a nuisance action for the inconvenience. However, a motorist who is injured from colliding with the boulder may bring a tort action for personal injuries.

Some nuisances can be both public and private in certain circumstances where the public nuisance substantially interferes with the use of an individual's adjoining land. For example, POLLUTION of a river might constitute both a public and a private nuisance. This is known as a mixed nuisance.

Private Nuisance   A private nuisance is an interference with a person's enjoyment and use of his land. The law recognizes that landowners, or those in rightful possession of land, have the right to the unimpaired condition of the property and to REASONABLE comfort and convenience in its occupation.

Examples of private nuisances abound. Nuisances that interfere with the physical condition of the land include vibration or blasting that damages a house, destruction of crops, raising of a water table, or the pollution of soil, a stream, or an underground water supply. Examples of nuisances interfering with the comfort, convenience, or health of an occupant are foul odors, noxious gases, smoke, dust, loud noises, excessive light, or high temperatures. Moreover, a nuisance may also disturb an occupant's mental tranquility, such as a neighbor who keeps a vicious dog, even though an injury is only threatened in the future.

An attractive nuisance is a danger likely to lure children onto a person's land. For example, an individual who has a pool on his property has a legal obligation to take reasonable precautions, such as erecting a fence, to prevent foreseeable injury to children.

Trespass is sometimes confused with nuisance, but the two are distinct. A trespass action protects against an invasion of one's right to exclusive possession of land. If a landowner drops a tree across her neighbor's boundary line she has committed a trespass; if her dog barks all night keeping the neighbor awake, she may be liable for nuisance.

Legal Responsibility A private nuisance is a tort, that is, a civil wrong. To determine accountability for an alleged nuisance, a court will examine three factors: the defendant's fault, whether there has been a substantial interference with the plaintiff's interest, and the reasonableness of the defendant's conduct.

Fault FAULT means that the defendant intentionally, negligently, or recklessly interfered with the plaintiff's use and enjoyment of the land or that the defendant continued her conduct after learning of actual harm or substantial RISK of future harm to the plaintiff's interest. For example, a defendant who continues to spray chemicals into the air after learning that they are blowing onto the plaintiff's land is deemed to be intending that result. Where it is alleged that a defendant has violated a statute, proving the elements of the statute will establish fault.

Substantial Interference The law is not intended to remedy trifles or redress petty annoyances. To establish LIABILITY under a nuisance theory, interference with the plaintiff's interest must be substantial. Determining substantial interference in cases where the physical condition of the property is affected will often be fairly straightforward. More challenging are those cases predicated on personal inconvenience, discomfort, or annoyance. To determine whether an interference is substantial, courts apply the standard of an ordinary member of the community with normal sensitivity and temperament. A plaintiff cannot, by putting his land to an unusually sensitive use, make a nuisance out of the defendant's conduct that would otherwise be relatively harmless.

Reasonableness of Defendant's Conduct If the interference with the plaintiff's interest is substantial, a determination must then be made that it is unreasonable for the plaintiff to bear it or to bear it without compensation. This is a balancing process weighing the respective interests of both parties. The law recognizes that the activities of others must be accommodated to a certain extent, particularly in matters of industry, commerce, or trade. The nature and gravity of the harm is balanced against the burden of preventing the harm and the usefulness of the conduct.

The following are factors to be considered:
- Extent and duration of the disturbance;
- Nature of the harm;
- Social value of the plaintiff's use of his property or other interest;
- Burden to the plaintiff in preventing the harm;
- Value of the defendant's conduct, in general and to the particular community;
- Motivation of the defendant;
- Feasibility of the defendant's mitigating or preventing the harm;
- Locality and suitability of the uses of the land by both parties.

ZONING boards use these factors to enact restrictions of property uses in specific locations. In this way, zoning laws work to prohibit public nuisances and to maintain the quality of a neighborhood.

Defenses In an attempt to escape liability, a defendant may argue that legislation (such as zoning laws or licenses) authorizes a particular activity. Legislative authority will not excuse a defendant from liability if the conduct is unreasonable.

A defendant may not escape liability by arguing that others are also contributing to the harm; damages will be apportioned according to a defendant's share of the blame. Moreover, a defendant is liable even where her actions without the actions of others would not have constituted a nuisance.

Defendants sometimes argue that a plaintiff "came to a nuisance" by moving onto land next to an already operating source of interference. A new owner is entitled to the reasonable use and enjoyment of her land the same as anyone else, but the argument may be considered in determining the reasonableness of the defendant's conduct. It may also have an impact in determining damages, because the purchase price may have reflected the existence of the nuisance.

Remedies Redress for nuisance is commonly monetary damages. An INJUNCTION or ABATEMENT may also be proper under certain circumstances. An injunction orders a defendant to stop, remove, restrain, or restrict a nuisance or abandon plans for a threatened nuisance. In public nuisance cases, a fine or sentence may be imposed, in addition to abatement or injunctive relief.

Injunction is a drastic remedy, used only when damage or the threat of damage is irreparable and not satisfactorily compensable only by monetary damages. The court examines the economic hardships to the parties and the interest of the public in allowing the continuation of the enterprise.

A self-help remedy, abatement by the plaintiff, is available under limited circumstances.

This privilege must be exercised within a reasonable time after learning of the nuisance and usually requires NOTICE to the defendant and the defendant's failure to act. Reasonable force may be used to employ the abatement, and a plaintiff may be liable for unreasonable or unnecessary damages. For example, dead tree limbs extending dangerously over a neighbor's house may be removed by the neighbor in danger, after notifying the offending landowner of the nuisance. In cases where an immediate danger to health, property, or life exists, no notification is necessary.

See also LAND-USE CONTROL; TORT LAW.

NULL 📖 Of no legal validity, force, or effect; nothing. 📖

The term *null* as used in the phrase *null and* VOID refers to something that binds no one or is incapable of giving rise to any rights or duties under any circumstances.

NUNC PRO TUNC 📖 [*Latin, Now for then.*] When courts take some action *nunc pro tunc*, that action has retroactive legal effect, as though it had been performed at a particular, earlier date. 📖

The most common use of *nunc pro tunc* is to correct past clerical ERRORS, or omissions made by the court, that may hinder the efficient operation of the legal system. For example, if the written record of a trial court's JUDGMENT failed to correctly recite the judgment as the court rendered it, the court has the inherent power to change the record at a later date to reflect what happened at trial. The decision, as corrected, would be given legal force from the time of the initial decision so that neither party is prejudiced, or harmed, by the error. The purpose of *nunc pro tunc* is to correct errors or omissions to achieve the results intended by the court at the earlier time.

NUNCUPATIVE WILL 📖 The oral expression of a person's wishes as to the disposition of his or her property to be performed or to take effect after the person's death, dictated by the person in his or her final illness before a sufficient number of WITNESSES and afterward reduced to writing. 📖

Such WILLS are invalid in certain states and in others are valid only under certain circumstances.

NUREMBERG TRIALS The Nuremberg trials were a series of trials held between 1945 and 1949 in which the Allies prosecuted German military leaders, political officials, industrialists, and financiers for crimes they had committed during World War II.

The first trial took place in Nuremberg, Germany, and involved twenty-four top-ranking survivors of the National Socialist German Workers' Party (Nazi Party). The subsequent trials were held throughout Germany and involved approximately two hundred additional defendants, including Nazi physicians who performed vile experiments on human subjects, concentration camp commandants who ordered the extermination of their prisoners, and judges who upheld Nazi practices.

World War II began in 1939 when Germany invaded Poland. Over the next few years, the European Axis powers (Germany, Italy, Albania, Bulgaria, Hungary, and Romania) successfully invaded and occupied France, Belgium, Luxembourg, Denmark, Norway, Greece, Yugoslavia, Czechoslovakia, Finland, and the Netherlands. But when ADOLF HITLER's troops invaded the Soviet Union, the Nazi WAR machine stalled. By the end of the war, the Axis powers were battered and beleaguered, and in 1945 they unconditionally surrendered to the United States, the Soviet Union, Great Britain, and France (the four Allied powers).

Although the surrender of the Axis powers brought the war to its formal conclusion, the Third Reich had left an indelible imprint on the world. During Germany's attempted conquest and occupation of Europe and Asia, the Nazis slaughtered, tortured, starved, and tormented over six million Jews and countless others—including Catholics, prisoners of war, dissenters, intelligentsia, nobility, and other innocent civilians. As part of their systematic effort to extinguish persons they deemed subversive, dangerous, or impure, the Nazis constructed concentration camps around Europe where they murdered their victims in gas chambers and incinerated their bodies in crematories. Persons who escaped this fate were deported to Nazi labor camps where they were compelled upon threat of death to work for the Third Reich.

The Allies had been discussing the idea of punishing war criminals since 1943 when U.S. president FRANKLIN D. ROOSEVELT, British prime minister Winston Churchill, and Soviet premier JOSEPH STALIN signed the Moscow Declaration promising to hold the Axis powers, particularly Germany, Italy, and Japan, responsible for any atrocities they committed during World War II. In 1944 Roosevelt and Churchill briefly entertained the idea of summarily executing the highest-ranking members of the Third Reich without a trial or legal proceeding of any kind.

However, by June of 1945, when delegations from the four Allied powers gathered in London at the International Conference of Military Trials, the U.S. representatives firmly believed that the Nazi leaders could not be executed without first being afforded the opportunity to defend themselves in a judicial proceeding. Principles of justice, fairness, and DUE PROCESS, delegates from the United States argued, required no less. U.S. leaders also feared that the Allies would be perceived as hypocritical for denying the vanquished powers the same basic legal rights that were denied to those persons summarily executed by Germany, Italy, and Japan during the war.

On August 8, 1945, the four Allied powers signed a convention called the Agreement for the Prosecution and Punishment of the Major War Criminals of the European Axis Powers, which set forth the parameters by which the accused would be tried. Under this convention, which is sometimes referred to as the London Agreement or Nuremberg Charter, the Allies would conduct the trials of leaders of the European Axis powers in Nuremberg, and would subsequently prosecute lower-ranking officials and less important figures in the four occupied zones of Germany. American military tribunals in the South Pacific, under the command of General Douglas MacArthur, tried accused Japanese war criminals.

The London Agreement also established the International Military Tribunal (IMT), which was a panel of eight judges, two named by each of the four Allied powers. One judge from each country actively presided at trial, and the other four sat on the panel as alternates. The four Allied powers also selected the prosecutors, who agreed to pursue a conviction against the defendants on behalf of the newly formed UNITED NATIONS.

Under the Nuremberg Charter, each defendant accused of a war crime was afforded the right to be represented by an attorney of his choice. The accused war criminals were presumed innocent by the tribunal and could not be convicted until their guilt was proven BEYOND A REASONABLE DOUBT. In addition, the defendants were guaranteed the right to challenge incriminating EVIDENCE, cross-examine adverse witnesses, and introduce exculpatory evidence of their own.

The court appointed interpreters to translate the proceedings into four languages: French, German, Russian, and English. Written evidence submitted by the prosecution was translated into the native language of each defendant. When considering the admissibility of particular documents or testimony, the IMT was not bound by technical rules of evidence common to Anglo-American systems of justice. The tribunal retained discretion to evaluate

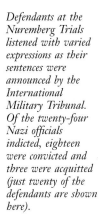

Defendants at the Nuremberg Trials listened with varied expressions as their sentences were announced by the International Military Tribunal. Of the twenty-four Nazi officials indicted, eighteen were convicted and three were acquitted (just twenty of the defendants are shown here).

HEARSAY and other forms of evidence that are normally considered unreliable in the United States and Great Britain.

The IMT made all of its decisions by a majority vote of the four judges. On issues that divided the judges equally, the president of the court, Lord Justice Geoffrey Lawrence from Great Britain, was endowed with the deciding vote. In all other situations, a vote cast by Lawrence carried no greater weight than a vote cast by Soviet judge Ion Nikitchenko, French judge Henri Donnedieu de Vabres, American judge FRANCIS BIDDLE, or any of the alternates. The IMT's decisions, including any rulings, judgments, or sentences, were final and could not be appealed.

Neither the defense nor the prosecution was permitted to challenge the legal, political, or military authority of the court. The IMT said that its JURISDICTION stemmed from the London Agreement that was promulgated by the Allies pursuant to their inherent legislative powers over the conquered nations, which had unconditionally surrendered. According to the tribunal, each Ally possessed the unqualified right to legislate over the territory that it occupied. By establishing the IMT, the court said, the Allies "had done together what any one of them might have done singly."

The IMT was given authority to hear four counts of criminal complaints: CONSPIRACY, crimes against peace, war crimes, and crimes against humanity. Count I encompassed conspiracies to commit crimes against peace, whereas count II covered persons who committed such crimes in their individual capacities. Crimes against peace included the planning, preparation, initiation, and waging of aggressive war in violation of international treaties, agreements, or assurances. Crimes against peace differed from other war crimes, the tribunal said, in that they represented the "accumulated evil" of the Axis powers.

Count III consisted of war crimes committed in violation of the laws and customs of war as accepted and practiced around the world. This count aimed to punish those individuals who were responsible for issuing or executing orders that resulted in the plundering of public and private property, the wanton destruction of European cities and villages, the murder of captured Allied soldiers, and the CONSCRIPTION of civilians in occupied territories for deportation to German labor camps.

Count IV consisted of crimes against humanity, including murder, extermination, enslavement, and other inhumane acts committed against civilian populations, as well as every form of political, racial, and religious persecution carried out in furtherance of a crime punishable by the IMT. This count aimed to punish the most notorious crimes committed by the Nazi regime, such as GENOCIDE and torture. Early in the trial, however, the IMT ruled that the court did not have authority to try the defendants for crimes they committed before 1939 when World War II began.

Many of the prospective Nazi defendants were dead or could not be found after the war. Adolf Hitler, the totalitarian dictator of Germany who was the emotional and intellectual catalyst behind most of the war crimes committed by the Nuremberg defendants, Heinrich Himmler, head of the SS (*Schutzstaffel*, or Blackshirts, the Nazi organization in charge of the concentration camps and the Gestapo, the German secret police), and Paul Joseph Goebbels, the Nazi minister of propaganda, had all killed themselves during the final days of the war. BENITO MUSSOLINI, totalitarian dictator of Italy, was shot and hung by his own people in Milan in April 1945. Other German officials such as Karl Adolf Eichmann, a lieutenant colonel in the SS who was the architect of Hitler's "final solution" to exterminate the Jewish population in Europe and Asia, and Dr. Josef Mengele, a physician who performed barbaric experiments on prisoners at the concentration camp in Auschwitz, Poland, eluded the Allies by fleeing Germany after the war.

Not all of the Nazi leadership was able to escape justice. Twenty-four Nazi officials were indicted under the Nuremberg Charter for war crimes. The tribunal convicted eighteen of the defendants and acquitted three defendants (Dr. Hjalmar H. G. Schacht, president of the German Central Bank, Hans Fritzsche, propaganda minister for German radio, and Franz von Papen, vice chancellor of Germany). One defendant (Dr. Robert Ley, leader of the Nazi Labor Front) committed suicide before the proceedings began; one defendant (Gustav Krupp von Bohlen und Halbach, a German military industrialist) was deemed mentally and physically incompetent to stand trial; and one defendant (Martin Bormann, Hitler's secretary and head of the Nazi Party Chancellery) was tried and convicted in absentia because his whereabouts were unknown.

The trial began on November 20, 1945, and concluded on October 1, 1946. Thirty-three witnesses testified for the prosecution. Eighty witnesses testified for the defense, including nineteen of the defendants. An additional 140 witnesses provided evidence for the defense through written INTERROGATORIES. The prosecution introduced written evidence of its own, including original military, diplomatic, and government files of the Nazi regime that fell into the hands of the Allies after the collapse of the Third Reich.

ROBERT H. JACKSON, an associate justice of the U.S. Supreme Court, led the prosecution team. President HARRY S. TRUMAN had asked Jackson to assemble a staff of U.S. attorneys to investigate alleged war crimes and present evidence against the defendants. Jackson was joined on the prosecution team by Roman Rudenko, François de Menthon, and Sir Hartley Shawcross, the chief prosecutors for Russia, France, and Great Britain, respectively. Each of the four powers employed a number of assistant prosecutors as well.

Jackson commenced the trial with an opening statement that is considered one of the most eloquent in the annals of jurisprudence. "The wrongs which we seek to condemn and punish," Jackson said, "have been so calculated, so malignant, and so devastating that civilization cannot tolerate their being ignored because it cannot survive their being repeated. . . . That four great nations, flushed with victory and stung with injury, stay the hand of vengeance and voluntarily submit their captive enemies to judgment of the law is one of the most significant tributes that power has ever paid to reason."

Hermann Goering was the most powerful surviving member of the German government to be tried at Nuremberg. Goering had been elected president of the Reichstag (the German parliament) in 1932. After Hitler was named chancellor of Germany in 1933, Goering was appointed minister of interior for Prussia where he created the Gestapo and established the first concentration camps. In 1935 Goering became chief of the Luftwaffe (the German air force), and two years later he was made commissioner of the Four Year Plan, an economic program designed to make Germany self-sufficient in preparation for the ensuing Nazi blitzkrieg. After Germany's invasion of Finland in 1939, Goering was elevated to Reich marshall, the highest military rank in Germany, and designated as Hitler's successor in the event of Hitler's death.

The IMT convicted the Reich marshall on all four counts and sentenced him to death. The prosecution demonstrated that Goering had helped plan and direct the invasions of Poland and Austria. Other evidence indicated that Goering had ordered the Luftwaffe to destroy a business district in Rotterdam, Netherlands, even though the city had already surrendered.

Goering was also implicated in the extermination of Polish intelligentsia, nobility, and clergy, the execution of British prisoners of war, the deportation of foreign laborers to Germany, the theft of art from French museums, and the suppression of domestic political opposition. Additionally, Goering admitted on CROSS-EXAMINATION that he was responsible for promulgating laws that had facilitated the persecution of Jews throughout Europe.

Rudolph Hess was another influential Nazi official prosecuted at Nuremberg. Hess was a longtime friend of Hitler. In 1923 the two joined forces in an unsuccessful attempt to incite a Nazi revolution in a Munich tavern. Although Hitler was arrested and convicted of treason for his role in the so-called beer hall putsch, German interest in the Nazi movement grew after the publication of *Mein Kampf*, a manifesto Hitler dictated to Hess while serving his prison term. *Mein Kampf* planted the seeds of Aryan supremacy, German nationalism, anti-Semitism, and totalitarian government, seeds that Hess later cultivated in his capacity as deputy führer to the Third Reich.

During the Nuremberg trial, the prosecution offered evidence that Hess had signed orders authorizing the persecution of European Jews and the ransacking of churches. Documents signed by Hess and meetings he attended reflected his support for Hitler's plan to invade Czechoslovakia, Poland, France, Belgium, Luxembourg, and the Netherlands. Hess originally asserted a defense of amnesia to these charges, claiming that he had forgotten the entire period of his life in which he had acted as deputy führer. However, Hess withdrew this defense upon realizing that he would not stand trial with the other defendants if he were diagnosed as incompetent. Hess was convicted of counts I and II and sentenced to life imprisonment.

Joachim von Ribbentrop, Germany's foreign minister during World War II, was convicted on all four counts and sentenced to death. When he took the witness stand, the prosecution asked him if he considered Germany's invasions of Poland, Denmark, Norway, Greece, France, and the Soviet Union "acts of aggression." In each case Ribbentrop answered in the negative, arguing that such invasions were more properly described as acts of war. Confronted with evidence that he had urged the German regent of Hungary to exterminate the Jews in that country, Ribbentrop responded only by saying that he did not use those words exactly.

Dr. Ernst Kaltenbrunner was the head of the Reich Central Security Office, the Nazi organi-

Robert H. Jackson was the Chief U.S. Prosecutor at the Nuremberg Trials. He and the three other Allied prosecutors sought convictions of accused war criminals on behalf of the United Nations.

zation in charge of the Gestapo and the SD (*Sicherheitsdienst*, Security Service, the German intelligence agency) and was second in command to Himmler at the SS. Kaltenbrunner faced a mountain of evidence demonstrating that he visited a number of concentration camps and had personally witnessed prisoners being gassed and incinerated. One letter signed by Kaltenbrunner authorized the execution of Allied prisoners of war, and another letter authorized the conscription and deportation of foreign laborers. Laborers who were too weak to contribute, Kaltenbrunner wrote, should be executed, regardless of their age or gender. Kaltenbrunner received a death sentence after being convicted under counts III and IV.

Alfred Rosenberg was the Nazi minister for the occupied Eastern European territories. Rosenberg told Axis troops that the accepted rules of land warfare could be disregarded in areas under his control. He ordered the segregation of Jews into ghettos where his subordinates murdered them. His signature was found at the bottom of a directive approving the deportation of forty-five thousand youths to German labor camps. Cross-examined about his role in the unlawful confiscation of Jewish property, Rosenberg claimed that all such property was seized to protect it from Allied bomb-

ing raids. Rosenberg was found guilty on all four counts and sentenced to death by hanging.

Hans Frank, the governor-general of Poland during German occupation, was sentenced to hang after being convicted on counts III and IV. Frank described his administration's policy by stating that Poland was "treated like a colony" in which the Polish people became "the slaves of the Greater German World Empire." The tribunal found that this policy entailed the destruction of Poland as a national entity, the evisceration of all political opposition, and the ruthless exploitation of human resources to promote Hitler's reign of terror. While on the witness stand, Frank confessed to participating in the Nazis' systematic attempt to annihilate the Jewish race.

Wilhelm Frick, the German minister of interior, was found guilty on counts I, II, and III and sentenced to be hanged. Frick had signed decrees sanctioning the execution of Jews and other persons held in "protective custody" at the concentration camps and had given Himmler a blank check to take any "security measures" necessary to ensure the German foothold in the occupied territories. The tribunal also determined that Frick exercised supreme authority over Bohemia and Moravia and was responsible for implementing Hitler's policies of enslavement, deportation, torture, and extermination in these territories.

Wilhelm Keitel, field marshall for the High Command of the armed forces, was sentenced to die after being found guilty on every count. On direct examination Keitel admitted that there were "a large number of orders" bearing his signature that "contained deviations from existing international law." He also conceded that a number of atrocities had been committed under his command during Germany's invasion of the Soviet Union. As a defense to these charges, Keitel asserted that he had been following the orders of his superiors when committing these crimes. Yet some witnesses testifying on behalf of the defense tended to undermine this assertion.

Alfred Jodl, chief of the operations staff for the armed forces, also received the death sentence after being convicted on every count. During the early stages of World War II, Jodl had been asked to review an order drafted by Hitler authorizing German troops to execute all Soviet military commissars captured during the Nazi invasion of Russia. Aware that this order was a violation of the customs, practices, and laws governing the treatment of prisoners during times of war, Jodl made no attempt to dissuade Hitler from issuing it. Jodl was also found responsible for distributing an order that authorized the execution of Allied commandos caught by the Axis powers and for mobilizing the German army against its European foes.

Julius Streicher, an anti-Semitic propagandist, was found guilty of count IV and sentenced to death. Author, editor, and publisher of *Der Stuermer*, a privately owned Jew-baiting newspaper, Streicher held no meaningful government position with the Axis powers during World War II. Yet the tribunal determined that circulation of Streicher's racist newspaper had fueled the Nazis' maniacal hatred of Jews and fomented an atmosphere in which genocide was acceptable and desirable. The prosecution introduced an article Streicher had published during 1942 in which he described Jewish procreation as a curse of God that could only be lifted through a process of political and ethnic emasculation.

Albert Speer, Nazi minister of armaments, received a prison term of twenty years after being convicted on counts III and IV. Speer had fascinated Hitler long before the war with his architectural prowess, designing buildings that were both immense and imposing. After the war began, however, Speer's primary obligation was to supply the German armed forces with military supplies, equipment, and weapons.

Thus, Speer became a lynchpin in the Nazi military empire. In an effort to maintain this empire, the prosecution demonstrated, Speer had repeatedly cajoled Hitler to procure foreign labor to work in his weapons factories.

Dr. Arthur Seyss-Inquart, an Austrian who was appointed by Hitler to govern Austria and the Netherlands during German occupation, was found guilty on counts II, III, and IV and sentenced to death for his confessed mistreatment of racial minorities in those territories, including the deportation of more than 250,000 Jews to Germany. Seyss-Inquart also assisted Hitler's takeover of Austria, Poland, and Czechoslovakia.

Baron Konstantin von Neurath, Reich protector of Czechoslovakia, was convicted on all four counts and sentenced to fifteen years in prison for participating in the Nazi militarization campaign. Hoping to immunize the Nazi regime from its obligations under INTERNATIONAL LAW, Neurath had advocated Germany's withdrawal from the LEAGUE OF NATIONS and denounced the Versailles Treaty that had formally concluded World War I. Neurath was also implicated in various brutalities committed against the Czechoslovakian civilian population.

Baldur von Schirach, governor of occupied Vienna and leader of the Hitler Youth, was convicted on count IV and sentenced to a twenty-year prison term. The IMT determined that Schirach had provided the visceral foundations for the militarization of Germany's youngest Nazis through psychological and educational indoctrination and had conspired with Hitler to deport Viennese Jews to Poland where most of them met their death. Fritz Sauckel, the plenipotentiary general for the allocation of labor, was convicted on counts III and IV and sentenced to death for his central role in the Nazi forced labor program that enslaved more than eleven million Europeans.

Erich Raeder served as Germany's naval commander and chief until 1943 when he resigned due to a disagreement with Hitler, and he was succeeded by Karl Doenitz. Both Raeder and Doenitz were indicted under counts I, II, and III for war crimes committed on the high seas, and both were convicted based in part on evidence that they had authorized German submarines to fire on Allied commercial ships without warning in contravention of international law. Doenitz was sentenced to a ten-year prison term, and Raeder received a life sentence. Walther Funk, Nazi minister of economics, also received a life sentence for financing Germany's aggressive warfare and for exploiting foreign laborers in German industry.

The IMT declared four Nazi organizations to be criminal: the SS, the SD, the Gestapo, and the Nazi Party. A team of Allied attorneys, including American Telford Taylor, subsequently prosecuted individual members of these organizations. Three Nazi organizations were acquitted: the SA (*Sturmabteilung*, the paramilitary organization also known as the Brownshirts or Stormtroopers), and the general staff and High Command of the German armed forces.

The Nuremberg trials made three important contributions to international law. First, they established a PRECEDENT that all persons, regardless of their station or occupation in life, can be held individually accountable for their behavior during times of war. Defendants cannot insulate themselves from personal responsibility by blaming the country, government, or military branch for which they committed the particular war crime.

Second, the Nuremberg trials established that individuals cannot shield themselves from liability for war crimes by asserting that they were simply following orders issued by a superior in the chain of command. Subordinates in the military or government are now bound by their obligations under international law, obligations that transcend their duty to obey an order issued by a superior. Orders to initiate aggressive (as opposed to defensive) warfare, to violate recognized rules and customs of warfare, or to persecute civilians and prisoners are considered illegal under the Nuremberg principles.

Third, the Nuremberg trials clearly established three discrete substantive war crimes that are punishable under international law: crimes against peace, crimes against humanity, and crimes in violation of transnational obligations embodied in treaties and other agreements. Before the Nuremberg trials, these crimes were not well defined, and persons who committed such crimes had never been punished by a multinational tribunal. For these reasons the Nuremberg convictions have sometimes been criticized as ex post facto justice.

The Nuremberg trials have also been criticized as "victor's justice." Historians have observed that the Allied nations that tried and convicted the leading Nazis at Nuremberg did not come to the table with clean hands. The Soviet Union had participated in Germany's invasion and occupation of Poland and had been implicated in the massacre of more than a thousand Poles in the Katyn forest. Bombing raids conducted by the United States and Great Britain during World War II left thousands of civilians dead in cities like Dresden, Germany, and Nagasaki and Hiroshima, Japan. President Roosevelt had implemented a relocation program for more than 100,000 Americans of Japanese descent that confined them to concentration camps around the United States.

However, the Nuremberg trials were not typical partisan trials. The defendants were afforded the RIGHT TO COUNSEL, plus a full panoply of evidentiary and procedural protections. The Nuremberg VERDICTS demonstrate that these protections were taken seriously by the tribunal. The IMT completely exonerated three defendants of war crimes and acquitted most of the remaining defendants of at least some charges. Thus, the Nuremberg trials, while not perfect, changed the face of international law, both procedurally and substantively.

See also TOKYO TRIALS.

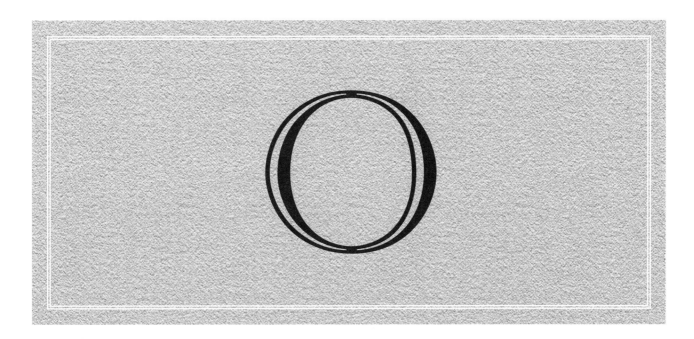

OATH 📖 Any type of ATTESTATION by which an individual signifies that he or she is bound in conscience to perform a particular act truthfully and faithfully; a solemn declaration of truth or obligation.

An individual's appeal to God to witness the truth of what he or she is saying or a pledge to do something enforced by the individual's responsibility to answer to God. 📖

Similarly an AFFIRMATION is a solemn and formal declaration that a statement is true; however, an affirmation includes no reference to God so it can be made by someone who does not believe in God or by an individual who has conscientious objections against swearing to God. Provisions in state statutes or constitutions ordinarily allow affirmations to be made as alternatives to oaths.

In order for an oath to be legally effective, it must be administered by a public official. The law creating each public office and describing the duties of the official ordinarily indicates who is authorized to administer the oath of office. A spoken oath is generally sufficient; however, a written and signed oath can be required by law.

The most famous oath prescribed by law in the United States is the oath repeated by the president-elect upon taking the office of the presidency.

OBITER DICTUM 📖 [*Latin, By the way.*] Words of an opinion entirely unnecessary for the decision of the case. A remark made or opinion expressed by a judge in a decision upon a cause, "by the way," that is, incidentally or collaterally, and not directly upon the question before the court or upon a point not necessarily involved in the determination of the cause, or introduced by way of illustration, or analogy or argument. Such are not binding as PRECEDENT. 📖

See also COURT OPINION.

OBJECT 📖 As a verb, to take exception to something; to declare or express the belief that something is improper or illegal.

As a noun, the thing sought to be accomplished or attained; aim; purpose; intention. 📖

One might, for example, object to the admission of particular EVIDENCE at a trial.

The object of a civil suit, for example, might be to be compensated in the form of DAMAGES for an injury incurred.

OBJECTION 📖 A formal ATTESTATION or declaration of disapproval concerning a specific point of law or procedure during the course of a trial; a statement indicating disagreement with a judge's ruling. 📖

Some laws provide that an APPEAL to a higher tribunal can be based only upon errors objected

Television and movies have made us familiar with the oath required of witnesses at trial, but many public offices require an oath to uphold the obligations and honor of that office. Here George W. Bush is sworn in as Governor of Texas by Texas Chief Justice Thomas Phillips.

to during the course of a trial conducted in a lower court. An ERROR that initially slips by without any objection by the party's counsel cannot subsequently be set forth as a reason for the appeals court to overturn the original decision in a particular case. The making of objections in open court during the course of a proceeding is important so that on appeal, the APPELLATE COURT can evaluate the record of the lower court action.

The Federal Rules of Evidence, the Federal Rules of Civil Procedure, and the Federal Rules of Criminal Procedure govern the making of objections in federal actions. Comparable state provisions apply to state proceedings.

See also CIVIL PROCEDURE; EVIDENCE.

OBLIGATION A generic term for any type of legal DUTY or LIABILITY.

In its original sense, the term *obligation* was very technical in nature and applied to the responsibility to pay money owed on certain written documents that were executed under SEAL. Currently obligation is used in reference to anything that an individual is required to do because of a PROMISE, vow, OATH, CONTRACT, or law. It refers to a legal or moral duty that an individual can be forced to perform or penalized for neglecting to perform.

An *absolute obligation* is one for which no legal alternative exists since it is an unconditional duty.

A *contractual obligation* arises as a result of an enforceable promise, agreement, or contract.

An *express obligation* is spelled out in direct and actual terms, and an *implied obligation* is inferred indirectly from the surrounding circumstances or from the actions of the individuals involved.

A *joint obligation* is one that binds two or more people to fulfill whatever is required, and a *several obligation* requires each of two or more individuals to fulfill the obligation in its entirety by himself or herself.

A *moral obligation* is binding upon the conscience and is fair but is not necessarily enforceable in law.

A *primary obligation* is one that must be performed since it is the main purpose of the contract that contains it, whereas a *secondary obligation* is only incidental to another principal duty or arises only in the event that the main obligation cannot be fulfilled.

A *penal obligation* is a PENALTY, such as the obligation to pay extra money if the terms or conditions of an agreement cannot be satisfied.

OBLIGEE The individual to whom a particular DUTY or OBLIGATION is owed.

The obligation might be to pay a DEBT or involve the performance or nonperformance of a particular act.

The term *obligee* is often used synonymously with CREDITOR.

OBLIGOR The individual who owes another person a certain DEBT or DUTY.

The term *obligor* is often used interchangeably with DEBTOR.

OBLITERATION A destruction; an eradication of written words.

Obliteration is a method of revoking a WILL or a clause therein. Lines drawn through the SIGNATURES of WITNESSES to a will constitute an obliteration of the will even if the names are still decipherable.

OBSCENE Offensive to recognized standards of decency.

The term *obscene* is applied to written, verbal, or visual works or conduct that treat sex in an objectionable or lewd or lascivious manner. Although the FIRST AMENDMENT guarantees freedom of expression, such constitutional protection is not extended to obscene works. To determine whether a work is obscene, the trier of fact applies the guidelines established by the Supreme Court in the case of *Miller v. California*, 413 U.S. 15, 93 S.Ct. 2607, 37 L.Ed.2d 419 (1973): whether the average person, applying contemporary community standards would find that the work depicting or describing sexual conduct when taken as a whole, appeals to the prurient interest; whether the work does so in a patently offensive way; and whether when taken as a whole, it lacks serious literary, artistic, political, or scientific value.

See also FREEDOM OF SPEECH; PORNOGRAPHY.

OBSCENITY The character or quality of being OBSCENE; an act, utterance, or item tending to corrupt the public morals by its indecency or LEWDNESS.

Obscenity is a legal term that applies to anything offensive to morals and is often equated with the term *pornography*. *Pornography*, however, is a more limited term, which refers to the erotic content of books, magazines, films, and recordings. Obscenity includes PORNOGRAPHY but may also include nude dancing, sexually oriented commercial telephone messages, and scatological comedy routines. U.S. courts have had a difficult time determining what is obscene. This problem has serious implications, because if an act or an item is deemed obscene, it is not protected by the FIRST AMENDMENT.

Until the mid-nineteenth century and the Victorian era in Great Britain and the United

States, sexually explicit material was not subject to statutory prohibition. The federal Comstock Law of 1873 criminalized the transmission and receipt of "obscene," "lewd," or "lascivious" publications through the U.S. mail. U.S. courts looked to the English case of *Regina v. Hicklin*, 3 L.R.-Q.B. 360 (1868), for a legal definition of obscenity. The *Hicklin* test was "whether the tendency of the matter charged as obscenity is to deprave and corrupt those whose minds are open to such immoral influences, and into whose hands a publication of this sort may fall."

This test permitted judges to look at objectionable words or passages without regard for the work as a whole and without respect to any artistic, literary, or scientific value the work might have. In 1930 Massachusetts courts declared both Theodore Dreiser's novel *An American Tragedy* and D. H. Lawrence's novel *Lady Chatterly's Lover* obscene. An important break from *Hicklin* came in a lawsuit over the U.S. publication of James Joyce's novel *Ulysses*. Both at the trial and APPELLATE levels, the FEDERAL COURTS held that the book was not obscene (*United States v. One Book Called "Ulysses,"* 5 F. Supp. 182 [S.D.N.Y. 1933], affirmed 72 F.2d 705 [2d Cir. 1934]). The courts rejected the *Hicklin* test and suggested a standard based on the effect on the average reader of the dominant theme of the work as a whole.

In 1957 the U.S. Supreme Court retired the *Hicklin* test in *Roth v. United States*, 354 U.S. 476, 77 S. Ct. 1304, 1 L. Ed. 2d 1498. Justice WILLIAM J. BRENNAN, JR., stated that obscenity is "utterly without redeeming social importance" and therefore was not protected by the First Amendment. He announced, as a new test, "whether to the average person, applying contemporary community standards, the dominant theme of the material taken as a whole appeals to a prurient [lewd or lustful] interest." The new test was applicable to every level of government in the United States.

The *Roth* test proved difficult to use because every term in it eluded a conclusive definition. The Supreme Court justices could not fully agree what constituted "prurient interest" or what "redeeming social importance" meant. Justice POTTER STEWART expressed this difficulty at defining obscenity when he remarked, "I know it when I see it" (*Jacobellis v. Ohio*, 378 U.S. 184, 84 S. Ct. 1676, 12 L. Ed. 2d 793 [1964]).

The Supreme Court added requirements to the definition of obscenity in a 1966 case involving the bawdy English novel *Fanny Hill*. In *Memoir v. Massachusetts*, 383 U.S. 413, 86 S. Ct.

HENRY HORENSTEIN/THE PICTURE CUBE

975, 16 L. Ed. 2d 1, the Court concluded that to establish obscenity, the material must, aside from appealing to the prurient interest, be "utterly without redeeming social value," and "patently offensive because it affronts contemporary community standards relating to the description of sexual matters." The requirement that the material be "utterly" without value made prosecution difficult. Defendants presented expert witnesses, such as well-known authors, critics, or scholars, who attested to the literary and artistic value of sexually charged books and films.

The Supreme Court did make conclusive rulings on two other areas of obscenity in the 1960s. In *Ginzburg v. United States*, 383 U.S. 463, 86 S. Ct. 942, 16 L. Ed. 2d 31 (1966), the Court held that "pandering" of material by mailed advertisements, designed to appeal to a prurient interest, could be prosecuted under the federal obscenity statute. Even if the material in publisher Ralph Ginzburg's *Eros* magazine was not obscene, the Court was willing to allow the government to punish Ginzburg for appealing to his prospective subscribers' prurient interest. In *Stanley v. Georgia*, 394 U.S. 557, 89 S. Ct. 1243, 22 L. Ed. 2d 542 (1969), the Court held that the First and Fourteenth Amendments prohibited making the private possession of obscene material a crime.

The failure of the WARREN COURT to achieve consensus over the *Roth* test kept the definition of obscenity in limbo. Then in 1973, aided by conservative justices LEWIS F. POWELL, JR., and WILLIAM H. REHNQUIST, Chief Justice WARREN EARL BURGER restated the constitutional definition of obscenity in *Miller v. California*, 413 U.S. 15, 93 S. Ct. 2607, 37 L. Ed. 2d 419. Burger explicitly rejected the "utterly without redeeming social value" standard:

Ambiguous language and shifting mores make obscenity laws difficult to interpret, and to prosecute. Courts must decide if the goods and services offered by an establishment violate "contemporary community standards" or if they have "redeeming social value."

The basic guidelines for the trier of fact must be (a) whether the "average person, applying contemporary community standards" would find that the work, taken as a whole, appeals to the prurient interest . . ., (b) whether the work depicts or describes, in a patently offensive way, sexual conduct specifically defined by the applicable state law, and (c) whether the work, taken as a whole, lacks serious literary, artistic, political, or scientific value.

Burger noted that the new test was intended to address " 'hard core' sexual conduct," which included "patently offensive representations or descriptions of ultimate sexual acts, normal or perverted, actual or simulated . . . masturbation, excretory functions, and lewd exhibitions of genitals."

In 1987 the Supreme Court modified the "contemporary community standards" criteria. In *Pope v. Illinois*, 481 U.S. 497, 107 S. Ct. 1918, 95 L. Ed. 2d 439, the Court stated that the "proper inquiry is not whether an ordinary member of any given community would find serious literary, artistic, political, and scientific value in allegedly obscene material, but whether a reasonable person would find such value in the material, taken as a whole." It is unclear whether the "reasonable person" standard represents a liberalization of the obscenity test.

In 1989 the Supreme Court unanimously held that the First Amendment's guarantee of free speech protected indecent, sexually explicit telephone messages (*Sable Communications of California, Inc. v. Federal Communications Commission*, 492 U.S. 115, 109 S. Ct. 2829, 106 L. Ed. 2d 93. The Court ruled that a federal law that attempted to ban "Dial-a-Porn" commercial phone services over interstate telephone lines (Pub. L. No. 100-297, 102 Stat. 424) to shield minors from obscenity was unconstitutional because it applied to indecent as well as obscene speech. The Court indicated, however, that obscene calls could be prohibited.

In 1996 President BILL CLINTON signed into law the Telecommunications Act of 1996. Title V of the act includes provisions of the Communications Decency Act of 1996 (CDA), codified at 47 U.S.C.A. § 223(b), as amended, 47 U.S.C.A. § 223(b). The CDA was designed to outlaw obscene and indecent sexual material in cyberspace, including the INTERNET. Section 223 makes it a federal crime to use TELECOMMUNICATIONS to transmit "any comment, request, suggestion, proposal, image, or other communication which is obscene or indecent,

knowing that the recipient of the communication is under 18 years of age, regardless of whether the maker of such communication placed the call or initiated the communication."

The AMERICAN CIVIL LIBERTIES UNION (ACLU) and twenty other plaintiffs immediately filed a lawsuit challenging the constitutionality of the CDA's provisions, especially that part of the CDA that deals with indecent material. The ACLU did not contest the prohibition on obscene material. In *American Civil Liberties Union v. Reno*, 929 F. Supp. 824 (E.D. P. 1996), the Supreme Court held that the CDA was unconstitutional because it violated the First Amendment (1997 WL 348012, No. 96–511, June 26, 1997).

CROSS-REFERENCES

Censorship; Dworkin, Andrea; Federal Communications Commission; Freedom of Speech; MacKinnon, Catharine; Mass Communications Law; Movie Rating; *Roth v. United States*; Theaters and Shows; X or XXX Rating.

OBSTRUCTION OF JUSTICE
A criminal offense that involves interference, through words or actions, with the proper operations of a COURT or OFFICERS OF THE COURT.

The integrity of the judicial system depends on the participants' acting honestly and without fear of reprisals. Threatening a judge, trying to bribe a witness, or encouraging the destruction of EVIDENCE are examples of obstruction of justice. Federal and state laws make it a crime to obstruct justice.

Obstruction of justice in the FEDERAL COURTS is governed by a series of criminal statutes (18 U.S.C.A. §§ 1501–1517), which aim to protect the integrity of federal judicial proceedings as well as agency and congressional proceedings. Section 1503 is the primary vehicle for punishing those who obstruct or who endeavor to obstruct federal judicial proceedings.

Section 1503 proscribes obstructions of justice aimed at judicial officers, grand and petit jurors, and witnesses. The law makes it a crime to threaten, intimidate, or retaliate against these participants in a criminal or civil proceeding. In addition, section 1503 makes it illegal to attempt the BRIBERY of an official to alter the outcome of a judicial proceeding.

Besides these specific prohibitions, section 1503 contains the Omnibus Clause, which states that a person who "corruptly or by threats of force, or by threatening letter or communication, influences, obstructs, or impedes, or endeavors to influence, obstruct, or impede, the due administration of justice" is guilty of the crime of obstruction of justice.

This clause offers broad protection to the "due administration of justice." Federal courts have read this clause expansively to proscribe any conduct that interferes with the judicial process.

To obtain a conviction under section 1503, the government must prove that there was a pending federal judicial proceeding, the defendant knew of the proceeding, and the defendant had corrupt intent to interfere with or attempted to interfere with the proceeding.

Two types of cases arise under the Omnibus Clause: the concealment, alteration, or destruction of documents; and the encouraging or rendering of false TESTIMONY. Actual obstruction is not needed as an element of PROOF to sustain a conviction. The defendant's endeavor to obstruct justice is sufficient. "Endeavor" has been defined by the courts as an effort to accomplish the purpose the statute was enacted to prevent. The courts have consistently held that "endeavor" constitutes a lesser threshold of purposeful activity than a criminal "attempt."

Federal obstruction of justice statutes have been used to prosecute government officials who have sought to prevent the disclosure of damaging information. The WATERGATE scandal of the 1970s involving President RICHARD M. NIXON is a classic example of this type of obstruction. A number of Nixon's top aides were convicted of obstruction of justice, including former attorney general JOHN N. MITCHELL. A federal GRAND JURY named Nixon himself as an unindicted coconspirator for the efforts to prevent disclosure of White House involvement in the 1972 burglary of Democratic National Committee headquarters at the Watergate building complex in Washington, D.C.

OCCUPANCY ⬙ Gaining or having physical possession of REAL PROPERTY subject to, or in the absence of, legal right or TITLE. ⬙

In a fire INSURANCE policy, for example, the term *occupancy* is used in reference to the purpose to which the land or building is devoted or adopted, as indicated in the policy.

OCCUPATION See MILITARY OCCUPATION.

OCCUPATIONAL DISEASE ⬙ A disease resulting from exposure during employment to conditions or substances that are detrimental to health (such as black lung disease contracted by miners). ⬙

An individual suffering from an occupational disease can seek compensation for his or her condition under WORKERS' COMPENSATION statutes or such federal legislation as the Black Lung Benefits Act of 1972, 30 U.S.C.A. § 901 et seq. Worker's compensation statutes typically require that the worker contract the disease during the COURSE OF EMPLOYMENT; that the disease be peculiar to the worker's job by virtue of how it is caused and manifested or how job conditions result in a particular hazard, unlike employment in general; and that there be a substantially greater risk of contracting the disease or condition on the job in a different, more serious manner, than in general public experiences.

OCCUPATIONAL SAFETY AND HEALTH ACT OF 1970 The Occupational Safety and Health Act, 29 U.S.C.A. § 651 et seq., makes it a federal MISDEMEANOR for businesses to risk negligently the lives or health of their workers.

The Occupational Safety and Health Act of 1970 created the Labor Department's Occupational Safety and Health Administration (OSHA) to serve as the federal government's workplace safety watchdog, and the Occupational Safety and Health Review Commission (OSHRC) to rule on cases, forwarded to it by the LABOR DEPARTMENT, of disagreements over the results of OSHA safety and health inspections.

The act authorizes civil fines up to $10,000 for instances where employers "willfully" expose workers to "serious" harm or death. Any act of CRIMINAL NEGLIGENCE can result in imprisonment of up to six months.

The Labor Department's assistant secretary for occupational safety and health has responsibility for overseeing OSHA. OSHA has its headquarters in Washington, D.C., and maintains ten regional offices. OSHA develops and promulgates occupational safety and health standards and issues regulations that enforce these standards. The heart of OSHA is its inspection responsibilities. OSHA inspectors conduct investigations and inspections to determine the status of compliance with safety and health standards and regulations. If an inspector visits a work site and finds that the employer is not in compliance with OSHA regulations, the inspector issues a citation and proposes penalties.

From its inception OSHA has been a controversial agency. Businesses have complained that OSHA regulations are often too bureaucratic, rigid, and hard to understand, making it difficult to comply with the standards. Organized labor, on the other hand, has charged that OSHA is not diligent enough in enforcing the regulations.

During the administration of President RONALD REAGAN, the number of OSHA inspectors was reduced by 25 percent, making it even more difficult to investigate ALLEGATIONS of injuries. In addition, President Reagan, by Execu-

Sources, Events of Exposure, and Nature of Resultant Occupational Illnesses or Injuries in 1994

Source of Injury or Illness

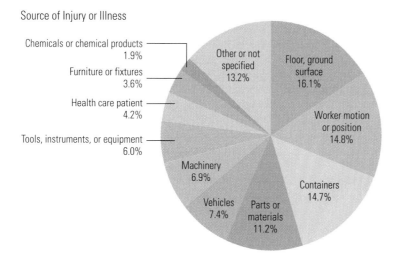

Event of Exposure

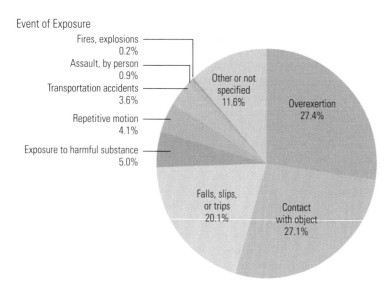

Nature of Injury

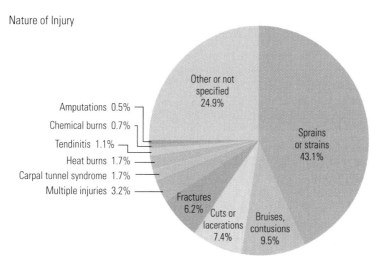

Source: U.S. Bureau of Labor Statistics, *Occupational Injuries and Illnesses in the United States by Industry*, annual.

tive Order No. 12,291 in 1981, permitted OSHA to certify that a company was in compliance with safety and health standards by reviewing paperwork submitted by the company.

OSHA standards and regulations touch every facet of workplace health and safety. The regulations establish maximum levels of exposure to lead, asbestos, chemicals, and other toxic substances. In addition, OSHA regulations specify the proper safety gear for workers. For example, construction workers who work on scaffolding or on structural steel must wear a safety harness.

OSHA works to improve health and safety through education and training programs. It also provides assistance to state occupational and health programs to maintain consistent national standards.

Employers have the right to dispute any alleged job safety or health violation found during an OSHA inspection, the penalties OSHA has proposed, or the time given by OSHA to correct any hazardous situation. Employees and union representatives may file a case challenging the propriety of the time OSHA has allowed for correction of any violation.

These cases are heard by OSHRC, an independent, quasi-judicial agency. A case arises when a citation is issued against the employer as a result of an OSHA inspection and the employer contests the citation within fifteen working days.

All cases that require a hearing are assigned to an administrative law judge (ALJ), who decides the case. The government has the burden of proving the case. A substantial number of the decisions of the ALJs become final orders of the commission. However, each decision is subject to discretionary review by the three members of the commission upon the direction of any one of the three, if done within thirty days of the filing of the decision. This means that a party dissatisfied with an ALJ decision does not have a right of APPEAL to the commission but must convince at least one commissioner to exercise discretion and agree to have the commission hear the appeal. When discretionary review is taken, the commission issues its own decision. Once a case is decided, any person adversely affected may file an appeal with the U.S. courts of appeals.

The principal office of the commission is in Washington, D.C. There are also three regional offices where commission judges are stationed.

CROSS-REFERENCES

Administrative Law and Procedure; Employment Law; Labor Law; Workers' Compensation.

O'CONNOR, SANDRA DAY

Sandra Day O'Connor was appointed to the U.S. Supreme Court in 1981, becoming the first female justice. O'Connor has established herself as a moderate conservative who prefers narrow, limited holdings.

Sandra Day was born on March 26, 1930, in El Paso, Texas. She grew up in a remote part of southeastern Arizona where her parents had a 160,000-acre ranch. She spent her winters in El Paso, where she lived with her grandmother while attending school. In 1950 she graduated from Stanford University with a major in economics. She then attended Stanford Law School, where she graduated third in her class in 1952. WILLIAM H. REHNQUIST, who would later become her colleague on the U.S. Supreme Court, ranked first in the same law school class.

After law school she married John O'Connor, an attorney. She hoped to join a law firm in Los Angeles or San Francisco, but none was willing to hire a woman attorney, although one did offer her a position as legal secretary. Instead O'Connor spent a year as a deputy county attorney in San Mateo, California. In 1953 she accompanied her husband, a member of the U.S. Army's Judge Advocate General's Corps, to West Germany. During the three years the couple spent in Germany, O'Connor worked as a civilian attorney for the Quartermaster Corps.

On their return from Germany in 1957, O'Connor and her husband settled in Phoenix, where she entered private practice. She soon became active in state and local government, serving as a member of the Maricopa County Board of Adjustments and Appeals (1960–1963) and the Governor's Committee on Marriage and the Family (1965). From 1965 to 1969 she served as assistant attorney general for Arizona.

In 1969 O'Connor was appointed to fill a vacancy in the Arizona Senate. She won election to a full term in 1970 and was reelected in 1972. After her reelection her colleagues elected her majority leader, making her the first woman in the country to hold such a position.

Sandra Day O'Connor

"THE PURPOSE OF STRICT SCRUTINY IS TO 'SMOKE OUT' ILLEGITIMATE USES OF RACE BY ASSURING THAT THE LEGISLATIVE BODY IS PURSUING A GOAL IMPORTANT ENOUGH TO WARRANT USE OF A HIGHLY SUSPECT TOOL."

During her years in the Arizona Senate, O'Connor voted in favor of the EQUAL RIGHTS AMENDMENT to the U.S. Constitution and supported the restoration of the death penalty and limitations on government spending. She also played an active role in Republican Party politics, serving as state cochair of the committee supporting the reelection of President RICHARD M. NIXON in 1972.

O'Connor's career shifted in 1974 with her election to the Maricopa County Superior Court. She became a respected trial judge and was appointed by Democratic Governor Bruce Babbitt to the Arizona Court of Appeals in 1979. In 1981 President RONALD REAGAN appointed her to the U.S. Supreme Court, replacing Justice POTTER STEWART.

Her decisions on the Court have revealed her to be a pragmatic conservative. She has written many concurring opinions that attempt to limit the majority's holding, suggesting ways that the Court could have decided an issue on narrower grounds. She has joined her conservative brethren in limiting the rights of defendants in CRIMINAL PROCEDURE cases and restricting federal intervention into areas reserved to the states. She has been an influential voice in reviewing challenges to AFFIRMATIVE ACTION programs. In her majority opinion in *City of Richmond v. J. A. Croson Co.*, 488 U.S. 469, 109 S. Ct. 706, 102 L. Ed. 2d 854 (1989), O'Connor struck down a set-aside program for minority contractors. She concluded that these types of affirmative action programs can only be justified to remedy prior government discrimination instead of past societal discrimination.

Her position on ABORTION has been consistent. O'Connor has refused to join some of her conservative colleagues in overruling *Roe v. Wade*, 410 U.S. 113, 93 S. Ct. 705, 35 L. Ed. 2d 147, the 1973 decision that defined the right to choose abortion as a fundamental constitutional right. In *Planned Parenthood of Southeastern Pennsylvania v. Casey*, 505 U.S. 833, 112 S. Ct. 2791, 120 L. Ed. 2d 674 (1992), she joined Justices ANTHONY MCLEOD KENNEDY and DAVID

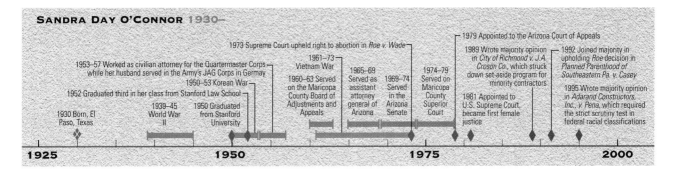

H. SOUTER in an opinion that defended the reasoning of *Roe* and the line of cases that followed it. She has supported the rights of states to regulate abortion as long as the regulations are not too burdensome.

O'CONOR, CHARLES Charles O'Conor achieved prominence as a New York attorney and as counsel for the prosecution in the trial of the notorious Tweed Ring.

O'Conor was born January 22, 1804, in New York City. After his admission to the bar in 1824, O'Conor practiced law in New York for twenty years, specializing in corporation law. He attended the New York Constitutional Convention in 1846 and served as U.S. district attorney from 1853 to 1854.

In 1871 O'Conor began a four-year term as special deputy attorney general for New York State. During his tenure he acted as counsel for the prosecution in the trial of William M. ("Boss") Tweed and his followers, who controlled a corrupt political machine in New York City. The trial resulted in the disbandment of the Tweed Ring.

The year 1872 was a presidential election year and O'Conor was nominated for the presidency by a faction of the Democratic party known as the Straight-Out Democrats. After his unsuccessful presidential campaign, O'Conor served, in 1877, as counsel during the investigation of the controversial RUTHERFORD B. HAYES-SAMUEL TILDEN election results.

O'Conor died May 12, 1884, in Nantucket, Massachusetts.

BIOGRAPHY

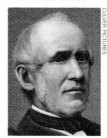

CULVER PICTURES

Charles O'Conor

OFFENSE A breach of law; a CRIME.

An offense may consist of a FELONY or a MISDEMEANOR. The term is used to indicate a violation of public rights as opposed to private ones. For example, MURDER is an offense whereas LIBEL is not.

OFFER A PROMISE that, according to its terms, is CONTINGENT upon a particular act, forbearance, or promise given in exchange for the original promise or the PERFORMANCE thereof; a demonstration of the willingness of a party to enter into a BARGAIN, made in such a way that another individual is justified in understanding that his or her assent to the bargain is invited and that such assent will conclude the bargain.

The making of an offer is the first of three steps in the traditional process of forming a valid contract: an offer, an ACCEPTANCE of the offer, and an exchange of CONSIDERATION. (Consideration is the act of doing something or promising to do something that a person is not legally required to do, or the FORBEARANCE or the promise to forbear from doing something that he or she has the legal right to do.)

An offer is a communication that gives the listener the power to conclude a contract. The question of whether a party in fact made an offer is a common question in a contract case. The general rule is that it must be reasonable under the circumstances for the recipient to believe that the communication is an offer. The more definite the communication, the more likely it is to constitute an offer. If an offer spells out such terms as quantity, quality, price,

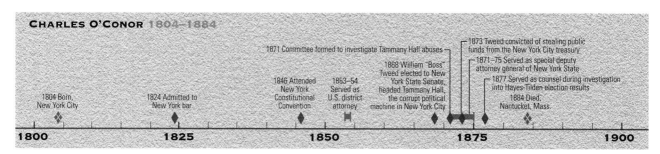

CHARLES O'CONOR 1804-1884

1804 Born, New York City

1824 Admitted to New York bar

1846 Attended New York Constitutional Convention

1853–54 Served as U.S. district attorney

1871 Committee formed to investigate Tammany Hall abuses

1868 William "Boss" Tweed elected to New York State Senate, headed Tammany Hall, the corrupt political machine in New York City

1873 Tweed convicted of stealing public funds from the New York City treasury

1871–75 Served as special deputy attorney general of New York State

1877 Served as counsel during investigation into Hayes-Tilden election results

1884 Died, Nantucket, Mass.

1800   1825   1850   1875   1900

OF COUNSEL A term commonly applied in the practice of law to an ATTORNEY who has been employed to aid in the preparation and management of a particular case but who is not the principal attorney in the action.

Of counsel is also sometimes used in reference to an attorney who is associated with a law firm, but is neither a partner nor an associate.

OF COURSE Any action or step that an individual might take during judicial proceedings without being required to ask the judge's permission or that will receive the judge's automatic approval if the individual does ask permission; that which is a matter of right.

and time and place of delivery, a court may find that an offer was made. For example, if a merchant says to a customer, "I will sell you a dozen high-grade widgets for $100 each to be delivered to your shop on December 31," a court would likely find such a communication sufficiently definite to constitute an offer. On the other hand, a statement such as "I am thinking of selling some widgets" would probably not be labeled an offer.

The question of whether a communication constitutes an offer can be significant. An offer may bind the offerer to the terms of the offer if the recipient of the offer responds by accepting the offer and giving the offerer a partial payment. If the offerer accepts the payment, a deal has been struck, and the offerer is legally obligated to follow through on the agreement. If the offerer fails to fulfill the terms of the offer, the offeree may seek a remedy in court.

There are many notable caveats to the general rules on offers. Generally, a simple price quote is not an offer. Advertisements are considered invitations for offers, not actual offers. However, an advertisement promising to pay an award may constitute an offer because only one person, or very few persons, will have the opportunity to accept the offer.

An oral offer cannot be enforced against the offerer for agreements concerning REAL ESTATE, CONTRACTS for the sale of GOODS priced at $500 or more, and transactions that cannot be completed within one year. Such agreements must be in writing to be enforceable. These restrictions on oral offers are derived from the STATUTE OF FRAUDS, 29 Car. II, ch. 3, a law passed by the British Parliament in 1677 and designed in part to prevent false claims that an offer was tendered.

If a person rejects an offer, it is considered terminated. Likewise, if the recipient of an offer changes its terms, the original offer is terminated and a new offer is created. This new offer is called a COUNTEROFFER, and the original offerer may accept it.

In offers between merchants, a counteroffer may constitute acceptance of the original offer. Courts often hold that a contract is created when the facts show that two merchants agreed to make a sale but the recipient of the offer added terms to the agreement. In many such cases, a contract will be created as to the original offer, and the additional terms may be enforced. For example, assume that a wholesaler writes to a retailer, "Will sell 750 Grade A Fancy Pears immediately. Also have Grade A Fancy Cherries." If the retailer writes back, "Will take 750 Grade A Fancy Pears and 10 bushels of Grade A Fancy Cherries," a court may find that a contract had been created for the sale of pears and cherries.

Courts find offer and acceptance more readily in communications between merchants because merchants are more sophisticated than non-merchants in the practice of making agreements. Nevertheless, a counteroffer between merchants that adds new terms will not be enforced if the offer expressly limited acceptance to the terms of the offer, if the additional terms materially alter the intent of the parties, or if notification of rejection of the counteroffer was given to the recipient of the offer by the original offerer.

If an offer indicates that it will terminate within a certain period of time, it cannot be accepted after the time has expired. The passage of a reasonable length of time may automatically terminate an offer. The determination of a reasonable length of time depends on the circumstances surrounding the offer. For example, if a wholesaler contacts a retailer offering to sell perishable produce, the retailer cannot wait six weeks and then accept the offer. Even if an item is nonperishable, an unusually lengthy response time may terminate an offer. For example, if the usual practice in the lumber business is a response time of less than two weeks, the offerer may refuse to honor the offer if the recipient of the offer does not respond within that time period.

Some offers may be made IRREVOCABLE. An irrevocable offer is one that cannot be revoked by the offerer and terminates only upon the passage of time or rejection by the recipient. There are three types of irrevocable offers: (1) where the recipient of the offer pays the offerer for the promise to keep the offer open; (2) where the recipient of the offer partly or fully performs his or her obligations under the offer; and (3) firm offers under section 2-205 of the UNIFORM COMMERCIAL CODE. A FIRM OFFER is an assurance by a merchant to buy or sell goods. The assurance must be in writing. No consideration is necessary to support the promise that the offer will remain open. A firm offer created under section 2-205 remains open no more than ninety days.

OFFERING See PUBLIC OFFERING.

OFFICE AUDIT ◫ A thorough examination and verification of the tax returns and financial records of an individual or firm by the INTERNAL REVENUE SERVICE in the office of the agent who is conducting the review. ◫

OFFICE OF MANAGEMENT AND BUDGET ◫ An agency of the federal government that evaluates, formulates, and coordinates management procedures and program objectives within and among departments and agencies of the EXECUTIVE BRANCH. It also controls the administration of the FEDERAL BUDGET, while routinely providing the president of the United States with recommendations regarding budget proposals and relevant legislative enactments. ◫

The Office of Management and Budget (OMB), formerly the Bureau of the Budget, was established in the Executive Office of the President pursuant to Reorganization Plan No. 1 of 1939 (5 U.S.C.A. app.), effective July 1, 1939. Its functions were reorganized and the office renamed OMB by Executive Order No. 11,541 of July 1, 1970. Since the reorganization the OMB has played a central role in analyzing the federal budget and making recommendations for changes in the budget. Its director, who is appointed by the president, is a key advisor on fiscal policy. The director often appears before congressional committees to explain budgetary proposals.

The OMB assists the president in developing and maintaining effective government by reviewing the organizational structure and management procedures of the executive branch to ensure that the intended results are achieved. It works to develop efficient coordinating mechanisms to implement government activities and to expand interagency cooperation.

The OMB assists the president and executive departments and agencies in preparing the budget and in formulating the government's fiscal program. It publishes the president's proposed *Budget of the U.S. Government* every year. Once Congress approves a budget, the OMB supervises and controls the administration of it. In addition, it advises the president on proposed legislation and recommends to the president whether to sign or VETO legislative enactments.

The office also assists in developing regulatory reform proposals and programs for paperwork reduction, especially reporting burdens of the public. The OMB helps in considering, clearing, and, where necessary, preparing proposed EXECUTIVE ORDERS and proclamations that will have an impact on the federal budget.

The OMB has assumed an oversight role in determining the effectiveness of federal programs. It plans and develops information systems that provide the president with program performance data, and it plans, conducts, and promotes evaluation efforts that assist the president in assessing program objectives, performance, and efficiency.

The office also keeps the president informed of the progress of government agency activities with respect to work proposed, initiated, and completed. It coordinates work among the agencies of the executive branch to eliminate overlap and duplication of effort and to ensure that the funds appropriated by Congress are expended in the most economical manner.

Finally, OMB works to improve the economy, efficiency, and effectiveness of the procurement processes by directing procurement policies, regulations, procedures, and forms for the executive branch.

OFFICE OF NATIONAL DRUG CONTROL POLICY The Office of National Drug Control Policy (ONDCP) was established by the National Narcotics Leadership Act of 1988 (21 U.S.C.A. § 1501 et seq.) and began operations in January 1989.

ONDCP develops and coordinates the policies and objectives of the federal government's program for reducing the use of illicit drugs. ONDCP seeks ways to combat the manufacture and distribution of illegal drugs, drug-related crime and violence, and drug-related health consequences. The director of ONDCP is charged with producing the National Drug Control Strategy, which directs the U.S. antidrug efforts and establishes a program, a budget, and guidelines for cooperation among federal, state, and local entities.

By law, the director also evaluates, coordinates, and oversees both the international and domestic antidrug efforts of the executive branch agencies and ensures that such efforts sustain and complement state and local antidrug activities. The director is commonly referred to as the "drug czar" because he or she advises the president regarding changes in the organization, management, budgeting, and personnel of federal agencies that could affect the U.S. antidrug efforts. The director is a member of the NATIONAL SECURITY COUNCIL and the Cabinet Council on Counternarcotics.

ONDCP's drug-control priorities include treatment, prevention, domestic law enforcement, and interdiction and international initiatives. It presumes that chronic, hard-core drug use is a disease and that anyone suffering from the disease needs treatment. ONDCP seeks to create a balance between sanctions for drug-related criminal activity and treatment of an addictive disease.

In the area of prevention, ONDCP seeks to reverse the upward trend in drug use and find ways to empower communities to address their drug problems. It develops and implements initiatives that attempt to prevent illicit drug use by young people and other high-risk populations.

Drug Use in the General U.S. Population

Current users are those who used drugs at least once within the month prior to the survey

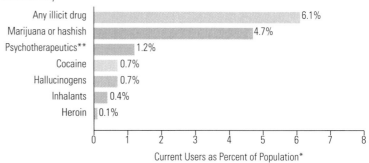

*Population includes ages 12 and over
**Includes tranquilizers, sedatives, analgesics, and stimulants.

Source: U.S. Substance Abuse and Mental Health Services Administration, *National Household Survey on Drug Abuse*, 1995.

ONDCP also emphasizes the need for strong, effective law enforcement efforts, including strong sanctions against drug offenders. Key priorities for domestic law enforcement are the disruption and dismantling of drug trafficking organizations, including seizure of their assets, and the investigation, arrest, prosecution, and imprisonment of drug traffickers. It seeks to attack drug trafficking organizations at every level, from the drug kingpin to the street-corner dealer, through a careful coordination of federal, state, and local law enforcement efforts.

In the international sphere, ONDCP views interdiction as an important component of national drug policy. It cooperates with other nations in building their law enforcement institutions, attacking drug production facilities, interdicting drug shipments in both source and transit countries, and dismantling drug trafficking organizations.

The director of ONDCP is supported by a number of organizational units. The Office of Demand Reduction undertakes and oversees activities to reduce the demand for drugs, including drug education, drug prevention, drug treatment, and related efforts for the rehabilitation of persons addicted to drugs. This office also conducts research on drug use and periodically convenes expert panels to assess state-of-the-art approaches to reducing the demand for drugs.

The Office of Supply Reduction seeks to reduce the availability, production, and distribution of illicit drugs in the United States and abroad. The Bureau of State and Local Affairs coordinates agency relationships and outreach efforts to state and local government agencies. The Counter-Drug Technology Assessment Center is the central counter-drug enforcement research and development organization of the federal government. It works to identify the scientific and technological needs of federal, state, and local law enforcement agencies.

See also DRUGS AND NARCOTICS.

OFFICE OF THRIFT SUPERVISION The Office of Thrift Supervision (OTS) was established as a bureau of the TREASURY DEPARTMENT in August 1989 as part of a major reorganization of the thrift regulatory structure mandated by the Financial Institutions Reform, Recovery, and Enforcement Act of 1989 (FIRREA) (12 U.S.C.A. § 1462a). The reorganization resulted from the savings and loan crisis of the 1980s, when a newly deregulated thrift industry invested in high-risk REAL ESTATE ventures, many of which collapsed. This led to enormous financial losses and the call for more federal regulation and oversight.

The OTS is authorized to charter federal thrift institutions and to serve as the primary regulator of the 1,700 federal- and state-chartered thrifts that belong to the Savings Association Insurance Fund. Its purpose is to maintain the safety, soundness, and viability of the thrift industry by adopting regulations that seek to prevent unreasonable lending risks, examining and supervising thrift institutions, and enforcing compliance with federal laws and regulations. In addition to overseeing thrift institutions, the OTS also oversees companies that own thrifts and controls the acquisition of thrifts by such holding companies.

The OTS is organized into five main divisions. The Washington Operations office develops national policy guidelines to clarify and implement statutes and regulations and establishes programs to implement new policies and laws. This division monitors the condition of the thrift industry and attempts to identify emerging supervisory problem areas.

The Regional Operations division examines and supervises thrift institutions through five regional offices located in Jersey City, Atlanta, Chicago, Dallas, and San Francisco. These offices also promote housing and other financial services in areas with the greatest need. The regional offices oversee the training and development of federal thrift regulators through accredited programs.

The Chief Counsel division provides a full range of legal services to the OTS, including drafting regulations, representing the agency in court, and taking enforcement actions against savings institutions that violate laws or regulations.

The staff of the Congressional Affairs division interacts with members of Congress, congressional staff, and committee members to accomplish the legislative objectives of the OTS. This division provides information to Congress about the office's supervisory, regulatory, and enforcement activities.

The Public Affairs division disseminates information, including policies, regulations, and key developments within the office. It also maintains an archive of business records and documented actions of the OTS and its predecessor, the Federal Home Loan Bank Board.

The OTS uses no tax money to fund its regulation. Its expenses are met through fees and assessments on the thrift institutions it regulates. The OTS is headed by a director appointed by the president and confirmed by the Senate to serve a five-year term.

See also SAVINGS AND LOAN ASSOCIATION.

OFFICER 📖 An individual with the responsibility of performing the duties and functions of an office, that is a duty or charge, a position of trust, or a right to exercise a public or private employment. 📖

A *public officer* is ordinarily defined as an individual who has been elected or appointed to exercise the functions of an office for the benefit of the public. *Executive officers,* such as the president or state governors, are public officers charged with the duty to ascertain that the law is enforced and obeyed. A *legislative officer,* such as a member of Congress, has the duty of making the laws. A public officer whose duties include administering justice, adjudicating controversies, and interpreting the laws is called a *judicial officer.* A *de jure officer* is one who is legally appointed and qualified to exercise the office. A *de facto officer* is an individual who appears to be legally qualified and appointed to an office but is not due to some legal technicality, such as failure to file a financial disclosure statement within the time prescribed by statute.

A public office must be created either by statute or by constitutional provision. Public officers are distinguishable from employees in that they are required to take an OATH of office and are appointed or elected to specified terms of office. The eligibility, duties, and compensation of public officers are defined by statute.

Removal from office occurs when an officer is dismissed from his or her position by a superior officer acting according to law. Sufficient cause must exist to justify the removal. When an individual is wrongfully removed from office, he or she may seek reinstatement.

A *military officer* is one who has been commissioned as such in the ARMED SERVICES.

An officer of a CORPORATION is someone, such as the president, vice-president, treasurer, or secretary, whose main duties are to oversee the efficient operation of the business.

See also OFFICERS OF THE COURT.

OFFICERS OF THE COURT 📖 An all-inclusive term for any type of court employee including JUDGES, CLERKS, SHERIFFS, MARSHALS, BAILIFFS, and CONSTABLES. 📖

An ATTORNEY is also regarded as being an officer of the court and must therefore comply with court rules.

OFFICIAL GAZETTE 📖 A compilation published weekly by the PATENT AND TRADEMARK OFFICE listing all the PATENTS and TRADEMARKS issued and registered, thereby providing notice to all interested parties. 📖

OFFSET 📖 A contrary CLAIM or demand that may cancel or reduce a given claim; a COUNTERCLAIM. A kind of bookkeeping entry that counters the effect of a previous entry. 📖

OF RECORD 📖 Entered on the appropriate official documents maintained by a governmental body and that are usually available for inspection by the public. 📖

A MORTGAGE is of record when it is entered in the appropriate records of the clerk in the area where the mortgaged property is located. When it is recorded, notice is thereby provided to anyone interested in purchasing the land that it is subject to certain ENCUMBRANCES. See also RECORDING OF LAND TITLES.

An *attorney of record* is the lawyer whose name is contained in the records of the court as the principal lawyer handling an action.

OLD-AGE, SURVIVORS, AND DISABILITY INSURANCE 📖 The system developed pursuant to the federal SOCIAL SECURITY ACT OF 1935 (42 U.S.C.A. § 301 et seq. [1935]) to provide government benefits to eligible retirees, disabled individuals, and surviving spouses and their dependents. 📖

Federal Old-Age, Survivors, and Disability Insurance (OASDI) benefits are monthly payments made to retired people, families whose wage earner has died, and workers who are unemployed because of sickness or accident. Workers qualify for such protection by having been employed for the mandatory minimum amount of time and by having made contributions to SOCIAL SECURITY. There is no financial need requirement. Once a worker qualifies for

There are many types of officers, and each has responsibilities and duties within the context of his office. This military officer, for example, would have no authority to arrest a civilian for speeding.

HERB SNITZER/THE PICTURE CUBE

protection, his or her family is also entitled to protection. The OASDI program is geared toward helping families as a matter of social policy.

The OASDI program is funded by payroll taxes levied on employees, their employers, and the self-employed. The rate of the contributions is based upon the employee's taxable income, up to a maximum taxable amount, with the employer contributing an equal amount. The self-employed person contributes twice the amount levied on an employee. In 1996 a tax rate of 6.2 percent was levied on earned income up to a maximum of $62,887 to fund OASDI.

Old-Age Benefits Old-age benefits were the cornerstone of the original Social Security Act, which was passed in 1935. More than twenty-five million Americans receive old-age benefits each month, and those payments amount to almost $20 billion a year. Because of the increasing median age of the adult population, these figures are constantly increasing.

To be eligible for Social Security old-age benefits, a person must have worked a minimum number of calendar quarters, which increases with the worker's age. Forty quarters is the maximum requirement. Once a person earns credit for the required number of calendar quarters, she or he is insured. Workers born before 1950 can retire at age 65 with full benefits based on their average income during working years. For those workers born between 1950 and 1960, the retirement age has increased to age 66. Workers born in 1960 or later will be awarded full benefits for retirement at age 67. A person may retire at age 62 and receive less than full benefits. A worker's spouse who has not contributed to Social Security receives, at age 65, 50 percent of the amount paid to the worker.

Survivors' Benefits Survivors' benefits are payments made to family members when a worker dies. The payments are intended to help ease the financial strain caused by the loss of the worker's income. Survivors can receive benefits if the deceased worker was employed and contributed to Social Security long enough to be considered insured.

When a wage earner dies, his or her spouse and unmarried minor children are entitled to receive benefits. In addition to monthly checks, the worker's surviving spouse, or if there is none, another eligible person, may receive a lump-sum payment of $255.

Disability Benefits A person who becomes unable to work and expects to be disabled for at least twelve months or who will probably die from the condition can receive Social Security payments before reaching retirement age. A worker is eligible for disability benefits if she or he has worked enough years under Social Security before the onset of disabilities.

A disability is any physical or mental condition that prevents the worker from doing substantial work. Examples of disabilities that meet the Social Security criteria include brain damage, heart disease, kidney failure, severe arthritis, and serious mental illness.

The Social Security Administration (SSA) determines whether a person's disability is serious enough to justify the awarding of benefits. The SSA determines whether the impairment is so severe that it significantly affects "basic work activity." If the answer is yes, the worker's medical data are compared with a set of guidelines known as the Listing of Impairments. If the claimant is found to suffer from a condition contained in this list, payment of the benefits will be approved. If the condition is less severe, SSA determines whether the impairment prevents the person from doing his or her former work. If not, the application will be denied. If so, a determination is made as to whether the impairment will prevent the applicant from doing other work present in the economy.

At this point SSA uses a series of guidelines that attempt to combine consideration of the applicant's residual functional capacity with the factors of age, education, and experience. The guidelines classify work into three types: sedentary work, light work, and medium work. If the SSA determines that an applicant can perform one of these types of work, it will deny benefits. A claimant may appeal this decision and ask for a hearing in which to present further evidence, including personal testimony. If the recommendation of the administrative law judge conducting the hearing is adverse, the claimant may appeal to the Social Security Administration's Appeals Council. If the claimant loses the appeal, she or he may file CIVIL ACTION in federal district court seeking review of the agency's adverse determination.

Three types of benefits are available to persons who meet the OASDI disability eligibility requirements: monthly cash payments, vocational rehabilitation, and medical insurance. Cash payments begin, provided proper application has been made, with the sixth month of disability. The amount of the monthly payment depends on the amount of earnings on which the employee has paid Social Security taxes and the number of eligible dependents. The maximum for a family usually equals roughly the amount to which the disabled employee is entitled as an individual plus allowances for two dependents.

Vocational rehabilitation services are provided through a joint federal-state program. Persons receiving cash payments for disability may continue to receive them for a limited time after they begin to work or near the end of a program of vocational rehabilitation. This period is referred to as the "trial work period" and may last as long as nine months.

Medical services are available through the MEDICARE program (a federally sponsored program of hospital and medical insurance) in which a recipient of OASDI disability benefits begins to participate twenty-five months after the onset of disability.

CROSS-REFERENCES

Disabled Persons; Elder Law; Health Insurance; Senior Citizens.

OLMSTEAD v. UNITED STATES

Olmstead v. United States, 277 U.S. 438, 48 S. Ct. 564, 72 L. Ed. 944 (1928), was the first case dealing with the issue of whether messages passing over telephone wires are within the constitutional protection against unreasonable SEARCHES AND SEIZURES.

In *Olmstead*, several individuals were convicted of a CONSPIRACY to violate the National Prohibition Act (41 Stat. 305) by illegally possessing, transporting, and importing intoxicating liquors, maintaining nuisances, and selling intoxicating liquors. The information leading to the discovery of the conspiracy was, for the most part, obtained through the interception of messages on the telephones of the conspirators by four federal prohibition officers. Wires were placed along the ordinary telephone wires from the homes of four of the defendants and along the wires that led to their main office of operation. The insertion of the wires was made without any trespass having been committed on any of the defendants' property since it was done in the basement of the large office building and in the streets near the residences.

The Supreme Court held that messages passing over telephone wires were not within the protection against unreasonable searches and seizures. The eavesdropper had to have physically trespassed in order for EVIDENCE procured by WIRETAPPING to be regarded as having been obtained unconstitutionally. The Court reasoned that, since there was no entry of the homes or offices of the defendants, there was no physical TRESPASS. In addition, in spite of the fact that the evidence leading to the conviction was obtained in violation of a state statute that made it a MISDEMEANOR to intercept telegraphic or telephonic messages, the Court indicated that

In Olmstead v. United States the Supreme Court held that placing wire taps on the phone lines of suspects was a legitimate way to collect evidence; the decision was later overruled. In Olmstead several people were convicted of a conspiracy to violate the National Prohibition Act.

BIOGRAPHY

Richard Olney

the statute did not declare that evidence obtained in such manner would be INADMISSIBLE, and it was not inadmissible under COMMON LAW.

Subsequently the *Olmstead* case was overruled, the physical trespass doctrine abandoned, and the holding in *Olmstead* is no longer the law. Under current law, in order for ELECTRONIC SURVEILLANCE to be constitutionally permissible, it must be done pursuant to the prior authorization by a court.

OLNEY, RICHARD

In the late nineteenth century, the Massachusetts-born attorney Richard Olney exerted a powerful influence over domestic and international affairs. From 1893 to 1895, Olney served as U.S. attorney general under President GROVER CLEVELAND and, from 1895 to 1897, as secretary of state. A nationalist with a forceful personality who took a broad view of federal power, Olney is remembered for two important actions during his public career that had long-lasting implications for U.S. law. First, as attorney general, he used the office in 1894 to break a strike by railway workers that hampered the delivery of mail nationwide. The outcome affected the rights of workers for more than a quarter of a century, thrust Olney into the national spotlight, and earned him the enmity of LABOR UNIONS. Second, after becoming secretary of state, he resolved a conflict between Venezuela and England that shaped U.S. foreign policy well into the twentieth century.

Born in Oxford, Massachusetts, on September 15, 1835, Olney was educated at Brown University and Harvard Law School. Admitted to the Boston bar in 1859, he established a successful law practice and earned recognition for his work with railroads. A brief political career followed with his election to the Massachusetts state legislature, where he served one

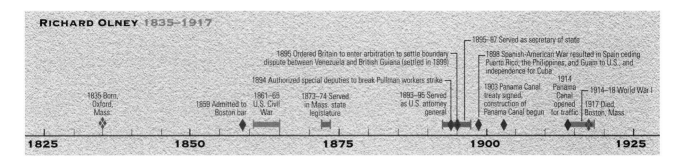

RICHARD OLNEY 1835-1917

1835 Born, Oxford, Mass.

1859 Admitted to Boston bar

1861-65 U.S. Civil War

1873-74 Served in Mass. state legislature

1893-95 Served as U.S. attorney general

1894 Authorized special deputies to break Pullman workers strike

1895 Ordered Britain to enter arbitration to settle boundary dispute between Venezuela and British Guiana (settled in 1899)

1895-97 Served as secretary of state

1898 Spanish-American War resulted in Spain ceding Puerto Rico, the Philippines, and Guam to U.S., and independence for Cuba

1903 Panama Canal treaty signed, construction of Panama Canal begun

1914 Panama Canal opened for traffic

1914-18 World War I

1917 Died, Boston, Mass.

1825   1850   1875   1900   1925

term between 1873 and 1874. In 1893 he was appointed U.S. attorney general at the start of the second and deeply troubled administration of President Cleveland. The president became mired in public controversies, and his new attorney general would be at the heart of one of the worst.

When Olney assumed his duties in the Department of Justice, the nation was suffering from an economic depression. The Pullman Company, a Chicago-based RAILROAD, cut its workers' pay to near-starvation wages but went on paying DIVIDENDS to its shareholders. In 1894 the company's laborers staged a strike that spread nationwide under the auspices of the nascent American Railway Union: everywhere, railroad workers refused to handle Pullman train cars. Tensions escalated when railroad owners began firing the workers, and violence was threatened. The General Managers Association, a trade organization representing railroads, appealed to the Cleveland administration for federal intervention.

Because the strike had prevented the delivery of U.S. mails, Cleveland and Olney had to intervene. Olney had little sympathy for the workers. His first idea was to use the U.S. Army to crush them. Instead he sent five thousand special deputies to restore order. When riots followed, Olney arrested and prosecuted union leaders on grounds of CONSPIRACY, and he won a sweeping federal court INJUNCTION to prevent workers from interfering with the railroads' operation. Appealing to the U.S. Supreme Court in 1895, union president Eugene V. Debs lost his case, and the strike was broken (*In re Debs*, 158 U.S. 564, 15 S. Ct. 900, 39 L. Ed. 1092). The Court's sanction of the injunction was a great boon to U.S. corporations, which thereafter sought court injunctions to break strikes until the practice was restrained during the 1930s. Nonetheless, Olney and Cleveland paid a high political price in the polls for their widely unpopular actions.

In 1895, toward the end of the Cleveland administration, the president appointed Olney secretary of state. At once Olney faced a foreign policy crisis: the conflict between Venezuela

"TODAY THE UNITED STATES IS PRACTICALLY SOVEREIGN ON THIS CONTINENT AND ITS FIAT IS LAW UPON THE SUBJECTS TO WHICH IT CONFINES ITS INTERPOSITION."

and Great Britain over the Venezuela-British Guiana boundary. As much a believer in U.S. supremacy as he was in federal power at home, Olney ordered Britain to enter ARBITRATION with Venezuela. His order relied on a broad reading of the MONROE DOCTRINE. As the basis of U.S. foreign policy in the nineteenth century, the Monroe Doctrine essentially preserved U.S. independence in the Western Hemisphere. Although the doctrine prohibited foreign intervention in Latin American nations, Olney believed it permitted U.S. intervention to stop European interference with Latin American affairs. Britain ultimately resolved its conflict with Venezuela through arbitration in 1899. But the broader impact of Olney's views came later. His interpretation came to be known as the Olney Corollary to the Monroe Doctrine and was influential in the foreign policy of President THEODORE ROOSEVELT.

Olney left office in 1897 at the end of the unpopular Cleveland administration. Returning to private practice, he was touted as a possible presidential candidate in 1904, but he did not run. He died in Boston on April 8, 1917.

OLOGRAPH See HOLOGRAPH.

OMBUDSPERSON 📖 A public official who acts as an impartial intermediary between the public and government or BUREAUCRACY, or an employee of an organization who mediates disputes between employees and management. 📖

The Swedish legislature first created the position of ombudsperson in the early 1800s; the literal translation of *ombudsperson* is "an investigator of citizen complaints." This official was considered to be a person of "known legal ability and outstanding integrity" and was chosen by the Swedish parliament to serve a four-year term.

Today, an ombudsperson addresses concerns (such as administrative abuse or maladministration) that citizens or groups have about organizations or bureaucracies. In these situations, the ombudsperson acts as an impartial mediator between the two parties, providing a less threatening type of dispute resolution. For the ombudsperson to help reduce friction between citizens and the government, he or she must be viewed as trustworthy and neutral; the process will not work if one party believes that the ombudsperson is taking the side of the other party. Ombudspersons are bound by the oath of the Ombudsman's Association, which requires neutrality and confidentiality, requirements that are necessary to create a trust between the persons involved in a dispute and the ombudsperson.

The power of the ombudsperson lies in his ability to investigate complaints of wrongdoing and then notify the public or the relevant government agencies, or both, of the findings. However, an ombudsperson cannot change or make laws, enforce any recommendations, or change administrative actions or decisions.

At the government level, the ombudsperson is appointed by the legislature of the state or county in which she serves. The ombudsperson typically has some law training, although a law degree is not required, and she must be free of any political loyalties because of the neutrality the job requires. The goal of the ombudsperson is to assist the communication between the public and the government and help create solutions to problems that arise between the two parties, rather than punishing the wrongdoer. These solutions are aimed at reducing the possibility of similar problems in the future.

Friction between the public and government often can be attributed to the way laws or legislative policies are enforced. In these cases, the ombudsperson can try to reduce the friction by finding a more satisfactory method of carrying out the law. For example, even though police officers may legally enter a workplace to arrest an employee on charges of a crime, this practice can embarrass the employee and threaten her job, even if charges are later dropped. In this situation the ombudsperson would most likely confer with the police department to see if arrests for nonfelonies could be made safely outside the workplace.

The ombudsperson's role in U.S. government is not clearly defined; not all states use an ombudsperson within their governmental agencies. Compared with ombudspersons in other countries, an ombudsperson in the United States has a larger role in the MEDIATION and negotiation of settlements. Government branches such as social and child welfare agencies, prisons, law enforcement agencies and consumer bureaus often have ombudspersons within their ranks.

Although ombudspersons generally work in government agencies, county governments, and city governments, companies also may employ an ombudsperson as a confidential, neutral contact with whom employees can discuss their concerns. In the mid-1990s more than two hundred private CORPORATIONS employed an ombudsperson. A corporate ombudsperson serves as the point of contact for dispute resolution in a corporation. The corporate ombudsperson, who is typically a senior official within the company, helps employees work through a variety of work-related conflicts, such as dissatisfaction with salary, unethical behavior such as THEFT or FRAUD, terminations, discrimination, and SEXUAL HARASSMENT. In recent years issues such as government contract compliance and WHISTLE-BLOWING also have been handled by corporate ombudspersons.

The corporate ombudsperson's position arose from corporations' desire to increase the job satisfaction of their employees, improve the communication between employees and management, and avoid litigation. As of 1992, there were more than one thousand corporate ombudspersons practicing. On average, a corporate ombudsperson will handle two hundred to three hundred cases per year and deal with two to eight percent of the corporate workforce.

A corporate ombudsperson works with employees and management by reviewing management decisions and intervening in employee-employee and employee-management disputes. Generally, the methods the corporate ombudsperson may use include responsive listening, investigation, mediation, direct resolution, and upward feedback to management. The ombuds-

No longer strictly a government functionary, today an ombudsperson may be employed by any type of organization or bureaucracy to hear complaints and resolve disputes.

J. PICKERELL/THE IMAGE WORKS

person allows an employee to voice her concerns and advises or counsels the employee on the best way to deal with the situation. If necessary, as is often the case in allegations of sexual harassment, for example, the ombudsperson can investigate the situation further.

Because of the variety of situations a corporate ombudsperson deals with and because corporate cultures vary from one company to another, there is no standard job description or authority level for corporate ombudspersons.

Other organizations that employ ombudspersons include hospitals, school districts, and universities. In the mid-1990s more than one hundred colleges and universities employed an ombudsperson, and more than four thousand hospitals offered ombudsperson services for patients. Many small businesses also have an office that handles client or citizen complaints and functions as an ombudsperson's office.

Ombudsperson confidentiality is important to the success of the office. If either party in a dispute believes that her concerns are not heard in confidence, communication with the ombudsperson will decline and the possibility of resolving a problem will also decline. Generally, communication with an ombudsperson is confidential. However, an ombudsperson is not required to maintain confidentiality regarding criminal behavior or conduct that threatens employee safety or company assets.

The question of whether an ombudsperson's communications with a party to a dispute are privileged (whether they may be protected from disclosure in court) is determined by courts on a case-by-case basis. Several cases have recognized an ombudsperson's privilege, including *Shabazz v. Scurr*, 662 F. Supp. 90 (S.D. Iowa 1987), which involved communications to a prison ombudsperson, and *Kientzy v. McDonnell Douglas Corp.*, 133 F.R.D. 570 (E.D. Mo. 1991), which involved a corporate ombudsperson.

See also ADMINISTRATIVE LAW AND PROCEDURE; ALTERNATIVE DISPUTE RESOLUTION.

OMNIBUS [*Latin, For all; containing two or more independent matters.*] A term frequently used in reference to a legislative bill comprised of two or more general subjects that is designed to compel the executive to approve provisions that he or she would otherwise reject but that he or she signs into law to prevent the defeat of the entire bill.

Laws governing the FEDERAL BUDGET are typically omnibus bills; for example, the Omnibus Consolidated Rescissions and Appropriations Act of 1996 (110 Stat. 1321).

ON DEMAND Payable immediately on request.

A note that is payable on demand is one that is to be paid the moment payment is requested by the individual who has legal possession thereof. See also COMMERCIAL PAPER.

O'NEILL, THOMAS P., JR. In many ways, Democrat Thomas P. ("Tip") O'Neill, Jr., epitomized the cigar-smoking, deal-making American politician of a bygone era. A tough, gregarious leader, O'Neill was the formidable Speaker of the U.S. House of Representatives from 1977 to 1986. He was a die-hard liberal whose commitment to America's poor and working class remained undiminished throughout his thirty-five years in Washington, D.C. When O'Neill died of cardiac arrest at age eighty-one on January 5, 1994, President BILL CLINTON eulogized him as one of the nation's most prominent and loyal champions of American workers and as a man who genuinely loved politics and people.

O'Neill was born December 9, 1912, in a working-class section of Cambridge, Massachusetts. His Irish Catholic father, Thomas O'Neill, Sr., was a bricklayer and member of the Cambridge City Council. His mother, Rose Tolan O'Neill, died when O'Neill was just one year old.

At an early age, O'Neill developed a passion for politics. When he was fifteen years old, he spent hours working on Democrat Alfred E. Smith's unsuccessful presidential campaign against HERBERT HOOVER. During his senior year at Boston College, O'Neill ran for public office for the first time. He entered the race for the Cambridge City Council and lost by a mere 150 votes.

BIOGRAPHY

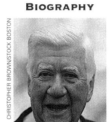

Thomas P. O'Neill, Jr.

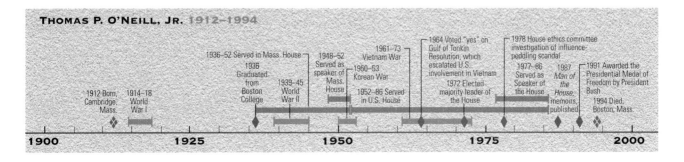

THOMAS P. O'NEILL, JR. 1912–1994

1900 · 1912 Born, Cambridge, Mass. · 1914–18 World War I · 1925 · 1936 Graduated from Boston College · 1936–52 Served in Mass. House · 1939–45 World War II · 1948–52 Served as speaker of Mass. House · 1950 · 1950–53 Korean War · 1952–86 Served in U.S. House · 1961–73 Vietnam War · 1964 Voted "yes" on Gulf of Tonkin Resolution, which escalated U.S. involvement in Vietnam · 1972 Elected majority leader of the House · 1975 · 1977–86 Served as Speaker of the House · 1978 House ethics committee investigation of influence-peddling scandal · 1987 *Man of the House*, memoirs, published · 1991 Awarded the Presidential Medal of Freedom by President Bush · 1994 Died, Boston, Mass. · 2000

This early defeat taught the young candidate a valuable lesson about politics. Taking his local support for granted, O'Neill had failed to campaign in his own North Cambridge neighborhood. The voters from his district resented his neglect and did not back him as strongly as expected. O'Neill never repeated this tactical error. After the city council loss, O'Neill's father reportedly observed, "All politics is local." For years, O'Neill quoted his father's maxim and applied it to his work.

In 1936, the year he graduated from college, O'Neill enjoyed his first victory at the polls. Using the political leverage of jobs and favors, he won a seat in the Massachusetts House of Representatives, from the North Cambridge district. O'Neill served in the state legislature for sixteen years. In 1952, he launched into national politics and was elected to the U.S. House of Representatives, beginning a congressional career that included an appointment as majority whip in 1971 and election as majority leader in 1972. He reached the pinnacle of legislative power in 1976 when he rose to the House speakership.

Outgoing and outspoken, O'Neill was known for his partisanship and for his skillful use of power. He embodied the liberal politics of the Democratic party during the late twentieth century. His support of federal social programs was unbending. As the political right grew in power, O'Neill fought conservative proposals such as a balanced budget because they threatened the education, housing, and welfare programs he cherished.

As Speaker of the House, O'Neill led Congress during the administrations of Presidents JIMMY CARTER, a Democrat, and RONALD REAGAN, a Republican. O'Neill did not respect Reagan's intellectual capabilities or his conservative policies. After clashing repeatedly with Reagan during his two terms in the White House, O'Neill called his fellow Irishman the least knowledgeable president he had ever worked with in thirty-five years in the nation's capitol. The two were polar opposites on nearly every political issue, particularly the government's role in American life.

O'Neill's legislative legacy includes a code of ethics for House members and a drive to IMPEACH President RICHARD M. NIXON. O'Neill also was among the first Democrats to speak out against the VIETNAM WAR during the 1960s. He once told an interviewer that the only vote in his congressional career that he regretted was his affirmative vote on the Gulf of Tonkin Resolution in 1964. (The resolution increased American troop involvement in Southeast Asia.)

"YOU CAN TEACH AN OLD DOG NEW TRICKS—IF THE OLD DOG WANTS TO LEARN."

Partisan to a fault, O'Neill had voted for the measure because he felt duty bound to support the Democratic president, LYNDON B. JOHNSON.

While in office, O'Neill shared a bachelor apartment in Washington, D.C. with Representative Edward Boland of Massachusetts. His wife, Mildred ("Millie"), and their five children stayed in the home district. According to Capitol Hill legend, the refrigerator in the men's apartment was stocked mostly with diet soft drinks, beer, and cigars.

O'Neill did not survive more than a quarter century in Washington, D.C., without some tarnish to his reputation. In 1978, he was criticized for accepting favors from Tongsun Park, an influence-peddling rice merchant from South Korea. An ethics committee investigation concluded that O'Neill had shown bad judgment in allowing Park to throw parties for him. The committee cleared O'Neill of any illegalities.

O'Neill retired from Congress in 1987. He subsequently spent most of his time in Washington, D.C., or at Cape Cod with his wife. O'Neill wrote a best-selling book about his experiences in Washington, entitled *Man of the House*, and starred in popular commercials for credit cards. He died January 5, 1994, in Boston, Massachusetts.

O'Neill was a throwback to an earlier era of backroom politics on Capitol Hill. The colorful Massachusetts congressman was a master at pressuring representatives to pass or block key legislation. O'Neill enjoyed a national reputation but remained loyal to the constituents back home. He is remembered as an unapologetic liberal, proud of his role in assisting the poor, the unemployed, and the least privileged Americans. He was one of the last and most highly regarded of the old-style American politicians.

ONE PERSON, ONE VOTE 📖 The principle that all citizens, regardless of where they

In Reynolds v. Sims, *the Supreme Court held that the right of suffrage can be denied by diluting the weight of a citizen's vote just as effectively as by prohibiting the free exercise of it.*

T PRETTYMAN/PHOTOEDIT

reside in a state, are entitled to equal legislative representation. 📖

This principle was enunciated by the Supreme Court in the case of *Reynolds v. Sims*, 377 U.S. 533, 84 S. Ct. 1362, 12 L. Ed. 2d 506 (1964). The Court ruled that a state's APPORTIONMENT plan for seats in both houses of a BICAMERAL state legislature must allocate seats on a population basis so that the voting power of each voter be as equal as possible to that of any other voter.

See also BAKER V. CARR; REYNOLDS V. SIMS.

ON OR ABOUT 📖 Near; approximately; without significant variance from an agreed date. 📖

The phrase *on or about* is used to avoid being bound to a more precise statement than is required by law. For example, when an individual seeks to purchase a home, the date when the transaction is closed and the legal TITLE and possession are transferred from seller to buyer is ordinarily scheduled on or about a particular date. The phrase is used to indicate that the parties recognize the fact that, although the exact date might not be convenient for both of them, the transaction should be completed as close to that date as is practicable.

ON POINT 📖 Directly applicable or dispositive of the matter under consideration. 📖

A statute or case is "on point" if it has direct application to the facts of a case currently before a tribunal for determination.

ONUS PROBANDI 📖 [*Latin, The burden of proof.*] In the strict sense, a term used to indicate that if no EVIDENCE is set forth by the party who has the burden of proof to establish the existence of facts in support of an ISSUE, then the issue must be found against that party. 📖

OPEN 📖 To make accessible, visible, or available; to submit to review, examination, or inquiry through the elimination of restrictions or impediments. 📖

To *open a judgment* means to render it capable of reexamination by removing or relaxing the bar of its finality. A JUDGMENT is ordinarily opened at the insistence of a party who is able to show GOOD CAUSE as to why the execution of the judgment would be inequitable.

To *open a court* is to formally announce, ordinarily through the BAILIFF, that the session has commenced and that the business before the tribunal will proceed.

The term *open* is also used as an adjective in reference to that which is patent, visible, apparent, or notorious, such as a defect in a product, or conduct such as LEWDNESS.

OPEN ACCOUNT 📖 An unpaid or unsettled account; an account with a balance that has not been ascertained, that is kept open in anticipation of future transactions. A type of CREDIT extended by a seller to a buyer that permits the buyer to make purchases without a note or security and is based on an evaluation of the buyer's credit. A contractual obligation that may be modified by subsequent agreement of the parties, either by expressed consent or by consent implied from the conduct of the parties, provided the agreement changing the contractual obligation is based upon independent CONSIDERATION. 📖

OPEN BID 📖 An offer to perform a CONTRACT, generally of a construction nature, in which the bidder reserves the right to reduce his or her bid to compete with a lower bid. 📖

OPEN COURT 📖 COMMON LAW requires a trial in open court; "open court" means a court to which the public has a right to be admitted. This term may mean either a court that has been formally convened and declared open for the transaction of its proper judicial business or a court that is freely open to spectators. 📖

OPEN-END CONTRACT 📖 An agreement that allows a buyer to make purchases over a period of time without a change in the price or terms by the seller. 📖

OPEN-END CREDIT 📖 A type of revolving account that permits an individual to pay, on a monthly basis, only a portion of the total amount due. 📖

This type of CONSUMER CREDIT is frequently used in conjunction with bank and department store credit cards.

OPEN-END MORTGAGE 📖 A MORTGAGE that allows the borrowing of additional sums, often on the condition that a stated ratio of collateral value to the DEBT be maintained. A mortgage that provides for future advances on the mortgage and which so increases the amount of the mortgage. 📖

OPENING STATEMENT 📖 An introductory statement made by the ATTORNEYS for each side at the start of a TRIAL. The opening statement, although not mandatory, is seldom waived because it offers a valuable opportunity to provide an overview of the case to the JURY and to explain the anticipated proof that will be presented during the course of the trial. 📖

The primary purpose of an opening statement is to apprise the trier of fact, whether jury or court, of the issues in question and to summarize the EVIDENCE that the party intends to offer during the trial. The Supreme Court has characterized an opening statement as "ordinarily intended to do no more than to inform the jury in a general way of the nature of the action and defense so that they may better be prepared to understand the evidence" (*Best v. District of Columbia*, 291 U.S. 411, 54 S. Ct. 487, 78 L. Ed. 882 [1934]).

Most practitioners and legal scholars agree that an effective opening statement is vital to the trial process. The importance of an opening statement has been established by studies that showed that 80 percent of jurors' ultimate conclusions with respect to the VERDICT corresponded with their tentative opinion after opening statements. This is because an effective opening statement establishes the facts of the case and sets forth a legal theory and explanation for why the attorney's client should prevail.

An opening statement may be either a matter of RIGHT or a PRIVILEGE depending on applicable state and local laws. A party may waive its option of presenting an opening statement because opening statements are not mandatory.

If a party chooses to give an opening statement, the party with the burden of proof will usually present its opening statement first. In a civil case, this means that the plaintiff's attorney presents an opening statement first. In a criminal case, the burden of proof rests on the prosecution. Therefore, the prosecution will be first to present an opening statement.

The defense may present its opening statement after the plaintiff or prosecution has given its opening statement. The defense also has the option of reserving the opening statement until after the plaintiff has presented its case. Courts have discretion to direct a different order of presentation of opening statements if it finds good reasons for such change in order.

Opening statements allow attorneys for each side to introduce themselves and to introduce the parties involved in the lawsuit. Additionally, attorneys will usually outline the important facts of the case during the opening statement to assist the jury in understanding the evidence that will be presented during the trial. An opening statement generally contains a brief explanation of the applicable law and a request for verdict. In a request for verdict, the attorney explains the verdict sought and explains the facts that will support the verdict. A well-planned opening statement serves as a road map of the trial.

Opening statements are often informal and narrative in form. The attorney tells the client's story and explains to the jury what the evidence will show. An opening statement, however, does not constitute evidence, and the jury cannot rely on it in reaching a verdict. The opening statement should be brief and general rather than long and detailed.

An attorney is limited in what he or she can say during an opening statement. An attorney may not discuss INADMISSIBLE evidence. This is especially true where the evidence was ruled inadmissible in a pretrial motion hearing. The attorney must reasonably believe that the matters stated will be supported by the evidence. In addition, statements that are purely ARGUMENTATIVE are not proper during opening statements. An attorney may not assert personal opinions, comment about the evidence, or comment about the CREDIBILITY of a WITNESS during an opening statement.

Objections by opposing counsel during an opening statement are appropriate where the attorney presenting the opening statement engages in improper conduct. If the attorney fails to object to the inappropriate conduct, the objection is deemed waived, and the attorney cannot complain of such misconduct later in the trial.

A court usually has the discretion to employ one of several remedies for misconduct during an opening statement. The most common remedy for misconduct during an opening statement is jury admonition, where the judge simply instructs the jury to disregard the improper statement. Where misconduct is more serious, however, the following remedies may be available: (1) counsel may be cited for misconduct or CONTEMPT; (2) a MISTRIAL may be declared; (3) a new trial may be ordered; (4) an appeal may be taken based on the misconduct.

An attorney can make damaging statements during the opening statement that legally bind the client. Such statements, known as "admissions," are not limited to the opening statement

In the Massachusetts trial of John Salvi III, accused of murdering two abortion clinic workers, prosecutor John Kivlan (pictured) noted in his opening statement that Salvi had been in possession of maps with abortion clinics highlighted. While not evidence in itself, the remark hinted at evidence to be presented during the trial.

AP/WIDE WORLD PHOTOS

but can occur throughout the litigation process. Attorneys must use caution during the opening statement to avoid making damaging ADMISSIONS.

The court may decide the case after the opening statement and before the jury ever has the opportunity to hear the evidence. A court can properly take the case from the jury where it is clear from the opening statement that the plaintiff cannot succeed on the merits or that the defendant has no valid defense. This is usually accomplished by an attorney bringing a motion for a DIRECTED VERDICT. Taking the case from the jury is an extreme measure and exercised with great caution. Courts favor allowing a case to be tried on its MERITS and rarely grant a directed verdict after the opening statement.

A strong opening statement will have a lasting impact on the trier of fact. It is often the jury's first introduction to the parties, the issues, and the trial procedure. The opening statement begins the process of persuasion, the ultimate goal of which is a favorable verdict.

OPEN LISTING 📖 A type of REAL ESTATE listing contract whereby any agent who has a right to participate in the open LISTING is entitled to a commission if he or she produces the sale. 📖

OPEN SHOP 📖 A business in which union and nonunion workers are employed. A business in which union membership is not a condition of securing or maintaining employment. 📖

The term *open shop* is frequently used to imply that the operator of this type of shop is, in effect, exercising discrimination against TRADE UNIONS and hampering their advancement through the employment of nonunion employees.

See also LABOR UNION.

OPERATION OF LAW 📖 The manner in which an individual acquires certain rights or liabilities through no act or cooperation of his or her own, but merely by the application of the established legal rules to the particular transaction. 📖

For example, when an individual dies INTESTATE, the laws of DESCENT AND DISTRIBUTION provide for the inheritance of the ESTATE by the HEIR. The property of the DECEDENT is said to be transferred by operation of law.

OPINION See COURT OPINION.

OPINION EVIDENCE 📖 EVIDENCE of what the WITNESS thinks, believes, or infers in regard to facts in dispute, as distinguished from personal knowledge of the facts themselves. The rules of evidence ordinarily do not permit witnesses to TESTIFY as to opinions or conclusions. 📖

When this type of evidence is expressed by an expert witness, it may be used only if scientific, technical, or specialized knowledge will aid the trier of fact in understanding the evidence or determining a fact in issue. In the event that the witness is not testifying as an expert, the witness's TESTIMONY is restricted to opinions or inferences that are rationally based upon his or her perception and are helpful to a clear understanding of the testimony or the determination of a fact in issue.

OPPRESSION 📖 The offense, committed by a public official, of wrongfully inflicting injury, such as bodily harm or imprisonment, upon another individual under COLOR OF OFFICE. 📖

Oppression, which is a MISDEMEANOR, is committed through any act of cruelty, severity, unlawful exaction, or excessive use of authority.

OPTION 📖 A privilege, for which a person has paid money, that grants that person the right to purchase or sell certain commodities or certain specified securities at any time within an agreed period for a fixed price.

A right, which operates as a continuing offer, given in exchange for CONSIDERATION—something of value—to purchase or lease PROPERTY at an agreed price and terms within a specified time. 📖

An option is a type of CONTRACT that is used in the STOCK and COMMODITY markets, in the leasing and sale of REAL ESTATE, and in other areas where one party wants to acquire the legal right to buy something from or sell something to another party within a fixed period of time.

In the stock and commodity markets, options come in two primary forms, known as "calls" and "puts." A CALL gives the holder of the option the choice of buying or not buying stock or a commodities FUTURES contract at a fixed price for a fixed period of time. A PUT gives the holder the option of selling or not selling stock or a commodities futures contract at a fixed price for a fixed period of time. Because an option only has value for a fixed period of time, its value decreases with the passage of time. Because of this feature, it is considered a "wasting" ASSET.

There are four parts to an option: the underlying security, the type of option (put or call), the strike price, and the expiration date. Take, for example, an "International Widget July 100 call." International Widget stock is the underlying security, July is the expiration month of the option, $100 is the strike price (sometimes referred to as the exercise price), and the option is a call, giving the holder of the call the RIGHT, not the OBLIGATION, to buy one hundred shares of International Widget at a price of $100. The holder of the call cannot buy the one hundred shares until the exercise date.

In the case of a commodity option, the right to purchase or sell pertains to an underlying physical commodity, such as a specific quantity of silver, or to a commodity futures contract. The period during which an option can be exercised is specified in the contract.

Stock option plans are used in business to reward employees. A stock option is a contract between the company and the employee giving the employee the right to purchase shares of company stock between certain dates at a price that is often fixed by the company or determinable by formula at the time the option is granted. For example, International Widget may issue an option to a key employee, which will allow the employee to purchase one hundred shares of stock at the FAIR MARKET VALUE at the grant date. The employee has five years in which to exercise that option. If the price increases above the grant-date fair market value, the employee will presumably exercise the option and realize an economic gain based on the spread between the fair market value at the grant date and the fair market value at the exercise date. If the price decreases after the option is granted, the employee will forgo exercising the option and thereby have no loss in economic value.

Options have a role in business outside the stock and commodity markets. In the law of CONTRACT, the option is a continuing OFFER to purchase or lease property. The offer is irrevocable for the stated period of time. Like most other contracts, the option contract is not terminated by the subsequent death or insanity of either party.

Options usually assume one of two forms. The seller can state to the purchaser, "If you pay me $500 today, I promise to sell Whiteacre to you for $50,000 on the condition that you pay the $50,000 within sixty days." If the purchaser pays the $500, a unilateral contract—an agreement in which there is a promise on only one side and a possibility of a performance by the other side—is created, and the offer is irrevocable. The seller of Whiteacre is obligated to perform if the purchaser pays the $50,000 within sixty days.

The second form of option contract is created when the seller states to the purchaser, "I offer to sell you Whiteacre for $50,000. This offer will remain open for sixty days if you pay $500 for this privilege." If the purchaser pays the $500, there is a collateral contract—an agreement made prior to, or simultaneous with, another agreement not to revoke the offer—and the seller is obligated not to revoke.

ACCEPTANCE of an option contract is operative when received by the offeror, rather than when sent. An option contract is interpreted strictly in favor of its creator and must be unequivocal and in accordance with the terms of the option. It is frequently said that "TIME IS OF THE ESSENCE" in an option contract, but this means only that the option cannot be exercised after the offer has lapsed.

An offer can be accepted only by the person or persons for whom it is intended. Therefore, no ASSIGNMENT—a transfer to another of any property—of an offer can be made. The prohibition is based on the concept that everyone has the privilege of choosing with whom to contract. Once an offer has ripened into a contract, however, the rights thereby created are usually assignable. For example, if Jane offers an option to Jack to purchase Whiteacre, Jack cannot accept the option and then assign it to Joe. Once Jack and Jane enter into a contract for the sale of Whiteacre, Jack can assign his contract rights to Joe.

ORAL CONTRACT An agreement between parties that is either partly in writing and partly dependent on spoken words or that is entirely dependent on spoken words.

An oral contract is enforceable unless its subject matter comes within the STATUTE OF FRAUDS, an English law adopted in the United States, that requires certain CONTRACTS to be in writing. For example, a contract to sell REAL PROPERTY, to be enforceable, must be in writing to comply with the statute. An oral contract to sell PERSONAL PROPERTY for an amount less than that set in the statute does not fall within its limits and, therefore, is enforceable without being reduced to a writing. The UNIFORM COMMERCIAL CODE (UCC) governs the enforceability of oral contracts in SALES transactions involving merchants.

Is a so-called "handshake agreement" between parties enforceable as an oral contract? It depends on what is being agreed upon.

ORDEAL 📖 One of the most ancient forms of trial in England that required the accused person to submit to a dangerous or painful test on the theory that God would intervene and disclose his or her guilt or innocence. 📖

Trials by ordeal were a pagan custom that took on added ritual when Christianity was introduced into England. There were various ordeals, and at different times certain ordeals were reserved for people of higher rank, whereas others were used for common people. All were based on the belief that supernatural forces would rescue the innocent from perils to which they were exposed and would allow the guilty to be physically harmed.

The *ordeal of water* was performed by casting the suspect into a pond or river. If the suspect floated to the surface without any action of swimming, she was deemed guilty. If the suspect sank, she was pulled out and pronounced innocent. The *hot water ordeal* required the accused to plunge his bare arm up to the elbow into boiling water without injury. In the *ordeal of the cursed morsel*, the suspect swallowed a piece of dry bread with a feather in it. If the suspect did not choke, he was found innocent. The *ordeal of the red-hot iron* required the accused to carry a heated poker weighing one, two, or three pounds over a certain distance. After that, the suspect's hand was bound, and in three days the bandages were removed. If the wound had not become infected, the suspect was pronounced innocent. A variation of this ordeal required the accused person to walk barefoot and blindfolded over nine red-hot plowshares placed at uneven distances. The ordeals of the red-hot iron and the plowshares were also called the *fire ordeals* and were often reserved for nobility.

Evidence from very early cases indicates that there were more acquittals than convictions by ordeal, but the severity of the methods may have encouraged cheating. It is impossible to tell exactly how compelling the psychological stresses of the ordeal were, but all were administered amidst the ritual of the church at the high moment of the mass. In time church leaders came to disapprove of the participation of clergymen in a somewhat pagan tradition, and in 1215 priests were forbidden to take part in trials by ordeal. In remote places, the practice continued for a time as priests disobeyed the order, but eventually trial by ordeal was eliminated. This made the criminal law of England unenforceable because the chief means of determining guilt or innocence had been abolished.

The people were reluctant to accept a system that permitted a judge to determine the facts in a criminal case. That would be replacing the voice of God with that of a mortal man. For a while, the law enforcers imprisoned persons with a general reputation for wrongdoing, banished those guilty of moderately serious crimes, and required pledges of security to ensure the peacefulness of persons accused of small crimes. When these measures proved unsatisfactory, judges began calling upon groups of people in the community to make decisions. As many as forty-eight neighbors might be asked whether the accused was guilty or innocent. Their opinions were based on what they knew or could find out about the case and not on the presentation of evidence or testimony. This procedure was a forerunner of the modern JURY.

ORDER 📖 Direction of a court or judge normally made or entered in writing, and not included in a JUDGMENT, which determines some point or directs some step in the proceedings. 📖

The decision of a court or judge is made in the form of an order. A court may issue an order after a MOTION of a party requesting the order, or the court itself may issue an order on its own discretion. For example, courts routinely issue scheduling orders, which set the timetable and procedure for managing a civil lawsuit. More substantive orders, however, typically are made following a motion by one of the parties.

A motion is an application for an order. The granting or denying of a motion is a matter of judicial discretion. When a motion is granted, the moving party (the party who requests the motion) is ordinarily limited to the RELIEF requested in the application. Although no particular form is required, a court order granting a motion should be sufficiently explicit to enable the parties to do whatever is directed. Though a court is not obligated to issue an opinion, in most cases a party is entitled to have the reasons for the decision of the court stated in the order. The order must be consistent with the relief requested in the motion, and it should set forth any conditions on which relief is awarded.

In trial courts the attorney for a party who obtains a favorable ruling usually has the responsibility of writing a proposed order. A copy of the proposed order is furnished to the other party so that he or she can propose amendments to it. It is then presented to the court for settlement and approval. Courts are free, however, to modify proposed orders or to write their own order. APPELLATE COURTS routinely write their own orders.

To take effect, an order must be entered, filed, or incorporated into the minutes of the court. An entry or filing must be made with the COURT ADMINISTRATOR within the prescribed time limits.

Aside from scheduling orders and other orders that deal with the administration of a case, there are several general categories of orders. An INTERLOCUTORY order is an order that does not decide the case but settles some intervening matters relating to it or affords some temporary relief. For example, in a DIVORCE case, a judge will issue an interlocutory order that sets the terms for temporary CHILD SUPPORT and visitation rights while the case is pending.

A RESTRAINING ORDER may be issued upon the filing of an application for an INJUNCTION forbidding the defendant to do the threatened act until the court has a HEARING on the application. These types of orders are also called TEMPORARY RESTRAINING ORDERS (TROs), because they are meant to be effective until the court decides whether to order an injunction. For example, if a neighborhood association seeks to prevent a land developer from cutting down a stand of trees, the association would seek an injunction to prevent the cutting and a TRO to forbid the developer from removing the trees before the court holds a hearing. If the association did not request a TRO, the developer could legally cut down the trees and effectively render the injunction request MOOT.

A final order is one that terminates the action itself or finally decides some matter litigated by the parties. In a civil lawsuit, the plaintiff may make many ALLEGATIONS and legal CLAIMS, some of which the court may dispose of during the litigation by the issuance of an order. When the court is ready to completely dispose of the case, it enters a final order. As part of the final order, the court directs that judgment be entered, which authorizes the court administrator to close the case in that court.

ORDER OF THE COIF ▥ An unincorporated national scholastic honor society in law. Its purpose is to foster excellence in legal scholarship and to recognize those who have attained high grades in law school or who have distinguished themselves in the teaching of law. There are more than sixty chapters located in law schools throughout the country. ▥

The honor society is named after the English Order of the Coif, the most ancient and one of the most honored institutions of the common law. The coif was a close-fitting cap of white linen that covered the ears and was tied with strings under the chin, like a baby's bonnet. It originated in the twelfth century as a head covering for men and became part of the ecclesiastic and legal headgear, lasting until the six-

teenth century. For a long period of time, English judges were selected only from the order.

The Order of the Coif honor society was formed in 1912 as a national organization. The national constitution sets requirements for election to membership and criteria for the creation of chapters at law schools. The order is a federated organization with authority in local matters vested in each chapter. Each chapter has its officers, and the national organization has an executive committee composed of three officers and three other members. Officers are elected every three years.

Law students who are graduating seniors are eligible for election to the Order of the Coif if they have completed 75 percent of their law studies in graded courses and their grade record ranks them in the top 10 percent of all graduating seniors of the chapter's school. A chapter may also elect members of the law school faculty if the chapter believes professors have exhibited qualities of scholarship consistent with the objectives of the order.

A chapter may each year elect to honorary membership one member of the legal profession who is recognized for his or her scholarship. Every three years the national executive committee may elect up to five honorary members who have attained national distinction for their contributions to the legal system.

In addition, every three years the Order of the Coif recognizes legal scholarship by conferring one or more awards on the author or authors of published legal works. The national executive committee also is empowered to establish other awards for the purpose of recognizing preeminent legal scholarship and leadership among law students, law professors, judges, and practitioners.

ORDINANCE ▥ A law, statute, or regulation enacted by a MUNICIPAL CORPORATION. ▥

An ordinance is a law passed by a municipal government. A municipality, such as a city, town, village, or borough, is a political subdivision of a state within which a municipal corporation has been established to provide local government to a population in a defined area.

Ordinances constitute the subject matter of municipal law. The power of municipal governments to enact ordinances is derived from the state constitution or statutes or through the legislative grant of a municipal CHARTER. The charter in large part dictates how much power elected officials have to regulate actions within the municipality. Municipalities that have been granted "HOME RULE" charters by the legislature have the most authority to act. If, however, a municipality enacts an ordinance that exceeds its charter or is in conflict with state or federal law, the ordinance can be challenged in court and ruled void.

Many ordinances deal with maintaining public safety, health, morals, and GENERAL WELFARE. For example, a municipality may enact housing ordinances that set minimum standards of HABITABILITY. Other ordinances deal with fire and safety regulations that residential, commercial, and industrial property owners must follow. Many municipalities have enacted noise ordinances, which prohibit prescribed levels of noise after certain hours of the evening.

Ordinances may also deal with public streets and sidewalks. They typically include regulations regarding parking, snow removal, and littering. Restrictions on pets, including "pooper scooper" and leash laws, are also governed by municipal ordinances.

One of the most significant areas of municipal law is ZONING. Zoning ordinances constitute a master plan for land use within the municipality. A municipality is typically divided into residential, commercial, and industrial zoning districts. Zoning attempts to conserve the value of property and to encourage the most appropriate use of land throughout a particular locality.

In the past, many U.S. municipalities enacted a variety of ordinances regulating public morals and behavior. Many, such as ordinances that prohibited spitting on a public sidewalk, have been repealed or are rarely enforced.

ORGAN DONATION LAW Dramatic developments in organ and tissue transplantation have allowed persons with life-threatening illnesses a chance to live. The successful transplantation of kidneys, livers, hearts, lungs, eyes, and skin has been enhanced by better surgical techniques and new drugs, such as cyclosporin, that prevent the body from rejecting a transplanted organ. Success, however, has led to an undersupply of organs for the estimated thirty thousand patients each year who need a transplant. Laws have been enacted at the state and local level that attempt to provide a better system of organ donation and distribution and to encourage individuals to volunteer to be organ donors.

The Uniform Anatomical Gift Act that was drafted in 1968 was the first effort at providing a national organ and tissue donation policy. The act created a uniform legal procedure for persons who wish to donate organs and for hospitals and medical institutions that want to accept them. Under this model act, which has been adopted in some form by all fifty states, a person of sound mind, who is at least eighteen years of age, may donate all or part of his or her own body. There are several ways for a donor to record the wish to make a donation. The donor may include the donation in a WILL. If part of a will, the provision becomes effective immediately upon death, unlike other provisions of the will, which need to go through PROBATE before they become effective. In practical terms, however, a will may be ineffective. TIME IS OF THE ESSENCE in organ donation, and if the will is not read for several days, it may be too late to make an effective donation.

The uniform act provides for a more common form of recording a person's intention to make an organ donation: a donor card that may be carried in a wallet. States also allow this donor information to be imprinted on a driver's license. When a person applies for a driver's license, she or he has the option of including a desire to donate organs. Despite the simplicity of this option, it has not generated the quantity of donors that proponents of the procedure expected.

A written donation must be signed by the donor and witnessed by at least two other people. A donation can be made orally, but it too must be witnessed by at least two other people. A dying patient can communicate his or her wish to donate organs to an attending physician, who can act as one of the witnesses. However, the attending physician cannot be the doctor who removes or transplants the organ.

A person can revoke in writing or orally her or his intent to make an organ or tissue donation. If a dying person is unable to communicate and has not expressed an intent to donate, a family member or GUARDIAN can make a GIFT of all or part of the person's body, within certain limitations. In general, even if a person has expressed the intent to donate, physicians still ask permission of a family member or guardian.

The uniform act forbids the sale of body parts. The recipient cannot pay for the donated organ but must pay for the cost of transportation and transplant. Organs and tissue can only be received by hospitals, surgeons, physicians, educational institutions involved in medical or dental research, a storage facility for these institutions, or any specified individual who needs the organ personally for therapy or transplantation.

A 1986 federal law (42 U.S.C.A. § 1320b–8) requires all hospitals participating in MEDICARE or MEDICAID to implement a "required request" policy. Hospitals are required to discuss with potential donors and their families "the option of organ and tissue donation and their option to decline."

SHOULD DYING BABIES BE ORGAN DONORS?

As many as half of the approximately 1,500 children waiting for organ transplants each year die before donors can be found. The shortage of donors has led to calls for permitting the organs of children born with the birth defect anencephaly to be donated before the children die. The issue has proved controversial, as doctors and medical ethicists debate the legality and morality of allowing the harvesting of organs from a person who is not legally dead.

Anencephaly is a birth defect that prevents the skull and brain from fully developing. While the heart and other internal organs of anencephalic infants often develop normally, most of the brain is missing. The anencephalic infant possesses a brain stem, which can keep breathing and heartbeat going temporarily. But because the cerebral cortex is missing, the infant has no thought or sensory functions and will never be conscious. Most of these infants die within hours or days of birth. Because of these bleak prospects, most of each year's 2,500 anencephalic pregnancies are aborted.

Some parents have forgone abortion but have sought to have their child's organs donated. Because the brain stem gradually fails after birth, an infant's heartbeat and breathing gradually slow until the infant dies of heart failure or stops breathing. The vital organs deteriorate, however, leaving them useless as transplants. The only way the organs can be used is if they are removed while the infant is still alive. This requirement cannot be met under current law because organ donation is premised on the dead donor rule: donors must be declared brain dead before their organs can be removed. An anencephalic infant exists in a gray area between life and death, but because the brain stem functions, he cannot be declared brain dead. Therefore, the harvesting of organs of anencephalic infants would require stretching the definition of death.

Some physicians, medical ethicists, and parents of anencephalic infants be-lieve that such a redefinition should occur and that organ retrieval from an anencephalic infant at birth should be permitted. They argue that an anencephalic infant's profound abnormality makes it permissible to make an exception to the dead donor rule. It is a unique abnormality: the infant never experiences consciousness.

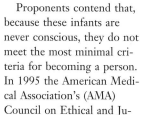

IN FOCUS

Proponents contend that, because these infants are never conscious, they do not meet the most minimal criteria for becoming a person. In 1995 the American Medical Association's (AMA) Council on Ethical and Judicial Affairs supported the idea of organ retrieval from anencephalic infants at birth on the basis that the infants' lack of consciousness meant that they could not suffer harm.

Proponents point out that it has been the parents of anencephalic infants who have sought to donate the babies' organs. As long as the harvesting of organs is done at the request of the parents and with their consent, the interests of the parents are not harmed. For these parents the desire to have some good come from the tragedy of giving birth to an anencephalic infant is the driving force in making their decision.

Finally, proponents note the shortage of organs for transplantation in children. Because of this shortage, many children die who might otherwise live a normal life if given a transplant. Some experts believe that using organs from anencephalic infants could mean up to an additional three hundred transplants a year. Faced with this prospect, proponents contend that society's interests are advanced by making a narrow exception to the dead donor rule.

Opponents are horrified at the idea of removing organs from a living infant. They contend that the dead donor rule is an important boundary in medical science. Crossing this line in the case of anencephalic infants, they contend, will cause a "slippery slope" effect. Physicians might ask to harvest organs from coma victims or from children with other severe, but nonfatal brain defects. Opponents argue that blurring the definition of brain death will have detrimental consequences to society greater than the benefit of obtaining organs from several hundred infants each year.

Critics further argue that anencephalic infants are human beings who deserve the protection of the law. They point out that, to be an organ donor, a person's entire brain must be declared dead. This means that the brain stem completely ceases to function and to produce electrical impulses and that the person has no reflexes or responses. Anencephalic infants do not meet all these criteria. They are not brain dead because the brain stem functions, they support their respiration independently, and they have responses and reflexes. These critics note that, only six months after its support of harvesting organs from anencephalic infants at birth, the AMA's Council on Ethical and Judicial Affairs reversed its decision, citing questions as to whether anencephalic infants are truly unconscious and whether they feel pain.

Though most of the critics ground their objections in ethical, moral, and religious concerns about the sanctity of human life, others have more pragmatic arguments. These critics argue that the debate itself over harvesting organs from anencephalic infants at birth harms the effort to recruit the general public as organ donors. The public may become fearful that the medical community is seeking ways to change the definition of death. The few hundred organs a year that could be gained through a change in law, these critics contend, is not worth the loss of thousands of potential donors.

Critics respect the desire of parents who wish to do something good through organ donation. Yet they contend that making parents feel better does not rank higher than society's interest in preserving human life. Unless a state passes a law that makes an exception to the dead donor rule, the use of anencephalic infants as organ sources immediately upon birth will not occur.

The 1984 National Organ Transplant Act (42 U.S.C.A. § 273 et seq.) initiated a national health care policy regarding organ transplantation. The act provided funds to help establish "qualified organ procurement organizations," banned the interstate sale of organs, and created a task force to study organ transplantation policy issues. The task force's 1986 report was an exhaustive examination of the medical, legal, social, and economic implications of organ procurement and transplantation. The 1986 required request law came from one of the task force's recommendations.

Despite these legal and medical mechanisms that seek to encourage organ donation, demand has continued to exceed supply. In 1996 it was estimated that eight people died every day waiting for a transplant that never came because of the donor shortage. In response, Congress enacted the Organ Donor Insert Card Act in 1996 (Pub. L. No. 104-91, 110 Stat. 1936). The act directed the secretary of the treasury to enclose with each tax refund check in 1997 an organ donor card. It was estimated that this would reach seventy million U.S. families and would result in increased donations.

The donation of an entire body to a medical school's anatomy department for educational use has had a long history. The Uniform Anatomical Gift Act applies to these donations as well.

CROSS-REFERENCES

Abortion; Death and Dying; Fetal Rights; Fetal Tissue Research; Health Care Law; Patients' Rights; Physicians and Surgeons.

ORGANIC LAW ▥ The FUNDAMENTAL LAW or CONSTITUTION of a particular state or nation, either written or unwritten, that defines and establishes the manner in which its government will be organized. ▥

ORGANIZATION ▥ A generic term for any type of group or association of individuals who are joined together either formally or legally. ▥

The term *organization* includes a CORPORATION, government, PARTNERSHIP, and any type of civil or political association of people.

ORGANIZED CRIME ▥ Criminal activity carried out by an organized enterprise. ▥

Modern organized crime is generally understood to have begun in Italy in the late nineteenth century. The secretive Sicilian group La Cosa Nostra, along with other Sicilian mafia, were more powerful than the Italian government in the early twentieth century. In 1924 BENITO MUSSOLINI's fascist government rose to power and Mussolini orchestrated a crackdown on the Italian mafia. Those mafiosi who were not jailed or killed were forced to flee the country. Many came to the United States, where they flourished in the art of bootlegging and other criminal activity. Since the 1920s organized crime has crossed ethnic lines, and is associated with no particular ethnic group.

Congress and many states maintain laws that severely punish crime committed by criminal enterprises. On the federal level, Congress passed the Organized Crime Control Act in 1970. The declared purpose of the act is to eradicate organized crime by expanding evidence-gathering techniques for law enforcement, specifying more acts as being crimes, authorizing enhanced penalties, and providing for the FORFEITURE of property owned by criminal enterprises.

The RACKETEER INFLUENCED AND CORRUPT ORGANIZATIONS ACT (RICO) (18 U.S.C.A. § 1961 et seq.) is the centerpiece of the Organized Crime Control Act. RICO is a group of statutes that define and set punishments for organized crime. The act's provisions apply to any enterprise that engages in racketeering activity. Racketeering is the act of engaging in a pattern of criminal offenses. The list of offenses that constitute racketeering when committed by an enterprise more than once is lengthy. It includes EXTORTION, FRAUD, MONEY LAUNDERING, federal drug offenses, MURDER, KIDNAPPING, gambling, ARSON, ROBBERY, BRIBERY, dealing in OBSCENE matter, COUNTERFEITING, EMBEZZLEMENT, OBSTRUCTION OF JUSTICE, obstruction of law enforcement, tampering with witnesses, filing of a false statement to obtain a PASSPORT, passport FORGERY and false use or misuse of a passport, PEONAGE, SLAVERY, unlawful receipt of WELFARE funds, interstate transport of stolen property, sexual exploitation of children, trafficking in counterfeit labels for audio and visual works, criminal infringement of COPYRIGHTS, trafficking in CONTRABAND cigarettes, white slavery, violation of payment and loan restrictions to LABOR UNIONS, and harboring, aiding, assisting, or transporting illegal ALIENS. RICO also includes forfeiture provisions that allow the government to take the property of parties found guilty of violations of the act.

Modern organized criminal enterprises make money by specializing in a variety of crimes, including extortion, BLACKMAIL, gambling, loan-sharking, political corruption, and the manufacture and sale of illicit narcotics. Extortion, a time-tested endeavor of organized crime, is the acquisition of property through the use of threats or force. For instance, a criminal enterprise located in a certain neighborhood of a city may visit shopkeepers and demand a specific amount of so-called protection money. If a shopkeeper does not pay the money, the criminal organization may strike at him, his property, or his family.

Blackmail is similar to extortion. It is committed when a person obtains money or value by accusing the victim of a crime, threatening the victim with harm or destruction of the victim's property, or threatening to reveal disgraceful facts about the victim.

Gambling and loan-sharking are other traditional activities of organized criminal enterprises. Where gambling is illegal, some organized crime groups act as the locus for gambling activity. In states where some gambling is legal and some gambling is illegal, organized crime groups offer illegal GAMING. Loan-sharking is the provision of loans at illegally high interest rates accompanied by the illegal use of force to collect on past due payments. In organized crime circles, such loans usually are made to persons who cannot obtain credit at legitimate financial institutions and who can serve the criminal enterprise in some way in the event they are unable to repay the loan. Loan-sharking not only provides organized criminal enterprises with money, it also helps enlarge the enterprise by bringing into the fold persons who owe a debt to the enterprise.

Political corruption has diminished as a focus of organized crime. In the first half of the twentieth century, some organized crime groups blackmailed or paid money to politicians in return for favorable legislation and favorable treatment from city hall. This sort of activity has decreased over the years as public scrutiny of political activity has increased.

The most recent major venture in organized crime is the manufacture and sale of illicit narcotics. This practice was prefigured in the activities of organized crime from 1919 to 1933. During this period ALCOHOL was illegal under the EIGHTEENTH AMENDMENT to the U.S. Constitution, and the manufacture and sale of liquor was a favorite activity of organized crime groups. The manufacture and sale of illegal liquors, or bootlegging, was extremely profitable, and it gave organized crime a foothold in American life. Many organized criminal enterprises now mimic bootlegging by fulfilling the demand for illegal drugs.

Violence often accompanies organized crime. Many crime syndicates use murder, torture, ASSAULT, and terrorism to keep themselves powerful and profitable. The constant threat of violence keeps victims and witnesses silent. Without them, prosecutors find it difficult to press charges against organized criminals.

The modern notion of organized crime in the United States has expanded beyond the prototypical paradigm of family operations. Organized crime now refers to any collection of persons in a continuing operation of criminal activity, including street gangs. To combat the violence and other illegal activity of street gangs, federal and state legislatures have passed laws pertaining specifically to street gangs. Many states provide extra punishment for persons in street gangs who are convicted of certain crimes.

On the federal level, a street gang is defined as an ongoing group, club, organization, or association of five or more persons formed for the purpose of committing a violent crime or drug offense, with members that have engaged in a continuing series of violent crimes or drug law violations that affect interstate or foreign commerce (18 U.S.C.A. § 521). Any person in a street gang convicted for committing or conspiring to commit a violent federal crime or certain federal drug offenses receives an extra ten years in prison beyond the prison sentence for the actual crime.

Organized crime is difficult to eradicate. It tends to occur in large cities where anonymity is relatively easy to maintain. The size and hereditary makeup of many enterprises make them capable of surviving the arrest and imprisonment of numerous members. Many organized crime participants are careful, efficient, and professional criminals, making them difficult to apprehend.

Another reason organized crime is so durable is that the participants are extremely dedicated. This is not only because the group looks after its own, but also because of the grave consequences of betrayal. Members of organized crime groups often take an oath of allegiance. For example, members of La Cosa Nostra stated, "I enter alive into this organization and leave it dead."

See also CAPONE, ALPHONSE; DRUGS AND NARCOTICS.

ORGAN TRANSPLANTATION The transfer of organs such as the kidneys, heart, or liver from one body to another.

The transplantation of human organs has become a common medical procedure. Typical organs transplanted include the kidneys, heart, liver, pancreas, cornea, skin, bones, and lungs. The organ most frequently transplanted is the cornea, followed by the kidney.

The first human organ transplants were performed in the early 1960s, when it became possible to use special tissue-matching techniques and immunosuppressive drugs that reduced the chance that a transplanted organ would be rejected by the host body. By the early 1980s, the new immunosuppressive drug cyclosporine led to great advances in the success rate of organ transplants.

Organ Shortages As organ transplants have become increasingly successful, the most significant problem related to them has become the shortage of available organs. A large gap separates the high demand for organs and their scarce supply. Experts estimated that by the late 1980s, three people were on transplant waiting lists for every available organ. Given the grossly inadequate supply of organs, many vexing ethical, legal, and political issues surround the question of what is the best way to harvest or procure organs.

A number of laws have sought to address the problem of organ procurement. The Uniform Anatomical Gift Act (8A U.L.A. 15-16 [1983]), drafted in 1968 and adopted in all fifty states, allows any COMPETENT adult to state in writing, including by signing a donor card or checking off an item on a driver's license application, whether he wishes to allow or forbid the use of her or his organs after death. The act also permits NEXT OF KIN to authorize donation. Such a program, termed encouraged voluntarism, relies on the free and autonomous choice of the individual or surviving family as the basis for organ donation.

Organ donation is also aided by brain-death statutes. These make it possible to declare as dead those who have lost whole-brain function but whose bodies are kept alive through artificial means. Such brain-dead persons become potential organ donors. In fact, most organs are obtained from accident victims.

The combination of encouraged voluntarism and brain-death statutes has not produced adequate numbers of organs. For example, a 1984 study estimated that of the 20,000 people each year who die of accidents or strokes and are medically suitable organ donors, only 3,000 served as donors. Experts have estimated that only three percent of those who serve as organ donors are actually carrying a donor card at the time they are pronounced dead.

A number of different problems contribute to this shortage of donated organs. Most people are fearful or uncomfortable with thoughts of death—particularly their own—and consequently do not contemplate organ donation. Others point out that some states have not yet enacted statutes that recognize brain death as the definition of death. Also, a general distrust of large, impersonal medical institutions keeps many people from committing to organ donation. Many people are afraid that if they carry an organ donor card, they will not receive adequate medical treatment in an emergency. Moreover, medical professionals are generally not required to present the option of organ donation to critically ill or injured patients and their families. As a result, even if a person has a donor card, it may go unnoticed.

When the system of encouraged voluntarism established by the Uniform Anatomical Gift Act failed to increase the number of available organs adequately, some individuals advocated establishing a legal market in organs. Some versions of an organ market would allow living individuals to sell one of their kidneys at a market price. More commonly, organ market advocates propose the sale of organs taken only from those who have died—that is, cadaveric organs—usually through "forward contracts" signed when the patient was living. However, the sale of organs has been barred by state and federal legislation, particularly the National Organ Transplant Act (42 U.S.C.A. § 274(e) [1985]), which states, "It shall be unlawful for any person to knowingly acquire, receive or otherwise transfer any human organ for valuable consideration for use in human transplantation if the transfer affects interstate commerce." Rather than creating an organ market, Congress has since sought to establish laws that establish "required request" protocols. These protocols would require major hospitals to ask a patient's family if it wishes to donate the patient's organs (Omnibus Reconciliation Act of 1986, Pub. L. No. 99-509, 100 Stat. 1874, 2009).

Some states have gone a step further, passing "presumed consent" laws that allow for the removal of organs unless the next of kin objects or it is known that the potential donor objected to such a procedure while alive. Some of these laws allow only the removal of corneas under such conditions; others apply only to unclaimed dead bodies. The huge demand for organs may lead to the wider passage of presumed consent laws and the creation of market incentives for organ donation.

Controversial Issues Organ transplants generate increasingly vexing legal and ethical questions as medical technology becomes more complex. Three controversial issues surrounding the subject are conception for organ donation, donor consent, and transplants from terminally disabled infants.

In some instances, a child is conceived expressly for the purpose of using her organs for transplantation in another person, usually a blood relative. In 1990, for example, a California couple gave birth to a child they had con-

ORGAN PROCUREMENT:
IS IT BETTER TO GIVE OR TO SELL?

In the early days of organ transplant surgery, during the 1960s and 1970s, the practice was seen as experimental and risky. Patients' bodies often rejected a transplant, and the survival rate in many cases was deemed too low to be acceptable. However, with the development of new surgical procedures and the wide use of new immunosuppressive drugs such as cyclosporine in the 1980s, organ transplantation became a common medical technique available to more and more people. In the 1980s, over 400,000 transplants were performed in the United States. The age range of heart transplant recipients has expanded from forty-five to over sixty at the upper limit, and to infancy at the lower limit.

Results such as these have caused such a demand for organ transplants that there are far more potential organ recipients than available organs. Those who are deemed medically suitable to receive organs are put on long waiting lists, and it is often months or years before they get the organs they need; many others are deemed medically unsuitable and are not even put on waiting lists. Some have criticized the term *medically unsuitable* as an arbitrary and uncertain medical judgment used simply to prevent raising the hopes of those who are unlikely to get a timely transplant.

What should be done about this dire shortage of organs available for transplantation? Three different organ procurement systems have been proposed as a means of alleviating the situation: an organ market, a presumed consent program, and a required request program. All three proposals have their advocates and detractors.

Organ Market

Although the sale of human organs was made illegal by the 1985 National Organ Transplantation Act (42 U.S.C.A. § 274(e)), an organ market remains a widely discussed alternative to the generally accepted approach of encouraged voluntarism. Its supporters claim that the system of encouraged voluntarism, which supplies organs free of cost through altruistic donation, has created a rapidly worsening organ shortage.

Typically, advocates of the market system are quick to note that they do not support a market in organs from living donors, nor do they envision donors and recipients haggling in hospital rooms. Instead, they focus on paying potential donors a fixed amount for signing a contract that authorizes the future removal of one or more of their organs at death. This may, for example, occur in the form of a uniform cash payment or tax credit to all individuals who agree to sign a donor form on the back of their driver's license application. This type of arrangement is called a forward market because payment for the organ occurs well before the organ is removed. The amount paid for such donor contracts could be adjusted up or down depending on the demand for organs.

Some of those who call for an organ market take the economist's perspective and claim that it is the best alternative because it would maximize social welfare. The benefits of such a system would include an increase in the supply of organs, and thus the saving of many more lives and the improved health of many more patients. More patients who have to undergo the expensive and time-consuming procedure of kidney dialysis, for example, would be able to instead receive a transplant. Moreover, firms and individuals engaged in the procurement business would have a direct financial incentive to increase public awareness of the facts surrounding organ donation and transplantation.

Advocates claim that a market would also produce a number of indirect benefits. Medical professionals would be able to choose from a greater number of available organs from the dead—termed cadaveric organs—and obtain higher-quality organs that more precisely match the tissue type of the recipient. With more closely matched organs would come less need to rely on living donors, thus avoiding the pain, loss of pay, and risks associated with donor surgery. Moreover, more organs would mean more transplant operations, and with increased frequency, the cost of those operations would fall as hospitals and their staffs become more proficient at conducting and managing them. Organ market supporters also argue that an undersupply of organs leads to a black market, and that this market will only become greater with time. Finally, an increase in the harvesting of cadaveric organs would eventually lead to greater social acceptance of the practice as part of the death process.

---

ceived solely in hopes that the baby's bone marrow cells would save the life of their teenage daughter, who was dying of cancer. Although the legality of such conceptions has not been challenged, the practice raises ethical questions relating to who may give informed consent for the donor child and whether such a practice may be considered CHILD ABUSE.

The problem of donor consent has arisen in lawsuits seeking to compel persons to donate organs to relatives. For example, in 1990, an Illinois family with a son who had leukemia brought a lawsuit seeking to compel the boy's half sister and half brother to submit to preliminary medical tests that would have established their suitability to serve as bone marrow do-

Critics see an organ market as not expanding the number of choices available but diminishing them, thereby undermining the ethical goal of individual autonomy and free choice. Even if sales were restricted to organs from those who are dead, they claim, the potential conflicts of interest on the part of physicians, patients, and families would erode the capability of individuals to make decisions about their own bodies. Critics also point out that if the sale of organs from living subjects were permitted, poor people would have economic incentives to sell their body parts, and as a result their own health could suffer.

Detractors of the market approach also claim that it would not increase the supply of organs and that the price of organs would be so high that few people would consent to give away their valuable organs. Some also claim that an organ market would result in lower-quality organs because poorer people, who are generally less healthy, would be more likely to sell organs for profit. Moreover, if organs had to be purchased, poor people would not be able to afford transplants. Market advocates counter that the total costs of organ transplantation would likely fall under a market system, making it more, not less, accessible to poor people.

Presumed Consent Program

The presumed consent system of organ procurement is currently used in many European countries. It means that medical professionals are presumed to have a deceased individual's and surviving family members' consent to remove needed organs, unless those individuals have earlier made known their objections to organ removal. Supporters of this system argue that it increases the supply of organs, makes the decision to remove organs much easier, and further removes the physician and hospital from liability.

Critics of the presumed consent system find fault with it for economic, legal, and ethical reasons. Looking at the program in terms of economics, they claim that it does not actually increase the number of organs harvested because it does not impose financial incentives for organ requests. As a result, medical staff still exhibit a reluctance to remove organs and that leads to a continuation of the organ shortage. Critics also claim that a presumed consent system is expensive to create and maintain. It requires the creation of large, centralized registries listing individuals' decisions regarding their own body, and these must be updated continuously. Mistakes inevitably occur, causing unwanted organ removal and expensive lawsuits.

Other critics of the presumed consent system find it legally suspect and charge that if it is implemented in the United States it will violate the Due Process Clause of the Constitution.

Those who find fault with the ethical premise of presumed consent argue that it removes the moral dignity surrounding donation by making it mandatory. It also detracts from the goal of free choice and autonomous behavior by precluding the individual from making no decision or from leaving the decision to others.

Required Request Program

A required request program is a more moderate approach to the problem of organ donation. It seeks to reform the existing system of encouraged voluntarism by requiring that family members or guardians be given the opportunity to make an organ donation when a death has occurred. Such a program would require hospitals to have a specially trained person to approach families and inquire about organ donation at the time death is pronounced. The request would be noted in writing on the death certificate to ensure that medical providers comply with the policy. The required request system would allow for exceptions in cases where a request would not be in the best interests of family members or guardians, with such exceptions also duly noted on the death certificate. Such a system, its advocates claim, would increase freedom of choice by informing individuals of their options.

Proponents of this system point to statistics that indicate that in the U.S. public, the level of altruism regarding organ donation is quite high. In some hospitals, for example, over 60 percent of the families who were asked to donate the organs of loved ones agreed to do so. The problem with the current system, they maintain, is that donor cards do not adequately tap this altruistic sentiment. They also note that a required request system would ensure that donor cards or written directives are honored. With time, such requests would become a routine part of the death process in medical facilities, making them less surprising and less intrusive to family privacy at the time of death.

Critics of the required request system say that it would not do enough to change an already flawed organ procurement system. Moreover, they argue that approaching families in the hours following the death of a loved one imposes too much psychological distress.

nors. A judge, noting the objections of the mother of the half siblings, ruled that such tests would be an invasion of the potential donors' right of PRIVACY. The Illinois Supreme Court later upheld this ruling (*Curran v. Bosze*, No. 70501 [Ill. filed Dec. 20, 1990]). In its opinion, the court outlined three critical factors in determining the best interests of the donating child: (1) the consenting parent must know the inherent risks and benefits of the procedure, (2) the primary caretaker of the child must be able to provide emotional support, and (3) there must be an existing, close relationship between the donor and the recipient.

The issue of organ donations made by terminally disabled infants came to national attention in 1992 when a Florida couple sought to have the organs of their anencephalic baby, Theresa Ann Campo Pearson, donated for use by other newborns. Anencephaly is a rare and always fatal gestational disorder in which the brain develops a stem, or lower brain, but not a cortex, or upper brain. Though the rest of the anencephalic infant's body is healthy, the disorder causes the child to die soon after birth. Theresa Ann's mother and father sought to have her declared brain dead, but a judge stated that under Florida statutes, a declaration of brain death may be made only if activity in all parts of the brain has ceased (Fla. Stat. ch. 382.009 [1992]). The judge noted that Theresa Ann had lower-brain activity. She died ten days after birth, without having donated her organs.

Critics of this decision have argued that because anencephaly is always fatal, the organs of children with this disorder should be used to save other children. Supporters note that if an exception were made for anencephaly, other severely disabled persons may be inappropriately targeted as a source for organs. Others argue that the life of one child, no matter how brief or unsatisfactory, cannot be taken to save another.

See also DEATH AND DYING; FETAL RIGHTS.

ORIGINAL INTENT ◫ The theory of interpretation by which judges attempt to ascertain the meaning of a particular provision of a state or federal constitution by determining how the provision was understood at the time it was drafted and ratified. ◫

Sometimes called original understanding, originalism, or intentionalism, the theory of original intent is applied by judges when they are asked to exercise the power of JUDICIAL REVIEW during a LEGAL PROCEEDING. (The power of judicial review is the power of state and federal courts to review and invalidate laws that have been passed by the legislative and executive branches of government but violate a constitutional principle.)

Not every judge adheres to the theory of original intent, and many adherents fail to apply it in a uniform and faithful manner. Judges who do attempt to apply this judicial philosophy generally agree that only through its application may courts be bound by the law and not their own views of what is desirable. They also generally agree that courts must apply original intent in order to preserve the representative democracy created by the federal Constitution.

Originalists observe that the democracy created by the U.S. Constitution is marked by three essential features: a SEPARATION OF POWERS, FEDERALISM, and a BILL OF RIGHTS. The Constitution separates the powers of the federal government into three branches, which help foster what is known as a system of checks and balances. Article I of the Constitution delegates lawmaking power to the legislative branch, which comprises the two houses of Congress. This lawmaking power authorizes members of Congress to pass LEGISLATION that reflects the values of their voting constituency, usually consisting of a plurality or majority of the adults residing in the representative's home state. If a representative makes policy that is inconsistent with the values of the representative's constituents, the representative will likely be voted out of office at the next election and replaced by someone who is more sensitive to popular will. Under this system, Congress remains perpetually accountable to the U.S. people, who, originalists point out, are the ultimate source of authority from which the Constitution derives its legitimacy.

The EXECUTIVE BRANCH is also held accountable to the U.S. public at the voting booth. Every four years, U.S. citizens are given the opportunity to determine who will be PRESIDENT of their country. They generally vote for someone who is perceived to represent their economic, societal, and personal interests on a variety of issues, including taxes, the WELFARE system, and the right to live and die free from governmental restraint.

Article II empowers the president to sign the congressional acts that he or she approves and VETO the rest, enabling the executive branch to influence national policy, if not make it. The president may also influence national policy by promulgating executive decrees (which are orders issued by the executive branch without congressional approval) that are intended to implement a constitutional provision, federal law, or TREATY. In addition, Article II charges the president with the responsibility of enforcing legislation that has been passed by Congress and signed into law.

Article III of the Constitution delegates federal judicial power to the U.S. Supreme Court and to other "inferior" FEDERAL COURTS that Congress may establish. Unlike the president and members of Congress, federal judges are largely unaccountable to the U.S. electorate. Once appointed to the bench by the president and confirmed by the Senate, a federal judge holds office for life, unless she or he retires or is removed for "treason, bribery, or other high crimes and misdemeanors" (U.S. Const. art. II, § 4).

Although Article III does not confer the power of judicial review, in *Marbury v. Madison*, 5 U.S. (1 Cranch) 137, 2 L. Ed. 60 (1803), the Supreme Court ruled that it is "emphatically the duty" of the federal "judicial department to say what the law is" by "resolving the operation" of congressional legislation that conflicts with the paramount law of the U.S. Constitution. *Marbury* thus emphasized the traditional role of courts as oracles of the law; however, it provided little guidance on how courts should interpret and apply the particular provisions of the Constitution.

Originalists attempt to provide this guidance. They argue that the interpretation of most written documents, legal or otherwise, involves a form of "communication" in which "the writer seeks to communicate with the reader" (Graglia 1992, 1023). Constitutional interpretation is no different, originalists say, because it involves the attempt of judges, as readers, to understand the meaning of a constitutional provision as conveyed by the Framers and ratifiers who authored it. Originalists believe that judges who fail to employ this method of interpretation transform courts into naked power organs (Weschler 1959, 27).

Originalists contend that judges who deviate from the original understanding of a constitutional provision are forced to replace that understanding with their own subjective sympathies, social preferences, and notions of reasonableness. When judges substitute their own value choices for those actually written in the Constitution, federal courts become super-legislatures that make decisions based on the personal will of judges and not the law of the land (*Day-Brite Lighting v. Missouri*, 342 U.S. 421, 72 S. Ct. 405, 96 L. Ed. 469 [1952]).

Originalists assert that judges who legislate from the bench violate the separation of powers by making law rather than interpreting and applying it. These judges also violate the principles of federalism, the second essential feature of U.S. constitutional democracy identified by originalists. Under these principles, courts must strike an appropriate balance between the sovereignties of state and federal governments, not allowing the smaller state governments to be wholly consumed by the ubiquitous federal government. Originalists contend that this balance impermissibly tips in favor of the federal government when federal courts invent new constitutional rights that state governments are then required to enforce.

Such rights have protected areas concerning homosexual behavior, ABORTION, CAPITAL PUNISH-MENT and individual PRIVACY. Justice CLARENCE THOMAS, an exponent of originalism, observed that "[t]he federal Constitution" is not meant to "address all ills in our society" (*Hudson v. McMillian*, 503 U.S. 1, 112 S. Ct. 995, 117 L. Ed. 2d 156 [1992] [Thomas, J., dissenting]). Nor is the Constitution meant, Thomas said, "to prohibit everything that is intensely undesirable" (*Bennis v. Michigan*, __U.S.__, 116 S. Ct. 994, 134 L. Ed. 2d 68 [1996] [Thomas, J., concurring]). Originalists claim that the Constitution must protect only the areas of life that are expressly referenced in or fairly implied by the explicit language of its text. In other words, where the Constitution stops speaking, the state governments may begin.

Respect for principles of federalism, then, is intimately connected with the third essential feature of U.S. Constitutional democracy identified by originalists, the Bill of Rights. The Bill of Rights protects certain freedoms from the popular will no matter how democratically the majority attempts to trample them. In all other areas, originalists assert, state and federal majorities are entitled to rule for no better reason than that they are majorities. Originalists explain that majority tyranny occurs if legislation invades areas properly left to individual freedom, and minority tyranny occurs if the majority is prevented from ruling where its power is legitimate.

Originalists argue that the JUDICIARY facilitates minority tyranny by improperly interpreting the Bill of Rights to guarantee liberties not contemplated by the language and intent of the Framers. To avoid this pitfall, originalists believe, judges must safeguard only the liberties that can be clearly derived from the Constitution. Originalists cite a series of cases in which the Supreme Court recognized a right to privacy as the antithesis of proper constitutional interpretation.

In *Griswold v. Connecticut*, 381 U.S. 479, 85 S. Ct. 1678, 14 L. Ed. 2d 510 (1965), the Court struck down a state law forbidding married adults to use contraceptives, because it violated their right to privacy guaranteed by the First, Third, Fourth, Fifth, Ninth, and Fourteenth Amendments. Although a majority of the Court recognized privacy interests that may be inferred from these several CONSTITUTIONAL AMENDMENTS, Justice Potter Stewart noted in a dissenting opinion that "no such general right of privacy" can be found in the express language of "the Bill of Rights" or "any other part of the Constitution." Originalists argue that courts cannot apply a general right to privacy in a politically neutral manner without protecting all sorts of illegal activities that are conducted in private, such as spousal abuse, PRICE-FIXING, and PROSTITUTION.

CROSS-REFERENCES

Bork, Robert Heron; Constitution of the United States; *Griswold v. Connecticut;* Jurisprudence; *Marbury v. Madison;* Penumbra; Scalia, Antonin.

ORIGINAL JURISDICTION 📖 The authority of a tribunal to entertain a lawsuit, try it, and set forth a JUDGMENT on the law and facts. 📖

Original JURISDICTION is distinguishable from APPELLATE jurisdiction, which is the power of a court to hear and enter judgment upon a case brought for review.

ORIGINAL WRIT 📖 A document formerly used to commence a lawsuit in English courts. 📖

Historically, the WRIT needed to start a personal action was a mandatory letter from the king, issued by the CHANCERY and sealed with the Great Seal. It was directed to the SHERIFF of the county where the wrong was supposed to have been committed and required the sheriff to command that the defendant either satisfy the plaintiff's claim or answer the charges that had been made. This form of writ has been replaced by the SUMMONS, which commences CIVIL ACTIONS today, but the summons is still sometimes called an original writ.

ORIGINATION FEE 📖 A charge imposed by a lending institution or a bank for the service of processing a loan. 📖

For example, a bank might charge an individual who has applied for a student loan an origination fee of one percent for processing the application and granting the loan.

ORPHAN'S COURT 📖 The designation of tribunals in a number of New England states that have PROBATE or surrogate JURISDICTION. 📖

Such a court ordinarily has the power to handle such matters as the establishment of WILLS, the administration and distribution of decedents' estates, the supervision of the guardianship of INFANTS, and the control of their property.

LIBRARY OF CONGRESS

James Otis, Jr.

OSTENSIBLE 📖 Apparent; visible; exhibited. 📖

Ostensible authority is power that a principal, either by design or through the absence of ordinary care, permits others to believe his or her AGENT possesses.

OTIS, JAMES, JR. James Otis, Jr., was a Massachusetts lawyer who became a leading colonial political activist in the 1760s. His constitutional challenge to British governance of the colonies in the *Writs of Assistance* case in 1761 was one of the most important legal events leading to the American Revolution. A brilliant speaker and writer, Otis faded from the revolutionary scene as he struggled with alcoholism and mental illness.

Otis was born on February 5, 1725, in West Barnstable, Massachusetts. His father, James Otis, Sr., was a prominent merchant and political figure in the colony. Otis graduated from Harvard College in 1743 and was admitted to the bar in 1748. He moved his law practice from Plymouth, Massachusetts, to Boston in 1750 and was appointed advocate general of the Boston vice-admiralty court in 1756. He served until 1761, when the furor over writs of assistance pushed Otis into becoming an opponent of the colonial government he served.

A writ of assistance was a general SEARCH WARRANT that allowed customs officers to command the assistance of any local public official in making entry and seizing CONTRABAND goods. Goods seized by use of the writ were brought before the vice-admiralty court, which determined if the goods had been imported lawfully. Smuggling had bedeviled the colonial government for many years, but the need for tax revenue during the course of the French and Indian War led to a crackdown. The use of the writ made revenue collection easier, but it upset the merchant community of Boston.

Otis resigned his position on the vice-admiralty court and agreed to represent the merchants in challenging the legality of the writs of assistance. At trial Otis argued that the writs were a form of tyranny. He coined the

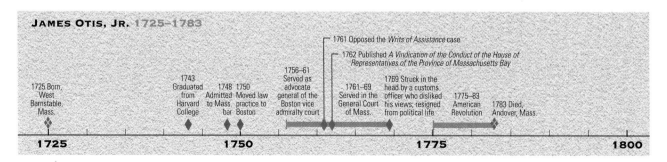

JAMES OTIS, JR. 1725–1783

- 1725 Born, West Barnstable, Mass.
- 1743 Graduated from Harvard College
- 1748 Admitted to Mass. bar
- 1750 Moved law practice to Boston
- 1756–61 Served as advocate general of the Boston vice admiralty court
- 1761 Opposed the *Writs of Assistance* case
- 1761–69 Served in the General Court of Mass.
- 1762 Published *A Vindication of the Conduct of the House of Representatives of the Province of Massachusetts Bay*
- 1769 Struck in the head by a customs officer who disliked his views; resigned from political life
- 1775–83 American Revolution
- 1783 Died, Andover, Mass.

1725   1750   1775   1800

phrase "A man's home is his castle" to describe the sanctity and privacy that a citizen deserved from his or her government.

More important, he argued that the writs were unconstitutional under British law. Though England did not have a written constitution, Otis referred to the accumulation of practices and attitudes throughout English history that set limits on the power of government. In his view there were traditional limits beyond which the Parliament or the king could not legitimately go. The writs exceeded these bounds and were therefore null and void. Though he lost the *Writs of Assistance* case, his theory caught the public's attention. It provided justification for an increasing number of protests against taxation without representation. The case also elevated Otis as a radical colonial leader.

In May 1761 he was elected to the General Court of Massachusetts. This body, which served as the provincial legislature, gave Otis a platform to expound his radical political views. In 1762 he published *A Vindication of the Conduct of the House of Representatives of the Province of Massachusetts Bay*. In the pamphlet he defended the legislature's refusal to pay for ships that England had sent to protect the colony from pirates. He wrote numerous papers to the other colonies and to the government in England arguing for political freedom. His ideas became a part of the address that the Stamp Act Congress of 1765 sent to the House of Commons protesting taxation of the colonies.

As the colonies moved closer to breaking away from England, Otis's influence faded, the result of alcoholism and mental illness. In 1769 he was struck in the head by a customs officer who disliked Otis's views. This injury left him mentally incapacitated and unable to continue in public life. For the remainder of his life, Otis had few lucid moments. He died on May 23, 1783, in Andover, Massachusetts, after being struck by lightning.

See also WRITS OF ASSISTANCE CASE.

BIOGRAPHY

OTTO, WILLIAM TOD William Tod Otto served as the REPORTER of decisions for the U.S. Supreme Court from 1875 to 1883. A distinguished lawyer, judge, and government administrator before his appointment as reporter, Otto is also noted for successfully arguing before the Supreme Court the case of *Murdock v. City of Memphis*, 87 U.S. (20 Wall.) 590, 22 L. Ed. 429 (1875), which resolved issues concerning the JURISDICTION of the Court.

Otto was born on January 19, 1816, in Philadelphia, Pennsylvania. He earned a bachelor's degree in 1833 and a master's degree in 1836 from the University of Pennsylvania. Otto studied law in Philadelphia and then moved to Brownstown, Indiana, to open a private practice. In 1844 he was elected a judge of Indiana's Second Circuit court, a position he held until his defeat in the election of 1852. From 1847 to 1852, Otto also taught law at Indiana University.

Despite his election defeat, Otto remained interested in public office. Although he lost an election in 1858 for Indiana attorney general, he had the good fortune of supporting ABRAHAM LINCOLN for president at the 1860 Republican convention. President Lincoln named Otto assistant secretary of the interior in 1863. In this post Otto administered Indian affairs. He left the department in 1871 to serve as arbitrator for claims against Spain from U.S. citizens living in its colony of Cuba.

In 1875 Otto argued *Murdock v. Memphis* before the Supreme Court. The case concerned congressional changes to section 25 of the JUDICIARY ACT OF 1789, which granted appellate authority to the Supreme Court over FEDERAL QUESTION cases from the state courts (those cases involving federal constitutional or statutory issues) but excluded questions of state law from review by the Court. This meant that state courts had the final and unreviewable authority over the interpretation of the state constitution and laws. However, in the 1867 reenactment of section 25, Congress omitted the provision containing this exclusion. *Murdock* raised the

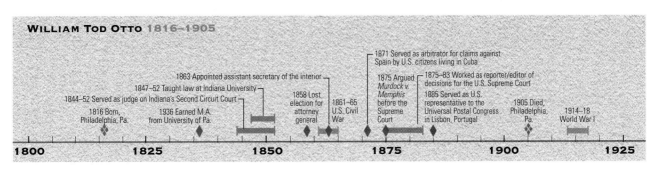

WILLIAM TOD OTTO 1816–1905

1871 Served as arbitrator for claims against Spain by U.S. citizens living in Cuba

1863 Appointed assistant secretary of the interior

1875 Argued *Murdock v. Memphis* before the Supreme Court

1875–83 Worked as reporter/editor of decisions for the U.S. Supreme Court

1847–52 Taught law at Indiana University

1844–52 Served as judge on Indiana's Second Circuit Court

1858 Lost election for attorney general

1861–65 U.S. Civil War

1885 Served as U.S. representative to the Universal Postal Congress in Lisbon, Portugal

1816 Born, Philadelphia, Pa.

1936 Earned M.A. from University of Pa.

1905 Died, Philadelphia, Pa.

1914–18 World War I

1800   1825   1850   1875   1900   1925

question of whether the U.S. Supreme Court could now review questions of state law. The Court agreed with Otto, concluding that Congress's failure to clearly state its intent to radically change the scope of federal jurisdiction prevented the Court from inferring intent.

Shortly after the *Murdock* decision, Otto was appointed reporter of decisions, succeeding John William Wallace. He was the first reporter to issue Supreme Court reports without his name appearing on the spine of each volume. Previous reporters had acted as their own publishers and distributors; thus they were entitled to use their names in marketing the volumes of court decisions. In 1874, however, Congress appropriated money for publishing the Court's opinions under government auspices. Otto, though hardly anonymous, assembled the reports for publication by the government.

Between 1875 and 1883, Otto edited seventeen volumes (91–107 *United States Reports*). He left the position to resume a private law practice and served as U.S. representative to the Universal Postal Congress in Lisbon, Portugal, in 1885.

Otto died on November 7, 1905, in Philadelphia.

OUTLAWRY 📖 A declaration under Old English law by which a person found in CONTEMPT on a civil or criminal process was considered an outlaw—that is, someone who is beyond the protection or assistance of the law. 📖

During the Anglo-Saxon period of English history, a person who committed certain crimes lost whatever protection he or she had under the law, forfeited whatever property he or she owned, and could be killed by anyone. If the crime committed was TREASON or a FELONY, a declaration of outlawry was tantamount to a conviction and ATTAINDER. Outlawry for a MISDEMEANOR did not, however, amount to a conviction for the offense. The Norman Conquest led to significant changes in the law governing outlawry, eventually leading to its abolition.

OUT-OF-COURT SETTLEMENT 📖 An agreement reached between the parties in a pending lawsuit that resolves the dispute to their mutual satisfaction and occurs without judicial intervention, supervision, or approval. 📖

An out-of-court settlement provides that the parties relinquish their rights to pursue judicial remedies.

OUTPUT CONTRACT 📖 In the law of SALES, an agreement in which one party assents to sell his or her total production to another party, who agrees to purchase it. 📖

This type of contract does not entail an ILLUSORY PROMISE, a purported agreement that actually means nothing because it leaves to one party the choice of PERFORMANCE or nonperformance, even if the quantity of goods that are the subject of the contract is indefinite. It is also known as an *entire output contract*, and it is subject to the UNIFORM COMMERCIAL CODE (UCC), a body of law adopted by the states that governs commercial transactions. See also REQUIREMENTS CONTRACT.

OUTSTANDING WARRANT 📖 An order that has not yet been carried out; an order for which the action commanded has not been taken. 📖

When the action ordered has been done, the WARRANT is said to have been executed.

OVERBREADTH DOCTRINE 📖 A principle of judicial review that holds that a law is invalid if it punishes constitutionally protected speech or conduct along with speech or conduct that the government may limit to further a compelling government interest. 📖

Legislatures sometimes pass laws that infringe on the FIRST AMENDMENT freedoms of RELIGION, speech, press, and peaceable assembly. When a legislature passes such a law, a person with a sufficient interest affected by the legislation may challenge its constitutionality by bringing suit against the federal, state, or local sovereignty that passed it. One common argument in First Amendment challenges is that the statute is overbroad.

Under the overbreadth doctrine, a statute that affects First Amendment rights is unconstitutional if it prohibits more protected speech or activity than is necessary to achieve a compelling government interest. The excessive intrusion on First Amendment rights, beyond what the government had a compelling interest to restrict, renders the law unconstitutional.

If a statute is overbroad, the court may be able to save the statute by striking only the section that is overbroad. If the court cannot sever the statute and save the constitutional provisions, it may invalidate the entire statute.

The case of *Brockett v. Spokane Arcades, Inc.*, 472 U.S. 491, 105 S. Ct. 2794, 86 L. Ed. 2d 394 (1985), illustrates how the overbreadth doctrine works. At issue in *Brockett* was an OBSCENITY statute passed by the state of Washington. The statute declared to be a moral NUISANCE any place where lewd films were shown as a regular course of business and any place where lewd publications constituted a principal part of the stock in trade. Lewd matter was defined as being OBSCENE matter, or any matter that appeals to the prurient interest. Under the statute the term *prurient* was defined as tending to incite LASCIVIOUSNESS or lust.

The Supreme Court in *Brockett* ruled that the Washington statute was overbroad because it prohibited lust-inciting materials. According to the Court, because lust is a normal sexual appetite, materials that include an appeal to lust enjoy First Amendment protection. Therefore, a statute that prohibits any material arousing lust is constitutionally overbroad.

The remedy in the *Brockett* case was not complete invalidation of the moral nuisance law. The Court directed that the reference to lust be excised from the statute and stated that the rest of the statute was valid. The statute, though originally overbroad, was still valid because it contained a severability clause and was still effective after its overbroad portion was struck.

CROSS-REFERENCES

Compelling State Interest; Freedom of Speech; Freedom of the Press.

OVERDRAFT 📖 A CHECK that is drawn on an account containing less money than the amount stated on the check. 📖

The term *overdraft* is also used in reference to the condition that exists when vouchers or purchase orders are drawn in amounts exceeding the amount that has been appropriated or budgeted. See also COMMERCIAL PAPER.

OVERHEAD 📖 A sum total of the administrative or executive costs that relate to the management, conduct, or supervision of a business that are not attributable to any one particular product or department. 📖

Expenses such as rent, taxes, insurance, lighting, heating, and other miscellaneous office expenses all fall under the category of overhead.

OVERREACHING 📖 Exploiting a situation through FRAUD or UNCONSCIONABLE conduct. 📖

OVERRIDE 📖 An arrangement whereby commissions are made by sales managers based upon the sales made by their subordinate sales representatives. A term found in an agreement between a REAL ESTATE agent and a property owner whereby the agent keeps the right to receive a commission for the sale of the property for a reasonable time after the agreement expires if the sale is made to a purchaser with whom the agent negotiated prior to the expiration of the agreement. 📖

OVERRULE 📖 The refusal by a judge to sustain an objection set forth by an attorney during a trial, such as an OBJECTION to a particular question posed to a witness. To make VOID, annul, supersede, or reject through a subsequent decision or action. 📖

A judicial decision is overruled when a later decision, made by the same tribunal or a higher court in the same system, hands down a decision concerning the identical QUESTION OF LAW, which is in direct opposition to the earlier decision. The earlier decision is thereby overruled and deprived of its authority as PRECEDENT.

OVERT 📖 Public; open; manifest. 📖

The term *overt* is used in CRIMINAL LAW in reference to conduct that moves more directly toward the commission of an offense than do acts of planning and preparation that may ultimately lead to such conduct.

OVERT ACT 📖 An open, manifest act from which criminality may be implied. An outward act done in pursuance and manifestation of an intent or design. 📖

An overt act is essential to establish an attempt to commit a CRIME. It is also a key element in the crime of TREASON and has become a component of federal and some state criminal CONSPIRACY laws. It also plays a role in the right of SELF-DEFENSE.

An attempt to commit a crime is an offense when an accused makes a substantial but unsuccessful effort to commit a crime. The elements of attempt include an intent to commit a crime, an apparent ability to complete the crime, and an overt act. An overt act is an act that is performed to execute the criminal intention and will naturally achieve that result unless prevented by some external cause. The act must directly move toward commission of the crime and must be more than acts of planning or preparation.

Defining when an act is more than preparatory has proved difficult. Several tests have been used to determine when an overt act has been committed. The "unequivocal" test states that a defendant's act, standing alone, is unequivocally consistent only with her or his intent to commit the allegedly attempted crime. This test has been criticized as too lenient on criminals because no act is truly unequivocal. A person who shoots someone several times can argue that she was only trying to injure the victim and that it was her skilled shooting and not luck that prevented the victim's death.

Some JURISDICTIONS favor the "substantial act" test. They permit an attempt conviction when a defendant with the requisite criminal INTENT performs a substantial act towards the commission of the crime. Under this test, for example, a prospective burglar can be convicted of attempted BURGLARY if apprehended in an alley with burglary tools, even though he had not determined which building he was going to burglarize.

The "probable desistence" test asks whether the defendant had gone so far down the road of crime that it is unlikely that she or he would have voluntarily desisted from completing the crime. One way of measuring this probability is to look at the past criminal record of an accused. Thus, an accused with a previous record may be convicted under this test, because her past propensity makes it unlikely that she would have stopped taking the acts leading to the crime.

The need for an overt act also is required in federal and some state criminal conspiracy prosecutions. A conspiracy is a voluntary agreement by two or more persons to commit an unlawful act or to use unlawful means to accomplish an act that is not in itself unlawful. Under federal law the overt act must be an independent act that comes after the agreement or conspiracy and is performed to effect the objective of the conspiracy. The overt act itself need not be a criminal act, because its sole function is to demonstrate that the conspiracy is operative. If, for example, two persons conspire to rob a bank and rent a getaway car, the rental is an overt act that in itself is perfectly legal. Some states, however, still adhere to the COMMON-LAW rule that an overt act is not required to prove a conspiracy.

An overt act that justifies the exercise of the right of self-defense is one that causes a REASON-ABLE PERSON to perceive a present intention to cause his or her death or great bodily harm.

The federal crime of treason contains an overt act requirement. Article III, Section 3, Clause 1, of the U.S. Constitution provides, "No Person shall be convicted of Treason unless on the Testimony of two Witnesses to the same overt Act." In such a case, an overt act means a step taken to execute a treasonable purpose, as distinguished from mere words or a treasonable sentiment, purpose, or design not resulting in action. It is an act in furtherance of the crime.

See also CRIMINAL LAW.

OWNER 📖 The person recognized by the law as having the ultimate control over, and right to use, property as long as the law permits and no agreement or COVENANT limits his or her rights. 📖

OYER AND TERMINER 📖 [*French, To hear and decide.*] The designation "court of oyer and terminer" is frequently used as the actual title, or a portion of the title, of a state court that has criminal JURISDICTION over felonious offenses. 📖

OYEZ 📖 [*French, Hear ye.*] A word used in some courts by the public crier to indicate that a proclamation is about to be made and to command attention to it. 📖

ABBREVIATIONS

A.	Atlantic Reporter
A. 2d	Atlantic Reporter, Second Series
AAA	American Arbitration Association; Agricultural Adjustment Act of 1933
AAPRP	All African People's Revolutionary Party
ABA	American Bar Association; Architectural Barriers Act, 1968
ABM Treaty	Anti-Ballistic Missile Treaty of 1972; antiballistic missile
ABVP	Anti-Biased Violence Project
A/C	Account
A.C.	Appeal Cases
ACAA	Air Carrier Access Act
ACF	Administration for Children and Families
ACLU	American Civil Liberties Union
ACS	Agricultural Cooperative Service
Act'g Legal Adv.	Acting Legal Advisor
ACUS	Administrative Conference of the United States
ACYF	Administration on Children, Youth, and Families
A.D. 2d	Appellate Division, Second Series, N.Y.
ADA	Americans with Disabilities Act of 1990
ADAMHA	Alcohol, Drug Abuse, and Mental Health Administration
ADC	Aid to Dependent Children
ADD	Administration on Developmental Disabilities
ADEA	Age Discrimination in Employment Act of 1967
ADR	alternative dispute resolution
AEC	Atomic Energy Commission
AECB	Arms Export Control Board
A.E.R.	All England Law Reports
AFDC	Aid to Families with Dependent Children
aff'd per cur.	affirmed by the court
AFIS	automated fingerprint identification system
AFL	American Federation of Labor
AFL-CIO	American Federation of Labor and Congress of Industrial Organizations
AFRes	Air Force Reserve
AFSCME	American Federation of State, County, and Municipal Employees
AGRICOLA	Agricultural Online Access
AIA	Association of Insurance Attorneys
AID	artificial insemination using a third-party donor's sperm; Agency for International Development

AIDS	acquired immune deficiency syndrome
AIH	artificial insemination using the husband's sperm
AIM	American Indian Movement
AIUSA	Amnesty International, U.S.A. Affiliate
AJS	American Judicature Society
ALEC	American Legislative Exchange Council
ALF	Animal Liberation Front
ALI	American Law Institute
ALJ	administrative law judge
All E.R.	All England Law Reports
ALO	Agency Liaison
A.L.R.	American Law Reports
AMA	American Medical Association
Am. Dec.	American Decisions
amdt.	amendment
Amer. St. Papers, For. Rels.	American State Papers, Legislative and Executive Documents of the Congress of the U.S., Class I, Foreign Relations, 1832–1859
AMVETS	American Veterans (of World War II)
ANA	Administration for Native Americans
Ann. Dig.	Annual Digest of Public International Law Cases
ANZUS	Australia–New Zealand–United States Security Treaty Organization
AOA	Administration on Aging
APA	Administrative Procedure Act of 1946
APHIS	Animal and Plant Health Inspection Service
App. Div.	Appellate Division Reports, N.Y. Supreme Court
Arb. Trib., U.S.-British Convention of 1853	Arbitration Tribunal, Claim Convention of 1853, United States and Great Britain
ARS	Advanced Record System
Art.	article
ASCS	Agriculture Stabilization and Conservation Service
ASM	available seatmile
ASPCA	American Society for the Prevention of Cruelty to Animals
Asst. Att. Gen.	Assistant Attorney General
AT&T	American Telephone and Telegraph
ATFD	Alcohol, Tobacco and Firearms Division
ATLA	Association of Trial Lawyers of America
ATTD	Alcohol and Tobacco Tax Division
ATU	Alcohol Tax Unit
AZT	azidothymidine
BALSA	Black-American Law Student Association
BATF	Bureau of Alcohol, Tobacco and Firearms
BCCI	Bank of Credit and Commerce International
BEA	Bureau of Economic Analysis
Bell's Cr. C.	Bell's English Crown Cases
Bevans	United States Treaties, etc. *Treaties and Other International Agreements of the United States of America, 1776–1949* (compiled under the direction of Charles I. Bevans) (1968–76)
BFOQ	bona fide occupational qualification
BI	Bureau of Investigation
BIA	Bureau of Indian Affairs; Board of Immigration Appeals
BJS	Bureau of Justice Statistics
Black.	Black's United States Supreme Court Reports
Blatchf.	Blatchford's United States Circuit Court Reports
BLM	Bureau of Land Management
BLS	Bureau of Labor Statistics
BMD	ballistic missile defense
BOCA	Building Officials and Code Administrators International
BPP	Black Panther Party for Self-Defense

Brit. and For.	British and Foreign State Papers
Burr.	James Burrows, *Report of Cases Argued and Determined in the Court of King's Bench during the Time of Lord Mansfield* (1766–1780)
BVA	Board of Veterans Appeals
c.	Chapter
C^{3}I	Command, Control, Communications, and Intelligence
C.A.	Court of Appeals
CAA	Clean Air Act
CAB	Civil Aeronautics Board
CAFE	corporate average fuel economy
Cal. 2d	California Reports, Second Series
Cal. 3d	California Reports, Third Series
CALR	computer-assisted legal research
Cal. Rptr.	California Reporter
CAP	Common Agricultural Policy
CATV	community antenna television
CBO	Congressional Budget Office
CCC	Commodity Credit Corporation
CCDBG	Child Care and Development Block Grant of 1990
C.C.D. Pa.	Circuit Court Decisions, Pennsylvania
C.C.D. Va.	Circuit Court Decisions, Virginia
CCEA	Cabinet Council on Economic Affairs
CCR	Center for Constitutional Rights
C.C.R.I.	Circuit Court, Rhode Island
CD	certificate of deposit
CDA	Communications Decency Act
CDBG	Community Development Block Grant Program
CDC	Centers for Disease Control and Prevention; Community Development Corporation
CDF	Children's Defense Fund
CDL	Citizens for Decency through Law
CD-ROM	compact disc read-only memory
CDS	Community Dispute Services
CDW	collision damage waiver
CENTO	Central Treaty Organization
CEQ	Council on Environmental Quality
CERCLA	Comprehensive Environmental Response, Compensation, and Liability Act of 1980
cert.	*certiorari*
CETA	Comprehensive Employment and Training Act
C & F	cost and freight
CFC	chlorofluorocarbon
CFE Treaty	Conventional Forces in Europe Treaty of 1990
C.F. & I.	Cost, freight, and insurance
CFNP	Community Food and Nutrition Program
C.F.R.	Code of Federal Regulations
CFTC	Commodity Futures Trading Commission
Ch.	Chancery Division, English Law Reports
CHAMPVA	Civilian Health and Medical Program at the Veterans Administration
CHEP	Cuban/Haitian Entrant Program
CHINS	children in need of supervision
CHIPS	child in need of protective services
Ch.N.Y.	Chancery Reports, New York
Chr. Rob.	Christopher Robinson, *Reports of Cases Argued and Determined in the High Court of Admiralty* (1801–1808)
CIA	Central Intelligence Agency
CID	Commercial Item Descriptions
C.I.F.	Cost, insurance, and freight
CINCNORAD	Commander in Chief, North American Air Defense Command
C.I.O.	Congress of Industrial Organizations

C.J.	chief justice
CJIS	Criminal Justice Information Services
C.J.S.	Corpus Juris Secundum
Claims Arb. under Spec. Conv., Nielsen's Rept.	Frederick Kenelm Nielsen, *American and British Claims Arbitration under the Special Agreement Concluded between the United States and Great Britain, August 18, 1910* (1926)
CLE	Center for Law and Education
CLEO	Council on Legal Education Opportunity
CLP	Communist Labor Party of America
CLS	Christian Legal Society; critical legal studies (movement), Critical Legal Studies (membership organization)
C.M.A.	Court of Military Appeals
CMEA	Council for Mutual Economic Assistance
CMHS	Center for Mental Health Services
C.M.R.	Court of Military Review
CNN	Cable News Network
CNO	Chief of Naval Operations
C.O.D.	cash on delivery
COGP	Commission on Government Procurement
COINTELPRO	Counterintelligence Program
Coke Rep.	Coke's English King's Bench Reports
COLA	cost-of-living adjustment
COMCEN	Federal Communications Center
Comp.	Compilation
Conn.	Connecticut Reports
CONTU	National Commission on New Technological Uses of Copyrighted Works
Conv.	Convention
Corbin	Arthur L. Corbin, *Corbin on Contracts: A Comprehensive Treatise on the Rules of Contract Law* (1950)
CORE	Congress of Racial Equality
Cox's Crim. Cases	Cox's Criminal Cases (England)
CPA	certified public accountant
CPB	Corporation for Public Broadcasting, the
CPI	Consumer Price Index
CPSC	Consumer Product Safety Commission
Cranch	Cranch's United States Supreme Court Reports
CRF	Constitutional Rights Foundation
CRS	Congressional Research Service; Community Relations Service
CRT	critical race theory
CSA	Community Services Administration
CSAP	Center for Substance Abuse Prevention
CSAT	Center for Substance Abuse Treatment
CSC	Civil Service Commission
CSCE	Conference on Security and Cooperation in Europe
CSG	Council of State Governments
CSO	Community Service Organization
CSP	Center for the Study of the Presidency
C-SPAN	Cable-Satellite Public Affairs Network
CSRS	Cooperative State Research Service
CSWPL	Center on Social Welfare Policy and Law
CTA	*cum testamento annexo* (with the will attached)
Ct. Ap. D.C.	Court of Appeals, District of Columbia
Ct. App. No. Ireland	Court of Appeals, Northern Ireland
Ct. Cl.	Court of Claims, United States
Ct. Crim. Apps.	Court of Criminal Appeals (England)
Ct. of Sess., Scot.	Court of Sessions, Scotland
CU	credit union

CUNY	City University of New York
Cush.	Cushing's Massachusetts Reports
CWA	Civil Works Administration; Clean Water Act
Dall.	Dallas' Pennsylvania and United States Reports
DAR	Daughter of the American Revolution
DARPA	Defense Advanced Research Projects Agency
DAVA	Defense Audiovisual Agency
D.C.	United States District Court
D.C. Del.	United States District Court, Delaware
D.C. Mass.	United States District Court, Massachusetts
D.C. Md.	United States District Court, Maryland
D.C.N.D.Cal.	United States District Court, Northern District, California
D.C.N.Y.	United States District Court, New York
D.C.Pa.	United States District Court, Pennsylvania
DCS	Deputy Chiefs of Staff
DCZ	District of the Canal Zone
DDT	dichlorodiphenyltricloroethane
DEA	Drug Enforcement Administration
Decl. Lond.	Declaration of London, February 26, 1909
Dev. & B.	Devereux & Battle's North Carolina Reports
Dig. U.S. Practice in Intl. Law	Digest of U.S. Practice in International Law
Dist. Ct. D.C.	United States District Court, District of Columbia
D.L.R.	Dominion Law Reports (Canada)
DNA	deoxyribonucleic acid
DNase	deoxyribonuclease
DNC	Democratic National Committee
DOC	Department of Commerce
DOD	Department of Defense
Dodson	Dodson's Reports, English Admiralty Courts
DOE	Department of Energy
DOER	Department of Employee Relations
DOJ	Department of Justice
DOS	disk operating system
DOT	Department of Transportation
DPT	diphtheria, pertussis, and tetanus
DRI	Defense Research Institute
DSAA	Defense Security Assistance Agency
DUI	driving under the influence; driving under intoxication
DWI	driving while intoxicated
EAHCA	Education for All Handicapped Children Act of 1975
EBT	examination before trial
ECPA	Electronic Communications Privacy Act of 1986
ECSC	Treaty of the European Coal and Steel Community
EDA	Economic Development Administration
EDF	Environmental Defense Fund
E.D.N.Y.	Eastern District, New York
EDP	electronic data processing
E.D. Pa.	Eastern District, Pennsylvania
EDSC	Eastern District, South Carolina
E.D. Va.	Eastern District, Virginia
EEC	European Economic Community; European Economic Community Treaty
EEOC	Equal Employment Opportunity Commission
EFF	Electronic Frontier Foundation
EFT	electronic funds transfer
Eliz.	Queen Elizabeth (Great Britain)
Em. App.	Temporary Emergency Court of Appeals

ENE	early neutral evaluation
Eng. Rep.	English Reports
EOP	Executive Office of the President
EPA	Environmental Protection Agency; Equal Pay Act of 1963
ERA	Equal Rights Amendment
ERISA	Employee Retirement Income Security Act of 1974
ERS	Economic Research Service
ESF	emergency support function; Economic Support Fund
ESRD	End-Stage Renal Disease Program
ETA	Employment and Training Administration
ETS	environmental tobacco smoke
et seq.	*et sequentes* or *et sequentia;* "and the following"
EU	European Union
Euratom	European Atomic Energy Community
Eur. Ct. H.R.	European Court of Human Rights
Ex.	English Exchequer Reports, Welsby, Hurlstone & Gordon
Exch.	Exchequer Reports (Welsby, Hurlstone & Gordon)
Eximbank	Export-Import Bank of the United States
F.	Federal Reporter
F. 2d	Federal Reporter, Second Series
FAA	Federal Aviation Administration; Federal Arbitration Act
FAAA	Federal Alcohol Administration Act
FACE	Freedom of Access to Clinic Entrances Act of 1994
FACT	Feminist Anti-Censorship Task Force
FAO	Food and Agriculture Organization of the United Nations
FAR	Federal Acquisition Regulations
FAS	Foreign Agricultural Service
FBA	Federal Bar Association
FBI	Federal Bureau of Investigation
FCA	Farm Credit Administration
F. Cas.	Federal Cases
FCC	Federal Communications Commission
FCIA	Foreign Credit Insurance Association
FCIC	Federal Crop Insurance Corporation
FCRA	Fair Credit Reporting Act
FCU	Federal credit unions
FDA	Food and Drug Administration
FDIC	Federal Deposit Insurance Corporation
FDPC	Federal Data Processing Center
FEC	Federal Election Commission
Fed. Cas.	Federal Cases
FEMA	Federal Emergency Management Agency
FFB	Federal Financing Bank
FGIS	Federal Grain Inspection Service
FHA	Federal Housing Authority
FHWA	Federal Highway Administration
FIA	Federal Insurance Administration
FIC	Federal Information Centers; Federation of Insurance Counsel
FICA	Federal Insurance Contributions Act
FIFRA	Federal Insecticide, Fungicide, and Rodenticide Act
FIP	Forestry Incentives Program
FIRREA	Financial Institutions Reform, Recovery, and Enforcement Act
FISA	Foreign Intelligence Surveillance Act of 1978
FMCS	Federal Mediation and Conciliation Service
FmHA	Farmers Home Administration
FMLA	Family and Medical Leave Act of 1993
FNMA	Federal National Mortgage Association, "Fannie Mae"
F.O.B.	free on board

FOIA	Freedom of Information Act
FPC	Federal Power Commission
FPMR	Federal Property Management Regulations
FPRS	Federal Property Resources Service
FR	Federal Register
FRA	Federal Railroad Administration
FRB	Federal Reserve Board
FRC	Federal Radio Commission
F.R.D.	Federal Rules Decisions
FSA	Family Support Act
FSLIC	Federal Savings and Loan Insurance Corporation
FSQS	Food Safety and Quality Service
FSS	Federal Supply Service
F. Supp.	Federal Supplement
FTA	U.S.-Canada Free Trade Agreement, 1988
FTC	Federal Trade Commission
FTS	Federal Telecommunications System
FUTA	Federal Unemployment Tax Act
FWPCA	Federal Water Pollution Control Act of 1948
GAO	General Accounting Office; Governmental Affairs Office
GAOR	General Assembly Official Records, United Nations
GA Res.	General Assembly Resolution (United Nations)
GATT	General Agreement on Tariffs and Trade
Gen. Cls. Comm.	General Claims Commission, United States and Panama; General Claims Commission, United States and Mexico
Geo. II	King George II (Great Britain)
Geo. III	King George III (Great Britain)
GM	General Motors
GNMA	Government National Mortgage Association, "Ginnie Mae"
GNP	gross national product
GOP	Grand Old Party (Republican)
GOPAC	Grand Old Party Action Committee
GPA	Office of Governmental and Public Affairs
GPO	Government Printing Office
GRAS	generally recognized as safe
Gr. Br., Crim. Ct. App.	Great Britain, Court of Criminal Appeals
GRNL	Gay Rights National Lobby
GSA	General Services Administration
Hackworth	Green Haywood Hackworth, *Digest of International Law* (1940–44)
Hay and Marriott	Great Britain. High Court of Admiralty, *Decisions in the High Court of Admiralty during the Time of Sir George Hay and of Sir James Marriott, Late Judges of That Court* (1801)
HBO	Home Box Office
HCFA	Health Care Financing Administration
H.Ct.	High Court
HDS	Office of Human Development Services
Hen. & M.	Hening & Munford's Virginia Reports
HEW	Department of Health, Education, and Welfare
HHS	Department of Health and Human Services
Hill	Hill's New York Reports
HIRE	Help through Industry Retraining and Employment
HIV	human immunodeficiency virus
H.L.	House of Lords Cases (England)
H. Lords	House of Lords (England)
HNIS	Human Nutrition Information Service
Hong Kong L.R.	Hong Kong Law Reports
How.	Howard's United States Supreme Court Reports
How. St. Trials	Howell's English State Trials
HUAC	House Un-American Activities Committee

HUD	Department of Housing and Urban Development
Hudson, Internatl. Legis.	Manley O. Hudson, ed., *International Legislation: A Collection of the Texts of Multipartite International Instruments of General Interest Beginning with the Covenant of the League of Nations* (1931)
Hudson, World Court Reps.	Manley Ottmer Hudson, ed., *World Court Reports* (1934–)
Hun	Hun's New York Supreme Court Reports
Hunt's Rept.	Bert L. Hunt, *Report of the American and Panamanian General Claims Arbitration* (1934)
IAEA	International Atomic Energy Agency
IALL	International Association of Law Libraries
IBA	International Bar Association
IBM	International Business Machines
ICBM	intercontinental ballistic missile
ICC	Interstate Commerce Commission
ICJ	International Court of Justice
IDEA	Individuals with Disabilities Education Act, 1975
IEP	individualized educational program
IFC	International Finance Corporation
IGRA	Indian Gaming Regulatory Act, 1988
IJA	Institute of Judicial Administration
IJC	International Joint Commission
ILC	International Law Commission
ILD	International Labor Defense
Ill. Dec.	Illinois Decisions
ILO	International Labor Organization
IMF	International Monetary Fund
INA	Immigration and Nationality Act
IND	investigational new drug
INF Treaty	Intermediate-Range Nuclear Forces Treaty of 1987
INS	Immigration and Naturalization Service
INTELSAT	International Telecommunications Satellite Organization
Interpol	International Criminal Police Organization
Int'l. Law Reps.	International Law Reports
Intl. Legal Mats.	International Legal Materials
IPDC	International Program for the Development of Communication
IPO	Intellectual Property Owners
IPP	independent power producer
IQ	intelligence quotient
I.R.	Irish Reports
IRA	individual retirement account; Irish Republican Army
IRCA	Immigration Reform and Control Act of 1986
IRS	Internal Revenue Service
ISO	independent service organization
ISSN	International Standard Serial Numbers
ITA	International Trade Administration
ITI	Information Technology Integration
ITO	International Trade Organization
ITS	Information Technology Service
ITU	International Telecommunication Union
IUD	intrauterine device
IWC	International Whaling Commission
IWW	Industrial Workers of the World
JCS	Joint Chiefs of Staff
JDL	Jewish Defense League
JOBS	Jobs Opportunity and Basic Skills
John. Ch.	Johnson's New York Chancery Reports
Johns.	Johnson's Reports (New York)
JP	justice of the peace

K.B.	King's Bench Reports (England)
KGB	Komitet Gosudarstvennoi Bezopasnosti (the State Security Committee for countries in the former Soviet Union)
KKK	Ku Klux Klan
KMT	Kuomintang
LAPD	Los Angeles Police Department
LC	Library of Congress
LD50	lethal dose 50
LDEF	Legal Defense and Education Fund (NOW)
LDF	Legal Defense Fund, Legal Defense and Educational Fund of the NAACP
LEAA	Law Enforcement Assistance Administration
L.Ed.	Lawyers' Edition Supreme Court Reports
LMSA	Labor-Management Services Administration
LNTS	League of Nations Treaty Series
Lofft's Rep.	Lofft's English King's Bench Reports
L.R.	Law Reports (English)
LSAS	Law School Admission Service
LSAT	Law School Aptitude Test
LSC	Legal Services Corporation; Legal Services for Children
LSD	lysergic acid diethylamide
LSDAS	Law School Data Assembly Service
LTBT	Limited Test Ban Treaty
LTC	Long Term Care
MAD	mutual assured destruction
MADD	Mothers against Drunk Driving
MALDEF	Mexican American Legal Defense and Educational Fund
Malloy	William M. Malloy, ed., *Treaties, Conventions, International Acts, Protocols, and Agreements between the United States of America and Other Powers* (1910–38)
Martens	Georg Friedrich von Martens, ed., *Noveau recueil général de traités et autres act es relatifs aux rapports de droit international* (Series I, 20 vols. [1843–75]; Series II, 35 vols. [1876–1908]; Series III [1909–])
Mass.	Massachusetts Reports
MCH	Maternal and Child Health Bureau
Md. App.	Maryland, Appeal Cases
M.D. Ga.	Middle District, Georgia
Mercy	Movement Ensuring the Right to Choose for Yourself
Metc.	Metcalf's Massachusetts Reports
MFDP	Mississippi Freedom Democratic party
MGT	Management
MHSS	Military Health Services System
Miller	David Hunter Miller, ed., *Treaties and Other International Acts of the United States of America* (1931–1948)
Minn.	Minnesota Reports
MINS	minors in need of supervision
MIRV	multiple independently targetable reentry vehicle
Misc.	Miscellaneous Reports, New York
Mixed Claims Comm., Report of Decs.	Mixed Claims Commission, United States and Germany, Report of Decisions
M.J.	Military Justice Reporter
MLAP	Migrant Legal Action Program
MLB	major league baseball
MLDP	Mississippi Loyalist Democratic party
Mo.	Missouri Reports
Mod.	Modern Reports, English King's Bench, etc.
Moore, Dig. Intl. Law	John Bassett Moore, *A Digest of International Law*, 8 vols. (1906)
Moore, Intl. Arbs.	John Bassett Moore, *History and Digest of the International Arbitrations to Which the United States Has Been a Party*, 6 vols. (1898)

Morison	William Maxwell Morison, *The Scots Revised Report: Morison's Dictionary of Decisions* (1908–09)
M.P.	member of Parliament
MPAA	Motion Picture Association of America
mpg	miles per gallon
MPRSA	Marine Protection, Research, and Sanctuaries Act of 1972
M.R.	Master of the Rolls
MS-DOS	Microsoft Disk Operating System
MSHA	Mine Safety and Health Administration
NAACP	National Association for the Advancement of Colored People
NAAQS	National Ambient Air Quality Standards
NABSW	National Association of Black Social Workers
NAFTA	North American Free Trade Agreement, 1993
NARAL	National Abortion Rights Action League
NARF	Native American Rights Fund
NARS	National Archives and Record Service
NASA	National Aeronautics and Space Administration
NASD	National Association of Securities Dealers
NATO	North Atlantic Treaty Organization
NAVINFO	Navy Information Offices
NAWSA	National American Woman's Suffrage Association
NBA	National Bar Association
NBC	National Broadcasting Company
NBLSA	National Black Law Student Association
NBS	National Bureau of Standards
NCA	Noise Control Act; National Command Authorities
NCAA	National Collegiate Athletic Association
NCAC	National Coalition against Censorship
NCCB	National Consumer Cooperative Bank
NCE	Northwest Community Exchange
NCJA	National Criminal Justice Association
NCLB	National Civil Liberties Bureau
NCP	national contingency plan
NCSC	National Center for State Courts
NCUA	National Credit Union Administration
NDA	new drug application
N.D. Ill.	Northern District, Illinois
NDU	National Defense University
N.D. Wash.	Northern District, Washington
N.E.	North Eastern Reporter
N.E. 2d	North Eastern Reporter, Second Series
NEA	National Endowment for the Arts
NEH	National Endowment for the Humanities
NEPA	National Environmental Protection Act; National Endowment Policy Act
NFIP	National Flood Insurance Program
NGTF	National Gay Task Force
NHRA	Nursing Home Reform Act, 1987
NHTSA	National Highway Traffic Safety Administration
Nielsen's Rept.	Frederick Kenelm Nielsen, *American and British Claims Arbitration under the Special Agreement Concluded between the United States and Great Britain, August 18, 1910* (1926)
NIEO	New International Economic Order
NIH	National Institutes of Health, the NIH
NIJ	National Institute of Justice
NIRA	National Industrial Recovery Act; National Industrial Recovery Administration
NIST	National Institute of Standards and Technology, the NIST
NITA	National Telecommunications and Information Administration
N.J.	New Jersey Reports

N.J. Super.	New Jersey Superior Court Reports
NLRA	National Labor Relations Act
NLRB	National Labor Relations Board
No.	Number
NOAA	National Oceanic and Atmospheric Administration
NOW	National Organization for Women
NOW LDEF	National Organization for Women Legal Defense and Education Fund
NOW/PAC	National Organization for Women Political Action Committee
NPDES	National Pollutant Discharge Elimination System
NPL	national priorities list
NPR	National Public Radio
NPT	Non-Proliferation Treaty
NRA	National Rifle Association; National Recovery Act
NRC	Nuclear Regulatory Commission
NSC	National Security Council
NSCLC	National Senior Citizens Law Center
NSF	National Science Foundation
NSFNET	National Science Foundation Network
NTIA	National Telecommunications and Information Administration
NTID	National Technical Institute for the Deaf
NTIS	National Technical Information Service
NTS	Naval Telecommunications System
NTSB	National Transportation Safety Board
N.W.	North Western Reporter
N.W. 2d	North Western Reporter, Second Series
NWSA	National Woman Suffrage Association
N.Y.	New York Court of Appeals Reports
N.Y. 2d	New York Court of Appeals Reports, Second Series
N.Y.S.	New York Supplement Reporter
N.Y.S. 2d	New York Supplement Reporter, Second Series
NYSE	New York Stock Exchange
N.Y. Sup.	New York Supreme Court Reports
NYU	New York University
OAAU	Organization of Afro American Unity
OAP	Office of Administrative Procedure
OAS	Organization of American States
OASDI	Old-age, Survivors, and Disability Insurance Benefits
OASHDS	Office of the Assistant Secretary for Human Development Services
OCED	Office of Comprehensive Employment Development
OCHAMPUS	Office of Civilian Health and Medical Program of the Uniformed Services
OCSE	Office of Child Support Enforcement
OEA	Organización de los Estados Americanos
OFCCP	Office of Federal Contract Compliance Programs
OFPP	Office of Federal Procurement Policy
OICD	Office of International Cooperation and Development
OIG	Office of the Inspector General
OJARS	Office of Justice Assistance, Research, and Statistics
OMB	Office of Management and Budget
OMPC	Office of Management, Planning, and Communications
ONP	Office of National Programs
OPD	Office of Policy Development
OPEC	Organization of Petroleum Exporting Countries
OPIC	Overseas Private Investment Corporation
Ops. Atts. Gen.	Opinions of the Attorneys-General of the United States
Ops. Comms.	Opinions of the Commissioners
OPSP	Office of Product Standards Policy
O.R.	Ontario Reports
OR	Official Records

OSHA	Occupational Safety and Health Administration
OSHRC	Occupational Safety and Health Review Commission
OSM	Office of Surface Mining
OSS	Office of Strategic Services
OST	Office of the Secretary
OT	Office of Transportation
OTA	Office of Technology Assessment
OTC	over-the-counter
OUI	operating under the influence
OWBPA	Older Workers Benefit Protection Act
OWRT	Office of Water Research and Technology
P.	Pacific Reporter
P. 2d	Pacific Reporter, Second Series
PAC	political action committee
Pa. Oyer and Terminer	Pennsylvania Oyer and Terminer Reports
PATCO	Professional Air Traffic Controllers Organization
PBGC	Pension Benefit Guaranty Corporation
PBS	Public Broadcasting Service; Public Buildings Service
P.C.	Privy Council (English Law Reports); personal computer
PCIJ	Permanent Court of International Justice
	Series A—Judgments and Orders (1922–30)
	Series B—Advisory Opinions (1922–30)
	Series A/B—Judgments, Orders, and Advisory Opinions (1931–40)
	Series C—Pleadings, Oral Statements, and Documents relating to Judgments and Advisory Opinions (1923–42)
	Series D—Acts and Documents concerning the Organization of the World Court (1922–47)
	Series E—Annual Reports (1925–45)
PCP	phencyclidine (no need to spell out)
P.D.	Probate Division, English Law Reports (1876–1890)
PDA	Pregnancy Discrimination Act of 1978
PD & R	Policy Development and Research
Perm. Ct. of Arb.	Permanent Court of Arbitration
Pet.	Peters' United States Supreme Court Reports
PETA	People for the Ethical Treatment of Animals
PGM	Program
PHA	Public Housing Agency
Phila. Ct. of Oyer and Terminer	Philadelphia Court of Oyer and Terminer
PHS	Public Health Service
PIC	Private Industry Council
Pick.	Pickering's Massachusetts Reports
PIK	Payment in Kind
PINS	persons in need of supervision
PIRG	Public Interest Research Group
P.L.	Public Laws
PLAN	Pro-Life Action Network
PLI	Practicing Law Institute
PLO	Palestine Liberation Organization
PNET	Peaceful Nuclear Explosions Treaty
POW-MIA	prisoner of war–missing in action
Pratt	Frederic Thomas Pratt, *Law of Contraband of War, with a Selection of Cases from the Papers of the Right Honourable Sir George Lee* (1856)
Proc.	Proceedings
PRP	potentially responsible party
PSRO	Professional Standards Review Organization
PTO	Patents and Trademark Office
PURPA	Public Utilities Regulatory Policies Act

PUSH	People United to Serve Humanity
PWA	Public Works Administration
PWSA	Ports and Waterways Safety Act of 1972
Q.B.	Queen's Bench (England)
Ralston's Rept.	Jackson Harvey Ralston, ed., *Venezuelan Arbitrations of 1903* (1904)
RC	Regional Commissioner
RCRA	Resource Conservation and Recovery Act
RCWP	Rural Clean Water Program
RDA	Rural Development Administration
REA	Rural Electrification Administration
Rec. des Decs. des Trib. Arb. Mixtes	G. Gidel, ed., *Recueil des décisions des tribunaux arbitraux mixtes, institués par les traités de paix* (1922–30)
Redmond	Vol. 3 of Charles I. Bevans, *Treaties and Other International Agreements of the United States of America, 1776–1949* (compiled by C. F. Redmond) (1969)
RESPA	Real Estate Settlement Procedure Act of 1974
RFRA	Religious Freedom Restoration Act
RICO	Racketeer Influenced and Corrupt Organizations
RNC	Republican National Committee
Roscoe	Edward Stanley Roscoe, ed., *Reports of Prize Cases Determined in the High Court of Admiralty before the Lords Commissioners of Appeals in Prize Causes and before the Judicial Committee of the Privy Council from 1745 to 1859* (1905)
ROTC	Reserve Officers' Training Corps
RPP	Representative Payee Program
R.S.	Revised Statutes
RTC	Resolution Trust Company
Ryan White CARE Act	Ryan White Comprehensive AIDS Research Emergency Act of 1990
SAC	Strategic Air Command
SACB	Subversive Activities Control Board
SADD	Students against Drunk Driving
SAF	Student Activities Fund
SAIF	Savings Association Insurance Fund
SALT I	Strategic Arms Limitation Talks of 1969–72
SAMHSA	Substance Abuse and Mental Health Services Administration
Sandf.	Sandford's New York Superior Court Reports
S and L	savings and loan
SARA	Superfund Amendment and Reauthorization Act
Sawy.	Sawyer's United States Circuit Court Reports
SBA	Small Business Administration
SCLC	Southern Christian Leadership Conference
Scott's Repts.	James Brown Scott, ed., *The Hague Court Reports*, 2 vols. (1916–32)
SCS	Soil Conservation Service
SCSEP	Senior Community Service Employment Program
S.Ct.	Supreme Court Reporter
S.D. Cal.	Southern District, California
S.D. Fla.	Southern District, Florida
S.D. Ga.	Southern District, Georgia
SDI	Strategic Defense Initiative
S.D. Me.	Southern District, Maine
S.D.N.Y.	Southern District, New York
SDS	Students for a Democratic Society
S.E.	South Eastern Reporter
S.E. 2d	South Eastern Reporter, Second Series
SEA	Science and Education Administration
SEATO	Southeast Asia Treaty Organization
SEC	Securities and Exchange Commission
Sec.	Section
SEEK	Search for Elevation, Education and Knowledge
SEOO	State Economic Opportunity Office

SEP	simplified employee pension plan
Ser.	Series
Sess.	Session
SGLI	Servicemen's Group Life Insurance
SIP	state implementation plan
SLA	Symbionese Liberation Army
SLBM	submarine-launched ballistic missile
SNCC	Student Nonviolent Coordinating Committee
So.	Southern Reporter
So. 2d	Southern Reporter, Second Series
SPA	Software Publisher's Association
Spec. Sess.	Special Session
SRA	Sentencing Reform Act of 1984
SS	Schutzstaffel (German for Protection Echelon)
SSA	Social Security Administration
SSI	Supplemental Security Income
START I	Strategic Arms Reduction Treaty of 1991
START II	Strategic Arms Reduction Treaty of 1993
Stat.	United States Statutes at Large
STS	Space Transportation Systems
St. Tr.	State Trials, English
STURAA	Surface Transportation and Uniform Relocation Assistance Act of 1987
Sup. Ct. of Justice, Mexico	Supreme Court of Justice, Mexico
Supp.	Supplement
S.W.	South Western Reporter
S.W. 2d	South Western Reporter, Second Series
SWAPO	South-West Africa People's Organization
SWAT	Special Weapons and Tactics
SWP	Socialist Workers party
TDP	Trade and Development Program
Tex. Sup.	Texas Supreme Court Reports
THAAD	Theater High-Altitude Area Defense System
TIA	Trust Indenture Act of 1939
TIAS	Treaties and Other International Acts Series (United States)
TNT	trinitrotoluene
TOP	Targeted Outreach Program
TPUS	Transportation and Public Utilities Service
Tripartite Claims Comm., Decs. and Ops.	Tripartite Claims Commission (United States, Austria, and Hungary), Decisions and Opinions
TRI-TAC	Joint Tactical Communications
TRO	temporary restraining order
TS	Treaty Series, United States
TSCA	Toxic Substance Control Act
TSDs	transporters, storers, and disposers
TTBT	Threshold Test Ban Treaty
TVA	Tennessee Valley Authority
UAW	United Auto Workers; United Automobile, Aerospace, and Agricultural Implements Workers of America
U.C.C.	Uniform Commercial Code; Universal Copyright Convention
U.C.C.C.	Uniform Consumer Credit Code
UCCJA	Uniform Child Custody Jurisdiction Act
UCMJ	Uniform Code of Military Justice
UCPP	Urban Crime Prevention Program
UCS	United Counseling Service
UDC	United Daughters of the Confederacy
UFW	United Farm Workers
UHF	ultrahigh frequency
UIFSA	Uniform Interstate Family Support Act

UIS	Unemployment Insurance Service
UMDA	Uniform Marriage and Divorce Act
UMTA	Urban Mass Transportation Administration
UNCITRAL	United Nations Commission on International Trade Law
UNCTAD	United Nations Conference on Trade and Development
UN Doc.	United Nations Documents
UNDP	United Nations Development Program
UNEF	United Nations Emergency Force
UNESCO	United Nations Educational, Scientific, and Cultural Organization
UNICEF	United Nations Children's Fund
UNIDO	United Nations Industrial and Development Organization
Unif. L. Ann.	Uniform Laws Annotated
UN Repts. Intl. Arb. Awards	United Nations Reports of International Arbitral Awards
UNTS	United Nations Treaty Series
UPI	United Press International
URESA	Uniform Reciprocal Enforcement of Support Act
U.S.	United States Reports
USAF	United States Air Force
U.S. App. D.C.	United States Court of Appeals for the District of Columbia
U.S.C.	United States Code
U.S.C.A.	United States Code Annotated
U.S.C.C.A.N.	United States Code Congressional and Administrative News
USCMA	United States Court of Military Appeals
USDA	U.S. Department of Agriculture
USES	United States Employment Service
USFA	United States Fire Administration
USICA	International Communication Agency, United States
USSC	U.S. Sentencing Commission
U.S.S.R.	Union of Soviet Socialist Republics
UST	United States Treaties
USTS	United States Travel Service
v.	*versus*
VA	Veterans Administration, the VA
VGLI	Veterans Group Life Insurance
Vict.	Queen Victoria (Great Britain)
VIN	vehicle identification number
VISTA	Volunteers in Service to America
VJRA	Veterans Judicial Review Act of 1988
V.L.A.	Volunteer Lawyers for the Arts
VMI	Virginia Military Institute
VMLI	Veterans Mortgage Life Insurance
VOCAL	Victims of Child Abuse Laws
WAC	Women's Army Corps
Wall.	Wallace's United States Supreme Court Reports
Wash. 2d	Washington Reports, Second Series
WAVES	Women Accepted for Volunteer Service
WCTU	Women's Christian Temperance Union
W.D. Wash.	Western District, Washington
W.D. Wis.	Western District, Wisconsin
WEAL	West's Encyclopedia of American Law, Women's Equity Action League
Wend.	Wendell's New York Reports
WFSE	Washington Federation of State Employees
Wheat.	Wheaton's United States Supreme Court Reports
Wheel. Cr. Cases	Wheeler's New York Criminal Cases
Whiteman	Marjorie Millace Whiteman, *Digest of International Law*, 15 vols. (1963–73)
WHO	World Health Organization
WIC	Women, Infants, and Children program
Will. and Mar.	King William and Queen Mary (Great Britain)

WIN	WESTLAW Is Natural; Whip Inflation Now; Work Incentive Program
WIU	Workers' Industrial Union
W.L.R.	Weekly Law Reports, England
WPA	Works Progress Administration
WPPDA	Welfare and Pension Plans Disclosure Act
WWI	World War I
WWII	World War II
Yates Sel. Cas.	Yates' New York Select Cases

BIBLIOGRAPHY

LEGAL REPRESENTATION

American Research Corporation. 1994. "How to Hire an Attorney." In *Consumer Guidebook: Law and Leading Attorneys.* Minnesota ed. Minneapolis: American Research Corporation.

Editors of *Court TV* and *The American Lawyer.* 1995. *The Court TV Cradle-to-Grave Legal Survival Guide.* 1st ed. Boston: Little, Brown.

Morgan, Thomas D., and Ronald D. Rotunda. 1993. *1993 Selected Standards on Professional Responsibility.* Westbury, N.Y.: Foundation Press.

LEGAL SERVICES CORPORATION

American Bar Association (ABA). 1995. *Arguments against Cutting the LSC.* Fact sheet. April. Chicago: ABA.

Heritage Foundation. 1995. *Why the Legal Services Corporation Must Be Abolished,* by Kenneth F. Boehm and Peter T. Flaherty. Backgrounder no. 1057. October 18.

LEGARE, HUGH SWINTON

Cain, Marvin R. 1978. "Return to Republicanism: A Reappraisal of Hugh Swinton Legare and the Tyler Presidency." *South Carolina History Magazine* 79.

Catalogue of the Library of the Honorable Hugh Legare. 1843. Washington, D.C. In the Caroliniana Collection, Univ. of South Carolina.

Catalogue of the Rare and Valuable Private Library of the Late Honorable H. S. Legare. 1848. Washington, D.C. In the Caroliniana Collection, Univ. of South Carolina.

Welsh, John R. 1971. "An Early Pioneer: Legare's 'Southern Review.'" *Southern Literary Journal* 3.

Wilson, James Grant, and John Fiske, eds. 1888–1889. *Appleton's Cyclopaedia of American Biography.* New York: Appleton.

LEGISLATIVE COURT

Braugh, Roger S., Jr. 1995. "Personal Injury and Wrongful Death Claims in Bankruptcy: The Case for Abstention." *Baylor Law Review* 47.

Cross, John T. 1993. "Congressional Power to Extend Federal Jurisdiction to Disputes outside Article III: A Critical Analysis from the Perspective of Bankruptcy." *Northwestern University Law Review* 87.

Fallon, Richard H. 1988. "Of Legislative Courts, Administrative Agencies, and Article III." *Harvard Law Review* 101.

LEGISLATIVE HISTORY

Kunz, Christina L., et al. 1992. *The Process of Legal Research: Successful Strategies.* 3d ed. Boston: Little, Brown.

LEGISLATURE

Hirsch, E. D., Jr., Joseph F. Kett, and James Trefil. 1988. *The Dictionary of Cultural Literacy.* Boston: Houghton Mifflin.

Maddox, Russell W., and Robert F. Fuquay. 1975. *State and Local Government.* 3d ed. New York: Van Nostrand.

LEMON LAWS

Clark, Barkley, and Christopher Smith. 1984. Cumm. Supp. 1995. *The Law of Product Warranties.* Boston: Warren, Gorham, and Lamont.

Gillis, Jack. 1996. *The Car Book.* 16th ed. New York: HarperPerennial.

Reitz, Curtis R. 1987. *Consumer Product Warranties under Federal and State Laws.* 2d ed. Philadelphia: American Law Institute–American Bar Association Committee on Continuing Professional Education.

LENIN, VLADIMIR ILYICH

Hall, Kermit L. 1989. *The Magic Mirror: Law in American History.* New York: Oxford Univ. Press.

LESSER INCLUDED OFFENSE

Holten, N. Gary, and Lawson L. Lamar. 1991. *The Criminal Courts: Structures, Personnel, and Processes.* New York: McGraw-Hill.

Torcia, Charles E., ed. 1992. *Wharton's Criminal Procedure.* 13th ed. Vol. 4. New York: Clark Boardman Callaghan.

_____. 1993. *Wharton's Criminal Law.* 15th ed. Vol. 1. New York: Thomson Legal.

LETTER RULING

Banoff, Sheldon I., and Richard M. Lipton, eds. 1995. "Letter Ruling Held Relevant Authority in Malpractice Case." *Journal of Taxation* 82 (April).

Kanter, Burton W., and Sheldon I. Banoff, eds. 1992. "Associate Chief Counsel Speaks Out on Letter Rulings." *Journal of Taxation* 76 (January).

Tien, Wendy, tax attorney, Internal Revenue Service. 1996. Interview, August 29.

LETTERS OF ADMINISTRATION

Evans, Daniel B. 1996. "Technology: Probate." *Probate and Property* (March–April).

LEVI, EDWARD HIRSCH

Cambridge Univ. Press Biography, Department of Justice, Gerald R. Ford Presidential Library, and Grolier American Presidency sites. World Wide Web.

LEXIS®

"LEXIS-NEXIS Background." 1997. LEXIS-NEXIS site. World Wide Web (May 8).

LIBEL AND SLANDER

Fenno, Edward T. 1995. "Public Figure Libel: The Premium on Ignorance and the Race to the Bottom." *Southern California Interdisciplinary Law Journal* 4.

Friedman, Jessica R. 1995. "Defamation." *Fordham Law Review* 64.

Hiemstra, Nathalie L. 1993. "*Masson v. New Yorker Magazine, Inc.:* A 'Material Alteration.'" *University of Miami Entertainment and Sports Law Review* 10.

"Jewell Box: An Archive on Richard Jewell and the Olympic Park Bombing." 1997. Creative Loafing Network site. World Wide Web (February 10).

"The Media and Richard Jewell: Rush to Judgment." 1997. Media Studies Center site. World Wide Web (February 10).

Ransom, Elsa. 1995. "The Ex-Public Figure: A Libel Plaintiff without a Class." *Seton Hall Journal of Sport Law* 5.

Stephens, Otis H., Jr., and John M. Scheb II. 1993. *American Constitutional Law.* St. Paul: West.

Stonecipher, Harry W. 1993. "A Survey of the Professional Person as Libel Plaintiff: Reexamination of the Public Figure Doctrine." *Arkansas Law Review* 46.

LIBERTARIANISM

Bergland, David. *Libertarianism in One Lesson.* Orpheus.

Libertarian Party. *10 Answers to Commonly Asked Questions about the Libertarian Party.* Libertarian Party.

Winter, Bill, director of communications, Libertarian party. 1994. Telephone interview, November 1.

LIBERTARIAN PARTY

Winter, Bill, director of communications, Libertarian party. 1994. Telephone interview, November 1.

Libertarian National Committee. Libertarian party promotional flyers. Washington, D.C.: Libertarian National Committee.

LIBERTY

Burris, Alan. 1983. *A Liberty Primer.* Rochester, N.Y.: Society for Individual Liberty.

LIBRARY OF CONGRESS

Library of Congress. Public Affairs Office. 1993. *Background and History.* September.

_____. 1996. *Facts about the Library of Congress.* March.

_____. 1996. *Twenty-five Questions Most Frequently Asked by Visitors.* May.

United States Government Manual, 1995–1996. Washington, D.C.: U.S. Government Printing Office.

LIMITED LIABILITY COMPANY

Callison, J. William, and Maureen A. Sullivan. 1994. *Limited Liability Companies: A State-by-State Guide to Law and Practice.* St. Paul: West.

Ribstein, Larry E., and Robert R. Keatinge. 1995. *Ribstein and Keatinge on Limited Liability Companies.* Colorado Springs: Shepard's/McGraw-Hill.

Wolf-Smith, Risa L., and Robert R. Keatinge. 1994. "Start with Limited Partnership Agreement." *Journal of Limited Liability Companies* 1 (summer).

LIMITED LIABILITY PARTNERSHIP

American Law Institute–American Bar Association (ALI-ABA) Committee on Continuing Professional Education. 1996. *Partnerships, LLCs, and LLPs: Uniform Acts, Taxation, Drafting, Securities, and Bankruptcy.* 12th ed. Vol. 1. Philadelphia: ALI-ABA.

Bromberg, Alan, and Larry Ribstein. 1995. *Limited Liability Partnerships and the Revised Uniform Partnership Act.* Boston: Little, Brown.

Callison, J. William. 1995. *Partnership Law and Practice.* New York: McGraw-Hill.

Dickerson, Claire Moore. 1991. *Partnership Law Adviser.* New York: Practising Law Institute.

LIMITED TEST BAN TREATY

Kegley, Charles W., Jr., and Eugene R. Wittkopf. 1993. *World Politics.* 4th ed. New York: St. Martin's Press.

Palmer, R. R. 1984. *A History of the Modern World.* New York: Knopf.

Sheehan, Michael. 1988. *Arms Control: Theory and Practice.* Cambridge, Mass.: Blackwell.

United States Arms Control and Disarmament Agency. 1982. *Arms Control and Disarmament Agreements.* Washington, D.C.: U.S. Government Printing Office.

LINCOLN, ABRAHAM

Cottrell, John. 1966. *Anatomy of an Assassination.* London: Muller.

Eisenschiml, Otto. 1937. *Why Was Lincoln Murdered?* New York: Crosset and Dunlap.

Good, Timothy S., ed. 1995. *We Saw Lincoln Shot.* Jackson: Univ. Press of Mississippi.

Hall, Kermit L. 1989. *The Magic Mirror: Law in American History.* New York: Oxford Univ. Press.

Pitman, Benn. 1954. *The Assassination of President Lincoln and the Trial of the Conspirators.* New York: Funk & Wagnall's.

Roscoe, Theodore. 1959. *The Web of Conspiracy: The Complete Story of the Men Who Murdered Abraham Lincoln.* Englewood Cliffs, N.J.: Prentice-Hall.

Stephens, Otis H., Jr., and John M. Scheb II. 1993. *American Constitutional Law.* St. Paul: West.

Tidwell, William A. 1995. *Confederate Covert Action in the American Civil War, April '65.* Kent, Ohio: Kent State Univ. Press.

Weichmann, Louis J. 1975. *A True History of the Assassination of Abraham Lincoln and the Conspiracy of 1865.* New York: Knopf.

LINCOLN, LEVI
Justice Department. 1985. *Attorneys General of the United States, 1789–1979.* Washington, D.C.: U.S. Government Printing Office.

Malone, Dumas. 1970. *Jefferson the President: First Term, 1801–1805.* Vol. 4. Boston: Little, Brown.

LINCOLN, ROBERT TODD
Donald, David Herbert. 1995. *Lincoln.* New York: Simon & Schuster.

Goff, John S. 1969. *Robert Todd Lincoln: A Man in His Own Right.* Norman, Okla.: Univ. of Oklahoma Press.

Mearns, David C., ed. 1948. *The Lincoln Papers.* Vol. 1. Garden City, N.Y.: Doubleday.

Oates, Stephen B. 1994. *With Malice toward None: A Life of Abraham Lincoln.* New York: Harper Perennial.

Sandburg, Carl. 1939. *Abraham Lincoln: The War Years.* 4 vols. New York: Harcourt, Brace.

LINDBERGH KIDNAPPING
Bradley, Craig M. 1984. "Racketeering and the Federalization of Crime." *American Criminal Law Review* (fall).

Silverman, Barbara Sheryl. 1983. "The Search for a Solution to Child Snatching." *Hofstra Law Review* (spring).

LIQUIDATED DAMAGES
Brizzee, David. 1991. "Liquidated Damages and the Penalty Rule: A Reassessment." *Brigham Young University Law Review* 1991.

Calamari, John D., and Joseph M. Perillo. 1987. *Contracts.* 3d ed. St. Paul: West.

Daniszewski, Robert M., and Jeffrey W. Sacks. 1990. "One View Too Many." *Boston Bar Journal* 34 (April).

LIQUORMART V. RHODE ISLAND
Stephens, Otis H., Jr., and John M. Scheb II. 1993. *American Constitutional Law.* St. Paul: West.

LITERARY PROPERTY
de Grazia, Margreta. 1992. "Sanctioning Voice: Quotation Marks, the Abolition of Torture, and the Fifth Amendment." *Cardozo Arts and Entertainment Law Journal* 10.

Diviney, Catherine A. 1987. "Guardian of the Public Interest: An Alternative Application of the Fair Use Doctrine in *Salinger v. Random House, Inc.*" *St. John's Law Review* 61.

Jaszi, Peter. 1991. "Toward a Theory of Copyright: The Metamorphoses of 'Authorship.' " *Duke Law Journal* 1991.

Peppe, Vincent H. 1988. "Fair Use of Unpublished Materials in the Second Circuit: The Letters of the Law." *Brooklyn Law Review* 54.

LITTLE-COLLINS, ELLA LEE
Collins, Rodnell. 1996. Telephone interviews, February 29, August 23, and October 2.

Malcolm X, with Alex Haley. 1973. *The Autobiography of Malcolm X.* New York: Ballantine Books.

LIUZZO, VIOLA FAUVER GREGG
Gentry, Curt. 1991. *J. Edgar Hoover: The Man and His Secrets.* New York: Norton.

Powers, Richard G. 1987. *Secrecy and Power: The Life of J. Edgar Hoover.* New York: Free Press.

Siegel, Beatrice. 1993. *Murder on the Highway: The Viola Liuzzo Story.* Four Winds Press.

LIVERY OF SEISIN
Bergin, Thomas F., and Paul G. Haskell. 1966. *Preface to Estates in Land and Future Interests.* Brooklyn: Foundation Press.

LIVINGSTON, HENRY BROCKHOLST
Friedman, Leon, and Fred L. Israel, eds. 1969. *The Justices of the United States Supreme Court, 1789–1969: Their Lives and Major Opinions.* New York: Chelsea House.

LIVINGSTON, ROBERT R.
Brandt, Clare. 1986. *An American Aristocracy: The Livingstons.* New York: Doubleday.

LLEWELLYN, KARL N.
Twining, William L. 1943. *Karl Llewellyn and the Realist Movement.* London: Weidenfeld & Nicolson.

LOBBYING
Browne, Steven A. 1995. "The Constitutionality of Lobby Reform." *William and Mary Bill of Rights Journal* 4.

Doherty, Carroll J., and the "Inside Congress" Congressional Quarterly Staff. 1996. *Congressional Quarterly Weekly Report* 54 (January 20).

Fuller, William P. 1993. "Congressional Lobbying Disclosure Laws: Much Needed Reforms on the Horizon." *Seton Hall Legislative Journal* 17.

Government Accounting Office. 1991. *Federal Lobbying: Federal Regulation of Lobbying Act of 1946 Is Ineffective.* July. Washington, D.C.: Government Accounting Office.

Jacobs, Jerald A., ed. 1989. *Federal Lobbying.* Washington, D.C.: Bureau of National Affairs.

Lane, Edgar. 1964. *Lobbying and the Law.* Berkeley, Calif.: Univ. of California Press.

Mack, Charles S. 1989. *Lobbying and Government Relations: A Guide for Executives.* New York: Quorum Books.

Schram, Martin. 1997. "Shakedown." *Mother Jones* site. World Wide Web (March 3).

Stone, Peter H. 1997. "Shining a Brighter Light on Lobbyists." In *National Journal.* February 5, 1996 Politics USA site. World Wide Web (March 3).

LOCHNER V. NEW YORK
Bieneman, Charles A. 1991. Review of *Judicial Power and Reform Politics: The Anatomy of Lochner v. New York,* by Paul Kens. *Michigan Law Review* 89.

Bork, Robert H. 1990. *The Tempting of America.* New York: Free Press.

Ely, James W., Jr., 1991. Review of *Judicial Power and Reform Politics: The Anatomy of Lochner v. New York,* by Paul Kens. *Vanderbilt Law Review* 44.

Kordana, Kevin A. 1995. "Law Firms and Associate Careers: Tournament Theory versus the Production Imperative Model." *Yale Law Journal* 104.

Shell, G. Richard. 1993. "Contracts in the Modern Supreme Court." *California Law Review* 81.

LODGE, HENRY CABOT

Garraty, John A. 1953. *Henry Cabot Lodge: A Biography.* New York: Knopf.

Lodge, Henry Cabot. 1902. *Fighting Frigate and Other Essays.* New York: Scribners.

LOGAN ACT

Kearney, Kevin M. 1987. "Private Citizens in Foreign Affairs: A Constitutional Analysis." *Emory Law Journal* 36 (winter).

Roth, Brad R. 1993. "The First Amendment in the Foreign Affairs Realm: 'Domesticating' the Restrictions on Citizen Participation." *Temple Political and Civil Rights Law Review* 2 (spring).

LONG-ARM STATUTE

Casad, Robert C. 1983. *Jurisdiction in Civil Actions.* Warren, Gorham and Lamont.

———. 1988. *Callaghan's Trial Practice Series: Jurisdiction and Forum Selection.* Callaghan.

Myers, Rosemary E. 1984. "Procedural Law." *New York University Law Review* 59.

Shreve, Gene R., and Peter Raven-Hansen. 1989. *Understanding Civil Procedure.* New York: Bender.

Tunick, David C. 1996. "Up Close and Personal: A Close-up Look at Personal Jurisdiction." *Creighton Law Review* 29.

LOOPHOLE

Burke, Debra. 1995. "Twenty Years after the Federal Election Campaign Act Amendments of 1974: Look Who's Running Now." *Dickinson Law Review* 99 (winter).

Wardle, Geoffrey M. 1996. "Political Contributions and Conduits after Charles Keating and Emily's List: An Incremental Approach to Reforming Federal Campaign Finance." *Case Western Reserve Law Review* 46 (winter).

LOYALTY OATH

Levinson, Sanford. 1986. "Constituting Communities through Words That Bind: Reflections on Loyalty Oaths." *Michigan Law Review* 84 (June).

Scanlan, John A. 1988. "Aliens in the Marketplace of Ideas." *Texas Law Review* 66 (June).

Senhauser, William B. 1987. "Education and the Court: The Supreme Court's Educational Ideology." *Vanderbilt Law Review* 40 (May).

Sullivan, Kathleen M. 1989. "Unconstitutional Conditions." *Harvard Law Review* 102 (May).

LURTON, HORACE HARMON

Friedman, Leon, and Fred L. Israel, eds. 1995. *The Justices of the United States Supreme Court, 1789–1969: Their Lives and Major Opinions.* New York: Chelsea House.

MACVEAGH, ISAAC WAYNE

Justice Department. 1985. *Attorneys General of the United States, 1789–1985.* Washington, D.C.: U.S. Government Printing Office.

MADISON, JAMES

Abney, David L. 1994. "Constitutional Interpretation: Moving toward a Jurisprudence of Common Sense." *Temple Law Review* 67.

Bailyn, Bernard. 1977. *The Great Republic.* Lexington, Mass.: Heath.

Hall, Kermit L., ed. 1992. *Oxford Companion to the Supreme Court of the United States.* New York: Oxford Univ. Press.

Levy, Leonard W. 1988. *Original Intent and the Framers' Constitution.* New York: Macmillan.

Madison, James. 1987. *Notes of the Debates in the Federal Convention of 1787.* Edited by Adrienne Koch. New York: Norton.

Meyers, Marvin, ed. 1981. *The Mind of the Founder: Sources of the Political Thought of James Madison.* Rev. ed. Hanover: Univ. Press of New England.

Rakove, Jack. 1990. *James Madison and the Creation of the American Republic.* New York: HarperCollins.

Wood, Gordon S. 1969. *The Creation of the American Republic, 1776–1787.* New York: Norton.

MAGNA CHARTA

Bailyn, Bernard. 1992. *The Ideological Origins of the American Revolution.* Enl. ed. Cambridge: Harvard Univ. Press.

Holt, J. C. 1965. Reprint 1992. *Magna Carta.* Cambridge: University of Cambridge.

Plucknett, Theodore. 1956. *A Concise History of the Common Law.* Boston: Little, Brown.

Trevelyan, G. M. 1982. *A Shortened History of England.* Middlesex, England: Penguin.

MAGNUSON-MOSS WARRANTY ACT

Schaefer, David T. 1996. "Attorney's Fees for Consumers in Warranty Actions—An Expanding Role for the UCC?" *Indiana Law Journals* 61 (summer).

MAIL COVER

Feld, Daniel E. 1982. "Validity, under Fourth Amendment, of 'Mail Cover.' " *American Law Reports* 57.

MAIL FRAUD

Henning, Peter J. 1995. "Maybe It Should Just Be Called Federal Fraud: The Changing Nature of the Mail Fraud Statute." *Boston College Law Review* 36.

Podgor, Ellen S. 1992. "Mail Fraud: Opening Letters." *South Carolina Law Review* 43.

MAINE, HENRY JAMES SUMNER

Hall, Kermit L. 1989. *The Magic Mirror: Law in American History.* New York: Oxford Univ. Press.

MAINTENANCE

Cornick, Matthew S. 1995. *A Practical Guide to Family Law.* St. Paul: West.

MALCOLM X

Carson, Clayborne. 1991. *Malcolm X: The FBI File.* New York: Carroll & Graf.

Estell, Kenneth. 1994. *African America: Portrait of a People.* Detroit: Visible Ink.

"Malcolm X Scores U.S. and Kennedy." 1963. *New York Times* (December 2).

Malcolm X, with Alex Haley. 1984. *The Autobiography of Malcolm X.* New York: Ballantine Books.

Myers, Walter. 1993. *Malcolm X: By Any Means Necessary.* New York: Scholastic.

MALICIOUS PROSECUTION

American Law Institute. *Restatement (Second) of Torts*, div. 7, ch. 29, topic 2, §§ 659–661. 1977. St. Paul: American Law Institute.

Cooper, David R. 1993. "Attorneys as Plaintiffs: Absolute Immunity for Ethics Complainants Bars Suit by Attorney for Malicious Prosecution (*Jarvis v. Drake*, 250 Kan. 645, 830 P.2d 23 [1992])." *Washburn Law Journal* 32.

Weber, Christopher W. 1994. "The Loss of Consortium-Malicious Prosecution Nexus: No Recovery for Loss of Spousal Consortium Absent Physical Injury and No Recovery for Malicious Prosecution beyond the Person Prosecuted: *Browning Ferris Industries v. Lieck*, 881 S.W.2d 288 (Tex. 1994)." *Texas Tech Law Review* 26.

Zbytowski, Jennifer S. 1995. "The Case against Section 1983 Immunity for Witnesses Who Conspire with a State Official to Present Perjured Testimony." *Michigan Law Review* 93.

MALPRACTICE

Mallen, Ronald E., and Jeffrey M. Smith. 1996. *Legal Malpractice*. 4th ed. St. Paul: West.

MANAGED CARE

HMO Information Home Page. 1996. WNET site. World Wide Web (November 14).

MANDAMUS

Louisell, David W., Geoffrey C. Hazard, Jr., and Colin C. Tait. 1989. *Pleading and Procedure, State and Federal: Cases and Materials*. 6th ed. Westbury, N.Y.: Foundation Press.

Wyler, Robert A. 1990. *Legalines: Civil Procedures*. 3d ed. Chicago: Harcourt Brace Jovanovich Legal & Professional Publications.

MANN, HORACE

Blanshard, Paul. 1963. *Religion and the Schools: The Great Controversy*. Boston: Beacon Press.

MANN, JAMES ROBERT

Grittner, Frederick K. 1990. *White Slavery: Myth, Ideology, and American Law*. New York: Garland.

Hall, Kermit L. 1989. *The Magic Mirror: Law in American History*. New York: Oxford Univ. Press.

Stephens, Otis H., Jr., and John M. Scheb II. 1993. *American Constitutional Law*. St. Paul: West.

MANN ACT

Grittner, Frederick K. 1990. *White Slavery: Myth, Ideology, and American Law*. New York: Garland.

Langum, David J. 1994. *Crossing over the Line: Legislating Morality and the Mann Act*. Chicago: Univ. of Chicago Press.

MANSFIELD, WILLIAM MURRAY, FIRST EARL OF

Hall, Kermit L. 1989. *The Magic Mirror: Law in American History*. New York: Oxford Univ. Press.

MARBURY V. MADISON

Levy, Leonard W. 1988. *Original Intent and the Framers' Constitution*. New York: Macmillan.

McCloskey, Robert G. 1960. *The American Supreme Court*. Chicago: University of Chicago Press.

Wills, Mary, ed. 1982. *The Federalist Papers*, by Alexander Hamilton, James Madison and John Jay. No. 78. New York: Bantam Books.

MARITAL COMMUNICATIONS PRIVILEGE

Pappa, Kristina K. 1995. "Note: Evidence—Privileged Communications." *Seton Hall Law Review* 25.

MARRIAGE

Hall, Kermit L. 1989. *The Magic Mirror: Law in American History*. New York: Oxford Univ. Press.

Stephens, Otis H., Jr., and John M. Scheb II. 1993. *American Constitutional Law*. St. Paul: West.

MARSHALL, JOHN

Friedman, Leon, and Fred L. Israel, eds. 1969. *The Justices of the Supreme Court, 1789–1969: Their Lives and Major Opinions*. New York: Chelsea House.

MARTIAL LAW

Currie, David P. 1987. "The Constitution in the Supreme Court: The Second World War, 1941–1946." *Catholic University Law Review* 37.

Koh, Harold Hongju. 1994. "America's Offshore Refugee Camps." *University of Richmond Law Review* 29.

McCleskey, Robert A. 1994. "Maybe Oil and Water Should Mix—At Least in Texas Law: An Analysis of Current Problems with Texas Ground Water Law and How Established Oil and Gas Law Could Provide Appropriate Solutions." *Texas Wesleyan Law Review* 1.

Mello, Michael A., and Donna Duffy. 1991. "Suspending Justice: The Unconstitutionality of the Proposed Six-month Time Limit on the Filing of Habeas Corpus Petitions by State Death Row Inmates." *New York University Law Review* 18.

Rumore, Samuel A., Jr. 1996. "Building Alabama's Courthouses: Russell County Courthouse." *Alabama Lawyer* 57.

MARTIN, LUTHER

Hall, Kermit L. 1989. *The Magic Mirror: Law in American History*. New York: Oxford Univ. Press.

MARTINDALE-HUBBELL LAW DIRECTORY

Martindale-Hubbell site. 1996. World Wide Web (November 11).

MARX, KARL HEINRICH

Inverarity, James M., Pat Lauderdale, and Barry C. Feld. 1983. *Law and Society: Sociological Perspectives on Criminal Law*. Boston: Little, Brown.

MASON, GEORGE

Stephens, Otis H., Jr., and John M. Scheb II. 1993. *American Constitutional Law*. St. Paul: West.

MASON, JOHN YOUNG

Hopkins, Joseph G. E., ed. 1977. *Concise Dictionary of American Biography*. 2d ed. New York: Scribner.

Justice Department. 1985. *Attorneys General of the United States, 1789–1985*. Washington, D.C.: U.S. Government Printing Office.

Morris, Richard B., ed. 1976. *Encyclopedia of American History*. New York: Harper & Row.

The National Cyclopaedia of American Biography 1898. New York: White.

MASS COMMUNICATIONS LAW

Sapranov, Walt, and Anne E. Franklin. 1997. "Summary of the Telecommunications Act of 1996." Gerry, Friend, and Sapranov law firm site. World Wide Web (March 5).

MASSIAH V. UNITED STATES

Howe, Patrick M. 1990. "Cleaning Up the Counsel Clause: Revisiting *Massiah v. United States.*" *University of San Francisco Law Review* 25.

Tomkovicz, James J. 1989. "The *Massiah* Right to Exclusion: Constitutional Premises and Doctrinal Implications." *North Carolina Law Review* 67.

MATTER OF LAW

Hall, Kermit L. 1989. *The Magic Mirror: Law in American History.* New York: Oxford Univ. Press.

MATTER OF RECORD

Jansen, Jenneane, attorney. 1996. Interview, October 31.

MATTHEWS, STANLEY

Stephens, Otis H., Jr., and John M. Scheb II. 1993. *American Constitutional Law.* St. Paul: West.

MCCARRAN-FERGUSON ACT OF 1945

Macey, Jonathan R., and Geoffrey P. Miller. 1993. "The McCarran-Ferguson Act of 1945: Reconceiving the Federal Role in Insurance Regulation." *New York University Law Review* 68.

Russ, Lee R., and Thomas F. Segalla. 1995. *Couch on Insurance.* 3d ed. Rochester, N.Y.: Clark Boardman Callaghan.

MCCARTHY, EUGENE JOSEPH

Eisele, Albert. 1972. *Almost to the Presidency: A Biography of Two American Politicians.* Piper.

McCarthy, Abigail. 1972. *Private Faces, Public Places.* New York: Doubleday.

McCarthy, Eugene. 1969. *The Year of the People.* New York: Doubleday.

MCKENNA, JOSEPH

Friedman, Leon, and Fred L. Israel, eds. 1969. *The Justices of the United States Supreme Court, 1789–1969: Their Lives and Major Opinions.* New York: Chelsea House.

MCKINLEY, JOHN

Friedman, Leon, and Fred L. Israel, eds. 1969. *The Justices of the United States Supreme Court, 1789–1969: Their Lives and Major Opinions.* New York: Chelsea House.

MCKINNEY ACT

Foscarinis, Maria. 1996. "Downward Spiral: Homelessness and Its Criminalization." *Yale Law and Policy Review* 14.

MCLEAN, JOHN

Cushman, Clare. 1995. *The Supreme Court Justices: Illustrated Biographies 1789–1995.* Washington, D.C.: Congressional Quarterly.

Witt, Elder, ed. 1990. *Guide to the U.S. Supreme Court.* 2d ed. Washington D.C.: Congressional Quarterly.

MCNABB-MALLORY RULE

LaFave, Wayne R., and Jerold H. Israel. 1984. *Criminal Procedure.* Vol. 1. St. Paul: West.

Rhodes, Mark S. 1985. *Orfield's Criminal Procedure under the Federal Rules.* 2d ed. Rochester, N.Y. Lawyer's Cooperative.

MCREYNOLDS, JAMES CLARK

Hall, Kermit L. 1989. *The Magic Mirror: Law in American History.* New York: Oxford Univ. Press.

Stephens, Otis H., Jr., and John M. Scheb II. 1993. *American Constitutional Law.* St. Paul: West.

MEDICAID

"Medicaid Reform." 1997. Twentieth Century Fund site. World Wide Web (January 17).

MEDICARE

"Medicare Reform." 1997. Twentieth Century Fund site. World Wide Web (January 5).

MEREDITH, JAMES HOWARD

Harris, Janet. 1967. *The Long Freedom Road: The Civil Rights Story.* Blue Ridge Summit, Pa.: McGraw-Hill.

Levy, Peter B. 1992. *Let Freedom Ring: A Documentary History of the Modern Civil Rights Movement.* New York: Praeger.

Weisbrot, Robert. 1990. *Freedom Bound: A History of America's Civil Rights Movement.* New York: Norton.

MERIT SYSTEMS PROTECTION BOARD

United States Government Manual 1996–1997. Washington, D.C.: U.S. Government Printing Office.

MEXICO AND THE UNITED STATES

U.S.-Mexico Binational Commission site. 1997. World Wide Web (March 19).

MICHIGAN V. TUCKER

Stephens, Otis H., Jr., and John M. Scheb II. 1993. *American Constitutional Law.* St. Paul: West.

MILITARY GOVERNMENT

Chapman, William. 1991. *Inventing Japan: An Unconventional Account of the Post-War Years.* New York: Prentice-Hall Parkside.

Craven, Avery. 1969. *Reconstruction: The Ending of the Civil War.* New York: Holt, Rinehart.

de Mulinen, Frederic. 1987. *Handbook on the Law of War for the Armed Forces.* Geneva: International Committee of the Red Cross.

Dolan, Ronald E., and Robert L. Worden. 1992. *Japan: A Country Study.* Federal Research Division, Library of Congress. Headquarters, Department of the Army. Washington, D.C.: U.S. Government Printing Office.

MILITARY LAW

Bishop, Joseph W., Jr. 1974. *Justice Under Fire: A Study of Military Law.* New York: Charterhouse.

Duignan, Kathleen A. 1996. "Military Justice." *Federal Lawyer* 43.

Falvey, Joseph L. 1995. "United Nations Justice or Military Justice." *Fordham International Law Journal* 19.

Fuger, Stanley J. 1992. "Military Justice." *Connecticut Bar Journal* 66.

Gilligan, Francis A. 1990. "Civilian Justice v. Military Justice." *Criminal Justice* 5 (summer).

Kohlmann, Ralph H. 1996. "Saving the Best-Laid Plans." *Army Lawyer* 3 (August).

Wiener, Frederick B. 1989. "American Military Law in the Light of the First Mutiny Act's Tricentennial." *Military Law Review* 126 (fall).

MILITIA

Fields, William S., and David T. Hardy. 1992. "The Militia and the Constitution: A Legal History." *Military Law Review* 136 (spring).

Mahon, John K. 1983. *History of the Militia and the National Guard.* New York: Macmillan.

Maslowski, Peter, and Allan R. Millett. 1994. *For the Common Defense: A Military History of the United States.* New York: Free Press.

Weigley, Russell F. 1967. *History of the United States Army.* New York: Macmillan.

MILLER, SAMUEL FREEMAN

Hall, Kermit L. 1989. *The Magic Mirror: Law in American History.* New York: Oxford Univ. Press.

Stephens, Otis H., Jr., and John M. Scheb II. 1993. *American Constitutional Law.* St. Paul: West.

MILLER, WILLIAM HENRY HARRISON

Justice Department. 1985. *Attorneys General of the United States, 1789–1985.* Washington, D.C.: U.S. Government Printing Office.

MILLET, KATHERINE MURRAY

Bullock, Alan, and R. B. Woodings, eds. 1983. *20th Century Culture: A Biographical Companion.* New York: Harper & Row.

Rose, Phyllis, ed. 1993. *Women's Lives.* New York: Norton.

MINIMUM WAGE

Levitan, Sar A., and Richard A. Belous. 1979. *More Than Subsistence: Minimum Wages for the Working Poor.* Baltimore and London: Johns Hopkins Univ. Press.

Linder, Marc. 1990. "The Minimum Wage as Industrial Policy: A Forgotten Role." *Journal of Legislation* 16.

Norlund, Willis J. 1988. "A Brief History of the Fair Labor Standards Act." *Labor Law Journal* 39.

Quigley, William P. 1996. " 'A Fair Day's Pay for a Fair Day's Work': Time to Raise and Index the Minimum Wage." *St. Mary's Law Journal* 27.

MINTON, SHERMAN

Hall, Kermit L. 1989. *The Magic Mirror: Law in American History.* New York: Oxford Univ. Press.

Stephens, Otis H., Jr., and John M. Scheb II. 1993. *American Constitutional Law.* St. Paul: West.

MISFEASANCE

Kionka, Edward J. 1988. *Torts.* St. Paul: West.

MISPRISION

Gould, Keri A. 1993. "Turning Rat and Doing Time for Uncharged, Dismissed, or Acquitted Crimes: Do the Federal Sentencing Guidelines Promote Respect for the Law?" *New York Law School Journal of Human Rights* 10.

Guerra, Sandra. 1996. "Family Values?: The Family as an Innocent Victim of Civil Drug Asset Forfeiture." *Cornell Law Review* 81.

Mosteller, Robert P. 1992. "Child Abuse Reporting Laws and Attorney-Client Confidences: The Reality and the Specter of Lawyer as Informant." *Duke Law Journal* 42.

MISREPRESENTATION

Kionka, Edward J. 1988. *Torts.* St. Paul: West.

MISSOURI COMPROMISE OF 1820

Hall, Kermit L. 1989. *The Magic Mirror: Law in American History.* New York: Oxford Univ. Press.

Stephens, Otis H., Jr., and John M. Scheb II. 1993. *American Constitutional Law.* St. Paul: West.

MISTAKE OF FACT

"Contracts." 1994. *SMH Bar Review.*

"Criminal Law and Procedure." 1994. *SMH Bar Review.*

Kionka, Edward J. 1988. *Torts.* St. Paul: West.

MISTAKE OF LAW

"Criminal Law and Procedure." 1994. *SMH Bar Review.*

Kionka, Edward J. 1988. *Torts.* St. Paul: West.

MITCHELL, JOHN NEWTON

Justice Department. 1985. *Attorneys General of the United States, 1789–1985.* Washington, D.C.: U.S. Government Printing Office.

MITIGATION OF DAMAGES

Kionka, Edward J. 1988. *Torts,* St. Paul: West.

Knapp, Charles L., and Nathan M. Crystal. 1987. *Problems in Contract Law: Cases and Materials.* 2d ed. Boston: Little, Brown.

"Torts." 1994. *SMH Bar Review.*

M'NAGHTEN RULE

Kaplan, John, and Robert Weisberg. 1991. *Criminal Law: Cases and Materials.* 2d ed. Boston: Little, Brown.

MODEL ACTS

Armstrong, Walter P., Jr. 1991. *A Century of Service: A Centennial History of the National Conference of Commissioners on Uniform State Laws.* St. Paul: West.

MONEY LAUNDERING

Mellinkoff, David. 1992. *Mellinkoff's Dictionary of American Legal Usage.* St. Paul: West.

Sulltzer, Scott. 1995. "Money Laundering: The Scope of the Problem and Attempts to Combat It." *Tennessee Law Review* 63.

MONOPOLY

Hall, Kermit L. 1989. *The Magic Mirror. Law in American History.* New York: Oxford Univ. Press.

MONTESQUIEU, CHARLES-LOUIS DE SECONDAT, BARON DE LA BREDE ET DE

Bergman, Matthew P. 1990. "Montesquieu's Theory of Government and the Framing of the American Constitution." *Pepperdine Law Review* 19 (December).

MOODY, WILLIAM HENRY

Friedman, Leon, and Fred L. Israel, eds. 1969. *The Justices of the United States Supreme Court, 1789–1969: Their Lives and Major Opinions.* Vol. III. New York: Chelsea House.

Witt, Elder, ed. 1990. *Guide to the U.S. Supreme Court.* 2d ed. Washington, D.C.: Congressional Quarterly.

MOORE, ALFRED

Friedman, Leon, and Fred L. Israel, eds. 1969. *The Justices of the United States Supreme Court, 1789–1969: Their Lives and Major Opinions.* New York: Chelsea House.

Witt, Elder, ed. 1990. *Guide to the U.S. Supreme Court.* 2d ed. Washington, D.C.: Congressional Quarterly.

MOOT COURT

Davis, Tracy Hamrick. 1995. "The Holderness Moot Court Bench." *North Carolina Law Review* 73 (January).

Mellhorn, Donald F., Jr. 1995. "A Moot Court Exercise: Debating Judicial Review prior to *Marbury v. Madison.*" *Constitutional Comment* 12 (winter).

MORAL LAW

McWilliams, Peter. 1993. *Ain't Nobody's Business If You Do.* Los Angeles: Prelude Press.

Tivnan, Edward. 1995. *The Moral Imagination: Confronting the Ethical Issues of Our Day.* New York: Simon & Schuster.

MORATORIUM

Amundson, Roland C., and Lewis J. Rotman. 1984. "Depression Jurisprudence Revisited: Minnesota's Moratorium on Mortgage Foreclosure." *William Mitchell Law Review* 10.

MORMON CHURCH

Acts, Resolutions and Memorials Passed at the Several Annual Sessions of the Legislative Assembly of the Territory of Utah. 1855. Salt Lake City: Caine.

Homer, Michael. 1996. "The Judiciary and the Common Law in Utah." *Utah Bar Journal* 9 (September).

MOTION

Practising Law Institute (PLI). 1993. *Motion Practice under the CPLR and the Uniform Rules of Court,* by L. Peter Parcher and William Fitzgerald. Litigation and Administrative Practice Course Handbook series.

MOTIVE

Candeub, Adam. 1994. "Motive Crimes and Other Minds." *University of Pennsylvania Law Review* 142 (June).

Pillsbury, Samuel H. 1990. "Evil and the Law of Murder." *University of California at Davis Law Review* 24.

MOTLEY, CONSTANCE BAKER

Gilbert, Lynn, and Gaylen Moore. 1981. *Particular Passions: Talks with Women Who Have Shaped Our Times.* New York: Potter.

Plowden, Martha Ward. 1993. *Famous Firsts of Black Women.* Gretna, La.: Pelican.

Stoddard, Hope. 1970. *Famous American Women.* New York: Cromwell.

MOVANT

Foremaster, Gary T. 1987. "The Movant's Burden in a Motion for Summary Judgment." *Utah Law Review* 1987.

MOVIE RATING

Cole, David. 1994. "Playing by Pornography's Rules: The Regulation of Sexual Expression." *University of Pennsylvania Law Review* 143 (November).

Katz, Michael. 1996. "The Precursor: Movie Ratings." *Broadcasting and Cable* 8 (May 19).

"The Ratings Game: Movies' Ratings Can Have Strong Effect on Box Office's Rental Performances." 1994. *Video Store* 16 (May 1).

MULTIDISTRICT LITIGATION

Whitman, M. Hamilton, and Diane Festino Schmitt. 1996. "Multidistrict Litigation: A Primer on Practice before the Panel." *The Business Line*—Newsletter of Ober and Kaler. World Wide Web (November 10).

MUNICIPAL CORPORATION

Mulcahy, Charles C., and Michelle J. Zimet. 1996. "Impact Fees for a Developing Wisconsin." *Marquette Law Review* 79.

Powell, Frona M. 1990. "Challenging Authority for Municipal Subdivision Exactions: The Ultra Vires Attack." *DePaul Law Review* 39.

MURDER

Hobson, Charles L. 1996. "Reforming California's Homicide Law." *Pepperdine Law Review* 23.

MURPHY, FRANCIS WILLIAM

Friedman, Leon, and Fred L. Israel, eds. 1969. *The Justices of the United States Supreme Court, 1789–1969: Their Lives and Major Opinions.* New York: Chelsea House.

Witt, Elder, ed. 1990. *Guide to the U.S. Supreme Court.* 2d ed. Washington, D.C.: Congressional Quarterly.

MUSIC PUBLISHING

Satorius, Daniel M., ed. 1993. *The Practical Musician.* St. Paul: Minnesota Continuing Legal Education.

NADER, RALPH

Nader, Ralph. 1965. *Unsafe at Any Speed: The Designed-in Dangers of the American Automobile.* New York: Grossman.

NATIONAL CONSUMER COOPERATIVE BANK

United States Government Manual, 1981–1982. Washington, D.C.: U.S. Government Printing Office.

NATIONAL CREDIT UNION ADMINISTRATION

United States Government Manual, 1981–1982. Washington, D.C.: U.S. Government Printing Office.

NATIONAL GUARD

Bovarnick, Jeff. 1991. "*Perpich v. United States Department of Defense:* Who's in Charge of the National Guard?" *New England Law Review* 26.

Breitenbach, Roy W. 1989. "*Perpich v. United States Department of Defense:* Who Controls the Weekend Soldier?" *St. John's Law Review* 64.

Rich, Steven B. 1994. "The National Guard, Drug Interdiction and Counterdrug Activities, Posse Comitatus: The Meaning and Implications of 'In Federal Service.' " *Army Law* 35 (June).

Theurer, Kenneth M. 1994. "Low-Level Conflicts and the Reserves: Presidential Authority under 10 U.S.C. sec. 673b." *University of Cincinnati Law Review* 62.

NATIONAL INDUSTRIAL RECOVERY ACT OF 1933

Badger, Anthony J. 1989. *The New Deal: The Depression Years, 1933–1940.* New York: Farrar, Straus & Giroux.

Boardman, Fon W. 1967. *The Thirties: America and the Great Depression.* New York: Walck.

Leuchtenburg, William E. 1963. *Franklin D. Roosevelt and the New Deal, 1932–1940.* New York: Harper & Row.

Rabin, Robert L. 1986. "Federal Regulation in Historical Perspective." *Stanford Law Review* 38.

Watkins, T. H. 1993. *The Great Depression: America in the 1930s.* Boston: Little, Brown.

NATIONAL MEDIATION BOARD

United States Government Manual, 1996–1997. Washington, D.C.: U.S. Government Printing Office.

NATIONAL SECURITY COUNCIL

United States Government Manual 1996–1997. Washington, D.C.: U.S. Government Printing Office.

NATIONAL TRANSPORTATION SAFETY BOARD

Atwood, Roy Tress. 1987. "Admissibility of National Transportation Safety Board Reports in Civil Air Crash Litigation." *Journal of Air Law and Commerce* 53 (winter).

Cook, Joseph T. 1992. "Let Safety Board Give the Facts." *The National Law Journal* 15 (October 26).

United States Government Manual, 1995–1996. Washington, D.C.: U.S. Government Printing Office.

NATION OF ISLAM

Carson, Clayborne. 1991. *Malcolm X: The FBI File.* New York: Carroll & Graf.

Estell, Kenneth. 1994. *African America: Portrait of a People.* Detroit: Visible Ink.

Karim, Benjamin, with Peter Skutches, and David Gallen. 1992. *Remembering Malcolm: The Story of Malcolm X from inside the Muslim Mosque.* New York: Carroll & Graf.

Malcolm X, with Alex Haley. 1984. *The Autobiography of Malcolm X.* New York: Ballantine Books.

NATIVE AMERICAN RIGHTS

Cox, Michael D. 1995. "The Indian Gaming Regulatory Act: An Overview." *St. Thomas Law Review* 7.

Getches, David H., Charles F. Wilkinson, and Robert A. Williams, Jr. 1993. *Federal Indian Law.* St. Paul: West.

Kelly, Joseph M. 1995. "Indian Gaming Law." *Drake Law Review* 43.

McNeil, Heidi L. 1994. *Indian Gaming—Prosperity, Controversy.* PLI order no. B4-7077. New York: Practising Law Institute.

Pevar, Stephen L. 1983. *The Rights of Indians and Tribes.* New York: Bantam Books.

NATURAL LAW

Berman, Harold J. 1983. *Law and Revolution: The Formation of the Western Legal Tradition.* Cambridge: Harvard Univ. Press.

Horwitz, Morton J. 1977. *The Transformation of American Law: 1780–1860.* Cambridge: Harvard Univ. Press.

Levy, Leonard W. 1963. *Jefferson and Civil Liberties: The Darker Side.* Chicago: Elephant Paperback.

Locke, John. 1980. (First printed in 1690.) *Second Treatise of Government.* Indianapolis: Hacket Publishing.

Wood, Gordon S. 1972. *The Creation of the American Republic: 1776–1787.* New York: Norton.

NAVIGABLE WATERS

"Annotated Federal Statutes of Limitation: Title 33—Navigation and Navigable Waters." 1995. *Southwestern University Law Review* 24.

Arnold, Alvin L. 1993. "Navigable Waters: Four Tests to Determine Navigability." *Real Estate Law Report* 22 (January).

Kullman, Aimee P. 1994. "Expanding the Scope of 'Navigable Waters' under the LHWCA." *Tulane Maritime Law Journal* 19 (winter).

NAVY DEPARTMENT

United States Government Manual, 1995–1996. Washington, D.C.: U.S. Government Printing Office.

NECESSITY

Goldberg, Stephanie B. 1993. "Necessity Defense Fails in Massachusetts." *American Bar Association Journal* 79 (October).

Pearson, James O., Jr. 1992. " 'Choice of Evils': Necessity, Duress, or Similar Defense to State or Local Criminal Charges Based on Acts of Public Protest." *American Law Reports.* 5th ed. Vol. 3.

Schulkind, Laura J. 1989. "Applying the Necessity Defense to Civil Disobedience Cases." *New York Law Review* 64 (April).

Stone, Stephanie. 1996. "No Surrender Requirement for Escapees Claiming Necessity Defense, Rules Texas." *West's Legal News* (January 12).

NELSON, SAMUEL

Friedman, Leon, and Fred L. Israel, eds. 1969. *The Justices of the United States Supreme Court, 1789–1969: Their Lives and Major Opinions.* New York: Chelsea House.

NEW DEAL

Fraser, Steve, and Gary Gerstle. 1989. *The Rise and Fall of the New Deal Order.* Princeton, N.J.: Princeton Univ. Press.

Freedman, Russell. 1990. *Franklin Delano Roosevelt.* New York: Clarion Books.

Schraff, Anne E. 1990. *The Great Depression and the New Deal.* New York: Watts.

Stewart, Gail B. 1993. *The New Deal.* New York: New Discovery Books.

NEW YORK TIMES V. SULLIVAN

Stephens, Otis H., Jr., and John M. Scheb II. 1993. *American Constitutional Law.* St. Paul: West.

NEW YORK TIMES V. UNITED STATES

Glendon, William R. 1993. "Fifteen Days in June That Shook the First Amendment: A First Person Account of the Pentagon Papers Case." *New York State Bar Journal* 65 (November).

Godofsky, Stanley, and Howard M. Rogatnick. 1987/1988. "Prior Restraints: The Pentagon Papers Case Revisited." *Cumberland Law Review* 18.

Practicing Law Institute (PLI). 1996. *The Pentagon Papers: Excerpts from the Record*, by William R. Glendon. Patents, Copyrights, Trademarks, and Literary Property Course Handbook series, PLI order no. G4-3963.

Seymour, Whitney North, Jr. 1994. "Press Paranoia—Delusions of Persecution in the Pentagon Papers Case." *New York State Bar Journal* 66 (February).

NINETEENTH AMENDMENT

Brown, Jennifer K. 1993. "The Nineteenth Amendment and Women's Equality." *Yale Law Journal* 102 (June).

Hillyard, Carrie. 1996. "The History of Suffrage and Equal Rights Provisions in State Constitutions." *Brigham Young University Journal of Public Law* 10.

Lind, Joellen. 1994. "Dominance and Democracy: The Legacy of Woman Suffrage for the Voting Right." *UCLA Women's Law Journal* 5 (fall).

NINTH AMENDMENT

Jackson, Robert H. 1958. *The Supreme Court in the American System of Government.* Cambridge: Harvard Univ. Press.

Levy, Leonard. 1988. *Original Intent and the Framers' Constitution.* New York: Macmillan.

Wills, Gary, ed. 1982. *The Federalist Papers*, by Alexander Hamilton, James Madison, and John Jay. New York: Bantam Books.

Yoo, John Choon. 1993. "Our Declaratory Ninth Amendment." *Emory Law Journal* 42.

NIXON, RICHARD MILHOUS

Ambrose, Stephen E. 1987. *Nixon: The Education of a Politician, 1913–1962.* New York: Simon & Schuster.

———. 1989. *Nixon: The Triumph of a Politician, 1962–1972.* New York: Simon & Schuster.

Brodie, Fawn M. 1981. *Richard M. Nixon: The Shaping of His Character.* New York: Norton.

Mankiewicz, Frank. 1973. *Perfectly Clear: Nixon from Whittier to Watergate.* New York: Quadrangle Books.

Nixon, Richard M. 1978. *R. N.: The Memoirs of Richard Nixon.* New York: Grosset & Dunlap.

———. 1990. *In the Arena: A Memoir of Victory, Defeat and Renewal.* New York: Simon & Schuster.

White, Theodore H. 1975. *Breach of Faith: The Fall of Richard Nixon.* Atheneum Publications.

Wicker, Tom. 1991. *One of Us: Richard Nixon and the American Dream.* New York: Random House.

Wills, Garry. 1969. *Nixon Agonistes: The Crisis of the Self-Made Man.* Boston: Houghton Mifflin.

NONCOMPETE AGREEMENT

Jordan, Thomas E. 1990. "The Application of Contract Law to Georgia Noncompete Agreements: Have We Been Overlooking Something Obvious?" *Mercer Law Review* 41 (winter).

NONFEASANCE

Kionka, Edward J. 1988. *Torts.* St. Paul: West.

Rowe, Jean Elting, and Theodore Silver. 1995. "The Jurisprudence of Action and Inaction in the Law of Tort: Solving the Puzzle of Nonfeasance and Misfeasance from the Fifteenth through the Twentieth Centuries." *Duquesne Law Review* 33.

NONPROFIT

Barrett, David W. 1996. "A Call for More Lenient Director Liability Standards for Small, Charitable Nonprofit Corporations." *Indiana Law Journal* 71 (fall).

NOTARY PUBLIC

Closen, Michael L., and G. Grant Dixon III. 1992. "Notaries Public from the Time of the Roman Empire to the U.S. Today and Tomorrow." *North Dakota Law Review* 68.

Regine, Lynn, et al. 1994. "Notaries Public." *Rhode Island Bar Journal* 43 (November).

NUCLEAR NONPROLIFERATION TREATY

Kegley, Charles W., Jr., and Eugene R. Wittkopf. 1993. *World Politics.* 4th ed. New York: St. Martin's Press.

Mandelbaum, Michael. 1995. "Lessons of the Next Nuclear War." *Foreign Affairs* (March–April).

Palmer, R. R. 1984. *A History of the Modern World.* New York: Knopf.

Sheehan, Michael. 1988. *Arms Control: Theory and Practice.* Cambridge, Mass.: Blackwell.

U.S. Arms Control and Disarmament Agency. 1982. *Arms Control and Disarmament Agreements: Texts and Histories of Negotiations.*

NUCLEAR REGULATORY COMMISSION

United States Government Manual, 1996–1997. Washington, D.C.: U.S. Government Printing Office.

NUISANCE

Prosser, William, and Page W. Keeton. 1984. *Prosser and Keeton on Torts.* 5th ed. St. Paul: West.

NUREMBERG TRIALS

Conot, Robert. 1983. *Justice at Nuremberg.* New York: Carrol & Graf.

Davidson, Eugene. 1966. *The Trial of the Germans.* New York: Macmillan.

Gilbert, Gustav. 1947. *Nuremberg Diary.* New York: Signet.

Green, L. C. 1995. "Command Responsibility in International Humanitarian Law." *Transnational Law and Contemporary Problems* 5.

Lippman, Matthew. 1991. "Nuremberg: Forty-five Years Later." *Connecticut Journal of International Law* 7.

Persico, Joseph. 1994. *Nuremberg: Infamy on Trial.* New York: Penguin Books.

Taylor, Telford. 1992. *The Anatomy of the Nuremberg Trials.* New York: Little, Brown.

OBSTRUCTION OF JUSTICE

Roush, Corey, and Rishi Varma. 1996. "Obstruction of Justice." *American Criminal Law Review* 33.

Stephens, Otis H., Jr., and John M. Scheb II. 1993. *American Constitutional Law.* St. Paul: West.

OCCUPATIONAL SAFETY AND HEALTH ACT OF 1970

United States Government Manual, 1996–1997. Washington, D.C.: U.S. Government Printing Office.

OFFER

"Contracts." 1994. *SMH Bar Review.*

Knapp, Charles L., and Nathan M. Crystal. 1987. *Problems in Contract Law: Cases and Materials.* Boston: Little, Brown.

OFFICE OF MANAGEMENT AND BUDGET

"Office of Management and Budget." *United States Government Manual, 1995–1996.* Washington, D.C.: U.S. Government Printing Office.

OFFICE OF NATIONAL DRUG CONTROL POLICY

Office of National Drug Control Policy site. 1996. World Wide Web (November 14).

United States Government Manual, 1995–1996. Washington, D.C.: U.S. Government Printing Office.

OFFICE OF THRIFT SUPERVISION

"Office of Thrift Supervision." *United States Government Manual, 1995–1996.* Washington, D.C.: U.S. Government Printing Office.

OMBUDSPERSON

Davidson, Howard A. 1994. "Applying an International Innovation to Help U.S. Children: The Child Welfare Ombudsman." *Family Law Quarterly* 28 (spring).

Kahana, Jeffrey S. 1994. "Re-Evaluating the Nursing Home Ombudsman's Role with a View toward Expanding the Concept of Dispute Resolution." *Journal of Dispute Resolution.*

Thompson, Brenda V. 1992. "Corporate Ombudsmen and Privileged Communications: Should Employee Communications to Corporate Ombudsmen Be Entitled to Privilege?" *University of Cincinnati Law Review* 61.

Wibberuneyer, Kevin L. 1991. "Privileged Communication Extended to the Corporate Ombudsman-Employee Relationship via the Federal Rule of Evidence 501." *Journal of Dispute Resolution.*

ORGAN DONATION LAW

Anencephalic Infants Organ Donor site. 1996. World Wide Web (March 18).

California, Irvine, College of Medicine site. World Wide Web (December 4).

"Health Law." 1996. Law and Leading Attorneys site. World Wide Web (December 4).

ORGANIZED CRIME

Jankiewicz, Sara. 1995. "Comment: Glasnost and the Growth of Global Organized Crime." *Houston Journal of International Law* 18.

ORGAN TRANSPLANTATION

Blair, Roger D., and David L. Kaserman. 1991. "The Economics and Ethics of Alternative Cadaveric Organ Procurement Policies." *Yale Journal on Regulation* 8 (summer).

Caplan, Arthur L. 1992. *If I Were a Rich Man Could I Buy a Pancreas? and Other Essays on the Ethics of Health Care.* Bloomington, Ind.: Indiana Univ. Press.

Naylor, Chad D. 1989. "The Role of the Family in Cadaveric Organ Procurement." *Indiana Law Journal* 65 (winter).

ORIGINAL INTENT

Bork, Robert H. 1971. "Neutral Principles and Some First Amendment Problems." *Indiana Law Journal* 47.

———. 1990. *The Tempting of America: The Political Seduction of the Law.* New York: Free Press.

Dworkin, Ronald. 1977. *Taking Rights Seriously.* Cambridge: Harvard Univ. Press.

———. 1990. Review of *Bork's Jurisprudence,* by Robert H. Bork. *University of Chicago Law Review* 57.

———. 1994. *Life's Dominion: An Argument about Abortion, Euthanasia, and Individual Freedom.* New York: Knopf.

Graglia, Lino. 1992. "Interpreting the Constitution: Posner on Bork." *Stanford Law Review* 44.

Hand, Learned. 1958. *The Bill of Rights.* Cambridge: Harvard Univ. Press.

Levy, Leonard. 1988. *Original Intent and the Framers' Constitution.* New York: Macmillan.

Pankratz, Jeffrey. 1992. "Neutral Principles and the Right to Neutral Access to the Courts." *Indiana Law Journal* 67.

Posner, Richard A. 1990. "Bork and Beethoven." *Stanford Law Review* 42.

Scalia, Antonin. 1989. "Originalism: The Lesser Evil." *University of Cincinnati Law Review* 57.

Weschler, Herbert. 1959. "Toward Neutral Principles of Constitutional Law." *Harvard Law Review* 73.

OTIS, JAMES, JR.

Hall, Kermit L. 1989. *The Magic Mirror: Law in American History.* New York: Oxford Univ. Press.

OTTO, WILLIAM TOD

Stephens, Otis H., Jr., and John M. Scheb II. 1993. *American Constitutional Law.* St. Paul: West.

OVERT ACT

Ferdico, John N. 1992. *Ferdico's Criminal Law and Justice Dictionary.* St. Paul: West.

TABLE OF CASES CITED

INDEX

BY NAME

INDEX

BY SUBJECT

References that include photos or
exhibits are printed in *italic* type.